Robert A. Mercure

D1503537

# Modern
# Business Law

# Modern
# Business Law

A. LINCOLN LAVINE, A.B., LL.B., J.D.

*Professor of Law and Chairman of the Law
Department, St. John's University, School of
Commerce; Member of the New York Bar*

*New York*
PRENTICE-HALL, INC.
1954

*Copyright 1954 by A. Lincoln Lavine. All rights reserved.
No part of this book may be reproduced, by mimeograph,
or any other means, without permission in writing from
the publisher.*

L. C. Cat. Card No.: 54-9414

## NOTE

The forms contained in this book have been carefully selected to cover the given situations and problems as completely as possible. They will be useful to lawyers for adaptation to specific situations in connection with which they are to be used. Laymen will find them informative on the contingencies and problems which should be considered, but should consult their own legal counsel before entering into any contract or business arrangement based on these forms.

PRINTED IN THE UNITED STATES OF AMERICA

# Preface

In selecting the title "Modern Business Law," the author hopes he is not guilty of a casual choice of language. Rather, in using the word "modern," he feels a sense of responsibility to an age in which sound barriers are shattered and hydrogen bombs are with us. Our entire economy is adjusting itself to a new world which shrinks with each new air travel speed record. If our economy is not to founder, the law, which regulates our economy, must keep pace with the rush of events. And that is exactly what the law is doing.

The result is interesting—and inevitable. Businessmen, like nations, can no longer afford to practice isolationism. No businessman can confine himself today to the old copybook rules of business, because business is no longer "just business." With the growing complexity of our economic structure, the modern businessman is beset by legal problems that relate to every part of his personal as well as his commercial affairs.

Just as a successful brain surgeon must have a sound familiarity with the functions of the entire human body, so the student of business law must understand the entire body of law by which our lives are governed. It will no longer suffice to have a smattering of the so-called "business law subjects"—Contracts, Negotiable Instruments, and so on. These must be related to the entire body of our law: the law relating to our homes and home life as well as to buying or selling the home; the basic law, or Constitution, under which we live; the wrongs we may commit, or that may be committed against us, as well as the rights and duties we must all observe; and the manner in which these wrongs are redressed by civil remedies and criminal punishment.

It is for these reasons that *Modern Business Law* is divided into three books: the first dealing with Rights and Duties and covering the conventional business law subjects; the second dealing with Wrongs, including a chapter on Torts and a chapter on Crimes; and the third dealing with Enforcement and embracing a chapter on Civil Procedure and a chapter on Criminal Procedure.

For the same reasons, the opening chapter of this book includes a fairly complete discussion of the basic constitutional principles to which all other law is subject: the basic powers and limitations of our Federal and state governments, habeas corpus, ex post facto laws, impairment of contract rights, eminent domain, searches and seizures, self-incrimination, double jeopardy, freedom of religion and of the press, equal protection, class legislation, and due process.

No businessman of today can ignore or escape the pressing problems in the field of labor and management. These are fully discussed in the chapter on Employer and Employee, which summarizes modern labor legislation and court decisions bearing on such industrial pressure devices as strikes, picketing, boycotting and sabotage on the part of labor, and lockouts, shutdowns and plant removals on the part of management; as well as the major types of social legislation, including minimum wage and workmen's compensation laws, and the more recent social security laws.

Stress has also been laid on the Regulation of Business, treated in Chapter 13. It is in this field that modern business finds it necessary to move forward with cautious tread, frequently not knowing whether a bold step will win commendation or a jail sentence. This discussion of legal rules as applied to modern business conditions embraces the laws and the court decisions bearing on restraint of trade, and the perplexing questions dealing with price fixing, business expansion and mere size as distinguished from monopoly; the distinction between co-operation and conspiracy; and the problems of unfair competition and unfair trade practices.

That the law is making a valiant effort to keep pace with the rush of events is attested by one of the most extensive pieces of legislation ever undertaken—the Uniform Commercial Code. It is now in process of adoption by the various states. In each state where it is adopted, it supersedes the Uniform Negotiable Instruments Law, the Uniform Sales Act, the Uniform Bills of Lading Act, the Uniform Warehouse Receipts Act, the Uniform Stock Transfer Act and the Uniform Trust Receipts Act, as well as the model statutes which have been based on the Uniform Conditional Sales Act and the Uniform Chattel Mortgage Act. Students of business law must be prepared for the new rules which this legislation invokes. *Modern Business Law* is annotated throughout the text to the more important changes effected by this new legislation. A digest of the Code is presented in the Appendix.

In his endeavor to select test questions and problems closely related to business practice, the author has borrowed liberally from the official C.P.A. examinations prepared by the American Institute of Accountants. For permission to use these, grateful acknowledgment is hereby made.

Likewise, in preparing the Court Cases for Review which follow each chapter, the author has sought as far as practicable to fetch live problems fresh out of the current stream of litigation. In this, he wishes to acknowledge valuable assistance from Professor John F. Middlemiss, of St. John's University.

A. LINCOLN LAVINE

# Contents

# Key to
# Case Citations

Throughout this book, numerous court decisions are cited in support of the text. They are given in the footnotes.

Without attempting to cover the vast variety of annotation symbols in use from the early days of the common law and in other English-speaking countries, it is believed that a simple key to the more important citation references may be useful. This will cover the major Federal and state courts.

**United States Supreme Court Reports.** The opinions of the United States Supreme Court (except for the earlier cases) are reported in volumes entitled *United States Supreme Court Reports*. The symbol is "U.S." The citation gives, in this order, the names of the parties, the volume number, the "U.S." symbol and the page number at which the case is reported. To illustrate (we shall use hypothetical cases only): The case of Jones against Smith, reported in volume number 200 of the *United States Supreme Court Reports*, at page 50, would be cited *Jones v. Smith*, 200 U.S. 50.

**Federal Reports.** The *Federal Reporter* gives the decisions of the Federal intermediate courts. The case of Brown against Green, reported in volume 100 of the *Federal Reporter*, on page 500, would be cited *Brown v. Green*, 100 Fed. 500. The more recent decisions of the Federal intermediate courts are reported in a Second Series of the *Federal Reports*, to get away from too high a volume number arrangement. The fact that the case involves the Second Series is indicated by "2d." Thus, the case of White against Black, reported in Volume 70 of the Second Series of the *Federal Reporter*, on page 600, would be cited *White v. Black*, 70 F.2d 600.

**State Reports.** Every state has its own system of courts, with a supreme court (by whatever name) at the top. Official citations from these courts are designated by an abbreviation of the state name. Thus, *Allen v. Baker*, 210 Ill. 150 would indicate that the case in question was decided by the highest court in the State of Illinois; *Carter v. Davis*, 98 Pa. 75 would show that the citation was from the highest court in the State of Pennsylvania, and so forth. In addition, a substantial number of states (for example, California, Illinois, Indiana, Missouri, Ohio and New York) have intermediate appellate courts. Some (for example, New York, Ohio and Pennsylvania) report selected cases from courts of initial jurisdiction, where the case was tried in the first instance. Thus *Edgar v. Franklin*, 212 App. Div. 68 would be a case decided by the New York Appellate Division; *Gage v. Henry*, 185 Misc. 90 would be a case that came from one of the miscellaneous lower courts of New York.

**Unofficial Reports.** In addition to the Official Reports, a National Reporter

System has come into use. These reports are not official, but they are comprehensive, and they frequently come off the press much sooner than the Official Reports. In some states (for example, Florida) the Unofficial Reports have recently superseded the Official Reports, which have ceased separate publication. The Unofficial Reports embrace more than one state. Their coverage is as follows:

*Atlantic Reporter* (*"A."*): Connecticut, Delaware, Maine, Maryland, New Hampshire, New Jersey, Pennsylvania, Vermont and Rhode Island.

*New York Supplement* (*"N.Y. Supp."*): New York cases only (except Court of Appeals).

*North Eastern Reporter* (*"N.E."*): Illinois, Indiana, Massachusetts, New York (Court of Appeals) and Ohio.

*North Western Reporter* (*"N.W."*): Iowa, Michigan, Minnesota, Nebraska, North Dakota, South Dakota and Wisconsin.

*Pacific Reporter* (*"P."*): Arizona, California, Colorado, Idaho, Kansas, Montana, Nevada, New Mexico, Oklahoma, Oregon, Utah, Washington and Wyoming.

*South Eastern Reporter* (*"S.E."*): Georgia, North Carolina, South Carolina, Virginia and West Virginia.

*Southern Reporter* (*"So."*): Alabama, Florida, Louisiana and Mississippi.

*Southwestern Reporter* (*"S.W."*): Arkansas, Kentucky, Missouri, Tennessee and Texas.

Wherever possible, this book gives both official and unofficial citations.

**Dates.** Dates are supplied with the citations only when they are deemed significant in connection with the case.

# Modern
# Business Law

# BOOK I
# Rights and Duties

*Legally speaking, each of us living in a civilized society is a bundle of rights and duties. A study of these rights and duties, and of the way they are enforced, constitute a study of the law.*

# 1
# Law in General

**Scope of This Chapter.** In this chapter we consider (1) the origin, nature and kinds of law; (2) the various classes of "unwritten" law, or law based on precedent and expressed in judicial decisions; (3) the codification of law into its basic forms, including constitutions, treaties and statutes; and (4) the substance of the law, consisting of rights and duties, and including (a) the natural rights of personal security, personal liberty and property, and (b) the conventional rights arising out of the so-called domestic relations and the wide range of rights created by contract.

## PART 1. NATURE, ORIGIN AND KINDS OF LAW

**Nature and Definition of Law.** Law is rule; such as a rule of action (*laws of physics, chemistry, economics*) or of conduct (*moral law, divine law, municipal law, international law*).

*Municipal law* deals with rules of conduct governing persons within a sovereign state, as distinguished from *international law* which deals with the conduct of nations and their respective peoples in their intercourse with one another. Municipal law is defined by Blackstone as "a rule of civil conduct prescribed by the supreme power in a state, commanding what is right, and forbidding what is wrong." The word "municipal" in this sense is derived from the Roman "municipium," and is intended to convey the idea of a complete, self-sustained governmental unit.

*The law of the land* is an expression commonly used to indicate the rules of human conduct by which a civilized community hears before it condemns, proceeds upon inquiry, and renders judgment only after trial, thereby safeguarding each person's life, liberty and property.

**Substantive and Adjective Law.** *Substantive* law tells us what our rights and duties are and what constitutes a violation of such rights and duties; *adjective* law tells us how we may enforce our rights and duties and redress our wrongs. If you and I enter into an oral agreement by which I am to render services and you are to pay me $500, the question of whether such an agreement is enforceable is one of substantive law. If we assume that I could enforce such an agreement, the question of how I should go about

3

enforcing it—how one brings the matter to suit, trial and judgment—would be a question of adjective law.

**Origin and Evolution of Law.** In the history of law, we perceive a common tendency. First we have custom, usage and tradition, reflecting an existing state of morality, followed by an effort to codify and crystallize the accumulated mass of custom and usage into codes or statutes. This tendency is reflected not only in the ancient law of the Hebrews, Greeks, and Romans, but in the English law on which our own is based. The tendency has been defined as a transition from "unwritten law" to "written law."

**Unwritten Law.** Law based on precedent alone is commonly referred to as *unwritten law*. Originally formulated by rulers, prophets and priests, it now takes the form of judicial decisions.

Actually, what we call "unwritten" law is today not only written, but printed and published, so that all may consult it. But in less enlightened times, unwritten law was in very truth unwritten. It reached back to the dark ages, when justice was administered by appeal to the supernatural. Examples were trial by *compurgation*, by *combat*, and by *ordeal*. In the first of these, the accused got a number of *compurgators* or "oath helpers" to swear that they believed him innocent, and if the oath was taken with due formality, the accused was thereby exonerated. In the second situation, a trial consisted of physical combat between two litigants, and the verdict went to the strongest lance or the mightiest club. In the last (ordeal), guilt or innocence was determined by holding a hot iron with the bare hands (whoever dropped it first was guilty); or by plunging one's arm into a cauldron of boiling water to determine, by the time it took to heal, whether one was innocent or guilty; or, as in the case of witchcraft, by the simple test of ducking the accused in a body of water: if she came out dead, she was innocent, and if she came out alive, she was guilty and burned at the stake.

When, however, reason began to dawn in the administration of justice, and some royal judge, in trying an issue between two litigants, pronounced a principle applicable to the facts and founded in logic, common sense, or a sense of fair play, a true legal precedent was established, to be followed subsequently if the same set of facts transpired.

As these precedents or legal principles grew, they furnished a pattern of unwritten law, inscribed at first only in the memories of judges and lawyers, and either recalled from personal experience, or transmitted by word of mouth.

Mere memory, however, became insufficient, and notes of these cases and legal principles found their way into the memoirs and private records of bench and bar. Some of these notes were compiled and published in the form of commentaries, such as those of Coke, Lyttleton, Blackstone and—in our own country—Kent. By means of these commentaries, together with various digests, Year Books, and so forth, the "unwritten" law took on more definite and coherent shape.

Not only were these precedents thus clarified and given permanence, but they came to be reported and published by official reporters from the transcribed opinions of the judges. Today they are to be found on our law shelves in the form of volumes published, bound and numbered in sequence, so that they may easily be referred to by volume number and page as a source of law and a guide for determining the application of legal principles to a given set of facts.

*Citation of cases.* To facilitate reference to judicial decisions and precedents, standard case citations in abbreviated form have been generally adopted throughout the country. Footnote citations used in this book will be furnished in the standard form, and where the dates of the decisions are deemed important they will be added after the citation. A key to the abbreviations used in these citations will be found after the preface.

Unwritten law embraces four subdivisions: (a) common law; (b) equity; (c) international law; and (d) the law merchant.

To these may be added two other branches of law in which precedent plays a dominant part: (e) admiralty law, and (f) business or commercial law.

**Common Law.** Common law is the earliest branch of unwritten law founded on ancient English usage and custom. It superseded the early Anglo-Saxon mummery which passed for justice and prevailed in England before the Eleventh Century. It likewise superseded the civil authority of the ecclesiastical courts established after the Norman Conquest, which had jurisdiction not only over ecclesiastical matters, but also over decedent estates, marriage and divorce. By the Lateran Council of 1215, Trials by Oath, Ordeal, and Combat were abolished altogether. Even before the Norman Conquest, however, the Saxons had a crude form of local justice administered by the *witan* or wise men, until the year 1166, when King Henry II convoked the Assize of Clarendon, followed ten years later by another known as the Assize of Northampton. Out of these sessions came far-reaching reforms, designed to suppress the haphazard justice of the local courts and to subordinate the ecclesiastical courts to a court of the King's own making. Thus was established a King's Bench, to administer King's Law, or *Common Law*, as a supreme and common standard of law for the kingdom.

*Stare decisis.* The keystone of the common law is *stare decisis*—the doctrine that constrains judges to stand by former decisions as far as possible, without following too slavishly the outworn dogma of the past.

The basic principles of the common law are still in effect. As reflected in judicial decisions, modified to suit the changing needs of changing times, and adapted to our own needs and institutions, it continues to serve as a fundamental branch of our law.

**Common Law Courts and Common Law Actions.** A court in which a common law remedy is sought is known as a *common law court,* or *court of law,* and the action in which such remedy is sought is known as a *common law action,* or, more briefly, a *law action.* The jurisdiction of a court of law extends to those matters which were originally recognized only at common law. Ordinary law actions have for their object the assessment of damages. For example, the ordinary breach of contract action is a law action in which a party sues for money damages. The same applies to tort actions (Ch. 20:1), such as actions for assault and battery, libel, slander, negligence, conversion, replevin, and so on.

**Equity.** Equity is that branch of unwritten law, founded in justice and fair dealing, which seeks to supply a more adequate remedy than that available at (common) law. Ordinary law actions, as stated, have for their object the assessment of damages for wrongs done, but a court of equity reaches beyond mere damages: It seeks to prevent the wrong itself, or, if it has already been committed, to requite it more fully than would be possible by a mere payment of money damages. As a system of jurisprudence, equity originated in applications for royal relief from the rigidity or inadequacy of the common law. If you wanted to prevent someone from doing you irreparable injury instead of suing him for the injury after it was done, or if you wanted to compel someone to carry out a contract instead of suing him for damages for the breach, you went to the Crown— the fountainhead of all justice—for a royal decree enjoining the threatened wrong or compelling specific performance of the contract. In time, the King referred these matters to his Chancellor, the "keeper of the King's conscience," who presently called in the assistance of Vice-Chancellors, so that a system of *chancery* emerged, whose object was to provide *equity,* or a more equitable form of relief than that available at common law. Among the more common equity actions, which provide remedies not available "at law," are the following:

*Injunction suits,* which consist of a writ or order commanding an act which the court regards as essential to justice (*mandatory injunction*), or restraining an act which it deems contrary to equity and good conscience;

*Specific performance,* wherein a party seeks to compel actual performance of a contract, instead of seeking money damages for the breach;

*Partition suits,* wherein two or more persons own an undivided interest in lands and seek to have separate interests apportioned among them;

*"Bills of peace,"* wherein it is sought to unite several controversies between the same parties to avoid a multiplicity of suits (as where a series of suits are threatened, all founded on the same facts and the same questions of law, so that the decision of one will determine all);

*Reformation,* wherein a bill in equity is brought to reform a contract so that it will express correctly the true intent of the parties;

*Rescission,* wherein a court is asked to annul a contract entered into through fraud or excusable error; and

*Actions involving a trust,* wherein one person has legal title to property which equitably belongs to another.

**Maxims of Equity.** In the course of its development since the early days of English chancery, equity has established certain fundamental principles, or maxims, among which are the following:

*He who seeks equity must do equity.* One who seeks equitable relief must do what is equitable as a condition for that relief. If I seek the return of a chattel which I was induced to sell through fraud, I must tender back the purchase price. If an infant buys an expensive watch and then decides he wants his money back, he must tender back the watch.

*He who comes into equity must come with clean hands.* One cannot obtain the aid of a court of equity in respect to any transaction, if his conduct in such transaction has been in any way unconscionable, inequitable or offensive to the dictates of natural justice. If, for example, I persuade you to breach a contract to buy Smith's home, and to buy mine instead, and then you breach my contract, too, I cannot seek the aid of a court of equity to compel specific performance of your contract with me.

*Equity aids the vigilant, not those who slumber on their rights.* This maxim is akin to the doctrine of *laches* (Ch. 22:5) that, if a person sleeps on his rights, his continued silence indicates acquiescence. The maxim is designed to promote diligence, penalize delay and discourage stale claims.

**International Law.** International law consists of a body of usage and custom arising out of the intercourse of nations and their peoples with one another, reinforced by treaties, the writings of jurists, international conferences and the declarations, resolutions and decisions of international tribunals.

(a) *Public international law* regulates the conduct of sovereign nations toward one another.

(b) *Private international law* governs the rights of citizens that may be acquired in one country and enforced in another by virtue of a doctrine of international reciprocity known as the *comity of nations.* Private international law is sometimes referred to as *Application of Foreign Law,* or *Conflict of Laws.* It applies not only internationally, but also among the several states of the Union.

**The Law Merchant.** The law merchant is that branch of the unwritten law which was originally founded on the customs of merchants, mariners and business men generally in their dealings with one another throughout the civilized countries of the world. The expansion of international trade following the Renaissance gave new impetus to the need of mercantile paper in place of hazardous gold shipments across pirate-infested waters and over robber-infested lands. Also, mercantile disputes called for legal remedies more suited to the needs of merchants and mariners than those prevailing in the ordinary courts. Mercantile courts—often presided over by arbiters chosen by the merchants and mariners themselves—dispensed quick justice based on the unique body of custom which had grown up outside the ordinary rules of law. In the beginning, the decisions of these *pie poudre* or "dusty foot" courts, as they were called, had no legal sanction. Later, they were recognized as a valid body of rules based on precedent, and were adopted as the law of the land.

This body of law based on mercantile precedent has come to be known as the law merchant. It embraces not only that branch of the law known as *bills and notes*, or negotiable instruments, but others as well, such as insurance and similar branches of mercantile law.

**Admiralty Law.** Admiralty jurisprudence arose out of the ancient law of the sea, which antedates even the civil law. It was upon this ancient law that the admiralty courts of England and the maritime courts of Europe were based. Admiralty law in the United States is based on general maritime law, as modified by American usages, statutes and decisions. The United States Constitution vests exclusive admiralty jurisdiction in the Federal courts; hence no state court can exercise admiralty jurisdiction.

Admiralty law was formerly restricted to the high seas and tide-waters, but it now includes all navigable waters of the United States, such as navigable lakes and rivers subject to Congressional control.

Admiralty jurisdiction may depend upon the subject matter of the claim, or the locality where the cause of action arose. Thus, if the subject matter of a contract is the chartering, towing or salvaging of a vessel, it is a maritime contract: a dispute in reference to it is triable in an admiralty court. The size of the vessel is immaterial, so long as it is capable of water transportation. In the case of a tort, such as the negligent falling of a beam or the snapping of a cable, or a crime, such as murder, if the injury or crime occurred on the high seas or a navigable river of the United States, it is triable in a Federal court; if it occurred on shore, it is not an admiralty case.

**Business or Commercial Law.** In recent years the terms *business law* and *commercial law* have come into general use to denote rules of law of primary concern to business and to the professions ministering to business. These, like the other rules of unwritten law, originated in judicial precedent or court decisions, many of which have been codified into statute. The study of commercial law normally excludes adjective law (page 3), and such noncommercial matters as international law, matrimonial rights and duties, and crimes or torts which have no relation to business.

**Written Law.** The codification of unwritten law, as outlined, takes the form of what some writers have referred to as "written law." It embraces constitutions, treaties and statutes. These we shall consider in Part 2.

## Questions

1. What is meant by "municipal law"? Is a farmer governed by it?
2. Distinguish between substantive and adjective law.
3. What is the meaning of unwritten law? Name four kinds of unwritten law.
4. How and where did the common law develop?
5. Give two types of common law actions.
6. What is meant by the doctrine of *stare decisis?*
7. Define equity. How does it differ from the common law?
8. Name and briefly describe seven remedies available only in an equity action.
9. State and explain three maxims of equity.
10. Distinguish between public and private international law. By what other designation is private international law known?
11. What is the law merchant?
12. What is meant by statutory law? How does it differ from the common law?
13. What does admiralty law embrace?
14. What is meant by the term "business law," or "commercial law"? Name three branches of the law not embraced within such designations.

## Problems

1. Brown, driving his automobile at an excessive rate of speed and in total disregard of traffic, runs down Black, who is confined to a hospital with consequent injuries for upwards of three months. When Black leaves the hospital, he sues Brown for damages, and to ensure an early disposition of the case, he brings his action in a court of equity. Brown seeks to have the case dismissed. What results, and why?
2. Jones, a former employee of Sno-Wite Laundry, now employed with a competitor, solicits the customers of the Sno-Wite Laundry. The Sno-Wite Laundry, desirous of obtaining an injunction against Jones, consults an attorney, and urges the importance of presenting the case to a jury. The attorney explains that jury trials are usually conducted in a common law court. The Sno-Wite Laundry thereupon requests the attorney to bring the injunction suit in a common law court. What was the attorney's response?
3. The President of the United States authorizes the Secretary of State to conclude a commercial treaty with a group of specified nations. After the treaty is concluded, Senator Smith attacks it as unconstitutional. Is Smith's position sound? Explain.
4. As the steamship Ubanga left the high seas and entered New York harbor, a member of the crew shot and killed one of the ship's officers, disappeared over the side of the vessel, and several months later was apprehended and brought to justice. What branch of law had jurisdiction of the case? Why?

## PART 2. CONSTITUTIONS, TREATIES AND STATUTES

**Dual Sovereignty.** A constitution is the basic law of the land, to which all other law must conform. Under our system of dual sovereignty, each state is sovereign except as to powers delegated to the Federal Government; and each state has a constitution of its own. Hence, the laws of each state must conform not only to the United States Constitution, but to the constitution of that particular state as well.

**Constitutionality.** Any act of Congress which fails to conform to the United States Constitution, and any state statute or municipal ordinance which fails to conform to both Federal and state constitutions, is "unconstitutional" and void. It is therefore of paramount importance that we understand the basic framework of the Constitution of the United States.

**Basic Framework of Constitution.** The Constitution of the United States does three things: (1) It prescribes the form and specifies the powers of the government it creates; (2) by way of guaranty and safeguard it limits the powers, not only of the government it creates (the Federal Government), but also, in certain respects, of the states themselves; and (3) it provides for amendments. Every act of Congress must find its authority in these powers. Every act of government, Federal, state or local, is subject to these limitations.

### Constitutional Powers and Functions

**Distribution of Powers and Functions.** The Constitution distributes all Federal powers and functions into three separate departments—executive, legislative, and judicial. For any of these departments to transgress upon the others is to violate the Constitution.

**Separation of Powers: Legislative v. Judicial.** Since under our Constitutional system the legislative branch makes the laws and the judicial branch interprets them, the former cannot say what the *application of the law* is to a particular situation, neither can the latter say what the law *ought to be* in such a situation. For example, it is unconstitutional for a state to pass a law impairing the obligation of a contract. However, the court cannot enjoin the enactment of such a law, because legislative bodies are exempt from judicial interference. All that the court can do, if an unconstitutional law is enacted, is to arrest its enforcement in any particular case. Legislative discretion, whether rightly or wrongly exercised, is not subject to judicial interference.[1]

**Separation of Powers: Executive v. Judicial.** Similarly, any act which bestows judicial functions upon the executive branch, or *vice versa*, is unconstitutional. Thus, an act of Congress gave the Secretary of War power to direct the alteration of any bridge which he deemed an obstacle to free navigation, and to impose penalties for non-compliance. The court declared this act unconstitutional because it invested an executive officer with judicial power.[2]

**Separation of Powers: Legislative v. Executive.** The constitutional powers vested in the executive department can neither be exercised nor

[1] *McChord v. Louisville & N.R. Co.*, 183 U.S. 483.
[2] *U.S. v. Rider*, 50 Fed. 406.

interfered with by the legislative branch, any more than the executive department can interfere with the legislative. The willingness of either department to accept dictation from the other is immaterial: neither can be relieved by the other of duties imposed under the Constitution. Thus, the National Industrial Recovery Act (N.I.R.A.), passed in 1933, permitted trade and industry to police themselves by drawing up codes of fair competition subject to approval by the President of the United States. The act was declared unconstitutional because it delegated legislative power to the executive department.[3]

**Congressional Powers: in General.** Congress possesses only such powers as are specifically delegated to it by the Constitution. Any act of Congress dealing with matters outside these powers is null and void. Congress may: (1) raise money by taxation and duties on a uniform basis throughout the country; (2) borrow money on credit; (3) regulate commerce among the states and with foreign nations; (4) establish uniform rules on naturalization; (5) enact bankruptcy laws; (6) coin and issue money and punish for counterfeiting; (7) fix standards of weights and measures; (8) establish post offices and post roads; (9) enact copyright and patent laws; (10) establish Federal courts inferior to the United States Supreme Court; (11) punish for crimes committed on the high seas and acts in violation of international law; (12) declare war; (13) raise and support armies; (14) provide and maintain a navy; (15) govern the district which is the seat of the government (District of Columbia); and (16) make all laws necessary and proper for carrying the foregoing powers into effect.

**Congressional Powers: Right to Delegate.** Congress has no power to delegate its purely legislative functions, such as the power to fix tax rates, prescribe terms of office, regulate hours of labor, appropriate moneys, define offenses and prescribe punishments. Congress may, however, create the agencies and prescribe the regulations and details for effectuating its legislation. An example is the Interstate Commerce Act, which set up a code of laws regulating interstate carriers, and an expert body of commissioners with power to act upon notice and hearing, and to issue orders supported by findings of fact sustained by evidence.[4]

**Limitations on Congressional Powers.** The Constitution of the United States imposes specific limitations on Congressional power. Congress may not: (1) suspend the writ of habeas corpus; (2) take away the property of a person condemned to death (bill of attainder); (3) pass criminal laws to govern acts committed prior to the enactment of the law (*ex post facto* laws); (4) tax exports; (5) give preference to any domestic port; (6) compel vessels doing an interstate business to pay duty; or (7) grant titles

---

[3] Also because it sought to regulate business that was not truly interstate, hence not within the jurisdiction of Congress. *Schechter Poultry Corp. v. United States,* 295 U.S. 495.

[4] *Interstate Commerce Commission v. Louisville & N.R. Co.,* 227 U.S. 88.

of nobility (an officeholder may not accept any present, office, or title from any foreign land or its head without the consent of Congress). The most important of these limitations are those which relate to the habeas corpus writ and to *ex post facto* laws.

**Suspension of Writ of Habeas Corpus.** The nature of the writ of habeas corpus is more fully discussed in Part 3 of this chapter. The framers of the Constitution guarded it jealously against encroachment, by providing that "The privilege of the writ of habeas corpus shall not be suspended, unless when in cases of rebellion or invasion the public safety may require it."

**Ex Post Facto Laws.** The provision against *ex post facto* laws applies only to penal and criminal statutes. Every law that makes an act done before the passage of such law criminal, which was innocent when done, is an *ex post facto* law and within the prohibition of this clause.

**Limitations on States.** In addition to prohibitions in respect to attainders, *ex post facto* laws and titles of nobility, no state may (1) make treaties, (2) issue money, (3) pass any law impairing the obligation of contracts, (4) lay import or export duties, (5) tax marine tonnage, (6) keep armies or warships in peacetime, or (7) engage in war unless actually invaded or in imminent danger.

By giving up powers in respect to war and treaty making, issuing money, laying import and export duties and maintaining army and navy strength in peacetime, the states divested themselves of the dominant rights of sovereignty, though retaining sovereignty in all other respects.

**Impairing Obligation of Contracts.** The Constitution preserves the integrity of contracts by providing that no state shall pass any law impairing the obligation of contracts. Thus, a statute abolishing existing debts would be unconstitutional; so would a city ordinance repudiating a bonded indebtedness. Once a franchise is granted, it cannot be revoked except in accordance with its terms. The prohibition of laws impairing the obligation of contracts is directed at the states: the limitation does not apply to Congress.

**Taxation.** The power to tax is essential to the very existence of a state. Hence, taxes may with constitutional impunity cut into property and contract rights provided their purpose is public and their imposition uniform. A fundamental distinction in taxing power should be noted between Federal and state governments: each state has the unlimited power to tax which goes with sovereignty, but Federal taxation must be limited to the specific purposes delegated by the United States Constitution.

Taxation must be for a truly public purpose. If the levy is on one group for the benefit of another, the tax is unconstitutional.

EXAMPLE: The First Agricultural Adjustment Act, passed by Congress in 1933, sought to restore the farmer's purchasing power by adjusting production to demand and compensating farmers who cut down their crops, out of a fund raised through taxes on processing the farm product. The act was declared unconstitutional on various grounds, one of which was that the tax was not collected for government support generally, but took from one group for the benefit of another.[5]

**Police Power.** Inherent in the very nature of government, though not specifically mentioned in the Constitution, is the dominant power of a sovereign state, known as the *police power,* to pass laws for the protection and promotion of the health, safety, morals and general welfare of the people. States, like individuals, have the natural right of self-preservation, hence the duty to protect their citizens and to provide for their safety and good order. Therefore if a law is attacked as unconstitutional on the ground that it interferes with personal liberty, personal security, property or contract, and if it can be shown that the law is necessary to promote the health, safety, morals or general welfare of the people, the attack must fail, because such a law can be sustained as a valid exercise of the police power.

EXAMPLES: Tenement house legislation, sanitary laws, emergency rent laws and laws fixing maximum or minimum prices for public necessities. These may impair the obligation of contracts without violating the Constitution.

Regulation under the police power is further discussed in Chapter 13.

**Eminent Domain.** The right of a sovereign power to take private property for a public purpose is known as the right of eminent domain. It is limited by the Fifth Amendment, which commands *just compensation* to the owner, and by the *due process clause,* referred to on page 18. The power of eminent domain may be exercised by a government directly, as where it condemns property for a post office, courthouse or public road, or it may be delegated to a corporation or individual together with the delegation of some public duty or function, as in the case of railroad, telegraph or telephone rights of way. There can be no right of eminent domain unless the purpose is truly public.

**Reserved Rights of States.** All sovereign power not delegated to the Federal Government is reserved to the states. That would seem to be axiomatic, but to leave no doubt on the subject the Tenth Amendment (the last of the so-called Bill of Rights) provides that "The powers not delegated to the United States by the Constitution, nor prohibited by it to the states, are reserved to the states respectively, or to the people." [6]

## Constitutional Guaranties and Safeguards

**In General.** Embedded in the Constitution are certain fundamental guaranties, safeguards and limitations, which serve as a bulwark to protect

---

[5] *United States v. Butler,* 297 U.S. 1.

[6] One of the grounds on which the First Agricultural Adjustment Act (page 12) was declared unconstitutional was that it invaded the reserved rights of states.

minorities against oppression, and which we may evaluate by contrasting them with the all too familiar procedure under a totalitarian regime. The dread knock on the door after midnight, the arrest without hint as to the nature of the alleged offense, the hustling off for star-chamber questioning, the summary sentence of death or imprisonment—these conditions, contrasted with our own, highlight the true meaning of liberty under a constitutional government.

The Constitution provides the following personal, civil and political rights and safeguards: personal liberty and security, freedom of religion, freedom of speech and the press, right of assembly and petition, equal protection of the laws, the prohibition of special privileges, immunities and class legislation, and the all-important "due process clause."

**Liberty and Security.** The so-called "natural" rights of personal liberty and personal security are discussed in Part 3. The guaranty of personal liberty, implicit in numerous provisions of the Constitution, is specifically mentioned in the Fifth Amendment, which provides that no person shall be deprived of life, liberty or property without due process of law, and in the Fourteenth Amendment, which reiterates the prohibition as to the states. Liberty and security are safeguarded not only by such constitutional provisions and restrictions as those relating to *habeas corpus* and *ex post facto* laws, but they are further fortified by provisions in respect to (1) searches and seizures, (2) presentment or indictment, (3) trial by jury, (4) assistance of counsel, (5) compulsory process for obtaining witnesses, (6) confrontation by hostile witnesses, (7) excessive bail and fines, and cruel and unusual punishments, (8) self-incrimination, and (9) double jeopardy.

**(1) Searches and Seizures.** The Fourth Amendment to the Constitution provides that "the rights of the people to be secure in their persons, houses, papers, and effects, against unreasonable searches and seizures, shall not be violated, and no warrants shall issue, but upon probable cause, supported by oath or affirmation, and particularly describing the place to be searched, and the persons or things to be seized."

A person's home and place of business cannot be invaded forcibly and searched by the curious and suspicious, or even by a disinterested officer of the law, unless he is armed with a search warrant.[7] Belief, however well founded, that an article sought is concealed in a dwelling house furnishes no justification for search of that place without a warrant.

A search warrant must be based upon specific information, not on a statement of belief or general conclusion.

**(2) Presentment or Indictment.** It is of the essence of a fair trial that a person charged with a crime shall be informed in advance of the nature of his alleged offence so that he may prepare a proper defense to the charge. The Fifth Amendment provides that "No person shall be held to

[7] *United States v. Veeder*, 246 U.S. 675.

answer for a capital, or otherwise infamous crime, unless on a presentment or indictment of a Grand Jury." A *presentment* is defined by Blackstone[8] as a written notice of an offence taken by a grand jury from their own knowledge or observation, and an *indictment* as "a written accusation, of one or more persons, of a crime or misdemeanor, preferred to, and presented by, a grand jury, upon oath." [9]

(3) **Trial by Jury.** The Sixth Amendment provides that in all criminal prosecutions the accused shall enjoy the right to a speedy and public trial, by an impartial jury. To ensure impartiality, the accused is entitled to challenge proposed jurors.

The Seventh Amendment guarantees the right to a jury trial in civil (as distinguished from criminal) cases, in all actions where the right existed at common law when the amendment was adopted. State constitutions generally guarantee the right to a jury trial in similar situations. Parties to a civil dispute may stipulate to waive their right to a trial by jury; and a statute may provide that if a jury trial is not demanded within a given time or in a given manner, it shall be deemed waived. There is no constitutional right to a jury trial in an equity case.

(4) **Assistance of Counsel.** The Sixth Amendment provides that in all criminal prosecutions, the accused shall have the right to have the assistance of counsel for his defense. A court in a criminal proceeding must advise the accused that he is entitled to such assistance, and may assign counsel at public expense if the accused so requests and is unable to afford counsel of his own.

(5) **Compulsory Process for Obtaining Witnesses.** There are many situations where a man's life or freedom may depend on his ability to compel the attendance of witnesses on his behalf. Such witnesses may be unwilling or afraid to attend, for one reason or another. The accused may compel the attendance of such witnesses by subpoena, and may obtain the assistance of the court for this purpose if needed.

(6) **Right to Be Confronted with Hostile Witnesses.** The Sixth Amendment guarantees to a person accused of a crime, the right to be confronted with the witnesses against him. This provision secures the accused in his right to be tried, so far as the facts are concerned, by only such witnesses as meet him face to face at the trial, give their testimony in his presence, and give the accused an opportunity of cross-examination.

(7) **Excessive Bail and Fines; Cruel and Unusual Punishments.** The Eighth Amendment provides that "Excessive bail shall not be required, nor excessive fines imposed." The determination of an "excessive" bail or fine is a judicial question. The discretion of the magistrate in fixing bail is usually guided by the prisoner's ability to give bail and the atrocity of the offense.

---

[8] 4 Comm. 301.
[9] 4 Comm. 302.

***Standards of cruelty; "third degree"; death.*** The constitutional prohibition of cruel and inhuman punishment embraces not only the obvious forms, such as torture, chains, or lingering death, but also all forms of punishment regarded by civilized standards as beyond the norm of decency as a penalty for violation of the law. Confessions tortured out of a prisoner by the "third degree" are frequently kept out of evidence because they are regarded as having been procured by cruel and inhuman methods. The punishment of death is not regarded as cruel or inhuman within the constitutional meaning of these terms.[10]

(8) **Self-Incrimination.** The Fifth Amendment provides that no person "shall be compelled in any criminal case to be a witness against himself." This privilege relates only to communications by a witness, not to facts which speak for themselves. A bankrupt is not deprived of his constitutional right by an order requiring him to surrender his books to a duly authorized receiver, since the constitutional privilege in respect to self-incrimination does not allow a person to appropriate property merely because it might tell an incriminating story.[11] Formerly, a bankrupt might refuse to answer questions on the constitutional ground that such testimony might tend to incriminate him. This he can no longer do. The Bankruptcy Act of 1938 provides that a bankrupt's testimony shall not be offered against him in any criminal proceeding: hence he cannot object that such testimony might incriminate him. Neither can he urge the objection when he applies for a discharge, because such testimony is voluntary; it is the *bankrupt* who wants his discharge.

(9) **Double Jeopardy.** The Fifth Amendment provides that no person shall be subject for the same offence to be twice put in jeopardy of life or limb. The Constitution does not define what constitutes double jeopardy, nor what constitutes an offence. The courts, however, have held that double jeopardy applies to the trial of all indictable offences and misdemeanors, but not to indictments themselves, because an indictment is not a trial. Neither is a hearing before a magistrate or police court regarded as a trial so far as concerns double jeopardy; nor a trial which ends in a disagreement. A man may be tried for the same offence fifty times, provided all prior trials ended in disagreement. If a jury acquits but the judge is dissatisfied with the verdict and sets aside the acquittal, such judicial act is without validity: the judge's decision must be reversed without subsequent trial, since such trial would constitute double jeopardy.

**Freedom of Religion.** The first of the ten amendments (Bill of Rights) provides: "Congress shall make no law respecting an establishment of religion, or prohibiting the free exercise thereof." The sixth article of the

---

[10] *Ex parte Kemmler*, 136 U.S. 436, 446-447, which upheld a New York statute providing for execution of the death penalty by electrocution.
[11] *Re Harris*, 221 U.S. 274.

Constitution further provides that "no religious test shall ever be required as a qualification to any office or public trust under the United States."

**Freedom of Speech and the Press.** The First Amendment provides that Congress shall make no law abridging the freedom of speech or of the press. No law may be passed which limits our right, by the spoken or written word, to criticise any public or private act. On the other hand, as the Supreme Court observes, freedom of speech and the press "does not permit the publication of libels, blasphemous or indecent articles or other publications indecent to public morals or private reputation." [12] The exercise of this right, as Mr. Justice Holmes has observed, may depend upon the circumstances of the utterance. "The most stringent protection of free speech would not protect a man in falsely shouting fire in a theatre and causing a panic . . ." [13]

**Right of Assembly and Petition.** The First Amendment guarantees the right of any and all persons, individually or collectively, to apply to any officer or department of government for relief or the redress of grievances —free of all penalty for having sought or obtained it.

**Equal Protection of the Laws.** The Fourteenth Amendment provides that no state shall "deny to any person within its jurisdiction the equal protection of the laws." It is a denial of equal protection to pass legislation which discriminates against some persons in favor of others (see page 12, First Agricultural Adjustment Act). In this sense, "persons" includes corporations. The law may discriminate, however, where real differences exist, such as differences in age, sex, professions and trade. For example, a labor law fixing maximum hours and discriminating as to age or sex is valid because it is based on real differences; but if it also sought to discriminate as to race, religion or politics, it would violate the equal protection clause.

**Privileges, Immunities, and Class Legislation.** The Fourth Article of the Constitution provides that "the citizens of each state shall be entitled to all privileges and immunities of citizens in the several states." For example, a state law giving priority to its own creditors is void.[14] The Fourteenth Amendment further provides that "no state shall make or enforce any law which shall abridge the privileges or immunities of citizens of the United States." Hence no statute may prevent a citizen from passing freely from one state to another or from doing business in any state other than his own.

*Who are citizens.* Persons are citizens of the United States if they are (1) born in the United States, or (2) born abroad of parents who are American citizens, or (3) duly naturalized. Persons may be naturalized

---

[12] *Robertson v. Baldwin,* 165 U.S. 275, 281.
[13] *Schenck v. United States,* 249 U.S. 47, 52.
[14] *Blake v. McLung,* 172 U.S. 239, 247; 176 U.S. 59.

(a) by personal compliance with civil naturalization laws, including five years' residence, declaration of intention and oath of allegiance, (b) by parent's naturalization, or (c) by military service in the armed forces of the United States. Formerly, a female alien acquired citizenship upon marriage to an American citizen. Under the act of Congress of 1922, as amended in 1930, 1931 and 1934, citizenship is not acquired by marriage, but if an alien spouse is otherwise eligible, he or she may become a citizen upon full compliance with the naturalization laws, without declaration of intention, and upon three years' residence prior to filing a petition, instead of the normal five-year period.

*Corporations are not citizens.* Although corporations have been judicially declared to be *persons,* they are not and cannot be citizens. Hence any state may refuse, limit, or regulate the right of corporations organized in other states to enter that state and conduct business therein (Chap. 12:8).

**Due Process.** All dominant government powers, including eminent domain, the police power and the power to tax, as well as all private rights and powers, are subject to the all-inclusive constitutional limitation of due process. The Fifth Amendment, as noted, provides that no person shall "be deprived of life, liberty, or property, without due process of law," and the Fourteenth Amendment applies the provision specifically to the states. The term "due process" has been given widely varying interpretations, but the concept corresponds roughly to that of "the law of the land," as defined on page 3. Thus, it would be a denial of due process to violate any of the constitutional privileges and safeguards referred to on pages 13 to 17.

The due process clause, because of its broad and all-inclusive character, especially as interpreted under the Fourteenth Amendment, has greatly extended the power of the Supreme Court, because the clause has been construed to mean that the Court may declare any statute unconstitutional if in the opinion of the Court it violates due process.

## Treaties

**In General.** Treaties are solemn contracts or "compacts" between or among two or more nations. Once adopted, they constitute international law so far as concerns the signatory nations and their respective citizens. Treaties between two countries are *bilateral;* among more than two countries, *multilateral.* The Constitution of the United States provides that treaties may be concluded only by the President with the approval of two thirds of the Senate.

**Types of Treaties.** Treaties are commonly classified as political, commercial and legal.

*Political treaties* deal with alliances, war, cessions of territory, the settlement of boundary disputes and similar matters.

*Commercial treaties* may govern such matters as tariffs, fisheries, navigation and monetary exchange.

*Legal treaties* may concern extradition of criminals, patent and copyright protection, and so forth.

**United Nations Charter.** Immediately after the Second World War, by a multilateral compact known as the United Nations Charter, an international organization was established to replace the League of Nations which had been established after the First World War and which had succumbed to nationalistic pressures. The Charter set up a General Assembly with representation by all member nations; a Security Council, with limited representation, to function continuously and to enforce measures for the preservation of peace as particular dangers arose; and a Secretariat, headed by a Secretary-General, to handle administrative functions. The purposes of the United Nations organization thus established are set forth in the Charter as the maintenance of international peace and security, the development of friendly relations among states, and the achievement of cooperation in solving international economic, social, cultural and humanitarian problems.

Under the United Nations Charter, member nations are required to register all treaties with that organization.

## Statutes

**Definition and Classification.** A statute is a formal enactment by a legislative body of some rule or rules of civil conduct. It is referred to as an *act* when adopted by Congress, a *statute* when adopted by a state and an *ordinance* when adopted by a municipal legislative body, such as a board of aldermen or common council. Statutes are *enabling*, if they grant power; *enlarging*, if they extend power; *restraining*, if they limit power; *disabling*, if they take power away or extinguish it; *corrective*, if they remove or correct hardships in existing law; or *declaratory*, if they declare the common law. Many statutes are substantially declarations in codified form of the previous common law on the subject.

**Uniform Statutes; Commercial Code.** Confusion caused by conflicting judicial decisions and statutes has led to the adoption of uniform statutes in various states throughout the country. The matters involved being of state, not Federal, jurisdiction, cooperative state action was necessary to ensure uniformity. This led to the appointment of a National Conference of Commissioners on Uniform State Laws under whose direction, from time to time, over sixty uniform statutes were formulated and adopted by numerous, and in some cases by all the different states throughout the country.

In the course of time, however, the uniform application of some of these statutes became entangled with conflicting judicial interpretations. Others were manifestly behind the march of commercial progress. As a result, the National Conference of Commissioners in cooperation with the American Law Institute formulated a comprehensive Uniform Commercial Code, for adoption by the different states in place of the uniform statutes which they were designed to supersede. A summary of the new provisions of the Commercial Code will be found at the end of this book.

## Questions

1. What is meant by "dual sovereignty" as applied to our system of government?

2. How would you explain the statement that our constitutional system is based on a "separation of powers"?

3. Under our system of constitutional government, may Congress delegate any of its functions? Discuss fully.

4. May the writ of habeas corpus ever be suspended? Explain.

5. What is meant by an *ex post facto* law? What is the constitutional provision in respect to it? Does it apply to all statutes, or only to some and not to others?

6. What are some of the things which the states are prohibited from doing under the United States Constitution?

7. Explain the constitutional provision with respect to the integrity of contracts. Are there any exceptions?

8. Can you name a fundamental distinction in taxing power between the Federal and state governments? What is a basic limitation with respect to the purpose for which a government may impose a tax?

9. What is meant by the "police power"? Name three types of laws which are permissible under the police power.

10. What is meant by the right of eminent domain?

11. To what extent is a state sovereign?

12. Supply the missing information indicated by the blanks in the following sentence: A home cannot be searched by the public authorities without a _____, which must usually contain _____.

13. What is the constitutional provision with respect to the requirement, in connection with a capital or other infamous crime, of a presentment or indictment? What is the reason behind such requirement?

14. What is the constitutional provision with respect to a person's right to a trial by jury? In what cases is a person not entitled to such right?

15. What assistance does the Constitution guarantee to a person accused of a crime?

16. What is the constitutional provision with respect to (a) compulsory process for obtaining witnesses, (b) the right to be confronted with hostile witnesses, (c) excessive bail and fines, (d) double jeopardy, and (e) self-incrimination?

17. What types of utterances and publications are not protected by the constitutional right of freedom of speech and of the press?

18. When may a law be discriminatory without violating the constitutional provision with respect to equal protection of the laws?

19. In view of the fact that the Constitution provides that "The citizens of each state shall be entitled to all privileges and immunities of citizens in the several states," how is it that a state may prevent an outside corporation from doing business in the state except upon prescribed conditions?

20. What is your idea of due process? Give an example of a violation of due process.

21. Define a treaty. Distinguish between bilateral and multilateral treaties.

22. What matters are usually included in (a) political treaties, (b) commercial treaties, (c) legal treaties?

23. Describe the framework and purposes of the United Nations Charter.

24. How would you define a statute? What are the functions of the following types of statutes: (a) enabling; (b) enlarging; (c) restraining; (d) disabling; (e) corrective; (f) declaratory?

25. What are the objectives of uniform statutes? Have these objectives been entirely fulfilled?

## Problems

1. The state of Kansippi passed a law requiring all transcontinental airplanes passing over the state to have certain markings. The day before the law was passed a jet-propelled plane operated by the Canadian-American Lines, and flying from Central Canada to Texas, passed over the state of Kansippi without having the markings prescribed by the Kansippi legislature. A week later the state legislature adopted another law requiring that the Canadian-American Lines be prosecuted for violating the first law. The second statute contained a definition of the word, "transcontinental," as including north and south traffic. The statute may be attacked on three grounds. What are they?

2. One of the state supreme courts, having reached the conclusion that telephone rate schedules in that state are excessive, adopts a judicial rule prescribing maximum rate schedules, which would leave the telephone company no profit. On what two grounds may such a statute be attacked?

3. Congressman Smith proposes a law delegating the following power to a newly created Atomic Authority: (a) to fix tax rates; (b) to prescribe the terms of office of the members of the board constituting the Authority; (c) to regulate hours of labor; (d) to appropriate moneys for needed developments and research; and (e) to define offenses and prescribe punishments in connection with the functions of the Atomic Authority. Is such proposed legislation constitutional? Give reasons.

4. Congressman Jones introduces a bill authorizing the President of the United States to suspend the writ of habeas corpus in connection with Communist activities whenever in his judgment such action seems desirable. Various members of Congress question the constitutionality of such a measure. What would be your opinion with respect to it?

5. The Mayor of an incorporated village, having difficulty with a private right of way leading from his garage to the street, causes an ordinance to be adopted for the improvement of such right of way. The ordinance imposes a small tax on all residents of the community for this purpose. What are your comments with respect to this ordinance?

6. J. Whittington Gotmoney has a sumptuous suburban home on a site which is wanted for a government post office. He fights condemnation proceedings, at considerable expense to himself and the Government, in consequence of which the court, upon termination of the proceedings, condemns the property and refuses to allow any award in connection with its acquisition for said public purpose. What do you think of the validity of these proceedings?

7. In the course of an investigation into alleged gambling activities, a police

detective is assigned to obtain evidence of alleged participation by one, John Ladyluck. The detective rings Ladyluck's doorbell, and notwithstanding the latter's protestations, searches his home from top to bottom. Considerable evidence of an incriminating nature is thus obtained. In criminal proceedings subsequently brought against Ladyluck, the latter's attorney objects to the use of the evidence thus discovered. The district attorney points out that the evidence clearly establishes Ladyluck is a criminal, not entitled to constitutional protection. How should the court rule?

8. Bart Gumshoe, an ex-convict suspected of burglary, is questioned by the police, then arrested and held for prosecution. The indictment charges him with "unlawful activities, and violations of the Penal Law." An attorney is assigned by the court to defend Gumshoe. What would his probable position be as to the indictment?

9. In view of the rising costs of government administration, a statute is passed vesting in judges of certain criminal courts broad authority to determine the facts as well as the law, thereby dispensing with the necessity of a jury for prosecutions of various enumerated types. The constitutionality of this statute is challenged. Will the challenge be judicially sustained?

10. An immigrant unfamiliar with the English language is picked up by the police and charged with larceny. The immigrant is wholly without funds and is unable to hire an attorney. At the trial the court provides an interpreter, but does not feel that the state should be charged with the expense of paying counsel fees on behalf of one who is not a citizen or taxpayer. What is your comment on this procedure?

11. Jed Gorilla is charged with criminal assault involving torture of his victim. Because of the atrocious nature of the offense the magistrate refuses to fix bail. Is the magistrate justified in his position?

12. Creakle is indicted for the crime of robbery. His attorney moves to quash the indictment, and the indictment being defective, the court grants the motion. Another indictment is then drawn up against Creakle. His attorney now pleads double jeopardy. Will the plea be sustained or rejected? Why?

13. Mary Jones is charged with smuggling a valuable gem into this country. The only proof against her is the possession of the gem and her inability or unwillingness to explain where she got it. She is therefore put on the witness stand and required to explain where and how she procured the gem. Her attorney objects to this procedure. How will the court rule, and why?

14. The state of Pennsylvania refuses to permit a New York corporation to do business in Pennsylvania without obtaining a license to do so and paying a fee in connection therewith. The position of the state of Pennsylvania is challenged on the ground that the Fourth Article of the Constitution provides that the citizens of each state shall be entitled to all the privileges and immunities of citizens in the several states. Does this position of the State of Pennsylvania violate the United States Constitution? Explain.

## PART 3. RIGHTS AND DUTIES

**Your Rights Are My Duties.** Every person is a "bundle of rights and duties." These are *reciprocal:* that is, your rights as to me are my duties toward you, and *vice versa*. Rights are either *natural* or *conventional,* also known, respectively, as *absolute* or *relative*. Natural or absolute rights are those supposed to spring from the nature of our existence. They embrace *personal security*, *personal liberty*, and *property*. Conventional or relative rights are those created by "convention"—literally, the *coming together* of individuals upon a united purpose; for example, rights arising out of the so-called *domestic relations,* and rights created by *contract.*

**Personal Security.** Personal security consists in the peaceable enjoyment of life, limb, body, health and reputation. It may be violated both civilly, as in negligence, assault and battery, libel, slander and malicious prosecution; criminally, as in homicide, arson, robbery, burglary, forgery and larceny. These violations, known respectively as torts and crimes, are discussed in Chapters 20 and 21 respectively.

**Personal Liberty.** Under our system of government, no man, save by express law, can be restrained of his liberty, prevented from going where he pleases, compelled to go where he does not want to, or be in any way imprisoned or confined. If an offender is apprehended, he must be given an immediate hearing before the proper magistrate. Only if reasonable probability of guilt appears may the offender be committed to prison and held for trial. Even then, pending trial, the offender (except in capital cases) may secure his liberty on *bail,* by the posting of a bond for appearance to stand trial.

*Habeas corpus.* Safeguarding the right of personal liberty is the writ of habeas corpus (literally, "have with you the body"): a court order available at all times, requiring one having custody of another's person to produce him on short notice for inquiry into the cause of detention. As noted on page 12, this constitutional writ can be suspended only in the most extreme emergencies. The character of the restraint or imprisonment which justifies a person in applying for the writ varies with the circumstances. The most common illustration is confinement under civil or criminal process. "Wives restrained by husbands, children withheld from the proper parent or guardian, persons under arbitrary custody by private individuals, as in a madhouse, as well as those under miltary control, may all become proper subjects of relief by the writ of habeas corpus." [15]

**Property.** The legal institution known as *property,* namely, the relationship of persons to things which gives persons exclusive control over things, is guaranteed by the United States Constitution, which provides that no person may be deprived of his property, even for a public purpose, save by due process of law and upon just compensation.

**Domestic Relations.** The so-called "domestic relations" include those of *husband and wife, parent and child, guardian and ward,* and *master and servant.* For the most part, they deal with matters outside the domain of commercial law. A brief reference to these relationships, however, will be useful, since at times they concern certain phases of business law. For example, banks, trust companies, accountants and others are frequently called upon to deal with matters affecting the legal rights and duties of husband and wife in respect to each other and to third parties, the

[15] *Wales v. Whitney,* 114 U.S. 564.

respective rights and duties of parents and their children, and the duties imposed by the law upon the various types of guardians representing the business interests of their wards.

**Husband and Wife.** The relationship of husband and wife arises out of a marriage, which is defined as "a contract under which a man and a woman reciprocally engage to live with each other during their joint lives, and to discharge toward each other the duties imposed by law on the relation of husband and wife." [16] Unlike an ordinary contract, the contract of marriage affects not only the parties themselves, but the state, which may therefore license, regulate and control the conditions under which a marriage will be recognized as valid. Most marriages entail civil formalities and religious solemnization. Some states, however, recognize "common-law marriages," or informal marriages contracted without civil or religious ceremony, and without prior license. Regardless of the form of marriage, the relationship thereby established creates certain mutual rights and duties.

*Duty of support.* The husband has the duty of support: the wife is by law her husband's agent in purchasing, for herself and household, necessities as gauged by the husband's income. However, some states have adopted statutes imposing upon the wife the duty of sharing in the burden of family support. In some cases, the husband's physical and financial condition, contrasted with the wife's, may place the duty of support on the wife.[17]

*Earnings of wife.* Under the common law, a husband was entitled to his wife's services whether rendered inside or outside the home. In most jurisdictions today, a wife's earnings derived from sources other than household duties belong to her. But a wife has no legal claim to compensation for services rendered by her in her husband's business.[18]

*Household savings.* Where the management of the household budget is entrusted to the wife, the law looks upon any savings she may effect as a household fund: in her possession, but belonging to the "head of the house." The court has gone even further and held that moneys saved by a wife out of her household allowance belong to the husband, unless otherwise agreed.[19]

*Contracts between husband and wife.* At common law, contracts between husband and wife were not recognized, since husband and wife were regarded as one, and one cannot contract with himself. Under modern statutes, however, husband and wife may freely contract with each

---

[16] 55 *Corpus Juris Secundum* 806. (Corpus Juris Secundum will hereafter be cited as "C.J.S.")

[17] *McLean v. McLean,* 69 N.D. 665, 290 N.W. 913.

[18] 41 C.J.S. 742, citing *Detroit & Security Trust Co. v. Gitre,* 254 Mich. 66, 235 N.W. 884; *Brittain v. Crowther,* 54 F. 295 (Neb.), 4th Cir. 341.

[19] *Fretz v. Roth,* 68 N.J. Eq. 516, 59 A. 676; *In re Ekins,* 126 Misc. 1, 213 N.Y. Supp. 162; *Kirsh v. Kirsh,* 118 N.Y. Law Journal 960 (October 21, 1947).

other, and if the contract is valid in all other respects, it will be enforced. (See Chap. 2:3.)

**Parent and Child.** A parent is the *natural guardian* of his children. Although the relationship is established by nature, it is regulated by law. As natural guardian, a parent has custody of his child's *person*, but not of his *property*. To exercise control over a child's property, the parent must first be appointed by the court as a *legal* guardian of the child. The rights and duties of parent and child (as with all rights and duties) are reciprocal: the duty to support, educate and protect go with the right to custody, control, services and earnings.

*Age and status of infancy.* An *infant* or *minor* is a person of either sex who has not attained the age of *majority* which marks the status of an adult. The age of majority varies in different states. At common law, and by statute in most states, the age is twenty-one years.[20] By common law precedent, which ignores a fraction of a day, an infant reaches the legal age of twenty-one the day before his twenty-first birthday. In some states, the female age of majority, at least for some purposes, has been fixed at eighteen. State statutes vary as to privileges accorded to infants at varying ages, including those in relation to contracts, wills, marriage, voting, and so on. Infants of sufficient age to understand the nature of their acts are liable for their torts and crimes; and in the purchase of necessaries, for their contracts (Chap. 2:3).

*Adoption.* Adoption is an act by which the relation of parent and child is created by law instead of by nature. It is usually effected by a court proceeding authorized by statute. Its effect is to create all the rights, duties and obligations existing between natural parents and children, and to sever completely the legal relationship between the adopted child and his former parents. An adopted child, however, has one advantage over other children: he may inherit from both his natural and his adopted parents.

*Duty to support.* The duty to support infant children is on the father, though the children have property of their own sufficient for such purpose, except that in the latter case the rule does not apply if the father has no means of his own or his estate is limited. If the father dies, the duty of support falls on the mother, except where the child has means of his own, or is able to earn a living. Where a child leaves home and remains away against the father's wishes, and without the father's fault or neglect, he forfeits the right to support; but if the father abandons the child, or drives him away by cruel treatment, he remains liable for the child's support.

*Duty to educate.* The common law imposed no duty on parents to educate their children. By virtue of our system of compulsory education, the duty to educate one's children is now largely a matter of statute. It has

[20] *Hutchison v. Till,* 212 Ala. 64, 101 So. 676.

been held in one case that a business or commercial education may in some circumstances be regarded as a "necessary" for which the parent may be held liable.[21] In another case, the court has held that a son, twenty years old, in good health, could not compel his mother (however extensive her property interests) to furnish him with the means of obtaining a professional education.[22] In still another case, the court, in referring to the rule that a proper education is a necessary, added that what is a "proper education" depends upon the circumstances of a particular case, so that even a college education may be "proper": "The court . . . should, in determining this fact, take into consideration the progress of society, and the attendant requirements upon the citizens of today." [23]

*Liability for torts.* For the torts of a child, whether willful or mischievous (as in the case of assault, breaking a neighbor's window, or setting fire to his land), or merely negligent (as by leaving a roller skate in the path of a pedestrian), a parent as such is not liable, unless the act of the child was committed on behalf or in the service of the parent, or under circumstances where the parent may be said to have been negligent in not preventing the tort. The infant himself, of course, is liable for his own torts, and may be compelled to respond in damages for them out of any property he may own, unless, at the time the tort was committed, he was not of sufficient age or capacity to be chargeable with malice or negligence.

*Right of custody and control.* At common law the primary right to the custody of a child is in the father. This is still the law in most jurisdictions, where the father has the primary duty of support. By statute in some states, the parents are joint guardians of their children and have an equal right to their custody. If the father is unfit, or dies, custody passes to the mother. If the parents live apart and are unable to agree as to custody, a court will decide the matter on the basis of what is best for the child.

*Right to punish.* Despite the trend away from corporal punishment, either parent may discipline the child, by chastisement if they deem it necessary; but if the parent wantonly inflicts cruel, merciless and unnecessary punishment upon the child, he may be prosecuted criminally for it. The child, however, has no civil action for damages in such case, though he may have sustained severe personal injuries in the course of punishment. A parent may delegate the right to punish a child to another person, for example, to a school teacher.[24]

*Marriage of child without parent's consent.* The common law established the age of consent to the marriage contract at 14 years for males

---

[21] *Cory v. Cooke,* 24 R.I. 421, 53 A. 315.
[22] *In re Ryder,* 11 Paige 185.
[23] *Esteb v. Esteb,* 138 Wash. 174, 182, 244 P. 264, 246 P. 27.
[24] *Rowe v. Rugg,* 117 Iowa 606, 91 N.W. 903.

and 12 years for females. Many of our states, by statute, have fixed this age at 18 for both sexes; some states, at 21 for both sexes, and others, at 21 for males and 18 for females. Marriages below the age of consent are generally deemed voidable by legal action on the part of the parents, hence valid unless declared void in court. Parents may thus assert control in such cases; in some states, not without prior annulment, in others, even before.

*Right to services and earnings of child.* The father's duty to support carries with it the right to services and earnings. This right the father may relinquish, lose or abandon. He may relinquish the right by expressly authorizing the child to make his own arrangement for employment elsewhere, or by employing the child and paying him for his services though not obliged to do so. He may lose the right by neglecting to provide for the child's support, or he may abandon it by allowing the child to shift for himself, as in the case of emancipation (see below).

Under some statutes, the parent must serve written notice on the child's employer that he makes claim to the wages earned, otherwise payment to the child is valid.

*Right to recover for injuries to child.* If a child sustains injuries through the wrongful act or omission of a third party, a parent may not only bring suit as guardian on behalf of the child, but also in his own name for any damages sustained, such as medical, hospital or nursing expenses, as well as "loss of services," though no actual services were being rendered by the child to his parent at the time of the injury.

*Emancipation of child.* A child is said to be legally "emancipated" if he is freed from the parent's custody and control, thereby simultaneously relieving the parent of his duty of support and entitling the child to his own earnings. Emancipation may be brought about: (1) by parental consent, (2) by entering the armed forces, (3) by marriage, (4) by parental failure of support, (5) by death of parents, and (6) by arrival at majority.

**Guardian and Ward.** Besides the natural guardianship of parents, other forms of guardianship include (1) legal guardian, (2) testamentary guardian, (3) guardian by deed, (4) special guardian, and (5) guardian *ad litem*.

**1.** *Legal guardian.* As previously stated, a parent, as natural guardian, has custody of his child's *person* but not of his *property*. If an infant has property, the court appoints a legal guardian (usually, but not necessarily, the parent). The legal guardian must give bond for faithful management, must keep true accounts and file periodic reports with the court, must conform to law as to proper depositaries of funds and proper forms of investment, must not sell or mortgage the ward's real property without court order, and must reasonably safeguard the ward's property on pain of damages for improvident losses.

**2.** *Testamentary guardian.* In most states a father and in some states a mother may by will appoint a guardian for a minor child, such guardianship extending to both person and property of the ward until the latter's majority.

**3. *Guardian by deed.*** A guardian by deed is similar to a testamentary guardian except that appointment is by deed instead of by will. Statutory provisions in some states, copying an early English statute, permit a father to appoint a guardian, by deed, for his infant child, until the latter attains full age.

**4. *Special guardian; "committees for the insane."*** A special guardian is one named by the court (usually an attorney at law) to protect the rights of an infant concerned in probate proceedings or having an interest in a decedent estate. A person appointed by a court to take over, manage and control the estate of an insane ward is sometimes referred to as a "committee." Such person, like a special guardian, is an officer of the court and is charged with the duty of protecting the interests of his insane ward.

**5. *Guardian ad litem.*** An infant may not sue or be sued in his own name. If court action is desired by or against an infant, a guardian *ad litem* or "guardian to the action" must first be designated by the court to sue or defend on behalf of the infant.

**Master and Servant.** The relationship of master and servant was originally domestic, because upon "indenture" of the servant or apprentice to a master, the latter was made to stand in the place of the parent. This domestic relationship has been almost completely superseded by the contractual relationship of employer and employee (Chapter 10).

**Contract-Created Rights and Duties.** The rights and duties arising out of contract-created relationships, including the manifold types of transactions originating in contract, such as sales, bailments, transportation (carriers), guaranty and suretyship, insurance, principal and agent, employer and employee, partnership, and so forth, will be considered at length in succeeding chapters.

**Wrongs, Civil and Criminal.** A wrong is the violation of some right or duty. Wrongs are either *civil* or *criminal*, although the same act may constitute both a civil and criminal wrong; for example, injuring a person by assault and battery, or by reckless driving. Civil wrongs invade private rights and duties, and hence concern individuals privately rather than the public as a whole. Such wrongs are therefore redressed by private actions, as in *Johnson v. Baker* or *Carr v. Rhodes*, wherein the remedy sought may be at common law for damages or in equity for other forms of redress. Among the more common civil wrongs are *torts* and *breaches of contract*. A criminal wrong, or crime, invades some public right or duty, hence is prosecuted by the people; thus, *People v. Jones*, or *People v. Smith*.

Torts are discussed in Chapter 20, and crimes in Chapter 21. Breaches of contract are discussed at the end of Chapter 2.

## Questions

1. What is meant by the statement that rights and duties are reciprocal?
2. What are the so-called natural rights?
3. What are the so-called conventional rights?
4. Describe the right of personal security. How may this right be violated?
5. Explain the right of habeas corpus. Give an illustration of two situations in which such a right may be exercised.
6. What is embraced within the so-called domestic relations?
7. To what extent may it be said that the law no longer limits a married woman in respect to her rights as a free agent?
8. Who has the duty of family support? Are there any exceptions to the rule in this respect?
9. Is a husband entitled to the earnings of his wife under any and all circumstances? Explain.
10. May a husband and wife freely enter into contracts with each other?
11. What is meant by the term natural guardian? What rights and duties are involved in the relationship between a natural guardian and his ward?
12. What is the effect of adoption so far as concerns the rights and duties of the adopted child's former and new parents, and the rights and duties of the adopted child?
13. On whom is the duty to support infant children? What, if any, are the exceptions to this duty?
14. Describe the parent's duty to educate his children. What types of education are included in this duty?
15. When, if at all, does the law impose liability for the torts of a child (a) upon the parent, (b) upon the child?
16. As between father and mother, who has the right of custody and control of the children under ordinary circumstances? When, if at all, does the law make exceptions to the rule?
17. To what extent, if at all, does the law permit a parent to punish his child?
18. To what extent may a parent regulate, control or prohibit marriage on the part of an infant child?
19. Under what circumstances, if any, does a parent have the right to services and earnings of his child?
20. If an infant child is injured through fault of another, who may sue for consequent damages?
21. What is meant by the emancipation of a child, and under what circumstances may it be brought about?
22. Apart from natural guardianship, name and describe five other classes of guardianship.
23. Distinguish between civil and criminal wrongs. Describe two types of civil wrongs.

## Problems

1. The town of Jonesboro passes an ordinance making all traffic violations punishable by imprisonment for not less than ten days nor more than thirty days. A stranger motoring through the town passes a partially concealed traffic light, is arrested, and sentenced to thirty days in jail. He is advised by counsel that the ordinance under which he is imprisoned is unconstitutional, and that

his only remedy is by an appeal, which, however, will afford him no relief, since he will be out of jail before the appeal can be heard. Has the motorist no other remedy?

2. John Smith is the proprietor of an antique shop. Mary Smith, his wife, an experienced interior decorator, assists him in running the shop. Both John and Mary Smith have their home at the rear of the shop. Mary Smith insists that she is entitled to compensation at the rate of $50 a week, that being the salary she has received for similar work during the five years prior to her marriage. Is Mary Smith legally entitled to such compensation? Explain.

3. Janie Blossom is a child motion picture star. Up to her tenth birthday her accumulated earnings amounted to $1,000,000. John Blossom, her father, insists that inasmuch as he is her father, and hence her natural guardian, he has a right to the custody of this money without the necessity of going through legal proceedings for this purpose. Is John Blossom's position sound? Give reasons.

4. Young Copperfield, aged 17, unwilling to submit to discipline by his father, runs away from home. Being mechanically inclined, he obtains a good position as an automobile mechanic. The father, relieved of the necessity of supporting his son, makes no objection, but writes to the boy's employer requiring the son's wages to be paid directly to the father. If the employer should refuse to pay over the boy's wages directly to the father, can the father compel the employer to do so? How do you support your answer?

5. Martin Murdstone, a mining engineer, while on an exploring expedition in South America, is lost in the heart of the jungle. His companions give him up for dead. His wife, Helen Murdstone, is left with a two year old infant, Frank, whom she is unable to support owing to ill health. William and Betsy Barkis, a childless couple, with the consent of the infant's mother, legally adopt Frank as their own child. Two months later, the infant's mother dies. In the meantime, Frank's father, contrary to the belief of his companions, has survived, and after acquiring valuable mining property in his own right, dies of jungle fever, leaving, in addition to his infant son, two brothers and a sister, who now claim to be entitled to the wealth left by their brother. The child's foster parents, on behalf of the child, insist that he is entitled to inherit his father's estate. How will the court decide this dispute and why?

6. James Johnson, an infant 19 years of age, borrowed an automobile belonging to a friend, and while driving the car recklessly through traffic, injured an infant pedestrian, Walter Brown, who thereafter personally brought suit for damages against (a) James Johnson and (b) John Johnson, his father. How should this case be decided and why?

7. Henry Hughes, in a violent fit of temper, chastises his ten year old boy for killing a cat with an air rifle. As a result the boy is rendered deaf in one of his ears. His mother, after taking the boy to a physician, brings him to an attorney's office for advice as to what the boy's remedies might be against his father. What advice do you think the attorney would give to the mother?

8. Harry White, aged 19, and Gladys White, aged 18, without the knowledge or consent of their respective parents, are married by a justice of the peace after procuring a license for such purpose. May the parents have such marriage annulled?

9. George Black, an infant 12 years of age, is injured through the negligence of Amos Brown. George's father brings suit as guardian ad litem for his boy, and he also brings a suit on his own behalf wherein he asks for damages sustained because of medical and hospital expenses incurred by reason of George's

injuries; also damages for loss of services. On the trial, the attorney for Amos Brown asks the court to charge the jury that in view of the fact established on the trial that George Black was too young to render services, and in fact had never rendered any services of material value to his father, the jury could not award damages for the alleged loss of services. How would the court rule on such an application?

10. Harold Green, an infant 20 years of age, under the last will and testament of his grandfather, James Green, has inherited a palatial summer home. Being in need of cash, he decides to sell the home. He procures a customer, Samuel Strong. Upon payment of the purchase price, he executes and delivers a deed to Strong conveying title to the property. Later, Samuel Strong sells the property to Robert Smith, but Smith's attorney, on the closing, refuses to allow his client to take title to the premises on the ground that the title is defective. What is your comment on this situation?

## COURT CASES FOR REVIEW

### How Did the Court Decide, and Why?

1. Plaintiff's wife instituted proceedings against him. Plaintiff, to avoid his obligation to support his wife, placed his real property in the name of a friend. Later, the friend refused to return the property. Plaintiff sued in equity to get the property back. *Bascombe v. Sargent*, 195 Misc. 328, 90 N.Y. Supp. 2d 113.

2. Green is arrested under a clearly unconstitutional ordinance. He seeks a release by court action, but such release is denied him. The question thereupon arose, whether his further remedy under the circumstances was by appeal, or otherwise. *Ex parte Green*, 114 Fed. 959.

3. Plaintiff, a child of eight, brought a damage suit through his father against his aunt for corporal punishment administered by the aunt. The punishment was not excessive. The mother had delegated authority to the aunt to administer the punishment. The question raised was whether a mother, while the father was alive and head of the family, could delegate such authority to another. *Rowe v. Rugg*, 117 Iowa 606, 91 N.W. 903.

4. Scott, of full age, and Sadie Lowell, 13 years and 11 months old, were married without the consent of the latter's parents. The father went to the husband's house, forcibly took his daughter away against her wishes, and kept her confined. The husband sued out a writ of habeas corpus. The referee found: (1) that the husband was industrious; (2) that he had a home and was able to support a family; and (3) that the girl was ready and anxious to return to and live with her husband. The respective rights of husband and wife were raised on appeal. *Spate v. Lowell*, 79 Minn. 166, 80 N.W. 877.

5. A minor son, without his father's consent, secured employment with a third person. The father, knowing of such employment, neither objected to it, nor made demand that the wages be paid directly to him. Later, the father sought to enforce his right to his son's earnings. *Culberson v. Ala. Constr. Co.*, 127 Ga. 599, 56 S.E. 765.

6. A minor, by an appropriate proceeding in the state in which she resided, obtained a decree of full emancipation, with power to perform all acts as fully as if she had attained majority. She then applied to a New York court for a decree directing her guardian to distribute and to deliver to her, assets in a New York estate. *In re Rayner*, 92 N.Y. Supp. 2d 105.

7. The charter of a bridge company required it to enlarge its draws when necessary for the accommodation of navigation. Later, the legislature sought

to determine whether such draws were suitable. The power of the legislature to do this was questioned in a court proceeding. *Com. v. New Bedford Bridge,* 2 Gray (Mass.) 339.

8. An act of the Mississippi legislature authorized the Governor, on proof that a bank had refused to pay its note, to issue a proclamation declaring the bank's charter forfeited. The validity of this measure was called into question. *Campbell v. State Union Bank,* 7 Miss. 625.

9. The State of New York adopted an emergency rent law effective January 24, 1945, fixing maximum commercial rents at a level of 15% above rents charged on March 1, 1943. Plaintiff sued to recover rent under a lease executed prior to the effective date of the emergency rent law. From a judgment dismissing its complaint, plaintiff appealed, challenging the constitutionality of the law as impairing the obligation of contracts. *Twentieth Century v. Waldman,* 294 N.Y. 571, 63 N.E. 2d 177.

10. A narcotics addict consented to the use of a stomach pump and emetic by state officers to recover contraband narcotics which were subsequently used by federal officers to procure a conviction, pursuant to which the addict was restrained. He sought a release on habeas corpus on the ground that his constitutional right to protection against unlawful searches and seizures had been violated. *In re Guzzardi,* 84 Fed. Supp. 294.

11. Certain law enforcement officers obtained a search warrant describing intoxicating liquors and articles for their manufacture. Armed with this warrant they seized a ledger and bills of account found in a search of the premises specified in the warrant. This seizure was challenged as unconstitutional. *Byars v. United States,* 273 U.S. 28.

12. A jury wished to look at a prisoner's face in order to compare his features with a photograph offered in evidence. The prisoner objected on the ground that his constitutional privilege of protection against self-incrimination had been violated. *Holt v. United States,* 218 U.S. 245.

# 2

# Contracts

**Scope of This Chapter.** In this chapter we consider (1) the formation of contracts, and its basic requisites, including (a) mutual assent, (b) competency of parties, (c) consideration and (d) valid subject matter, with additional comment on Sunday contracts and the effect of invalid subject matter; (2) the classification and form of contracts; (3) contracts which must be in writing under the statute of frauds and the extent to which written contracts may be modified by oral testimony; (4) the operation and effect of contracts, including (a) their interpretation, and (b) the extent to which they may be transferred by *assignment* or superseded by *novation;* (5) the termination or discharge of contracts, (a) by performance, (b) by agreement, (c) by operation of law, and (d) by breach; (6) damages for breach of contract; and (7) agreements by which disputes may be settled by arbitration.

### PART 1. FORMATION AND REQUISITES: MUTUAL ASSENT

**Definition and Nature.** A contract is defined as an agreement upon sufficient consideration to do or refrain from doing some lawful thing. The agreement must create an obligation. This obligation takes the form of a binding promise, expressed in words or implied from conduct. To be binding, the promise must have been given in exchange for something of value, such as an act (paying money, delivering merchandise, rendering service), or a promise to do the act, or else the giving up of some right, privilege, or benefit. Such a thing of value is termed *consideration* (page 50).

**Requisites of Contract.** There are certain requisites which every contract must have; if it lacks any one of these, it is void. These requisites are: *mutual assent, parties* with capacity to contract, *consideration* and *valid subject matter.* To these, the additional elements of *time* and *form* are sometimes added. In the sense that every contract involves the element of time, it may be said that time is a requisite of every contract. More accurately, however, time is a condition, express or implied, governing the performance of every contract. Nor is it requisite to a contract that it be in any particular form, except with respect to the requirement that

33

certain contracts, to be enforceable, must be evidenced by a writing, and that in certain jurisdictions contracts, for some purposes, they must be under seal.

These requisites or elements of a contract may be illustrated in the following example:

**In consideration of the sum of $250** in hand paid by **Richard Green to Harry**
        *[Consideration]*                               *[Parties]*
**Brown**, receipt whereof is hereby acknowledged, **it is hereby mutually agreed**
                                      *[Mutual Assent]*
that Harry Brown is to ship and deliver to Richard Green at his said address, **1,000 pounds of Rio coffee,** superfine blend, **not later than 12 o'clock noon,**
   *[Subject Matter]*                                   *[Time]*
**June 1, 1954.**

The *form* of the contract given in the above example may be oral or written.

**Mutual Assent.** Mutual assent consists of two things: an offer and an acceptance. The offer itself must conform to certain requisites. The acceptance must meet the offer exactly, otherwise the assent is not mutual: no contract results.

**Requisites of Offer.** An offer, to serve as the basis for a contract, (a) must be seriously intended as such, (b) must be communicated to the person who is to accept it, and (c) must be definite and certain.

**Offer Must Be Intended as Such: Invitations to Trade.** An offer must be intended as the basis of a valid obligation. This excludes offers involving social functions, such as theater or dinner parties, and so on. It also excludes "invitations to trade." Price lists, circular letters and most advertisements are construed as invitations to trade.[1] So are most offers to sell an indefinite quantity of merchandise.

EXAMPLE: A storekeeper contracts with a newspaper to publish an advertisement of its merchandise, including items priced at $15 each. The price is erroneously published as $5 instead of $15. The storekeeper, refusing to pay for the advertisement, asserts a claim against the newspaper for losses sustained through having to sell his articles at $5 instead of $15. The claim is unfounded. The storekeeper was not obliged to accept such losses. His advertisement did not constitute an offer but only an invitation to trade.

**Offer Must Be Communicated.** One cannot accept an offer of which he has no knowledge.

A *particular offer* is one made to a particular person or persons. An offer made to one person cannot be accepted by another.

A *general offer* is one addressed to the public, as by a newspaper advertisement, poster, bulletin, and so on. Offers of reward are frequently thus made. A general offer of reward for the doing of an act is not accepted where one does the act without knowledge of the offer.

---

[1] *Nickel v. Theresa Farmers Coop. Ass'n*, 247 Wis. 412, 20 N.W. 2d 171.

EXAMPLE: Carter publishes an offer of reward for information leading to the discovery of the murderer of his brother. Martin, without knowledge of the reward, gives the desired information. Later, upon learning of the reward, he sues to recover it. His suit must fail.

**Signing without Reading.** If an offer is brought to the attention of an offeree in such a way that a person of ordinary intelligence would be presumed to have knowledge of it, communication of such an offer will be presumed. Hence, if one accepts a written offer, as by signing a paper, and later claims he had no fair opportunity to read it, he is bound by his acceptance and cannot shelter himself behind the defense of ignorance, even if in fact he did not read the offer he accepted. Inability to read what one signs because of defective eyesight is no defense if one signs notwithstanding.

*Signature procured by fraud.* If a signature is procured by fraud, the offeree is not bound. Hence, a contract procured by trickery is unenforceable.

EXAMPLE: In *Wilcox v. American Telephone & Telegraph Co.,*[2] a farmer was induced by the Company's agent to sign a paper represented to be a receipt. In reality the paper was a document giving the Company a right to erect poles on the farmer's land. The court refused to recognize the document because of the trickery, though the farmer had an opportunity to read it. Had the farmer signed through ignorance, but without trickery, he would have been bound.

*Inconspicuous type.* If an offer contains terms so inconspicuous that the average person would be unlikely to see them, such terms may be presumed not to have been communicated. Matter printed in small type on the back or at the foot of a letterhead or billhead, or in the margin of office stationery, may be deemed excluded because insufficiently communicated, unless attention is called to it in the body of the writing.

**Offer Must Be Definite and Certain.** Vague and indefinite offers cannot furnish the basis for acceptance; otherwise it would be difficult to determine whether a breach was committed.

EXAMPLES:
(1) B hires A on a salary of $40 a week plus a "fair share of the profits of the business."
(2) A buyer agrees "to give the 'R. S.' brand cement the preference" in his sales for the year 1948, and in consideration thereof, the seller agrees "to sell said brand of cement to the first party during the year 1948 at the price of 95 cents a bbl. f.o.b. Haverstraw, New York." Each of these proposals, viewed as an offer, is too vague and indefinite to furnish the basis for an acceptance.

**Form of Offer.** Offers may be oral or written. Oral offers are those made by word of mouth: face to face, by telephone or by radio. Written offers are those made by letter, telegram, advertisement, or other written

---

[2] 176 N.Y. 115.

medium, as by presenting a formal contract for signature (see Form 1, Letter Contract).

FORM 1

**LETTER CONTRACT**

**PERFECT PLASTIC CORPORATION**
1000 Main Street
Newark, New Jersey

August 18, 1954

Mr. Robert Blake,
45 Chestnut Street,
Mapleville, N.J.

Dear Sir:

This letter will confirm our understanding that you are to be employed as a salesman of plastic products manufactured by us including any other articles which we may deem necessary to further the sale of such products, upon the following terms:

1. Your territory is to include the entire State of New Jersey.

2. You are to devote all your time, attention and energy to the performance of your duties as such salesman, subject to direction and instruction from us. During the period of your employment with us, you are not either directly or indirectly to represent or be employed by any other person, firm, association or corporation.

3. You are to sell our products at such prices as we shall fix. We agree that such prices will not differ materially from the prices at which similar goods are sold by competitors.

4. You are to receive ten per cent (10%) commissions on all sales made by you, said commissions to be paid on or about the first day of the month following receipt of payment from your customers; except for a drawing account of fifty ($50) dollars a week, which shall be paid you on Monday of each week and which shall be deducted from your commissions. We are to pay all travelling expenses reasonably and necessarily incurred by you in connection with your duties outside of the City of Newark.

5. All sales shall be either on a cash basis or on the basis of credit not to exceed thirty (30) days from the date of delivery. A discount of two per cent (2%) may be allowed on payments made within ten (10) days from the date of delivery. Your commissions shall in all cases be figured on the net amounts received from your customers.

6. Your employment is to commence on the first day of September, 1954. It may be terminated by either of us upon sixty (60) days written notice.

If the foregoing terms are satisfactory, kindly return this letter with your signature at the foot hereof as indicated, retaining the enclosed signed copy. This letter will constitute the entire agreement between us.

Very truly yours,

PLASTIC PRODUCTS CORPORATION

By: *William Whitney*
General Sales Manager

WW:RS

I hereby accept the foregoing employment upon the terms hereinabove set forth.

*Robert Blake*

Dated *August 19, 1954*

**Disposition of Offer.** Three things may happen to an offer: It may be *revoked, rejected* or *accepted.* We shall consider the effect of each of these upon the offer.

**Revocation of Offer.** An offer may always be revoked (withdrawn) before it is accepted, with three exceptions: (1) In all states a promise to hold an offer open for a given time (namely, an *option*) is binding provided the promise is based on consideration; (2) in some states (New York, for example) a *written* option is binding without consideration (page 60); and (3) in a few states (reflecting the common law rule) an option under seal is binding because a seal, under the common law, imports consideration.

EXAMPLE: *A* offers to sell *B* three dozen hats of a given description, at a given price, on given terms. *A* also agrees that the offer is to remain irrevocable for two weeks. The offer may be revoked at any time before it is accepted, with the exceptions noted above.

An offer may be revoked in the following ways:

*Expressly.* If I have made you an offer and no longer wish to be bound by it, I owe you the duty of communicating my revocation to you. But whether I have communicated the revocation or not, if you learn (no matter how) that the offer is no longer open, you cannot accept it.[3] General offers may be revoked in the same way they were made. For example, today I advertise a $50 reward in a newspaper for the return of a lost ring, and tomorrow I advertise a revocation in the same newspaper; you see the first advertisement but not the second, then find the ring. You cannot collect the reward.

*By lapse of specified time.* When a time is fixed for acceptance, the offer is deemed revoked by lapse of such time. However, with the exceptions noted, one may revoke an offer even before expiration of the time fixed for acceptance.

*By lapse of reasonable time.* An offer automatically lapses if not accepted within a reasonable time. What constitutes a reasonable time depends on the circumstances.

*By death or insanity.* An offer (unless first accepted) lapses upon death or insanity of the offeror or offeree. There can be no offer without a mind behind it.

**Rejection of Offer.** An offer is extinguished by rejection. It cannot thereafter be accepted unless renewed.

EXAMPLES: (1) *Flat rejection: A* offers to buy 100 barrels of flour from *B* at $15 a barrel on twenty days' credit. *B* refuses.

(2) *Rejection by counteroffer: A* offers to buy 100 barrels of flour from *B* at $15 a barrel on twenty days' credit. *B* first replies, "I accept your order and will ship the goods, *but on ten days' credit*"; and later, after *A* receives this letter, *B* writes again, "I have reconsidered, and will allow twenty days' credit.

---

[3] *Masonic Temple v. Ebert,* 199 S.C. 5, 18 S.E. 2d 584.

Am shipping the goods." *A* need not accept the goods. *B*'s first counteroffer rejected *A*'s offer.

**Acceptance.** Acceptance of an offer constitutes a meeting of minds and results in a contract. But the acceptance must be unqualified, and must conform with the terms of the offer. Thus, if the offer specifies that acceptance must be made in some particular way, as by mail, telegraph, cable, and so on, it must be made in that way.[4] If the offer specifies no mode of acceptance, it may be accepted in any way, provided the acceptance is actually communicated to the offeror.[5]

**Offer and Acceptance by Mail, Telegraph, Cable, and so on.** Offers, acceptances, revocations and rejections by mail, telegraph, cable, and so on, can be understood better if we consider the following hypothetical situations, in which *A* and *B* have no way of intercommunication except by messenger:

(a) *A* sends an offer to *B* by messenger, and before *B* accepts, *A* sends another messenger to revoke the offer. The second messenger arrives with his revocation before *B* accepts. The revocation is communicated—the offer is withdrawn—*B* can no longer accept.

(b) If *B* gives the first messenger an acceptance while *A*'s second messenger is on his way with a revocation but before he actually delivers it to *B*, there is a contract, and the revocation, when it arrives, is too late.

(c) If *A*'s first messenger departs right after delivering the offer without waiting for an acceptance and *B* sends his own messenger to accept the offer, the acceptance is not effective until it is actually delivered to *A*; and if *B*'s messenger tarries on the way or loses the message and *A* in the meantime sends his messenger back to *B* with a revocation, there can be no acceptance after the revocation is delivered: *B* must look to his own messenger for redress.

(d) If *A*'s offer stipulates that it can be accepted only by delivering an acceptance to *A*'s messenger, *B* cannot accept through a different messenger.

(e) If *A*'s offer stipulates that he is not to be bound by an acceptance unless and until *A*'s messenger returns and delivers the acceptance to him, there is no contract until the acceptance is actually brought back to *A* by *A*'s messenger.

The foregoing hypothetical situations may now be adapted to offers by mail, wire or cable. If I employ any of these agencies to communicate an offer and if I do not prescribe a particular mode of acceptance, you may accept by the same or any other agency. If you accept by the *same* agency (*my* agent), the acceptance becomes effective when it is delivered

---

[4] *Folz v. Evans*, 113 Ind. App. 596, 49 N.E. 2d 358.

[5] This is also the modern rule reflected in the provision of the Uniform Commercial Code (Article 2, Sales, sec. 2-206) that acceptance may be "in any manner and by any medium reasonable in the circumstances." (See digest of Code in Appendix.)

to such agency,[6] that is, when it is mailed or delivered to the telegraph or cable company, as the case may be. If I *mail* you an offer and you *wire* an acceptance, I am not bound if your wire is lost in transmission; you must look to *your* agent for redress.[7] An offer by mail may be withdrawn or rejected so long as it has not already been thus accepted.

EXAMPLES:

(1) *A* wires an offer to *B* at 9 A.M. which is received by *B* at 11:15 A.M. *B* wires an acceptance at 12:45 P.M. which reaches *A* at 4:15 P.M. At 2 P.M., however, *A* had wired a revocation which reached *B* at 3 P.M. Is there a contract?

There is. *A*'s revocation was communicated two hours and fifteen minutes after *B*'s acceptance.

(2) *A* in New York makes an offer by mail to *B* in Buffalo. *B* posts an acceptance and later wires a withdrawal of the acceptance. *B*'s wire reaches *A* before the letter. Is there a contract?

Yes. *B*'s wire, though it reached *A* first, could not destroy the contract which arose on posting the acceptance (unless *A* acquiesced in *B*'s withdrawal).

(3) *A* in New York air mails an offer on Monday to *B* in San Francisco, which *B* receives on Tuesday morning. Immediately on receiving *A*'s offer, *B* sends a night letter accepting *A*'s offer, which reaches *A* on Wednesday. On Tuesday afternoon, however, *A* wires *B* withdrawing his offer. That wire reaches *B* Tuesday night, ten hours after *B* sent his night letter. Is there a contract?

No. When *B* accepted by night letter (telegraph company) instead of by mail, he chose his own agent, or agency, to deliver his acceptance, and such acceptance was not complete until it actually reached *A*. Had *B* accepted by air mail, or even by ordinary mail, acceptance would have been complete on posting. (Had *A* specified that acceptance must be by air mail only, there could have been no acceptance at all except by air mail.)

(4) On October 10th *A* mails an offer to *B* to sell 150 tons of Steel Filings, Second Grade, at $66.50 a ton, "subject to actual receipt of your acceptance at this office by mail not later than the 21st inst." *B* receives this offer on October 12th. He mails an immediate acceptance which, however, is lost in the mails. Is there a contract?

There is not. The offer required actual receipt of acceptance.

*Acceptance after rejection.* On principle, the offeree's rejection, like his acceptance, should become effective on delivery to the offeror's agency. This, however, is not the rule. "Rejection by mail or telegram does not destroy the power of acceptance until received by the offeror but limits the power so that a letter or telegram of acceptance started after the sending of the rejection is only a counteroffer unless the acceptance is received by the offeror before he receives the rejection." [8]

EXAMPLE: *A* makes *B* an offer by mail. *B* immediately mails a letter of rejection. Then, within the time permitted by the offer, *B* accepts. This acceptance creates a contract if received before the rejection.

---

[6] *L. & E. Wertheimer v. Wehle-Hartford Co.*, 126 Conn. 30, 9 A. 2d 279; *State of Ohio ex rel. Squire v. Eubank*, 295 Mich. 230, 294 N.W. 166; *Dick v. Vogt*, 196 Okl. 66, 162 P. 2d 325; *McKinney v. Croan* (Tex.) 188 S.W. 2d 144, 145.

[7] See page 38, note 5.

[8] *Restatement of Law of Contracts*, sec. 39.

**Auctions.** Auctions are governed by the following rules relating to offer and acceptance: the auctioneer merely calls for offers; the bidder makes the offer; and acceptance is complete when the hammer falls.

**Silence No Acceptance.** An offeror cannot compel an offeree to speak or act, on penalty of construing silence as acceptance.

EXAMPLE: A stationery store voluntarily delivers a package of analysis paper at the office of an accountant, with a sealed letter stating that unless the paper is returned in 10 days the accountant will be deemed to have accepted it at the price stated. The package and letter are accepted by the accountant's clerk as a matter of routine. Assuming that there have been no prior transactions in which the accountant has accepted and used paper in this manner (which might create an inference of acceptance based on prior conduct), the accountant is not liable for the paper; neither is he required to answer the letter or return the package. (Of course, if the accountant reads the letter and uses the paper, he voluntarily accepts the terms stated in the letter.)

**Agreements to Agree.** An agreement to reach an agreement is no agreement at all. Mutual assent must be voluntary. The law cannot *compel* a *voluntary* assent. Hence an agreement to agree has no force in law.

**Agreement to Formalize Agreement.** Where the parties have informally reached substantial agreement on terms with the intention of embodying such agreement into a formal contract, the informal agreement is binding though the formal agreement is never drawn up or executed.[9] To this rule, however, there are several exceptions:

(a) Where parties do not intend the informal agreement to be binding unless and until the formal agreement is executed.

(b) Where the informal agreement is insufficient in law, as in the cases governed by the statute of frauds (pages 85-88).

An informal writing, if sufficiently definite as to terms, may constitute a binding contract though it provides for a subsequent formal writing.

EXAMPLE: A document entitled "Articles of agreement," duly executed, states that the parties have agreed to execute a formal lease of specified premises, for a specified term, at a specified rental; the lease to contain "the usual and proper covenants" as to possession, surrender and delivery, warranty, re-entry and so on, "in brief, all the usual and formal clauses to the mutual satisfaction of the parties." Such writing is binding though it is never followed by a formal lease. It expresses with sufficient definiteness the intention of the parties. Since mutual assent is substantially complete, the expression "to the mutual satisfaction of the parties" obviously refers to the choice of mutually satisfactory words to express their assent.

---

[9] *Cowin v. Salmon*, 244 Ala. 285, 13 So. 2d 190; *Clarke v. Fiedler*, 44 Cal. App. 2d 838, 113 P. 2d 775; *Socony-Vacuum Oil Co. v. Elion*, 126 Conn. 310, 11 A. 2d 5; *Micheletti v. Fuggitt*, 61 Nev. 478, 134 P. 2d 99; *Moran v. Fifteenth Ward Building & Loan Ass'n*, 131 N.J. Eq. 361, 25 A. 2d. 426; *North American Managers v. Reinach*, 177 Va. 116, 12 S.E. 2d 806.

## Questions

1. "A contract is a promise which creates a binding obligation." Comment on this statement, and explain the difference between a promise which is binding and one which is not.

2. What are the requisites of every contract? Are these requisites necessary regardless of the form, nature, subject or importance of the contract? Explain.

3. What constitutes mutual assent?

4. Name three requisites of a valid offer.

5. Distinguish between a valid offer and an invitation to trade.

6. Distinguish between a particular and a general offer.

7. By whom must a particular offer be accepted in order to constitute mutual assent?

8. Can you accept an offer of which you have no knowledge?

9. If you sign an agreement without reading it, can you disclaim liability under the agreement if you were unaware of its contents?

10. With reference to Question 9, explain the relevance of (a) signatures procured by fraud, and (b) inconspicuous type.

11. Why must an offer be definite and certain?

12. What are the different ways in which an offer may be made?

13. What three things may happen to an offer?

14. When may an offer be revoked, and when not?

15. In what four ways may an offer be revoked?

16. If an offer is rejected, may the rejection be withdrawn and the offer then accepted without further action on the part of the offeror?

17. Does every acceptance of an offer constitute a meeting of minds? Explain.

18. If an offer is made by mail, telegraph or cable, does it have to be accepted that way? Explain.

19. When goods are sold at auction, who makes the offer, who accepts it, and how is the acceptance indicated?

20. "Silence gives consent." Comment on this statement with respect to the law of contracts.

21. Is "an agreement to reach an agreement" binding? Explain.

22.** If an offer is made by mail, when is the offer completed? If an acceptance is to be made by mail, when is the acceptance completed? May either the offer or the acceptance be withdrawn? Explain.

## Problems

1.* Prepare a simple contract with the essential elements arranged in separate paragraphs. Point out the essential elements.

2.* A retail storekeeper contracted with a newspaper to publish an advertisement in which certain articles were listed at the price of $15 each. The newspaper negligently and erroneously printed the price of these articles as $5 each. The newspaper sued the storekeeper for the contract price of the advertisement. The storekeeper set up a counterclaim that he was obliged by law to sell the articles at $5 instead of at $15 and that he thereby incurred a heavy loss. Was his counterclaim a valid defense?

---

** Official question, New York Board of C.P.A. Examiners. All questions and problems from this source will be similarly marked throughout the book.

* Official problem, American Institute of Accountancy. All questions and problems from this source will be similarly marked throughout the book.

3.** *C* published an offer of a reward for information leading to the discovery of the murderer of his brother. The reward was payable on conviction of the criminal. *M*, without knowledge of the reward offered and being in fear of death, gave the desired information. *M*, on regaining his health, sues to recover the reward. Will he succeed? Explain.

4.* On May 1, 1927, Shearman signed and sealed a formal written offer to sell to Allen at any time on or before May 15, 1927, certain merchandise at a specified price. On May 5, 1927, Shearman wrote Allen that the offer was canceled and withdrawn. Upon receipt of that letter on May 6, 1927, Allen formally accepted the offer and thereafter sued to enforce the contract. What decision would you render in the action?

5.* *A* in writing offers to sell to *B* three dozen hats. The description of the hats, the price of them and the terms of the proposed sale are all set forth in the offer and are all sufficiently definite for a contract. *A* also states in the offer as follows:

I agree that this offer will remain open for two weeks and that I cannot revoke it until the expiration of that time.

At the end of one week *A* writes *B* that he revokes the offer. In reply *B* writes to *A* that he accepts the offer to sell as stated in *A*'s original letter. This letter is received by *A* before the expiration of the two weeks. Is there a contract?

6.* *A* sent an order by mail to *B* for 100 barrels of flour at $15 a barrel on twenty days' credit. *B* replied, saying, "I accept your order and will ship the goods, but on ten days' credit." *A* received this letter and made no reply. After *A*'s receipt of the letter, *B* wrote again, saying: "I have reconsidered the matter and will allow twenty days' credit. Am shipping the goods." *A* refused to receive or pay for the goods. Is *A* liable?

7.* *X* wrote to *Y* offering to sell *Y* 2000 three-inch boiler tubes for $2.25 each. *Y* replied, "I will buy 1200 tubes at your price." *Y* claimed that a contract was made and that *X* was bound to deliver the 1200 tubes. Was he?

8.** *A* wired an offer to sell oil to *B*. The telegram was sent at 9 A.M. and received by *B* in due course at 11:15 A.M. *B* wired his acceptance at 12:45 P.M., and it reached *A* in due course at 4:15 P.M. At 2 P.M. of the same day, *A* had wired a revocation of his offer, which reached *B* at 3 P.M. When, if at all, was a contract completed in this case?

9.* *A*, in New York, wrote *B* in Buffalo, offering certain goods for sale at a certain price. *B* wrote a letter to *A* accepting the offer and posted it in Buffalo. Before *A* received the letter he received a telegram from *B* stating that he withdrew the acceptance. Was a valid contract made? Explain the principles involved.

10.* On January 31, 1921, Travis & Wood, commission merchants at Buffalo, N.Y., wrote a letter to Vassar & Camp at New York, offering to sell 500 gallons of linseed oil at a certain price per gallon. The letter was received by Vassar & Camp on February 2, 1921, and on the same day they mailed a reply to Travis & Wood, accepting the offer and giving directions as to shipment. On February 3, before the receipt of the acceptance, Travis & Wood telegraphed, revoking the offer. Was the revocation effectual to prevent the consummation of the agreement?

11.* August 1, 1927, *A* in Baltimore by letter to *B* in New York offers to sell to *B* 500 bushels of potatoes. The price, description, terms, and place of delivery are all set forth in the letter and are sufficiently definite for a contract. On August 2, 1927, the price of potatoes rises, and *A* wires *B* that he revokes his offer of August 1, 1927. A few minutes before receiving this wire B had put in the mail a letter to A properly addressed and stamped in which he accepted A's offer. A does not receive this letter from B until after B has received A's wire. Was there a contract between A and B?

12.* At 11:30 A.M. Shaw wired Brauer, "Subject prompt reply will engage you to make audit $2200 fee." Brauer received this wire at 12:16 P.M. At 12:28 P.M. Brauer wired Shaw accepting the offer. At 1 P.M. Shaw had not received Brauer's wire and Shaw wired Brauer revoking his offer. At 1:43 P.M. Shaw received Brauer's wire accepting the offer. Was there a contract?

13.* A document entitled "Articles of Agreement," duly executed, stated that the parties to it agreed to execute a formal lease of certain specified real estate for a specified term of years at a specified rental. The document provided for "the usual and proper covenants" as to possession, surrender and delivery, warranty, re-entry and the like and recited that the lease was to contain "in brief, all of the usual and formal clauses to the mutual satisfaction of the parties." Did the phrase "to the mutual satisfaction of the parties" make the document indefinite, a mere agreement to agree, and thus unenforceable as a contract?

14.* A stationery company wrote to a certified public accountant that "We have quite a few pads of slightly defective but completely usable analysis paper which we now offer you at 45 cents per pad." The accountant wrote in reply: "I accept your offer and I will take one dozen pads." Do these two letters constitute a valid contract?

15.* Mason and Dana were negotiating and Mason's attorney prepared a long and carefully drawn contract which was given to Dana for examination. Five days later and prior to its execution, Dana's eyes became so infected that it was impossible for him to read. Ten days thereafter and during the continuance of the illness Mason called upon Dana and urged him to sign the contract, but without in any way misrepresenting the contents of it, and Dana signed without reading it. In a subsequent suit by Mason, Dana claimed that the contract was not binding upon him because he had not and could not have read it prior to his signing it. Is Dana's claim a valid defense?

16.* A stationery supply store voluntarily, and without request by the accountant, delivered by messenger to the accountant's office a package of analysis paper, together with a sealed envelope containing a letter stating that the paper was to be paid for at the price stated or returned within ten days. The package and letter were accepted as a matter of routine by the accountant's reception clerk, who did not know and had no way of knowing their contents. Is the accountant under any legal obligation to answer the letter or to return the package if he makes no use of the analysis paper?

17.* A calls B on the telephone and says: "I have fine apples at $5.00 a barrel." B says: "I will take two barrels."

(a) Is this a good contract?

(b) What effect, if any, would be created if the same words had been expressed on a signed letter by A to B with B's signed reply?

(c) What additional effect, if any, would be created by a more formal expression of the same conversation in a "memorandum of agreement" signed by both parties and properly witnessed?

18. Smith is a wholesale dealer in television equipment. Davis is a retail dealer in television sets and equipment. Both parties are friends. Smith agrees to sell Davis a quantity of television equipment, the nature, number and price of which are to be subsequently agreed upon and embodied in a written con-

tract. Thereafter Smith fails and refuses to enter into the specific agreement in question, in spite of repeated requests by Davis that he do so. May Davis hold Smith to his agreement?

## PART 2. REALITY OF ASSENT

**In General.** Mutual assent must consist of a real meeting of minds. Factors which may mar or even destroy the reality of mutual assent are *fraud, mistake, duress,* and *undue influence.*

**Fraud: Defined.** Both common law and equity have hesitated to define fraud, for fear, as the court declared in *Stonemets v. Head,*[10] that "were courts to cramp themselves by defining it with a hard-and-fast definition, their jurisdiction would be cunningly circumvented at once by new schemes beyond the definition." Nevertheless the cases teem with definitions of fraud. In the law of contracts, fraud is defined as a "reckless or intentional misrepresentation of material fact inducing one to contract to his injury."[11]

**Classifications of Fraud.** There are numerous classifications of fraud. These are by no means universally accepted as meaning the same thing in different jurisdictions. Among the more common classifications and distinctions are the following:

(a) *Fraud in the factum* (also known as fraud in the *procurement,* fraud in the *execution,* and fraud in the *inception*), which is said to exist when, by trickery, a person is made to sign a different instrument from the one intended, so that there is really no meeting of minds at all. The instrument in such case is a nullity; the contract is void, not *voidable* (see page 83). For an example, see page 35.

(b) *Fraud in the treaty* (also known as fraud in the *inducement,* or *antecedent* fraud) is fraud occurring during the negotiations which precede the making of the contract. The contract itself is the one intended to be made, but the reality of assent is marred by the antecedent fraud. Hence the contract is valid, but *voidable* at the option of the defrauded party.

(c) *Actual fraud* (as distinguished from *constructive fraud*) is fraud based on a misrepresentation of fact with intent to deceive.

(d) *Constructive fraud* (also known as *legal fraud,* or *fraud in law*) is based, not on a misrepresentation of fact, but on a false violation of duty. It exists—regardless of intent to deceive—as a matter of law declared by the court, not as a matter of fact determined by a jury. It frequently results from violation of a fiduciary relationship.

EXAMPLES:

(1) It becomes desirable for the *XYZ* Corporation to buy certain oil wells. The directors form a separate corporation (in which they are secretly inter-

---

[10] 248 Mo. 243, 154 S.W. 108.
[11] 17 C.J.S. 504.

ested) which buys the oil wells and resells them at a profit to the *XYZ* Corporation. Such conduct of the directors constitutes constructive fraud.

(2) A depositor having a balance of $22,505 with a trust company lost his memory following an illness. An official of the trust company, knowing all the facts but concealing his official position, induced the depositor to contract to pay $10,000 for revealing the location of the deposit. This, said the court, was constructive fraud.[12]

(*e*) *Actionable fraud.* Regardless of the numerous forms which deception may take, the broad term "actionable fraud" applies to misrepresentation as distinguished from breach of duty. For actionable fraud, certain elements are essential and certain remedies available.

**Elements of Actionable Fraud.** The elements of actionable fraud are: (a) misrepresentation, (b) its materiality, (c) knowledge of its falsity or ignorance of its truth, (d) intent that it should be acted on and (e) rightful reliance by the defrauded party (f) to his damage or injury.

(**a**) *Misrepresentation in general.* Misrepresentation may take the form of words, conduct, or silence when there is a duty to speak. In the latter case it is known as *concealment*.

*Words.* "The plainest case of a false representation is the telling of a deliberate lie. . . . A representation need not be a direct lie in order to constitute actionable fraud; the false representation may consist in a deceptive answer, or any other indirect but misleading language." [13]

*Conduct.* "Actions speak louder than words." The court has held that a nod, a wink, a shake of the head or a smile may constitute fraud under certain conditions.

EXAMPLES: (1) selling a crate of ostensibly high quality peaches, with rotten fruit hidden underneath; (2) covering up defective material or workmanship by the use of plugs, putty, paint, and so on; (3) turning a log of mahogany over to hide a hole in it; (4) turning back an automobile speedometer; (5) pointing to a high number on a typewriter (suggesting recent manufacture) which has been affixed by a dealer to a secondhand machine.

*Silence (concealment).* Mere silence does not constitute concealment unless there is a duty to speak. Ordinarily, where persons deal at arm's length, there is no duty to speak except where a deliberate failure to answer a question gives a misleading impression or where one under no duty to speak volunteers a misleading statement.

EXAMPLES:

(1) *A* induces *B* to transfer title to certain lost sheep which *A* knew had been found, but *B* did not. Had no questions been asked nor answers given, there would have been no fraudulent concealment. *A* volunteered the opinion, however, that the sheep would never be found. The court held that *A* was guilty of fraud.[14] (Had *B* stated, "I suppose those sheep will never be found,"

---

[12] *Gierth v. Fidelity Trust Co.,* 93 N.J. Eq. 163, 115 A. 397.
[13] 137 C.J.S. 225.
[14] *Bench v. Sheldon,* 14 Barb. 66.

*A*'s failure to reply would likewise have amounted to fraudulent concealment.)

(2) *B*, a violin expert, buys a famous old violin from *A* (who has no knowledge of its true value) at a price far less than its value. If *A* asks no questions and *B* volunteers no representations, the transaction must stand; but if the buyer makes a misleading statement, the transaction is tainted with fraud.[15]

Where parties deal, not at arm's length, but in relationships involving faith and confidence (principal and agent, attorney and client, partner and copartner, and so on), full disclosure is required whether questions are asked or not: failure to speak amounts to concealment.

(b) *Materiality.* The misrepresentation must be material. The test is this: Did the misrepresentation induce the contract, or, conversely, would the contract have taken place without it?

(c) *Knowledge of falsity, or reckless ignorance of truth,* which courts refer to as "scienter," is essential to hold a person liable for fraud, but knowledge is not essential as a basis for avoiding a contract. Knowledge of falsity, calling for proof of a state of mind, is often difficult to prove; but the law will presume knowledge where one has the means of knowing.

EXAMPLE: The director, vice president, and general manager of a casualty company, who was also half owner, to induce plaintiff to buy his stock, furnished a written statement of the company's financial position showing a surplus of $112,201.34. Relying on the statement, plaintiff bought the stock. Later, an examination by the state insurance department showed, as of the date of the prior statement, a deficit of $47,943.01 instead of the reported surplus. The difference lay in the reserve for outstanding claims. Defendant, on the trial, offered no proof of how he had determined the reserve. From all the circumstances, a jury would be justified in concluding that defendant had knowledge of the falsity of his statement.

*Recklessness of the truth* is equivalent to fraud. "One who . . . states a fact to be true when he has no knowledge on the subject, and thus misleads the other to his injury, is as much liable in law as for a fraud, as if he had wilfully misstated a fact to be true when he knew it to be false." [16]

*Honest error.* Misrepresentation based on honest and reasonable error is not fraudulent, and the person who makes it is not liable for fraud, though a contract based on it may be avoided or rescinded, as in the case of mutual mistake (pages 48-49).

EXAMPLE: The vice president of a corporation signed a statement prepared in the usual course of business by a trusted employee. The truth or falsity of the statement was unknown to him, but he assumed it was true. Actually, it was false. The court held that the vice president was not so reckless as to be personally liable for the misrepresentations contained in the statement.[17] A contract based on such misrepresentations, however, may be avoided or rescinded.

(d) *Intent to deceive.* The representation, to be actionable, must have been made with intent to deceive the other party and cause him to act on

[15] *Long v. Krause,* 105 Neb. 538, 181 N.W. 372.
[16] *James v. Piggott,* 70 W.Va. 435, 439.
[17] *Ray County Savings Bank v. Hutton,* 224 Mo. 42, 123 S.W. 47.

it. This excludes false statements made in jest or casual representations made without intent to induce action.

(e) *Rightful reliance.* There can be no deception where there is disbelief; neither can one claim injury from a misrepresentation on which he did not rely. Under the earlier decisions, the right to rely depended on the exercise of common prudence and diligence in view of all the circumstances, but the later cases tend to condemn the liar rather than his victim. In any event, where the facts are peculiarly within the knowledge of the person making the representation and the representation is not transparently false, the other party has a right to rely on it. This right is not lost though the other party makes an investigation of his own.

EXAMPLE: *A* owns a stationery business with an average annual profit of $3000. By falsely representing his net profit as $10,000, he sold his business to *B*, who would not have bought it but for the misrepresentation. In an action by *B* for rescission, *A* defends on the ground that *B* had made inquiries of other persons and could have discovered the truth had he been more diligent. Such defense must fail. The facts were peculiarly within *A*'s knowledge, and *B* had a right to rely on *A*'s representation. *A* could not complain that *B* failed to discover *A* was a liar.

(f) *Damage or injury.* In all cases of actionable fraud, one must show loss or injury if he is to recover damages for the fraud.

EXAMPLE: *A* sells *B* 100 shares of *XYZ* common at $50 a share on the false representation that he had secret information from the president of the *XYZ* Company of a forthcoming extra dividend. After buying the stock, *B* resells it at a profit, then discovers *A*'s fraud. An action by *B* against *A* based on the fraud would fail of damage.

**Statement of Opinion *versus* Statement of Fact.** Mere expressions of opinion, however false, cannot constitute actionable fraud. In this category may be classed "dealers' talk," "puffing," "boosting," and the like, commonly indulged in by salesmen anxious to make a sale.

A *misrepresentation of the law* is construed as a statement of opinion, rather than fact, unless the misrepresentation is deliberately made by one who is supposed to know the law to one ignorant of it.[18]

**Expression of Expectation *versus* Misrepresentation of Present Intention.** An expression of expectation, such as that "gross sales are certain to reach $1,000,000 by 1960," or that "this motor will outperform any other on the market," are mere statements of opinion, and as such furnish no basis for actionable fraud. On the other hand, by the weight of authority in this country,[19] promises made as a means of deception, with no intention of keeping them, constitute a false representation of one's state of mind and may therefore be classed as fraud.

---

[18] *Ramos v. Pacheco,* 64 Cal. App. 2d 304, 148 P. 2d 704, 708; *Lone Star Olds Cadillac Co. v. Vinson,* Civ. App. (Tex.), 168 S.W. 2d 673.
[19] 17 C.J.S. 510.

EXAMPLE: Plaintiff owned 60%, defendant 10%, of the stock of a baking company. Defendant told plaintiff he intended to start a baking company of his own 500 miles away. Thereupon plaintiff bought defendant's stock. Immediately thereafter defendant started a competing company in the same city. Defendant's alleged intention was obviously contrary to his true intention: The sequence of events would not be consistent with a mere change of mind. An action for rescission based on fraud would probably succeed.

**Remedies of Defrauded Party.** A defrauded party may elect to affirm or disaffirm a fraudulent contract, but he cannot do both: If he does the one, he waives the other; that is, he cannot treat a contract as both valid and void. However, his affirmance merely bars a subsequent rescission; it does not bar a suit for damages based on the fraud. Neither does it bar the defrauded party from "sitting tight," refusing to perform, and—in case he is sued—urging the fraud as a defense. If the defrauded party prefers to rescind, he may do so by giving notice to this effect, or, if he desires complete relief, he may pray for rescission in a court of equity. The Court sums up the remedies of a defrauded party as follows:

(1) He may rescind the contract by promptly tendering back all that he has received under it. He may then bring an action at law upon the rescission to recover back what he has paid or (2) defend an action brought against him on the contract, setting forth the fraud and rescission as a defense. (3) He may bring an action in equity for rescission, the tender may be made in the complaint and must be kept good at the trial, and the court will adjust the relief as equity requires upon the facts established. (4) He may affirm the contract and sue for his damages. (5) If sued upon the contract, he may counterclaim his damages.[20]

**Warranties** *versus* **Representations.** Warranties are assurances which are part of a contract. Hence the important thing about a warranty is whether it is performed. A representation is a statement which induces a contract. Hence the important thing about a representation is whether it is true or false. "A warranty differs from a representation in that a warranty must always be given contemporaneously with, and as part of, the contract; whereas a representation precedes and induces to the contract. And, while that is their difference in nature, their difference in consequence or effect is this: that, upon breach of warranty (or false warranty), the contract remains binding, and damages only are recoverable for the breach; whereas, upon a false representation, the defrauded party may elect to avoid the contract, and recover the entire price paid." [21]

**Mistake.** A mistake is a misunderstanding of fact. Mistakes may be *mutual* and *unilateral*.

**Mutual Mistake.** A mistake is mutual when made by both parties. In

---

[20] *Wood v. Dudley*, 188 App. Div. 136, 176 N.Y. Supp. 494.

[21] *Black's L. Dic.*, 3d Ed., 1833. This distinction, expressing the common law rule, has been modified by statute; for example, in respect to sales (Chapter 4) and insurance (Chapter 8).

such case, there is no real meeting of minds, hence no real contract; and either party may avoid or rescind. Mutual mistakes may relate to:

*Terms of contract,* such as price, cash or credit, delivery or no delivery, and so on;

*Existence of subject matter,* as where *A*, owner of a mill in Maine, meets *B* in New York and sells him the mill, both *A* and *B* being unaware that the mill was destroyed by fire the night before; or where a contract, based on a survey, is made for the sale of a timber tract which, unknown to both parties, has been stripped between the time of survey and sale;

*Identity of parties,* as where two parties enter into a contract, each believing the other to be someone else;

*Identity of subject matter,* as where the owner of two houses on Prospect Street agrees to sell "my house on Prospect Street," neither party meaning the same house as the other;[22]

*Nature of the subject matter,* as where I sell you a bar of silver which both of us believe to be sterling, but which actually is not;

*Quantity of subject matter,* as where I sell you, out of a stock pile, a box supposed by both of us to contain a dozen silver knives and forks, which actually contains but half a dozen.

The foregoing instances relate to *fact.* Mutual mistake involving *opinion* is usually no ground for avoiding or rescinding a contract; such as mutual mistake about quality, or value, or as to the law.

EXAMPLES:

(1) Both buyer and seller of a stone thought it was of small value, whereas in reality it was precious. The court held the contract binding.[23]

(2) A contract is made to sell lands. Both parties know that a neighbor has been crossing the lands for seventeen years, but both assume that no legal right of way can be established in less than twenty years. Both are mistaken: the law of that state has reduced the period to fifteen years. The mistake being one of law, not of fact, the buyer would be liable on his contract.

**Unilateral Mistake.** When a mistake is made by one party to a contract, but not by the other, it is unilateral. Such mistakes do not as a rule furnish the basis for avoidance or rescission, especially where the mistake is made through inexcusable carelessness. Thus, in *Steinmeyer et al. v. Schroeppel,*[24] an error of about $400 was made in a lumber contract. It appears that the mistake was made through inexcusable carelessness. Said the Court: "There was no evidence tending to prove any special circumstances excusing the blunder." The Court then concludes: "If equity would relieve on account of such a mistake, there would be no stability in contract, and we think the Appellate Court was right in concluding

[22] *Kyle v. Kavanaugh,* 103 Mass. 356.
[23] *Wood v. Boynton,* 64 Wis. 265, 25 N.W. 42.
[24] 226 Ill. 9, 80 N.E. 564.

that the mistake was not of such character as to entitle appellants to the relief prayed." A similar result was reached in a Texas case.[25]

There are, however, situations which furnish the basis for avoidance or rescission, though the mistake be unilateral, as in the following:

(a) *Taking unconscionable advantage of inadvertent error,* especially where one has not changed his position by acting on the error.

EXAMPLE: If a building contractor orders a list of lumber, and the lumberman erroneously computes the bill to his disadvantage, the lumberman is not bound by his mistake, though it be unilateral, so long as the contractor has not yet changed his position by acting on the bill, as by submitting a bid based upon it.[26]

(b) *Unilateral mistake known to the other party.* If one party makes a mistake and the other party knows it, he cannot take advantage of such mistake unless the mistake is one of opinion, not fact. For example, in the lumber case above, if the contractor knew that the lumberman had miscalculated, he could not take advantage of it even if he had acted upon it before the lumberman discovered it. But if the lumberman believed he was getting a good price, and the contractor knew the contrary, that would have no effect on the contract.

(c) *Mistake equivalent to fraud.* Where a unilateral mistake is obvious to the other party and good faith would require him to correct the error, failure to correct it amounts to fraud.[27]

EXAMPLE: A diamond merchant's clerk sells a gem to Williams for $650. The price tag reads $6500. If Williams is fully aware of the clerk's error, his failure to correct it amounts to fraud: suit for rescission is in order.

However, a superior knowledge of values imposes no duty to speak. As noted on page 45, "Silence (concealment)," a failure to speak where there is no duty to speak does not constitute fraudulent concealment.

EXAMPLE: After selling Y an oil painting worth $1200 for $75, X sues to recover the painting or, in the alternative, the sum of $1125 as the balance of its true value. Although Y knew that the painting was valuable, he owed X no duty to speak. (If, however, Y had spoken, and had thereby misled X as to the true value of the painting, the transaction would have been vulnerable.)

**Duress.** Duress is coercion causing action or inaction contrary to the victim's will.[28] It may take various forms: physical force, imprisonment, bodily harm, or the threat of any of these. Under the common law, a threat of imprisonment was not duress unless such imprisonment were illegal or wrongful. This is no longer the rule. Likewise, threats of crim-

---

[25] *Brown v. Levy* (Tex. Civ. App.), 69 S.W. 255.
[26] *Ex parte Perusini Const. Co.,* 242 Ala. 632, 7 So. 2d 576; *Garsick v. Dehner,* 145 Neb. 73, 15 N.W. 2d 235, 237; *Steiner v. Fecycz,* 72 Ohio App. 18, 50 N.E. 2d 617; *Martens & Co., Inc. v. City of Syracuse,* 183 App. Div. 622, 626-627, 171 N.Y. Supp. 87.
[27] *Harding v. Robinson,* 175 Cal. 354, 166 P. 808.
[28] 17 C.J.S. 525.

inal prosecution constitute duress regardless of guilt or innocence, so long as they induce a contract against a party's will. However, the threat of civil suit (page 28) does not constitute duress.

*Threats involving relatives.* Threats involving a victim's near relatives by blood or marriage, such as wife, husband, parent, child or other near relative constitute duress, whether the threatened prosecution or imprisonment is lawful or not and regardless of the guilt or innocence óf the relative.[29] So is a threat to publish defamatory matter concerning a near relative, since its execution might entail mental pain, distress and injury to victim and relative alike. In all cases such threats, to constitute duress, must have directly influenced the victim in making or not making a contract.

*Effect of duress.* Since mutual assent, from its very nature, must be voluntary, any influence which makes assent involuntary renders the contract voidable at the option of the victim.

**Undue Influence.** Undue influence is the exertion of influence upon a person by means not amounting to duress, yet negativing the idea of voluntary assent. Courts of equity view with disfavor contracts induced by undue influence. Such influence may result from:

*Relationship of parties,* as in the case of *guardian and ward, trustee and beneficiary, principal and agent, attorney and client, physician and patient,* or

*Weakness of mind,* resulting from inferior capacity or physical condition.[30]

## Questions

1. "Once parties reach a mutual assent, there can be no inquiry as to the manner in which it was reached." Is this a correct statement of the law? Give your reasons.

2. "Any misrepresentation of a fraudulent nature constitutes cause for cancellation of a contract." Is this a correct statement of the law? Explain.

3. (a) Define fraud "in the factum." (b) What are the other terms for this type of fraud? Explain what is meant by these terms. (c) Is a contract based on this type of fraud absolutely void regardless of the wishes of the parties, or only voidable, that is, valid unless voided by the defrauded party?

4. Distinguish between actual and constructive fraud. Give an illustration of each.

5. What is meant by the term "actionable fraud"?

6. Name, explain and illustrate the elements of actionable fraud.

7. Distinguish between a statement of fact and a statement of opinion with respect to their bearing on fraud.

8. Distinguish between an expression of expectation and a misrepresentation

---

[29] *Hutchinson v. Hutchinson,* 48 Cal. App. 2d 12, 119 P. 2d 214—*Ramos v. Pacheco,* 64 Cal. App. 2d 304, 148 P. 2d 704; *Coleman v. Crescent Insulated Wire & Cable Co.,* 350 Mo. 781, 168 S.W. 2d 1060; *Motor Equipment Co. v. McLaughlin,* 156 Kan. 258, 133 P. 2d 149, 155; *Morrill v. Amoskeag Sav. Bank,* 90 N.H. 358, 9 A. 2d 519.

[30] *Cook v. Hollyday,* 185 Md. 656, 45 A. 2d 761.

of one's present intention, and explain the importance of this distinction in connection with actionable fraud.

9. Name and explain the remedies of a defrauded party.

10. Distinguish between a warranty and a representation as applied to contracts generally.

11. Distinguish between mutual and unilateral mistakes.

12. How does mutual mistake generally affect a contract?

13. What is the general rule with respect to the effect of a unilateral mistake on a contract? Are there any exceptions?

14. Define duress. What forms may it take?

15. What is the effect of duress on a contract?

16. Define undue influence. What is its general effect on a contract?

## Problems

1. I. M. Swift presents a document to U. R. Slow, representing it to be a petition for the elimination of a grade crossing. Actually, the paper is a contract to purchase an electric washing machine. Slow, who is nearsighted and has misplaced his glasses, signs the paper. Later, when an attempt is made to deliver the washing machine, Slow refuses to accept it. The question arises whether this contract is valid, void or voidable. How would you answer the question?

2. White is induced to hire Black for one year as a radio mechanic at $60 a week, on Black's representation that he has had three years' experience in this field. White, upon learning that this representation was false, discharges Black, who sues White for breach of contract. What type of fraud, if any, may White set up as a defense?

3. Arthur buys 500 shares of stock from Bacon on the latter's representation that the Board of Directors of the Corporation has secretly declared an extra dividend, which representation is false. When the alleged dividend fails to materialize, Arthur confronts Bacon with the misrepresentation. Bacon learns through a friend connected with the Corporation that the Corporation in the meantime has acquired valuable assets and that in consequence the stock has become more valuable than it was when Bacon sold it to Arthur. Without divulging this information to Arthur, Bacon buys the stock back from Arthur at the price paid for it by Arthur, and then resells the stock to Chase at a profit of $5000. On learning these facts, has Arthur any remedy against Bacon?

4.* B, a violin expert, ascertained that A owned an old violin of famous make, worth many thousands of dollars. In talking with A, B found that the violin had been in A's family for many years but that A had no knowledge of its true value. B, after some persuasion and by offering what to A seemed an excessive price ($350), succeeded in buying the instrument. Later A heard of the true facts and, tendering a return of the purchase price, sued to recover the violin. What, in your opinion, would be the result?

5.* Norton, owner of a pulp mill in Maine, negotiated with Burns for the sale of the mill. Burns lived in New York City, where Norton arranged to meet him. Norton left Maine on October 2nd, met Burns in New York, and on October 5th they executed the contract of sale. On October 4th the mill was destroyed by fire, a fact unknown to both parties when the contract was signed. What are the rights of the parties?

6.* Wickham, a New York businessman, had title to a large timber tract in the Northwest which he honestly believed contained approximately 5,000,000 feet of lumber, such belief being based on reports of competent timber experts. Wickham contracted to sell the tract to Monroe, both believing the reports in

Wickham's possession to be correct. Actually, unknown to either party, the tract had been stripped of good timber between the time of Wickham's survey and the time of sale. What was Wickham's position?

7. Brown is in the lumber business. Smith is a building contractor and, being about to erect a building, left at the office of Brown a list containing various items of lumber needed. In the price submitted by Brown a mistake in addition of $400 was made by Brown's bookkeeper. Smith accepted the bid. What are the rights of the parties in the following circumstances:

(a) The mistake was made through inexcusable carelessness.

(b) Smith knew that Brown's figure was due to a mathematical miscalculation.

(c) The mistake was not due to inexcusable carelessness and before Smith had done anything further, Brown notified Smith of the mistake.

8.* An accountant's secretary, in transcribing her notes, erroneously wrote to a prospective client that the per diem charge for a a senior accountant was $25 (instead of $35, which had been dictated to her) and she signed the accountant's name and mailed the letter. The client immediately wrote to the accountant engaging him "at the rates specified in your letter." The accountant satisfactorily performed the work and now seeks to charge the client $35 per diem, which is the prevailing rate, of which the client was fully aware at all times. Can the accountant succeed?

9. A contract is made to sell lands. Both parties know that a neighbor has been crossing the lands for seventeen years, but both assume that no legal right of way can be established in less than twenty years. Both are mistaken: the law of that state has reduced the period to fifteen years. On discovering his mistake as to the law, the buyer seeks to withdraw from the contract. May the seller compel the buyer to take title? Explain.

10. A diamond merchant's clerk sells a gem to Franklin for $120. The price tag reads $1200. Franklin is fully aware of the clerk's error when he buys the gem. May the diamond merchant, upon discovering the error, sue to rescind the transaction?

11.* X lawfully came into possession of an oil painting which he sold to Y for $75. Afterwards, X found that the painting was a valuable one, worth at least $1200. He tried to collect $1125 from Y. Could he? Discuss the principle involved.

12.* State whether a contract between Allen and Benson is valid, voidable, or void in *each* of the following cases, in each case assuming consideration, legality of subject matter, legal capacity to contract, and complete compliance with the statute of frauds:

Allen obtains the contract by threatening Benson that if Benson does not make the contract

(a) Allen will sue Benson for a debt which Allen alleges Benson owes to him;

(b) Allen will have Benson arrested for an alleged defalcation;

(c) Allen will publish defamatory matter concerning Benson's wife.

## PART 3. PARTIES

**Number and Competency.** There must be at least two parties to every contract, both of whom must be in existence when the contract is made. All parties are presumed to have capacity to contract, so long as they have a whole and mature mind capable of intelligent assent. Where these qualities are absent, the law makes exceptions. *Examples:* infants; insane persons; drunkards; convicts; aliens; and corporations. Married women, under the common law, were likewise disqualified.

**Infants.** The general status of an infant has already been defined (page 25). Infants have the *right* to make contracts and to hold adults to them, but they are not *liable* on their contracts, with the following qualifications:

*Necessaries.* Infants are liable for necessaries, but only to the extent of their reasonable value.[31] Hence even for necessaries, an infant is not, strictly speaking, liable on *his* contract, but on the one that the law makes for him. Necessaries embrace food, clothing, shelter, medical attendance, ordinary education and similar fundamentals of living unless they duplicate those already furnished.[32] Beyond these basic requirements, what constitutes a necessary depends on the infant's station in life. A purchase classed as a necessary to the millionaire's son may be a luxury to the son of a day laborer. A classical or professional education may be a necessary to one infant and a luxury to another.

EXAMPLE: An infant contracted for a correspondence course in steam engineering. After receiving some instruction and making some payments, he dropped the course. In a suit on the contract, it was urged that education is a necessary. Said the court: "A proper education is a necessary, but what is a proper education depends on circumstances. A common school education is doubtless necessary in this country. . . . A classical or professional education, however, has been held not to come within the term. . . . Still, circumstances . . . may exist where even such an education might properly be found a necessary. . . . In the absence of all facts relating to any of these subjects we think that a course of instruction in 'Complete Steam Engineering' . . . was not a necessary. . . ."[33]

*Luxuries: disaffirmance.* An infant's contracts for anything other than necessaries are valid but voidable at his option, and the infant may exercise this option by disaffirming the contract at any time during infancy or promptly after reaching majority. Where a contract is executed and the infant has performed, he cannot rescind or disaffirm without returning or accounting for the value received by him.[34]

*Ratification.* Upon attaining majority, an infant may ratify any contract which he has the right to disaffirm. Once an infant ratifies, he cannot disaffirm.[35] Ratification may be *express* (that is, in words, oral or written);

[31] *Sumner v. Hall*, 273 Ky. 138, 116 S.W. 2d 309; *In re Dzwondiewicz's Estate*, 231 Mich. 165, 203 N.W. 671; *O'Donniley v. Kinley*, 220 Mo. App. 284, 286 S.W. 140; *Quinley v. Desautels*, 45 R.I. 106, 120 A. 65.

[32] *Utterstrom v. Myron D. Kidder, Inc.*, 124 Me. 10, 124 A. 725; *Chabot v. Paulhus*, 32 R.I. 471, 79 A. 1103; *Worman Motor Co. v. Hill*, 54 Ariz. 227, 94 P. 2d 865, 124 A.L.R. 1363; *Thrall v. Wright*, 38 Vt. 494.

[33] *International Text Book Co. v. Connelly*, 206 N.Y. 188, 195-196.

[34] *Weeks v. Berschauer*, 140 Kan. 244, 36 P. 2d 81, 83; *Merchants' Credit Bureau v. Kaoru Akiyama*, 64 Utah 364, 230 P. 1017.

[35] *Lee v. Thompson*, 124 Fla. 494, 168 So. 848; *First Nat. Bank v. Guenther*, 125 Neb. 807, 252 N.W. 395; *Smith v. Williams*, 141 S.C. 265, 139 S.E. 625.

or *implied* (as by an act done after reaching majority indicating approval, or by failing to disaffirm promptly upon reaching majority).

EXAMPLE: Six weeks before his twenty-first birthday, an infant buys an automobile for $2000 on a down payment of $100, balance on credit. Upon attaining majority, the infant may ratify the contract orally, by letter, by affirmative act (reselling the car or continuing to make payments), or by using the car and failing to disaffirm.

**Business contracts.** Some states have adopted statutes making infants who engage in business liable on their business contracts. These statutes reflect a rising standard of necessaries to self-supporting infants. (If, for example, the correspondence school case cited under "Necessaries" in this section were to be tried today, a majority of states would probably class such education as a necessary to a self-supporting infant or one in moderate circumstances.)

**Contracts of marriage.** A minor's contract to marry is voidable at the minor's option. But if the marriage is consummated, and the minors are of legal age (which in many states is fixed at eighteen for both males and females), it is not subject to annulment on the ground of infancy.

**Infant misrepresenting age.** Infants, as previously noted (page 26), are liable for their torts. There is no good reason why an infant who misrepresents his age should not be liable for deceit. Yet not all states are agreed on this. In many states, the courts refuse to allow a tort to be used as a lever for enforcing an infant's contract.

In many other states, however, an infant is liable in a separate action for deceit. This is especially true in states which have statutes providing that a minor cannot disaffirm his contract if he misrepresents his age to an adult who relies on the misrepresentation. Among such states are Iowa, Kansas, Utah and Washington.

**Infancy no defense to adult.** It is the infant, not the adult, who may plead infancy as a defense. Where the infant, however, is guilty of fraud in inducing the contract (as in misrepresenting his age), the defrauded adult may avoid the contract.[36]

**Infancy "a shield, not a sword."** "If an infant pays money on his contract and enjoys the benefit of it and then avoids it when he comes of age, he cannot recover back the consideration paid. On the other hand, if he avoids an executed contract when he comes of age on the ground of infancy, he must restore the consideration which he had received. The privilege of infancy is to be used as a shield and not as a sword. He

---

[36] *Western Union Telegraph Co. v. Ausbrooks*, 148 Tenn. 615, 257 S.W. 858; *Welch v. King*, 279 Mass. 445, 181 N.E. 846; *Hammassapoulo v. Hammassapoulo*, 134 S.C. 54, 131 S.E. 319; *Cheney v. Cheney*, Civ. App., 82 S.W. 2d 1024, reversed on other grounds *Cheney v. Coffey*, 131 Tex. 212, 113 S.W. 2d 162, rehearing denied 131 Tex. 212, 114 S.W. 2d 533; *Horney v. Downs*, 209 Ky. 255, 272 S.W. 728.

cannot have the benefit of the contract on one side without returning the equivalent on the other." [37]

**Married Women.** The legal status of women, formerly and now, has already been discussed on pages 24-25. Though in Florida married women must obtain court orders to become "free dealers," and in Pennsylvania they are not liable on surety contracts or accommodation paper, generally speaking the common law disabilities of married women in the United States, as to contracts and civil rights have been removed.

**Insane Persons.** Insanity has many definitions, but as to contractual capacity, persons are insane if derangement of mind prevents the giving of intelligent assent. Persons may be *adjudged* or declared insane after inquiry and the appointment of a guardian or *committee* to look after their affairs. Prior to such adjudication, contracts with insane persons are *voidable;* thereafter, *void* (page 83). Though a person judicially declared insane is not liable on express contracts thereafter personally made by himself, his estate is liable for the reasonable value of necessaries furnished to him or his family.

**Drunkards.** Intoxication is ordinarily no defense to a contract, unless fraudulently procured, or unless it is so extreme as to negative the capacity for intelligent assent.

A confirmed drunkard may be adjudicated an incompetent, the same as an insane person. In such case, all contracts made by such an incompetent, other than through the guardian or committee appointed for him, are void. Where such contracts are made with innocent persons unaware of the incompetent's condition, the court will hold the estate of the incompetent drunkard for the reasonable value of goods furnished or services rendered.

**Convicts.** "At common law, conviction of treason or other felony placed the convict in a state of attainder, resulting in forfeiture of his estate, corruption of his blood, and civil death or loss of civil rights." [38] These extreme consequences of criminal conviction have been largely abolished. In the absence of statute, the doctrine of civil death on conviction has been abandoned. In some jurisdictions, a person sentenced to life imprisonment is deemed civilly dead. If sentenced to a lesser term, his civil rights are suspended during the term. Likewise in the absence of statute, a convict may enter into contract, but his ability to enforce it may be limited or impaired by his confinement, or by statute.

**Aliens.** Contracts with aliens are fully enforceable. Contracts with enemy aliens are suspended upon declaration of war; if made after war is declared, they are void. As to existing contract rights, every resident,

---

[37] *Rice v. Butler*, 160 N.Y. 578.
[38] 18 C.J.S. 101.

whether citizen or alien, may freely resort to our courts, but the right of an alien to do so may be curtailed, regulated, or entirely withheld by statute (such as the Trading With The Enemy Act). By Act of Congress all property rights of an enemy alien, including contract rights, may be taken over by the Alien Property Custodian or corresponding officer of the United States Government.

**Corporations.** A corporation is an artificial person under the law and as such may make contracts the same as natural persons. However, corporations from their very nature labor under certain disabilities and limitations more fully discussed in the chapter on corporations.

## Questions

1. In the absence of proof, one way or the other, what is the general presumption as to the capacity of parties to enter into a contract? What, if any, are the exceptions to this rule?

2. Is the following statement (a) entirely right, (b) entirely wrong, or (c) partly right and partly wrong: "Infants have no right to make contracts or to hold adults to them, and they are not liable on their contracts except for necessaries"? Explain your answer.

3. What alternatives may an infant adopt, on reaching his majority, with respect to contracts made by him during his infancy?

4. Distinguish between an express and an implied ratification of an infant's act. Give an example of each.

5. What is the rule with respect to an infant's liability for his torts? Does this apply to fraudulent misrepresentation by an infant that he is an adult? Explain and illustrate your answer.

6.* When, if at all, may a creditor enforce a contract with a minor?

7. When may a minor enforce a contract with an adult?

8. Under what circumstances, if any, are the following persons liable on their contracts: (a) married women, (b) insane persons, (c) drunkards, (d) convicts, (e) aliens, (f) corporations?

9. What is the meaning of the expression, "Infancy is a shield, not a sword"?

10. As used in connection with contracts made by infants, what does the term "necessaries" embrace? Is the term definite and fixed, or otherwise? Explain.

## Problems

1. An infant bought a suit of clothes for $100, payable in four quarterly installments of $25 each. He paid $25 down, and $25 additional three months after his majority. He made no further payments. In an action on the contract, the infant's defense was that a $100 suit represented a luxury to him, and that he was willing to rescind the contract and return the suit. Would the infant's position be sustained in court?

2. An infant buys a second-hand automobile for his pleasure, pays the full price, then trades the car in for a new one with another dealer. The new car is demolished in a wreck. The infant then demands the return of his second-hand car from the second dealer, who refuses on the following grounds: (1) The infant is unable to return the new car, except as junk, and (2) The second-hand

car has been sold to an innocent third party. What are the rights of the parties?

3. An infant buys a diamond ring on credit. He represents his age as over 21. On learning the truth, the jeweler seeks to rescind the contract and recover the ring. Will he succeed? Explain.

4. Suppose in the preceding case that the infant had not misrepresented his age, and that the jeweler's suit was based on the purchaser's infancy and the fact that the diamond ring was not a necessity. How would the court decide the case?

5. Mr. and Mrs. Smith, joint owners of a parcel of land, contracted to sell it to Henry Brown, who paid a deposit of $250 on the purchase price of $5000. Title was to be delivered and the balance of the price paid in sixty days. Thirty days after the contract was made, Mrs. Smith was adjudicated insane, and Mr. Smith was appointed her committee. On the closing date, Mr. Smith refused to deliver title, contending and later proving that his wife was insane at the time of the contract. At the trial Brown urges that since Mrs. Smith was not adjudicated insane until after the contract was executed, the deed should have been delivered on the closing date. How would the court decide the issue?

6. Fred Ryan and Bob Reynolds met for dinner in a nightclub to discuss a prospective partnership. The parties indulged liberally in alcoholic refreshments, and at the close of the evening agreed upon the partnership, including its terms and conditions. The next day Ryan refused to proceed with the partnership on the ground that his judgment the night before had been influenced by the refreshments. Reynolds sued Ryan for breach of contract. Who would succeed, and why?

7. John and Harriet Smith formed a partnership in the retail sale of infants' wear. After the business had prospered for several years, John Smith died. The business then folded up, leaving many debts and practically no assets. John Smith personally left no assets, but Harriet Smith had a substantial estate of her own. Acting on the partnership principle that partners are personally liable for the debts of an insolvent partnership, the creditors seek to hold Harriet Smith for the partnership debts. She pleads non-liability because of her marital status. Who will succeed? Why?

8. An infant, working in a community where ownership of an automobile was essential to his job, purchased a car from a second-hand dealer at a price of $1,000, which was twice what the car was worth. Half of this price he paid at the time of purchase. The other half he agreed to pay in six weeks. On failure and refusal to make the latter payment, the second-hand dealer sues. How should the case be decided, and why?

9. Heinrich and Carl Schultz were brothers engaged in the manufacture of hardware in Berlin, Germany. Carl Schultz emigrated to the United States, and Heinrich remained in Berlin. During World War II, Carl and Heinrich, through South American agents, entered into a contract calling for shipment of merchandise from Berlin to San Francisco via Buenos Aires. This contract was breached by Carl throughout the war. Heinrich now sues Carl for breach of contract. How will the court decide, and why?

## PART 4. CONSIDERATION

**Nature and Necessity.** Consideration is something of value given for a promise. Without it, a promise is *nudum pactum*—a naked pact, without force in law. A promise supported by consideration is binding; that is, a contract.

EXAMPLE: *A*, by written contract, buys *B*'s drygoods store, pays $2000 down, and agrees to pay the balance of $2500 on or before February 1, 1955. On February 1, 1955, *A* secures *B*'s agreement to postpone payment until April 1, 1955, but immediately thereafter *B*, ignoring his promise, sues *A* for the balance. The suit will succeed: *B*'s promise was "naked"—not supported by consideration.

**Act *v.* Promise as Consideration.** The thing of value called for by a promise may be either an act or a promise to do the act.

If an act is called for as consideration for a promise, only the act, not a promise to perform it, will constitute consideration to bind the promise.

EXAMPLE: A promise to pay $50 "if you can deliver the coal to my bin by Friday" becomes obligatory, not upon a *promise to deliver* the coal, but by the *act* of delivery itself. This is known as a *unilateral contract* (page 83).

On the other hand, if a promise or commitment to do the act is called for, the making of such promise or commitment constitutes the consideration to support the other promise; that is, each promise immediately becomes obligatory because of the other. This is known as a *bilateral contract* (page 83).

**What May Constitute Consideration.** Anything of value given for a promise may constitute consideration. "Value" may take the form of a benefit to the promisor or a sacrifice to the promisee.

*Benefits as consideration* may include money, property or services, or the promise thereof.

*Detriment or sacrifice as consideration* may consist in the promisee's giving up some right, or promising to give it up, whether such sacrifice benefits the other party or not.

EXAMPLE: If an uncle promises his nephew $5000 for refraining from liquor, tobacco, swearing and gambling until the nephew becomes of age, the uncle must pay if the nephew makes these sacrifices.[39]

**Mutuality of Obligation.** If one party to a contract is bound and the other is not, the contract is unenforceable for lack of mutuality of obligation: Both parties must be bound, or neither is.[40]

EXAMPLE: Cooper's Glue Factory writes Schlegel Manufacturing Co., "We are instructed to enter your contract for your requirements in 1927, deliveries to be made as per your orders during the year." The Schlegel Company signs its name to the letter. After some deliveries, the Cooper Company stops further shipments, and the Schlegel Company sues. *Held*, no contract. The agreement lacked mutuality. The Schlegel Company in signing the letter did not obligate itself to do anything.[41]

[39] *Hamer v. Sidway*, 124 N.Y. 538.
[40] *Friedman v. Decatur Corporation*, 77 U.S. App. D.C. 326, 135 F. 2d 812; *Heisley v. Allied American Mut. Fire Ins. Co.*, 71 Ga. App. 107, 30 S.E. 2d 285; *Duclos v. Turner*, 204 Ark. 1000, 166 S.W. 2d 251; *Stephen L. Guice & Co. v. Perkowski* (La.) App., 12 So. 2d 692.
[41] *Schlegel Manufacturing Co. v. Cooper's Glue Factory*, 231 N.Y. 459.

**Options and Mutuality.** An option is a promise to hold an offer open. Like any other promise, it is ineffective without consideration. In a limited sense, options dispense with mutuality since one of the parties may be bound or not, as he sees fit, while the other is absolutely bound. This is especially true where a statute provides that a *written option* is binding without consideration.[42] In reality, however, an option (where there is consideration) is mutually obligatory: One party is obligated to furnish a consideration and the other to hold an offer open.

**Good v. Valuable Consideration.** With respect to the enforceability of contracts, it is sometimes necessary to distinguish between *good* and *valuable* consideration.

*Good consideration* is consideration based on sentiment, or a moral (as distinguished from a legal) obligation. For example, a promise to pay a debt outlawed by the statute of limitations is a promise based on a moral, rather than on a legal obligation, hence based on good, not valuable consideration.

*Valuable consideration* is something representing a material benefit to the promisor or some sacrifice or detriment by the promisee. The word "consideration," standing alone, generally means valuable consideration.

With certain exceptions (page 61), good consideration will support an executed but not an executory (unperformed) contract. Only valuable consideration will support an executory contract.

EXAMPLE: Hawkins, upon reaching the age of 65, retires from Culver's employ. Immediately thereafter Culver promises Hawkins $100 a month for life. Culver makes the payments for four years, then stops. Since Culver's promise was based on good consideration only, the contract, so far as it is still executory, cannot be enforced. Neither may Culver rescind the contract so far as it is executed: The payments already made, stand.

**Executory and Executed (Past) Consideration.** Consideration to be furnished in the future, as the thing of value supporting a promise, is executory. If the consideration, unsolicited, is given first and *then* the promise is given for it, such promise is based on *executed*, or *past* consideration.

EXAMPLE: Following a storm, you repair the roof of my house in my absence and without my knowledge or consent. On my return I promise to reimburse you and to compensate you for your time and trouble. Such a promise is based on past consideration.

Executed or past consideration will not support a promise; that is, a promise based on past consideration is not binding.

---

[42] The Uniform Commercial Code provides that a signed offer by a merchant to buy or sell goods, containing an assurance that it will be held open, needs no consideration to be irrevocable for a specified time, or if no time is specified, for a reasonable time, in no event to exceed three months. (See Appendix.)

The foregoing rule may be changed by statute. Some statutes provide, for example, that a *written* promise based on past consideration is binding.

**Adequate Consideration.** The court is not concerned with the question of whether or not the thing supplied as consideration was adequate. The adequacy of consideration is left to the parties. Hence, a large contract can be bound by a small consideration.[43] Only where the consideration is so ridiculously inadequate as to suggest fraud, will the courts interfere to set aside a contract for lack of consideration.[44]

**Moral Obligation v. Legal Obligation.** A moral obligation will not constitute consideration, unless it is also a legal one. For example, if you voluntarily pay my debt to Smith, my moral obligation to repay you would not constitute consideration.[45] If, however, I did repay you, the transaction would stand: Good consideration supports an executed contract (page 60). Where a moral obligation was formerly a legal obligation, a *written* promise may in certain cases convert it into a legal obligation again.

EXAMPLE: A claim barred by the statute of limitations, or discharged in bankruptcy, leaves only a moral obligation, yet a subsequent *written* promise to pay such claim is enforceable.

**Fulfilling a Duty No Consideration.** Fulfilling or promising to fulfill a duty already in existence represents no sacrifice of a right, hence cannot constitute consideration.

*Pre-existing contract obligation.* If a person is obligated by contract to do a certain thing for a certain price, he has no further right to promise the same thing for a higher price, since the doing of that thing is no longer his to bargain away.

EXAMPLE: An accountant engaged to make an audit at specified per diem rates uncovers a defalcation whereby he saves his client $25,000. When the audit is concluded, the grateful client promises the accountant an additional $5000 for his services. Should the client refuse to pay the additional fee, the accountant could not compel payment, because he was already obligated by contract to render the service for which he was promised extra payment.

*Agreement to accept part payment in full.* Payment of a lesser sum than that actually due on a liquidated debt will not constitute considera-

---

[43] *Alabama Mills v. Smith,* 237 Ala. 296, 186 So. 699—*Gray v. Gray,* 246 Ala. 627, 22 So. 2d 21; *Hanks v. McNeil Coal Corp.,* 114 Colo. 578, 168 P. 2d 256; *Affiliated Enterprises v. Waller, Super.* (Del.) 1 Terry 28, 5 A. 2d 257; *Franklin Fire Ins. Co. v. Noll,* 115 Ind. App. 289, 58 N.E. 2d 947; *Featherstone v. Walker,* 43 N.M. 181, 88 P. 2d 271; *Williston Sav. & Loan Ass'n v. Kellar* (N.D.), 2d 30; *Matthews v. Matthews,* 24 Tenn. App. 580, 148 S.W. 2d 3.

[44] *Woods v. Griffin,* 204 Ark. 514, 163 S.W. 2d 322; *Sova v. First Nat. Bank of Ferndale,* 18 Wash. 2d 88, 138 P. 2d 181, 190.

[45] *Lanfier v. Lanfier,* 227 Iowa 258, 288 N.W. 104; *Succession of Burns,* 199 La. 1081, 7 So. 2d 359; *Fender v. McCain,* 144 Neb. 58, 12 N.W. 2d 541; *White Mountain Nat. Bank v. Malloy,* 93 N.H. 197, 37 A. 2d 785; *In re Knisley's Estate,* 12 Ohio Supp. 140.

tion for a promise to accept such payment in full satisfaction. To make such payment is but to discharge an existing obligation.[46]

EXAMPLE: Peter Winter, being financially embarrassed, gave his creditors notes in payment of their respective claims. On due date, the creditors surrendered their notes upon payment of 50% of their respective face values. Such payments would furnish no consideration for a discharge of the full amounts due, unless each creditor (1) made a gift of the balance, or (2) gave a binding release (page 111), or (3) accepted the payment as part of a composition (page 63). However, as noted in the paragraph immediately following, if the payments were made before maturity, the debts would be fully discharged.

*An agreement to accept part payment in advance of due date,* as payment in full, is binding, because prepayment may constitute consideration for accepting less than the amount due.[47]

*An agreement to accept part payment plus something additional,* as payment in full, is binding.[48]

EXAMPLE: Geller owes Gordon $650, which is past due. He offers Gordon $150 plus an automobile worth approximately $400 in full satisfaction of the debt. If Gordon accepts, the debt is discharged: The parties may fix what value they please on the automobile as adequate consideration.

*Promise to extend payment.* If a creditor promises to extend payment of a debt, the promise is not binding on the creditor unless he gets something for it in addition to that which he is already entitled to receive.

EXAMPLES:
(1) A promise to extend payment of a debt for one month if the debtor will agree "to surely pay it then," is not binding, because the creditor is entitled to payment anyway.
(2) A promise to extend the time of payment for three months of a note that bears no interest, if the maker will pay interest at 5% from and after due date, is not binding, because the holder is entitled *by law* to interest *after due date.* (Such legal interest exceeds the rate of 5% in most states.)

*Forbearance to sue.* Forbearance or sacrifice of the right to sue constitutes valuable consideration. However, your promise to pay me $100 in consideration of my forbearance to sue you would be unenforceable unless there was an honest dispute between us. If I have no colorable right to sue, I forbear nothing by withholding suit.

*Withdrawing from suit in consideration of secret preference.* If one of the creditors of an insolvent estate withdraws from a pending suit brought on behalf of all the creditors, in consideration of the debtor's promise to pay his claim in full, the debtor's promise, being based on the illegal consideration of an unlawful preference, is unenforceable.

---

[46] *Mutual Home & Savings Ass'n v. Welker* (Ohio), 42 N.E. 2d 167, 170.
[47] *Jones v. Vennerberg,* 133 Neb. 143, 274 N.W. 494, 496; *Levine v. Blumenthal,* 117 N.J. Law 23, 186 A. 457, affirmed 117 N.J. Law 426, 189 A. 54.
[48] *Tucker v. Dolan,* 109 Mo. App. 442, 84 S.W. 1126.

**Composition with Creditors.** An agreement among creditors and with a debtor to compromise for less than the amounts due them is more than a mere promise to accept a smaller sum for a larger sum due, because it involves mutual forbearances among the creditors, as well as their promises to the debtor. These forbearances furnish consideration because they represent not only mutual sacrifices, but also a mutual exchange of benefits among the creditors in not pressing their respective claims against the debtor, thereby eliminating the mad scramble among creditors which inevitably results in less being available for all.

**Voluntary Subscriptions.** Voluntary subscriptions standing by themselves are in effect promises to make gifts. The rule that mutual promises to subscribe supply mutual consideration is not uniform. The English view is that such promises are gratuitous, hence not binding. The view most commonly held in this country is that a subscription is an offer to contract which becomes binding as soon as the work toward which the subscription was promised has been done or begun, or as soon as liability is incurred in reliance on the subscription. The consideration for the subscription or promise may consist in the procurement or making of other similar promises, or in the assumption by the promisee, express or implied, of the obligation to undertake or further the object of the subscription.

EXAMPLE: A party subscribed to a university endowment fund by giving a note payable on his death. The obligation to pay the note was contested on the ground of no consideration. The court held that by accepting the note the university assumed the obligation to keep the endowment fund intact and to apply the income from it to payment of salaries and other expenses. The assumption of such obligation, said the court, supplied consideration to support the note.[49]

**Consideration in Contracts under Seal.** Under the common law, contracts under seal were binding regardless of consideration. In this country, only a small minority of states observe the common law rule.[50] In a majority of states,[51] the distinction between sealed and unsealed contracts has been abolished by statute. In several states[52] where contracts under seal import consideration the law allows proof to the contrary, upon the establishment of which the contract is unenforceable.

## Questions

1. Explain the nature of consideration.
2. What is meant by a "naked pact"?

[49] *In re Griswold's Estate*, 113 Neb. 256, 202 N.W. 609.
[50] Florida, Maine, Pennsylvania, South Carolina, Vermont, Virginia and one or two others.
[51] Alaska, Arizona, Arkansas, California, Colorado, Idaho, Indiana, Iowa, Kansas, Kentucky, Minnesota, Mississippi, Missouri, Montana, Nebraska, Nevada, New Mexico, New York, North Dakota, Ohio, Oklahoma, South Dakota, Tennessee, Texas, Utah, Washington, West Virginia, Wyoming.
[52] Alabama, Illinois, Michigan, New Jersey, Oregon and Wisconsin.

3. "Consideration may consist of an act or promise to do the act." Illustrate this statement.

4.** (a) Can a large contract be bound by a small consideration?

(b) Name four things that will constitute valuable consideration.

5. Distinguish between, and illustrate, (a) a benefit, and (b) a detriment or sacrifice, as consideration for a contract.

6. May a contract be enforceable if one party is bound by it and the other not? Explain your answer.

7. What is an option? When does an option lack mutuality and when not?

8. Distinguish between and illustrate good and valuable consideration.

9. Distinguish between and illustrate executory and executed, or past, consideration.

10. What is the attitude of the courts in respect to the adequacy of consideration?

11. When, if at all, will a moral obligation constitute consideration?

12. "Fulfilling or promising to fulfill a duty already in existence cannot constitute consideration." Give four examples of this statement.

13. Are creditors who agree with one another and with the debtor to accept part payment, as payment in full, bound by such agreement? Explain your answer.

14. When are voluntary subscriptions binding, and when not?

15. What is the general rule today with respect to the necessity for consideration in contracts under seal?

## Problems

1. Lambert buys Dollard's grocery store for $5,000. He pays $2,500 on February first, and agrees to pay the balance on May first. On May first, Lambert asks for an additional month's extension, to which Dollard agrees. Two days later Dollard sues Lambert for the balance. Lambert's defense is the 30-day extension. How did the court decide, and why?

2.* A entered into the following agreement with the R. S. Cement company:

Memorandum of agreement made this 6th day of July, 1905, between A, first party, and R. S. Cement company, second party, to wit., first party agrees to give the "R. S." brand cement the preference in his sales of cement for the year 1905, and in consideration thereof, second party agrees to sell said brand of cement to the first party during the year 1905 at the price of 95 cents a bbl. f.o.b. Haverstraw, New York.

A ordered several shipments of cement which were duly delivered and paid for. Subsequently the market price for cement rose and the cement company notified A that it would furnish no more cement under the agreement. A then purchased his cement elsewhere during the remainder of the year at higher market prices, and he sought to recover from the cement company as damages the difference between the cost of the cement purchased by him at the prevailing market price and what the cement would have cost at the price provided in the agreement. Could he recover?

3. Mildred Bloom goes shopping for a television set. She sees just the set she wants in the Grand Department Store. Later, while shopping in the Modern Department Store, she sees a set she likes better. The clerk in the Grand store had promised to keep the set for her several days until she made up her mind. The clerk in the Modern store refused to make such promise unless Miss Bloom left a deposit of $25, which she did. The next day, Miss Bloom decided

she preferred the set in the Grand store. She first went to the Modern store and demanded back her $25 deposit, which was refused; then she went to the Grand store and learned that the set there had been sold. She now wants to know whether she can hold the Grand store for breach of the option, and the Modern store for return of the deposit. What are her rights?

4.* State in each of the following cases whether or not Culver is legally bound by his promise, and state the principles of law on which your answer is based:

(a) Hawkins, upon reaching the age of sixty-five years, retired from the employ of Culver, and immediately thereafter Culver promised to pay Hawkins $100 each month as long as Hawkins lived. Culver had no established pension plan and at no time prior to his retirement had Hawkins expected or had any reason to expect a pension.

Culver made the payments for four years but then discontinued them although Hawkins was still alive.

(b) Culver signed a subscription list by which he promised to give $100 to the Central Church toward the cost of a new organ. Other subscribers signed before and after him. The Central Church purchased the organ but Culver refused to pay the $100.

5. Hunter owes Flint $1,000. The debt is eight years old. Hunter meets Flint on the street and promises to pay the debt within thirty days, notwithstanding that it has lapsed and is legally uncollectible. May Flint hold Hunter on his promise?

6. Silver is adjudicated a bankrupt and in due course is discharged in bankruptcy. He writes Joyce, stating: "I want you to know that notwithstanding my discharge in bankruptcy, I intend to pay my $500 debt to you as soon as I get back on my feet, which I am sure will be within the coming year." During the succeeding year, Silver enters into a very profitable business which nets him a surplus of $50,000 by the end of the year. Joyce seeks to hold Silver on his promise. Can he do so?

7. An accountant, engaged to make an audit at specified per diem rates, uncovers a defalcation whereby he saves his client $10,000. When the audit is concluded, the grateful client promises the accountant an additional $500 for his services, but later refuses to pay this additional fee. Can the accountant compel payment?

8. Mulcahy owes Crawford $500. He goes to Crawford's home, tenders $400 in cash, and says, "This is all I have. Will you take it and forget the rest?" Crawford takes the money and says, "All right, let's forget the balance." The next day Crawford sues Mulcahy for $100. Will his suit succeed?

9. Merry owes Morgan $1,000, which is not due until July 1st. On June 1st, Morgan goes to Merry's place of business and says, "If you can spare $900 in cash now, you can save yourself $100. I need cash that bad." Merry gives Morgan $900, but on July 1st, Morgan insists that he is entitled to the additional $100. Omitting all question of usury, can Morgan recover the additional $100?

10. Gray owes Hands $1,200, which is past due. He offers Hands $200 and an automobile worth approximately $500, in full satisfaction of the debt. Hands accepts, but later seeks to compel Gray to pay him an additional $500. Can he compel such payment?

11. Arthur owes Baker $500. Baker insists on immediate payment. Arthur pleads for an additional month in which to pay. Baker says, "Very well, I will give you the extension, provided you agree to surely pay it then." Arthur agrees. The day after this conversation, Baker telephones Arthur, "I must insist

on immediate payment," and several days later, on Arthur's insistence that Baker stick to the extension, the latter brings suit. Will he win?

12. Chase holds Dalton's note for $2,000, which is due. The note bears no interest. Chase agrees to extend the note for three months if Dalton will agree to pay the legal interest during that period. Dalton agreed to do so. The next day Chase revokes his extension and insists on immediate payment. Can he compel immediate payment?

13. Ewing owes his creditors $100,000, but has only $50,000 in assets with which to pay them. He calls in his creditors and discloses his financial position. The creditors agree with one another, and with Ewing, to accept one-year notes for half the amounts respectively due them, in full satisfaction of Ewing's debts. A week later Flagg, one of the creditors, repudiates the agreement and sues Ewing for the full amount. Ewing's defense is the creditor's agreement. Flagg insists that the agreement is unenforceable for lack of consideration. How would the court decide, and why?

14.* Kenyon was a businessman in the city of X. He signed a subscription list by which he agreed to contribute $1,000 toward the purchase of a building for the local chamber of commerce. Other subscribers for the same amount signed this list both before and after Kenyon signed it, and Kenyon knew of these other subscriptions. The building was purchased in accordance with, and in reliance upon, this subscription list. Could Kenyon be compelled to pay the amount of his subscription?

15. Gordon enters into a written agreement with the Vacuum Tube Corporation to give the latter's products preference in selling its vacuum tubes in his store for the year beginning August 1st, in consideration of which the Tube Corporation agrees to sell Gordon all his requirements in vacuum tubes during said period, at a fixed schedule of prices. For the first six months, the Vacuum Tube Corporation makes all deliveries ordered by Gordon, but on February 1st, it advises Gordon that all subsequent deliveries are subject to a 15 per cent price increase. Gordon thereupon purchases his vacuum tubes elsewhere at higher market prices, and at the end of the contract period sues the Vacuum Tube Corporation for the additional cost of his tubes. How will the court decide, and why?

16.* A entered into a contract to erect a house for B at a cost of $10,000. During construction, A notified B that the price of a certain material called for by the specifications had advanced so that it could not be used unless B would agree to pay $600 more. B agreed, but when the house was completed, refused to pay the extra $600; so A brought suit. Did B have a defense?

17. Harvey agrees to work for Ives as plant superintendent at an annual salary of $5,000, payable monthly. At the end of three months, Harvey receives an offer of a similar position elsewhere at a salary of $7,500 a year. Ives persuades Harvey to remain in his employ, on the promise that he will pay him the difference at the end of the year. This, however, Ives fails to do. Harvey sues Ives. How will the court decide, and why?

## PART 5. VALID SUBJECT MATTER

**In General.** It is axiomatic that the law will not enforce an agreement to do what the law says must not be done. Whether the wrong be criminal, as in the case of homicide, robbery, arson or burglary, or civil, as in the case of a tort or a breach of contract, an agreement to commit the wrong, or to do an act founded upon it, is just as lacking in legal sanction as the wrong itself. A wrongful act, and hence an agreement either to do it, or founded upon it, may be declared to be wrongful by judicial precedent (common law), by statute, or by both; but even where not declared wrongful at common law or by statute, it may lack validity because it is contrary to public policy.

**Agreements Involving Commission of Crime.** Not only is an agreement entailing or encouraging the commission of a crime unlawful, and sometimes criminal in itself (see Chapter 21:1), but any agreement to protect or indemnify a person against the consequences of a criminal act committed by himself is invalid and unenforceable.

EXAMPLES:
(1) A policy of insurance protecting Brown against loss sustained by reason of his own burglarious activities is illegal and unenforceable, though if it indemnified Brown against loss resulting from burglary by others, it would be valid and enforceable.
(2) A newspaper publisher, to induce a reporter to break into the home of a public official and remove therefrom certain documents, agrees to pay the reporter a substantial bonus if successful, and to protect him against loss or criminal prosecution if caught in the act. Not only is the agreement to pay the bonus unenforceable, but if the reporter is caught in the act and prosecuted, he cannot compel the newspaper to fulfill its agreement to indemnify the reporter against loss or prosecution, and the newspaper itself may be criminally liable.

**Agreements Involving Civil Wrongs.** An agreement to commit a tort, such as assault and battery, libel, slander or trespass, or to infringe another's patent, copyright or trade-mark, or to induce a person to breach his contract with another, or to indemnify a person if he sustains loss in the deliberate commission of any of these acts, is unenforceable for lack of valid subject matter.

EXAMPLES:
(1) *A*, a news reporter, has exclusive news rights in connection with a polar flight. *B*, another newsman, obtains passage on the plane on condition that he will send no radio reports of the flight. *B* and a certain newspaper, with full knowledge of *A*'s rights, agree that *B* is to send news reports by radio, for which the newspaper is to pay $5,000. If *B* performs and the newspaper refuses to pay, the court will refuse to enforce *B*'s claim against the newspaper.
(2) The Smith Film Company agrees to pay Simpson $5,000 if he can persuade his daughter to abandon her contract with the Jones Film Company and to accept a contract with the Smith Company instead. Simpson persuades his daughter to abandon her contract with the Jones Company and to accept a contract with the Smith Company, but the Smith Company refuses to compensate Simpson. The latter has no recourse under his contract with the Smith Company, because it was founded on a tortious interference with another's contract. In addition, the Jones Company has a cause of action against Simpson and the Smith Company. (See Ch. 20:5.)

Among the more common civil wrongs are those entailing the commission of a fraud.

**Agreements to Defraud Others.** We have noted in Part 2 above that where one party, by fraud, induces another to enter into a contract, such contract is unenforceable because there was no real assent to the bargain. The law goes further and holds that where both parties, without fraud as to each other, enter into an agreement to defraud others, such agreement is invalid because of invalid subject matter.

EXAMPLES:
(1) Plaintiff agreed to sell defendant a quality of domestic sardines with foreign labels. Both parties understood the situation, neither committing fraud on the other. *Held,* that plaintiff could not recover on such contract.[53]
(2) Crump is hired by an auctioneer at $50 a week to boost prices by making pretended bids. At the end of the week, the auctioneer refuses to pay Crump's salary. Crump has no recourse, since the employment contract is invalid.[54]

**Agreements to Breach Fiduciary Duty.** Where one owes a special duty of fidelity or trust toward another, such as that of an agent toward his principal, a partner toward his co-partner, a trustee toward his beneficiary, an attorney toward his client, or a guardian toward his ward, any contract involving a dereliction of such duty is void and unenforceable.

EXAMPLES:
(1) A secret agreement between a buyer and the agent for a seller that if the agent will persuade his principal to sell below a given figure, the buyer will give the agent half of the amount thus saved.
(2) An agreement by a prospective buyer to compensate an attorney for advising his client to sign a certain contract to sell.

**Agreements Contrary to Public Policy.** In a broad sense every wrong, civil or criminal, is contrary to public policy. In a more limited sense, acts or transactions are deemed contrary to public policy if—regardless of statute or precedent—their effect is detrimental to the public welfare. Many such transactions are now prohibited by statute. Many others are refused sanction by the courts. Agreements to engage in such transactions are therefore void and unenforceable. Transactions of this character may involve: (1) interference with public service; (2) interference with justice; (3) interference with marital relations; (4) restraint of trade or employment; and (5) miscellaneous social and economic abuses.

**Interference with Public Service.** Included in this category are agreements to influence legislative, executive or administrative action by bribery or other means; agreements to obtain public contracts by improper offers of rewards; agreements to stifle competition for public work; agreements involving interference with public elections, such as to procure a large attendance by some voters and a small attendance by others, or to guarantee a favorable count, or to procure the nomination or election

---

[53] *Materne v. Horwitz,* 101 N.Y. 469, 5 N.E. 331.
[54] 17 C.J.S. 549.

of certain persons to office; and generally any agreement which tends to corrupt or diminish integrity in the administration of government.

**Interference with Justice.** The true administration of justice requires that persons with a grievance, or charged with a crime, or sued in a civil action, should have a free opportunity to select their own counsel without the pressure of salesmanship. It requires that such counsel be qualified by training, experience and the maintenance of proper professional standards to represent them in their legal difficulties, loyally, effectively, and without fear or favor. It requires that judges render fair, impartial and honest decisions; that juries, properly chosen, be permitted to have the facts of a criminal prosecution or civil dispute fully and fairly presented to them, by witnesses who testify truthfully to the facts within their knowledge, and that they render a true and just verdict upon the facts as so presented. Any agreement tending to interfere with the integrity or effectiveness of such judicial procedure is unlawful and void.

*Champerty and maintenance* (Ch. 21:3), which tend to encourage lawsuits regardless of their merit, and to lower professional legal standards, constitute crimes, and agreements based on them are unenforceable.

*Ambulance chasing,* or the active seeking out and procurement, by attorneys personally, or by others hired for such purpose, of matters requiring legal attention, constitutes a crime. Any agreement based on it is unenforceable.

*Production, suppression or tampering with evidence.* Agreements to compensate witnesses for testifying to, denying or suppressing certain facts are prohibited by law, hence unenforceable. The law, however, allows the payment of fixed witness fees, and permits a party to compensate expert witnesses, such as physicians or handwriting experts, for time consumed in testifying, or to compensate ordinary witnesses for time lost while away from business. On the other hand, if an agreement to pay a witness fee is made contingent upon a given result, it is unlawful and void.

**Interference with Marital Relations.** A contract not to marry, or having a tendency to restrain marriage, is contrary to public policy and unenforceable. So, also, is a contract to promote or encourage a divorce. However, a contract of separation is valid if made in prospect of immediate separation or after the separation takes place. An agreement on alimony, support and property rights is valid if made as part of a separation agreement or as part of impending divorce proceedings. Marriage brokerage contracts are void: They stimulate, not marriages in general, but mercenary marriages.

**Restraint of Trade.** The statutes and cases dealing with restraint of trade are more fully discussed in Chapter 13. Agreements which restrain the free play of competition are contrary to public policy and void. Some restraint of trade, however, is inevitable and unavoidable.

*Reasonable restraint of trade.* The purchaser of a retail store having a local trade, such as a grocery, drugstore or dairy, may protect the store's good will by exacting from the seller an agreement not to open a new store within reasonable limits necessary to protect the purchase, such as for a given period of years, within a radius of a given number of blocks, and so on.

*Unreasonable restraint of trade.* If in the above illustration the purchaser exacted a promise from the seller not to compete anywhere in the United States, such a restraint would be unreasonable because unnecessary to protect the buyer's good will. But a nationwide restraint would not be unreasonable if the sale involved a nationwide chain of stores.

*Tests of reasonableness.* The basic test of reasonableness is whether the restraint is necessary to protect the purchase. The courts in applying this test have tended to hold that where the restraint is unlimited as to time and space, or even as to space alone, the restraint is unreasonable.

EXAMPLES:

(1) An accountant, retiring from practice and selling his assets and good will, agrees not to engage in the public practice of accounting anywhere for ten years. *Agreement invalid:* restraint unreasonable, not necessary to protect purchaser.

(2) A retail furniture dealer with no trade outside the county, in selling his business agrees not to re-engage in the furniture business for five years, anywhere in the state. *Agreement invalid:* restraint unreasonable, not necessary to protect purchaser.

(3) The owner of a grocery chain in Cleveland, Ohio, in selling his entire business, agrees not to re-engage in the grocery business anywhere for ten years. *Agreement invalid:* space unlimited; not necessary to protect purchaser.

**Business Monopolies.** A contract may be in reasonable restraint of trade as between the parties, yet may be invalid if it is detrimental to the public interest. A business monopoly, for example, tends to restrain trade to the public detriment. Agreements to form such monopolies are illegal, not only under the Sherman and Clayton Acts (Ch. 13:2), but under various state antitrust statutes.

**Government Monopolies.** Government monopolies, such as the post office, and government-protected monopolies, such as patents, copyrights, trade-marks and trade names (Chapter 16, Parts 3 and 4), being in the public interest, are lawful.

**Price Fixing.** Congress or the state legislatures may fix maximum and minimum prices in the public interest, but price-fixing agreements among business concerns, with certain exceptions (Ch. 13:2), are prohibited by law.

*Patents and copyrights.* If the owner of a patent grants a license to manufacture under the patent, he may restrict the price at which the licensee may sell the articles thus manufactured. Likewise, the owner of a copyright may restrict the price at which a licensee may sell the copyrighted matter. But no further restriction is permitted: Once the patented article or copyrighted matter itself is sold, the buyer is under no restriction as to its resale price.

**Restraint of Employment: Trade Secrets.** The law looks with disfavor on contracts which prohibit employees from seeking similar employment after terminating their contracts.

EXAMPLES:

(1) A contract restrained a manager on terminating his services from engaging in the clothing business for five years in any place where the employer had stores. In refusing to enforce the agreement, the court pointed out the difference between such restrictions and those which accompany the sale of a business. In the latter case, said the court, "the restrictions add to the value of what the vendor wishes to sell, and . . . what the vendee purchases. In such cases also the parties are presumably more nearly on a parity in ability to negotiate than is the case in the negotiation of agreements between employer and employee." [55]

(2) The articles of copartnership of a firm of accountants provided that any partner who voluntarily withdrew from the firm would not practice accountancy within four years thereafter, and within 100 miles of any city in which the firm had an office. The court held this covenant void and ineffective; that it would in effect prevent plaintiff from practicing on a national scale; and that its true purpose was to prevent voluntary withdrawals from the firm.[56]

However, an agreement not to engage or accept employment in a competing business is valid, where necessary to protect the employer against disclosure of trade secrets obtained in confidence during the course of employment.

**Unlicensed Transactions.** The subject of unlicensed transactions in violation of law is discussed in Chapter 21, Part 3. For services rendered as part of an unlicensed transaction, compensation may be refused with impunity.

EXAMPLES:

(1) In a state requiring real estate brokers to be licensed, Jones acts as broker in the sale of Smith's home upon an agreed commission of 5 per cent. On Smith's refusal to pay the commission, Jones sues; but since it appears that Jones has no license, his suit will fail.

(2) A corporation, pursuant to contract, rendered architectural services in fitting up a restaurant. The restaurant refused to pay, and the corporation sued. The court denied recovery on the ground that the plaintiff was not licensed (in fact, being a corporation, could not be licensed under the state law prohibiting corporations from practicing architecture).[57]

*Restrictions on professions.* The professions in particular are subject to legal restrictions: (1) Licenses to practice are required, to maintain professional standards of fitness. (2) Solicitation of clients, patients, and so

---

[55] *Samuel Stores, Inc. v. Abrams,* 94 Conn. 248, 108 A. 541.

[56] *Lynch v. Bailey et al. (Touche, Niven, Bailey & Smart),* 275 App. Div. 527, 90 N.Y. Supp. 2d 359, affirmed 300 N.Y. 615, 90 N.E. 2d 484.

[57] *American Store Equipment, etc. Corporation v. Jack Dempsey's Punch Bowl, Inc.,* 174 Misc. 436, 21 N.Y. Supp. 2d 117, affirmed 258 App. Div. 794, 16 N.Y. Supp. 2d 702.

on is prohibited, not only as incompatible with professional dignity, but also on the theory that professional fitness rather than "go-getting" ability should govern the practice. (3) Professional service sets up a *fiduciary relationship* (Ch. 9:3) which imposes higher standards of dealing than those in the common marts of trade.

**Stifling Competition for Public Contracts.** "Agreements not to compete with another in making bids, to withdraw a bid for a public or quasi-public contract, to share in the result or profits, or other agreements having a direct tendency to prevent bidding or competition, are against public policy." [58]

EXAMPLE: *A* and *B*, road-building contractors, agree that if *A* will refrain from bidding on one public road, *B* will refrain from bidding on the other. The agreement is void.

**Miscellaneous Social and Economic Abuses.** The complexity of our social and economic structure has called forth a variety of measures designed to curb social and economic abuses, such as those dealing with public safety, sanitation, true weights and measures, false labels, business licenses and the maintenance of proper professional and technical standards. These are discussed in Chapter 21. Contracts in contravention of measures dealing with these abuses are invalid and unenforceable. Of a similar nature are contracts which conflict with usury, wagering and Sunday statutes.

Usury is discussed in Chapter 16, Part 2. Sunday laws are discussed on pages 76-78.

**Wagering Contracts.** A wagering contract is one based on pure chance. In such transactions, what one party gains the other must necessarily lose. Among the more common examples are games of cards, dice, lotteries and betting on the outcome of an event. Formerly, under the common law, and now in the so-called "common law states," wagering contracts were and are permitted. Other states have passed laws against them. Characteristic of such laws are those passed in New York, where money lost on a bet or wager may be recovered by the loser, whether in the hands of a stakeholder, or the winner, but the winner cannot recover from the loser. If more than $25 is lost on a game by a player or spectator, the loser may get it back if he acts within three months; otherwise, the Overseer of the Poor may sue for the winnings, plus three times as much by way of penalty.

*Speculations on rise and fall of market.* Transactions on a stock or produce exchange, or transactions involving the purchase and sale of securities generally on the basis of pure chance, that is, on the rise or fall of the market, are wagering contracts and are unenforceable. However, the law permits the buying and selling of "futures," and of stock "on margin,"

---

[58] 17 C.J.S. 582.

on the theory that unless an intent *not to make future delivery* is shown, it will be presumed.

*"Puts" and "calls"* (options to buy or sell stock at a given figure within a given time) are not necessarily gambling contracts.

EXAMPLE: In *Story v. Salomon*,[59] defendant agreed to buy from or sell to bearer, at any time within thirty days, 100 shares of Western Union stock at 77½. The court held that in the absence of proof that the parties were merely speculating upon the fluctuations in price of the stock without intent of delivery or acceptance, the transaction could not be deemed a wager but would be presumed to be legal.

## Questions

1. Under what circumstances may one enter into a contract of insurance against the consequences of committing a crime?

2. Are any of the following agreements valid: (a) to commit assault and battery; (b) to defraud a third party; (c) to indemnify a person against the consequences of his negligence?

3. "Any contract causing or encouraging dereliction of fiduciary duty is void." Give three illustrations.

4. Under what circumstances will the following agreements be held void: (a) to induce the adoption of a given course of legislative, executive or administrative action; (b) to obtain public contracts; (c) to obtain unity of action among competing bidders on a public contract; (d) to further the nomination or election of persons to public office; (e) to influence the result of any other election?

5. Are the following agreements valid or void: (a) an agreement to compensate an expert for testifying in court; (b) an agreement by a lawyer to pay a commission for obtaining a client?

6. Are the following agreements valid or void: (a) an agreement which encourages marriage; (b) an agreement, for a consideration, to procure a matrimonial mate; (c) an agreement encouraging or promoting a divorce?

7. What is the basic test in determining the extent to which the buyer of a business may restrain the seller from opening up a similar establishment after the sale?

8. Does the law make any distinction between an agreement by a seller not to reopen a similar establishment, and an agreement by an employee not to work for a competing establishment on termination of his employment? Explain.

9. When, if at all, may a manufacturer enforce a contract in which he fixes a minimum resale price?

10. A stockbroker asks you whether transactions on a stock or produce exchange, or transactions involving the purchase and sale of securities generally on the rise or fall of the market, are enforceable or not. How would you answer him?

## Problems

1. The Risky Insurance Company issues a policy indemnifying the assured against loss or damage resulting from "any and all violations of law by the

---

[59] 71 N.Y. 420.

assured, whether committed by others, by himself, or by any member of the assured's immediate family." Comment on the validity of this policy.

2. The *Go-Gettem Press* sends a reporter to the home of Dorothy DeLite, an actress, to obtain her photograph in connection with a newspaper story. The reporter is refused admittance. The editor then requests the reporter to obtain a pass key to Miss DeLite's apartment, and to endeavor to obtain a photograph of her in her absence. The newspaper indemnifies the reporter against loss or criminal prosecution if caught in the act. The reporter is caught in the act and prosecuted, and he seeks to compel the newspaper publisher to indemnify him against the consequences of prosecution. Will he succeed?

3. Stupendous Studios, of Hollywood, hires an agent to persuade Antonio Basso, a famous singer, to terminate his contract with an opera company and to enter into a contract for several productions with Stupendous Studios. The agent succeeds in getting Basso to terminate his agreement with the opera company. The agent was promised $5,000 if he succeeded in his mission. He now demands payment by Stupendous Studios, which is refused. The opera company sues Basso, the agent, and Stupendous Studios, and the agent sues Stupendous Studios. How will these lawsuits be decided? Give reasons for your answer.

4. Samuel Slick submits an expensive display advertisement for publication in a farm journal, consisting of a striking illustration bearing the legend, "How to double your money instantly. Send One Dollar for this amazing secret." In line with its policy, the advertising department demands proof of Slick's ability to supply a proper answer to such inquiry. Slick exhibits the answer, which is as follows: "Catch suckers the way we do." The farm journal then runs the advertisement. Slick fails to pay for the advertisement, and the farm journal sues him. Will it recover?

5. Jones is injured in an automobile accident. Kiley, his friend, urges Jones to sue for damages. He offers, for a commission, to procure an attorney for Jones. Jones agrees, and Kiley procures an attorney, who brings suit on behalf of Jones and recovers a substantial judgment. Jones refuses to pay Kiley the promised commission. Can Kiley hold Jones on his promise?

6. In the above case, Jones needed a physician to testify to his injuries. Jones' attorney persuaded a physician to testify on Jones' behalf, on the latter's promise that the physician would be paid 10 per cent of the amount of any judgment recovered on the trial. Jones obtains a $10,000 judgment but refuses to pay the physician anything. The physician sues Jones for $1,000. Will he recover?

7.**

New York, July 15, 1929.

For value received, the bearer may call on the undersigned for one hundred (100) shares of the capital stock in the Western Union Telegraph Company, at 200, any time in thirty (30) days from date.

Or the bearer may, at his option, deliver the same to the undersigned at 200, any time within the period named, one day's notice required.

All dividends declared during the time are to go with the stock in either case, and this instrument is to be surrendered on the stock's being either called or delivered.

JOHN JONES.

(a) Give legal reasons for approving or disapproving the above instrument.

(b) If it should be shown that neither party intended to deliver or accept the shares, but merely to pay the differences according to the rise or fall of the market, what would be the status of the instrument?

8. Lane was hired by the Busy Building Corporation to assemble a group

of plots on which to build a forty story building. He spends the better part of a year assembling the plots by purchasing them from different owners through different agents. Lane's commission was to be 5 per cent of a maximum aggregate purchase price of $500,000. The actual cost was $400,000. At the end of his task, Lane submits his bill, which the Busy Building Corporation refuses to pay unless it is cut in half. Lane sues for his commission. The Busy Building Corporation interposes the defense that Lane had no brokerage license, which was the fact, Lane having forgotten to renew it during the period in question. How should the court decide, and why?

9.* Jones and Chambers were both road-building contractors. Bids were called for by the State of New Jersey for the building of a certain state road in that state. Jones proposed to Chambers that Chambers refrain from bidding in consideration of Jones' refraining from bidding against Chambers on another road soon to be built, and an agreement was entered into to that effect. Jones, however, entered a bid on both jobs and was awarded both contracts. Chambers sued Jones for the profits made under the second contract, alleging breach of the agreement between them. Could Chambers recover?

10.* Bishop, a public accountant, desiring to retire from practice, sold all his assets including his good will to Palmer for a stated sum. As a part of the sale Bishop covenanted that he would not engage in the public practice of accounting anywhere for a period of ten years. Is this agreement by Bishop valid?

11.* A corporation entered into a contract whereby it agreed to plan and supervise the construction and decoration of a restaurant. The state law which was applicable to this contract permitted such work to be done only by licensed architects. The corporation fully performed all of the services required of it by this contract, but the restaurant refused to pay for the services on the true ground that the corporation was not a licensed architect. Is the restaurant's refusal to pay legally justifiable?

12.* A retail furniture dealer has a business with customers throughout a certain county, but makes no sales outside that county. He sells his entire business and agrees with the purchaser that for a period of five years he will not engage in the furniture business anywhere in the state. Is such agreement enforceable under common law?

13.* Chandler, owner of a chain of grocery stores in Cleveland, Ohio, sold his entire business to Davison. The contract of sale contained an agreement by Chandler not to engage in the grocery business for a period of ten years. Could Davison enforce the agreement mentioned? What would have been the effect if Chandler had agreed not to engage in the grocery business in Cleveland, Ohio, and vicinity for a period of ten years?

14. In an election contest for the office of sheriff, Martin, the losing candidate, promises a hostile witness a free trip to Florida if he will go and stay there until the hearing is over. On his return, the witness presents his bill to Martin for traveling expenses, which Martin refuses to pay. What recourse, if any, has the witness?

15. Norton hires a broker to sell his house. The broker procures Ottaway as a purchaser. To save lawyer's fees, Norton and Ottaway agree to let the broker draw up the contract and handle the details of closing title, for which they promise the broker a fee of $100 in addition to his brokerage commission. When the transaction has been consummated, Norton tenders the broker his commission for procuring a purchaser, but neither of the parties is willing to pay anything toward a fee for drawing up the contract and attending to the

details of closing. The broker sues Norton and Ottaway for $100. Will he succeed? Explain.

## PART 6. SUNDAY LAWS; EFFECT OF INVALID SUBJECT MATTER

**In General.** The law governing Sunday business activities, including Sunday contracts, is multifarious in the extreme. Not only do the numerous state laws vary from one state to another, but local Sunday ordinances within each state are far from uniform. We shall limit our discussion of Sunday laws to the rules which may be said to have the widest acceptance.

**Common Law Rule.** At common law, any Sunday act or agreement not otherwise unlawful is valid; that is, any Sunday act or agreement is valid if it is not prohibited by statute.

**Agreement on Weekday for Action on Sunday.** If a statute prohibits the doing of an act on Sunday, an agreement, regardless of when it is made, is invalid if it calls for the doing of such act on Sunday.

EXAMPLE: Plaintiff, a band master, agreed on a weekday with defendant, the proprietor of a seaside resort, to give a series of daily concerts, seven days the week, during July and August, at a fixed price for the season. Plaintiff sued for an unpaid balance. *Held*, since the Sunday services, which were prohibited by law, and which were neither necessary nor charitable, were part of the contract, plaintiff could not recover.[60]

**Agreement on Sunday for Action on Weekday.** If a statute prohibits the making of business contracts on Sunday, such contracts, if made on Sunday, are invalid, though they call for performance on a weekday; but if the *making* of such contracts on Sunday is not forbidden, they will be enforced, unless they call for performance on a Sunday of acts forbidden on that day.

EXAMPLES:
(1) The statute in a given state prohibits the making of business agreements on Sunday (except for works of charity or necessity). A used car dealer sells an automobile to Roberts on Sunday, for $1,000, which Roberts pays. The car is to be serviced and delivered the next day. Should the dealer refuse to deliver the car, Roberts would have no recourse against him.
(2) A farmer, on Sunday, hires a helper for the summer at $5 a day and board, exclusive of Sundays. The statute prohibits Sunday labor, also "pursuing one's usual business or vocation on Sunday." The helper presents himself ready for work the following day, but the farmer repudiates the contract. Since the statute does not prohibit the making of such contract on Sunday, the helper may hold the farmer for the breach.[61]

---

[60] *Stewart v. Thayer*, 168 Mass. 519, 47 N.E. 420. It should be noted that this contract was entire ("fixed price for the season"), not severable, hence was entirely bad. (See page 84.)
[61] See *Johnson v. Brown*, 13 Kan. 529; *Merritt v. Earle*, 29 N.Y. 115 (aff'g 31 Barb. 38).

**Negotiation Begun on Sunday, Concluded on Weekday.** Where an agreement forbidden to be made on a Sunday is negotiated on that day but consummated on a weekday, it is deemed made on a weekday, and if otherwise lawful, is valid and enforceable.

EXAMPLE: Defendant, a property owner, negotiated on Sunday with plaintiff, a real estate broker, offering to pay a commission for procuring a purchaser. Plaintiff later (on a weekday) procured a purchaser, and the deal was consummated, but defendant refused to pay the commission on the ground that the contract was negotiated on Sunday. *Held*, that "what was said on the Sunday in question amounted only to an offer by the defendant and a contract did not arise until the plaintiff produced a customer who was ready, able and willing to purchase the property, which event does not appear to have occurred on a Sunday." [62]

**Sunday Activities Most Commonly Prohibited.** Among the Sunday activities most commonly prohibited by statute are those relating to work, labor, or the prosecution of one's business or occupation.

*Work or labor.* Many states prohibit Sunday work or labor; and where such prohibition is not statewide, it is frequently imposed by local ordinance.

*Business or occupation.* Where the statute prohibits a person from conducting his business or occupation on Sunday, or pursuing his "avocation," or his "worldly employment," it is immaterial "whether the act or acts which constitute such employment are one or many." [63] A person may be guilty of violating such act though it is done by a partner, agent or employee and not by himself, provided the act is done with his knowledge and consent.

*"Keeping open."* Many statutes forbid the opening or keeping open of any establishment or of certain particular establishments. It is no defense in such case that the front door is actually locked, if persons wishing to enter for business purposes are afforded access.

*Acts done in exercise of ordinary calling.* Where the statute merely prohibits acts done in the exercise of one's "ordinary calling," a person who engages on Sunday in some other business than that of his "ordinary calling" is not violating the statute, unless such other business activity is likewise prohibited on Sundays.

**Exceptions to Sunday Laws.** Common exceptions to the Sunday laws are those relating to works of necessity or charity, to persons observing the Sabbath on another day than Sunday, and contracts of marriage.

*Works of necessity.* What constitutes a necessity depends on the facts. Works of necessity are not, however, limited solely to transactions and services which are urgent and cannot be delayed. Nor are they matters the suppression of which would be merely inconvenient. They are mat-

---

[62] *Isenberg v. Williams*, 27 N.E. 2d 726 (Mass.).
[63] *Friedeborn v. Com.*, 113 Pa. 242, 245, 6 A. 160.

ters, rather, the omission of which "would work severe hardship or loss or unusual discomfort or inconvenience." [64] Here no convenient yardstick can be applied. More often than not, the temper of the community will determine the liberality or strictness with which the word "necessity" is construed. Commonly accepted as clearly matters of public necessity are medical and surgical attendance, emergency repairs and steps necessary to save things from serious loss or destruction, church affairs and subscriptions, drugs, mortuary and burial services, restaurants, dairy, delicatessen, and similar establishments, Sunday newspapers, and (subject to local regulation) motion picture and other entertainment. Beyond these, what constitutes a public necessity is subject to local interpretation.

*Works of charity.* As applied to a Sunday law, charity includes anything "which proceeds from a sense of moral duty, or a feeling of kindness and humanity," [65] such as the furtherance of religious or philanthropic enterprises by contributions of money, services or talent.

*Observing the Sabbath on another day.* Some Sunday laws except persons who observe the Sabbath on another day than Sunday. Unless the statute makes such exception, such persons are not excused from observing the Sunday laws.

*Mutual promises to marry* made on Sunday and marriages consummated on that day are valid.

**Effect of Invalid Subject Matter: General Rule.** Courts generally refuse to recognize contracts tainted with illegal subject matter, and will turn a deaf ear to pleas for relief based on non-performance of such contracts.

EXAMPLES:
(1) Plaintiff was made ill by eating sausage purchased from a retailer on Sunday in violation of the statute. He sued for breach of implied warranty of wholesomeness and fitness for human consumption (Ch. 4:3). *Held*, as a participant in the illegal transaction, he could not found a suit upon it.[66]
(2) Plaintiff sold defendant a dog on Sunday. The balance due remaining unpaid, plaintiff sued to recover the dog. *Held*, plaintiff, as a party to the illegal transaction, had no standing in court in reference to it.[67]

**Effect of Invalid Subject Matter: Exceptions to Rule.** There are certain exceptions to the rule that contracts tainted with illegality afford no basis for relief. The most common exceptions are: (1) transactions in which the illegal purpose has not been consummated; (2) transactions in which the parties are not equally at fault (*in pari delicto*); (3) transactions declared illegal for the purpose of protecting their victims; (4) transactions in which the proceeds of an illegal transaction are in the hands of a third party or stakeholder; and (5) transactions which are only partly tainted with invalid subject matter.

---

[64] *McAfee v. Com.*, 173 Ky. 83, 190 S.W. 671, 673.
[65] 60 Corpus Juris 1056. (Corpus Juris will hereafter be cited as C.J.)
[66] *Johnston v. Swift & Co., of Illinois*, 191 So. 423 (Miss.).
[67] *Foster v. Behre*, 7 N.J. Misc. 623, 146 A. 672.

(1) *Illegal transaction not consummated.* The law encourages parties to withdraw from illegal contracts not yet carried out. If I give you money to invest in an illegal enterprise and the money is not yet so invested, I may repudiate the transaction and recover the money. If the illegal purpose has been partly though not fully consummated, the general rule is that money or property contributed toward such purpose can not be recovered.

(2) *Parties not* **in pari delicto.** Where parties to an illegal agreement are not equally at fault, the party less at fault may seek relief through court action if public policy will be served by granting rather than denying such relief. Thus a party brought into an illegal agreement through fraud, or duress, or undue influence, is either not at fault at all, or less at fault than the other party; that is, the parties are not *in pari delicto.*

EXAMPLE: Plaintiff sued to recover money paid defendant on the false representation that it was needed to bribe public officials in procuring plaintiff's appointment as a state highway maintenance police officer. Defendant moved to dismiss on the ground that the alleged contract was void. *Held*, that where parties to an illegal contract are not *in pari delicto*, or equally guilty, and public policy is advanced by allowing recovery to the more excusable party, the court will grant such party relief, "especially where he has been fraudulently induced to become a party to such transaction." [68]

*"Confidence games."* In a so-called "confidence game," one person swindles another by getting him to part with something of value in a pretended joint swindle of a third party. While in a minority of cases the victim is allowed no relief on the ground that he and his co-swindler are *in pari delicto*, the majority of cases have permitted recovery either because public interest will be better served thereby, or on the ground of "repentance and repudiation of the transaction before it was fully executed." [69]

(3) *Transactions declared illegal, to protect victims.* Where a transaction is declared illegal for the purpose of protecting possible victims, the latter, for whose benefit the statute was passed, may seek relief thereunder. For example, usury statutes passed to protect needy persons from exorbitant interest charges frequently permit such persons not only to recover the exorbitant interest paid, but to refuse repayment of the loan. (As a rule, parties to such transactions are not *in pari delicto.*)

(4) *Proceeds of transaction in hands of third party or stakeholder.* The courts distinguish between situations where the proceeds of an illegal transaction are in the hands of one of several parties associated in the transaction, and situations where such proceeds are in the hands of a third party or stakeholder. In the former case, "Courts will not divide the spoils

---

[68] *Johnson v. Harman,* 328 Ill. App. 585, 66 N.E. 2d 498.
[69] 17 C.J.S. 662.

of an illegal transaction." [70] In the latter case, the law permits recovery by the person for whose benefit the third party holds the money or property, on the theory that the suit is not based on the illegal contract, but on the independent contract of the third party to deliver over the money or property entrusted to him.

**Winner's rights against third party.** Where the loser pays over a gambling debt to a third party (for example, to the winner's attorney), the latter cannot refuse to turn over the money to the winner on the plea that the original transaction was illegal. "In such cases the action is not based on the illegal contract, but on the independent contract of such third person to deliver over the property received by him. . . ." [74]

(5) *Contracts only partly affected by invalid subject matter.* If a contract is *severable* (made up of separate obligatory parts or installments), the invalidity of one part will not necessarily invalidate the rest. But if the contract is *entire*, the illegality of any part taints the whole. Thus, in the *Dempsey's Punch Bowl* case cited on page 71, the contract was to furnish work, labor and materials *and unlicensed architectural services.* The court ruled that the contract was entire and indivisible because there was "no means of segregating the good from the bad portions of the contract." Since part of the contract was bad, it was all bad. (See band concert example on page 76.) On the other hand, had the contract been to furnish unlicensed architectural services on one alteration job for $5,000, and only work, labor and materials on another job for $10,000, or a total contract price of $15,000, the invalidity of the first job would not have tainted the rest of the (divisible) contract.

## Questions

1. What is the rule governing weekday contracts to be performed on Sunday?

2. What is the rule governing Sunday contracts to be performed on weekdays?

3. What is the rule governing Sunday contracts where such agreements are forbidden by statutes and where negotiation of such contracts is begun on a Sunday and concluded on a weekday?

4. Name four common exceptions to Sunday laws.

5. Under the usual statutes and ordinances governing such matters, are contracts made on Sunday for the following purposes valid or not: (a) theatrical entertainment; (b) the purchase of groceries; (c) the purchase of drugs; (d) the operation of a restaurant; (e) conducting a church bazaar; (f) the operation of a shoe store; (g) the exchange of vows in a marriage ceremony; (h) the exhibition of motion pictures for profit?

6. What is the general rule governing the attitude of courts with respect to a suit to recover monies paid on an illegal contract?

---

[70] 17 C.J.S. 664.

[71] *Wise v. Radis,* 74 Cal. App. 765, 242 P. 90; *Matta v. Katsoulas,* 192 Wis. 212, 212 N.W. 261.

7. What provision does the law make with respect to withdrawal by a party from an unconsummated, illegal contract?

8. Name five exceptions to the rule governing the attitude of the court in respect to suits based on contracts the subject matter of which is tainted with illegality?

9. What is the meaning of the expression, "The parties were not *in pari delicto*"? Give an example.

10. What is the rule of recovery by a victim of a "confidence game"?

## Problems

1. After attending a Sunday baseball game, Potter buys a second-hand automobile for $1,000. He pays $500 down on the purchase price and agrees to pay the rest the next day. In driving it on a trial run, he discovers a leaky carburetor and faulty transmission. The following day he demands his $500 back. The dealer insists on receiving the balance of the purchase price. Each of the parties brings suit against the other. How will the court decide these suits, and why?

2. On leaving church one Sunday morning Quimby spies Roberts, a broker, and asks, "Do you think you can get $35,000 for my house?" Roberts replies, "I think so." Quimby then says, "Well, go ahead and get it." Three days later Roberts procures a purchaser, ready, willing and able to buy Quimby's house at his price. Quimby refuses to pay Roberts the commission on the ground that the contract was negotiated on a Sunday. How will the court decide?

3. Sloan agrees on a Sunday to rent his hall to a Benevolence Society for a charity ball the following Sunday evening. He cancels the agreement the next day, and when sued for the breach, pleads that the contract was negotiated on a Sunday and was unenforceable. Was Sloan's position sound?

4. Plaintiff got sick eating black market meat, knowingly bought as such. He sued the butcher for negligence, and also for breach of implied warranty that the food was fit for human consumption. How would the court decide, and why?

5. Clem Toddy, temporarily confined to the Federal penitentiary, asks his friend, Hank Upson, to dispose of Toddy's whiskey still, hidden in the backwoods a mile from Toddy's shack. Upson receives an offer from Varley to buy the still for $500. He accepts a deposit of $100 and tells Varley that as soon as he gets Toddy's approval, Varley can have the still on payment of the balance. The next day, Varley tells Upson he has changed his mind and demands back the $100 deposit, which Upson refuses. Varley sues Upson for the $100. Will he recover?

6. Wing, a manufacturer of toys, hires York as a sales agent on a drawing account of $50 a week, plus 10% commissions on net sales. He also gives York $1,000 in cash "to establish good will in the trade." York is prosecuted for attempted bribery of a purchasing agent. On the trial it comes out that this was York's first offense and that he had not yet paid out any bribe monies. York is given a suspended sentence. On being released, he sues Wing for $300, representing six weeks' drawing account. Wing counterclaims for $1,000, representing the cash he turned over to York. How will these suits be decided, and why?

7. Suppose, in the last case, that before York had entered upon his duties, Wing asked York to return the $1,000, and on York's refusal, brought suit for its return: what would be your opinion as to the outcome of the suit?

8. Zell, an immigrant, unfamiliar with the English language, is induced to

indorse a note for the accommodation of Allen. The note is not paid, and Zell, sued as an accommodation indorser, is advised by Brown, an alleged friend, to turn over his savings temporarily to the latter, in view of the threatened judgment. Allen, however, pays the note before trial. Zell then demands the return of his savings, and on Brown's refusal, brings suit. Brown sets up illegality as a defense. How would the court decide?

9. I. M. Smoothe, a "confidence man," strikes up a friendship with Simon Simple, then tells him of a plan to issue fake securities to a wealthy widow, whereby both Simple and Smoothe would be greatly enriched. Simple's share of the expense in the scheme, Smoothe tells him, is only $500, which Simple pays. Simple and Smoothe were to meet in the widow's apartment, but when Simple goes there, he learns that both Smoothe and the alleged widow have disappeared. Later, Simple locates Smoothe and sues him for the return of his money. Will he succeed?

10. Carter owes Dalton $1,000 on a gambling debt incurred in a state where gambling is and always has been illegal. Dalton hires Edwards to collect the debt, and Carter, unaware that he has a good defense to the suit, pays Edwards the amount of the debt. Edwards refuses to transmit the collection to Dalton on the following grounds: (a) illegality of the gambling debt, and (b) illegality of hiring a layman to practice law. Can Dalton compel Edwards to turn over the money?

## PART 7. CLASSIFICATION AND FORM OF CONTRACTS: STATUTE OF FRAUDS

**Classification of Contracts in General.** Contracts may be variously classified as follows:

(a) As to manner of showing intent: *express* and *implied*.

(b) As to whether the thing agreed to be done has or has not been done: *executed* and *executory*.

(c) As to whether the contract consists of an exchange of promises or a promise on one side only: *bilateral* and *unilateral*.

(d) As to collective liability where there are several promisors: *joint* and *joint and several*.

(e) As to enforceability: *valid, void, voidable* and *enforceable*.

(f) As to whether all parts of the contract are interdependent, or susceptible of division and apportionment: *entire* and *divisible*.

(g) As to form or formality: *contracts of record, specialties,* and *parol (simple)* contracts.

(a) **Express and Implied Contracts.** An *express* contract is one wherein the intent of the parties is shown by words, oral or written.

An *implied* contract is one wherein the intent of the parties is shown by conduct, as where (without mentioning compensation) *A* renders and *B* accepts valuable services.

*Quasi contracts* are obligations in the nature of contract implied or imposed by law. Strictly speaking, they are not contracts at all, because—unlike either express contracts or contracts implied in fact—they do not rest on the express or implied assent of the parties but are imposed by law to prevent injustice. They are really a fiction of equity aimed at ensuring that no person shall enrich himself unjustly at the expense of another.

EXAMPLES:
(1) Where money is improperly received, there is an implied obligation to account for it.
(2) Where money is improperly paid, there is an implied obligation to return it.
(3) Where an infant contracts for necessaries he is not, strictly speaking, liable on *his* contract for the agreed price, but on the contract implied by law for the reasonable value (page 54).

**(b) Executed and Executory Contracts.** An *executed* contract is one that has already been performed; an *executory* contract, one not yet performed. If one party has performed and the other not, or if both have partly performed, the contract is partly executory and partly executed.

**(c) Bilateral and Unilateral Contracts.** A contract consisting of an exchange of promises is said to be *bilateral*. A promise given for an act already done, or an act to be done without promise on the other side to do it, is termed a *unilateral* contract. (See page 59.) Strictly speaking, it is not a contract at all, since in the former case it is based on past consideration (page 60), and in the latter it lacks mutuality (page 59).[72]

**(d) Collective Liability: Joint v. Joint and Several Contracts.** Where two or more promisors obligate themselves on a contract as one so that they are liable together or not at all, the contract is *joint*. Where they obligate themselves, both individually, and collectively as a unit, the contract is *joint and several*.

EXAMPLE: Fifty persons sign an agreement, "We hereby agree," and so on. Such an obligation is joint, and in case of dispute all must be sued together, or none. If they signed, "We and each of us agree," or "*I* hereby agree," the contract would be joint and several: all, or *any one*, could be sued in case of dispute.

**(e) Valid, Void, Voidable, and Enforceable Contracts.** A *valid* contract is one having all legal requisites. A *void* contract lacks one or more requisites to validity, hence is invalid. In a *voidable* contract, one of the parties may (if he wishes) avoid the contract on some ground, such as fraud, infancy, duress, and so on, but unless and until such contract is thus avoided, it remains valid. An *enforceable* contract is not necessarily the same as a valid contract: Many contracts are valid but unenforceable for some procedural reason (such as oral contracts required by law to be evidenced by a writing, or contracts outlawed by the statute of limitations).

---

[72] The distinction between unilateral and bilateral offers and acceptances in connection with sales contracts is done away with under the Uniform Commercial Code. (See Appendix, Art. 2. Sales.)

(f) **Entire and Divisible (Severable) Contracts.** A contract is *entire* when all its parts are so interdependent that they must stand or fall together, so that failure or illegality of one part renders the whole invalid. A contract is *divisible* or *severable* when it is susceptible of division or apportionment, so that failure or illegality of one part does not destroy the whole. The test is usually whether a single consideration or price is fixed for the whole contract (in which case the contract is entire) or whether separate considerations are apportioned to the separate parts (in which case the contract is divisible).

EXAMPLES:

(1) Hecht buys from McCormick a team of horses for $650, a set of harness for $185 and a wagon for $75. Before delivery, the harness is stolen. McCormick tenders the team and wagon, which Hecht rejects because of the missing harness. The rejection is unwarranted, because the contract is divisible: Hecht must accept the team and wagon, but may sue for breach as to the harness.

(2) In the *Dempsey's Punch Bowl* case (page 71), where the contract to alter premises was held illegal because it included unlicensed architectural services, plaintiff urged that its architectural services, if any, amounted only to about 5% or 10% of the entire services rendered. The court ruled, however, that "there is no means of segregating the good from the bad portions of the contract, in this case. The contract was entire and indivisible: to plan, construct and furnish a complete unit. If the plaintiff had sold the interior furnishings and decorations, the contract could have been separated at least to the extent of permitting recovery for the merchandise sold. Here however were only services, ideas and supervision. They cannot be separated into different classes —legal and illegal."

(g) **Form of Contract.** Although form is sometimes included among the contract requisites (pages 2-3), a contract need not be in any particular form unless the statute so provides, as in the case of instruments required to be under seal or agreements required to be in writing.

A contract which lacks validity in itself does not acquire validity by being written or under seal: formality adds nothing to futility.

EXAMPLE: *A* telephones *B*, "I have fine apples at $5.00 a barrel." *B* says, "I will take two barrels." Since *A*'s mere invitation to trade (page 34) cannot be accepted as an offer, there is no contract. To cast this futility into a writing, with formal language, witnesses, seal, and so on, would not cure a failure of contract requisites (in this case, mutual assent).

From the standpoint and in the order of their formality, contracts are *of record, under seal,* and *parol* or *simple.*

**Contracts of Record.** A contract of record is one entered into before some court "of record." Two leading examples are *judgments* and *recognizances.* A judgment is the official determination of a court of justice, but it is enforceable by execution only in the state where rendered. For the purpose of enforcing a judgment in another jurisdiction, it is treated as a contract. The most common form of recognizance is a *bail bond.*

**Contracts under Seal (Specialties).** A contract under seal, or *specialty* (also sometimes called a *covenant*) is a contract solemnized by adding to one's signature a seal ("L.S.," the word "seal," a disc, scroll or other symbol). Under the common law, such contracts possessed greater force than ordinary contracts, and this is still true, as we have seen, in various states today, particularly in respect to consideration (page 63) and the statute of limitations (Ch. 22:5). The force of a seal, however, is on the wane.

The two most common types of specialties are *deeds* (Ch. 14:2) and *bonds* (Ch. 3:2).

**Parol or Simple Contracts.** A parol or simple contract is one neither of record nor under seal. It may be oral, unless required by law to be evidenced by a writing.

**Statute of Frauds: Nature, Origin, and Purpose.** The "statute of frauds" is the name given to a group or collection of statutory provisions relating to agreements that are unenforceable unless evidenced by a memorandum in writing. The underlying purpose of the statute of frauds is to minimize the possibilities of fraud and perjury and to promote certainty in making and enforcing contracts. Memory is fallible; writings are specific. Hence the various states in this country have adopted statutes based upon the English statute of frauds, providing that no action may be brought on certain specified contracts unless the agreement upon which such action is brought, or some memorandum or note of it is in writing, signed by the party to be charged, or by some person authorized to sign it.

The English statute of frauds was adopted by Parliament in 1676. Its most important provisions were embodied in the fourth and seventeenth sections. The *fourth section* covered (a) contracts for more than one year, (b) contracts for the sale of realty, (c) contracts of guaranty and suretyship, (d) promises of executors or administrators to be personally liable for estate debts and (e) contracts in consideration of marriage. The *seventeenth section* covered contracts for the sale of personal property. These provisions have been adopted without substantial change throughout this country. Additional provisions have been adopted by the different states, requiring various other forms of agreements to be evidenced by a writing. These provisions are not uniform throughout the country. The more common ones are reflected in the New York statute. (See pages 87-88.)

**Contracts Not to Be Performed within One Year.** A contract not to be performed within one year from the date of its *making* is unenforceable unless it is in writing and signed by the party to be charged.

*One year to begin in future.* A one-year oral contract made today but to begin next week is unenforceable because it cannot be performed within one year from the date of *making*.

*No period specified: possibility of performance within year.* A contract which fixes no definite time for performance but which is capable of performance within a year, need not be in writing; for example, an agreement to repurchase bonds "at any time buyer is in need of money," or to cut and deliver timber *within* two years. A contract for the maintenance, support or education of a person, for life or other indefinite period (without specifying a definite purpose the achievement of which would have to take more than a year) is deemed a contract possible of performance within a year, because of the possibility of death within the year.

*No period specified: impossibility of performance within year.* An oral agreement which specifies no period of performance but must of necessity take more than one year to perform is void.

EXAMPLES OF VOID CONTRACTS:
(1) An oral agreement involving educational training for a specific purpose that must of necessity take more than one year to achieve.[73]
(2) An oral agreement to do something after the expiration of a written agreement that still has more than a year to go.

*No period specified: improbability of performance within year.* An oral contract which is possible of performance within one year is not void under the statute of frauds merely because it is not likely, or not expected, to be performed within that time, or even because it is probable that it will not be so performed. The question is not what the probable, expected, or actual performance of the contract may be, but whether, according to the reasonable interpretation of its terms, it requires that it should not be performed within the year.[74]

EXAMPLE: An oral agreement to pay a sum of money for life, payments to start within a year from the date of contract, is enforceable because, regardless of probabilities, death *might* come within the year.

*No period specified: where parties clearly intend performance to take more than a year.* Where the situation is such that the parties clearly intended the contract to take more than a year, an oral agreement is within the statute and void. The proof of intent is not what the parties orally *say* they intended, but what the facts unmistakably show. Probability or improbability of performance within the year, as we have seen, is usually immaterial; but where the improbability "is so great or of such a character as to show unmistakably that the parties intended the agreement to last more than one year," the contract, if oral, is void.[75]

EXAMPLE: An agreement by a water company to furnish water to a village free of charge "so long as such waterworks exist."

**Contracts for Sale of Realty.** A contract for the sale of *any interest in* real property (except leases for not more than one year) must be evidenced by a writing. This includes not only land but also buildings, stand-

---

[73] *Fitzgerald v. Upson,* 74 S.W. 2d 1061, affirmed 129 Tex. 211.
[74] 37 C.J.S. 561.
[75] 37 C.J.S. 562.

ing timber, growing crops, real fixtures (Ch. 14:1) and anything else annexed to land as part of the realty.

**Contracts of Guaranty and Suretyship.** An agreement to answer for another's debt, default or failure of duty, must be in writing to be enforceable.

*Promise to "answer for" v. promise to pay.* A promise to answer for another means that the latter is obligated in the first instance. If *A* says to *B*, "Let *C* have groceries and I will pay if he does not," such promise is to *answer for C*, because *C* is liable in the first instance. But if *A* says, "Let *C* have groceries and I will pay," such promise, though oral, would be binding, because only *A* is liable: *C* is not liable at all.

**Special Promise by Executor or Administrator.** If an executor or administrator promises that estate obligations will be met, such promise is in no way extraordinary: The law will enforce estate obligations in any event. But if an executor or administrator promises the creditors that he will *personally* make good their claims against the estate, such promise is unenforceable unless it is in writing.

**Promises in Consideration of Marriage.** A promise in consideration of marriage is unenforceable unless in writing. This does not mean mutual promises to marry, but an agreement the consideration of which is marriage. For instance, if *A* says to *B*, "If you will marry *C*, I will pay you $50,000," and *B* marries *C*, *B* cannot recover on *A*'s promise unless it is in writing, since the promise was made in consideration of marriage.

**Seventeenth Section: Contracts for Sale of Personal Property.** The seventeenth section of the English statute of frauds, as noted on page 85, covered contracts for the sale of personal property. A corresponding provision has been widely adopted in this country. The statute of frauds in relation to the sale of personal property is further discussed in the chapter on Sales.

**Additional Contracts Governed by Statute of Frauds.** In addition to the foregoing provisions of the statute of frauds, which are directly derived from the English statute, various new provisions have been added to the old ones rendering agreements unenforceable unless they are evidenced by a writing in each instance. These provisions vary in the different states, but the following requirements of the New York statute are typical:

*Agreements not to be performed before the end of a lifetime.* An oral agreement to bequeath property, to make a testamentary provision, or to do anything else which cannot be performed before the end of the life of the person making the promise, is unenforceable. The purpose of this provision is obvious. Suits for breach of contract to bequeath property, or to make a testamentary provision, are naturally brought against the estate of the person who is alleged to have made and violated the contract. Such person, at the time of the suit, has died: His mouth is stopped, and he cannot defend or dispute the claim that he made the promise sued on. By requiring a writing to prove such a promise, the law reduces the temptation to frauds and perjuries.

EXAMPLES:
(1) An oral agreement between husband and wife regarding disposition of the proceeds of an insurance policy covering the husband's life.
(2) An oral promise allegedly made by a decedent, that plaintiff would be compensated out of the proceeds of the decedent's estate for taking care of decedent's sister.

*Contracts to establish a trust in real property,* with the exception of *implied* or *resulting* trusts (Ch. 19:3), have always required a writing since the statute of frauds came into existence, inasmuch as such contracts concern an interest in real property. However, the statute of frauds in a number of states now also covers contracts to establish a trust in personal property.

*Contract to convey or assign trust in personal property.* If I hold $50,000 worth of securities in trust for you, an oral conveyance or assignment of your interest as beneficiary of that trust would be unenforceable.

*Subsequent or new promise to pay debt discharged in bankruptcy.* If a person, notwithstanding his discharge in bankruptcy, promises one of his creditors to pay a certain debt, such promise is unenforceable unless it is evidenced by a writing.

*Subsequent or new promise to pay debt barred by the statute of limitations.* If a person, notwithstanding that a certain debt he owes is outlawed by the statute of limitations, promises to pay the debt, such promise is unenforceable unless it is evidenced by a writing (Ch. 22:5).

*Agreement to modify or discharge sealed instrument.* In states still recognizing the efficacy of a seal, an oral agreement to modify or discharge a contract under seal is ineffective, unless it has been executed.

*Contracts to arbitrate* a controversy between the parties must be in writing to be enforceable.

**Form of Memorandum; Signature.** No particular form of memorandum is prescribed by the statute of frauds.[76] The memorandum will suffice if it (a) sufficiently identifies the subject matter of the contract, (b) names or identifies the parties, (c) states the consideration, (d) embodies the terms of the contract and (e) contains the signature of the party to be charged or his duly authorized agent. The memorandum may consist of a single writing, or several writings, such as an exchange of letters or telegrams.[77] The memorandum may be very brief.

---

[76] *Bartlett-Heard Land & Cattle Co. v. Harris,* 28 Ariz. 497, 238 P. 327; *Goetz v. Hubbell,* 66 N.D. 491, 266 N.W. 836.
[77] *Fey v. Loose-Wiles Biscuit Co.,* 147 Kan. 31, 75 P. 2d 810, 813.

EXAMPLES:

(1) In *Page v. Cohen*,[78] a brief extract from the minutes of a lodge, signed by the Secretary, was held sufficient.

(2) In *Bayles v. Strong*,[79] the following was held a sufficient memorandum to charge the seller with an agreement to sell real property (that is, standing timber): "Setauket, N.Y., Feb. 14, 1901. Received from Thomas N. Bayles two hundred and twenty-five dollars for locust at Oakwood. Selah B. Strong." It will be noted that this latter memorandum designated the subject matter, named the parties, stated the consideration, set forth the terms (obviously cash), and was signed by the party to be charged.

The writing need not be signed by both parties, but only by the one to be charged. If both are to be charged, both must sign, since the right of action is against only the one or ones who sign.

EXAMPLE: A written agreement for the sale of land was drawn by the proposed purchaser and sent to the landowner, who did not sign it but returned it with a letter signed by him, stating, "The inclosed agreement, of this date, is satisfactory. I will sell you the land described in it on the terms which are stated in it." This is an enforceable contract. The proposal or offer embodied in the written agreement for the sale of land was duly accepted by the owner. The acceptance was evidenced by a signed memorandum (the letter) which incorporated the written agreement into the letter by specific reference to such agreement, the result being the same as if the written agreement had been physically embodied in the letter. As stated, a written memorandum, under the statute of frauds, need not be signed by both parties, but only by the party "sought to be charged," in this case, the owner.

**Writing Must Show All the Terms.** The writing must *fully* embody the terms of the contract.[80] If it omits any material part of the understanding, it is insufficient to satisfy the statute of frauds.

EXAMPLE: Berman orally ordered of Hirsh 2250 men's suits of various sizes, styles, materials and prices. The oral agreement further stipulated terms of shipment and delivery. Hirsh signed a written memorandum specifying the number, sizes, styles, materials and prices, but omitted reference to shipment and delivery. In a suit for breach of contract, Hirsh successfully pleaded the statute of frauds, because the written memorandum did not embody all the terms of the understanding.[81]

**Equity and the Statute of Frauds: Part Performance of Land Contract.** Equity will not permit the statute of frauds to be utilized as an instrument for achieving a fraudulent or inequitable result. Hence, where

[78] 80 Misc. 237.

[79] 104 App. Div. 153.

[80] *Santoro v. Mack*, 108 Conn. 683, 145 A. 273; *F. & W. Grand Five-Ten-Twenty-Five Cent Stores v. Eiseman*, 160 Ga. 321, 127 S.E. 872; *Gaskill v. Jacobs*, 38 Idaho 795, 225 P. 499; *Patterson v. Beard*, 227 Iowa 401, 288 N.W. 414, 125 A.L.R. 393; *Cassity v. Cassity*, 147 Kan. 411, 76 P. 2d 862; *Farrell v. Simons*, 180 Okl. 600, 71 P. 2d 688.

[81] *Berman Stores v. Hirsh*, 208 App. Div. 622 (reversed on evidentiary grounds, 240 N.Y. 209).

an oral agreement to sell real property has been partly performed (as where the buyer has paid part of the price, taken possession and made improvements), equity will compel specific performance, and the seller will be compelled to deliver the deed.

**Full Performance by One of the Parties.** The doctrine of part performance is a creature of equity and applies only to land contracts. In all other oral contracts governed by the statute of frauds, there must be full performance by one of the parties to compel performance by the other.

**Unjust Enrichment.** Even where the contract does not concern real property and where one of the parties has only partly performed under an oral contract governed by the statute of frauds, the law will not permit the other party to be unjustly enriched by pleading the statute; and this is all the more so where one of the parties has fully performed.

EXAMPLES:
(1) If I pay you $100 as a deposit on a two-year, oral contract, you may refuse performance by pleading the statute, but the law will imply a promise on your part to repay me the amount of my deposit. (See page 82, "Quasi contracts.")
(2) If a farm hand is orally hired for eighteen months and discharged without pay at the end of a month, the fact that the contract is oral will not defeat the employee's right to recover the reasonable value of his services.

**Parol Evidence Rule.** Once parties have reduced an oral agreement to writing, they are bound by the writing and are not allowed to offer any proof of the oral agreement contradicting the terms of the writing. This rule has four exceptions:

(1) *Oral proof of invalidity* does not merely contradict a writing; it *goes to the existence* of a written contract and destroys it. For example, oral proof showing fraud, mutual mistake, lack of consideration, duress or illegality, would have the effect, not of altering or varying the written contract, but of showing that *there was no contract really in existence.*

(2) *Oral proof of a condition precedent,* that is, that the parties orally agreed that a certain condition was to have been fulfilled before the written agreement was to become effective, is permissible. To establish oral proof of such a condition, and its nonfulfillment, would also be not to vary the terms of a written contract, but to show that there was really no contract in existence, since its existence depended upon the fulfillment of the condition.

(3) *Oral proof to clear up ambiguity, omissions, or obscurity* is not only permissible, but necessary. If a contract contains words that might mean one of several things, there is no way to prove what was really intended, except by oral evidence. The same applies to omissions in a contract, or to portions that are blurred, erased, or obscure in meaning.

(4) *Oral proof of subsequent modification upon consideration* is permissible. If you and I enter into a written agreement, and subsequently,

without consideration, we orally agree to modify the terms of the written agreement, this subsequent oral agreement, lacking consideration, is no contract at all, and leaves the written agreement unaffected. But if such oral agreement is upon consideration, it is a valid contract. Its subject matter is to modify a prior written agreement. Written contracts (except those required to be in writing under the statute of frauds) may thus be modified or discharged at will by mutual agreement of the parties, even though such mutual agreement be oral, provided there is consideration for the contract of modification or discharge.

## Questions

1. How would you classify contracts with respect to (a) the manner of showing intent, and (b) whether the thing agreed to be done has or has not been done?

2. Distinguish between bilateral and unilateral contracts. Give an illustration of each.

3. With respect to collective liability, how would you distinguish between joint promisors and joint and several promisors? Illustrate the distinction.

4. Distinguish valid, void, voidable and unenforceable contracts. Give an illustration of each.

5. Distinguish between entire and divisible contracts. Give an illustration of each.

6. Define and illustrate (a) contracts of record, (b) specialties and (c) parol (simple) contracts.

7. Define and illustrate a quasi-contract.

8. Are all oral contracts also parol contracts?

9. Are all parol contracts also oral contracts?

10. When and where was the statute of frauds first adopted? What was the underlying basis for such statute?

11. Is the following statement true or false: "Any contract which takes longer than one year in the performance is unenforceable unless evidenced by a writing"? Explain.

12. Are there any exceptions to the rule that a contract for the sale of any interest in real property must be evidenced by a writing?

13. Does a promise to discharge another person's obligation have to be in writing?

14. "All promises by an executor or administrator with respect to estate obligations must be evidenced by a writing." Is this a correct statement of the law? Comment fully.

15. Is it true, or not true, that promises made in connection with matrimony must be evidenced by a writing or they will be unenforceable? How would you explain the law in this connection?

16. Does the statute of frauds require that the memorandum which evidences agreements must be in a prescribed form?

17. In reference to contracts required by the statute of frauds to be evidenced by a memorandum in writing, what in substance must such memorandum contain or set forth?

18. In reference to the memorandum in writing required by the statute of frauds, must such writing be signed by both parties to the contract, to be enforceable? Explain.

19. Does equity ever intervene so as to provide exceptions to the rule that certain contracts must be evidenced by a writing in order to be enforceable? Comment fully.

20. Explain what effect the following may have in respect to the statute of frauds: (1) full performance by one of the parties; (2) unjust enrichment.

21. What is the parol evidence rule? Name and explain four exceptions.

## Problems

1. Flint, a farm hand, asks Gage, a farmer, "Do you need help?" Gage replies, "I can always use help. You're just in time for milking." Flint works for a week, then asks for his pay. Gage denies that there is any pay due, since there ,was no specific agreement between the parties. If you were the court sitting in this case, how would you rule, and why?

2. Hoe buys a diamond ring in Irving's jewelry store. He takes the ring home with him, promising payment in a week. Would you class this contract as executed, executory, or partially executed and partially executory?

3. Johnson hires Knox as his plant manager on an oral contract for two years. At the end of a month, Johnson, without cause, discharges Knox, and when sued for a month's wages defends on the ground that an oral contract which cannot be performed within one year from the date it is made is unenforceable. What is Knox's position?

4. Horatio Lubbock offers a reward of $500 for the return of a lost briefcase containing important papers. Specify which of the following classes of contracts this might fall into: (1) voidable, (2) unilateral, (3) executed, (4) entire, (5) specialty, (6) parol, (7) implied, (8) joint, (9) divisible, (10) executory, (11) express, and (12) valid.

5. Two hundred persons sign an agreement reading as follows: "In consideration of the procurement by the trustees of the Pleasant Valley Church of similar subscriptions from other members of the Church, we hereby agree to contribute the sum or sums respectively set opposite our signatures hereinbelow, said contributions to be for the procurement of a new church bell." Is the obligation thus expressed joint, or joint and several?

6. Manning is arrested and jailed for drunken driving. A friend deposits $1,000 in court as security for an undertaking that Manning would appear to answer the charge on a given date, in the meantime to be at liberty. From the standpoint of formality, what type of contract was thereby consummated? How is this particular obligation commonly designated?

7. Nevins telephones Orwell "I have just got in a fine lot of flounder which I expect to price at around 30¢ a pound." Orwell says, "Fine, I'll take two barrels." Assuming that this conversation was reduced to writing, signed by both parties, and sworn to before a notary, would such transaction constitute a valid and enforceable contract?

8. On Wednesday morning, the Photo Engraving Corporation hires Price for one year at an annual salary of $10,000, starting the following Monday. When Price reports for duty on Monday he is told by the President of the Company that the management has decided on another man for the position. Price, in the meantime, has rejected another opening, which has since been filled. Has Price a cause of action against the Photo Engraving Corporation?

9. The Crouch Estate has 2,000 acres of timberland. A violent storm fells many of the trees, which threaten to rot unless removed. The executor of the Crouch Estate makes an oral agreement with the Davis Lumber Mill whereby the latter is to remove all the trees without charge within a period of not

over eighteen months, and to keep the timber. Three months later the Lumber Mill people, without having removed a stick of timber, advise the executor of the Crouch Estate that they have "dropped the project." What remedy, if any, has the executor of the Crouch Estate?

10.* In 1930, John Adams orally promised his brother Henry that he would advance to Henry all cash needed by Henry to enable the latter to take a university course in accountancy, obtain a certificate as a C.P.A. and equip an office for the public practice of accountancy. Henry orally agreed to repay these advances out of the first fees collected by him in his practice as a C.P.A. John made these advances, amounting in total to $6,000, and Henry completed the course, became a C.P.A. in 1935, and began to practice as such. After collection of his first fees, Henry refused to repay any part of the advances, relying upon the statute of frauds.

(a) Upon what provision in the statute of frauds did Henry rely?

(b) Does the statute of frauds bar a recovery by John?

11.* A, following his discharge in bankruptcy, again entered business and wrote to B requesting that B sell him a certain quantity of goods to be delivered in monthly installments, A to have thirty days in which to pay for each installment. B replied, refusing to extend credit to A unless A's former indebtedness to B were liquidated. A then wrote agreeing to pay the former indebtedness in monthly payments until paid in full. B then extended the requested credit to A in the contract for A's new purchases. Subsequently, A defaulted in an installment payment and B sued to recover the balance of the old debt. Could he recover?

12.** John Doe, doing business as a merchant, borrowed money from his bank, which he failed to repay prior to his becoming insolvent. He subsequently went through bankruptcy and was discharged. Believing himself morally, if not legally, indebted to the bank, he, subsequent to the date of his discharge, executed and delivered to the bank a note in payment of his debt. When the note became due, Doe declined to pay it, on the ground that the note was executed without consideration, since it was given to cover a debt that he owed to the bank prior to his discharge in bankruptcy. The bank brought suit to enforce payment of the note. Will it succeed?

13.* Jones ordered Cleary, a tailor, to make him a suit of clothes at a cost of $80. Cleary made the suit, but Jones refused to accept it and defended Cleary's action at law, pleading as a defense the statute of frauds. Was this a good defense?

14.** B sued H for money damages for failure of H to manufacture and deliver 2,250 men's suits of various sizes and models. H signed a memorandum showing number of suits ordered, size and price; the styles and materials were identified by letters, figures and lot numbers used by H in his business, and the writing contained all the terms which ordinarily enter into a contract to manufacture and sell except that it contained no statement of the time of shipment or delivery. H delivered no goods, nor did B make any payments on account. H pleaded as a defense the statute of frauds. Who is entitled to judgment? Why?

15. Quick orally agrees to sell his farm to Ritter. Title is to close in sixty days. In the meantime Ritter, who has paid part of the purchase price, is given possession of the farm and allowed to make a number of substantial improvements. The title proves to be clear, but Quick, having changed his mind, tenders a return of the down payment and seeks to cancel the contract. May he do so?

16. Stone and Thornton orally agree to form a partnership in the sale of

household appliances. Each is to contribute $5,000 toward the establishment of the business; each is to have a drawing account of $75 a week; and profits are to be divided equally. After this agreement is reduced to writing and signed by both parties, Stone persuades Thornton that in view of the fact that he, Stone, has had more experience in the business, he ought to receive 60% of the profits, and Thornton 40%. Thornton agrees. Stone then suggests that the contract be amended accordingly, but Thornton says, "Never mind, let's shake hands on it." At the end of the year, Thornton insists on half the profits, and Stone sues for an accounting, demanding 60% of the profits. On the trial Stone seeks to testify about the subsequent oral agreement, but Thornton's attorney objects. Will the objection be sustained or overruled?

17.* In August, 1941, X and Y duly made a legally valid written contract whereby X agreed to audit the books and accounts of Y for the calendar year 1942 for a fee fixed by this contract. At the time of the making of this contract and as a part of the negotiations leading up to it, X and Y orally agreed that said contract was to be effective only in the event that Y procured certain additional capital from Z prior to January 1, 1942. If Y is unable to procure such capital, is the written contract legally binding?

## PART 8. OPERATION AND EFFECT OF CONTRACTS

**Construction and Interpretation of Contracts.** The operation and effect of a contract often depend upon judicial interpretation and construction, particularly where the meaning of a contract is in dispute. The following rules of construction and interpretation have been laid down by the courts:

(1) *Object of courts.* The object of the courts is to ascertain the *true intent* of the parties from what was *actually said or written.*

(2) *Ordinary words.* Ordinary words are interpreted in their ordinary grammatical sense, except where such interpretation would be absurd. For example, where a policy of insurance on a stock of goods in a store provides that the policy is to become null and void "if the said property shall be sold and conveyed," it would be absurd to give the words "sold and conveyed" their ordinary grammatical meaning, because the purpose of the store is to sell merchandise. The kind of sale referred to in the policy was obviously a sale of the store.

(3) *Technical and trade words.* Technical and trade words are given their technical and trade meaning.

(4) *Handwriting, typewriting, print; words and figures.* Where hand-written and typewritten words conflict, the handwriting prevails; where typewritten and printed words conflict, the typewriting prevails; where words and figures conflict, the words prevail.

(5) *Legal intent presumed.* Where one construction will make a contract legal and the other not, the parties will be presumed to have intended a legal contract. For an example, see page 73, the "put" and "call" case (*Story v. Salomon*). The court in that case said that if the contract could be construed *either* as legal *or* as a gamble, the court would presume that the parties intended to obey the law.

(6) *Ambiguous words.* Ambiguous words will be construed against the party who drew the contract and selected the words. Thus, if a clause in an insurance policy may be construed two ways, one in favor of the company, which drew the contract, and another in favor of the policy-holder, the latter construction will prevail.

(7) *General words followed by specific.* If general words are accompanied by specific, the specific will control, as if the general words had not been used at all.

EXAMPLE: If a contract reads, "performance is excused in case of fire, flood, hurricanes, tornadoes *or other conditions beyond our control,*" the general words "or other conditions beyond our control" are limited by the specific words "fire, flood, hurricanes, tornadoes," and only contingencies of the latter nature will excuse performance, so that if the actual contingency that arises to prevent performance is a strike, it will not excuse performance.

(8) *No time for payment specified.* Where no time is specified for payment under a contract, performance is a prerequisite to payment. Thus, in the absence of other provision, the law would require the last payment under a building contract to be made upon completion.

(9) *No provision for termination.* A contract containing no provision for termination is terminable at will.

**Different Jurisdictions: Which Law Governs.** When a contract is made in one state and sued on in another, all questions involving the validity of the contract itself are governed by the law of the state where the contract was made and to be performed, and all questions involving remedies and procedure—such as the effectiveness of a seal (page 85), the applicability of the statute of frauds (page 85), or of the statute of limitations (Ch. 22:5)—are governed by the law of the state where suit is brought. When a contract is made in one state but is to be performed in another, many states[82] hold that the law which governs the validity of the contract is the law of the state where the contract was to have been performed. Parties to a contract may stipulate as to the law of which state shall govern in case of dispute. It should be noted that the Uniform Commercial Code seeks to do away with this rather complicated and confusing conflict of jurisdictions, by providing that if a state embraces any phase of a transaction, it thereby acquires exclusive jurisdiction. (See Appendix.)

**Contract Obligations: Duty Not to Interfere.** Ordinarily, only the parties to a contract are obligated by its terms. However, any person who induces a party to violate the terms of his contract is liable to the other party for *tortious interference with contract* (Ch. 20:5, subd. "Wrongful Interference With Contracts").

**Contract Rights of Outside and Subsequent Parties.** Under the com-

---

[82] Among them, the following: Arkansas, Georgia, Illinois, Iowa, Kentucky, Michigan, Missouri, Nebraska, New York, Oklahoma, Pennsylvania, Washington, and Wyoming.

mon law, only the parties to a contract were interested in it, and only a party to a contract could sue on it. These limitations have been broadened so that parties may acquire contract rights (a) as third party beneficiaries and (b) as undisclosed principals. Subsequent parties, also, may acquire an interest in a contract, as by: (c) operation of law, (d) assignment, (e) negotiation and (f) novation.

**Third Party Beneficiaries.** It is the rule in a majority of the states[83] that if I make you a promise *for the benefit of a third party*, the latter, though not a party to our contract, may hold me to my promise, *provided you (the promisee) are obligated to him.*

EXAMPLES:

(1) Holly lent Fox $300, on Fox's promise to repay that amount to Lawrence, to whom Holly owed that sum. On Fox's failure to repay the amount as promised, Lawrence sued Fox, whose defense was that he made no promise to *Lawrence*. The court held Fox liable, because (a) Holly, to whom Fox made the promise, was obligated to Lawrence and (b) the promise was made for the benefit of Lawrence.[84]

(2) *A*, who contemplates buying a home from *X*, a realtor, asks *X* to get a new tenant for *A*'s apartment. *X* procures *B*. The landlord of *A*'s apartment promises *B* that he will pay the realtor's commission. Such promise, *made to B*, is not binding, since *B* is not obligated to the realtor.

(3) Morgan, a patent attorney, rendered services to Forbes on patent applications for a cigarette cut-off device. Thereafter Forbes gave Ebco Machine Corporation the right to manufacture the device, and the Corporation, without mentioning Morgan's name, agreed to pay for future legal services in prosecuting the patent applications. Morgan, with knowledge of this agreement, continued to render services on the patent applications, for which he later billed the Corporation. The Corporation refusing to pay, Morgan sued. The court, in dismissing the complaint, pointed out that an outside third party has no right to sue on a contract unless it is made for his benefit, and that this contract was solely for the benefit of Forbes, not Morgan or any other third party.[85]

**Undisclosed Principals.** If I, representing an undisclosed principal, make a contract with you, my undisclosed principal may step forward at any time and claim the benefit of the contract; and you, on the other hand, upon disclosure of the principal, may elect to hold him. To this rule there are certain exceptions discussed in the chapter "Agency" (Ch. 9:4). If a person wants to make sure that he is not dealing with an undisclosed principal, he may so provide in the contract.

**Subsequent Parties in General.** Persons subsequent to the original parties may acquire an interest in a contract and become subject to its

---

[83] Including Alabama, Arkansas, California, Colorado, Connecticut, Florida, Illinois, Indiana, Iowa, Kansas, Kentucky, Mississippi, Missouri, Nebraska, New Jersey, New York, North Carolina, Ohio, Oregon, Pennsylvania, Tennessee, Texas, Utah, Wisconsin and Wyoming.

[84] *Lawrence v. Fox*, 20 N.Y. 286.

[85] *Morgan v. Ebco Machine Corporation*, 239 App. Div. 346, 267 N.Y. Supp. 369.

obligations. Frequently, contracts so provide, though the law generally implies it in the absence of such provisions; for example: "This contract shall inure to the benefit of, and be binding upon the parties hereto, *their heirs, executors, administrators and assigns.*"

**Privity of contract** is said to exist between two or more parties or their successors when such parties have an enforceable right or liability in respect to one another by reason of such contract.

**Subsequent Parties by Operation of Law.** In case a person dies, or goes into bankruptcy, his personal representatives acquire his contract rights and discharge his contract obligations.

**Death.** If the decedent has left a will in which he has named an executor, the latter, as personal representative for the estate, acquires the decedent's contract rights and discharges his contract obligations. If the decedent has left no will, his administrator (Ch. 19:2) serves as personal representative. Personal contracts (promises to marry, to render personal services, and so on) die with the person; other contracts survive.

EXAMPLE: If a decedent had made a contract with X to deliver 1,000 bushels of wheat at $1.00 a bushel, X could compel the decedent's personal representatives to fulfill the contract or pay damages out of the decedent's assets; and if the decedent had delivered the wheat but had not been paid, his personal representatives could compel payment.

**Bankruptcy.** If a person goes into bankruptcy, his assets, including his contract rights, are acquired, through operation of law, by the trustee in bankruptcy (Ch. 18:3).

**Assignment: Nature and Parties.** To *assign* a contract is to transfer one's rights under it. Such transfer may be effected, (a) by act of parties, as where one person transfers his contract rights to another, and (b) by operation of law, as in the case of death or bankruptcy.

The party who transfers his rights is the *assignor;* the party to whom they are transferred, the *assignee.*

**Assignment v. agreement to assign.** An assignment is an executed transfer. It corresponds to a gift. An agreement to assign is a contract. It is unenforceable in the absence of any contract requisite. However, assignments, like gifts, may be invalid under certain conditions.

**Assignment: Form and Requisites.** An assignment need not be in any form. It may be oral; or it may be indicated by indorsing on the contract, "Assigned," with the assignor's signature or initials; or it may be in more formal terms. Unless required by statute, a written assignment need not be signed, provided it is accepted and acted upon.

An assignment, like a gift, requires no consideration. It must, however, effect a *present transfer* to a *specific assignee* in existence.

EXAMPLE: An assignment of War Bonds to a corporation not yet in existence effects no present transfer and is invalid.

**Rights of Assignee.** An assignee acquires only such rights as the assignor has and is subject to any defenses which the other party to the contract might have urged against the assignor.

EXAMPLES:

(1) If I agree to sell you a carload of grain for $1000, you may transfer your rights under the contract to Robinson, who acquires, by assignment, the same rights you had to compel me to deliver the carload of grain for $1000; or I may transfer my contract to Franklin, who thus acquires, by assignment, the right to compel you to pay $1000 for a carload of grain.

(2) If in making the above contract you were guilty of fraud, duress or similar conduct giving me a defense against you should you sue me for non-performance, I can urge the same defense against Robinson or any subsequent assignee, because you cannot assign any greater rights than you possess; and the same would apply to me and my assignee if I had been guilty of similar misconduct in making the contract with you.

(3) If *A* owes *B* money, and assigns a lease to secure the debt, *B* as assignee gets no greater rights under the lease than *A*. Like *A*, *B* takes the lease subject to all its terms, covenants and conditions.

*Assignee's right to sue.* Formerly, an assignee had to sue in the assignor's name. This is no longer true.

**Obligations of Assignor and Assignee.** In the ordinary assignment, the assignor, as an original party to the contract, remains liable for its performance, and the assignee merely acquires the assignor's rights (subject to any defenses), without himself becoming liable for performance, because there is no *privity* between him and the other party to the contract; that is, they are "contract strangers" to each other.

*Assumption v. assignment.* If the assignee assumes the contract, he is liable, because in effect he is making a promise to the assignor for the benefit of the other party to the contract, to whom the assignor is obligated (see Third Party Beneficiaries, page 96).

EXAMPLE: If, in the example given above, Robinson also agreed to *accept* the grain, or if Franklin agreed to *deliver* the grain, we would have an assumption as well as an assignment; and the assignee in each case would be liable as well as the assignor.

Under the Uniform Commercial Code, unless the contrary is stipulated an assignment of rights carries with it a delegation and assumption of the assignor's duties. (See Appendix.)

**Liabilities not Assignable.** If, by contract, I become obligated to you for $500, I cannot, without your consent, shuffle off such obligation by transferring it to Brown. If I attempt to do so, I remain personally liable so far as you are concerned, unless you consent to the arrangement, in which case we have a *novation* (see below).

**What Contracts Assignable.** Generally speaking, all mercantile contracts are assignable. For example, if *A* agrees to sell *B* 200 drums of oil, with deliveries at the rate of two drums a day and *B* then sells his business to *C* before the drums are fully delivered, *A* has no right to refuse further deliveries because of the transfer. However, to the rule that all contracts are generally assignable, there are certain exceptions:

(a) *Contracts creating a personal relationship,* such as a contract to marry, a contract of agency, partnership or guaranty, or a contract to render personal services.

(b) *Contracts prohibiting assignment,* or containing provisions that they cannot be assigned without consent of the other party.

(c) *Illegality of contract,* or of a coupon or certificate issued in connection with it, such as sweepstake, lottery or other tickets or certificates issued in connection with a gambling event.

**Notice of Assignment.** If a creditor assigns an account, the assignee should notify the debtor promptly of the assignment; otherwise, should the debtor, ignorant of the assignment, pay his creditor and should the creditor then disappear, the assignee would have no remedy.

**Subsequent Parties: Negotiation.** A contract obligation in the form of a negotiable instrument is transferable by indorsement and delivery or, where the obligation is to bearer, by delivery alone. An assignee, as we have noted, takes subject to all defenses available against the assignor (page 98), but this is not true where rights in commercial paper pass by negotiation to innocent third parties. This subject is more fully discussed in the chapter on negotiable instruments, which follows this chapter.

**Novation.** Novation is the substitution of a new contract, or a new debtor or obligor, for an existing one. In reality it is a contract consisting of two stipulations; one to extinguish an existing obligation or to release an existing debtor, the other to substitute a new one in place of the old. Since novation creates a new contract, it requires the assent of both parties to the original contract. This is what is really meant by the statement that liabilities cannot be assigned (page 98).

EXAMPLE: *A* is obligated to *X* by contract. He may not, without *X*'s consent, shift his obligation to *B*, even though *B* is willing to assume it. If, however, *X* consents to release *A* upon condition that *B* assume the obligation, a novation takes place. The consideration supporting such new contract or novation is the obligation assumed by *B* in place of *A*.

Four elements must be present to constitute a novation: (1) a previous valid obligation, (2) agreement of all parties, (3) extinguishment of the old contract, and (4) validity of the new one.

## Questions

1. What, in general, is the object of the courts when they construe and interpret contracts?

2. What is the rule governing the interpretation of ordinary words? Give an example.

3. "Technical and trade words are to be construed in accordance with their

ordinary meaning as defined in the dictionary." Is this a correct statement of the law? Explain, giving an example.

4. In construing inconsistencies in a contract, which will prevail in the following situations: (a) where handwritten and typewritten words conflict; (b) where typewritten and printed words conflict; (e) where words and figures conflict?

5. What presumption is raised by the court where one construction will make a contract legal and the other not? Give an example.

6. Where two parties sign a contract prepared by the attorney for one of the parties, and the contract contains words that may have several meanings, one of which favors one of the parties, and the other, the other party, what rule will the court adopt in construing such ambiguous words?

7. Give an example of the following rule: "If general words are accompanied by specific, the specific will control as if the general words had not been used at all."

8. When a contract contains no provision for termination, when is it terminable?

9. When a contract is made in one state and sued on in another, and the law governing contracts is not uniform in both states, which state law will govern a dispute in the following situations: (a) where the validity of the contract itself is involved; (b) where the question at issue involves a remedy, or some rule of procedure?

10. When a contract is made in one state but is to be performed in another, what is the prevailing rule with respect to the law of which state will govern the validity of the contract? May parties to a contract stipulate as to the law of which state shall govern in case of a dispute?

11. If I make you a promise for the benefit of a third party, under what circumstances may such third party, though not a party to our contract, hold me to my promise?

12. What is meant by "privity of contract"?

13. Does the death of a party to a contract terminate all his rights and liabilities under the contract? Explain.

14. Is an assignment of a contract valid if made without consideration?

15. What rights does an assignee of a contract acquire? To what defenses is such assignee subject?

16. Does an assignor remain liable on the contract which he assigns?

17. When, if at all, is an assignee liable on the contract assigned to him?

18. What contracts, generally speaking, are assignable? Name three exceptions.

19. If a creditor assigns an account, what should the assignee do to protect himself?

20. Define novation. How does it differ from assignment? What four elements must be present to constitute a novation?

## Problems

1.** As a bookkeeper or auditor you are examining a contract prepared upon a printed form with some typewriting and some pen writing thereon, and you conclude that the document has been carelessly drawn because:

There are conflicts between figures and words.

There are conflicts between printing, typewriting and manuscript.

There are portions of the contract which are ambiguous, and constructions which could be placed upon some portions of it would make the contract absurd or illegal in those respects.

(a) What would be your opinion as to the consideration to be given to (1) the absurd construction, (2) the illegal construction, (3) the ambiguous statement, (4) technical or trade words, (5) conflicts between figures and words, (6) conflicts between print and writing, (7) conflicts between pen writing and typewriting?

(b) Having given seven short answers to the above, state briefly the principle of construction upon which your opinions are based.

2.* A contract for the construction of a building recites that the consideration to be paid by the owner shall be "the cost of materials, wages, and direct expenses plus ten percentum of the sum of such costs. Direct expenses shall include the salary of a full-time superintendent and his assistants, the expense of a field officer, employees' compensation insurance, public liability insurance, travel expense, and two percentum per month of the cost of equipment used for wear and tear." Would fire insurance premiums upon equipment be a direct expense to be included?

3.** The Apex Importing Company sold to Kerwin certain goods to be shipped during a certain month from a certain country. The goods were purchased with the understanding that "sellers are not to be responsible for strikes, fires, accidents or anything beyond their control."

Owing to embargoes imposed by the government of the country from which shipment was to have been made, shipment could not be made.

Defendant contended that its failure to deliver was due to something beyond its control, and that the contract was entered into because of a mutual mistake and could not be enforced.

In whose favor will the decision be given? Why?

4.* A contract executed and delivered in California is the subject matter of a suit in New York. What laws will govern the validity of the contract, and what laws will govern the remedy? State the rule in such cases.

5.* Jones lent Smith $50. At the time Jones stated that he owed Fisher $50 which he had promised to pay the next day. Smith, in consideration of the loan, promised Jones that he would pay the $50 to Fisher the next day, which, however, he failed to do. Fisher sued Smith on Smith's promise to Jones. Could he recover?

6.** Jones, who rents the apartment in which he lives, holds under a lease running to May 1, 1932. In December, 1931, he calls on Young, a realtor, from whom he expects to purchase a home, to secure a tenant to take over the lease of Jones from January 1, 1932. Brown is secured by the realtor to take over the lease but the landlord refuses to accept Brown and the deal falls through. One week later, the landlord agrees to give a new lease to Brown directly and promises Brown to pay the realtor's commission. The landlord refuses to pay the realtor his commission and the latter brings suit against the landlord. What holding, and why?

7.* Doran, by a written contract, agreed to sell to Best 200 drums of acid of certain specifications, at the rate of two drums *per diem*, title to pass upon delivery. After delivery the acid was to be sampled and tested and the price fixed according to daily market quotations. Best sold his business, including the contract with Doran, to Trimble, but Doran refused to make deliveries to Trimble who thereupon sued Doran for damages. Is Doran liable?

8. Forbes made a five-year contract with the Newtown Public School District to transport school children by bus to and from school. The contract

provided that Forbes was to furnish a safe, sanitary and comfortable bus adequate for the purpose, and to maintain discipline among the children while en route. Forbes died, and the executor of his estate insisted on the right to continue the contract. The school refused to accept the executor's tender of performance. Thereupon the executor sued the School District on its contract with Forbes. How did the court decide?

9. Glenn enters into a contract with the Hardy Steamship Corporation for the purchase of two reconditioned ships at $200,000 each. He then makes a contract with the Overseas Trading Corporation whereby the latter agrees to buy both ships for $750,000. Before the ships are delivered to or paid for by Glenn, the latter dies. The executor of Glenn's estate tenders the purchase price to the Hardy Steamship Corporation, which refuses delivery because of Glenn's death. The Overseas Trading Corporation also tenders the sum of $750,000 to the executor of the Glenn estate, demands delivery of the ships, and on failure to receive delivery, sues the Glenn estate. What position should the executor for the estate take in both situations?

10. Irwin agrees to sell a carload of grain to Jenkins for $1,000. Jenkins assigns the contract to Kraft. When Kraft demands delivery, Irwin refuses to deliver the grain because of fraud committed by Jenkins in procuring the contract from Irwin. Kraft, however, had no knowledge of such fraud. In a suit by Kraft against Irwin, who will win? Explain.

11. Larson, a contractor, agrees to build a home for Morton at an over-all cost of $35,000. Larson assigns the contract to the Modern Construction Corporation which, however, subsequently goes into bankruptcy without having built the house. Morton sues Larson for breach of contract. Larson's defense is that his liability under the contract was terminated upon his assignment of the contract to the Modern Construction Corporation. How should the court decide?

12. Nesbit owes the Oliver Corporation $5,000. The Oliver Corporation is in immediate need of that amount of cash, but being unable to collect it from Nesbit, borrows the money from the Generous Finance Corporation, to which the Oliver Corporation assigns, as security, its $5,000 claim against Nesbit. Later, Nesbit pays the Oliver Corporation. The President of the Oliver Corporation cashes Nesbit's check and disappears. The Oliver Corporation has no other assets. The Generous Finance Corporation then sues Nesbit, whose defense is that he had no knowledge of the assignment. How should the court decide, and why?

## PART 9. TERMINATION OR DISCHARGE: PERFORMANCE

**In General.** A contract is discharged when it ceases to have any binding effect as a contract, though it may be survived by some form of legal liability, such as for damages in case of a breach. Contracts may be discharged by performance, agreement, operation of law and breach. In this part we deal with discharge by performance. In Parts 10, 11 and 12 of this chapter, we deal with discharge by agreement, operation of law and breach, respectively.

**Discharge by Performance, Generally.** Questions most frequently arising in connection with the performance of contracts are: (a) time of performance, (b) satisfactory performance, (c) performance by payment and (d) tender of performance.

**Time of Performance.** If a contract specifies no time for performance, it must be performed within a reasonable time. What constitutes a reasonable time depends on the circumstances. If the contract specifies a time for performance, it must be performed within that time; if not, the other party may offset, against payment, any damage caused by the delay, or if time is "of the essence," he may reject performance entirely.

*Time of the essence.* Time is "of the essence" when failure to perform on time gives the other party a right to cancel the contract. At common law, time was presumed to be of the essence. In equity and by the modern rule, the presumption is the other way around unless (1) the parties clearly stipulate that time is of the essence, or (2) it is evident that nonperformance within the time fixed will defeat the purpose of the contract (as in the case of merchandise ordered for a voyage and not delivered until after departure).

**Satisfactory Performance: in General.** In the absence of specific provision, performance is deemed satisfactory if it should satisfy the ordinary, reasonable person under the circumstances. This is a question of fact in each case, to be determined by a jury.

**Satisfactory Performance: Compliance with Conditions.** Performance of a contract, to be satisfactory, must comply with its conditions. Conditions may be *precedent, subsequent,* and *concurrent.*

*Conditions precedent* are those that must either come to pass, or be performed by the other party, before a party is required to perform.

*Conditions subsequent* are those that follow performance and must be complied with by the party on whom they are imposed, else his rights and benefits under the contract will be defeated or impaired.

*Conditions concurrent* are those that are mutually dependent and are to be performed at the same time. Examples: simultaneous contributions of capital investment between prospective partners as conditions for the creation of the firm; simultaneous delivery and payment as conditions for a sale.

**Satisfaction Guaranteed.** Where a party guarantees satisfaction, the other party must be reasonable in protesting dissatisfaction, unless performance involves personal taste, fancy or judgment. In the latter situation, the question is not whether the other party's taste, fancy or judgment are reasonable, but whether they are real or spurious; that is, whether they are urged in good faith. Some jurisdictions go further and hold that one must not be capricious in exercising his judgment, taste or fancy; but the weight of authority is that when *A* agrees to perform a contract to *B*'s satisfaction and the work involves personal judgment, taste, fancy, and so on, *B* has an arbitrary right to reject performance. Certainly where *B*'s judgment is neither spurious nor capricious, he may reject performance regardless of what the ordinary reasonable person might have done under like circumstances.

EXAMPLE: If one agrees to paint a portrait, do a bust, design a dress or fit a suit of clothes to another's satisfaction and the latter is dissatisfied, the law will not inquire into the reasonableness of such dissatisfaction.

**Performance to Third Party's Satisfaction.** Parties may agree that performance shall be to the satisfaction of an outsider, such as an architect (in building contracts), an umpire, judge, arbitrator or referee. In such cases, performance must satisfy such third party or there is no liability, unless fraud or collusion can be shown in arriving at a decision.

**Substantial Performance.** Under the common law, performance of an express contract had to be complete to the last detail or one could not recover on the contract but had to resort to the doubtful remedy of a suit based on an implied contract. This frequently resulted in hardship, and in the course of time the rule was superseded by the doctrine of "substantial performance": that if (a) a *bona fide* effort is made toward full compliance with the terms of the contract, (b) there has been no wilful or intentional departure from such terms and (c) the deviations, defects or omissions are minor only, recovery will be allowed for substantial performance, with an offset for any damage sustained because of such deviations, defects or omissions.

EXAMPLE: Smith, a contractor, alters and repairs Brown's store, but Brown refuses to pay him because certain doors are not well hung and one door does not fit its casing; otherwise, the job is well done. The court would allow recovery in such case under the doctrine of substantial performance, with a set-off to Brown for the reasonable cost of curing the defects.

**Performance by Payment.** Numerous questions arise in connection with the performance of a contract by payment. These have been largely settled by the courts.

*Debt defined.* A debt is a sum of money due upon contract, express or implied.

*Payment: when due.* Payment agreed to be made at a particular time is due then. When no time is fixed, payment is due immediately on demand, or within a reasonable time. When a debt is payable within a specified term, it is not due until the last day of the term.

*Payment: place where due.* If payment is tendered at the wrong place, drastic legal consequences may ensue, as where an installment contract provides that if any installment is not paid when due, the entire unpaid balance becomes due; or where the full amount of a mortgage may fall due in case interest is not paid on or by a given date. The following rules are therefore important:

(1) Parties may agree by contract on where payment shall be made; in such case, payment must be made there.

(2) If parties have not agreed on the place of payment, a debt is payable where the creditor resides, or has his place of business, or wherever he may be found.

(3) It is ordinarily the duty of the debtor to seek the creditor for the purpose of making payment.

(4) If a contract is made outside the debtor's state, it will be presumed (in the absence of agreement) that payment is due there.

(5) If the contract is made in the debtor's state, he is not obliged to seek his creditor outside the state, but the latter must arrange to receive payment in the debtor's state.

*Medium of payment.* A debt must be paid in legal tender (page 108) if the creditor insists. The medium of payment is frequently stipulated: by money, or by credit instrument, such as check, draft, note, trade acceptance or similar instrument; this depends on the terms of the contract. If the contract requires payment in money, only such payment will extinguish the debt, unless the requirement is waived and a substitute accepted. If the contract is silent on the medium of payment, payment in money is usually implied. If, instead, a check is given in payment, and it is neither actually nor impliedly accepted as payment, the law presumes that the acceptance is conditional only; so that if the check is not paid, the original debt survives. But a creditor may impliedly (and sometimes unwittingly) accept a check as payment; for example, where, on receiving a check, he acknowledges "receipt of your check *in payment*," or where he negotiates the check to someone else. If a check is accepted as payment, either expressly, impliedly, or by waiver of money payment, and the check is not paid when presented, the creditor must sue on the check, since the original debt is deemed discharged by acceptance of the check. If the check is lost, the creditor is at a disadvantage in proving his case.

Where a creditor accepts a check as conditional payment, subject to collection, he must not unreasonably delay presenting the check for payment. If he does, and the bank has become insolvent in the meantime, the consequent loss falls on the creditor.

*Certified checks.* Certified checks are not substitutes for money, unless the parties agree to accept them as such. When a debtor sends a certified check in payment of a debt, which the creditor has not expressly agreed to accept as payment, and the bank becomes insolvent before the check is paid, the loss falls on the debtor. But where the debtor sends his *uncertified* check in payment, and the *creditor* has it certified, he thereby accepts the certification as payment, and in case the bank becomes insolvent before the check is paid, the loss is the creditor's.

*Cashier's check.* Where a creditor accepts a cashier's check as payment, and the bank fails, the creditor has no further claim against the debtor.

EXAMPLE: An investment company sells certain bonds to Clark, and accepts in payment a cashier's check drawn on Clark's bank. The bonds are thereupon delivered to Clark, whose bank fails before the check can be cashed. The investment company has no further recourse against Clark.

*Promissory notes.* When a debtor gives his own promissory note in payment of a debt, the same rule applies as that governing payment by check, that is, it is not deemed payment unless specifically or impliedly accepted as such. If the note is paid, the debt is discharged; if not, the original debt survives. If the note is accepted as payment, and when due, it is not paid, the creditor must sue on the note, not on the original debt, and if the note is lost, the creditor is at a disadvantage in proving his case.

A somewhat different principle applies, however, when a debtor gives the note, check or draft of a *third person* in payment of a debt. In such a case, if the debt was incurred before the instrument was given, the rule is the same as if the instrument were made by the debtor himself, that is, payment is conditional unless otherwise agreed. But if such instrument is given *at the same time the debt is incurred,* the law will presume that it was accepted as unconditional payment, so that if the instrument is not paid, the creditor must sue on the instrument itself, since the original debt was discharged.

*Payment by mail.* If a debtor sends money by mail to pay a debt, he does so at his own risk, unless directed to do so by the creditor.

Where payment is made by mail, it is not effective unless received. Hence if payment is due on a given date (for example, an insurance premium), and the debtor remits by mail, he is in default if the remittance is lost in the mails, or if delivery is delayed beyond the due date.

*Exceptions:* (1) Where the creditor expressly or impliedly directs or consents that payment be made by mail; or (2) where payment by mail is according to the usual course of dealing between the parties, from which creditor's assent to such remittance may be inferred.

*Application of payments: principal and interest.* "Where partial payments are made, the rule is to apply the payments in the first place to the discharge of the interest then due. If the payment exceeds the interest then due, the surplus goes toward discharging the principal, and interest is to be computed thereafter on the balance of the principal. If the payment is less than the interest, the surplus of interest must not be taken to augment the principal, but interest continues on the former principal until the payments, taken together, exceed the interest due, and then the surplus is to be applied toward discharging the principal, and interest is to be computed on the balance of the principal as before." [86]

*Application of payments to different accounts.* Where a debtor owes several debts to the same creditor, the following rules govern payments on account:

(1) "A debtor paying money to a creditor to whom he owes several debts may direct the application of the payment because the money is his and he may do as he will with it and control its application. But the

[86] 33 C.J. 250.

debtor must exercise his option as to the application when he makes the payment. After that the money has ceased to be his and is no longer subject to his control. Then it belongs to the creditor, and he is master of it, and may control its application." [87]

Therefore, when a debtor owes several debts to the same creditor, and makes a payment on account, he should specify to which account he wants the payment applied. Otherwise, the creditor may apply it to whichever account he prefers; and if one of the accounts bears no interest and the others do, he will be likely, in the absence of direction from the debtor, to apply the payment to the account bearing no interest.

(2) The creditor need not specify immediately to which account he intends to apply the payment; he has a reasonable time in which to do this. He must make his election, however, before controversy and suit on the subject.

(3) After appropriation is made, it cannot be changed, except (a) with the consent of the debtor, (b) for fraud of the debtor, or (c) where the wrong account has clearly been credited in error.

(4) Where payments are made on open account and neither debtor nor creditor designates or applies the payment to any given item, the law will presume that it is to be applied to the earliest item of the account,[88] though a court may make any disposition which accords with "intrinsic equity and justice." [89]

**Tender of Performance.** Tender is an offer to do what one is required to do under a contract. When it squares unconditionally[90] with the requirements of a contract, it is "good tender," but if it deviates from the contract in any respect, it is not. Tender is necessary where acts to be performed are mutual and dependent. It enables the tendering party, in case of breach, to show that he was ready to do his part, and it places the other party more clearly in default.

Tender is not good if coupled with demand for a receipt. If a seller makes a partial tender, the buyer is not bound to sever the tender, take what is due and reject what is nontenderable, but may reject the improper tender in its entirety.

EXAMPLE: By contract between *H* and *C*, *H* agrees to sell fifty warps of cotton yarn, deliveries 10% weekly. *H* makes one delivery of eight warps, then suspends delivery for eight weeks because of an embargo, then ships the re-

---

[87] *Bank of California v. Webb, et al.,* 94 N.Y. 467, 472. To the same effect: *Lazarus v. Freidheim,* 51 Ark. 371, 11 S.W. 518; *Huffman v. Cauble,* 86 Ind. 591; *Thomas v. Beaufort Bank,* 183 N.C. 508, 112 S.E. 27; *Fargo First Nat. Bank v. Roberts,* 2 N.D. 195, 49 N.W. 722; *Baum v. Trantham,* 42 S.C. 104, 19 S.C. 973, 46 Am.S.R. 697.
[88] *Lehigh Coal, etc. Co. v. McLeod,* 114 Me. 427, 96 A. 736; *Smith v. Lewiston Steam Mill,* 66 N.H. 613, 34 A. 153; *Huger v. Bocquet,* 1 S.C.L. 497.
[89] *Camp v. Smith,* 136 N.Y. 187.
[90] *Hanlon v. Manger,* 85 Mont. 31, 277 P. 433.

maining forty-two warps, which *C* refuses to accept. *C*'s rejection of the tender was sustained by the court.[91]

*Legal tender* is money a creditor must accept in payment of a debt. Congress determines what coins and notes constitute legal tender. Prior to 1933 legal tender consisted of nickels and copper coins up to twenty-five cents, dimes, quarters or half dollars up to ten dollars, and gold coins, silver dollars, United States notes, gold certificates and United States Treasury notes to any amount. By various acts in 1933, Congress caused all gold coins and gold certificates to be withdrawn from circulation and made all other existing coins and currency, together with Federal Reserve and National Bank notes, legal tender for the payment of private debts to any amount.

## Questions

1. What are the different ways in which a contract may be discharged?

2. If a contract specifies no time for performance, within what time must it be performed, and how is such time determined?

3. (a) What is meant by the expression, "Time is of the essence"? (b) When is time "of the essence"?

4. In the absence of specific provision, what constitutes satisfactory performance?

5. Name and describe three types of conditions that may be connected with the performance of a contract.

6. (a) Where a party guarantees satisfaction, may the other party arbitrarily reject performance on the ground that he is not satisfied? (b) Suppose performance involves some question of taste, fancy or judgment, would your answer be the same? Comment fully.

7. What is the rule with respect to performance where parties agree that performance shall be to the satisfaction of a third party, such as an umpire, judge, arbitrator or referee?

8. What was the doctrine of substantial performance under the common law, and what is the modern rule governing substantial but not complete performance of a contract?

9. Define debt.

10. When no time for payment is fixed by contract, when is payment due?

11. If parties to a contract have not agreed as to the place of payment, and payment is to be made personally by cash, and not by check or otherwise through the mails, must the debtor make payment at the place where the creditor resides, or must the creditor seek out the debtor and receive payment at the place where the debtor resides?

12. How would you answer the previous question where the creditor resides in one state and the debtor in another state?

13. If a contract requires payment in money, would such provision include payment by check?

14. If a contract is silent as to the medium of payment, may the creditor insist on payment in money?

15. (a) If a debtor gives a check in payment of a debt, when will such check

---

[91] *Herx & Eddy v. Carlson*, 210 App. Div. 417, 206 N.Y. Supp. 179.

be deemed payment, and when not? (b) How could such question become a practical one?

16. When, if at all, may a certified check or a cashier's check be deemed a legal substitute for money?

17. (a) When, if at all, may a promissory note be deemed to constitute payment of a debt? (b) How could this question become of practical importance?

18. What circumstances would determine who bears the loss where a debtor sends money by mail to pay a debt, and the money is lost in the mails?

19. Where payment is due on a given date on penalty of losing a valuable right if not made on time, is the right lost if the debtor makes timely remittance by mail, which delays delivery beyond the due date?

20. Where the principal of a debt is overdue, and interest has accumulated, how is a payment on account apportioned as between principal and interest?

21. Where a debtor owes several debts to the same creditor, how are payments on account apportioned: (a) Where the debtor specified how the payment is to be applied; (b) Where neither debtor nor creditor designates how the payment is to be applied?

22. Define (a) tender, (b) good tender, (c) legal tender.

23. When is tender necessary?

24. Is there any advantage in making tender where the law does not require it?

25. Is tender good if coupled with demand for a receipt? Where a receipt is refused, what should a debtor do?

## Problems

1. Paterson orders a special assortment of rare orchids for his daughter's wedding on the morning of June 15th. The flower shop mistakes the date and delivers the orchids on the morning of June 16th, when they are refused. The flower shop is unable to resell the orchids and seeks to hold Paterson for the purchase, subject to a deduction for late delivery. How will the court decide?

2. The Cosmopolitan Museum places an order with a noted sculptor for a full size reproduction of a famous Greek statue. The contract stipulates that the figure is to be approved by the Museum's Committee on Design and Sculpture. The figure is duly delivered to the Museum and placed on public view. It is declared by critics to be a first-class work of art. The Committee on Design and Sculpture, however, rejects the statue as unacceptable. May the sculptor hold the Museum for the contract price of the statue?

3. The Peace Society conducts a prize contest for the best five-thousand-word essay on "Peace—How to Attain It." Under the terms of the contest the choice of the judges, selected by the Peace Society, is to be final. The prize money for the contest is supplied by a well-known soap company. One of the contestants is the son of the President of the soap company. His essay is selected by the judges as the best. Other candidates who have submitted essays protest the decision. Should the contest be brought into the courts, what would be the outcome?

4.** Jones, a contractor, contracted with Souter to alter and repair a store owned by the latter. He finished the work, but several defects appeared therein. It was shown that the roof was not well supported, that certain doors were not well hung, that one door did not fit its casing. Except for these defects, the work had been well done. Souter refused to pay for any of the work. Jones brought suit on the contract for the compensation that had been agreed on, less the amount of damages caused by these defects.

Decision for whom, and why?

5. The Delightful Air Conditioning Company agrees to install an air conditioning system in the executive offices of the Apex Advertising Agency. The Agency is to have a free summer trial of the system, and to pay for it on October 1, if the system proves satisfactory. The installation meets with all the terms and specifications of the contract, and the executive offices were admittedly comfortable during the warmest days of the summer. The Agency, however, refuses to accept and pay for the installation, insisting that it is not satisfactory, and requesting removal of the installation, whereupon the Air Conditioning Company sues. How should the court charge the jury?

6.** Smith owes Jones four debts as follows:

$100 which is barred by limitation
200 which is past due but not barred
300 which is currently due
400 which has not yet become due

(a) Smith pays Jones $300, without designating how it is to be applied. How may Jones apply it?

(b) Smith pays Jones $300, stating that it is for the debt currently due. Does Smith's designation of the debt to be discharged control?

(c) Discuss and compare your answers.

7.* X, a dealer, makes numerous sales to Y, and at the end of each calendar month X sends Y an itemized statement. Some but not all of the charges by X bear interest. Because of unsettled disputes, a few of the items listed on the statement of April 30, 1939, had been billed for over five years. Y is about to make a payment on account. Has Y the right to compel X to apply this payment to items of principal or interest specified by Y, at the time of payment? Or has X the right to apply this payment as X desires, (a) if Y specifies the application, (b) if Y does not specify? If X has a right to apply the payment as X desires, within what time should he exercise it, and what notice if any should X give Y concerning the application made by X?

8.* An investment company sold certain bonds to Clark but refused to take Clark's check in payment although Clark offered the check in time to enable the vendor to have it certified before delivery of the bonds. Clark refused to give a check already certified, but by agreement between the parties the vendor delivered the bonds to a bank in which the vendee had a balance sufficient to cover the purchase price and accepted that bank's cashier's check and the bank immediately delivered the bonds to the vendee. Thereafter, but before the cashier's check could be cashed, the bank failed. Can the vendor recover the purchase price from the vendee?

9.** Debtor A owes his creditor X a number of separate obligations, incurred at different times, which total $1,800. Debtor A sends X a check for $1,000.

(a) What principles govern creditor X in applying this check to the obligations owed him by A?

(b) One of the debts owed has been barred by the statute of limitations. Part of the payment received is applied in partial payment of this debt. What principles govern the right of X to sue for the balance still owed on the debt barred?

10. Quill is indebted to The Quality Ink Company in the amount of $500. He sends The Quality Ink Company his ninety-day note for $500, with a letter stating, "I hope you can give me this accommodation." The Company responds, stating, "We beg to acknowledge receipt of your $500 note in payment of

your indebtedness, and we are pleased to extend the accommodation requested." Quill's letter and note are lost by The Quality Ink Company. In the meantime, Quill dies. The Quality Ink Company sues Quill's estate on the original indebtedness. How will the court decide?

### PART 10. TERMINATION OR DISCHARGE: AGREEMENT

## In General

**Discharge by Agreement.** Parties may "agree to disagree," that is, to sever their contract relationship. This may be done by the terms of the original agreement or by subsequent agreement; and in the latter event, (a) by modification, novation or merger, (b) by cancellation and release or (c) by accord and satisfaction.

**Discharge by Original Agreement.** A contract may provide by its own terms for its own discharge upon certain contingencies; as, that it shall be automatically discharged by unauthorized assignment, by failure to comply with certain conditions, by labor disputes, or by *force majeur* (contingencies beyond human control).

**Discharge by Modification, Novation, Merger.** Parties to an unperformed contract may, upon mutual assent, consideration[92] and the other contract essentials, modify an existing contract in any respect. When they do so, they thereby discharge the old terms as thus modified.

*Novation* is similar to modification, except that novation imports the substitution of a substantially new contract or new parties (page 99). The effect, however, is the same: to discharge the superseded terms or parties.

*Merger* takes place (in the contract sense of the term) when one form of contract is superseded by another form of *the same contract*. For example, if an oral agreement is superseded by a writing, or an unsealed written agreement by one under seal (the terms of the contract remaining unchanged), the earlier contract is said to be *merged* into the later one. A reversal of this process formerly was regarded as legally ineffective. For example, a written contract could not be discharged by an oral one, or a contract under seal by an unsealed writing. It is now generally recognized (except in those states which still attach importance to a seal) that this is no longer the rule, provided the later contract is supported by consideration. In many states, the old rule is abolished by statute.

**Cancellation and Release.** Either party to a contract, for cause, may cancel or rescind it, and both parties, by mutual assent, may terminate it and release each other from further obligations under it.

A *release* is an instrument discharging an obligation. It is often, but not necessarily, under seal, except in those states which still recognize the

---

[92] Under the Uniform Commercial Code, contracts may be modified without consideration. (See Appendix.)

common law efficacy of a seal. If the release discharges all claims of whatsoever nature, it is known as a *general release* (see Form 2).

FORM 2

## RELEASE *

KNOW ALL MEN, that I, John Doe, residing at No. 11½ Broadway, Borough of Manhattan, City of New York, in consideration of one ($1.) dollar, lawful money of the United States of America, heretofore paid to me by Richard Roe, residing at No. 37½ Broadway, Borough of Manhattan, City of New York, the receipt whereof is hereby acknowledged, do hereby remise, release, and forever discharge the said Richard Roe, his heirs, executors, and administrators, of and from all, and all manner of, action and actions, cause and causes of action, suits, debts, dues, sums of money, accounts, reckonings, bonds, bills, specialties, covenants, contracts, controversies, agreements, promises, variances, trespasses, damages, judgments, extents, executions, claims and demands whatsoever, in law or in equity, that against the said Richard Roe, I, the said John Doe, ever had, now have, or that my heirs, executors or administrators hereafter can or may have, by reason of any matter, cause or thing whatsoever from the beginning of the world up to and including the day of the date of this release.

IN WITNESS WHEREOF, I have hereunto set my hand and seal, in the City of New York, on this 1st day of May, 1952.

In the presence of    John Doe (L.S.)
    John Doe, Jr.
    Richard Roe, Jr.

---

* Reprinted from *Modern Annotated Forms of Agreement* by Saul Gordon. Published by Prentice-Hall, Inc. Copyright, 1940, 1947, by Saul Gordon.

A *mutual release* is a discharge by each of two or more parties to the other or others, the consideration for each discharge being the discharge or discharges given by the others.

*Release and receipt distinguished.* A release extinguishes a right. A receipt is merely an admission. The person obtaining such admission has a right to assume that it is correct unless the contrary is proved, and the burden of proving the contrary is on the signer of the receipt. "As otherwise stated, a receipt is evidence that an obligation has been discharged, but a release is itself a discharge of it; a receipt is only *evidence* that a debt has been paid, whereas a release is the extinguisher itself." [93] A release, once given, cannot be disturbed except for fraud, mutual mistake, or duress; a receipt, being merely evidence, may, if it is incorrect, be contradicted by the true facts, whatever they are, unless the signer who seeks to contradict his admission is estopped (Ch. 22:5) from so doing.

*Release without consideration.* Under the common law a release, being necessarily under seal, could not be questioned for lack of consideration. In states which have abolished the common law sanctity of a seal, releases became exposed to challenge for lack of consideration. As against this,

---

[93] 53 C.J. 1197.

statutes have been passed rendering a release in writing, with or without seal, binding regardless of consideration.[94]

**Discharge by Accord and Satisfaction.** An *accord* is an agreement between parties to a dispute, to accept a new arrangement in place of the disputed one. It often takes the form of agreeing upon a given sum as due, in place of conflicting claims on the amount due. When the accord is carried out, it is said to be *satisfied*. There must be a *genuine dispute* about an *unliquidated claim*, or the accord and satisfaction, lacking consideration, will not be binding, and the creditor may sue for any unpaid balance.

EXAMPLES:

(1) When a physician, attorney, or accountant sends a bill for $500 for services, the claim is unliquidated unless there has been prior agreement on the bill. If the patient or client sends a check for $350 indorsed, "In full payment," cashing the check constitutes an accord and satisfaction: subsequent efforts to collect the difference must fail.[95]

(2) If in Example (1) the creditor, before cashing the check, strikes out the words "In full payment" or adds words of his own to qualify the debtor's language, the attempt to cancel or modify the debtor's terms will be ignored: the check will be deemed cashed on the *debtor's* terms. The result is an accord and satisfaction.

**Undisputed claims; no genuine dispute.** If, in Example (1) above, the claim were undisputed, cashing the check would constitute an agreement, without consideration, to accept as full payment, less than the full amount due (see page 61, "Agreement to accept part payment in full"). Cashing the check in such case would therefore not constitute an accord and satisfaction, and the creditor could sue for the difference.

An accord presupposes a prior dispute. In the absence of a genuine dispute, there can be no accord and satisfaction.

EXAMPLES:

(1) You leave $1,000 in cash with me for safe keeping. When you demand your money, I send you a check for $500 indorsed, "In full of all claims." Cashing such check would not constitute an accord and satisfaction, since there was no genuine dispute.

(2) X, without agreement on compensation, asks Y to sell certain merchandise for him, which Y does. Y deducts 10% from the proceeds of the sale, and sends X the balance by check indorsed, "Less 10% commission." Cashing such check would not constitute an accord and satisfaction, since there was no genuine dispute.

---

[94] For example, the New York statute provides that an agreement to change, modify or *discharge* an obligation shall not be invalid because of the absence of consideration, provided the agreement or release is in writing, signed by the party to be bound.

[95] *Jenkins v. National Mut. Building & Loan Ass'n of New York*, 111 Ga. 732, 36 S.E. 945; *Hamilton v. Stewart*, 108 Ga. 472, 34 S.E. 123; *Northern Bank & Trust Co. v. Harmon*, 126 Wash. 25, 217 P. 8; *Wildstein v. Greenberg & Sons*, (Pa.) 5 Schuylkill Reg. 285.

*Mere retention of a debtor's check* will not in some states (New York, for example) constitute an accord and satisfaction, although in other states (Illinois, for example) failure to return the check within a reasonable time spells out an accord and satisfaction. The New York rule[96] reflects the majority view.

*Accord without satisfaction.* An accord not followed by a satisfaction leaves the creditor free to press his original claim.[97] The same rule holds where satisfaction is only partial.

EXAMPLE: Kromer, having obtained a judgment against Heim, agreed to accept a portion in cash, and for the balance, an assignment of a patent. After receiving the cash, Kromer rejected the patent assignment. *Held*, Kromer could enforce the judgment by execution for the unpaid balance.[98]

*Statutory changes.* The foregoing rules on accord and satisfaction may be modified by statute. For example, some statutes provide that if an accord is in writing, and it is not followed by a satisfaction, the other party has the option of pressing his original claim or insisting on the accord's being carried out.

**Account Stated *v.* Accord and Satisfaction.** An *account stated* should not be confused with an accord and satisfaction. It represents acquiescence or admission rather than compromise, simplifies proof by reason of such admission, and prevents subsequent challenge of the facts thus admitted.

EXAMPLES:

(1) *A* sends *B* a bill, which *B* approves as correct. Later, *B* refuses to pay the bill on the ground that some of the goods mentioned in it were not up to quality. *A* may ignore *B*'s contention and sue *B* on an account stated.

(2) During a period of several years *X* and *Y* have sold merchandise and made payments to each other but they have not agreed as to the status of their accounts. Each furnishes to the other an itemized statement of his account, and the statement of each contains items not shown in the statement of the other. *X*'s statement shows *Y* owes him $1540. *Y*'s statement shows that *X* owes him $220. *Y* writes to *X* that he admits he owes a balance of $250, and *X* writes to *Y* that he will agree to this balance, although neither party has furnished a fully revised statement. These statements and letters constitute an accord and satisfaction rather than an account stated, since they involve a disputed or controverted claim, rather than a mere agreement upon the accuracy and correctness of a creditor's statement.

---

[96] *In re Riley*, 266 App. Div. 160, 43 N.Y. Supp. 2d 753.

[97] In a case tried by the author in 1922 as attorney for the plaintiff, on an original claim for $1,258, the parties had arrived at an accord in the amount of $600. Defendant paid $300 on account of the accord but made no further payment. Plaintiff therefore sued for the amount of the original claim, less $300 paid on account, or $958. Judgment went for plaintiff, from which defendant appealed. Following affirmance and execution, defendant ultimately paid over $1100 in satisfaction of judgment, interest and costs, although the claim could have been satisfied by payment of an additional $300 on the original accord. *Pace & Pace v. Coastwise Lumber & Supply Co.*, New York City, Manhattan Municipal Court, Index No. 47980—1922.

[98] *Kromer v. Heim*, 75 N.Y. 574.

## Questions

1. Give three illustrations showing how a contract may be discharged by the terms of the original agreement.

2. In what three ways, broadly, may a contract be discharged by subsequent agreement?

3. Is there anything necessary to validate an amendment to a contract besides the mutual agreement of the parties for such purpose?

4. What difference, if any, is there between an ordinary amendment to a contract and a novation?

5. Define and illustrate a *merger*, in the contract sense of the term.

6. What is the basic difference between a cancellation and a release as applied to a contract?

7. Define (a) release, (b) mutual release, (c) general release. Distinguish between a release and a receipt. Is a release valid without consideration?

8. (a) Define accord. (b) What is the essential prerequisite to an accord? (c) Give an illustration of an accord based upon such prerequisite, and one not so based.

9. (a) Distinguish between an accord and a satisfaction. (b) Is an accord ever enforceable without a satisfaction?

10. Distinguish between an account stated and an accord and satisfaction. Give an example of each.

## Problems

1. Thomas obtains judgment against Ullman in the amount of $5,000. Ullman, before deciding whether to appeal, writes Thomas, "Will you take your judgment half in cash, and the rest in a $2,500 note which I hold and will be glad to indorse over to you?" Thomas replies that he will, and upon receipt of this reply, Ullman mails Thomas a certified check for $2,500, together with the note duly indorsed. Thomas cashes the check, returns the note, and insists on the balance in cash. Will Thomas succeed in collecting the balance in cash, or must he wait to collect the note when it matures?

2. Over a period of many years the Magic Mirror Corporation sold mirrors to the Bon Ton Shop at various times and in various quantities. The Magic Mirror Corporation billed the Bon Ton Shop monthly, and the Bon Ton Shop made payments from time to time until about six months ago, when the Magic Mirror's statement in the amount of $682.95 was disputed by the Bon Ton concern, which insisted that the balance amounted only to $135.68. After considerable correspondence, the Magic Mirror Corporation writes, "If you will send your check in the amount of $300 without further delay, we will accept it as payment in full." The Bon Ton Shop agrees to this proposal but fails to make the payment. The Magic Mirror Corporation thereupon sues the Bon Ton Shop, basing its action on an account stated. Is this suit well founded?

3.* *A* owes *B* $500. There is no dispute as to the amount owed or about *A*'s liability to pay the $500 to *B*. *A* pays *B* $300, and *B* gives to *A* a receipt for the $300 in which he states that he accepts the $300 in full discharge of *A*'s obligation to pay the $500. Later *B* sues *A* for the remaining $200. Can he recover?

4.** A physician sends a bill for $500 to a patient as a reasonable value of services rendered, no amount having been agreed on previously. The patient sends $350 with a note claiming that the charge is excessive but requesting the physician to return the check if it is not satisfactory. The physician fails to do so but notifies the patient that he intends to hold him responsible for the full balance of $150. The patient failing to pay the balance, the physician sues. Can he recover? Give reasons.

5.** Smith & Jones, Certified Public Accountants, completed an engagement for which the fee was not prearranged; they submitted a bill to their client for $1,500, which represented the reasonable value of the services rendered. Doe, the client, on receiving the bill, sent a check for $850, which he indorsed "in full satisfaction of Smith & Jones Claim." Smith & Jones deposited and collected the check, then sued for the balance. What defenses, if any, had Doe? Give reasons for your answer.

6.* Jordan was a salesman on commission with a drawing account. In March, 1932, he was discharged, and a dispute arose between him and his employer as to the amount due him. On April 7, 1932, the employer gave Jordan a check for $390, marked "Final" on its face and endorsed "Payment in full for commissions earned or to be earned and/or all claims to date." Jordan added to this "Also subject to Mr. Jordan's letter of 4/7/32," endorsed the check and cashed it. In his letter of April 7, 1932, Jordan wrote his employer that he was "compelled to receive this check under protest subject to adjustment of my account." Did Jordan's acceptance of this check constitute an accord and satisfaction?

## PART 11. TERMINATION OR DISCHARGE: OPERATION OF LAW

**In General.** Under certain conditions the law—independently of the parties themselves—operates to terminate or discharge a contract. This result may be brought about in various ways. The law may excuse performance, as in certain cases involving impossibility. It may present one of the parties with a right to declare a termination upon the other party's unauthorized attempt to alter the contract. It may in certain cases declare a contract terminated or waived in favor of another contract which is to supersede it, as in the case of merger. Or it may bar the remedy for enforcement, as in cases affected by the statute of limitations or by a discharge in bankruptcy.

**Discharge by Impossibility: in General.** Contracts may be impossible of performance when made, or the impossibility may arise thereafter. In the former case, the question is not whether the contract is discharged but whether it comes into existence. In the latter case, the contract may under certain conditions be discharged (or, to be strictly accurate, performance may be excused) by the fact that performance has become impossible.

**Impossibility at Time of Making.** If a contract, when made, is impossible of performance, and both parties know it, there can be neither intention nor expectation of performance, hence no contract. If neither party knows of the impossibility, there is also no contract, because of the mutual mistake. If one party knows it and the other not (as where a person promises payment out of a fund he knows does not exist, but which the other party believes does exist), the promisor is bound.

**Impossibility Arising After Contract Is Made.** The earlier cases held that when one undertakes a duty by contract, he undertakes the risk of performance and will therefore not be excused by impossibility, because he might have anticipated and provided against it in the contract. This rule was more rigorous than realistic. It has given way to the more modern rule that intention controls. The intention may be expressed in the contract, implied from the facts, or implied in law.[99]

*Intention expressed.* Parties may expressly provide in the contract that impossibility arising from specified causes shall or shall not excuse performance.

*Intention implied from circumstances.* The circumstances may indicate, as an implied condition of the contract, that the parties acted on the assumption that certain conditions, such as life, health or subject matter, would continue to exist, or else that they embarked upon an absolute undertaking regardless of such conditions.

*Continued existence of life and health: personal service contracts.* Contracts for personal services are based on the assumption of continued life and well-being; hence impossibility because of death, insanity, sickness or other physical disability excuses performance of *personal service contracts.*

*Continued existence of subject matter: in general.* Where the circumstances show that a contract is impliedly based on the assumption—as a condition of the contract—that its subject matter will continue to exist, impossibility through destruction of the subject matter will excuse performance.[100]

*Preventable v. unpreventable destruction of subject matter.* A distinction should be made, however, between preventable and unpreventable destruction of subject matter. If a party makes a contract obviously resting on the assumption that things will remain as they are, impossibility inherent in the nature of things and not subject to personal control will excuse performance; but impossibility which is personal, rather than objective, will not excuse performance. In the former group are cases involving destruction of subject matter or prevention of performance by fire, war, or the so-called "acts of God," such as flood, lightning, rain, hail, snow, tornado, hurricane, and so on. In the latter class are situations which depend in whole or in part on personal deficiency.

EXAMPLES *of impossibility excusing performance* (*unpreventable*):

(1) Contract to move barn: barn destroyed by lightning before it could be moved.

(2) Agreement to give series of concerts at music hall, which was destroyed by fire before the concerts could be given.

(3) Defendants, after agreeing to sell and deliver a particular consignment of cotton consisting of 621 bales, delivered only 460 bales, the other 161 bales hav-

---

[99] *Lloyd v. Murphy* (Cal. App.), 142 P. 2d 939, subs. op. 25 Cal. 2d 48, 153 P. 2d 47; *Niblett Farms v. Markley-Bankhead, Inc.,* 202 La. 982, 13 So. 2d 287.

[100] *Leonard v. Autocar Sales & Service Co.,* 392 Ill. 182, 64 N.E. 2d 447.

ing been destroyed by fire without defendants' fault. Plaintiff sued. Judgment for defendants. The parties, by their contract, obviously contemplated the continued existence of the cotton.[101]

EXAMPLES *of impossibility not excusing performance* (*preventable*):

(1) Insolvency, financial stringency, great difficulty or inconvenience, unexpected expense, and so on.

(2) Lack of sufficient labor supply.

(3) Failure of expected source of raw materials or supply.

(4) Booth contracted with a railroad company to sell and deliver 400 tons of rails made of iron with steel caps. He then contracted with the Spuyten Duyvil Rolling Mill Company for manufacture of the steel caps. The rolling mill was destroyed by fire, the caps could not be delivered, and Booth lost his contract with the railroad company. Booth sued the rolling mill for consequent damages, and the rolling mill pleaded impossibility as an excuse. The court rejected the excuse, saying: "There was no physical or natural impossibility, inherent in the nature of the thing to be performed, upon which a condition that the mill should continue can be predicated. The article was to be manufactured and delivered, and whether by that particular machinery or in that mill would not be deemed material." [102]

**Absolute undertaking: no implied conditions.** If a party undertakes to do a given thing by a given time, without other qualification, he is bound regardless of subsequent impossibility affecting the subject matter of the contract, because he thereby impliedly assumes the risk of impossibility. In such cases, neither the so-called "acts of God," nor of the enemy, will excuse performance, because the promisor has impliedly assumed these risks.

EXAMPLES:

(1) A contract to manufacture and deliver 5,000 sweaters within a given period, rendered impossible by a strike.

(2) A contract to ship 300 barrels of apples at a certain time, rendered impossible because the harbor froze over.

**Impossibility because third party disappoints.** If a party makes a contract which cannot be performed without the consent or co-operation of a third party, he is not excused because of inability to secure such consent or co-operation.

EXAMPLE: Dunbar Molasses Co. as seller contracted to sell to Canadian Industrial Alcohol Co., Ltd., as buyer, 1,500,000 gallons of molasses "of the usual run from the National Sugar Refinery." Deliveries were to begin three months after date of seller's contract with the refinery. Shortly after deliveries began, the refinery, for economic reasons, curtailed its output, so that the seller was unable to fulfill its contract with the buyer. There was no failure of sugar crop, no fire or strike at the refinery. Buyer sued seller. *Held*, the fact that the refinery disappointed the seller is no reason why the buyer must suffer.[103]

**Intention implied in law: doctrine of "frustration."** In recent years, the courts have liberalized the rule that intention governs the question of

---

[101] *Dexter v. Norton*, 47 N.Y. 62.

[102] *Booth v. Spuyten Duyvil Rolling Mill Co.*, 60 N.Y. 487.

[103] *Canadian Ind. Alcohol Co. v. Dunbar Molasses Co.*, 258 N.Y. 197.

whether impossibility excuses performance or not. Where "the true intent of the parties was thwarted by the happening of subsequent events over which they had no control and which were unforeseen at the time," said the Court recently,[104] equitable relief will be applied and performance excused. "The doctrine of frustration," said the Court, "is one born of compelling necessity, rooted in truth, and stems from actuality."

**Impossibility Created by Party Himself.** If a person is unable to perform because of impossibility created by himself, he cannot plead such impossibility as an excuse for nonperformance; as when a person agrees to sell a horse and then shoots the horse, or agrees not to leave his employment without giving two weeks' notice and then commits a crime for which he is sentenced to jail and is consequently unable to give the required two weeks' notice.

**Impossibility Created by Law.** Where performance of a contract becomes illegal, it will be excused.[105]

EXAMPLE: *A*, by lease of a wooden structure to *B*, agrees to rebuild it promptly in case of destruction by fire. If the structure is destroyed by fire, but in the meantime a municipal ordinance has prohibited wooden structures in the zone where the building was located, performance of the agreement to rebuild is excused.

**Discharge by Alteration.** If one party to a written instrument alters it without the other's consent, the other party may, if he wishes, declare the contract discharged.[106] The alteration, however, must be *intentional* and *material*. An alteration is material if it changes the legal effect of a contract; otherwise not.

When a party intentionally makes an alteration which he *thinks* is material, but which really has no legal effect, the rule is not uniform. Some states permit the other party to void the contract if he so wishes, but the majority rule is that "if the change is immaterial, the motive, even though fraudulent, will be immaterial." [107]

**Discharge by Merger.** As noted on page 111, merger, in the law of contracts, takes place when one form of contract is superseded by another form of the same contract, such as an oral by a simple written contract, or a simple written contract by one under seal. Although the substitution results from an agreement of the parties, the superseded contract is terminated by operation of law, in that the earlier obligation is deemed to have been waived in favor of the later one.

· **Statute of Limitations.** Situations in which legal remedies may be

---

[104] *Farlou Realty Corporation v. Woodsam Associates*, 49 N.Y. Supp. 2d 367, 371-2.
[105] *Hood v. Southern Production Co.*, 206 La. 642, 19 So. 2d 336; *Fast Bearing Co. v. Precision Development Co.* (Md.), 44 A. 2d 735; *Cinquegrano v. T. A. Clarke Motors*, 69 R.I. 28, 30 A. 2d 859; *Takahashi v. Pepper Tank & Contracting Co.*, 58 Wyo. 330, 131 P. 2d 339.
[106] *Lowe v. Henson* (Tex. Civ. App.), 190 S.W. 2d 423.
[107] 3 C.J.S. 926.

barred by the lapse of time are discussed in Chapter 22. The law in such situations does not really discharge the obligation, but refuses to assist the tardy party: it will neither compel performance, nor afford a remedy for non-performance.

**Discharge in Bankruptcy.** Discharges in bankruptcy are discussed in Chapter 18. They are not to be confused with insolvency, or with assignments for the benefit of creditors.

*Insolvency v. Bankruptcy.* Insolvency is a financial status, bankruptcy a legal one. (Ch. 18:2.) Insolvency alone furnishes no legal ground for discharge. A discharge in bankruptcy, however, discharges the bankrupt from all his contract obligations, with certain exceptions noted in Chapter 18.

*Assignment for benefit of creditors.* Under state debtor and creditor laws, an insolvent may transfer all his assets to an assignee for the benefit of his creditors. This, however, does not discharge the assignor of his debts, except to the extent that the debts are paid, or the creditors consent to a discharge. At one time, under the statutes of some of the states, an assignor could obtain a court order discharging him of all his debts if he complied with the statute. These statutes have either been repealed or superseded by the National Bankruptcy Act (Chapter 18).

## Questions

1. State the effect of impossibility upon an agreement under the following circumstances: (a) When the agreement is made, it is impossible of performance and both parties know this to be the fact. (b) Neither party knows of the impossibility. (c) One party knows of the impossibility, but the other does not.

2. What is the effect upon an agreement where the parties expressly provide that impossibility arising from specified causes shall or shall not excuse performance?

3. Under what circumstances will impossibility due to death, insanity, sickness, or other physical disability excuse performance?

4. When will destruction of the subject matter of a contract excuse its performance, and when not? Illustrate.

5. In relation to excuses for non-performance of a contract, what is meant by the so-called "acts of God"? Do they excuse performance in all cases? Explain.

6. Give two examples each of (a) impossibility excusing performance, and (b) impossibility not excusing performance.

7. What is the effect of subsequent impossibility where a party undertakes to do a given thing by a given time, without other qualification?

8. "Where a contract is rendered impossible of performance because of the default of a third party on whom the promising party relied, such impossibility will excuse performance." Is this statement true, false, or partly true and partly false? Explain.

9. What is the effect on a contract of impossibility created by (a) the promisor, (b) the promisee?

10. How does impossibility resulting from a change of law affect a contract?

11. What is the effect on a written contract where it is altered by one of the parties without the consent of the other, and where the alteration was: (a) intentional but not material; (b) material but not intentional?

12. Give an example of a contract discharged by merger.

13. Under what circumstances will insolvency result in the discharge of a contract?

## Problems

1. Yardley agrees to build a church in accordance with a set of plans and specifications. The contract price is $450,000. Yardley dies during the course of construction, after having received $200,000 under the contract. Another builder is hired to complete the construction, which he does at a cost of $300,000, which experts agree was a reasonable charge under the circumstances. The church, after paying the new builder, seeks to hold Yardley's estate liable for $50,000. May it do so?

2.* Hughes was a bookkeeper for the Sutton mills, receiving his salary monthly under a contract providing that if he left without giving two weeks' notice he should receive nothing for wages accrued during the current month. On June 14, 1930, Hughes was arrested, convicted and sentenced to jail. The damage to the Sutton mills from want of notice was greater in amount than one half of Hughes's salary for June. Can Hughes recover his salary for the period from June 1 to June 14?

3. Allen & Co. agree to build a private roadway for Burns at a cost of $500. The road is to follow a line laid out on a survey. The road builders encounter an enormous boulder along the line prescribed, which would require extensive blasting and greatly increase the cost of the road. The builders therefore advise Burns that it is "impossible to build the roadway at the figure given in view of this obstacle." Burns insists that the roadway be constructed at the agreed cost, and upon failure of the road builders to complete the task, sues them for breach of contract. How will the court decide, and why?

4. Agricultural Wonders, Inc., manufacturers of weed-killing agents, agree to ship and deliver to Walter Brown, a wealthy wheat farmer, 100 drums of Death-to-Weeds within six months from the date of his order. Owing to unsettled conditions in Europe, Agricultural Wonders, Inc. is unable to obtain an essential ingredient in making the weed killer, and is therefore unable to fill the order, in consequence of which Brown sustains a $10,000 loss through excessive weed damage to his wheat crop. Brown sues Agricultural Wonders, Inc. How will the suit be decided?

5. Craig agrees to move Dobson's barn for $300, the work to begin next Tuesday. Craig gets his men and equipment on the job, only to learn that the barn was struck by lightning an hour or two before he got there, and completely destroyed by the ensuing fire. Craig seeks to recover $50 from Dobson on the ground that that was the damage he sustained in getting his equipment and men ready to move the barn. Will Craig succeed?

6. Earle contracted with the Free-Flow Valve Company to sell and deliver 500 valves with brass valve heads. He then contracted with the Grand Brass Works for manufacture of the brass valve heads. The brass works went on strike, the valve heads could not be delivered, and Earle lost his contract with the valve company. Earle sued the brass works for consequent damages, and the brass works pleaded impossibility as an excuse. How did the court decide, and why?

7. The Red River Fruitgrowers contracted to ship 500 cases of tomatoes

"within three days from the date of this shipping memo." The next day a storm prevented the freighter from loading the tomatoes, and the following day the tomatoes froze in subzero weather and thereafter spoiled. The buyer rejected the shipment and sued the Red River Fruitgrowers for breach of contract. How did the decision go, and why?

8. On September 30, the Hartford Housefurnishing Company leases a second-hand electric refrigerator to Gill at a rental of $25 per month, with the understanding that Gill has a thirty-day option in which to purchase the refrigerator at a price of $200. The leasing agreement is oral. On October 2, after the refrigerator had been installed for several days, Gill insists on having the agreement reduced to writing. This, accordingly, is done, the writing being dated October 2 and signed by both parties. On October 31, Gill seeks to exercise his option and tenders the amount of the purchase price which the Hartford Housefurnishing Company rejects on the ground that the time for exercising the option has expired. How would the court decide, and why?

## PART 12. BREACH OF CONTRACT

**What Constitutes Breach.** A contract is commonly breached by failure to perform it. It may also be breached by making performance impossible (page 119) and by renunciation or "anticipatory breach."

*Anticipatory breach.* If a party to a contract *unqualifiedly* announces in advance of performance date that he will not perform, he commits an anticipatory breach, and the other party need not wait for the performance date but may sue at once.

EXAMPLES:

(1) *A*, having contracted on Februray 1 to sell 100 bbls. flour for delivery on July 1, notifies *B* on March 1 that he will not deliver. *B* may sue at once.

(2) If, in (1), *A* is adjudicated a bankrupt on March 1, he thereby commits an anticipatory breach, as if he had announced on that date that he would not, perform. *B* may file his claim without waiting for the performance date.

A minority of states[108] dissent from the anticipatory breach doctrine, holding that a mere refusal of performance before the time for performance arrives cannot form the basis for damages.

**Remedies for Breach.** Remedies for breach of contract include: (1) discharge, (2) damages, (3) *quantum meruit*, (4) specific performance and—where the parties so provide—(5) arbitration.

**(1) Discharge by Breach.** If you and I make a contract, and I breach it, you are thereby discharged; that is, you are under no obligation to proceed further with the contract.

EXAMPLE: If prepayment is required under a contract of sale as a condition for delivery, the seller is discharged by failure to make such prepayment.

**(2) Damages.** Damage is recompense for a wrong. In a breach of contract, it represents the loss *directly and naturally* resulting from the breach. It therefore excludes speculative, remote or possible losses which cannot

---

[108] Including Massachusetts, Nebraska and North Dakota.

be shown to have directly resulted from the breach. Damages may be *general, special* and *liquidated.*

*General v. special damages.* "General damages are such as might accrue to any person similarly injured, while special damages are such as did in fact accrue to the particular individual by reason of the particular circumstances of the case." [109]

EXAMPLE: You agree to manufacture for me 1,000 dresses in given styles and sizes, at $1.00 a dress. The market value of such dresses, manufactured, is $1.25 a dress. However, I have a special customer who is willing to pay $1.50 a dress. In case of your breach, my general damages would be the difference between the contract price and the market price, or $250. But if, when we made our contract, you knew of my special customer who was willing to pay $1.50 a dress, and if, in my complaint, I plead my special damages and the facts giving rise thereto, I may recover not only general damages of $250, but additional special damages of $250 because of the special circumstances affecting my case.

*Liquidated damages.* "Liquidated damages constitute the compensation which the parties have agreed must be paid in satisfaction of the loss or injury which will follow from a breach of contract. They must bear reasonable proportion to the actual loss. *Seidlitz v. Auerbach,* 230 N.Y. 167, 129 N.E. 461. Otherwise an agreement to pay a fixed sum, upon a breach of contract, is an agreement to pay a penalty, though the parties have chosen to call it 'liquidated damages,' and is unenforcible." [110]

*Nominal damages.* When a wrong is established but no real damage shown, a jury may award *nominal* damages, sometimes fixed at six cents (Ch. 22:1).

*Measure of damage: in general.* As a rule, the measure of damage for breach of contract is the loss which the injured party can *prove* he sustained because of the breach. In a contract of sale the measure of damage is the difference between the contract price and the market price at the time of the breach.

*Measure of damage: breach of employment contracts.* The measure of damage for breach of a contract of employment is the sum or sums which the employee would have been paid had the contract not been breached, less what the employee has earned or should have earned for the balance of the contract period.

**Mitigating Damages.** The law requires an injured party to *mitigate,* not *aggravate* his damage; that is, to keep the damages down.

EXAMPLES:
(1) Wood contracts with Long, a shirtmaker, for 1,000 men's shirts. Long manufactures and delivers 500 shirts. Wood pays for them and at the same time asks Long not to manufacture any more shirts, because he cannot dispose of more. If Long sues Wood for the breach, he may include, as damage, the profit he would have made on the additional shirts, plus any extra expense he

[109] *Black's L. Dic.,* p. 314.
[110] *Wirth & Hamid Fair Booking v. Wirth,* 265 N.Y. 214, 223, 192 N.E. 297.

has already been put to because of Wood's order, such as the cost, less salvage, of the material needed to make up the extra 500 shirts, and so on; but Long must not aggravate the damage by proceeding to manufacture the additional shirts and by charging the cost thereof as additional damage.

(2) If I hire you for a year and discharge you at the end of six months, you must mitigate the damage by trying to find another position (though not a different type of position, nor a position in a different locality).

(3) **Quantum Meruit.** The term *quantum meruit* means "as much as he deserves." If you hire me for a year by an express contract and discharge me without pay at the end of the month, I need not sue on the express contract, but may sue you on the *implied contract* that where one accepts services or benefits from another, he will compensate the latter by an amount representing the *reasonable value* of the services or benefits received. (See page 90, second example.)

(4) **Specific Performance.** Where damages at common law would be inadequate, either because there is no yardstick to measure the loss, or because a party, to receive full justice, is entitled to acquire *the thing contracted for*, a court of equity will decree the *specific performance* of the contract. Contracts of this nature usually involve *land* and *unique chattels* not readily obtainable on the open market, such as antiques, heirlooms, famous paintings, manuscripts and first editions of books, ancient coins and relics, patents, copyrights, or shares of stock in a closely held corporation.

**Injunctions in Lieu of Specific Performance.** As previously noted (page 71), the law looks with disfavor on contracts which prohibit employees from seeking similar employment after terminating their contracts. However, where the services are exceptionally unique and extraordinary, a court of equity, though powerless to compel specific performance, may accomplish the same end through the remedy of injunction (page 6). For example, a court of equity cannot compel an actor to play or a singer to sing; but it can decree that they shall not play or sing for *someone else* until they specifically perform their contracts. No such injunction will be granted unless the services are truly unique and the contract is free from taint of any sort.

EXAMPLES:

(1) On breach of contract by a teacher for services in a school of music, the court denied an injunction because the services were not so special or extraordinary that they could not be supplied elsewhere and another teacher found to take defendant's place without materially impairing the school's efficiency.[111]

(2) In 1914, Hal Chase, then regarded as the foremost first baseman in professional baseball, "jumped" from the American League (Chicago Club) to the Federal League (Buffalo Club). The Chicago American Club sought an injunction restraining Chase from playing with the Buffalo Club. The court held that ordinarily, a player with the unique and extraordinary talents of Chase could be restrained from violating a contract that he would not work for an-

---

[111] *Columbia College of Music, etc. v. Tunberg,* 64 Wash. 19, 116 P. 280.

other during a specified term, but in this case, the plaintiff was engaged in maintaining an unconscionable monopolistic arrangement with players and other ball clubs, hence he did not come into a court of equity with "clean hands" (see page 7).[112]

(5) **Arbitration.** In addition to the usual remedies for breach of contract, many contracts contain a provision that in case of dispute, the parties will submit their differences to arbitration, instead of resorting to litigation. Where a contract contains no such clause, the parties may submit their dispute to arbitrators by an agreement known as a *submission*.

*Irrevocability of arbitration agreements and submissions.* Public policy favors arbitration, which not only saves parties the expense of litigation, but the public the expense of a trial. Hence in states where arbitration is governed by statute, arbitration agreements and submissions are generally irrevocable except by mutual consent or by operation of law (as in the case of death, insanity or destruction of the subject matter of the arbitration).

*Arbitrators.* The agreement or submission may provide for an arbitrator agreeable to both sides, or it may provide that each is to select an arbitrator, the two to select a third, or umpire. In the latter event, the designation must be in writing.

*Arbitration proceedings.* The arbitrators must first be sworn by an officer authorized by law to administer an oath, faithfully and fairly to hear and examine the matters in controversy and to make a just award to the best of their understanding. The arbitrators then appoint a time and place for the hearing, cause notice of it to be given to each of the parties, and may adjourn the hearing from time to time, but not beyond the day, if any, fixed in the submission for rendering the award. The procedure and circumstances under which hearings are held may be prescribed and limited by the terms of the written submission, in which event, the arbitrators must abide by such terms in proceeding with their hearings. Otherwise, the arbitrators may adopt their own procedure, which may be informal.

*The award.* The determination or decision of the arbitrators is known as the *award*. To be enforced, the award must be in writing and signed by the arbitrators making it; must be made within the time limit, if any, fixed in the contract or submission; must be acknowledged or proved and certified in like manner as a deed to be recorded (Ch. 14:2); and must be either filed with the clerk of the court or delivered to one of the parties. Upon application of either party, the award must be confirmed by the court, unless it is vacated, modified or corrected.

*Judgment on the award.* Upon the granting of an order confirming,

---

[112] *American League Baseball Club of Chicago v. Chase*, 86 Misc. 441, 149 N.Y. Supp. 6.

modifying or correcting an award, judgment may be entered accordingly with the same force and effect as if the dispute had been tried in court.

## Questions

1. Name the different circumstances which may constitute a breach of contract.

2. Define and illustrate *anticipatory breach*.

3. Name the remedies for breach of contract.

4. Define (a) damages, (b) general damages, (c) special damages, (d) liquidated damages, and (e) nominal damages.

5. State the general rule governing the measure of damage for breach of contract.

6. State the rule governing the measure of damage for breach of an employment contract.

7. What is meant by (a) *mitigating* damages; (b) *aggravating* damages?

8. What is the meaning of the expression *quantum meruit*, and how does it apply as a remedy for breach of contract?

9. Define and explain the principle of *specific performance*.

10. Under what circumstances may the law substitute an injunction for the remedy of specific performance?

11. How may parties provide for arbitration?

12. "Either party may withdraw from an arbitration, with or without the consent of the other party." Is this statement true, false, or partly true and partly false?

13. What provision does the law generally make with respect to the number of persons who may be selected as arbitrators and the manner of their selection? What does an agreement to arbitrate usually provide in this connection?

14. What must the arbitrators do before they proceed to take testimony?

15. When may arbitrators adopt their own procedure for taking testimony, and when are they governed by mandatory requirements in this connection?

16. Define *award*. What does the law usually require as to the form of an award in order that it may be binding on the parties and serve as a basis for court approval?

17. Upon what ground may an award be (a) vacated, (b) modified?

18. Upon the granting of an order confirming, modifying or correcting an award, what may the successful party do to convert the award into a binding mandate?

## Problems

1. Hill receives an order from a municipal waterworks commissioner for 100 water valves of a special size and specification, to be delivered by June 1. On February 1, the commissioner advises Hill that the proposed waterworks system has been abandoned and that the valves will not be needed. Hill nevertheless completes the manufacture of the valves, and on June 1 tenders full delivery, which is rejected. He then sues the municipality for the full contract price of the valves. How will the court charge the jury?

2. You agree to build me ten two-story houses at an aggregate price of $150,000, all to be completed for October occupancy. A clause in the contract provides that "For each workday beyond October 1 that the builder fails to have all said houses fully completed, the owner is to be allowed a deduction

from the contract price of $1,000." Nine of the houses are completed by October 1, but the tenth house is not completed until October 15, which is ten working days beyond October 1. In making payment for the houses I insist on withholding $10,000 as a proper deduction from the contract price. You sue me for that amount. Who will win, and why?

3. A seller breaches his contract to deliver 1,000 crates of eggs at $4.80 a crate. Eggs on the market are $6.00 a crate. Owing to the unusual bargain presented to this buyer, he insists on delivery of the eggs and sues the seller for specific performance. How will the court decide?

4.* X owns 48% of the capital stock of a corporation conducting a profitable but highly competitive business, Y holds 49%, and Z holds 3%. X enters into a legally binding contract with Z for the purchase of Z's stock. Z, without excuse, breaches his contract and refuses to deliver the stock. What can X legally do about it?

5. Ives is a tea taster. He has learned no other trade or profession. He is employed by the Tastea Corporation as a tea taster, on a five-year written contract, at $8,000 a year. At the end of a year he is discharged without cause. He seeks employment as a tea taster, but is unable to secure another such position for the next four years. Many other forms of employment, however, were open to him, but he declined to accept any other position than that of tea tasting. At the end of four years, Ives sues the Tastea Corporation for $32,000. How should the case be decided, and why?

6. The Metropolitan School of Music hires Miss Jennings to serve on its teaching staff for one year at an annual salary of $6,500. After signing the contract, Miss Jennings receives an offer from another school at an annual salary of $7,500. She notifies the Metropolitan School that she has decided to accept the other offer, whereupon the Metropolitan School seeks an injunction to restrain Miss Jennings from accepting such other employment. Miss Jennings is unquestionably an accomplished musician with an extraordinary gift as a teacher. Similar teachers are available, but at a substantially higher salary. Will the Metropolitan School obtain the injunction?

7. Kane and Lane get into a dispute over a bill, and finally decide to submit the matter to Maine, a mutual friend, as arbitrator. The matter is fully threshed out at a luncheon conference, at the end of which Maine states, "Well, I think Lane is right." Kane refuses to abide by the decision, and Lane seeks the advice of counsel as to whether, if these facts were fully set forth in an affidavit, a judgment could be entered in favor of Lane and against Kane. How should Lane be advised?

8. A chain store proprietor signs a contract with a jobber which contains a clause that all disputes under the contract are to be settled by arbitration. A dispute arises under the contract, and the chain store proprietor refuses to be bound by the arbitration clause. The jobber wants to know whether he can compel specific performance of the arbitration clause, or must sue for breach of contract. What is your opinion?

## COURT CASES FOR REVIEW

### How Did the Court Decide, and Why?

1. A plastering contractor, after negotiations with a construction company, sent the company a letter stating that "our bid" for plastering the main floor of one type of house was $505, and of another type of house, $575. The company wrote the contractor on a purchase order form, requesting entry of an order for plastering a number of houses of both types in accordance with the con-

tractor's letter. The contractor did not reply, and except for delivering a large number of laths to the building project, did nothing until five months later, when he renounced the contract. Suit followed. *Westland Const. Co. v. Chris Berg, Inc.,* 35 Wash. 2d 824, 215 P. 2d 683.

2. Buyer sent seller two purchase orders. Each bore on its face a request that seller sign and return one copy, and on its back the terms and conditions of the order. One of these called for arbitration of all disputes, and another provided that the order and all its terms became binding unless the seller advised otherwise within ten days. The orders were neither signed nor returned. Instead, the seller sent the merchandise ordered, with his own memorandum of sale. The buyer, claiming that the merchandise was defective, demanded arbitration, which the seller rejected. *Albrecht Chemical Co. v. Anderson Trading Corp.,* 298 N.Y. 437, 84 N.E. 2d 625.

3. Defendants employed plaintiff to render legal and executive services in real estate development operations. The contract provided that defendants at the end of the year would pay plaintiff, in addition to a specified salary, a fair, reasonable and just share of the profits of the business. Defendants refused to pay any share of the profits and plaintiff sued. *Gray v. Aiken,* 205 Ga. 649, 54 S.E. 2d 587.

4. A contract granted defendant an exclusive agency for shoes manufactured by plaintiff. It provided that the price to be paid plaintiff should be on the basis of actual cost of manufacture plus a general average of profit, minus a 20% deduction, and that the contract should continue in force as long as sales made on defendant's account amounted to a yearly average of $35,000. In a subsequent suit, the validity of the contract was called into question. *Red Wing Shoe Co. v. Shepherd Safety Shoe Corp.,* 164 F. 2d 415.

5. A production manager was hired under a one-year contract at a specified annual salary plus a given bonus if the manager saved the employer more than $7,000 in the manufacture of wagons and other articles. On suit by plaintiff, defendant challenged the enforceability of the contract. *Chew v. Leonard,* 228 N.C. 181, 44 S.E. 2d 869.

6. Plaintiff made an inadvertent error in a bid on public work. Before the city board had considered any bids, plaintiff notified the board of its mistake, and of its desire to withdraw the bid. The city readvertised for new bids, the lowest of which was higher than plaintiff's bid. The city having retained plaintiff's deposit against the difference, plaintiff sued for return of the deposit. *W. F. Martens & Co., Inc. v. City of Syracuse et al.,* 183 App. Div. 622, 171 N.Y. Supp. 87.

7. The widow of decedent wrote her niece enclosing an assignment, for the niece's signature, of the niece's one-half interest as an heir at law. The widow wrote that she did not know the amount of the estate, but called attention to the fact that decedent had lost "so much money in stock" that she (the widow) would have to go to work. The niece, on reading the letter, signed the assignment. The inventory, however, subsequently showed that the estate consisted of assets worth approximately $14,000. The validity of this assignment was attacked on the widow's accounting. *Appeal of Robie,* 141 Me. 369, 44 A. 2d 889.

8. Defendant signed a contract for the sale of a real estate parcel and later repudiated the contract on the ground that she was intoxicated when the contract was signed. The following facts were established in the trial: (1) Defendant was not enfeebled by the habitual use of intoxicants; (2) She pursued a remunerative employment; (3) The bargain was not shown to have been

improvident; (4) The sale exposed her to the loss of living quarters, which were difficult to obtain. Plaintiff sued for specific performance. *Seminara v. Grisman*, 137 N.J. Eq. 307, 44 A. 2d 492.

9. An infant purchased and received possession of a bicycle at a price paid partly at the making of the contract, with provision for payment of the remainder in future weekly installments; title to pass upon the completion of the stipulated payments. Having used the bicycle for a time, and having paid the accrued installments, the infant returned the bicycle before it was fully paid for, and claimed the right to rescind the contract and recover the amounts paid thereon. *Rice v. Butler*, 160 N.Y. 578.

10. Plaintiff, an infant, bought a truck trailer on time, received a certificate of title thereto, and executed a chattel mortgage securing the payment of subsequent installments. On default of the latter, the seller repossessed itself of the trailer and, acting under the power reserved to it in the mortgage, sold the trailer to a third person and conveyed both title and possession. Plaintiff sought rescission and demanded a return of the purchase price. Defendant claimed that plaintiff's failure to surrender his certificate of title precluded his rescission of the contract. *Freiburghaus v. Herman Body Co.*, 102 S.W. 2d 743 (Mo. App.).

11. A son, during infancy, conveyed his real estate to his father, expending or wasting the consideration therefor before his arrival at full age. Having nothing with which to replace the consideration received for his property, the infant on arriving of age sought to disaffirm his deed without restoring or offering to restore the consideration. Rescission was sought three years after arrival at full age when the infant made re-entry and the father sued in trespass. *Green v. Green*, 69 N.Y. 553.

12. Defendant orally promised to pay for damages allegedly done by his dog. The dog was not known to be vicious. Defendant repudiated the promise, and plaintiff sued. *Pirello v. Roach*, 32 Erie (Pa. Com. Pl.) 147.

13. Defendant's parents owed plaintiff a bill for furniture. Defendant signed an agreement to pay the debt in consideration of plaintiff's promise not to sue her parents. Thereafter plaintiff demanded payment, which was refused. Plaintiff sued. *Hofmann v. De Felice*, 136 Conn. 187, 70 A. 2d 129.

14. Plaintiff arranged to remove scrap metal from defendant's premises. He was not obligated to remove and pay for any particular amount of scrap metal, and defendant was under no obligation to permit plaintiff to remove any definite amount of scrap. The enforceability of this contract was challenged. *Larkins v. St. Paul & Tacoma Lumber Co.*, 35 Wash. 2d 711, 214 P. 2d 700.

15. A contract entered into in August, 1948 prohibited the resale within six months of a new automobile of a type for which the demand then greatly exceeded the supply. The contract was attacked as an invalid restraint of trade. *Becker-Mills, Inc. v. Bosher*, 68 D. & C. (Pa. Mun.) 115.

16. A contract between an attorney and a layman provided for an equal division of attorney's fees to be received in a contemplated or pending litigation. The layman's share was for services rendered by him in searching out an important witness to testify on the trial. The attorney refused to pay the stipulated compensation, and the layman sued. *Porter v. Jones*, 176 F. 2d 87.

17. The seller of a candy business agreed not to go back into that business, then breached his agreement. Plaintiff's suit was based on the breach. *Barner v. Boggiano*, 32 Tenn. App. 351, 222 S.W. 2d 672.

18. A layman solicited decedent's heir for authorization to appear on his behalf in administration proceedings and to employ counsel to represent the

heir. He obtained a power of attorney or assignment providing for payment of all expenses, including attorney's fees and court costs, upon an agreed compensation based on a percentage of the heir's distributive share. The validity of this arrangement was challenged. *In re Reilly's Estate,* 81 Cal. App. 2d 564, 184 P. 2d 922.

19. Defendant caused the arrest of plaintiff's daughter on a criminal charge. The daughter threatened to prosecute defendant for conspiring with another to have her wrongfully arrested. Defendant and the daughter then agreed to withhold respective prosecutions. As part of this agreement defendant agreed to employ plaintiff, who was fully informed of the facts, though he took no part in the agreement. Plaintiff sued for breach of the contract of employment. *Cantales v. Mazzei,* 190 Misc. 292, 73 N.Y. Supp. 2d 902.

20. A covenant in an employment contract prohibited a store manager from engaging in similar business activity, after leaving the employer's business, for a period of two years and within a 25-mile area surrounding any store owned by the employer. The covenant was breached and the employer sued. *Jewel Paint & Varnish Co. v. Walters,* 339 Ill. App. 335, 89 N.E. 2d 835.

21. A rule requiring women who married to leave the employer's service within 30 days, adopted by arbitrators under a bargaining contract with a union, was challenged as void, on grounds of public policy. *Standard Oil Co. v. Review Bd. of Ind. Employment Sec. Division,* 119 Ind. App. 576, 88 N.E. 2d 567.

22. A father bought postal savings certificates in the names of his son and his daughter, pursuant to an oral agreement by the children to hold the certificates in trust for the father. The transaction was in violation of the law permitting a person to have only one account, not to exceed $2,500. The children refused to honor their agreement, and the father sued to recover the moneys. *Zorich v. Zorich,* 119 Ind. App. 547, 88 N.E. 2d 694.

23. A husband and wife entered into an agreement that the wife would enter any appearance required in a Florida divorce proceeding, and that she would lose her rights under a trust agreement if she opposed any divorce proceeding. The wife sought to avoid the effect of this agreement. *Staedler v. Staedler,* 6 N.J. 380, 78 A. 2d 896.

24. On Thursday, August 1, 1946, a soldier received orders to leave Atlanta, Ga., and report to Fort Dix, N.J., for discharge, by Monday, August 5. He proceeded at once to Philadelphia and in the face of a severe housing shortage, he began hunting for a home for his wife and three children. On Saturday, August 3, the soldier found a house and on Saturday evening at 9:30, closed on terms for its purchase; but no lawyer being available, a broker drew up an agreement Sunday morning, which the soldier signed. Thereafter the sellers refused to convey title, pleading the Sunday statute. The soldier sued for specific performance, and the sellers moved to dismiss his complaint. *Chadwick v. Stokes,* 162 F. 2d 132.

25. Plaintiff entered into a written agreement with defendants to remodel a house for $3,075, payable as follows: $150 on signing of contract; $1,000 upon delivery of materials and starting of work; $1,500 on completion of rough carpentry and plumbing; and $425 on completion of job. When the "rough work" was done, plaintiff asked for the third installment of $1,500, but defendants would not pay it, so plaintiff stopped work and brought suit for the entire balance of $1,925. *New Era Homes Corporation v. Forster,* 299 N.Y. 303, 86 N.E. 2d 757.

26. Plaintiff sued for commissions in procuring a lease. The defense was

that the salesman who negotiated the lease was not duly licensed, and that the statute required that he possess one to function as such salesman. The statute, however, did not specifically provide that such transactions were unlawful in the absence of a license; neither did it provide that recovery could not be had thereon if the statute was violated. *Firpo v. Murphy, et al.*, 72 Cal. App. 249, 236 P. 968.

27. Defendant asked plaintiff to sign a note as surety. The note was made by defendant's brother. Defendant orally promised plaintiff he would make good any loss plaintiff might suffer by signing the note as surety. Plaintiff signed as surety, and as a result was required to pay the bank which held the note a substantial balance due on it. Suit was brought against defendant to make good such balance paid by plaintiff, and defendant set up the statute of frauds as a defense. A motion was made to dismiss the suit. *Gilinsky v. Klionsky*, 140 Misc. Rep. 724, 251 N.Y. Supp. 570.

28. A corporation was in need of money. Defendant, a large stockholder, director and vice-president of the corporation, asked plaintiff to loan the corporation $1,500. To induce plaintiff to make the loan it was orally agreed between plaintiff and defendant that plaintiff was to buy 6,000 shares of stock in the corporation, pay $1,500 therefor to the corporation, and in the event the stock became worthless, defendant would buy it and pay plaintiff $1,500 for it. The stock became worthless, plaintiff tendered it to defendant and demanded $1,500, and defendant refused. Plaintiff sued and defendant set up the defense of the statute of frauds. *Kilbride v. Moss*, 113 Cal. 432, 45 P. 812.

29. Children orally agreed to share equally the proceeds of their father's estate, in consideration of their equally sharing his expenses during his lifetime. The question at issue was whether such an agreement was enforceable under the statute of frauds as not performable within one year from the date of its making. *Meltzer v. Koenigsberg*, 99 N.Y. Supp. 2d 143, aff'd 277 App. Div. 1050, 100 N.Y. Supp. 2d 592.

30. A woman bought some kitchen cabinets under an oral contract. After expressing her approval of the cabinets she requested the seller to store them for a length of time. The question was whether the cabinets could be deemed to have been received and accepted by the purchaser, thereby dispensing with a writing. *H. W. Myers & Son v. Felopulos*, 76 A. 2d 552 (Vt.).

31. A contract between brothers and their wives provided that in case of the sale of a hotel in which they were interested, defendants were to pay plaintiff and her husband, one-quarter of the net profits resulting from the sale. Title to the hotel was transferred by defendants to a corporation controlled by them. Contending that such transfer constituted a sale, plaintiffs claimed one-quarter of the profits resulting from the transfer. *Altman v. Altman*, 8 N.J. Super. 301, 72 A. 2d 536.

32. A bill of sale of a restaurant business required the sellers to pay liquidated damages of $500 a month for violation of a covenant not to engage in the restaurant business within a "radius" of 500 yards for 10 years. A dispute arose as to whether the 500 yards meant a direct air line distance, or a distance of 500 yards measured along the usual and customary route which human beings could travel on streets and sidewalks. *Mead v. Anton*, 33 Wash. 2d 741, 207 P. 2d 227.

33. An employment contract gave a motion picture producer the right to suspend the contract if an actor, by reason of mental or physical disability, or otherwise, should be incapacitated from fully performing the contract. The actor was unable to perform the contract due to military service. The employer

contended that it was thereby given the right to suspend the contract. *Autry v. Republic Productions,* 30 Cal. App. 2d 144, 180 P. 2d 888.

34. A professional football player was hired to play football for the defendant. A printed provision in the contract specified compensation at $300 per game. There was also an insertion in handwriting that the compensation was to be $3600 for the season. The question arose as to whether the player was entitled to receive the full sum of $3600 for the entire season, whether or not he participated in all the games played. *Tollefson v. Green Bay Packers,* 256 Wis. 318, 41 N.W. 2d 201.

35. Defendant employed plaintiff to print a book entitled "Beginners' Bird Guide," which defendant was under contract to publish for a professor specializing in ornithology at Rutgers University. It was understood that the finished colors of the plates would be reasonable approximations only but that the colors themselves were not to be interchanged. A substantial number of printed volumes showed variations in color from the original master sheets and from the final press sheets which had been submitted. The book was on that account rendered unmerchantable and unfit for the purpose intended. Plaintiff sued for work, labor and services in printing the book. Defendant counterclaimed for its advertising and shipping expenses, for lost profits and for the value of the color drawings prepared by the author and retained by plaintiff. Plaintiff claimed substantial performance. From a judgment in favor of plaintiff, defendant appealed. *Duenewald Printing Corporation v. G. P. Putnam's Sons,* 276 App. Div. 26, 92 N.Y. Supp. 2d 553.

36. A bathhouse owner contracted with a slate company for the installation of a Spanish tile roof. The work being in some respects unfinished and defective, the owner stripped the tiles from the roof and refused payment to the contractor, who brought suit. *Brandin Slate Co. v. Bannister,* 30 So. 2d 877 (La. App.).

37. Plaintiff contracted to haul all the pulp wood cut upon a certain tract at a compensation of 85¢ per cord, of which 25¢ per cord was to be held back until completion of the contract. There were 8345 cords cut. Plaintiffs hauled all the wood except 7½ cords which had been concealed by snow and overlooked. Defendants withheld payment at the rate of 25¢ per cord, claiming that plaintiffs had not completed their contract. *Drew et al. v. Goodhue,* 74 Vt. 436, 52 A. 971.

38. Defendant engaged plaintiff to make vocal phonograph records, on an agreement to pay a stipulated sum for every record which it declared satisfactory. Defendant declared most of the records unsatisfactory but was willing to allow plaintiff another opportunity to make satisfactory records. It was admitted that plaintiff possessed a highly cultivated voice of exceptional tone and quality, which she could use with expression, feeling and ability. On proof of these facts, plaintiff demanded judgment. *Lyon v. Starr Piano Co.,* 107 Misc. 334, 177 N.Y. Supp. 662.

39. In a mortgage foreclosure suit brought after expiration of the six-year limitation period, the question arose whether the mortgage indebtedness had become outlawed by the statute, or was revived by a $2,000 payment which had been made within six years. At the time of payment, over $58,000 interest was due in addition to unpaid principal. No specific instruction was given as to how the $2,000 payment was to be applied, but the mortgagor's letter forwarding the check inquired as to the possibility of changing the mortgage rate. The mortgagee contended that he applied the payment on principal, thereby reviving the debt. *Woolley v. Hoffman,* 99 N.Y. Supp. 293.

40. Defendant, who had contracted to haul coal for plaintiff, advised plaintiff that he had discovered he could not legally do so. Plaintiff replied, "We are very sorry that you cannot continue to haul coal under our contract," and suggested an arrangement for the sale of coal. The suggested arrangement was never consummated. Later plaintiff sought to hold defendant on the contract and defendant pleaded mutual rescission. *Underhill Coal Min. Co. v. Irwin*, 60 D. & C. (Pa. Com. Pl.) 226.

41. Plaintiff contracted to excavate and construct a cement sidewalk and curb in front of defendant's property. The contract was made in September. The agreed price was $420. Plaintiff was to start work within a week and finish it before cold weather set in. Plaintiff did nothing until December, then excavated a strip 12 feet wide and 8 feet deep along the front of the premises. Nothing further having been done by the following March 2, defendant notified plaintiff that he cancelled the contract. Plaintiff sued for $158.60 as the reasonable value of the work done. Defendant counterclaimed for the value of the dirt removed. The lower Court allowed judgment for plaintiff in the full amount less $25 for the dirt. Defendant appealed. *Kelley v. Hance,* 108 Conn. 186, 142 A. 683.

42. Dr. Fuller sent Mrs. Kemp a bill for $670 for services rendered. Mrs. Kemp disputed the value of Dr. Fuller's services and sent him a check for $400 "in full payment." Dr. Fuller cashed the check and brought suit for the balance of the account. *Fuller v. Kemp*, 138 N.Y. 231.

43. Plaintiff contracted to paint a portrait of defendant's father, at an agreed price of $500 for the canvas "if my work is found to be to the entire satisfaction of all concerned." The defendant refused to accept the portrait when completed because it was not satisfactory. Plaintiff sued on the contract price. *Wolff v. Smith*, 303 Ill. App. 413, 25 N.E. 2d 399.

44. Plaintiff sued defendant for failure to perform a contract to purchase Italian lire for him. Payment for the lire was to have been made in cash on a specified day. Plaintiff told a representative of the defendant that he had the cash ready to pay. The representative replied that the trust company had not bought the lire. The truth was that defendant had sufficient lire on hand to satisfy its commitment. Plaintiff sued. The defense was, insufficient tender, to which plaintiff replied that tender is waived where the other party evades it. *Monello v. Hanover Trust Co.*, 252 Mass. 563, 148 N.E. 136.

45. Plaintiff contracted to provide the necessary materials and labor for certain alterations and additions to defendant's residence, including the rebuilding of a private chapel involving specially designed mill-work, the materials for which were duly ordered by plaintiff. Without fault of either party, the residence was destroyed by fire. The special mill-work had been completed by the concern from whom plaintiff had ordered it, but had not been delivered, accepted or approved by the architect. Defendant paid plaintiff for work done and materials installed in the residence before the fire, but refused payment for the mill and cabinet work which had not been delivered at the time of the fire. For the latter, plaintiff brought suit. *Matthews Construction Company v. Brady*, 104 N.J.L. 438, 140 A. 433.

46. On or about February 1, 1926, defendant agreed to purchase 1,500 net tons of Scotch coke, to be imported by plaintiff, at a price of $12 per ton unloaded at New Haven, Conn., and shipped by rail to Hartford, Conn. The coke was to be delivered in February. It did not arrive in New Haven until March 8, and defendant rejected delivery. After some negotiations, defendant agreed to accept the coke at New Haven and pay $6.50 per ton for it. There-

after plaintiff sued on the original contract price less a down payment. *Riverside Coal Company v. American Coal Company*, 107 Conn. 40, 139 A. 276.

47. A student registered for a correspondence course in air conditioning, then discontinued the course. The school sued the student for a balance of tuition due. On the trial the school proved the contract, the breach, and the balance due, but was unable to prove a connection between such balance and the loss sustained by the school as the result of the breach. *Air Conditioning Training Co. v. Knouse*, 46 So. 2d 665 (La. App.).

48. A lumber company exclusively contracted to supply a lime company with wood slabs for fuel to the limit of its mill production capacity. It thereafter breached its contract by delivering slabs to a chemical company. Wood slabs were extremely difficult to obtain and the market for them was highly uncertain. The lime company sued the lumber company for specific performance. *White Marble Lime Co. v. Consolidated Lumber Co.*, 205 Mich. 634, 172 N.W. 603.

49. A contract was entered into for the purchase of stock. The sole purpose of the contract was to obtain control of a patent owned by the company. The contract was breached by the seller and the buyer sued for specific performance. *U.S. Fire Apparatus Co. v. G. W. Baker Mach. Co.*, 10 Del. Ch. 421, 95 A. 294, rev. on other grounds 11 Del. Ch. 386, 97 A. 613.

50. A contract for the construction of a fishing vessel provided that any dispute between the builders and the purchasers should be referred to a named person, and that the decision of the latter should be final and binding. The purchasers brought action against the builders for breach of contract and the loss of profits which would have been earned if the vessel had been built according to contract. The evidence disclosed that though the builders had insisted upon compliance with the provision for arbitration, the purchasers had not complied with such provision nor attempted to do so. The purchasers insisted on judgment. *Gonsalves v. Hodgson*, 38 Cal. 2d 91, 220 P. 2d 560.

# 3

# Negotiable
# Instruments

**Scope of This Chapter.** This chapter covers the nature and types of negotiable instruments, with particular emphasis on how they function legally in the business world of today. In Part 1 we consider the nature of such instruments, and what makes them negotiable. In Part 2 we deal with the various types of negotiable instruments in common use today. In Part 3 we analyze the process of putting commercial paper into circulation, first by issue, and then by negotiation. In Part 4 we deal with the defenses which may relieve a person from liability on an instrument to which he has put his signature, and in Part 5 we discuss the liabilities of the various parties connected with such instrument: the maker of a promissory note, the drawer of a bill of exchange, the drawee against whom the bill is drawn, and the indorsers on either a bill or a note; also the extent to which an individual, a partner or a corporation may be held on an accommodation signature, and the liability of parties on negotiable documents of title such as bills of lading and warehouse receipts. In Parts 6 and 7 we consider the presentment of an instrument for acceptance or for payment, and the steps which must be taken if an instrument is dishonored by non-acceptance or non-payment. In Part 8 we deal with the discharge of a negotiable instrument, and in Part 9 with that most familiar of negotiable instruments, the check.

## PART 1. NATURE AND REQUISITES

**Origin of Negotiable Instruments: the Law Merchant.** Modern business is characterized by an enormous expansion of credit and a corresponding use of readily transferable ("negotiable") credit instruments as a substitute for money.

Credit instruments are not, however, a recent invention, but an outgrowth of mercantile customs from time immemorial. They were known in early Rome. There is even evidence that some forms of negotiable instruments were in use many centuries ago among the Chinese.

The expansion of international trade following the Renaissance gave new impetus to the need of mercantile paper in place of hazardous gold shipments across pirate-infested waters and over robber-infested lands. Also, mercantile disputes called for legal remedies more suited to the needs of merchants and mariners than those prevailing in the ordinary courts. As noted on page 8, these mercantile disputes were originally decided informally in tribunals selected by the merchants and mariners themselves, for quick determination in accordance with the mercantile customs that had grown up outside the ordinary rules of law. These customs, in the course of time, acquired legal sanction, became part of the law of the land, and became known as the law merchant. They embraced mercantile or credit instruments, such as bills of exchange and promissory notes, as well as insurance and other branches of mercantile law.

**Uniform Negotiable Instruments Law; Uniform Commercial Code.** As with many other branches of the law, the vast body of precedent, much of it conflicting, which grew out of the thousands of judicial decisions on the subject of negotiable instruments, made it necessary to crystallize and codify these precedents into statute form. In 1895, a Uniform Negotiable Instruments Law was framed, and it was ultimately adopted by all the states. By 1940 it was evident that the uniformity of this and other commercial statutes was largely eroded by conflicting decisions, resulting in the formulation by 1952 of a Uniform Commercial Code for submission to the legislatures of the different states. (See Appendix.)

**Nature of Negotiability.** Negotiability is that quality which permits a written obligation to pass freely from hand to hand as a credit instrument or substitute for money. This quality distinguishes negotiation from assignment. To assign a contract is to pass title to it subject to any burdens or defenses connected with its origin. A negotiable instrument is not thus burdened. It travels freely on its own. It is acceptable on its face.

**Negotiable Instruments and Ordinary Contracts Distinguished.** Four characteristics distinguish negotiable instruments from ordinary contracts:

(1) *The right of transfer.* Not all contracts may be assigned (see page 99). Negotiable instruments, on the other hand, may be freely transferred.

(2) *Manner of transfer.* A contract may be transferred by any words, oral or written (page 97). A negotiable instrument is transferred by indorsement and delivery, or, in some cases, by delivery alone.

(3) *Rights of the transferee.* The rights of a transferee by assignment, i.e., the rights of an *assignee*, can never be greater than the rights of his assignor. The assignee merely steps into the assignor's shoes. If the party obligated to the assignor has any defense to the contract, or any offset against the assignor, he may urge such defense or offset as successfully

against the assignee as against the assignor with whom he contracted. This is not true, however, of transfer by negotiation. The transferee of a negotiable instrument, if he is a holder in due course (page 160), acquires his rights in such instrument free from many defenses which might be urged between the original parties.

EXAMPLES: I give you a nonnegotiable note. The note is (1) based on fraud, or (2) without consideration, or (3) procured through duress, or (4) given for merchandise not as warranted (thus furnishing an offset on the price), or (5) given for a consideration that fails (unfit merchandise, for example). Any of these facts constitutes a defense not only against you, the payee, but against any subsequent assignee of the note. But if the note were negotiable, and you transferred it to a "holder in due course," he could compel me to pay regardless of such defenses or offsets.

(4) *Consideration.* In respect to consideration, a negotiable instrument differs from an ordinary contract in three ways:

(a) There is no presumption of consideration in an ordinary contract, such as a nonnegotiable instrument, but every negotiable instrument is deemed *prima facie* (that is, unless and until the contrary is shown) to have been issued for a valuable consideration.

(b) An ordinary contract based upon past consideration is unenforceable in most jurisdictions, but a negotiable instrument is valid though based upon past consideration.

(c) The assignee of a contract lacking consideration acquires no greater rights than his assignor. As noted in (3) above, however, this is not true where a negotiable instrument is acquired by a holder in due course.

**Requisites of Negotiability.** The Negotiable Instruments Law provides that an instrument to be negotiable must conform to the following requisites:

(a) It must be in writing and signed by the maker or drawer;

(b) It must contain an unconditional promise or order to pay a sum certain in money;

(c) It must be payable on demand, or at a fixed or determinable future time;

(d) It must be payable to order or to bearer; and

(e) Where the instrument is addressed to a drawee, he must be named or otherwise indicated therein with reasonable certainty.

**Instrument Must Be in Writing.** The word "instrument" necessarily signifies a writing. The instrument may be handwritten in ink or pencil, typewritten, lithographed, engraved, printed, or stamped.

**Instrument Must Be Signed by Maker or Drawer.** A note is signed by a "maker," a draft (bill of exchange) by a "drawer." The signature must be intended as such, and must consist of a name, an initial or initials, a mark ("X"), or a trade, assumed, or fictitious name. It may be written, typewritten, mimeographed, lithographed, or printed.

No person is bound on an instrument unless his name is on it.

*Signature by agent.* If an agent, John Mason, signs for a principal, Henry Brown, he should sign, "Henry Brown, by John Mason, Agent," not "John Mason, Agent." Otherwise, he may become personally liable to a holder in due course. However, as to a payee, the rule is somewhat different. Where a person signs as agent without disclosing his principal and the payee knows that he is acting as agent and does not intend to bind himself individually, the agent is not personally liable to the payee if he was authorized to sign for the principal; and the principal is not liable in such case either, since his name is not on the instrument. If the agent signs without authority, he is personally liable. If he signs for a non-existent or incompetent principal, he is also liable.

An agent's authority to execute and deliver negotiable instruments need not be in writing.

*Signature by procuration.* A signature "by procuration" serves as notice that the agent has only limited authority to sign and that the principal is not bound if the agent exceeds his authority.

*Signature by corporation.* A signature in the corporate name only, or in a corporate name by an officer or agent, is binding on the corporation if actually or ostensibly authorized. There are cases which hold, however, that where a note is signed, not in the name of a corporation, but in the name of an officer, with an addition of the office he holds, the officer is personally liable. This is true even where the corporate name is printed in the margin of the instrument.

**Unconditional Promise or Order.** The promise (note) or order (bill) must not depend on any contingency, such as a promise or order to pay out of a particular fund. But a promise or order to pay is not conditional merely because it is coupled with an instruction to "charge" the payment to a particular fund or account. Neither is the unconditional character of a promise affected by a guaranty indorsed on the instrument, or by a provision adding costs of collection and attorney's fees in case of suit. Where the promise or order is subject to a contingency, it is immaterial that the contingency afterwards happens: the instrument is nonnegotiable. A promise or order conditional upon the terms of another instrument or contract renders the instrument nonnegotiable, but a mere reference to some other instrument or contract is immaterial.

**Sum Certain in Money.** "Money" means an acceptable medium of exchange, not necessarily legal tender. It excludes gold or silver bullion, bonds, notes, checks (certified or uncertified), goods, "solvent cash notes," scrip, and so on. The promise or order may be to pay in a particular kind of money, or in coin, or some particular kind of coin, such as "gold dollars" or "United States gold coins." The instrument need not be payable in American money.

A sum is certain even though payable in installments, with interest on unpaid installments and with a promise that on default in payment of either the whole becomes due. A provision adding taxes, however, makes the sum uncertain and the instrument nonnegotiable.

**On Demand.** An instrument is payable on demand:

(a) If it so states; or

(b) If it is payable "on presentation" or "at sight"; or

(c) If it expresses no time for payment.

(d) If a person issues, accepts, or indorses an instrument after it is overdue, the instrument, as to him, is payable on demand. Thus, if I indorse a note today that was due yesterday, such note, as to me, is payable on demand.

**"Fixed or Determinable Future Time."** An instrument must be payable at a fixed future time or at a *determinable* future time (one that is certain to come): "Thirty days after my death," for example, but not "thirty days after my marriage" or "thirty days after receiving a share of my father's estate." [1]

**"Time note."** A note payable in the future, as distinguished from a demand note, is known as a "time note."

**"To Order or to Bearer."** These are known as *words of negotiability*. An instrument payable *to a person* instead of to his order is not negotiable, but if it is payable *to a person or his order*, or *to a person or bearer*, or *to the order of a person*, or simply *to bearer*, the instrument is negotiable.

The instrument need not follow the exact language of the statute. Hence, the words "negotiable and payable without defalcation," following a promise to pay "to John Smith," would probably suffice as words of negotiability.

An instrument payable in the alternative ("to the order of James G. Kelly *or* Charles Perkins") is not negotiable.

An instrument is payable to bearer:

(a) When it so provides; or

(b) When it is payable to a person or bearer; or

(c) When it is payable to cash; or

(d) When it is intentionally made payable to a fictitious or nonexistent person, or to a bookkeeping account (such as Payroll, Petty Cash, Sundries, and so on); or

(e) When the payee's name does not purport to be the name of any person; or

(f) When the only or last indorsement is in blank (page 158).

But an instrument payable to a particular bearer ("Pay **to bearer,** Claude Nelson") is not negotiable.

---

[1] The Uniform Commercial Code provides that an instrument must be payable at a "definite" time instead of at a fixed or "determinable" future time. Hence, in jurisdictions which adopt the Code, an instrument payable at a given time after death will no longer be negotiable.

**Specific Designation of Drawee.** If an instrument is addressed to a drawee, he must be named or otherwise indicated therein with reasonable certainty. A bill of exchange addressed "To Whom It May Concern" would therefore not be negotiable.

**Factors Which Affect Negotiability.** Any factors which violate the foregoing requisites necessarily prevent negotiability. A negotiable instrument must not contain a promise or order to do any act in addition to the payment of money, such as a promise to deliver merchandise or render services. Four exceptions to this rule are:

(1) A provision which authorizes the sale of collateral securities in case the instrument is not paid at maturity.

(2) A provision which authorizes a confession of judgment if the instrument is not paid at maturity.

(3) A provision which waives the benefit of any law intended for the advantage or protection of the obligor.

(4) A provision which gives the holder an election to require something to be done in lieu of payment of money.

**Factors Which Do Not Affect Negotiability.** Negotiability is not affected by unessential omissions or by the inclusion of matter which does not affect the promise or order.

*Unessential omissions.* An instrument is negotiable though the following be omitted: (a) date, (b) "value received," (c) place where instrument was drawn, (d) place where instrument is payable, and (e) provision for interest.

*Language not affecting the promise or order,* and not constituting a promise or order to *do* something additional, does not affect negotiability.

EXAMPLES:
(1) A statement of the transaction which gave rise to the instrument.
(2) A provision that the article sold is to remain as security until the instrument is paid.

**Examples of Negotiability.** Following are examples of language which does not violate the rules of negotiability:

(a) Promise to pay in wheat or money, *at holder's option.*

(b) "The obligation of the acceptor hereof arises out of the purchase of goods from the drawer."

(c) "In case this note is collected by an attorney . . . the maker hereof agrees to pay a reasonable attorney's fee."

(d) Promise to pay $50,000 "in successive semiannual payments of not less than $1,000 each for eight years, balance on demand thereafter."

(e) "With interest on unpaid principal at the rate of 6% per annum payable semiannually."

(f) "Pay to the order of . . . on account of contract between you and the undersigned."

(g) "On account of 14,789 bags Cuban centrifugal sugar as per contract 4/25/48."

(h) "The piano for which this note is given shall remain the seller's property until note is paid with interest."

(i) "I promise to pay . . . for the amount of the second installment on machine purchased this date."

(j) "Thirty days after the death of William Smith, I promise to pay to the order of . . . ."

**Examples of Nonnegotiability.** Following are examples of language which renders an instrument nonnegotiable:

(a) "Pay to C. Jones." (*Not payable to order or bearer.*)

(b) Promise to pay "ten ounces in gold." (*Not payable in money.*)

(c) "I have this day borrowed $5,000 from Alfred K. Brown, which sum is subject to and payable on demand." (*Not payable to order or bearer.*)

(d) "I, *A*, hereby acknowledge my indebtedness to *G* for services rendered by him, for which I promise to pay him the sum of $10,000." (*Not payable to order or bearer.*)

(e) "Sixty days after my arrival in London, I promise to pay to the holder, James Gray, $500 for value received." (*No certain maturity, and not payable to order or bearer.*)

(f) "I promise to pay James Jones or order $1,000 when he becomes twenty-one years of age." (*No certain maturity.*)

(g) Promise to pay $12,000 in twelve equal monthly payments of $1,000 each, with interest on unpaid installments, "together with all taxes assessed upon said sum against said payee or holder of this note." (*Sum not certain.*)

(h) "As security for this note, I agree to deposit pass book No. 15043, issued by your compound-interest department in my name, and to deposit therein $18 on the 15th of each month until the face amount of this note has been deposited." (*Promise to make deposits is promise to do additional act.*)

**Factors Which Destroy Negotiability.** An instrument that is negotiable may lose its negotiability in three ways: (1) by restrictive indorsement (page 158); (2) by arrival at maturity (page 160); and (3) by discharge (page 200).

**Validity v. Negotiability.** The mere omission of a requisite to negotiability will not destroy the validity of an instrument. Instruments may lack negotiability, yet be fully enforceable as contract obligations. In *Matter of Nellis*,[2] the maker signed a paper designated "Demand Note," which read as follows: "This is to certify that I, William J. Collins of New York City, have this day and date borrowed in cash and received in cur-

---

[2] 126 Misc. 638, 214 N.Y. Supp. 378.

rency the sum of Five Thousand Dollars from one of my friends, Alfred K. Brown of Albany, N.Y., which sum is subject to and payable on demand, with interest at the rate of 6% per year." The Court held that this was not a negotiable promissory note because there was no promise to pay to order or to bearer. However, from the fact that the paper was designated "Demand Note," and that it clearly implied a promise to repay monies, the Court further held that the paper was a good *promissory note*, hence that there was no good reason why the payee could not collect it.

**Ambiguous Instruments: Rules of Construction.** The Uniform Negotiable Instruments Law provides that when the language of an instrument is ambiguous, or there are omissions therein, the following rules of construction apply:

(a) When the sum payable is expressed in words and also in figures and there is a discrepancy between the two, the sum denoted by the words is the sum payable; but if the words are ambiguous or uncertain, reference may be had to the figures to fix the amount.

(b) When the instrument provides for the payment of interest, without specifying the date from which interest is to run, the interest runs from the date of the instrument, and if the instrument is undated, from the issue thereof.

(c) When the instrument is not dated, it will be considered to be dated as of the time it was issued.

(d) When there is a conflict between the written and printed provisions of the instrument, the written provisions prevail.

(e) When the instrument is so ambiguous that there is doubt whether it is a bill or note, the holder may treat it as either at his election.

(f) When a signature is so placed upon the instrument that it is not clear in what capacity the person making the same intended to sign, he is to be deemed an indorser.

(g) When an instrument containing the words, "I promise to pay," is signed by two or more persons, they are deemed to be jointly and severally liable thereon. (See page 83.)

**Presumption as to Date.** Where an instrument or its acceptance (page 184), or any indorsement on it, is dated, such date is deemed *prima facie* (that is, unless the contrary can be shown) to be the true date it was made, drawn, accepted or indorsed.

### Questions

1. Describe briefly the origin of our law governing negotiable instruments.
2. Is there any similarity between the statute on negotiable instruments in your state and similar statutes in other states? Explain.
3. Explain the meaning of the word, "negotiability."
4. Name and explain four characteristics which distinguish negotiable instruments from ordinary contracts.
5. What are the five requisites of negotiability?

6. Can a person be liable as maker or drawer of a negotiable instrument without having signed it? Explain.

7. When, if at all, is an agent liable on a negotiable instrument, and when not?

8. How should a negotiable instrument made by a corporation be executed so as to bind the corporation? Under what circumstances may an officer executing such an instrument be personally liable on it?

9. Does a negotiable instrument have to be payable in legal tender?

10. Is an instrument negotiable if it is payable in installments? Would your answer be the same if the instrument provided: (a) for interest on unpaid installments; (b) that on default in payment of either principal or interest, the whole amount becomes due?

11. Is an instrument negotiable if it contains a provision adding taxes?

12. An instrument is payable on demand if it so states. Name three other situations in which an instrument is payable on demand.

13. An instrument is payable to bearer when it so provides. Name five other situations in which an instrument is payable to bearer.

14. A negotiable instrument must not contain a promise or order to do any act in addition to the payment of money. Name four exceptions to this rule.

15. To whom may a bill of exchange be addressed?

16. Name five items which may be omitted from an instrument without affecting its negotiability.

17. How will the following affect the negotiability of an instrument: (a) The instrument contains a statement of the transaction which gave rise to it; (b) The instrument contains a provision that the article sold is to remain as security until the instrument is paid?

18. Name three ways in which an instrument may lose its negotiability.

19. Distinguish between the validity of a negotiable instrument and its negotiability.

## Problems

1. Prepare a negotiable instrument and indicate each of its essential elements.

2.*

Detroit, Mich., July 5, 1929.

Sixty days after date I promise to pay to the order of O. R. King six hundred dollars at the Citizens' National Bank, Detroit, Michigan. Value received.

Frederick Thompson,<br>By James Thompson,<br>Attorney-in-fact.

Actually James Thompson had no authority from Frederick Thompson to execute the above note. From whom can a holder in due course recover?

3.* The R.I. Company gave the following note in payment for goods purchased:

$7,500.

Albany, N.Y., June 1, 1920.

Three months after date we promise to pay to the order of A.B. Corporation seventy-five hundred dollars at the Albany Trust Company. Value received.

JOHN SMITH, Pres.<br>ELMER H. BROWN, Treas.

The note was written on a blank note across the margin of which appeared the words "R.I. Company." The note was discounted for the payee by the

Citizens National Bank and upon nonpayment thereof the bank brought suit against Smith and Brown. Could the bank recover?

4.*

New York, October 1, 1917.

One month after date I promise to pay to John Smith Five Hundred Dollars for value received, negotiable and payable without defalcation or discount.

(Signed) HENRY JONES

Is the above note negotiable or not? Give reasons.

5.* A promissory note, otherwise negotiable, contained a promise to pay the sum of $50,000 "in successive semiannual payments of not less than one thousand dollars each, for a period of eight years from date, and the balance then due to be payable on demand thereafter, with interest on the principal unpaid at the rate of six per cent per annum, payable semiannually, together with all taxes assessed upon said sum against said payee or the holder of this note." Explain whether or not the foregoing provision affected the negotiability of the note.

6.* Is the following a negotiable instrument?

Topeka, Kansas
Jan. 10, 1927

To George W. Brown, Topeka, Kansas:

Pay to the order of Fred L. Jones $2,000 on account of contract between you and the undersigned.

(Signed) James A. Smith

Accepted

(Signed) George W. Brown.

7.** State whether the following document is, or is not, negotiable. If not, what does it lack to make it negotiable?

New York, May 1, 1925.

Sixty days after my arrival in London, I promise to pay to the holder James Gray, $500 for value received. William Smith.

8.* Bowman, a resident of Middleport, N.Y., purchased a piano from the X Piano Company of Buffalo for $300, giving the X Piano Company $50 in cash and the following note:

Buffalo, N.Y., May 29, 1906.

$250.

On or before one year after date I promise to pay to the order of X Piano Company Two Hundred and Fifty Dollars at 418 Main Street, Buffalo, N.Y. Value received with interest.

The piano for which this note is given shall remain the property of X Piano Company until the note with interest is paid.

On June 3, 1906, the payees endorsed the note and transferred it to Buffalo National Bank for value.

On August 6, 1906, Bowman paid to the Piano Company $50 on account of the note and on December 1, 1906, the further sum of $100. Both of these payments were accepted. Neither payment ever came into the hands of the Buffalo Bank.

In May, 1907, the note having been presented for payment, was refused, and the bank sued for the full amount. Could it recover?

9.* Is the following a negotiable instrument?

Boston, Mass., July 1, 1920. One year after date, for value received, the Y.Z. corporation promises to pay to the order of Adam Brown three thousand dollars with interest at the office of the Y.Z. corporation, Boston, Mass., or at the option of the holder thereof upon the surrender of this note, to issue to the holder hereof in lieu thereof thirty shares of the preferred stock of said *Y.Z.* corporation and to pay to the holder hereof in cash the interest then due upon said sum. The *Y.Z.* corporation, by *Y.Z.*, President.

10.** *X* executes a promissory note to *Y*, in which the following clause is inserted: "In the case this note is collected by an attorney, either with or without suit, the maker hereof agrees to pay a reasonable attorney's fee."

The following indorsement appeared on the note: "For value received we hereby guarantee payment of the within note, including interest and cost at maturity, or at any time thereafter demanded." Is such a note negotiable?

11.* Are the following notes negotiable or not? Give reasons.

(a) No date, nor place.
I promise to pay to bearer One Hundred Dollars.

Signed *A.B.*

(b) January 5, 1917.
Due *A.B.* or order on demand One Hundred Dollars.

Signed *C.D.*

(c) Chicago, Sept. 5, 1916.
On or before Dec. 1, 1916, I promise to pay to *C.D.* or order One Hundred Dollars.

Signed *A.B.*

(d) New York, April 10, 1916.
On.................I promise to pay to the order of *C.D.* One Hundred Dollars.

Signed *A.B.*

12.** *A* for value made, executed and delivered to *G* the following: New York, N.Y., January 23, 1927. I, *A*, hereby acknowledge my indebtedness to *G* for services rendered by him, for which I promise to pay him the sum of Ten Thousand ($10,000.00) Dollars, and in the event of my death I hereby authorize and direct the payment of the same out of the funds of my estate. Signed *A*.

(a) Is the instrument a promissory note?
(b) Is it negotiable or nonnegotiable?
(c) When is it due and payable?
Give reasons for each answer.

13.** Brown wrote the following, which Collins signed:

Demand Note, New York City, September 19, 1918. Made this 19th day of September, 1918, as follows: This is to certify that I, William J. Collins of New York City, have this day and date borrowed in cash and received in currency the sum of Five Thousand Dollars from one of my friends, Alfred K. Brown of Albany, N.Y., which sum is subject to and payable on demand, with interest at the rate of 6% per year.
When the note is paid in full, I am to surrender the same and receipt it in full.

WILLIAM J. COLLINS.

(a) Is the instrument a negotiable promissory note? Explain.
(b) If Brown sued Collins thereon to recover the sum due, would he succeed? Give reasons.

14.* *A* made the following promissory note to *B*:

"January 31, 1909. I, *A*, hereby acknowledge my indebtedness to *B* for services rendered by him for which I promise to pay to *B* the sum of ten thousand dollars; and in the event of my death I direct the payment of this sum out of the funds of my estate. (Signed) *A*."

In 1911, before *A*'s death, *B* made demand for payment; payment was refused and suit brought. Could *B* recover?

15.* Is an instrument made payable to "James G. Kelly or Charles Perkins" negotiable?

16.** Plaintiff, before maturity, purchased from the Benz Manufacturing Company several trade acceptances, a copy of one of which is as follows:

Trade Acceptance

Acceptance Number: No. 1           New York, N.Y., Sept. 30, 1932
To John Sharp, P. O. 1934 Franklin St., Syracuse, N.Y.:
Sixty days after date pay to the order of ourselves at New York, N.Y., the sum of..........Two Hundred..........Dollars. Accepted at Syracuse Trust Company of Syracuse. Firm: J. Sharp. The obligation of the acceptor hereof arises out of the purchase of goods from the drawer.

Benz Manufacturing Company, C. H. Strum, Gen'l Mgr.

Defendant, an acceptor, contends that the instrument is not negotiable because of the words "the obligation of the acceptor hereof arises out of the purchase of goods from the drawer." What holding, and why?

17.* Is the following a negotiable instrument?

New York, June 1, 1921

I hereby certify that James K. Sloane has deposited with me Five Hundred Dollars which I promise to pay to his order on demand with interest from date on the return to me of this instrument and of my guarantee for the note for Five Hundred Dollars dated June 1, 1921, made by said James K. Sloane to Thomas J. Smith.

(Signed) Edward F. Wilson.

18.* Belknap, for an adequate consideration, gave the following written instrument to Pinney on August 5, 1932:

New York, N.Y.

Thirty (30) days after date I promise to pay to the order of Albert Pinney One Thousand Seven Hundred Fifty Dollars ($1,750) at Liberty Trust Company. Value received. Interest at 6%.

Robert Belknap<br>James Silliman<br>Agents of New York Turbine<br>Company.

Against whom, when, and for what amount will Pinney be entitled to enforce this instrument?

19.* In what particulars is the following paper not in the usual form?

Boston, Mass.

I, Thomas H. Green, promise to pay to James Malone or order Two Hundred Dollars. Value received.

(Signed) THOMAS H. GREEN.

20.* Are the following instruments negotiable?

(a) "March 1, 1920. I promise to pay to the order of John Smith & Co. on August 30, 1920, in the city of New York, the sum of $340 for the amount of the second installment on machine purchased of them on this date. William Brown."

(b) "New York, May 1, 1920. Sixty days after date, I promise to pay to John Smith $5000 for value received. William Brown."

21.* You are treasurer of the A corporation with power to sign commercial paper. Draw and sign a negotiable promissory note binding upon the corporation as maker.

22.** (a) What are the essential elements of a negotiable instrument?
(b) State which of the following are negotiable:

(1) April 18, 1939—One year from date, I promise to pay C. Jones one hundred dollars. (Signed) F. Smith.

(2) On or before April 18, 1939, I promise to pay to the order of C. Jones ten ounces of gold. (Signed) F. Smith.

(3) Thirty days from date I promise to pay to the order of C. Jones 100 bushels of wheat or one hundred dollars at his election. (Signed) F. Smith. Dated March 19, 1939.

23.* Does the inclusion, by the maker, of the following clause in a promissory note payable in installments make it nonnegotiable: "In the event of my failure to pay any of such installments at the time above specified therefor, all of the remaining principal and interest shall, at the option of the holder hereof, be immediately due and payable, without notice"?

24.* State in each of the following cases whether the negotiability of an otherwise negotiable instrument would be destroyed if:

(a) It were written in pencil.

(b) It contained the following promise: "I promise to deliver to John Smith or order 100 tons of gold-bearing ore from the North Star mine."

(c) It contained the following promise: "I promise to pay James Jones or order $1000 when he becomes 21 years of age."

(d) It contained the following promise: "I promise to pay Richard Rose $100" at a specified date.

25.* A promissory note, properly dated and signed, read as follows: "One year from date, for value received, I promise to pay to the order of the Mercantile Bank the sum of two hundred sixteen dollars ($216), there having been deposited herewith as collateral security pass book No. 15043 issued by your compound-interest department in my name, and I agree to deposit in said compound-interest account the sum of eighteen dollars ($18) on the fifteenth day of every month hereafter until a total of the face amount of this note shall have been deposited." Is this note negotiable?

26.* A dealer in raw sugar made a sale to a refiner who accepted a draft for the goods and delivered it to the vendor. The draft was in the usual commercial form except that the direction to charge the account of the vendor was followed by the words: "On account of 14,789 bags Cuban centrifugal sugar as per contract 4/25/39." Does the addition of these words render the draft nonnegotiable?

27. A court is called upon to charge the jury as to the rules of law applicable in the following situations:

(a) A promissory note provides as follows: "Thirty days after date I promise to pay to the order of Nicholas Farnham the sum of One Hundred Dollars ($1000)."

(b) A draft reads in part as follows: "Pay to the order of William Jenkins Thirty-Five Twenty-Five Dollars ($25.00)." It is the contention of the drawer that he had crossed out the words Thirty-Five in pencil, or had intended to do so, and that the payee-holder knew of such intention. The payee-holder disputes this. There is no pencil mark visible through the words "Thirty-Five."

(c) An instrument dated July 1, 1954 and payable September 1, 1954 provides for the payment of interest without specifying the date from which interest is to run. The question arises whether interest runs from the date of the instrument, from its due date, or from the date of actual issuance, which was July 10th.

(d) The instrument sued on is not dated.

28. An instrument is payable to "Bearer, William Farnsworth." The ques-

tion arises whether this instrument is (a) valid, and (b) negotiable. What is your opinion?

## PART 2. TYPES OF CREDIT INSTRUMENTS

**In General.** Broadly, negotiable instruments fall into two classes: *Promissory notes* and *bills of exchange* (*notes* and *bills*, for short). Notes take various designations and forms, such as bank notes, certificates of deposit and bonds. Variations of bills include drafts, checks, bank drafts, trade acceptances, money orders, letters of credit, and banker's acceptances. In addition to bills and notes, there are certain types of instruments possessing negotiability or quasi negotiability and commonly designated *documents of title*, such as bills of lading, warehouse receipts and trust receipts.

FORM 3

## PROMISSORY NOTE BEARING INTEREST FROM DATE OF MAKING

---

$1,500           New York City, New York,
May 1st, 1952.
      Two months after date, I promise to pay to the order of Richard Roe & Company————————————————————Fifteen Hundred ————————————————————Dollars at the Koe National Bank of New York, with interest.

Value received.

                                          John Doe

---

**Promissory Notes.** (See Form 3.) In a promissory note one party, the "maker," promises to pay a sum of money to another party, the "payee," or to his order, or to bearer. The promise need not be expressed; it may be implied from any language that imports a promise to pay or repay money. A note may be signed by a single individual, or it may be joint, or joint and several, with corresponding collective liability (see page 83).

*Note to maker's order.* A note drawn to the maker's own order is not complete unless indorsed by him.

*Note payable at bank.* A note payable at a bank is equivalent to an order on the bank to pay the money on due date.

*Simple* v. *collateral note.* A simple note is an ordinary, unsecured note. A collateral note is one which recites that it is secured by some form of collateral, with authority to the payee in case of default to sell the collateral and apply the proceeds to the payment of the note.

*Bank note.* A bank note is a note issued by a bank or banker authorized to do so, payable to bearer on demand and intended to circulate as money.

*Judgment note.* A judgment note is one which authorizes a confession of judgment on behalf of the maker in case of default, namely, a formal statement on which a judgment may be entered without trial; so that a judgment may in such case be entered against the maker without suit for the amount of the note with interest, attorney's fees and costs.

FORM 4

**BILL OF EXCHANGE (Sight Draft)**

| | | | |
|---|---|---|---|
| $ 500.00 | Chicago, Ill., | *July 1* | , 19 |
| *At sight* | | | Pay to |
| the order of | *Chester J. Moran* | | |
| *Five Hundred and 00/100* | | | Dollars |
| Value received and charge the same to account of | | | |
| To *Benjamin Bellamy* | | | |
| | | | *Frank Gleason* |
| No. 8 | *Des Moines, Iowa* | | |

**Due bill.** A due bill is an acknowledgment of indebtedness in a specified sum, from which a promise to pay may be inferred. If the requisites of negotiability are present, the due bill is negotiable. For example: "Jan. 7, 1955. Due A.B. or order, on demand, One Hundred Dollars. Signed, C.D." If the due bill specifies no due date, it is payable forthwith, though no demand was made.

**Certificate of deposit.** A certificate of deposit is a writing signed by a bank acknowledging receipt of a sum of money payable to the depositor or his order at a time specified in the certificate. It enables one to make a temporary interest-bearing deposit in a bank for safekeeping, without opening a savings or checking account; and if it has the requisites, it may be used as a negotiable instrument. For example:

"First National Bank

Milwaukee, Wis.—May 1, 1955
This is to certify that John Doe has deposited with this bank one thousand dollars ($1,000) payable six months from date, with interest at four per cent per annum upon return of this certificate properly indorsed

B—Cashier"

**Bond.** A bond is an acknowledgment under seal of an obligation to pay a fixed sum of money. The obligation may be conditional, as in the case of an indemnity or penalty bond, or it may be unconditional, as in the case of a simple bond for the payment of a definite sum of money to bearer or a named obligee on demand or on a day certain, with interest at fixed intervals. The latter type of bond is commonly issued by business or municipal corporations and by governments generally for the purpose of long term loans.

*Bearer bonds* (usually with interest coupons attached) are negotiable by delivery. If bearer bonds are lost or stolen, the finder or thief may pass good title to an innocent purchaser for value.

*Registered bonds* are transferable only by indorsement, and by registration of the transferee's name on the books of the government or corporation issuing the bonds; hence, not negotiable.

Some statutes permit the owner of a bearer bond to render it nonnegotiable by writing his name on it, with a statement that he owns it.

**Bills of Exchange.** (See Form 4.) A *bill of exchange* or *draft* consists of a written order addressed and signed by one party (the drawer) to another party (the drawee) requiring the latter to pay a third party (the payee), or his order, a sum of money. If the drawee "accepts," he becomes the acceptor. Such an instrument, having three parties, is called a *three-party draft.*

*Two-party draft.* A draft made payable by the drawer to himself as payee (for collection purposes) is known as a *two-party draft.*

A *domestic or inland bill or draft* is one drawn and payable in the same state; all others are *foreign.*

A *sight draft* is a bill of exchange payable at sight, or on demand, as distinguished from a *time draft* which is payable at a fixed time *after date* (that is, after the date of the instrument), or *after sight* (that is, after the instrument has been presented to the drawee for acceptance).

A *documentary sight draft* is one which is accompanied by documents, such as bills of lading or warehouse receipts (page 153) in connection with which the draft is drawn.

**Checks.** A check is a bill of exchange drawn on a bank and payable on demand. Checks are further discussed on pages 205-212.

**Bank draft.** A bank draft is a check by one bank on another. It is distinguishable from a *cashier's check* which is drawn by a bank upon itself, signed by the cashier, and payable to another.

**Trade acceptances.** (See Form 5.) A trade acceptance is a two-party time draft, drawn by a seller upon a purchaser, payable to the seller as payee, and accepted by the purchaser as evidence that the goods shipped are satisfactory and that the price is due and payable. A trade acceptance has two advantages over a note: (1) It gives the seller a better assurance of payment, because it carries proof of the transaction for which it was accepted, and the acceptor's satisfaction therewith; (2) it is more readily discountable through banking channels, because it is rediscountable at a Federal Reserve bank provided its maturity is not more than ninety days.

**Money orders.** A money order is an order for the payment of a specified sum of money to the order of a specified person, drawn by a post office or express office, and payable respectively at any other post office or express office. Only one transfer by indorsement is permitted on a money order.

*Letters of credit.* A letter of credit is a letter, either generally or specifically addressed, requesting that money be advanced or credit given to the bearer, and promising or guaranteeing repayment of the moneys advanced.

*Traveller's letters.* Letters of credit are frequently used by travellers

FORM 5

## TRADE ACCEPTANCE

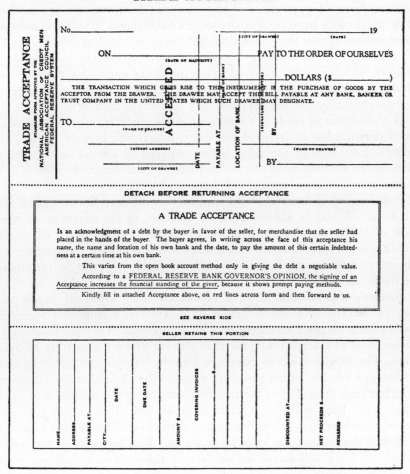

who, upon presenting the letters to express offices, banks or similar institutions, may obtain funds as and when needed, up to the full amount specified in the letter, by signing checks or drafts for the particular amounts required.

*Traveller's checks.* Traveller's checks are a simplification of traveller's letters of credit. They consist of checks in convenient denominations purchased by a traveller from a bank or express company, payable to the order of the traveller upon his signature in the presence of the person who sells the checks, and upon his countersignature in the presence of the person cashing it. Traveller's checks are popular because they are readily acceptable in this country or abroad and can be easily cashed.

*Commercial letters of credit.* Letters of credit are also frequently used by merchants, particularly exporters. The purchaser may be unwilling to pay for a shipment in advance; the seller may be unwilling to ship without assurance of payment. A letter of credit facilitates the transaction. The purchaser's bank notifies the seller's bank that a letter of credit has been opened against the transaction, and the seller's bank utilizes the credit by drawing a draft on the purchaser's bank, accompanied by shipping documents, which may be delivered to the purchaser upon acceptance of the draft. The seller is protected by having a responsible source of payment; the purchaser, by making payment only against the documents of title.

A *clean letter of credit* is a statement that a credit for a certain sum has been drawn upon in favor of the seller, which will be paid against the seller's draft; that is, the seller is not required to present any shipping documents but may simply draw his draft. A clean letter of credit is as a rule confined to transfers of funds between branch establishments.

A *documentary letter of credit* requires that the draft drawn against the credit established be accompanied by evidence of the shipment, such as bills of lading, invoices, and so on. Frequently documentary letters of credit contain specific conditions in respect to the quality and quantity of the merchandise, a specified time within which shipment and delivery must be made, and so on.

*Banker's acceptances.* Closely connected with letters of credit are banker's acceptances: drafts drawn by a seller on a bank and accepted by the bank on prior arrangement with a purchaser. They are most commonly used in foreign trade; for example, say you are importing Belgian linen. The Belgian concern refuses to ship the linen on open account and insists on a letter of credit issued by a responsible American bank, against which it may draw a draft for the bank's acceptance as assurance of payment. Your bank will issue a letter of credit and either charge your account, if satisfactory, or require collateral to cover. The Belgian exporter will then ship against the letter of credit and draw his draft on the bank, which the bank will accept on satisfactory shipment in accordance with the letter of credit.

**Documents of Title.** A document of title is one which confers upon the holder the right of ownership, possession or transfer in respect to merchandise therein specified. Strictly speaking, documents of title are not negotiable instruments since they do not call for the payment of money. They are sometimes called *quasi-negotiable instruments*. They are invested by statute (*Uniform Bills of Lading Act* and *Uniform Warehouse Receipts*

*Act*) with certain characteristics of negotiability (pages 300-301 and 318). Two examples are *bills of lading* and *warehouse receipts*. Other evidences of ownership possessing quasi-negotiable characteristics are *trust receipts* and *certificates of stock*.

**Bills of Lading.** A bill of lading is a receipt issued by a carrier for merchandise shipped. "Order bills of lading" are said to be negotiable; "straight bills of lading," not. The word "negotiable," in this connection, does not have the same meaning as when applied to instruments for the payment of money.

An *order bill of lading* is one which recites that goods are consigned *to the order of* a person named therein, hence is negotiable by indorsement and delivery.

A *straight bill of lading* is one which recites that goods are consigned to *a specified person,* hence is not negotiable.

Bills of lading are discussed more fully in pages 316 to 319 inclusive.

**Warehouse Receipts.** A warehouse receipt is a receipt issued by a warehouseman against goods accepted for storage. If deliverable to the order of a person named therein, the instrument is negotiable by indorsement and delivery and may be freely bought, sold or pledged. (See pages 300-301.)

**Trust Receipts.** A trust receipt is an instrument of commerce by which a bank advancing money to enable a customer to purchase goods takes the bill of lading for such goods in its own name and thereafter surrenders possession to the customer under an agreement that the title to the goods shall remain in the bank and that the proceeds of the sale shall be applied to the repayment of advances made by the bank on account of the original purchase price. The trust receipt secures the bank in connection with the merchandise thus surrendered to the customer. (See pages 274-275.)

**Certificates of Stock.** A certificate of stock represents ownership, not an unconditional promise or order for the payment of money. However, under the Uniform Stock Transfer Act it possesses negotiability to the extent that if it is indorsed in blank by the owner, an innocent purchaser for value gets good title though the certificate was lost, stolen, or procured from the owner by fraud, duress, mistake, or otherwise without his true consent.

EXAMPLE: If a stockholder loses his certificate after indorsing it in blank, and the finder (or a thief) sells it to an innocent purchaser for value, the latter gets good title under the Uniform Stock Transfer Law.

However, the Uniform Stock Transfer Act has no application where a finder or thief alters the stock certificate before transferring it: an innocent purchaser for value gets no title in such case. (See page 171, *"Alteration of stock certificate."*

The Uniform Commercial Code extends the negotiability of stock certificates.

## Questions

1. Broadly speaking, into what two classes do negotiable instruments fall? Name some of the common designations or forms of each class.

2. Define the nature of a *document of title* and give three examples.

3. What, in substance, do the following instruments contain, and designate the parties to such instruments: (a) promissory note; (b) bills of exchange.

4. Where a note is drawn to the maker's own order, when does it become complete?

5. What is the effect of a note payable at a bank?

6. Distinguish between a simple and a collateral note.

7. What is the nature of (a) a *bank note;* (b) a *judgment note;* (c) a *due bill;* (d) a *certificate of deposit?*

8. Define bond; bearer bond; registered bond.

9. Is there any difference between a bill of exchange and a draft? Distinguish between a *three-party draft* and a *two-party draft.*

10. Distinguish between a *domestic or inland* bill and a *foreign* bill of exchange.

11. Distinguish between a *sight draft* and a *time draft.* What is a *documentary sight draft?*

12. Define *check.* Distinguish between a check and a *bank draft.*

13. Define and explain: (a) trade acceptance; (b) money order; (c) letter of credit; (d) commercial letter of credit; (e) clean letter of credit; (f) documentary letter of credit.

14. Distinguish between traveller's letters of credit and traveller's checks.

15. Define: (a) bill of lading; (b) order bill of lading; (c) straight bill of lading.

16. Distinguish between warehouse receipts and trust receipts.

17. Is a certificate of stock a negotiable instrument? Does it possess any element of negotiability?

## Problems

1. A debtor writes to his creditor as follows: "Confirming telephone conversation of this morning, this is to assure you that I will pay you or anyone else you may designate the sum of Five Hundred Dollars not later than September 15 next. Very truly yours, George Baker." Does this constitute a negotiable instrument of any sort, and if so, what?

2. Silas Crabtree, a wealthy recluse, hires a housekeeper and a handyman for a period of three weeks while he is confined to his bed. Still in a weak condition, he gives each of them a letter, addressed to his bank and signed by himself, reading as follows: "Gentlemen: Please pay bearer One Hundred Dollars." May these letters be considered as negotiable instruments? If so, what would be their nature? If not, why not?

3.*

$5000                                                                No. 657

### THE FIRST NATIONAL BANK

Newark, N.J., Jan. 15, 1929

E. R. Cater has deposited in this bank Five Thousand Dollars payable to the order of himself on the surrender of this certificate properly endorsed, with interest at 4½%.

J. H. Benedict, *Cashier.*

Is the foregoing a negotiable instrument? What is it called? What is its use?

4.** Whitely owned "bearer bonds" and certificates of stock of a corporation. The certificates were indorsed by him in blank. He lost the securities in a railway accident. The finder sold the bonds and the stock to Westfall. Westfall acted in good faith and without knowledge of the facts relating to Whitely's loss. What interest does Westfall acquire in the securities?

5.* Backus, in the excitement of a railroad accident, lost unregistered coupon bonds and stock certificates endorsed in blank which he had been carrying in a brief case. These were found by another passenger who made no attempt to ascertain or find the loser but two weeks later sold the bonds and the certificates. The purchaser paid full value for them and had no knowledge of Backus' loss. Did the purchaser become the legal owner of the bonds and the certificates?

## PART 3. ISSUE AND NEGOTIATION

**Birth of Liability.** Issue marks the birth of liability. Until an instrument is issued, it has no more effect than any other undelivered contract.

**Issue Defined.** The statute defines issue as "the first delivery of an instrument, complete in form, to a person who takes it as a holder." Emphasis is placed on two requisites governing the issuance of an instrument: (1) It must be complete in form; and (2) it must be delivered.

**Date of Issue.** The date of delivery of an instrument is the date of its issue, regardless of the date on the instrument or the absence of any date. The payee acquires title as of the date of issue.

*Antedating or postdating an instrument* does not alter the fact that the payee acquires title when the instrument is actually issued.

EXAMPLE: If Jones issues a thirty-day note on May 1 and postdates it May 10, his death on May 3 does not invalidate the note, though it is dated a week later.

**Right to Supply Missing Date.** Where an undated instrument is expressed to be payable a fixed period after date or after sight, any holder may insert the true date of issue or acceptance, and the instrument becomes payable accordingly. A wrong date, if inserted, is deemed the true date only as to a holder in due course.

EXAMPLE: I give you an undated note payable ninety days after date; or I draw a draft upon William Smith in your favor as payee, payable ninety days after "sight" (that is, ninety days after its acceptance by Smith), and Smith accepts without dating his acceptance. You or any subsequent holder may insert the correct date of issue or acceptance, respectively. If you insert the wrong date, it will be deemed the true date only as to a holder in due course.

**Instrument Must Be Complete in Form.** Valid issue requires that the instrument be complete in form. No liability arises on an incomplete instrument, except where the law presumes authority to complete the instrument.

*Filling in blank spaces.* Where an instrument is wanting in any material particular, the person in possession of it has *prima facie* authority to complete it by filling up the blanks. In order that such instrument may be enforced against a person who becomes a party to it before it is completed, it must be completed strictly in accordance with the authority given, and within a reasonable time; otherwise such person will not be liable, except to a holder in due course.

EXAMPLE: Jones gives his bookkeeper two signed notes with the amounts and names of the payees' blank. He instructs the bookkeeper to fill in the names of two creditors as payees, with the correct amounts as shown by invoices on file ($100 and $200, respectively). The first note is negotiable; the second, not. The bookkeeper mistakenly fills in the amounts of $1,000 and $2,000, respectively, on the two notes. The first creditor negotiates the first note to Smith, for value, before maturity, and without knowledge by Smith of the mistake; and the second creditor transfers the second note to Brown, likewise for value, before maturity, and without notice of the error. Jones would be liable to Smith, but not to Brown, because Smith, whose note is negotiable, is a holder in due course, but Brown, whose note is nonnegotiable, is not a holder in due course.

*Signature on blank paper, delivered.* Where a person signs his name on a blank paper which he delivers with instructions to convert it into a negotiable instrument, he is liable on it only if it is filled in pursuant to authority; except that as to a holder in due course, he is liable on it whether it was filled in pursuant to instructions or not.

**Delivery: Instrument Complete in Form.** As stated, issue means the first delivery of an instrument, complete in form, to one who takes it as a holder. If such an instrument is delivered to one not as holder (an agent or custodian, for instance), it is as if the maker or drawer still had it in his own possession. When such instrument is no longer in the hands of a person who makes, draws, accepts or indorses it, a valid delivery will be presumed in the absence of proof to the contrary. If proof to the contrary is shown, namely, that there was no real delivery, or that the delivery was conditional, or for a special purpose, there is no liability. However, if the instrument gets into the hands of a holder in due course, no such proof may be shown, for as to him, delivery of a completed instrument is conclusively presumed.

EXAMPLE: Bacon makes a nonnegotiable note payable to bearer and leaves it on his desk. A gust of wind blows it out of the window. Johnson finds it and transfers it for value to Hall. Hall cannot collect the note, because as to him, Bacon may show that there was no delivery. But if the note were negotiable and Johnson transferred it to a holder in due course, the latter could collect it, because as to him, delivery would be conclusively presumed.

**Incomplete Instrument: No Presumption of Delivery.** When an *incomplete* instrument leaves one's possession, there is no presumption of delivery. Lack of delivery in such case may be shown even as against a holder in due course.[3]

EXAMPLE: Taking the preceding example, if, when Bacon left the note on his desk, it was incomplete as to amount, or due date, or in any other respect, even a holder in due course could not hold Bacon on the note.

*Signature on blank paper, not delivered.* When a person scribbles his name on a blank sheet of paper, and someone, without authority, fills in a negotiable instrument over the signature and negotiates it, no liability attaches to such signature, even when an innocent person gives value for the bogus instrument. No presumption of delivery can arise in such case.

**Issue v. Negotiation.** Strictly speaking, an instrument is not "negotiated" until it leaves the hands of the payee, or person to whom it is issued. If I make a note to your order and deliver it to you, the note is issued, but it is not yet negotiated. In other words, as between you and me (the "immediate" parties), the instrument is still an ordinary contract.

Negotiation is the subsequent transfer by the payee to a third party, by the latter to a fourth, and so on. Such transfer creates certain rights and obligations peculiar to the law governing negotiable instruments.

**Negotiation: Definition and Process.** The statute defines negotiation as so transferring an instrument "as to constitute the transferee the holder thereof." Only the entire amount of an instrument can be negotiated.

An instrument, if payable to order, is negotiated by indorsement and delivery; if payable to bearer, by delivery alone.

**Indorsement: What Constitutes.** Indorsement is writing one's name, with or without additional words, either on the instrument itself or, if it is too crowded, on an *allonge*, or paper attached to the instrument. One usually indorses on the back of the instrument; but as stated on page 142, if one puts his signature anywhere on the instrument he is deemed to be an indorser unless he clearly indicates his intention to be bound in some other capacity.

*Typewritten indorsements* are valid.

*Words of negotiability unnecessary.* An indorsement need not contain words of negotiability ("order" or "bearer").

*Misspelled names.* Where the name of a payee or indorsee is wrongly designated or misspelled, he may so indorse the instrument, adding, if he wishes, his proper signature.

**Indorsement v. Guaranty.** An indorsement is governed by the Negotiabile Instruments Law; a guaranty is not. Thus, an indorser is discharged if the holder fails to make proper presentment (Part 6) and to serve notice of dishonor (Part 7). A guarantor is not thus protected.

---

[3] Under the Uniform Commercial Code, this distinction is rejected: non-delivery even of an *incomplete* instrument is a personal defense, ineffective against a holder in due course.

**Kinds of Indorsements.** Indorsements may be *in blank, special* or *"full,"* *restrictive, qualified, conditional,* and *irregular* or *anomalous.*

**Indorsement in Blank.** An indorsement in blank, or "general" indorsement, specifies no indorsee and consists merely of the indorser's signature. Such an indorsement makes the instrument payable to bearer; that is, i may be negotiated by delivery without further indorsement.

EXAMPLE: A mere signature, "Walter Watson," on the back of an instrument, constitutes an indorsement in blank.

**Special Indorsement.** A special, or "full" indorsement, specifies a person to whose order the instrument is payable.

EXAMPLE: "Pay to the order of Sarah Jane Moore. Walter Watson."

The effect of a special indorsement is to require the indorsee's signature (Sarah Jane Moore) before the instrument can be further negotiated. In this respect it has an advantage over an instrument indorsed in blank. If the latter is lost or stolen, an innocent purchaser of it for value and before maturity may collect the instrument from the maker, and the indorser (Watson) would then have no remedy except against the finder or thief. This is because a blank indorsement converts the instrument into bearer paper negotiable by delivery; and delivery, as to a holder in due course, is conclusively presumed (page 156). A special indorsement has the added advantage that it provides a record of payment where the holder of an instrument uses it to pay a debt.

**Restrictive Indorsement.** A restrictive indorsement is one which "restrains the negotiability of the instrument to a particular person or for a particular purpose." [4] It (1) prohibits further negotiation, or (2) makes the indorsee the indorser's agent, or (3) vests title in the indorsee in trust for or to the use of another.

EXAMPLES:
(1) "Pay to Sarah Jane Moore only. Walter Watson."
(2) "Pay to the Transcontinental Trust Company for collection. Walter Watson."
(3) For distribution, Estate of Franklin Jones. Walter Watson."

A restrictive indorsement serves notice on all subsequent parties of the purpose specified in the indorsement.

EXAMPLE: If Moore, payee of a note, indorses it "Pay to Neil Bartlett for collection," he serves notice that he has not parted with title to the instrument but has merely made Bartlett his agent for collection. If Bartlett indorses to Fred Downs, and Fred Downs collects the note, he holds the proceeds as trustee for Moore.

**Qualified Indorsement.** A qualified indorsement is one which qualifies the indorser's liability and limits his function principally to that of an

---

[4] 10 C.J.S. 704.

assignor. Such an indorsement, however, in no way limits the further negotiaton of the instrument.

EXAMPLE: "Without recourse. Walter Watson."

The statute says that if an indorser wishes to qualify his liability to a subsequent holder, he must use the words "without recourse" or words "of similar import." [5] Words of assignment, the courts hold, are not words "of similar import."

EXAMPLE: The payee of a note, before maturity, wrote on the back of it: "I hereby assign all my right and interest in this note to Richard Fay in full. (Signed) Henry C. Witte." The maker defaulted and Fay sued Witte as indorser. Witte denied liability, claiming that he was a qualified indorser. The Court held that if an indorser wishes to qualify his liability, he must use the words "without recourse" or words "of similar import," adding: "This indorsement contains no such words." [6]

The foregoing decision represents the majority rule. The courts in some states[7] hold that words of assignment constitute a qualified indorsement.

**Conditional Indorsement.** A conditional indorsement renders the indorser liable only upon a specified condition or conditions.

EXAMPLES: "Pay to Dixie Cotton Company against my receipt for thirty-two standard bales cotton, Snow White brand"; or "Pay to King Coffee Growers Ass'n upon delivery of warehouse receipt for twelve sacks of Blended Ambrosia Coffee."

**Irregular (Anomalous) Indorsement.** An irregular or anomalous indorsement is one made by a third person (other than the payee or holder), who writes his name (with or without additional words) on the back of an instrument for a purpose other than to transfer title to the instrument. Such indorsement, which transfers no title in the instrument, is distinguishable from a *regular* indorsement, which transfers title. The usual purpose of such an indorsement is to lend credit by way of accommodation.

EXAMPLE: Tompkins makes a note payable to the order of the First National Bank, and before delivery Chase writes his name on the back of it.

**Mixed Classification of Indorsements.** The foregoing classifications of indorsements are not necessarily mutually exclusive. For example, a restrictive or qualified indorsement may be either in blank, or special, as in the following illustrations:

*Restrictive* (*in blank*): "For deposit only." *Frank White*
*Restrictive* (*special*): "Pay to the order of Transcontinental Trust Company, for deposit only." *Frank White*

---

[5] *Stover Bank v. Welpman* (Mo.), 284 S.W. 177, transferred 323 Mo. 234, 19 S.W. 2d 740; *Kennedy v. Hudson*, 224 Ala. 17, 138 So. 282; *Walter v. Kilpatrick*, 191 N.C. 458, 132 S.E. 148; *Smith v. Fulton*, 51 Ohio App. 12, 199 N.E. 218; *Copeland v. Burke*, 59 Okl. 219, 158 P. 1162; *Howard v. Kincaid*, 54 Okl. 271, 156 P. 628.

[6] *Fay v. Witte*, 262 N.Y. 215, 186 N.E. 678.

[7] Including California, Illinois, Michigan and North Carolina.

*Qualified (in blank):* "Without recourse." *Frank White*
*Qualified (special):* "Pay to the order of Sarah Jane Moore, without recourse." *Frank White*

**Indorsement by Infant or Corporation.** The Uniform Negotiable Instruments Law provides that infants or corporations may pass title to an instrument by indorsement, notwithstanding that from want of capacity they may not be liable on it.

EXAMPLE: A note payable to Allen is indorsed by him to Ball, an infant, and by Ball to Cole. The maker defaults, and Cole sues Allen and Ball as indorsers. Ball's defense is infancy; Allen's, that Cole acquired no valid title because of Allen's infancy. Ball's defense is good; Allen's bad.

A similar rule would apply where a corporation indorses an instrument without power to do so and hence without liability (Ch. 12:8), or without consideration so that the indorsement amounts to an accommodation and is unenforceable (Ch. 12:8).

**Transfers and Holders in Due Course.** The essence of negotiability, as noted on page 136, is that an instrument shall circulate freely; that one may take the instrument on its face, without concern as to possible personal defenses to which assignees are subject (page 98). One who acquires an instrument with these immunities of negotiability is known as a *holder in due course.*

**When Person Is a Holder in Due Course.** A holder in due course is one who acquires a negotiable instrument under the following conditions:

(1) *That it is complete and regular on its face.* If one takes a note in which some material item (such as maturity, amount or signature) is omitted, incomplete or irregular, he is not a holder in due course. A purchaser of an instrument with unfilled blanks is put on inquiry, and takes his chances if he fails to inquire.

(2) *That he became the holder of the instrument before it was overdue and without notice that it had been previously dishonored if such was the fact.* If one takes a note on June 15 which was due the day before, he cannot be a holder in due course.

(3) *That he took the instrument in good faith and for value.* If the person who takes a negotiable instrument either knows, or suspects, or has reason to know or suspect some condition or circumstance which might justify a refusal to pay the instrument—such as that the instrument was issued without consideration or procured through fraud—he cannot be said to have taken the instrument in good faith. Knowledge or notice of an agent in this connection, is knowledge or notice of the principal.[8] (See Ch. 9:4.)

(a) *Value.* Anything constituting consideration (page 59) constitutes value. Giving another instrument for the one acquired constitutes

---

[8] *International Harvester Co. v. Carruth* (La.), 23 So. 2d 473.

giving value for it. If I give your note to my bank and take for it a certificate of deposit payable after your note is due, the bank has given me value and is a holder in due course. The Uniform Negotiable Instruments Law provides that "value is any consideration sufficient to support a simple contract. An antecedent or pre-existing debt constitutes value, and is deemed such whether the instrument is payable on demand or at a future time."

(b) *Holder for value.* Ordinarily, a person must give value for an instrument to be a holder for value. However, the Negotiable Instruments Law provides that where value has at any time been given for the instrument, the holder is deemed a holder for value in respect to all parties who became such prior to that time.

(c) *Pledgee as holder for value.* When a note is taken as collateral security for a debt, the transferee is a holder for value to the extent of the debt secured.

(4) *That at the time the instrument was negotiated to the holder, he had no notice of any infirmity in the instrument or defect in the title of the person negotiating it.* Notice of infirmity or of defect in title means actual knowledge of it, or knowledge of such facts that one's action in taking the instrument amounts to bad faith. "Infirmities" may be obvious from an inspection of the instrument, such as errors, omissions or other irregularities on its face, or they may not be apparent from an inspection, such as defects in the title of a prior holder.

**When transferor's title is defective.** The title of a person who negotiates an instrument is defective when he obtains the instrument, or any signature to it, by circumstances amounting to fraud, duress or other unlawful means or for an illegal consideration or in breach of faith.

**Rights of Holder in Due Course.** As a holder in due course, the purchaser of a negotiable instrument may acquire rights greater than the vendor had. A holder in due course may enforce collection of the instrument against prior parties regardless of their claims, defenses and offsets against one another (except for *real* or *absolute* defenses, such as forgery, and so on, explained in Part 4). The maker, for example, may have given the note to the payee without getting anything for it; or he may have a claim or offset against the payee equal to or greater than the amount of the note itself; or one of the indorsers may have a claim against his indorsee. All these claims, counterclaims and offsets of prior parties against one another are of no concern to a holder in due course. He may say, in effect, "This instrument which I hold provides on its face for payment of a certain sum, by a certain person or persons, and at a certain time; and that is all that concerns me. I am not interested in the history of the instrument; in any personal defenses or disputes as between prior parties to the instrument; in any questions as to whether the instrument was originally given for an inadequate consideration, or for no consideration at all; or whether it was procured through fraud, duress, or without actual delivery. All these matters do not concern me. I am interested only in what I read within the four corners of the instrument. So far as I am concerned, the instrument is a 'courier without luggage, whose countenance is its passport.' "

**No Holder in Due Course of Nonnegotiable Instrument.** Rights in a nonnegotiable instrument, like rights in any other contract, pass by assignment, subject to any defenses (page 98). Hence there can be no holder in due course of a nonnegotiable instrument.

**No Holder in Due Course of Stale Demand Instruments.** When an instrument payable on demand is negotiated an unreasonable length of time after its issue, the holder is not deemed a holder in due course. The Uniform Negotiable Instruments Act provides that in determining what is an unreasonable time, regard is to be had to the nature of the instrument, trade usage in connection therewith, and the facts of the particular case.

**Acquiring Rights of Holder in Due Course without Being One.** A person may acquire the *rights* of a holder in due course without being one, provided he was not a party to any fraud or illegality affecting the instrument.

EXAMPLE: You are a holder in due course of a note procured by the payee through fraud. Being a holder in due course, you were unaware of the fraud when you took the note. You indorse the note to me. I know of the fraud; hence I am not a holder in due course. But I acquire, by assignment, your right as holder in due course to collect the note regardless of the fraud, provided I had no part in the fraud.

Any other rule than the above would unjustly limit the marketability of an instrument in the hands of a holder in due course.[9]

## Questions

1. What is the act which creates liability on a negotiable instrument?

2. You are asked to explain what is meant by issue in connection with a negotiable instrument. How would you explain it? What are the two requisites governing the issuance of an instrument?

3. Is the following statement right or wrong: "The date of an instrument is the date of its issue"? Explain.

4. "The payee acquires title as of the date of issue." Is this statement right or wrong?

5. What is the effect of antedating or postdating an instrument so far as concerns the date when the payee acquires title?

6. "No liability can arise on an incomplete instrument." Is this statement always true, never true, or true only under certain circumstances, and if so, what are they?

7. "Where a person signs his name on a blank paper which he delivers

---

[9] However, the Uniform Commercial Code provides that anyone who as prior holder had notice of a defense or claim against the instrument cannot improve his position by taking it from a holder in due course.

with instructions to convert it into a negotiable instrument, he is liable on it whether it was filled in pursuant to instructions or not." Is this satement always true, never true, or true only under certain circumstances, and if the latter, what are the circumstances?

8. "When an instrument, complete in form, is no longer in the hands of the person who makes, draws, accepts or indorses it, a valid delivery will be presumed." Is this statement always true, never true, or true only under certain circumstances, and if the latter, what are the circumstances?

9. "If I make a note to your order and deliver it to you, the note is thereby issued and negotiated." Is this statement entirely true, entirely false, or partly true and partly false? Explain.

10. Are the following statements true or false; if false, correct them:

(a) Typewritten indorsements are valid.

(b) An indorsement must contain words of negotiability, such as "order," or "bearer."

(c) Where the name of the payee or indorsee is wrongly designated or misspelled, it cannot be indorsed until properly corrected by the person who made the mistake.

11. "An indorsment is a guaranty applied to a negotiable instrument." Is this statement true or false; if the latter, correct it.

12. What are the different kinds of indorsement? Specify which of them is illustrated by the following:

(a) Pay to the order of Frank Farley. James Marvin.

(b) Without recourse. Samuel Dobbs.

(c) For deposit only. William Moore.

(d) A mere signature on the back of the instrument.

(e) Pay to Tom Blake only. Benjamin Randell.

(f) An indorsement by a person who writes his name on the back of an instrument for a purpose other than to transfer title to it.

(g) Pay to Ajax Elevator Corporation upon delivery of 500 bushels Supreme Buckwheat. Carver Grain Company.

(h) Pay to the Main Street National Bank for collection. Mary Monahan.

13. Is the following statement entirely true, entirely false, or partly true and partly false: "Neither infants nor corporations may pass title to an instrument by indorsement."

14. Having considered the different types of indorsements, what would you say as to the effect of each type?

15. A negotiable instrument has been indorsed in blank and delivered to you for value. How would you protect yourself against the consequences which might be entailed by the loss of such an instrument?

16. An instrument has been delivered to you for value, and you wish to transfer it for value to Swift. How could you do this and at the same time avoid liability on the instrument?

17. A businessman asks you to explain the purpose of the immunities granted to a holder in due course. What would you tell him?

18. A person cannot become a holder in due course unless he acquires a negotiable instrument under four conditions. Name and explain these conditions.

19. What, in general, are the rights of a holder in due course, as distinguished from other transferees of a negotiable instrument?

20. May a person become a holder in due course of a non-negotiable instrument?

21. May a person become a holder in due course of a demand instrument? Would you qualify your answer in any way?

22. May a person ever become a holder in due course of a negotiable instrument, if at the time he acquires title he has knowledge of some defect in the title of a prior holder?

## Problems

1.** On May 15, Jones purchased a bill of goods from Gray. Gray agreed, as a matter of accommodation to Jones, to accept a thirty-day note, dated May 10. Jones made the note and delivered it to Gray on May 1. Two days thereafter Jones met a violent death. Gray is now confronted with the problem, since he holds a note dated seven days after the death of the maker, does this fact invalidate the note? Explain.

2. Allen gives Baker an undated note payable 90 days after date. He dies three days later. Baker is now confronted with the problem of making this note mature notwithstanding Allen's death. What is your opinion?

3. Suppose Baker indorses the undated note to Chase, who wishes to insert the correct date of issuance on the note. May he do so?

4. Carter draws a draft on Davis in favor of Eagan, as payee. The draft is payable 90 days after sight. Davis accepts the draft without dating his acceptance. Eagan antedates the acceptance by 30 days, and discounts it with the bank, which seeks to hold Davis 60 days later. Davis refuses to pay the draft when presented, and the bank sues. May the bank hold Davis?

5. Jones gives his bookkeeper two signed notes with the amounts and names of the payees blank. He instructs the bookkeeper to fill in the names of two creditors as payees, with the correct amounts as shown by invoices on file ($100 and $200, respectively). The first note is negotiable; the second, not. The bookkeeper mistakenly fills in the amounts of $1,000 and $2,000, respectively on the two notes. The first creditor negotiates the first note to Smith, for value, before maturity, and without knowledge by Smith of the mistake; and the second creditor transfers the second note to Brown, likewise for value, before maturity, and without notice of the error. Is Jones liable either to Smith or Brown?

6. Franklin signs his name on a blank paper which he delivers with instructions to convert it into a negotiable instrument. If the instrument is not filled in pursuant to authority, may Franklin disclaim liability to anyone who may become the holder of the note?

7. Grimes makes a nonnegotiable note payable to bearer and leaves it on his desk. A gust of wind blows it out of the window. Harvey finds it and transfers it for value to Irving. May Irving collect the note?

8. If, in problem 7, the note were negotiable, would your answer be the same? Explain.

9. Suppose, in problem 7, that when the note in question was left on the desk, it was incomplete as to amount, or due date, or in any other respect, would the note be collectible if it got into the hands of: (a) a holder in due course; (b) a holder not in due course?

10. Jackson scribbles his name with his fountain pen on a blank sheet of paper while conversing in a telephone booth. Kerwin, who follows Jackson into the booth, finds the paper with Jackson's signature on it, fills in a negotiable instrument over the signature, and negotiates it to an innocent person for value. Is Jackson liable on the instrument?

11. Lane makes and delivers a promissory note payable to Morse, who has

his secretary typewrite his indorsement on the instrument, after which he delivers the instrument for value to Nolan. On due date, Nolan presents the note to Lane for payment, and Lane refuses payment on the ground that the note was not properly indorsed to Nolan. Is the defense valid?

12. Suppose, in problem 11, that Morse had signed his name on the reverse of the instrument after the indorsement, "Pay to John Nolan." Would such an indorsement render the instrument nonnegotiable in the hands of John Nolan?

13. Suppose, in problem 11, that Morse had indorsed the instrument "Pay to the order of John Bolan," and then, after signing his name, had delivered it for value to John Nolan. Would Nolan be able to collect the note?

14. A note payable to Allen is indorsed by him to Ball, an infant, and by Ball to Cole. The maker defaults, and Cole sues Allen and Ball as indorsers. Ball's defense is infancy; Allen's, that Cole acquired no valid title because of Allen's infancy. Is either of these defenses good?

15.** A indorses B's note in favor of C for $1,000. At the same time he guarantees in writing the payment of another note by B to C for the same amount. Neither note is presented at maturity, and neither is paid by B. C sues A for the amount of the two notes. Can he recover, and if so, how much? Give reasons for your answer.

16.* A note payable to Moore or order is endorsed "Pay to Neil Bartlett for collection" over Moore's signature. It is then endorsed "Pay to Fred Downs" over Bartlett's signature. Downs collects the amount of the note from the maker. To whom does the money belong?

17.* On October 14, 1937, X steals two legally valid negotiable notes payable to bearer (one due October 21, 1937, and one due November 22, 1937) and corporate bearer bonds with the November 1, 1937, coupons attached. On October 22, 1937, X sells both notes and the bonds to Y, who pays full value and has no knowledge, either actual or constructive, of the theft by X.

(a) Can Y collect from the maker on either or both of these notes?

(b) Can Y collect from the corporation on the November 1, 1937, coupons?

18.* Give an example of a case in which a holder with notice is a holder in due course.

19.** Mr. White purchased a used automobile from the Used Motor Car Corporation and gave in part payment therefor his negotiable promissory note payable sixty days after date. The car was guaranteed to be in perfect running order. The seller sold White's note before maturity to X, who became an innocent holder for value and without notice. The car was grossly misrepresented and proved to be worthless; White refused to pay the note at maturity on the ground that he was defrauded. X had negotiated this note before maturity to C, who had knowledge of the fraud practiced on White. Can C recover from White on this note? Give reasons for your answer.

20.* Allen, by fraud, induces Bates to issue a negotiable promissory note to him. Allen then sells the note to Cameron, who is a holder in due course. Cameron in turn negotiates the note to Davis who, while not a party to the fraud, has full knowledge of it. Can Davis recover from Bates? State the rule involved and the reason for it.

21.* A sold his automobile to B, warranting it to be a 1918 model in good mechanical condition. B gave A his note in payment of the purchase price, of which note C became the holder in due course. B, after a few days, found that the automobile was a 1917 model and in such defective condition that its actual value was but a small proportion of the purchase price paid by him, of all of which X had knowledge. X subsequently purchased the note from C. Could he enforce the note against B?

22.** In the consummation of a business transaction between $X$ and $Y$, $Y$ gave $X$ his promissory note payable in six months. Thirty days after receiving the note, $X$ sold it to his bank and accepted in payment thereof a negotiable certificate of deposit, payable in six months. This certificate of deposit was paid by the bank and a demand made on $Y$ for payment of his note. $Y$ then claimed that $X$ obtained the note from him by fraud. He further contended that the bank is not a holder in due course, because the certificate of deposit was not payable until after the maturity of the note. Can the bank enforce payment of the note by $Y$?

## PART 4. DEFENSES

**In General.** If there is any reason why a party is excused from liability on an instrument, he is said to have *a defense* to it. Under this head we consider defenses available to parties primarily liable. Such defenses may not be available to parties secondarily liable. For example, forgery, infancy or insanity would constitute a defense by a maker (who is primarily liable) against even a holder in due course; but an indorser would be liable in such case on his warranties of genuineness and capacity of prior parties (pp. 176-7). Defenses available to parties secondarily liable are considered in connection with presentment, dishonor and protest (Parts 6 and 7).

Defenses available to parties primarily liable are either *personal* ("nominal") or *real* ("absolute").

**Personal ("Nominal") Defenses.** Personal defenses to a negotiable instrument are those which are personal to the original parties or their assignees but which are cut off and become unavailable against a holder in due course. These defenses are really contract defenses. When I make you a promise, based on some consideration furnished by you, I am bound to you by contract, unless I have a good defense. Any defense which I may have against you, I have against your assignees also. In such case, if I promise to pay you money, I am not liable to you or to any subsequent assignee who derives his title from you, because I have a good contract defense. In other words, the payee and all subsequent holders *except holders in due course* are subject to such defenses. These personal or contract defenses may be enumerated and illustrated as follows:

(a) *Lack of consideration.* A promise given without consideration is unenforceable.

EXAMPLE: Allen, without consideration, gives Baker a note. Allen could successfully resist payment against Baker or any subsequent holder except a holder in due course. However, in the case of a negotiable instrument, unlike that of an ordinary contract, consideration is presumed unless the contrary is shown.

(b) *Failure of consideration.* If a negotiable instrument is given for a consideration which failed, the effect is the same as if no consideration were given in the first place.

EXAMPLE: Baker sells Allen a secondhand machine with a sixty-day guaranty, for which Allen gives his ninety-day note. The machine proves worthless after a ten-day trial. Allen may resist payment of his note as against Baker or any subsequent holder except a holder in due course.

(c) *Breach of contract.* If the consideration given for an instrument is a contractual obligation, which is not discharged, such breach of contract constitutes a personal defense on the instrument.

EXAMPLE: Allen gives Baker a thirty-day note for which Baker, a mason, agrees to erect a retaining wall. Baker defaults. Neither Baker nor any subsequent holder except a holder in due course may compel Allen to pay the note.

(d) *Counterclaim.* If I am obligated to you on an instrument, but you are also obligated to me on another transaction, I may interpose such counterclaim as a setoff against my obligation to you or to any subsequent assignee of the instrument.

EXAMPLE: Baker agrees to ship 500 Swiss watches to Allen at $20 per watch, for which Allen gives Baker his note for $10,000. When the shipment arrives, it is found to be fifty watches short. Upon suit on the note, Allen may successfully interpose a setoff for $1,000 against Baker or any subsequent holder except a holder in due course.

(e) *Fraud (in the inducement).* As noted on page 44, fraud in the inducement is fraud occurring during negotiations which precede the making of the contract. Such contract is voidable at the option of the defrauded party, and the maker or acceptor of a negotiable instrument may urge such fraud as a defense against all parties except a holder in due course.

EXAMPLE: Baker, after tampering with the speedometer, sells a secondhand automobile to Allen upon the fraudulent representation that the car has gone only 10,000 miles. Allen gives his note for the car. Upon discovering the facts, Allen may resist payment of the note as against Baker or any subsequent holder except a holder in due course.

But where an instrument is issued through the fraud of a third party, *not the payee,* and the payee, without notice of the fraud, gives value for the instrument, he or any subsequent holder not a party to the fraud may enforce payment of the instrument.[10]

EXAMPLE: Black, purporting to represent a charity, gets Green to draw a check for $100 to the order of White, then cashes the check with White, who knows nothing of Black's fraud. Black disappears. White deposits the check, but Green, having discovered the fraud, stops payment. In a suit on the check by White, Green's defense of *Black's fraud* will be unavailing.

---

[10] *Farmer's Sav. Bank of Ruthven v. Grange,* 199 Iowa 978, 203 N.W. 37; *Cook v. Parker,* 22 Cal. App. 2d 539, 71 P. 2d 591; *Williams v. Garrett,* 32 Ga. App. 762, 124 S.E. 811; *Utah State Nat. Bank v. Stringer,* 44 Idaho 599, 258 P. 522; *Kansas City Wholesale Grocery Co. v. Ridgeway,* 115 Kan. 685, 224 P. 38.

(f) *Duress.* As noted on page 50, duress is coercion in any form causing action or inaction contrary to the victim's will, and renders a contract voidable at the victim's option.

EXAMPLE: If Baker obtains a note from Allen by threatening to expose Allen's wife as a shoplifter, neither Baker nor any subsequent holder except a holder in due course can compel Allen to pay the note.

(g) *Blank spaces wrongly filled in.* As previously noted (page 156), when an instrument is wanting in any material particular, the person in possession of it is presumed to have authority to complete it by filling in the blanks. If he disobeys instructions and fills the blanks in wrongly, such fact will constitute a defense against the payee or any subsequent holder, except a holder in due course.

(h) *Nondelivery (of complete instrument).* As noted on page 155, unless a person has issued (hence delivered) an instrument, or caused it to be delivered, he is not liable on it; except that if the instrument is complete in form and gets into the hands of a holder in due course, delivery as to such holder will be conclusively presumed.

(i) *Payment.* If I obligate myself to you on an instrument, then pay it, such payment constitutes a good defense on the instrument as against you or any subsequent assignee, but not against a holder in due course.

EXAMPLE: Allen gives Baker his thirty-day note for $100 for a loan in that amount. Ten days later, Allen pays Baker the full amount of the loan but fails to pick up the note. If Baker has transferred the note, neither he nor any subsequent holder *except a holder in due course* can force Allen to pay the note again.

**Absolute ("Real") Defenses.** Absolute or real defenses are such as can be urged against *any* holder of a negotiable instrument, including a holder in due course. These defenses are:

(a) *Forgery.* The Negotiable Instruments Law provides that when a signature is forged, or made without the authority of the person whose signature it purports to be, it is wholly inoperative. No right to retain the instrument, or to give a discharge for it, or to enforce payment against any party to it, can be acquired through such a signature, unless the party against whom it is sought to enforce the instrument is estopped from urging the defense of forgery or want of authority.

EXAMPLE: Swift, Jr., without authority, signs his father's name to a check payable to the order of Bates, who negotiates it to Clyde. Though Clyde were ignorant of the forgery and gave value for the check, he could not compel Swift, Sr. to pay it, because one is not liable on an instrument he did not make. But if Clyde had sought to verify the signature and Swift, Sr. (to protect his son) had assured Clyde that the signature was genuine, Swift, Sr. would be estopped from later urging forgery or want of authority as a defense.

(1) *Forged indorsements: in general.* No title to a bill or note passes by a forged indorsement. Hence the payee of a check whose signature has been forged may (in the absence of negligence or estoppel) recover the amount of the check (a) from the drawer, or (b) from an indorsee (*bona fide* or otherwise) to whom the check was paid by the drawee bank, or (c) from the drawee bank which paid the check to anyone claiming under the forged indorsement.[11]

(2) *Forged indorsements: fictitious or nonexistent payee.* Under the Negotiable Instruments Act, where a bill or note is payable to the order of a fictitious or nonexistent person and *such fact is known to the person making it so payable,* the instrument is payable to bearer. But if an impostor gets someone to make or draw an instrument in favor of a fictitious payee and then, impersonating such payee, indorses and cashes the instrument, the maker or drawer is not liable because he had no knowledge that the payee was fictitious, hence no intention that the instrument was to be deemed payable to bearer.

EXAMPLE: An impostor, purporting to represent "Lieut. Parks" as the alleged head of a tuberculosis camp, obtained from American Raw Silk Co. a check made out to the order of "Lieut. Parks," and then cashed the check with United Cigar Stores Co., after indorsing it, "Lieut. Parks." United Cigar Stores Co. was ignorant of any wrongdoing. American Raw Silk Co., upon ascertaining that both "Lieut. Parks" and the camp were nonexistent, stopped payment of the check. In a suit by United Cigar Stores Co. against American Raw Silk Co., the Court held for American Raw Silk Co.: Only where the maker or drawer *knows* that the payee is fictitious may an instrument payable to a fictitious payee be treated as payable to bearer. "This check, intended to be paid to Lieut. R. F. Parks, in charge of a tuberculosis fund for the Navy, has never been indorsed by Parks, or anyone assuming to be Parks, in any of these negotiations . . . judgment directed in favor of defendant, dismissing the complaint with costs." [12]

(3) *Indorsement by impostor v. indorsement by thief or swindler.* When an instrument is delivered to an impostor who pretends to be someone else and the impostor indorses the check in the name of the payee and cashes it, the transaction constitutes a fraud, but the impostor's indorsement is not a forgery, because the person who indorsed the instrument was the same person who (mistakenly) was made the payee. Consequently, as between the drawer and the bank, the loss must necessarily fall on the drawer.

Where, however, a properly drawn and legally valid check is in the hands of the payee, and a thief or swindler gets hold of it and cashes it by indorsing the payee's name, no rights can arise by such indorsement, since

---

[11] 10 C.J.S. 1088-1089.

[12] *United Cigar Stores Co. v. American Raw Silk Co.*, 184 App. Div. 217, aff'd 229 N.Y. 532.

it is a forgery. If the drawer's account has been charged, he may compel the bank to restore the credit. The payee, however, may not compel the bank to pay him the amount of the check, since a bank is under no contractual duty to him (page 205); but the payee may compel the bank to return the check, and he may then present the check for payment. If the bank dishonors the instrument by refusing to pay it, the payee may hold the drawer (page 176).

(b) *Material alteration.* Any alteration is material which changes the date, the sum payable, the time or place of payment, the number or relation of the parties, or the medium of payment, or which adds a place of payment where none is specified, or alters the effect of the instrument in any respect. Material alteration of an instrument without the assent of all parties liable thereon voids the instrument except as against a party who makes, authorizes or assents to the alteration, and except as against subsequent indorsers (who, by indorsing, warrant the regularity and genuineness of the instrument). However, though even a holder in due course may not enforce such alteration against the maker or drawer who did not authorize or assent to it, he may enforce the instrument "according to its original tenor" (that is, as it was before the alteration).

(1) *Alteration v. filling in blank spaces.* To alter an instrument is to change something already in it. This is very different from the act of wrongly filling in a blank space. As previously noted (page 155), where a missing date is supplied or other blank space filled in contrary to instructions, the maker or drawer may become liable on such instrument, changes and all, to a holder in due course.

(2) *Negligence inviting alteration.* The early English rule, that a person is liable on an altered instrument where he has executed it so negligently "that it can readily be altered without giving it an appearance calculated to excite the suspicion of a prudent man," is by no means the uniform rule in this country. Some states hold that the maker or drawer is liable (to a holder in due course) only where a party wrongly filled in blanks that are so obvious as to suggest that the filling in was impliedly authorized. Other states hold that a person owes no duty to guard against a crime. It is probable that most courts would agree that if blank spaces are so negligently left as to invite alteration and to justify belief that the filling in was regular and authorized, a holder in due course could collect an instrument so altered. (See page 211.)

(3) *Immaterial alteration accompanied by filling in.* Where an immaterial alteration is accompanied by the unauthorized filling in of a blank space, the drawer or maker is liable (to a holder in due course) notwithstanding.

EXAMPLE: Foster signs and delivers to his secretary, a salary check with the amount (in words) blank, and the marginal amount (in figures) filled in at $50. The secretary writes "Five Hundred Dollars" in the blank space, raises the figures to $500, cashes the check at the bank, and disappears. As between Foster and the bank, Foster is liable. The marginal figures on an instrument are not a part of the instrument but are regarded as "merely a memorandum for convenience." [13] Hence the alteration was immaterial, and the filling in of the blank space (as to the bank, which was a holder in due course) was impliedly authorized.

(4) *Alteration of stock certificate.* The rules governing alteration of negotiable instruments are not applicable to certificates of stock. Although a *bona fide* purchaser of a lost or stolen stock certificate *indorsed in blank* gets good title under the Uniform Stock Transfer Act (page 153), this rule does not apply where theft and forgery intervene between the true owner and a *bona fide* purchaser.

EXAMPLE: A certificate of stock issued to Lovett & Co. is indorsed by them in blank and sold to Whitestone & Co. A thief steals the certificate, erases the name Lovett & Co., also the indorsement, substitutes the name Adolph Zitman as stockholder, and indorses in that name to Brown & Co., an innocent pledgee. As between Whitestone & Co. and Brown & Co., the former will succeed in establishing the right to the stock.[14]

(c) *Incompetence (contractual incapacity).* Incapacity to contract, such as that arising out of infancy or insanity, is a real defense, good against a holder in due course.

(d) *Illegality.* Mere illegality is no defense against a holder in due course. For example, it is illegal in many states for a corporation selling original issue stock to take a note in payment, or anything else except money, property, or services; yet the maker of such a note cannot urge such illegality as a defense against a holder in due course. But where a statute specifically declares a given type of transaction, or instrument given for it, *void*, such fact is a real defense, good even against a holder in due course. Examples:

(1) *Gambling transactions.* Some states expressly make gambling transactions, including instruments given in connection therewith, void; others do not. In the former, the fact that the instrument was given for a gambling debt is a real defense, good against a holder in due course; in the latter states, this would not be true. In any event, if an instrument has a valid inception, the fact that it was later negotiated in payment of a gambling debt would furnish no defense to payment.

EXAMPLES:
(1) Green gives White a check for $30 in payment of a poker debt. White gives the check to his landlord for rent. Green in the meantime stops payment of the check, and the landlord sues him. Judgment for Green. The check was void at its inception.[15]

---

[13] *Vinson v. Palmer*, 45 Fla. 630, 636, 34 So. 276.
[14] *National Surety Co. v. Indemnity Co. of North America*, 237 App. Div. 485, 261 N.Y. Supp. 605.
[15] *Larschen v. Lantzes*, 115 Misc. 616, 189 N.Y. Supp. 137.

(2) If the check had been given originally by Green to his landlord for rent and the landlord had given the check to White in payment of a poker debt, such fact would have furnished no defense to Green in an action on the check by White.

(2) *Sunday instruments.* In states which have statutes declaring Sunday business transactions void, instruments given on Sunday in connection with such transactions are likewise void, provided the fact of Sunday issuance is apparent on the face of the instrument. But if an instrument, though given on Sunday, is dated as of a weekday, the person so dating it is estopped, as to a holder in due course, from setting up as a defense the fact that it was actually issued on a Sunday.

(3) *Usury.* Some statutes merely render usury illegal and provide penalities for it. Most states, however, declare usurious transactions, and instruments given in connection with them, void at their inception. In the former states, usury is no defense against a holder in due course. In the latter, a holder in due course is subject to the defense of usury, on the principle that otherwise it would be easy to defeat the statute by transferring the instrument to an actual or pretended holder in due course.

(e) *Fraud (in the execution).* When one's signature is procured by trickery, without actual intent by the signer to make or draw a negotiable instrument, no liability arises, even to an innocent holder for value.

EXAMPLES:

(1) A printed receipt is presented to Brown for signature, and while Brown is adjusting his spectacles, a promissory note is substituted instead.

(2) White scribbles his name on a blank sheet of paper, and Black, without White's knowledge, fills in a negotiable instrument over the signature (pages 156-157).

(f) *Nondelivery (of incomplete instrument).* Although delivery of a complete instrument is conclusively presumed (page 156), this is not true of an incomplete instrument. Nondelivery of such an instrument is a real defense. (See pages 156-157.)[16]

## Questions

1. Explain fully the distinction between personal or "nominal" defenses and absolute or "real" defenses.

2. Name and illustrate nine personal defenses to liability on a negotiable instrument.

3. Name and illustrate five absolute or "real" defenses to liability on a negotiable instrument.

4.* In what respects must a negotiable instrument be changed in order that the change will constitute a material alteration?

5. What is the liability of one whose signature is procured by trickery,

---

[16] Under the Uniform Commercial Code, nondelivery of an incomplete instrument is a personal defense, the same as nondelivery of a complete instrument, and will not avail as against a holder in due course.

without intent of the signer to make or draw a negotiable instrument (a) to a person not a holder in due course; (b) to a holder in due course?

6. Is infancy a real or a nominal defense?

7. "Where a missing date is supplied or other blank space filled in contrary to instructions, the maker or drawer cannot be held by anyone, including a holder in due course." Is this statement true, false, or partly true and partly false?

## Problems

1.* McDonald becomes the holder in due course of a note purporting to have been made by Knapp and bearing endorsements in blank by Abbott, Perrin and Pringle. The maker's name was forged. When due the note was duly presented for payment, payment refused, and notice of dishonor given to all parties. Could McDonald collect and from whom?

2.* A note nonnegotiable in form is executed and delivered by A to B and endorsed by B to C. A refuses to pay it when due, claiming want of consideration. C brings suit against A, averring that he was a holder in due course. Can A successfully defend the action if want of consideration is established? Give reasons.

3.* Suppose that the above note had been negotiable, would A's defense of want of consideration be a bar to C's recovery or not? Give reasons and state the rule applicable to the principle involved in this and the foregoing question.

4.* On December 1, 1910, A gives to B the following instrument:

January 30, 1911, after date I promise to pay to B Four Hundred Dollars at 25 Broad St., New York, N.Y.

(Signed) A

B endorsed the instrument to X before maturity for value. A, the maker, did not pay on the due date and defended suit by X on the ground of lack of consideration. Could X recover?

5.* Taylor held Thompson's note for $400. Taylor was indebted to Thompson on an open account for $400. Taylor transferred the note to King in the usual course of business for value. When due, King presented the note to Thompson, who refused payment on the ground that Taylor owed to him, Thompson, an amount equal to the note. Did Thompson, the maker, have a good defense?

6.** A drew a check in favor of B or order, leaving the amount blank. He authorized B to fill it in for a sufficient amount to pay a claim which he (A) owed X, the exact amount of which was not known at the time the check was drawn. It was understood between A and B, however, that in no event should the amount inserted in the check exceed $200. B fraudulently filled in the check for $800 and gave it to C in payment of a bill of goods which he (B) purchased from C. To what amount is C entitled?

7.* Best made a promissory note jointly with Kelly for Kelly's accommodation. Kelly altered the note into the note of a corporation, in which both were officers, forging other signatures and causing Best's signature to appear as that of a personal endorser of the note. The X Bank, a holder in due course, sued Best personally upon this endorsement. Could it recover?

8.* Rowe, private secretary for Foster, brought to Foster a cheque for signature payable to cash. The cheque was made out in figures for $50.00, but no words were inserted in the space left for writing. Rowe raised the cheque to $500.00, which Foster's bank paid. Was the bank liable?

9.* A certificate of stock for 100 shares of the capital stock of the Bond &

Share Company, issued to Lovett & Co., was endorsed by Lovett & Co. in blank and then sold for value to Whitestone & Co. who did not fill in their firm name or otherwise alter the certificate. Thereafter it was stolen from Whitestone & Co. The thief erased the name of Lovett & Co. as the stockholder and their signature as endorser, inserted the fictitious name of Adolph Zitman as stockholder, wrote Zitman's name as endorser, and pledged the certificate with Brown & Co., who received it for value in good faith and without notice or knowledge of the theft or alteration. Does the loss fall upon Whitestone & Co. or upon Brown & Co.?

10.* *A* gave to *B* a negotiable promissory note for $100, the note being payable to "*B* or bearer." The note was transferred several times by delivery only, without endorsement, and came into the hands of *R* as a note for $1000, the alteration not being at all apparent on the face of the instrument. What can *R* do with reference to enforcement?

11.** Fogarty gave Benson his check for a valid obligation. Benson transferred this check to Smollett in payment of a gambling debt. Subsequently, Benson alleged to Fogarty that he had lost the check, and asked him to stop payment on it. Later, Fogarty learned what had actually happened, and issued a second check in payment to the attorney for one Casety, to whom Smollett had transferred the original check for a legal consideration.

Benson sues Fogarty for payment of the original debt, contending that Fogarty was under no obligation to pay the check to Casety, since the check, having been transferred from Benson to Smollett in payment of a gambling debt, was void, even in the hands of a holder in due course.

Fogarty contends that his indebtedness to Benson was discharged by his acceptance and transfer of the check.

Decision for whom, and why?

12.** John Green and Richard White took part in a game of poker. In the game Green lost $60, $30 of which was won by White. At the time the game broke up, Green had but $30 in his pocket, which he gave to one of the other players whom he did not know so well as he did his friend White. To the latter he gave a check for $30. White, in turn, indorsed the check, making it payable to William Smith, his landlord, to whom White delivered the check in payment of rent.

At the opening of banking hours next morning Green notified the bank to stop payment on the check, which was done. Upon refusal by the bank to pay the check, Smith undertook to enforce its collection from the payee bank, and to that end instituted a suit. Can Smith recover from the bank? Answer fully and give reasons.

13.* *B* signed a promissory note in blank, leaving it on his desk. During *B*'s absence from his desk *A* took the note, filled it in for two hundred dollars and sold it for value to *C*, who knew nothing about the method by which *A* came into possession of the note. Could *C* recover on the note from *B*?

14.* Black made and delivered a legally valid promissory note, entirely in his own handwriting, payable at "No. 22 Mira Vista Ave.," which was his residence. The note was transferred several times by endorsement, and someone without authority added "People's Trust Co." in printed characters on the face of the note directly under the handwritten designated place of payment. Thereafter, but prior to maturity, Brown acquired the note by purchase for value and without actual knowledge of the alteration. At maturity, Brown presented the note at the People's Trust Company, which was not at the stated address, and the note was not paid. Can Brown recover from Black on this note?

## PART 5. LIABILITIES OF PARTIES

**Parties Liable.** As previously stated, no person can be liable on a negotiable instrument unless his name is on it. All parties to an instrument are liable on it in some way. The nature and extent of such liability depends on the instrument itself (amount, date when due, whether with or without interest, and so on) and on the *capacity in which a party affixes his signature.* On a note, a party may affix his signature in the capacity of maker or indorser; on a bill, in the capacity of drawer, drawee-acceptor or indorser. In these capacities, a party's liability may be *priamry or secondary.*

**Primary and Secondary Liability.** A party is *primarily* liable on an instrument if he is absolutely bound to pay it; that is, if he has to pay it in the first instance. All other parties are *secondarily* liable.

*Parties primarily liable.* The maker is primarily liable on a note, the acceptor on a bill. They are the parties to whom the instrument must first be presented for payment. Their liability is absolute, not conditional.

*Parties secondarily liable.* The indorsers are secondarily liable on a note; the drawer and indorsers, on a bill. They are the parties who must pay the instrument if the party primarily liable does not. Their liability, therefore, is conditional.

**Maker's Liability.** The maker of a note engages to pay it according to its terms. He admits (1) the existence of the payee and (2) his capacity then to indorse.

EXAMPLE: For the use of a truck owned by John Able and Tom Beck, I give them a note payable to "Able & Beck," which is thus indorsed to Carter for value. The Court would reject my refusal to pay the note based on the defense (1) that there was no such firm as "Able & Beck," or (2) that they could not indorse in such capacity.

**Drawee-Acceptor's Liability.** A drawee is not liable on a bill unless and until he accepts it. The acceptor of a bill engages to pay it according to its terms, and admits:

(a) *As to the drawer:* (1) his existence, (2) the genuineness of his signature, and (3) his capacity and authority to draw the instrument.

(b) *As to the payee:* (1) his existence, and (2) his capacity then to indorse.

EXAMPLES:

(1) An acceptor may not refuse payment on the ground (a) that a drawer's name is fictitious or (b) forged or (c) that the drawer was insane, or had no authority to draw the draft—though all these propositions be true.

(2) On a bill drawn in favor of the *XYZ* Corporation as payee, the acceptor may not refuse payment on the ground (a) that there is no such corporation or (b) that the bill was indorsed for such corporation by an unauthorized person.

But the acceptor does not admit the genuineness of any part of the draft itself except the drawer's signature. Thus, proof of a material alteration in the body of a bill furnishes a complete defense to the acceptor. If he has paid the bill in ignorance of the alteration, he may recover such payment from the party receiving it. If an acceptor pays a bill to a holder who has derived title through a forged indorsement, he may recover such payment from the holder upon discovering the forgery.

**Conditions of Secondary Liability.** The conditions of secondary liability are (1) those imposed by a party himself (for example, by an indorser in the way he indorses) and (2) those imposed by law, which must be complied with before the drawer or indorsers can be held (presentment, notice of dishonor, notice of protest, and so on).[17]

As stated, the parties secondarily liable on a bill are the drawer and indorsers; on a note, the indorsers.

**Drawer's Liability.** The drawer of a bill admits (1) the existence of the payee, and (2) his capacity then to indorse; and engages (1) that on due presentment (Part 6) the instrument will be accepted, paid, or both, according to its terms, and (2) that if the instrument be dishonored (page 193) and necessary proceedings on dishonor taken (pages 193-196), he will pay the amount of it to the holder or any subsequent indorser compelled to pay it. (A drawer may insert a provision in an instrument disclaiming or limiting his liability to the holder.)

**Indorser's Liability: General v. Qualified Indorsers.** From the standpoint of liability, all indorsers may be classed as (a) *general* or *unqualified*, and (b) *qualified*. Both classes of indorsers are liable on substantially similar warranties, but qualified indorsers do not undertake to pay on default of the party primarily liable.

**Liability of General Indorser.** A general or unqualified indorser, whether his indorsement is in blank, special or full, restrictive, conditional or irregular (as an accommodation), warrants *four* things and undertakes *two*.

He *warrants* to all subsequent holders in due course:

(1) *That the instrument is genuine and in all respects what it purports to be* (for example, that the instrument is not forged or that a person signing it as an agent is duly authorized).

(2) *That he has a good title to it* and that all prior transferors had good title.

---

[17] Throughout this chapter the importance is stressed of making proper presentment and of giving due notice where an instrument is dishonored by non-acceptance or non-payment, because under existing law, failure to make such proper presentment or to give such due notice will discharge the drawer in the case of a bill, and the indorsers in the case of a bill or a note. It should be observed, however, that under the new Uniform Commercial Code, presentment for payment and notice of dishonor will not be necessary to charge the indorser of a note, unless he has added such requirement to his signature. U.C.C. Sec. 3-501. (See Appendix.)

(3) *That all prior parties had capacity to contract* (which would prevent the indorser from setting up as a defense against a subsequent holder in due course, that the maker of a note was an infant, lunatic or idiot).

(4) *That the instrument was valid and subsisting at the time he indorsed it.* (If, for example, a note is issued by a partnership or corporation for the accommodation of a third party, the indorser may not urge such fact in defense of his liability, because he has warranted the instrument to be valid and subsisting at the time of his indorsement.)

A general indorser further *undertakes:*

(a) That on due presentment (Part 6) the instrument will be accepted, paid, or both.

(b) If not, and if the necessary proceedings on dishonor are taken (pages 193-196), he will pay the instrument.

**Liability of Qualified Indorser.** A qualified indorser makes the same warranties as a general indorser except (4) above; and as to that, he merely warrants that *so far as he knows* the instrument is valid. Nor does he undertake that the instrument will be paid at maturity.

Thus, a person who indorses "without recourse" escapes liability on the instrument only (a) when the instrument is invalid and he had no knowledge of invalidity at the time of his indorsement, or (b) where the instrument is valid but defaulted by the maker or acceptor.

EXAMPLES: Cook, who indorses the following six notes "without recourse," is liable to the holder, for the reasons indicated, on notes (1) to (5) inclusive, but not on note (6):

(1) A note on which the maker's signature is forged. (*Warranty that the instrument is genuine and what it purports to be.*)

(2) A note signed, "John Doe, by A. B., Attorney-in-fact," which John Doe never authorized. (*Warranty that the instrument is genuine and what it purports to be.*)

(3) A note payable to the order of Jones, as payee, indorsed by Jones in blank and stolen from him by Smith, who negotiated the instrument to Cook. (*Warranty of title.*)

(4) A note made by an infant. (*Warranty that all prior parties had capacity to contract.*)

(5) A note given by Atkins to Cook for a usurious consideration. (*Warranty that, so far as he knew, the instrument was valid. Cook knew the note was invalid.*)

(6) A note valid in all respects, defaulted by the maker at maturity. (*Cook did not undertake that the note would be paid at maturity.*)

**Liability of Indorser on Negotiable Instrument.** The term *indorsement* normally applies to negotiable paper only. Strictly speaking, there can be no indorsement of nonnegotiable paper, and the writing of one's name on such an instrument by way of transfer constitutes an assignment under the law of contracts. There is considerable conflict in the various jurisdictions as to the liability incurred by such assignment. In some jurisdictions, the liability is prescribed by statute. In others,[18] the indorsement of itself creates no liability on the part of the indorser (assignor) to the assignee, but merely transfers the assignor's rights. In still other jurisdictions,[19] the indorser is liable to the indorsee either as maker or as guarantor. In several states,[20] the indorser is liable only if by due diligence the note cannot be collected from the maker.

**Liability of Person Negotiating by Delivery.** When one negotiates an instrument by delivery alone, without indorsement, his liabilities are the same as those of a *qualified indorser,* except that his warranties run in favor of no one but the person to whom he delivers the instrument.

EXAMPLE: *A* gives *B* a note for $100 payable to "*B* or bearer." The note is transferred several times by delivery only, and gets into the hands of *R* as a note for $1000. *R* may hold *A* for $100 only (according to the "original tenor" of the note), but he may hold his immediate transferor (whether the latter had anything to do with the alteration or not) for the other $900, because one who negotiates an instrument by delivery only, warrants (to his immediate transferee) the genuineness of the instrument.

If a person indorses an instrument which is negotiable by delivery only, he incurs all the liabilities of an indorser.

*Agent negotiating instrument without indorsement.* When a broker or other agent negotiates an instrument without indorsement, he incurs all the liabilities of a qualified indorser unless he discloses the name of his principal and the fact that he is acting only as agent.

**Order of Liability among Indorsers.** In the absence of agreement, indorsers are liable to one another in the order of their indorsement. Thus, if the holder of a note, on the maker's default, elects to hold only the last of five indorsers instead of all five together, the last indorser may recover against the fourth, the fourth against the third, and so on. But where (as in *Empire Trust Co. v. Bartley & Co.*)[21] the indorsers of a note agreed among themselves that each would pay one third of the amount without recourse to the others, one indorser could recover against the other two after discharging more than one third of the note, since the indorsers by special agreement assumed among themselves the relationship of *cosureties* (page 343). Without such agreement they would have been liable in the order of their indorsement.[22]

**Striking Out Indorsement.** The holder may at any time strike out any indorsement not necessary to his title. The indorser whose name is thus stricken out, and all indorsers subsequent to him are thereby relieved from liability on the instrument.

---

[18] Including Illinois, Pennsylvania and Montana.
[19] Including Maryland, Massachusetts, New York, Vermont and Tennessee.
[20] Connecticut and Indiana.
[21] 258 App. Div. 249, 16 N.Y. Supp. 2d 248.
[22] *Ray v. Livingston,* 204 N.C. 1, 167 S.E. 496; *Harris v. Jones,* 23 N.D. 488, 136 N.W. 1080; *Whitten v. Kroeger,* 183 Okl. 327, 82 P. 2d 668.

EXAMPLE: If *F*, the holder of a note indorsed by *B, C, D* and *E*, strikes out *C*'s indorsement, he releases not only *C*, but *D* and *E* as well.

**Instrument Negotiated Back to Indorser.** When an instrument is negotiated back to a prior party, he may reissue and renegotiate it. But he is not entitled to enforce payment of the instrument against any intervening party to whom he was personally liable.

**Liability of Accommodation Party.** An accommodation party is one who signs an instrument as maker, drawer, acceptor or indorser, without receiving value therefor, and for the purpose of lending his name to some other person. Accommodation paper is any type of bill or note to which an accommodation party puts his name.

When a person, not otherwise a party to an instrument, places his signature thereon in blank before delivery, he is liable as indorser in accordance with the following rules:

(a) If the instrument is payable to the order of a third person, he is liable to the payee and to all subsequent parties.

(b) If the instrument is payable to the order of the maker or drawer or is payable to bearer, he is liable to all parties subsequent to the maker or drawer.

(c) If he signs for the accommodation of the payee, he is liable to all parties subsequent to the payee.

An accommodation party, of course, is not liable to the party accommodated.

*Knowledge by holder.* An accommodation party is liable to a holder for value even if the latter, when he took the instrument, knew the former to be an accommodation party.

*Absence of consideration immaterial: wives as accommodation parties.* The very nature of an accommodation signature denotes absence of consideration. Such absence is therefore no defense to liability where a married woman, without consideration, adds her signature to her husband's on a note, except when she is exempted by statute (see page 56).

EXAMPLE: A farmer, owing money for feed, gives, in payment, a note signed by himself and his wife. In a suit on the note, the wife could not escape liability on the ground that her signature was gratuitous and that the holder knew it (except in states where married women are exempt by statute from suretyship or accommodation liability).

*Alterations in liability of accommodation party.* An accommodation indorser, like a surety, is discharged if his risk is altered without his consent.

EXAMPLES:

(1) Following an accommodation indorsement, a collateral agreement is entered into between maker and holder (but without the accommodation indorser's knowledge or consent), which provides that if any one of a series of notes is defaulted, all become due. Such an agreement varies the accommodation indorser's liability and therefore discharges him.

(2) If one of two accommodation parties is released without the other's consent, the latter is discharged.

(3) If the holder, by renewal note or otherwise, gives the maker a valid extension of time in which to pay the note, without an accommodation party's consent thereto, the latter is discharged, unless the holder reserves his rights against the accommodation party, in which event the latter may promptly pay and then bring immediate suit against the maker for reimbursement (page 341).

*Accommodation paper transferred after maturity.* Ordinarily, one who takes an instrument after it is overdue is not a holder in due course and is subject to all defenses which may be urged against an ordinary assignee, unless he acquired the instrument from a holder in due course (page 162). This rule likewise applies to persons taking accommodation paper after maturity, so that an accommodation party may urge absence of consideration against such transferee, unless the latter acquired the instrument from a holder in due course. The rule is the same where the *party accommodated* transfers the instrument after maturity, but in such cases a minority of states[23] have held that such transferee may not hold the accommodation party if he knew him to be such when he took the instrument.

*Rights of accommodation party.* When an accommodation party pays the instrument, he may proceed against the party accommodated and all parties prior to him, for recovery of the amount paid.

**Partnership and Accommodation Paper.** A partner has no right to execute accommodation paper in the name of the firm. Where the accommodation character of such paper is obvious, or where the person to whom the note is given knows or ought to know from the circumstances that the instrument is not given for partnership purposes, he cannot hold copartners on such instrument without their previous acquiescence, subsequent ratification, or estoppel.

**Corporations and Accommodation Paper.** A corporation has no power to execute or indorse accommodation paper. A corporation may, however, be estopped (page 877) from contending that it had no such power, where it has made a practice of issuing and later honoring such paper.[24]

**Liability on Negotiable Document of Title.** When a person, by indorsement and delivery, negotiates a document of title, such as a warehouse receipt or a bill of lading, he warrants:

(a) That the receipt or bill of lading is genuine.

(b) That he has a legal right to negotiate it.

(c) That he knows of no fact which would impair the validity or worth of the document.

(d) That he has a right to transfer title to the goods.

(e) That the goods are merchantable or fit for a particular purpose (whenever such warranties would be implied without receipt or bill).

---

[23] Including Alabama, Connecticut, Illinois, Maine and Maryland.
[24] *Jacobus v. Jackson,* 211 N.Y. 154.

## Questions

1. When is a party *primarily* liable on an instrument?

2. When are parties *secondarily* liable on an instrument?

3. When a maker signs a note he engages to pay it according to its terms. He also admits two things. What are they?

4. When does a drawee become liable on a bill?

5. The acceptor of a bill engages to pay it according to its terms. He also admits three things with respect to the drawer, and two things with respect to the payee. What are they?

6. Does the acceptor admit the genuineness of any part of the draft? Explain.

7. When the drawee has accepted a bill of exchange, may he later set up the defense that there was a material alteration in the body of the bill before he accepted it?

8. If an acceptor pays a bill to a holder who has derived title through a forged endorsement, may he recover such payment from the holder upon discovering the forgery?

9. When a person draws a bill of exchange, what two things does he admit with respect to the payee? What two things does the drawer engage to do?

10. What four things does a general indorser warrant? What two things does he undertake?

11. Does a qualified indorser make the same warranties as a general indorser? Explain.

12. Does a qualified indorser undertake that the instrument will be paid at maturity?

13. State the conditions under which a qualified indorser escapes liability on the instrument.

14. What is the liability of a person who negotiates an instrument by delivery alone?

15. Indorsers may become liable to one another under certain circumstances. State the circumstances and the order in which the indorsers may become liable to one another.

16. What is the effect upon the liability of a group of indorsers, where the name of one of them has been stricken out by the holder?

17. What are the rights of an indorser when an instrument has been negotiated back to him by a subsequent party?

18. Define (a) accommodation party; (b) accommodation paper.

19. When a person, not otherwise a party to an instrument, places his signature thereon in blank before delivery, what is his liability: (a) if the instrument is payable to the order of a third person; (b) if the instrument is payable to the order of the maker or drawer, or is payable to bearer; (c) if he signs for the accommodation of the payee? What is the effect upon the liability of an accommodation party who receives no consideration for his signature?

20. What are the rights of an accommodation party where he pays the instrument?

21. May a partner ever bind his firm by accommodation paper? Explain.

22. May a corporation ever be bound by accommodation paper executed in its name? Explain.

23. When a person, by indorsement and delivery, negotiates a document of title, such as a warehouse receipt or a bill of lading, what does he warrant?

## Problems

1. You engage two mechanics, Allen and Brown, to overhaul your motor at a cost of $150. They agree to accept a 30-day promissory note in payment. On completion of the work you execute and deliver to these mechanics a 30-day note for $150 payable to the order of "Allen and Brown." Allen and Brown thus indorse the note to White for value. When White presents the note on due date, you refuse payment on the ground that you have since discovered there was no such firm as "Allen and Brown." In case of suit, how would the court hold?

2. Green draws two drafts on the same drawee: one in favor of the Beauty Decorators Company, Inc., and another payable to the order of Household Utilities Corporation, which indorses the draft for value to Perkins. The drawee refuses to honor either draft, and the holders require Green to make good. Green refuses to make good on the first draft, on discovering that there is no such corporation as Household Utilities Corporation, and on the second draft on the ground that it was indorsed by the assistant secretary who had no authority to indorse drafts on behalf of the corporation. In case of suit, how would the court dispose of Green's defenses?

3. After accepting a bill of exchange drawn on you as drawee, you discover that there was a material alteration in the body of the bill. You refuse payment on due date because of this discovery. Can the holder enforce payment against you?

4. As acceptor of a bill of exchange, you pay it on due date, then discover that the holder had derived title through a forged indorsement. May you recover such payment from the holder?

5.* On the balance sheet of a merchant there appears an item, "notes receivable $5,695.50." You find these notes on hand or in bank for collection. You also find that the merchant has discounted at his bank notes previously received by him not yet due amounting to $11,000.00.

(a) Since these discounted notes are no longer held by the merchant, has he any further responsibility or liability?

(b) If so, describe its nature and what effect it may have on the balance sheet.

6.* Dupont drew a check on the X bank for $1.22 payable to the order of Alice Nugent. This check was fraudulently raised to $3,881.22, and the name of the payee changed to Alfred Nugent. Thereafter, this check was endorsed by Alfred Nugent and deposited by him in the B bank. The B bank endorsed it, guaranteeing all prior endorsements, and collected $3,881.22 from the X bank. Prior to the discovery of the fraud, Alfred Nugent closed his account with the B bank and disappeared. Upon whom does the loss fall and why?

7.** Brown receives from Jones and Smith two notes that are identical in amount, maturity and all other respects, except that Jones has indorsed the one generally, whereas Smith has indorsed the other without recourse.

Compare or contrast Brown's rights against the respective indorsers:

(a) If either or both notes are found to be forgeries.

(b) If either or both notes were made or indorsed by parties incapacitated therefor.

(c) If either or both indorsers did not have good title.

(d) If, though the notes were invalid for any reason, the indorsers had no knowledge of that fact.

(e) If either or both makers become insolvent.

8.* Burns loaned a sum of money to Atkins, but at a usurious rate of interest. He took a note payable to bearer for the amount of the loan and interest. Burns then sold the note to Wilson but endorsed "without recourse." Wilson could not recover the face amount of the note from Atkins because of the usury and so attempted, by suit, to recover from Burns, the endorser. Could he recover?

9.*

Boston, Mass.<br>January 2, 1927

Ninety days after date I promise to pay to the order of X.Y. Five Hundred Dollars with interest.

(Signed) John Doe<br>By A.B.<br>Attorney-in-fact.

Endorsed in blank "without recourse." X.Y.

The foregoing note passes in due course to William Smith. The note being unpaid at maturity, Smith sues. John Doe is not liable as maker because A.B. had no authority to sign as agent or attorney-in-fact. X.Y. interposes the defense that he is not liable as he endorsed "without recourse." Is such defense good?

10.* Royce becomes the holder of a negotiable promissory note in regular form made by A to B and bearing several full endorsements. He endorses the note to Church for value, but "without recourse." When Church endeavors to collect upon maturity of the note, it is discovered that A is an infant and refuses to pay. Church then sues the endorsers, including Royce. Has Royce any defense?

11.** Smith is the holder in due course of a negotiable promissory note made by A and indorsed by Brown, Green, Black and White. Smith is personally acquainted with Green and, not desiring to hold Green liable as an indorser, cancels Green's signature. Smith then sues the maker and all the indorsers except Green. Against whom will Smith obtain a judgment? Explain.

12.** You desire to borrow $1,000 from the X bank. As maker you execute a promissory note for that sum due ninety days from date of execution. The X bank refuses to accept the note until you have it indorsed by a responsible indorser. You secure B, who indorses the note. You then take the note to the X bank which discounts it for you. B neither gave nor received any consideration for his indorsement. When the note matures, you are unable to pay. Has X bank the right to recover from B? Give reasons.

13.* A made a note for the accommodation of B. B, before maturity, transferred it for value to C, who, at the time of taking the note knew that A was an accommodation party. Upon maturity, the note not being paid, C sued A thereon. Can he recover?

14.** The White Yarn Knitting Company borrowed $1,500 from the bank on its note. The loan was purely an accommodation. After the note was executed by the officials of the Knitting Company, A and B, both of whom were stockholders and directors in the Knitting Company, consented to indorse the note, by partial payments, to the sum of $800. At that time A, without the knowledge of B, requested the bank to release him as indorser, which the bank did for a consideration of $200. The Knitting Company failed to pay the balance of the note and the bank commenced action against B as indorser. Will the bank succeed?

15.** E gives F a note due in six months from date, such note being indorsed by two friends of E. At maturity E makes payment on account and asks for an extension of sixty days. *F* grants the request and *E* gives a new note for the balance due in sixty days from date. In the new note, *E* inserts the words "that the original note with the indorsers stands as collateral." Does *F*'s action in granting *E* the extension discharge the indorsers on the original note?

16.** *B*, a member of the firm of *A* and *B*, indorses the firm name on a promissory note for the accommodation of his brother, who is entering into business. Before the note is due, *A* discovers what his partner has done, and tells him that he is not going to be responsible for it but fails to notify the payee of the note. Is *A* liable together with his partner *B*? Explain.

17.*** (a) Allen, without receiving any consideration and for the accommodation of Brown, signs a promissory note payable to Brown, who endorses it for value to Cox. When Cox took the note he knew that Allen received no value and was only an accommodation party. Brown is irresponsible and Cox sues Allen on the instrument. Can Cox recover from Allen? If not, why? If so, why?

(b) Amos, who was 17 years old, gave a note in payment for goods to Blue, who endorses it to Coty for value before maturity. The note is not paid at maturity. Coty sues Amos and Blue. Both Amos and Blue set up the infancy of Amos as a defense. Can Coty recover from Amos, or Blue, or both, or neither? Explain.

18.* (a) *A* makes a note to *B* or order. It is duly indorsed by *B*, *C*, *D*, and *E*, the last indorsing it over to *B*, the original holder. Default and due notice, etc. *B* sues the maker and all the indorsers. Advise all parties. (b) Where a negotiable instrument is ambiguous, what are the rules of construction and interpretation as to:

(1) Conflict of words and figures.

(2) Instrument providing for payment of interest without specifying date from which interest is to run.

(3) Undated.

(4) Conflict between written and printed provision.

(5) Instrument containing words "I promise to pay," signed by two persons.

## PART 6. PRESENTMENT

**Presentment: Definition and Types.** An instrument is *presented* when it is placed before a person obligated or to become obligated on it with the request that he honor the obligation.

Presentment may be (1) for acceptance, and (2) for payment.

**Presentment for Acceptance.** Presentment for acceptance relates only to bills of exchange (drafts). If I draw a draft on you as drawee, that does not make you liable on the instrument. I must first *present* the draft to you for *acceptance*. If you accept, the instrument is *honored*. If you refuse or neglect to accept, the instrument is *dishonored by nonacceptance*.

*General v. qualified acceptance.* A general acceptance is one which assents without change to the drawer's order. A qualified acceptance is one which varies the effect of a bill as drawn, as by changing the time, place or amount of payment, or by imposing a condition upon the acceptor's liability. An acceptance to pay at a particular place is a general acceptance

---

*** Official problem, both American Institute and New York Board.

unless it expressly states that the bill is to be paid there and not elsewhere.

**Bills Which Must Be Presented for Acceptance.** Presentment for acceptance is not necessary, and a drawee may pay a draft when due without prior presentment for acceptance, except in the following cases:

(a) Bills payable "after sight": If a bill is payable 30 days after sight, it cannot mature until it has been "seen," and accepted;

(b) Bills expressly stipulating that presentment for acceptance be made; and

(c) Bills payable elsewhere than at the drawee's residence or place of business.

**Presentment for Acceptance: Time and Manner of Making.** When presentment for acceptance is necessary, the holder must make it within a reasonable time after issuance, and in any event before it is overdue, or the parties secondarily liable (drawer and indorsers) are discharged.

Bills may be presented for acceptance at a reasonable hour on any business day, and up to twelve o'clock noon on Saturdays (except when Saturday falls on a legal holiday).

The bill must be presented to the drawee or some person authorized to accept or refuse acceptance on his behalf.

In a partnership, presentment may be made to any partner. In other situations, the following rules govern:

(a) When a bill is addressed to two or more drawees, not partners, presentment must be made to them all, or to any one having authority to accept for all.

(b) When the drawee is dead, presentment may be made to his personal representative (page 753).

(c) When the drawee has been adjudged a bankrupt or is insolvent, or has made an assignment for the benefit of creditors, presentment may be made to him or to his trustee or assignee.

**Presentment for Acceptance: When Excused.** Presentment for acceptance is excused and a bill may be treated as dishonored by nonacceptance:

(a) When the drawee is dead or has absconded or is a fictitious person or a person not having capacity to contract by bill.

(b) When after the exercise of reasonable diligence, presentment cannot be made.

(c) When, although presentment has been irregular, acceptance has been refused on some other ground.

**Acceptance: How Made.** The Negotiable Instruments Law provides that the drawee must accept in writing, and on the face of the bill, if the holder requires it; otherwise the holder may treat the bill as dishonored. It is customary for the drawee to accept by writing "Accepted" across the face of the bill followed by date and signature.

Under certain circumstances, however, the drawee may be deemed to have accepted without a writing, as where an intention to accept may be spelled out from the fact of retaining, destroying or refusing to return a bill.

**Time Allowed Drawee to Accept: Effect of Retention, Destruction or Refusal to Return Bill.** There is a conflict of authority on whether or not a drawee's mere retention of the bill beyond the period allowed for acceptance constitutes an acceptance. The weight of authority is that it does not; the circumstances must show an intention to accept. The Uniform Negotiable Instruments Law provides[25] that where a drawee destroys the bill or refuses within twenty-four hours after presentment, or within such other period as the holder may allow, to return the bill to the holder, accepted or not accepted, he will be deemed to have accepted the bill. The court has held, however, that this relates to the affirmative act of destruction or refusal, not to the negative act of failing to return the instrument.[26] The Uniform Law[27] provides further that where a bill is duly presented for acceptance and is not accepted within the prescribed time, the person presenting it must treat the bill as dishonored by nonacceptance, or he loses the right of recourse against the drawer and indorsers. The Uniform Commercial Code resolves this seeming conflict by treating a failure to return as a dishonor.[28]

**Promise to Accept.** An unconditional promise in writing to accept a bill before it is drawn is deemed an actual acceptance in favor of every person who, on the faith of such promise, receives the bill for value. The bill must be drawn, however, strictly in accordance with the terms of the promise to accept. Immaterial variations may be ignored.

EXAMPLE: A bank agreed to pay a check for $1035. The check as written called for $1035 "with exchange." *Held*, the acceptance was valid, since the variation was immaterial; the bank was not liable to pay exchange on the check drawn on it and payable over its counter.[29]

The Uniform Commercial Code, wherever adopted, will supersede the foregoing rule, because it requires that acceptance must be written on the draft.[30]

**Who May Accept Bills.** Only the drawee may accept. There are, however, two exceptions to this rule. These relate to *referees in case of need*, and *acceptances "supra protest" for honor*.

**Referee in Case of Need.** A "referee in case of need" is a person named

---

[25] Section 137.
[26] *Matteson v. Moulton*, 79 N.Y. 627. "In the absence of statutory provisions changing the rule, the weight of authority favors the position that mere retention alone will not bind the drawee as acceptor." 10 *C.J.S.* 664, citing *Hibbard v. Parciak*, 94 Conn. 562, 109 A. 725; *Southern Creosoting Co. v. Chicago & A.R. Co.* (Mo.), 205 S.W. 716; *Mitchell Livestock Auction Co. v. Bryant State Bank* (S.D.), 275 N.W. 262.
[27] Section 150.
[28] U.C.C. Sec. 3-410.
[29] *Iowa State Sav. Bank of Fairfield v. City Nat. Bank of Tipton*, 183 Iowa 1347, 168 N.W. 148.
[30] U.C.C. Sec. 3-410.

in a bill to whom presentment may be made in case the instrument is dishonored by nonacceptance or nonpayment. The holder may or may not resort to such person, at his option.

**Acceptance for Honor "Supra Protest."** If a bill has been dishonored by nonacceptance *and is not yet overdue*, it may be accepted (with the holder's consent) by any person not already a party to the instrument, for the honor of a person liable on it or for whose account the bill is drawn. The acceptor for honor may do this either because he is indebted to the drawer, or as an act of friendship, or (as in most cases) because the drawer has designated a "referee in case of need," to save protest fees or avoid risking injury to the drawer's credit.[31]

*How executed.* An acceptance for honor must be in writing, signed by the acceptor for honor, and it must indicate that it is such an acceptance.

*Liability.* The acceptor for honor is liable to the holder and all parties subsequent to the party for whose honor the bill has been accepted, on the following engagement: that he will pay the bill according to the terms of his acceptance provided (1) the drawee has not paid it, and (2) the bill has been presented for payment and protested for nonpayment, and due notice of dishonor has been given to the acceptor for honor.

**Presentment for Payment: in General.** Presentment for payment relates to both bills and notes. An instrument is presented for payment to the person primarily liable on it: maker of note, acceptor of bill. If such person is absent or inaccessible, presentment may be made to any person found on the premises. The instrument must be exhibited to the person from whom payment is demanded, and when it is paid, it must be delivered up to the party paying it.

Presentment for payment is necessary if the parties secondarily liable are to be held.

EXAMPLE: An audit of Brown's books shows a past due note for $10,000 made by Wilson and indorsed by James. Wilson is wholly bankrupt. James is a wealthy man. The note was never presented for payment. What is the note worth? Nothing. James is discharged by Brown's failure to make presentment.

But failure to make presentment for payment does not discharge the party *primarily* liable, because he is absolutely liable in any event. He merely need not pay interest accruing after maturity if he was ready, willing and able to pay at the proper time and place.

*Accommodation maker primarily liable.* An accommodation maker, though known to be such to the holder, is, as to the latter, primarily liable; hence he remains liable notwithstanding nonpresentment.

**Presentment for Payment: Time.** All instruments not payable on demand must be presented for payment on due date. If due date falls on a

---

[31] Acceptance for honor has been eliminated from the new Commercial Code, as obsolete. (See page 900.)

Saturday, Sunday or legal holiday, presentment must be made on the next succeeding business day. If Friday is a legal holiday and an instrument falls due on that day, the following Monday is regarded as the next succeeding business day.

When an instrument is payable a given number of days after date or after sight or after the happening of a specified event, the date of payment is determined by excluding the day or event from which the time is to run and by including the day of payment.

*Demand instruments* must be presented for payment *within a reasonable time after issue,* except that a demand bill may be presented for payment *within a reasonable time after its last negotiation.* The Negotiable Instruments Law provides that in determining what is a "reasonable time" or an "unreasonable time," regard is to be had to the nature of the instrument, the usage of trade or business (if any) with respect to such instruments, and the facts of the particular case. Court decisions throughout the country have varied widely as to reasonable and unreasonable periods.

EXAMPLES:

(1) Delays in presenting sight bills or drafts of four days (Mass.), six days (Mich.), seven days (Pa.), eleven days (Pa.), one month (N.Y.), thirty-five days (Ill.), seven weeks (Tex.), two months (N.Y.), and three months (La.) have been held not unreasonable in view of given circumstances; but delays of five days (Ky.), ten days (N.Y.), sixteen days (W.Va.), twenty-one days (Mich.), one month (N.C.), more than one month (U.S.), one year or more (U.S.), two years (La.) and two and one-half years (Tex.) were declared unreasonable in view of other circumstances.

(2) Delays in presenting notes for periods ranging from four days to nine and one-half years have been held not unreasonable under given circumstances, though similar ranges of delay under other conditions were held unreasonable.

**Demand instruments presented on Saturday.** An instrument payable on demand may be presented for payment on a Saturday up to twelve o'clock noon (unless the entire day is a legal holiday).

**Proper hours.** An instrument payable at a place of business must be presented during the usual business hours; at a person's home, before the usual hours of rest.

The time within which checks must be presented for payment is discussed on pages 206-207.

**Presentment for Payment: Place.** Presentment for payment is made at the proper place:

(a) When a place of payment is specified in the instrument and it is there presented.

(b) When no place of payment is specified but the address of the person to make payment is given in the instrument and it is there presented.

(c) When no place of payment is specified and no address is given and the instrument is presented at the usual place of business or residence of the person to make payment.

(d) In any other case if presented to the person to make payment wherever he can be found or if presented at his last known place of business or residence.

**Presentment for Payment When Instrument Payable at Bank.** Making an instrument payable at a bank is equivalent to an order to the bank to pay it for the account of the person primarily liable on it. However, presentment for payment must be made during banking hours unless the person to make payment has no funds there to meet it at any time during the day, in which case presentment at any hour before the bank is closed on that day, is sufficient.

**Presentment for Payment Where Principal Debtor is Dead.** Where the person primarily liable on the instrument is dead and no place of payment is specified, presentment for payment must be made to his personal representative (page 753) if such there be, and if with the exercise of reasonable diligence he can be found.

**Presentment for Payment Where Several Persons are Primarily Liable.** Where several persons are primarily liable on an instrument and no place of payment is specified, presentment may be made to any one of them if they are partners; otherwise, it must be made to all.

**When Presentment for Payment is not Required to Charge the Drawer.** Presentment for payment is not required to charge the drawer when he has no right to expect or require that the drawee or acceptor will pay the instrument; for example, where the drawee has neither funds of the drawer with which to pay the draft, nor any obligation to pay it.

**When Presentment for Payment is not Required to Charge the Indorser.** Presentment for payment is not required to charge an indorser when the instrument has been made or accepted for his accommodation and he has no reason to expect that the instrument will be paid if presented.

**When Presentment for Payment may be Dispensed with.** Presentment for payment is dispensed with:

(a) If with the exercise of reasonable diligence, presentment cannot be made.

(b) When the drawee is a fictitious person.

(c) By waiver of presentment, express or implied (pages 196-197).

**When Delay in Making Presentment for Payment is Excused.** Delay in making presentment for payment is excused when it is caused by circumstances beyond the control of the holder and not due to his own fault. When the cause of delay ceases to operate, presentment must be made with reasonable diligence.

**Payment for Honor.** Where a bill has been protested for nonpayment, any person may pay it "supra protest" for the honor of any person liable on the bill or for the honor of the person for whose account it was drawn. This provision is eliminated under The Uniform Commercial Code, as obsolete. (See page 900).

## Questions

1. What is meant by the "presentment" of an instrument? For what purpose may an instrument be presented?

2. To what types of instrument does presentment for acceptance relate?

3. If I drew a draft on you as drawee, under what circumstances would you become liable on the instrument?

4. In respect to acceptance, distinguish between "honoring" and "dishonoring" an instrument.

5. Distinguish between general and qualified acceptance of an instrument. To which class would an acceptance to pay at a particular place belong? Is there any exception to your last answer?

6. Is presentment for acceptance necessary in all cases?

7. "Presentment for acceptance must be made not later than the next day after the bill is issued." Is this statement correct or incorrect? Explain.

8. If a bill is presented for acceptance beyond the time allowed by law, what is the effect on the drawer and the indorser?

9. At what hour of the day must a bill be presented for acceptance? Will your answer depend in any way upon which day the instrument is presented?

10. To whom must a bill be presented for acceptance:
    (a) when the bill is drawn on a particular drawee,
    (b) when it is addressed to two or more drawees, not partners,
    (c) when the drawee is dead,
    (d) when the drawee has been adjudged a bankrupt, or is insolvent, or has made an assignment for the benefit of creditors?

11. Name three situations in which presentment for acceptance will be excused.

12. Does the law prescribe how presentment for acceptance must be made? Explain.

13. May an intention to accept an instrument be spelled out from any of the following situations: (a) retaining the bill, (b) destroying the bill, and (c) refusing to return the bill? Explain your answers.

14. Under what circumstances may a promise to accept a bill before it is drawn be deemed an actual acceptance?

15. "Only the drawee may accept a bill." Name two exceptions to this rule.

16. To whom is an instrument presented for payment in respect to the types of paper requiring such presentment?

17. How is presentment for payment made if the person to whom it should be made is absent or inaccessible?

18. When an instrument is presented for payment, what must be done with it (a) before payment, and (b) after payment?

19. Where presentment for payment is necessary, what is the effect of not making it?

20. Does failure to present an instrument for payment to the person who is primarily liable on it have any legal effect with respect to such person?

21. When must time instruments be presented for payment? Would your answer depend in any way on the fact that the instrument became due on (a) an ordinary weekday, (b) a Saturday, (c) a Sunday, (d) a legal holiday other than Friday, (e) a legal holiday which fell on a Friday?

22. When must a demand instrument be presented for payment? Explain your answer. What is the rule with respect to demand instruments presented on Saturday?

23. What are the proper hours for presenting an instrument for payment: (a) at a place of business, and (b) at a person's home?

24. What is the proper place for presenting an instrument for payment:

(a) when a place of payment is specified in the instrument,

(b) when no place of payment is specified but the address of the person to make payment is given in the instrument,

(c) when no place of payment is specified and no address is given, and

(d) in any other case?

25. What is the duty of a bank at which a note is made payable and in which the maker has sufficient funds on deposit, when the note is presented there for payment?

26. Where the person primarily liable on an instrument is dead and no place of payment is specified, how must presentment for payment be made?

27. How must presentment for payment be made where several persons are primarily liable?

28. What is the rule with respect to presentment for payment of a bill of exchange where the drawer has no right to expect or require that the drawee or acceptor will pay the instrument?

29. When is presentment for payment not required to charge an indorser?

30. Under what circumstances may presentment for payment be dispensed with?

31. When will delay in making presentment for payment be excused?

## Problems

1. On March 1, Loft draws a thirty day draft on Martin in the amount of $1,000, payable to the order of Nearing. On the same day, Loft delivers the draft to Orr, who indorses it to Paterson. Six weeks later Paterson presents the draft to Martin for acceptance, and Martin refuses to accept it. Paterson now wants to know what his rights are under the circumstances. What would you tell him?

2. A draft drawn on three parties, not partners, is presented for acceptance to one of them, who refuses acceptance on the ground that the instrument was presented a day late, which is not the fact. The holder, treating the instrument as dishonored by non-acceptance, seeks to hold the drawer and two indorsers on the draft. May he do so?

3. Ryan gives Stone his promissory note for $1,000, without interest, payable at the Sterling Bank. On due date, Stone presents the note for payment to Ryan at his office, and Ryan refuses payment. Stone sues Ryan for $1,000, with accrued interest from due date. Ryan's defense is improper presentment. How will the court decide?

4. An audit of Tracy's books shows a past due note for $10,000, made by Ury and indorsed by Vernon. Ury is bankrupt, Vernon is a wealthy man. The note was never presented for payment. The auditor seeks to evaluate the note. What value will he give it?

5.* Beach drew a bill of exchange on Washburn as drawee and gave it to the payee for adequate consideration. The payee personally presented it to Washburn who immediately became enraged and tore up the bill. Against whom has the payee any right of action on the bill?

6.* On January 7, 1932, Baldwin drew a bill of exchange on Clute payable March 7, 1932, to the order of Dillingham. On January 12, 1932, Dillingham presented the bill to Clute who refused to accept it. On the same day, Dillingham protested the bill for nonacceptance. On January 27, 1932, Everett, who desired to protect Baldwin's credit, accepted this bill.

(a) What is the technical name for this kind of acceptance?

(b) How must such an acceptance be made?

(c) Just what did Everett, by this acceptance, engage to do?

7.** In the following circumstances, state the respective rights and obligations of (a) the maker, (b) the payee, (c) the holder, (d) the bank:

John Smith gave his promissory note for $1,000, due February 15, 1944, payable at the Citizens Bank, to Henry Brown, who, for value, endorsed and delivered it to William Jones. Through an oversight, it was not presented for payment until February 25, 1944, when, as on February 15 and thereafter, Smith had more than $1,000 on deposit in the Citizens Bank.

8. Adams, a farmer, orders a quantity of feed from the Farmers' Supply Corporation and offers in payment a thirty day draft for $832.41, drawn on Kanine Kennels, Frank Brown, Prop. Farmers' Supply Corporation agrees that it will take the draft on confirmation by Kanine Kennels. He then writes Kanine Kennels for confirmation, and Frank James, on behalf of Kanine Kennels, replies that the draft, if drawn, will be duly accepted. Farmers' Supply Corporation thereupon takes the draft, and forwards it to Kanine Kennels for acceptance. The latter, however, now advises that a check of its account with Adams shows no outstanding balance in favor of Adams which will entitle him to draw on Kanine Kennels in the stated amount, for which reason Kanine Kennels refuses to accept the draft. What are the rights, if any, of Farmers' Supply Corporation in respect to Kanine Kennels?

9. Carr draws a ninety day, $2,000 draft on Dorn, to the order of John Erwin and Sons, to whom the draft is delivered. Three days later Dorn's plant is destroyed by an explosion. At the time of the accident the insurance on the plant had expired, leaving Dorn wholly insolvent. A week later Dorn suffers a stroke and dies. On due date Erwin and Sons, without having made an attempt to present the draft for acceptance, demand payment of Carr, who denies liability under the circumstances. Thereupon John Erwin and Sons bring suit against Carr. Who will succeed, and why?

10. An audit of Fine's books shows a past due note for $5,500 made by Graham and indorsed by Hand. Graham is bankrupt, Hand is a man of means. The note was never presented for payment. To what extent should the auditor treat the note as an asset in checking Fine's balance sheet?

11. Jones issues a demand note payable to the order of Kraft. Larson, a holder in due course, presents the note for payment on the morning of August 1, which day falls on Saturday. The note not being paid, Larson, after serving notice of dishonor on Kraft on the following Monday, sues Jones and Kraft, who set up improper presentment as a defense. Who will get judgment, and why?

12. A thirty day note falls due on a Friday, which happens to be a legal holiday. The holder, who is away for the weekend, does not present the note for payment until the following Monday. The maker defaults. The holder then sues both maker and indorser, and the latter sets up improper presentment for payment as a defense. Will the indorser's defense succeed?

13. Morse draws a sight draft on Null. The draft is made payable to the order of Ottaway. Thirty days after receiving the draft, Ottaway presents it to Null for payment, which is refused. Morse as drawer is now called on to make good. Morse's defense is improper presentment. Apart from any other defense, what would you say as to this particular defense urged by Morse?

14. A finance company holds two notes. The first note specifies no place

of payment but gives the address of the person to make payment. The second note specifies no place of payment and gives no address of the person to make payment. Where should the finance company present these instruments for payment?

15. Assume that the same finance company holds three additional instruments. The first instrument is a promissory note which the finance company has been unable to present for payment notwithstanding the exercise of reasonable diligence. The second instrument is a draft drawn on a fictitious person. As to the third instrument, presentment is waived. What is the requirement in each of these cases with respect to presentment under the circumstances?

16. Sutton makes and delivers his promissory note to Thomas, payable on September 1. Thomas, before maturity, indorses the note for value to Ulrich. Two days before maturity, Thomas, who is a friend of Sutton's, writes to Ulrich, advising him that Sutton is pressed for funds; that he is sure Sutton will pay if Ulrich will withhold presentment for ten days. Ulrich replies, agreeing to do so. Ten days later he presents the note for payment, and upon default, notifies Thomas of the default and then brings suit against Sutton and Thomas. Thomas defends on the ground of improper presentment and failure to give proper notice of dishonor. Judgment for whom?

## PART 7. DISHONOR AND PROTEST

**Dishonor and Protest, Defined and Distinguished.** *Dishonor* consists in nonacceptance of a bill, or nonpayment of a bill or note. *Protest* is a formal attestation of dishonor. The word is often loosely used to mean taking the necessary steps to charge secondary parties (drawers and indorsers) with liability in case an instrument has been dishonored. Technically, however, a certificate of protest is a formal statement by a notary public, attested by his seal, or by a respectable resident of the place of dishonor in the presence of two or more witnesses, to the effect that presentment of a specific instrument was duly made at a given time and place to a given person, and payment or acceptance demanded and refused. *Notice of protest* is notice given by a notary to parties secondarily liable, of the fact that the instrument in question was duly presented, dishonored and protested.

**When protest necessary.** Only foreign bills of exchange (page 150), including checks, need be protested, though other instruments are often protested as a matter of business practice. Proof of presentment and dishonor is sometimes difficult when an instrument is drawn and payable in different states. Protest facilitates proof, because certificates of protest under the seal of a notary are commonly made "self proving" by statute.

**Notice of Dishonor; Nature and Purpose.** *Notice of dishonor* is notice given orally[32] or in writing, personally, by mail, by wire, or even by tele-

---

[32] *O'Neal v. Clark*, 229 Ala. 127, 155 So. 562, 94 A.L.R. 589; *Caine v. Foreman*, 106 Cal. App. 636, 289 P. 929; *Blue Ribbon Garage v. Baldwin*, 91 Conn. 674, 101 A. 83; *Winn v. Perryman*, La. App. 160 So. 804; *McShane v. Dingley*, 132 Me. 429, 172 A. 264; *Harr v. Edsall*, 121 Pa. Super. 19, 183 A. 67; *Carroll v. Fidelity Trust Co.*, 6 Tenn. Civ. App. 101; *Hall v. First State Bank of Hawley*, Tex. Civ. App., 4 S.W. 2d 253; *Harris v. Citizens Bank & Trust Co.*, 172 Va. 111, 200 S.E. 652; *Lawhead v. Nelson*, 113 W.Va. 453, 168 S.E. 659.

phone[33] to all parties secondarily liable (drawer of bill and indorsers of bill or note), identifying the instrument and advising that it has been dishonored. By giving notice of dishonor, the holder perfects his rights against the parties secondarily liable; by failing to give it, he discharges them, and his only recourse then is against the party primarily liable.

**Parties Benefited by Notice of Dishonor.** Where notice is given by or on behalf of the holder, it inures to the benefit of all subsequent holders and all prior parties who have a right of recourse against the party to whom it is given. Where notice is given by or on behalf of a party entitled to give notice, it inures to the benefit of the holder and all parties subsequent to the party entitled to give notice.

**Notice of Dishonor: to Whom Given.** Except when notice of dishonor is waived or dispensed with, it must be given to the drawer of a bill and to each indorser of a bill or note.

**Death.** When any party is dead, and his death is known to the party giving notice, the notice must be given to a personal representative, such as an executor or administrator (page 757), if there be one and if with reasonable diligence he can be found. If there is no personal representative, notice may be sent to the last residence or last place of business of the deceased.

**Bankruptcy, and so on.** Where a party has been adjudged a bankrupt or an insolvent or has made an assignment for the benefit of creditors (page 705), notice may be given either to the party himself or to his trustee or assignee.

**Partners and joint parties.** When the parties to be notified are partners, notice to any one partner is notice to the firm even though there has been a dissolution.

EXAMPLE: Fox, for value, gives a promissory note to Amos and Bell, partners, who indorse the note to Cody before maturity. Fox fails to pay the note at maturity and Cody, the holder, gives notice of dishonor to Amos only. The firm of Amos and Bell had been dissolved by mutual consent before maturity of the note, which fact the holder, Cody, knew, and Amos had become financially irresponsible. The holder, Cody, seeks to recover from Bell, who disclaims liability for want of legal notice. Cody can recover from Bell. Where the indorsers are partners, notice to any one partner is notice to all, though the firm is dissolved.

Notice to joint parties who are not partners must be given to each of them, unless one has authority to receive notice for the others.

**Accommodation parties.** An accommodation maker, as pointed out on page 187, is deemed primarily liable; hence he is not entitled to notice of dishonor. An accommodation indorser, however, is entitled to notice of dishonor.

**Form and Contents of Notice.** A notice of dishonor need not be in any

---

[33] *Yonkers Nat. Bank v. Yerks & Co., Inc.,* 142 Misc. 640, aff'd 234 App. Div. 885.

particular form, so long as it conveys the following information: (a) description of instrument, (b) the fact of presentment and demand, (c) the fact of dishonor and (d) intent to look to the party secondarily liable for payment.

**Time for Giving Notice of Dishonor.** The time for giving notice of dishonor depends on whether parties reside in the same or different communities, as follows:

*Where the Parties Reside in the Same Community:*

(1) If given at the recipient's place of business: It must be *received* before the close of business on the *day after* dishonor.

(2) If given at the recipient's residence: It must be *received* before the usual hours of rest not later than the *day after* dishonor.

(3) If sent by mail: It must be mailed so as to *reach* the recipient in "usual course" on the *day after* dishonor.

*Where the Parties Reside in Different Communities:*

(1) If mailed: It must be deposited so as to go by mail not later than the *day after* dishonor.

(2) If given otherwise: It must be received within the same time as if mailed on the day after dishonor.

**Successive Notices.** Each indorser, after receiving notice of dishonor, has the same time to give notice to prior parties that the holder has after dishonor. Thus, when a note held by *X* is indorsed by *A, B, C* and *D* in that order, and when *X* serves notice of dishonor on *D* only, *D* has the same time to serve notice on *C* (if he elects to notify *C* only) that *X* had to notify *D*; *C* would have the same time to notify *B* that *D* had to notify *C*, and so on.

**Delay in Giving Notice: When Excused.** Delay in giving notice of dishonor is excused when the delay is caused by circumstances beyond the control of the holder and not imputable to his default, misconduct, or negligence. When the cause of delay ceases to operate, notice must be given with reasonable diligence.

**Place for Giving Notice of Dishonor.** When a party has added an address to his signature, notice of dishonor must be sent to that address; but if he has not given such address, then the notice must be sent as follows:

(a) Either to the post office where he is accustomed to receive his letters; or

(b) If he lives in one place, and has his place of business in another, notice may be sent to either place; or

(c) If he is sojourning elsewhere, notice may be sent to him there.

But when the notice is actually received within the time specified by law, it will be sufficient, though not sent in accordance with the above requirements.

**Notice by Mail: Presumption of Delivery.** When notice of dishonor is duly addressed and deposited in the post office, the sender is deemed to have given due notice, notwithstanding any miscarriage in the mails. Notice is deemed to have been deposited in the post office when deposited in any branch post office or in any letter box under the control of the post office department.

**When Notice is Dispensed With.** Notice of dishonor is dispensed with when, after the exercise of reasonable diligence, it cannot be given to or does not reach the parties sought to be charged. What constitutes reasonable diligence would be a question of fact in each case.

**When Notice to Drawer is not Required.** Notice to the drawer is not required in any of the following cases:

(a) When the drawer and drawee are the same person.

(b) When the drawee is a fictitious person or a person not having capacity to contract.

(c) When the drawer is the person to whom the instrument is presented for payment.

(d) When the drawer has no right to expect or require that the drawee or acceptor will honor the instrument.

(e) When the drawer has countermanded payment.

**When Notice to Indorser is not Required.** Notice to an indorser is not required in any of the following cases:

(a) When the drawee is a fictitious person or a person not having capacity to contract, and the indorser was aware of the fact at the time he indorsed the instrument.

(b) When the indorser is the person to whom the instrument is presented for payment.

(c) When the instrument was made or accepted for his accommodation.

**Nonpayment Following Nonacceptance.** Where due notice of dishonor by nonacceptance has been given, notice of a subsequent dishonor by nonpayment is not necessary, unless in the meantime the instrument has been accepted.

**Waiver of Protest.** A waiver of protest, whether in the case of a foreign bill of exchange or other negotiable instrument, is deemed to be a waiver not only of a formal protest, but also of presentment and notice of dishonor. Waivers of protest are frequently insisted upon by businessmen to dispense with the necessity, in case of suit, of proving presentment and notice of dishonor.

Notice of dishonor may be waived, either before the time of giving notice has arrived or after the omission to give due notice. The waiver may be express or implied. Express waivers may be oral or written. What constitutes an implied waiver is a question of fact.

Mere knowledge by an indorser of a maker's actual or prospective inability to pay does not of itself spell out a waiver.

*Waiver implied.* The following acts would spell out a waiver when notice of dishonor had not been given: (1) Payment of instrument by indorser, in whole or in part. (2) Admission or acknowledgment of liability after maturity. (3) Indorser's agreement, before time for presentment, to collect the instrument. (4) Preventing maker or drawee from paying, as when an indorser strips a corporate maker of its assets, or where a drawer, at the indorser's request, stops payment of a check. (5) Indorsing a renewal note.

*Waiver not implied:* The Brown Corporation, by John Brown, its president, signs a note payable to "ourselves," and both the corporation and Brown individually indorse the note before delivery. Before maturity, The Brown Corporation, by Brown its president, makes an assignment for the benefit of creditors. The note is not paid at maturity. Unless notice of dishonor is given to Brown, he is not liable. As an irregular or accommodation indorser (page 159), he was entitled to notice of dishonor. His prospective knowledge of the Corporation's inability to pay and his subsequent knowledge of its default did not spell out a waiver.

When the waiver is embodied in the instrument itself, it is binding upon all parties; but when it is written above the signature of an indorser, it binds him only.

**Rights of Party Secondarily Liable Who Pays Instrument: Reissue.** When the instrument is paid by a party secondarily liable thereon, it is not discharged; but the party so paying it is remitted to his former rights as regards all prior parties. He may, if he wishes, strike out his own and all subsequent indorsements, and again negotiate the instrument, except:

(a) When it is payable to the order of a third person and has been paid by the drawer.

(b) When it is made or accepted for accommodation and has been paid by the party accommodated.

## Questions

1. How would you explain and distinguish the following terms in relation to a negotiable instrument: dishonor; protest; notice of dishonor; notice of protest?

2. When and for what purpose is notice of dishonor given? How may it be given?

3. "Where notice of dishonor is given by or on behalf of the holder, it inures exclusively to the benefit of the holder." Is this statement correct or incorrect? Explain.

4. To whom is notice of dishonor given: (a) in the case of a promissory note; (b) in the case of a bill of exchange?

5. When a party entitled to notice of dishonor is dead, to whom may such notice be given?

6. When a party has been adjudged bankrupt, or insolvent, or has made an assignment for the benefit of creditors, to whom may notice of dishonor be given?

7. Where the parties reside in the same community, what time limit does

the law place on the giving of notice of dishonor: (a) if given at the recipient's place of business; (b) if given at the recipient's residence; (c) if sent by mail?

8. Where the parties reside in different communities, what time limit does the law place for giving notice of dishonor: (a) if the notice is mailed; (b) if the notice is given otherwise?

9. Where a party holds a negotiable instrument indorsed by four prior parties, and serves notice of dishonor on the last indorser only, what right has the last indorser with respect to the other indorsers, and within what time may such right be exercised?

10. Is delay in giving notice of dishonor ever excusable under the law? Explain.

11. What is the proper place for giving notice of dishonor: (a) when a party has added an address to his signature; (b) when he has not given such address?

12. When is notice of dishonor dispensed with?

13. There are five situations in which notice of dishonor need not be given to the drawer of a bill of exchange. What are they?

14. There are three situations in which notice of dishonor need not be given to an indorser. What are they?

15. Does an instrument which waives protest have any effect on the necessity for presentment and notice of dishonor?

16. There are five situations in which the law will spell out a waiver of notice of dishonor. What are they?

17. When an instrument is paid by a party secondarily liable thereon, is the instrument discharged? Explain.

## Problems

1. Bronson draws a draft on Chase to the order of Drake, has it indorsed by Earle and Flood, and then delivers it to Drake for value. Chase duly accepts the draft, but on due date, when Drake presents it for payment, refuses to pay it. Drake now wants to know if any or all of the following parties may be Earle and Flood.

2. The indorser of an instrument adds his business address to his indorsement. Later the instrument is dishonored. The holder mails a notice of dishonor to the indorser, addressing it to the indorser's home. The indorser refuses payment, and when sued, exhibits the notice and the envelope in which it came. What would be the court's ruling, and why?

3. A bill of exchange was dishonored by non-acceptance. The drawer and three indorsers duly received notice of such dishonor. Later the holder presented the draft to the drawee for payment, which was refused. The holder, without serving further notice of dishonor, seeks to hold the drawer and indorsers. May he do so? Explain.

4.* Among the notes receivable of E.F., whose books are being examined, are two promissory notes past due. The maker of both is A.B., whose financial responsibility is doubtful. One of the notes bears the endorsement of B.C., who is known to be "good." What steps should have been taken by E.F. on the dates when each of these notes fell due to protect his rights?

5.* A received from B a negotiable promissory note for $2,500 payable on demand to the order of B and endorsed by B to the order of A. Six months later the maker of the note became insolvent. Has B any defense to an action by A against him as endorser? Explain fully.

6.* Barr and Nelson, copartners, received in the course of business a note made by Nash. Barr endorsed the note in the firm name. The note not being paid at maturity was protested by the holder and notice given to Barr. In a suit against Barr and Nelson as endorsers, Nelson defended on the ground that he had not had notice. Was his defense good?

7.** Jordan was the holder in due course of a promissory note made by *A* and indorsed by Conroy, White and Holden. This note was duly presented to the maker at maturity and payment was refused. Thereupon Jordan caused the notary public, who protested the instrument, to send written notices of dishonor to each of the indorsers. These notices were mailed in envelopes, properly addressed and stamped, to each of the indorsers, but, owing to the miscarriage of the mail, such notices were never received by any of the indorsers. In the suit brought by Jordan against the maker and each of the indorsers, the indorsers set up as a defense the fact that they had never received any notice of dishonor. Will the indorsers succeed in this defense? Give reason.

8.* The X Dress Corporation made a promissory note payable to the order of "ourselves." Brown was president of that corporation and as such he signed the note. The note was endorsed before maturity by the maker corporation and by Brown individually. Prior to the due date of the note, the X Dress Corporation made an assignment of its assets for the benefit of creditors and said assignment was executed by Brown as president. The note was not paid at maturity, and the maker corporation and Brown individually were sued. Notice of dishonor of the note had not been given to Brown. Can Brown be held as endorser?

9.*** Fox, for value, gives a promissory note to Amos and Bell, partners, who indorse the note to Cody before maturity. Fox fails to pay the note at maturity and Cody, the holder, gives notice of dishonor to Amos only. The firm of Amos and Bell had been dissolved by mutual consent before maturity of the note, which fact the holder, Cody, knew, and Amos had become financially irresponsible. The holder, Cody, seeks to recover from Bell, who disclaims liability for want of legal notice. Can Cody recover from Bell? Why?

10.* Formal notice of presentment and dishonor of a promissory note was not mailed or otherwise given to an indorser. Upon the trial of an action brought against him, the testimony showed that the indorser had said to at least one witness that the maker "is having trouble with his creditors and I don't believe he will be able to meet this note at maturity." It further appeared that the indorser had arranged with the maker a plan whereby the maker could pay the note in installments. Is the defense of lack of notice an effective bar to the action against the indorser?

11.* A corporation duly executed and issued a legally binding negotiable promissory note, on which the president of the corporation was an accommodation indorser. Prior to maturity of the note, the president initiated and conducted bankruptcy proceedings for the corporation with the result that when the note matured the corporation was without funds, its business suspended, its place of business closed, and its property in the hands of a receiver. Upon due presentation of this note, the corporation failed to pay it but no notice of dishonor was given to said indorser, who still was president. Can the president be held liable on his indorsement? What rule or principle of law is involved?

12. Coburn, a holder in due course of a promissory note made by Arthur and indorsed by Brennan, presents the note for payment, which is refused. On

---

*** Official problem, both American Institute and New York Board.

the same day, he serves notice of dishonor by mail on Brennan. Owing to a mail robbery, the notice is never delivered, and when Coburn sues Brennan as indorser, the latter sets up failure to receive notice of dishonor as a defense. Assuming that Coburn can prove that he mailed the notice in question, is he entitled to recover?

13. Atwater, an indorser of a promissory note, resides at Stamford, Conn. He has a brokerage office on Wall Street, New York City. He also maintains a residence on Park Avenue, of the same city, where he resides during the winter, although rarely to be found at such address. Atwater, on indorsing the note, added his Park Avenue address to his signature. Following presentment and default by the maker, the holder of the note serves notice of dishonor on Atwater at his brokerage office, and sends a copy to his Stamford residence. No other notice is sent. The maker is insolvent. At the time of the default, Atwater was residing at Stamford. Atwater refuses to pay the note. The holder sues and Atwater sets up improper notice of dishonor as a defense. Judgment for whom?

## PART 8. DISCHARGE

**Discharge in General.** A party primarily liable on an instrument is discharged by any act which discharges the instrument. The reverse is also generally true: An act which discharges the party primarily liable generally discharges the instrument.[34] However, parties secondarily liable may be discharged by acts or omissions which do not necessarily discharge the instrument.

**Discharge of Instrument.** A negotiable instrument may be discharged in various ways: (1) It may be paid in due course; (2) It may be cancelled or destroyed by the holder; (3) It may be renounced by the holder; (4) The principal debtor may himself become the holder; and (5) The instrument may be discharged by any act which would discharge a contract.

**Payment in Due Course.** The Negotiable Instruments Act provides that an instrument is discharged by "payment in due course by or on behalf of the principal debtor" or "by the party accommodated, where the instrument is made or accepted for accommodation." A negotiable instrument is payable in money only, unless the holder is willing to accept a check, draft, new note or other consideration.

*Renewal note.* A renewal note may be accepted in payment of the old one, but if the old note is made to stand as security for the new, it is not deemed paid until the new one is paid.

*Interest.* Unless the instrument provides for interest, no interest is payable until after due date.

EXAMPLE: A note made on January 15, due April 15, and not paid until September 15 would carry interest at the legal rate from April 15 to September 15, but not from January 15 to April 15 unless the note provided for interest.

---

[34] This does not include discharge by operation of law, as in bankruptcy or by the statute of limitations.

**Intentional Cancellation or Destruction by Holder.** The Negotiable Instruments Law provides: "A cancellation made unintentionally, or under a mistake or without the authority of the holder, is inoperative; but where an instrument or any signature thereon appears to have been cancelled the burden of proof lies on the party who alleges that the cancellation was made unintentionally, or under a mistake or without authority."

**Renunciation.** The holder may expressly renounce his rights against any party to the instrument, before, at or after its maturity. Such renunciation must be in writing, unless the instrument is delivered up to the person primarily liable on it, or unless the oral renunciation is based upon an executed consideration.

EXAMPLES:

(1) Jones executes and delivers a note to Brown. Before maturity, Brown meets Jones on the street and says, "Forget about that note. I know how things are with you, and I don't want to add financial hardship to your other troubles." Before maturity, however, Brown dies. If the executor, finding Jones' note among Brown's papers, demands payment, Jones is liable on it: The oral renunciation was ineffective.

(2) If a holder orally agrees to release an indorser on the latter's agreement to turn over valuable property to the holder, and the property is turned over and accepted, the renunciation, though oral, is valid.

**Principal Debtor Becoming Holder.** An instrument is discharged when the principal debtor becomes the holder of it, at or after maturity. If he becomes the holder of the instrument before maturity, he may further negotiate it, as if it were any other instrument, or as if he were any other holder.

*Presumption of payment.* If a past due note, indorsed by the payee but not marked paid, is found by an executor or administrator among the deceased maker's effects, payment of the note will be presumed.

**Acts Which Would Discharge Contract.** The Negotiable Instruments Law provides that a negotiable instrument will be discharged by any "act which will discharge a simple contract for the payment of money." This provision, of course, relates to situations where the rules of negotiability do not conflict with the ordinary rules of contract. Thus, fraud or duress may furnish the basis for avoidance or discharge in contract, but may be unavailing against a holder in due course. However, such acts or factors as bankruptcy, the statute of limitations, novation, or release, which would discharge an ordinary contract, would likewise discharge a negotiable instrument.

**Discharge of Parties Secondarily Liable.** As we have already noted (page 176), the liability of secondary parties on a negotiable instrument is quite different from that of a primary party. The latter is absolutely liable. The obligation is his in the first place. He incurs the debt and is unconditionally obligated to pay it. Secondary parties, on the other hand, obligate themselves conditionally. They will pay *if* the principal debtor does not. They will pay *if* proper presentment is made, and *if*, on default, due notice thereof is given them as required by law. If these conditions, or any of them, fail, secondary parties are discharged. And of course they are discharged by any act which discharges the instrument, such as those we have already considered. In addition, there are certain other acts that will discharge a secondary party, such as: (1) striking out his name from the instrument, (2) discharge of a prior party, (3) valid tender of payment made by a prior party, (4) release of the principal debtor, (5) binding extension of time to a primary party, and (6) binding agreement by a holder modifying the original agreement.

**Striking out Name from Instrument.** As noted on page 178, the holder of an instrument may strike out any indorsement not necessary to his title, and the indorser whose name is thus stricken out and all indorsers subsequent to him are thereby relieved from liability on the instrument.

**Discharge of a Prior Party.** If, in the order named, *A, B* and *C* are the indorsers of a note, a discharge of the maker by the holder would also discharge *A, B* and *C,* who have a legal right to fall back on the maker; a discharge of *A* would also discharge *B* and *C,* who have a right to fall back on *A,* and so on.

**Valid Tender of Payment Made by Prior Party.** As to parties secondarily liable, tender, if valid, has the same effect as payment.

EXAMPLE: X, the maker of a $500 note bearing three indorsements but making no provision for interest, tenders payment of $500 to the holder on due date. The holder, insisting upon interest, rejects tender. The indorsers are discharged.

**Release of the Principal Debtor.** If the holder releases the maker, he thereby releases the indorsers unless he expressly reserves his rights against them. But if, in releasing the maker, he cuts off the indorser's rights against the maker, his reservation of rights against the indorser is worthless: The law releases the indorser.

EXAMPLE: In *Spies v. National City Bank,*[35] the holder ·obtained judgment against the maker of a note. It then sold the judgment for 50% of its face amount to a dummy acting for the maker. The holder also reserved all rights against the indorser for the unpaid 50%. The legal effect of the arrangement, however, was to cut off the rights which the indorser would otherwise have had against the maker if he paid the note. The court therefore held that the indorser was discharged.

**Binding Extension of Time to Primary Party.** The Negotiable Instruments Act provides that parties secondarily liable are discharged by "any agreement binding upon the holder to extend the time of payment, or to postpone the holder's right to enforce the instrument, unless made with the assent of the party secondarily liable, or unless the right of recourse against such party is expressly reserved."

---

[35] 174 N.Y. 222.

**Binding Agreement by Holder Modifying Original Agreement.** Any binding and material modification in the original terms of the instrument made between holder and party primarily liable, without the consent of parties secondarily liable, discharges the latter. It matters not that the modified terms are more favorable to the debtor; parties secondarily liable have a right to be consulted before any agreement on which they are obligated is changed without their consent.[36]

EXAMPLE: The holder and maker of a $5,000 demand note with interest at 6% enter into a binding agreement (without the indorser's consent) reducing the interest rate to 5%. The indorser is thereby discharged.

## Questions

1. "A party primarily liable on an instrument is discharged by any act which discharges the instrument."
(a) Is the reverse of the foregoing statement also true; that is, does an act which discharges the party primarily liable also generally discharge the instrument?
(b) May parties secondarily liable be discharged by acts or omissions which will not necessarily discharge the instrument? Explain.
2. Name five ways in which a negotiable instrument may be discharged.
3. Is interest ever collectible on an instrument unless the instrument so provides? Explain.
4. If a past due note, indorsed by the payee but not marked as paid, is found by an executor or administrator among the deceased maker's effects, what presumption will the law permit under the circumstances?
5. Parties secondarily liable on an instrument are discharged if proper presentment has not been made and due notice of dishonor given. Name six other acts which will discharge a secondary party.
6. What is the effect on the liability of parties to an instrument where the holder strikes out an indorsement not necessary to his title?
7. What is the effect on the liability of parties secondarily liable, where a valid tender of payment is made, and rejected by the holder?
8. What is the effect on the liability of any indorsers where the holder releases the maker without reservation?
9. (a) What is the effect on parties secondarily liable, where an agreement is made without consulting such parties, binding the holder to extend the time of payment?
(b) Are there any circumstances under which a holder may make such an agreement and still retain his rights against parties secondarily liable?
10. What is the effect on parties secondarily liable where the holder and the party primarily liable enter into a binding agreement involving a material modification in the original terms of the instrument, without the consent of parties secondarily liable? Give an illustration.

---

[36] This is the prevailing rule in this country. "The rule in England and in Massachusetts seems to be quite the contrary, in which jurisdictions it has been held that if the alteration or modification of the contract was for the benefit of the person whose performance is guaranteed, or is not against the interests of the guarantor, the modification would not destroy the guaranty." *Katz v. Leblang,* 243 App. Div. 421, 277 N.Y. Supp. 850. See also *Gould v. Keith,* 9 Cal. App. 2d 284, 49 P. 2d 623; *Baumer v. Du Pont,* 338 Pa. 193, 12 A. 2d 566.

## Problems

1. On the maturity date of a note, the maker tenders a renewal note for an additional period of 90 days. The holder accepts the renewal date with the proviso that the old note is to stand as security for the new. The new note is not paid when it falls due and the holder now wants to know whether he can proceed against the maker on the old note with interest to date. The maker contends that the old note was discharged by the renewal note. What is your opinion?

2. A note made on January 15, due April 15, is not paid until September 15. Assuming the note says nothing about interest, can the holder collect interest and if so, for what period?

3. Hastings executes and delivers a note to Igoe. Before maturity Igoe meets Hastings on the street and says, "Forget about that note. You have troubles enough without having to worry about this note." Before maturity, Igoe dies. The executor finds Hastings' note among Igoe's papers and demands payment. Hastings wants to know if he is liable on the instrument in view of Igoe's renunciation. What do you think?

4. Alden, Barr and Crane are the indorsers of a note made by Williams. The holder, a friend of Williams, knows that Williams has had considerable financial trouble and writes him a letter discharging him from liability on the instrument. The question now arises as to the liability of Alden, Barr and Crane. How would you decide such a question if it were submitted to you for determination?

5. The indorsers on the back of an instrument are as follows: Warren Jones, Harold Kreb, Frank Lane and James Morton. Morton indorses and delivers the instrument to Timothy Nixon, who strikes out the name of Harold Kreb, the second indorser. What effect has this action on the liability of the other indorsers? Explain.

6. Cole, the maker of a $500 note bearing three indorsements but making no provision for interest, tenders payment of $500 to the holder on due date. The holder, insisting upon interest, rejects the tender. Are the indorsers in any way thereby affected?

7. The holder of a note bearing an indorsement obtains judgment against the maker. The maker, pleading poverty, receives a satisfaction of judgment and a general release, without reservations, in payment of 50% of the amount of the judgment. When the holder seeks to hold the indorser for the other 50%, the latter denies liability. In the suit by the holder against the indorser, how would the court decide? Give reasons.

8. The holder and the maker of a $500 demand note with interest at 6% enter into a binding agreement (without the indorser's consent) reducing the interest rate to 5%. Does this in any way affect the indorser? Explain.

9.* Styles made a note to Johnson dated January 1, 1924, and due April 1, 1924. The note contained no provision as to interest. The note was not paid by Styles when due but it was allowed to run until September 1, 1924, when Styles paid it. Could Johnson collect any interest?

10.* Thompson gave a promissory note, indorsed by Sherwood, to Babcock. This was a demand note for $5,000 with interest at six per cent. Later, without Sherwood's knowledge, Babcock made a valid agreement with Thompson reducing the interest rate to five per cent. Upon Thompson's failure to pay the note, Sherwood contended that he had been discharged from liability because Babcock had changed Thompson's agreement. Is his contention sound?

## PART 9. CHECKS

**Checks Distinguished from Other Drafts.** A check, as noted on page 150, is a bill of exchange drawn on a bank and payable on demand. However, certain points of difference are to be noted between checks and ordinary bills of exchange or drafts:

(a) A check, unlike bills of exchange generally, is always drawn on a bank or banker.

(b) It is not necessary that the drawer of a bill have funds in the hands of the drawee, but writing a check in such a case would be a fraud, and in most states, a crime.

(c) Checks need not be presented for acceptance (certification) and, unlike bills generally, are not usually so presented.

(d) The death of the drawer of a check revokes the authority of the bank to pay, whereas the death of the drawer of a bill does not have this effect.

(e) Laches or delay of the holder of a check in presenting it for payment discharges the drawer only in case he has sustained injury by the delay, whereas the rule is otherwise for bills of exchange.

(f) A check is not due until payment is demanded, and the statute of limitations runs only from that time. This is not true of an ordinary bill.

(g) When a check is accepted (certified) at the request of the holder, the drawer and all indorsers are discharged (page 207); presentment for acceptance by the holder of a bill of exchange does not have this effect.

(h) By accepting (certifying) a check, the drawee (bank) warrants that sufficient funds are on hand to pay the instrument, and that such funds are being set aside for such purpose (page 207); acceptance of an ordinary bill of exchange entails no such warranties by the drawee.

**Right to Compel Payment: Drawer v. Payee.** It is the drawer, not the payee, who has a right of action against a bank for refusal to pay a check. The drawer is a creditor of the bank; the payee is not. A check, unless and until it is certified, does not operate as an assignment of the drawer's funds. If the bank refuses to pay, the payee has his recourse against the drawer (page 176), and the drawer, if the refusal is unwarranted, has his recourse against the bank.

EXAMPLES:

(1) X, by fraud, gets a check for $100 from Y, payable to the order of A, then cashes the check with A, who is innocent of the fraud. Y, learning of the fraud, stops payment. Later, Y becomes insolvent. If A seeks to hold the bank, he will fail. The bank owes him nothing. The check did not operate as an assignment of Y's funds in the bank.

(2) A swindler forges the payee's name to a check, and the bank pays the check. The payee's recourse is limited to the following: He may recover the check from the bank, present it for payment, and then, if payment is refused, he

may hold the drawer. The bank may not debit the drawer's account with the amount paid to the swindler.

**Time Within Which Checks Must be Presented for Payment.** The Negotiable Instruments Law provides that "A check must be presented for payment within a reasonable time after its issue or the drawer will be discharged from liability thereon to the extent of the loss caused by the delay." The usual cause of such loss is insolvency of the bank after the check is issued and before it is presented. If no loss is caused by the delay, the drawer remains liable.

EXAMPLE: Morse gives Winter his check on the X bank. Winter holds the check for three months before presenting it for payment. In the meantime, the bank has failed. Morse, however, had withdrawn his money before the bank failed. He therefore suffered no loss because of Winter's delay, and Winter may hold Morse on the check.

The statute does not define "a reasonable time." The generally accepted rules are:

(a) If the payee and drawee bank are in the same place, the check should be presented not later than during banking hours on the next business day after receipt of the check.

(b) If the payee is in one place and the bank in another, the check should be forwarded for presentment not later than the business day after its receipt, and should be presented not later than the next business day after its receipt by the forwarder's agent.

The foregoing rules may be modified by special circumstances. In rural communities, a somewhat longer time may be allowed for presentment. Under other circumstances, a reasonable time may require exceptional diligence.

EXAMPLE: Ingle gives his check on the First National Bank to Case. An hour later Case is informed that a run has started on the bank. He immediately sends his clerk to the bank with Ingle's check. The clerk holds his place in the line until noon, then goes to lunch, after which he goes to the end of the line. At 2 P.M., before the clerk reaches the teller's window, the bank closes its doors and does not reopen thereafter. Others who took their places in the line that morning behind Case's clerk were paid while the clerk was eating his lunch. In a suit by Case against Ingle, the question whether Case would recover would depend upon whether presentment, under these special circumstances, was made within a reasonable time.

*Effect of unreasonable delay: drawer v. indorser.* Although the drawer of a check is not discharged by unreasonable delay in presentment unless he sustains loss by the delay, this rule does not apply to indorsers. Checks, unlike time paper, are not intended to go into circulation, but are issued with a view to prompt payment. If, instead, a check is negotiated, the payee-indorser and all subsequent indorsers are discharged by any unreasonable delay in presentment after the last negotiation, whether the indorsers have suffered loss through such delay or not.

*Stale checks under Uniform Commercial Code.* The Uniform Commercial Code allows thirty days as a reasonable period within which checks may be presented for payment, to charge the drawer in case of nonpayment, and seven days, to charge an indorser.[37] Moreover, under the Code, a bank is under no obligation to pay a check presented more than six months after its date, but may do so and charge its customer's account if it acts in good faith.[38]

**Certification of Check: Effect of.** Certification of a check corresponds to the acceptance of a bill. It makes the drawee bank primarily liable to the holder, who otherwise has no claim upon the bank (page 205). Like any other acceptor, the certifying bank not only engages to pay the instrument according to its terms, but guarantees the genuineness of the drawer's signature and his capacity and authority to draw the instrument. Certification, however, goes further than an ordinary acceptance; it warrants that funds on deposit are sufficient to pay the check and are being set aside for such purpose.

The bank indicates certification by writing or stamping upon the check such words as "Certified," "Accepted," "Good," or words of similar import, usually accompanied by the date.

Certification constitutes an equitable assignment of the drawer's funds, which are charged accordingly.

If the bank fails after certification and before payment, its assets are impressed with a trust in favor of the payee to the amount of the check, and the payee has a corresponding preference.

**Holder v. Drawer Procuring Certification.** Where the *holder* of a check procures it to be certified, the drawer and all indorsers are discharged from liability. Where the *drawer* of a check procures it to be certified, he remains liable thereon; and if the bank fails or refuses to pay, the drawer may be held for the amount of the check.

EXAMPLE: A creditor gets two checks from his debtor on a Saturday morning before Labor Day. One of the checks has been certified at the behest of the debtor; the creditor has the other check certified later that morning. The following Tuesday morning the bank fails to open and goes into liquidation. The creditor may hold the drawer on the first check, but as to the second, the drawer is discharged.

The foregoing rule will be inapplicable wherever the new Uniform Commercial Code is adopted: the Code does away with the distinction between certification at the request of the drawer and at the request of the holder. The drawer is relieved of liability in either situation.[39]

---

[37] U.C.C. Sec. 3-503.
[38] U.C.C. Sec. 4-404.
[39] U.C.C. Sec. 3-411.

**Effect of Refusal to Certify Check.** On principle, it would seem that refusal to certify a check should constitute dishonor and render the drawer liable to the holder, because the drawer of a bill guarantees that it will be accepted. Under the Uniform Negotiable Instruments Act, the provisions applicable to bills are applicable to checks unless otherwise provided, and the statute does not otherwise provide. Yet several leading cases have held that a bank's refusal to certify does not constitute dishonor; that the holder may not on that account proceed against the drawer; that as a matter of right, a check is presentable for payment only; and that a bank has no obligation under the law to certify a check, but that its only obligation is to pay it.[40]

**Authority to Certify.** The authority of a bank to certify checks is customarily vested in the cashier. The directors of a bank have no power, merely by reason of their being directors, to certify checks so as to bind the bank, unless the bylaws give them such authority. "The president, the cashier, and, according to some authorities, the teller may, by virtue of their positions, bind the bank by certifying checks when presented to them in due course of business; and it has been held that the authority of one certifying a check for the bank might be shown by evidence of a course of dealing as between himself, his principal, and the bank's customers." [41] However, the authority of an officer to certify checks does not extend to checks drawn by himself.

**Certification of Overdraft.** Where a bank mistakenly certifies an overdraft, an innocent holder thereof may collect, but not the depositor himself, who remains liable for such overpayment.

EXAMPLE: In *Rankin v. Colonial Bank*,[42] plaintiff was given two checks drawn on defendant bank. He took one to the main office of the bank where it was certified, and then took the second check to a branch office where the teller, not knowing of the certification of the first check which had made the account too short to meet the second, certified the second check. It was held that where the second check had not passed out of the plaintiff's hands and no third parties were involved, the bank was liable for certification only up to the amount of the actual balance.

**Certifying Raised Checks and Raising Certified Checks.** When a bank certifies a raised check, or when a check is raised after certification and is then paid, the bank can recover, because the bank is not bound to know the handwriting or genuineness of the filling up of the check, but only the signature of the drawer.

**Stopping Payment.** The drawer of an uncertified check can stop payment at any time before the bank's acceptance (certification), and the bank is bound by such revocation and has no right to pay the check after

---

[40] *Wachtel v. Rosen*, 249 N.Y. 386, 164 N.E. 326; *National Produce Bank of Chicago v. Dodds*, 205 Ill. App. 444.
[41] 7 C.J. 706.
[42] 31 Misc. 227, aff'd 60 App. Div. 629.

being thus notified. If it does pay the check after proper notice to stop payment, the bank is liable to the drawer, but the drawer in such case is liable to the holder for the amount of the check unless he has a valid defense against the holder.

If the bank pays a check before the regular banking hours, and the drawer immediately thereafter (but before banking hours) notifies the bank to stop payment, the bank is liable to the drawer, because he had a right to stop payment at any time before due presentment and payment, and there was no *due* presentment and payment.

**Payment of Check after Drawer's Death.** The death of a drawer automatically revokes any outstanding drafts upon his account with a bank. However, a bank is not liable for payment of a check after the drawer's death if it had no reasonable opportunity to ascertain the fact of such death. In some states, banks are given a period of grace after a depositor's death within which they may honor his checks though they know him to be dead.

**Right to Recover Proceeds from Payee.** When a bank pays a decedent's check to the payee, the bank's immunity does not cover the payee. The fact remains that death automatically revoked the decedent's order on the bank. The check itself did not operate as an assignment of the decedent's funds (page 205). Though payment by the bank under these circumstances does not render the bank liable to the estate, such payment, made without the authority of an existing drawer, remains unauthorized, subject to recovery by the estate. Of course, if the check was given in payment of a legitimate claim against the decedent, such claim, unpaid by the drawer while alive, would remain a legitimate claim against the estate, and could be set off against any claim by the estate for the amount of the check. If, on the other hand, the check was issued through fraud or mistake, or for inadequate consideration, or for a consideration that failed (page 166), or for no consideration at all, the estate would have a right to recover the proceeds, just as the drawer, had he lived, could have rightfully stopped payment.

EXAMPLE: X gives his favorite nephew a check for $5,000 as a graduation gift. The following morning, before the check is presented for payment, X dies. If the bank, unaware of X's death, pays X's check when the nephew presents it, the bank is not liable to X's estate, but the nephew is. The check was not a gift of $5,000, but of an order for that sum, and the order, or check, did not constitute an assignment of the funds (page 205), hence the gift lacked the essential of delivery (page 655, subd. d) and was revocable either by the drawer before death or by his estate after his death.

**Check Delivered to Impostor.** Where a drawer delivers an instrument to an impostor whom he believes to be someone else, he must bear the consequent loss as between himself and either the drawee or a *bona fide* holder, since the impostor obtained the money by fraud but not by forgery. (See page 169, "Indorsement by impostor *v.* indorsement by thief or swindler.")

EXAMPLES:

(1) An impostor, posing as Dorne, a creditor, obtains a check from Cole drawn on the Metropolitan Bank and payable to cash. He cashes the check at the bank and then disappears. As between Cole and the bank, Cole must stand the loss: he intended to deliver the check to the person who stood before him though he was mistaken about the impostor's identity.

(2) Suppose the imposter had negotiated the check to an innocent tradesman for value, and the latter was unable to collect the check because Cole had stopped payment in the meantime. In such case the tradesman could collect the amount of the check from Cole.

(3) Suppose the impostor, purporting to represent a charity, got a check from Cole payable to the order of *A*, then cashed it with *A*, who was innocent of any fraud, then disappeared. If *A* sought to hold Cole on the check, Cole's defense of fraud would be good as against *A*, because *A* would not be a holder in due course, but an immediate party (the payee). If *A* sought to hold the bank instead of Cole, his suit would likewise fail, since the bank would be under no duty to *A*.

(4) Suppose the impostor, purporting to represent a charity, got a check from Cole payable to the order of the impostor, who then indorsed and cashed it with *A*, an innocent third party. *A* could hold Cole if the bank refused payment, since fraud (in the inducement) is no defense against a holder in due course (page 167, subd. "e").

**Duty of Depositor to Examine Statements and Vouchers.** When banks furnish depositors with statements of their accounts and supporting vouchers, it is the duty of the depositor to examine them without unreasonable delay and to object to any item that he may consider incorrect. If he fails to do this, the account will be deemed correct in the absence of fraud or concealment. A depositor is not concluded by such statements or vouchers as to matters which he cannot reasonably be expected to know. For example, a depositor in most states is not required to ascertain whether *indorsements* are genuine or false; he is not presumed to know, and in fact seldom does know, the signature or indorsement of the payee.

What constitutes an unreasonable delay by the depositor is a question of fact. The statute may fix a depositor's deadline in such cases. For example, the New York statute[43] provides: "No bank shall be liable to a depositor for the payment by it of a forged or raised check, unless *within one year* after the return to the depositor of the voucher of such payment, such depositor shall notify the bank that the check so paid was forged or raised." The New York statute goes further, and establishes a *two-year* deadline as to forged *indorsements* in the case of checks drawn on banks.[44] The Uniform Commercial Code extends the deadline to three years, though the depositor may become liable to the bank, regardless of the

---

[43] Negotiable Instruments Law, sec. 326.
[44] Negotiable Instruments Law, sec. 43.

lapse of time, if he has been negligent in discovering and reporting such forgeries.[45]

**Check Altered through Drawer's Negligence.** We have already noted (page 170, subd. b (2), "Negligence inviting alteration") that when a person in drawing an instrument leaves blank spaces so negligently as to invite alteration and justify the holder in assuming that the filling in was regular and authorized, a maker or drawer may be liable to a holder in due course if the instrument is wrongly altered. When the drawer of a check has prepared it so negligently that it can be altered easily without giving a suspicious appearance and the bank, following alteration, pays the check, the drawer may be prevented by his own negligence from recovering against the bank. This does not mean that a check must be so drawn as to make it impossible for a wrongdoer to tamper with it. As the court said in a leading case: "Now, while the drawer of a check may be liable where he draws the instrument in such an incomplete state as to facilitate or invite fraudulent alterations, it is not the law that he is bound to so prepare the check that nobody else can successfully tamper with it." [46]

**Indorsement of Corporate Checks.** A corporation may authorize any officer or employee to indorse on its behalf checks payable to its order. However, such authority to indorse cannot be enlarged or extended; for example, authority to indorse restrictively (page 158) does not imply authority to indorse in blank (page 158). Thus if a corporate employee with authority to indorse restrictively, cashes corporate checks for his own use by indorsing in blank, the corporation is not bound and may recover the amounts thus cashed. "Any person taking checks made payable to a corporation, which can act only by agents, does so at his peril and must abide by the consequences if the agent who indorses the same is without authority, unless the corporation is negligent * * * or is otherwise precluded by its conduct from setting up such lack of authority in the agent * * *." [47]

EXAMPLE: In the Corn Exchange Bank case just cited, Standard Steam Specialty Company authorized its stenographer to indorse and deposit incoming checks by stamping them, "Pay to the order of the Greenwich Bank. The Standard Specialty Co." followed by the words in her own handwriting, "Percy H. Pinder, Treasurer." The stenographer instead indorsed numerous incoming checks wholly in her own handwriting, "Standard Steam Specialty Company, Percy H. Pinder, Treasurer." She also indorsed her own name thereon, then cashed these checks with various merchants and kept the money.

[45] U.C.C. Sec. 4-406 (a).
[46] *Critten v. Chemical National Bank*, 171 N.Y. 219. See also *Laseter v. Hill*, 218 Ala. 240, 118 So. 252, denying *certiorari*, 22 Ala. App. 485, 118 So. 250; *Greenfield Savings Bank v. Stowell*, 123 Mass. 196, 25 Am. R. 67; *Herington Bank v. Wangerin*, 65 Kan. 423, 70 P. 330, 59 L.R.A. 717; *Fordyce v. Kosminski*, 49 Ark. 40, 3 S.W. 892, 895; *Holmes v. Trumper*, 22 Mich. 427, 435.
[47] *Standard Steam Specialty Co v. Corn Exchange Bank*, 220 N.Y. 478.

The merchants deposited these checks in their own bank (Corn Exchange Bank), which ultimately paid out the proceeds to the merchants. In sustaining a suit against the Corn Exchange Bank to recover the proceeds of these checks, the Court said: "The business man who authorizes his clerk to take his checks to his bank for deposit does not vest in her so dangerous a power as to preclude him from setting up her lack of authority if she indorses his name thereon in blank and innocent persons cash the checks for her without inquiry."

**Issuing Fraudulent Checks, Drafts or Orders.** Penal statutes commonly provide that if a person knowingly issues a check, draft or order against insufficient or nonexistent funds in a bank, he is guilty of a misdemeanor; and if he obtains money or property thereby, he is guilty of larceny and punishable accordingly.

## Questions

1. There are at least eight points of difference between checks and ordinary bills of exchange or drafts. How many can you name?

2. "Where a bank refuses to pay a check, either the drawer or the payee may bring suit against the bank for such refusal, if unwarranted." Is this statement wholly true, wholly false, or partly true and partly false? Explain.

3. What does the Negotiable Instruments Law provide with respect to the time within which a check must be presented to the bank for payment? What is the penalty for a failure to present the check within such time?

4. Do conditions and circumstances, such as the nature of a community, have any bearing upon the rule governing the time within which checks should be presented for payment? Explain.

5. What is the effect of an unreasonable delay in presenting a check for payment, (a) upon the drawer, and (b) upon an indorser?

6. What is the nature and effect of the certification of a check, and what constitutes such certification?

7. What difference does it make, from the standpoint of the liability of parties concerned, whether the holder or the drawer procures certification of a check?

8. What are the usual officers of a bank vested with authority to certify checks? Have the directors of a bank, as such, the power to certify checks?

9. Where a bank mistakenly certifies an overdraft, may an innocent holder collect on the check? If such check is paid to an innocent holder, what effect does this have on the liability of the depositor?

10. What is the legal position of a bank which has (a) certified a raised check; (b) paid a check which was raised after certification?

11. When may the drawer of an uncertified check stop payment on the instrument? What is the effect if a bank pays such check after receiving notification to stop payment on it?

12. "A bank is always liable for the payment of a check after the drawer's death." Comment on the legal validity or invalidity of this statement.

13. Explain the duty of a depositor with respect to the examination of a bank statement and return vouchers.

14. State the rule with respect to checks altered through the drawer's negligence.

15. What is the usual penal provision (a) where a person knowingly issues

a check against insufficient or non-existent funds; (b) where he obtains money or property thereby?

## Problems

1.** *A* sold to *B* a case of dry goods and accepted *B*'s check in payment therefor. The check was drawn on the Overseas National Bank and was in due course presented by *A* for payment. Although there were sufficient funds in the bank to pay the check, the bank refused payment without giving any reason. Can *A* enforce the collection of the check against the bank? Give reasons.

2.* *A* delivered his check to *B* for $150 in payment for a horse and later gave notice to the bank on which it was drawn not to pay it. What are *B*'s rights (a) against the bank and (b) against *A*?

3.* Ingle gave a check for $142 drawn on the First National Bank of the town of *X* to Case, who received it on the morning of November 19, 1930. Case sent his clerk to the First National Bank, on which a run had started at 9 A.M. The clerk took his place in line, which he held until 1 P.M. when he left and went to lunch. Upon his return he took his place at the end of the line, but the bank stopped paying at 2 P.M., before the clerk had reached the paying teller's window, and the bank did not reopen thereafter. Other persons who took places in the line after the clerk had joined it in the morning had their checks cashed. Ingle had sufficient funds in the bank to meet all checks drawn by him. Can Case recover in an action against Ingle?

4.* In counting the cash in a mill office you find as part of the cash checks which have been received from customers subsequent to the last bank deposit, which was made a week prior to your visit. The checks are drawn on various widely scattered banks, including the mill's own bank, which is three miles away on a trolley line.

(a) What does the law require the holder of checks to do?

(b) What danger, if any, may this mill incur in the collection of these checks when it makes its next deposit?

5.** *A* draws a check payable to *C* who indorses to *D* 500 miles away. *D* indorses the check to *X* in the same place. All the parties act promptly except *X* who deposits the check three days after its receipt in a local bank, which forwards it to the drawee's bank. In the meantime the drawee has failed and afterwards declares dividends amounting to 50%. *X* brings suit to recover. Will he recover and why?

6.* Andrew J. Morse drew a check on the *A.B.* Bank to the order of Samuel Winter in payment for goods purchased. Winter held the check more than three months before presenting it for payment. During that time the *A.B.* Bank failed. Morse had, however, withdrawn his deposits before the failure. Was Morse released from liability on the check?

7.** *A* gave his check payable to order of cash to *X* in the sum of $300 for goods sold and delivered. *X* immediately rushed to the Butchers Bank on which the check was drawn and had it certified. A week later the Butchers Bank became bankrupt, and *X* was unable to collect anything on the check. *X* tells *A* that he can have the check back, and that *A* should give him cash for the goods sold. *A* refuses to do this and *X* sues *A* for $300. How would you dispose of the case? Explain.

8.** *A* is the payee of a certified check of which *X* is the drawer and which has been certified by the bank at the instance of *X* before delivery. One day after the check is issued *A* indorses it to *B*, who presents it to the bank for payment on the day on which he receives it. An hour before *B* arrives at the bank, the bank has closed its doors due to insolvency. What are the rights of *B* against *X*? Give reasons.

9.* *Y* gave *X* a check for $1,500 in payment of a debt. The check was drawn on the Union Trust Company. *X* had the cheque certified by the Union Trust Company. On the following day when *X* was about to deposit the check in his own bank, *X* learned that the Union Trust Company had failed at the opening of business that morning. *X* then claimed that *Y* must make good for the check. Was *X* correct in his contention?

10.** *W* gave his check for $500 to *B* drawn on *N* Bank. *B* presented the check to *N* Bank for certification, which was refused. *B* immediately sued *W* to recover $500 without putting the check through for collection in the regular way. (a) Can *B* recover? Give reasons. (b) Was *N* Bank obliged to certify the check when it was presented for certification? Give reasons.

11.** Henry Green, who is a cashier of the Springtown National Bank, draws his individual check against his own account in the bank, and then certifies it as cashier. Can the holder of such a check enforce it against the bank? Give reason for answer.

12.** Jones, in order to take up an out of town draft, draws his check on the bank for the required amount, although his balance in the bank, subject to check, is less than the amount needed. The bank by mistake certifies the check. Can the bank collect the amount of the overdraft from its depositor? Give reasons.

13.** A bank certified a check that had been altered by changing the date and the name of the payee, and by raising the amount. Then subsequently the bank paid the check on presentation. Shortly after having paid the check the bank sued for the amount thus paid. Can the bank recover? Or does the certification of the check amount to a warranty of the genuineness of the body of the check, as well as of the payee and amount?

14.** Green drew his check to Jones in payment of merchandise purchased. Jones, in order to obtain an additional amount of money, raised the check after it had been certified. He then induced Black to cash the check at the increased amount. Has the bank any right to recover against Black? Explain.

15.** When a bank pays a check drawn upon it, to the holder thereof, before the regular hour for the beginning of business, and the drawer of the check immediately thereafter, though before the hour for the opening of business, requests the bank not to pay the check, is the bank in any way liable to the drawer?

16.* *X* represents to *Y* that he is soliciting money for a charity and succeeds in getting *Y* to draw a check payable to *X* for $100. *X* indorses the check to *A*, an innocent third party, who has no notice of any defenses. *X* receives from *A* for the check $100, which *X* keeps. *X*, as a matter of fact, did not represent the charity. After the check has passed to *A*, *Y* learns that he has been defrauded by *X*, and he therefore stops payment on the check. The bank on which the check is drawn does not pay the check when it is presented by *A*. *A* sues *Y* on the check, and *Y* defends on the ground that the check was originally obtained from *Y* by fraud. Is the defense valid?

17.* In the preceding question assume that *Y*, after the transactions mentioned and before suit is filed, becomes insolvent so that it will be futile for *A* to try to collect anything from him. If such were the case, could *A* recover from the bank on which the check was drawn?

18.* *A* opened an account with the *X* Trust Company in November, 1919, by a deposit of $75,000. On December 29, 1919, the bank paid out of the account

$5,000 on a check on which *A*'s signature had been forged. On January 2, 1920, *A* receipted for a statement of the account by the bank and for eighteen vouchers or canceled checks attached thereto, one of which was the forged check. Since *A* customarily delegated to his secretary the work of examining statements and keeping the check-book, the forgery was not immediately discovered. In March, 1921, the forgery was discovered by *A* through the report of the bank of an overdraft of the account. The bank refused to make good on the forged check and *A* sued. Did the bank have any defense?

19.** *K*, the drawer of a check on the West Side National Bank, prepares it negligently so that it can be easily altered. Alterations are made by raising the check from five dollars to sixty-five dollars. Can *K* recover from the bank by notifying it within a year? If so, why? If not, why not?

20.** *A* has an ordinary checking account in a bank, with a credit balance of $2,000. He owes *B* $1,000 and gives him a check for that amount on the bank, which the bank declines to pay.

(a) Among *A*, *B* and the bank, who then is indebted to whom?

(b) Give reasons for your answer.

21.** Shortly before the close of banking hours on Saturday before Labor Day, a creditor receives from his debtor two checks, one of which has been certified before its delivery to the creditor. Certification of the other check is secured by the creditor but too late for the deposit of either check in the creditor's bank until after Labor Day. At this time the bank on which both checks were drawn does not open for business and has been taken over by the Banking Department.

State the position of the creditor with regard to each check, giving reasons therefor.

22.* A certified public accountant who had completed his professional work for an out-of-town corporate client, delivered his report to the president of the corporation in the latter's office. The president thereupon told him that the corporation's check for his fee would be given to him in half an hour and that the accountant could have it certified on his way to the railroad station, or, if the accountant preferred, a check already certified would be given to him in three-quarters of an hour. Disregarding entirely all matters of personal convenience, which offer should the accountant accept?

23.* The legal holder of a properly drawn check presented it to the bank on which it was drawn and demanded that the bank certify it, which the bank refused to do. At no time was the check presented for payment, but, within what would have been a reasonable time for such presentation, the holder formally notified the drawer that certification had been refused and demanded that the drawer pay the amount of the check. On the facts stated, must the drawer immediately pay the holder?

24.* On a Saturday afternoon, *X* signed a check for $7,000 and gave it to the payee as a gift. On the next day, *X* was killed in an accident. On the following Monday morning, the payee cashed the check at the bank on which it was drawn, said bank having neither actual nor constructive notice of *X*'s death.

(a) Can *X*'s estate recover from the bank the amount of this check?

(b) Can *X*'s estate recover the amount of it from the payee?

## COURT CASES FOR REVIEW

### How Did the Court Decide, and Why?

1. Suit was brought against the signers of the following instrument:

Dolls. 166 51/100                                        Brooklyn, Aug. 13th, 1903.
   Three months after date we promise to pay to the order of Wm. Kerby one hundred & sixty-six 51/100 dollars at the Union Bank, value received & interest.

Andrew Ruegamer, Jr.,<br>
Daniel W. Moore,<br>
Leon Raunheim,<br>
"As Trustees, etc.

Defendants pleaded that they signed in behalf of creditors, not as individuals, and proved on the trial that plaintiff knew defendants were acting for certain creditors. Judgment went for defendants and plaintiff appealed. *Kerby v. Ruegamer*, 107 App. Div. 491, 95 N.Y. Supp. 408.

2. The Village of Itasca was indebted to the plaintiff. Plaintiff's agent presented notes at the regular meeting of the Village Board of Trustees. In the presence of plaintiff's agent, the Trustees, by a motion duly passed, authorized the Village President and Clerk to sign the notes for the Village. The President and Clerk thereupon signed the notes in their representative capacities. Plaintiff thereafter brought suit against the President and Clerk personally, on the ground that they were not the duly authorized agents of the Village. Defendants claim that only the Village is liable, or, if the motion conferred no power to bind the Village, then the notes are a nullity. *Greenlee v. Beaver*, 334 Ill. App. 572, 79 N.E. 2d 822.

3. The Reimann Mfg. Co. authorized its officers to execute and deliver a promissory note. The note was indorsed as follows:

Reimann Furniture Mfg. Co.<br>
Rich L. Reimann<br>
L. D. Reimann.

After maturity, the note was sold and assigned to plaintiffs. Suit was commenced against the corporation, which made no appearance, and also against the two Reimanns. Defendants Reimann allege that they signed the instrument in a representative capacity for the defendant corporation, not with any intention of assuming personal liability. *Murphy v. Reimann Mfg. Co.*, 183 Or. 474, 193 P. 2d 1000.

4. Defendant's superintendent fraudulently prepared requisitions for supplies, and induced the defendant to draw several checks against them, payable to the order of fictitious payees. The superintendent then indorsed the checks in the names of the fictitious payees, and cashed them with plaintiff. On learning the facts, defendant stopped payment on the checks, and the plaintiff brought suit. *Hillman v. Kropps Forge Co.*, 340 Ill. App. 606, 92 N.E. 2d 537.

5. Cecelia Donohoe gave her son Richard the following note, the italicized portion being in Mrs. Donohoe's handwriting:

$13,070.86                                                    August 30th, 1910
   *I, Cecelia W. Donohoe,* after date, *August 30th,* promise to pay to the order of *Richard Donohoe, Thirteen Thousand and Seventy Dollars and 86/100* Dollars without defalcation, value received, *with interest at 6%* . . . Witness *my* hand seal.
   (Seal)

Hester Johnson,<br>
Notary Public

The contention was that the note was not signed by Cecelia Donohoe and hence was not enforceable. *In re Donohoe's Estate*, 271 Pa. 554, 115 A. 878.

6. The Snyder Planing Mill Company agreed to erect a barn for Lightner at a contract price of $3,500, but was adjudged a bankrupt before it completed the barn. Lightner had to complete the barn at his own expense. Prior to the bankruptcy, the Planing Mill had drawn two drafts on Lightner, one for $1,000 and one for $1,500. Both drafts and Lightner's acceptances were identical except as to the amount and date. The one for $1,500 read as follows:

Hutchinson, Kansas, Aug. 10, 1903.

G. W. Lightner, Offerle, Kansas—Dear Sir: Pay to the order of the First National Bank of Hutchinson, Kansas, on account of contract between you and the Snyder Planing Mill Co. $1,500.

The Snyder Planing Mill Co.
Per J. F. Donnell, Treas.

Accepted. G. W. Lightner

The drafts were discounted with the First National Bank of Hutchinson. Lightner refused to pay these two drafts on the ground that the Planing Mill had not completed its contract and the balance due it was considerably less than the amount of the two drafts. The bank, claiming to be a holder in due course, contended it was not subject to such defense. Lightner contended that the bank was not a holder in due course because the draft was non-negotiable, since (1) no specific time of payment was mentioned, and (2) the order, based on a transaction referred to in the draft, was conditional. *First National Bank of Hutchinson v. Lightner*, 74 Kan. 736, 88 Pac. 59.

7. Davis and his wife executed a $4,000 promissory note, secured by a deed of trust on their home, to Turley Mortgage Company, a mortgage broker, which was to sell the note to the New York Life Insurance Company and turn the proceeds over to Davis and his wife. Turley Mortgage Company negotiated the note to defendant bank instead, and Davis and his wife received nothing. The bank knew nothing of the true purpose of the note. In a suit to enjoin the bank from foreclosing the trust deed on their home, Davis and his wife contended that the bank was not a holder in due course because the note was not negotiable, since it contained the following provision: "Upon breach of any promise made in this note or in the deed of trust securing it, at the option of the holder the entire indebtedness hereby evidenced shall become due then or thereafter as the holder may elect regardless of the date of maturity. Notice of the exercise of such option is hereby expressly waived." *Davis et ux. v. Union Planters National Bank & Trust Co. et al.*, 171 Tenn. 383, 103 S.W. 2d 579.

8. A father conveyed 115 acres of land to his son, subject to a life estate in the father. The son then made and delivered the following note:

For value received I promise to pay Elizabeth Gamble, or order, the sum of fifteen hundred dollars in twelve months after I shall become the legal owner of one hundred and fifteen acres of land conveyed to me by my father, H. V. Davis, reserving to him, H. V. Davis, a life estate in said land, by which at his death I am to become possessed of and the owner in fee of said one hundred and fifteen acres, situated in the southeast corner of section 30, in township 18 north, range 11 east of the third P.M., Champaign County, Illinois.

Emmons Davis.

In a subsequent suit on this note, defendants contended that the instrument was not a negotiable promissory note, because it was not payable at a fixed or determinable future time, but on the contingency of acquiring title to land, which might never occur. *McClenathan v. Davis,* 243 Ill. 87, 90 N.E. 265.

9. Plaintiff, having farmed land belonging to his father, received the following note:

$500.00                                                                                                                  June 14, 1932
For services rendered Value received I promise to pay Henry C. Meyers five hundred dollars one year from date with 6 per cent interest from date until paid.

Three years later the father died without having paid the note. Plaintiff sued the father's estate. The lower court found in favor of the estate, which contended that past consideration would not support such an instrument. Plainiff appealed. *Meyer v. Meyer,* 379 Ill. 97, 39 N.E. 2d 311.

10.

Bellville, Texas, September 9, 1944, No. 5333. This certifies that Will J. Jackson has deposited with the First National Bank of Bellville 4,400 Dol's 00 cents. Dollars $4,400.00, payable to the order of himself or Maggie Reese in current funds on the return of the certificate properly indorsed, 6 months after date with interest at the rate of 1 per cent per annum. No interest after maturity. (signed) H. O. Fisher, V.P. and Cashier.

Jackson died intestate prior to the maturity of the above instrument which he had kept under his exclusive control. Maggie Reese claims that Jackson agreed that she was to be paid the deposit in case of his death. The heirs of Jackson claim that this is a negotiable certificate which forms a part of Jackson's estate. *Reese v. First Nat. Bank of Bellville,* 196 S.W. 2d 48 (Tex. Civ. App.).

11. A written instrument recited:

Having been cause of a money loss to my friend Geraldine H. Hickok, I have given her three thousand dollars. I hold this amount in trust for her, and one year after date or thereafter on demand I promise to pay to the order of Geraldine H. Hickok, her heirs or assigns, three thousand dollars with interest.

The note was signed by the obligor. The exact nature of this instrument was the subject of this suit. *Hickok v. Bunting* 67 App. Div. 560, 73 N.Y. Supp. 967.

12. The payee of a note indorsed and transferred it to another in consideration of the latter's promise to pay the payee the amount of the note. As evidence of the transferee's indebtedness to the payee, he indorsed the note with the following words: "I hereby assume and agree to pay the principal of the within note," and signed such indorsement. Later the question was raised whether such indorsement itself constituted a promissory note payable on demand. *Clarke v. Marlow,* 20 Mont. 249, 50 P. 713.

13. Plaintiff surrendered certain stock to decedent, receiving from the latter an instrument containing the following words: "Good for $1,000 . . . for ten shares Kinloch Jockey Club stock surrendered to the undersigned . . . by the owner of said stock, J. Kessler and for which I am liable. Joseph D. Lucas." The question arose whether this instrument constituted a promissory note. *Kessler v. Clayes,* 147 Mo. A. 88, 125 S.W. 799.

14. Before signing an order for goods, defendant signed certain notes for the purchase price. While these notes lay on the counter and during the defendant's temporary absence, the seller's agent took them. A dispute having arisen, and suit having been brought on these notes, defendant contended that the notes had not been issued. *Sheffer v. Fleischer,* 158 Mich. 270, 122 N.W. 543.

15. The maker of a note delivered it to his servant for delivery to the payee. The servant delivered it to the payee, but the maker had died in the meantime. The question then arose whether the maker's estate was liable on the note. *Daggett v. Simonds*, 173 Mass. 340, 53 N.E. 907.

16. Harry C. Witte made the following instrument:

Albany, New York, Jan. 13th, 1931

November 1st, after date We promise to pay to the order of Harry C. Witte, Two Thousand Five Hundred Dollars ($2,500.00) at the Central Bank of Albany, New York, with interest.

Value received.

Harry C. Witte, Inc.
By: Harry C. Witte, Pres.

Before maturity, Witte indorsed the note as follows: "I hereby assign all my right and interest in this note to Richard Fay in full, Harry C. Witte," and negotiated the instrument to Fay for a valuable consideration. The note was thereafter protested for non-payment, and due notice thereof given to Witte, who refused to pay. Suit followed. The lower court found that Witte's "assignment of the note" constituted an indorsement without recourse. Fay appealed. *Fay v. Witte*, 262 N.Y. 215, 186 N.E. 678.

17. Defendants arranged for work to be done by a plumbing concern. To finance payment, they made arrangements for an FHA loan. They signed a note in which the amount, date, and monthly installments were left blank, and delivered the note to their plumber, who brought it to the bank, where the cashier completed the note in conformity with the terms of defendants' written loan application, and paid the plumber the face value of the note after the plumber had indorsed it. Defendants refused to pay the note on the ground that the plumber fraudulently completed and negotiated it before completing the agreed work. The bank sued. *First Nat. Bank of Springfield v. Di Taranto*, 9 N.J. Super. 246, 175 A. 2d 907.

18. On January 11, 1946, defendants issued two checks for $3,006.90 each, drawn on a Missouri bank, payable to the order of L. B. Silver, a licensed broker, who was instructed to deposit the checks in a bank to pay for two carloads of grapes. Silver received the checks on January 12, 1946. On January 14, 1946, he was drawn into a gambling game known as "crap shooting," in the course of which he indorsed and delivered the foregoing checks to one S. Elder for money lost in the game. On January 15, 1946, the checks were indorsed to the plaintiff, who had no knowledge of the way Elder got the checks. On the same day defendants, learning the facts, stopped payment on the checks. In the suit which followed, defendants claimed that the transfer of the checks was illegal, hence that no title passed either to Elder or to the plaintiff; also that plaintiff acquired the checks after they were past due and no longer negotiable. *Alchain v. Fadles*, 240 Mo. App. 610, 212 S.W. 2d 78.

19. Katz delivered eight negotiable bonds to plaintiffs, a firm of stockholders, to sell for his account. Plaintiffs sold the bonds and credited the purchase price to Katz's account. Thereafter the bonds were returned to plaintiffs as stolen, though the purchasers had acquired them without notice of this fact. The bonds were immediately exchanged for like bonds of unquestionable title, in accordance with the rules of the New York Stock Exchange. The defendant insurance company claimed the stolen bonds because it had paid the loss to the owner following the theft, and the plaintiffs claimed the stolen bonds because they had replaced them with like bonds of unquestionable title. *Gruntal v. U.S. Fidelity & Guaranty Co.*, 254 N.Y. 468, 173 N.E. 682.

20. Bruce Redding, desiring to purchase plumbing supplies, made out a check for $500 to the order of Herman T. Hymowitz. He gave the check to Hymowitz, who indorsed it in blank, laid it on his desk, and went into a back room to telephone the bank on which the check was drawn. Told that Redding's check was "no good," he returned to find that Redding had taken the check and left the store. Later, Redding appeared at plaintiff's store, introduced a man as Hymowitz, and cashed the check. Plaintiff, as holder of the check, now sues Hymowitz on his prior indorsement. *Gimbel Bros. v. Hymowitz,* 160 Pa. Super. 327, 51 A. 2d 389.

21. Plaintiff signed her name on a blank check drawn on defendant bank. The check was stolen, and the amount of $250 was inserted, together with a date and the name of a fictitious payee. The check was then indorsed in the name of the fictitious payee and cashed at plaintiff's bank, which debited plaintiff's account accordingly. Plaintiff insists that the bank had no right to charge her account with the amount of a check that had never been delivered. *Weiner v. Pennsylvania Co. for Insurance,* 160 Pa. Super. 320, 51 A. 2d 385.

22. Gaines was an agent for the plaintiff, a money-lending concern. He sent plaintiff a list of 32 persons, representing that their applications for loans had been duly approved. Plaintiff drew checks on defendant bank aggregating $4,953.57, payable to the persons named on the list, and delivered the checks to Gaines. Actually, the names on the list were fictitious. Gaines forged the names of these non-existing payees, indorsed his name on each check, and cashed the checks. Thereafter plaintiff sued the drawee bank to recover the amount of the checks. *Citizens Loan & Security Co. v. Trust Co. of Georgia,* 79 Ga. App. 184, 53 S.E. 2d 179.

23. Moore purchased a truck from Deaton and gave Deaton his check for $1,550 drawn on the Sulphur Springs State Bank. Deaton deposited the check in the plaintiff bank, which permitted Deaton to draw out the money the same day. The next day Deaton asked Moore to pay him the face value of the check, stating that he had not drawn any money against it, but had deposited it for collection. As proof, he exhibited a deposit slip, with the words "For Collection" written across its face in lead pencil. Deaton suggested that Moore could give him the cash and stop payment on the check, which Moore did. In due course the check, having been forwarded through regular banking channels, was returned to the plaintiff bank marked "Payment stopped." Plaintiff now sues Moore on the check. *First Nat. Bank of Quitman v. Moore,* 220 S.W. 2d 694 (Tex. Civ. App.).

24. Defendant signed and delivered to Bennett a check for $800 drawn on the Peoples Bank, as the purchase price of an automobile. Bennett indorsed the check in blank and cashed it at the plaintiff bank. On learning that Bennett did not have title to the car, defendant stopped payment on the check. Plaintiff bank, claiming the right of a holder in due course, demanded that defendant pay the amount of the check. Defendant refused on the ground that he had a right to stop payment on the check; that plaintiff bank should have accepted the check for collection only, and that the loss was due to plaintiff's negligence in not doing so. *Bank of Fort Mill v. Rollins,* 217 S.C. 464, 61 S.E. 2d 41.

25. The defendant was treasurer of the Domestic Furnace Co. which purchased most of its materials from the Fox Furnace Company. Customers of the Domestic Furnace Co. were in the habit of signing promissory notes for the amount of their purchases. These would then be indorsed in blank by the Domestic Furnace Co. and defendant, and delivered to the Fox Furnace Co. as supplier. Plaintiff became the owner of twelve such promissory notes, each indorsed by defendant. The notes were defaulted, and suit was brought against

defendant, who claimed that he was induced by an officer of the Fox Furnace Company to sign his name on the back of the notes solely because they wanted to keep his name and address on record for identification. Defendant contended that his indorsement was thus procured through fraudulent representations to the effect that he, defendant, was not thereby making himself personally liable on the notes. *Heating and Plumbing Finance Corp. v. Braun,* 76 N.E. 2d 920.

26. Bill Boyd purchased two automobiles from Ray Rudolph and paid for them with a check and cash. The check was drawn on the Dees Bank. It was presented by Rudolph to the Bank of Marshall County. The cashier of the latter bank telephoned the drawee bank, ascertained that Boyd's account was sufficient to pay the check, and cashed it. The cashier, however, neglected to have Ray Rudolph, the payee, indorse the check. The check, with stamped notation, "All prior endorsements guaranteed," was forwarded back through several intermediate banks to the Dees Bank, where it was marked "Paid" and charged to Bill Boyd. When Boyd discovered that the automobiles had been stolen, he brought suit for the amount of his check, against the Dees Bank and the other banks through which the checks had passed. From a judgment in favor of Bill Boyd, the Bank of Marshall County now appeals. *Bank of Marshall County v. Boyd,* 308 Ky. 742, 215 S.W. 2d 850.

27. Defendant issued and delivered his check for $700 to a person purporting to be Wallace Gross, in payment for a car. Upon apparent identification and a telephone call to defendant verifying the issuance of the check, plaintiff cashed the check. Thereafter, defendant stopped payment, alleging that the indorsement was made by an impostor and not by the payee named in the check. *Greenberg v. A & D Motor Sales,* 341 Ill. App. 85, 93 N.E. 2d 90.

28. Defendant made a note for $198.55 to Aviation Industries Inc. in payment for tuition at the payee's aviation school. The note was purchased by plaintiff for $129.06. Suit was instituted on defendant's default. The defense was an alleged failure of consideration and that plaintiff obviously was not a holder in due course in view of the price paid for the note. The lower court concluded that the plaintiff was not a holder in due course because of disparity between the face value of the note and the price paid for it, and that the defense was available against plaintiff. Plaintiff appeals. *Credit Adjustment Co. v. McCormick,* 198 Okl. 348, 178 P. 2d 610.

29. Defendant gave plaintiff, his fiancée, a $5,000 promissory note as a present. Plaintiff put the note in a safe-deposit box. Upon the engagement being broken, plaintiff sued defendant on the note. *Suske v. Straka,* 229 Minn. 409, 39 N.W. 2d 745.

30. Defendant agreed to purchase a bar dispensing unit from Economizer Products, Inc. He gave a promissory note which recited that in the event any of the terms and conditions of a conditional sales contract which accompanied the note were not fully complied with, the note, at the option of the holder, became due and payable without demand and notice. The note was indorsed by Economizer Products, Inc. to plaintiff, for value. At the time the note was executed, defendant was insane, but not legally adjudicated as such. The unit was never used, and defendant had offered to return it. Plaintiff sued on the note. *Hillsdale Nat. Bank v. Sansone,* 8 N.J. Super. 497, 73 A. 2d 362.

31. Defendant lost his job as an insurance salesman. Through an error, his salary checks were mailed to him for nineteen months after his employment terminated, and he cashed each check. Upon discovery of the overpayments, plaintiff threatened defendant with civil suit and criminal prosecution. Defendant sent a note to the plaintiff in repayment of the checks. He made several

payments on the note until the statute of limitations on the original claim had run, then refused to make any more payments. Plaintiff brought suit on the note for the unpaid balance. Defendant now alleges lack of consideration and duress, and counterclaims for the payments already made. *Prigmore v. Hardware Mut. Ins. Co. of Minn.*, 225 S.W. 2d 897 (Tex. Civ. App.).

32. During a period of shortage and delayed deliveries, William Huson represented to plaintiff that he could obtain a new automobile for him from defendant. Plaintiff gave Huson as a downpayment, a check for $600.00 payable to defendant's order. Huson gave the check to defendant in part payment of his own personal debt to the latter, stating that the money had been loaned to him for that purpose. When plaintiff inquired as to the delivery date of his new car, these facts came to light, and plaintiff sued defendant for moneys had and received. *Alpert v. City Motor Sales,* 194 Misc. 909, 90 N.Y. Supp. 2d 479.

33. Hunter was indebted to plaintiff, a loan organization, which held a chattel mortgage on his car. He agreed to sell the car to defendant. He therefore went with defendant to plaintiff's office to secure a release from plaintiff, and to substitute defendant as debtor on the car. Plaintiff released Hunter and transferred the automobile to defendant, who executed a chattel mortgage from defendant to plaintiff, securing a note made by defendant to Hunter, and indorsed by Hunter to plaintiff. Two days later, the car left the road and was demolished. Plaintiff, as holder in due course, now sues defendant on his note, and defendant denies that plaintiff is a holder in due course, because of (1) plaintiff's participation in the transaction, and (2) inherent defects in the automobile. *Citizens Loan Corp. v. Robbins,* 40 So. 2d 503 (La. App.).

34. On October 23, 1946, Therrien, an impostor, sold a car to defendant, a used car dealer, which gave Therrien a check for $1,200, post-dated to October 25, 1946, to allow time for checking Therrien's title. The day after the sale defendant discovered that the automobile was stolen, and stopped payment on the check. The impostor changed the "5" in "October 25" by drawing a line in a different color ink through the numeral "5," to make it resemble the numeral "8," thereby changing the date of the check to October 28, 1946. He then cashed the check with the plaintiff. Plaintiff, claiming that he is a holder in due course, sues defendant on its check. *Medeiros v. Fellsway Motors, Inc.*, 326 Mass. 656, 96 N.E. 2d 170.

35. Plaintiff's bookkeeper, whose duty it was to make out checks for the payment of bills, prepared a batch of checks payable to various dealers with whom the plaintiff did business, and presented them to one of plaintiff's officers for signature. The bookkeeper included in the batch a check drawn to "Swift," corresponding to "Swift & Co.," one of the dealers. After the checks were signed, the bookkeeper removed the spurious check to "Swift," inserted an initial so that the payee became "C. Swift," a fictitious name, which he indorsed, then wrote in his own name and cashed the check at defendant bank, on which the check was drawn. Plaintiff's account with the bank was debited accordingly. Plaintiff brings suit against the bank to recover the amount of the check. *Gutfreund v. East River Nat. Bank,* 251 N.Y. 58, 167 N.E. 171.

36. Defendant, a private New York banker, received a letter which purported to come from Marsh, an Army officer who was at a hotel in Washington, and which requested defendant to discount pay vouchers for himself and another officer named Shipton. Defendant ascertained that there were such officers, and that they were regularly stationed as stated in the letter. He wrote Marsh that he would discount the vouchers. He received the vouchers and sent checks for the amounts, one to the order of Marsh in his official capacity,

and another to the order of Shipton in his official capacity. The checks were sent to the Washington Hotel, each in an envelope addressed to the recipient in his official capacity. The checks were collected through a Washington Bank which guaranteed the indorsements. The person receiving and signing the checks proved to be an impostor. Plaintiff bank sued on a note given by defendant and defendant counterclaimed for the Marsh and Shipton checks which he claimed should not have been charged to his account because they were indorsed and collected by an impostor. *Mercantile National Bank v. Silverman,* 148 App. Div. 1, 132 N.Y.S. 1017, aff'd 210 N.Y. 567, 104 N.E. 1134.

37. An impostor stole an automobile from Heinz Rettig along with Rettig's registration certificate and operator's license. He displayed these papers to plaintiff who then bought the automobile for $1,450, and received a check drawn on defendant bank, payable to Heinz Rettig. Using the same registration and license papers for identification, the impostor presented the check to defendant bank, which cashed the check and debited plaintiff's account. Plaintiff sues defendant to recover the amount of the check, on the ground that it was the bank's duty to pay the check only to the true owner of the automobile, Heinz Rettig. *Santa Maria v. Industrial City Bank & Banking Company,* 326 Mass. 440, 95 N.E. 2d 176.

38. John Gilreath, employed with a manufacturing company, had access to funds. When an alleged shortage was discovered, a criminal charge was lodged against him, and he was indicted by the grand jury. The plaintiff, a bonding corporation, was surety for the manufacturing company. Through its agents, negotiations were conducted with the brothers of John Gilreath. Defendant, one of the brothers, was assured by plaintiff's agents that the matter could be disposed of if John Gilreath executed a promissory note and the brothers indorsed it. The agreement was that the brothers would be bound only if the plaintiff should succeed in securing a dismissal of the criminal charge. Plaintiff attempted but failed to have the charges dismissed. Suit on the note followed. *Liberty Mut. Ins. Co. v. Gilreath,* 191 S.C. 244, 4 S.E. 2d 126.

39. The Sweet Coal Company drew a negotiable trade acceptance on defendant, payable to itself. Defendant accepted the instrument and returned it to the Sweet Coal Company, which sold the instrument to plaintiff bank, by indorsement, "For Deposit Only, Sweet Coal Co. of Utah, by V. W. Sweet, Pres." The bank sued defendant on the instrument. Defendant contended that plaintiff was not a holder in due course because of the restrictive indorsement, and set up failure of consideration as a defense, based on non-delivery of the goods for which the trade acceptance was given. *Continental Nat. Bank & Trust Co. v. Stirling,* 65 Idaho 123, 140 P. 2d 230.

40. On September 19, defendant drew a draft on the Cairo Cotton Oil Mill, Inc., as drawee, payable at sight to the Liberty Central Trust Company, and on the same day deposited the bill with the Liberty Central Trust Company and received credit thereon. The Liberty Central Trust Company indorsed the bill the same day and sent it to plaintiff bank. Plaintiff received the draft two days later, which was on a Friday morning, called the drawee over the telephone, and was informed that the bill would be paid. Friday had been declared a holiday by the Mayor of Cairo. Plaintiff bank was therefore closed at noon that day, and at noon on Saturday. The following Monday plaintiff bank, not having received a remittance from the drawee, telephoned again and was informed by the drawee that it would not pay the draft. Plaintiff caused the draft to be presented by a notary at the drawee's office, where payment was refused. The bill was duly protested and notice of protest given. Defendant drawer now argues that the act of the plaintiff in telephoning the drawee on

Friday constituted an election to make presentment in such manner and at such time; that such presentment was insufficient; that thereby defendant drawer was discharged; and that, having been discharged, defendant drawer's liability could not be reinstated by any subsequent act of plaintiff. Plaintiff conceded that the telephone communication on Friday was not a legal presentment, but insisted that it was entitled to a reasonable time after negotiating the draft within which to make presentment, and that defendant drawer was not discharged until after plaintiff had failed to make such presentment within a reasonable time. *Cairo National Bank of Cairo, Illinois v. Blanton Co.*, 287 S.W. 839 (Mo. App.).

41. Defendant drew four trade acceptances on Capital Park Building Company, as drawee, payable to "ourselves." The drawee accepted the instruments on presentation. Defendant indorsed the trade acceptances in blank and transferred them to the Olympia National Bank. The bank failed before the trade acceptances fell due. Its affairs were taken over by the Comptroller of the Currency. The trade acceptances were never paid. About six years later they were sold to plaintiff, who sued on them. Defendant set up as a defense that it was never served with any notice of protest or of the failure of the drawee-acceptor to pay the acceptance on due date. *Legal Discount Corporation v. Martin Hardware Co. et al.*, 199 Wash. 476, 91 P. 2d 1010.

42. During the course of a building operation, the general contractor became indebted to a subcontractor, who in turn was indebted to a materialman. The subcontractor drew a written order on the contractor directing him to pay a specified sum of money to the materialman. The order or draft when presented by the materialman for payment was refused by the contractor. There was no question, however, that the contractor owed the money to the subcontractor. Suit on the draft followed in due course. *Wisconsin Lime, etc., Co. v. Lelivet*, 182 Ill. App. 436.

43. In response to an inquiry as to whether a bank would pay a check drawn on it by Elliott in a certain sum, the bank replied, "Elliott has deposited with us $1,790.00 to pay check drawn by him." The bank later denied that it had accepted the check. *Elliott v. Ft. Stockton First State Bank*, 135 S.W. 159 (Tex. Civ. App.).

44. The payee of a note deposited it with a bank, which indorsed it and sent it to another bank in another state for collection. Upon default, the latter, by its agent, sent notice of dishonor to the first bank, and in the same envelope, in care of the first bank, enclosed a notice of dishonor addressed to the first indorser, which the first bank received but neglected to send to the first indorser for several weeks thereafter. The first indorser claimed that on these facts he was discharged from liability. *Vaughan v. Potter*, 131 Ill. App. 334.

45. William E. Neal, payee on a note, indorsed and transferred it to plaintiff before maturity. After default, plaintiff's attorney wrote to Neal's law firm, stating that the note was due and unpaid, and that they were commencing suit against Neal and the makers. Other than this, plaintiff had had no personal contact with Neal or the makers. Neal's defense is (1) failure of presentment, and (2) insufficient notice of dishonor. *Aisted v. Grim*, 35 Wash. 2d 883, 215 P. 2d 877.

46. On the day an instrument fell due the holder, knowing that the instrument would be dishonored on presentment, served notice of dishonor and shortly thereafter, on the same date, presented the instrument for payment, when the instrument was in fact dishonored. Notice of dishonor was challenged

as insufficient under the circumstances. *Pierce v. Cate*, 12 Cush. (Mass.) 190.

47. A note fell due on Saturday in a city having no postal delivery. The notary, being unable to gain admittance to the indorser's house because the latter was away from home, mailed the notice, and it was received by the indorser on the following Tuesday. The question arose as to whether the notary had used due diligence as a matter of the law in giving the indorser notice of non-payment. *Lenhart v. Ramey*, 2 Oh. Cir. Ct. 135.

48. At the solicitation of a trust company which was promoting an insurance company, defendant subscribed to stock in the insurance company and gave the trust company a demand note in payment for the subscription, depositing the insurance stock with the trust company as collateral. Subsequently the trust company, through its president and treasurer, agreed to take back the stock in satisfaction of the note. Defendant assigned the certificate of stock in blank and handed it over to an officer of the trust company. Two years after its date, the note was transferred by the trust company to a subsequent transferee, who sought to hold defendant on the note. *Carrington v. Turner*, 101 Md. 437, 61 A. 324.

49. The indorsers of a bill of exchange held by a bank claim discharge thereon by virtue of the fact that the drawer gave the bank a stock of merchandise, which the bank accepted, to be applied pro-rata toward the discharge of the drawer's debts. The goods were actually sold by the bank and the proceeds applied pro-rata toward the extinguishment of the drawer's obligations. *Ford v. Decatur Branch State Bank*, 6 Ala. 286.

50. The payee of a check put it in the hands of a bank for collection. The drawee bank, upon receiving the check by mail, marked it "Paid," sent a draft to the collection bank for the amount of the check, and surrendered the check to the drawer after charging the item to his deposit account. The drawee bank failed, and its draft was dishonored. The question then arose as between the drawer and the payee, whether the drawer's obligation to the payee had been discharged under the circumstances. *O'Leary v. Abeles*, 68 Ark. 259, 57 S.W. 791.

51. Plaintiff was given two checks drawn on defendant bank. He took one to the main office of the bank, where it was certified, and then took the second check to a branch office where the teller, not knowing of the certification of the first check (which had made the account too short to meet the second), certified the second check. The second check being still in the plaintiff's hands, and payment thereon having been refused, plaintiff brought suit against the bank on its certification. *Rankin v. Colonial Bank*, 31 Misc. 227, 64 N.Y. Supp. 32, aff'd 60 App. Div. 629, 69 N.Y. Supp. 1144.

52. Standard Steam Specialty Company authorized its stenographer to indorse and deposit incoming checks by stamping them, "Pay to the order of the Greenwich Bank. The Standard Specialty Co.," followed by the words, in her own handwriting, "Percy H. Pinder, Treasurer." The stenographer indorsed numerous incoming checks wholly in her own handwriting, "Standard Steam Specialty Company, Percy H. Pinder, Treasurer," under which she indorsed her own name, then cashed these checks with various merchants, and kept the money. The merchants deposited these checks in their own bank (Corn Exchange Bank), which ultimately paid out the proceeds to the merchants. Plaintiff sued the Corn Exchange Bank to recover the proceeds of these checks. *Standard Steam Specialty Co. v. Corn Exchange Bank*, 220 N.Y. 478.

# 4

# Sales

**Scope of This Chapter.** In this chapter we summarize the nature and elements of sales and contracts to sell personal property, the requirements of the statute of frauds governing sales, the question of when title passes, the warranties, express and implied, that go with a sale, the remedies available to seller and purchaser, and the more important legal aspects of installment selling, particularly those related to conditional sales, chattel mortgages and trust receipts.

## PART 1. NATURE AND ELEMENTS

**Modern Trends in Buying and Selling.** The pattern of business law is nowhere more nicely cut to the needs of the market place than in the law of sales. Essentially, business is concerned with producing, buying and selling the millions of things men need and want. With the vast expansion of business has come a vast acceleration in the exchange of goods. With this advance has come a steady improvement in business standards. *Caveat emptor,* "Let the buyer beware," is no longer a safe guide. In the law of sales, as in other branches of business law, a more enlightened business code has slowly but surely been making itself felt. New business techniques, new forms of credit, new types of secured transactions have brought forth new statutes and new judicial rulings governing the purchase and sale of merchandise and personal property generally. It is as important that we should follow these changing rules, adapted to changing conditions, as that we should understand the basic rules making up the law of sales.

**Law Governing Sales: Uniform Sales Act; Uniform Commercial Code.** Up to 1954, all but ten states had adopted the Uniform Sales Act which formulates the rules governing sales of personal property. On all matters not covered by the statute, the rules of the common law apply. (See pages 5 and 19.) In addition to the Uniform Sales Act, various other uniform statutes, more or less allied to the subject of sales, have been adopted by various states; notably, a Uniform Conditional Sales Act, a Uniform Stock Transfer Act and a Uniform Bills of Lading Act. In another decade, it is likely that the latest uniform legislation on sales and other branches of commercial law, namely, the Uniform Commercial Code,[1] will have found its way to the statute books of most of our states.

**Sale v. Contract to Sell.** The Uniform Sales Act distinguishes between a sale and a contract to sell as follows:

"A *sale* of goods is an agreement whereby the seller *transfers* the property (title) in goods to the buyer for a consideration called the price."

"A *contract to sell* goods is a contract whereby the seller *agrees to transfer* the property (title) in goods to the buyer for a consideration called the price."

The distinction is between an actual present transfer (sale) and an agreement to transfer in the future (contract to sell). The former is sometimes called an *executed sale*, and the latter, an *executory sale*.

*Importance of distinction.* The distinction between a sale and a contract to sell may become important. A sale of "future goods" (page 229) passes no title; it merely operates as a contract to sell such goods. A sale vests immediate title in the buyer, including the benefits and risks of ownership.

**Absolute v. Conditional Sale.** An absolute sale is one where the transfer of title is complete and unqualified. The buyer becomes the absolute owner. A conditional sale is one where the transfer is subject to a condition. This may be a condition precedent, as where title does not pass (although possession may have passed), until the buyer first complies with certain conditions, such as the payment of the full purchase price, etc. Or it may be a condition subsequent, as where title passes to the buyer, subject to the seller's right to reclaim the title, if certain conditions are not complied with.

**Voluntary v. Involuntary Sale.** A voluntary sale is one made by or under the authority of the owner. An involuntary sale, also referred to as a forced or judicial sale, is one made pursuant to law and regardless of the owner's wishes; as, for example, in the case of a sheriff's sale, an executor's sale, a guardian's sale, or a sale under foreclosure. Under a voluntary sale, the owner impliedly warrants that he has title. Under an involuntary sale, no warranty of title is implied.

**Sale, Exchange and Gift Distinguished.** A sale is the transfer of title to personal property for money; an *exchange*, or *barter*, is the transfer of title in one chattel for title in another. The Uniform Sales Act governs both sales and exchanges.

A sale is distinguishable from a gift in two respects. (1) A sale involves the transfer of title, but not necessarily an immediate transfer of possession; a gift is invalid without an immediate transfer of possession. (2) A sale necessarily involves a consideration, or price; the essence of a gift is a transfer without consideration. (See page 655.)

---

[1] See pages 893-903.

**Sale v. Bailment.** A sale or exchange involves the transfer of title, a bailment the transfer of possession. Hence if I give you iron ore in exchange for pig iron to be smelted from that ore, the transaction is a bailment because I retain title throughout; but if you may give me *any* pig iron for my ore, I part with title to the ore in exchange for pig iron, and the transaction is an exchange. (See page 284.)

**Sale v. Consignment.** A sale transfers title with or without immediate possession. A consignment transfers possession, either (a) for the purpose of shipment or transportation, or (b) for the purpose of sale. In (a), the parties involved are the *shipper* and *carrier*, and the rights and obligations of the parties are governed by the law of *carriers*. In (b) the parties are known as *consignor* and *consignee*, and the rights and obligations of the parties are governed by the law of *agency* and of *sales*.

In the ordinary case, a consignee is the agent of the consignor in the sale of goods. Since he does not own the consignment, he is liable for conversion (page 803) if he uses the proceeds; but since he is authorized to sell, an innocent purchaser for value gets title, regardless of what the consignee does with the money.

**Divisible v. Indivisible Contract of Sale.** The distinction between entire and divisible contracts has already been pointed out (page 84). A sale or a contract to sell calling for a single delivery, or a single, lump-sum price, would be construed as entire, or indivisible, though it contained a large assortment of items. On the other hand, a sale or a contract to sell is divisible if it has separate and distinct parts and creates separate and distinct obligations; as, for example, when a vendor sells, under the same contract, a horse, a cow and an automobile, involving different delivery dates and separate prices for each item.

**Essentials of Sales Transaction.** The essentials of a sales transaction correspond to those of any other contract, whether executed (as in a sale) or executory (as in a contract to sell). There must be (a) parties having capacity to contract, (b) consideration (price), (c) subject matter (possessing not only validity, but actual or potential existence), and (d) mutual assent (including intent to pass title). With respect to these essentials, the Uniform Commercial Code embodies substantial changes in line with modern practice. Some of these have already been noted in the chapter on Contracts (pages 38, 60, 83 and 111).[2]

**Price.** A sale without price is ineffectual. The price may be fixed or "fixable"—that is, the parties may agree on a definite basis for determining the price in the future—for example, the market price on a given day, or a price to be fixed by an arbitrator, umpire, or other third party. But a contract which provides that the parties are to agree on a price later is

---

[2] See also pages 893-903.

unenforceable, because the minds of the parties have not completely met.[3]

EXAMPLE: The National Chemical Company gives the Agricultural Improvement Company a memorandum confirming that the former has sold to the latter 2,500 pounds of powder for a selective weed-killing solution "at a price to be determined between us, subject to market fluctuations, to be not less than $4.65 a pound in the event of decline, nor more than $4.85 in the event of advance." Such transaction constitutes neither a sale nor a contract of sale, since it lacks the essential of an ascertained or ascertainable price.

If a contract merely says nothing about price, the law presumes that the parties intend a reasonable price. Such price, being ascertainable, renders the contract enforceable.

**Existence of Subject Matter: "Future Goods."** "Future goods" are goods which are not yet in existence, or which the seller does not yet own. Such goods, as stated, cannot be the subject of a present or executed sale (page 227). Future goods are included in the designation "unascertained" goods, which are distinguishable from "specific" goods in determining when title passes. (See pages 238-240.)

The Uniform Sales Act provides that "Where the parties purport to effect a present sale of future goods, the agreement operates as a contract to sell goods."

EXAMPLE: "The Champion Chain Corporation hereby sells its entire output for the next three months, a guaranteed minimum of 500 tons, at $585 a ton, to Universal Chain Co., Inc." Such transaction would be construed, not as a sale, but as a contract to sell.

**Potential Existence.** Despite the Uniform Sales Act provision that there can be no *present sale* of goods not in existence, the doctrine of "potential existence," long recognized at common law, still prevails in many states in respect to the natural growth or increase of things owned by the seller. Thus, a farmer who owns a peach orchard may sell, *now*, the next crop of such orchard: title to the peaches passes automatically when the crop comes into existence. But where there is not even potential existence, no title can pass either under a present sale, or a contract of sale: the buyer's remedy, should the seller default, is to sue for the breach.

EXAMPLE: John Low, about to sail on a fishing voyage, signed an agreement to sell his expected catch to plaintiff at 5¼ cents a pound, and received $1,500 on account. During the voyage, John Low went into bankruptcy, and defendant was appointed receiver. On the schooner's return, plaintiff, claiming title to the fish caught, tendered the balance of the purchase price and demanded delivery, which was refused. The court, ruling that no title had passed, held for defendant, because "the sellers, at the time of the sale, had no interest in

---

[3] The Uniform Commercial Code provides that a reasonable price will be presumed, and the contract will be binding accordingly, even if "the price is left to be agreed upon by the parties and they fail to agree." (U.C.C. Sec. 2-305.)

the thing sold. There was a possibility that they might catch halibut; but it was a mere possibility . . . coupled with no interest."[4]

**Destruction of Subject Matter.** The Uniform Sales Act provides that "where the parties purport to sell specific goods, and the goods without the knowledge of the seller have *wholly perished* at the time when the agreement is made, the agreement is void." Similarly, the Act provides that when there is a *contract to sell* specific goods, and subsequently, before the risk passes to the buyer, the goods *wholly perish*, without fault of either buyer or seller; the contract is thereby avoided.

EXAMPLE: X, a New York dealer, buys twenty-five barrels of specially graded and packed apples from an Oregon producer, and resells them to Y under a contract specifying an agreed price on delivery at Y's place of business in New York. The apples were shipped to X from Oregon but (through no fault of either X or Y) were totally destroyed before reaching New York. Since title, at the time of loss, was still in X (the contract having specified delivery to Y), the loss falls on X. Neither X nor Y has any claim against the other, the contract in such case being void.

In case of substantial *partial* destruction, the buyer may treat the contract as avoided, or he may insist on taking title to so much as has not deteriorated or been destroyed. In the latter event, he pays the full price if the sales contract is indivisible (page 84), or a proportionate price if the contract is divisible.

**Destruction of Source of Supply.** The law distinguishes between (1) a case where a given source of supply is contemplated, and its continued existence implied, and (2) the case of a seller who merely agrees to sell, privately relying on a given source of supply, which subsequently fails him. In (1), destruction of the source of supply excuses performances; in (2) it does not. (See pages 117-118.)

EXAMPLES:
(1) A contract was made for the sale of specific bales of cotton. The cotton was destroyed by accidental fire before title had passed to the buyer. The court held that the seller was not liable to the buyer for damages for non-delivery, because the parties impliedly contemplated the continued existence of the specific bales of cotton.[5]
(2) In *Booth v. Spuyten Duyvil Rolling Mill Co.*, referred to on page 118, plaintiff agreed to sell steel caps which he expected to procure from a manufacturer whose mill was destroyed by fire before plaintiff could get his caps. The court held that the destruction of the mill did not relieve plaintiff from his obligation to deliver.

**Statute of Frauds.** We have already referred to the provisions of the statute of frauds as originally embraced within the seventeenth section of the English statute, dealing with contracts for the sale of personal property (see Ch. 2, page 85). An agreement to sell personal property ("goods, wares and merchandise"), including *choses in action* (page 652) as well

---

[4] *Alfred Low & Co. v. Pew*, 108 Mass. 347.
[5] *Dexter v. Norton*, 47 N.Y. 62.

as tangibles, of a specific value or over, is unenforceable unless in writing. The maximum value at which oral contracts of sale are permissible varies widely.[6]

*Part delivery, part payment, or sale at auction.* An oral contract to sell personalty may exceed the allowable maximum price, yet be enforceable under any of the following circumstances:

(a) Where, at the time of the contract, the buyer receives and accepts the whole or any part of the goods sold; or,

(b) Where, at the time of the contract, the buyer pays the whole or any part of the purchase price; or,

(c) Where, if the sale is by auction, the auctioneer at the time of the sale enters a memorandum in his sale book specifying the nature and price of the goods sold, the terms of sale, the name of the purchaser, and the name of the person on whose account the goods were sold.

*Several articles at different prices.* Where several articles are bought at different prices, each less than, but all together aggregating more than, the maximum price limit fixed by the statute of frauds, a writing is required if the various items are *part of the same transaction;* otherwise not.[7]

EXAMPLES:

(1) In *Bradley v. Parker,*[8] defendant went into the plaintiff's shop and bargained for various articles. No one article was of the value of £10, but the total amount of the bill was £70. Some were severed from a larger bulk, and some were marked in order to satisfy the purchaser that the same were afterwards sent home to him. The purchaser, rejecting delivery, pleaded the statute of frauds, and the shopkeeper sued. The court held that the various purchases were part of an entire transaction; that if it were not thus construed, "we should entirely defeat the object of the statute. For then persons intending to buy many articles at one time, amounting in the whole to a large price, might withdraw the case from the operation of the statute by making a separate bargain for each article."

(2) But in *Aldrich v. Pyatt,*[9] the court held that where several articles are purchased, the circumstances may show an intent to make *separate contracts.* In such a case, if the value of each article is less than the maximum prescribed

---

[6] $30 in Arkansas and Missouri; $50 in Alaska, Colorado, The District of Columbia, Georgia, Maryland, Minnesota, Mississippi, Nevada, New Mexico, New York, Oklahoma, Oregon, South Carolina, Vermont, Washington, Wisconsin and Wyoming; $100 in Connecticut, Hawaii and Michigan; $200 in Montana; $500 in Alabama, Arizona, California, Idaho, Illinois, Indiana, Kentucky, Maine, Massachusetts, Nebraska, New Hampshire, New Jersey, North Dakota, Pennsylvania, Rhode Island, South Dakota, Tennessee and Utah; and $2500 in Ohio. Oral sales are unenforceable regardless of value in Florida and Iowa. In Louisiana there is no statutory limitation up to $500, nor over that amount if the contract is provable by witnesses. Oral sales are enforceable regardless of value in Kansas, North Carolina, Texas, Virginia and West Virginia. The Uniform Commercial Code sets the maximum, in terms of *price* (not value), at $500.

[7] *Weeks v. Crie,* 94 Me. 458, 48 A. 107; *Standard Wall Paper Co. v. Towns,* 72 N.H. 324, 56 A. 744; *Wertheimer v. Klinger Mills, Inc.,* 216 Ind. 481, 25 N.E. 2d 246, 249.

[8] 2 B. & C. 37.

[9] 64 Barb. 391.

by the statute of frauds, there neeu be no writing, acceptance, or payment to make the purchases enforceable.

*Sale v. work, labor, and services.* Where goods are manufactured by the seller especially for the buyer, and are not suitable for sale to others in the ordinary course of the seller's business, the transaction is treated, not as a contract of sale, but as one for work, labor or services (to which the statute of frauds does not apply).

EXAMPLES:
(1) Order to have tailor make up a suit of clothes.
(2) Furniture ordered in particular styles.
(3) Contract to cut, shape, sew and make carpet for designated rooms.

The Uniform Commercial Code considerably relaxes the requirements of what the written memorandum must contain to satisfy the statute of frauds. The Code declares a memorandum sufficient if it (1) contains evidence enough to justify a court in holding that a contract for the sale of goods has been entered into, (2) is signed by the party to be charged, or his agent, and (3) specifies the *quantity* of goods. The *price* need not be specified.

## Questions

1. How would you distinguish between a sale and a contract to sell, and when may such a distinction become important?
2. Distinguish between an absolute and a conditional sale, and illustrate the distinction.
3. (a) Distinguish between a voluntary and an involuntary sale.
   (b) Is an involuntary sale known by any other designation?
   (c) Give four examples of such sale.
4. Distinguish between a sale and an exchange.
5. In what two ways does a sale differ from a gift?
6. Distinguish between a sale and a bailment.
7. (a) Distinguish between a sale and a consignment. (b) What two purposes may a consignment serve?
8. Distinguish between a divisible and an indivisible contract of sale, and illustrate the distinction.
9. If a contract of sale is silent as to price, is such contract enforceable?
10. "Where the subject matter of a contract has neither actual nor potential existence, the contract cannot be enforced." Is this statement (a) right, or (b) wrong, or (c) partly right and partly wrong? Explain.
11. Is it true that all contracts for the sale of personal property of a fixed minimum value are unenforceable unless evidenced by a writing? Explain fully.
12. What limit, if any, does the law place on oral contracts which primarily represent work, labor and services rather than the sale of a chattel?

## Problems

1. Hygrade Clothing Products, Inc., ships 200 bolts of woolen cloth to a clothing manufacturer subject to an agreement confirmed by an exchange of

letters: (1) that each bolt has enough material for ten suits of clothes; (2) that the manufacturing company is to make up and deliver to the Hygrade company five suits of clothes out of each bolt in certain sizes and styles; and (3) that the manufacturing company could keep the rest of the cloth as consideration for the work done. On the day the material arrives at the factory, a fire breaks out and destroys the entire plant, including the bolts of cloth shipped by the Hygrade company. The manufacturer was in no way responsible for the fire. There is no insurance. The Hygrade company sues the clothing manufacturer for the value of 1,000 suits of clothes. Judgment for whom, and why?

2. Rice, a manufacturer, and Stone, a wholesaler, of radio tubes and equipment, are intimate friends. Stone sends a written order to Rice for two gross of radio tubes, stating: "As for the price, we will leave that until we can get together." Rice ships the tubes, but Stone having changed his mind after a quarrel with Rice, refuses to accept them. Rice sues Stone. Judgment for whom, and why?

3. Suppose in the above illustration, Stone had written Rice: "As for the price, I will leave that to you. I know you will do your best to be reasonable." Would this change your answer in any way?

4. In the following cases will the court sustain the contract:
   (a) Contract for the sale of ice at a price "to net the seller not more than $1 a ton profit"?
   (b) A contract of sale wherein the price is left "to be settled by some future agreement, or to be determined by what is reasonable under the circumstances"?
   (c) A contract at the market price on a certain day?
   (d) A contract at "10¢ less than the market price on any day thereafter which the seller shall name"?
   (e) A price to be determined upon the valuation of a third party?

5. Blow, the owner of a fishing schooner, enters into an agreement with the Coastal Fisheries which recites that "in consideration of the sum of $500 hereby paid and received, the party of the first part hereby sells to the party of the second part all the halibut that may be caught by the master and crew of the schooner Nancy Ann on the voyage on which she is about to proceed." The schooner, after making a large catch of halibut, founders upon the rocks and the halibut becomes worthless. Coastal Fisheries sues to recover the money paid, and Blow defends on the ground that title to the fish having passed before the loss, such loss must fall upon Coastal Fisheries. How should the case be decided, and why?

6. The Transcontinental Truck Company agrees to sell to the Unlimited Delivery Corporation 80 trucks of a specified model for delivery within ninety days from the date of contract. Prior to the expiration of this period the Unlimited Delivery Corporation cancels the order and upon being sued, sets up the defense that the contract was unenforceable because the trucks were not in existence at the time when the contract of sale was executed. Is this a good defense? Explain.

7. Carson sells to Dawson a cargo of grain on the steamer "Advance," en route from New Zealand to Edinburgh, Scotland. The cargo, however, without Carson's knowledge, had previously been sold at an intermediate port by the master of the vessel pursuant to authority previously given him. Dawson sues Carson for breach of contract of sale. How should the court decide and why?

8. Defendants agree to sell and deliver to plaintiff 621 bales of cotton. Defendants delivered to plaintiff 460 bales of cotton. The remaining 161 bales

were accidentally destroyed by fire without fault of defendants. Cotton having risen in value, plaintiff sued to recover the increase on the 161 bales. How did the court decide, and why?

9. A farmer agrees with a dairy association to sell "the entire production of milk from my dairy at Sweetgrass Farm, containing 209 head of Holsteins and 36 head of Jerseys, with minimum 3.6% butterfat, at $3.50 per hundred-quart can." A drought followed by a sandstorm causes the loss of most of the farmer's cattle. The dairy association sues the farmer for breach of contract. Judgment for whom, and why?

10. Hubert, an automobile racer, orders a racing car of special design with particular specifications made up by him as to motor and chassis. When the manufacturer delivers the car, Hubert refuses to accept it. The manufacturer sues, and Hubert defends on the ground that the order was not confirmed by writing. Judgment for whom, and why?

11.** On the 31st day of October, 1930, an agreement was entered into by which Mr. Bacon, among other things, agreed to deliver 36,000 tons of iron ore to the Bay Iron Company, for which the company agreed to pay Mr. Bacon in pig iron, at the rate of one ton of pig iron for every eight tons of ore delivered. Was this a contract to sell? Give reason.

12. In a state where the maximum value at which an article may be purchased orally is $500, Mrs. Jones enters a department store, and buys the following articles in different departments: (1) a pair of shoes for $12.50; (2) a lamp shade for $15; (3) a television set for $300; (4) a gateleg table for $75; (5) two woolen blankets for $50; and (6) an electric washing machine for $265. Assuming that the purchases were all made on credit, and that the purchase slips signed by Mrs. Jones have been lost, can the department store hold Mrs. Jones to her purchases if she refuses to take delivery of any of these items?

13. If the following transactions are entirely oral, without payment on account or delivery in any form, can they be enforced: (1) an order to have a tailor make up a suit of clothes for $100; (2) an order to a cabinet maker to have furniture made up and delivered according to specifications; (3) an order to make up 1,000 plastic trays from a given mold, in a size and style similar to standard trays on the market, to retail at 25 cents a tray (assume a $50 minimum under the statute of frauds)?

## PART 2. PASSING TITLE

**Title v. Possession.** Title is ownership. It does not necessarily include possession, because one may have the ownership but not the right of possession; as when one pawns a ring. To "pass title" is to transfer ownership.

**Bill of Sale.** A bill of sale is a written instrument transferring title to personal property. Such instrument is merely formal evidence of the title transfer. Title may be transferred without it. A bill of sale should not be confused with a contract to sell. The latter is the agreement to transfer title; a bill of sale is the evidence of the sale itself. While not essential to the transfer of title, it is useful, and sometimes important, in disclosing the terms and conditions of the sale, time of transfer, what passes with the transfer, and other important details. Some transactions require a bill of sale for purposes of registration; for example, the sale of a motor vehicle. Form 6 is a specimen bill of sale.

## FORM 6

### BILL OF SALE

KNOW ALL MEN BY THESE PRESENTS, That I, William Marsters, residing at No. 130 Chestnut Street, in the City of Rochester, State of New York (herein called the "Seller"), for and in consideration of the sum of Five Hundred ($500) Dollars lawful money of the United States to me in hand paid, at or before the ensealing and delivery of these presents by Elmer Osgood, residing at 12 Ranier Street of the City of Rochester, State of New York (herein called the "Buyer"), the receipt whereof is hereby acknowledged, have bargained and sold, and by these presents do grant and convey unto the Buyer, his heirs, executors, administrators, and assigns all those items of furniture and household belongings located in the Seller's dwelling at 12 Ranier Street, Rochester, New York more specifically set forth in the following schedule, to wit:

*Schedule*

1 living room set, consisting of—
  1 divan
  2 club chairs
1 dining room set, consisting of—
  1 mahogany table
  6 side chairs
  1 mahogany sideboard
1 second-hand Silvertone piano

TO HAVE AND TO HOLD the same unto the Buyer, his heirs, executors, administrators and assigns forever.

And I do, for my heirs, executors, administrators and assigns covenant and agree, to and with the Buyer, to warrant and defend the sale of the aforesaid chattels hereby sold unto the Buyer, his heirs, executors, administrators and assigns, against all and every person and persons whomsoever.

IN WITNESS WHEREOF, I have hereunto set my hand and seal the 23rd day of November in the year One Thousand Nine Hundred and Fifty-four.

Signed, sealed and delivered }
in the presence of       }                    *William Marsters*
*Joan Terry*
State of New York
             ss.:
County of New York

On the 23rd day of November, 1954, before me came William Marsters, residing at No. 130 Chestnut Street, Rochester, New York, to me known and known to me to be the individual described in, and who executed the foregoing instrument, and acknowledged to me that he executed the same.

                           *John Jones*
            Notary Public, State of New York
            Residing in New York County
            N.Y. Co. Clks. No. 134, Reg. No. 2R603
            Commission expires March 30, 1957

The two major questions involved in passing title are: (a) Who may pass title; and (b) When does title pass?

## A. Who May Pass Title

**Only the Owner May Pass Title: Exceptions.** Ordinarily, only the owner may pass title. Hence if I lose my watch or a thief steals it, the finder or thief cannot pass title, even though he sells the watch to an innocent person for value. However, there are a number of situations where a vendor in wrongful possession, having neither title nor authority to sell, may nevertheless pass title. These are situations where, to quote the Uniform Sales Act, "the owner of the goods is by his conduct precluded from denying the seller's authority to sell." Such situations include, among others, the following: (1) transfer of money or bearer instruments; (2) sale by one having possession or other evidences of title; (3) sale by one having voidable title; (4) duplicate sale of same merchandise; and (5) sale by conditional vendee.

**Transfer of Money or Bearer Instruments.** Where money is transferred by one not the owner, to an innocent party who gives value for it, title to the money passes to such third party, even if the person from whom he obtained such money stole it from the true owner. The same applies to a negotiable instrument—such as a check or a promissory note—which is made payable to bearer, or indorsed in blank by the lawful holder. If the latter loses the instrument, or it is stolen from him, the thief who passes it along to an innocent third party for values, passes good title.

**Sale by One Having Possession or Other Evidences of Title.** When the owner intrusts possession of goods to an agent or dealer apparently clothed with authority to sell or to a person whose common business it is to sell, such as a factor or commission merchant (pages 389 and 418), with instructions *not to sell* except upon prior approval, or subject to further directions, or upon some other condition, a sale by such agent contrary to instructions will not prevent title from passing to a purchaser in good faith and for value. This rule of law has been confirmed by statute in most of our states. Because of the wide authority granted to factors or commission merchants in selling goods ostensibly their own but in reality belonging to others, statutes have been widely adopted to protect the title of innocent purchasers dealing with such factors. A typical law[10] provides: "Every factor or other agent, entrusted with the possession of any bill of lading, custom-house permit, or warehouseman's receipt for the delivery of any merchandise, and every such factor or agent not having the documentary evidence of title, who shall be entrusted with the possession of any merchandise for the purpose of sale, or as a security for any advances to be made or obtained thereon, shall be deemed to be the true owner thereof, so far as to give validity to any contract made by such agent with any other person, for the sale or disposition of the whole or any part of

---

[10] *New York Personal Property Law*, sec. 43 ("Factors Act").

such merchandise and any money advanced, or negotiable instrument or other obligation in writing given by such other person upon the faith thereof."

**Possession of documents or "indicia" of title.** When a person is intrusted with a negotiable document of title, such as a bill of lading or warehouse receipt calling for delivery to the order of a person whose name is indorsed on the document, or when a person is intrusted with any other evidences or "indicia" of title, such as a bill of sale or certificate of ownership, such person may pass title to an innocent purchaser in good faith and for value, though the documents or "indicia" were surrendered by the holder contrary to the owner's instructions. The owner's only recourse in such case is against the custodian who violated instructions.

**When possession not conclusive evidence of title.** Possession is only prima facie, not conclusive, evidence of authority to pass title. In some situations the true owner may rebut the presumption of title which goes with ownership. Among these situations are (a) sales on memorandum, and (b) sales by one procuring possession through larceny, trick, or the finding of a lost article.

(a) **Sale on memorandum.** In a sale "on memorandum," the court in some states refuses to bar the owner's title, even as against an innocent party purchaser.

EXAMPLE: In *Green v. Wachs*,[11] Green, a jeweller, gave Vollman, a dealer, an emerald cut diamond, which Vollman was to show his customers and sell, if possible, but only on prior approval by Green. Vollman confirmed this arrangement by a signed memorandum. He then passed the diamond on to another dealer, Cohn, who passed it on to still another dealer, Arnow, who sold it to two people named Wachs and Mann. The money paid for the stone never reached Vollman or Green. Green, standing on the signed memorandum and insisting that he was still the owner, sued Wachs and Mann for the return of the diamond. The court found for Green, holding that "even an innocent purchaser for value, such as these defendants, had no better right to the stone than did Vollman."

(b) **Possession through larceny, trick or finding.** A person who procures possession by larceny, trick or the finding of a lost article (except money or bearer instruments) cannot pass title in such article to a third party, however innocent, and regardless of value given for it by the latter.

EXAMPLES:

(1) A person representing himself to be manager of a corporation purportedly bought goods for it and sold them to an innocent third party. As a matter of fact, there was no corporation. The court held that this was larceny by trick, and no title passed thereby.[12]

(2) *A* bought an automobile from the *X* Motor Sales Co., giving in payment a check drawn on an outside bank; title and possession to pass when the check

---

[11] 254 N.Y. 437, 173 N.E. 575.
[12] *Wyckoff v. Victory*, 75 Hun. 409.

had cleared. In the meantime, *A* asked permission to use the car on a short business trip, which was granted. The check came back, but not *A*, who had left for another state, where he sold the car to *B*, who sold it to *C*. Though both *B* and *C* were innocent purchasers for value, *X* Motor Sales was allowed to recover the car from *C*.[13]

**Sale by One Having Voidable Title.** When a person acquires a chattel through fraud, his title is voidable, at the seller's option; but if, before the seller rescinds, the fraudulent buyer resells the chattel to an innocent purchaser for value, the latter gets good title notwithstanding the voidability of his vendor's title. As already noted, however, this rule would not apply to a *void* title, as in the case of a person who procures possession by larceny, trick, or the finding of a lost article.

**Duplicate Sale of Same Merchandise.** A buyer of merchandise who leaves it with the seller risks a possible resale (deliberate or by mistake) to a second buyer who, if innocent of the facts, may acquire title as against the first buyer. (The seller in such case would be liable to the first buyer for conversion.)

**Sale by Conditional Buyer.** Under a conditional sales contract (page 266), the seller transfers *possession* to the buyer, but retains *title* in himself pending final payment. If, in the meantime, the buyer resells the chattel, the second buyer acquires title as against the original owner, unless the latter has publicly filed the conditional sales agreement (page 266).

## B. When Title Passes

**Importance of Ascertaining When Title Passes.** When goods in the process of sale are lost, damaged or destroyed, the loss falls on the owner unless the other party is to blame for it. If, at the time of loss, title has not passed, the loss falls on the seller as owner; if title has passed, the loss falls on the buyer as owner. Hence it is frequently important to determine at what point in the transaction title passes.[14]

**When Title Passes: General Rule.** Title passes when the parties intend it to pass. When parties fail to express their intention as to when title shall pass, it becomes necessary to invoke rules of law. These rules are prescribed by the Uniform Sales Act.

**Specific *v*. Unascertained Goods.** The Uniform Sales Act in prescribing rules as to when title passes in the absence of express agreement, distin-

---

[13] *Packard Florida Motors Co. v. Malone*, 208 La. 1058, 24 So. 2d 75.

[14] The Uniform Commercial Code, in Article 2 dealing with Sales, substantially minimizes the importance of determining when title passes. "Each provision of this Article with regard to the rights, obligations and remedies of the seller, the buyer, purchasers or other third parties applies irrespective of title to the goods except where the provision refers to such title" (Sec. 2-401). The official Comment to this section is that the Article "deals with the issues between seller and buyer in terms of step by step performance or non-performance under the contract for sale and not in terms of whether or not 'title' to the goods has passed."

guishes between *specific* and *unascertained* goods. *Specific* or *ascertained* goods are goods selected or set aside either by the buyer, or by the seller with the buyer's consent. *Unascertained* goods are goods not yet selected or in existence, such as a lot of 500 dresses ordered by the buyer subject to his selection, or a lot of 500 suits of clothes to be made up on specifications to be furnished by the buyer.

**Passing of Title: Specific Goods.** The question as to when title passes to specific goods depends upon whether the goods are *in a deliverable state*.

**(a)** *Specific goods in deliverable state.* Under an unconditional contract to sell specific goods in a deliverable state, title passes when the contract is made, even though delivery or payment be deferred. If, however, delivery or payment is stipulated as part of the contract before the bargain is closed, title does not pass until such delivery or payment is made.

EXAMPLE: The *M* Company, a boatbuilder, selected certain mahogany lumber in the *Y* Company's yard, and bought and paid for it. The *Y* Company agreed to load the lumber on a railroad freight car. Before the *Y* Company had the opportunity to do so, the lumber was destroyed by fire without the *Y* Company's fault. If delivery on board the freight car was stipulated *after* the contract was closed, the loss would fall on the *M* Company as owner, because title would have passed on the closing of the contract to sell specific goods in a deliverable state. If delivery on board the freight car was stipulated *before* the contract was closed, the loss would fall on the *Y* Company as owner, because title would not pass until such delivery was made. In either event, if the *Y* Company had loaded the lumber on the freight car before the fire occurred, the loss would have fallen on the *M* Company as owner.

**(b)** *Specific goods not in a deliverable state.* Title to specific goods not in a deliverable state passes when the goods are put into a deliverable state; for example, title to a machine which the seller has agreed to rebuild does not pass until the seller has rebuilt the machine.

**(c)** *Goods sold "on sale or return."* Title to goods sold "on sale or return" passes immediately, but may revest in the seller at the buyer's option exercised within the time fixed in the contract, or, if no time has been fixed, within a reasonable time.

EXAMPLE: *A* buys goods from *B* on the understanding that *B* shall take back any goods unsold at the end of the season. If, during the season, the goods are destroyed by fire the loss falls on *A*, whether the fire occurred through *A*'s fault or not, since he was the owner when the fire occurred.

**(d)** *Goods sold on approval.* When goods are sold on approval, title passes when the buyer signifies his approval within the time agreed, or if no time has been agreed upon, within a reasonable time.

EXAMPLE: In August, *A* delivers a secondhand roadmaking machine to *B* on approval. No time is fixed for its return if unsatisfactory. The machine having been neither paid for nor returned by the end of the year, *A* sues *B* for the purchase price. Judgment would go for *A*. By failing to return the machine within a reasonable time, *B* signified his approval.

(e) *Fungible goods.* Fungible goods are goods consisting of a uniform mass, no part of which can be ascertained or sold except by weight or measure, such as peas, beans, oats, wheat, corn, barley, flour, wine, oil, gasoline, sand or bricks. Such goods, when sold by weight or measure, are deemed specific goods, and if they are in a deliverable state, title to them passes upon the making of the contract.

EXAMPLE: *R* buys 400 bushels of corn out of a quantity of 400 bushels owned by *M* and stored in a grain elevator. *R* pays for the corn and gets a receipt. He then gives the receipt to his agent, with an order on the grain elevator in connection with arrangements to ship the wheat the following morning. If, before the order is presented to the grain elevator company, the elevator and contents are destroyed by fire, the loss must fall on *R*, since he became the owner of the corn when the contract was made. The transaction was equivalent to a contract to sell specific goods in a deliverable state.

**Passing of Title: Unascertained Goods.** In a contract to sell unascertained goods, title passes when the goods are ascertained and "unconditionally appropriated to the contract"; that is, when the goods are definitely set aside for the buyer, or selected, marked or designated, either by the buyer, or by the seller with the buyer's consent.

EXAMPLE: A department store orders a quantity of razor blades from a jobber, with instructions that the store's trade name is to be imprinted on the blades. If, after such imprint is made, the blades are destroyed or damaged without the jobber's fault, the loss falls on the department store: title passed on the unconditional appropriation of the blades to the contract (by stamping).

**Delivery.** Though unconditional appropriation to the contract may take place without delivery, such appropriation is conclusively established when delivery actually takes place.

**Delivery to a common carrier.** Delivery to a common carrier is delivery to the buyer, because the carrier is deemed to be the *buyer's agent*, with the following exceptions: (1) when the buyer names a particular carrier and the seller ships by another; (2) when the seller is required by contract or custom to make actual delivery to the buyer; (3) when the seller is required to deliver at a particular place, as at the buyer's dock or railroad siding; (4) when the seller is required to pay the freight up to a given point, as in f.o.b. contracts (see below); (5) when the seller is required by contract or custom to make arrangements with the carrier to protect the buyer (as by declaring the value of shipment, or as in "C.I.F." contracts), and fails to do so; (6) when the seller ships a larger or smaller quantity than that ordered; and (7) when the seller reserves title, as by retaining the bill of lading.

**Goods sold by sample or description.** When goods are bought by sample, or by description (as in the case of goods ordered from a catalog), title passes when goods of the description ordered or goods corresponding to the sample are unconditionally appropriated to the contract.

EXAMPLE: A sporting goods store orders a quantity of canoe paddles from an illustrated catalog, the name of the store to be imprinted on the paddle blades. The manufacturer selects the paddles ordered from his stock, has the name of the store imprinted as requested, and is about to ship the paddles when they are destroyed by a fire for which the manufacturer was in no way responsible. The loss in such case must fall on the buyer: title had passed to him, since goods of the description ordered had been unconditionally appropriated to the contract.

**F.O.B. Shipments.** When goods are shipped f.o.b. ("free on board") at a given point, such as the shipping point, or destination, or an intermediate point, the seller pays the cost of transportation up to that point, and the buyer from that point on; and title passes upon delivery to the carrier at the point specified. However, when goods are shipped f.o.b. shipping point, "sight draft, bill of lading attached, with the privilege of examining the goods on arrival," they are not unconditionally appropriated to the contract until payment or tender of the price.

**C.O.D. Shipments.** The fact that a shipment is c.o.d. (cash on delivery) does not alter the rule that title passes upon delivery to the carrier: it merely requires payment before surrender of *possession*.

EXAMPLE: *A* ships goods to *B* by carrier instructed not to deliver without payment. The carrier negligently delivers to *B* without payment. If *B* resells to *C*, a *bona fide* purchaser for value without notice, neither *A* nor the carrier can recover the goods from *C*. Title passed to *B* on delivery to the carrier. For violating the instruction not to deliver possession without payment, the carrier is liable to *A*.

**C.I.F. Shipments.** The letters "c.i.f." mean "cost, insurance and freight." A c.i.f. contract is one for the sale and delivery of goods at a price to cover the cost of the merchandise, freight and insurance. Under a c.i.f. contract, title passes when the seller completes his contract. "Unless there is something in a c.i.f. contract to indicate to the contrary, the seller completes his contract when he delivers the merchandise called for to the shipper,[15] pays the freight thereon to point of destination, and forwards to the buyer bill of lading, invoice, insurance policy, and receipt showing payment of freight." [16]

EXAMPLE: A contract for the sale of antimony, to be shipped from Hamburg to New York, called for the following: (1) shipment—promptly from Hamburg, (2) duty—for account of buyers, (3) insurance—for account of sellers, (4) payment—net cash against shipping documents payable upon arrival of steamer, (5) no arrival, no sale. The shipment reached New York within the contract time. The invoice, freight receipt, bills of lading and other documents

---

[15] Presumably the Court refers here to the carrier, not the shipper.
[16] *Seaver v. Lindsay Light Co.*, 233 N.Y. 273, 135 N.E. 329. To the same effect: *Smith Co., Ltd., v. Marano*, 267 Penn. St. 107.

were not forwarded by the seller to the buyer but were tendered to the buyer after the goods had arrived. The insurance policies were issued to bearer "for account of whom it may concern," and were never tendered to the buyer. The bills of lading were through bills and did not contain the name of the buyer as assignee. When the antimony arrived in New York, the buyer refused to accept it. In a suit for the price, the question was whether or not this was a true c.i.f. contract, under which title would have passed to the buyer on shipment at Hamburg. The Court, in reversing judgment for plaintiff in the Court below, held: "The finding that the instrument constituted a c.i.f. contract was a conclusion of law without evidence to support it. As title to the goods was not transferred, an action for the purchase price cannot be maintained * * *." [17]

**Auction Sales.** In an auction sale title passes when the hammer falls, unless the right is reserved, under the terms of sale, to determine whether the bid shall be accepted.[18] Title passes with the falling of the hammer though the buyer is required to deposit secured notes before he can take the property away and has not done so.[19] Hence, loss of goods sold at auction, but retained temporarily by the seller under arrangement with the buyer, falls upon the buyer, the seller being a mere bailee, and the sale having been completed.[20]

## Questions

1. "A bill of sale is a contract to sell personal property." Is this statement true or false? Explain.

2. When, if at all, is a bill of sale necessary in order to pass title to personal property?

3. "Only the owner may pass title." Name five exceptions to this rule.

4. Name two exceptions to the rule that a person who is entrusted with possession of personal property is presumed to be the owner so far as concerns innocent purchasers for value.

5. What is meant by (a) "specific" goods, and (b) "unascertained" goods?

6. When does title pass: (a) to specific goods in a deliverable state; (b) to specific goods not in a deliverable state?

7. Distinguish between goods sold "on sale or return" and goods sold "on approval," with particular reference to the question as to when title passes in each case.

8. What is meant by fungible goods? Give five illustrations.

---

[17] *Cundill v. A. W. Millhauser Corporation*, 257 N.Y. 419, 178 N.E. 680. In pointing out why the contract did not conform to c.i.f. requirements, the Court said: "The contract as written did not conform to the regular c.i.f. contract form. Under such a contract, the insurance should be for the benefit of the buyer as the title passes on shipment and the risk of the voyage is on the buyer. Here the provision of the contract was 'Insurance—For account of sellers.' The terms of the contract as to payment were also in conflict with the terms of a c.i.f. contract. The contract of sale reads: 'Payment—Net cash against shipping documents payable upon arrival of steamer.' * * *. So also the words, 'No arrival, no sale,' are repugnant to the idea of a c.i.f. contract."

[18] *City of New York v. Union News Co.*, 222 N.Y. 263, 118 N.E. 635.

[19] *Forbes v. Hunter*, 223 Ill. App. 400.

[20] *Stanhope State Bank v. Peterson*, 205 Iowa 578, 218 N.W. 262.

9. What is meant by "unconditionally appropriating goods to a contract"? What is the clearest example of such appropriation?

10. When does title pass to unascertained goods?

11. When does title pass to goods shipped by common carrier? Name seven exceptions.

12. When does title pass to goods sold by sample or description?

13. When does title pass on: (a) f.o.b. shipments, (b) c.o.d. shipments, and (c) c.i.f. shipments?

14. When does title pass in an auction sale?

## Problems

1. Kraft entrusted a watch to Lake, with instructions to pawn it. Lake in turn entrusted the watch to Manson with the same instructions. Manson sold the watch to Nolan and disappeared with the proceeds. Kraft, discovering the watch in Nolan's possession, claims it. Nolan disputes the claim. How would the court decide such dispute?

2.* Miller, a diamond cutter, gave a diamond on memorandum to Falk, the written memorandum expressly providing that title was to remain in Miller until Miller approved of a sale by Falk. Falk, representing that he was the owner and without showing the written memorandum, sold the diamond to Porter for cash and then disappeared without accounting to Miller. Miller now sues Porter to recover possession of the diamond. For whom should judgment be rendered?

3. Dunn bought a two carat diamond from Church, in the name of the Elite Jewelry Shop, which he purported to represent. He then sold the diamond to Folsom, purportedly on behalf of the Elite Jewelry Shop, and disappeared with the proceeds. Folsom was unaware of the fact that Dunn had no connection with the Elite Jewelry Shop and relied on Dunn's possession of the diamond as evidence of his right to dispose of the gem. Church now seeks to reclaim the diamond from Folsom. Can he do so?

4. West sold merchandise to a dealer. The terms were supposed to be cash, but on the dealer's fraudulent representations, West let him have a bill of sale to the merchandise on ten days' credit. The dealer then sold the goods to Yates for cash. West shipped the goods to Yates but insisted on prepayment before making delivery. Yates sues West for conversion. The question now arises, did Yates acquire a good title? If you were sitting as judge in this case, how would you decide and why?

5. The Universal Motor Corporation orders fifty typewriters from the International Typewriter Exchange, Inc. Upon condition of prepayment, which is made, the Typewriter Exchange agrees to substitute *elite* for pica type on each machine prior to delivery. Before such substitution can be made, the Typewriter Exchange is adjudged a bankrupt. The Universal Motor Corporation files a claim with the trustee in bankruptcy either for the return of the prepaid purchase price, or in the alternative, for the delivery of the typewriters properly equipped. The trustee in bankruptcy insists that the Universal Motor Corporation is merely a general creditor and must take its chances with all other creditors. Who is right, and why?

6. Suppose in the previous question that the International Typewriter Exchange, Inc., instead of agreeing to a substitution of type in advance of delivery, had agreed as a condition to the contract that it would cause the substitution of type to be made within three months after delivery. Would this affect your opinion in any way, and if so, how and why?

7. The Durable Rubber Company sells the Everyday Shoe Store a quantity of rubbers with the understanding that the rubbers could be returned if they were not in all respects as represented. The rubbers were received June 20th, and the bulk of them, unsold, were returned December 8th on the ground that there had been numerous complaints by customers in respect to those which had been sold. The Durable Rubber Company sued for the purchase price. On the trial the judge directed a verdict for plaintiff notwithstanding defendant's request that the matter be submitted to the jury. Defendant appealed. What was the outcome of the appeal?

8. Peabody buys a second-hand automobile on approval for a week. Before the week has elapsed, the automobile is stolen without Peabody's fault and cannot be recovered. Upon whom will the loss fall? Why?

9. Suppose in the previous case that Peabody had bought the automobile from a friend with the following understanding expressed by the seller: "Try it for a while. If you are satisfied with the car, all right. If not, I will buy it back at what you paid for it." If the car were stolen during the first week, would your answer be the same as in the previous question?

10. The Bon Ton Dress Company sends its buyer to the Supreme Dress Manufacturing Company to make a selection of merchandise for its new store. The buyer inspects numerous garments of various sizes and styles, marking his initials on the price tags and stating to the sales representative of the manufacturing concern, "We will send for these tomorrow." Before the close of business on that day a fire breaks out without fault of the manufacturing company, destroying the entire lot of dresses selected. Upon whom must the loss fall, the buyer or the seller?

11. Marvin in New York orders 1,000 bags of coffee from Félipe Bros. in Rio de Janeiro to be shipped from Rio to New York. The coffee is duly delivered to the steamer at Rio; but it is rendered worthless during transit by salt water damage. The insurance company covering the shipment has become insolvent. Marvin refuses to accept and pay for the shipment. Félipe Brothers sue. Judgment for whom, and why?

12. Under a c.i.f. contract, a quantity of automobile parts is shipped by steamer from New York to Marseilles. The seller delivers the merchandise to the carrier, pays the freight to the point of destination and forwards to the buyer a bill of lading, invoice and receipt showing payment of freight. The steamer is lost in a fog and never heard from. The shipment was not insured, the seller assuming that the buyer had arranged for insurance and the buyer assuming that such arrangements had been made by the seller. Upon whom must the loss fall?

13. The Jefferson Fruit Exchange of New York City orders 500 barrels of apples from the Pacific Fruit Growers of Seattle, Washington, to be shipped f.o.b. Chicago. The fruit is completely spoiled en route from Chicago to New York City. Omitting the question of railroad liability, upon whom must the loss fall in the first instance, the buyer or the seller?

14. Peters attends an auction sale and bids on a radio alarm clock, which is finally "knocked down" to him for $25. Before he can pick up the clock, a fire breaks out, ultimately destroying or ruining every article in the store, including the clock. The proprietor seeks to hold Peters for the purchase price of the clock, and Peters denies liability. Who is right and why?

15. The Shady Outlet Store, owned by Samuel Fox, sells Philip Golden an ivory chess set for $60. Golden pays the purchase price and asks the proprietor to keep the set for him until he calls for it on his return from a trip on the

road. The following day the store is sold by the proprietor, including stock, fixtures, good will, etc., to Maxwell Bailey. No notice of the sale is given to the creditors. Bailey, upon taking possession, unaware that the chess set had already been sold, resells it to a customer. Thereafter Fox's creditors file a petition in bankruptcy and he is adjudicated a bankrupt. The trustee sets aside the sale to Bailey and sells out the entire stock at a trustee's sale. Assets realized for the estate amount to $980 which, after administration expenses, court costs, etc., are reduced to $300 as against total liabilities of $3,000. Upon Golden's return from the road, he learns of the facts and is told by the trustee in bankruptcy that if he will file a proof of claim, he may ultimately receive a 10% dividend on the $60 paid by him for the chess set. Golden, after ascertaining the identity and whereabouts of the second purchaser of the chess set, consults you as to his rights. What would you advise?

## PART 3. WARRANTIES

**Nature of Warranty.** A warranty, under the common law, was defined as "an express or implied statement of something which a party undertakes shall be part of a contract; and though part of the contract, yet collateral to the express object of it." If I sell you a horse, the express object of the transaction is to transfer title in the horse. However, as collateral to the express object of this contract, I may make certain statements, either before or at the time of the sale, to induce you to buy the horse. Such statements, whether made expressly, or implied by law, would constitute warranties.

**Warranty Distinguished from Condition.** Under the Uniform Sales Act, the word "condition" is used in the sense designated under the common law as a "pure condition": a stipulated contingency upon which the contract depends, without promise that the contingency shall occur. If it does occur, the parties are bound, otherwise not, though the buyer may waive the condition and accept the merchandise. To quote the Uniform Sales Act: "Where the obligation of either party on a contract to sell or a sale is subject to any condition which is not performed, such party may refuse to proceed with the contract or sale, or he may waive performance of the condition."

A warranty, on the other hand, as construed under the Uniform Sales Act, corresponds to what was known under the common law as a "promissory condition": a promise, express or implied, forming an essential part of the contract itself, and not, as in the case of a pure condition, collateral to it. Here the seller does not merely agree to perform *if* the condition happens: he promises that the condition *shall happen.*

A promissory condition may be treated as a warranty, and upon its breach, the seller is not relieved from performance, but may be held by the buyer for breach of warranty.

**Warranty v. Representation.** In a broad sense, every warranty is a representation, but not every representation is a warranty. A representation is an antecedent statement made to induce a sale or contract of sale; a warranty is part of the contract itself. A breach of warranty constitutes a breach of contract; a fraudulent representation constitutes a tort.

EXAMPLE: The owner of a typewriter, to induce a sale, stated that he had personally paid $85 for it. The bill of sale contained the following clause: "This machine is warranted to be in good working order and to be made up of its original parts. No parts have been supplied in reconditioning same." The first statement, which induced the making of the contract, was a representation; the second, a warranty.

(For further distinctions between warranties and representations, see page 48.)

**Warranty v. Guaranty.** A warranty is a statement made on behalf of one's self in connection with a sale or other transaction. A guaranty is an undertaking to answer for another's obligation, that is, to make it good if the other defaults (page 333).

**Classification of Warranties.** Warranties may be *express* or *implied*.

*Express warranty.* Basically, an express warranty is one created by words, oral or written. The Uniform Sales Act defines it as follows: "Any affirmation of fact or any promise by the seller relating to the goods is an express warranty if the natural tendency of such affirmation or promise is to induce the buyer to purchase the goods, and if the buyer purchases the goods relying thereon."

*Implied warranty.* An implied warranty is one deducible from conduct or circumstances. A warranty may also be implied in law from considerations of public policy. The most common example is a *warranty of title*. Every person impliedly warrants that he owns what he sells, with the exception of goods sold at forced or judicial sales, such as executors', administrators', auctioneers' or sheriffs' sales. Other examples of implied warranties are those in sales by sample, description, and for a particular purpose (page 249).

## Express Warranties

**Usual Scope of Express Warranty: Quality.** An express warranty usually concerns itself with *quality*, since an express warranty of *title*, as a rule, is not necessary: the law implies it. However, express warranties of title are not uncommon.

**Rules Governing Express Warranties.** From the decisions of the courts in respect to express warranties, we may gather the following rules:

1. *A warranty, to be effective, must have been intended as such.* In order that a seller may be bound by his warranty, it must appear from all the facts and circumstances surrounding the statement, that the seller's representation was intended to operate as a warranty.

EXAMPLE: Winter sells Horn a second-hand car. He rejects Horn's request for a ninety-day guaranty, but adds: "You can depend on it, the car will give you years of satisfaction." Two months later the axle breaks, and Horn sues Winter on the latter's statement as a warranty. In view of the facts, the court would hold that Winter's statement was not intended as a warranty.

**2. The intention to warrant depends, not upon the seller's true state of mind, nor upon any particular words, but upon the ordinary reasonable interpretation of the language used.** If the *effect* of a seller's language is to spell out a warranty in the light of what the ordinary, reasonable person under the facts and circumstances would have construed as such, the seller is bound, regardless of his true intent.

EXAMPLES:
(a) Plaintiff agreed to furnish defendant beef that had not been "heated" before killed; the beef to be thoroughly chilled, in first class condition, and merchantable in every respect. The word "warranty," however, was nowhere used. A portion of the beef was heated before killed. The court held that the word "warranty" need not be used, to constitute an express warranty. The agreement to furnish beef that had not become heated before killed amounted to a warranty.[21]
(b) Seller's agent, to induce the buyer to purchase a typewriter, called the latter's attention to the fact that the machine was of a certain number. This number suggested that the machine was of recent date, and therefore of greater value, because it included certain recent improvements—a fact which was known to the parties although not gone into any further by them. On the strength of this number, which was merely called to the buyer's attention, the latter purchased the machine. The machine was in fact of an earlier date, and the number had been altered. The Court held that this constituted a warranty, even though no particular words of warranty were employed.[22]

**3. The buyer cannot take advantage of a warranty unless he relied upon it. There is therefore no warranty against obvious defects.** If I purport to sell you a brand new automobile, and you inspect it before buying, you cannot rely on my statement that the car is new, if it is obviously old.

However, the rule is different if a warranty is made against *future consequences* from defects. The defects may be obvious, and known to the buyer, but the *consequences* may not be.

A merchant may sell hose which is defectively dyed, and obviously so. He may warrant, however, that the defective dyeing will cause no harm to the wearer. If the defective dyeing should result in an injury to the skin, the merchant would be liable.

**4. The warranty must represent statements or promises made at the time of the sale or immediately prior and leading up thereto. It therefore excludes statements made after the sale.** If, *after an article is sold*, the seller makes misrepresentations in respect to it, the buyer cannot claim to have been injured, since the deal has been closed, and the statements have played no part in inducing the sale.

---

[21] *Fairbank Canning Co. v. Metzger*, 118 N.Y. 260.
[22] *American Writing Machine Co. v. Bushnell*, 9 Misc. 462, 30 N.Y. Supp. 228.

EXAMPLE: Plaintiff sued defendant for an alleged breach of warranty on the sale of a horse. The testimony showed that the representations were made after the sale was complete and the horse delivered to the buyer. The Court held that there was no ground for breach of warranty.[23]

**5. *No oral warranties can be claimed if the contract is written.*** This is but a re-statement of the *parol evidence rule:* you cannot vary or alter the terms of a written instrument by parol testimony, except where such parol testimony deals with something separate and distinct from the subject matter of the written agreement, or clears up some ambiguity or uncertainty in the writing, or supplements what is left incomplete.

**6. *No warranties will be implied with reference to matters that are covered by an express warranty.*** The law will not *imply* anything as to matters about which the parties have *expressly* agreed. An express warranty of quality, since it covers that particular point, excludes any claim that a contrary warranty was implied.

EXAMPLES:

(a) If cotton fabric is sold under a warranty that it contains no impurities, no warranty will be implied as to anything else with respect to the quality of the merchandise, since the specific warranty in respect to quality excludes any implied warranty which goes further than what is expressed.

(b) An express warranty that "Gleamo" is guaranteed to impart a high polish to all brass surfaces without injury to the metal excludes an implied warranty that the polish will be equally efficacious and noninjurious when applied to silver.

But if an implied warranty is claimed with respect to something not covered by the express warranty contained in the writing, this rule would not apply.

EXAMPLE: If I sell a horse and give a written warranty as to the health and soundness of the animal, this does not exclude a warranty that I *own* the horse.

**7. *Statements of opinion do not constitute warranties.*** Sales talk, "boosting," and other expressions of opinion, rather than facts, do not constitute warranties. Examples are such phrases as, "We estimate," "It is expected," "It is believed," "It is estimated," "It appears," "There seems to be," "Experts have estimated," etc.

## Implied Warranties

**Classification of Implied Warranties.** There are two kinds of implied warranties: those dealing with *title*, or *ownership*, and those which deal with questions of *quality*, such as genuineness, identity, merchantability, fitness for intended use, or conformity to sample.

**Implied Warranty of Title.** As stated (page 246), every person impliedly warrants that he owns what he sells. The Uniform Sales Act provides that

---

[23] *Cady v. Walker,* 62 Mich. 157, 28 N.W. 805.

"unless a contrary intention appears" every seller impliedly warrants: (1) That in case of a sale, he has a right to sell the goods, and in case of a contract to sell, that he will have such right when title is to pass; (2) That the buyer "shall have and enjoy quiet possession" (*i.e.*, that no one will lawfully dispute the buyer's title or right of possession); and (3) That at the time of sale, the goods will be free from "any charge or encumbrance in favor of any third person," *i.e.*, that no other person has a rightful claim or lien against the goods.

*Exceptions to implied warranty of title.* Parties to a sale may stipulate that the seller does not warrant title. Also, as noted on page 246, the Uniform Sales Act provides that the seller's warranty of title does not apply to forced or judicial sales, such as sales by a sheriff, auctioneer or mortgagee.

**Implied Warranty of Quality: *Caveat Emptor v. Caveat Venditor.*** The common law implied no warranties of quality. A person bought "as is," and took the risk as to the quality of what he bought. The doctrine applied was *caveat emptor:* Let the buyer beware. Opposed to this doctrine of the common law was the civil law rule of *caveat venditor:* Let the *seller* beware: "A sound price implies a sound quality."

The *caveat emptor* doctrine still applies to ordinary sales, particularly those where the buyer has a full opportunity for inspection and where the parties deal at "arm's length." Especially in the case of defects which are obvious, not hidden, a buyer with full opportunity to inspect is bound by his bargain.

**Exceptions to the *Caveat Emptor* Doctrine.** The Uniform Sales Act makes the following exceptions to the doctrine of *caveat emptor*, invoking, in effect, the doctrine of *caveat venditor* in such cases: (1) sale by sample, (2) sale by description, and (3) sale for a particular purpose.

**Sale by Sample.** When goods are sold by sample, the seller impliedly warrants (a) that the bulk shall correspond with the sample in quality, (b) that the buyer shall have a reasonable opportunity of comparing the bulk with the sample, and (c) that if the seller is a dealer in goods of that kind, the goods shall be free from any defect rendering them unmerchantable which would not be apparent on reasonable examination of the sample.

**Sale by Description.** When goods are sold by description, there is an implied warranty that the goods will correspond to the description.

EXAMPLE: Smith orders a raincoat described in a mail-order catalog as handmade and waterproof. There is an implied warranty that the raincoat shipped will conform to that description.

**Sale for Particular Purpose.** When goods are sold for a particular purpose and the purpose is either made known by the buyer to the seller, or should be known by the seller from the nature and circumstances of the purchase, and *where the buyer relies on the seller's skill or judgment,* there is an implied warranty that the goods shall be reasonably fit for such purpose.

*Food: fitness for human consumption.* A person who sells food impliedly warrants that it is fit for human consumption[24] unless the food is boxed or packaged under some patent or other trade name, in which case the law holds that if the buyer calls for such package by trade name, he relies on his own judgment.[25] The implied warranty of fitness for human consumption applies only as between seller and buyer, not as between seller and a third party to whom the buyer resells.

EXAMPLE: A lunchroom waitress who bit into a nail baked into a cake sued the company which baked the cake. The suit was dismissed on the ground that the company warranted nothing as to a consumer with whom it had no direct dealing.[26]

*Mechanical products.* In purchasing mechanical products, buyers are prone to rely on the seller's skill and judgment, unless they make their own selection by brand or known make. In the former situation, buyers may rely on an implied warranty of fitness for the particular purpose intended; in the latter, not, since the buyer substitutes his own judgment for the seller's.

EXAMPLES:
(1) A certified public accountant, relying on a salesman's knowledge of the particular purpose for which it was intended, buys a calculating machine, after explaining such purpose. If the machine proves unfit for the purpose in question, the certified public accountant may rely on the implied warranty of fitness.
(2) A farmer buys (from a dealer) a "Challenge Tractor," which proves unfit for his purpose. Since he used his own judgment in selecting the make, he must stand on it.

*Implied warranty Under Commercial Code.* The Uniform Commercial Code embodies a substantial modification of the foregoing exclusion of third parties from the benefits of a seller's warranties. "A warranty," it provides,[27] "whether express or implied extends to any natural person who is in the family or household of the buyer or who is his guest or one whose relationship to him is such as to make it reasonable to expect that such person may use, consume or be affected by the goods and who is injured in person by breach of the warranty."

## Questions

1. Explain just what is meant by a warranty in connection with the law of sales.

[24] *Baum v. Murray,* 23 Wash. 2d 890, 162 P. 2d 801.
[25] *Botti v. Venice Grocery Co.,* 309 Mass. 450, 35 N.E. 2d 491.
[26] *Chysky v. Drake Bros. Co.,* 235 N.Y. 468, 139 N.E. 576.
[27] U.C.C. Sec. 2-318.

2. "Express warranties are those which relate to quality; implied warranties, those which relate to title." Is this statement true, false, or partly true and partly false?

3. Explain and illustrate each of the following statements: (a) A warranty, to be effective, must have been intended as such. (b) The intention to warrant depends, not upon the seller's true state of mind, nor upon any particular words, but upon the ordinary reasonable interpretation of the language used. (c) The buyer cannot take advantage of a warranty unless he relied upon it. There is therefore no warranty against obvious defects. (d) The warranty must represent statements or promises made at the time of the sale or immediately prior and leading up thereto. It therefore excludes statements made after the sale. (e) No oral warranties can be claimed if the contract is written. (f) No warranties will be implied with reference to matters that are covered by an express warranty. (g) Statements of opinion do not constitute warranties.

4. Name two exceptions to the rule that a seller impliedly warrants that he owns what he sells.

5. What is meant by the doctrines of (a) *caveat emptor*, and (b) *caveat venditor?*

6. In what respect has the doctrine of caveat emptor been modified by statute in a sale of goods
   (a) by description?
   (b) by sample?
   (c) by description and sample?
   (d) in respect to fitness in the absence of description or sample where seller knows the buyer's purpose and the buyer relies on the seller's skill or judgment?
   (e) in respect to fitness in the absence of description or sample where the seller does not know the buyer's purpose and there is no reliance on the seller's skill or judgment?

7. Is a seller liable to third parties under any of the circumstances referred to in the previous question?

8. What is the rule as to implied warranty of fitness (a) where goods are sold by brand or trade-mark; (b) in the case of defects which are obvious on the buyer's examination?

9. When may a buyer of a mechanical product rely on an implied warranty of fitness for the purpose for which such product is intended, and when may he not so rely?

## Problems

· 1. The Universal Chemical Products agrees with a textile concern that "upon successful conclusion of experiments now being conducted in our laboratory with a new fast Prussian blue dye suitable for rubberized cotton, we shall be pleased to furnish you an average of two standard size drums per month at $18.60 for as long a period as you may desire." The experiments are not successful. The textile concern, claiming that it has gone to considerable expense in the manufacture of special fabrics for treatment with the new dye and in advertising and other respects, sues Universal Chemical Products for breach of warranty. Will it succeed? Explain.

2. National Auto Parts Corporation writes The Condor Motor Car Company: "We are perfecting a new type of dual windshield wiper which will not only furnish two complete arcs of visibility, but which will automatically heat the windshield and prevent freezing and blurring of vision during cold

weather. The price will be $6.29 net. If you are interested, we suggest that you order well in advance owing to expected rush of orders." The Condor Motor Car Company orders 5,000 windshield wipers, but the order is not filled, the National Auto Parts Corporation claiming that the experiments on the device proved a disappointment, and that the device was not available for the purposes claimed. The Condor Motor Car Company sues the National Auto Parts Corporation. Judgment for whom, and why?

3. A dealer in second-hand printing presses writes to the Ludlum Press: "We have received eight comparatively new hand presses which we think you will be interested in. While it is not our policy to guarantee or warrant performance of second-hand presses, we would call your attention to the fact that all these presses bear high serial numbers indicating recent manufacture. We suggest an early visit." The Ludlum Press, upon inspection, makes the purchase. The presses prove unsatisfactory. It appears that the manufacturer's serial numbers are forged, although the dealer was unaware of this fact. Upon suit by the Ludlum Press for breach of warranty, the dealer defends on the ground that the sale was without warranty. How should the court decide, and why?

4. Jordan, a furrier, sold a quantity of furs to Kaplan, a manufacturer of ladies coats, at a bargain price. The fur was defectively dyed, and obviously so, and Kaplan had a full and complete opportunity of inspection; but Jordan assured Kaplan that the defective dye was harmless. Subsequently a judgment was procured against Kaplan by a customer, owing to a skin injury sustained by her in wearing one of Kaplan's coats with a fur neckpiece made from the fur supplied by Jordan. Kaplan in turn sues Jordan for breach of warranty. How should the case be decided, and why?

5. Walker sells a horse to Cady. A few days later Cady complains to Walker that the horse is apparently ill with a wind gall. Walker assures Cady that this is not so, and warrants the animal against such defect. It turns out, however, that Cady is right. He sues Walker for breach of warranty. Judgment for whom, and why?

6. Gerhaghty buys a second-hand automobile from Shank for $500. He later sells the car to Pinney who sells it to Sims. The car was in fact stolen by Shank, but this fact was not known to any of the other parties. The true owner recovers the car from Sims who sues and recovers the purchase price which he paid to Pinney. Pinney thereupon sues Gerhaghty who defends on the ground that no warranty of title was contained in the bill of sale. How should the case be decided, and why?

7. A merchant in Peoria, Illinois, orders a quantity of wheelbarrows by number and description from a mail order catalog. The description contains the words, "wheels equipped with noiseless tires." Upon delivery, it appears that the wheels are equipped with iron tires which are not noiseless. The wheelbarrows have been paid for in advance. May the merchant return the wheelbarrows and recover the purchase price? Explain.

8. The Durable Cotton Mills orders 100 bales of cotton "as per sample exhibited at your Charlestown office May 10th." The merchandise is delivered, duly accepted, and a receipt given therefor. Several weeks later, however, in the course of use, the merchandise clearly appears not to conform to sample. The cotton mills endeavors to return the merchandise, but the seller refuses to accept such return. In a suit by the cotton mills, who should succeed?

9. The Hand Truck Manufacturing Company orders a quantity of metal rods from the Universal Steel Corporation. The letter accompanying the order states: "We have been doing business for many years with the National Steel

Company which has supplied all our needs for metal rods as framework in the construction of our hand trucks. We understand, however, that you put out a less expensive grade of rod and if the same proves satisfactory in all respects, rest assured of our continued business." Numerous complaints arising out of the use of the metal rods thus ordered and a number of lawsuits cause considerable loss of business and expense to the Hand Truck Manufacturing Company, which sues the Universal Steel Corporation for breach of warranty. How should the case be decided and why?

10. Plaintiff orders a package of Bully Breakfast Food. The food is tainted and plaintiff becomes ill. Can he hold the grocer who sold him the package? Give the reason for your answer.

11. The purchasing agent of a chain of drug stores buys a large quantity of Silken Strands, a hair dye, in various colors. Numerous lawsuits are brought against the proprietor of the drug stores, based upon claims for personal injuries arising from the use of the hair dye which is alleged to contain a harmful metallic ingredient. The proprietor of the drug stores sues the manufacturer of the hair dye. How should the court decide, and why?

## PART 4. REMEDIES

**Rights, Duties and Remedies in General.** The rights of each party to a sale or contract to sell correspond to the duties of the other party, and his remedies are designed to ensure performance of those duties. Basically, it is the duty of the buyer to pay the price, and of the seller to deliver title and possession. Breach of these respective duties by either party gives the other certain remedies.

### Seller's Remedies

**Basis and Summary of Seller's Remedies.** A seller may part with title and retain possession until he is paid; or he may part with possession and retain title until he is paid, as in the case of a conditional sale (page 266); or he may part with both title and possession before he is paid. If the buyer defaults, the seller's remedies will depend on whether he has parted with title, possession or both.

The seller's remedies against the buyer include: (1) lien; (2) stoppage in transit; (3) resale; (4) rescission; (5) action for the price; and (6) damages.

**1. Seller's Lien.** A lien is a charge imposed on property by which such property becomes security. As more fully explained on pages 685-689, the law distinguishes between *possessory* and *charging* liens: in the former, the person who has the lien has possession of the property, in the latter he has not. A seller's lien is possessory: an unpaid seller in such case parts with title, but not with possession, and the lien continues only so long as the seller retains possession.

EXAMPLE: A dealer sells you an automobile, but retains possession of it until you pay the price. Should he deliver the car and send you a bill, he would lose his lien: his only remedy then would be to sue for the price.

A seller's lien cannot exist where the unpaid seller retains title as well as possession: one cannot have a lien against his own property.

In addition to possession, the requisites of a seller's lien are:

(a) *Goods sold without stipulation as to credit.* Credit implies faith. It would be inconsistent to say to a buyer, "I trust you, hence I give you credit, but I have no faith in you, hence I retain a lien."

(b) *Goods sold on credit, but credit has expired.* A seller on credit may transfer possession as seller but retain it as the buyer's agent or bailee. If in such case the term of credit expires, the seller may exercise his lien though he has parted with possession as seller.

EXAMPLE: Baker buys a motor launch from Stone, receiving a bill of sale against Baker's thirty-day note. Stone is to procure and install new parts, for which purpose he is to keep the launch in his wharf without charge. Baker fails to pay the note and Stone, claiming a lien, refuses to surrender the launch. Should Baker sue for the launch, his suit would fail unless the note was paid.

(c) *Goods sold on credit, but the buyer becomes insolvent.* Insolvency may have the same effect as if a stipulated period of credit had expired. Though the seller parts with actual possession, equity may revive the lien in such cases under certain conditions. *Stoppage in transit* is an example.

**2. Stoppage in Transit.** Though the seller, upon delivery to a carrier, parts with possession, the law under certain conditions revives his possessory lien and gives him the right to stop the goods in transit. The basis of this right is equity, which projects an equitable lien over goods no longer in the seller's possession, to prevent an insolvent buyer from getting something for nothing.

*Conditions.* The conditions for exercising the right of stoppage in transit are: (1) goods sold on credit, (2) insolvency of buyer, (3) goods still in transit.

Once the goods cease to be in transit and come into the buyer's actual possession, it is too late for stoppage in transit.[28]

EXAMPLE: Jones sold a carload of lumber to Silsbee Company to be shipped f.o.b. destination, New Hartford, N.Y. The day before the lumber arrived the Silsbee Company was adjudicated a bankrupt and a receiver appointed. The receiver having taken possession of the lumber as an asset of the bankrupt, Jones was unable to recover it.[29]

*Ways of exercising the right to stop.* The unpaid seller may exercise his right of stoppage in transitu either by obtaining actual possession of the goods or by giving notice of his claim to the carrier or other bailee in whose possession the goods are. Such notice may be given either to the person in actual possession of the goods or to his principal. In the latter case the notice, to be effectual, must be given at such time and under

---

[28] *Henderson Co. v. Webster,* 178 Ark. 553, 11 S.W. 2d 463; *Weyerhaeuser Timber Co. v. First Nat. Bank,* 150 Or. 172, 38 P. 2d 48.

[29] *In re Arctic Stores,* 258 Fed. 688.

such circumstances that the principal, by the exercise of reasonable diligence, may prevent a delivery to the buyer.[30]

Notice by wire has been held sufficient.[31]

*Duty of carrier; expense of redelivery.* "When notice of stoppage in transitu is given by the seller to the carrier, or other bailee in possession of the goods, he must redeliver the goods to, or according to the directions of, the seller. The expenses of such redelivery must be borne by the seller." [32] A carrier who delivers the goods in the face of a stoppage notice is liable to the seller for the consequent loss.

EXAMPLE: *A* in Chicago sold goods to *B* in Boston and shipped them by express. While the goods were still in the express company's possession *A*, learning that *B* was insolvent, notified the express company to return the goods to *A*, but the express company, upon payment of the express charges, delivered the goods to *B*. For consequent loss, *A* may hold the express company.

*Duty when negotiable document of title issued.* If the carrier has issued a negotiable or order bill of lading (page 318), or if a bailee (such as a storage warehouse) has issued a warehouse receipt, such carrier or bailee "shall not be obliged to deliver or justified in delivering the goods to the seller unless such document is first surrendered for cancellation." [33] Criminal penalties may attach for so doing.

EXAMPLE: Rummell & Co. sold *A* & Co. on credit 500 cases of varnish which they had stored in Blanchard's warehouse. They delivered the warehouse receipt to *A* & Co., who became bankrupt before calling for the varnish or paying for it. Rummell & Co. thereupon demanded the varnish of Blanchard, who refused to give it up except upon surrender of the warehouse receipt. In a suit by Rummell & Co., the court sustained Blanchard.[34]

Under the Uniform Commercial Code,[35] the seller's remedies on discovering the buyer's insolvency are considerably broadened. The seller in such situation may reclaim the goods not only while they are in transit, but even after they have come into the buyer's possession, and within ten days thereof, provided they have not in the meantime passed to a good faith purchaser. Moreover, if misrepresentation of solvency has been made to the seller in writing within three months before delivery, the seller is not even bound by the ten-day limitation.

**3. Resale.** When the seller exercises his right of lien or of stoppage in transit, he may resell the goods in any of the following situations:

(a) When they are of a perishable nature;

---

[30] Uniform Sales Act, sec. 59, subd. (1).
[31] *Interstate Window Glass Co. v. New York, N.H. & H.R. Co.,* 104 Conn. 342, 133 A. 102.
[32] Uniform Sales Act, sec. 59, subd. (2).
[33] Uniform Sales Act, sec. 59, subd. (2).
[34] *Rummell & Co. v. Blanchard,* 216 N.Y. 348.
[35] U.C.C. Sec. 2-702.

(b) When the seller expressly reserves the right of resale in case of the buyer's default;

(c) When the buyer has defaulted in payment for an unreasonable time.

The Uniform Sales Act provides[36] that upon such resale, the seller "shall not thereafter be liable to the original buyer upon the contract to sell or the sale or for any profit made by such resale, but may recover from the buyer damages for any loss occasioned by the breach of contract or the sale."

The Uniform Commercial Code goes even further. It eliminates the foregoing conditions to the seller's right of resale, and makes such remedy available upon *any* breach by the buyer, including an anticipatory breach (page 122).[37]

**4. Rescission.** For the buyer's default, the seller may rescind. There are two kinds of rescission: absolute and qualified. To rescind a contract absolutely is to treat it as if it had never existed, so that no rights or claims survive it: The seller has no cause of action against the buyer for damages, and resumes title and possession as if he had never parted with them. In qualified rescission, the seller likewise resumes title and possession, but he does not rescind the entire contract, because he reserves the right to hold the buyer for any loss resulting from his default.

*Requisites for absolute rescission.* The seller may rescind a contract absolutely, where (a) the goods have not been delivered and the buyer has repudiated the contract, or (b) the buyer has manifested his inability to perform his contract, or (c) he has materially breached it.

*Requisites for qualified rescission.* The right of qualified rescission does not exist unless (a) the seller has a right of lien, or (b) has stopped the goods in transit. In either case, the seller may re-assume title as well as possession, provided (1) he has expressly reserved the right to do so on the buyer's default, or (2) the buyer has been in default an unreasonable time. Not only does the buyer in such case lose all rights under the contract or the sale, but the seller may hold the buyer for damages because of the default.

**5. Action for Price.** When the seller has transferred both title and possession, he is in no position to assert a lien, stop goods in transit, or resell them; neither is rescission effective as a remedy. He must therefore sue for the purchase price.

**6. Damages for Nonacceptance.** When the buyer wrongfully neglects or refuses to accept and pay for the goods, the seller may maintain an action against him for nonacceptance. The measure of damages, as defined by the Uniform Sales Act, is "the estimated loss directly and naturally resulting in the ordinary course of events, from the buyer's breach

---

[36] Section 60, subd. (1).

[37] U.C.C. 2-706, Comment 1.

of contract." Ordinarily, when there is a market for the goods, this means the difference between the market and the contract price at the time of the breach. The seller must "mitigate," not "aggravate" damages (page 123) after notification of nonacceptance. He may include prospective profit, provided his proof is more than mere speculation.

**Seller's Alternative Remedies.** A seller often finds himself in a position where he may resort to one of several alternative remedies. For example, suppose an ice dealer sells 7,000 tons of ice to a buyer, who agrees to pay for and remove it by a given date. Two months prior to such date, the buyer notifies the seller that he will not take the ice. The seller is now faced with a choice of alternative remedies:

(a) He may await performance date and upon the buyer's refusal to take delivery then, sue for the price (page 256).

(b) He may treat the buyer's notification as an anticipatory breach (page 122) and sue for damages for nonacceptance (page 256).

(c) Having a seller's lien for the unpaid price, he may exercise his right of resale (page 255).

(d) For the same reason (seller's lien), he may rescind the transaction (page 256).

**Protecting Sale Through Shipping Documents.** When shipping goods to a purchaser, the seller may retain title in himself until the purchase price is paid, by drawing a bill of exchange on the buyer for the price and transmitting it with the bill of lading to a bank or other agent for collection. On payment of the bill of exchange, the bill of lading is delivered. Or the seller may send both bill of exchange and bill of lading direct to the purchaser, with the understanding that delivery of the bill of lading is conditional only, and is not to be deemed absolute until the bill of exchange is paid. When the purchaser pays the bill of exchange, the conditional delivery of the bill of lading becomes absolute, and title thereby passes automatically to the buyer. "Where the seller of goods draws on the buyer for the price and transmits the bill of exchange and bill of lading together to the buyer to secure acceptance or payment of the bill of exchange, the buyer is bound to return the bill of lading if he does not honor the bill of exchange, and if he wrongfully retains the bill of lading he acquires no added right thereby." [38]

**Fraudulent Transfers.** A transfer of one's property is fraudulent if its object is to cheat someone and its intent to avoid some obligation of the party making the transfer. Among the tests to determine whether a transfer is fraudulent are: (a) good faith of transaction, (b) prejudice to creditors, (c) intent, (d) existence and sufficiency of consideration, (e) relationship between transferor and transferee.

*Seller retaining possession after sale.* When the seller, after an absolute

[38] Uniform Sales Act, sec. 20, subd. (4).

sale, retains possession of the merchandise without valid reason, such retention is presumed to be fraudulent. If the fraud is established, judgment creditors (page 861) may have the alleged transfer set aside and the property applied to the payment of their judgments.

*Fraudulent or preferential transfers while insolvent* constitute acts of bankruptcy (page 714) and may be set aside by the trustee in bankruptcy. When a document of title is transferred during solvency but the property itself is retained and not transferred until later when the transferor is insolvent, such transfer is fraudulent as to creditors.

EXAMPLE: A stockholder, while solvent, executes and delivers to his wife, as a gift, a bill of sale for the stock, but retains the stock certificate and continues to vote the stock until three years later when, being insolvent, he indorses the stock certificate to his wife without consideration, and has it transferred to her on the books of the corporation. Such transfer is void. Under the Uniform Stock Transfer Act, title to stock can be transferred only by delivery of the certificate. Hence, the bill of sale is ineffective to transfer the stock in any event. Regardless of such requirement, however, the husband's retention of the certificate and voting privileges makes the transfer presumably fraudulent as to creditors. The subsequent actual transfer of the certificate does not cure the situation, because it was made while the husband was insolvent.

**Bulk Sales.** Many of our states have adopted statutes designed to prevent dishonest merchants from buying up large quantities of merchandise without paying for it and then selling it to third parties and making off with the proceeds. The New York "Bulk Sales Act" is similar to others. It provides that sales in bulk are void against creditors unless the following requirements are observed:

(a) The seller, at least ten days before the sale, must make and deliver to the purchaser a full and detailed inventory showing each article to be included in the sale, and, so far as possible, its cost price to the seller.

(b) The buyer must retain this inventory in his possession for at least ninety days thereafter, subject to inspection by any creditor of the seller.

(c) The buyer must demand and receive from the seller a written list of names and addresses of the seller's creditors, with the amount of indebtedness due to each of them; and the seller must certify this list under oath to be a full, accurate and complete list of his creditors and of his indebtedness.

(d) At least ten days before taking possession of or paying for the merchandise or fixtures sold, the buyer must notify each creditor personally or by registered mail of the proposed sale, giving the price, terms and conditions of the sale.

The statute further provides that any purchaser of such merchandise who fails to conform to the above requirements shall, upon application of any of the seller's creditors, be deemed to hold the merchandise as a receiver and shall be accountable for it to such creditors.

Similar laws are now on the statute books in reference to chattel mortgages placed on goods in bulk, or on merchandise and fixtures used in the conduct of a person's business. (See pages 273-274, "Fraudulent chattel mortgages.")

## Buyer's Remedies

**Basis and Summary of Buyer's Remedies.** A buyer's rights and remedies correspond to the seller's duties, and their breach. It is the seller's duty (a) to deliver the goods at the agreed time and place, or, if no time or place is agreed upon, within a reasonable time and at the seller's place of business or residence, or wherever the goods are; and (b) to make good all warranties, express or implied. The buyer's remedies, like the seller's, depend upon whether the seller has parted with title alone, or possession alone, or both title and possession. The buyer's remedies against the seller include: (1) conversion, (2) breach of contract for failure to deliver and (3) various remedies connected with breach of warranty. In addition, in exceptional situations, equity will grant the buyer (4) specific performance.

**1. Conversion.** Where a person unlawfully exercises a property right over goods not his own, the owner may sue him in *conversion*. The owner's measure of damages is usually the value of the goods at the time of the conversion. If the owner seeks the return of the chattel itself, he sues in *replevin*. Hence where title to goods has passed to the buyer but the seller unlawfully refuses to deliver possession, the buyer may sue him in conversion or replevin.

EXAMPLE: Plaintiff purchased and paid for a certain number of tons of hay out of a certain stack. The purchaser sued in replevin for the hay purchased. The defense was, no title had passed because the hay had not been identified or delivered. The court held that since hay was fungible (page 240), actual segregation and delivery were unnecessary to the passing of title, and the buyer was entitled to his hay.[39]

**2. Breach of Contract for Failure to Deliver.** Whether title has passed or not, the buyer may sue the seller for damages for failure to deliver. The *measure of damages* is "the loss directly and naturally resulting in the ordinary course of events" from the seller's breach. Ordinarily, when there is a market for the merchandise, this means the difference between the contract price and the market price at the time of the breach (delivery date).[40]

*Buyer's failure to give instructions.* When shipments are to be made upon the buyer's instructions and the buyer fails to give instructions, he cannot cancel the contract because of the seller's failure to deliver.

EXAMPLE: Kent agreed to sell and deliver 200,000 yards of sheeting to be manufactured by Iselin, and Silberstein agreed to take four monthly deliveries

---

[39] *Logan v. Cross*, 101 Or. 85, 198 P. 1097.
[40] *Consolidated Pipe Line Co. v. British American Oil Co.*, 163 Okl. 171, 21 P. 2d 762.

of 50,000 yards each beginning in September. The contract contained the words "shipping instructions later." No delivery having been made in September, Silberstein cancelled the contract. Kent, claiming that he had notified Silberstein of readiness and willingness to deliver, but that Silberstein had failed to give shipping instructions, sold the goods in open market for Silberstein's account, at a loss of $12,765.77, for which he sued Silberstein. The court gave judgment to Kent: Silberstein, having failed to give shipping instructions, could not cancel the contract for failure to ship.[41]

*Failure to deliver right quantity.* When the seller delivers a *larger quantity* than ordered, the buyer may (1) reject the entire shipment, or (2) accept the right quantity and reject the rest, or (3) accept the entire shipment at the contract rate. When the seller delivers a *smaller quantity* than ordered, the buyer may (1) reject the entire shipment or (2) accept the shorter shipment and sue for damages resulting from failure to deliver the right quantity.

*Periodic deliveries.* When the seller fails to make periodic deliveries in full as agreed, but eventually makes up the shortages by subsequent overshipments which are accepted by the buyer, the latter cannot counterclaim for damages resulting from the previous short shipments, because by accepting the short shipments in the first place without objection, he waived any damage he might have sustained because of the shortages.

EXAMPLE: Under a contract calling for periodic deliveries of coal, *K* sued *Y* for failure to take an undelivered balance. *Y* counterclaimed because *K* had failed to make certain periodic deliveries in full as per contract, though the shortages were later made up. The counterclaim was dismissed. *Y*, by failure to protest the shortages, and by accepting subsequent overages to balance the shortages, had waived any damages due to previous failure to deliver the right quantity.[42]

**3. Breach of Warranty.** For breach of warranty, the buyer is given any one of the following optional remedies:

(a) Accept or keep the goods and set up against the seller the breach of warranty by way of recoupment in diminution or extinction of the price.

(b) Accept or keep the goods and maintain an action against the seller for damages for the breach of warranty. The measure of damages in such case is the same as in the case of a seller's failure to deliver (page 259).

(c) Refuse to accept the goods, if title has not passed, and maintain an action against the seller for damages for the breach of warranty.

(d) Rescind the contract to sell, or the sale, and refuse to receive the goods, or if the goods have already been received, return or offer to return them to the seller and recover the price or any part of it which has been paid.

*Election and waiver of remedies.* When the buyer has claimed and been

---

[41] *Kent v. Silberstein*, 241 N.Y. 440, 150 N.E. 509.
[42] *Wm. C. Atwater & Co. v. Panama & Co.*, 255 N.Y. 496, 175 N.E. 189.

granted a remedy in any one of these ways, he will be deemed to have waived the other remedies.[43]

EXAMPLE: Smith contracted to sell and deliver at Jones' place of business, by truck delivery on a given date, certain goods of specific quality. At the time and place in question, the goods were delivered and paid for. On that date, the market price of the goods was substantially higher than the contract price. The next day Jones examined the goods, found them to be not as specified, returned them, notified Smith that he rescinded the contract, and replaced the goods by others bought in the open market. Jones then sued Smith to recover the price, plus the additional sum paid in buying on the open market. Such suit would have to be dismissed: Having elected option (d) above, Jones waived option (b).

*When buyer cannot rescind.* Where the goods have been delivered to the buyer, he cannot rescind the sale if he knew of the breach of warranty when he accepted the goods, or if he failed to notify the seller within a reasonable time of his election to rescind, or if he failed to offer to return the goods to the seller in substantially as good condition as they were at the time the property was transferred to the buyer.

*Measure of damage for breach of warranty.* The measure of damages for breach of warranty is the loss directly and naturally resulting from the breach. In the case of a breach of warranty of quality, such loss is usually the difference between the value of the goods at the time of delivery, and the value they would have had if they had corresponded with the warranty.

*Additional remedies under Uniform Commercial Code.* In addition to the foregoing remedies, the Uniform Commercial Code gives the buyer, on breach by the seller in any of the above respects, a "security interest" in any rejected goods in his possession, to cover the account paid by him, plus expenses. To realize on such interest, the buyer may resell such goods in like manner as an aggrieved seller, but he is not allowed to profit on such resale.[44]

**Right to Examine Goods.** The Uniform Sales Act makes the following provisions in respect to the buyer's right to examine the goods:

(a) *Right to examine before delivery.* Unless otherwise agreed, when the seller tenders delivery of goods to the buyer, he is bound, on request, to afford the buyer a reasonable opportunity of examining the goods for the purpose of ascertaining whether they are in conformity with the contract.

(b) *Right to examine goods after delivery.* When goods, which he has not previously examined, are delivered to the buyer, he is not deemed to have accepted them unless and until he has had a reasonable opportunity to examine them for the purpose of ascertaining whether they are in conformity with the contract.

---

[43] *Yancey v. Jeffreys,* 39 Ariz. 563, 8 P. 2d 774.
[44] U.C.C. Sec. 2-711, Comment 2.

(c) *C.O.D. shipments.* On c.o.d. shipments, the buyer is not entitled to an examination before paying the price, unless otherwise specifically agreed. "When the agreement of purchase is that the buyer will pay the purchase price by sight draft to be attached to the bill of lading, he is not entitled to an inspection of the property before paying the draft, and he cannot refuse to accept the property because such inspection is refused." [45] A similar rule would apply when the contract calls for acceptance of a time draft on delivery.

EXAMPLE: Early in August the *A* Company, in New York, accepted a draft payable September 1 in favor of the *B* Company, of Norway, against a shipment of cod-liver oil. The oil when tested (the testing process took ten days) proved to be of lower grade than that specified. The *A* Company notified the *B* Company by cable of the defects, offered to return the oil, and on September 1 refused to pay the draft (which was still held by the *B* Company). The *B* Company refused to accept a return of the oil and sued for the price, claiming that the *A* Company had accepted the oil. The *B* Company's position would be sustained, since the transaction called for draft acceptance on delivery, which constituted a waiver of the right of examination before acceptance. However, such waiver would not bar an action by the buyer for damages notwithstanding acceptance (see next paragraph).

**Damages Notwithstanding Acceptance.** The Uniform Sales Act provides that unless otherwise agreed, the buyer's acceptance of the goods does not discharge the seller from liability in damages or other legal remedy for breach of warranty (page 260) unless he fails to notify the seller of the breach within a reasonable time after discovery.

**4. Specific Performance.** The Uniform Sales Act provides that "Where the seller has broken a contract to deliver specific or ascertained goods, a court having the powers of a court of equity may, if it thinks fit, on the application of the buyer, by its judgment or decree direct that the contract shall be performed specifically, without giving the seller the option of retaining the goods on payment of damages." However, specific performance of a contract of sale of personal property is rare, and the courts will grant it only in unusual circumstances. If damages are an adequate remedy, a court of equity will never grant specific performance. In the case of the sale of goods, damages are, as a rule, an adequate remedy. (For situations in which specific performance may be granted, see page 124.)

## Questions

1. Name six remedies of the seller against the buyer.

2. Which of the above remedies are available to the seller (a) when he still has possession of the merchandise; (b) when he has parted with possession; (c) regardless of whether or not he has parted with possession?

3. Under what circumstances may a seller who has parted with title, refuse to part with possession?

---

[45] *Plumb v. J. W. Hallauer,* 145 App. Div. 20, 30 N.Y. Supp. 147.

4. Under what circumstances may a seller require the return of his merchandise while it is in transit to the buyer?

5. A seller wishing to be prepared in case he desires to exercise the right of stoppage in transit, asks you to explain exactly how such right must be exercised. What would you tell him?

6. An unpaid seller having exercised the right of stoppage in transit, consults you as to what he may do with the merchandise. How would you advise?

7. A grain dealer consults you as to three transactions involving the purchase of various quantities of wheat. In none of the transactions has the merchandise been delivered to the buyer. In the first transaction, the buyer has repudiated the contract; in the second, the buyer has manifested his inability to perform his obligations under the contract; and in the third, the buyer has committed a material breach of the contract by failing to make the required deposit. The grain dealer desires to know what he may do in respect to these transactions. How would you advise him?

8. If, in the preceding case, the seller, after giving notice of his election to rescind, resells the merchandise at a loss, can he hold the first buyer for the loss?

9. A seller consults you in reference to two transactions:

(1) In the first transaction, the seller has transferred both title and possession to the goods under a contract calling for payment of the price at a specified date. The buyer has failed to pay on such date.

(2) In the second transaction, title to the merchandise has passed, but the seller has not parted with possession. The buyer has defaulted in the terms of the contract.

What advice would you give as to the seller's remedies?

10.* Under the Uniform Sales Act, what are the remedies of the seller when the buyer refuses to accept the goods contracted to be sold?

11.* How may a seller ship goods to a purchaser, retaining title in himself until the purchase price is paid? How is title then passed when the purchaser makes payment?

12. Name and explain four remedies of the buyer against the seller.

## Problems

1. A buyer wrongfully neglects and refuses to accept and pay for goods ordered by him. The seller consults you as to his remedies. The seller advises you that the buyer would not be greatly disturbed if the seller exercises his vendor's lien, because the buyer is not interested in possessing the goods. The seller further does not wish to exercise, for the time being, the right of resale, nor is he interested in rescission or in an action for the price. How would you advise the seller as to what other remedy may be available to him?

2. The buyer of a department store asks you what his remedies are in the case of a breach of warranty in connection with goods bought under the following circumstances: (1) goods not delivered nor paid for where the breach of warranty is discovered at the time of attempted delivery; (2) goods delivered but not paid for; (3) goods delivered and paid for before discovery of the breach of warranty.

How would you advise him?

3. A wholesale hardware merchant orders a quantity of wire nails. After the nails are delivered and various customers have purchased the same, the hardware dealer discovers that the nails are of an inferior quality and contrary to an express warranty of merchantability subject to which the nails were bought.

The hardware merchant sues the manufacturer in an action for damages. Thereafter he decides to rescind the entire contract. He tenders the return of the nails, which the manufacturer refuses to accept. Is the manufacturer justified in his refusal? Explain.

4.* Park sold certain goods to Markoe, shipping them by express and forwarding a negotiable bill of lading therefor to Markoe. Markoe was insolvent and while the goods were in transit he made an assignment of his property, including the bill of lading, for the benefit of his creditors. Park, on being advised of the facts and before the goods were delivered, exercised a right of stoppage in transitu by proper notice to the express company. Markoe's assignee claimed the goods by reason of holding the bill of lading, maintaining that the transfer to him of the document ended Park's right of stoppage in transitu. To whom should the goods be awarded?

5. Plaintiff, in securing employment with defendant as a traveling salesman for the period of two years, was required to give a bond for faithful performance in the penal sum of $10,000, and as collateral security for such bond, deposited certain bonds owned by him. Upon his resignation, plaintiff demanded the return of the bonds, which was refused. Plaintiff sued for specific performance. Upon the trial, it appeared that plaintiff had possession of and sold other similar bonds during the preceding year. How was the case decided?

6. A dealer in toys sells a quantity of Daisy Dimple Dolls to the Modern Department Store of Turnpike Landing, Mo., on thirty days' credit; likewise a quantity of electric trains to the Progressive Department Store at Tatum, Texas, without terms as to credit. Prior to shipment, the toy dealer learns that the Modern Department Store is insolvent. He also refuses to ship the electric trains to the Progressive Department Store until he receives payment in advance. Both buyers sue the dealer for conversion, alleging that title had passed in both transactions. Assuming that the dealer admits that title has passed in both cases, can he be compelled to deliver the merchandise and to take his chances on a lawsuit for the purchase price?

7. Goods are shipped from New York to Springfield, f.o.b. Chicago, on thirty days' credit. The buyer decides to arrange for truck delivery from Chicago, and makes corresponding arrangements with the Illinois Trucking Company for this purpose. The truckman picks up the shipment at Chicago, and reports to the home office of the Illinois Trucking Company at Chicago before proceeding to Springfield. The home office of the Illinois Trucking Company has in the meantime received a wire from the seller requesting the trucking company to withhold delivery owing to the buyer's insolvency. The proprietor of the trucking company asks you to advise him what he must do under the circumstances. What advice would you give?

8. Suppose in the previous question that the buyer had resold the merchandise to an innocent third party for value, and that such second purchaser had employed the Illinois Trucking Company to pick up the shipment at Chicago. Assuming that the seller's notice reached the freight office in Chicago prior to the delivery of the merchandise to the Illinois Trucking Company, could the second purchaser require delivery of the merchandise to him?

## PART 5. INSTALLMENT SALES AND SECURED TRANSACTIONS

**Installment Buying: Conditional Sales and Chattel Mortgages.** The enormous growth in our industrial output has been made possible by installment selling. This in turn has been made possible by such legal devices as conditional sales and chattel mortgages,[46] which enable the sellers of merchandise to part with possession yet retain title as security, while the buyer gets immediate use but is not required to make immediate payment of the full price. In an ordinary sale on terms requiring subsequent payments of stated amounts at stated intervals (such as thirty, sixty, ninety and 120 days after delivery), title passes to the buyer, and if the payments are not made, the seller must sue for the price. Often as not the seller in such case gets an uncollectible judgment. In a conditional sale, however, or in a sale secured by a chattel mortgage, the seller retains title until fully paid. The thing sold stands as security; it may not be resold to a third party until paid for, and it may be retaken by the seller if the buyer defaults in his payments.

**Secured Commercial Transactions.** Directly or indirectly, a large part of our commercial credit is employed in consumer financing. However, consumer purchases on the installment plan are only part of the picture, because the retailer himself frequently requires financing in purchasing his supplies from the dealer, and the dealer in turn may be financed by a manufacturer, finance company or bank, either through an unsecured loan, or by giving trust receipts on his merchandise to cover advances. Thus conditional sales, chattel mortgages and trust receipts represent variations of instrumentalities employed in secured commercial transactions.

*Uniform Commercial Code.* The framers of the Uniform Commercial Code have recognized this interrelationship by covering the problems inherent in secured financing as a unit, whether the subject matter be consumer goods, equipment, farm products, inventory or accounts receivable. In this way they have drawn together the various provisions now found in statutes dealing separately with conditional sales, chattel mortgages and trust receipts. Article 9 of the Uniform Commercial Code, dealing with secured transactions, is intended in large part to supersede the present Uniform Conditional Sales Act, the Uniform Trust Receipts Act, and the various statutes relating to chattel mortgages. The Article is designed to fit more closely the needs of secured financing, not only in the field of installment selling, but in all commercial fields where inventory and accounts receivable financing becomes vital to meet such present day competitive conditions as those prevailing in the automobile, radio and television industries. A brief reference to this Article will be found on page 904, in the Appendix at the end of this book. Until the Commercial Code is widely adopted, of course, the present law remains in force; and to understand what may be the law of tomorrow in this important segment of our economy, it is necessary to have a clear understanding of the law of today.

---

[46] Chattel mortgages are discussed on pages 271-274.

## Conditional Sales

**Conditonal Sale Defined.** The Uniform Conditional Sales Act defines a conditional sale as any contract for the sale of goods under which possession is delivered to the buyer and title is to vest in him subsequently upon the payment of part or all of the price, or upon the performance of any other condition, or the happening of any other contingency. (See Form 7.)

*Parties to conditional sale.* The seller and buyer under a conditional sale are frequently referred to, respectively, as *conditional vendor* and *conditional vendee.*

**Conditional Sale v. Chattel Mortgage.** In a conditional sale, the seller parts with possession, but reserves title until the buyer has performed the conditions of the sales contract, which usually consist in making a given number of payments. A chattel mortgage, strictly speaking, is a lien on a chattel, or group of chattels. It may be given in connection with a transaction having nothing to do with a sale, such as a loan, where the borrower gives the lender a lien on a chattel as security for the loan. As part of an installment sale, chattel mortgages are employed in somewhat roundabout fashion. The seller gives the buyer a bill of sale, and the buyer, as security, gives the seller back a chattel mortgage, which says, in effect, "Here is your chattel back again. It's yours, though I keep it and use it; but if I make all the agreed payments, it ceases to be yours and becomes all mine again."

**Conditional Sale v. Lease with Option to Purchase.** Frequently a seller desiring to avoid the statutory restrictions governing conditional sales and imposed for the protection of the buyer, gives the transaction the appearance and effect of a lease with an option to purchase. The Uniform Conditional Sales Act, however, in defining a conditional sale, includes "any contract for the bailment or leasing of goods by which the bailee or lessee contracts to pay as compensation a sum *substantially equivalent to the value of the goods,* and by which it is agreed that the bailee or lessee is *bound to become,* or *has the option of becoming* the owner of such goods upon full compliance with the terms of the contract." [47]

**Filing Conditional Sales Agreement.** A conditional vendor should file the conditional bill of sale or a copy of it, else an innocent third party who buys the chattel from the conditional vendee may acquire good title as against the conditional vendor. It is not necessary for the document to be "recorded," that is, to be copied into permanent record books (as in the case of deeds and mortgages).

EXAMPLE: Brown sells a television set to Green for $500; terms, $50 down, balance, $50 monthly; title retained until final payment. Green, after the initial

---

[47] Sec. 1.

payment, resells the set for $100 to White, who believes Green to be the true owner. Green disappears. If Brown has complied with the law in respect to filing, he may reclaim the set from White; otherwise not.

**Risk of Loss or Injury.** Ordinarily, damage to, or loss or destruction of a chattel must be borne by the owner. However, under the Uniform Conditional Sales Law, a conditional vendor's title is regarded as nominal only, for the protection of the seller. If a chattel is lost, damaged or destroyed while in the conditional vendee's possession, the loss is borne by the conditional vendee.

**Removal or Sale without Notice.** A conditional vendee may neither remove the chattel from the filing district where he bought it, nor sell his interest in the conditional sales contract, without first giving the seller written notice of the proposed removal or sale. If he does, the seller may retake the chattel and exercise the same remedies as if the conditional vendee had defaulted in one of the payments.

**Fraudulent Injury, Concealment, Removal or Sale.** The preceding paragraph relates to innocent removal or the sale of his interest by a conditional buyer. If the buyer, before discharging the contract, maliciously or with intent to defraud injures, destroys or conceals the goods, or removes them to a different filing district without written notice to the seller, or sells or mortgages the goods under the pretense that he is the full owner, he is guilty of a crime and subject to fine and imprisonment.

**Retaking Possession.** If the buyer defaults in any of the payments, the

FORM 7

## CONDITIONAL SALE CONTRACT

The undersigned seller hereby agrees to sell, and the undersigned buyer hereby agrees to buy, subject to the terms and conditions hereof, the following personal property, hereinafter for convenience referred to as "goods" (delivery and acceptance of which is hereby acknowledged by buyer), viz.:

Make or Trade Name          Year          Model Number
Motor Number          Chassis Number          together with extra equipment as follows:

For the total Time Purchase Price of......................$..............................
which is made up as follows:

(1) Cash Price ...........................................$..............................
(2) Cash Down Payment...............$..............................
(3) Trade-In (Down Payment in Goods)...$..............................
    (Make................Model....................)
    (Motor................Serial................)
(4) Total Down Payment.............................$..............................
(5) Unpaid or Deferred Balance.......................$..............................
(6) Insurance—Fire, Theft, and Combined
    Additional Coverage.....$..............................
    $................Deductible Collision....$................$..............................

**(7)** Principal Balance ................................ $..............................

**(8)** Finance Charge ................................ $..............................

**(9)** Total Time Balance .............................. $..............................

which buyer expressly agrees to pay at the office to be hereafter designated, of MANUFACTURING ACCEPTANCE CORPORATION, in ................ instalments of $................each and................instalment(s) of $................each in accordance with the Schedule of Payments hereinafter set out, with interest thereon after maturity at the highest lawful contract rate, and if this contract be placed with an attorney for collection, then, unless the same be in violation of some statute, an additional sum shall be paid by the buyer as attorney's fees, equal to fifteen per cent (15%) of the amount then unpaid, or if such amount be in violation of any such statute, then as large an amount, if any, as shall by law be permitted.

The terms, covenants and conditions of this agreement are as follows, viz.:

(1) Title to said property shall not pass to the purchaser until said time balance is fully paid in cash or until seller shall have obtained judgment against buyer for the unpaid balance of said purchase price.

(2) This contract may be assigned by the seller from time to time, and the legal holder of this contract from time to time shall be entitled to all of the rights of the seller hereunder. No waiver or extension of any payment, term, provision, covenant or condition should be considered as a payment or waiver of any default hereunder, nor be construed as a permanent waiver thereof. The failure of the seller to insist on prompt payment of any instalment when due hereunder or the accepance of any delinquent payment shall not constitute a waiver of any subsequent default and seller shall have the right to repossess or exercise any other remedy reserved to it hereunder upon any subsequent default. No transfer, renewal, extension or assignment of this contract, or any interest hereunder, by the seller, voluntarily or involuntarily, or any loss, injury, destruction of or to the goods herein described, shall release the buyer from any obligation hereunder.

(3) No warranties either expressed or implied have been made by seller unless endorsed hereon in writing.

(4) The buyer shall at buyer's own cost and expense, keep said goods in first class order, repair and running condition and free from all taxes, liens, encumbrances, and charges for keep, repairs, storage, maintenance and accessories.

(5) Buyer agrees to procure, pay all premiums thereon and deliver to seller, an insurance policy or policies, issued by an insurance company satisfactory to seller, naming as beneficiaries or assureds buyer, seller and seller's heirs, administrators, successors and assigns, as their interests may appear, under which the property covered hereby is insured against loss or damage by collision, fire and theft thereof. Buyer expressly agrees that in the event of the failure of buyer to procure such policy or policies of insurance and to keep the premiums paid thereon, during the life of this agreement, seller and seller's heirs, executors, administrators, successors and assigns are hereby authorized to procure such policy or policies, and to pay all premiums thereon which be not paid when due. All amounts so paid by seller as premium on said insurance shall be added to the amounts due hereunder, and shall become due and payable with the instalment next due hereunder after such payment by seller. Failure of buyer to repay such sum or sums so paid by seller as premiums on such policy or policies when due, shall constitute a material breach of this agreement. The proceeds of any insurance, whether paid by reason of loss, injury,

returned premiums or otherwise, shall be applied toward the replacement of the goods or the payment of this obligation at the option of the seller.

(6) Time is of the essence of this contract, and if the buyer shall default in any payment required by buyer to be made hereunder or in complying with any of the terms, covenants and conditions hereof, or if seller shall deem the said goods in danger of misuse, abuse, confiscation, or believe that the said goods are being depreciated in excess of the payments made by buyer hereunder, or believe buyer to be insolvent, then in any such event, seller may declare the entire amount then remaining unpaid hereunder to be due and immediately payable and sue therefor, or declare this contract void and through legal process or otherwise, without notice or demand, take immediate possession of said goods. Said goods when retaken may be retained by seller and all payments made by buyer may, without demand, for performance of this agreement and without notice of default to buyer, be retained by seller as liquidated damages for breach hereof, for loss in value of said goods, and as rent for the use thereof. Buyer expressly agrees that seller may take possession of any other property in, upon or attached to said goods so retaken from buyer, and hold the same temporarily without any liability to buyer therefor. In the event any other property in, upon or attached to said goods is so taken by seller and not removed by buyer within five (5) days after demand therefor, seller may place the same in storage for the account of and at the expense of buyer. The rights given the seller by this contract shall be in addition to all rights given the seller by virtue of any statute or rule of law.

(7) Buyer hereby expressly releases and forever releases and discharges Seller, its successors and assigns, and their agents and employees of and from any and all damages and claims for damages resulting from trespass or otherwise growing out of the repossession of said goods.

(8) Any notice given to buyer hereunder may be given by delivering a copy thereof to buyer personally or by sending a copy thereof by United States Registered Mail postage prepaid, and addressed to buyer at his address given herein or at such other address as shall have been last given to seller by buyer, and such notice shall have been deemed to have been duly given when so mailed.

(9) The goods hereinabove described shall be kept, when not in use, at number..... ........
..............................................,
unless the buyer shall secure the consent in writing of the seller to a change in the place of storage or housing of such goods.

(10) Purchaser agrees to and does waive and

release any and all rights, existing or that may be acquired, in or to the payment of any penalty, forfeit or damages for failure by the seller or holder of this contract, upon payment or satisfaction of this contract, to file a satisfaction certificate in compliance wih any law or statute requiring the filing of same, except for failure to file such certificate within a reasonable time upon written demand delivered by the purchaser or by registered mail to the holder of this contract.

Executed in quadruplicate, one of which was delivered to and retained by the buyer

this................................day of..................................................................., 19.......

....................................................................................(Seal)

By........................................................................
(Official Title, if Company)

........................................................................................
Seller's Address.  Street.  City, State)

_____(Seal)

SIGN           (Buyer's Signature—Individual,
                          Corporate or Firm Name)
.............................................................
(Witnesses to Buyer's and Seller's Signature)          IN

ATTEST:                                 INK    By........................................................................
(Seal of Buyer if                                                  (Official Title, if Company)
a Corporation)

........................................................................................
(Buyer's Business Address.
Street, City, State)

.............................................................                ........................................................................................
(Buyer's Secretary)                                              (Buyer's Residence Address.
Street, City, State)

## MAKE CERTAIN THAT DEALER'S RECOMMENDATION, ASSIGNMENT AND GUARANTY ON REVERSE HEREOF IS SIGNED

### SCHEDULE OF PAYMENTS

| | |
|---|---|
| $....................1 mo.  after date of contract | $....................10 mos. after date of contract |
| $....................2 mos.  after date of contract | $....................11 mos. after date of contract |
| $....................3 mos.  after date of contract | $....................12 mos. after date of contract |
| $....................4 mos.  after date of contract | $....................13 mos. after date of contract |
| $....................5 mos.  after date of contract | $....................14 mos. after date of contract |
| $....................6 mos.  after date of contract | $....................15 mos. after date of contract |
| $....................7 mos.  after date of contract | $....................16 mos. after date of contract |
| $....................8 mos.  after date of contract | $....................17 mos. after date of contract |
| $....................9 mos.  after date of contract | $....................18 mos. after date of contract |

(In states where acknowledgment or affidavit is necessary for filing or recording, Notary Public will insert necessary acknowledgment or affidavit in this space.)

### DEALER'S RECOMMENDATION, ASSIGNMENT AND GUARANTY
To YELLOW MANUFACTURING ACCEPTANCE CORPORATION:

To induce you to purchase the within contract, the undersigned submits an accompanying statement which the undersigned believes to be substantially true, unless otherwise hereinafter stated, and certifies that said contract arose from the sale of the goods described in said contract, warranting that the title to said goods was at the time of the sale and is now vested in the undersigned free of all liens and encumbrances and that the undersigned has the right to assign such title.

For value received, the undersigned does hereby sell, assign and transfer to the YELLOW MANUFACTURING ACCEPTANCE CORPORATION, its successors or assigns, his, its or their right, title and interest in and to the within and foregoing contract and the goods covered thereby and authorizes said YELLOW MANUFACTUR-

ING ACCEPTANCE CORPORATION, its successors or assigns, to do every act and thing necessary to collect and discharge the same.

In consideration of the purchase of the said contract, the undersigned does hereby guarantee payment of all deferred payments as and at the respective times specified therein and covenants, in the event of the failure of the buyer to make any payment at the respective times and in the manner in said contract provided, or to perform any term, provision, covenant or condition provided by said contract to be made or performed by the buyer at the respective times and in the manner in said contract provided, to pay upon demand the full amount remaining unpaid to YELLOW MANUFACTURING ACCEPTANCE CORPORATION, its successors or assigns. The liability of the undersigned shall not be affected by any indulgence, compromise, settlement, extension of credit, or variation of terms effected by or with the buyer or any other person interested. Notice of acceptance of this guaranty, notices of non-payment and non-performance, notices of amount of indebtedness outstanding at any time, protests, demands, and prosecution of collection, foreclosure and possessory remedies, and the right to remove any legal action from the court originally acquiring jurisdiction, are hereby expressly waived. In the event of repossession of the property covered by within contract for default by buyer, YELLOW MANUFACTURING ACCEPTANCE CORPORATION, its successors or assigns, may, at its election, sell the repossessed equipment at public or private sale and apply the proceeds thereof against the unpaid balance under the written contract or tender the repossessed equipment to the undersigned and the undersigned will pay to YELLOW MANUFACTURING ACCEPTANCE CORPORATION, its successors or assigns the amount of any deficiency established by any such sale or repurchase said property from YELLOW MANUFACTURING ACCEPTANCE COPÔRATION, its successors or assigns in the event of tender thereof at a price equal to the unpaid balance of deferred payments at the time of such repossession, including interest, plus any and all costs of repossession. It is expressly agreed that in case of non-payment of either principal or interest when due, suit may be brought by the holder hereof against any one or more or all of us at the option of the holder, whether such suit has been commenced against the maker or not, and that in any such suit the maker may be joined with one or more or all of us, at the option of the holder.

.................................................................

(Seller's Signature)

.................................................................

(Official Title, if Company)

## GUARANTY

In consideration of the making of the within contract by the seller therein and/or the purchase thereof by YELLOW MANUFACTURING ACCEPTANCE CORPORATION, the undersigned does hereby guarantee payment of all deferred payments as specified therein and covenants in default of payment of any installment or performance of any requirement thereof by buyer to pay full amount remaining unpaid to the seller, his or its heirs, executors, administrators, successors or assigns upon demand. The liability of the undersigned shall not be affected by any indulgence, compromise settlement, extension of credit, or variation of terms effected by or with the buyer or any other person interested. Notice of acceptance of this guarantee, notices of non-payment and non-performance, notices of amount of indebtedness outstanding at any time, protests, demands, and prosecution of collection, foreclosure and possessory remedies, and the right to remove any legal action from the court originally acquiring jurisdiction, are hereby expressly waived. It is expressly agreed that in case of non-payment of either principal or interest when due, suit may be brought by the holder hereof against any one or more or all of us at the option of the holder, whether such suit has been commenced against the maker or not, and that in any such suit the maker may be joined with one or more or all of us, at the option of the holder. WITNESS:

.................................................................

.....................................................................(L.S.)

(Guarantor)

(Address)

.................................................................

seller may retake possession of the goods. Unless the goods can be retaken without breach of the peace, they must be retaken by legal process.

**Buyer's Right to Redeem.** Although there is considerable diversity of statutory provision on the subject, in states which have adopted the Uniform Conditional Sales Act the buyer has a right to redeem the goods unless the seller, before retaking, gave the buyer (a) advance notice of his intention to retake and (b) an opportunity to make good the default before the retaking, and the buyer failed to make good notwithstanding. If the buyer did not receive such notice, he has ten days after the retaking within which to redeem, by making good the default plus expenses of retaking.

**Resale after Retaking.** Under certain conditions, resale by the seller after retaking is compulsory. If the buyer (having a right to do so) does not redeem the goods within ten days after the retaking, and if he has paid in at least half the purchase price at the time of retaking, the seller *must* sell the goods at public auction after posting public notice and giving the buyer written notice of the sale. If the buyer has not paid in at least half the purchase price at the time of retaking, he has ten days after the retaking within which to serve a written request, personally or by registered mail, demanding a resale, in which event a resale, upon public notice and notice to the buyer, must be had.

**Proceeds of Resale: Deficiency.** The proceeds of the resale must be applied (a) to payment of the expenses of the sale, (b) to payment of the expenses of retaking, keeping, and storing the goods and (c) to satisfaction of the balance due under the contract. Any surplus remaining must be paid to the conditional buyer. If there is a deficiency, the seller may recover it from the buyer.[48]

EXAMPLE: Laufer sold furniture to Burghard for $515.39 on conditional sale. After default, with $343 remaining due, Laufer retook possession of the furniture and resold it. (a) If the net proceeds amounted to $400, Laufer must account to Burghard for $57, less expenses of sale, retaking, and so on. (b) If the net proceeds amounted to $200 Laufer need not account to Burghard for any of the proceeds and may recover the deficiency from Burghard.

**Rights of Parties When There Is No Resale.** When resale is not compulsory, the seller may retain the goods as his own property without obligation to account to the buyer. When resale is required but not held, the buyer may recover his actual damages from the seller, and in no event less than one fourth of the sum of all his payments, with interest.

## Chattel Mortgages

**Nature of Chattel Mortgage.** As already noted (page 266), a chattel mortgage takes the form of a conditional transfer of title, intended to

---

[48] Statutory amendments in some states have softened these provisions in the case of small purchasers in noncommercial transactions.

operate, however, not as an actual transfer of ownership, but rather as a lien in favor of the lender (chattel mortgagee), which may ripen into absolute ownership if the giver of the mortgage (chattel mortgagor) fails to comply with its conditions. In this respect it resembles, at least in form, a real estate mortgage transaction as it originally existed under the common law, when the borrower simply gave a deed as security for the debt (page 691).

**Chattel Mortgage v. Pledge.**[49] Although the basic function of both a chattel mortgage and a pledge is to secure an obligation, the two transactions are by no means identical. In a chattel mortgage, the debtor retains possession but transfers technical ownership, while in a pledge, the debtor retains ownership but transfers possession. In a chattel mortgage, the creditor does not have possession of the chattel and hence must file public notice to protect his interest, while in a pledge, the pledgee's possession itself constitutes notice to the world that he has some interest in the chattel, hence he need give no other public notice.

**Property Which May Be Subject to Chattel Mortgage.** Only personal property can be made the subject of a chattel mortgage. We have already noted (page 227) that one cannot effect a present sale of something unless such thing is in actual or potential existence. Similarly, the subject matter of a chattel mortgage must be in actual or potential existence.

**Fixtures.** Where fixtures are no longer personal, that is, where they become part of the realty (page 637), they cannot be made the subject of a chattel mortgage.

EXAMPLES:
(1) The Crown Realty Corporation borrows money on two automatic elevators located in one of its apartment houses, and gives a chattel mortgage covering these elevators to secure the loan. The elevators have been in service for several years. Since the elevators are clearly a part of the realty, the lender's chattel mortgage is void.

(2) Frigidaire Sales Corporation sold Katz a number of electric refrigerators subject to a chattel mortgage, with the stipulation that the refrigerators were to be so installed as to be removable without damage to the premises. The court held the chattel mortgage valid, because the status of the refrigerators as personalty had been preserved by contract.[50]

**Property Not Yet Owned or in Existence.** Except where the law allows for "potential existence," one cannot mortgage something that he does not yet own, or that is not yet in existence. One cannot mortgage a book he hopes to write, an invention he hopes to patent, or an automobile he hopes to buy. But under the doctrine of "potential existence" he may mortgage his next crop of fruit or vegetables if he owns the orchard or the farm, though not if he acquires them after the execution of the mort-

---

[49] For a more complete distinction, see pages 296-297.
[50] *Frigidaire Sales Corporation v. Katz*, 29 Ohio N.P., N.S., 595.

gage. He may mortgage coal to be mined from an existing mine which he now owns, or sand to be dug from an actual pit which he owns, but neither of these if he expects to acquire them after the mortgage.

**Continuous Mortgages Covering Future Advances.** Merchants sometimes borrow on inventories or equipment, giving the lender a chattel mortgage which covers not only existing stock or equipment for existing advances, but *after-acquired* merchandise for *future* advances as well. This is done to eliminate the necessity for repeated mortgages. To the extent that such further advances are actually made and such additional merchandise or equipment is actually acquired, such mortgages are in most states valid not only between the lender or borrower but as to third parties as well, provided the rights of third parties arose *after* the additional advances and purchases were made, and provided, of course, due notice of the chattel mortgage was given by filing or recording.

**Filing or Recording Chattel Mortgage.** As pointed out on page 297, a chattel mortgage, unlike a pledge, does not in and of itself constitute notice of the creditor's rights in the chattel. Hence the creditor, if he wishes to protect his rights, must give public notice of his lien on the chattel. This he does by filing the chattel mortgage or a true copy of it in a prescribed public place. Failure to do this may give an innocent purchaser a prior right as against the chattel mortgagee, though the debtor himself remains liable.

EXAMPLE: Morse sold Larkin an electric refrigerator for $300, against a chattel mortgage providing for twelve monthly payments of $25 each. Larkin made a down payment of $25, and ten days later sold the refrigerator for $200 to Griffin, who assumed that Larkin was the true owner. Larkin then disappeared. If, prior to the sale to Griffin, Morse had filed his chattel mortgage, he could reclaim the refrigerator, otherwise not.

*Refiling of chattel mortgage.* The filing of a chattel mortgage, in most states, is effective for one year only. If the mortgage remains unsatisfied at the end of a year, it should be refiled.

*Filing v. recording.* To *file* a document in a public office is to place it in official custody. To *record* a document is to copy it off into a public book or "*liber.*" Some statutory provisions for constructive notice relating to chattel mortgages and conditional bills of sale require that they be filed; others, that they be recorded.

**Fraudulent Chattel Mortgages.** Similar to the provisions of the *Bulk Sales Act* (page 258) is the statutory provision, now common,[51] that a chattel mortgage on goods in bulk or on merchandise and fixtures pertaining to the conduct of the mortgagor's business is void unless the following steps are taken: (1) The mortgagor, at least five days before executing the mortgage, must make up a full inventory showing each article included in the mortgage and its cost price. (2) The mortgagee must demand and

---

[51] An example is the New York Lien Law, sec. 230-a.

receive from the mortgagor a sworn list of names and addresses of the mortgagor's creditors, specifying the amount due each creditor. (3) The mortgagee, at least five days before the mortgage is executed, must notify every creditor personally or by registered mail of the proposed mortgage and its terms.

**Foreclosure of Chattel Mortgage.** Normally, the foreclosure of a mortgage is a judicial procedure, in which the mortgagee asks the court to "foreclose" or shut out all claims except his own. On receiving a judgment, he may sell the property (at public sale and on notice to the mortgagor), and out of the proceeds pay himself what is due him, then turn over the surplus to the mortgagor, or, in case of a deficit, hold the mortgagor for the difference. In the case of a chattel mortgage, however, the mortgagee is technically the owner. In some states where the mortgage contains a power of sale to the mortgagee, he may sell the chattel without a judicial proceeding, provided the mortgagor surrenders possession of it; otherwise he must sue the mortgagor in replevin to regain possession, and then exercise his power of sale. The usual procedure, even in situations permitting sale without foreclosure, is to foreclose anyway, thereby avoiding the necessity of an extra suit in replevin.

## Trust Receipts

**Origin of Trust Receipts.** Businessmen have used trust receipts in financing imports for half a century. The practice has been for the foreign seller to draw a draft on the importer's bank for the purchase price, accompanied by order bills of lading (page 318) covering the merchandise. The importer's banker thereupon met the draft, took title to the bills of lading as security, and delivered possession to the importer for a special purpose only, such as to re-ship, to store, to process, or to sell for the purpose of paying off the banker's advance. The importer, on receiving the bills of lading from the bank, then signed a trust receipt acknowledging that title remained in the banker, and agreeing to limitations embodied in the trust receipt restricting the importer's rights in connection with the goods.

In more recent years, the use of trust receipts has been extended to the financing of installment sales of automobiles, refrigerators, radios, and so on. Manufacturers, or finance companies and banks on their behalf, have developed the practice of financing dealers' purchases and taking trust receipts to cover advances on the purchase price.

**Nature of Trust Receipts.** The general nature of a trust receipt has already been indicated (page 265). Like conditional sales and chattel mortgages, trust receipts are employed in financing commercial transactions. The lender retains title to secure the loan, and the borrower receives possession, coupled with the power to sell and the duty to account as trustee for the proceeds, up to the amount of the advance. (See form of trust receipt on pages 267-270.)

*Trust receipt distinguished from chattel mortgage.* In a trust receipt transaction, the lender obtains title from the seller, entrusts the borrower with possession as trustee pending resale, and charges the borrower as trustee with the proceeds of resale up to the amount of the loan. In a chattel mortgage, the seller passes title to the borrower, and takes it back conditionally as a mortgage pending full payment of the purchase price.

EXAMPLE OF TRUST RECEIPT TRANSACTION. Billings, a dealer, finances the purchase of automobiles for resale by borrowing $25,000 from the bank, which takes a bill of sale or a bill of lading for the automobiles direct from the manufacturers and entrusts possession to Billings against the latter's trust receipt.

EXAMPLE OF CHATTEL MORTGAGE TRANSACTION. Billings buys a quantity of automobiles from the manufacturer, receiving credit for all or part of the purchase price by giving back a series of notes secured by a mortgage on the cars.

Many courts regard trust receipts as merely a different form of chattel mortgage.

**Uniform Trust Receipts Act: Major Purposes.** The major purposes of the Uniform Trust Receipts Act were to limit the property on which, and the creditors to whom, a trust receipt might be issued; to limit the purposes for which such receipt might be used; to protect the lender against claims of the borrower's creditors; and to protect the borrower's purchasers against the lender's claims.

## Questions

1. A contract provides for the sale of goods, possession to be delivered to the buyer upon the execution of the contract, and title to vest in him upon compliance with certain of its terms. The seller had obtained title by borrowing the purchase price from the bank and agreeing to repay the bank on reselling the merchandise. The seller and buyer each kept one copy of the contract between them. The question now arises whether the latter contract constituted (a) a chattel mortgage, (b) a trust receipt, or (c) a conditional sale. How would you decide this question?

2. How would you explain the difference between a conditional sale and a chattel mortgage?

3. When does the law view a lease with an option to purchase as a conditional sale?

4. What is the purpose of filing a conditional sales agreement in a prescribed place of registration? Explain and illustrate your answer.

5. Where an article sold under a conditional bill of sale is lost or destroyed while in the conditional vendee's possession, through no fault of the vendee, who bears the loss, the seller or the buyer?

6. What are the rights of a conditional vendor when the conditional vendee removes the chattel from the filing district where he bought it without first giving the seller written notice of the proposed removal or sale?

7. Does it make any difference whether the removal referred to in the previous question is deliberate or innocent? Explain.

8. (a) When may a seller retake possession of a chattel sold under a conditional bill of sale? (b) When may the buyer redeem it?

9. If a seller retakes possession under a conditional sale, is he (a) always compelled to resell the chattel at public auction, or (b) never compelled to do so, or (c) sometimes required to resell and sometimes not? Explain.

10. Where a chattel is resold by the conditional vendor after retaking, what disposition must be made in the case of (a) a surplus and (b) a deficiency?

11. Explain two differences between a chattel mortgage and a pledge.

12. Is the following a correct statement of the law: "Fixtures cannot be made the subject of a chattel mortgage"? Explain.

13. Is the following a correct statement of the law: "Property not yet owned or in existence can never be made the subject of a chattel mortgage"?

14. To what extent, if at all, is a chattel mortgage covering future advances valid?

15. What is the difference between filing and recording a chattel mortgage and what is their effect?

16. (a) What is the name of the statute governing chattel mortgages on goods in quantity, or on merchandise and fixtures pertaining to the conduct of the mortgagor's business? (b) What is its purpose, and what does it provide?

17. Explain the nature and mechanism of a trust receipt.

18. How does a trust receipt differ from a chattel mortgage?

19. What were the major purposes of the Uniform Trust Receipts Act?

## Problems

1. A contract with a dealer in safes provided that a safe should be placed in the possession of the other party, who should pay "rent" therefor in six equal monthly installments. It provided further that if this should be done, the manufacturer would sell the safe for one dollar; that if default should be made in payment, the manufacturer might terminate the lease, retake the safe, and retain the rent paid. Before the six payments were made, there was a default and the dealer sought to reclaim the safe. What was the disposition of the court and why?

2. Deep Freezers, Inc. sell a unit to Black for $600 on the following terms: down payment, $100; balance in ten equal monthly installments; title in the meantime to remain in the seller. Black, after making the initial payment, resells the unit to White, who believes Black to be the true owner. Black then disappears. Deep Freezers, Inc. seek to recover the unit from White. Will they succeed? If not, why not? If so, under what circumstances?

3. Jones buys a second-hand automobile from Reliable Motors, Inc. The price is $800, payable in various installments; title in the seller until full payment is made. After making two payments, the car is completely demolished in an automobile accident through no fault of Jones. The question now arises, who is to bear the loss?

4. Baker buys a new automobile under a conditional bill of sale. His employer is about to move his plant to a distant state, and Baker is to go with him. Baker is in doubt whether he can take his new car with him before completing payments on it. How would you advise?

5. Evers discovers coal on his Pennsylvania farm. He borrows $5,000 for mining machinery, and gives the bank a chattel mortgage on the mining ma-

chinery and on the coal to be mined. Is the chattel mortgage (a) wholly valid, (b) wholly void, or (c) partly valid and partly void?

6. Fuller sold Gray an electric dishwasher and took back a chattel mortgage on it. He instructed Hall, his attorney, to file the chattel mortgage, which the latter promised but forgot to do. Later, Gray, without having fully paid for the dishwasher, sold it to Hall. Fuller now seeks to reclaim the dishwasher from Hall, who sets up as a defense that the chattel mortgage had not been filed. How would the court decide and why?

7. Allen, proprietor of a sporting goods store, being pressed by his merchandise creditors, borrows $10,000 from Brundage and gives him a chattel mortgage on the entire contents of the store, including merchandise, trade fixtures and good will. Allen, who sailed for South America, is not heard from further. Brundage, on failure to obtain payment of the loan, takes possession of the store and after several months is made defendant in a proceeding to void the chattel mortgage. How would the court decide and why?

8. Frost borrows $1,000 from Gill to buy a second-hand car, and gives Gill a one-year note, secured by a chattel mortgage on the car he expects to buy. Frost defaults on the note, and Gill seeks to foreclose on the car. How would the court decide and why?

## COURT CASES FOR REVIEW

### How Did the Court Decide, and Why?

1. In a contract of sale the price was left "to be settled by some future agreement, or to be determined by what is reasonable under the circumstances." The parties failed to reach an agreement. In a subsequent suit, the court left it to the jury to determine the price in accordance with such method. One of the parties appealed on the ground that the contract was invalid and the case should have been dismissed. *Valpy v. Gibson*, 4 C.B. 837.

2. In the following situation the question arose as to whether a valid contract of sale existed: The parties fixed the price at ten cents less than the market price on any day thereafter which the seller should name. *McConnell v. Hughes*, 29 Wis. 537.

3. Plaintiff bought a quantity of grape roots for which he paid the purchase price. When the goods were delivered they were found to be dead and worthless. The buyer tendered them back, but the seller rejected the tender. *Stone v. Frost*, 61 N.Y. 614.

4. A quantity of grain was stored in an elevator. The owner sold 400 bushels of it. He delivered to the buyer a receipted bill of sale for that amount, and an order for its delivery, signed by the person depositing the grain and drawn upon the elevator. The grain was destroyed before the buyer obtained actual possession of it. The buyer sued to recover the price paid, on the ground that no delivery had been made to him. *Russell v. Carrington*, 42 N.Y. 118.

5. Plaintiff sold to defendant his entire flock of turkeys consisting of about 100 turkey hens and 600 turkey toms at specified prices for specified grades. Defendant was to call for and cart away all the turkeys on November 13, 1940. Two days earlier a blizzard killed about half the turkeys and damaged the rest. Defendant refused to accept or pay for any of the turkeys. Plaintiff sued for the price. *Radloff v. Bragmus et al.*, 214 Minn. 130, 7 N.W. 2d 491.

6. A contract for the manufacture and sale of church furniture required the manufacturer to install it. After the contract was concluded and the furniture identified, but before it was installed, a dispute arose as to whether the furniture

belonged to the manufacturer or to the church. *Second Baptist Church v. Myers*, 193 S.W. 1147 (Tex. Civ. App.).

7. Defendant sold a horse to plaintiff for $125. The agreement of sale provided that the horse could be returned within two weeks, if there was "anything the matter with him." The horse proved unsound, and on the last day of the two weeks, at 9:20 in the evening, the plaintiff returned the horse. He sued to recover the purchase price. *Cornell v. Fox*, 95 App. Div. 71, 88 N.Y. Supp. 482.

8. A ring was sold in New York City, to be delivered to the buyer's address in Greenwich, Conn. The box arrived empty at Greenwich. In other words, the ring had not been delivered to the buyer's address. Could the seller recover the value of the ring from the express company, or had title passed from the seller to the buyer? *Conroy v. Barrett*, 95 Misc. 247, 158 N.Y. Supp. 549.

9. Under a contract for the sale of lumber, the buyer selected the sample piles from which his lumber was to be taken and directed that when ready, the lumber should be delivered on the seller's dock, and notice of readiness to deliver given, so that the lumber could be promptly inspected by the buyer and delivered following such inspection. The lumber was destroyed by fire after it was made ready for delivery on the seller's dock, and notice given, but before defendant had inspected it, taken it away or exercised any control over it. The question arose as to who was to stand the loss. *Cooke v. Millard*, 65 N.Y. 352.

10. On a sale of 500 bags of cocoa to be shipped from Bahia to New York, the cocoa became wet during transit. A dispute arose as to whether the loss had to be borne by the buyer or the seller. *Mee v. McNider*, 109 N.Y. 500.

11. Braun, a Philadelphia coal dealer, contracted to sell and deliver a quantity of coal to McNeal at Burlington, New Jersey. Braun shipped the coal by barge. The barge arrived safely alongside McNeal's wharf at Burlington, but sank before it could be unloaded. McNeal refused to pay and Braun sued. *McNeal v. Braun*, 53 N.J.L. 617.

12. On June 22, 1948 McClain sold an automobile to Harris for $850. McClain gave Harris a bill of sale to the automobile and took a check in payment of the purchase price. The next day Harris sold the automobile to McClure for $675 and indorsed over to McClure the bill of sale which Harris had received from McClain. Payment of the check given by Harris was refused for insufficient funds, whereupon McClain sued McClure to recover possession of the automobile. *J. L. McClure Motor Co. v. McClain*, 34 Ala. App. 614, 42 So. 2d 266.

13. A brewing company agreed to sell its products to a wholesale beer distributor at prices to be announced by the brewing company, f.o.b. its plant. The distributor requested shipment of specified quantities of beer as soon as a specified common carrier by truck would accept such shipment for sure delivery. Thereafter delivery was made to the carrier and in a subsequent dispute the court submitted to the jury the issue as to the intent of the parties with respect to the place of delivery and the passing of title. This action by the court was objected to and an appeal taken on the ground that the question should never have been submitted to the jury. *Storz Brewing Co. v. Brown*, 154 Neb. 204, 47 N.W. 2d 407.

14. A seller told the buyer of a radio receiving set that the set could "get" any station in Rome clearly at any time. Events proved this statement to be without foundation. The seller, claiming such representation as sales talk, sued to recover the unpaid balance of the purchase price when the buyer tendered

return of the radio. *V. Valente Inc. v. Mascitti*, 163 Misc. 287, 295 N.Y. Supp. 330.

15. Plaintiff bought a threshing machine from defendant, at the same time signing an order which contained the following: "The Pitts Agricultural Works warrant said machine to be of good materials and to be well made; to do good work in threshing and cleaning grain, if properly managed. The condition of warranty is that notice of any defect is to be given the Pitts Agricultural Works at Buffalo, New York, within one week, after putting the machine in operation." Plaintiff alleged an oral warranty by the defendant's agent, that the machine was as well made as any other, was capable of doing good work, was made of good material, and would work perfectly in all particulars. The machine was defective in that the cylinders became easily heated, and grain was carried over with the straw. *Bucy v. Pitts Agricultural Works*, 89 Iowa 464.

16. The seller's agent, in the sale of an automobile, stated that it had been used by him as a demonstration car, and had run about 500 miles; that it was in first-class condition; that its value new was $1,600. The car was bought for $900, the buyer getting a receipt reading, "1 second Yale Touring Car, $900." After the car was in use two months, the crankshaft broke. The buyer sued. *Morley v. Consolidated Mfg. Co.*, 196 Mass. 25, 81 N.E. 993.

17. Plaintiff, a woman who was unfamiliar with furs, was shown a coat with a fur collar. She asked defendant's salesman what kind of fur it was, and whether it was dyed fur, and was told that it was black fox, and not a dyed fur. Plaintiff wore the coat, and as a result, her neck and body broke out in eruptions due to poisonous and irritating substances contained in the fur collar. Plaintiff sued for breach of warranty. *Flynn v. Bedell*, 242 Mass. 450, 136 N.E. 252.

18. Defendant, a manufacturer of mineral waters, supplied the plaintiff, a small shopkeeper, with mineral water in bottles for sale in her shop. The bottles were returnable to the defendant when empty. While the plaintiff was replacing in its case a bottle supplied by the defendant, the bottle, being defective, burst, and injured the plaintiff, who brought suit against the defendant for damages. The defendant urged, among other defenses, that there could be no implied warranty of sale in respect to the bottles, since the bottles were not sold, but were to be returned to the defendant. *Geddling v. Marsh*, 1 K.B. (Kings Bench) 668.

19. Anna Rinaldi and Maria Savarese went shopping together in defendant's meat market. Mrs. Rinaldi bought a loin of pork and Mrs. Savarese a can of chicken salad. The pork was infected with trichina, and the chicken salad was tainted. In consequence both Mrs. Rinaldi and Mrs. Savarese became ill. Both sued the proprietor of the market. *Rinaldi v. Mohican Co.*, 171 App. Div. 814, aff'd 225 N.Y. 70.

20. Plaintiff was made ill by eating macaroni purchased in packages at a grocery store. He sued the proprietor of the store on the theory of breach of implied warranty of fitness for human consumption. The customer had asked for and received a particular brand of macaroni. *Botti v. Venice Grocery Co.*, 309 Mass. 450, 35 N.E. 2d 491.

21. An automobile owner purchased anti-freeze for his automobile from an operator of a filling station. The latter had purchased the anti-freeze from an authorized distributor for a manufacturer. The automobile owner sued the manufacturer and distributor for damages allegedly caused to his automobile by the anti-freeze, based upon the alleged breach of either an express or an implied warranty that the anti-freeze was fit for the purpose intended. *Jordon v. Brouwer*, 86 Ohio App. 505, 93 N.E. 2d 49.

22. The buyer of an electric refrigerator which the seller had agreed to put in running order, retained and used it for more than a month pending the seller's attempt to make it work satisfactorily. On plaintiff's suit for the price, defendant urged non-acceptance. *Kaminsky v. Levine*, 106 Pa. Super. Ct. 278, 161 Atl. 741.

23. On April 3, 1949, the seller's employees replaced a burned-out rod in a reconditioned automobile motor which seller had sold two months before under a ninety-day warranty. A month later another rod burned out, and was replaced by the seller within a month. Still another rod burned out on June 13, 1949. The buyer sued to recover the purchase price and damages under the warranty, and the seller defended on the ground that the ninety-day guaranty had expired. *Smith v. Walsh*, 53 So. 2d 295.

24. During the summer and fall of 1946, plaintiff sold and delivered to defendant a quantity of waste baskets in sealed cartons. In December, 1946, because of alleged latent defects in the baskets, defendant offered to return the waste baskets on hand, but made no attempt to do so and continued to sell them up to the date of the trial in April, 1948. On plaintiff's suit for the price of the baskets which remained unpaid, defendant counterclaimed, tendering the return of all the baskets received but not disposed of, and demanding recovery of all moneys paid plaintiff. *Reno Sales Co., Inc. v. Pritchard Industries, Inc.*, 178 F. 2d 279.

25. The issue before the court in the following case was whether stoppage in transit was timely under the following circumstances: A bill of lading was cancelled on the arrival of the goods, by marking across its face the word, "Cancelled by Delivery." The goods were refused by the buyer on examination, and the bill of lading was returned by the buyer to the seller after the cancellation was stricken from the bill by the buyer. *Northern Grain Co. v. Wiffler*, 168 App. Div. 95, 153 N.Y. Supp. 723, reversed, 223 N.Y. 393, 119 N.E. 393.

26. Plaintiff sought to repossess an automobile under the following circumstances: The automobile was sold under a conditional sales contract designating a husband as the purchaser obligated to make the payments, but accompanied by a certificate of ownership in the wife's name, the car being likewise registered in her name. The wife was not mentioned in the conditional sales contract, nor obligated for any part of the payments. The conditional seller assigned the contract to plaintiff. The wife sold the car for cash to defendant. *Associates Discount Corp. v. Davis Motor Sales*, 275 App. Div. 745, 87 N.Y. Supp. 2d 757.

27. Alderdyce sold Young a truck under a conditional sales contract. Alderdyce filed an incomplete copy of the contract in another county. Young sold the truck to Mary and Charles Starkey, who, to secure a $500 loan, gave plaintiff a chattel mortgage, which was duly recorded. Alderdyce assigned his conditional sales contract to Murphy Transportation Co., which, on default in payment, had the truck seized by a sheriff. Plaintiff sued the sheriff in replevin. *Union Bank & Trust Co. v. Willey, Sheriff* (Murphy Transportation Co., intervener), 237 Iowa 1250, 24 N.W. 2d 796.

28. Plaintiff sold an automobile to Little under a conditional sales contract, which plaintiff filed. Little had the motor number changed by one Leo Parks. The car was later brought to plaintiff's repair shop and plaintiff, in checking over the car, noticed the changed number and made a notation of it on his copy of the conditional sales contract, but made no effort to correct the original on file. Later, Little delivered the car to Parks, who sold it to defendant, an innocent purchaser for value. Plaintiff sued defendant in replevin. *Shepard v. Van Doren*, 40 N.M. 380, 60 P. 2d 635.

29. A conditional sales contract covering a tractor and trailer was filed in

Florida, where the sale occurred. While they were being temporarily used in delivering merchandise in Wisconsin, the tractor and trailer became disabled and were placed in a Wisconsin garage for repairs. The conditional sales contract was not refiled in Wisconsin. The tractor and trailer were seized under a writ of attachment against the conditional purchaser. The conditional seller in Florida insists that his right of possession is superior to that of the attaching creditor and brings suit accordingly. *Confidential Loan & Mortgage Co. v. Hardgrove*, 259 Wis. 346, 48 N.W. 2d 466.

30. Defendant executed and delivered to plaintiff a promissory note secured by a chattel mortgage on an automobile. The chattel mortgage was filed for record in the county where defendant lived and the automobile was located. Later, while a renewal note was due and unpaid, defendant moved to another county, took the automobile with him, and gave another chattel mortgage to a second party to secure a note given to the latter. *Peabody State Bank v. Hedinger*, 170 Kan. 237, 224 P. 2d 1014.

31. Plaintiff bought a car on the installment plan, but defaulted in three installment payments. The conditional sales contract provided that defendant could retake the car in case any payment was defaulted. Without plaintiff's knowledge or consent, defendant took possession of the car by removing it from a vacant lot behind plaintiff's house. Plaintiff sued for conversion. *Ikovich v. Silver Bow Motor Car Co.*, 117 Mont. 268, 157 P. 2d 785.

32. Plaintiff leased a rock crusher to Fisher at a monthly rental of $175, with the understanding that when the total rental paid amounted to $800, Fisher was to own the rock crusher. The entire agreement was oral. After Fisher had paid only $200, he turned the rock crusher over to defendant to satisfy a debt. Defendant assumed that Fisher was the owner of the crusher. Plaintiff thereupon brought suit against Fisher and the defendant. *Billiter v. Ledbetter-Johnson Contractors, Inc. et al.*, 60 Ga. App. 1, 2 S.E. 2d 677.

33. Post borrowed $2,500 from the Fidelity Corp. of Michigan, to buy two cars. Before obtaining actual delivery of the cars, he gave the Fidelity Corp. a chattel mortgage on them. The mortgage failed to state the motor or serial numbers, since they were unknown in advance of delivery. Following delivery the cars were attached by a creditor of Post's. Immediately upon such attachment Post phoned the motor and serial numbers to the Fidelity Corp. which inserted them in the chattel mortgage, filed the mortgage, and then proceeded to contest the attachment. *Fidelity Corp. of Michigan v. Post*, 273 Mich. 697, 263 N.W. 775.

# 5

# Bailments

**Scope of This Chapter.** In this chapter we deal with the rights, duties and obligations arising out of the transfer of possession of personal property, for whatever purpose, legally designated as a bailment. We consider the nature, essentials and classifications of bailments, and the rights, duties and liabilities involved in each classification, whether the bailment is gratuitous, or whether it is one for mutual benefit, as in the case of a pledge, the hiring of a chattel, or the hiring of service. In the latter category we consider contracts for alteration or repair, and contracts involving warehousemen and innkeepers.

## PART 1. NATURE AND REQUISITES

**General Nature of Bailment.** If I leave personal property with you, such as a watch, a garment, a machine, raw material and the like, with the understanding that you are to keep it for me, or to do some work on it, or to get the benefit of it while it is in your custody, such a transaction constitutes a bailment. Our rights and obligations in such a case will be governed by the specific understanding between us, or, in the absence of such understanding, by the general rules which make up the law of bailments. If the purpose of bailment is to transport the property in question, we have to consider not only the general rules of bailment, but certain special rules as well, commonly designated as the *law of carriers*, which we discuss in the next chapter.

**Bailment Defined: Parties.** A bailment is the delivery and acceptance of personal property for some particular purpose, upon condition that the property be redelivered when it has served its purpose, or that it be kept until reclaimed, or that it be otherwise dealt with according to agreement.

The persons concerned in a bailment are the *bailor*, who delivers the chattel, and the *bailee*, who accepts it.

**Essentials of Bailment.** Three elements must be present to give rise to a bailment: (1) A valid existing chattel; (2) Transfer of possession; and (3) Acceptance of possession.

**Valid Existing Chattel.** No rights can arise out of an illegal bailment. Thus, an attempt by the owner to reclaim forbidden narcotics or illegally purchased food or drink stored in a warehouse will receive no legal support. Also, there can be no bailment of future goods (page 229).

**Transfer of Possession.** Unless the owner transfers possession, there can be no bailment. Giving custody to an employee does not constitute transfer of possession: The employee's possession is the employer's possession. Transfer of possession may be actual, as by delivery of the thing itself, or constructive, as by delivery of a bill of lading, warehouse receipt or the key to a store.

**Acceptance of Possession.** The duties and responsibilities of a bailee cannot be thrust on a person without his knowledge or consent. Hence delivery without acceptance is insufficient to constitute a bailment.

EXAMPLES:
(1) During your absence, I leave a package on your doorstep with a note asking you to deliver it to the postman. If the package is stolen before you return, you incur no liability: Without your acceptance, no bailment arose.
(2) Some jewelry left in clothing sent to the cleaners got into the hands of employees who, without the cleaner's knowledge, made off with it. As to the jewelry, there was no acceptance by the cleaner, and no bailment.[1]
(3) A customer enters a clothing store and waits on himself. Knowing that there is no one but himself to watch his garment, he lays it aside while trying on new ones. His garment is lost. The proprietor is not liable. There was no bailment—no delivery and acceptance.[2]

Acceptance of possession, however, may be implied from the circumstances.

EXAMPLES:
(1) A customer took off her cloak and, there being no other place to put it, laid it on a counter directly in front of a clerk who was waiting on her with a cloak in her hands for the customer to try on. While she was trying on the cloak, her own cloak disappeared. *Held*, that there was an implied acceptance by the clerk of the customer's cloak as a bailment.[3]
(2) A dentist's patient left her coat in the dentist's reception room, which contained no closet or other appropriate place to deposit wraps. She had done the same thing on previous visits. On this occasion, the coat disappeared. She was unable to see the coat while in the dentist's chair. The court held that under the circumstances, the dentist undertook voluntary custody of the coat as an accommodation to his patient and as part of the service for which he was being paid; hence he was liable for the loss of the coat.[4]

In addition to the foregoing elements, every bailment contract must have the usual contract requisites (pages 33-34).

**Bailments Distinguished from Similar Transactions.** Bailments are frequently difficult to distinguish from similar transactions.

Suppose I deliver to you a television set, with the understanding that

---

[1] *Copelin v. Berlin Dye Works*, 168 Cal. 715.
[2] *Wamser v. Browning King & Co.*, 187 N.Y. 87.
[3] *Bunnell v. Stern*, 122 N.Y. 539.
[4] *Webster v. Lane*, 125 Misc. 868, 212 N.Y. Supp. 298.

you are to keep it for a year, to pay me $20 a month for its use, and, at the expiration of that period, if all payments have been made, you are to get title to the property. Is this a bailment—*i.e.*, a rental agreement— or is it a conditional sale? If it is a bailment, and you sell it to an innocent third party, I can still reclaim it. If it is a conditional sale, and I have not filed a copy of the agreement in the public record office prescribed by statute, the innocent third party would get a good title.

Or suppose a farmer delivers wheat to a miller, with the understanding that he is to get back flour. Without fault of the miller, a fire destroys the mill, including the wheat. If this is a bailment, the loss falls on the farmer, because it is *his* property that is destroyed. If it is not a bailment, and title passed to the miller, the loss falls on him.

Again, suppose a merchant delivers a thousand yards of cloth to a clothing manufacturer, who agrees, in turn, to deliver two hundred cloth garments to the merchant within a given time. Suppose, in the meantime, the manufacturer goes into bankruptcy. If the merchant has parted with title, he is a general creditor, and must take his chances with the other general creditors. But if the transaction is a bailment, the merchant still owns the cloth, and may reclaim it.

*The test.* The test of a bailment is this: If the *identical* chattel delivered is to be returned to the owner or some person designated by him, in the *same or altered form*, it is a bailment. If there is no obligation to restore the *specific* chattel, but the bailee is at liberty to return an *equivalent* chattel, or its equivalent in *money*, the transaction is, respectively, an exchange or a sale.

Bailments are thus distinguishable from sales, exchanges, gifts, conditional sales and the consignment of goods to a factor or commission merchant.

**Bailment *v.* Sale or Exchange.** The distinction between a bailment and a sale or exchange has already been briefly noted (page 228). A bailment is rarely confused with a sale, because the latter, unlike a bailment, involves a money price; but the distinction between a bailment and an exchange is somewhat less distinct, because both bailments and exchanges involve the transfer of chattels exclusively.

Bearing in mind the previous test, an exchange involves the transfer of one chattel in return for another, a bailment the return of an identical chattel, though it may have been considerably altered in the interim.

For example, in the case of the miller and the farmer, or the merchant and the clothing manufacturer, if the flour was to be milled from the *identical wheat delivered*, or the garments were to be made from the *identical cloth furnished*, the transaction would be a bailment, since it would involve redelivery of the owner's property, even though in altered form.

But if the miller were at liberty to furnish flour from *any* wheat, or the clothing manufacturer was not required to furnish garments from the *particular cloth* forwarded by the merchant, the transaction would be an exchange, and not a bailment.

In *Norton v. Woodruff*,[5] Wilson, a miller, contracted to take Harvey's wheat, and to return one barrel of flour for every five bushels of wheat. After the wheat was delivered but before delivery of the flour, the mill burned down without Wilson's fault. Harvey sued for the value of the flour. The court, in granting judgment for Harvey, pointed out that the wheat, when destroyed, was Wilson's, since the transaction was an exchange, not a bailment. The contract called for flour against wheat, not flour to be milled *from Harvey's wheat.*

*Raw material "contracted out" for manufacture or finishing.* A considerable amount of work is done today by "contracting out" raw material for manufacture or finishing. In such cases, the contractor, who is to do the work, becomes a bailee, though he uses material of his own in the course of manufacture.

EXAMPLE: In *Mark v. Snell*,[6] rough castings were delivered to be manufactured into shears. The blades were to be furnished by the manufacturer. The court held that the transaction amounted to a bailment.

Where the manufacturer's contribution, however, is not merely "accessorial," but represents the major part of the product, the latter will not be regarded as a bailment, but as the manufacturer's property subject to contract.

EXAMPLE: Burkan orders 500 suits of men's clothing, to be made up by Block in various sizes and models, Burkan to furnish the linings. The suits are almost finished when they are wholly destroyed by a fire caused through no one's fault and not covered by insurance. Since the transaction is a manufacturing contract rather than a bailment, the merchandise belongs, not to Burkan, but to Block, who must stand the loss.

**Money and Securities Deposited in Bank.** Where money is deposited in a bank, although the depositor is entitled to the return of the same *amount* deposited, he cannot as a rule demand the return of the *identical* money deposited; unless, of course, the deposit is a *special* one, such as a special deposit of gold, silver, securities, etc., where the identical deposit must be returned. In the latter case, the transaction amounts to a bailment.

If money or securities be deposited in a vault maintained by a bank or safe deposit company, and the same be negligently lost, destroyed or stolen, the bank or safe deposit company is deemed a bailee, and is liable accordingly.

**Fungible Bailments.** There is an exception to the rule that the identical thing delivered must be returned, in the same or altered form, in order that

---

[5] 2 N.Y. 153.
[6] 140 N.Y. 193.

the transaction may be deemed a bailment. This exception exists where the bailment consists of fungible goods (page 240). It is often impractical, in such cases, to return the identical goods delivered to the bailee, where such goods are merged with other goods, since it is not possible to identify each pea, bean or oat delivered by the bailor to the bailee. Redelivery, in such cases, must take the form of quantity or measurement, rather than identity. Nevertheless, a transaction of this character constitutes a bailment, not an exchange.

**Bailment v. Conditional Sale.** The basic distinction between a bailment and a conditional sale is in the object of the transaction. In the former, the object is to transfer possession only, in the latter, to transfer title in compliance with the conditions of the contract. However, as noted on page 266, the Uniform Conditional Sales Act treats a bailment or lease with option to purchase as equivalent to a conditional sale, if the bailee or lessee contracts to pay as compensation a sum substantially equivalent to the value of the goods, and the bailee or lessee is bound to become, or has the option of becoming the owner on fully complying with the terms of the contract. Thus, the television transaction referred to on page 283 would clearly be a conditional sale, under the uniform statute mentioned. If you sold the set before it was paid for to an innocent purchaser for value, the latter would get good title, so far as I was concerned, unless I had duly observed the filing requirements (pages 266-267).

**Bailment v. Agency.** When a bailor parts with possession, he assumes no control over the bailee beyond that which the contract provides. So long as the bailment continues, the bailee may exercise complete control over it within the terms of the contract. The bailor is not responsible to third parties for the bailee's acts in connection with the bailment. On the other hand, where a principal intrusts a chattel to an agent, the latter is subject to the principal's control and direction. The chattel is in effect still in the principal's possession, since the possession of the agent is the possession of the principal. Moreover, the principal is liable to third parties for damage or injury occasioned to them by negligent misuse of the bailment during the course and scope of the agency.

**Bailment v. Consignment.** Where goods are delivered by one person to another to sell on behalf of the person delivering them, the transaction is a bailment—an agency to sell on consignment—and title remains in the principal or consignor. However, an ordinary bailment differs from a consignment in two respects: (1) A bailment ordinarily involves the delivery and acceptance of a chattel for some particular purpose, the chattel to be returned to the owner in the same or altered form when it has served the purpose. A consignment does not contemplate a return of the goods, but their sale to third parties by the consignee and an accounting for the proceeds of the sale. (2) Since a bailment contemplates possession, whether for safe keeping, or as a pledge, or for use by the bailee, or for some service to be rendered (such as repairs, storage or transportation), there is no ostensible authority to sell, and an unauthorized sale by the bailee, even to an innocent third party for value, will not deprive the owner of his title. In a consignment, on the other hand, since the primary object is to sell, an innocent third party purchaser for value gets good title as against the owner even if the consignee, such as a factor or commission merchant, was instructed not to sell until further notice, or to sell only upon certain terms, which were violated.

## Questions

1. What three elements must be present to give rise to a bailment? Give an example of each of these.
2. What is the essence of the distinction between a bailment and an exchange?
3. "Neither money nor securities deposited in a bank may constitute a bailment." Is this statement true, false, or sometimes true and sometimes false? Explain.
4. State in simple language the test of a bailment as distinguished from similar transactions. How does this test apply to fungible goods?
5. What is the basic distinction between a bailment and a conditional sale?
6. Is a bailment or lease with option to purchase ever treated as equivalent to a conditional sale, and if so, under what circumstances?
7. What is the basic distinction between a bailment and an agency? A bailment and a consignment?

## Problems

1. Makemoney delivers a large quantity of black market meat to a cold-storage warehouse where, owing to defective refrigeration, the meat spoils. Makemoney sues the warehousemen. These facts having been duly presented upon the trial, what disposition should the court make of the case?
2. Jones delivers a suit to one of the pressers in a tailor shop, for the purpose of having the suit pressed. He accidentally leaves a $100.00 bill in one of the pockets of his suit. The tailor employs ten men to press clothes by machine. When the suit is returned to Jones, the money is missing. Jones sues the tailor. On the trial, it appears conclusively that the tailor personally never saw the suit or the money. Judgment for whom and why?
3. Briggs enters a restaurant, hangs up his hat and coat on a hook near a table, seats himself at the table, gives the waiter his order, finishes his meal, pays the check, and then discovers that his coat and hat have disappeared. The proprietor of the restaurant disclaims liability and Briggs brings suit for the value of his coat and hat. Who will succeed and why?
4. The Robinson Clothing Store advertises a sale of men's coats. Martin enters the store, removes his coat and, owing to the crowd of customers seeking to be waited on, and the fact that all the salesmen are busy at the time, Martin tries on a number of overcoats himself, and finally decides to leave the store without waiting for a salesman. When he looks for his overcoat, however, he finds it has disappeared. The Robinson Clothing Store disclaims responsibility and Martin brings suit. Will he recover? Give reasons.
5. I. M. Sharp, a "confidence" man, telephones Rosenheim's, a wholesale

jewelry store, which had been supplying merchandise to Stacey's, a leading department store, and says: "This is Stacey's jewelry department. Please send over a gross of Rand watches, ladies size, model 6198, at ten o'clock tomorrow morning." The next morning, at a little past ten, Sharp goes to the clerk in charge of the jewelry department at Stacey's, and says: "I am from Rosenheim's. We sent a gross of watches to you by mistake." The clerk replies: "Yes, I know. They have just come up from our receiving department. We never ordered them," and hands over the watches to Sharp, who signs a receipt in Rosenheim's name, and then disappears with the watches. Rosenheim sues Stacey's. Judgment for whom and why?

6. Piper leaves a package with the clerk of a cigar store, requesting the clerk to keep the package for him, and stating that he will return in an hour. The package is left on the counter, where any person might readily pick it up, and a customer makes off with it while the clerk is waiting on other customers. Piper sues the proprietor of the cigar store, who sets up as a defense that he was under no obligation to Piper, since there was no consideration for the clerk's promise to keep the package. How should this defense be disposed of and why?

7. The Midwest Grain Corporation deposits 1,000 tons of wheat with the Twentieth Century Grain Elevator Co. for winter storage. Several months later the Midwest Grain Corporation demands delivery of the wheat. The Twentieth Century Grain Elevator Co. stands ready to deliver the quantity of wheat stored, but not the precise wheat left for storage. The Midwest Grain Corporation sues in replevin. On the trial, the Twentieth Century Grain Elevator Co. proves that the wheat tendered was equivalent in quantity, quality and value to that which was stored. How should the court decide, and why?

8. The Wideview Television Co., Inc., makes a contract with Blossom, by the terms of which Blossom is to pay the company $10.00 a week for 20 weeks, during which time he is to have the use of a Wideview television set. It is agreed in the contract, which is signed by both parties, that the payments are to be "as and for rent, and are not to be considered as payments on account of purchase." It is further stipulated that "the lessor (the company) upon default in any of the payments by the lessee (Blossom), is to have the immediate right to repossess itself of the said property wheresoever found, and in such event the lessee shall have no further claim in respect thereto." Blossom makes 12 payments and then defaults. The company sends a man around to Blossom's home to seize the television set, and Blossom refuses to give it up. An action in replevin is brought by the company. How should the case be decided and why?

9. Green sends to Fashion Fabricators, Inc., a thousand yards of gabardine to be manufactured into raincoats. Fashion Fabricators, Inc., make up the raincoats, using a large quantity of their own material, including sateen and plaid fabrics, the total value of which is in excess of the value of the gabardine. The garments are about to be shipped from the company's warehouse, when a storm blows away part of the roof, and the raincoats are rendered worthless by the rain. Green sues: (1) for breach of contract; (2) replevin as to the gabardine; (3) conversion for failure to return the gabardine manufactured into garments after making demand therefor. The company counterclaims for the value of the labor and materials, and denies breach of contract, replevin and conversion. How should the case be decided, and why?

## PART 2. RIGHTS, DUTIES AND LIABILITIES

**Nature of Bailment as Determining Rights and Duties.** Certain rights and duties govern all bailments, others vary in accordance with the type of bailment. It is therefore necessary to note the major classifications of bailments.

**Major Classifications of Bailments.** The modern classification of bailments is based on benefit to the parties, the first two being gratuitous, the third not:

(a) *Bailments for the sole benefit of the bailor*, as where the bailee gratuitously keeps something for the bailor, or renders some gratuitous service in connection with bailor's chattel.

(b) *Bailments for the sole benefit of the bailee*, as where the bailor gratuitously lends something to the bailee.

(c) *Bailments for mutual benefit*, which are further classified and described on pages 296 to 303.

### Rights, Duties and Obligations
### Common to All Bailments

**In General.** Rights, duties and obligations common to all bailments embrace: (a) the bailee's duty to fulfill the purpose of the bailment, (b) the bailor's duty to deliver a safe chattel, (c) the bailee's right and duty to protect the chattel, and (d) the bailee's duty to return the chattel.

**Bailee's Duty to Fulfill Purpose of Bailment.** One who undertakes a bailment, whether gratuitously or for reward, must fulfill its purpose.

EXAMPLE: If I leave a dog with you on your promise to take care of him in my absence, I can hold you liable for any damage I sustain in case you abandon the dog while I am away. This is true even where you get no benefit from the transaction: My sacrifice in parting with possession in reliance on your promise is the consideration which supports your promise (page 59). However, if I have not yet parted with possession, I cannot hold you to your *gratuitous promise* to take care of the dog, should you change your mind.

**Bailor's Duty to Deliver Safe Chattel.** Whether he receives any benefit or not, if a person lends or leases a chattel to another for some purpose, the chattel must be safe. If it is not, and the bailee suffers damage in consequence, the bailor is liable.

EXAMPLE: A contract for the leasing of an airplane provided that the plane was to be used exclusively for civil pilot training. The court held that this imposed a corresponding duty on the bailor to ensure that the plane was safe, suitable and airworthy.[7]

However, a bailor for mutual benefit is in this respect held to a stricter responsibility than a gratuitous bailor. The former is liable for not disclos-

---

[7] *Dufort v. Smith*, 37 Luz. L. Reg. Rep. (Pa.) 315.

ing defects of which he knew *or should have known;* the latter only for
defects actually known to him.

**Bailee's Right and Duty to Protect Chattel.** The bailee not only has the
right but the duty to protect the bailment against damage, loss, theft or
destruction.

*Duty to insure.* Because the bailee is charged with the responsibility of
returning the chattel, he has an "insurable interest" (page 353) in it. However, a mere gratuitous promise to insure, unconnected with the liability
or responsibility of a bailee, will not render one liable for loss through failure to insure.

EXAMPLE: *A* and *B* were joint owners of a vessel. *A* voluntarily undertook to
get the vessel insured, but neglected to do so. The vessel having been lost at
sea, it was held that no action would lie against *A* for the nonperformance
of his promise, although *B* had relied on that promise to his loss, because there
was no consideration for the promise.[8]

*Duty to take legal steps.* Likewise, though not the owner of the chattel.
the bailee may sue third parties who seek to appropriate, damage or interfere with it in any way.[9]

**Bailee's Duty to Return Chattel.** A bailee must return the chattel to
the bailor when it has fulfilled the purpose of the bailment. Failure to do
so, upon the bailor's demand, subjects the bailee to a suit for *conversion,*
or for *replevin* (pages 803, 847). For example, if a bailee to whom is entrusted possession of property belonging to another, sells such property,
or uses it contrary to the terms of the bailment, he commits conversion.
Similarly, when the bailee redelivers the property *to the wrong person,*
even though he does so in good faith and without negligence, he commits
conversion.[10]

EXAMPLE: In *Doyle v. Peerless Motor Car Co. of New England,*[11] the bailee
of an automobile delivered it to the owner's chauffeur under an order signed
by the owner's daughter. The court held that the bailee was guilty of conversion unless the order was authorized by the owner, since the bailee is liable
for conversion on delivery of property to an unauthorized person, though he
acts in good faith and exercises a high degree of care.

## Rights, Duties and Liabilities
## Dependent Upon Nature of Bailment

**Particular Rights, Duties and Obligations.** In addition to the foregoing
rights, duties and obligations common to all bailments, the following
rights, duties and obligations depend upon whether the bailment is (a)

---

[8] *Thorne v. Deas,* 4 Johns. 84, 99.
[9] *Grand Rapids & I. Ry. Co. v. Resur,* 186 Ind. 563, 117 N.E. 259.
[10] *Baer v. Slater,* 261 Mass. 153, 158 N.E. 328.
[11] 226 Mass. 561, 116 N.E. 257.

for the sole benefit of the bailor, (b) for the sole benefit of the bailee, or (c) for mutual benefit:

(1) Degree of care a bailee must use.

(2) Bailee's right to use bailment.

(3) Duty to reimburse bailee for expenses.

(4) Right to terminate bailment.

**Bailee's Duty to Exercise Care.** Regardless of degree, a bailee must exercise some measure of care in connection with the bailment. Failure to exercise care is negligence. If a bailment is lost, damaged or destroyed without negligence or fault on the bailee's part, the bailee is not liable, except where he is an "insurer" of the goods.

EXAMPLE: *A* hires a "Drive-Your-Self" automobile at $1.00 an hour. Through no fault of his, the car is damaged in collision with *B*. Since the damage occurred without *A*'s fault, *A* is not liable for such damage. (Note: If *B* was negligent, he would be liable to the owner for damage to the car, and to *A* for any damage to him as bailee.)

**When Bailee is Liable as Insurer.** For a consideration or "premium," one may contract to assume the role of insurer, that is, one may agree to be liable regardless of negligence. In addition, the law itself, as a matter of public policy, fixes the responsibility of an insurer on certain classes of persons, that is, it renders them liable regardless of negligence in connection with property in their custody. Examples are innkeepers (page 303) and carriers of goods (page 314).

**Liability Regardless of Negligence, Where Bailee Deviates.** Where a bailee deviates from his contract of bailment, as by transferring the bailment to someone else, or changing the place of storage, and loss or damage results from such deviation, the bailee becomes liable regardless of negligence. For example, if a bailor entrusts a chattel to a bailee for the purpose of having it repaired, and the bailee, without the bailor's knowledge or consent, delegates the performance of his undertaking to someone else, in consequence of which the bailment is damaged, lost or destroyed, the original bailee is liable regardless of the question of negligence. So, also, if the owner of an automobile contracts with the proprietor of a garage to keep his car in a certain garage, and the garageman, without the bailor's consent, removes the car to another garage where it is damaged by the falling of the roof, the garage keeper is liable regardless of negligence.

**Degree of Care a Bailee Must Use.** A bailee must use either slight, great or ordinary care, depending upon the nature of the bailment.[12]

(a) *In a bailment for the sole benefit of the bailor*, the bailee, who is

---

[12] This doctrine, however, is being generally superseded by the doctrine that the test is whether "due care" has been exercised under a given set of circumstances.

merely accommodating the bailor, is required to exercise but *slight care,* hence is liable only for *gross negligence.*

(b) *In a bailment for the sole benefit of the bailee,* the latter is being accommodated, hence he must exercise *great care* and is liable for *slight negligence.*

(c) In a bailment for *mutual benefit,* neither party is being accommodated. The bailee must exercise ordinary care and is liable for ordinary negligence.

What constitutes gross, slight or ordinary negligence depends on the facts of each case. The following examples may be illustrative:

(1) When a watch is left at a shop for repair, and the same night the shop is destroyed by fire, the shop owner's liability will depend upon whether, from the facts, he exercised ordinary care.

(2) If a bank accepts from a customer, for safekeeping, a package of money and securities, and the package is stolen by the bank's cashier who has previously had a good reputation, the liability of the bank will depend upon whether, from the facts, it exercised ordinary care.

(3) *A*, as security for a loan, gives *B* a watch, which *B* puts in his safe. If burglars break into the safe and remove its contents, *B*'s liability for the watch will depend upon whether the facts spell out lack of ordinary care, that is, ordinary negligence.

(4) If, in example (3) above, the watch had been placed in a trunk instead of a safe, and removed therefrom by burglars, a court might well hold that *B* had exercised less than ordinary care, and was liable. If, however, *B* were a gratuitous bailee, a jury might find that *B* had exercised the "slight" care required of such bailee.

(5) *A* gave *B* a bag of gold coins to keep for him as an accommodation. *B* placed the bag of coins with his own money in a locked trunk, whence it was stolen by burglars. The Court held that *B*, as a gratuitous bailee, exercised the degree of care required of him.[13]

(6) In *More v. Fisher,*[14] the court held that where a truck was used by a cleaner to pick up and deliver articles of clothing, it was lack of ordinary care to leave the truck unguarded in a public street in Chicago, even though it was locked and left for not more than five minutes.

(7) Jones, on an automobile trip from New York to Boston, agrees to take a valuable parcel for his friend Smith and to deliver it to Smith's son in Providence. Jones stops at Bridgeport for dinner, parks his car at the curb, takes his own property out, but leaves Smith's parcel in the car, whence it is stolen. Although Jones is a gratuitous bailee, a jury might well find that he failed to exercise the slight care required of him, that is, that he was grossly negligent, hence liable.

(8) Zindle, a jeweler, gave Mrs. Chapman, a prospective customer, a diamond brooch, worth $5,200, to wear on trial. Mrs. Chapman wore the brooch with other expensive pieces of her own jewelry, to all of which she gave what women of her social standing regarded as reasonable care. Nevertheless, the brooch was lost or stolen. Since this was a bailment for mutual benefit

---

[13] *Hargis v. Spencer,* 254 Ky. 297, 71 S.W. (2nd) 666.
[14] 245 Ill. App. 567.

(prospective purchase), and ordinary care was exercised, Mrs. Chapman was not liable for the loss.

(9) Brown, a farmer, borrows a team of horses from his neighbor. One of the horses steps into a hole in Brown's pasture and is lamed. Though Brown might not have been liable had he hired the use of the team, the fact that the bailment was for his sole benefit should have made him exceptionally careful, and a jury might well hold that he was guilty of slight negligence and liable accordingly.

**Bailee's Right to Use Bailment.** The bailee's right to use the bailment is as follows:

(a) *In a bailment for the sole benefit of the bailor,* the bailee has no right to use the bailment unless use will not affect it, or is necessary to preserve it.

EXAMPLE: Reading a book will not affect it; exercising a horse or milking a cow is necessary to preserve such bailment.

(b) *In a bailment for the sole benefit of the bailee,* use by the latter is naturally permitted, since it is the object of the bailment. But if the bailee uses the bailment for a different purpose than that agreed upon, he is liable to the bailor for any loss, damage or destruction to the bailment, though it occurred without his fault.

EXAMPLE: If a person borrows a car to move his trunk, then uses it for a short pleasure trip, he is liable if the car is damaged on the pleasure trip, though the accident is not his fault.

(c) *In a bailment for mutual benefit,* use by the bailee depends upon the purpose of the bailment. For example, a musician who rents a piano to practice on it is in a different position from a warehouseman who merely stores the piano and has no right to use it.

**Duty to Reimburse Bailee for Expenses.** In a bailment for the sole benefit of the bailor, the bailee is entitled to reimbursement for any reasonable expense he incurs in accommodating the bailor by keeping the bailment for him. In a bailment for the sole benefit of the bailee, or for mutual benefit, the bailee may compel reimbursement only for extraordinary, not ordinary expense. If a contractor, for example, leases a drilling machine, he must bear the expense of replacing any drills he breaks, but not of replacing essential parts of the machine that require replacement through no fault of his own.

**Bailee's Lien: Right to Terminate Bailment.** The subject of liens is discussed in Chapter 17. A bailee's lien is his right to retain possession of the bailment until some charge or obligation in connection with it is discharged or satisfied. (See page 685.) The right to terminate a bailment, or to assert a lien in respect to it, depends upon the nature of the bailment.

(a) In a *bailment for the sole benefit of the bailor,* the latter may at any time require the return of his chattel, and the bailee may at any time require the bailor to take it back, unless the bailee has undertaken to keep the chattel for a prescribed period. The bailee has no claim or lien in connection with the bailment, since he undertook it without reward.

(b) In a *bailment for the sole benefit of the bailee,* since the bailor receives no value for the use of his chattel, nor consideration for his promise to let the bailee use it, he may require the bailee to return the chattel at any time; and of course the bailee has no lien in connection with it.

(c) In a *bailment for mutual benefit,* the rights of the parties, including the right to terminate the bailment, depend upon their contract and the type of bailment it creates. For example, in a pledge (page 296) or hire of service (page 299), the purpose of the contract would be defeated and the rights of the bailee infringed if the bailor could terminate the bailment at will. Moreover, when a bailee renders service in connection with a chattel, he acquires a *possessory lien* in respect to it, that is, a right to retain possession until his charges for the service have been paid.

## Questions

1. What is the modern classification of bailments? On what is such classification based?

2. Name four rights, duties and obligations which are common to all bailments.

3. In what two ways may a bailee be called upon to discharge his duty to protect the bailment?

4. What liabilities may a bailee incur on failing to return the bailment?

5. Name four rights, duties and liabilities which may vary with the nature of the bailment.

6. Can you think of a situation, other than by express contract, in which a bailee is required to exercise no care at all with respect to a bailment? Explain.

7. In the absence of an express contract, can you think of any situations in which a bailee is liable regardless of negligence? Explain.

8. Relatively speaking, what degree of care is a bailee required to exercise in the following transactions: (a) bailment for the sole benefit of the bailor, (b) bailment for the sole benefit of the bailee, or (c) bailment for mutual benefit?

9. What right has a bailee to use a bailment in the following situations: (a) bailment for the sole benefit of the bailor, (b) bailment for the sole benefit of the bailee, and (c) bailment for mutual benefit? Explain fully.

10. Where a bailee incurs expenses in connection with a bailment, is the bailor required to reimburse the bailee for such expenses, and if so, under what conditions and to what extent?

11. Under what conditions may a bailor or bailee terminate (a) a bailment for the sole benefit of the bailor, (b) a bailment for the sole benefit of the bailee, or (c) a bailment for mutual benefit?

## Problems

1. Davis agrees to take care of Parker's dog while the latter is out of town. When Parker brings the dog to Davis' apartment, the latter refuses to take the dog. Has Parker any cause of action against Davis? Give reasons.

2. Suppose that Davis accepted the dog, but finding him to be very active, and something of a nuisance, especially on the street, refused to be bothered with a leash, and allowed the animal to run about freely, so that the dog got in front of an automobile which ran him over and killed him. The dog had a high pedigree and cost Parker $500. Parker, upon his return, sues Davis for the value of the dog and Davis' defense is that he was under no legal obligation to take care of the dog. Who would get judgment and why?

3. Couch borrows an expensive camera from Crump, who cautions Couch to be very careful with it and not lose it, because it would be difficult to replace. Couch says, "Don't worry, I will get it back to you safe and sound." The camera is stolen from Couch without fault of the latter. Crump sues Couch for the value of the camera. Judgment for whom and why?

4. Barker borrowed an ax from Baxter, his neighbor. The ax head was loose, but Baxter neglected to call Barker's attention to this fact. While Barker was using the ax, its head flew off and hit Barker's infant son, seriously injuring him. Barker sues Baxter on behalf of his son. How should the case be decided and why?

5. Foster borrowed his friend Brown's automobile, with permission to use it during Brown's absence on a six months' cruise. The Active Finance Company sought to replevy the car on the ground that Brown still owed the final installment on the purchase price. Foster opposed the Finance Company's proceeding to replevy the car. The Finance Company claims that Foster has no legal standing in the dispute, since he has no legal interest in the car. How should the court decide and why?

6. Williams delivers a watch to Roach, a jeweler, for repair. The jewelry store is broken into by a burglar who takes the watch among other articles of jewelry. The watch had already been repaired. Williams sues Roach, who counter-claims for the value of his services. Judgment for whom and why?

7. Larkin leaves a suit of clothes with Silverman, his tailor, to be cleaned and pressed. Silverman is busy with an unusual rush of work, and sends Larkin's suit with others to be serviced by neighboring tailor. That evening a fire of unknown origin destroys the latter's shop, including Larkin's suit. May Larkin hold either tailor responsible? Explain.

8. Clarke borrows the use of an automobile from Carter, stating that he wishes to move a trunk from his office to his home. While moving the trunk, Clarke decides to pay a friendly call at the same time, but in doing so runs into a telegraph pole to avoid collision with a truck, which was being recklessly driven by a drunken driver. Clarke was not negligent. Carter sues Clarke for damage to the car. Judgment for whom and why?

9. Brown, a furrier, agrees to store an ermine wrap for his daughter-in-law during the summer months without charge. He prepares the garment for storage as is customary, and stores it in his warehouse, which is properly equipped as to temperature, but which is not burglar-proof. It is customary for furriers to adopt the precaution of installing a burglar alarm in and about their warehouses and safes containing expensive garments. A burglar breaks into Brown's warehouse and steals his daughter-in-law's ermine wrap. The

daughter-in-law sues Brown and the court charges the jury: "If you find that the defendant failed to exercise the caution usually exercised under similar circumstances, that is, the ordinary reasonable precaution which furriers adopt under like conditions, you must find the defendant guilty of negligence, and liable accordingly." The jury brings in a verdict for the plaintiff and Brown appeals. Should the judgment be sustained or reversed? Give reasons.

10.* A banker accepts from his customer, for safekeeping, a package of money and securities marked with the depositor's name. The package is subsequently stolen by the banker's cashier, who had previously borne a good reputation. Is the banker responsible? If so, upon what principle?

11.* X stores goods with Y, a warehouseman. The goods are stolen from the warehouse without negligence on the part of Y. Is Y liable for the goods? If so, why? If not, why not?

12.** A borrowed $75 from B, giving to B as security for the loan a valuable Swiss watch. B placed the watch in his office safe. Burglars entered B's office, broke open the safe and took its contents including the watch. Is B liable for the loss of the watch?

13. Hicks and Wicks, farmers, are neighbors. Hicks borrows $500 from Wicks and leaves as security three cows and two horses. One of the cows takes sick and Wicks has to pay $35 to a veterinary for doctoring the beast. The loan was for one month, during which time the cattle and horses cost Wicks $28.00 for upkeep. Hicks pays the $500 with interest within one month, and demands the return of his cattle and horses. Wicks refuses to accept the money and to return the animals, claiming $500 with interest, and $63 besides. Judgment for whom and why?

## PART 3. BAILMENTS FOR MUTUAL BENEFIT

**Further Classification of Mutual Benefit Bailments.** Bailments for the mutual benefit of bailor and bailee may take one of the following forms:

(1) Pledge
(2) Hire of use
(3) Hire of service, including
      (a) Labor, skill and materials
      (b) Custody
      (c) Transportation.

**Pledge Defined: Essentials.** A pledge is the bailment of personal property as security for the discharge of an obligation.

EXAMPLES:
(1) Pawn of watch to secure loan.
(2) Deposit of stocks or bonds as collateral security on a note.

The essentials of a pledge are: (a) an obligation to be secured, (b) the parties, *pledgor* and *pledgee*, (c) the thing pledged, (d) transfer of possession, (e) a contract, express or implied, governing the pledge, (f) reservation of title in the pledgor, and (g) the pledgor's right of redemption.

**Pledge Distinguished from Chattel Mortgage.** A pledge differs from a chattel mortgage in at least three respects:

(1) *Nature of security.* The security of a pledge is *possessory*, whereas

the security of a chattel mortgage lies in its character as a "charging lien" (page 688), which does not depend upon possession. Thus, in a pledge, possession is in the obligee or creditor as security, the obligor or debtor retaining title. In a chattel mortgage, possession is usually in the mortgagor or debtor, the mortgagee or creditor retaining title, not possession, as security for the debt.

(2) *Necessity of public notice, by filing.* The pledgee's possession is sufficient notice that he claims some right in respect to the pledge. A chattel mortgage, however, is a charging lien: The creditor, in lieu of possession, must file the lien in a prescribed public place if he wishes to give public notice of his rights.

(3) *Rights on default.* In the case of a pledge, nonpayment or default does not work an automatic forfeiture; title remains in the pledgor until the pledgee, by selling the goods (on notice to the pledgor or not, as the contract may provide), divests the pledgor of title. In the case of a chattel mortgage, nonperformance causes an automatic forfeiture, that is, the mortgagee's title, reserved as security, becomes absolute.

**Pledge Distinguished from Liens Generally.** A pledge is limited to the security afforded by possession. Liens are broader; they may extend to situations not dependent upon possession (page 688). In the case of a pledge, transfer of possession by way of security is the objective. In the case of a lien, transfer of possession is an incident, not an objective: Possession is transferred for some purpose other than security, such as for alteration, repair, storage or transportation; the lien arising incidentally in case the service rendered is not paid for.

**Common Types of Pledge: Pawn and Collateral.** Among the more common illustrations of pledge are (a) the *pawning* of chattels, and (b) the deposit of stocks and bonds as *collateral security*.

Although a "pawn" is technically synonymous with a pledge, the term is commonly used in relation to the pledge of chattels with a pawnbroker as security for a loan.

A pawn is clearly distinguishable from a deposit of securities as collateral in that the very thing pawned must be returned when it is redeemed, whereas the identical securities pledged as collateral need not be returned upon redemption (page 298).

**Pawnbrokers.** Pawnbrokers lend money on the deposit of chattels as security. Because they frequently deal with the financially unfortunate, their business is strictly regulated by statute. A pawnbroker cannot conduct his business without a license, must give bond, keep prescribed records (for police and other purposes), issue receipts against chattels pledged, and charge no more than a fixed interest rate. Pawnbrokers are prohibited from buying second-hand articles offered as pledges, and from selling the chattels of defaulting pledgors unless they remain unclaimed for at least a year and then only at public auction after published notice.

*Collateral security.* Technically, *collateral security* is any form of pledge accompanying and securing a debt. By common usage, the term has come to mean stocks and bonds deposited to secure a debt.

*Income on collateral security* belongs to the pledgor, but it may be collected by the pledgee and applied to reduction of the debt. "The pledgee has the right to retain possession and control of the pledge with the income and benefits in addition thereto, until the debt is paid, and it is the pledgee's duty to collect dividends on the stock and apply them to the reduction of the indebtedness." [15]

**How Stock is Pledged.** A pledge of stock is usually made by depositing the stock certificate with the pledgee, duly indorsed in blank by the pledgor. Such indorsement consists of the pledgor's signature to an assignment, which usually carries with it a power of attorney delegating authority to transfer the stock on the books of the corporation. The assignment and power of attorney may be either printed, typewritten or handwritten on the back of the certificate itself, or it may be executed on a separate paper attached to the certificate, known as a *fly-power*, which has the same effect as an indorsement on the back of the certificate.

**Pledgee's Right to Sell or Repledge Stock.** Pledgees of stock (usually stockbrokers) are customarily empowered by law to sell or repledge stock pledged with them to secure advances on margin or similar transactions. The pledgee need not return the identical stock certificate or certificates deposited by the pledgor or customer. A bank, for example, need not retain for return to a borrower the identical securities it receives as collateral, so long as it has on hand, at all times, an equivalent quantity of the securities pledged to answer the borrower's redemption.

*Pledgee's right to assign or repledge his interest.* Unless prohibited by the terms of the pledge, a pledgee may assign or repledge his interest.[16]

**Bonds Deposited as Pledge v. Bonds Deposited for Safekeeping.** If a person deposits bonds with a bank as collateral for a debt, and also bonds for safekeeping, and the debtor defaults, the bank cannot apply, in satisfaction of the debt, the bonds deposited for safekeeping, even though the bonds deposited as collateral are insufficient to cover the debt. A deposit of bonds for safekeeping constitutes a special deposit, which cannot be set off against a depositor's indebtedness.[17]

**Procedure on Pledgor's Default.** The pledgee's procedure on the pledgor's default may be prescribed by the terms of the pledge. Otherwise, it is prescribed by law, including the requirement of a public sale on notice, the disposition of any surplus, and the pledgor's liability for a deficiency.

---

[15] *Brightson v. Claflin*, 225 N.Y. 469, 122 N.E. 458.

[16] 49 C.J. 963.

[17] *First-Mercer Nat. Bank of Harrodsburg v. Tewmey's Assignee*, 246 Ky. 139, 54 S.W. 2d 672.

*Rights of third parties.* A *pledgor's creditor* may proceed against the property pledged, to the extent of the pledgor's interest; that is, to the extent of his right of redemption. Such creditor may pay the debt secured by the pledge and then levy upon the property. A *pledgee's creditor* may proceed against the pledged property only to the extent of the pledgee's possible interest in case of the pledgor's default; that is, his remedy is limited to the pledgee's remedy of selling the chattel upon the pledgor's default subject to the terms of the pledge.

**Hire of Use.** When one rents a chattel, such as a car, a printing machine or a typewriter, he hires the use of it. The bailor or lessor, in such case, warrants that the chattel leased is fit for the purpose for which it is hired. If it is not, the bailor is liable for resulting loss sustained by the bailee. The bailee, on the other hand, must exercise reasonable care in the use of the chattel; he must pay, for such use, the rental agreed upon, or, in the absence of an agreed rental, the reasonable value of the hiring; and he must return the chattel in the same condition as it was in when the hiring commenced—reasonable wear and tear excepted. He has no right to use the chattel for any other purpose than that specified in the hiring.

**Hire of Service: in General.** As noted on page 296, the hire of service includes (a) *labor, skill and materials* applied to a bailment, as when a bailor delivers raw materials for manufacture by a bailee, or a watch to be repaired by a jeweler, or a motor by a mechanic; (b) *custody,* as when valuables are left with a safe deposit company, or merchandise with a warehouse, or personal belongings with an innkeeper; and (c) *transportation,* which is more fully considered in relation to the law governing *carriers* (pages 300-331 inclusive).

**Hire of Service: Labor, Skill and Materials.** When the bailee adds or uses material in the manufacture or repair of a chattel, such material becomes part of the chattel, and title to it immediately vests in the bailor. For example, if a garageman installs new cylinders in an automobile, title thereto automatically vests in the bailor, and the garageman cannot thereafter remove the cylinders, even though he is not paid for his services. His proper remedy is to assert his lien by retaining the automobile as a whole. But if the chattel in question is made up *completely of materials furnished by an artisan or manufacturer,* there is really no bailment; as where a tailor makes up a suit of clothes, or a sculptor erects a monument, in both cases from materials wholly supplied by the tailor or sculptor.

**Hire of Service: Custody, in General.** The hire of custodial services embraces a wide variety of bailees, such as *agistors* (animal keepers, dog and cat hospitals, and so on), *livery stable* and *garage keepers, airplane hangars, warehousemen, wharfingers* (persons who keep wharves for the storage of goods), and *hotel, boarding-* and *lodginghouse keepers.* The law governing keepers of motor vehicles, watercraft and aircraft, although considerably revised by statute, derives largely from the common law governing livery stables. The most common type of bailees furnishing custody are warehousemen and innkeepers.

**Warehousemen: in General.** A warehouseman is a bailee engaged in the business of storing goods for profit. Like all bailees, a warehouseman must redeliver the identical merchandise stored, except that the proprietor of a grain elevator, being engaged in the storage of *fungible* goods (page 240), is required merely to return grain of equivalent quantity and quality.

**Warehouse Receipts.** Warehouse receipts (see Form 8) may be issued by any warehouseman. The importance of this type of document of title and the need for a uniform application of legal rules in connection with its wide commercial use have led to the general adoption of a Uniform Warehouse Receipts Act. The act provides that warehouse receipts need not be in any particular form, but every such receipt must embody certain specific items in its written or printed terms.

*Negotiable and nonnegotiable receipts.* The Uniform Act defines a negotiable receipt as one in which it is stated that the goods received will be delivered to the bearer, or to the order of any person named in the

FORM 8

### NEGOTIABLE WAREHOUSE RECEIPT
*(Courtesy Lawrence Warehouse Company)*

## FORM 8 (cont'd)

## NEGOTIABLE WAREHOUSE RECEIPT

(Reverse Side)

receipt. A nonnegotiable receipt is one in which it is stated that the goods received will be delivered to the depositor, or to any other specified person. A nonnegotiable receipt must be plainly marked, "Nonnegotiable," or "Not Negotiable"; otherwise a holder for value who believes the receipt to be negotiable may, at his option, treat the receipt as imposing upon the warehouseman the same liabilities he would have incurred had the receipt been negotiable.[18]

**Liabilities of Warehousemen.** Unlike innkeepers and carriers of goods, warehousemen are not insurers (page 291), that is, they are not liable unless negligent. Hence a warehouseman is not liable for goods stolen

---

[18] The Uniform Commercial Code definition is more flexible and up-to-date. The Code provides (Sec. 6-102) that a document of title is negotiable (a) if it provides for delivery to bearer or to the order of a named person; (b) if it runs to a named person, and the issuer conspicuously marks it negotiable; or (c) where recognized in overseas trade, if it runs to a named person "or assigns." Any other document, says the Code, is nonnegotiable.

from his warehouse without his negligence. The law does, however, impose upon warehousemen certain liabilities arising out of the nature of the bailment:

(a) A warehouseman must not and may not be compelled to deliver up the goods stored except against the warehouse receipts previously issued for them.

(b) If a receipt is lost or destroyed, a court, upon proper proof of the facts and the filing of a bond to secure the warehouseman, may order the goods delivered without a receipt; but if such receipt, negotiable in form, turns up in the hands of an innocent holder for value, the warehouseman may be liable to such person notwithstanding, in which event he is protected by the bond.

(c) Negotiable receipts must be cancelled when the goods are delivered; else the warehouseman is liable to any subsequent innocent holder of the receipt for value.

(d) A warehouseman who issues a fictitious receipt is guilty of a crime punishable by fine and imprisonment.

(e) If the proprietor of a grain elevator fails to keep on hand at all times an equivalent quantity of grain to answer the demands of depositors, he is guilty of conversion (page 803).

**Warehouseman's Lien.** A warehouseman has a lien for storage charges against all goods brought into the warehouse by the owner or his agent. If a thief or other unauthorized person deposits goods in a warehouse, the owner is not liable for storage nor subject to a warehouseman's lien. But if possession was entrusted to a person who, under the law, would have implied authority to pledge the goods (page 419), such person, so far as concerns a warehouseman's lien, would be deemed to have implied authority to store the goods.

**Innkeepers: in General.** Under the common law, an "inn" was a place which furnished travellers not only with lodging, but with food, drink and a stable for the care of their horses. Unless all these services were supplied, the place was not, legally speaking, an inn, and the rules of law governing innkeepers, including the benefit of an innkeeper's lien on the traveller's belongings, were inapplicable. Thus, though innkeepers have been entitled to a lien on a guest's belongings from the earliest days of the common law, no such right existed in favor of boarding- and lodginghouse keepers until supplied by statute. Today, however, with the change in customs and modes of travel, it is not necessary for a hotel or similar establishment to supply food, drink and stable or garage accommodations in order to qualify under the law as an inn, so long as it receives transient guests (as distinguished from nontraveling or resident guests), and furnishes them with lodging.

*Innkeeper's lien unique.* An innkeeper's lien, which extends to a guest's entire belongings on the premises, is unique in that it is superior to all other claims. An innkeeper may therefore hold a guest's baggage as security for an unpaid bill even though such baggage does not belong to the guest or is covered by conditional sale or chattel mortgage. However, this rule does not apply if the hotel proprietor knew that the baggage did not belong to the guest.

**Special Duties and Liabilities of Innkeeper.** An innkeeper's liability is unique because he comes into direct contact with the public and guests would be at his mercy if he were not charged with special responsibility. Among the more important duties and liabilities of an innkeeper are: (a) duty to serve all, (b) liability for safety of guests, (c) liability as insurer of guests' property.

**Innkeeper's Duty to Serve All.** An innkeeper must, without discrimination, serve all proper persons who apply for accommodation, and for failure to do so he is liable in damages to the person rejected.

**Liability for Safety of Guests.** An innkeeper's liability for the safety of his guests is that of using ordinary care; and if a guest is injured while on the premises, but without the innkeeper's negligence, the innkeeper is not liable.

**Liability as Insurer of Guests' Property.** As to a guest's *property*, an innkeeper is an *insurer;* that is, if such property is lost or stolen while on the premises, the innkeeper is liable whether he was negligent or not. However, an innkeeper's liability as an insurer of his guests' property is subject to the following exceptions: (a) *acts of God* (floods, hurricanes, earthquakes, fire caused by lightning, and so on); (b) *acts of the public enemy;* (c) *loss due to guest's own fault* (as where a guest fails to lock the door of his room); (d) *statutory limitations.*

**Statutory Limitations on Innkeeper's Liability.** As a rule, hotels may limit their liability for guests' valuables by complying with certain statutory requirements. Thus, if a hotel provides a safe where guests may deposit their valuables, and posts proper notices to this effect, the hotel proprietor (unless he is guilty of negligence) is not responsible if a guest fails to heed the notice and his valuables are lost or stolen. Statutes also commonly protect a hotel proprietor against liability for valuables in excess of a given maximum ($500 in New York and New Jersey, $250 in Illinois), so that if such articles are deposited in the safe and lost, the hotel proprietor is not liable above the statutory maximum.

## Questions

1. How would you define a pledge?
2. Name seven essentials of a pledge.
3. In what three respects does a pledge differ from a chattel mortgage? Explain fully.
4. Distinguish between a pledge and liens, generally.
5. Name two of the more common types of pledge.

6. How would you distinguish between a pawn and a deposit of securities with respect to the return of the identical bailment?

7. What are some of the ways in which the law regulates pawnbrokers?

8. Give a brief description of the steps by which stock is pledged as collateral security.

9. Under what circumstances are pledgees of stock, such as stockbrokers, empowered to sell or repledge stock not their own, and what is their duty in this connection when the pledgor discharges his obligation and demands a return of his stock?

10. What is meant by a "hire of use"? Give two illustrations.

11. What is meant by a "hire of service"? Name three major types of service in this connection.

12. What are some of the major types of custodial services which may be rendered by a bailee for the hire of service?

13. "Like all bailees, a warehouseman must deliver the identical merchandise stored." Name one exception to this rule.

14. Distinguish between a negotiable and a non-negotiable warehouse receipt.

15. With respect to the responsibility for property entrusted to them, is there any distinction between warehousemen and innkeepers? Explain.

16. Explain the liabilities of a warehouseman in respect to the following: (a) what is required before goods stored can be returned, (b) duty in respect to innocent third parties acquiring a negotiable warehouse receipt, (c) duty in respect to cancellation of receipt, (d) liability for fictitious receipt, and (e) quantity of grain which proprietor of grain elevator must keep on hand.

17. What are the more important duties and liabilities of an innkeeper?

## Problems

1.* B, a depositor in the Cotton Exchange Bank, borrowed $5,000 from the bank, for which he gave his negotiable promissory note payable sixty days from its date. B, as sole collateral security for the payment of the said note pledged with the bank five $1,000 bonds, on an agreement that such bonds be sold if default should be made in the payment of the note, and that the net proceeds of such sale should be applied to the payment of the debt. B failed to pay the note at maturity. The net proceeds of the sale of the bonds amounted to $4,000, and B was still indebted to the bank in the sum of $1,000 and interest. B had on deposit for safekeeping with the bank two Liberty Bonds for $1,000 each. Has the bank a legal right to sell these bonds and apply the proceeds to the payment of B's indebtedness without B's consent or a judgment of the Court? Give reasons.

2. Kraft buys an automobile on the installment plan, and signs a paper that he is not to obtain title to the car until all the installments are paid. The conditional bill of sale is duly filed. Kraft, after storing his car with the Mammoth Garage, defaults in his payments on the car, and also fails to pay the storage charges. The vendor of the automobile seeks to reclaim the vehicle from the Mammoth Garage, which refuses to give it up until the storage charges are paid. The vendor sues the garage. Judgment for whom and why?

3. Rand owes Sand $1,000 for which he has pledged 50 shares of preferred stock worth $5,000. Hand, a creditor of Rand, secures judgment against him for $3,500, and issues execution to the sheriff, who, learning of the preferred stock left with Sand, offers Sand $1,000 with interest and demands the stock. Sand refuses. What are the rights of the parties?

4.* X stores goods with Y, a warehouseman. The goods are stolen from the warehouse without negligence on the part of Y. Is Y liable for the goods? If so, why? If not, why not?

5. A traveling salesman visiting New York leaves his suitcase in the checkroom of the Sycamore Hotel where, however, he is not stopping. Later he returns and demands his suitcase, which in the meantime has been stolen. Assuming that these are the only facts presented on the trial, who would get judgment, and why?

6. The Cosmopolitan Hotel is a first-class boardinghouse catering to a high type of lodgers, and selecting its boarders with care and discrimination. No lodgers are taken for less than a period of one week. During the night, in the absence of one of the lodgers, his room is broken into by a burglar and valuable articles are taken therefrom. No negligence can be shown on the part of the hotel. The lodger sues the hotel for the value of the articles stolen. The Court charges the jury that an innkeeper is an insurer, and directs judgment for the plaintiff. Was the charge correct? Give reasons.

7. Bowman, a well-to-do and respectable citizen, delivers 500 cases of bonded liquor to the Worldwide Warehouse for storage. Two months later, Bowman demands redelivery of the liquor, but is unable to present his warehouse receipt, on the ground that the same has been lost, mislaid or stolen. Bowman insists, however, that as a respectable citizen, he is entitled to redelivery of the liquor, and upon the warehouseman's refusal, he brings suit. Upon the trial, he brings ample proof of the delivery of the liquor. May the warehouseman be compelled to redeliver the liquor under the circumstances? Explain.

8. Plaintiff sued the proprietor of a hotel to recover for loss of his wife's wrist watch stolen from his room while he was a guest at the hotel. The hotel proprietor defended on the ground that the watch involved was ornamented with diamonds and hence was an item of jewelry which should have been deposited in the safe. How did the court decide, and why?

## COURT CASES FOR REVIEW

### How did the Court decide, and why?

1. Swindlers ordered goods from a manufacturer to be sent to a dealer; then telephoned the dealer in the manufacturer's name that the goods had been sent by mistake and would be called for; then called for and disappeared with the goods. The manufacturer sued the dealer. *Krumsky v. Loeser*, 37 Misc. 504, 75 N.Y. Supp. 1012.

2. Plaintiff hung up his overcoat on a hook in the box of a theatre occupied by him while watching a performance. The overcoat disappeared. Plaintiff sued the proprietor of the theatre. *Pattison v. Hammerstein*, 17 Misc. 375, 39 N.Y. Supp. 1039.

3. A furnace repairer obtained a chain from defendant for the removal of a furnace case weighing slightly less than six tons. The chain broke while the case was suspended, causing severe injuries to the repairer's employee. The latter, as bailee, sued the foundry company, which interposed two defenses: (1) The chain had a six ton manufacturer's rating; and (2) It had been purchased from a reliable manufacturer. *Reynolds v. American Foundry & Mach. Co.*, 239 P. 2d 209.

4. Plaintiff took his automobile to a parking lot. He informed the attendant that his car contained considerable personal property. Assured by the attendant that "it would be all right," he paid the necessary charges and received a

parking lot ticket. The ticket purportedly excluded liability for personal property loss. The contents of the car were stolen, and plaintiff sued. *Parkrite Auto Park v. Badgett*, 242 S.W. 2d 630.

5. Plaintiff's airplane was delivered to defendants for servicing and repair. Defendants were cautioned to remove the ignition key. This they failed to do. As a result, the plane was stolen from the hanger and destroyed in a subsequent crash. Upon suit by the owner, defendants pleaded: (1) Liability for theft and destruction was not within the contemplation of the parties; and (2) The loss of the plane was not the natural and proximate result of the alleged breach. *Lewis v. Jensen*, 39 Wash. 2d 301, 235 P. 2d 312.

6. A retailer of fur coats from time to time had returned unwanted merchandise by express to a wholesaler without declaring its full value, having on those various occasions relied upon the wholesaler's statement that he carried insurance against losses in transit of merchandise being returned to him by retailers. The wholesaler had never in the past protested this practice. Following his usual custom, the retailer returned by express a valuable consignment of coats which was ultimately lost. The wholesaler now brings suit against the retailer because of the latter's failure to declare their true value. *B. Ordiver & Sons v. Kay*, 212 Miss. 475, 54 So. 2d 729.

7. The proprietor of a parking lot required car owners to surrender their keys on parking. He had also erected signs of non-liability for fire and theft, and he orally informed car owners of such non-liability. Under these circumstances, a car owner parked his car in the lot in question. The car was stolen, and the owner sued the parking lot proprietor. *Miller's Mut. Fire Ins. Ass'n of Alton, Ill. v. Parker*, 234 N.C. 20, 65 S.E. 2d 341.

8. Plaintiff delivered her fur coat to defendant for storage. She was given a receipt limiting the furrier's liability for loss during storage. At the same time, it was agreed that defendant would make certain alterations and repairs in the coat, at an agreed price. After the repairs had been completed and while the coat was being transported to the warehouse for storage, it was lost. The owner demanded full value, and on rejection by defendant, brought suit. *Lumberman's Mut. Ins. Co. v. F. Z. Cikra, Inc.*, 155 Ohio St. 421, 99 N.E. 2d 81.

9. A contract between a sawmill operator and a fuel dealer provided that the dealer should furnish equipment for converting mill refuse into sawdust fuel. Title to the equipment was to remain in the dealer during the two year term of the agreement, after which it was to pass to the mill operator. A separate clause provided that if the mill operator had not delivered to the dealer a total of 26,000 units of fuel at the end of the two year period, the operator was to continue until 26,000 units had been delivered. In a subsequent action between the parties by reason of the failure of the mill operator to deliver the required number of units within the specified time, it became important to ascertain if title had passed to the mill operator at the end of the two year term. *Lloyd v. Ridgefield Lumber Ass'n*, 38 Wash. 2d 723, 231 P. 2d 613.

10. Plaintiff checked a parcel in defendant's parcel room. The parcel contained valuable furs. Plaintiff received a small cardboard check, printed on one side. The charge was ten cents. On the check, among other printed matter, there appeared in red letters a quarter of an inch high, the word "CONTRACT," and directly underneath in fine black type, legible on close inspection but crowded into a space less than one inch in width, the following: This CONTRACT is made on the following conditions and in consideration of the low rate at which the service is performed, and on acceptance by the depositor, expressly binds both parties to the CONTRACT. Charge—10 cents for every

24 hours or fraction thereof, for each piece covered by this contract. Loss or damage—no claim shall be made in excess of $25.00 for loss or damage to any piece." Defendant delivered the parcel to the wrong party, and plaintiff sued. *Klar v. H. & M. Parcel Room*, 270 App. Div. 538; aff'd 296 N.Y. 1044.

11. Plaintiff bought a diamond and sapphire ring from a manufacturing jeweller. On losing one of the diamonds, she arranged with the jeweller to leave the ring at his hotel so as to have the missing diamond replaced. Plaintiff brought the ring to the hotel, but the jeweller being out, she left the ring with the hotel cashier, who placed the ring in an envelope, wrote the jeweller's name on it, and left it on her desk within easy reach of persons passing her window. The ring was lost or stolen, and plaintiff sued the proprietor of the hotel. *Peet v. Roth Hotel Co.*, 191 Minn. 151, 253 N.W. 546.

12. Plaintiff consigned goods to Union Grocers, Inc., subject to an agreement that plaintiff was to be paid for the goods as and when they were sold, pending which, title, control and direction were to remain with the plaintiff. Union Grocers, Inc., on receiving the goods, placed them in a warehouse, which issued its negotiable receipt for them to Union Grocers, Inc. The latter pledged the negotiable warehouse receipt with defendant bank as security for a loan, on which it later defaulted. The bank seized the goods. Plaintiff, claiming it had never parted with title to the goods, sued defendant for damages. (*Lippincott Distributing Co. v. Peoples Commercial & Savings Bank et al.*, 137 Ohio St. 399, 30 N.E. 2d 691.)

# 6

# Transportation

**Scope of This Chapter.** In this chapter we consider the rights, duties and liabilities of all parties concerned in the hire of transportation, commonly known as the law of carriers. In Part 1 we consider the different types of carriers, and the laws, Federal and State, which regulate their activities from the standpoint of the general public. In Part 2 we deal with the rights, duties and liabilities of common carriers of goods, and of the shippers who deal with them, including a discussion of shipping documents such as express receipts and bills of lading, as well as the respective liabilities of initial and connecting carriers; and in Part 3 we consider the respective rights and obligations of the parties concerned in the transportation of passengers and their baggage.

## PART 1. CARRIERS: CLASSIFICATION AND REGULATION

**In General.** Ages before the dawn of history, transportation had become one of the most important factors in human affairs. Long before the invention of the wheel, when chattels were crudely dragged from place to place on sticks, or carried on the backs of slaves or of pack animals, certain rules probably had to be devised to govern the rights of those who entrusted their persons or their property to others for transportation.

Where such transportation deals with chattels alone, the general principles of bailment for hire apply; for transportation of chattels is merely one form of bailment for the hire of service.

Transportation, however, deals not only with the carriage of goods, but of persons as well. From the sedan chair to the airplane express, we find it necessary, in our varied affairs, to employ hundreds of forms of conveyances to take us from place to place. The rules applicable to this form of transportation are not controlled by the law of bailments alone.

**Carriers Defined and Classified.** A *carrier* is a bailee for hire engaged in the business of transportation. Carriers are commonly classified as (a) *private carriers*, (b) *common carriers*, (c) *carriers of goods*, and (d) *carriers of passengers*.

**Private v. Common Carriers.** A private carrier is one who undertakes to supply transportation in special instances and upon special arrangement, who does not hold himself out as ready to serve all who apply, and whose business is not of such general public concern as to be affected with a public interest. Examples are: private delivery services, truckmen and moving vans.

A common carrier is one who undertakes for hire to transport persons and goods for anyone who may choose to employ him.

Two liabilities which distinguish common carriers from private carriers are:

(a) *Liability for refusal to serve all who apply.* A private carrier may select whom he chooses to do business with. A common carrier is bound to serve all who apply, and for a refusal, without just cause, to serve any and all who apply, he is liable in damages.

(b) *Liability for loss or injury.* A private carrier is liable only as an ordinary bailee for hire, that is, only if he is guilty of negligence. A common carrier, in the transportation of goods, is charged with the risk of an insurer, that is, he is liable regardless of negligence.

The question of whether one is to be classed as a common carrier does not depend upon the carrier's desires in the matter, but upon the nature of the services he purports to render. If a person undertakes to engage in a business which is "affected with a public interest"—which touches the public on a wide scale—he must be prepared to serve all who apply, without discrimination. He must be prepared to subject himself and his business to public regulation in the public interest. Such a person, engaged in transportation, is known as a common carrier.

**Carriers of Goods v. Carriers of Passengers.** The distinction between carriers of goods and carriers of passengers is not merely a distinction between transporting things and transporting persons, but in the legal duties and responsibilities arising out of such distinction, notably in the liability for loss, damage and injury (page 314).

**Types of Common Carriers.** Common carriers include many forms of quasi-public service in the field of transportation; among them, railway, express, steamship, public ferry, stage coach, omnibus and public trucking concerns, and carriers by air.

**Regulation of Carriers: Basis and Purpose.** Carriers—particularly common carriers—by reason of the extent to which they are affected by a public interest and constitute "public utilities," are peculiarly subject to public control. It is the purpose of government regulation of carriers to insure a proper discharge of their functions, not only through the usual remedies available by court action, but under the supervision and control of administrative bodies established with a view to maximum service at minimum cost compatible with a fair rate of return on the investment.

To achieve these objectives, regulatory bodies maintain a system of physical inspection, prescribe standard account and record forms, and require periodic reports on forms prescribed for such purpose.

**Interstate v. Intrastate Regulation.** To the extent that carriers engage in interstate commerce, they are subject to Federal regulation under the Commerce Clause (page 572). To the extent that they do business wholly within a single state, they are subject to regulation by that state. Where *intra*state shipments also affect interstate commerce, Federal regulation is supreme if Congress has provided it, otherwise states may pass laws regulating such commerce.

**Federal Regulation: Interstate Commerce Commission.** The basic Federal statute regulating carriers is the Interstate Commerce Act of 1887, which created the Interstate Commerce Commission. This has been supplemented by various acts strengthening and extending the authority of the Interstate Commerce Commission. The Hepburn Act of 1906 provided for the enforcement of the Commission's orders. The Transportation Act of 1920 enlarged the Commission's powers over carriers under its jurisdiction, and authorized the Commission not only to regulate interstate rates, but intrastate rates as well when necessary to remove discrimination against interstate commerce. The Motor Carrier Act of 1935 gave the Commission jurisdiction over interstate and foreign transportation of passengers and property by motor carriers. The Transportation Act of 1940 conferred jurisdiction on the Commission over water carriers operating coastwise, and upon intercoastal and inland waters of the United States, thereby relieving the Maritime Commission of some of its functions when that body was transferred to the Department of Commerce. In 1942, the Interstate Commerce Commission was given jurisdiction over forwarders as well as handlers of freight.

**Functions and Activities of Interstate Commerce Commission.** As indicated, the functions and activities of the Interstate Commerce Commission have considerably broadened. Originally created to ensure just and reasonable charges for transportation, to prohibit unjust discrimination and to prevent undue or unreasonable preferences in the transportation of passengers or property by rail or water, its jurisdiction has been extended to include express companies, pipelines, sleeping car companies and the transportation of persons and property by motor carriers engaged in interstate or foreign commerce.[1] Among the various functions and activities of the Commission are the following:

(1) *Procuring information as basis for regulation.* The Commission requires common carriers to make annual reports on forms officially presented, with a view to maximum service at minimum cost compatible with a fair rate of return on the investment.

[1] The Commission had jurisdiction over telephone and telegraph communication until 1934, when it was transferred to the Federal Communications Commission.

(2) *Utilization of information.* To implement the foregoing objectives, the system of information so established and maintained is designed to achieve the following:

(a) Standardization and regulation of accounting practices.

(b) Standard minimum rates, free from discrimination.

(c) Control over capitalization and financing.

(d) Maintenance of safe and adequate facilities, including terminals and docks, rolling stock, equipment and appliances.

(e) Maintenance of safe and adequate management, and a personnel sufficient in number and training to operate the service up to the required standards.

**Federal Bill of Lading Act.** The Federal Bill of Lading Act,[2] effective January 1, 1917, provided for the use of non-negotiable and negotiable bills of lading[3] in interstate and foreign commerce. The Interstate Commerce Commission has prescribed a standard form of bill which must be used in all interstate shipments. The rules of the Commission, set forth on the reverse of such bills, govern all such shipments.

**Commerce by Air.** The Civil Aeronautics Board,[4] established in 1940, performs four principal functions: (1) It regulates the economic aspects of air transportation (certificates and permits, mail and business rates, reasonable and adequate service, avoidance of preferences and discrimination, unfair or destructive competition, consolidations, mergers, etc.); (2) It promulgates safety standards in the form of Civil Air Regulations; (3) It investigates and analyzes aircraft accidents; and (4) It fosters international air transportation.

**State Regulation.** Intrastate carriers are regulated by state statutes, which have set up regulatory bodies variously known as railroad, public utility and public service commissions, with objectives similar to those of the Interstate Commerce Commission—limited, of course, to intrastate traffic. Intrastate highways and intrastate motor traffic thereon are likewise controlled by state statutes, through highway commissions and similar bodies.

**Certificate of Public Convenience and Necessity.** Carriers which fall into the classification of public utilities are not permitted to embark upon a new venture, or open up new territory, without obtaining, from the appropriate public utility commission, a certificate of "public convenience and necessity." Unless such certificate is made a prerequisite to the rendering of a public service, needless duplication and confusion might follow, the investing public might be exposed to loss, and public convenience would be sacrificed rather than furthered.

**Uniform Bills of Lading.** We have already referred to the Uniform

---

[2] Also known as the Pomerene Act.
[3] Referred to in the Act as "straight" and "order" bills, respectively.
[4] Not to be confused with the Civil Aeronautics Commission.

Bills of Lading Act adopted by the various states. The Act itself prescribes a standard form of bill of lading applicable to intrastate shipments.

**Uniform Commercial Code.** Part 3 of Article 7 of the Uniform Commercial Code is designed to supplant the Uniform Bills of Lading Act, though it retains many of the earlier provisions. The new provisions are made necessary by new developments in the field of commerce. Transportation by air is an example. The use of ordinary bills of lading in connection with air transport is frequently impracticable because the goods may arrive at their destination ahead of the documents of title, so that no one can take delivery from the carrier. For this type of transportation the Commercial Code has adopted a new type of bill of lading, called a *destination bill*, issued at the point of destination instead of at the place of shipment. Similar provisions in the new Code bring the law of transportation closer to new commercial needs and methods.

## Questions

1. Define (a) private carrier, (b) common carrier. Give two practical distinctions between private and common carriers.
2. When is a carrier subject to State regulation, and when to Federal?
3. Summarize briefly the jurisdiction, functions and activities of the Interstate Commerce Commission.
4. What is the basis and purpose of government regulation of carriers?
5. What was the purpose of the Federal Bill of Lading Act and how was it achieved?
6. What governmental body has jurisdiction over commerce by air, and what are its principal functions?
7. What is a "certificate of public convenience and necessity" and what is the occasion for its issuance?

## Problems

1. The Exclusive Bus Corporation obtains a franchise to operate a bus service in a midwestern city. The company offers a special fare to members of an exclusive club. John Q. Citizen challenges the company's right to do this. The company, on the other hand, insists that having elected to consider itself as only a private carrier, it may select whom it chooses to serve. How would the court rule in such a situation?
2. William Smith, a resident of Cooper's Corners, owns a second-hand truck, which he uses in making deliveries to and from the railroad station and in and about the village. One day a cow runs into the truck, causing it to swerve into a tree, upset, and ruin fifty crates of eggs which Smith was delivering for Farmer Brown. The latter sues Smith. He is unable to prove that Smith was negligent, but insists that such proof is unnecessary because of the nature of Smith's occupation. How will the court decide?
3. The Interurban Electric Railway Co. operates a passenger service between several cities in Massachusetts. The Interstate Commerce Commission issues an order requiring the company to furnish certain reports. Must the company comply with the order?

## PART 2. COMMON CARRIERS OF GOODS

**Duties and Liabilities of Carriers in General.** The law governing common carriers of goods involves, primarily, a consideration of their duties and liabilities, particularly in respect to the following: (1) When a carrier's liability begins, (2) The duty to serve all, (3) Liability for loss, (4) Shipping documents, such as bills of lading and express receipts, (5) Rules governing delivery, (6) Initial and connecting carriers, and (7) When a carrier's liability ends.

**When Carrier's Liability Begins.** The liability of a carrier begins when the goods are delivered to it or to its authorized agent at the proper place for the purpose of transportation. However, if anything remains to be done by the shipper before the goods are sent on their way, the carrier's liability during that interval is the liability of an ordinary bailee, so that if loss occurs during such period, without negligence of the carrier, there is no liability. For example, if, during such interval, the goods left with the carrier were stolen, or destroyed by fire, without fault of the carrier, the latter would not be liable, whereas if the delivery in such case had been absolute, the carrier would have been liable regardless of negligence.

The factors which may prevent delivery from being absolute and, hence, which may prevent the relationship of shipper and carrier from coming into existence, may vary with the circumstances. Among these are: (1) failure to give shipping directions; (2) directions to hold until further notice; and (3) failure to prepay freight.

**Failure to Give Shipping Directions.** When a shipper delivers goods to a carrier for transportation, but fails to give shipping directions, he in effect makes the carrier a warehouseman; since one cannot be said to have assumed the duty of transportation without knowing where and to whom the goods are to be shipped.

**Directions to Hold Until Further Orders.** Where a shipper delivers merchandise with directions to hold until further orders, such delivery will not render the carrier liable as such. In effect, this is really the situation where the shipper delivers, but fails to give shipping directions. However, as soon as the shipper delivers shipping instructions, the relationship of shipper and carrier arises, and the carrier from then on becomes liable as insurer.

**Failure to Prepay Freight.** Where, as is usually the case, the contract of shipment requires the freight to be prepaid, or where a regulation of the Interstate Commerce Commission requires collection of freight rates on a prepaid consignment before it is forwarded, a carrier is not liable as insurer until such payment is made.

**Issuance of Receipt or Bill of Lading Immaterial.** The formal execution or issuance of a receipt or bill of lading is not necessary to establish the relation of carrier and shipper. Actual delivery and acceptance are sufficient to bind the carrier as such.

**Duty to Serve All.** A common carrier of goods must serve all who apply, on payment or tender of the proper charges; and such charges must be uniform. For a failure to discharge such duty, a common carrier may be liable in damages. However, the duty to serve all indiscriminately does not apply to the following goods:

(a) Goods not of the character that the carrier transports (a taxicab driver cannot be forced to carry a horse, cow or piano, nor a railroad company to transport steel rails on a milk train).

(b) Goods not tendered at the proper time and place.

(c) Goods not properly packed.

(d) Dangerous goods.

(e) Goods injurious to public health.

(f) Perishable goods where the carrier has no immediate means of transportation.

**Carrier's Liability as Insurer.** Common carriers are insurers of goods in transit; that is, they are liable for loss, damage or destruction of merchandise entrusted to them for transportation, regardless of negligence. Common carriers are not, however, insurers of passengers; that is, they are not liable for injury to passengers unless it is occasioned by the carrier's negligence.[5] The reason is obvious. Common carriers have complete control of the subject matter which they transport. If their liability for loss were to depend on negligence, it might be difficult to establish such liability, since the person suffering the damage or loss is in no position to establish its cause: he is not there when the loss occurs. A passenger, of course, is on the site when the injury occurs. He must prove negligence, though the burden of such proof is slight.

EXAMPLE: The Black Paint Company receives an order to ship a barrel of paint via The ABC R.R. Co. When the barrel reaches its destination, it is empty. If the Black Paint Company can prove that the barrel was full when shipped, the consignee (to whom title passed on delivery to the carrier) can hold the carrier for the loss without proving how it happened.[6]

**When Carrier is Excused from Liability as Insurer.** A common carrier of goods is excused from liability as insurer if loss, damage or destruction is due to one of the following causes:

(1) *Acts of God,* such as floods, snowstorms, hurricanes, cyclones, lightning or fires caused by lightning, and any other extraordinary natural causes beyond the carrier's control.

---

[5] *Missouri Pac. R. Co. v. Baum,* 196 Ark. 237, 117 S.W. 2d 31; *White v. Chappell,* 219 N.C. 652, 14 S.E. 2d 843; *Lentz v. Carolina Scenic Coach Lines,* 208 S.C. 278, 38 S.E. 2d 11; *Sine v. Salt Lake Transp. Co.,* 106 Utah 289, 147 P. 2d 875; *Cleveland v. Danville Traction & Power Co.,* 179 Va. 256, 18 S.E. 2d 913.

[6] *Krulder v. Ellison,* 47 N.Y. 36.

(2) *Acts of a public enemy,* during a period of organized warfare.

(3) *Fault of the shipper,* such as improper packing, misdirection of merchandise, failure to indicate delicate or fragile contents, and so on.

(4) *Acts of public authorities,* as in the case of seizure by law enforcement or health officers, or of due process, as by attachment, stoppage in transit, and so on.

(5) *Inherent nature of goods,* including perishables, livestock, and merchandise subject to natural deterioration.

**When Carrier May Limit Liability.** In many states, carriers are prohibited by constitutional or statutory provision from limiting their liability for loss of goods through negligence. This is because it is contrary to public policy to bargain away the duty to be careful. These state provisions affect *intrastate* shipments only. *Interstate* shipments are governed by Federal statute. Under the Carmack Amendment to the Hepburn Act as subsequently further amended,[7] although a carrier cannot *exempt* itself from liability for negligence,[8] it may, by agreement upon a maximum valuation, *limit* its liability for negligence, provided:

(a) The shipper receives consideration for the limitation (usually a lower rate).

(b) The shipper is given an option to ship without such limitation, though at a higher rate.

(c) The limitation is reasonable and just; that is, it bears a fair relation to the reduced rate.

EXAMPLES:

(1) An express company may contract to place a maximum valuation and liability of $50 for any parcel received for interstate shipment, regardless of whether the loss is negligent or not.

(2) If *A* ships goods worth $500 upon an agreement limiting the railroad company's liability for loss to an amount not exceeding $250, *A* is bound by his bargain in cases of loss.

(Both the above examples are subject to the three conditions just stated.)

*Customary practice in limiting liability.* Where carriers are permitted to limit their liability regardless of negligence, the practice is to charge the *usual* rate for *limited* liability, and a *higher* rate for an unlimited risk.

**Shipping Documents: Express Receipts and Bills of Lading.** A shipping receipt may be a mere acknowledgement by the carrier of the receipt of goods. Where it is that and no more, it does not constitute a contract between shipper and carrier, other than the bailment necessarily implied from the circumstances. But where the receipt contains provisions for transportation, it constitutes the contract by which the goods are to be

---

[7] By the Cummins Acts.

[8] It may, for a consideration, exempt itself from liability as an insurer. For a case dealing with this subject, see *S. S. Ansaldo San Giorgio 1 v. Rheinstrom Bros. Co.,* 294 U.S. 494.

shipped, and the parties are bound by its terms. Typical of the former are express receipts, and of the latter, bills of lading.

**Express Receipts.** An express receipt constitutes barely more than the words imply: it acknowledges receipt. Contractually, it promises nothing beyond what the law implies from the nature of a bailment for the hire of service—in this case, transportation. Furthermore, the receipt limits the carrier's liability for loss to specific contingencies. An express receipt thus differs from a bill of lading, which is a contract to transport and deliver.

*Uniform express receipts.* Uniform express receipts are prescribed by the Interstate Commerce Commission. For intrastate shipments, they may be approved by state regulatory bodies, such as public service and public utility commissions. The Court has held [9] that a provision in an express receipt exempting the express company from liability for loss, damage or delay caused by acts of God, public enemies, riots, strikes, and so on (unless caused by the carrier's own negligence), is not inconsistent with public policy or Federal transportation laws; and that a shipper is presumed to have known and assented to such conditions contained in a uniform express receipt issued and accepted in connection with the shipment.

**Bill of Lading: Nature and Contents.** A bill of lading is an instrument in writing signed by the carrier or his agent, describing the freight so as to identify it, stating the name of the consignor and the terms of the contract for transportation, and agreeing or directing that the freight be delivered to a specified person or his order at a specified place.

Every bill of lading must embody within its written or printed terms at least the following: (a) date of issue, (b) name of person from whom goods have been received, (c) place where goods have been received, (d) place to which goods are to be transported, (e) statement whether goods received will be delivered to a specified person or to the order of a specified person, (f) description of goods or of packages containing them, and (g) signature of carrier.

A negotiable bill of lading must have the words "order of" printed immediately before the name of the person upon whose order the goods are deliverable.

*Law governing bills of lading.* The rules of the common law governing bills of lading have been largely superseded by statute, including the Uniform Bills of Lading Act applicable to intrastate shipments and the Federal Bills of Lading Act (Pomerene Act) applicable to interstate and foreign commerce.

**Bill of Lading as Receipt.** When possession of goods is transferred from one person to another, the latter cannot be held responsible unless the

---

[9] *Feniger v. American Railway Express Co.,* 226 Mich. 106.

fact of transfer and delivery to him can be established. The clearest proof of such transfer and delivery is a signed receipt. A bill of lading serves as a signed receipt and fixes liability on the carrier for custody and transportation.

**Bill of Lading as Contract.** Any instrument issued by a carrier upon receiving goods for shipment, to the extent that it contains stipulations about transportation, constitutes a contract governing the shipment. Its terms, therefore, bind both parties and determine their rights and liabilities. Thus the holder, under a bill of lading, may require the carrier to complete its terms on shipment and delivery, and the carrier may hold the shipper to the provisions and limitations of the bill, such as, for example, a limitation in liability (page 315).

*Formal acceptance or knowledge of contents by shipper unnecessary.* Neither formal acceptance nor knowledge by the shipper of the contents of the bill of lading is necessary to bind the shipper to its terms and provisions. ". . . as a general rule, in the absence of controlling statutes providing otherwise, if a formal bill of lading is executed by the carrier, delivered to the shipper and accepted by him as evidence of the terms of shipment, valid stipulations embodied therein limiting the carrier's liability will be binding on the parties, and no formal assent to the limitation of liability by signature to the bill of lading, or otherwise, is essential on the part of the shipper. . . ." [10]

EXAMPLE: *A* ships goods on a bill of lading which contains references to a classification under which the goods are sent. The goods are destroyed while in transit. The carrier offers to pay only a small part of the value of the goods by reason of a limitation in liability in the bill of lading. The shipper, claiming that he had no knowledge of the limitation in liability and that his attention had not been called to it by the shipper, insists on full payment. The carrier's position in such a situation will be sustained.

**Bill of Lading as Evidence of Kind and Quantity of Goods.** A bill of lading is *prima facie* evidence (page 868) of the receipt by the carrier of the kind and quantity of goods therein described. It is customary to insert in a bill of lading recitals to the effect that the goods were received in good or apparently good condition. This is not conclusive, but unless the contrary can be shown, the presumption will stand. If the goods are intended to be negotiated, and they reach the hands of a *bona fide* transferee for value, the recital of good condition, as to him, may become binding on the carrier.

**Bill of Lading as Evidence of Title.** A bill of lading is known as a *document of title* (page 152). By this is meant that the bill serves as documentary evidence of title and provides proof of ownership of the merchandise therein described. It is in effect a symbol of the title to the

---

[10] 13 C.J.S. 176.

goods themselves, particularly in the case of an order bill; so that a transfer of the bill of lading constitutes a transfer of title to the goods therein described.

**Negotiable (Order) Bills v. Nonnegotiable (Straight) Bills.** The Uniform Bills of Lading Act defines a negotiable or order bill as one "in which it is stated that the goods are consigned or destined to the order of any person named in such bill." It defines a nonnegotiable or straight bill as one "in which it is stated that the goods are consigned or destined to a specified person." Strictly speaking, no bill of lading or other document of title is "negotiable" in the sense used in connection with negotiable instruments, since documents of title do not involve orders or promises to pay sums certain in money. However, the essence of negotiability, as noted on page 136, is that an instrument shall pass readily from hand to hand, free from restrictions that characterize ordinary assignments. In this respect negotiable bills of lading present four points of distinction from ordinary bills:

(1) *As to defect in transferor's title:* The transferee of a nonnegotiable bill acquires only such title as the transferor has. A bona fide transferee of a negotiable bill of lading (that is, one to whom a bill is negotiated for value, without notice) acquires good title though the transferor's title was defective, as where the original owner was deprived of possession of the document by loss, theft, fraud, accident, mistake, duress or conversion.[11]

(2) *As to judicial process:* Once goods are shipped against a negotiable bill of lading, such goods cannot be attached or levied upon in legal proceedings against the shipper, and while the goods are in the possession of a carrier or other bailee, unless the bill of lading is first surrendered or its negotiation enjoined. This is not true of a nonnegotiable bill.[12]

(3) *As to stoppage in transit:* When a negotiable bill has been issued, the unpaid seller cannot, by stoppage in transit (page 254), defeat the rights of a purchaser for value in good faith to whom such bill has been negotiated, nor is the carrier obliged to deliver the goods or justified in delivering them unless such bill is first surrendered for cancellation.[13] This is not true of a nonnegotiable bill.

(4) *As to liens:* Liens or claims of a seller, shipper or prior transferor are invalid against a purchaser in good faith and for value to whom a negotiable bill of lading has been negotiated. The purchaser enjoys no such immunity when the bill of lading is nonnegotiable.

**Authority to Issue Bill of Lading.** The Uniform Bills of Lading Act makes it a criminal offense punishable by imprisonment not exceeding five years, or by fine not exceeding $5000, or both, for any officer, agent or employee of a carrier to issue a bill of lading, knowing that all

---

[11] Uniform Sales Act, sec. 38.
[12] Uniform Sales Act, sec. 39.
[13] Uniform Sales Act, sec. 42.

or any part of the goods for which the bill is issued has not been received by such carrier. Since no one is authorized to issue a bill of lading except against actual receipt of the goods, the common law rule, still in force in some states, is that a carrier is not liable on an unauthorized bill, even to one who in good faith has given value in reliance upon the description contained in the bill. This rule, however, has been modified by statute. The Federal Uniform Bills of Lading Act, applicable to interstate shipments, and the Uniform Bills of Lading Act, applicable to intrastate shipments in the states which have adopted the act, provide in effect that when a bill of lading is issued by an agent or employee acting within the scope of his actual or apparent authority, the carrier is liable thereon to "one who has given value in good faith relying upon the description therein of the goods," notwithstanding the nonreceipt of the goods therein described.

EXAMPLE: Hart, captain of a ship, contrary to orders, signs a bill of lading for goods not received. If the shipment is interstate or to a foreign country, or intrastate in a jurisdiction which has adopted the Uniform Bills of Lading Act, the carrier is liable to an innocent third person who in good faith dealt with Hart in reliance upon the bill of lading. The carrier would not be liable to such third person in jurisdictions where the common law rule obtains.

**Rules Governing Delivery.** A common carrier of goods must make delivery at the proper time, to the proper person, and at the proper place.

(a) *Time of delivery.* If a carrier undertakes to deliver within a specified time, it is liable for any loss due to delay, regardless of cause. If no time for delivery is specified, it must be made within a reasonable time.

(b) *Delivery to the right person.* A carrier is liable for mistake in delivery to the wrong person. Fraud practiced on the carrier is no excuse, because a carrier of goods is an insurer.

(c) *Place of delivery.* The place of delivery may be governed by the bill of lading, or by custom. It has been the custom for express companies to deliver to the consignee's door and for railroad companies to deliver to their freight offices; but competition with motor transport has induced railroad companies in many instances to inaugurate personal delivery service.

(d) *C.O.D. shipments.* When a carrier agrees to collect on delivery, it is liable for loss resulting to the shipper from a failure to collect on delivery.[14]

**Initial v. Connecting Carriers.** When a shipment of goods must necessarily pass over the lines of more than one carrier, the carrier to which goods are delivered in the first instance is known as the *initial carrier.* When the initial carrier passes the goods along to the next carrier beyond its lines, such carrier and all subsequent similar carriers are known as

---

[14] *Okin v. Railway Express Agency,* 24 N.J. Misc. 8, 44 A. 2d 896.

*connecting carriers.* The rules of liability governing initial and connecting carriers, though uniform as to *interstate* shipments, are not uniform as to *intrastate* shipments.

**Liability of Initial and Connecting Carriers.** The rules governing the liability of initial and connecting carriers may depend upon whether the shipment is interstate or intrastate.

*Interstate shipments.* Under the Carmack amendment to the Interstate Commerce Act, as amended, connecting carriers are treated as agents of the initial carrier, and the latter is liable for any loss or damage occurring during the shipment, whether on its own line or on that of the connecting carrier. If the initial carrier is required to pay such loss, it may recover such payment from the connecting carrier. A stipulation in a bill of lading that the initial carrier will not be liable for loss occurring on the lines of a connecting carrier is specifically forbidden by statute. Under the *Motor Carrier's Act* of 1935, the Federal rule making initial carriers liable in the first instance applies to shipments by truck as well as to shipments by rail.

*Intrastate shipments.* Under the common law, when an initial carrier delivered the goods in good condition to the connecting carrier, his liability ceased and the shipper or his consignee had to look to the connecting carrier for any loss or damage occurring thereafter, unless the initial carrier accepted the goods for *through transportation,* in which case the courts held that the carrier assumed complete liability for the shipment throughout. As to *intrastate* shipments, this is still the rule in some states. In other states, the rule has been modified by statute. In New York, for example, the statute provides[15] that "Any one of two or more corporations owning or operating connecting roads within this state, or partly within and partly without the state, shall be liable as a common carrier, for the transportation of passengers or delivery of freight received by it to be transported by it to any place on the line of a connecting road; and if it shall become liable to pay any sum by reason of neglect or misconduct of any other corporation it may collect the same of the corporation by reason of whose neglect or misconduct it became liable."

**When Carrier's Liability Ends.** The liability of a carrier ends when the goods have been delivered to the consignee, or, where actual delivery is not required, as in the case of railroad companies and carriers by water, when the carrier's duty *as carrier* has been discharged. Thereafter, if the goods remain in the carrier's possession, such custody is no longer that of an insurer liable regardless of negligence, but of an ordinary bailee liable only for negligence.

*When carrier's duty is discharged.* The courts of the country are not in agreement on when a carrier's duty is discharged following completion of transit. There are three distinct views on the subject, known, respec-

---

[15] *Railroad Law,* section 70.

tively, as the Massachusetts Rule, the New Hampshire Rule and the New York Rule.

(1) *Massachusetts Rule:* When transit is completed, and the carrier has placed the goods in his warehouse awaiting delivery to the consignee, the carrier's duty as such is ended, though no notice is given to the consignee. Thereafter, the carrier is liable as warehouseman only.[16]

EXAMPLE: Goods shipped by rail, while in the railroad's warehouse awaiting delivery to the consignee, are destroyed by fire, without negligence on the part of the railroad. The loss falls on the consignee, though no notice of arrival was sent.

(2) *New Hampshire Rule:* Merely placing goods in the railroad warehouse does not discharge the railroad, which remains liable as an insurer until the consignee has had a reasonable time after their arrival to inspect the goods and take them away in the common course of business.[17]

EXAMPLE: In the previous example, liability under the New Hampshire Rule would fall on the railroad unless the consignee had a reasonable time after their arrival to inspect the goods and take them away in the common course of business.

(3) *New York Rule:* Liability of the carrier as insurer continues until the consignee has been notified of the receipt of the goods and has had a reasonable opportunity thereafter to take the goods away. (Differs from the New Hampshire Rule only in the necessity of notice.) [18]

EXAMPLE: In the previous example, liability under the New York Rule would fall on the railroad unless the consignee had received notice of arrival and had had a reasonable opportunity thereafter to take the goods away.

## Questions

1. Generally speaking, when does the relationship of shipper and carrier begin?

2. Name and explain three conditions which may prevent a shipper from holding a carrier liable as such, notwithstanding delivery of merchandise for shipment.

3. "A common carrier of goods must serve all who apply on payment or tender of the proper charges." Is this statement always true, or are there any exceptions? Explain.

4. "Common carriers are insurers of goods in transit." Explain this statement, and give five exceptions.

5. "Where a shipment is interstate, the carrier is not allowed to limit its

---

[16] This rule is supported by decisions in the following states: Illinois, Indiana, Iowa, Massachusetts, Missouri, New Jersey, Ohio and Tennessee.

[17] This rule is supported by decisions in the following states: Arkansas, Connecticut, Kansas, Kentucky, Minnesota, New Hampshire, Pennsylvania, South Carolina, Vermont, Washington, West Virginia and Wisconsin.

[18] This rule is supported by decisions in the following states: Alabama, California, Maryland, Michigan, New York, North Carolina and Oregon.

liability for negligence." Is this statement entirely true, entirely false, or partly true and partly false? Explain fully.

6. Explain and distinguish: (a) shipping receipt, (b) bill of lading, and (c) express receipt.

7. Every bill of lading must embody within its written or printed terms at least seven items. What are these items?

8. A bill of lading serves four distinct functions. What are they?

9. Distinguish between negotiable and non-negotiable bills of lading in respect to (a) defect in transferor's title, (b) judicial process, (c) stoppage in transit, and (d) liens.

10. Is there any distinction between negotiable and order bills of lading? Non-negotiable and straight bills of lading?

11. Distinguish between an initial and a connecting carrier.

12. What is the rule governing liability of an initial carrier for loss of any interstate shipment occurring on the lines of a connecting carrier? Does this rule also apply to an interstate shipment? Explain.

13. When does a carrier's liability to a shipper end? Is the rule in this respect uniform throughout the United States? Explain.

## Problems

1. A carrier receives and accepts merchandise for shipment. Before the merchandise can be loaded, it is lost. These facts are admitted by the carrier. The shipper, however, is unable to prove either negligence, or issuance of a receipt or bill of lading. On suit for the loss, who will win, and why?

2. Oriental antiques worth $10,000 are shipped by express from San Francisco to New York. In consideration of a 10% reduction in shipment charges, the shipper agrees to a valuation of $100 for the shipment, which is thereafter lost in transit. The shipper insists that the carrier must make good the full value of the loss, and the carrier insists that its liability is limited to $100. How would the court resolve such dispute?

3. The Metropolitan Novelty Company delivers a quantity of toys at the freight office of the ABC Railroad with the tag marked "hold until further orders." That evening, the entire freight office, including the freight delivered by the Metropolitan Novelty Company, is destroyed by a fire of unknown origin. There is no proof of negligence on the part of the ABC Railroad. The Metropolitan Novelty Company seeks to hold the ABC Railroad liable and the latter denies liability under the circumstances. How should the case be decided and why?

4. Carter ships goods from Chicago to Buffalo via the Great Lakes. A terrific storm comes up, the worst in 20 years. The ship becomes disabled and sinks. Carter sues the steamship company. Judgment for whom and why?

5. Plaintiff delivers a quantity of jewelry worth $3,000 to the National Express Company. The express receipt contains this clause: "It is hereby expressly agreed that in case of loss or detention of or damage to the property herein described, the holder hereof will not claim a sum exceeding $50.00 therefor unless the value of said property is stated." No value was stated. The jewelry was lost through defendant's negligence. Plaintiff sues for $3,000. Judgment for whom and why?

6. The Kansas City Feed Company ships goods on a bill of lading which contains references to a classification under which the goods are sent. The goods are destroyed while in transit. The carrier offers to pay only a small

part of the value of the goods by reason of a limitation in liability in the bill of lading. The shipper, however, claims that it had no knowledge of the limitation in liability, and that the carrier had not called the shipper's attention to such limitation. How would the court resolve this dispute?

7. A shipper delivered goods to a railroad company for shipment. The train was derailed by train wreckers and the goods stolen. Can the shipper recover the value of the goods from the railroad company? If so, why? If not, why not? Explain.

8. The X Bank loaned $2,000 to I. M. Bent against a straight bill of lading made out to James Upright. Bent represented himself to be James Upright and assigned the bill of lading to the bank in that name. Actually, the bill of lading had been purloined from Upright's office by a dishonest employee who was in collusion with Bent. Upon discovery of the facts, and Bent having disappeared, a dispute arises between Upright and the bank as to who is entitled to the merchandise described in the bill of lading. How would the court decide the dispute?

9. Goods are shipped against a negotiable bill of lading. While in the hands of the carrier, a creditor of the shipper gets out a writ of attachment which the sheriff seeks to levy upon the goods in the carrier's hands. The carrier refuses to surrender the goods unless the bill of lading is first surrendered. The bill of lading is still in the shipper's possession. What may the creditor do to prevent the bill of lading from getting into the hands of an innocent third party?

10. Goods are shipped over the XYZ Railroad to plaintiff at Cross Corners, Iowa. Plaintiff resides ten miles from the station. He hires the Dandy Delivery Company to call for the goods at the freight office of the railroad. The Dandy Delivery Company calls for the goods, pays the freight, signs the freight receipt, but owing to the fact that one of the delivery horses is lame, decides to leave the goods at the freight office until the next morning. During the night some marauders set fire to the freight office, and plaintiff's goods are destroyed. Plaintiff sues the railroad company. Judgment for whom and why?

## PART 3. PASSENGER CARRIERS

**Definition.** A common carrier of passengers is one engaged in transporting for hire any and all *persons* who apply. Such carriers include steam and electric railways, steamship lines, ferries, omnibuses, street railways, stage coaches, taxicab companies, air lines, and similar agencies of transportation.

**Duty to Serve All.** A common carrier of passengers must carry all who present themselves in a proper condition for transportation, and are ready, able and willing to pay their fare.

By "proper condition" is meant that they must be fit to travel. A common carrier has the right to refuse transportation to one who is obviously intoxicated, or who is known to be infected with a contagious disease.

**Accommodations.** A carrier of passengers must provide accommodations usual in the type of service offered. Under ordinary conditions, every passenger is entitled to a seat, and if he is unable to obtain one, he may quit the train at the next stop without paying his fare; but he cannot both ride and refuse to pay. Under extraordinary conditions such as war, emergencies, or unsurmountable traffic conditions (subway congestion, for example), the right to accommodations is subject to such conditions.

*Footstools for boarding or alighting.* Is a railroad company required at all station stops to provide footstools for each car to assist passengers in boarding or alighting? The answer to this question depends upon the circumstances in each case. Where the duty of reasonable care and safety requires a footstool for such purpose, the railroad company must provide one; otherwise not.

**Right to Prescribe Time, Place and Manner of Paying Fares.** "In the absence of a statute to the contrary, a carrier may make and enforce reasonable regulations as to the time, place, and mode of payment of fare. As a general rule, the time of taking the fare, whether at the carrier's station or office, or in the car or other vehicle, is immaterial, but the carrier may demand prepayment of fare, and, if it does not, it must be presumed to rely on its lien on the passenger's baggage or on his integrity." [19] The carrier may insist on cash, but the passenger need not tender the exact fare, though the carrier may prescribe reasonable rules as to the maximum amount for which it will make change.

**Duty to Protect Passengers.** A common carrier of passengers is bound to protect its passengers from injuries, violence or ill treatment on the part of its employees, and from dangerous conditions due to overcrowding, and so forth. A carrier of passengers is not, however, liable for injuries resulting from the conduct of a fellow passenger, unless the carrier had notice thereof, or reason to anticipate it, and had an opportunity to prevent the injury.

**Liability for Injuries.** A common carrier of *passengers* is not an insurer, and therefore differs in this respect from a common carrier of goods.

The liability of a carrier for injuries to passengers exists only in case of negligence. If no negligence can be shown, the carrier cannot be held liable. However, a common carrier of passengers must exercise the highest degree of care for the lives and safety of its passengers. To ensure that this liability is properly discharged, regulatory bodies, state and Federal, prescribe rules, conditions, safety devices and appliances, and maintain periodic inspections.

Even, however, where the carrier is guilty of negligence, the rule in most states is that if the passenger is guilty of contributory negligence, there can be no recovery.

**Exemption from Liability for Injuries to Passengers.** In some states, a carrier of passengers may exempt itself from all liability for injuries caused by the negligence of its servants or agents. But there must be a special consideration for such contract of exemption. If the passenger has paid the

[19] 13 C.J.S. 1148.

usual fare, an agreement exempting the carrier from such liability would be ineffectual.

A carrier of passengers thus differs from a carrier of goods, since the latter, as we have seen, may in no case *exempt* itself from liability for loss *due to its own negligence*.

**Liability to Passengers on Free Pass.** Where a passenger travels on a free pass, the carrier owes him the same degree of care as in the case of a passenger who pays his fare.

However, if the free pass contained printed stipulations exempting the carrier from liability, whether due to negligence or not, there is sufficient consideration for such an agreement, and unless the injury is wilful or wanton, there is nothing contrary to public policy in such an agreement.

**Liability to Passengers at Reduced Fare.** The courts have held that where a person is killed while traveling on a reduced fare ticket providing for complete exemption to the carrier, such exemption will be sustained and the carrier freed from liability for negligence. But if the ticket provided for no such exemption, the carrier would be liable as in the case of an ordinary ticket.

**The Passenger Ticket.** The ordinary passenger ticket is not a contract in itself, but is in the nature of a receipt. It is evidence of the right to transportation furnished to the passenger in consequence of a contract to carry; and the passenger must therefore exhibit the ticket whenever required by the conductor. If he fails to do so, he may be required to pay full fare, or be ejected; and if he later proves that he had a ticket, which he was unwilling to exhibit, he will nevertheless have no redress for being ejected.

**Right to Eject Passengers.** A carrier may eject passengers for infringing any reasonable rules and regulations established by the carrier, such as the one already mentioned (requiring the passenger to exhibit his ticket or pay full fare), annoying fellow passengers, or any other reasonable regulation of the carrier. However, in ejecting such passengers, the carrier must use proper and reasonable means. For example, a tramp may not be recklessly thrown from a train while in motion, and if he is, he may hold the carrier liable for resulting injury.

A passenger may resist wrongful ejection, using such force as may be necessary for this purpose. However, he is not required to offer such resistance. He may pay his fare under protest, or suffer wrongful ejection and thereafter obtain his redress.

**Passengers' Baggage: What Constitutes.** Baggage includes articles which persons traveling usually take with them for their pleasure, convenience or comfort, according to the habits and wants of the class to which they belong. As stated by the court in *Merrill v. Grinnell*:[20]

The sportsman who sets out on an excursion for amusement in his department of pleasure, needs, in addition to his clothing, his gun and fishing ap-

[20] 30 N.Y. 594.

paratus; the musician, his favorite instrument; the man of letters, his books; the mechanic, his tools. In all these cases, and in a vast number of others, unnecessary to enumerate, the articles carried are necessary, in one sense, to the use of the passenger. He cannot attain the object he is in pursuit of, without them, and the object of his journey would be lost, unless he was permitted to carry them with him. Yet, under pretense of carrying these articles, it by no means follow that the carrier is bound to carry a box of guns, a pianoforte or organ, a library, or the tools and machinery of a machine shop.

**Duty to Transport Baggage.** When a carrier undertakes to transport a passenger, he also undertakes to transport a reasonable amount of baggage, as previously defined; and when such baggage is checked, the carrier is an insurer against all losses other than those due to the expected perils, such as acts of God, the public enemy, public authority, acts of the shipper, or loss arising from the inherent nature of the goods. Thus, while a carrier may not be liable for injury to a passenger in the absence of negligence, he may be liable for loss or damage to his baggage, though negligence be wanting.

**Articles in Possession of Passenger.** When a passenger retains possession of articles or packages, such as handbags or luggage, the carrier's liability as insurer does not attach, because the carrier has no control over such baggage.

**Right to Limit Liability.** A carrier of passengers, as to baggage, is in the same position as a carrier of goods, and has the same right to *limit* liability by contract. In other words, the carrier may place a maximum valuation on the baggage, or, for a special consideration, agree to be liable for a higher valuation.

However, it is now practically uniform law throughout the country that a carrier cannot *exempt* itself from liability for the loss of baggage due to its own negligence, although it may do so as to loss not resulting from negligence.

**Baggage Check v. Bill of Lading.** A baggage check or receipt differs from a bill of lading, in that the latter is the contract between the parties, whereas a baggage check or receipt is merely a protection to the passenger, and a means of enabling him to identify his baggage.

Hence, while the provisions of a bill of lading, limiting the value for which a carrier will be liable, are binding upon the parties, the provisions of a baggage check or receipt containing such limitation are not binding on a passenger unless he has had actual notice of such provisions.

In the case of steamship tickets, however, the courts have held that whether passengers read them or not, the stipulations on them limiting liability for baggage loss or damage are binding, since an ocean trip is a more deliberate and less common transaction than a railroad trip, and the opportunity for becoming acquainted with the conditions of the voyage is supposed to be sufficient for the passenger to become subject to the terms and conditions under which he hires transportation.

**When Relationship of Carrier and Passenger Begins.** The relation of carrier and passenger begins when the person who intends to become a passenger enters, or is directed to, a place of waiting, within a reasonable time before departure.

Hence entering a carrier's waiting room, vehicle, station, etc., makes one, to all intents and purposes, a passenger; so that if the passenger is injured while thus awaiting transportation, due to the carrier's negligence, the carrier can be held liable. Payment of fare is not essential as a condition for recovery under these circumstances.

**When Relationship Ceases.** The relationship of passenger and carrier ceases when the journey is concluded and the passenger has left the carrier's premises; unless the relationship is sooner terminated, as by the passenger's voluntary relinquishment of his rights, or his forcible ejection for misconduct.

If a passenger, for example, is rightfully ejected from a train, he ceases to be a passenger then and there. If, thereafter, he attempts to board the train, and is injured in so doing, he cannot hold the railroad liable, because he was a trespasser when the injury occurred.

Where passengers are required to alight during the course of transit, the relationship of passenger and carrier continues so long as the passenger remains within the confines of the carrier's station. If injury occurs during the course of such halt in the journey and while the passenger is still on premises provided by the carrier, the carrier continues to be chargeable as such, namely, for a high degree of care toward its passengers. The rule has been summarized as follows:

. . . a passenger does not lose his character as such by merely temporarily alighting at an intermediate station, with the express or implied consent of the carrier, for any reasonable and usual purpose, such as the procuring of refreshments, the sending or the receiving of telegrams, or for the purpose of exercising by walking up and down the platform, or for relief from fatigue of travel, or even from motives of curiosity. This is an absolute right of the passenger, so long as his object in alighting is not inconsistent with his character as passenger.[21]

### Questions

1. "A common carrier of passengers must carry all who present themselves for transportation, and are ready, able and willing to pay their fare." Is this statement wholly true, wholly false, or partly true and partly false? Explain.
2. Discuss the following statement: "Every passenger is entitled to a seat."
3. What is the rule governing footstools for boarding or alighting?
4. "A carrier of passengers may demand prepayment of fare." Is this statement wholly true, wholly false, or partly true and partly false?
5. "A carrier may insist on a cash fare, and the passenger must tender the exact fare." Is this statement wholly true, wholly false, or partly true and partly false?

---

[21] 13 C.J.S. 1075-1076.

6. What is the rule governing a carrier's duty to protect passengers from: (a) injuries, violence or ill-treatment on the part of its employees; (b) dangerous conditions due to overcrowding; (c) injuries resulting from the conduct of fellow passengers?

7. "A common carrier is liable for injuries to passengers regardless of negligence." Is this statement wholly true, wholly false, or partly true and partly false?

8. Are the following statements wholly true, wholly false, or partly true and partly false?

(a) "Where a passenger travels on a free pass, the carrier owes him the same degree of care as in the case of a passenger who pays his fare."

(b) "Where a person is killed while riding on a reduced fare ticket, his estate cannot hold the carrier liable regardless of negligence."

(c) "A passenger ticket is a contract."

9. What is the rule regarding the right of a carrier to eject passengers?

10. What constitutes baggage?

11. What is the rule governing a carrier's duty to transport baggage?

12. "A carrier is liable for loss of baggage whether in the passenger's custody or otherwise, regardless of negligence." Is this statement true, false, or partly true and partly false?

13. Distinguish between a baggage check and a bill of lading.

14. When does the relationship of carrier and passenger begin, and when does it cease?

## Problems

1. Abou Ben Ali, a native of India, while traveling in this country, garbed in his native costume, applies for a ticket from Los Angeles to New York. The railroad company, disapproving of Ben Ali's garb, and thinking it might annoy fellow travellers, refuses to sell him a ticket. Ben Ali sues. Judgment for whom and why?

2. A tramp stealing a ride on a freight car is discovered by a railroad employee and kicked off the car while the train is in motion. The tramp sustains a fracture of two ribs and a dislocated shoulder. He sues the railroad company, which defends on the ground that plaintiff was a trespasser, and the company had a right to eject him. Judgment for whom and why?

3. John Burly, a passenger on board the *M, L & N* Railroad, who had been steadily drinking after boarding the train, became obstreperous and abusive. George Gentle, a newly-wed bridegroom who protested against Burly's foul language, was severely beaten and permanently disabled by Burly. The train porter, a man past middle age, failed to interfere with or attempt to restrain Burly, because of the latter's size and powerful physique. Burly is finally overpowered and ejected when the porter is able to summon additional help. On suit for damages by Gentle against the railroad company, how would you charge the jury if you were the judge?

4. Toward midnight, as a passenger train approached one of the glacier parks in northern Montana, a bear leaped on the track, causing a wreck. Have any of the passengers who sustained consequent injuries any claim against the railroad company?

5. Ransom, a travelling salesman representing a firm of silversmiths, packs a considerable quantity of sample plate, partly in his trunk and partly in a suitcase. He checks the trunk at the railroad station, but takes the suitcase with him. Upon retiring for the night, he slips the suitcase under his berth in a

sleeping car, whence it is stolen. The trunk also is stolen. He sues the railroad company. How should the case be decided and why?

## COURT CASES FOR REVIEW
### How Did the Court Decide, and Why?

1. A showman contracted with a railroad company for the hire of two baggage cars for the transportation of theatrical properties under an agreement that the railroad company would not be liable for loss even though caused by the railroad's negligence. For a subsequent loss allegedly caused by the railroad's negligence, the showman brought suit, contending that the contract provision as to negligence was ineffective. *McKeon v. N.Y., N.H. & H.R.R. Co.*, 177 App. Div. 462, 164 N.Y. Supp. 312.

2. Plaintiff, a cattle shipper, engaged the services of defendant to transport his animals in a freight car on the assurance of defendant's representative that they would be picked up by the evening freight train. The train in question, however, did not stop. As a result, some of the cattle were injured by the overnight confinement. Plaintiff sued. *Chicago, Rock Island & Pac. Ry. Co. v. Stallings*, 132 Ark. 446, 201 S.W. 294.

3. A buyer of cotton seed oil sued the shipper and the railway for loss of oil through leakage because of an outlet valve on a tank car which was alleged to have been improperly set. The shipper sought to place the responsibility on the railway company and vice versa. It appeared that the greater part of the cotton seed oil was lost through leakage from the railway tank car because of the shipper's negligence in not loading the car properly. The shipper, on the other hand, claimed that such loss could have been saved if the railway's employees, who discovered the leak and attempted to remedy it, had been supplied with proper tools and had been instructed in the opening of the dome covers on tank cars. *Blytheville Cotton Oil Co. v. Kurn*, 155 F. 2d 467.

4. A shipper sued a railroad for loss due to deterioration of meat during shipment. The shipper had given icing orders to the railroad on the morning on which the meat was loaded into a comparatively warm car. The loading was done by the shippers under a "shippers load and count" bill of lading. *Standard Hotel Supply Co. v. Pennsylvania R. Co.*, 65 F. Supp. 439.

5. A shipper brought suit against a railroad company for damage to a carload of rice bran during shipment. The shipper contended that the rice bran was damaged by spoilage due to excessive delay in shipment. The carrier contended that any spoilage to the carload of rice bran was the result of excessive moisture in the bran when it was loaded, and the fact that the bran had not been properly kiln dried. The shipper offered no proof that the bran had been properly kiln dried, and the carrier offered no proof that it had not been so dried. *Kaplan Rice Mill v. Texas & N.O.R. Co.*, 26 So. 2d 42.

6. An initial motor carrier placed freight inside the door of the connecting motor carrier's warehouse for delivery to the consignees, and left the freight bills and manifests in the connecting carrier's office. All this was done after warehouse office hours, but in accordance with established practice. Shortly thereafter, a fire destroyed the merchandise. The connecting carrier disclaimed liability, on the ground that there had been neither formal delivery, nor formal receipt of the merchandise. The question arose as to whether the liability lay with the initial or connecting carrier. *Great Coastal Exp., etc. v. Fidelity & Guaranty Fire Corp.*, 46 A. 2d 93.

7. Plaintiff left merchandise with a railroad company as initial carrier, for shipment to a distant point outside the state. The initial carrier in turn de-

livered the merchandise to defendant connecting carrier, subject to a bill of lading relieving such carrier from any damage caused by an "Act of God." While the freight cars were in the defendant's yards in Springfield, Mass., the nearby Connecticut River began to rise, overflowed its banks and did considerable damage to plaintiff's property. In bringing suit, plaintiff claimed that defendant's agents had notice of the river's rising and should have moved the cargo to higher ground. *Standard Brands, Inc. v. Boston & M.R.R.*, 29 Fed. Supp. 593.

8. Three days after the arrival of merchandise at the railroad depot, a heavy freshet occurred in a nearby river which overflowed the freight house and destroyed the goods. Plaintiff, who was unaware that the merchandise had reached the depot, sued for damages. *Sprague v. N.Y.C.R.R. Co.*, 52 N.Y. 637.

9. Plaintiff sued for injuries sustained by her in a fall on alighting from a train. There was a seventeen-inch-high step at the point where the passenger alighted. There was no footstool. She carried a night bag in her right hand, and a purse and knitting bag under her left arm, but retained her hold on the hand rail with her left hand and, misjudging the distance, stepped straight forward, rather than letting herself down. *Ellis v. Southern Pac. Co.*, 50 N.M. 76, 169 P. 2d 55.

10. A passenger who was drinking whiskey on a bus, was told by the driver either to surrender the liquor or get off the bus. Because of intoxication or mental illness, he was confused. He finally left the bus, alighting at night at a point on a heavily traveled state highway. Shortly thereafter, he was struck and killed by an oncoming truck. His estate brought suit for his death, alleging negligence of the carrier. *Houston v. Strickland*, 184 Va. 994, 37 S.E. 2d 64.

11. A shipper and a carrier entered into an agreement for the transportation of horses. The agreement provided that the cargo, although worth much more, was to be valued at $200, and in the event of a loss, even though caused by the carrier's negligence, the shipper's claim would be limited to $200. Following a loss caused by the carrier's negligence, the shipper brought suit for the true value of the horses. *Hart v. Penn. R.R. Co.*, 112 U.S. 331.

12. Plaintiff, an artist, residing at 27 West 67th Street, New York City, shipped a valuable painting to Colorado for exhibition. Later, the painting was delivered by the exhibitor to defendant express company for return to plaintiff. The express company delivered the painting at 27 West 27th Street, New York, which was a hotel entrance. The painting was received by a hotel employee and receipted for by him on plaintiff's behalf, but without plaintiff's knowledge. It remained in the hotel unclaimed for some time thereafter, when it was lost, plaintiff having no knowledge of the shipment until a year later. Plaintiff sued the express company. *Hassam v. Platt*, 163 App. Div. 366, 147 N.Y. Supp. 544.

13. A person was killed while traveling as a passenger on defendant's railroad on a ticket for which he had paid a reduced fare. The ticket contained a provision that the holder assumed all risks of accidents and damage to his person or property, including those caused by the negligence of the company, its agents, servants and employees. In a subsequent action against the company for wrongful death, plaintiff urged that the provisions on the company ticket were void as being against public policy. *Anderson v. Erie R.R. Co.*, 223 N.Y. 277.

14. A bus passenger was ordered off the bus at a rest stop, along with other passengers. The bus driver turned out his lights and the passengers entered a café and restaurant in front of which the bus had drawn up. Plaintiff sought to return to the bus. She was unfamiliar with the premises, which were dark

and unilluminated. She wore bifocal glasses. In attempting to make her way back to the bus from the outside of the restaurant building, and due to the darkened condition of the premises, she did not see an obstruction at the walkway in front of the door to the café. As she started to step down, she caught her foot on the edge of the projection and fell to the hard driveway. She sued the bus company for the personal injuries thus sustained. The question turned on whether, at the time of the accident, defendant owed plaintiff the high degree of care which a carrier owes to a passenger, that is, whether, at the time, the defendant occupied the status of carrier toward the plaintiff. Defendant's position was that at the time of the accident plaintiff was neither in transit, nor on premises which belonged to the defendant. *McBroom v. S.E. Greyhound Lines*, 193 S.W. 2d 92.

15. After a bank had discounted drafts with bills of lading attached, the sheriff, in execution of a judgment against the consignor, seized the grain in shipment. The bank thereupon sued the sheriff for damages for conversion. *National Bank of Ashtabula v. Bradley*, 264 F. 700.

# 7

# Suretyship and Guaranty

**Scope of This Chapter.** In this chapter we consider the rights, duties and liabilities which arise when one person agrees to make good another's obligation to a third party. In Part 1 we consider the nature and basis of suretyship, various suretyship classifications and distinctions, certain unique characteristics of the suretyship contract, and the extent to which suretyship is governed by the statute of frauds. In Part 2 we consider the various grounds or defenses on which a surety may disclaim liability under his contract, and the various remedies he may have when called on to make good under his contract. We also briefly consider the subject of surety bonds.

## PART 1. NATURE AND BASIS

**Origin and Nature of Suretyship.** The device by which one person lends the credit of his word to support the obligation of another is of ancient origin. It was a common device in Biblical times, though viewed with disfavor as of dubious wisdom.[1] Its essence is the plighted word given to support the obligation of another, where the latter has no property to serve as security. The distinction was referred to in the earlier texts as that between *real* and *personal* security. The giving of property to secure an obligation, as in the case of a mortgage or pledge, was referred to as *real* suretyship. The giving of a person's *promise* to secure the obligation of another was designated as *personal* suretyship, now referred to simply as *suretyship*.

**Contracts Involved.** Every guaranty or suretyship involves two contracts. The first, or *principal contract*, is the one secured; the second, which secures the first, is the contract of guaranty or suretyship. It is a

---

[1] "He that is surety for a stranger shall smart for it: and he that hateth suretyship is sure." *Proverbs*, XI:15.

*contingent* or *collateral* contract, that is, it does not become effective unless the first contract is breached or defaulted.

**Parties Involved.** Every guaranty or suretyship involves at least three parties. In the principal contract, creating the primary obligation, the primary or *principal debtor* or *obligor* becomes obligated to a *creditor* or *obligee.* In the secondary contract, creating the guaranty or suretyship, the secondary debtor, known as a *guarantor* or *surety,* promises the creditor to make good upon the principal debtor's default.

**Promise to Pay *v.* Promise to Answer for.** A promise to pay the creditor for some benefit bestowed on another creates but one contract. To create a guaranty or suretyship there must be a promise to *answer* for another.

EXAMPLES:
(1) Jones writes Smith: "Deliver the following merchandise to Brown, and send me the bill." This involves but a single promise to pay, and creates but a single contract (for Brown's benefit), wherein Jones is debtor and Smith creditor.
(2) Jones writes Smith: "Deliver the following merchandise requested by Brown, and *if he does not pay,* I will." This involves a promise to answer for another. It creates, first, a *principal contract* (between Smith and Brown), and secondly, a contract of guaranty or suretyship, wherein Jones agrees to answer for Brown, that is, to pay Smith *if Brown defaults.*

**Guaranty and Suretyship: Defined and Distinguished.** In substance, guaranty and suretyship are one and the same. Both involve obligations to answer for the debt, default or miscarriage of another. Debt refers to money obligation, default to breach of contract obligation, and miscarriage to breach of some duty, as where one promises to make good for another's negligence, embezzlement, and so on.

In practice, the words "guaranty" and "suretyship" are used interchangeably, not only by laymen, but by lawyers and courts as well. However, certain technical distinctions are sometimes made between suretyship and guaranty:

(a) *Time when obligation accrues.* A surety becomes liable simultaneously with his principal, upon the same undertaking, the same consideration, and usually the same instrument, whereas a guarantor becomes liable at a different time from that which marks the origin of the principal's liability, and likewise by a different instrument and often upon a separate consideration from that on which the principal is bound. Principal and surety, in other words, are usually bound on the same identical contract, and the surety is thus definitely obligated from the start, as if he were a co-principal. The guarantor's undertaking, on the other hand, is separate and collateral. The liability assumed by him does not come into actual existence unless and until the principal defaults.

(b) *Necessity of notice.* A surety, being obligated on the same undertaking with the principal, is chargeable with knowledge of the principal's default. He is therefore liable without notice immediately upon such default, as in the case of a surety bond on which *both* principal and surety are jointly and severally "held and firmly bound." A guarantor is usually entitled to notice of the principal's default.

(Except where otherwise noted, we shall use the words "guaranty" and "suretyship" interchangeably throughout the remainder of this chapter.)

**Guaranty of Collection v. Guaranty of Payment.** A *guarantor of collection* virtually says, "I will pay if the principal debtor *cannot*." Before the creditor can hold a guarantor of collection, therefore, he must show that the principal *cannot pay;* that is, he must first exhaust his legal remedies against the principal. A *guarantor of payment*, however, says in effect, "I will pay if the principal debtor *does not*." His liability is fixed when the debt is due and the principal *does not pay*, regardless of his ability or inability to pay.

**Guaranty v. Indemnity.** The object of a contract of guaranty is to induce the extension of credit. The object of an indemnity agreement is to assume, for a money consideration, the risk of loss if credit is extended. A contract of guaranty is a promise to make good a specific debt or default. A contract of indemnity, however, is an undertaking, for a given consideration, to *save a person harmless* in respect to dealings, past, present, or contemplated, with some other person. It is not, as in guaranty, a promise to answer for the default of such other person, but rather an undertaking to make good any losses incurred by the creditor in dealing with such person. The consideration that the indemnitor gets is some money or other benefit paid by the creditor to the indemnitor for assuming the risk, not, as in the case of guaranty, *the mere act itself*, or creditor's sacrifice, *in extending the credit.* If the indemnitor pays a loss, he does so, not on account of the debtor's default, but on account of his own separate obligation (for which he has been paid) to assume the risk of losses. Hence, if a loss occurs, the indemnitor has no recourse against the debtor for reimbursement, unless so expressly agreed; whereas if a guarantor pays the principal debtor's obligation, he may proceed against the principal debtor for reimbursement, as a matter of law.

**Single v. Continuing Guaranty.** A *single* guaranty is one limited to a single transaction.

EXAMPLE: I promise to answer for your payment of a $2000 automobile. You buy a $1900 automobile. Though my risk is lessened, my obligation is varied: I am not liable.

A *continuing* guaranty is one that is not limited to a single transaction but covers a succession of liabilities for which, as and when they accrue, the guarantor becomes liable.

EXAMPLE: I promise a dealer to answer for your obligations in buying automobile accessories "up to" $1000, or "not exceeding" $1000. The language in both instances implies a continuing guaranty covering any liabilities from $1 up to $1000.

**General v. Special Guaranty.** A *general* guaranty is one addressed to no particular person but to the world at large, such as, "To whom it may concern." Such a guaranty may be enforced by anyone to whom it is presented and who acts on it. A *special* guaranty is one addressed to a particular person, who alone can take advantage of it and to whom alone the guarantor is liable.

**Guaranty v. Warranty.** Although the terms *guaranty* and *warranty* are used interchangeably in a loose sense, they are, strictly speaking, distinguishable. A guaranty is an undertaking to answer for the default of another. A warranty, ordinarily, relates to one's own obligation. It is "an undertaking that the title, quality, or quantity of the subject matter of a contract is what it has been represented to be." [2]

**Characteristics of Suretyship Contract.** A suretyship contract differs from an ordinary contract in that it depends for its existence on another or principal contract. If the principal contract is void, or is varied without the surety's consent, the contract of suretyship is void or extinguished. Moreover, suretyship always arises out of an express contract. Unlike many other obligations, the obligation of suretyship is never implied by law. Also, as we shall see, if the contract is *really* one of suretyship, it must be created by a *signed promise in writing*.

**Requisites of Suretyship Contract.** As with all contracts, a suretyship contract must have the usual contract requisites: Parties having contractual capacity, mutual assent, consideration, and valid subject matter.

*Parties.* As with all non-necessity contracts, an infant's contract of suretyship is voidable by the infant. The law also places limitations on the right to bind a partnership or a corporation by contracts of suretyship (pages 476 and 553).

*Mutual assent.* The rules governing mutual assent, already considered in the chapter on Contracts, apply to contracts of guaranty and suretyship, as they do to all contracts. Offer and acceptance must jibe, or there is no contract.

EXAMPLE: Jones writes Smith: "I will make good for all Brown's purchases up to $1000. Is this satisfactory?" Smith, without replying, lets Brown have $1000 credit. If Brown defaults, Jones is not liable: his acceptance called for prior commitment.

*Consideration.* As pointed out in the chapter on Contracts, consideration need not benefit the promissor, so long as it represents a *sacrifice* on the part of the promisee. In a contract of guaranty or suretyship, the promisee (creditor), by the sacrifice of extending or agreeing to extend credit to the principal debtor, supplies consideration to bind the promise

---

[2] 38 *C.J.S.* 1134.

of the guarantor or surety, though the latter may not be benefited by the extension of credit.

*Subject matter.* The subject matter of a contract of guaranty or suretyship is *the principal contract that it guarantees.* If the principal contract is void, so is the secondary one, that is, the suretyship contract. If the principal contract is merely voidable (for example, if the principal is an infant), the secondary contract is nonetheless binding.

EXAMPLES:

(1) If X guarantees A's promise to pay for merchandise at black market prices, the illegality of the principal contract renders the contract of suretyship illegal.

(2) But if X guarantees the legitimate obligation of B, an infant, he is liable notwithstanding B's infancy. Such infancy does not render the principal contract void for illegality, but voidable for incompetency.

## Suretyship and the Statute of Frauds

**General Rule.** The statute of frauds provides that a special promise to answer for the debt, default or miscarriage of another must be in writing or it is not enforceable. But the promise must be strictly one of suretyship or the rule will not apply. There must be a principal debtor who remains primarily liable and a promise made by one person to another to answer for a third party. As noted on page 87, a promise to *pay* for another, as distinguished from a promise to *answer for* another, is binding, though oral. Transactions resembling but not actually constituting suretyships are enforceable, though not evidenced by a writing. Such transactions include (1) indemnity agreements, (2) promises not made to the creditor, (3) situations where the promise is wholly or partly for the benefit of the promissor, and (4) novations.

(1) **Indemnity Agreements.** As noted on page 334, an indemnity agreement is not, strictly speaking, an agreement to answer for *another's obligation,* but to hold a person harmless in respect to his dealings with another. The object is to assume a risk, usually for a consideration. An indemnity agreement is therefore an original, not a collateral, undertaking. Although there is a conflict of authority as to whether contracts of indemnity must be in writing, such conflict arises from the fact that in some situations a contract purporting to indemnify is really an undertaking to answer for the debt of another, hence subject to the statute of frauds, whereas in other cases the indemnity agreement is truly an original undertaking, hence not subject to the statute. Where the main object of the indemnity is not to answer for another, but to benefit the indemnitor, the indemnity is an original agreement, and no writing is essential to its validity.[3]

---

[3] *New York Guarantee Trust Co. v. Koehler,* 195 F. 669, 115 C.C.A. 475, reversing C.C., 187 F. 192.

EXAMPLE: A promise by a bank depositor to reimburse a fellow depositor if he suffers any loss by not withdrawing his funds from the bank has been held to be a promise to answer for another, hence void unless in writing;[4] but a similar promise made by an officer of the bank for his own interest has been held to be an original undertaking, hence valid though not in writing.[5]

(2) **Promise Not Made to Creditor.** Frequently, indemnity agreements take the form of promises to hold some person harmless, other than the creditor. Such promises are not agreements to answer for another, but original undertakings, binding though oral.

EXAMPLE: If I encourage you to contract a debt and orally assure *you* (not the creditor) that I will back you up financially if you default, there is no suretyship; my promise is binding.

(3) **Benefit to Promissor.** Where the promise to answer for another is largely or even partly for the promissor's own benefit, the promise is more in the nature of an original undertaking, and is binding though oral. The benefit to the promissor, however, must be direct, not indirect; if the latter, the undertaking is collateral, not original, and must be in writing.

EXAMPLE: *Direct benefit: promise binding, though oral.* The promise of an agent to make good the debts of his customers, for higher commission (page 389).

EXAMPLE: *Indirect benefit: promise not binding, if oral.* A stockholder's or officer's oral guaranty of a corporate debt, where the corporation continues as the principal debtor.

(4) **Novation.** Where the promise constitutes a novation (page 99), it is not really a guaranty; the promissor merely takes the place of the original debtor. Such a promise is binding though oral.

EXAMPLE: My promise to assume Brown's debt to you in consideration of your releasing Brown would be binding though oral.

## Questions

1. There are two contracts involved in a suretyship. What are they?
2. Who are the three parties involved in suretyship?
3. Distinguish between a promise to pay another's obligation and a promise to answer for it.
4. (a) In what respect are contracts of guaranty and of suretyship similar? (b) Give two technical distinctions between them.
5. Distinguish between a guaranty of collection and a guaranty of payment.
6. How does a contract of guaranty differ from one of indemnity?
7. Distinguish between (a) a single and a continuing guaranty; (b) a general and a special guaranty; (c) a guaranty and a warranty.
8. Name three outstanding characteristics of a contract of suretyship that differentiate it from an original contract.

---

[4] *Trento v. De Benedetti,* 283 Ill. App. 182.
[5] *Dillard v. Walker,* 204 N.C. 16, 167 S.E. 636.

9. "Contracts of suretyship made by infants are void." Is this statement true, false, or partly true and partly false?

10. How will a contract of suretyship be affected by the fact that the principal contract is (a) void, and (b) voidable?

11. Name four types of transactions resembling suretyship which need not be evidenced by a writing in order to be binding.

## Problems

1. Fenwick, a friend of Warren's, writes the Watkins Furniture Company: "Henry Warren advises me that you require someone to guarantee his purchase from you of furniture in the sum of $850.00. This is to advise you that I will go as far as $500 if that is satisfactory." The Furniture Company, without further word, let's Warren have $500 worth of furniture on credit. Warren defaults. The Furniture Company promptly sues Fenwick on his guaranty. Judgment for whom and why?

2. Ropes writes the Planet Motor Corporation as follows: "I understand that the Apex Auto Sales Company has arranged to handle your cars upon condition that they secure a proper guaranty of their account with you upon the basis of a $10,000 maximum credit. You may consider this my guaranty accordingly." The Sales Company runs up a balance of $15,000 which it cannot meet. The Planet Motor Corporation sues Ropes on his guaranty to the extent of $10,000. Judgment for whom and why?

3. Bell guarantees a lease in the following language: "For a valuable consideration, I hereby guarantee payment of the within rent throughout the term of this lease." This guaranty was indorsed on the lease. The tenant fails to pay the rent. The landlord sues Bell on his guaranty, and Bell sets up that he never actually received any consideration for his guaranty. Judgment for whom and why?

4. Perkins wants to go into business for himself. He desires to buy $5,000 worth of merchandise, but is fearful lest he cannot succeed in disposing of it. Porter, his father-in-law, says to him, "Go ahead and buy the stuff and if you find you cannot pay, I will make good the account." Perkins buys the merchandise and then finds he cannot pay. Porter is sued, and sets up the statute of frauds in defense. Judgment for whom and why?

5. Wilkins is asked to become surety on a bond. He hesitates to do so unless he can get Carpenter to indemnify him against loss, which Carpenter orally agrees to do. Wilkins becomes liable as surety, and then seeks to hold Carpenter to his agreement. Carpenter pleads the statute of frauds. Judgment for whom and why?

6. Manning, in payment of a $500 debt, tenders his creditor a $500 note made by John Smith. The creditor asks Manning to endorse it, but Manning replies, "I never endorse paper, but my word is as good as my bond. If that note is not paid, I will make it good." The note is not paid. The creditor sues Manning, who sets up the statute of frauds as a defense. Judgment for whom and why?

7. Smith owes Rayon Distributors, Inc., $1,000. The latter threatens to sue, and also to attach a quantity of merchandise valued at $5,000 belonging to Smith but stored in a warehouse in the name of Henry Rogers, another creditor of Smith's. Rogers orally persuades Rayon Distributors, Inc., to withhold suit, saying, "I will guarantee to hold the merchandise as security not only for my account but also for yours." Upon Smith's refusal to pay, and Rogers' refusal

to deliver up the merchandise, Rayon Distributors, Inc., sues Rogers, who sets up the statute of frauds. Judgment for whom and why?

8. A firm of public accountants made an agreement with a corporation by its president to examine its books. After the examination had begun, the accountants refused to continue unless the president personally guaranteed that they would be paid. This he agreed to do. After the accountants had completed their work, they demanded payment of the president personally, the corporation in the meantime having become insolvent. Who should prevail?

9. White was planning to withdraw his account from a certain bank when Graham, a substantial depositor, orally promised to reimburse White if he suffered any loss by not withdrawing his funds from the bank. Thereafter the bank became insolvent, resulting in a serious loss to White, who then brought action against Graham on his promise. How should the court decide?

## PART 2. DEFENSES AND REMEDIES; SURETY BONDS

**Suretyship Defenses and Remedies in General.** A surety is said to have a defense if he has good ground for disclaiming liability. Where he has incurred the liability, the law provides him with certain remedies by which he may minimize such liability, or transfer the burden of it to someone else.

### Suretyship Defenses

**Grounds for Suretyship Defenses.** The defenses available to a surety fall into four classes: (1) Defenses based on infirmity of the surety's contract; (2) Defenses based on infirmity of the principal contract; (3) Defenses based on varying the surety's risk; (4) Defenses based on discharge.

(1) **Infirmity of Surety's Contract.** If the contract of suretyship is itself defective, either as to form or requisites, no liability arises. The requirements as to form under the statute of frauds have already been considered on pages 336 to 337. The contract requisites as they apply particularly to suretyship and guaranty are discussed on pages 335 to 336.

(2) **Infirmity of Principal Contract.** As noted on page 336, if the principal contract is void, the suretyship contract is void for illegal subject matter; but if the principal contract is merely voidable, the suretyship contract is nonetheless binding, unless such voidability is due to the creditor's misconduct.

EXAMPLE: A surety for an infant principal is not relieved of liability if the infant disaffirms, but if the principal successfully avoids liability because of the creditor's fraud, or duress, the surety is likewise relieved of liability for the same cause.

(3) **Varying the Surety's Risk.** A surety is said to be a favorite of the law. His liability is *strictissimi juris:* Strictly limited to the letter of his obligation. By this is meant, not that he is entitled to favored or preferential consideration, but that, inasmuch as he has assumed a liability without

benefit to himself, such liability must be strictly or literally construed. Consequently, a surety has a right to insist on strict performance of the contract that he has guaranteed. Any variance without the surety's consent, whether detrimental to the surety or not, discharges him. Examples of such variances are:

(a) *Variance in parties*. A guarantees performance by B. The contract is actually performed by B and Company. A is discharged.

(b) *Variance in extent of principal's commitment*. A tenant leases part of a building. The lease is guaranteed by X. Later, without X's knowledge or consent, the tenant obtains the rest of the building at an additional rental. X is discharged from all liability.

(c) *Variance in amount, place, time or manner of making payments*. A sues B for breach of B's contract obligation requiring ten equal monthly payments of $100 each to A, at A's office, none of which were paid. The contract is guaranteed by X. Upon the trial, the case is settled for $800 by stipulation requiring four payments of $200 each at the office of A's attorney. X is discharged.

(d) *Change in duties of principal*.[6] A surety for an agent who is to make sales only is not liable after authority is given to the agent to make collections also.[7]

(e) *Surrender of security*. X guarantees A's debt to B in the amount of $10,000, secured by a $10,000 mortgage on A's house. Upon A's request, without X's consent, B surrenders the mortgage to A.

(f) *Change of security*. If, in the previous example, B, without X's consent, exchanges the mortgage for other security, the result is the same: X is discharged.

(g) *Taking additional security*. If, in Example (e), B took additional security without modifying the existing debt and mortgage, the surety would not be released; but if such additional security affected the surety's risk in any way, as by extending the time of payment, the surety would be discharged.

(h) *Taking note for debt*. Where the creditor, without the surety's acquiescence, takes a note for an existing debt, the surety's liability on the guaranteed debt depends upon whether the debt was in any way affected by the note.

For example, Black orders merchandise from Brown. Ford guarantees payment. Black then gives Brown a demand note as further assurance of payment. Later, Black defaults on Brown's demand for payment of the ntoe. Brown sues Ford as surety and Ford's defense is that Brown discharged him by taking the note from Black. Such defense would fail, unless Brown, in taking the note, made some commitment which affected the debt.

(i) *Change beneficial to principal debtor*. It is not necessary that the variance be prejudicial to the surety in order that he be discharged. The surety may be discharged even where the change was beneficial to the principal debtor. For example, Thorne borrows $10,000 from Ward, and as security, gives Ward a bond and mortgage guaranteed by Gray. Later, without Gray's knowledge, Ward agrees to reduce the interest specified in the bond and mortgage. Though such variance lightens Gray's risk, he is discharged by the variance: The risk is no longer the same as the one he guaranteed.

---

[6] *Fidelity Mut. L. Assoc. v. Dewey*, 83 Minn. 389, 86 N.W. 423.

[7] *Tradesmen's Nat. Bank v. National Surety Co.*, 169 N.Y. 563.

**(4) Defenses Based on Discharge.** A surety may disclaim liability not only where the contract, his own or the principal's, is ineffective or where the principal contract has been varied without the surety's consent, but also where some act in and of itself, such as performance or release of the obligation, spells out a discharge.

(a) *Performance* by the principal debtor automatically releases the surety.

(b) *Release of the surety* by the creditor naturally discharges the surety.

(c) *Release of the principal debtor* by the creditor likewise discharges the surety, since the creditor cannot excuse performance on the one hand and insist on responsibility for nonperformance on the other.

*Voluntary v. involuntary release.* To discharge the surety, a release of the principal debtor must be voluntary. If it is involuntary, as in the case of a release by operation of law, it will not discharge the surety.

EXAMPLE: A discharge in bankruptcy, being involuntary (as to the creditor), will not discharge the surety, but a composition agreement, being voluntary, will.

*Qualified release: reservation of rights against surety.* A creditor in discharging the principal debtor may expressly reserve all his remedies against the surety, "in which case the latter will be in a position to pay immediately and, then, to proceed against the principal debtor." [8]

*Release v. suspension of remedy.* Where the creditor's remedy against the principal debtor is suspended by operation of law (as in the case of war between the creditor's and the debtor's countries), the surety is not thereby discharged.

(d) *Death or insolvency.* A surety is not discharged by the death or insolvency of the principal. Neither will the death of a surety release his estate from obligations incurred up to the date of his death. As to unmatured, contingent obligations that might arise under the surety's contract after his death, the liability of the estate will depend upon whether or not the suretyship contract was revocable at the surety's option during his lifetime. If it was, all contingent obligations ceased on death, otherwise not.

**Delay by Creditor in Proceeding against Principal.** Ordinarily, mere delay by a creditor in pursuing his remedies against the principal will not discharge the surety, because the surety, if he fears for the future solvency

---

[8] *National Park Bank v. Koehler,* 204 N.Y. 174, 179-180. See also, *Schwitzerlet-Seigler Co. v. Citizens, etc., Bank,* 155 Ga. 740, 118 S.E. 365; *Mueller v. Dobschuetz,* 89 Ill. 176; *Clagett v. Salmon* (Md.), 5 Gill. & J. 314; *Potter v. Green* (Mass.), 6 Allen 442; *Boatmen's Sav. Bank v. Johnson,* 24 Mo. A. 316; *Stirewalt v. Martin,* 84 N.C. 4; *Weddington v. Jones,* 41 Tex. Civ. App. 463, 91 S.W. 818; *Brown v. Vermont Mut. F. Ins. Co.,* 83 Vt. 161, 74 A. 1061.

of the principal, may always protect himself by stepping forward and promptly paying the debt himself. He is then in a position himself to turn around and hold the principal debtor forthwith. However, in some cases a surety's obligation is conditioned on an express or implied obligation by the creditor to proceed against the principal debtor promptly upon default; and in such cases, if the creditor fails to act promptly and the surety is unable to hold the principal debtor because of the delay, the surety will be discharged.

## Remedies of Surety

**Remedies v. Defenses.** The *remedies* of a surety, as distinguished from his *defenses*, deal with his efforts to relieve himself of the burdens of suretyship, not by *denying* the obligation but by seeking to *shift its burden*, in whole or in part. A surety's principal remedies are (1) subrogation, (2) indemnification, (3) exoneration, and (4) contribution.

(1) **Subrogation.** To "subrogate" is, literally, to substitute one person in the place of another. If the principal debtor's obligation to the creditor is in any way protected by security, either by the deposit of collateral or by a lien on the principal debtor's property, the guarantor, upon discharging the principal debtor's obligation, is entitled in equity to have the security transferred from the creditor to himself, because in discharging the principal debtor's obligation, the guarantor becomes "subrogated" to all the rights of the creditor against the principal debtor. This is what is meant by the expression, "The guarantor steps into the creditor's shoes."

(2) **Reimbursement or Indemnity.** Unless a surety pays the *entire debt* owed by the principal debtor to the creditor, he is not entitled to the equitable remedy of subrogation; that is, he has no equitable claim against the collateral or lien held by the creditor to secure the debt. However, the law raises an implied promise on the part of the principal debtor to indemnify the surety or guarantor to the extent of his loss in making good the principal debtor's obligation. Surety companies make it a practice, before issuing a bond, to require the principal debtor to execute a specific agreement indemnifying the surety company against loss in assuming the risk. Under the remedy of *indemnification*, if a guarantor pays only a *part* of the principal debtor's obligation, he is entitled to sue the principal debtor at *common law* (not in equity) for recovery of the amount of money that he has actually paid the creditor for the principal debtor's benefit.

(3) **Exoneration.** To exonerate a person is to relieve him from a burden. Where the principal debt has matured, the surety may bring an action in equity to compel the principal to pay the debt. "The jurisdiction in this class of cases rests upon the fact that there is a debt due which it is

the duty of the principal debtor, in exoneration of his sureties, to pay forthwith." [9]

(4) **Contribution.** Where there are two or more sureties, and only one of them makes good the default, he may compel contribution from his cosureties. Where two or more guarantors are jointly and severally obligated on a guaranty, each guarantor, upon paying more than *his proportionate share* of the guaranty, may compel the coguarantor or coguarantors to contribute their respective shares *of the excess*, "but in no case can the surety seeking contribution recover more than the excess he has paid beyond the amount which, as between himself and the cosureties, it was his duty to pay." [10]

EXAMPLE: Suppose Brown, Smith and Black are coguarantors on a $3000 principal obligation. If Brown makes good $1000 out of the principal amount, he can recover no contribution from Smith or Black, because $1000 is his ratable liability in any event. But if he pays $2000, he can compel contribution of $1000, or the excess over his proportionate share of the guaranty, from Smith and Black; and if he has paid the entire principal amount, he can compel Smith and Brown to contribute $2000, or the amount of the excess over his own ratable liability.

## Surety Bonds

**Definition.** A *bond* is the formal acknowledgment of an obligation, usually under seal. A *surety bond* acknowledges an obligation to make good the performance by another of some act or duty. The person who executes the bond is known as the *obligor*, corresponding to the *surety*, and the person to whom the obligation is incurred is known as the *obligee*, corresponding to the *creditor*.

**Single Bond v. Bond with Condition: Surety Bonds.** A *single bond* simply acknowledges indebtedness, without reciting any condition that might extinguish the indebtedness. A *bond with a condition* acknowledges an obligation in a specified sum and then recites a condition that may extinguish the liability. A surety bond is a bond with a condition. It usually takes the form of a conditional acknowledgment of indebtedness. First, in the "preamble," it recites the terms of the principal contract and the principal duty or principal obligation secured. Then, in the "obligatory" part, it acknowledges the "penal sum" in which the obligor, his heirs, representatives and assigns, are bound to the obligee. Finally, the bond concludes with the "condition," upon fulfillment of which the obligation is to be deemed discharged, namely, performance by the principal.

**Surety Companies: Nature of Surety Business.** Surety companies—

---

[9] *Holcombe v. Fetter*, 70 N.J. Eq. 300, 301.
[10] 50 *C.J.* 298.

that is, corporations organized for the purpose of engaging in the business of becoming sureties upon bonds and undertakings—occupy a somewhat different status from that of gratuitous sureties. Strictly speaking, when a company is engaged in assuming risks for compensation, it is engaged in the business of insurance rather than in the making of special promises to answer for another's debt, default or miscarriage. Hence the rule of *strictissimi juris* (page 339) is not so readily enforced in the case of surety companies as in the case of gratuitous sureties. Thus, where a creditor or obligee, upon the principal's default, fails to give a gratuitous surety prompt notice of such default, and the suretyship contract provides for such notice, the surety would be discharged, whereas the failure to give such notice to a surety company, notwithstanding a provision for such notice in the bond, would not discharge the company unless the delay was unreasonable or resulted in some prejudice to the company.

**Classification of Surety Bonds.** Surety bonds are now commonly issued by surety companies instead of being given by gratuitous sureties as a matter of accommodation. Surety bonds may be classified as (1) business bonds, (2) official bonds and (3) judicial bonds.

**(1) Business Bonds.** Business bonds are given to secure business obligations, as distinguished from official bonds, given in connection with the holding of public office, and judicial bonds, given in connection with a judicial proceeding. Business bonds include (a) *fidelity bonds,* and (b) *contract* bonds.

**(a)** *Fidelity bonds: nature and purpose.* Fidelity bonds guarantee the faithful performance of duties on the part of business officers, agents and employees in positions of trust, and protect employers against loss sustained through dishonest or criminal acts of employees. Fidelity bonds are frequently required by banks, financial institutions, fraternal and benevolent societies, and organizations generally that entrust to employees the handling of substantial funds or property.

*Fidelity bonds: conditions of liability.* Although, as stated, surety companies are not entitled to the same degree of stringency of performance as in the case of gratuitous sureties, they may insist on a strict performance of the conditions in the bond. The duties of the employee may not be materially enlarged nor the fidelity risks materially varied without the surety company's consent.

*Full disclosure as to previous record.* A surety company is entitled to full disclosure by the obligee in respect to all facts pertinent to the risk, especially where inquiry is made as to such facts. The writing of a fidelity bond being in the nature of insurance, the obligee must make full disclosure to the surety company of any facts within his knowledge bearing upon prior dishonesty or irregularity on the part of the prospective employee.

*Duty of employer upon discovering irregularity.* Upon discovering any dishonesty or material default on the part of the employee, the obligee or employer must notify the surety company with reasonable promptness in the light of all the circumstances, and must likewise promptly discharge the employee. If during the course of employment the employee is guilty of any act of dishonesty or infidelity that comes to the knowledge of the employer, a failure to notify the surety company of such default within a reasonable time may defeat recovery on the bond,[11] especially where the bond requires prompt notification of such default and where a failure to give such notice has prejudiced the rights of the surety company. Where, however, failure to give prompt notice does not prejudice the rights of the surety company, the latter will not be discharged on its bond, unless a specific time limit for notice has been fixed in the bond and such notice has not been given. Some states fix a minimum time limit which a fidelity company may impose. However, where an employer continues an employee in his service after the latter has committed a default and the employer fails to notify the surety company of the default or where the employer notifies the surety company but does not discharge the employee and the employee is then guilty of a second default, the surety company will be discharged from liability as to the second offense, but not as to the first.

(b) *Contract (performance) bonds.* Contract bonds, also referred to as performance bonds, guarantee the faithful performance of a contract. They most frequently concern *construction* and *supply* contracts. In the former case, they are sometimes referred to as *completion bonds.* Contract bonds are now required in practically all government contracts—Federal, state, county and municipal—and are becoming of increasing importance in contracts between private individuals.

EXAMPLE: The liability of a surety in connection with a private building contract is to make good to the obligee for a failure of the principal to complete or to complete within a given time or in accordance with the terms and specifications of the building contract, depending on the terms and conditions of the bond. The bond may provide for notice to the surety of the principal debtor's default as a condition for holding the surety liable, in which event notice must be given. Or the bond by its terms may render the surety liable forthwith upon default of the principal debtor or builder.

(2) **Official Bonds.** Many statutes require that a public officer, before he assumes his official duties, shall furnish a bond for the proper performance of his office. A "public officer," in this sense, means every person holding a government office or position and required to take an official oath. Not every public officer, of course, is required to furnish a bond, and no public officer may be required to furnish a bond unless a statute so provides.

---

[11] *Miners Sav. Bank of Pittston v. Royal Indemnity Co.,* 326 Pa. 428, 9 A. 2d 543.

(3) **Judicial Bonds.** Judicial bonds are those given in connection with a judicial proceeding. Among the more common judicial bonds are:

*Bail bonds,* given on behalf of a person subject to imprisonment by judicial process, and guaranteeing compliance with all orders of the court, such as appearance upon a given day to stand trial, and so on.

*Fiduciary bonds (judicial),* prescribed in proceedings wherein some judicial appointee has the care and custody of another's property. Examples of such appointees are guardians, administrators, executors and receivers.

*Court undertakings.* The liability of surety companies on a court undertaking depends upon the nature of the bond issued. An *attachment bond* is one wherein a surety company guarantees that if an attachment proves to be unwarranted, damages up to the amount stated may be recoverable by the owner of the property attached. An *injunction bond* is one wherein the surety or bonding company agrees to indemnify the person against whom the injunction was procured from damage sustained by him if the injunction should prove unfounded upon the final trial or hearing of the issues. An *appeal bond* is one wherein the bonding company guarantees a sum, usually to include a judgment with interest and costs, in case the judgment should be affirmed on appeal. An appeal bond usually operates as a stay to prevent the judgment creditor from proceeding against the judgment debtor until the appeal can be determined, and in consideration of such stay, the successful litigant or person stayed is indemnified if the appeal should prove unwarranted by an affirmance.

## Questions

1. A surety's ground for disclaiming liability may be based on some infirmity in his contract of suretyship. Name three other classes of defenses that are available to a surety.

2. Give nine ways in which a surety's risk may be so varied as to release him from his liability.

3. Name four acts or circumstances that will serve as a basis for a surety's discharge.

4. How does a delay by a creditor in proceeding against the principal affect the liability of a surety?

5. What are the four principal remedies of a surety?

6. What is meant by a surety bond?

7. Distinguish a single bond from a bond with a condition.

8. Name three classifications of surety bonds.

9. Give two examples of business bonds, and name the functions of each.

10. Name three of the more common types of judicial bonds, and explain their purpose.

## Problems

1. Fowler, an infant, purchases an automobile on installment. Cummings guarantees the account. The automobile is wrecked, and Fowler refuses to pay

the balance due. The dealer sues Cummings on his guaranty. Cummings defends on the ground that the principal contract being unenforceable, he is not liable on the guaranty. Judgment for whom and why?

2. The Superior Dairy Company makes a contract with Satisfied Cows, Inc., for the purchase of 12,000 cans of pure milk covering a period of one year. The contract provides that 1,000 cans are to be delivered each month, deliveries to be made daily, and payments to be made weekly. Gardner guarantees payment by the Superior Dairy Company. Subsequently both parties to the contract agree that since both the market and the supply of milk will be greater in the summer than in the winter, deliveries are to be made at the rate of 1,500 cans per month for the months of May to October, inclusive, and 500 cans monthly for the balance of the year; payments to be made weekly as originally agreed. Gardner is not advised of this change. The Superior Dairy Company fails to pay the balance due during the last month of the contract period, and Contented Cows, Inc., sues Gardner on his guaranty. Judgment for whom and why?

3. Vann and Mann are jointly and severally liable as co-sureties on a debt of $20,000. The principal debtor defaults. The creditor sues Vann, who settles for $10,000. Vann sues Mann for 50 per cent of this amount. Judgment for whom and why?

4. One of two sureties on a debt of $5,000 succeeds in settling the case for $3,500, obtaining a complete release of the obligation. He then sues the principal debtor for the principal amount. How should the court decide and why?

5. Billings, after furnishing a bond for his faithful performance, secures a position as Assistant Cashier with the Occidental Bank. One month later the cashier dies, and Billings is given his place. Shortly thereafter Billings disappears with $10,000 of the bank's funds. The bank sues the bonding company. Judgment for whom and why?

6. George Gray, an employee of the Fearless Finance Company, works his way up from the position of office boy to treasurer of the company. As office boy he had committed an indiscretion involving the theft of $3.00 worth of stamps, after which, having been given a good lecture, he turned over a new leaf. Upon being appointed treasurer, Gray was required to furnish a bond, upon an application jointly executed by Gray and the Finance Company. Nothing was said about Gray's indiscretion as an office boy. Six months after Gray assumes his duties as treasurer, he embezzles $50,000 of the company's funds, spends it, and commits suicide. The Fearless Finance Company sues the surety company on its bond, and the latter, learning of the indiscretion involving the theft of the stamps, refuses to make good on the bond. Judgment for whom and why?

7. Allen became a surety for Bronson, an infant principal, with respect to the latter's obligation to Clay. Bronson defaulted and was sued, but was able to show that his contract had been induced through fraud. Clay then brought action against Allen as surety. Who prevailed, and why?

8. A tenant leased part of a building. His obligation was guaranteed by Dedalus. Later, the tenant leased the remainder of the building from the landlord, without Dedalus's knowledge or consent. The tenant then defaulted. Has Dedalus a good defense in a subsequent action brought against him by the landlord?

## COURT CASES FOR REVIEW

### How Did the Court Decide, and Why?

1. A written financing agreement was executed by a corporation's president under which the plaintiff agreed to lend money to the corporation. A resolution was signed by the directors and stockholders ratifying the agreement and guaranteeing payment of the loan. In a subsequent action by the lender against the stockholders as guarantors, the latter interposed the defense that there was no consideration shown which might bind them to the contract. *McMillan v. Dozier*, 257 Ala. 435, 59 So. 2d 563.

2. A Georgia citizen was waylaid and murdered. The executor of his estate published a reward of $500 for information leading to the arrest and conviction of the killer. The mother of the deceased contacted a private detective and gave him a written guaranty of the executor's published reward. The detective unearthed sufficient evidence to cause the arrest and conviction of a second son of the decedent's mother for the murder of his own brother. When the mother refused to pay the reward money to the detective, the latter brought suit. *Campbell v. Mercer*, 108 Ga. 103, 33 S.E. 871.

3. Defendant, who was president, director and sole stockholder of Pluto Corporation, guaranteed payment of loans made by plaintiff to the Pluto Corporation. Defendant pledged stock in the Pluto and another corporation as security for his guaranty. The loans were defaulted, and without further proceedings against the Pluto Corporation, plaintiff sought recovery under defendant's guaranty by sale of the collateral and judgment against defendant. Defendant's position was that plaintiff was first required to exhaust his remedies against the principal debtor. *General Phoenix Corporation v. Cabot*, 300 N.Y. 87, 89 N.E. 2d 238.

4. The decedent during his lifetime executed a written guaranty to the plaintiff, a mercantile concern, making himself responsible for the nonpayment of any merchandise sold by the plaintiff to a certain third party. The guarantor further agreed that his promise would be binding upon him until he had given plaintiff written notice of its revocation. After the death of the deceased, plaintiff extended credit to the third party in the form of merchandise, and the latter neglected to pay for it. Plaintiff thereupon brought this action against the executor of the guarantor's estate. *Jordan Marsh & Co. v. Dobbins*, 122 Mass. 168.

5. The holder of a promissory note brought an action against one of three sureties named therein. The latter was able to show that the principal debtor and one of the sureties other than himself had, without his consent, made a valid agreement with the creditor by which the time of payment was extended. *Short v. Shannon*, 211 S.W. 463 (Tex. Civ. App.).

6. The agent of plaintiff insurance company converted to his own use the sum of $1,200 in collected premiums. Plaintiff's superintendent of agencies agreed that the agent might continue in plaintiff's employ if he made good the shortage and posted a surety bond against possible future defalcations. The shortage was made good and a bond was signed and posted by several of the agent's friends as sureties. The latter knew nothing about the agent's previous default. Subsequently, the agent again misappropriated his company's funds. Upon payment being demanded and refused, the company brought suit against the sureties. *Connecticut General Life Insurance Co. v. Chase et al.*, 72 Vt. 176.

7. At the request of M. E. McKee, a shoemaker, defendant wrote plaintiff, a

leather goods dealer, the following: "I will be responsible for what stock M. E. McKee has had and may want hereafter, to the amount of $500.00." Subsequently, plaintiff delivered leather on various orders which exceeded $1,000, but the indebtedness was reduced to approximately $400. When payment of the balance was demanded and refused, plaintiff brought this action against defendant. *Gates v. McKee*, 13 N.Y. 232.

8. Defendant wrote a letter to plaintiff on behalf of one Jacob Posner, guaranteeing the payment ". . . of any goods you may sell him, hoping you will comply with my request and attend to it at once. . . ." The goods were referred to as a "full line of samples . . . suitable for Spring and Summer." During an extended period of four years, Posner received and paid for the merchandise as ordered. Subsequently, when he defaulted in payment, plaintiff brought this action against defendant on his guaranty. *Schwartz et al. v. Hyman*, 107 N.Y. 562.

9. Defendant signed a suretyship agreement under a misconception arising from an allegedly fraudulent statement by the plaintiff and another, that the agreement was merely a recommendation for the plaintiff to sell the creditor's product. The surety contended that he could not read without glasses, and that he signed without getting his glasses to read the agreement. The creditor had no knowledge of this alleged fraud. *J. R. Watkins Co. v. Lankford*, 256 S.W. 2d 788.

10. Plaintiff was surety on performance bonds given by defendant on street construction and maintenance contracts awarded defendant by several cities. Defendant defaulted and plaintiff made good, after which plaintiff sued defendant for indemnification of loss sustained in making good defendant's default. The defense was that no contract of indemnity had ever been entered into between plaintiff and defendant. *American Bonding Co. v. Alcatraz Construction Co.*, 202 F. 483.

# 8

# Insurance

**Scope of This Chapter.** In this chapter we consider the major legal aspects of insurance. In Part 1 we deal with the insurance contract itself: the parties to the contract, including the different classes of insurance companies; the question of when insurance contracts come into existence (mutual assent); the consideration for the contract (premiums and assessments); the subject matter of the contract (necessity and kinds of insurable interest, exclusion of crimes, torts and deliberate losses, as by suicide); and the form of the contract (when a writing is mandatory, the formal contract, or policy, and so forth). In Part 2 we consider marine and fire insurance, in Part 3, life insurance, and in Part 4, casualty insurance, including accident and health, liability, automobile, burglary and title insurance. Finally, in Part 5, we consider the law in relation to insurance agents, brokers and adjusters, and in respect to the payment, avoidance and forfeiture of insurance benefits.

## PART 1. THE INSURANCE CONTRACT

**Nature of Insurance Contract.** Insurance is indemnification against the risk of loss, by distributing the loss over a group. If each of a hundred persons owns a vessel, the loss of any single vessel might spell financial ruin for the owner. But if all agree to contribute a fund out of which to reimburse any one owner upon whom such loss might fall, the weight of the loss is distributed over the group and all are assured against total loss from the contingency named. It is this characteristic, chiefly, that distinguishes insurance from gambling.

*Insurance v. wager.* If you toss a coin and I offer to pay you a dollar if it falls heads, you to pay me a dollar if it falls tails, one or the other of us must lose. The loss of one is the gain of the other. The transaction is a pure wager. But if you in common with many others pay me a given sum on my agreement to assume the risk of loss which any of you may sustain from a given cause, the transaction is of benefit to all; you are all assured against the risk of loss, and I make a profit measured by the aggregate of your contributions minus the aggregate of losses that I pay out.

**Contract Essentials.** Insurance contracts, like all contracts, must conform to the general rules in respect to contract essentials. These we have already considered in the chapter on Contracts. Our present concern is with the particular application of these rules to insurance transactions.

**Parties.** The parties to a contract of insurance are the *insurer,* who assumes the risk, and the *insured* or *assured,* whose risk is assumed. Insurers are frequently referred to as *underwriters.* Generally, any person or group of persons, individual or corporate, may be an insurer, provided there is contractual capacity (page 53). The bulk of insurance business is now done by corporations. Some states require insurers to be incorporated, because corporations can be more effectively regulated than private individuals. An exception is generally made in the case of "American Lloyds," unincorporated associations engaged chiefly in writing marine, fire and similar risks. In some states, individuals may be insurers provided they are duly licensed and comply with the statutory requirements.

*Classification of insurance companies.* Insurance companies may be *stock, mutual* or *mixed.*

*Stock companies* are corporations that issue stock. The stockholders, as a class, are separate and distinct from the policyholders. They are entitled to any profits available for dividends.

*Mutual companies* issue no stock. The policyholders automatically become members of the company. Thus the members, collectively, are the insurers, and each member, individually, is the insured. Profits after necessary expenses, reserves, and so on, are distributed as dividends among the members.

*Mixed companies are partly stock and partly mutual.* Profits are distributed in part to the stockholders and in part to the policyholders.

**Mutual Assent.** As in all contracts, the contract of insurance becomes effective when the minds of the parties meet. Usually, the offer takes the form of an application for insurance, signed by the insured, with information necessary to enable the insurer to pass on the request. The unconditional acceptance of the application completes the contract. Sometimes, however, the acceptance is conditional; for example, where it provides that the contract shall not be deemed effective until the premium is paid and the policy delivered (page 356). Statements in an accepted application bind the applicant.

**Consideration.** The consideration for the insurer's promise to indemnify is the payment or promise of payment, by the insured, of a *premium* or *assessment.*

*Premium and assessment distinguished.* A premium is a periodical sum of money agreed to be paid to the insurers as consideration for assuming the risk. An assessment is a sum of money, to be determined by the financial requirements of the insurer, that the insured is obligated to contribute as the need arises.

*Premiums: medium of payment.* Premiums are payable in cash, by check or by note of the policyholder, as may be agreed. However, an agent authorized to collect premiums has no implied authority to collect anything but cash.

*Premiums sent by mail: risk of nondelivery.* Ordinarily, when one elects to transmit something through the mails, he thereby designates the mails as *his* agent, and the risk of nondelivery or delayed delivery is on the sender. However, if the sender uses the mails at the request of the recipient or in response to the latter's offer, the post office is thereby designated as the recipient's agent, and delivery is complete upon deposit in the mails. Hence, if a premium is sent by mail, nondelivery or delayed delivery is at the risk of the insured, unless the company or its authorized agent requested or directed payment by mail or unless such payment was impliedly authorized by a long course of conduct acquiesced in by the company.

**Subject Matter.** The subject matter of an insurance contract is the assumption of a risk and the indemnification against loss that may be suffered by one exposed to it. The law places no limitation upon the character of the risk assumed, except to require:

(a) A risk to the person insured—*an insurable interest.*

(b) Legality of the transaction.

(c) That the loss must not be deliberate.

(d) Existence of the subject matter involving the risk.

(e) Compliance with statutory provisions in respect to licensing and similar requirements.

**Insurable Interest: What Constitutes.** Regardless of the nature of the insurance or the subject matter of the policy, the person to whom a policy of insurance is issued must have an insurable interest in the subject matter of the insurance or the transaction is a gamble and unenforceable. One has an insurable interest in the subject matter insured if he stands to gain by its preservation and to lose by its loss, damage or destruction.

EXAMPLE: If, for a consideration, I promise to pay you a sum of money in case it rains tomorrow, and you have no financial interest at stake in tomorrow's weather, such a transaction is clearly a gamble. But if you have some interest at stake in tomorrow's weather, some risk of loss—as, for example, by reason of conducting some open air event which would mean loss to you in case of rain—you have an insurable interest in the weather, and an assumption of that risk by another would constitute a valid insurance transaction.

**Insurable Interest in Life.** If a person is so related by blood, marriage, or business to another as to justify a reasonable expectation of benefit or advantage from continuance of the latter's life and loss or detriment from its termination, he has an insurable interest in such life. Husband and wife have each an insurable interest in the other's life. A father has an insurable interest in the lives of his children, since they might some day support him. Partners have an insurable interest in one another's lives. An employer has an insurable interest in the life of his employee, and vice versa. A creditor has an insurable interest in his debtor's life, and a surety in the life of his principal. A person has an unlimited interest in his own life, which will support a policy taken by him in favor of himself or his estate or in favor of another person as beneficiary, even though the beneficiary has no insurable interest in such life.

*Corporations: insurable interest in lives of officers, and so on.* A corporation has an insurable interest in the life of its president, general manager, principal stockholder or other person or officer on whose efforts the success of the corporation's business depends.[1] In case such officer retires or is removed or otherwise severs his connection with the company, the right of the corporation to keep up the premiums and collect the insurance is upheld in some states but not in others.

**Insurable Interest in Property.** A person has an insurable interest in property when he has such right, interest or relation to it that he will be benefited by its preservation and continued existence and will suffer a direct pecuniary loss from its destruction or injury by reason of the peril insured against. Persons held to have an insurable interest in property include: the holder of any legal or equitable title, such as a trustee and the beneficiary of a trust; a tenant in common (page 617) of real property, or a part owner of personal property; a partner; a stockholder; an ordinary tenant; a life tenant (page 615); a remainderman or a reversioner (page 616); the holder of a mortgage or any other kind of lien (page 684); any bailee, such as a carrier, warehouseman or pledgee; and a purchaser of real property under a contract of sale, though title has not yet closed or passed.

*Mortgagor and mortgagee.* A mortgagor of property (*i.e.,* the owner) has an insurable interest therein to the extent of its full value, since he remains the owner notwithstanding the mortgage. He loses his insurable interest when, after foreclosure proceedings, he loses his right to redeem, or "equity of redemption" (page 697), except where he remains liable on the mortgage debt (pages 696-697). In case of loss, he may recover the full amount thereof, if he was insured up to that amount.

The mortgagee (*i.e.,* the holder of the mortgage) has an insurable interest in the mortgaged property to the extent of the mortgage debt, but only so long as the debt remains unpaid. However, a mortgagee recovers nothing in case of loss unless there is an agreement to this effect between the mortgagor and the mortgagee, or a policy issued to or for the benefit

---

[1] *U.S. v. Supplee-Biddle Hardware Co.,* 265 U.S. 189.

of the mortgagee. In the absence of agreement, a mortgagee has no lien on the insurance proceeds.

**Insurable Interest: Some Distinctions between Life and Property.** In respect to insurable interest, there are two important distinctions between life and property insurance:

(a) *Expectation of benefit v. legal right.* In the case of life insurance, a mere expectation of benefit is sufficient, without legal right. In the case of property insurance, there must be either a legal right or interest in the property itself, or else an expectation founded on a legal right.

EXAMPLES:

(1) A sister may be dependent on her brother for support, without legal right to such support, yet such expectation alone is enough to give the sister an insurable interest in her brother's life.

(2) The foster parent of a child orphaned by his mother and abandoned by his father may have a reasonable expectation of benefit from the foster child in subsequent years, sufficient, as an insurable interest, to support an insurance policy taken out by the foster parent on the life of the foster child.

(3) Plaintiff took out a policy of insurance on the hull and equipment of the steamer Falcon. Plaintiff's sole interest was that he owned 36 shares of stock in the corporation that owned the Falcon. There was a loss, and defendant refused payment to plaintiff on the ground that he had no insurable interest. The Court held for plaintiff.[2]

(b) *Time when insurable interest must exist.* In the case of life insurance, the insurable interest must exist at the time the policy is issued, but need not exist at the time of the death or loss.[3] In the case of property (such as fire or marine) insurance, if there is no insurable interest in existence at the time of the loss, there can be no recovery.

EXAMPLES:

(1) To secure a debt, X gives Y a mortgage on X's home. Y takes out a policy of insurance on X's life, also a policy of fire insurance on X's home. Later X pays the debt and the mortgage is canceled. Y keeps up the premiums on both policies. Still later, X dies in a fire that destroys his home. Y may recover on the life but not on the fire insurance policy.

(2) A creditor may recover on a life policy covering the debtor's life notwithstanding payment of the debt.

(3) A policy on the life of a spouse is payable notwithstanding divorce.[4]

**Beneficiary need not have insurable interest.** Only the person who procures a policy of insurance need have an insurable interest in the life of an insured. A beneficiary may even be a stranger to the insured.

EXAMPLE: X insured his life for the benefit of Y, a friend. He then, with Y's consent, assigned the policy to Z, a stranger, for $1000. Upon X's death, the company refused payment to Z on the ground that neither Y nor Z had

---

[2] *Riggs v. C. M. Ins. Co.,* 125 N.Y. 7.

[3] Some policies, however, require that an insurable interest continue throughout the life of the policy. A few states have adopted statutes to such effect.

[4] *Edgington v. Equitable Life Assur. Soc.,* 236 Iowa 903, 20 N.W. 2d 411.

an insurable interest in the life of X. Held: for Z. A beneficiary need not have an insurable interest in the life of the insured.[5]

**Legality of Transaction.** The business of insurance is valid so long as it does not represent a mere gambling transaction, as in the case of betting on a risk without insurable interest.

**Crimes.** It is lawful to insure a risk based on the crimes of *others*, but not on the crimes of the insured. For example, a person may be insured against the risk of loss through burglary but not against the risk of loss through his own crimes.

**Torts.** Insurance is payable regardless of the fact that the loss was occasioned by a tort, so long as the tort was not wilful or deliberate. For example, a life insurance policy is payable though the loss of life is due to the insured's negligence. Likewise, fire insurance is payable notwithstanding an employee's negligence.

**Deliberate Losses: Suicide.** Losses caused by the deliberate acts of the insured are not recoverable; for example, there can be no recovery for fire losses if the fire was caused by the insured's deliberate act. If a policy of life insurance were to stipulate for payment in the case of suicide, it would be contrary to public policy and void. However, if a policy is silent on the subject of suicide, or even if it provides that the insurer is not to be liable in case of suicide, the law permits recovery under certain conditions (pages 368-369).

**Existence of Subject Matter.** A contract of insurance is invalid where the subject matter is not in existence at the time the risk attaches and such fact is known to one of the parties. For example, if a ship is lost at sea and the owner, knowing it, insures the vessel with an insurer ignorant of the fact, the policy is void. But if both parties were ignorant of the loss, the policy would be valid. Marine risks are sometimes accepted on this basis. (See page 359.) If a policy of life insurance is taken out by a creditor on the life of a debtor, and the debtor, unknown to both parties, has in the meantime died, the insurance is valid notwithstanding.[6]

**Licensing and Other Requirements.** Every state regulates the conditions under which it will permit insurance to be conducted. Statutes generally declare insurance policies void if issued within the state unless the insurer has complied with statutory requirements. These include procurement of a license, payment of a license fee, and compliance with regulations in respect to capital, surplus, reserves, liabilities, investments, deposits, and so on. Supervision is exercised by a state superintendent of insurance who, through his representatives, makes periodic audits and

---

[5] *St. John's v. Insurance Co.*, 13 N.Y. 31; *Smith v. Coleman*, 184 Va. 259, 35 S.E. 2d 107.

[6] *E. J. Riegel v. American Life Ins. Co.*, 140 Pa. 123, 21 A. 392.

inspections and requires periodic reports to insure compliance with the law.

**Insurance Contracts and the Statute of Frauds: Policies.** The law does not require ordinary contracts of insurance to be in writing. Even an oral contract of insurance for a term of years need not be in writing, because such a contract *may* be performed within a year by the happening of the event insured against; that is, the contract is not one that by its terms *must* take longer than a year to perform (page 85). In some jurisdictions, however, the statutes expressly require a contract of insurance to be in writing. Georgia is an example. In New York, the statute of frauds requires that every agreement, the performance of which is not to be completed before the end of a lifetime, must be in writing to be enforceable. This would seem to include contracts of life insurance. Other states prohibit the issuances of certain kinds of insurance unless a copy of the form of the policy has been filed with the insurance commission. Since no copy of a form can be filed unless it is in writing, this amounts to a requirement that the contract of insurance be in writing.

A *policy* is the formal contract of insurance, embodying its full terms and conditions.

**Form of Insurance Contract: Standard Provisions.** Formerly, different policies issued by different companies throughout the country varied widely in coverage, risks included and excluded, technicalities (often in fine print) resulting in avoidance or forfeiture, and tricky clauses generally. Ultimately, the various state legislatures devised standard provisions that must be incorporated into policies before the insurer will be allowed to do business. (See page 360.)

**When Contract Effective.** Ordinarily, life insurance companies stipulate that the contract is not effective until the policy is delivered and the premium paid. This is not the rule, however, with property insurance. In fire insurance, for example, if there has been a complete meeting of the minds on the terms of the risk, the insurer becomes liable even if a fire breaks out before the policy is delivered. This is usually evidenced by a brief written memorandum or commitment in the form of a "binder" (page 360).

**Assignability of Insurance Contracts, Generally.** As already pointed out (page 99), a contract is not assignable if it creates a personal relationship or if its terms prohibit assignment. Some policies are construed as creating a personal relationship, others not. Many policies specifically prohibit a change of interest. This subject is more fully discussed on pages 363 and 370.

**Forms of Insurance.** As noted on page 352, the law places no limitation upon the character of the risk assumed, given the validity of its subject matter and the existence of an interest therein on the part of the person assured. Insurance first took the form of indemnity against *marine* losses.

*Fire* insurance came much later, and *life* insurance still later. *Accident* and *health* insurance were naturally derived from life insurance. So extensively has insurance developed, that it now covers practically every form of risk known to business. (See pages 372 to 376.)

## Questions

1. What is the nature of an insurance contract and how does it differ from an ordinary wager?

2. Name three types of insurance companies.

3. What is the consideration for the insurer's promise to indemnify the insured? How does it differ from an assessment? Who bears the risk of loss if it is sent by mail?

4. The law places no restrictions upon risks that may be protected by insurance, except to require compliance with certain requisites. Name five such requisites.

5. What is meant by an insurable interest?

6. When may a person have an insurable interest in (a) life, (b) property?

7. With respect to insurable interest, name and illustrate two important distinctions between life and property insurance.

8. How does a deliberate loss affect the beneficiary's right to recover?

9. "An insurance contract based on non-existent subject matter is invalid." Is this statement true, false, or partly true and partly false?

10. "Insurance contracts must be in writing." Is this statement true, false, or partly true and partly false?

11. When do the following forms of insurance ordinarily become effective: (a) life; (b) fire?

## Problems

1. A number of young men mutually agree to contribute, to a joint fund, certain initiation fees, annual dues and assessments; each giving a guaranty that he will not be married within two years from the date of initiation; and each to receive $1,000 at the time of his marriage. Five years later one of the group, upon his marriage, demanded $1,000 under the agreement, which was refused. Upon suit for the sum stated, who would succeed, and why?

2. *A* owns a ship. He has twenty children, the eldest of whom is twenty-five years of age. *B* is a person who will inherit the ship provided he survives *A* and the twenty children; and he is ninety years old. Has he an insurable interest in the ship?

3. An insured mails $29.80 in cash to his insurance company in payment of a quarterly premium due that day upon expiration of a thirty-day grace period. Both the letter and the cash are lost. Assuming that the insured can prove he mailed the premium on the day in question, can the insurance company cancel the policy?

4. John promises to pay William $100 if it should not rain the next day, in consideration of William's promise to pay John that sum if it does rain. The next day it does rain, but William refuses to honor his promise. Can John compel William to make the promised payment?

5. Barr buys a $10,000 mortgage on property owned by Cole. He takes out a fire insurance policy on Cole's property, with himself as beneficiary. A fire destroys the entire premises, but the insurance company refuses to make good

on Barr's policy, claiming that Barr had no insurable interest in the property. Is the company's position sound?

6. Stevens took out a $50,000 policy of insurance on the life of Currin who was indebted to Stevens in the sum of $30,000. Upon Currin's death, the insurance company refused to pay the face amount of the policy on the ground that it exceeded the debt. Upon suit by Stevens, who should succeed?

7. Mary Bailey took out a policy on the life of her husband, payable upon his death to "his wife." Subsequently Mary Bailey was divorced by her husband, who shortly thereafter died. The insurance company refused payment to Mary Bailey, who thereupon sued the company. How did the court decide?

8. Plaintiff took out a policy on the life of her fiance and paid the first premium. Before the parties were married, the fiance died. Did plaintiff have an insurable interest in the life of her fiance?

9. Crocker, an admirer of the exploits of Major Speed, a jet pilot, takes out a $10,000 policy of insurance on his own life and makes Major Speed the beneficiary. In all other respects, Major Speed is a total stranger to Crocker. On Crocker's death, the insurance company refuses to pay the insurance money to Major Speed, on the ground that the Major had no insurable interest in Crocker's life. Can Major Speed enforce payment?

10. A policy of insurance provided for payment to a furrier in case of loss by burglary up to the value of $50,000. The furrier's warehouse was burglarized and he suffered a severe loss for which he sought compensation. The insurance company interposed the defense that since burglary was a crime, the contract was void for invalid subject matter. How should the Court rule?

11. (a) Ezra Perkins has for thirty years, as motorman, conductor and general passenger agent, operated the Tompkins Corners Trolley line, whose rolling stock consists of a single trolley car, and whose capital stock is wholly owned by the local banker. Fearing that an accident to the trolley car might deprive him of his livelihood, Ezra takes out a policy of fire insurance on the trolley car. Should the policy be issued and the car be destroyed by fire, would Ezra collect the insurance? (b) Would your answer be the same if Ezra instead of the local banker owned the capital stock of the trolley line?

## PART 2. MARINE AND FIRE INSURANCE

**Beginnings of Modern Insurance.** Modern insurance, as we know it, originated in marine risks. Its use on any extensive scale dates from the middle ages, when the merchants of such maritime Italian states as Venice, Florence and Genoa, conducting a flourishing international trade, freely resorted to maritime insurance upon a mutual indemnity basis. The term "policy" is derived from the Italian *"polizia."* From Italy, the practice of insurance and of the other mercantile customs commonly referred to as the "law merchant" spread to England and the rest of Europe.

*Lloyd's coffee house.* In 1688, an inn, maintained by one Edward Lloyd and known as Lloyd's coffee house, was popularly patronized by seafaring men and merchants engaged in foreign trade. Merchants gathered at Lloyd's, with a vessel about to embark for a foreign port, would pass around a slip containing a designation of the vessel, its cargo, the name of the master, character of the crew, and voyage contemplated; and those present who desired to insure the venture, would "underwrite" it, *i.e.,* would write their names or initials underneath the data on the slip, with the amount for which each was willing to be liable in case of loss. Lloyd's survives to this day as an outstanding insurance organization, with branches throughout the world.

*Early assumptions of fire risks.* Fire insurance came later. But it was not until 1710 that the first of the fire insurance companies (The Sun Fire Office) was established. Even then, it was not before the beginning of the nineteenth century that fire insurance attained any substantial proportions.

## Marine Insurance

**Nature of Marine Insurance.** Marine insurance protects against hazards known as *perils of the sea*—fire, shipwreck or piracy. The term *perils of the sea* does not include the ordinary action of wind and wave, wear and tear, or loss due to delays occasioned thereby.

**Time v. Voyage Policies.** A *time* policy is one that fixes the duration of the risk in terms of a fixed period, such as from noon of May 1, 1954 to noon of May 1, 1955. A *voyage* policy is one in which the duration of the risk is measured by the limits of the voyage; for example, from New York to Bordeaux.

**Seaworthiness: Original Defects.** A fundamental warranty in marine insurance is that the vessel is seaworthy. If this warranty is untrue, the insurer will not be liable.

EXAMPLE: If a vessel founders from a leak, the underwriter is liable for the loss, or not, depending respectively on whether the loss is due to violence from without or weakness from within.

**"Lost or Not Lost."** Where a policy contains a provision for insurance of a vessel "lost or not lost," the underwriter assumes not only the risk of future loss, but also the risk of loss that may already have occurred. Of course, if the assured has knowledge of the loss at the time when the policy is issued, he cannot recover from an underwriter who assumed the risk without such knowledge. The stipulation for insurance on a "lost or not lost" basis covers situations where the location of the vessel is unknown and knowledge of possible loss is unavailable.

**General Average v. Particular Average.** The amount of loss for which a marine insurer is liable is fixed in the policy. From earliest days, however, it has been the custom to resort to the "general average." Where goods are *jettisoned*—thrown overboard to lighten and save the ship—they are sacrificed for the benefit of cargo and ship as a whole, that is, such loss works to the benefit of the owners of the ship and the rest of the cargo not jettisoned. It is therefore customary to incorporate, into marine policies, a *general average* provision, whereby the underwriter undertakes to collect, from the owners of the vessel and of cargo saved by jettison of particular goods, a contribution to make good the loss on the particular goods, thus averaging up the loss. *Particular average* relates to the actual insurance paid by the underwriter on the particular thing insured.

**Proofs of loss.** Payment of loss will not be made without proofs of loss. These must give full particulars of the nature, amount and cause of damage, sworn to by the master and crew of the vessel. Bills of lading and similar documents must be submitted to prove title. An investigation is usually made by the government surveyor of the port or by experts chosen by both sides. If the parties cannot agree as to the amount of damage, the damaged goods are sold at auction and the amount is determined in that way.

## Fire Insurance

**Standard Fire Policy.** In many states, a standard fire policy is prescribed by statute or by a commissioner of insurance with statutory authority. New York pioneered such a statute, and many other states have adopted the New York standard fire policy merely by reference to such form. The purpose of such statutes is threefold: (1) To protect the insured against obscure or tricky language offering escape from liability in case of loss, (2) to secure uniformity in insurance contracts, and (3) to protect insurance companies against fraud and imposition on the part of the insured and the perils of alleged oral waivers by their local agents.[7] Most of the legal principles referred to in this discussion are embodied in such standard clauses.

**Definition and Coverage.** A fire insurance contract indemnifies the insured against property loss by fire. It covers not only direct loss due to fire, but also loss accompanying or resulting from a fire, such as damage by smoke, water or chemicals.

**Friendly v. hostile fire.** A fire kindled or employed for ordinary purposes, as for lighting, heating or manufacturing, is said to be of *friendly* origin, and unless otherwise provided in the policy, loss or damage resulting from such a fire is not recoverable. A *hostile* fire is one that breaks out where not desired or intended or that is intended for a legitimate purpose but becomes uncontrollable.

EXAMPLE: In *Mode v. Fireman's Fund Ins. Co.*,[8] the Court held that a fire policy did not cover loss resulting from the fact that an article of value was accidentally thrown into an incinerator fire, which was of friendly origin.

**Binders.** As pointed out on page 356, a contract of fire insurance may take effect before the policy is delivered. Usually, the meeting of the minds is evidenced by a "binder" or "binding slip." This consists of a written memorandum giving temporary protection pending delivery of the policy. The binder sets forth the essential terms of the insurance contract, including location of property, amount of insurance, premium,

---

[7] 44 *C.J.S.* 1026, and cases therein cited.
[8] 62 Idaho 270, 110 P. 2d 840.

and so on. It is subject to the conditions to be subsequently incorporated into the policy.

**Valued v. Open Policy.** A *valued* policy specifies the value of the property insured. An *open* or *unvalued* policy leaves the value open, to be determined at the time of the loss. Policies may be both valued and open: Valued, to the extent that the insurance company agrees to pay a specific amount in case of total loss, and open, to the extent that it agrees to pay, in the event of a partial loss, an amount to be fixed at the time of loss. Fire insurance policies are usually of the latter type, or else entirely open. A valued policy does not imply that the amount payable is the amount that will be paid in case of loss, but rather that such amount will be paid in case of *total* loss.

*Amount recoverable: fire v. life.* In a fire insurance policy, only the actual loss sustained is recoverable; in a life insurance policy, the loss sustained is the principal sum specified in the policy. The purpose of stating a specific amount of insurance in a fire policy is to fix a maximum recoverable.

*Option to restore or rebuild.* Fire insurance companies are generally given the option to restore or rebuild destroyed property. The usual standard clause provides that it shall be optional with the company "to take all or any part of the articles at ascertained or appraised value, or to rebuild or replace property, lost or damaged, within a reasonable time, on giving notice within thirty days after receipt of proofs (of loss)." Such an option enables the insurer to protect himself against the necessity of contesting inflated or fraudulent awards. It also tends to discourage arson, which is motivated usually by the prospect of a cash payment.

**Other Types of Fire Policies: Blanket, Specific and Floating.** *Blanket* or *compound* policies insure for a gross sum and cover several kinds of property in one or more localities without apportionment among them. A *specific* policy covers a specific item of property in a specific amount or various items in specific amounts apportioned among them. *Floating policies* cover property of a transitory nature, and not necessarily the same identical property. For instance, a merchant may insure his stock with the understanding that it is to be replaced by other material of the same kind. In case of loss, he may recover on the stock on hand at the time of the loss, regardless of what was on hand at the time the policy was issued.

**Co-insurance.** The standard co-insurance clause is designed to induce owners to insure their property at a higher percentage of its value. The tendency is to insure property at less than its full value, because most fires result in partial loss. Thus, the owner of a $30,000 house might normally be tempted to save insurance premiums by insuring the house for half or two-thirds of its value. A co-insurance clause provides that if the owner will insure his property up to a given percentage of its value (usually 80 per cent), he will be given the benefit of a lower premium, and if he insures for less than the fixed percentage, he must himself bear a proportion of any loss, that is, he must be a co-insurer on such loss. In the latter case, he may recover only such percentage of the loss as the actual amount of insurance bears to 80 per cent of the value of the property.

EXAMPLE: A storekeeper has a stock of merchandise worth $10,000, on which he has a fire insurance policy for $6000 with an 80 per cent co-insurance clause. Fire destroys $4000 worth of his merchandise. The storekeeper will recover $3000. Under the 80 per cent co-insurance clause, he was required to insure the stock for 80 per cent of its value, that is, for $8000. Instead, he insured the stock for $6000. He may therefore recover only such percentage of the loss as the actual insurance ($6000) bears to 80 per cent of value ($8000); that is, 6000/8000, or three fourths of the $4000 loss, namely, $3000.

**Concurrent Insurance: Pro Rata Clause.** Where property is insured in more than one company and the total concurrent insurance exceeds the general loss, the standard *pro rata clause* applies; that is, the insured can collect from each company only its proportionate or *pro rata* liability to the total amount of insurance.

EXAMPLE: The owner of a building worth $50,000, believing his loss by fire will not exceed $20,000, takes two standard policies with 80% co-insurance clauses, one in the *A* Company for $12,000, and the other in the *B* Company for $8000. He sustains a fire loss of $20,000. Under the 80% co-insurance clause, he should have insured for 80% of value, or $40,000. He actually insured for $20,000, or half. He will therefore recover half the loss, or $10,000. Under the pro rata clause, he will recover this sum as follows: Three-fifths from the *A* Company and two-fifths from the *B* Company.

**Occupancy of Premises.** The standard fire policy provides that if a building described in the policy, whether intended for occupancy by the owner or the tenant, becomes vacant or unoccupied and remains so for ten days, the *entire policy*, unless otherwise provided by agreement *indorsed on the policy or added to it*, shall be void. In such cases, it does not matter that the fire occurred after occupancy was resumed; the policy is voided.

EXAMPLE: The holder of a policy containing the standard vacancy clause left her New York home vacant for several months while she visited friends in Philadelphia. Two days after she returned, the house burned down. The Court held that the violation of the occupancy provision voided the policy. The insured's return before the fire was immaterial.[9]

A policyholder desiring to leave the premises unoccupied without violating the vacancy clause should beware of relying on the oral permission of an insurance agent, though he be the one who issued the policy. In such a case, the Court has held that the policyholder has no right to

---

[9] *Couch v. Farmer's Fire Insurance Co.*, 64 App. Div. 367.

rely on such permission, since the occupancy clause provides that such permission must be indorsed on the policy by proper authority.[10]

Recent decisions have inclined toward a more liberal interpretation of the vacancy clause, the courts holding that temporary absence of the occupants with an intention to return will not render the building "vacant" or "unoccupied." [11]

**Assignability of Policy: Change of Interest.** As noted on pages 99 and 356, a contract is not assignable if it involves a personal relationship or if its terms prohibit assignment. A fire insurance policy involves a personal relationship in that the insured's character, habits, experience and background may be material to the risk.[12] Moreover, fire policies almost invariably provide that the entire policy shall be void upon assignment without the company's written consent indorsed on the policy.

*Assignment after loss.* Once a fire loss takes place, the policyholder has a specific claim or *chose in action* (page 652) against the company, and this he may assign, subject, however, to any defense by the insurance company (page 98). The insured may not, however, assign any excess of insurance over the loss. To that extent, the policy remains a personal and nonassignable contract.

*Change of interest: alienation clause.* The "alienation clause" of the standard policy provides that the policy shall be void "if any change other than by the death of an insured take place in the interest, title, or possession of the subject of insurance (except change of occupants without increase of hazard), whether by legal process or judgment, or by voluntary act of the insured or otherwise." Even without the alienation clause, it is obvious that the seller, having parted with his insurable interest when he parted with title, would be unable to recover any loss under the policy (page 354), and that the buyer could acquire no right by assignment, to a personal contract between the seller and the insurance company; in short, that a fire insurance policy, unlike a fixed covenant in a deed, does not "run with the land."

*Seller's choice as to unexpired insurance.* A seller of premises covered by unexpired insurance has the choice (1) of obtaining a credit from the insurance company for the unearned premium, which usually means sacrificing a discount upon the basis of a shorter rate, or (2) arranging to obtain the insurance company's consent to an assignment of the policy to the buyer, in which case he will receive payment from the purchaser of the full value of the unexpired insurance.

[10] *Walsh v. Hartford Fire Insurance Company*, 73 N.Y. 5.

[11] *Foley v. Sonoma County Farmers' Mut. Fire Ins. Co.*, 18 Cal. 2d 232, 115 P. 2d 1, prior opinion, Cal. App., 108 P. 2d 939; *Republic Ins. Co. v. Watson* (Tex. Civ. App.), 70 S.W. 2d 441, 443.

[12] *National Union Fire Ins. Co.*, Pittsburgh, Pa., *v. Epstein*, 48 Ariz. 345, 61 P. 2d 1010; *Neiman v. Hawkeye Securities Fire Ins. Co.*, 205 Iowa 119, 217 N.W. 258; *Baughman v. Camden Mfg. Co.*, 65 N.J. Eq. 546, 56 A. 376.

*Change of interest by operation of law.* Except where the change of interest results from death, any change by operation of the law, without the insurer's consent, voids the policy.

EXAMPLES: (1) A sheriff's sale of property pursuant to a judgment, (2) a foreclosure sale of the insured premises, (3) transfer of property to a trustee or assignee in bankruptcy proceedings. (Bankruptcy alone, or transfer of *possession* to a receiver, will not void the policy.)

Although death of the insured will not void the policy, the executor or administrator, to avoid possible dispute in case of loss during the administration of the estate, should arrange with the company for a prompt transfer of all fire policies to the name of the estate.

*Joint ownership: change of partnership interests.* Where persons are jointly interested in the insured property, as in the case of joint owners, partners, cotrustees, and so on, a transfer from one to the other or others has no effect on the policy. "It is only where a stranger is to be brought into contractual relations with the insurance company that the consent of the latter is essential." [13] Thus, the admission of a new partner voids the policy.

EXAMPLE: The Home Insurance Co. issued a policy to Verdier on his stock of hardware. Verdier took in Brown, a new partner, and gave him a three-tenths interest in the firm property, which was subsequently damaged by fire. The Court held that the transfer of interest to Brown voided the policy.[14]

However, the subsequent *withdrawal* of a partner from the insured firm does not, in most jurisdictions, void the policy, even where the withdrawing partner sells his interest to an outsider, because the outsider thereby gains no right to become a partner but merely to demand an accounting (page 472).[15]

Prudent partners, to avoid forfeiture of insurance policies on partnership property in case of partnership changes, insist upon the insertion of a provision in the policy, after the partnership name, of the phrase, "as now or hereafter may be constituted."

**Cancellation of Policy.** Both insurer and insured have the right to cancel a fire policy at will. The standard cancellation clause usually reads: "This policy shall be cancelled at any time at the request of the insured; or by the company giving five days' notice of such cancellation." Where the company elects to cancel, it must remit the unearned portion of the premium paid by the insured.

**Disputed Clauses in Fire Policy.** As noted on page 95, ambiguous words and clauses in a contract are construed against the party who drew the contract and selected the words. Hence, in case of dispute as to the

---

[13] *Hoffman v. Aetna Ins. Co.,* 32 N.Y. 405.

[14] *Germania Fire Ins. Co. v. Home Ins. Co.,* 144 N.Y. 195.

[15] A contrary rule prevails in Texas. In California, the Court has held that such transfer voids the policy only as to the interest of the retiring partner.

meaning of a clause in a fire insurance policy, the doubt is generally resolved in favor of the insured and against the company, which drew up the policy.

## Questions

1. Distinguish a "time policy" from a "voyage policy."
2. How does the seaworthiness of a vessel affect a policy of marine insurance?
3. What is meant by the expression "lost" or "not lost" as applied to a marine policy?
4. Distinguish between general average and particular average in a policy of marine insurance.
5. What are the three purposes of the adoption of the standard fire policy?
6. What is the purpose of a binder?
7. Distinguish between a valued policy and an open policy.
8. How do fire and life policies differ with respect to the amount recoverable?
9. Distinguish between blanket, specific and floating policies of fire insurance.
10. What is the nature and purpose of the standard co-insurance clause?
11. What is the standard pro rata clause in insurance?
12. How does the occupancy of premises affect the usual fire insurance policy?
13. What choice has a seller of real estate with respect to his unexpired insurance?
14. What is the standard fire policy provision with respect to cancellation?
15. When words and clauses in a fire policy are ambiguous, in whose favor is the doubt resolved?

## Problems

1. A vessel which was covered by marine insurance founders from a leak caused by a weakness from within the hold of the ship, resulting in a severe loss to the owner. The insurance company resists payment on the policy. May the owner recover?
2. On May 1, while a vessel was at sea, the owner obtained a policy of marine insurance with respect thereto, "lost or not lost." Unknown to either party was the fact that the ship had foundered at sea during a terrific storm and that both the ship and the entire cargo were lost. In an action on the policy, the company defends on the ground that it was liable only for future, not past losses. How would you decide?
3. A marine insurance policy on a vessel and its cargo contained a general average clause. While at sea, mountainous waves and high winds shifted some of the cargo in such a way that the entire vessel and its contents were in imminent danger of being lost. In order to lighten the ship, part of the goods were jettisoned and the vessel made port in good condition with the balance of the merchandise intact. When the owner of the jettisoned goods filed a claim with the insurance company for the value of his goods, the company sought to collect, from the owners of the vessel and of the cargo which had been saved, a contribution to make good the loss on the jettisoned goods. What is the company's position in this connection?

4. A valuable fur piece owned by Mrs. Jones and fully covered by fire insurance was accidentally thrown by her into the incinerator of the apartment house where she resided, and was destroyed by the consuming flames. When the insurance company refused to make good the loss, she brought suit. How should the case be decided?

5. The owner of a building worth $100,000, believing his loss by fire will not exceed $40,000, takes out two standard fire policies with 80 per cent coinsurance clauses, one in the A Company for $24,000, and the other in the B Company for $16,000. He sustains a fire loss of $40,000. How much, if anything, will he recover from each of the respective companies?

6. The Alert Fire Insurance Company issued a policy to Henry Brown on his stock of hardware. Later Brown took his son into the firm and gave him a 15 per cent interest in the firm property, which was subsequently damaged by fire. The company refused to pay the loss. Was its refusal justified? If so, why? If not, why not?

7. The A and B Company, a partnership, had its stock insured against loss by fire. Subsequently B withdrew from the partnership and sold his interest to C. Thereafter a fire occurred and did considerable damage to the stock. In a subsequent action for recovery on the loss, the insurance company denied liability. Is its position legally maintainable? Explain.

8. Albert signs a contract of sale agreeing to convey a house and lot to Best for a consideration of $25,000, title to close thirty days later. Best pays $2500 an account at the time the contract is signed, and immediately thereafter takes out a policy of fire insurance for $18,000 covering the house. Five days later, the house is completely destroyed by fire. The insurance company resists payment on the ground that Best was not the owner of the house. Is the company's position sound?

9. Green obtains a policy of fire insurance on his store through Hemingway, his broker. The policy is issued by the A Company. It contains a provision to the following effect: "Unless otherwise provided by agreement in writing added hereto, this Company shall not be liable for loss or damage occurring while the assured shall have any other contract of insurance, whether valid or not, on property covered in whole or in part by this policy." Later Green, desiring additional protection, has his broker procure the issuance of another policy of insurance with the B Company covering the same store. The policy issued by the B Company has a provision substantially identical with that contained in the A Company's policy. While both policies are in force, a fire completely destroys Green's store. Both insurance companies resist payment. Upon the trial, Green contends that the insurance companies waived the effect of the provision in question because knowledge of the broker as to the existence of another policy was knowledge imputable to the insurance company in each instance. How should the court dispose of this contention?

## PART 3. LIFE INSURANCE

**Definition and Purpose.** Life insurance results from a contract whereby the insurer, for a named sum to be paid annually or at other intervals, stipulates to pay a larger sum at the insured's death. Thus, the purpose of a life insurance policy is to assume the risk of loss caused by the insured's death and to make compensation for such loss to a person designated by the insured, known as the *beneficiary*.

**Types of Life Insurance.** Among the more common types of life insurance are the following:

*Ordinary life (straight)*. An ordinary life, or straight, policy calls for payment of premiums straight through life, and the payment of a fixed sum to the beneficiary on the insured's death.

*Limited payment life.* A limited payment life policy calls for a limited number of premium payments, the insured being fully protected not only during the period of payments but for the rest of his life thereafter.

*Endowment.* An endowment policy provides for payment of a fixed sum to the insured upon conclusion of a given period of premium payments. The sum is payable either to the insured himself or, if he dies before the period of premium payment expires, to his beneficiary.

*Term policies* provide for insurance for a fixed term of years. In consideration of a low premium, the policy does not provide for any accumulations or permit the holder to take out a paid-up policy at the end of the term. Term policies are usually taken where the insured has not decided upon a permanent form of insurance, but desires to be covered in the meantime.

*Tontine policies* are those in which each policyholder agrees, in common with the other policyholders under the same plan, that no dividend return, premium or surrender value shall be received for a term of years, called the "tontine period." The entire surplus from all sources is allowed to accumulate to the end of that period, and is then divided among all who have maintained their insurance in force.

**Standard Provisions.** As previously noted (page 356), standard provisions that must be incorporated into life policies have now been generally adopted. A common statutory provision is that no policy of life insurance may be delivered or issued for delivery unless it contains provisions for the following: (a) a grace period; (b) incontestability after two years; (c) making the policy the entire contract between the parties, including the application (if a copy of it is indorsed on or attached to the policy); (d) adjustment of payment in accordance with the insured's true age, if his age was misstated; (e) divisibility of surplus; (f) nonforfeiture privileges and options, and a specification of the reserve basis to be adopted in determining nonforfeiture benefits; (g) loan privileges; and (h) the privilege of reinstatement under certain conditions and upon certain terms.

**Thirty-Day Grace Period.** State statutes throughout the country generally impose a thirty-day grace period for the payment of premiums beyond the actual due date. A typical provision is the following:

A grace of thirty days from the day when it would otherwise be payable shall be granted for the payment of every premium after the first, during which time the insurance shall continue in force.

**Risks Which May and May Not Be Excluded.** Statutes generally prohibit life insurance companies from excluding risks other than those connected with military or naval service, suicide within two years from the date the policy is issued, and aviation.

**Incontestability.** The "incontestable clause" of a life insurance policy is a provision to the effect that after a policy has been in force for a given length of time (the most common period is two years), the policy cannot be contested by the insurance company for misstatements by the insured or for any other reasons except those specified in the policy, such as nonpayment of premiums or breach of some other specified condition.

*Fraud.* Whether, notwithstanding an incontestable clause, an insurance company may urge the defense of fraud depends upon the time from which the policy becomes incontestable. If it becomes incontestable from the date of issue, fraud is a good defense; if after a given interval, fraud is not a good defense, since the company might have ascertained the fraud during the interval. (See pages 381-382.)

*Other defenses.* Other defenses which may be good notwithstanding incontestability are: (1) That the risk is not covered by the policy; (2) lack of insurable interest; (3) defenses arising after loss, such as failure to file proof of death within a required period, and (4) suicide.

*Proof of death.* Failure to file proof of death within the time prescribed in the policy may defeat recovery, notwithstanding incontestability. Proof of death is ordinarily made out on forms prescribed by the company. Where direct proof is lacking, circumstantial proof may be offered. Absence for a fixed period may raise a presumption of the fact of death but not of the date when it occurred.[16]

**Suicide.** We previously noted that a policy that affirmatively provides for payment in case of suicide is void for illegal subject matter. However, the question as to when suicide is a good defense is another matter.

*No suicide clause in policy: sanity v. insanity.* In the absence of a suicide clause in the policy, self-destruction by the insured *while insane* will not defeat recovery. Self-destruction *while sane* defeats recovery in most jurisdictions unless the policy is payable to beneficiaries other than the insured's family or personal representatives, and even then recovery is barred if it can be shown that the insured, at the time he took out the policy, intended to commit suicide and thereby defraud the company.[17]

*Suicide Clauses in Policy.* The effect of a suicide clause in a policy depends upon its language. The words "death by self-destruction," or "died by his own hand," in a suicide clause, are construed in most jurisdictions to mean intentional, not accidental, self-destruction *while sane;* that is, such language, in most states, does not bar recovery if the insured committed suicide while insane, unless the policy specifically says that it does.

---

[16] *Hogaboam v. Metropolitan Life Ins. Co.*, 248 Wis. 146, 21 N.W. 2d 268.
[17] 45 *C.J.S.* 923.

Regardless of the language of a suicide clause, suicide will not bar recovery after a specified period of incontestability unless the incontestable clause (page 368) excludes death from suicide.

*Statutory provisions.* In a few states, the statute provides that regardless of suicide clauses in a policy, suicide shall not constitute a defense unless the insured contemplated suicide when he took out his policy.

**Policy as Constituting the Entire Contract.** Every life policy must contain a clause that the policy constitutes the entire contract between the parties or, if a copy of the application is indorsed upon or attached to the policy when issued, a provision that the policy and application shall constitute the entire contract between the parties.

EXAMPLE: *A* applies for a life insurance policy and makes certain false statements on the application blank. The company issues a policy but tries to avoid payment of subsequent loss on the ground of *A*'s fraud. It nowhere appears in the policy that *A* made the false statements, but the company can produce the original application blank to prove the fraud. *A*'s beneficiary can collect on the policy and the insurance company will be unable to adduce the evidence of the false statements in question, since the statements contained in the application were obviously not embodied in the policy.

**Age of Insured.** Formerly, a misrepresentation of the insured as to his age would defeat recovery on the ground of fraud or, at least, breach of warranty. This rule has been modified by statute in many states, some allowing the company an offset for the amount of premiums that should have been paid had the age been correctly stated and others holding the company liable for the amount of insurance that the premium paid would have purchased at the true age.

**Nonforfeiture Privileges.** In the early days of life insurance, if a policyholder defaulted in the payment of his premium, he forfeited all previous payments, though a substantial part of them went into the reserve for payment in case of death. Standard policies now generally contain a provision specifying the reserve basis used in determining nonforfeiture benefits. After a given number of premiums have been paid (usually the first three annual payments), a reserve is accumulated that, after deduction of operation expenses, furnishes the basis for various options that must be extended to the insured in lieu of forfeiture, viz:

(a) *Cash surrender* in an amount equal to the reserve less handling expense.

(b) *Extended insurance,* usually in the form of additional term insurance (page 367) in the same amount as the original policy and for as long a term as the surrender value will buy.

(c) *Paid-up insurance* for an amount that the insured's reserve or surrender value will buy.

**Loan Value.** The standard provision most commonly in use is to the effect that after three full years of premium payment, a policyholder may borrow up to the amount of the policy reserve, less proper charges and deductions, upon assignment or pledge of the policy as security. Loan values during each of the first twenty years are shown in a table set forth in the policy. When the insured obtains a loan, his policy remains in force, provided he keeps up the premium payments. Interest is charged against the loan, and, if the policyholder dies, the company pays the principal sum, minus the amount of the loan, with an adjustment for interest prepaid or accrued.

**Reinstatement.** A typical provision dealing with reinstatement is that "the policy will be reinstated at any time within three years from the date of default, unless the cash surrender value has been exhausted by payment or unless the period of extended insurance has expired, upon the application of the insured and the production of evidence of insurability, including good health, satisfactory to the insurer and the payment of all overdue premiums and the payment or reinstatement of any other indebtedness to the insurer upon said policy with interest . . ."

**Divisible Surplus: Dividend Options.** The insurer must annually ascertain and distribute any divisible surplus accruing on the policy. The divisible surplus is calculated after a proper allowance (a) for the mortality rate, and the required reserve against it, (b) the interest rate and (c) operating expenses. In paying dividends, insurance companies usually give the policyholder various options:

(a) Payment in cash.

(b) Dividends to be applied toward reduction of premium.

(c) Amount of dividend to be left with the company at interest.

(d) Dividend to be applied toward the purchase of additional insurance, thereby increasing the face value of the policy.

**Notice of Premium Due.** Under the standard policy, insurance companies must notify policyholders when a premium is about to become due. Such notice must be given in writing not less than fifteen nor more than forty-five days prior to due date, or the policy will remain in force for at least a year after default. The notice must also state the penalty for failure to pay the premium on due date or within the grace period.

**Assignability.** A policy of life insurance is a *chose in action:* A right to have a certain sum of money paid on death. It differs from a policy of property insurance in that the loss insured against is one that is certain to happen. A substantial part of the value of a life policy lies in the right of the owner to certain immediate and marketable benefits inherent in the policy. If the insured has named himself as beneficiary and has paid the premiums, all value that lies in the policy is his. If he has named another as beneficiary, with right of revocation, his right to assign the policy is unimpaired. If he has not reserved the right of revocation, he must get the beneficiary's consent if he wishes to assign the policy. If, having an insurable interest in the life of another, he has insured such life for his own benefit and has paid all the premiums, the policy is his own property and he may freely assign it. Practically all life policies, however, contain a clause to the effect that: "No assignment of this policy shall take effect until written notice thereof shall be given to the company."

**Termination of Risk.** A life insurance policy may be terminated (a) by *expiration*, as in the case of a term policy; (b) by *lapse*, through default in premium payment; (c) by *payment of the loss;* or (d) by *forfeiture*. The subject of forfeiture, including policy cancellations, is discussed on pages 381 to 383.

## Questions

1. What is the purpose of life insurance?
2. Name five types of life insurance.
3. What are the eight standard provisions ordinarily contained in a contract of life insurance?
4. Statutes generally prohibit life insurance companies from making exceptions as to the risks covered by their policies. Name three types of risks that may be legally excluded.
5. What is meant by an incontestable clause in a life insurance policy?
6. Name five forms of defenses that may be urged by a life insurance company in resisting payment.
7. How is recovery on a life insurance policy affected by the suicide of the insured?
8. How does a misrepresentation of the age of the insured affect recovery on the policy?
9. Name three options that must be extended to the insured in lieu of forfeiture.
10. What is meant by the loan value of an insurance policy?
11. Under what circumstances may a policy of life insurance be reinstated after default?
12. In paying dividends what options do insurance companies usually give a policyholder?
13. When may a life policy be assigned?
14. Name four ways in which a life policy may be terminated.

## Problems

1. Chapman takes out a policy of life insurance, but after ten annual payments he drops the policy because of unemployment, and discontinues further premium payments. The company had sent the usual premium notice, but after Chapman's default, it does nothing further in the matter. Chapman, greatly in need of money, relates these facts to you. Is there anything you can tell Chapman to help him?
2. The ABC Life Insurance Company issues a policy on the life of Baker, excluding, however, "loss of life due to heart disease, tuberculosis and surgery." Baker dies of heart disease. The company refuses payment. What is the beneficiary's position?
3. Darling assigns a $10,000 policy on his life to Ewing, to cover a loan. He asks Ewing to keep the assignment a secret, which Ewing does, notifying no one of the transaction. Darling dies without paying the loan, and the insurance

company refuses Ewing's demand for payment. What are Ewing's rights, if any?

4. Nutley takes out a policy of insurance on his life, making his wife the beneficiary. Later, Nutley becomes insane, and while in that condition he commits suicide. The insurance company resists payment on the ground that the policy excluded death from suicide as a risk. Is the position of the insurance company well taken?

5. Suppose in the previous case that Nutley committed suicide while sane, two years and three months after the policy was issued; and that the policy contained the following provision: "This policy, after the lapse of two years from the date of its issuance shall be incontestable, provided all premiums that have become due shall have been paid, and except in the case of fraud and suicide." Would your answer be the same if the insurance company resisted payment?

6. In her application for insurance, an applicant stated: "I am in sound condition mentally and physically, and have never had any bodily or mental infirmity or deformity." Upon her death, the insurance company resisted payment, and upon the trial, the following facts were shown: Thirty years before, the applicant had received an internal injury. Subsequent to the issue of the policy, an operation disclosed an abnormality which had existed from birth. Were these facts of themselves sufficient to establish intentional falsification or fraudulent intent to void the policy?

7. Anderson applies for a life insurance policy and makes false statements on the application blank. The company issues a policy but tries to avoid payment of subsequent loss on the ground of Anderson's fraud. It nowhere appears in the policy that Anderson made the false statements, but the company can produce the original application blank to prove the fraud. May Anderson's beneficiary collect on the policy? If so, why? If not, why not?

## PART 4. CASUALTY AND OTHER FORMS OF INSURANCE

**In General.** The risks to which mankind is exposed are numerous and multifarious. Today, most of these may be provided against by one form of insurance or another. The most common of these—apart from fire and life insurance, which we have already discussed—is casualty insurance.

### Casualty Insurance

**In General.** The term *casualty insurance* is broadly applied to all forms of insurance covering loss or damage resulting from accident or unanticipated contingency, except fire and the elements. Although frequently used to designate health and accident insurance, the term "is more properly applied to insurance against the effects of accident resulting in injuries to property." [18]

**Accident and Health Insurance.** Accident policies insure against the contingency of accidental injury or accidental death. Many policies combine accident and health insurance. Sick benefits are frequently paid by fraternal orders under an arrangement that amounts to health insurance.

---

[18] 44 *C.J.S.* 476.

It is immaterial to recovery that the accident insured against was due to the insured's negligence, so long as it was not deliberate.

*Total disability.* The term *total disability*, unless otherwise defined in the policy, means permanent inability of the injured to earn a living at his usual and regular calling. Thus, if a prize fighter loses an arm, he has sustained total disability, though he may obtain other employment.

**Liability Insurance.** Liability insurance furnishes indemnity against loss or damage sustained by persons other than the insured, for which the insured might become liable. Originally, it related only to an employer's liability for injuries or accidental death of employees during the course of their employment. (See page 450.) Liability insurance now covers many forms of liability that the insured may incur toward others, such as owner's liability to a tenant or others; a contractor's liability toward employees and others injured or killed during the course of some building or other construction; automobile liability to passengers, pedestrians and other car owners; the liability of a physician, dentist or hospital to a patient; and many others. The insurable interest in this type of risk is the loss that the insured may sustain by reason of his liability toward the person or persons who may suffer the damage or injury in question.

Liability insurance is most widely resorted to in connection with the ownership and operation of automobiles.

## Automobile Insurance

**Hazards Covered.** Automobile insurance protects against the hazards incident to the ownership and operation of an automobile. These include (1) fire and theft, (2) collision and (3) liability for death or personal injury (frequently referred to merely as "liability"), or for property damage caused by negligent driving on the part of the insured or his agent. All these forms of insurance may be combined in a single policy.

**Fire and Theft.** Policies insuring the owner against fire damage to his car or loss of it through theft normally cover both the car and its usual equipment, but not personal belongings unless specially provided for. Such policies also exclude loss during the course of illegal or extra-hazardous use.

*Cars bought on time.* Purchasers of a car under a conditional sale or chattel mortgage (pages 266 to 273) are usually required to protect the conditional vendor or chattel mortgagee by keeping the car insured against loss by fire, theft or collision. Loss, damage or destruction of the car before it is paid for thus protects the vendor, but not the purchaser, unless the latter is also covered by the policy. Moreover, the purchaser may become liable to the insurance company for the balance of the purchase price.

EXAMPLE: Brooks buys a car for $2,500 under a conditional sales contract which requires him to keep the car insured for the benefit of the owner against loss by fire, theft or collision. After Brooks has paid in $1,250, a fire completely destroys the car. The vendor recovers the full amount of the loss sustained by him ($2,500 less $1,250), and Brooks recovers nothing unless he is covered by the policy; in addition to which Brooks may be required by subrogation (page 377) to make good to the insurance company for the amount it has paid the vendor.

**Collision Insurance.** This type of insurance covers the owner for damage to his own car from collision with another car or with anything else. Negligence is usually immaterial. Thus, if the owner of a car sustains damage by contact with another car through no fault of the latter, or by hitting a rock in the road, or running into a wall, he is reimbursed for such damage through collision insurance, whether he was guilty of negligence or not. Deliberate collisions, of course, are excluded.

*What constitutes "collision."* Jurisdictions vary widely as to what constitutes a "collision." In some states the courts hold that "collision" covers all impacts, whether with movable or stationary objects; in others, the courts exclude contact with stationary objects, such as roadways or obstructions thereon or therein, walls, trees, posts, embankments, ditches or excavations. These differences may be resolved by the language of the policy itself.

*Deductible clauses.* Most collision policies contain "deductible clauses"; that is, if the policy holder agrees to deduct or make no claim for collision damage up to a given figure, such as $50 or $100, he is given the benefit of a substantially lower premium.

**Liability and Property Damage Insurance.** A person who drives a car— his own or another's—is exposed to the risk that his negligent driving may cause injury or death to a pedestrian or passenger, or damage to a car or other property belonging to another, for all of which he may be held liable in a civil suit. As to such liability, a driver may be protected by liability and property damage insurance. If the driver is also thereby exposed to criminal liability, the insurance will not help him: one cannot insure himself against the consequences of his crimes.

*Negligence immaterial.* It is no defense to the insurance company that the driver was guilty of negligence, because liability for negligence is the very purpose of such insurance.

*"Permissive user" clause.* If a car owner wishes to be protected against liability for negligence when his car is being driven by someone other than himself, he must see to it that the policy adequately covers such contingency. Such a provision ("permissive user" clause) usually includes the owner's agents or employees, or specified or unspecified members of his family.

*"Drive any other car" clause.* What is sometimes referred to as a "drive

any other car clause" is a policy provision that protects a driver even when the accident occurred while he was driving a car not his own. Such insurance may become especially important where such other car is not insured by its owner under a "permissive user" clause, so that either such non-owning driver, or the owner himself, would be personally liable.

*Amount of coverage.* The amount of damage for which an insurance company is liable is optional with the policy holder, and his premium varies accordingly. Usually, there is a maximum for each person injured and for the total in each accident. Thus, a $5,000/$10,000 coverage means that the company will be liable up to $5,000 for each person injured, but not in excess of $10,000 for any one accident.

*Notice of accident: right to conduct litigation.* All liability and property damage policies contain a provision fixing a time limit for notifying the insurance company of any accident, and failure to comply relieves the insurance company of its liability under a policy. The company also reserves the right to defend the suit. If the policy holder insists on the right of defending the suit himself, he thereby relieves the company of its liability.

*Right to sue insurance company.* Ordinarily, a person injured or damaged in an automobile accident must seek recourse against the owner of the offending car himself, not the company with which he may be insured. Only where the injured party procures a judgment against the insured owner and such judgment is not paid, may the injured party sue the company direct.[19]

Where the insurance company wrongfully refuses to defend and the insured thereby sustains loss by way of judgment or the cost of defending, he may sue the company for such loss.

### Other Forms of Insurance

**In General.** In addition to the forms of insurance already discussed, there are various other types in common daily use. Among these are burglary insurance, title insurance and a miscellaneous group dealing with risks relating to fidelity, credit, rent, unemployment, boiler explosions, plate glass, rain, hail, tornadoes, windstorms.

**Burglary Insurance.** Burglary insurance protects property owners from loss by burglary. To exclude "inside jobs," burglary policies usually provide that payment shall be made only when loss results from unlawful, violent and external entry into buildings where the property is kept, of which violent and external entry there must be some visible mark or evidence, such as the breakage of a window or the forcing of a lock. A

---

[19] A few states permit the injured party to sue the insurance company direct, in advance of any judgment against the insured.

burglary insurance policy may prescribe the conditions and safeguards upon which liability is based. In the absence of such conditions and safeguards, the company will not be liable.

EXAMPLE: An indemnity company insured a bank against felonious abstraction of money and securities from its safes and vaults, provided they were closed with a time lock; otherwise, only in case forcible entry was made by the use of tools, explosives, chemicals or electricity directly on the vaults. The policy also covered damage to furniture and fixtures in the course of such entry. The bank was feloniously entered by key and the vault opened by someone who knew the combination, there being no time lock. Ledgers and other articles were taken. On suit by the bank, the Court disallowed recovery. The circumstances of the entry were not those covered by the policy, nor could the books and other articles be classed as furniture and fixtures.[20]

**Title Insurance.** Title insurance protects purchasers of real property from loss due to defective title and from the expense of lawsuits arising therefrom. In connection with such policies, title companies generally furnish title searches in advance of the title closing. Frequently, a title policy contains exceptions or specified conditions in respect to which the company will not be liable. If these exceptions and conditions cover matters that would render the title unmarketable, the policy is of doubtful value. (See page 622.)

**Miscellaneous Types of Insurance.** In the miscellaneous group of insurance risks already referred to are the following:

*Fidelity insurance*, protecting against losses from fraud or dishonesty of agents or employees, already considered in connection with the discussion of fidelity bonds (page 344);

*Credit insurance*, protecting against loss in connection with credit risks;

*Rent insurance*, protecting against rent losses;

*Unemployment insurance*, for the payment of benefits to employees during periods of unemployment (page 453);

*Boiler insurance*, protecting against property loss from boiler explosions;

*Plate glass insurance*, protecting against loss from breakage or destruction of plate glass;

*Rain and hail insurance*, protecting from losses occasioned by rain and hail; and

*Tornado and wind insurance*, protecting against losses resulting from windstorms.

**Reinsurance.** Underwriters not infrequently "reinsure" their risks in

---

[20] *Rosenthal v. American Bonding Co.*, 207 N.Y. 162. See also, *Citizens' Nat. Bank of Hot Springs v. Union Indemnity Co.*, 158 Ark. 398, 250 S.W. 329; *Wakem & McLaughlin, Inc., v. Royal Indemnity Co.*, 241 Ill. App. 427; *Jackson Steam Laundry v. Ætna Casualty & Surety Co.*, 156 Miss. 649, 126 So. 478; *Schoenfeld v. Royal Indemnity Co.*, 76 Pa. Super. 299; *Northwestern Casualty & Surety Co. v. Barzune*, Tex. Civ. App., 42 S.W. 2d 100, error dismissed.

whole or in part with other companies, so as to avoid a concentration of risk beyond the point of safety. If an entire railroad system, for example, insures with the *A* Company, the latter, to limit its liability on a single risk that may run into many millions of dollars, may reinsure this risk with a number of other companies, thereby spreading the risk in case of loss. Companies with relatively limited resources may elect to reinsure an overly heavy burden of risks to avoid an excessive drain on their resources in case of loss.

**Subrogation.** We have already noted the right of a surety, upon making good the debtor's obligation, to be subrogated to the creditor's claim against the debtor, including any lien, pledge or collateral held by the creditor to secure the debt (page 342). In a loose sense, a fire, marine or indemnity insurance company is similarly said to be subrogated to the rights of the insured to the extent ("pro tanto") that it has made good the loss to the insured.

EXAMPLES:

(1) A fire insurance company, upon paying to a home owner the fire loss caused by sparks from a locomotive, is subrogated to the home owner's claim against the railroad company for negligence in causing the loss.

(2) *A* carries collision insurance with the *X* Indemnity Company, covering damage to his automobile. *B* negligently runs into *A*'s car, damaging it to the extent of $200. The *X* Indemnity Company, upon paying *A*'s loss, is subrogated to *A*'s claim against *B* for $200.

## Questions

1. What is meant by casualty insurance? What risks does it usually cover?
2. Define total disability as generally interpreted by the courts.
3. What contingencies are embraced in liability insurance?
4. What are the three hazards usually covered by automobile insurance?
5. The courts in the different states differ as to what constitutes a collision. How do casualty companies generally resolve this situation?
6. What is meant by a deductible clause?
7. (a) Define a "permissive user" clause.
   (b) Define a "drive any other car" clause.
8. What is meant by the expression $5,000/$10,000 coverage?
9. What is the effect upon an automobile policy if the insurer (a) fails to notify the company of the accident, or (b) insists upon the right to conduct his own litigation?
10. Under what circumstances may suit be brought directly against a casualty company by (a) the insured himself, or (b) the person injured by the insured?
11. Name two of the more common types of insurance in vogue today in addition to marine, life, fire, health, accident and automobile insurance.
12. Define (a) reinsurance; (b) subrogation.

## Problems

1. A prize fighter carried an accident and health insurance policy which among other features contained a total disability provision. While negligently

driving his car at an excessive rate of speed, he struck a telephone pole, demolished his car and sustained serious personal injuries which necessitated amputation of his right arm. His prize fighting days over, he turned to another enterprise which netted him $10,000 a year. When the insurance company refused to pay him the benefits of the total disability clause, he brought suit. The defenses were: (1) The insured was negligent in causing the accident; and (2) He was now earning a substantial livelihood. How should the case be decided?

2. The owner of an automobile covered by fire and theft insurance discovered that a valuable oil painting had been stolen from the trunk of his car while it was parked in his garage. He presented his claim to the insurance company, which rejected it. In a subsequent suit by the owner, how was the case decided, and on what ground?

3. Brown buys a car for $2,500 under a conditional sales contract which requires him to keep the car insured for the benefit of the conditional seller against loss by fire, theft or collision. After Brown has paid in $1,000, a fire completely destroys the car. What are the respective rights of the buyer, the seller and the insurance company?

4. The owner of an automobile, who had imbibed a bit too freely, drove up a sidewalk and into a telephone pole. Damage to the car was estimated at $500. Although the car owner was covered by collision insurance, the company refused payment on the foregoing facts. How would you judge the matter?

5. Earle carries collision insurance with the X Indemnity Company covering damage to his automobile. Sauter negligently runs into Earle's car, damaging it to the extent of $200. The X Indemnity Company pays Earle's loss, and then brings action against Sauter for the amount thus paid out. How should the case be decided?

### PART 5. AGENTS, BROKERS AND ADJUSTERS; PAYMENT, AVOIDANCE AND FORFEITURE

### Agents, Brokers and Adjusters

**In General.** The rules applicable to agents and brokers generally are considered in Chapter 9. However, certain rules particularly applicable to insurance agents and brokers are worthy of note at this point. These rules, for the most part, have been created by statute to fit the requirements of the insurance business and to protect the public against overly technical practices. To that extent, the rules of the common law in respect to agents have been modified and extended, and should be borne in mind in connection with the principles discussed in Chapter 9.

**Insurance Agent v. Insurance Broker.** An insurance *agent* is customarily employed by an insurance company to solicit risks and effect insurance on its behalf. An insurance *broker*, as pointed out on page 413, acts as a middleman between insurer and insured. Under employment by no special company, he solicits insurance from the public, and having secured an order, places it with a company selected either by the insured or by the broker acting as the insured's agent. An insurance agent, therefore, usually represents the company, whereas an insurance broker represents the insured.

It is not always easy to determine whether an "insurance man" is agent for the company or for the insured. The use of the word "agent" or "broker" is not necessarily the test. Their *acts*, and not their names, determine.[21] Neither is the matter determined by a provision in the policy that the person who writes the insurance shall be deemed the insurer's agent and not the company's. Statutes in some states and decisions in others hold that such provisions must yield to the actual facts of each case, which alone determine the question whether a person is agent for the company or for the insured.

**Dual Agency of Insurance Broker.** Under the common law, agents cannot serve in a dual capacity, that is, on behalf of principals with conflicting interests (page 403). The interests of insurer and insured may, and often do, conflict, yet an insurance broker frequently finds himself in a situation where, in connection with the same risk, he may be acting first for the company, then, later, for the insured, or vice versa. "It is possible for an insurance broker, although first employed by one party to the insurance contract, to become during the progress of the negotiations the agent of the other; and in that event he may acquire rights, have powers, and incur obligations respecting both insurer and insured. The same person may be both an insurance agent and an insurance broker, and at different times act in both capacities; he may be the agent for insured, although as to the procuring of the insurance he also represents the company. Whether in a particular case or particular matter one acts as agent for the company or for insured depends on the intention of the parties, which is to be determined from the facts and circumstances of the case." [22]

In the field of fire insurance, brokers generally do business on a free lance basis. When they place insurance for a customer, they are agents for the latter, not for the company. But once they issue the policy, with due authority to do so, they bind the company as its agents, and payment of the premium to the broker is payment to the company.

EXAMPLES:

(1) Simpson orally applies to Alexander, a licensed fire insurance broker, for insurance on a building owned by Simpson. Alexander delivers the policy and collects the premium. In selecting the insurer for Simpson, Alexander was Simpson's agent. In delivering the policy and collecting the premium, Alexander was the company's agent.

(2) Suppose that Alexander had insured Simpson's building with two companies, each policy being in half the amount of the total insurance desired and each policy providing that the same might be declared null and void, at the insurer's election, if there was any other insurance on the premises and

---

[21] *Tri-City Transp. Co. v. Bituminous Casualty Corporation*, 311 Ill. App. 610.
[22] 44 *C.J.S.* 802-803.

such fact was not duly indorsed on the policy. Suppose further that such fact was not indorsed on either policy and that thereafter, a fire having totally destroyed the building, both companies successfully resisted payment. Since in selecting the insurers, Alexander was Simpson's agent, Simpson's only recourse would be against Alexander for incompetence.

**When Broker Deemed Authorized to Receive Premium.** Any insurance company that delivers a policy to a broker who has requested it on behalf of some insured, is deemed to have authorized the broker to receive on its behalf payment of any premium due on such policy. This abolishes the old rule that when a policyholder paid a premium to his broker and the broker failed to remit to the company, the latter was not bound, on the theory that the broker was agent for the insured, not for the insurer. Even where the policy contains a restriction upon the broker's authority to collect premiums, such provision may be deemed to have been waived by subsequent conduct.

EXAMPLE: A licensed broker procures a new policy from the company, delivers it to the assured and collects the premium. He notifies the company that he has collected the premium, then fails to remit to the company after being billed for the amount of the premium. Although the policy contained a provision that the broker was to be deemed the assured's agent, the facts spelled out a waiver of such provision.[23] The company is bound by the payment, must seek recourse against the broker and cannot collect again from the assured.

**General Agencies.** It is customary in the insurance business, particularly in the fire insurance business, for general agents to be authorized by various companies to solicit and accept insurance on their behalf and to issue policies subject to subsequent cancellation by the company. "A general agent of an insurance company is usually one who is authorized to accept risks, agree on and settle the terms of the insurance contracts, issue policies by filling out blank instruments which are furnished him for that purpose, and to renew policies already issued, as distinguished from a soliciting agent who merely procures applications, forwards them to some other officer by whom the policies are issued, collects the premiums, and delivers the policies. An agent may be a general agent as to his powers, although he represents the company only in a particular locality or within a limited territory, and in the latter aspect is called a 'local agent.' . . . In the absence of notice . . . of any limitations on such agent's authority, a general agent may bind the company by any acts, agreements, or representations that are within the ordinary scope and limits of the insurance

[23] *Globe & Rutgers F. I. Co. v. Lesher, Whitman & Co.*, 126 Misc. 874, 215 N.Y. Supp. 225; *Casper v. American Equitable Assur. Co. of New York*, 143 Misc. 916, 257 N.Y. Supp. 632. See also, *Continental Casualty Co. v. Monvoison*, La. App., 195 So. 785, 787; *Creech v. Massachusetts Bonding & Insurance Co.*, 160 Va. 567, 169 S.E. 545, 547; *Pagni v. New York Life Ins. Co.*, 173 Wash. 322, 23 P. 2d 6; *Halls v. Rhode Island Ins. Co.*, 193 Wis. 16, 213 N.W. 649.

business intrusted to him, although they are in violation of private instructions or restrictions on his authority." [24]

Restrictions on a general agent's authority are binding on the policyholder if they are brought to the policyholder's attention, as where they are contained in the policy itself. In such cases, notice to the general agent does not constitute notice to the company.

EXAMPLE: A policy containing a double indemnity clause provides for modification only upon home office approval. The policyholder mails to the local agent his notice of election to eliminate the double indemnity provision. After the agent receives the notice but before the home office gets it, the policyholder dies. The double indemnity provision is still in effect.

## Payment, Avoidance and Forfeiture

**Payment.** In the absence of waiver or subsequent modification, payment under an insurance policy must be made at the time specified in the policy, or, in the absence of specific provision on the point, within a reasonable time after submission of proof of liability and loss.

*Notice and proof of loss.* The notice and proof of loss required depend on the policy provisions, the nature of the risk and the loss sustained. In the case of life insurance, a death certificate is generally required. In the case of fire insurance, a schedule of items damaged or destroyed, and the monetary loss thereby sustained, is usual. In all cases, the time limit specified in the policy for the giving of notice should be rigidly complied with.

**Avoidance and Forfeiture Distinguished.** *Avoidance* generally means resisting an obligation when it accrues, such as the obligation to pay premiums, the obligation to pay losses, and so on. *Forfeiture* means cancellation by the insurer. It usually relates to a declaration by the insurer that the policy is terminated because of some act, omission, or breach of condition by the insured.

**Grounds for Avoidance and Forfeiture.** The courts hesitate to work a forfeiture against the insured wherever it is possible to avoid doing so without violating the rules of contract. Ordinarily, covenants will be construed strictly against the insurance company which frames them, and liberally in favor of the insured (page 95). However, an insurer may cancel a policy or, upon receiving proof of loss, may refuse payment, on the following grounds: (1) fraud; (2) concealment; (3) breach of warranty, representation or condition.

**Fraud.** Contracts of insurance are no exception to the rule rendering .all contracts tainted with fraud voidable at the option of the defrauded party. Fraud is particularly important in contracts of insurance. The in-

---

[24] 44 *C.J.S.* 822-823.

sured has peculiar knowledge of the facts affecting the risk. The insurer must assume the risk based upon the insured's representation as to such facts. The law therefore places upon the insured an obligation to exercise the highest degree of faith in procuring the insurance contract. Fraud will not, however, furnish ground for avoiding a life insurance policy unless the false statements complained of are embodied in, attached to or otherwise made part of the policy. (As to the relationship between incontestability and fraud, see page 368.)

**Concealment.** "A concealment in the law of insurance is the designed and intentional withholding of any fact, material to the risk, which insured in honesty and good faith ought to communicate. As a general rule a failure by insured to disclose conditions affecting the risk, of which he is aware, makes the contract voidable at insurer's option. However, the modern practice of requiring applicant to answer questions prepared by insured [25] has relaxed this rule to some extent, since information not asked for is presumably deemed immaterial." [26]

**Warranties and Representations.** Both warranties and representations are statements made by the insured in procuring a contract of insurance. The two, however, are distinguishable.

*Warranties,* under the common law, are statements usually embodied in the policy itself. Whether material or not, a warranty must be literally true, or the policy may be voided.

*Representations* are oral or written statements made at or before the execution of a contract and not necessarily made part of the policy. Representations, though untrue, will not void the policy unless they induced the risk and were material to it.

EXAMPLE: A representation, by the applicant for a fire policy, that the only out-building on the premises is a red barn will not furnish ground for avoidance if the barn happens to be green; the color is immaterial to the risk.

**Modern Rule Governing Warranties and Representations.** The modern rule governing warranties and representations is designed to counterbalance the advantage given to insurance companies because of the rule that a warranty must be literally true, regardless of its materiality. The New York statute, for example, provides: "No breach of warranty shall avoid an insurance contract or defeat recovery thereunder unless such breach materially increased the risk of loss, damage or injury within the coverage of the contract"; that is, unless the breach of warranty was material. This provision also furnishes a counterweight to the provision commonly contained in insurance policies that all statements made therein shall be presumed to be warranties, not representations.

**Warranties in Fire Policies.** Owing to the character of the risk, the

---

[25] So in the original. Presumably the word intended is "insurer."
[26] 45 *C.J.S.* 153.

insured under a fire policy is required to subscribe to certain warranties as part of the contract. Among the more common warranties are the following:

(a) That there will be no change in title or possession of the property insured.

(b) That no additional insurance will be placed on the property without the written consent of the insurer indorsed on the policy.

(c) That the premises will not be left vacant for longer than a certain period.

(d) That the insured will not do anything to increase the risk.

**Breach of Condition.** For the breach of any condition made part of the insurance contract, the insurer may avoid payment or cancel the policy. Subject to statutory restrictions, a party has a right to say under what conditions he agrees to assume a risk. If these conditions are violated, the obligation becomes ineffective. Among the conditions that may be embodied in a policy are those that give an insurer the right of cancellation, either absolutely or upon certain contingencies.

*Waivers.* An insurance company may waive the breach of any condition in a policy or of any warranty or fraudulent representation by the insured. However, such waivers must be pursuant to the policy itself and to the standard provision that the policy constitutes the entire contract between the parties (page 369). For this reason, waivers by insurance agents are not generally binding.

*Nonforfeiture clause.* The right of a life insurance company to forfeit a policy is subject to the nonforfeiture clause imposed by statute. (See page 369.)

*Limitation of action clauses.* Time limits for suit are commonly incorporated into life, health and accident policies, in the form of standard clauses. The New York statute, for example, provides that no action can be maintained to recover on a forfeited policy of life or total disability insurance unless it is instituted within two years from the date of default. This does not apply to actions to recover one's cash surrender value or the amount of any paid-up or extended insurance. A similar provision governs health and accident policies.

## Questions

1. Distinguish an insurance agent from an insurance broker.

2. Under what circumstances may an insurance broker act in a dual capacity?

3. When is the insurance broker deemed to be authorized by the insurance company to receive a premium on its behalf?

4. What is meant by a general agent of an insurance company?

5. What factors determine the nature of the notice and proof of loss to be furnished by a policy holder, and the time limit for submitting the same?

6. Distinguish between avoidance and forfeiture in connection with an insurance policy.

7. Upon what three grounds, generally, may a policy be cancelled or payment be refused?

8. What constitutes concealment in the law of insurance?

9. Distinguish between warranties and representations as applied to the law of insurance. What is the modern rule governing warranties and representations in connection with the issuance of an insurance policy?

10. Name four of the more common warranties applicable to fire insurance policies.

## Problems

1. A businessman applied for insurance to a general agent. He left the selection of the companies to the agent, with instructions to maintain the insurance in an amount stated. The agent complied. Thereafter, the agent upon notice from certain companies to cancel, purported to waive for the insured the period of notice of cancellation, and immediately wrote new policies in other companies for the assured. A loss occurred prior to the expiration of the period of notice for cancellation and before notices of cancellation were actually received by the assured. In subsequent litigation it became important to ascertain if the old policies had been cancelled and the new policies had become effective. How would you decide?

2. A licensed broker procures a new fire policy from the insurance company, delivers it to the assured and collects the premium. He notifies the company that he has collected the premium, but through the neglect of a clerk, he fails to remit to the company after being billed for the amount of the premium. The policy contained a provision that the broker was to be deemed the assured's agent. A loss occurs after the final date for the payment of the premium. May the assured collect from the company? Why or why not?

3. Adams, a fire insurance broker, insured Slattery's building with two companies, each policy being in half the amount of the total insurance desired, and each policy containing a provision that the same might be declared null and void, at the insurer's election, if there were any other insurance on the premises and such fact were not duly indorsed on the policy. It appeared that such fact was not indorsed on either policy. Thereafter, a fire occurred which destroyed the entire building. May the assured collect from either or both companies, and if so in what amount? If not, why not?

4. An insurance policy on the life of Dr. Peterson had been in effect for some five years. During that time, he had been in the habit of paying the quarterly premiums due even after the lapse of the grace period of 30 days. On one of these occasions after he had been confined to a hospital for a serious ailment, he remitted a payment of his premium, after having stated to the company, at the latter's request, that he was in good health. Shortly thereafter, he died. The company resisted payment. For whom would you decide?

5. A young man signed an application for a life insurance policy which contained a provision that no insurance was to be considered in effect until the first premium was paid and the application had been accepted by the home office of the insurance company. A week later, he paid the first premium and obtained a receipt which stated that the insurance was to be considered in effect from the date of the signing of the application. Prior to the issuance of the policy, he died. The company had never formally accepted the application. The company refused payment. Was the beneficiary entitled to the proceeds? If so, why? If not, why not?

6. The ABC Insurance Company issued a policy on the life of Coram. A

month later Coram was found dead in his garage, from carbon monoxide fumes. He was sitting in his car, with the motor running, and the doors slightly ajar. No notes were found. The policy provided that no sum was to be payable in the event of suicide. Was the company justified in its refusal to pay? If so, why? If not, why not?

7. Tracy signed an application for life insurance. He answered "No" to an inquiry as to whether he had ever been ill. Actually, as a boy, he had been ill with pneumonia, but he himself was unaware of the fact, and neither of his parents, who were dead, had mentioned the fact to him. On Tracy's death, the insurance company learned from a public record of the prior illness, and refused payment on the policy. Can the beneficiary compel payment?

## COURT CASES FOR REVIEW

### How Did the Court Decide, and Why?

1. Decedent, prior to his death, took out a policy upon his life for the benefit of his wife and children. The policy provided that if the insured died by his own act, whether voluntary or otherwise, it was to become void. The insured accidentally took poison which caused his death. The insurance company contested payment. *Penfold v. Ins. Co.*, 85 N.Y. 317.

2. The stockholders of a corporation took out a policy of insurance on the lives of the president and the secretary-treasurer of the corporation. The validity of the policy was subsequently challenged for lack of insurable interest. *Mickelberry's Food Products Co. v. Haeussermann*, 247 S.W. 2d 731.

3. The insured died as the result of a brain hemorrhage occurring when he sneezed violently after sniffing into his nose accumulated whiskers which he was endeavoring to blow out of his electric razor. The insured's policy contained a double indemnity provision for accidental death. The insurance company contended that the very nature of the cause of death showed that it was not due to an accident but to a pre-existing physical disease causing a thinning of the walls of the insured's blood vessels, and submitted evidence in support of such contention. *Hughes v. Provident Mut. Life Ins. Co. of Philadelphia* (Mo. App. 1953), 258 S.W. 2d 290.

4. A trucking contractor, who had placed his insurance with an agent on an open account for several years and had carried fire, theft, collision, public liability and property damage insurance on all of his vehicles, telephoned the agent and requested him to cover a new trailer and dolly with the usual insurance. The agent, however, failed to procure the insurance. This the plaintiff did not ascertain until after he had requested an adjustment upon the trailer and dolly which had been destroyed by fire. Thereupon, the contractor instituted an action against the agent for damages. *Brown v. Cooley*, 247 P. 2d 868.

5. An insurance company wrote its agent to return an insured's automobile liability policy for *pro rata* cancellation. Subsequently, but before the agent notified the insured of the cancellation, the latter was involved in an accident. The only business that the insured had theretofore given the agent had been some insurance on the insured's home. In an action by the insured against the company, the latter interposed the defense that the notice of cancellation forwarded by it to the agent was binding on the insured. *Clapperton v. U.S. Fidelity & Guaranty Co.*, 92 A. 2d 336.

6. The insured's application for a life insurance policy stated that he was in good health and that he had neither consulted nor been treated by any physician within the past five years. In a subsequent suit upon the policy, it appeared that the applicant had made eleven visits to a physician during a nine months'

period prior to his application for the policy. However, it was also shown that the insurance company had had its own physician examine the insured before issuing the policy now sued upon. *Sambles v. Metropolitan Life Ins. Co.*, 158 Ohio St. 233, 108 N.E. 2d 321.

7. Decedent was insured under an automobile accident policy expressly excluding chauffeurs. The insured's death resulted from an accident, which occurred while he was driving a truck in the course of his employment as a machine shop foreman, at which time he held a chauffeur's license. The company refused payment of the policy on the ground of the exclusion specified in the policy. *Great Northern Life Ins. Co. v. Cole*, 248 P. 2d 608.

8. A fire insurance policy, which was issued on a dwelling and its contents in different amounts at a gross premium, contained a warranty clause against "other insurance." Thereafter the insured obtained a loan from a finance company which, to protect its loan, required the insured to take out another fire insurance policy payable to the finance company and covering the contents of the dwelling. Upon repayment of the indebtedness, the finance company turned over the policy to the insured. In a subsequent action by the insured on the first insurance policy, the company resisted payment. *Oates v. Continental Ins. Co.*, 72 S.E. 2d 886.

9. A liability and workmen's compensation insurance company unjustifiably refused to defend an insured in a suit for injuries brought by the insured's employees against the insured and the owner of the ship wherein the injuries occurred. Later, the company offered to undertake the defense if, contrary to the policy, its liability was limited to $25,000. The insured made a reasonable settlement direct with the plaintiffs at a figure under $25,000 then sued the insurance company for reimbursement of the amount paid in settlement. The company resisted payment on the ground that the policy disclaimed liability for any settlement made without the company's consent. *Cardinal v. State*, 304 N.Y. 400, 107 N.E. 2d 569.

10. It was the duty of an insurance company's agent to make out requests for removal permits when any insured whose personalty was covered by a fire policy moved from one house to another. Such requests when made out by the agent were usually granted by the company as a matter of course, because the company relied on the agent's judgment as to whether the hazard had been increased. The insured moved to a new house and advised the agent of the change. The agent either advised the insured that the removal made no difference, or failed to make out the request and transmit it to the company. At any rate, no removal permit was issued for attachment to the policy. Thereafter, the insured sustained a loss, and upon being refused payment by the company, instituted suit. *Thomas Jefferson Fire Ins. Co. of Louisville v. Barker* (Ky. 1952), 251 S.W. 2d 862.

11. The owner of an automobile covered by defendant's insurance policy granted permission to his son to use his car. The son in turn permitted a minor to operate the car without his father's express or implied permission, which resulted in an accident involving personal injuries to third parties. The minor sought a declaratory judgment against the insurance company, claiming that he was an "insured" within the meaning of the policy. *Norris v. Pacific Indem. Co.*, 247 P. 2d 1.

12. An automobile ran off a highway bridge and landed upside down at the bottom of a stream. A provision in the policy previously issued to the owner stated that any damages to his car from collision due to upsets were excluded. Under these circumstances, the company refused to pay, resulting in suit. *Harris v. American Casualty Co.*, 83 N.J.L. 641, 85 A. 194.

# 9

# Principal and Agent

**Scope of This Chapter.** In this chapter we deal with a triangle of legal relationships involving principal, agent and third parties. In Part 1 we consider the nature of the agency relationship, the different types of agency, the distinctions between agency and similar relationships, and the question who may be principals and who agents. In Part 2 we consider the different ways in which an agency may come into existence, including a discussion of powers of attorney, implied agencies, the marital relationship and agency, what agency contracts must be in writing, the ratification of unauthorized agencies, agency by estoppel and agency by necessity. In Part 3 we take up the respective duties and obligations toward one another of principal, agent, and third parties, with the rights of each corresponding to the duties of the others. In Part 4 we discuss agency as it affects third parties, including the principal's liabilities to third parties for an agent's contracts and his liabilities for torts and crimes committed by an agent on his behalf; also the agent's own liabilities to third parties for his agency contracts and torts, as well as the liabilities of third parties to either principal, agent or both. In Part 5 we outline the functions, rights, powers, duties and limitations of brokers, auctioneers and factors (commission merchants), and in Part 6 we consider the different ways in which an agency may be terminated.

## PART 1. THE AGENCY RELATIONSHIP

**Agency and Modern Business.** Years ago, when business was largely a one-man affair, there was little occasion to be concerned with the subject of agency. A man planted and harvested his own grain, raised his own vegetables, butchered and consumed his own cattle, sheared his own sheep, prepared the wool, clothed himself in his family homespun, made his own shoes, built his own home—in short, was a complete self-sustaining unit, depending as little as possible upon the agency of others.

As business progresses and becomes more diversified, however, the law of agency grows increasingly important. We have grown to depend upon one another for the thousand wants of our existence. In other words, our existence depends upon the agency of others. Each of us, at one time or another, must play the part of principal. Each of us, from time to time, must act as agent. Each of us, necessarily, must act as third party in dealing with agents.

**Agency Defined.** Agency is a relationship wherein one person, known as *agent*, acts for another, known as *principal*, in dealing with *third parties*.

**Classifications and Distinctions.** Agencies may be variously classified and distinguished as follows: (a) as to scope of authority: *general* and *special;* (b) as to manner of appointment: *express* and *implied;* (c) as to reality of appointment: *actual* and *ostensible;* and (d) as to nature of employment. The law also distinguishes between an *agent* and a *servant*, an *agent* and an *independent contractor*, an *agent* and a *trustee*, and an *agent* and a *subagent*.

**General v. Special Agents.** A *general* agent has broad authority to represent his principal, as distinguished from a *special* agent whose authority is limited to a specific task or to a series of routine tasks. As more fully discussed on pages 406 and 408, a principal is bound by the acts of a *general* agent even though the latter exceeds his authority, provided such acts are usual and customary in that type of agency and the third party is unaware that the agent has exceeded his authority; whereas a third party dealing with a *special* agent can hold the principal only to the extent of the special agent's *actual authority*.

EXAMPLES:

(1) Smith owns several stockyards. He puts Green in charge of one of them with instructions to hire only a certain number of men. Green hires more than this number of men. Smith is liable for the wages of the extra men. Green was a general agent. The extra men were unaware of Smith's instructions to Green.

(2) An agent was appointed solely to take orders for merchandise. He collected $500 from a customer and disappeared. Since the customer was dealing with a special agent, the principal was not bound by the agent's unauthorized collection.

**Express and Implied Agencies.** When an agent's authority is created by a written contract, as by a *power of attorney* (page 396), or by an oral appointment, the agency is *express*. When the authority is inferred from the circumstances, the agency is *implied*.

**Actual and Ostensible Agent.** An agency, express or implied, is sometimes referred to as *actual* to distinguish it from an *ostensible* agency, or one created by law, regardless of the principal's wishes, to prevent injustice; as in the case of an agency by *estoppel* (page 399).

**Agents Classified as to Nature of Employment.** Among the more common types of agents classified as to the nature of their employment are:

(a) *Salesmen,* engaged to sell real or personal property for their principals.

(b) *Brokers,* also engaged to negotiate the sale of real or personal property, but with functions usually broader than those of an ordinary salesman. Brokers are to be distinguished in a number of respects from ordinary agents (see page 413).

(c) *Proxies,* or persons appointed to vote for a principal at some meeting or conference; for example, a *stockholder's proxy.*

(d) *Delegates,* or persons designated by a body of persons to represent them in some assembly or convention.

(e) *Attorneys at law,* or persons specially qualified to represent other persons, known as clients, in matters of a legal nature.

(f) *Auctioneers,* or persons authorized or licensed by law to sell lands and goods for other persons at public auction.

(g) *Factors or commission merchants.* A factor or commission merchant is an agent who sells or disposes of merchandise consigned to him by the principal, usually in the agent's own name, for a commission called *factorage.* The relation of a commission agent to his principal is the same as that of any agent to his principal, with certain exceptions. Factors may be either *domestic* or *foreign,* according as they reside and do business in the same or a different state or country with the principal.

(h) *Mercantile agents.* A mercantile agent is one employed to furnish information on the credit, character, financial standing, responsibility and reputation of merchants.

(i) *Del credere agents.* A *del credere* agent is one who for a higher commission guarantees the accounts of his customers. Although a special promise to answer for the debt of another must be in writing (pages 336 and 337), this rule does not apply to a *del credere* agent (page 337).

**Additional Classifications and Distinctions.** Other classifications and distinctions in respect to agents are as follows:

(a) *Agent v. servant.* See page 431, "Employees and Agents Distinguished."

(b) *Agent v. independent contractor.* An agent is subject to the control and supervision of the one who employs him; but this is not true of an independent contractor. Hence, for the contracts and torts of an agent in the course of his employment, a principal, who has the right to control him, is liable; but for the contracts and torts of an independent contractor who has complete charge and supervision of the work that he does for another, the latter is not liable.[1]

EXAMPLES:

(1) A certified public accountant, making a balance sheet audit of a coal dealer's business, engaged an engineer at his own expense to survey coal piles and report to the accountant the quantity in each pile. To do this, the engineer purchased certain supplies. Such purchases cannot be charged to the coal dealer. The engineer was an independent contractor.[2]

---

[1] *Dean v. Ketter,* 328 Ill. App. 206, 65 N.E. 2d 572.
[2] Some authorities hold that a public accountant is himself an independent contractor.

(2) If I hire you to build me a garage, and in the course of construction a third party is injured through your carelessness, I am either liable or not, depending, respectively, upon whether you are my agent, or an independent contractor.

(c) *Agent v. trustee.* There are three differences between an agent and a trustee: (1) An agent has no title to the property he handles. A trustee has the legal (but not equitable) title to the property in his custody. (2) An agent acts in the principal's name. A trustee acts in his own name. (3) An agency may generally be revoked by the principal at any time (see page 422). A trustee, as a rule, retains his authority until the purpose of the trust is fulfilled, and can be removed only for cause.

(d) *Agent v. subagent.* An agent derives his authority directly from the principal; a subagent, from an agent expressly or impliedly authorized to appoint subagents.

(e) *Agent v. escrow holder.* An agent acts for a principal in dealing with third parties. He cannot act for both principal and third party, if their interests conflict. An escrow holder acts for two adverse parties in accepting and holding some instrument or thing of value, such as a deed, document of title, money or securities, deposited by one of the parties for delivery to the other upon the happening or fulfillment of a condition. An agent's authority may generally be revoked at any time by the principal. An escrow holder's authority is irrevocable, except upon the consent of all parties. The parties to an escrow transaction are *grantor, grantee* and *escrow holder,* also known as *donor, donee* and *depositary.*

(f) *Attorney at law v. attorney in fact.* An attorney at law is a person specially qualified to represent other persons, known as clients, in matters of a legal nature. An attorney in fact, in a strictly legal sense, means an agent acting under a special power created by some instrument or deed, such as a "power of attorney." In a loose sense, however, the term is frequently employed to mean all agents except attorneys at law. The act of designating an attorney in fact is sometimes referred to as *procuration;* such attorney in fact is sometimes referred to as an *agent by procuration.*

**Who May Be Principal.** The general rule as to the capacity of parties to appoint agents is reflected in the doctrine that whatever a person may do himself, he may do through another.[3]

(a) *Infants,* under the earlier rulings, were deemed incapable in law of appointing agents. Hence the general rule prevailed that an infant could not be a principal. This is no longer the rule in a majority of states. In most states the appointment of an agent by an infant principal is valid, but voidable, at the option of the infant, unless such appointment is a necessity

---

[3] *Jefferson Standard Life Ins. Co. v. Guilford County,* 226 N.C. 441, 38 S.E. 2d 519, 525; *Hodge v. Feiner,* Mo. App., 78 S.W. 2d 478, aff'd 338 Mo. 268, 90 S.W. 2d 90, 103 A.L.R. 483.

and not a luxury to the infant, in which case it is valid and enforceable against the infant.

(b) *Corporations* are not only competent to act as principals, but, being fictitious persons, they cannot act except through human agency.

(c) *Married women* under the common law were incapable of entering into contracts on their own behalf. This rule has been generally superseded by statute, so that married women have the same contractual powers as all other adult persons. Hence a married woman has the same power to appoint an agent as her husband has.

(d) *Insane persons,* as we have noted in the chapter on contracts (page 56), are mentally incapable of contracting. Contracts made by insane persons after they have been adjudged insane by a court, are void; prior to such adjudication, voidable. This rule applies to all contracts, including contracts of agency.

(e) *Unincorporated clubs* and other voluntary associations, such as churches, political organizations, and so on, are not competent principals, not being legal entities; but their members may be held as principals if they have acted jointly in the appointment of an agent. In other words, members of such associations may be joint principals.

**Who May be Agent.** Any person may be an agent (except infants of tender years, lunatics, imbeciles, and so on). One may be legally incompetent to make a contract, yet act as agent, because the agent's contracts are not his own, but his principal's. An infant is only a medium, or conduit, through whom the transaction passes or flows. Therefore, only the legal capacity of the principal is material in such a case. So far as the agent is concerned, the only requirement on his part is that he possess sufficient physical and mental capacity to exercise the authority delegated to him. A person is disqualified to act as agent under the following conditions:

(a) When the agent has a personal interest adverse to his principal's.[4]

(b) When the agent acts for several principals with conflicting interests.[5]

(c) When the agent and third party have mutual interests that might conflict with the principal's.

EXAMPLE: Baker is a manufacturer, Potter a dealer, and Aiken a purchasing agent. Potter, unaware that Aiken is also Baker's secret partner, asks Aiken to purchase a quantity of plastic products from Baker, on the most favorable terms obtainable. Aiken has no right to act for Potter without disclosing his secret connection with Baker.

(d) When agents do not possess qualifications or licenses required by law, as in the case of attorneys at law, auctioneers, brokers, and so on.

---

[4] See page 403, "Loyalty and good faith."

[5] See page 403, "Loyalty and good faith," and page 413, "Brokers serving conflicting interests."

## Questions

1. Explain, in a general way, the distinction between a general agent and a special agent. What is the importance of the distinction?

2. What is meant by an *ostensible agent?* How does he differ from an actual agent?

3. Name nine types of agents classified as to the nature of their employment.

4. How would you distinguish between an agent and an independent contractor? In what way may the distinction become important?

5. Give three differences between an agent and a trustee.

6. In what way does an agent differ from a subagent?

7. Explain the distinction between an agent and an escrow holder.

8. "An attorney at law and an attorney in fact can never be one and the same." Is this statement true or false? Explain.

9. To what extent, if at all, are the following competent to act as principals and liable as such: (a) infants, (b) corporations, (c) married women, (d) insane persons, and (e) unincorporated clubs?

10. "No person may act as agent unless he is legally competent to make a contract." Is this a correct statement of the law? Explain.

11. Under what circumstances may a person legally competent to act as agent be disqualified from so acting?

## Problems

1. The X. Y. Z. Company, a chain store organization, appoints Jones as its manager in a midwestern community, with strict orders to purchase nothing for the store on credit. Jones purchases, on credit, a quantity of electric fans for use during the summer months. The X. Y. Z. Company refuses to pay and the electric fan concern sues. Judgment for whom and why?

2. The Universal Drug Shops, Inc., is engaged in selling books, rubber goods, fountain pens, cigars and cigarettes, candy, etc., these commodities being sold in respective departments in charge of a department head. Incidentally, the store also makes up and sells drugs on prescription. The prescription clerk, noting a shortage in the supply of rhubarb root, orders $100.00 worth, which is far in excess of the drug store's needs. The rhubarb is delivered and accepted by the prescription clerk, but when the general manager of the store sees the consignment, he promptly orders it returned to the sellers. The sellers refuse to accept the return, and sue for goods sold and delivered. Judgment for whom and why?

3. Packard, the owner of a small country home, decides to build an annex. He hires Post, a native carpenter, to do the work on plans which he draws up himself and gives to the carpenter, saying, "Please rush this work through by July 1, so that when I come back from abroad I will find it done." The carpenter proceeds with the work, and owing to negligent construction, a beam falls and injures the caretaker, who, upon Packard's return, sues both Post and Packard in negligence. The carpenter work was in complete charge of Post, but Post had agreed that the work was to be subject to Packard's acceptance and approval. How should the case be decided and why?

4. An agent was appointed solely to take orders for merchandise. He collected $325.50 from a customer and disappeared. Is the principal bound by the agent's unauthorized collection?

5. The Mullen Company hires Bronson to "use his best efforts" to sell

Mullen electric razors. Bronson has been similarly hired by the Franklin Company to sell Franklin electric razors. Bronson's idea is that some customers might prefer Mullen razors and others, Franklin razors. It appears that Bronson is 19 years old. Is Bronson qualified to act in these circumstances?

## PART 2. HOW AGENCY MAY BE CREATED

**In General.** An agency may be created (a) by appointment, (b) by ratification, (c) by estoppel, and (d) by necessity. The first two are by *act of the parties*, the last two by *operation of law*.

**Agency by Appointment.** A principal appoints an agent by written, oral or implied contract. The first two create an *express* agency, the last, an *implied* agency.

FORM 9

GENERAL

### Power of Attorney

KNOW ALL MEN BY THESE PRESENTS, that........................................................................

..........................................................................................................................................
(Set forth Name and Address)
(hereinafter referred to as the "Principal") has made, constituted and appointed, and by these presents does make, constitute and appoint..................................................

..........................................................................................................................................
(Set forth Name(s) and Address(es) distinctly)
a specimen of whose signature(s) appears in the lower left corner hereof, the true and lawful attorney(s)-in-fact of, for and in the name, place and stead of the Principal to do each and all of the following acts and things:

1. Open, maintain and/or reconcile any one or more deposit or other accounts either in the name of the Principal or otherwise with ———— BANK OF NEW YORK, (see footnote),* (hereinafter referred to as the "Bank");

2. Deposit with the Bank to the credit or for the account of the Principal any moneys, checks, drafts, promissory notes or other instruments for the payment of money; also, to endorse for deposit, collection, transmission and remittance, or otherwise, any and all such instruments and to deliver the same to the Bank for any of the indicated purposes;

3. Draw, make, execute and deliver any and all checks, drafts, promissory notes and other instruments for the payment of money payable by or at the Bank, and give any orders or directions by letter, telegram or otherwise for the withdrawal, transfer or other disposition of any funds at any time(s) held by the Bank on deposit or otherwise for or to the credit of the Principal, inclusive of any such instruments, orders or directions made payable to or for the account or benefit of the said attorney(s, or any of them);

4. Deposit with the Bank to the credit or for the account of the Principal any and all stocks, bonds or other securities or valuables registered in the name of or purporting to be owned by the Principal, and to endorse and cause all or any such securities to be transferred into the name of the Bank, or that of any nominee(s) of the Bank, or otherwise;

5. Purchase or otherwise acquire from or through the Bank any stocks, bonds, or other securities or valuables;

6. Sell, assign, transfer, substitute, pledge, withdraw or otherwise dispose of any stocks, bonds or other securities or valuables at any time(s) held by or in the possession or control of the Bank, and/or any one or more of its subsidiaries or affiliates, for or

---

\* NOTE: If it is desired that this Power of Attorney shall be applicable only to some particular office(s) or branch(es) of the Bank, please so indicate in the space provided therefor above.

on behalf of the Principal and to collect and dispose of any interest, dividend or other payments thereon; also, to give any orders or directions by letter, telegram or otherwise for the withdrawal, exchange, transfer, sale or other disposition of any such stocks, bonds or other securities or valuables, inclusive of any such orders or directions to or for the account of the said attorney(s, or any of them);

7. Discount and/or negotiate with the Bank any promissory notes, drafts or other instruments for the payment of money;

8. Borrow money from and incur indebtedness to the Bank either through loans, advances, renewals or other forms of credit which may be extended at any time or from time to time by the Bank, with or without security, and to make and enter into such agreements in reference thereto as may be acceptable to the Bank;

9. Apply to and cause to be issued by or at the instance of the Bank any letters or the Bank may require in connection therewith;

10. Sign and deliver to the Bank any Trust or Bailee Receipts and any relative other forms of credit, and to sign and deliver such indemnity or other agreements as Statements of Trust Receipt Financing or other documents;

11. Pledge, assign, mortgage or otherwise transfer, hypothecate, and deliver to the Bank as security for all or any liabilities of the Principal to the Bank now existing or hereafter arising, any promissory notes, drafts or other instruments for the payment of money, stocks, bonds, accounts, bills receivable, or any other securities or property purporting to be owned or held by or for the account of the Principal;

12. Give any directions and make any agreements concerning the extension, renewal, discharge or collection of any promissory notes, checks, drafts or other instruments for the payment of money, or for the insurance, delivery, sale, pledge or other disposition of any documents, merchandise or other property, which may be now or hereafter in the possession or under the control of the Bank;

13. ................................................................................................................................................
(Here insert any such further authority as is desired)

And the Principal hereby gives and grants unto said attorney(s) (severally, collectively or otherwise as hereinafter stated) full power and authority to do and perform each and every act and thing whatsoever deemed by any such attorney or attorneys so acting to be necessary or proper to be done in and about the premises as fully and effectually to all intents and purposes as the Principal might or could do if personally present, with full power of substitution, delegation and revocation, hereby ratifying and confirming all and whatsoever the said attorney or attorneys so acting, or any substitute or substitutes, or delegate or delegates, shall lawfully do, or cause to be done, in or about the premises by virtue hereof.

It is understood that, unless terminated by operation of law, this Power of Attorney may be revoked only by notice in writing signed by the Principal and delivered to the Bank, and that any substitution or delegation hereunder shall be revoked only by notice in writing signed by the Principal and/or any such attorney or attorneys so acting; and, for the purpose of inducing the Bank to act hereunder, the Principal hereby agrees that the Bank, its successor or assigns, shall be saved harmless from any loss suffered or liability incurred by it or them in acting hereunder until notice of any such termination or revocation shall have been received by the Bank.

If more than one attorney-in-fact has been hereinbefore appointed. each and all of the aforesaid powers, discretionary and otherwise, may be exercised severally, collectively or otherwise as follows:

— Each may act alone.     — Any.......................................or more may act collectively.

— ................................................................................................................................................

IN WITNESS WHEREOF, the Principal** having heretofore stricken out and omitted the paragraphs hereof numbered......................................................., has caused this instrument to be duly executed this....................day of..........................................19..........
Specimen signature(s) of
Attorney(s)-in-fact named above.

** If TWO OR MORE PARTIES execute this Power of Attorney, the word "Principal" as used therein shall be deemed to refer to those parties collectively and severally. If a PARTNERSHIP, one or more of the General Partners should sign in its behalf. If a CORPORATION or ASSOCIATION, a duly certified copy of the By-Law or Resolution under authority of which it has been executed should accompany the delivery hereof.

[Acknowledgment to be used if PRINCIPAL is an INDIVIDUAL]

STATE OF...............................................................⎫
⎬ ss.:
COUNTY OF...........................................................⎭

On the         day of         , 19    , before me personally
came         , to me known to be the person
described in, and who executed, the foregoing instrument, and acknowledged that he
(she) executed the same.
(Notary's Seal
to be affixed)

.....................................................................................

NOTARY PUBLIC, COUNTY OF ...................................

MY COMMISSION EXPIRES ..........................., 19........

[Acknowledgment to be used if PRINCIPAL is a PARTNERSHIP]

STATE OF...............................................................⎫
⎬ ss.:
COUNTY OF...........................................................⎭

On the         day of         , 19    , before me personally
came         ,to me personally known, and known
to me to be a member of the firm of         , and
known to me to be the individual described in, and who executed, the foregoing instrument in the name of the said firm, and he (she) duly acknowledged to me that he
(she) executed the same for and in behalf of the said firm.
(Notary's Seal
to be affixed)

.....................................................................................

NOTARY PUBLIC, COUNTY OF ...................................

MY COMMISSION EXPIRES ..........................., 19........

[Acknowledgment to be used if PRINCIPAL is a CORPORATION]

STATE OF...............................................................⎫
⎬ ss.:
COUNTY OF...........................................................⎭

On the         day of         , 19    , before me personally
came         , to me known, who, being by me duly
sworn, did depose and say that he (she) resides
that he (she) is         of
the corporation described in, and which executed the above instrument; that he (she)
knows the seal * of the said corporation; that the seal affixed to said instrument is such
corporate seal; that it was so affixed by order of the Board of Directors of said corporation, and that he (she) signed his (her) name thereto by like order.
(Notary's Seal
to be affixed)

.....................................................................................

NOTARY PUBLIC, COUNTY OF ...................................

MY COMMISSION EXPIRES ..........................., 19........

---

(* If such corporation have no seal, that fact must be stated in place of the statements required respecting the seal.)

*Power of attorney.* When the agent's authority is evidenced by a written instrument, such instrument is known as a *power of attorney.* This is not necessarily the same as a contract. The agency contract, setting forth the rights, duties, powers and liabilities of the parties, may be drawn up separately from the power of attorney, which is but the evidence of the agent's authority. A power of attorney may be *formal,* as in the case of a duly acknowledged instrument under seal, or informal, as in the case of a simple letter of authority.

*General v. special power of attorney.* A general power of attorney confers complete and exclusive authority upon an agent to do everything for the principal which the principal may do himself. It is furnished only in rare cases, as where one leaves on an extended journey, beyond easy means of communication, and desires an agent to attend to all his affairs in his absence. A special power of attorney limits the authority conferred to some special purpose or purposes, such as powers of attorney authorizing an agent to convey a deed to real property on behalf of the owner, or to manage and operate a store, or to collect moneys, etc.

*Formal v. informal power of attorney.* General powers of attorney are usually couched in formal language. They are also usually "acknowledged," that is, declared under oath before a notary or other competent officer to have been duly executed. For an example of such power of attorney, see Form 9.

Informal powers of attorney may consist of letters or memoranda of authority, without the formality of acknowledgment. The following is an illustration of an informal power of attorney.

Boston, Mass.<br>September 1, 19——

Mr. George Wharton,
1000 Flagler Street,
Miami, Florida.

DEAR SIR:

This will be your authority to act as my agent in the management of premises 500 Collins Avenue, Miami Beach, Florida; and I hereby authorize you, until further notice, to collect and receipt for, on my behalf, all rental payments due and to become due from tenants of said premises, and to take such steps and make such expenditures as may be necessary for the proper and economical management of the premises in question.

Very truly yours,<br>HENRY MASTERSON.

A common illustration of an informal special power of attorney is a stockholder's "proxy," conferring authority on one to represent the stockholder at a corporate meeting. A proxy need not, as a rule, be acknowledged, but it should be witnessed.

*Purposes for which power of attorney may be given.* Ten purposes for which a power of attorney may be given are: (1) to execute commercial paper, (2) to collect debts of a business, (3) to collect dividends, (4) to manage, lease and sell real estate, (5) to sell shares of stock, (6) to solicit and accept subscriptions and collect the proceeds thereof, (7) to acknowledge documents, (8) to institute suit, (9) to appoint subagents, (10) to sign receipts.

**Agency by Oral Appointment.** By far the large majority of agency transactions are conducted through oral appointment. Consciously or otherwise, we are constantly acting through agents orally appointed as occasion may arise. Such oral authority is adequate in all but the limited number of situations discussed below.

**Implied Agency.** An agency may be implied from conduct or circumstances evidencing an *intention* to create the relationship. This is what is meant by an agency implied *in fact*, as distinguished from an agency implied *in law*, as in the case of an agency by *estoppel* (discussed on page 399). Words, whether oral or written, are not the only means of conveying intent. There are a thousand different ways in which a person may by conduct indicate an intent to constitute another his agent.

EXAMPLES:
(1) A party agreed to pay an interpreter for his services in carrying on negotiations with another who spoke a different language. Did this make the party liable for material misrepresentations by the interpreter? The court held that it did.[6]
(2) If the holder of a note or other evidence of debt makes it payable at the office of another person, to whom possession of the paper is given, does this constitute the latter the holder's agent? The court has repeatedly held that it does.[7]

*Marital relationship no basis for implied agency.* Except for the implied agency of a wife in purchasing household necessities, an agency will not be implied from marital relationship alone.[8]

EXAMPLE: A husband went to a third party and stated that his wife wanted certain repairs done to her building. The repairs were accordingly made, without the wife's knowledge or acquiescence. The wife refused to pay for the repairs, claiming she never authorized her husband to order them. *Held*, for the wife.[9]

**Agency by Appointment: the Statute of Frauds.** The general provisions of the statute of frauds have already been considered (pages 85-90). An agency contract may be oral, except when it comes within the provisions of the statute of frauds. For example, an agency contract not to be performed within one year from the date of making must be evidenced by a writing (page 85). *If an agent's duties involve making contracts governed by the statute of frauds, must the contract of agency*

---

[6] *Bonelli v. Burton*, 61 Or. 429.
[7] See 2 C.J. 622-3 and cases there cited.
[8] *Rodgers v. Saxton*, 305 Pa. 479, 158 A. 166.
[9] *Aarons v. Klein*, 29 Misc. 639, 61 N.Y. Supp. 119.

*itself be in writing?* The answer to this question depends on the reading of the applicable statute of frauds. For example, if the statute of frauds in a particular state provides that a contract to sell real property must be signed by the party to be charged, "or his lawful agent thereunto authorized," the contract thus authorizing the agent need not be in writing, because the statute does not so provide. But if the statute reads "or his lawful agent thereunto authorized *in writing*," such authorization itself must also be in writing.

**Agency by Ratification.** Ratification, in agency, is the approval of an unauthorized act done by an agent without authority. If one person acts for another without authority or in excess of his authority, such lack of authority may be cured by a subsequent ratification, which may be written, oral, or implied, as by accepting the benefits of an act with full knowledge of the facts. The following rules apply to ratification:

(a) Whatever one may lawfully do he may ratify.

*Crimes and torts.* Since one cannot lawfully commit a crime, he cannot ratify it. Hence if Brown's bookkeeper forges Brown's name to a check and cashes it, Brown's subsequent ratification will not wash out the crime, though it may render Brown liable on the check. But one may ratify a *tort*, which is a private wrong (page 789), so as to assume liability for it; for example, if Allen procures money under false pretenses by dishonestly representing himself to be Brown's agent, Brown may ratify the tort so as to be liable for it. (But this would not cure the crime of obtaining money under false pretenses.)[10]

(b) The principal must be competent to ratify. If a person is not competent to act as principal in appointing an agent, he is incompetent to ratify an act done on his behalf. A corporation is not competent to ratify an act performed on its behalf before the corporation came into existence, because one cannot act as agent for a nonexistent principal. However, a corporation can *adopt* such an act so as to become liable on it (page 501).

(c) The act must have been done in the name and on behalf of the person who ratifies it. For example, if, without authority, you purport to act for Brown, the act cannot be ratified by Smith.

(d) The ratification must be with full knowledge of the facts. If you knew that I was anxious to sell my automobile for any price it would fetch, and you proceeded to sell the car for me without my knowledge or authority, and by fraudulent representations, and if I then ratified the sale, I would not be liable in a subsequent action for fraud unless I was aware of the fraudulent representations at the time of ratification.

(e) Ratification must cover the entire act. One cannot ratify the favor-

---

[10] *Daughters of American Revolution v. Schenley*, 204 Pa. 572, 54 A. 366; *Henry v. Heeb*, 114 Ind. 275, 16 N.E. 606, 5 Am.S.R. 613; *Owsley v. Philips*, 78 Ky. 517, 39 Am.R. 258; *Kelchner v. Morris*, 75 Mo. App. 588; *Workman v. Wright*, 33 Ohio St. 405, 31 Am.R. 546; *Henry Christian Bldg., etc., Assoc. v. Walton*, 181 Pa. 201, 37 A. 261, 59 Am.S.R. 36, 636.

able portion of an unauthorized act and reject the unfavorable: he must ratify all or nothing.

**Agency by Estoppel.** Agency may be based on the principle of estoppel (page 877). If I permit you to pose as my agent, and a third party acts on the belief that you are my agent and extends credit or makes some other sacrifice in dealing with you, the law will prevent or *estop* me from now stepping forward and denying that you are my agent. The effect is the same as if an agency actually existed: to all intents and purposes it exists, because the law will not permit the contrary to be shown.

**Agency by Necessity.** An agency by necessity is one implied in law where a situation exists or an emergency arises which makes it necessary to presume an agency as a matter of public policy. Examples are:

(a) The implied agency of a wife to pledge her husband's credit in purchasing necessities for the household.

(b) The implied agency of a child to pledge a parent's credit in purchasing necessities when the parent fails to supply them.

(c) The implied agency created by marine emergencies whereby the master of a vessel may obligate the owner for repairs or towage in a distant port, or may *jettison* (page 359) part or all of a ship's cargo.

(d) The implied agency in emergencies to contract for medical, hospital or first aid expenses. Where life, limb and health are at stake as the result of some accident, such as a railroad wreck, and authority from the principal cannot be obtained or time does not permit the delay in procuring it, an executive employee, superintendent or other representative may obligate his principal or employer by incurring the necessary medical, hospital or first aid expenses.

## Questions

1. (a) What are the different ways in which an agency may be created? (b) Which of these are by acts of the parties, and which by operation of law?

2. Give a short, simple definition of a power of attorney.

3. Distinguish between (a) a general and a special power of attorney, and (b) a formal and an informal power of attorney. Illustrate the distinction in each case.

4. Name ten purposes for which a power of attorney may be given.

5. Distinguish between an agency implied in fact and an agency implied in law. What is the common designation for the latter type of agency?

6. When, if ever, will the law imply an agency from the fact of marriage?

7. "Where an agent's duties include making contracts that must be in writing under the statute of frauds, such contracts are not binding on the principal unless the agent's authority is also evidenced by a writing." Is this statement true, false, or partly true and partly false? Explain.

8. Which of the following statements are true, and which false?

(a) One cannot ratify a previously authorized act.

(b) One cannot ratify a crime.

(c) One cannot ratify a tort.

(d) One may become liable for a tort by ratifying the act which constitutes the tort.

(e) If a person ratifies an act without having inquired into all the facts, he is liable though his ratification was without full knowledge of the facts.

9. What is the underlying basis for an agency by estoppel?

10. What is an agency by necessity? Give three illustrations.

## Problems

1. In a New York-to-Rome deal by telephone, Dalton authorizes a firm of Italian brokers to sell a consignment of motor oil for his account, at $75 per 50-gallon drum. The negotiations on Dalton's behalf are conducted through an interpreter, who mistakenly quotes the price as $57 a drum. The brokers execute the order, but Dalton refuses to honor it. The brokers sue Dalton for the regular brokerage charges in such transactions. Dalton's defense is that he is not responsible for the interpreter's mistakes, and that the brokers should sue the interpreter. How should the court decide, and why?

2. During his wife's absence in Europe, Keating orders certain repairs to their home, which is owned by the wife, who had not authorized the repairs and knew nothing about them until she returned from Europe. The wife refuses to pay for the repairs. Is she liable for them?

3. Brooks, on behalf of Mason, hires Dodd under a two-year written contract. At the end of six months, Dodd is discharged without cause. He sues Mason, whose defense is as follows: (a) Brooks himself had no written contract, and (b) The statute of frauds in his state provides that a contract of hiring for a period of over a year must be in writing, signed by the party to be charged, or by his lawful agent. How will the court rule?

4. William Lightfinger signs his firm's name to a check in payment of a personal debt. The firm discovers the forgery, but is persuaded not to prosecute, on Lightfinger's plea of family trouble and promise of restitution. The check is, therefore, duly honored and paid. A fellow employee, however, who is unfriendly to Lightfinger, presents the facts to the district attorney, who proceeds to prosecute. The defense interposed that no forgery was committed, by reason of the firm's ratification of Lightfinger's act. How should the case be decided, and why?

5. John Highstrung lends money to Walter Dubb against the latter's note due on November 1. Dubb, on November 1, calls at the Highstrung home, and finding Mr. Highstrung out, leaves the money with Mrs. Highstrung, requesting her to see that Mr. Highstrung returns the note. Mr. and Mrs. Highstrung, as a matter of fact, were not on speaking terms. The next day, Mrs. Highstrung disappears with the money. Highstrung sues on the note, and Dubb defends on the ground that payment was duly made. Judgment for whom, and why?

## PART 3. DUTIES AND OBLIGATIONS

**In General.** The rights, duties and liabilities of principal and agent as to each other, and the powers an agent possesses in dealing with third parties, depend in large part on their contract. Often, however, there is no express contract between the parties, or else it is silent on questions that subsequently arise. In such cases the law speaks.

If I gratuitously promise to act as your agent, and then change my mind, neither of us becomes obligated to the other. On the other hand, once I embark upon the agency, you are entitled to assume that I will discharge my duties as agent with reasonable fidelity and care. If I fail to do so, I am liable to you for consequent loss, and the fact that my services were gratuitous will furnish no defense.[11]

Rights and duties being *reciprocal* (page 22), the duties and obligations of a principal to his agent represent the agent's rights against his principal; and the duties and obligations of an agent to his principal represent the principal's rights against the agent.

## Duties and Obligations of Principal to Agent

**Major Duties and Obligations.** Among the major duties and obligations of a principal to his agent are the duty (a) to *compensate* the agent, (b) to *reimburse* him for expenses, (c) to *indemnify* him against risks, and (d) to pay *damages* for breach of the agency contract. In addition, (e) certain obligations of the principal, or rights of the agent, are secured by an agent's *lien*.

**Duty to Compensate Agent.** Unless otherwise agreed, or unless the services rendered are obviously gratuitous, a principal must compensate his agent. The amount of compensation depends upon the bargain of the parties or, in the absence of bargain, upon reasonable value based upon custom, nature of services rendered, and so on.

EXAMPLES:
(1) Arthur agrees to supervise the construction of a garage for $250. The work takes longer than Arthur anticipated. Arthur is nevertheless bound by the agreed compensation.

(2) If, in example (1), nothing was said about compensation, Arthur would be entitled to a reasonable compensation based on custom, experience and the value of his services.

(3) An insurance agent advises the beneficiary of a policy to pay the premium lest the policy lapse for nonpayment by the policyholder. As a result, the beneficiary, on the policyholder's death, collects a substantial payment. If the insurance agent now seeks compensation for his advice, he will not succeed: His services were obviously gratuitous, and without express or implied agreement as to compensation.

*Contingent compensation.* If an agent is hired on the contingency that there is to be no compensation unless a given result is achieved, the agent is bound by such bargain regardless of time expended or the value of his services, unless failure to achieve the result is the principal's fault.[12]

EXAMPLES: (1) Hull is hired to find a purchaser for McLean's yacht at a price of not less than $100,000. His compensation is to be 10% of the sales price

[11] *Carmichael v. Lavengood*, 112 Ind. App. 144, 44 N.E. 2d 177, 180.

[12] *Berwin v. Cable Raincoat Co.*, 311 Mass. 483, 42 N.E. 2d 729; *Clarkson v. Standard Brass Mfg. Co.*, 237 Mo. App. 1018, 170 S.W. 2d 407, 414; *Smith v. Duracraft Products Co.*, 75 Ohio App. 556, 62 N.E. 2d 731; *Cauthorn v. Allen*, 184 Okl. 489, 104 P. 2d 247.

if he is successful. He is unable to find a purchaser. Though he has spent three months of diligent effort and has incurred several hundred dollars in personal expenses in quest of a purchaser, Hull may recover neither compensation nor reimbursement.

(2) A real estate agent hired by a seller found a purchaser on the seller's terms. The agent had signed an agreement not to claim commissions if the deal for any reason fell through. The deal fell through because the seller could not give good title. The agent was entitled to his commissions: Failure to achieve the result was the principal's fault.

*Drawing accounts.* In the absence of an agreement specifically providing that a drawing account is to be deemed nothing more than a loan or advance to be returned in any event, a drawing account is equivalent to a salary. Thus, if a salesman is guaranteed a drawing account of $25 a week against commissions to be earned, and he earns no commissions, he need not repay the sums received unless the agreement specifies that the drawing account is in effect a loan or advance to be repaid if not earned.[13] A salesman is not a debtor to his principal for the deficiency of his commissions; the drawing account is offset only against commissions actually earned.[14]

**Duty to Reimburse Agent.** An agent is entitled to be reimbursed by his principal for all expenses expressly or impliedly authorized and incurred during the course of the agency.

**Duty to Indemnify Agent.** A principal must idemnify his agent against risks reasonably and necessarily assumed or to be assumed by him in the conduct of the agency.

EXAMPLES:
(1) An agent may be compelled to pay damages or fines innocently incurred in following the principal's instructions. If these were not so obviously illegal as to put the agent on notice of their illegality, the principal must indemnify the agent for losses incurred in assuming such risks.

(2) An agent who acts for an undisclosed principal may become personally liable at the option of the third party (page 410). For such risk, the agent may require indemnification, either before or after becoming personally obligated.

**Agent's Right to Damages for Breach of Contract.** A principal who violates his contract with his agent sustains the usual penalty of damages for breach of contract, subject to the rule which excludes speculative damage and requires a party to *mitigate* the damage (page 123). Thus, an agent under a five-year contract who was discharged without cause at the end of the first year cannot collect damages for four idle years without having attempted to procure other employment.

**Agent's Lien.** An agent has a lien for reimbursement and indemnity on account of advances, expenses and losses,[15] but not ordinarily for services,

---

[13] *Miller v. The Blaisdell Machinery Co.,* 83 Misc. 35, 144 N.Y. Supp. 792.

[14] *N.W. Mut. Life Ins. Co. v. Mooney,* 108 N.Y. 119.

[15] *Caughlan v. State,* 22 Ala. App. 220, 114 So. 280; *Jessen Liquor Co. v. Phoenix Distillery Co.,* 171 Iowa 505, 153 N.W. 148; *Arwshan v. Meshaka,* 288 Mass. 31, 192 N.E. 162; *Newhall v. Dunlap,* 14 Me. 180, 31 Am.D. 45.

except where such lien is specially created by contract. The lien attaches to the principal's money or property *in the agent's hands* in connection with which the advances were made, expenses incurred, or losses sustained; that is, the lien is *possessory* (page 685), not *charging* (page 688).

## Duties and Obligations of Agent to Principal

**Major Duties and Obligations: in General.** Among the major duties and obligations of the agent to his principal are (a) loyalty and good faith, (b) obedience, (c) skill, care and diligence, and (d) the duty to account.

**(a) Loyalty and Good Faith.** Unlike most business relations wherein parties deal "at arm's length," an agent's relationship to his principal is "fiduciary," that is, it involves a high degree of faith and trust. Hence an agent owes the highest degree of loyalty and good faith toward his principal. For violation of such duty, an agent is deprived of his right to compensation, reimbursement, indemnification or lien. Thus:

(a) An agent must not serve two masters with conflicting interests. But an agent may represent both buyer and seller where he has nothing to do with the price and merely brings the parties together, as is frequently the case with brokers (see page 413).

(b) An agent must not have a personal interest adverse to his principal's; as where a principal instructs an agent to buy certain property which the agent secretly owns himself.

(c) An agent must not engage in a business competing with the principal's, unless this is done with the principal's knowledge and consent.

**(b) Obedience.** An agent must obey his principal's instructions. If his duties are "ministerial" (routine) he must obey instructions to the letter; if discretionary, he must use his best judgment.

EXAMPLES:

(a) If an agent is instructed to remit by express and he remits by check, he becomes liable for the loss if the dealer becomes insolvent before payment.

(b) An agent was instructed to remit by mail in $50 and $100 bills. Instead, he sent $5, $10 and $20 bills, thus increasing the size of the package, which was lost. The agent was held responsible for the loss.[16]

(c) If an agent without authority to do so, pledges his principal's goods, and the principal is unable to release the goods from the pledge because the agent had possession of the documents of title and was ostensibly authorized to pledge the goods (see page 419), the principal may hold the agent for damages resulting from the latter's breach of duty. (If the agent pledged his principal's negotiable paper, the principal would in most cases not be bound by such pledge, since an agent's authority to pledge and indorse negotiable paper is not usually implied.)

**(c) Skill, Care and Diligence.** The degree of skill, care and diligence which an agent must use depends on the nature of the task. Ordinarily,

---

[16] *Wilson v. Wilson*, 20 Pa. 393.

when one undertakes a particular agency, he impliedly warrants that he has the necessary skill and will exercise the necessary care and diligence to perform the task properly. For example, if a certified public accountant or a lawyer undertakes to advise his client in a matter with which he is not familiar, or in which he is not qualified, he is responsible to his client for consequent loss.

*Malpractice* is the illegal or neglectful practice of one's profession. If a lawyer or accountant undertakes to advise professionally on a matter outside the scope of his knowledge, experience and training, such as in respect to the law or professional practice in another state, he may be liable to his client for consequent loss.

EXAMPLES:

(1) A certified public accountant of the State of New York advised a client as to a proper accounting system for the State of Illinois, and in so doing, failed to provide for certain records required by Illinois law. The certified public accountant is liable for consequent damage to his client.

(2) A New York attorney, assuming that the Connecticut law was the same as that in New York, advised his client on the refiling of a chattel mortgage in Connecticut. The refiling was ineffective, and the client lost a $15,000 lien. The attorney was held liable for the consequent loss.[17]

(3) A depositor leaves two bonds with a bank for sale and credit to his account. The bank, through an irresponsible employee, loses the bonds by mailing them unregistered to another bank. The bank clearly failed to exercise the skill, care and diligence required by the circumstances, and is liable to the depositor for the loss.

*An agent is not an insurer* of the services he renders, unless he guarantees a result by express contract.[18] If, for example, a lawyer fails to win his case, or a physician to effect a cure, neither can be held liable if reasonable skill, care and diligence were exercised.

(d) **Duty to Account.** The agent's duty to account is broader than the mere rendering of accounts. It embraces the duty to render unto the principal that which is, or in good faith should be, the principal's. An agent who collects money for a principal should notify the principal promptly of the collection and either remit forthwith or at such time as is customary and agreed upon between the parties.

*Intermingling funds.* If an agent is permitted to retain the principal's funds for some time, he should keep them in a separate account from his own. If he fails to do so and the intermingled fund is lost, even without his negligence, the agent is liable for the entire loss. In this respect an agent's duty is similar to that of a trustee. (See page 761.)

*Secret profits.* If an agent directly or indirectly earns or obtains any

---

[17] *Degan v. Steinbrink*, 202 App. Div. 477, 195 N.Y. Supp. 810, affirmed 236 N.Y. 669, 142 N.E. 328.

[18] *Northern Pac. Ry. Co. v. Minnesota Transfer Ry. Co.*, 219 Minn. 8, 16 N.W. 2d 894.

secret profit or advantage out of his agency, he must account for it (turn it over) to the principal.

## Questions

1. In the absence of express agreement, is a principal obligated to pay his agent for services rendered?

2. In the absence of statute, is a principal obligated to pay an agent for overtime or extra effort, beyond the compensation agreed upon between the parties? Explain.

3. To what extent is a principal obligated to reimburse his agent?

4. What is meant by the principal's duty to indemnify his agent? Give two situations where such duty may arise.

5. Under what circumstances does an agent have a lien in respect to money or property in his possession belonging to the principal?

6. Give three situations in which it may be said that an agent has violated his duty of loyalty and good faith toward his principal.

7. Must an agent at all times obey his principal's instructions to the letter? Explain.

8. "An agent must at all times exercise the highest degree of skill, care and diligence in the discharge of his duties on behalf of his principal." Is this statement true or false? Explain.

9. "An agent is always an insurer of the services he renders." Is this statement true or false? Give reasons for your answer.

10. Explain what is meant by an agent's duty to account.

## Problems

1. Billings hires Chase to build a private road from the highway to his summer cottage, a distance of about 200 feet. The contract price is $500. Owing to unexpected boulders in the roadway, the work takes twice as long as expected. Chase submits a bill for $1000. Will Billings have to pay it? Explain.

2. A real estate agent hired by a seller found a purchaser on the seller's terms. The agent had signed an agreement not to claim commissions if the deal for any reason fell through. The deal fell through because the seller could not give good title. Was the agent entitled to his commissions?

3. Richard Emmett, Esq., an attorney, is retained by three manufacturing companies to effect a merger. He does so. The Government prosecutes the merger as a combination in restraint of trade and the same is dissolved. Emmett spent six months in perfecting the merger. He submits a bill to the manufacturing companies for services, but they refuse to pay. He sues. Judgment for whom, and why?

4. The Handy Remedy Company designates Cox as its New York agent for the sale of patent bunion plasters at a net sale price of $1.00 per gross. Cox organizes a bunion plaster corporation and markets the plasters through the corporation, paying the Handy Remedy Company $1.00 per gross for all plasters sold, and selling the bunion plasters to the trade at $1.50 per gross. The difference he credits to his corporation. The Handy Remedy Company, discovering these facts, consults you as to its right. What would you advise, and why?

5. Miller and Seabury desire to consolidate a group of parcels for the purpose of constructing an office building. The corner parcel is owned by William

Miser. The firm, knowing that if they approached Miser, he would suspect the purpose of the purchase and "jack up" the price, hires Kenilworth to make the purchase in his own name. Kenilworth buys the parcel in his own name for $50,000, making a down payment of $5,000 cash, under an agreement to pay the balance in thirty days. Before the expiration of the thirty days, Miller and Seabury decide that they do not want the parcel. Miser sues Kenilworth, who sets up that he was only a dummy, and was acting for Miller and Seabury. Judgment for whom, and why?

6. Brown lists his property with Sharpe for sale, at a price of $15,000. Sharpe procures a purchaser at this figure, and a contract of sale is duly executed, by which title is to close in 30 days. In the meantime, Sharpe finds another purchaser, named Mann, who is willing to pay $20,000 for the property. Sharpe goes to the first purchaser, and buys his contract for $500, taking an assignment of it to himself. He then has the deed made out to the second purchaser, which he gets Brown to execute, and on the day of closing, procures the purchase price in the form of two certified checks: one to Brown for $15,000, and one to himself for $5,000. Brown discovers the facts, and sues Sharpe for $5,000. Judgment for whom, and why?

7. An agent dealing with The Clark Company was instructed by his principal as follows: "If you take that firm's order, better insist on cash or a certified check." The agent, a man of considerable judgment and experience, who had long dealt with The Clark Company, took an uncertified check, which was returned unpaid. The principal seeks to hold his agent for the amount of the unpaid check. May he do so? Explain.

## PART 4. AGENCY AND THIRD PARTIES

**Principal's Liability on Contracts Generally.** A principal is liable to third parties on contracts made by his agent:

(a) When the contract was expressly or impliedly authorized.

(b) When the contract, though originally unauthorized, was subsequently ratified.

(c) When the contract, though neither authorized in the first instance nor subsequently ratified, was made under circumstances from which the third party had a right to assume that the agent was duly authorized. Such circumstances are to be considered in the light of the distinction between general and special agencies.

**Principal's Liability on Contract: General Agencies.** The extent to which a principal is bound by an agent's contracts on his behalf in dealing with third parties depends upon whether the agency is *general* or *special* (page 388). On contracts made through a general agent, a principal is liable even when the agent exceeds his actual authority, provided (a) the agent was *apparently* authorized to make the commitment, that is, the unauthorized acts are such as similar agents usually have authority to perform, and (b) provided the third party is unaware that the agent is exceeding his authority.

EXAMPLE: A wholesaler appoints Barkus as his general agent for the sale of flour in Chicago, with instructions not to sell below market price and not to warrant quality. Barkus sells to Carter below market price, with a warranty of quality. The flour is not of the quality warranted by Barkus. The wholesaler is not only bound by the lower price but by the warranty of quality. Barkus, as a general agent, was apparently authorized to act as he did, and Carter was unaware that Barkus was deviating from his instructions.

**Authority to Make Collections.** Mere authority to sell or solicit does not carry with it a presumption of authority to make collections, unless the agent has possession of the goods or other "indicia" (page 237) of authority.

EXAMPLES:

(1) On July 7 a stranger called at the office of Dunham, a public accountant, exhibited the card of a well-known stationery house, and obtained an order for analysis paper. The next day Dunham received the analysis paper with an invoice payable in thirty days. On July 15 the stranger called and asked Dunham whether he would pay then for the paper. Dunham paid in cash and the stranger receipted the bill. The stranger was a solicitor who received a commission on any order accepted and filled. He disappeared without accounting for the collection. Under the circumstances, the stationery house can collect from Dunham. The stranger had neither possession of the goods sold nor "indicia" of authority.

(2) Zilberman, a wholesale dealer in hardware, hired Bromberg to take orders from customers. Bromberg got an order for hardware from Friedman. After the hardware was delivered, Bromberg, without authority, collected the money, gave Friedman a receipt in Zilberman's name, and disappeared. Zilberman, having received no money from Friedman, sued the latter, whose defense was that payment to Zilberman's agent was payment to Zilberman. The court gave judgment to Zilberman, holding: "Bromberg had no real or apparent authority to collect . . ." [19]

**Authority to Indorse and Cash Checks.** An agent authorized to make collections has no implied authority to collect anything but money,[20] unless such authority is established by custom or prior practice. If an agent is given authority to take checks, he has no implied authority to collect and cash them.[21]

EXAMPLES:

(1) An agent authorized to collect rents received a check payable to the order of the principal, which he indorsed in the principal's name and cashed at the bank. The agent then disappeared with the proceeds. The principal sued the bank. Said the Court: "The authority which Leonard had as agent to collect the rent and transact other business for Beare gave him no legal authority to endorse (the) check for Beare and his endorsement thereof was just as ineffectual to pass title as if he had forged Beare's name." [22]

(2) Hoven sold a horse to Turner, with instructions to pay Hoven's agent, who delivered the horse. Turner gave the agent a check to the order of Hoven.

---

[19] *Zilberman v. Friedman*, 54 Misc. 256, 104 N.Y. Supp. 363.
[20] *Lindsey v. Drs. Keenan, Andrews & Allred* (Mont.), 165 P. 2d 804.
[21] *Merchants' & Manufacturers' Ass'n v. First Nat. Bank*, 40 Ariz. 531, 14 P. 2d 717; *Wilson v. Johnson*, 98 Kan. 66, 157 P. 413; *Waldo v. Fuller*, 18 Ohio Cir. Ct. (N.S.) 184; *Kay v. Wayne County*, 274 Mich. 90, 264 N.W. 300.
[22] *Robinson v. Chemical National Bank*, 86 N.Y. 404, 407.

The agent indorsed Hoven's name on the check, and Turner, at the agent's request, guaranteed the indorsement, whereupon the bank cashed the check and the agent disappeared with the proceeds. As among Hoven, Turner and the bank, the loss falls on Turner. The bank had no right to cash the check on the agent's unauthorized indorsement, and was therefore liable to Hoven; but Turner, who guaranteed the indorsement, is liable in turn to the bank.

**Authority to Hire Subagents and Employees.** Whether a principal becomes liable to subagents and employees who are hired by a general agent, depends upon whether such delegation of authority is within the actual or apparent scope of the agent's authority (page 406); that is, whether subagents and employees have a right to assume that the agent is authorized to hire them. This, in turn, may depend upon such factors as: (1) nature of duties to be performed; (2) necessity of hiring skilled assistance, such as the services of a lawyer, accountant or engineer; (3) trade usage; (4) status of agent, that is, whether the agent is a single individual or a large organization with a staff of assistants, and so on; (5) location of agent with reference to location where services are to be rendered (that is, hiring a New York lawyer for a Chicago case, which would necessarily imply authority to retain Chicago counsel).

**Duties That Cannot be Delegated.** There are certain duties which an agent must perform himself and cannot delegate. Many public servants are in this class.

EXAMPLES:

(1) The President of the United States, members of Congress and the judiciary, and numerous other public officials cannot delegate to others certain constitutional functions entrusted to them.

(2) Private agents hired for their special fitness cannot delegate their professional duties to others: a noted surgeon hired to perform a delicate operation must do so himself; a skilled trial lawyer hired to conduct an important lawsuit cannot delegate the task to a subordinate.

**Principal's Liability on Contract: Special Agencies.** The principal is not liable on any contract negotiated through a special agent (page 388) unless the agent has been expressly authorized to make the contract. If a third party dealing with a special agent is in doubt about the agent's actual authority, he should verify it.

**Principal's Liability on Contract: Disclosed v. Undisclosed Principals.** A disclosed principal is one whose identity is revealed by the agent to the third party at the time of the contract. An undisclosed principal is one whose identity is not thus revealed, even though the third party knows that the agent is acting for someone else. When the principal is undisclosed at the time of the contract and the third party later ascertains his identity, he has the option of holding either the agent or the undisclosed principal, but not both.

**When Undisclosed Principal Is Not Liable.** There are three situations in which an undisclosed principal is not liable for the acts of his agent:

(1) *Fully executed contracts.* A principal is not liable on a contract which has been fully executed by the agent.

EXAMPLE: The agent of an undisclosed principal gave his personal notes, which were accepted as payment by the seller of land. This, said the Court, constituted a fully executed purchase contract, so that when the notes fell due and the agent failed to pay, the principal was not liable on the contract though he received the benefit of it.[23]

(2) *Contracts under seal.* Ordinarily, a principal cannot be bound by a contract under seal unless his name is on it. In some states, however, if the seal is unnecessary to the contract, the undisclosed principal will be liable though his name is not on the contract. An undisclosed principal is liable on a sealed instrument in any event where the statute has abolished the legal effect of a seal.

(3) *Negotiable instruments.* No person can be a party to a negotiable instrument unless he appears thereon to be such.[24] However, as pointed out on page 138, when an agent signs for an undisclosed principal and the payee knows it and that the agent does not intend to bind himself individually, the agent, if he has been authorized thus to sign, is not personally liable to the payee; but the principal in such case is not liable, either, since his name is not on the instrument.

**Principal's Liability for Agent's Torts.** A principal is liable for his agent's torts if they are committed during the course of the agent's duties and within the scope of his actual or apparent authority. This is true though the agent, in committing the tort, violated the principal's instructions.

*Torts held to be within scope of employment (principal liable):* (1) When an agent, to collect from a debtor, threatened unlawful imprisonment. (2) When a floorwalker followed a customer suspected of theft to the street, and forcibly compelled him to re-enter the store. (3) When an agent, with power to remove trespassers, attempted to remove one peaceably, but became involved in an altercation which resulted in wrongful killing. (4) When a subway guard, under the mistaken belief that a passenger had dropped a bad coin in the turnstile, detained and assaulted the passenger. (5) When, in selling merchandise, the agent made fraudulent representations, though instructed by the principal not to do so.

*Torts held to be outside scope of employment (principal not liable):* (1) When an agent, in collecting a disputed account, made a wilful and malicious assault on a bystander. (2) When an agent shot trespassers under a general authority to remove them. (3) When an agent, to make sales to a city, offered bribes to city officials without the principal's knowledge. (4) When a cashier, without authority or instructions to do so, caused

---

[23] *Ranger v. Thalman,* 84 App. Div. 341, affirmed 178 N.Y. 574. See also *Humphrey v. Bussey,* 99 Fla. 1249, 128 So. 841.

[24] Uniform Negotiable Instruments Law, sec. 18.

loss to a depositor by negligently and improperly undertaking to draw up legal instruments (bond and mortgage).

*Liability for torts: agency by estoppel.* A principal may be liable for the torts of a person who is not really his agent, if the principal is estopped from denying the agency.

EXAMPLE: A department store advertised itself as furnishing dental services through a dentist in charge. Actually the dentist was on his own. A customer suffered injury due to the dentist's negligence in the treatment of her teeth. The court held that the department store was estopped from denying that the dentist was its agent, and was liable for the dentist's negligence.[25]

**Principal's Liability for Agent's Crimes.** The principal is not liable for an agent's crimes, though committed during the course of the agency, unless the principal authorized, directed, aided or acquiesced in their commission. But a principal may become liable for negligence in hiring a criminal without proper investigation. An employer may be held liable for labor violations by his superintendent or foreman, though he neither authorized, directed, nor knew of the violation.

**Notice to Agent: When Binding upon Principal.** When a principal's liability depends upon his receiving notice, he may be bound by notice given to his agent in respect to matters within the scope of the agency.

EXAMPLES:
(1) A third party gave notice to an agent who purchased a note, that it was tainted with usury. This was held to constitute notice to the principal.[26]
(2) A railroad ticket agent was infected with smallpox. He knew it. This knowledge was also held to be chargeable to the railroad company.[27]

**Agent's Liability to Third Parties.** In addition to the agent's liability for breach of duties common to all persons, whether in contract, tort or crime, an agent may become personally liable to third parties in various ways connected with his function as agent:

(a) *Agent acting for nonexistent or incompetent principal.* If an agent purports to act for a principal who in fact is nonexistent or contractually incompetent (such as an infant in connection with a luxury, or an insane person), the agent himself becomes liable to the third party.

(b) *Agent acting for undisclosed principal.* As previously noted (page 402), an agent acting for an undisclosed principal may render himself personally liable to a third party at the latter's option.

(c) *Misrepresenting extent of authority.* When an agent misrepresents the extent of his authority and a third party, relying thereon, seeks to hold the principal but is unable to do so, the agent may become personally liable to the third party for his misrepresentation.

---

[25] *Hannon v. Siegel-Cooper Co.*, 167 N.Y. 244.
[26] *Sheppard v. White*, 78 Ill. App. 428.
[27] *Missouri etc. R. Co. v. Raney*, 4 Tex. Civ. App. 517.

EXAMPLE: An agent is authorized by a storekeeper to have the show counters revarnished at a cost not to exceed $50. He orders additional painting work for the rest of the store at a contract price of $250. If the agent's acts are held not to be within the apparent scope of his authority, and the painter, in consequence, is unable to hold the principal, he may hold the agent for misrepresenting the extent of his authority.

(d) *Agent's liability for monies wrongfully received.* An agent may likewise be personally liable to third parties for monies wrongfully paid to him through fraud, mistake, or for any other reason which gives the third party a right to recover the money back, provided the agent at the time of demand for the return of such money stands in his original position and has not yet turned the money over to his principal.

(e) *Obligations personally assumed.* An agent may obligate himself expressly in connection with the subject matter of an agency, as in a case where he guarantees the principal's obligation, or where he receives money or property from a third person for his principal, on his personal promise that it will be returned under certain conditions.

(f) *Agent's liability for torts.* An agent is personally liable for any torts committed by him, whether in the course of the discharge of his duties or otherwise. For example, if an agent knowingly commits fraud on behalf of his principal, the agent may be personally liable as well as the principal.

**Liability of Third Party to Principal.** Just as a principal, whether disclosed or undisclosed, is bound by his agent's contracts, so a third party is bound to the principal by the same contracts, whether the principal be disclosed or undisclosed. However, a third party may stipulate in his contract that the person with whom he is dealing represents that he is acting as principal, not as agent; and in such cases the third party will not be liable if the agent is really acting for an undisclosed principal.

EXAMPLE: Williams, in making a purchase from Brown, fails to disclose the fact that he is acting for Green. Brown has had previous unsatisfactory dealings with Green and does not wish to do business with him. Unless Brown obtains a stipulation in the contract that Williams is not acting for Green, or that Williams is acting for himself only, Brown must deliver the merchandise on Green's request.

**Liability of Third Party to Agent.** The agent's contracts are not his own, but his principal's. Therefore, the third party's liability on such contracts is to the principal, not to the agent. Of course if the third party commits a tort against the agent, such as assault and battery, negligence, libel, slander, and so on, the mere fact that the injury is to an agent does not prevent the latter from redressing his wrong.

## Questions

1. Under what three types of circumstances is a principal liable to third parties on contracts made by his agent?

2. Does authority to sell or solicit ever carry with it a presumption of authority to make collections? Explain.

3. "An agent authorized to make collections has no implied authority to collect anything but money." Is this statement true, false, or partly true and partly false?

4. What are some of the circumstances which determine whether a principal becomes liable to subagents and employees hired by a general agent?

5. Name two classes of agents who cannot delegate their duties to others.

6. When a person makes a contract with another without knowing that the latter was acting for a principal, what may he do on discovering such fact?

7. Name or illustrate three situations in which an undisclosed principal is not liable for the acts of his agent.

8. When is an agent liable for his torts, and when not? Illustrate.

9. May a person be liable for the torts of one not his agent? Explain.

10. "Crime is personal, and no person is liable for the crime of another." Is this statement true, false, or partly true and partly false?

11. Name and explain six situations in which an agent may become personally liable to third parties in connection with his functions as agent.

## Problems

1. Smiley, a book agent representing Cosmopolitan Classics, exhibits a "dummy" set of ten volumes bound in leather, and obtains an order thereon from Oliver, who signs an order blank agreeing to pay $25 on delivery of the books. The next day Smiley calls on Oliver and offers him a 10 per cent discount for cash against future delivery of the books. Oliver pays $22.50 to Smiley, who disappears. Later, Cosmopolitan Classics delivers the books and demands the price, which is refused on the ground of prior payment. May Cosmopolitan Classics hold Oliver?

2. An Iowa manufacturer of agricultural implements sends an agent to California with instructions to collect a $12,000 past due account from one of its dealers. The agent, after an unsuccessful attempt to collect the account, hires a California lawyer who sues the dealer and obtains judgment. The judgment, however, is worthless, the dealer being insolvent. The lawyer now submits his bill, which the manufacturer refuses to pay on the ground that the agent for collection had no authority to hire a lawyer without specific instructions to do so. Is the manufacturer liable?

3. In the following cases, the question arose whether the principal was liable for the agent's acts. If you were the judge, how would you hold?

(a) An agent, to collect from a debtor, threatened unlawful imprisonment.

(b) A floorwalker followed an innocent customer suspected of theft to the street and forcibly compelled him to re-enter the store.

(c) An agent, with power to remove trespassers, attempted to remove one peaceably, but became involved in an altercation which resulted in a wrongful killing.

(d) A bus driver, under the mistaken belief that a passenger had dropped a bad coin in the receptacle, assaulted the passenger.

(e) An agent made fraudulent representations in making a sale, though he had been instructed not to do so.

(f) An agent, in collecting a disputed account, made a willful and malicious assault on a bystander.

(g) An agent shot trespassers under a general authority to remove them.

(h) An agent, to make sales to a city, offered bribes to city officials without the principal's knowledge.

4. Long hires Short to collect antiques by visits to rural homes. Short bargains for and purchases many antiques, but is caught stealing a few without attempting to pay for them. Prosecution is instituted against Long and Short. Long's defense is that he neither authorized nor condoned Short's offense. How did the court decide?

5. Bailey, a jobber, has a quantity of woolen fabrics which he is holding for his customers during the busy season. Grimm, a dealer in woolens whom Bailey dislikes because of a prior deal, hires Loft to purchase a quantity of woolens on Grimm's behalf. Loft places an order for the woolens, which Bailey accepts, but when Bailey learns on whose behalf the order was placed, he refuses to fill it. May Grimm hold Bailey on the contract?

## PART 5. BROKERS, AUCTIONEERS, AND FACTORS

**Particular Rules Applicable to Particular Agencies.** So far we have considered the basic rules governing all classes of agents. However, there are particular rules applicable to particular types of agency. These rules arise out of the peculiar nature and public importance of the services rendered by these agents. Chief among these are brokers, auctioneers and factors.

### Brokers

**General Nature and Distinctions.** The general function of a broker has already been defined (page 388). Although a broker, broadly speaking, is an agent, his functions may be distinguished from those of other agents.

*Brokers v. ordinary agents.* Every broker is an agent, but not every agent is a broker. An ordinary agent usually acts for but one principal, whereas a broker acts as a negotiator between two or more parties to a transaction.

*Brokers serving conflicting interests.* As with agencies generally, a broker must not serve two masters with conflicting interests. For example, he may act for both buyer and seller to the point of bringing them together; but if he is hired by the one to negotiate the purchase, and by the other to negotiate the sale, he cannot well discharge his duties of loyalty and good faith toward both by procuring the highest price for the seller and the lowest price for the buyer. Hence a broker in such a position will have no claim against either buyer or seller, regardless of services rendered.

*Broker v. factor.* Though both broker and factor may be agents to sell, a broker, unlike a factor, is not usually entrusted with possession, control and disposition of the property concerned, nor may he bind the principal by buying or selling the property in his own name.

*Brokers are special agents.* A broker has no authority, except with the principal's consent, to change any of the principal's terms, such as price, time of payment, rate of interest, and so on; nor, ordinarily, has he the implied authority to make warranties or to sell on credit.

**Kinds of Brokers.** There are numerous types of brokers, depending on the nature of the brokerage handled. Among the most common types of brokers are: (a) real estate brokers, (b) stockbrokers, and (c) insurance brokers.

**Real Estate Brokers.** A real estate broker is one authorized to negotiate the purchase or sale of real property. He cannot conduct his business without first procuring a brokerage license. The license must be in force throughout the entire period during which services are rendered.

EXAMPLE: A broker spent many months in consummating a transaction. He was licensed when hired, also when his efforts culminated successfully; but his license had run out in between, and was not renewed for several weeks. *Held*, he was barred from recovering his commissions.[28]

*Right to commissions: necessity of contract.* Regardless of the value of his services, a broker, in the absence of a contract of hiring, express or implied, is not entitled to commissions.[29] "Where there is no employment or binding contract for the payment of commissions and the broker acts as a mere volunteer, he is not entitled to compensation for his services, although such services are the efficient cause of bringing the parties together and result in a sale or other contract between them." [30]

EXAMPLE: Lowenthal employed Oppenheimer to sell certain real estate. Oppenheimer brought the property to the attention of prospective purchasers, Barnett and another, who bought the property and in so doing, told Lowenthal, the owner, that Gregory, another broker, had brought about the sale. The seller, acting on such belief, paid commissions to Gregory. Oppenheimer, the first broker, sued the purchasers. The court, in dismissing the complaint, held that the purchasers "intended to dispense with Oppenheimer for the sole purpose of having Gregory get the commissions; but they had a legal right to do this. Oppenheimer did not represent them, and they were under no legal obligations to him." [31]

**Lien.** A real estate broker ordinarily has no lien, since he is not vested with possession of the property, but is hired to buy or sell. Moreover, real property is not usually subject to a possessory lien (page 685).

*"Subject to prior sale."* Real estate brokers are usually hired subject to the understanding, express or implied, that authority is automatically terminated in case of a prior sale. (This does not apply to an exclusive

---

[28] *Bendell v. De Dominicis*, 251 N.Y. 305, 167 N.E. 452.

[29] *Peebles v. Sneed*, 207 Ark. 1, 179 S.W. 2d 156, 158; *Klipfel v. Bowes*, 109 Colo. 17, 120 P. 2d 959; *Galloway v. McKinley*, 73 Ga. App. 381, 36 S.E. 2d 485; *Consolidated Realty Co. v. Graves*, 291 Ky. 456, 165 S.W. 2d 26; *Case v. Harrison*, 192 Miss. 531, 6 So. 2d 582, 586; *A. J. Meyer & Co. v. Schulte* (Mo.), 189 S.W. 2d 183, 189; *Williams v. Engler*, 46 N.M. 454, 131 P. 2d 267; *Foreman v. Reynolds*, Ohio App., 58 N.E. 2d 688; *First Trust Joint Stock Land Bank of Chicago, Ill., v. Ferguson*, 187 Okl. 48, 104 P. 2d 427; *Guenther v. Equitable Life Assur. Soc. of U.S.*, 23 Wash. 2d 65, 159 P. 2d 389.

[30] 12 *C.J.S.* 135-136.

[31] *Oppenheimer v. Barnett*, 131 App. Div. 614, 116 N.Y. Supp. 44.

brokerage, that is, where the principal agrees to hire no other broker.)

*"Ready, willing and able."* A broker is not entitled to a commission unless the customer he produces is ready, willing and able to meet the seller's terms.

*"Procuring cause."* When various brokers claim to have contributed to the result, only the broker who has been the *immediate procuring cause* of the transaction is entitled to commissions.

*Seller's inability to give good title.* A seller's inability to give good title does not excuse him from paying his broker's commission, unless it was so agreed in good faith between seller and broker.

*"No commission unless deal consummated."* When the contract contains a provision that "should the deal not be consummated and title not passed *for any reason whatever,* there shall be no commission considered earned," or similar language, the owner is not thereby excused from paying commissions if he arbitrarily and without reason refuses to consummate the sale in accordance with the terms he gave the broker.[32]

**Stockbrokers.** A stockbroker is one employed to buy and sell shares of stock and securities generally for customers who thus employ him. He differs from a dealer in securities in that the latter acts as an independent contractor, not as an agent, and therefore owes no fiduciary duty to the customer, except such as may be imposed by statute. Stockbrokers are frequently, though not necessarily, members of a securities or stock exchange.

*Stock bought on margin: stockbroker's right to sell.* When a stockbroker buys stock for a customer and carries it for him on margin, it is impliedly agreed, in the absence of express provision to the contrary, that if the stock depreciates, the "margin" shall be replenished and kept good upon demand, and upon failure to do so, that the stock may be sold upon reasonable and customary notice.[33]

*Stockbroker's right to repledge.* The right of a pledgee, including a stockbroker, to repledge a customer's securities has been summarized as follows: "A broker who has bought stock for a customer with money advanced by himself and who holds it in his own name as pledgee . . . may, so long as he has not been paid or tendered the amount of his advances, repledge it to the extent of his lien thereon as security for his own debt to a third person without being guilty of conversion or breach of contract, provided the broker has the stock under his control, and can resume possession by paying the amount borrowed thereon, not exceeding the amount owed by the customer . . ."[34] Pledging stock with a bank

[32] *Stern v. Gepo Realty Corporation,* 289 N.Y. 274, 45 N.E. 2d 440.

[33] *Gruman v. Smith,* 81 N.Y. 26, 28; *Stenton v. Jerome,* 54 N.Y. 480; *Krinsky v. Whitney,* 315 Mass. 661, 54 N.E. 2d 36; *Durant v. Block,* 11 N.J. Misc. 919, 930; 169 A. 848, affirmed 113 N.J. Law 509, 174 A. 889; *Goldfarb v. Bruner,* 46 Ohio App. 213, 188 N.E. 362; *Markham v. Jaudon,* 41 N.Y. 235.

[34] 12 *C.J.S.* 78-79.

as security for a loan, with the right to withdraw the same, does not put the stock out of control of the broker.[35]

*Stockbroker's right to transfer or break up certificate.* When stock is deposited with a broker as collateral to secure a purchase on margin, the broker, to facilitate repledging or selling the collateral in case it becomes necessary to cover the margin, has a right to transfer the collateral to a nominee selected by him. For the same reason, the broker is not required to keep or return the identical stock certificate pledged, so long as he has available at all times and returns to the customer a certificate for the same number of shares as that pledged.

*Penalty for pledging or disposing of customer's securities without lien.* If a customer's securities have been paid for in full so that the stockbroker has no lien on them, and the broker pledges or disposes of such securities without the customer's consent, or if, having a lien on them, he pledges or disposes of them for a larger amount than the customer owes, the broker is guilty not only of conversion, but also, in most states, of a felony. In New York, for example, he would be subject to a fine of not more than $5000, imprisonment for not more than two years, or both.

*When broker becomes insolvent: rights of customer as to deposited securities.* When a stockbroker becomes insolvent and is adjudicated a bankrupt, cash customers who can identify their securities may reclaim them. All other customers share ratably ahead of general creditors, but subject to claims having a higher priority.

*Bucketing.* Stockbrokers are strictly forbidden to trade for their own account against their customers' orders. Such practice, known as "bucketing," constitutes a felony, conviction of which is punishable by fine and imprisonment.

*Stock exchange transactions.* Under the Securities Exchange Act of 1934 no stockbroker may effect a transaction in any security on any national securities exchange, unless such security is registered under the act.

*Over-the-counter securities.* No stockbroker may deal in or attempt to sell over-the-counter securities on an interstate basis, unless he has duly registered under the Securities Exchange Act.

**Insurance Brokers.** We have already noted the status and functions of an insurance broker, together with his usual powers and limitations and the manner in which he differs from an insurance agent. (See pages 378-380.)

## Auctioneers

**Definition.** An auction is a public sale of property to the highest bidder. An auctioneer is a person authorized and licensed to conduct an auction.

**Auctioneer's Status as Agent.** An auctioneer, in making a sale, is pri-

---

[35] *Harris v. Friedman*, 245 Mass. 479, 139 N.E. 788.

marily the seller's agent. As such, he owes the usual duties of an agent to his principal: loyalty, good faith, obedience to instructions and a proper degree of skill, care and diligence in the discharge of his duties. Once the hammer falls, however, the auctioneer also becomes the purchaser's agent. When he enters a memorandum of the sale in his notebook, he binds the seller on behalf of the purchaser; and when he accepts a deposit, he is responsible therefor to the buyer if the seller refuses or fails to complete the sale. Both seller and buyer are bound by the auctioneer's announcement as to the identity of the property and the terms and conditions of sale.

**Authority of Auctioneer.** "An auctioneer is a special agent, and without further authority than that which comes from his position as auctioneer he cannot bind the parties by any contract other than that which is actually made, and a contract which is beyond his authority is not binding on the owner." [36]

However, an auctioneer has certain powers which are necessarily implied from the nature of his duties. He may determine the point at which the highest bid is deemed reached, and he may close the bidding by accepting the bid. He may bind the parties by notations in his memorandum book, and he may accept and hold deposits and final payment on the sale, for the account of the seller and to the credit of the purchaser.

On the other hand, an auctioneer's powers are subject to definite limitations. Being a special agent, he may not depart from the specific terms of sale. He has no authority to warrant the property he sells. Unless otherwise authorized, he must accept only cash in payment. He has no implied authority to delegate his power to sell.

**Manner of Making and Accepting Bids.** Bids are usually made orally, in the hearing of others; but cases have supported bids spoken privately to the auctioneer, or by wink, nod or sign. Secret signs between bidder and auctioneer are forbidden.

Acceptance of a bid may be by any established means, usually by the falling of a hammer.

**Withdrawal of Bid.** As previously noted (page 40), bids are mere offers to buy. They are not binding unless accepted. Hence a bidder may always withdraw his bid before it is accepted.

**Withdrawal of Property.** "Until the hammer falls and a bid is accepted . . . the seller may withdraw his property from sale; and he may withdraw it before any bidding, even where the sale is without reserve." [37]

**"Chilling" and "Puffing," Effect of.** To "chill" a sale is to stifle or discourage bidding. Any practice which prevents fair, free and open bidding vitiates the sale.

"Puffing" is bidding without intention to purchase, for the purpose of

---

[36] 7 C.J.S. 1248.
[37] 7 C.J.S. 1253.

raising the price. Puffers are sometimes employed by sellers in questionable auction sales. Generally, puffing is forbidden by law. Like chilling, it vitiates the sale, being a species of fraud. A puffer may not resort to law to compel payment for his services, since the law will not encourage one who assists in a sham.

**Licenses and Other Regulations.** Many states require auctioneers to procure a prescribed license. Among the more common state and municipal regulations governing auctioneers are the following:

*Posting bond* against damages sustained through dishonesty or fraud in conducting an auction sale.

*Responsible seller.* Ordinances frequently require that the seller must have been in an established business for a minimum period prior to sale.

*Night auctions.* State statutes prohibiting night auctions are designed to prevent the sale of fake jewelry and gems in the glitter of artificial light.

*Records.* State statutes generally require auctioneers to keep full records of their transactions with persons on whose behalf sales are conducted, the names and addresses of buyers, collections and proceeds of sales, and similar information. These records must be open for police inspection.

## Factors

**In General.** We have already briefly referred to the nature and function of a factor or commission merchant (page 389). Generally, his rights, duties and liabilities are similar to those of other agents. Certain rules particularly applicable to factors or commission merchants are worthy of note. These relate to the factor's power to sell, pledge or mortgage the owner's property, or to trade or exchange it for other property; the factor's duty to insure the principal's property and to account to the principal; and the factor's lien.

**Power to Sell and Collect.** An ordinary agent sells in the name of his principal, not his own. He may or may not have express or implied authority to collect (page 407). A factor, however, having possession of the merchandise he sells, or of the documents of title to the merchandise, is often the ostensible owner of the merchandise, and therefore, unless forbidden by contract or custom, has authority to sell his principal's goods in his own name, and to collect the proceeds, subject to his duty to account therefor to his principal.

*Power to trade owner's property for other property.* Since a factor's power is to sell, he has no implied power to barter or trade his principal's goods for other goods.

*Del credere function.* Del credere agencies (page 389) are most commonly found in businesses which employ commission merchants or agents whose relatively independent financial status enables them to guarantee the accounts of their customers upon the usual arrangement for higher commissions.

**Factor's Acts: Rights of Third Parties.** Under the common law, if a third party bought goods from an agent who was not authorized to sell, he ran the risk that the principal might repudiate the sale and reclaim the goods. If, in such cases, the agent had in the meantime disappeared, or was unable to respond in damages, the loss would fall on the buyer. The hardship of this rule led to the general adoption of statutes known as "factor's acts." These provide in substance (see page 236) that if a factor or other agent is entrusted with the possession of goods, or of documents of title to them (such as bills of lading, warehouse receipts, custom house permits, and so on), for purposes of sale or as security for advances, such factor is deemed to be the true owner of such goods or documents of title, so far as concerns innocent third parties who are unaware of the true ownership. Thus, third parties who give money or negotiable instruments or other written obligations in payment of such merchandise, or as an advance on the security of it, are protected against a subsequent claim by the true owner that the agent was not authorized to make the sale or pledge, though such may have been the fact. In short, owners in such cases are estopped from denying the factor's authority to sell or pledge.

**Limitation upon Power to Pledge or Mortgage.** Not all states are agreed on what facts will estop the owner from reclaiming his goods. This is especially true of unauthorized pledges. Some states hold that if a factor is authorized to sell only, mere possession of the goods by the factor is not enough to justify an innocent pledgee in believing that the factor is also authorized to pledge the goods. Generally, a factor's power to pledge or mortgage the owner's merchandise is limited to situations involving money advanced by the factor in connection with the goods, or claims involving other sums due him, or money advanced by third parties to enable the factor to buy the merchandise for his principal. The factor has no power to pledge his principal's goods for his own individual debts, and if he does so, the owner may reclaim the goods free from the pledge.[38]

*Notice of factorship.* Factor's acts, as a rule, do not protect persons who have notice of the factorship.

*Goods obtained through fraud or theft.* When the agent or factor obtained possession of the goods by theft, or with the preconceived idea of defrauding the owner, a pledgee (such as a pawnbroker, for example) is not protected by a factor's act: The owner may reclaim his property without reimbursing the pledgee.

[38] *Imperial Valley Long Staple Cotton Growers' Ass'n v. Davidson*, 58 Cal. App. 551, 209 P. 58; *Tropical State Bank v. Sunshine Motor Co.*, 137 Fla. 703, 188 So. 595; *International Trust Co. v. Webster Nat. Bank*, 258 Mass. 17, 154 N.E. 330; *De Bates v. Searls*, 52 S.D. 30, 216 N.W. 586, affirmed 52 S.D. 603, 219 N.W. 559; *Jacob E. Decker & Sons v. Milwaukee Cold Storage Co.*, 173 Wis. 87, 180 N.W. 256.

*Negotiable paper.* Authority to sell negotiable paper does not imply authority to pledge it. The owner may reclaim such paper, even from an innocent pledgee, when there was no authority to pledge it.

*Owner's right to redeem.* In some states, the owner is given a right to redeem property pledged by a factor, even though the pledgee was ignorant of the factorship, but only upon reimbursement of the money advanced.

EXAMPLE: The owner of a diamond ring entrusted possession of it to an agent for sale. The agent pawned the ring. The owner, tendering the amount of the loan, demanded the ring regardless of the contract between the factor and the pawnbroker. The Court sustained the owner: The factor's contract was good as against everybody but the true owner.[39]

**Duty to Insure.** It is the duty of the factor to insure the goods when such obligation is imposed upon him by custom or usage, or by the principal's instructions, or by agreement implied from a course of dealing. In such cases, if the factor fails to use reasonable prudence or diligence to effect the insurance, or fails to inform his principal of his inability to effect it, he becomes liable as insurer himself.

**Duty to Account.** A factor or commission merchant owes a special duty to his principal or consignor in the matter of keeping and rendering accounts. Generally, he has complete possession and control of the principal's goods. He arranges its disposal, and he receives the proceeds therefrom. Frequently he buys the merchandise for the principal in the first instance and then sells it without the principal's ever having seen it. The law therefore imposes upon a commission merchant the duty of keeping regular and accurate accounts of all his transactions on behalf of the principal. He must give the principal the fullest opportunity to inspect these accounts.

**Factor's Lien.** A factor has a general lien on goods consigned to him by his principal, or on the proceeds of such goods, for all commissions, advances and expenditures properly incurred in the course of the relation of principal and factor. (See page 686.)

### Questions

1. How does a broker differ from (a) an ordinary agent, and (b) a factor?
2. "A broker may not serve two masters." Is this statement true, false, or partly true and partly false?
3. What are the three most common types of brokers?
4. The right of a real estate broker to commissions may depend upon a number of conditions. Can you name them?
5. In what respect does a stockholder differ from a dealer in securities?
6. Under what conditions may a stockbroker sell a customer's stock without the customer's consent?
7. State the rule with respect to a stockholder's right to repledge.

---

[39] *Mann v. R. Simpson & Co.*, 286 N.Y. 450, 36 N.E. 2d 658.

8. What is the nature and extent of an auctioneer's authority?

9. What is the basic distinction between a factor and most other agents? What is the nature of the so-called "factor's acts"?

10.* (a) May a stockbroker use as collateral for his bank loan securities deposited by, or purchased for, a customer, which the broker is holding for the customer's debt?

(b) Are there any limitations on the stockbroker as to the use of his customer's securities?

## Problems

1.* Brown, a licensed real estate broker, notified Jones that certain real property could be purchased from the Security Bank. Jones, who knew that Brown would be entitled to a commission, falsely told him that he was not interested in purchasing the property. Immediately thereafter Jones signed a contract with the bank for the purchase of this property, falsely representing to the bank that no broker had brought about the sale. Brown was unable to collect a commission. If Brown has any legal rights against Jones, on what principle of law would they be based?

2.* Waldron placed an order with a stockholder to purchase some stock on margin, depositing as collateral certificate No. 137 for 200 shares of X Stock and certificate No. 78 for 300 shares of Y Stock, both endorsed in blank. Nothing further was said by the parties and nothing in writing was signed by either of them except a simple order and a simple receipt, neither of which contained any qualifications or conditions whatsoever.

(a) Has the stockbroker the legal right to have these certificates transferred at once to a nominee selected by the stockbroker without Waldron's knowledge or consent?

(b) After some months of profitable trading, during which it was not necessary for the stockbroker to utilize any of the collateral originally deposited, Waldron closes the account, receiving a check for the balance due him. The stockbroker refuses to return the two stock certificates originally deposited with him but offers to return various certificates aggregating 200 shares of X Stock and various certificates aggregating 300 shares of Y Stock. Is Waldron legally obliged to accept this offer by the stockbroker?

3.** A real estate agent, on behalf of the seller, finds a purchaser for the property, but after the contract is signed, the purchaser refuses to accept the deed, because the seller cannot give a perfect title. Is the agent entitled to commission? Explain.

4. The owner of a precious stone gave it to an agent with directions to sell it for the best possible price. Instead, the agent pawned it and retained the loan advanced thereon. In a subsequent action by the owner against the pawnbroker for the return of the ring, who should prevail and why?

5. The owner of a parcel of real estate retained the services of a licensed broker to sell the property for a specified price. The broker succeeded in obtaining a prospective purchaser agreeable to the seller and a contract between them was duly executed. At the closing of the transaction, however, it developed that the title was unmarketable because of a marginal encroachment, so that the deal fell through and the down payment was refunded to the purchaser upon demand. The broker thereupon demanded his commission from the seller, and upon the latter's refusal, brought suit. Judgment for whom and why?

## PART 6. TERMINATION OF AGENCY

**How Agency May Be Terminated.** An agency may be terminated either by the acts of the parties themselves or by operation of law. With one exception, the principal and agent always have the *power* (though not necessarily the right) to terminate their relationship. With the same exception, the relationship may be terminated by operation of law. The exception relates to agencies "coupled with an interest" [40] (see page 423).

**Termination by Act of Parties.** An agency may be terminated by act of the parties in any of the following ways:

(a) *By original agreement between the parties.* The agreement creating the agency may contain a specific provision calling for termination of the agency after the lapse of a given time or upon the happening of a given contingency; or the agency may be terminated by the fulfillment of its purpose, as in the case of an agency to sell a horse, which is terminated by the sale of the horse.

(b) *By subsequent agreement of the parties.* After entering into a contract of agency, both principal and agent may mutually agree to terminate it.

(c) *By revocation on the part of the principal.* A principal generally has the *power* to revoke an agency, even though he has not always the *right* to do so. In the latter event, he would be subject to damages for wrongful revocation.

EXAMPLE: Adams, agent for Prentice, was about to close an unusually large order for Prentice and to earn a substantial commission thereon, when Prentice revoked the agency, though it still had a month and a half to run. Adams' authority to go ahead with the deal was thereby automatically terminated, since a principal has the power to terminate the agency at any time. Adams may, however, hold Prentice for damages due to the wrongful termination.

A principal may rightfully revoke an agency if the agent violates his duties to his principal (pages 403-405).

(d) *By renunciation or abandonment on the part of the agent.* An agent always has the *power*, although he may not always have the *right*, to renounce or abandon his agency. If he renounces in violation of his agreement, he is liable for damages.

An agent may, however, rightfully renounce or abandon his agency when: (1) the principal violates the agency agreement, as by refusing to pay agreed compensation, to repay disbursements, or to indemnify the agent; (2) the agency is gratuitous; or (3) the agency is terminable at the will of either party.

**Termination by Operation of Law.** An agency may be terminated by operation of law in any of the following ways:

(1) *Illegality of subject matter.* A liquor agency, for example, is termi-

---

[40] *D'Amato v. Donatoni*, 105 Vt. 496, 168 A. 564.

nated by the passage of an antiliquor law; a foreign agency is terminated by a state of war between the principal's country and the agent's.

(2) *Destruction or loss of subject matter.* An agency to sell a horse would be terminated by death of the horse prior to its sale; an agency to sell a gem would be terminated by loss of the gem.

(3) *Death or incapacity of the parties.* The death of a principal automatically terminates the agency; the death of an agent has a like effect. Insanity is in most cases equivalent to "mental death," or a destruction of contractual capacity; hence it would have the same effect as death. Disability may have a like effect. If a prize fighter, after appointing a manager as his agent, lost his arms and legs in an accident, the agency would be automatically terminated.

(4) *Dissolution of business.* Dissolution of a corporation under the law amounts to corporate death and automatically terminates the authority of officers, agents and employees of the corporation. Similarly, dissolution of a partnership terminates the authority of agents acting for the firm.

(5) *Bankruptcy or insolvency.* If a principal is adjudicated a bankrupt, his status as principal is terminated and so, in consequence, is the agency. State insolvency laws may have a similar effect.

**Contracts Providing for "Irrevocable Agency" and "Permanent Employment."** A contract providing for an "irrevocable agency" is no more irrevocable than any other ordinary contract so far as concerns the *power* of the principal to revoke or of the agent to renounce the agency;[41] but if the revocation or renunciation is wrongful, it will entail damages for breach of the contract. Likewise, contracts for "permanent employment" are not specifically enforceable, since such an agreement is construed as merely an employment at the will of either party, not an employment for life.[42]

**Agency Coupled with Interest.** An agency coupled with an interest is one which gives the agent an interest in the subject matter of the agency itself, as distinguished from a mere interest in connection with the agency.

EXAMPLE: If I hire you to make collections for me, either upon salary or commission, you have an interest merely in connection with the agency, or in connection with its proceeds. But if I owe you $500 and Brown owes me $1000, and I make you my agent to collect my claim against Brown, with instructions to pay yourself out of the proceeds of the collection and to remit the surplus to me, you have an interest in the *subject matter* of the agency itself, namely, an agency *coupled with an interest.*

*Agency as security.* The foregoing example illustrates an agency by way of security for the performance of an obligation on the part of the principal. Such an agency cannot be terminated by the principal without the

---

[41] *State ex rel. Everett Trust & Sav. Bank v. Pacific Waxed Paper Co.,* 22 Wash. 2d 844, 157 P. 2d 707, 710; *Cooper v. Cooper,* 206 Ala. 519, 91 So. 82; *Roth v. Moeller,* 185 Cal. 415, 197 P. 62; *Staats v. Mangelsen,* 105 Neb. 282, 180 N.W. 78.

[42] *Arentz v. Morse Dry Dock & Repair Co.,* 249 N.Y. 439, 164 N.E. 342.

agent's consent. It may, however, be terminated by the principal's death unless the security is supported by a transfer of interest, as by the assignment of an account[43] of some other interest "engrafted" on the subject matter of the agency itself.[44]

EXAMPLE: *A* gives *B*, a creditor, authority to sell goods and collect rents, and to pay himself (*B*) the debt *A* owes him. *A* dies before the goods are sold or the rents collected. Such death will terminate the agency unless the authority was accompanied by the assignment of an interest in the goods or rents. Even without such assignment, however, *A*, if he lived, could not terminate the authority without *B*'s consent.

A transfer of interest as security need not be formal; it may be accomplished by wire or even implied.

EXAMPLE: French, while out on his yacht, runs short of funds and wires Thorne to raise $3000 on the yacht as security, with authority to sell the yacht if the money is not paid in three months. Thorne raises the money but French, after failing to repay the debt, wires Thorne that the authority to sell the yacht is revoked. The agency being coupled with an interest, the attempted revocation is ineffectual.

*Power coupled with duty: escrow agents or holders.* An agency coupled with an interest may take the form of a power coupled with a duty, as when an agent is entrusted with property to be held in escrow for the benefit of third parties. In such case, the agency is irrevocable until the terms of the escrow agreement are fulfilled.

EXAMPLE: The debtor of a bank offered to compromise his indebtedness by the payment of $2074.10. The state superintendent of banks accepted on condition (1) that the debtor deposit the money in escrow and submit to an audit, and (2) that the Court approve the transaction. After the money was deposited, the debtor died, and his executor demanded return of the deposit. The agency, however, having been created under an escrow agreement, was not terminable by death.

*Power of attorney to sell collateral.* Creditors, in making loans secured by collateral, frequently require that the deposit of collateral be accompanied by a power of attorney given to the creditor to sell the collateral as agent for the debtor in case the debt is not paid, and to apply the proceeds, or so much thereof as may be necessary, to the payment of the debt. Banks frequently lend money on notes thus secured. Such power of attorney is not terminable by the will of the principal (borrower) alone, or by his death.

**Notice of Termination.** When a principal revokes or an agent renounces the agency, the notice required for such termination may be such as is fixed in the agency contract or, if none is specified, reasonable notice under the circumstances. Such notice, however, will not bind third parties

---

[43] *Shepard v. McNail*, 122 Mo. App. 418.
[44] 2 C.J.S. 1176.

unless they, too, receive it. Third parties have a right to assume, unless they are otherwise informed, that the authority of the agent with whom they have been dealing continues to exist. In the absence of notice, they are entitled to hold the principal responsible for acts done by the agent within the apparent scope of his prior authority, even though the principal has actually terminated the agent's authority.

*Necessity of notice to third parties where principal dies.* Ordinarily, the principal's death automatically revokes the agent's authority (page 423). Whether a third party, unless notified, is bound by such termination, is a question on which the courts of the country are not in entire agreement. The majority of states hold that he is,[45] a minority that he is not.[46]

EXAMPLES:

(1) A landlord appointed an agent to collect rents. Later, he died. Thereafter a tenant, unaware of the landlord's death, paid his rent to the agent, who absconded with it. The tenant was forced to pay rent over again to the executor.[47]

(2) The payee of a negotiable note indorsed it in blank and delivered it to an agent for collection. The maker paid the note while it was in the agent's possession after the payee's death, and without knowledge of such death. The court held that such payment discharged the debt.[48]

## Questions

1. Name four ways by means of which an agency may be terminated by act of the parties.

2. Give three situations wherein an agent may rightfully renounce or abandon his agency.

3. An agency may be terminated by operation of law in any one of five different ways. Name them.

4. Does a contract providing for "irrevocable agency" or "permanent employment" connote irrevocability or lifetime employment?

5. What is meant by "an agency coupled with an interest"? Give three illustrations.

## Problems

1. Dalton, a commission merchant, agrees to sell Earl's output of chalk dolls, for a commission of 40 per cent. Dalton has a consignment of 1,000 dolls unsold on his premises. While he is negotiating with a customer for a sale, Earl dies. May Dalton continue his negotiations? Explain.

2. Perkins owes Watson $500. He says to Watson, "I have no money, but I have an important breach of contract action against the Lovelace Baking Corporation, which I can turn over to you for collection. You can then pay yourself what I owe you, and give me the difference." Perkins executes a power of

---

[45] This, also, is the view adopted by the American Law Institute (*Restatement, Agency*).

[46] Including Missouri, Nebraska, Ohio, Oklahoma and Pennsylvania.

[47] *Farmers Loan & Trust Co. v. Wilson*, 139 N.Y. 284.

[48] *Deweese v. Muff*, 57 Neb. 17.

attorney for this purpose to Watson. Watson retains his brother, an attorney, to prosecute the suit. Before the case comes to trial, Perkins dies. His estate directs Watson's brother, the attorney, to return the papers, advising that it desires to retain an attorney of its own. Watson and his brother refuse to turn the case over to the estate's attorney, and the estate applies to the court for relief, contending that the agency was revoked by death. How should the court decide, and why?

3. Chase draws a check on his account with the Yonkers Trust Company, payable to the order of Henry Smith. Henry Smith presents the check for payment, and the bank pays the check. One hour before the check was paid, Chase died. Chase's estate contests the payment on the ground that the bank was not authorized to make it after its depositor had died, claiming that the death of the principal automatically terminates the authority of the agent. How should the case be decided, and why?

4. The Jefferson Motor Car Company, pursuant to contract, gives Van Pelt an irrevocable power of attorney to sell its motor cars in the state of California as its exclusive agent for five years. One hundred models are shipped to Van Pelt, but before any orders can be taken, the company withdraws the agency, and demands the return of the models, at its own cost. Van Pelt refuses to ship the models, claiming a lien. The company sues for conversion. Judgment for whom and why?

5. Watson authorizes two brokers to find a purchaser for his property. One of the brokers sold the land. The other broker was not notified of the sale, and he, also, shortly after the first sale, finds a purchaser, who is ready, willing and able to buy on the owner's terms. Watson, of course, is no longer able to deliver title. The second broker sues him for services. Judgment for whom and why?

## COURT CASES FOR REVIEW

### How Did the Court Decide, and Why?

1. A steward was employed by a club to conduct its restaurant, and furnish all such food, cigars, etc., as might be required by the club, without any liability on the part of the club. The steward ran up a bill for meat. Monthly statements for the meat were delivered to the club, whose bookkeeper delivered them to the steward, who paid the bills by his personal checks. On an unpaid bill, suit was brought against the club as principal. *Reis v. Drug & Chemical Club*, 55 Misc. 276, 105 N.Y. Supp. 285.

2. A trucker agreed with a gas company to unload pipe from a railroad car at a specified price per car. He hired his own help and used his own equipment. For negligence in unloading one of the cars, suit was brought against the gas company. *Arkansas-Louisiana Gas Co. v. Tuggle*, 201 Ark. 416, 146 S.W. 2d 154.

3. The members of a college class voted to publish a book. They elected a business manager of the publication. When it came to paying for the cost of the publication the question arose as to who was legally liable for the expense. *Willcox v. Arnold*, 162 Mass. 577, 39 N.E. 414.

4. Plaintiff sued defendant for injuries sustained in a collision between her own car, which was being driven by her husband, and defendant's car. The jury found both defendant and plaintiff's husband guilty of negligence, but gave the wife (a passenger) a verdict for $1527.09 damages. The Superior Court reversed on the ground of the implied agency of the husband in driving

the car owned by his wife. Plaintiff appealed. *Rodgers v. Saxton*, 305 Pa. 479, 158 A. 166.

5. A prospective purchaser called the office of a firm of realty brokers with reference to the purchase of certain listed property. The broker informed the purchaser that they would send a man to consummate the purchase. The broker's agent closed the transaction and the purchaser, at the agent's request, made out a check payable to the agent, rather than to the brokerage firm. The proceeds of the check were not paid over to the brokerage firm and the latter brought suit against the purchaser on the ground that she had no right to make the check payable to the agent. *Peterson v. Millman*, 108 Cal. App. 2d 41, 238 P. 2d 117.

6. A buyer placed an order with a salesman for a wholesale beef establishment for 30,000 pounds of mutton in weekly shipments of 3,000 pounds or more. The buyer mailed a purchase order to the sellers which substantially recited the terms of the sale. The sellers' first weekly shipment substantially complied with the order. The sellers then informed the buyer that they would do their utmost to complete the transaction. On the sellers' default the buyer commenced suit for breach and the sellers thereupon repudiated the agreement on the ground of the salesman's lack of authority to accept the order. *Moses v. Archie McFarland & Son*, 230 P. 2d 571 (Wash.).

7. An agent contracted in the name of his alleged principal. The latter was able to establish that the agent was without authority to make the contract and that in consequence no obligation was imposed on the principal. The agent, however, acted in good faith and actually believed he had the authority to bind the principal. The question arose as to whether the third parties had any recourse against the agent. *Copeland v. Swiss Cleaners*, 255 Ala. 519, 52 So. 2d 223.

8. Plaintiff sold materials subsequently used on school construction jobs. Plaintiff at the time believed the buyer to be the principal in the transaction, and had no notice at the time of the sale that the buyer was a purchasing agent for the general contractor who constructed the schools. The plaintiff charged the materials to the agent and attempted to collect from him, but upon discovering the facts, brought suit against the general contractor, whose defense was that plaintiff, having extended exclusive credit to the agent, and having sought to collect from him, had elected to hold the agent, and consequently had waived any rights against the undisclosed principal who was the real contractor. *Imperial Val. Box Co. v. Reese*, 105 Cal. App. 2d 401, 233 P. 2d 629.

9. An insurance company hired a doctor to care for the company's injured employees. The doctor hired a specialist, and the insurance company repudiated the doctor's authority to do so and refused to pay the specialist's bill. It was contended on behalf of the plaintiff that the defendant was estopped from repudiating the doctor's authority to hire a specialist, inasmuch as the doctor had previously employed a specialist and the insurance company had paid such specialist for his services. *Lorie v. Lumbermen's Mut. Casualty Co.* (Mo. App.), 8 S.W. 2d 81.

10. Two agents took over the management of their principal's property. They caused title to be taken in the name of one of their clerks. Then they had another "dummy" buy the property, at a sale under a deed of trust, and thereafter, they bought the property themselves. The principal, on discovering the facts, sued for rescission. The agents counterclaimed for commissions. The clerk allowed rescission, but the further question remained as to the agents' counterclaim for commissions. *Witte v. Storm*, 236 Mo. 470, 139 S.W. 384.

11. An agent was employed to sell a plantation for his principal. It was provided that $50,000 should be paid in cash. This purchase price was to be made up in a certain way. In arranging the payment, a small balance of account between the parties was disputed, and it threatened to disrupt the deal. The agent, fearful of losing a substantial commission, undertook to pay this balance himself, so that he would not lose his commission. He thereafter sought reimbursement for this balance from the principal, on the ground that he had benefited his principal by rescuing the transaction and preventing it from falling through. *Woodlief v. Moncure*, 17 La. Ann. 241.

12. A manufacturer employed an agent to fill orders for engines, agreeing to allow the agent a commission on all monies realized from the sales. The agent secured orders and forwarded them according to agreement. The manufacturer failed to ship the engines within a reasonable time, and the sales were lost in consequence. The agent sued his principal for commissions lost through the principal's delay. *Stevenson v. Morris Mach. Works*, 69 Miss. 232, 13 So. 834.

13. Certain premises were rented by an agent on behalf of his principal for an illegal purpose. Rent was paid in advance to the agent. The principal refused to make the lease, and the tenant sued the principal on the ground that the latter became bound when his agent accepted the rent. *Stover v. Flower*, 120 Iowa 514, 94 N.W. 1100.

14. Plaintiff assigned insurance policies to defendant as agent, with instructions to collect on the policies and pay the proceeds to plaintiff's creditors. The agent settled with his principal's creditors on the basis of seventy cents on the dollar. The surplus he claimed for himself on the ground that he had created it through his own efforts, and that so long as the creditors were satisfied, the plaintiff had no further interest in the surplus. The plaintiff sued the agent for the surplus. *Ash v. A. B. Frank Co.*, 142 S.W. 42 (Tex. Civ. App.).

15. An agent was employed to examine land and determine what valuation his principal should place upon it in exchange for other property. The agent, in good faith, gave the principal his opinion. As a result, the principal suffered loss for which he sought to hold the agent accountable. *Durward v. Hubbell*, 149 Iowa 722, 128 N.W. 953.

16. A principal authorized two brokers to sell a parcel of real estate. One of the brokers sold the land. The other was not notified of the sale, and shortly thereafter made a contract to sell the same parcel to plaintiff. Plaintiff sued for damages. *Ahern v. Baker*, 34 Minn. 98, 24 N.W. 341.

17. Defendant orally engaged plaintiff, a real estate broker, to sell his farm land at $40 an acre. He agreed to pay plaintiff a commission of $500. Plaintiff interested a third party in the purchase of the land, and had him discuss it with defendant. The latter then told the purchaser that if plaintiff were out of the picture, the purchaser could save some money; and eventually the property was sold to the purchaser at $37.50 per acre. Defendant refused to pay commissions on the ground that plaintiff was not the procuring cause of the sale and that the agreement had been terminated prior thereto. From a judgment in favor of defendant, plaintiff appeals. *Dahlgren v. Olson*, 228 Minn. 379, 37 N.W. 2d 438.

18. Plaintiff, after accepting a sub-contract on stone work, soon found out that it was a losing proposition and demanded more money from defendant, the general contractor. Defendant's superintendent stated that "he would see that they got paid what it was worth to do the job." Plaintiff thereupon completed the work. Defendants, however, refused compensation beyond the price originally contracted for, and plaintiff brought suit on two grounds: (1) That

defendant's superintendent had authority as an agent to modify the written contract previously entered into; and (2) That the oral modification was ratified by defendant's acceptance of completion by plaintiff. Defendant showed on the trial that it did not know of the statement by its construction superintendent until after completion. *Ferro Concrete Construction Co. v. United States for Use and Benefit of Luchini, et al.,* 112 Fed. (2d) 488.

19. Defendant engaged plaintiff as a broker to obtain a financially responsible lessee for a twenty-one-year term. It was stipulated that no commission would be paid until the final execution of the lease. Plaintiff produced a person of doubtful financial responsibility, whereupon defendant refused to execute the lease unless plaintiff agreed to take a portion of his commissions as and when the lessee paid the rents, to which plaintiff agreed. Without waiting for his commissions to accrue out of rentals, plaintiff brought an action for his full commissions, claiming that the second agreement failed of any new or additional consideration. *Saum v. Capital Realty Development Corp.,* 268 N.Y. 341, 197 N.E. 303.

20. A store manager was empowered by the owner to employ and discharge help, but not to choose a successor as manager without the owner's approval. Subsequently, the manager hired a successor without the owner's approval, at a fixed salary plus a percentage of the store's gross. The owner refused to recognize the successor as the new manager, and to pay his salary and commissions, whereupon the new manager brought suit. *Gaddie v. Collins of Ky.,* 248 S.W. 2d 722 (Ky.).

21. The general agent of a farming partnership delivered a crop of peanuts to a purchaser, who charged back the value of supplies he had delivered to the partnership, giving a promissory note for the balance. The countercharge and note were accepted by the general manager, with the knowledge of one of the partners. Three years later, when payment of the note was not forthcoming, the partnership instituted an action for the entire value of the peanut crop. *Raines v. Graham,* 85 Ga. App. 815, 70 S.E. 2d 125.

# 10

# Employer and Employee

**Scope of This Chapter.** In this chapter, with the basic rules of principal and agent in the background, we consider the rights, duties and obligations that arise out of the employer-employee relationship. In Part 1 we consider the common law rights and duties of employers and employees in respect to each other, whether based on their contract, or on court precedent. In Part 2 we take up the subject of labor disputes and labor legislation, including the basic statutes applicable to such disputes, with particular reference to collective bargaining, strikes, picketing, boycotts, sabotage, lockouts, strikebreaking and labor espionage. In Part 3 we summarize the major aspects of social legislation during the first half of this century, particularly the laws dealing with wage liens, priorities and preferences, the establishment of minimum wages and maximum hours of employment, the prohibition of child labor, the assurance of workmen's compensation notwithstanding disability or death during employment, and the system designated as social security and embracing such matters as old age retirement benefits, unemployment insurance, public assistance to the needy aged, and various forms of health and welfare services.

## PART 1. COMMON LAW RIGHTS AND DUTIES

**Basis of Common Law Rights and Duties.** When one hires another, the parties usually agree upon their respective rights and duties. These may concern wages, hours of labor, work to be done, period of employment and similar matters. However, contracts rarely anticipate all possible questions that may arise in the course of employment. Questions not covered by the agreement frequently lead to litigation and must be decided by the courts. Other questions involve the so-called "natural" rights and duties, which exist regardless of contract, such as the right of personal security, involving a safe place to work, safe tools and safe fellow-workers, or the duty of loyalty which is implicit in the employer-employee relationship. All these questions, unless and until they become the subject of statutory regulation (and often even then) must be decided by the courts on the basis of prior decisions. That is, they are governed by common law instead of by statute, and the rights and duties so established are the common law rights and duties of the parties.

**Employees and Agents Distinguished.** The distinction between an agent and an employee is frequently not easy to draw. In theory, an agent has broader authority and responsibility than an ordinary employee, and is usually empowered to bind his principal by contract, where an employee is not. In practice, however, the terms *agent* and *employee* are used interchangeably. Employees in certain businesses necessarily bind their employers by contract, and their duties may call for the widest discretion. It is for this reason that many of the rights, duties and liabilities of principal and agent (pages 400 to 405) correspond with those of employer and employee.

**Employees Distinguished from Independent Contractors.** We have already distinguished between an agent and an independent contractor (page 389). A similar distinction exists with respect to an employee.

**Mutual Rights and Duties.** The relationship of employer and employee necessarily arises out of a contract. The rights and duties of the parties may be fixed in the contract, or based on the nature of the relationship. The amount of compensation, for example, is usually fixed in the contract; the nature and degree of care required of the parties are determined by the nature of their relationship.

**The Contract of Employment.** An employment contract, like all others, may be express or implied. If express, it may be oral or written, except where performance is to take more than a year, in which event it must be written (page 85). If the contract is implied, it is based on conduct and custom; it may consist of a nod of the head, or merely the performance and acceptance of services. As noted in the chapter on Contracts, the law will imply a contract to prevent unjust enrichment, so that if one works for another without a specific understanding as to compensation, the law will enforce payment of a reasonable compensation based on the circumstances.

On the other hand, when the contract is express instead of implied, and performance has not yet begun, it cannot be enforced unless the usual contract requisites are present (page 33). This is sometimes overlooked with unfortunate results. For example, in *Harris-Cortner v. Morgan*,[1] an employer hired an employee with the statement that if the employee proved "satisfactory" and was himself satisfied, his salary would be "advanced" at the beginning of the new season. The court held the contract invalid and unenforceable for indefiniteness and consequent lack of mutual assent.

An employment agreement should therefore fix, at the very least, the

[1] 214 Ala. 599, 108 So. 449.

duration of employment, the nature of the employee's duties, his working hours, and his compensation. These are usually specified. If not, and the agreement is executory, it will not be enforced, and if executed, it will be spelled out by the courts from the surrounding circumstances. Usually implied in the contract of employment, executory or executed, are such conditions as fitness or competency of the employee, obedience to instructions, and diligence in performing the task.

**Duration of Employment.** A hiring under a contract which specifies no period of employment is a hiring at will, terminable at the option of either party. A hiring at so much per day, month or year is likewise construed in most states[2] as a hiring at will, not as a hiring for the period measuring the pay, unless the period of employment is otherwise indicated.

EXAMPLE: Little is hired as a bookkeeper at a salary of $2500 a year. Business being slack, he is discharged at the end of six months. He sues for breach of a yearly hiring. His suit will be dismissed.

*Implied renewal of contract.* Where a contract of employment expires and the employee, with the employer's consent, holds over and continues his duties, the law may imply a renewal for the same period and on the same terms.

**Duties of Employment.** The nature of an employee's duties may be specified in the contract or fixed by custom. In neither event is an employee required to discharge duties for which he was not employed. If he is employed as a superintendent, he cannot be required to perform ordinary labor. If he is employed as a general worker, he may be required to do the usual variety of tasks that present themselves in such establishment, but not tasks that require special skill. If he is employed as a bookkeeper, he cannot be required to handle freight, and vice versa.

**Compensation: in General.** The obligation to compensate is implied from the fact of hiring, but the amount and form of compensation are usually fixed in the hiring contract. Compensation may be wholly contingent on results, as in the case of a profit-sharing arrangement or a sales agency operating exclusively on commissions. It may be fixed and definite, as in the case of a specified salary or wage. It may be measured on a time basis (so much per day, week or month), or by "piece work" (so much per item of work turned out). In the absence of agreement, express or implied, the law makes compensation payable at the end of the job, or upon completion of services.

*Extra work; overtime.* There is no obligation to pay an employee for extra work or overtime unless it is expressly provided for in the hiring, established by custom, implied from the hiring contract,[3] or required by statute (see page 450).

---

[2] Exceptions are Arkansas, Georgia, New Jersey, North Carolina and Wisconsin.
[3] 56 C.J.S. 526-527.

*Tips or gratuities.* Except where prohibited by statute, an employee's compensation may consist of, or include, tips or gratuities. In the absence of agreement to the contrary, tips belong to the employee.

*Drawing accounts.* The rule as to drawing accounts is the same with employees as with agents (page 402). A drawing account is payable absolutely, even where it exceeds commissions earned, and the employer cannot compel the employee to return any part of it, unless there is an agreement specifically requiring it.[4]

*Forfeitures and deductions.* An employee's right to compensation is not absolute: it depends on a proper discharge of his duties. An employer is not required to pay for services not rendered. If the employee is hired for a given task and refuses to do it, or to take orders connected with it, or to discharge his duties in a proper manner, he forfeits his right to compensation. If he is guilty of dishonesty, disloyalty, negligence or other misconduct, causing loss or damage to the employer, his right to compensation may be subject to forfeiture or deduction.

*Part performance: quitting job.* If a person is hired by the week or month and quits before the end of the period, the question arises whether he is entitled to pay for the period worked, or to no pay at all. In some cases the answer is obvious. If an employee is hired for a month and quits at the end of an hour, he will obviously find it difficult to establish a right to compensation. If he quits an hour before the end of the month, he will be clearly entitled to compensation for substantial performance. In the ordinary case, however, an employee hired for and to be paid at the end of a given period can recover nothing if he quits during the period. The contract in such case is deemed "entire," that is, wages are payable as an entire sum upon entire performance.

*Negligence or misconduct.* If an employee causes loss to his employer through negligence or misconduct, as by careless or deliberate waste or destruction of property, or by insulting a customer or assaulting a fellow employee, the employer may recover resulting damage from the employee, or may deduct it from the employee's paycheck.

*Illegality.* As noted in Chapter 2, no one can found a right on an illegal act. If an employee labors on an illegal task, knowing it to be such, he can recover no compensation regardless of the effort bestowed. Thus, a person employed in violation of a Sunday law, or to repair an obviously illegal gambling machine, will be unable to recover for his labors.

**Employer's Duty of Care.** Each person owes to all others the duty to be careful. The nature and extent of such duty are determined by the circumstances. An employer's duty of care toward his employees is governed not only by the fact of employment, but by the nature of the task. An employer, except as provided by statute, is not an insurer of

---

[4] *Zuby v. Height,* 188 N.Y. Supp. 88; *Southern Molasses Co. v. Boutcher,* 172 La. 691, 135 So. 27; *Anagnosti v. Almy,* 252 Mass. 492, 147 N.E. 854.

the employee's safety. He is required to do only what an ordinarily prudent man would do under the circumstances.

The subject of care, and the lack of it, are more fully discussed on pages 806 to 812, in the chapter on Torts. So far as concerns the relationship of employer and employee, the former's duty of care toward the latter usually concerns (1) a safe place to work, (2) safe tools and equipment, (3) a duty to caution and instruct, and (4) adequate and competent co-workers.

**Assumption of Risk.** Many types of employment are inherently dangerous and known to be such by persons accepting them. Examples are animal training and aerial performances in a circus, the manufacture and distribution of explosives, and industries affected by occupational diseases such as those caused by dust, fumes and gases. Under the common law, persons accepting such employment are held to assume its risks, except those which the employer, by due care, could or should remove or minimize. The assumption of risk doctrine has been considerably modified by statute in many industries (page 451).

**Fellow-Servant Rule.** Under the common law if an employee is injured through the negligence of a fellow-employee, the latter only is liable. The rule has been commonly justified on two grounds: (1) The negligence of a fellow-employee is one of the risks incident to employment and assumed by an employee; and (2) The rule is calculated to make persons in a common employment watchful of one another, thereby promoting care in the performance of their duties, with consequent benefit to the public.

The fellow-servant rule is inapplicable in the following situations:

(1) *Statutory regulation.* The fellow-servant rule has been superseded by statute in many occupations.

(2) *Faulty hiring.* The employer is liable if he has knowingly or negligently hired careless or incompetent fellow-employees.

(3) *Superiors v. fellow-servants.* Where the act causing injury is committed by an employee's superior, it is deemed the act of the employer rather than that of a fellow-employee.

(4) *Common employees v. fellow-employees.* Many big organizations employ thousands of employees in different branches and departments. Such employees do not come within the fellow-servant rule. If a clerk in one department is injured through the negligence of a truck driver on duty in another department, the employer would be liable as well as the truck driver.

**Duties of Employee.** As already indicated, the duties of an employee, like those of his employer, are governed by the contract of employment, whether expressly specified, or implied from the nature of the task. In addition, an employee, in relation to his employer and all others, must exercise the due care required by the circumstances.

**Sufficiency of Performance.** Whether the employee has rendered the services required under the contract is a question of fact in each case. If the contract is not specific on this point, the test is not performance to the employer's absolute satisfaction, but performance which should satisfy a reasonable employer under the circumstances.

**Obedience to Instructions.** The very nature of the contract of employment calls for obedience to the lawful and reasonable demands of the employer. "No man has a legal or moral right, while continuing in the employ of another, to refuse to do the work he is employed to do." [5] As previously stated, however, the employee is not required to discharge duties other than those for which he was employed.

**Compelling Performance.** "You can lead a horse to water but you cannot make him drink." Except where involuntary servitude is tolerated, there is no such thing as compelling specific performance of a labor contract. If an employee refuses to discharge the duties for which he was employed, the employer's remedy is to sue for damages because of the breach.

**Skill, Care and Diligence.** The skill, care and diligence required of an employee correspond to those exacted from an agent in the discharge of his duties toward his principal (pages 403-404).

**Loyalty and Good Faith.** To the extent that an employee's position is similar to that of an agent, his duties of loyalty and good faith reflect those due from an agent to his principal (page 403). Among the questions which frequently arise in this connection are: (1) Whether and to what extent an employee's time and effort must be devoted exclusively to the employer's interests; (2) The duty not to divulge trade secrets; and (3) An employee's inventions and discoveries while on duty for the employer.

**Duty to Serve Employer Exclusively.** An employee is not required to serve his employer exclusively unless his contract so requires. He may therefore take such outside jobs as will not interfere with a proper discharge of his regular duties. A provision in a contract that the employee shall give his entire time to the job is construed as meaning that he must give his full day's work to his employer. It does not mean that he may not have some time, after his full day's work, to further his own personal affairs or other business.[6] However, an employee may not engage in work which competes with that of his employment, because in so doing he violates his duty of loyalty and good faith.

**Trade Secrets.** An employee, not only during his employment, but after its termination, is under obligation not to divulge his employer's trade secrets. A trade secret has been defined as "A plan or process, tool or mechanism, or a compound known only to its owner and those of its

---

[5] 56 C.J.S. 477, citing *In re Grand Jury*, 62 F. (D.C., Cal.) 834.
[6] *Long v. Forbes*, 58 Wyo. 533, 136 P. 2d 242.

employees to whom it is necessary to confide it." [7] Trade secrets are to be distinguished from "know-how." In the absence of contract or fraud, a former employee who goes into business for himself may use the knowledge, training and talent he has developed in working for his former employer. The distinction between trade secrets and "know-how" is sometimes finely drawn. In *New Rochelle Coal & Lumber Co. v. Pugliese*,[8] a former employee solicited his former employer's fuel oil customers, but because he had retained the list of customers in his memory instead of physically appropriating it, the court denied an injunction to restrain him from such solicitation.

**Inventions.** As between employer and employee, the right to an invention made by an employee in the course of his general employment is determined by the contract of employment. In the absence of a contrary understanding, the mere existence of an employer-employee relationship does not entitle the employer to ownership of an invention made by an employee in the course of his employment, though the employee uses the employer's time and facilities in developing his invention. If an employer desires to safeguard such right, he must provide for it in the contract of employment.

However, if an employee is hired to invent something, or is assigned the duty of solving a particular problem, the resulting invention belongs to the employer.

**Shop rights.** Although an employee is entitled to his own invention, even where made on his employer's time and with the use of his employer's equipment, equity in such cases extends to the employer a limited right in such invention, known as a *shop right*. The "shop rights" doctrine is to the effect that where an employee finds or improves a method or device for doing his work, or discovers, invents or perfects a trade secret by use of his employer's time, property or equipment, he assents to the employer's use of such invention or improvement, and grants to the employer a free, irrevocable, non-assignable and non-exclusive license to use the invention or improvement, though the employee retains the right to the invention itself. If the employee develops the invention or improvement on his own time and without use of the employer's property or equipment, there is no shop right.

**Termination of Employer-Employee Relationship.** The relationship of employer and employee may be terminated pursuant to the contract itself, as where the contract expires by its own terms, or it may be terminated by mutual agreement of the parties, or by unilateral act of either employer or employee, as where an employer discharges the employee, or the employee quits. Where the hiring was for an indefinite term, the employer may discharge the employee, or the employee may quit,

---

[7] *Louis Milani Foods v. Scharf*, 335 Ill. App. 569, 82 N.E. 2d 75.
[8] 86 N.Y. Supp. 2d 757.

without recourse by either party, unless there was an agreement and failure to give notice. Where the hiring was for a definite term, and the discharge or abandonment was without cause, the employer or employee, as the case may be, may recover reasonable damages suffered in consequence. The measure of an employer's damages for wrongful abandonment is the reasonable and necessary expense incurred in replacing the services wrongfully terminated. The measure of an employee's damages for wrongful discharge is the difference between the amount earned in fact and what would have been earned under the contract.[9] Although a discharged employee must mitigate his damage by seeking other and similar employment (page 124) at a place reasonably convenient to the employee, the burden of proof in such cases is on the employer, not the employee: that is, the employer must prove that such employment was available.[10]

## Questions

1. What is meant by the common law rights and duties applicable to the relationship of employer and employee?

2. In theory, what is the difference, if any, between an employee and an agent?

3. What four conditions are usually specified in a contract of employment?

4. What three conditions are usually implied in a contract of employment?

5. What is the rule governing extra compensation for overtime, in the absence of statute or an express agreement?

6. "An employer is entitled to all tips, in the absence of agreement to the contrary." Is this statement true, false, or partly true and partly false?

7. What is the rule with respect to an employee's drawing account when the same exceeds commissions earned?

8. Under what circumstances may an employee's right to compensation be subject to forfeiture or deduction?

9. Where an employee is hired for and is to be paid at the end of a given period, to what wages, if any, is he entitled if he quits employment during the period? Explain.

10. The employer's duty of care to his employee usually embraces what four items?

11. Explain (a) the fellow-servant rule, (b) the assumption of risk doctrine.

12. Where an employee refuses to discharge the duties for which he was hired, what remedy has the employer?

13. Are the following statements true, false, or partly true and partly false? Explain.

(a) "An employee is required to serve his employer exclusively, unless the contract specifies otherwise."

(b) "An employee is under obligation not to divulge his employer's trade secrets."

(c) "In the absence of agreement to the contrary, an employee's inventions belong to his employer."

14. What is the "shop rights" doctrine?

---

[9] *Crillo v. Curtola,* 91 Cal. App. 2d 263, 204 P. 2d 941 (Cal. App.).

[10] *Martin v. Board of Education of Lincoln County,* 120 W. Va. 621, 199 S.E. 887.

## Problems

1. A salesman's contract for one year provided that he was "to devote his entire time and attention to the business of the employer," and that he was not to "engage, directly or indirectly, in any other business than that of the employer during the life of this agreement." The salesman complied with the terms of his agreement, to the extent that he took orders during the morning hours, in which he was more successful than other employees working the entire day; but the employer, learning that the salesman spent his afternoon hours playing cards and shaking dice, discharged him before the year expired. The salesman sues for breach of contract. Judgment for whom and why?

2. Jones is hired as a clerk at a salary of $3,000 a year. At the end of six months, because of lack of business, he is discharged. He sues for breach of a yearly hiring. Judgment for whom and why?

3. Roe is employed by Smith on a commission basis, with a weekly drawing account of $100. His commissions for the first five weeks amount to $300. He claims, however, that he is entitled to $500. Smith insists that Roe owes him $200. Who is right?

4. Farrell is hired as a bookkeeper on a salary of $300 per month. At the end of a week, he demands his salary on the basis of one fourth of the amount of his monthly salary. The employer insists that the bookkeeper's salary is not due until the end of the month. Who is right?

5. In a line of business not covered by the Wage and Hour Law, Robinson is employed at a salary of $60 per week. His normal working hours are from 9 A.M. to 5 P.M. Nothing is said about overtime. Robinson, however, during the second week of his employment, is required to work ten hours overtime. He insists that he is entitled to extra pay for this overtime. May he collect it?

6. A circus tiger claws his trainer, who sues the circus owner for injuries due to the maintenance of an unusually ferocious and dangerous beast. Will the trainer succeed?

7. During a period when farm labor is scarce, Rogers, a farmer, hires Lamb for the harvesting season, and Lamb agrees that he will stay throughout the season. A few days later, however, Lamb threatens to quit. Rogers seeks a court order restraining Lamb from breaching his contract. In support of his position Rogers urges that Lamb's breach would cause irreparable injury. Can Rogers obtain the desired relief?

8. Davis is employed under an agreement to devote his entire time and effort to his employer's business. Davis, who has a large family to take care of, has a night job from which he earns extra money. The employer, on learning of the night work, insists that Davis must discontinue it for fear that it may interfere with his work during the day. The employer makes no claim, however, that such work has interfered with the daytime tasks assigned to Davis. What are the respective rights of Davis and his employer?

9. Black is employed in a cotton mill. During slack intervals on the job, he works on an invention for turning out a stronger fibre. He ultimately obtains a patent which the employer claims belongs to him because it was developed by Black during working hours. Is the employer entitled to the invention?

10. Blake is hired for one year on a weekly salary of $100. At the end of six months he is discharged without cause. He sues his employer for $2,500, representing six months' salary. The case comes up for trial six months after Blake was discharged, during which period Blake had been able to earn only $1,500. How should the court instruct the jury under the circumstances?

## PART 2. LABOR DISPUTES AND LABOR LEGISLATION

**Transition in Status of Labor.** With the transition from handicraft to factory methods of production, the basis of bargaining between employer and employee underwent a radical change. For the large majority, skill was no longer at a premium. Anyone who could push a button or pull a lever was eligible for the assembly line. The ranks of the workers were swelled by the unskilled. The employee's personal contact with his employer gave way to a system where thousands could be employed for years in a single industry without ever seeing their employer.

**Growth of Trade Unions.** As the mechanization of industry spread, the supply of labor tended to outstrip the number of available jobs. In consequence the worker, in bargaining for his job, found himself at a disadvantage. To redress this disadvantage, trade unions, previously organized on a limited scale, began to assume more formidable proportions. The enormous expansion of mass-production industries in the early decades of the present century brought large-scale industrial unions to the fore. The adoption of legislation favorable to labor during the thirties and forties greatly accelerated the growth of unionism throughout the country.

**Industrial Disputes.** In the ensuing test of economic strength, each side —labor and management—sought to increase its bargaining power. Each sought to exert pressures of various sorts against the other. These pressures have precipitated industrial disputes, at times violent, the adjustment of which has increasingly taxed the courts and legislatures.

**Law Applicable to Industrial Disputes.** In the absence of statute, the law applicable to industrial disputes is necessarily based on judicial precedent and reasoning. In no field of litigation is there a wider range of judicial opinion than in the field of labor disputes. Most labor situations, however, are now governed by statute. Federal regulation of labor disputes is of course basically uniform throughout the country, but such regulation is limited to cases affecting the flow of interstate commerce. State regulation of *intrastate* industrial disputes is far from uniform.

## Labor Legislation

**Summary.** The principal Federal acts dealing with industrial disputes during the past few decades are the Norris-LaGuardia Act, the Railway Labor Act, the National Labor Relations Act, and the Labor-Management Relations (Taft-Hartley) Act.

**Norris-LaGuardia Act (1932).** Under this act, "yellow-dog" contracts (under which an employee binds himself not to join a union) cannot be enforced in a Federal court, nor may Federal courts issue injunctions to prevent workers from striking, picketing, holding mass meetings or encouraging other workers to strike, unless the employer can prove (a) that he will suffer substantial and irreparable injury if an injunction is not issued, (b) that unlawful acts are threatened and will be committed unless restrained, and (c) that public officers charged with the duty to protect his property are unwilling or unable to furnish adequate protection. One accused of contempt of court for violating a labor injunction may demand a jury trial before another judge than the one issuing the temporary injunction.

**Railway Labor Act (1934).** The purpose of this act was to avoid interruption of interstate commerce by promoting orderly and peaceful settlement of railroad labor disputes. The Act was designed, through a National Mediation Board, to safeguard the rights of railroad employees to self-organization and collective bargaining, and to seek adjustment of disputes through a National Railroad Adjustment Board.

**National Labor Relations Act (1935).** This act seeks to safeguard the right of labor to bargain collectively, by creating a National Labor Relations Board. The Board has the power to prevent interference by employers with the workers' right to organize or to bargain; to prevent employer domination through a company union; to prevent discrimination by an employer against a worker for labor union activities; and to conduct elections among workers to determine employee representation and the appropriate union for collective bargaining.

**Labor-Management Relations (Taft-Hartley) Act (1947).** This act grew out of alleged pro-labor one-sidedness in the National Labor Relations Act, which it amended. Among its provisions are the following:

(1) *Reorganization:* To meet criticisms that the National Labor Relations Board was acting as both judge and prosecutor, the Board was provided with an independent General Counsel having exclusive authority to issue complaints.

(2) *Unhampered rights of employees:* Except as to union shop requirements (see next paragraph), employees may join or refrain from joining any union, without restraint or intimidation.

(3) *Union shop v. closed shop:* The closed shop (hiring only union members) is banned: workers need not belong to a union to get a job, but must join after they get it ("union shop"), where such arrangement is supported by a majority vote of workers.

(4) *Unfair labor practices by unions* as well as by management are prohibited, including: (a) Coercion by unions or employers in the selection of bargaining representatives; (b) Discrimination, under the open shop (hiring both union and nonunion men), against nonunion employees; (c) Union refusal to bargain; (d) Illegal strikes and boycotts (pages 441 to 444); (e) Discriminatory or excessive initiation fees for joining a union; and (f) "Featherbedding" (page 444).

(5) *Free speech* is guaranteed to employers in expressing views on

labor problems to their employees, so long as they contain "no threat of reprisal or force or promise of benefit."

(6) **Unions must file reports** on money taken in, and what was done with it.

(7) **Communists** are prevented from holding union offices, and union officers must take oaths that they are not communists.

(8) **Unions of foremen or other supervisory personnel** are not embraced within the benefits of the Act.

(9) **Compulsory check-offs,** under which employers must deduct union dues from union wages and turn them over to the unions, are abolished, each worker having a right to decide for himself whether he will permit a check-off on his wages.

(10) **Strikes which may create national emergencies:** See page 442.

(11) **"Cooling-off" period:** See page 442.

(12) **Union liability:** Employers may sue unions for breach of collective bargaining agreements.

**State Statutes.** The foregoing Federal statutes, as stated, apply only to businesses affecting interstate commerce. However, many states have adopted laws modeled after the Norris-LaGuardia and National Labor Relations acts, so that intrastate as well as interstate industrial disputes are now largely governed by statute.

## Industrial Pressure Devices

**Summary.** The foregoing regulatory statutes have been necessitated by the results of the unrestricted play of labor-management pressures. In the course of industrial disputes, each side has exerted various pressure devices against the other. On the part of labor, these have included (a) strikes, (b) picketing, (c) boycotts and (d) sabotage, and on the part of management, (e) lockouts, including shutdowns and plant removals, (f) strikebreaking, (g) blacklisting, (h) espionage, and (i) "yellow-dog" agreements.

**Strikes.** A strike is defined as a concerted cessation of work by wage earners in support of some common purpose. The usual strike is one where wage earners quit work in support of a demand of their own. Where they quit work to support the demands of others, the stoppage is known as a *sympathetic* or *sympathy* strike. If a sympathy strike spreads to a wide area of unrelated trades or industries, it is known as a *general strike*. If it is based on a dispute between employee groups of various trades—such as carpenters and metal workers, or bricklayers and stone masons—as to which has the right to do a given job or control a given situation, it is known as a *jurisdictional strike*. Where strikers not only quit work but in effect take possession of the employer's plant, live there, and physically prevent the employer and others from coming in, their action is known as a *sit-down strike*. Sympathy and jurisdictional strikes are outlawed under the Labor-Management Relations Act. General strikes have been condemned as wholly lacking in legitimate motive or purpose. Sit-down strikes have likewise been declared illegal.[11]

*Strikes over labor-saving devices.* The courts are far from agreed on the question whether a union may call a strike because the employer has utilized labor-saving machinery. The weight of authority appears to support the view expressed by the Court of Appeals of the State of New York, that "For a union to insist that machinery be discarded in order that manual labor may take its place and thus secure additional opportunity of employment is not a lawful labor objective." [12]

*National emergencies.* The Labor-Management Relations Act sets up a special procedure in the case of a strike or threatened strike which might create a national emergency. The principal features of this procedure are the appointment by the President of the United States of a board of inquiry whose report is to be made public, coupled with authority to procure an injunction against the strike, followed by a 60-day period for collective bargaining and, if necessary, a further 15-day period for a secret ballot of employees under the auspices of the National Labor Relations Board.

*"Cooling-off" period.* Where there is danger of work stoppage toward the expiration of a collective bargaining contract covering employees in an industry affecting interstate commerce, the Labor-Management Relations Act provides a "cooling-off" period of 60 days prior to such work stoppage. Neither party to a dispute under such contract may terminate or modify it without (1) First serving a written notice on the other party 60 days prior to the expiration of the contract, of the proposed termination or modification; (2) Offering to meet and confer with the other party for the purpose of negotiating a new or modified contract; (3) Notifying the Federal Mediation and Conciliation Service and corresponding state agencies of the existence of the dispute; and (4) Continuing without work stoppage under all the terms and conditions of the existing contract, for at least 60 days after serving the written notice.

*Strikes by government employees.* The Labor-Management Relations Act provides that any employee who strikes against the United States Government or a government corporation shall be discharged, and forfeits his civil-service status.

*Picketing.* To "picket" a place is to patrol it, or parade in front of it, usually with placards, posters or similar devices designed to influence employees and the general public; the former, to refrain from working in the establishment, the latter, to refrain from patronizing it. Picketing usually accompanies a strike as a supporting pressure, in the nature of a

---

[11] *N.L.R.B. v. Fansteel Metallurgical Corporation,* 306 U.S. 240 (1938).

[12] *Opera on Tour v. Weber,* 285 N.Y. 348, 34 N.E. 2d 349, certiorari denied, 314 U.S. 615 (1941).

primary boycott (see below). Where it is organized and conducted by persons or groups not connected with the establishment, for the purpose of unionizing it, supplanting a union already there, or for some other purpose, it is sometimes referred to as "outsider" or "stranger" picketing. Court decisions on picketing have been conflicting in the extreme. Under the earlier decisions, all picketing, whether by the employees concerned or by outsiders, and whether peaceful or otherwise, was regarded as illegal by the courts. The more recent decisions, however, tend to distinguish between direct and "stranger" picketing, upholding the former and condemning the latter, and to sustain "peaceful picketing"—free from violence, libel and fraud—as a constitutionally protected form of free speech.[13]

**Mass picketing.** Although some cases have held that mass picketing was not necessarily inconsistent with peaceful picketing, the majority of decisions have followed the reasoning of the Supreme Court that "All persuasion used under such circumstances was intimidation," [14] and that mass picketing violated the constitutional guaranties of liberty and property, hence could not be legalized by state statute.[15]

**Boycott.** The boycott (named after Captain Boycott, an Irish land agent against whom the practice was first employed) is a concerted refusal to deal with a person, business or industrial establishment. It may be promoted or furthered by striking, picketing, advertising, the adoption of a union label, notices or editorials in the press or other publications, or by word of mouth. A *primary* boycott is one in which only those directly concerned participate, such as employees seeking to redress a grievance. A *secondary* boycott is one where pressure is brought to bear on others than those directly concerned. Thus, a strike by employees seeking a higher wage is in effect a primary boycott. If the strikers seek to influence outsiders not to deal with their employer, they thereby pursue a secondary boycott. From the outset the courts, with but a few exceptions, have condemned the boycott, especially the secondary boycott, the latter being regarded as an unfair conscription of neutrals. In the latter part of the nineteenth and the opening years of the twentieth century, labor organizations resorted extensively to boycotting until it was successfully challenged by employers in two leading cases, the Danbury Hatters' Case,[16] and the Bucks Stove and Range Case.[17] Under the National Labor Relations Act as amended by the Labor-Management Act, and under many of the state statutes, secondary boycotts are outlawed. There must be a community of interest between the boycotters

---

[13] *Thornhill v. Alabama*, 310 U.S. 88 (1940).

[14] *American Steel Foundries Co. v. Tri-City Central Trades Council*, 257 U.S. 184 (1921).

[15] *Truax v. Corrigan*, 257 U.S. 312 (1921).

[16] *Lowe v. Lawlor*, 208 U.S. 274 (1908).

[17] *Gompers v. Bucks Stove and Range Co.*, 221 U.S. 418 (1911).

and those whom they seek to help. However, the Labor-Management Relations Act expressly reserves the right of any person to refrain from entering the premises of another whose employees are engaged in a valid strike.

**Sabotage.** The word "sabotage" (from the French *sabot*, or wooden shoe, causing one to "drag his feet") is used to cover all forms of deliberate impediments to production, either by damaging or destroying the means of production, or by slowing it down. There are numerous forms of sabotage, some merely costly to the employer, others dangerous to life and limb. Among its forms are the following: limiting the daily number of bricks to be laid, doors to be hung, or radiators to be installed; limiting the width of a painter's brush to cut down painting efficiency; slowing down a worker's pace (if done in concert, this is sometimes miscalled a "slow-down strike"); soaping railroad tracks on a grade to impede transportation; mixing cement in improper proportions, thereby weakening building, bridge and other constructions, with resultant hazard to life and limb. This form of labor pressure is now generally condemned by most unions and the public generally.

**Featherbedding.** The Labor-Management Relations Act provides[18] that it shall be an unfair labor practice "to cause or attempt to cause an employer to pay or deliver or agree to pay or deliver any money or other thing of value, in the nature of an exaction, for services which are not performed or not to be performed."

**Lockouts, Shutdowns and Plant Removals.** Employers faced with threatened unionization, strikes or other labor pressures have adopted, as countermeasures, threatened or actual plant shutdowns, accompanied by "lockouts" or mass discharge of employees, with threatened or actual refusal of re-employment, and in many cases, removal of plants to non-union communities. This form of labor pressure was especially available to concerns having out-of-town plants, or organized on a nationwide basis.[19] Until recent years, lockouts enjoyed the same legal status as strikes. In recent years, labor legislation has tended to restrict lockouts if they interfered with labor's right to organize. Under the National Labor Relations Act and its state counterparts, lockouts, shutdowns and plant removals, actual or threatened, constitute an unfair labor practice unless the shutdown or plant removal results from economic necessity or other cause not connected with the exercise of a labor pressure.

**Strikebreaking.** To counteract strikes and reinforce lockouts, employers have in many cases replaced striking employees with non-union substi-

---

[18] Sec. 8 (b) (6).

[19] Examples are the Tubize Chatillon Corporation lockout at Hopewell, Va. in 1934, and the Great Atlantic & Pacific Tea Company shutdown at Cleveland, Ohio in the same year.

tutes (opprobriously referred to by striking employees as "scabs"). Frequently, in such cases, employers have drawn upon professional substitutes, known as "strikebreakers," supplied by concerns organized for this purpose. Strikebreaking may take various forms, some of them now prohibited by Federal statute in industries affecting interstate commerce, and by state statute in others. Among these are anti-union propaganda, the use or threat of violence, separate solicitation or persuasion of employees, discriminatory reinstatements, and the employment of strikebreaking agencies. Many states[20] make it a penal offense for an employer or employment agency to advertise for help during the existence of a strike without stating the fact of its existence.

**Blacklisting.** Employers and employers' associations have in times past maintained mutual exchanges or "clearing houses" of information, designated as "black lists," concerning discharged or former employees known to be active in labor unions, strikes, or labor agitation generally. This information has been imparted to prospective employers to warn them against hiring such employees. It has effectually prevented hiring in many cases. Under the common law it was difficult to base a successful suit on the practice of blacklisting, because of the secrecy maintained by employers, the difficulty of proving libel or slander, and the difficulty of proving loss or damage. The practice, however, has been outlawed in a majority of states. In many of these,[21] blacklisting has been made criminal by statute. In many other states,[22] however, the practice is undisturbed by statute. The National Labor Relations Act contains no express provision outlawing the practice of blacklisting, but the Supreme Court has held that a combination to blacklist workmen was subject to prosecution under the Sherman Anti-Trust Act.[23] Also, a threat to blacklist has been held to constitute an unfair labor practice.[24] In some states "Little Wagner" or State labor relations acts declare blacklisting an unfair labor practice.[25]

**Espionage.** Labor spies have been frequently employed in the past, either from within or outside a business organization, to report on labor

---

[20] Including California, Colorado, Connecticut, Illinois, Indiana, Maine, Massachusetts, Minnesota, Montana, New Hampshire, Nevada, Oklahoma, Oregon, Pennsylvania, South Dakota, Tennessee, Virginia, Washington, Wisconsin, Wyoming.

[21] Including Arizona, Arkansas, California, Colorado, Connecticut, Florida, Illinois, Indiana, Iowa, Kansas, Maine, Minnesota, Mississippi, Missouri, Montana, Nevada, North Carolina, North Dakota, Oklahoma, Oregon, Texas, Utah, Virginia, Washington, and Wisconsin. The statute in Arizona, however, has been declared unconstitutional for vagueness.

[22] Including Delaware, Georgia, Idaho, Kentucky, Louisiana, Maryland, Massachusetts, Michigan, New Hampshire, New Jersey, Ohio, Pennsylvania, Rhode Island, South Carolina, South Dakota, Tennessee, Vermont, West Virginia, and Wyoming.

[23] *Anderson v. Ship Owners*, 272 U.S. 359 (1926).

[24] 2 N.L.R.B. 117, enforced in 90 F. 2d 1017 (1937).

[25] Examples are Minnesota, New York and Wisconsin.

meetings, labor plans, projected strikes and labor disaffections generally, with a view to adopting timely countermeasures, and of furnishing to employers, as a basis for dismissal, the names of employees active in such matters. Espionage by an employer on the legitimate activities of employees constitutes an unfair labor practice under the National Labor Relations Act. However, when the espionage is conducted for the purpose of checking improper or unwarranted activities, or conduct which the employer has a right to forbid, such as the solicitation of union membership during working hours, the courts will sustain the employer.[26]

**Yellow-Dog Contracts.** The so-called "yellow-dog" contract, as noted on page 439, relates to an agreement not to join a union as a condition for being hired. This type of employer pressure proved quite effective during the period of its active use. A majority of states have adopted statutes similar to the Norris-LaGuardia Act (page 439) aimed at outlawing contracts of this type. By prohibiting acts interfering with the right to unionize, the National Labor Relations Act has necessarily prohibited contracts of this nature.

## Questions

1. What is a "yellow-dog" contract?
2. What was the purpose of the Norris-LaGuardia Act?
3. Name three conditions that must be established before a Federal injunction can be issued against striking employees.
4. What is the function of the Railway Labor Act?
5. Name four powers of the National Labor Relations Board.
6. Give ten provisions of the Labor-Management Relations (Taft-Hartley) Act.
7. Name four pressure devices exerted on the part of labor against management, and five now or formerly exerted by management against labor.
8. Name four different types of strikes.
9. Name the three types of strikes condemned as illegal.
10. What is the attitude of most state jurisdictions with respect to the right of a union to call a strike because the employer has utilized a labor-saving device?
11. Summarize the procedure set up in the Labor-Management Relations Act in case of a strike or threatened strike which might create a national emergency.
12. What are the four provisions of the "cooling-off" period covering employees in an industry affecting interstate commerce?
13. Distinguish between direct picketing and stranger picketing? What is the attitude of most courts toward mass picketing?
14. What provision is made with respect to boycotts under the Labor-Management (Taft-Hartley) Act?
15. What is meant by featherbedding?
16. What is the legal status of (a) lockouts, shutdowns and plant removals; (b) strikebreaking; (c) blacklisting; (d) labor espionage?

---

[26] *N.L.R.B. v. J. L. Brandeis & Sons,* 145 F. 2d 556 (1945).

## Problems

1. The employer of a large manufacturing concern engaged in interstate commerce maintains a policy of hiring no employees unless they first sign a contract that they will not join a union. In violation of their agreement, the employees of this establishment join a union, call a strike and picket the employer's place of business. The employer applies to the Federal Court for an injunction restraining the employees from continuing to strike, and from picketing his establishment. Judgment for whom and why?

2. A union representing the employees of the Atlas Corporation, engaged in interstate commerce, calls a strike in violation of a collective bargaining agreement with the corporation. As a result, the employers sustain a $100,000 loss, for which the corporation brings suit against the union. Judgment for whom and why?

3. The letter carriers of a midwestern city organize a union and make demands on the postmaster for higher wages and shorter hours. Upon being refused, they institute a strike and remain away from their employment for two weeks. The strike proves a failure, whereupon the men seek to return to their erstwhile positions, but are informed by the postmaster that they have been discharged. They then institute reinstatement proceedings before the National Labor Relations Board. What is the decision and why?

4. Carroll's Meat Market is a thriving establishment, but of late has been having labor trouble. The employees call a strike and seek to dissuade the public from patronizing the concern, but to no avail. They then visit Dalton's Wholesale Products, Inc., upon which Carroll depends for his meats, and demand that Dalton stop selling meat to Carroll, but are met with a refusal. However, they do succeed in persuading Dalton's employees to threaten a strike unless Dalton stops dealing with Carroll. Carroll and Dalton both seek an injunction. Will they succeed? Explain.

5. The employees of a large organization engage in a sit-down strike for better working conditions. They are finally dislodged by police with the aid of tear-gas, and are subsequently discharged from their jobs. In a suit brought by them for reinstatement, how should the National Labor Relations Board decide, and why?

## PART 3. SOCIAL LEGISLATION

**Nature and Purpose.** The term "social legislation" is applied in a loose sense to all legislation which seeks to improve, protect or advance the interests of a particular social group, on the ground that such group is somehow at a disadvantage, and that legislation to redress the disadvantage is not only morally just, but in the interest of society as a whole. Social legislation may be directed to a given age group, such as children up to or older persons beyond a given age; to an economic group, such as selected classes of employees; or to physically handicapped groups, such as the blind, the crippled or the insane.

**Legal Basis: Police Power.** Social legislation may be inspired by the dictates of decency or the maintenance of civilized standards, but legal support for it under our constitutional restrictions against class legislation must be found in the police power (page 13), that is, the legislation must be truly necessary for the protection of public health, safety, morals and the general welfare. Thus, child labor is abolished or severely restricted, not merely because of its morally pernicious character, but because of its deleterious effect upon the future of the country. Sweatshops are legislated against, not merely because of their unsanitary and constricting effect on the sweated workers, but because of their demoralizing effect on the public. Collective bargaining legislation is justified not only on the moral ground that the individual worker is at a disadvantage in bargaining with his employer, but on the broader social ground that such legislation is in the public interest because it tends to retard work stoppages and labor strife. Laws dealing with workmen's compensation, and with impoverished old age and unemployment, apart from their benevolent basis, are justified under the police power because they deal with evils which create serious fiscal and administrative problems and threaten the public weal.

In our discussion of social legislation, we shall briefly review the major measures adopted during the first half of the present century, including: (a) Wage laws creating liens, priorities and preferences; (b) Minimum wage laws; (c) Child labor; (d) Workmen's compensation laws; and (e) Social security laws.

### (a) Wage Laws Creating Liens, Priorities and Preferences

**Purpose.** In an attempt to offset the consequences of financial insecurity to which workers and their families may be subjected when their wages are threatened by business irregularities or failures, laws have been passed creating various liens, priorities and preferences.

**Liens.** Under the common law (that is, in the absence of statute), a worker, as such, has no lien to secure payment for work done, but must go to the trouble of a lawsuit to collect unpaid wages. It is only when he works on a chattel as an independent contractor that he is given a lien on the chattel.

EXAMPLES:
(1) The proprietor of a jewelry store requests one of his employees, a watchmaker, to repair a watch in stock. The employee repairs the watch, then is told the store is about to close down for lack of business. If the employee is unpaid, his only remedy at common law is to sue for his wages.
(2) Say the employee then opens a watch repair shop. His first customer, on calling for his repaired watch, pleads poverty and promises to pay for the repair in a few weeks. The watchmaker, protected by an artisan's lien, may retain possession of the watch until he is paid.

Statutes have been passed in various states conferring on employees, for unpaid labor, liens against specified assets of the employer.

**Priorities and Preferences.** Debtor and creditor laws in many states give priority to wage claims on the liquidation of an insolvent debtor's assets. The National Bankruptcy Act likewise gives wage claims priority over the claims of general creditors. (See page 724.) Court actions based on wage claims are frequently given trial priority over other actions. State laws throughout the country grant wage earners personal exemption from legal process in respect to wages, wearing apparel, jewelry and other personal effects, and various occupational exemptions, such as those affecting tools and implements of trade.

*Penalties for withholding wages.* Labor laws in some states impose criminal penalties for withholding or delaying payment of wages justly due.

### (b) Minimum Wage Laws

**Background.** Minimum wage legislation was originally invoked in connection with women and children in industry. In 1923, Congress passed a law fixing minimum wages for women and children in the District of Columbia. The Supreme Court declared the act unconstitutional on the ground that it interfered with the liberty of contract.[27] Similar decisions followed with respect to similar statutes in other states,[28] and still other states repealed their corresponding statutes.[29] In the post-depression period following the financial panic of 1929, new minimum wage laws were adopted in seven states. One of these was New York, where a minimum wage law for women was declared unconstitutional by the Court of Appeals,[30] on the ground that it interfered with the liberty of contract. The decision was sustained by the United States Supreme Court.[31] In the following year, this trend was reversed in the case of *West Coast Hotel Co. v. Parrish*,[32] in connection with a minimum wage law for women and minors adopted by the State of Washington. Under that law, a chambermaid employed by the West Coast Hotel Company brought suit to recover the difference between the wages paid her and the legal minimum of $14.50 for a 48-hour week. The hotel company challenged the constitutionality of the law. The United States Supreme Court, overruling its prior opinions, sustained the constitutionality of the statute, declaring, in an opinion by Chief Justice Hughes, that nothing could be closer to the public welfare (upon which the police power is based) than the health of women and their protection against industrial exploitation.

**Fair Labor Standards Act.** With this background of constitutionality, Congress in the following year (1938) adopted the Fair Labor Standards

---

[27] *Adkins v. Children's Hospital*, 261 U.S. 525 (1923).

[28] Arizona: *Murphy v. Sardell*, 269 U.S. 530 (1925); Arkansas: *Donham v. West Nelson Manufacturing Co.*, 273 U.S. 657 (1927); Kansas: *Topeka Laundry Co. v. Court of Industrial Relations*, 119 Kans. 12, 237 Pac. 1041 (1925).

[29] Nebraska, Texas and Utah.

[30] *People ex rel. Tipaldo v. Morehead*, 270 N.Y. 233, 200 N.E. 799 (1936).

[31] *Morehead v. People ex rel. Tipaldo*, 298 U.S. 587 (1936).

[32] 300 U.S. 379 (1937).

Act (popularly referred to as the Wage and Hour Law). It provides a minimum wage as base pay and time and a half for overtime for workers engaged in interstate commerce or in producing goods for interstate commerce. The minimum base wage, under a 1949 amendment, became 75 cents an hour. The Act also fixed maximum base-pay hours on a graduated scale, beginning with 44 hours a week the first year and ultimately going down to 40 hours a week. In respect to all goods affecting interstate commerce, the Act prohibits the employment of children under fourteen years of age, but permits the employment of children between the ages of fourteen and sixteen years, except in mining and manufacturing. The constitutionality of this Act was upheld by the United States Supreme Court in 1941.[33]

### (c) Child Labor

**Laws Regulating Child Labor.** Child labor laws were originally introduced in this country in conjunction with compulsory education laws, prohibiting employment of children under a given age during the school term. These were supplemented by factory laws limiting the employment of children as to age, hours and overtime. Court decisions from time to time have declared various child labor laws unconstitutional. As a result, a child labor amendment to the United States Constitution has been pending for a number of years, awaiting approval by the requisite number of states. In the meantime, as previously noted, the *Wage-Hour Law* established an important child labor provision in the field of interstate commerce, which was sustained by the Supreme Court.

### (d) Workmen's Compensation

**Nature and Purpose.** The underlying basis of workmen's compensation is an assurance of compensation notwithstanding disability through injury. The emphasis is on compensation rather than damage. The latter measures loss through someone's fault. No fault is attached to workmen's compensation. The law recognizes it as a legitimate burden upon industry: an element of cost as important, at the very least, as the cost of maintaining plant and equipment.

**Employers' Liability *v.* Workmen's Compensation.** Under employers' liability acts the theory of recovery is damage for actionable wrong, with the employer deprived of certain common law defenses. On the other hand, "Compensation laws proceed upon the theory that the injured workingman is entitled to pecuniary relief from the distress caused by his injury, as a matter of right, unless his own willful act is the proximate cause." [34]

---

[33] *United States v. Darby*, 312 U.S. 100.
[34] *Lewis & Clark v. Industrial Acc. Bd.*, 52 Mont. 6, 155 P. 268, 269.

Liability and Compensation Laws in United States. As an example of the employers' liability type of statute, we have the Federal Employers' Liability Act of 1908,[35] enlarging the remedies of employees against railroad companies engaged in interstate commerce, by modifying or limiting the assumption of risk, contributory negligence and fellow-servant rules. As an example of Federal workmen's compensation acts, we have the Federal Employee's Compensation Act of 1916, as amended and extended,[36] which provides workmen's compensation benefits for civil officers and employees as well as for members of the Army, Navy, Air Force and Coast Guard reserve.

State workmen's compensation laws vary widely in many details. Basically, however, they are fairly uniform as to types of employment and types of injuries covered, and as to major benefits bestowed. Compensation laws are compulsory in some states, elective in others. Methods of insuring the risks are substantially uniform.

Coverage: Personnel. Workmen's compensation laws are primarily designed to protect workers in hazardous occupations. The statutes in most states specifically designate the employments classed as hazardous under the act. Since these designations are usually broad, a majority of American workers are protected by workmen's compensation. Most states, however, exclude domestic servants, agricultural workers and employees of non-profit enterprises. About half the states exclude workers in establishments employing fewer than a specified number of persons. Independent contractors and casual workers are excluded, but not all courts are agreed on the definition of a casual worker. In *Bates v. Nelson*,[37] an employee was hired to work in a store and filling station and to do odd jobs around the employer's residence, such as putting up and taking down storm windows and screens. The court held that such employment was not "casual," and that the employee was entitled to compensation for injuries sustained in falling from a ladder while putting up storm windows on the employer's home. On the other hand, in *Schindler v. McFee*,[38] a roofer was hired to put a roof on an owner's warehouse. He inspected the roof from time to time, and made repairs when needed, with or without consulting the owner, who subsequently paid the roofer. The court held that the roofer was engaged in casual employment, precluding recovery of compensation for injuries sustained while replacing a jack on the warehouse chimney.

Coverage: Injuries. Employees engaged in hazardous occupations are entitled to the benefits of workmen's compensation provided: (1) the injuries are the result of an accident, (2) they arise out of and during

---

[35] 45 U.S.C.A., secs. 51-59.
[36] Including the Longshoremen's and Harbor Workers' Act, 33 U.S.C.A. 901-950.
[37] 240 Iowa 926, 38 N.W. 2d 631.
[38] 69 Idaho 436, 207 P. 2d 1158.

the course of employment, and (3) they are not wilful or intentional, nor due to the employee's intoxication while on duty.

**Medical and Surgical Care.** Practically all compensation laws provide medical and surgical care following injury. In about half the states, medical and surgical attendance is limited to periods ranging from two to one hundred months.

**Compensation Benefits.** Compensation is fixed in accordance with schedules based upon (1) wages paid, (2) extent of injury or incapacity and (3) in case of death, decedent's wage scale and the number and status of his dependents.

**Methods of Insuring Risks.** Each employer must insure the risks incurred by him and imposed by law for the payment of workmen's compensation benefits. This insurance may take three forms:

(1) Insurance with a stock or mutual insurance company;

(2) Insurance with a state insurance fund; and

(3) Self-insurance, where the employer can furnish proof of financial ability to pay the compensation himself, accompanied by the deposit of adequate security with the state commission to support such proof.

### (e) Social Security

**Basic Objective.** The basic objective of social security legislation is to alleviate the principal causes of economic insecurity. These include old age, unemployment, physical handicaps and dependent children.

**Social Security Act: Program and Scope.** The Social Security Act embraces three major programs: (1) *Social Insurance*, including (a) old-age benefits to retiring workers, their families and survivors and (b) unemployment insurance; (2) *Public Assistance to the Needy*, including (a) old-age assistance, (b) aid to the needy blind and (c) aid to dependent children; and (3) *Health and Welfare Services*, including (a) child welfare service, (b) services for crippled children, (c) maternal and child health services and (d) public health services. The first two program groups are administered by the Social Security Administration, the third by the various states. Most widely known of these programs are the insurance features: old age and survivors' insurance, and insurance against unemployment.

**Old-Age and Survivors' Insurance.** The purpose of old-age and survivors' insurance is to provide monthly benefits for workers and their families upon old-age retirement or death. The benefits are built up by premium payments in the form of a special tax imposed equally on worker and employer, at varying rates fixed by Congress. The 1950 amendment continued an existing 3 per cent rate (1½ per cent each for employer and employee) for each of the years 1951 through 1953, and prescribed a 4 per cent rate for 1954-1959, a 5 per cent rate for 1960-1964, a 6 per cent rate for 1965-1969 and a 6½ per cent rate for 1970 and after. The tax is based on wages paid by each employer to an employee, up to $3600 per annum. Self-employed persons provide the entire tax, but pay at a somewhat smaller rate than the combined employer-employee rate.

*Worker's social security account.* The Social Security Board keeps a social security account for each individual worker. A worker who is about to be employed obtains a social security card from the Social Security Board, with his name and number stamped or printed on the card. For each three-month period ending March 31, June 30, September 30, and December 31, every employer is required to make out a report to the Collector of Internal Revenue, giving the name of each employee, his social security number, and his wages for the period. Each worker's wages, as reported by his employer, are credited to his individual "social security account." When a worker files a claim, the wages credited to his account are used to compute the amount of his benefit.

*Employments covered.* The original Social Security Act covered most classes of employment, with certain specified exceptions, some of which have been eliminated by amendments extending the range of social security. For example, the 1950 amendment extended social security to domestic servants, farm workers and even self-employed tradesmen.

*Eligibility for benefits: "quarters of coverage."* A worker, to be eligible for benefits, must have worked in a covered employment for at least a given period. This period is measured in "quarters of coverage." A quarter of coverage is a three months' period beginning the first day of January, April, July or October, in which a person has received $50 or more in wages, or for which he has been credited with $100 or more of self-employment income. A worker is eligible for benefits to himself or his family only if he has had at least six "quarters of coverage," which need not have been consecutive.

*Benefits.* Monthly benefits fall into two classes: (1) retirement payments and (2) survivor payments. In addition, if no one is eligible for survivor payments on the worker's death, (3) lump-sum payments may be made.

**Unemployment Insurance.** This part of the Social Security Act seeks to encourage states to set up systems of unemployment insurance in accordance with certain prescribed standards. If a state passes an unemployment insurance law conforming to the prescribed standard, the Federal Government undertakes to collect a special payroll tax from employers (not to be confused with the old-age insurance tax). The employers of that state are given a credit of 90 per cent against the unemployment tax levied by the Federal Government. Thus, the Federal Government imposes a 3 per cent unemployment tax on all employers subject to the Act. As to the employers of any state which has adopted an unemployment insurance law meeting the Federal requirements, the Federal Government allows the employers in such state, in filling out their tax returns, to deduct a credit for the state unemployment tax paid by them, up to 90 per cent of the Federal tax, remitting the remainder to the Federal Government.

*Tax on employers only.* The unemployment insurance tax, based on the employer's payroll, is paid by the employer alone. The employee contributes nothing.

*Who must make Federal returns.* Employers in covered establishments need not make Federal unemployment insurance returns unless they employ eight or more persons during at least twenty weeks of the year. However, many states[39] impose an unemployment insurance tax in establishments having but one employee or more, others[40] three or more, still others[41] four or more, and several,[42] six or more. Twenty-three states[43] prescribe the Federal minimum of eight or more employees.

**Old-Age Assistance.** The Social Security Act provides for Federal grants to states which have old-age pension laws approved by the Social Security Administration. Old-age assistance has nothing to do with old-age insurance. It is furnished to needy persons of advanced age, as a noncontributory pension.

## Questions

1. What is the nature and purpose of social legislation? What is its legal basis? Name five major types of such legislation.

2. In what three respects have statutes provided wage earners with remedies not available under the common law, in connection with money due for services rendered?

3. State the main provisions of the Fair Labor Standards Act (Wage and Hour Law).

4. What are the major restrictions found in child labor statutes?

5. What is the underlying basis of the Workmen's Compensation Law?

6. What is the basic distinction between employers' liability and workmen's compensation acts?

7. Name four classes of persons not covered by Workmen's Compensation.

8. In order that an employee, who is engaged in a hazardous occupation and who sustains injuries, may be entitled to the benefits of Workmen's Compensation, three conditions are necessary. What are they?

---

[39] Including Arkansas, California, Delaware, Idaho, Maryland, Massachusetts, Minnesota, Montana, Nevada, Pennsylvania, Utah, Washington and Wyoming.

[40] Arizona and Ohio.

[41] Including Connecticut, Louisiana, New Hampshire, New Jersey, New York, Oregon, and Rhode Island.

[42] Illinois and Wisconsin.

[43] Including Alabama, Colorado, Florida, Georgia, Indiana, Iowa, Kansas, Kentucky, Maine, Michigan, Mississippi, Missouri, Nebraska, North Carolina, North Dakota, Oklahoma, South Carolina, South Dakota, Tennessee, Texas, Vermont, Virginia, and West Virginia.

9. The schedules for payment of compensation in all applicable cases are based upon what three elements?

10. What are the three forms of insurance available to an employer desiring Workmen's Compensation?

11. What is the basic objective of social security legislation?

12. What are the three major programs embraced by the Social Security Act?

13. Name the three types of benefit payments under the Social Security Act.

14. Who must make Federal returns with respect to unemployment insurance?

## Problems

1. I. M. Sloe, an employer, finds difficulty in managing his business profitably. He owes Needham, an employee, two weeks' wages. When Needham presses Sloe for his wages, Sloe discharges him. Has Needham any remedy besides suing for his wages?

2. Thomas & Sons are endeavoring to establish a new business. Feeling their way, on a conservative and economical basis, they hire employees at an initial salary below the legal basis established by law. Prosecuted for violating the minimum wage law, Thomas & Sons challenge the constitutionality of the statute, on the ground that it interferes with their right freely to contract with whom and on what basis they please. Will they sustain their legal position?

3. A local merchant, finding himself rushed during the Christmas week, requires his employees to work overtime for a period of three consecutive weeks. He refuses, however, to pay anything for overtime. One of the employees asks whether the employer has not violated the Fair Labor Standards Act. What do you think?

4. A salesman was killed while riding a motorcycle for a corporation dealing in lumber, coal and feed. His widow filed a claim with the employer for benefits under the Workmen's Compensation Act, for herself and the minor children. Should she receive an award?

5. A laundry using power-driven machinery hired claimant to solicit business for the firm. While so engaged, claimant was injured and filed a claim for compensation under the Workmen's Compensation Act. Should his claim be honored?

6. Frank Meany, an expert mechanic employed with the Higrade Machine Works, objects to any deduction from his wages for either old-age benefits or unemployment insurance. His employers, unwilling to lose the benefit of Meany's services, accede to his wishes, but nevertheless contribute their share toward the deductions required under the law. What, if any, are the legal consequences of this situation?

## COURT CASES FOR REVIEW

### How Did the Court Decide, and Why?

1. A letter purporting to be written on the letterhead of "Archbishop of North America" of the Russian Orthodox Greek Catholic Church and addressed to "Father Simeon" recited that the writer was asking the addressee's superiors "to have you with me in America. Please come. Here is really not as bad, as said. You will receive free quarters and a salary of not less than 180 rubles per month. . . . The government now does not advance money. We

will get later, I hope." The promises embodied in the foregoing letter were subsequently made the subject of a suit for breach of contract. *Nikulnikoff v. Archbishop, etc., of Russian Orthodox Greek Catholic Church,* 142 Misc. 894, 255 N.Y. Supp. 653.

2. An employee was hired for a year at an annual salary of $3,000 plus commissions. He was guaranteed at least $6,000 for the first year. There was to be a settlement at least once a year. The employee began work on October 16, 1945. He was continued in service after the expiration of the first year, but was discharged on February 1, 1947 for reasons of economy. He sued on the ground that his contract had been renewed for a year, and breached. *Smith v. Shallcross,* 165 Pa. Super. 472, 69 A. 2d 156.

3. The secretary of a labor union sued to recover on claims for wages assigned to him by a group of union billposters and theater ushers. The employees were to be paid by the week. They worked Monday, Tuesday and Wednesday of the week. On Thursday there was a strike by one or two other unions with which their unions were affiliated. An audience of 2,000 attended the theater Thursday night, but there was no performance because of the absence of ushers. The ushers did not report for work Friday or Saturday either. *Solotaroff v. Willner-Edelstein Amusement Co.,* 85 Misc. 445, 147 N.Y. Supp. 938.

4. Plaintiff employee broke his arm. He was working near a pile of lumber more than four feet high, when part of the pile fell and one of the larger pieces knocked him to the ground. He sued for the injuries sustained. The jury gave him judgment, and defendant appealed. *Smith v. United Lumber Co.,* 71 W.Va. 741, 77 S.E. 330.

5. Two dining car waiters, during a lull between meals, engaged in horseplay with a revolver, which went off and killed a third waiter. Suit was brought against the railroad company for failure to ensure decedent a safe place to work. *Lavender v. Illinois Cent. R. Co.,* 358 Mo. 1160, 219 S.W. 2d 353.

6. The owner of an airplane employed a mechanic who assisted the pilot on takeoffs and weather observations, and who occupied the co-pilot's seat where, if necessary, he could exercise equal control of the flight. The plane crashed and the mechanic lost his life, allegedly because of the pilot's negligence. *Baruch v. Sapp,* 178 F. 2d 382.

7. In a suit to establish the rights of an employer to the inventions of its employees, the evidence disclosed the following facts: There was an established practice whereby employees were required to assign to their employer inventions developed during the course of employment. Plaintiff employee not only knew of the practice, but acquiesced in it. Problems covered by inventions were assigned to him, and his inventions were made during the period of his employment. He used his employer's facilities and indicated that the work he was doing was for the employer's benefit, and that his inventions would be assigned. *Marshall v. Colgate-Palmolive-Peet Co.,* 175 F. 2d 215.

8. An employee-inventor worked privately on a new tire-demounter device. He did all his work on the device at his home, and not on the employer's time. He refused to give his employer a bill of materials or to take a model of the demounter to his employer's plant, and he insisted that he was the owner of the invention. The employer disputed this, and sued. *Gemco Engineering & Mfg. Co. v. Henderson,* 151 Ohio St. 95, 84 N.E. 2d 596.

9. The legality of a picket line was attacked under a New Jersey statute which prohibited picketing, except in furtherance of lawful strikes. The dispute hinged on whether a walk-out of four out of sixteen employees constituted

a strike. *Gevas v. Greek Restaurant Workers Club*, 99 N.J. Eq. 770, 134 A. 309.

10. An employee was discharged for refusal to work overtime. He petitioned the National Labor Relations Board for reinstatement, contending that his work had ceased as the result of a "current labor dispute," which would entitle him under the law to reinstatement. *C. G. Conn, Ltd. v. N.L.R.B.*, 108 F. 2d 390.

11. Picketing employees obstructed a plant gate in such a way as to leave the plant manager to understand that he could not enter the plant without taking physical risks. The employees were discharged, but the N.L.R.B. ordered them reinstated. The order was appealed to the Courts. *N.L.R.B. v. Perfect Circle Company*, 162 F. 2d 566.

12. A union of liquor-distributor employees engaged in a work stoppage. The object was to exert pressure on the distillery whose products the distributor was handling, so that the distillery would come to terms with a "sister union." This conduct was attacked as a secondary boycott, hence an unfair labor practice under the Labor-Management Relations Act. The union contended that the boycott was primary, not secondary, on the ground that the distillery and its distributors were "allies," and that this established a "community of interest" between them. *N.L.R.B. v. Wine, Liquor & Distillery Workers Union, Local 1, etc.*, 178 F. 2d 584.

13. A claim was filed under the Fair Labor Standards Act on behalf of an employee of a wholesale poultry and egg concern. The concern sold only in intrastate commerce, with the exception of isolated transactions. *Gerdert v. Certified Poultry & Egg Co.*, 38 F. Supp. 964.

14. A claim was filed under the Workmen's Compensation Law in behalf of a decedent employee, who died from drinking poison out of a bottle labeled whiskey—a "joke" perpetrated by fellow-employees during working hours but immediately preceding New Year's, when considerable drinking of liquor was going on in anticipation of the approaching holiday. It was contended by defendant that the death did not arise "out of and in the course of" employment. *McCarthy v. Remington-Rand*, 275 App. Div. 866, 88 N.Y. Supp. 2d 456.

15. A non-striking employee left his work and procured other employment when a striking union extended its picket line to the area in which he was employed. He made no effort to return to the strikebound plant until the strike was settled. However, he made application for unemployment compensation. *Urbach v. Unemployment Compensation Board of Review*, 169 Pa. Super. 569, 83 A. 2d 392.

# 11

# Partnerships and Other Associations

**Scope of This Chapter.** In this chapter we consider the nature and characteristics of a partnership, as distinguished from other business associations; the advantages and disadvantages of the partnership form of doing business as against the corporate form, and certain risks which one assumes when he enters a partnership. We also consider how partnerships may arise, intentionally and otherwise; firm names, assets, good will and capital; the rights, duties, powers and liabilities of partners, not only as to one another, but as to the outside world; and the different ways in which a partnership may be dissolved and its affairs wound up. We conclude the chapter with a brief discussion of limited partnerships and other business associations.

### PART 1. NATURE AND CREATION

**Role of Partnership in Modern Business.** Notwithstanding the many advantages of doing business in corporate form (pages 496 to 497), partnerships retain a stubborn hold on the business life of the community. In some fields, particularly where complete liberty and equality of action are desired, as well as freedom from corporate taxation, and from public supervision and the routine of corporate elections, business men find the partnership form of organization better adapted to their needs. In yet other fields, the law prohibits the corporate form of organization—as in the legal and medical professions. Finally, without intending it, persons are constantly undertaking the obligations of partnership, frequently paying an unexpected price for their experience.

*A hypothetical case.* A retired merchant, in exchange for advice, is given a half interest in a new business, with the right to supervise management and share in the profits. He has no idea of becoming a partner; indeed, it is stipulated between the parties that he is not to be regarded as such. A year later, however, the business goes on the rocks. Losses are heavy. All parties except the "retired" merchant being insolvent, the creditors press their claims against the latter alone, and recover in full; and the merchant learns, at a heavy cost, that the meaning of partnership is to be derived, not from inner intention, but from outward conduct.

**Law Governing Partnership: Uniform Partnership Act.** As with other branches of substantive law, a uniform statute embracing certain standard rules governing partnerships, known as the Uniform Partnership Act, has been adopted by many states. The rules of the common law apply to all partnership questions not covered by the Uniform Act or by separate state statutes.

### Nature and Characteristics of Partnership

**Definition and Characteristics of Partnership.** The Uniform Partnership Act defines partnership as "an association of two or more persons to carry on as co-owners a business for profit." The essential characteristics of a partnership are:

(a) *Association as individuals.* A partnership is an association of persons as individuals, not (as in the case of incorporators) an association whose individualities become merged into a corporate entity. Although a partnership may be treated as an entity for certain purposes, it remains, for most purposes, an association of individuals as such.

(b) *Voluntary association.* Persons cannot be forced into partnerships. Parties have a right to select the persons with whom they are to associate themselves in business. The fiduciary character of the relationship between partners and the risk of liability by each partner for the acts of the other partners within the scope of the partnership emphasize the highly voluntary character of the association.

EXAMPLE: A partner may assign his interest in the firm to an outsider, but he cannot, by doing this, make the assignee a partner without the consent of the other members of the firm.

(c) *Co-ownership.* Partners must have a *proprietary interest*, not only in the profits as such, but in the enterprise which is the subject-matter or object of the partnership.

(d) *Association must be one for profit.* If the object of the association is anything other than profit, it is not a partnership. For example, joint enterprises for charitable, eleemosynary, religious, or other nonprofit purposes, cannot be called partnerships.

(e) *Mutual agency of partners.* Each partner is agent for the others and for the firm in respect to all partnership acts. Hence partners occupy a fiduciary relationship toward one another, with everything that such relationship implies (pages 403 and 404).

(f) *Mutual liability of partners.* Since each partner, as to partnership acts, is agent for the others and the firm, each partner, as well as the firm, is a principal as to all partnership acts, in tort or in contract. This makes each partner financially responsible for such acts; if his copartners and the firm become insolvent, he may become exclusively responsible.

**Who May be Partners.** Generally speaking, any person who is competent to make a contract may become a partner. Therefore, the only limitations upon a person's capacity to unite with others in a partnership are those which apply to contracts generally.

*Infants as partners.* Infants may be partners, subject to their right to disaffirm (page 54), but once debts are incurred, the infant may not withdraw his investment until creditors are paid, unless remaining assets are sufficient to pay such debts.

*Corporations as partners.* The view of a majority of our courts (although some states have held to the contrary) is that a corporation, from its very nature, does not have the power to become a partner (pages 551-552). There are two exceptions to this rule:

(1) Corporations may be authorized by statute to become partners.

(2) A corporation may become a partner by estoppel (page 877).

EXAMPLE: A corporation enters into partnership with X, who contributes $50,000 toward the firm capital. At the end of the year, the corporation tenders the return of his capital, but refuses to divide a $25,000 profit on the ground that as a corporation, it had no authority to become a partner. The corporation in such case would be estopped to deny the partnership.

*Partnerships as partners.* A partnership or firm may enter as such into partnership with other firms, provided all firm members consent. Thus, the AB Company, consisting of A and B, may become a partner of the CDE Company, consisting of C, D and E, on consent of all five. In adjusting profits and other rights and liabilities in respect to each other, the two firms will be treated as separate entities, but as to outside creditors of the combined partnership, A, B, C, D and E will be liable as members of a single firm.

**Sharing Profits as Wages or Bonus.** Employees who share profits in the form of wages or bonus are not on that account partners. Thus, a manager hired at a fixed salary plus 15% of the profits is not on that account liable to creditors as a partner. However, his contract may require him to conduct himself in such manner that third parties may have reason to believe that he is a partner. To protect himself against such liability, such employee, before signing his contract of employment, would be well advised to request provisions in the contract to the following effect:

(a) That the employee is hired as such and is not a partner.

(b) That profits are received as salary or bonus, not as profits.

(c) That the employee is not required to contribute to capital or losses.

(d) That the employee is to receive a minimum guaranteed salary in any event.

(e) That the employee's name is not to appear on firm stationery or anywhere else in such way as to suggest membership in the firm.

(f) That the employee is not to be held out in any other way as a partner.

**Sharing Profits as Rent.** Ordinarily, the leasing of premises for a share of profits as rent, or in addition to rent, does not make the landlord liable as a partner. However, if the agreement, whether designated as a "lease" or by any other name, gives the owner of the property the rights, duties and powers of a partner, so that he clearly appears to be such to outsiders, he may be held liable as a partner.

**Other Forms of Nonproprietary Profits.** In addition to the foregoing forms of nonproprietary profits, the Uniform Partnership Act provides that no presumption of partnership shall arise from the receipt of profits as an annuity to a widow or representative of a deceased partner, or as consideration for the sale of the good will of a business or other property by installments or otherwise.

**Sharing Losses.** Under the common law, an agreement to share profits implied an agreement to share losses. This rule, as noted, no longer prevails where profits are not shared as such. However, although an agreement to share losses does not necessarily constitute a partnership, a true partnership does imply an agreement to share losses.

As noted on page 487, a special or limited partner may limit his losses to the amount of his investment.

**Partnerships as Between the Parties v. Partnerships as to Third Parties.** The test of a partnership as between the parties themselves is not necessarily the same as the test applied in deciding whether third parties may invoke the doctrine of estoppel against an ostensible partner (page 464). Evidence of any real intent to form a partnership may be wholly lacking, yet parties may so conduct themselves as to lead third parties to believe, and reasonably so, that a partnership exists. In such a situation, persons may have no claim upon one another as partners, yet may be chargeable as copartners in respect to third parties.

**Differences between Partnership and Corporation.** Partnerships differ from corporations in at least five important respects: (1) as to liability for debts of the business; (2) as to liability of the owners of the business for the acts of one another; (3) as to continuity of the business and the effect of death, bankruptcy or the sale of one's interest in the business; (4) as to the necessity of obtaining permission to do business; and (5) as to the right to practice a profession. (See pages 496 and 497.)

**Advantages of Partnership.** Offsetting its disadvantages as contrasted with the corporate form of doing business, partnerships present the following advantages: (1) relative liberty and equality of action in place of formal requisites for voting and elections at meetings of stockholders and directors, (2) lighter tax burdens, (3) relative freedom from public supervision, annual reports, and so on, and (4) freedom to unite professional skills in fields forbidden to corporations, as in the practice of law, medicine, architecture, and so on. (See, also, page 497.)

**Risks of Partnership.** Since the chain of partnership is no stronger than its weakest link and any partner may become liable for the acts of all, a prospective partner must weigh the following risks:

(a) One's own financial ability to withstand and survive reverses.

(b) The financial resources of prospective copartners.

(c) The age and health of prospective copartners. (Death dissolves a partnership; ill health of a copartner may handicap or ruin the firm.)

(d) Integrity of prospective copartners. (Equal access to firm funds and other assets, together with the power to borrow, may, if one partner is dishonest, lead to the ruin of all.)

(e) Ability, capacity, training, skill and experience of prospective copartners. (Enthusiasm is no substitute for qualifications.)

(f) Disposition of prospective copartner and his ability to get along with others. (Dissension frequently leads to dissolution.)

**Partnership v. Joint Venture.** In a partnership, persons associate as co-owners for the continued prosecution of an enterprise for profit. In a joint venture, there is merely co-ownership for a given limited purpose, without the usual powers, duties and responsibilities that go with a partnership. In the following situations, (a) is a joint venture, (b) a partnership:

(a) *A* and *B* unite their money and services in purchase and resale of a certain lot of machinery for their joint profit.

(b) *A* and *B* enter into an agreement whereby each contributes $2,000 and his services in establishing and carrying on a shoe store for their joint profit.

**Partnership v. Joint-Stock Association.** A joint-stock association is an unincorporated enterprise resembling a partnership in that it consists of an association of individuals as such rather than as shareholders of an entity such as a corporation. Members of a joint-stock association, like members of a partnership, are liable for its debts, and may sue and be sued together as individuals. However, joint-stock associations resemble corporations rather than partnerships in that they may issue shares of stock against capital, enjoy the corporate advantage of continuous succession, and manage their affairs through directors and officers. (See pages 497-498.)

## Partnership Classifications

**Kinds of Partnerships.** Partnerships are either (1) *ordinary* or (2) *limited*. The latter are also known as *special* partnerships. They are discussed on pages 487 to 489, inclusive.

Ordinary partnerships are either *universal* or *general*. A universal partnership, like a universal agency, is rare, being largely theoretical.

**General v. Special Partnerships.** General partnerships are created for the usual partnership purposes. The term *general* partnership is commonly used in contradistinction to the term *special partnership* (page 487). General partnerships are either *trading* or *nontrading*.

*Trading* partnerships are those formed for ordinary business or industrial purposes.

*Nontrading* partnerships are those formed for professional or quasi-professional purposes (law, accountancy, brokerage, and so on).

The practical effect of the distinction between trading and nontrading partnerships is that third persons are entitled to assume that members of a trading firm have wider authority than members of a nontrading firm.

**Kinds of Partners.** Partners may be classified as general, limited or special, secret, silent, dormant and nominal.

**General Partner.** A *general* or *active* partner is one who takes an active part in the management of the business and whose liability is unlimited. General partners may not only be members of an ordinary partnership, but also of a special or limited partnership; that is, the term *general partner* may indicate those members of a limited partnership whose powers, authority and liability are not limited, as they are in the case of the special partners who are members of the firm.

**Limited or Special Partner.** A *limited* or *special* partner is a member of a limited partnership whose powers, authority and liability are limited by statute, in contrast to those of the general partners who are members of such firm.

**Secret (Undisclosed) Partner.** A *secret* partner is one whose connection with the firm is not disclosed. He may be active in the conduct of the business, and if his connection with the firm becomes disclosed, third parties may hold him liable, like any other general partner. A secret partner is sometimes known as an *undisclosed* partner. His liability is similar to that of an undisclosed principal (page 408).

EXAMPLE: Tompkins and Sheehan form a manufacturing firm, conducted in Tompkins' name. Tompkins buys manufacturing material on credit from a seller who knows nothing of the partnership. Later the firm fails. The seller, on learning the facts, may hold Sheehan as well as Tompkins.

**Silent Partner.** A *silent* partner is one who has no voice in the management. Unless he is also a special partner, his liability for firm obligations is the same as that of any other partner.

**Dormant Partner.** A *dormant* or *sleeping* partner is one who is both secret and inactive. His liability or liabilities to third parties are the same as those of a general partner, if his connection with the firm is discovered.

The fact that he is a dormant partner does not prevent him from asserting himself as an active partner and taking part in managing the firm's business, unless he is prevented from so doing by the partnership agreement.

**Nominal (Ostensible) Partner.** A *nominal* or *ostensible* partner is one who appears to the world as a partner and who may be charged with the liabilities of a partner whether or not he has an actual interest in the firm.

*Partner by estoppel.* A nominal or ostensible partner is sometimes known as a *partner by estoppel.* This is another illustration of the doctrine of equitable estoppel referred to on page 877. Thus, where a person, intentionally or through culpable negligence, holds himself out or permits himself to be held out as a partner, he may share liability as a partner (without sharing profits) to anyone thereby misled. Where such holding out is public, he renders himself liable as a partner whether anyone has been misled or not.

**Subpartner.** A *subpartner* is a person who forms a partnership with one of the partners, to share, with the latter, his interest in the firm. The arrangement is a joint venture (page 462) rather than a partnership, and the subpartner, by his arrangement, does not become a member of the main firm.

## How Partnerships May Arise

**In General.** As already indicated, a partnership may be created by contract, express or implied, or by estoppel. An express contract of partnership may be oral or written. It need not be written except when the statute of frauds applies. A written contract governing the rights, duties and powers of the partners is known as "articles of copartnership."

**Articles of Copartnership.** Many a business firm, successful in other respects, has foundered for lack of a full agreement among the partners in respect to matters that normally arise in the course of a partnership business. The articles of copartnership should err on the side of resolving at the outset every possible point of difference, among them, the following (see Form 10):

(1) *Date when partnership effective.* It is wise to name the day specifically upon which the partnership is to begin, because the rights and liabilities of partners as to one another become effective on such date. If the date is not designated, the date of the agreement will be deemed the beginning date of the partnership.

(2) *Names and addresses of partners.* These may be important in deciding whether notices to partners have been proper in case of demands. or disputes requiring notice.

(3) *Firm name.* This is important not only so as to identify the partnership, but also because the firm name may become a valuable asset.

(4) *Nature, purpose and scope of partnership activity.* This should be stated in fairly precise language, because it may be of importance in

case one partner endeavors unfairly to compete with the partnership business.

(5) *Location of place of business and field of operations.* This may be of importance in case a question arises as to the rights of any of the partners to transact business in prohibited competitive communities.

(6) *Duration of partnership.* This should be specifically provided for so that no questions may arise among the partners themselves as to the period of time during which the parties may assert their rights as partners or remain subject to the firm's obligations.

(7) *Payment of interest.* If interest is to be paid on capital invested, the articles should so provide, otherwise none is payable.

(8) *Profits and losses: how computed and shared.* In the absence of specific provision to the contrary, profits and losses will be shared equally. The manner of computing such profits and losses may become important, especially where partners first deduct uneven drawing accounts.

(9) *Drawing and salary accounts.* This question should not be left to conjecture, but should be specifically provided for.

(10) *Time to be devoted to the business.* While this is a difficult thing to regulate, it is well to make some provision for it in the articles of co-partnership. Many partners have outside interests. If so, it may be wise to reserve the right to engage in outside activity, so as to rebut any presumption to the contrary.

FORM 10

## AGREEMENT OF PARTNERSHIP—SHORT FORM

AGREEMENT, made in the City of New York, State of New York, on May 1st, 1952, between John Doe, residing at No. 11½ Broadway, Borough of Manhattan, City of New York (herein called the "First Party"), and Richard Roe, residing at No. 37½ Broadway, Borough of Manhattan, City of New York (herein called the "Second Party"),

WHEREIN IT IS MUTUALLY AGREED, AS FOLLOWS:

1. That the parties hereto shall, as partners, engage in and conduct the business of buying, selling and dealing in dry goods, at wholesale and retail.

2. That the name of the partnership shall be John Doe & Co.

3. That the term of the partnership shall begin on May 1st, 1952, and shall end on April 30th, 1954.

4. That the place of business of the partnership shall be located at No. 57½ Broadway, Borough of Manhattan, City of New York.

5. (a) That the capital of the partnership shall be the sum of ten thousand ($10,000) dollars; and each party shall contribute thereto, contemporaneously with the execution of this agreement, the sum of five thousand ($5,000) dollars in cash.

(b) That neither party's contribution to the capital of the partnership shall bear interest in his favor.

6. That the capital of the partnership, and all other moneys of, as well as all instruments for the payment of moneys to, the partnership, shall be deposited in the name of the partnership, in the Koe Trust Company, in the Borough of Manhattan, City of New York; and all moneys credited therein to the partnership shall be subject to withdrawal only by check made in the name of the partnership, and signed jointly by the parties hereto.

7. (a) That neither party shall, without the written consent of the other, advance any moneys to the partnership in excess of the amount of his aforesaid contribution

to the capital thereof; but any such advance that shall be made by either party, with the written consent of the other, shall bear interest at the rate of six (6%) per cent. per annum.

(b) That if either party shall, with the consent of the other, become indebted to the partnership, such indebtedness shall bear interest at the rate of six (6%) per cent. per annum.

8. That each party shall devote all of his time and attention to the business of the partnership, and shall not, during the term of this partnership, either directly or indirectly, engage in any other business.

9. (a) That full and accurate accounts of the transactions of the partnership shall be kept in proper books; and each party shall cause to be entered in the said partnership books a full and accurate account of all of his transactions in behalf of the partnership.

(b) That the books of the partnership shall be kept at the place of business of the partnership, and each party shall, at all times, have access to, and may inspect and copy, any of them.

10. That each party shall be entitled to draw one hundred ($100.) dollars a week from the funds of the partnership.

11. That neither party shall, without the written consent of the other party, make, execute, deliver, endorse or guaranty any commercial paper, nor agree to answer for, or indemnify against, any act, debt, default or miscarriage of any person, partnership (other than that of the parties hereto), association or corporation.

12. (a) That, at the end of each calendar year, a full and accurate inventory shall be prepared, and the assets, liabilities and income, both gross and net, shall be ascertained, and the net profits or net loss of the partnership shall be fixed and determined.

(b) That the net profits or net loss shall be divided equally between the parties hereto, and the account of each shall be credited or debited, as the case may be, with his proportionate share thereof.

13. That, at the termination of this partnership, by the expiration of its term, or by reason of any other cause, a full and accurate inventory shall be prepared, and the assets, liabilities and income, both gross and net, shall be ascertained; the debts of the partnership shall be discharged; and all moneys and other assets of the partnership then remaining shall be divided in specie between the parties, share and share alike.

14. (a) That if any disagreement shall arise between the parties as to the conduct of the partnership business, or as to its dissolution, or as to any other matter, cause or thing whatsoever not herein otherwise provided for, the same shall be decided and determined by arbitrators; and each party shall appoint one such arbitrator, and both of such arbitrators shall appoint a third arbitrator, and the decision of two of such arbitrators, when made in writing, shall be conclusive upon the parties hereto.

(b) That the appointment of the arbitrators by the respective parties hereto shall be made, as follows: The party seeking arbitration hereunder shall serve a notice in writing upon the other party hereto, setting forth the disagreement or disagreements that he desires to be arbitrated, as well as the name of his arbitrator; and, thereupon, the other party hereto shall, within five (5) days after the receipt of such notice, serve upon the party seeking arbitration a notice in writing stating the name of his arbitrator.

(c) The failure of a party to appoint an arbitrator shall authorize the other party to make an appointment for the one so in default.

(d) If the two arbitrators appointed hereunder shall fail, within five (5) days after the second of the arbitrators shall have been appointed, to select a third arbitrator, then, and in any such event, any judge of the Supreme Court of the State of New York, County of New York, upon application made by either party hereto for that purpose, shall be authorized and empowered to appoint such third arbitrator.

(e) The award to be made by the arbitrators hereunder shall be made within five (5) days after the third arbitrator shall have been appointed.

IN WITNESS WHEREOF, the parties hereto have hereunto set their hands and seals, the day and year first above written.

In the presence of                    John Doe      (L. S.).
John Doe, Jr.
Richard Roe, Jr.                 Richard Roe      (L. S.).

(11) *Powers of partners and limitations, if any.* This provision is important if the partners are to be protected from the excessive exercise of authority on the part of their associates. Particularly is this true of the right to sign or countersign checks.

(12) *Management and control.* It is important to define very clearly how the business shall be managed and controlled, what vote shall be required on questions of policy, i.e., whether unanimous, two-thirds, majority, and so forth.

(13) *Books of account, inventories and statements.* Rights of partners cannot be determined unless proper books of account be kept, showing the status of the business and the profits, if any, to be distributed. The articles should provide for equal access to the books by all partners, although the law usually implies this.

(14) *Retirement of partners and notice thereof.* Provision for the retirement of any partner, notice thereof, etc., may be important, to avoid embarrassment to the business.

(15) *Dissolution and right to continue business upon withdrawal of any partner.* Although the law prescribes the rights of the parties in this respect upon dissolution, it may be well for the parties to provide for this contingency in accordance with their own mutually expressed desires, rather than to leave the rights of surviving partners to be determined by operation of the law.

(16) *Distribution of surplus upon dissolution.* The law governs the rights of parties in this event also; but the partners may desire to make special provision for distribution upon dissolution.

(17) *Disposition of firm name, good will, and so forth.* Provision should be made for the disposition, on dissolution, of the firm name, good will, partnership property and affairs, including, in the case of professional firms, the disposition of working papers, arrangements with clients, and so on.

(18) *Liquidating partners.* To avoid possible dispute and litigation, provision is sometimes made for the partner or partners who are to liquidate the partnership affairs following dissolution.

(19) *Provision for arbitration.* Especially where no provision for a majority rule can be made, as in the case of two partners, or in the case of an even number of partners who may divide equally on some question of policy, it may be important to provide for some means of arbitrating differences other than resort to law, since the latter may prove costly and fatal to the partnership.

**Implied Contracts of Copartnership.** Wholly apart from express contracts of copartnership and from partnerships by estoppel (page 464), persons may so conduct themselves as to create a partnership by the established standards of legal intent, though actually unaware that they have entered into a contract of copartnership.

**Facts Justifying Inference of Copartnership: "Outside" v. "Inside" Parties.** As indicated on page 461, the facts may justify no inference of partnership among the participants in a business venture, yet may justify such inference by third parties:

EXAMPLE: Brown lends Green $5000 for use in a business, the loan being evidenced by Green's two-year note. It is agreed that the business is to belong to Green exclusively, but that for his loan and his management services, Brown is to receive one-half the profits pending payment of the note. The business fails, and Black, a carpenter contractor who had been hired by Brown, seeks to hold Brown liable as a partner. Black may succeed because as to him, though not as to Green, the facts may justify a presumption of partnership.

## Questions

1. How does the Uniform Partnership Act define a partnership?
2. Name the six essential characteristics of a partnership.
3. What are the two exceptions to the general rule that corporations may not become partners?
4. If a prospective employee of a partnership is to share profits in the form of wages or bonus, what provisions should be set forth in his contract of employment in order to protect him against the liability of a partner as to third parties?
5. Name five distinguishing features between a partnership and a corporation.
6. Name four advantages of a partnership as contrasted with the corporate form of doing business.
7. What six risks should be studied by a person before forming a partnership with another?
8. Distinguish between a partnership and (a) a joint venture; (b) joint-stock association.
9. Name and differentiate the various types of partnerships.
10. Name and differentiate the various kinds of partners.
11. In what different ways may a partnership come into existence?
12. What is meant by "articles of copartnership"?
13. List the more important provisions that should be included in the articles of copartnership, and explain their importance.
14. "The test as to whether a partnership exists applies equally to all, including those alleged to be partners, and those dealing with the latter." Is this statement true, false, or partly true and partly false?

## Problems

1. A landlord rented premises to a partnership as tenant, the lease providing that the monthly rental would be equal to 25 per cent of the net profits of the tenant's business. Subsequently, the tenant failed; whereupon the latter's creditors instituted suit against the landlord for the firm's debts on the ground that he and the tenant were partners. Judgment for whom and why?
2. Atkins, Brown and Carter, partners, agree that Carter shall not be liable for losses. Eggers, an unpaid creditor who is unaware of the arrangement, sues all three for the debt. How will the Court decide and why?

3. Davis advanced money to Dalton for the purchase of stock upon an agreement that profits were to be divided, but that losses were to be borne by the purchaser. Later, the question arose as to whether the arrangement was a partnership. How would you decide such question?

4. Larson, who had invested $50,000 in a partnership, demanded interest thereon upon dissolution of the firm. His partner objected. The articles of copartnership were silent as to interest on capital invested. Should Larson receive interest on his capital? Explain.

5. Smith and Jones opened a hardware business, each making an original investment of $25,000. Smith's initiative and superior sales ability produced profits for the firm five times as great as those produced by Jones. Smith argued that his income from the firm should be at least twice that of Jones. The articles of copartnership were silent as to profits. Should Smith's request be complied with?

6. Seven persons associated themselves together to manufacture cheese at a factory owned by three of them, who received a certain sum for the use of the factory. The association adopted no name, and was known by several different names. Losses, if any, and expenses were to be paid by five of the associates, and then the net profits were to be divided equally among the seven. Comment on whether the arrangement constituted a partnership.

7. Smiley and Lamb, each of whom had his own business, were owners in common of several parcels of real property. Lamb was forced into bankruptcy by his creditors. The trustees attached Lamb's interest in the real estate owned in common by Smiley and Lamb, and then sought to charge Smiley with Lamb's debts on the basis of a copartnership. How would you decide this issue?

## PART 2. RIGHTS, DUTIES AND LIABILITIES OF PARTNERS

**Factors Involved.** The rights, duties, powers and liabilities of partners are determined by the articles of copartnership, and, in the absence thereof, by general rules of law. These rules may relate to (1) the attributes and assets of a firm, (2) the partners in respect to one another, and (3) the firm in its dealings with third parties.

### Firm Attributes and Assets

**In General.** The rights, duties, powers and liabilities of partners are governed in large part by the attributes and assets of the partnership, which must be first considered before discussing the specific rights, duties, powers and liabilities of partners. These attributes and assets include: Firm name, good will, capital, and firm property.

**Firm Name.** A firm name may consist of the actual names of all or of one or more of the partners, or of a fictitious name. The law places no restrictions on firm names except as to registration and misleading firm names.

**Registration: Fictitious Firm Names.** For years, statutes have forbidden the use of fictitious names unless a certificate is duly filed disclosing the true parties interested. Such statutes apply to individuals and copartners alike. (See page 838, "Business licenses," and so on.) The statutes of some states go further and require the filing of registration certificates for all partnerships.

**Misleading Firm Names.** Statutes commonly provide that no person may conduct business in the name of a partner not interested in the firm; and when the designation "and company," "and Co." or similar designation is used, it must represent an actual partner. Two exceptions are generally made:

(1) Where an established business continues to be conducted by some or any of the partners, or their assignees, appointees or successors in interest.

(2) Where a pre-existing firm or corporation about to discontinue or which has discontinued its business and name, consents to the use of the latter.

*Similarity of names.* A firm must not use a name so nearly like that of a business already in existence as to mislead the public. Where it does, the firm already in existence may procure an injunction against the use of the name, together with any damages sustained.

**Right to Hold Property in Firm Name.** Formerly, a firm could not hold real or personal property or sign firm contracts in the firm name; all firm property had to be held and all firm contracts signed in the names of the partners as individuals. This is no longer the law. To this extent, a partnership is an "entity."

**Suits in Firm Name.** Unlike a corporation, which is a true entity, partners generally can neither sue nor be sued in their firm name, but must sue or be sued in their individual names. In some states, however, a partnership that has a president or treasurer may sue or be sued in the name of such officer. In other states, the statute specifically permits a partnership to sue or be sued in the firm name.

**Disposition of Firm Name upon Dissolution.** When a firm dissolves, the firm name may be disposed of in the following manner: (a) If no provision is made as to the use of the firm name, any partner may use it provided the public is not misled; (b) the right to use the firm name may be sold as a business asset, or a retiring partner may give or sell to a continuing partner or partners the right to use the former firm name; (c) upon death of a partner, the Court may order a sale of the firm's good will and assets, in which event the firm name must be accounted for.

**Good Will.** Good will has been defined as "the probability that the old customers will resort to the old place." It is a partnership asset, but not part of a firm's "stock in trade." Thus, if the "assets" of a firm are purchased, they include good will; but if only the "stock in trade" is purchased, good will is not included.

**Capital.** Partnership capital is the aggregate of the sums, either in money or agreed value of property, contributed by the partners for the transaction of the partnership business. General partners may contribute cash, property or services as capital. Special or limited partners may contribute only cash or property as capital.

*Partnership capital v. partnership property.* Partnership capital differs from partnership property in at least three respects:

(1) As to amount: Partnership capital is fixed in amount and cannot be changed except by consent of the firm. Partnership property may vary in amount from time to time, and may be more or less than partnership capital.

(2) As to undivided profits: Partnership capital does not necessarily include undivided profits, although the partnership agreement may provide that undivided profits will, at the option of the partners, become part of the capital. Partnership assets necessarily include undivided profits.

(3) As to distribution upon dissolution: Capital is regarded as an obligation to the partners, repayable, upon dissolution, in proportion to the amounts contributed, before net assets are figured and distributed. Net assets, *in the absence of agreement to the contrary*, are distributed to the firm equally upon dissolution, like profits, and regardless of unequal contributions of capital.

*Capital v. loans or advances.* When a partner lends or advances money to his firm, such loan or advance is not regarded as capital, but as an obligation to be repaid ahead of capital (page 483). Loans or advances generally bear interest, capital contributions do not. (See page 471.) However, by long standing rule, adopted by the Uniform Partnership Act, a partner (unless otherwise agreed) receives interest on the capital contributed by him from the date when repayment should be made.

**Partnership Property.** Partnership property includes: All property originally contributed by the partners to make up the capital of the firm; all property subsequently acquired by the firm, either with firm funds, or by services and transactions on behalf of the firm; and undivided profits. Partnership property also includes any property, profits or proceeds, directly or indirectly acquired through the use of firm property, firm time or firm knowledge, which in good conscience should go to the firm.

**Rights of Partners in Firm Property Generally.** The property rights of a partner are his rights in specific partnership property, his interest in the partnership, and his right to participate in the management.

**Partner's Right in Specific Partnership Property.** A partner is co-owner with his partners of specific partnership property. He holds as a *tenant in partnership*, corresponding to a tenancy in common held by co-owners in a joint venture. However, a tenancy in partnership, unlike a tenancy in common, is subject to the claims of partnership creditors and cannot be "partitioned" (in the case of real property), or distributed (in the case of personal property), between or among the partners, unless firm debts are first paid and firm claims satisfied.

EXAMPLE: Two sons, Robert and William MacFarlane, having inherited a manufacturing establishment from their father, went into possession, conducted the business and, for two years, divided profits equally. Then Robert sued for partition of the real property owned by the business. William defended on the ground that the business was a copartnership, and hence that partition could not be had until firm affairs were wound up, creditors paid and partners' interests adjusted. William's position was well taken.

A partner's interest as a tenant in partnership gives him an equal right with his copartners to possess and use specific partnership property *for partnership purposes*. He has no right to possess such property for any other purpose without the consent of his copartners. Hence, a partner's right in specific property is not assignable without the consent of his copartners. Neither is it subject to attachment or execution (pages 858 and 861), except on a claim against the firm. For the same reason, a partner's right in specific property is not subject to dower, curtesy or allowances to widows, heirs or next of kin.

**Partner's Interest in Partnership.** A partner's interest in the firm itself, as distinguished from specific property owned by the firm, is the partner's share of the profits and surplus; that is, it is an interest in everything that the firm owns and earns, subject to the claims of creditors. Such interest is personal property, though the firm as such owns nothing but real property.

*Conveyance of partner's interest in firm: effect of.* A conveyance by a partner of his interest in the firm does not of itself dissolve the firm. Nor does it entitle the assignee, during the continuance of the partnership, to interfere in the management of the partnership business. Such assignee or purchaser, including a purchaser at a sale under execution issued on a judgment against a partner, acquires no partnership rights whatsoever, except to receive profits and surplus after firm creditors are satisfied.

### Rights, Duties, Powers and Liabilities of Partners As to One Another

**In General.** Rights and duties being *reciprocal* (page 22), the right of each partner as to the others represents a corresponding duty of the others to respect and conform to such right. Such rights and duties may be prescribed in the articles of copartnership, or they may be imposed by law in the absence of express agreement. If a partner violates any of the terms in the articles of copartnership, or those imposed by law, he must respond in damages to his copartners for consequent loss.

**Good Faith.** As in agency, so in partnership—the relationship between partners is fiduciary, that is, based on faith. This is because of the mutual agency of partners. Hence, a partner must account to his copartners for any personal profit, advantage or secret commission earned out of his partnership connection. No partner may take unfair advantage of his copartners.[1]

EXAMPLE: In *Meinhard v. Salmon*,[2] Salmon obtained a lease in his own name, but Meinhard contributed his share of the funds toward the venture and agreed to bear his share of any loss. Prior to the expiration of the lease, Salmon, without the knowledge of Meinhard, obtained a new lease to the premises and, in addition, several adjoining parcels, in the name of a corporation owned by Salmon. *Held*, that Meinhard, who was thus excluded, was entitled to impress a trust to the extent of one half the stock of the corporation.

**Loyalty to Firm Interests.** A partner's loyalty to his firm corresponds to the loyalty required of an agent toward his principal (page 403). He must not serve interests which conflict with those of the firm, have a personal interest adverse to the firm's, or engage in a competing business.

**Care and Skill.** A partner, in the discharge of his duties, must exercise that degree of care, skill, diligence and economy that the circumstances require. Anything less than this, resulting in loss to the firm, will render the partner liable for such loss.

**Accounts and Their Inspection.** Partners must keep true and accurate accounts of partnership transactions, and these must at all reasonable times be open to the inspection of all other partners at the place of business.

**Right to Share in Management, Knowledge and Control of the Business.** No partner may control or monopolize the management of the partnership business to the exclusion of others. But partners may provide in the articles of copartnership for differing degrees of responsibility and authority. Otherwise, each partner has an equal voice with the others in the management of the business, and a majority governs. (For acts requiring unanimous consent, see page 476.)

EXAMPLE: Smith, Howe and Rogers are partners engaged in the dry-goods business. Smith and Rogers wish to add a grocery department. Howe objects. Unless otherwise agreed in the articles of copartnership, the wishes of Smith and Rogers prevail.

**Profits and Losses.** As noted on page 465, in the absence of agreement to the contrary, partners share profits and losses equally, regardless of unequal capital contributions.

EXAMPLE: Jones, Johnson and Perry form a partnership. Jones contributes $5000, Johnson $3000 and Perry $1000. The articles of copartnership are silent on the division of profits. Jones, Johnson and Perry will share profits equally.

*Definition of profits.* The word "profits" is an elastic term.[3] Profits may be arrived at in various ways, depending upon the items to be deducted

---

[1] *Stephens v. Stephens*, 298 Ky. 638, 183 S.W. 2d 822.
[2] 249 N.Y. 458, 164 N.E. 545.
[3] There are literally hundreds of judicial definitions of the terms *profit* or *profits*.

from income in figuring profits. For this reason it is important, in drawing up articles of copartnership, to agree upon a definition of profits.

*Interest on profits left in business.* Unless so agreed, partners who leave profits in the firm are not entitled to interest thereon.

*Sharing losses in proportion to profits.* Where profit distribution is unequal, losses are shared in the same proportion, unless the partners have otherwise agreed.

**Right to Compensation.** A partner is not entitled to extra compensation for extra services rendered by him for the firm unless the partnership agreement so provides. This does not apply to a surviving partner (page 482).

EXAMPLE: *A* and *B* are partners in the hardware business. If *A*, because of *B*'s illness, is required for several months to assume an extra burden in conducting the partnership business, he will not on that account be entitled to extra compensation.

**Right to Return of Advances with Interest.** A partner, as already noted (page 471), is entitled to the return of loans or advances ahead of the firm's obligation to return capital investments, and he is entitled to interest on such loans or advances.

**Right to Return of Capital.** Upon dissolution, a partner is entitled to the return of his capital investment, after outside debts and advances by partners have been taken care of.

**Right to Have Partnership Property Applied to Partnership Debts.** The assets of a firm are not only a trust fund for the benefit of creditors; they also furnish a "buffer" to protect a partner's individual assets from the claims of creditors. (See pages 484-485.)

**Right to Contribution from Copartners.** The Uniform Partnership Act provides that the partnership must indemnify every partner for payments made and personal liabilities incurred by him on behalf of the firm in the ordinary and proper conduct of its business or in the preservation of its interests.

### Rights, Duties, Powers and Liabilities of Partners: As to Third Parties

**Mutual Agency of Partners.** Each partner is a general agent for every other partner and for the firm, while acting within the scope of the partnership. Hence the firm and its partners are bound by the acts of any partner on behalf of the firm, not only when such acts are actually authorized, but also if they are not authorized but are within the *apparent* scope of the firm business. (See page 406.)

*Agreements among partners not binding upon third parties.* Agreements among the partners themselves, fixing their duties and liabilities and limiting their powers, are not binding upon third parties unless they have knowledge of such agreements or have acquiesced in them.

EXAMPLE: The articles of copartnership of the firm of *A & B* provide that no written agreement shall be binding upon the firm unless it is signed by both partners. Such a provision is ineffective as to third parties unless they have knowledge of or have acquiesced in it.

**Power to Hire Agents, Servants and Employees.** When a partner hires third parties on behalf of the firm, either as agents, servants or employees, the latter are entitled to assume that the partner is authorized to hire them, regardless of whether he is actually so authorized or not. Hence, they may hold the firm for the compensation promised. But if a partner, in making such contracts of hiring, exceeded his powers, his copartners may hold him liable to the extent of any damage thereby sustained.

**Power to Convey Real Property.** Where real property stands in the firm name, a conveyance by one of the partners in the firm name, unless it was actually or apparently authorized, may be rescinded by the firm and the property recovered, provided it has not passed from the purchaser to an innocent third party.[4]

EXAMPLE: The Acme Coal Company, a partnership consisting of *A*, *B* and *C*, owns a coal shed and the land on which it stands. *A*, for a valuable consideration, signs the firm's name to a conveyance of the property to the Bates Coal Company. If *A* is actually authorized to do this or if such conveyances so executed are customary with such concerns, the conveyance stands; otherwise, the Acme Coal Company can recover the property unless the Bates Coal Company has reconveyed it to an innocent third party.

Where title to the property is in the names of all the partners themselves, a conveyance executed by all the partners passes all their rights in such property.

*Power to mortgage real property.* "A partner cannot make a valid mortgage or deed of trust of his copartners' interests in firm real estate without their assent or ratification, or circumstances estopping them to dispute it, even though the mortgage be made in the partnership name and to secure a partnership debt, but in jurisdictions where equity treats firm realty as personal property,[5] equity will sustain a mortgage upon firm realty given by one partner to secure a past or future firm indebtedness." [6]

**Power to Buy on Credit.** Regardless of whether or not a partner is actually authorized to make purchases for the firm on credit or whether his authority to make such purchases is limited to a given amount, third parties have a right to assume such authority within the customary limits fixed by usage in similar lines of business. This applies, however, to *trading* rather than *nontrading* firms (page 463). A partner in a nontrading firm has no implied power to bind the firm by purchases on credit.

**Borrowing Money.** In most trading partnerships, it is customary to bor-

---

[4] Uniform Partnership Act, sec. 10.
[5] Citing Alabama, Colorado and Texas cases.
[6] 47 *C.J.S.* 857.

row money for the conduct of the business. Hence, whether a partner
be actually authorized to do so or not, he may bind his firm by borrowing money on its behalf, and for this purpose he may make, indorse, draw
and accept firm paper in the firm name. Such transactions being customary, third parties are entitled to assume that a trading partner has such
authority. However, third parties have no right to assume such authority
in the case of a nontrading partnership, because it is not customary.

*Borrowing money on individual paper.* If a partner borrows money
against a note, draft or other instrument that shows on its face that it is
not firm paper, the firm is not bound, even if the partner signs or indorses
the firm name. Even if the money is used for firm purposes, only the borrowing partner (if the firm is nontrading) is liable to the payee, though
such partner may compel his copartners to make good their share of the
proceeds of the loan.

**Accommodation Paper and Contracts of Guaranty and Suretyship.**
As already pointed out (page 180), a partner has no implied right to
execute or indorse accommodation paper in the name of the firm. Third
parties are supposed to know this. Neither has a partner implied authority
to bind his firm by a guaranty or suretyship. However, if the partner has
been expressly authorized by his firm to do any of these acts or if they
are in furtherance of the partnership business, the firm will be bound.

**Partnership Gifts.** Partners may unanimously agree to give away what
they wish to, as long as firm creditors are not thereby prejudiced ("one
must be just before he is generous"), but no partner, alone, has the
*implied* power to make a gift of partnership property. Such gift may,
however, be binding so far as concerns the partner's own interest in the
property.[7]

**Acts Requiring Unanimous Consent.** The Uniform Partnership Act provides that, unless authorized by the other partners or unless the partners
have abandoned the business, one or more but less than all the partners
have no authority to:

(a) Assign the partnership property in trust for creditors or on the
assignee's promise to pay firm debts.

(b) Dispose of the good will of the business.

(c) Do any other act which would make it impossible to carry on the
ordinary business of the firm.

(d) "Confess a judgment" (that is, sign and swear to a paper which permits a creditor to enter up a judgment against the firm without a lawsuit).

(e) Submit a partnership claim or liability to arbitration or reference
(page 125).

**Noncontract Liabilities of Partners: Torts and Crimes.** Not only are
general partners, as distinguished from special or limited partners, liable

---

[7] 47 C.J. 856-7.

for debts and other contract obligations that any member may incur within the actual or apparent scope of his authority, but they are likewise liable for torts committed during the course of the partnership.

EXAMPLE: Brown, of the firm of Brown and Green, borrows $1000 from White on a firm check drawn against a non-existent account. On discovering the facts, White may hold Green as well as Brown, since Brown committed the tort of fraud while acting as a partner.

However, partners are not liable for one another's *criminal* acts unless they participate in, approve, connive at, acquiesce in, or aid and abet the offense. Thus, in the example above given, Green would not be liable criminally (see page 212) for the issuance of the check.

**Liability of Deceased Partner's Estate.** A deceased partner's individual property is subject to levy for all obligations of the firm incurred while he was a partner, but only after firm assets are first applied toward payment of firm debts and after the estate of the deceased partner has paid off all his personal debts (see page 484).

**Liability of Incoming Partner.** A person admitted into a firm is liable for all existing firm obligations, but this liability can be satisfied only out of partnership property.[8] In other words, the liability of an incoming partner for pre-existing firm debts is not personal but is limited to his interest in the firm's assets. This is because the debts of the old firm are properly chargeable as against the partnership assets, and there ought to be no transfer of such obligation personally to an incoming partner, unless the latter has agreed personally to assume it.

EXAMPLE: C is admitted to the firm of A and B on contributing $5000 as capital. Prior to C's admission the firm had incurred a $50,000 obligation, which the firm assets are now insufficient to cover. C's liability in such case is not personal. He stands to lose no more than his interest in the firm's assets.

**Liability of Retiring Partner.** A retiring partner's liability for debts of the firm depends upon whether such debts were incurred before or after retirement.

*Debts incurred before retirement.* A retiring partner is liable for all existing obligations of the firm. Although partners may agree among one another that the retiring partner is to be freed of existing firm debts, such agreement is not binding upon creditors unless they acquiesce.

EXAMPLE: One of three members retires from a firm, the remaining members assuming all responsibility for the then outstanding debts. Before these debts are paid, the new firm becomes insolvent. As to such debts, the retiring partner remains liable.

*Debts incurred after retirement.* A retiring partner is not liable for firm debts incurred after his retirement, provided he has given proper notice of his retirement. Such notice must be *actual* as to all parties who

---

[8] Uniform Partnership Act, sec. 17.

have previously extended credit to the firm and who have no other knowledge of his retirement, and *constructive* (notice by advertisement) as to all others. Under the common law, creditors were entitled to actual notice of retirement even if they had not previously extended credit to the firm, as long as they had previously "dealt with" the firm, but under the Uniform Partnership Act, actual notice is required only as to creditors who have "extended credit to the partnership prior to dissolution and had no knowledge or notice of the dissolution."

**Retirement of secret partner.** When a *secret* partner retires, he need not notify creditors. Since they did not know of the secret partner's connection with the firm, they are not hurt by not being informed that such connection has ceased to exist.

## Questions

1. "No person may conduct a business in the name of a partner not interested in the firm." Give two exceptions.

2. Name three ways in which a firm name may be disposed of upon dissolution.

3. Describe three respects in which partnership capital differs from partnership property.

4. What is a "tenancy" in partnership? How does it differ from a tenancy in common?

5. Name eleven reciprocal rights and duties existing among partners toward one another.

6. Assuming that nothing is said about the matter in the articles of copartnership, may a partner engage in another business, (a) the same as, (b) similar to, or (c) different from, the partnership business?

7. If one partner puts in twice as much capital as the other, and the articles of copartnership are silent on the point, what is the partner's profit position with respect to his copartner?

8. What is the general rule with respect to the power of a partner to bind the firm? Would the nature of the partnership affect your answer in any way? Explain.

9. What is the rule governing the liability of a firm for the torts of its partners?

10. What is the rule governing the liability of a firm for the crimes of any of its partners?

11. What is the liability of the following for the debts of a partnership: (a) Estate of a deceased partner; (b) Incoming partner; (c) Retiring partner?

12. Name six partnership acts requiring unanimous consent.

## Problems

1. Burton, a plumber and steamfitter, decides to open a store for the sale of plumbing supplies. His wife is to tend the store while he goes out on jobs. He puts up a sign, "John Burton & Co.," and likewise proposes to file a certificate under that name. Is Burton within his legal rights?

2. Clements acquired the interest of Shea in the firm of Shea & Schnorr by purchase at a sale under execution issued on a judgment against Shea indi-

vidually. Subsequently Shea & Schnorr gave a chattel mortgage on firm property to Jessup, a firm creditor. The question then arose as to who had the superior right, Clements, or Jessup. What do you think?

3. Adams, during the course of his duties as a member of the manufacturing firm of Adams and Benson, learns that certain property adjoining the firm's own plant is available for purchase. The property is ideally suited for much-needed expansion of the firm's plant facilities. Adams buys the property in the name of a dummy, then causes the latter to resell it to the firm of Adams and Benson at a $10,000 profit, which is turned over to Adams in due course. Later, on learning these facts, Benson consults counsel as to his remedies under the circumstances. What will counsel advise him?

4. The articles of copartnership of the firm of Jenks & Roper provide that no written agreement shall be binding upon the firm unless it is signed by both partners. Kane makes a written agreement with Jenks only, and seeks to enforce it. May he do so?

5. The Acme Coal Company, a copartnership consisting of Ayer, Black and Church, owns a coal shed and the land on which it stands. Ayer, for a valuable consideration, signs the firm's name to a conveyance of the property to the Bates Coal Company. What are the two factors, either one of which will make the conveyance binding on the Acme Coal Company?

6. Harris, of the warehousing firm of Gatesby & Harris, issues, without Gatesby's knowledge, a false warehouse receipt to Nash & Son, who borrow $4,000 on it from Robbins. On discovering the facts, Robbins seeks to have Gatesby and Harris both indicted. What is the legal position of each of these partners?

## PART 3. DISSOLUTION OF PARTNERSHIP

**Meaning of Dissolution.** The Uniform Partnership Act defines the dissolution of a partnership as "the change in the relation of the partners caused by any partner ceasing to be associated in the carrying on as distinguished from the winding up of the business."

*Partnership not terminated by dissolution.* On dissolution, the partnership is not terminated but continues until partnership affairs are wound up.

**Voluntary v. Involuntary Dissolution.** A partnership is voluntarily dissolved when its dissolution is brought about by agreement of the partners; otherwise, the dissolution is involuntary. Voluntary dissolution may be brought about by the terms of the *original* agreement—as by provision for a time limit, completion of the purpose set forth in the partnership agreement, or an event, condition or contingency on the happening of which the partnership is to terminate—and by *subsequent* agreement.

Where no time is specified for its duration, a partnership may be terminated at the will of any member.

**Involuntary Dissolution: How Brought About.** Involuntary dissolution of a partnership may be brought about automatically by operation of law, as in the case of death, bankruptcy or illegality, or it may be judicially decreed at the instance of a partner or someone standing in his place.

**Dissolution upon Death of Partner.** Death dissolves the partnership unless the partnership agreement specifically provides to the contrary.

Upon the death of a partner, his personal representative (page 753) stands in his place. The voluntary character of a partnership forbids a rule that would compel persons to accept a new partner against their will. The executor or administrator of a deceased partner's estate has merely the right to require that the surviving partner or partners wind up the affairs of the firm within a reasonable time and pay over to the estate the deceased partner's share of firm assets and profits after payment of firm debts.

**Dissolution through Bankruptcy.** Unless the partnership agreement provides to the contrary, the bankruptcy of a partner automatically dissolves the firm. Since upon the bankruptcy of a partner a trustee stands in his place, the rule of dissolution is similar to that in the case of a partner's death.

**Dissolution because of Illegality.** "A partnership is dissolved when the further prosecution of the enterprise has become illegal, or when one of the partners becomes so situated that it is illegal for him to continue in the partnership business." [9]

EXAMPLE: If one of the members of a law firm is elected a judge, so that it becomes illegal for him to practice law, the firm is thereby dissolved.

**Dissolution by Judicial Decree.** Ordinarily, only a partner is entitled to apply for a judicial decree of dissolution. As noted on page 472, the purchaser or assignee of a partner's interest in a firm, including a purchaser at an execution sale on a judgment against a partner, acquires no partnership rights whatsoever, except to receive profits and surplus after firm creditors are satisfied. He may, however, apply for a decree of dissolution when the partnership is one at will, or for a specified term which has elapsed, or for a particular undertaking which has been completed.

On application by or on behalf of a partner, the court must decree a dissolution in any of the following cases:

(1) *Insanity:* Where a partner has been adjudged a lunatic, or is shown to be of unsound mind.

(2) *Incapacity:* In case of relatively permanent, not temporary incapacity, showing that the partner lacks the necessary health, strength, diligence or skill required to conduct his duties as partner, a court will decree, dissolution.

(3) *Misconduct:* A court will decree dissolution for misconduct which tends "to affect prejudicially the carrying on of the business," [10] but will not "enter into a consideration of mere partnership squabbles." [11]

---

[9] 47 *C.J.* 1115.
[10] Uniform Partnership Act, sec. 32 (1) (c).
[11] *Cash v. Earnshaw*, 66 Ill. 402.

EXAMPLES OF PREJUDICIAL MISCONDUCT:
(1) Persistent violations of the articles of copartnership.
(2) Abandonment of the business by a partner.
(3) Excluding a copartner from participation.
(4) Repudiating a copartner's lawful interest.
(5) Dishonesty.
(6) Habitual drunkenness.
(7) Acts leading to a state of "irreconcilable discord."

(4) *Futility:* If a partnership is being carried on at a heavy loss, or if it becomes evident that further prosecution of a partnership must inevitably lead to loss or failure or that its purpose is unattainable, a dissolution may be decreed to avoid carrying on a useless project or incurring certain loss.

(5) *Other circumstances:* A court may decree dissolution in any other situation which would make it equitable to do so.

**Power v. Right of Partner to Withdraw.** A partner cannot be compelled to remain in a firm longer than he desires to do so, even though, in withdrawing, he violates his contract; but in the latter case, he is liable to the firm for consequent loss. A partner at will may retire when he pleases. Hence, in a partnership organized without mention of duration, any partner may retire at any time and receive the value of his interest in the firm.

**Notice of Retirement.** We have already pointed out the notice that a retiring partner must give to third parties if he desires to avoid liability for future obligations of the firm (page 477). As to his copartners, a retiring partner must give such notice as the articles of copartnership require. In the absence of such provision, he should give reasonable notice. Such notice need not be written. Even a partner at will must give such notice as may be required in the *articles*, or reasonable notice in the absence of specific provision.

**Expulsion of Partner.** Unless such right is specified in the *articles*, partners may not expel one of their members, even though all but the objectionable member agree upon such expulsion. However, partners have the *power* to accomplish the same result by dissolving the firm and forming a new one that excludes the undesirable partner. If this is done contrary to agreement and without justification, the partner excluded may hold the others liable in damages.

**Effect of Dissolution: Surviving and Liquidating Partners.** Immediately upon dissolution, all authority of the partners ceases insofar as *new business* is concerned. For the purpose of winding up the affairs of the firm, however, partners continue in authority, not as partners, but as trustees in respect to firm assets, the discharge of firm debts, and a proper distribution of assets remaining after payment of such debts. If a surviving or liquidating partner continues the partnership or conducts new business not necessary or incidental to winding up the affairs of the firm, he only, and not firm assets, will be charged thereby, except as to persons without knowledge or notice of the dissolution.

A surviving partner, in winding up the affairs of the firm, is chargeable as a trustee in respect to firm assets. He may not appropriate the good will for himself but must account for it as a firm asset.

*Receivership.* Where liquidating partners are at odds in the process of winding up, the Court may appoint a receiver, provided the dispute is real and the petitioner not a mere troublemaker.

*Compensation.* Liquidating partners may be allowed compensation for liquidating services, provided they have not dealt inequitably with the firm.

**Partnership Remedies.** The remedies of a firm against outsiders are the same as those of ordinary persons against one another. However, the remedy of partners *as to one another* can be obtained only in equity, because the relationship between partners is fiduciary. If a partner sues his firm or the firm sues a member, we have an instance where an individual is suing himself, or being sued by himself, to the extent that the firm includes himself; and if a partner who thus sues should recover a judgment, he might be called upon as a partner to help satisfy his own judgment. Thus, simple actions at law between a firm and its members are usually inadequate to determine the balance of remedies among them. For this reason, partnership remedies must be sought by way of an accounting in equity rather than by way of damages at law. However, suits between partners which in no way involve the partnership may be brought in an ordinary law court.

EXAMPLE: If Martin and McBride are partners, and Martin personally furnishes supplies to McBride in connection with a separate business in no way involving the partnership, Martin may sue McBride at law for any unpaid balance.

The usual partnership remedies include: (a) accounting and dissolution, (b) injunction and (c) receivership.

**Accounting and Dissolution.** A partner's interests and rights in the firm may be ascertained and made available by an accounting. A demand for an accounting is usually, but not necessarily, joined to a demand for dissolution. A partner may have an accounting without dissolution where he is wrongfully excluded, where the right exists by agreement, where secret profits or property have been acquired with the aid of partnership funds or property, and whenever other circumstances render it just and reasonable. However, one cannot have a dissolution without an accounting, because dissolution is followed by distribution, which cannot be had without an accounting.

**Injunction.** In unusual cases, a partner may demand an injunction, as, for example, where, upon demand for an accounting and dissolution, there is danger that a copartner may monopolize the management of the firm, control or "doctor" its books, papers, records and credits, do away with assets, or otherwise render an accounting ineffectual without an injunction.

**Receivership.** As already pointed out (page 482), the Court may appoint a receiver where circumstances require. A receiver is an officer of the Court. He must give bond, must conserve the assets and wind up the affairs of the firm satisfactorily and expeditiously and must render an accounting upon the discharge of his duties.

**Order of Distribution of Firm Assets.** In the voluntary dissolution of an *ordinary* partnership, assets are distributed in the following order:

(1) To creditors other than partners.

(2) To partners for liabilities other than for capital and profits.

(3) To partners for liabilities in respect to capital.

(4) To partners for liabilities in respect to profits.

In the case of a *limited* partnership, a different order of distribution is adopted. (See page 489.)

**Adjustment of Liabilities as Among Partners.** The adjustment of liabilities as among the partners may be fixed by agreement, but, if not, it is governed by the following rules:[12]

(a) Each partner must be repaid his contributions, whether by way of capital, or advances to the partnership property; and

(b) Each partner is entitled to share *equally* in the profit and surplus remaining after all liabilities, *including those to partners*, are satisfied; and

(c) Each partner must contribute toward the losses, whether of capital or otherwise, sustained by the partnership, *according to his share in the profits.*[13]

EXAMPLE: Suppose *A*, *B* and *C* are partners. *A* contributes $10,000 to the capital, *B* $5,000, and *C* his skill. The partnership is terminated by the expiration of the time specified in the articles of copartnership. After all debts and liabilities to third parties are paid, $3,000 remains. There have been no capital withdrawals. The question would thus arise as to how the $3,000 should be divided:

(1) In the absence of agreement to the contrary, *A*, *B* and *C*, sharing equally in the profits, must share equally in the losses. The combined loss being $12,000 ($15,000 capital contributed, less $3,000 remaining), *A*, *B* and *C* are each liable for $4,000, or one third of such loss. *A* is credited with $10,000 originally contributed, less $4,000, or $6,000. *B* is credited with $5,000 originally contributed, less $4,000, or $1,000. *C* is credited with nothing contributed, less $4,000, or a net charge of $4,000 owing to the firm.

(2) Assuming that *C* is insolvent, we must treat *C*'s debt as a loss to be borne equally between *A* and *B*, so that the total loss to *A* and *B* each ($4,000 plus $2,000) is $6,000. Deducting $6,000 from the $10,000 originally contributed by *A*, gives him $4,000; and charging $6,000 against the $5,000 originally con-

---

[12] Uniform Partnership Act, sec. 18 (a).

[13] *Whitcomb v. Converse*, 119 Mass. 38.

tributed by *B*, leaves a net debt owing by *B* in the sum of $1,000, which goes toward discharging the firm obligation to repay *A* $4,000, the balance due him on capital. In other words, the remaining $3,000 asset of the partnership, plus $1,000 due from *B*, goes to *A*.

*Adjustment of losses: profit ratio fixed by agreement.* Where the profit ratio is fixed by agreement, adjustment of losses must follow the profit ratio.

EXAMPLE: Brown, Coates and Danforth, partners, share profits by agreement in the ratio of one-fourth, one-third and five-twelfths, respectively. On dissolution, firm liabilities exceed firm assets by $24,000. Coates, without contributing to the loss, moves to Europe, beyond legal process. Brown and Danforth must share the $24,000 loss in the ratio of one-fourth to five-twelfths, or $9,000 to $15,000, respectively.

*Adjustment of losses: liability for interest.* As previously noted (pages 471 and 474), loans and advances bear interest but capital contributions, unless so agreed, do not, until they become fixed obligations upon accounting and dissolution. From then on, all partners must contribute equally, in the absence of contrary agreement, not only to the principal of balances due to outside creditors and to partners for capital and advances, but also to accrued interest on such balances. This liability applies as much to a partner who contributes only skill and services as to any other partner.[14]

*Priority of advances in distribution of assets.* Where one of the partners makes an advance beyond his capital contribution, the advance, on liquidation and final settlement, is repayable ahead of capital contributions.

**Personal Liability of Partners for Firm Debts.** Partners are personally liable for the debts of the firm, *provided firm assets are insufficient to satisfy such debts.* Such liability, as previously noted (page 477), survives the death of a partner, so that his estate is correspondingly liable.

**Marshaling Assets.** The term *marshaling assets*, important in partnerships, means making them available in a given order of priority in connection with various classes of claims. It is an equitable doctrine. As applied to partnership, it means that upon application in a proper case, a court of equity may require that firm assets must first be made available for payment of firm debts, and the partners' individual assets for the payment of their respective individual debts. If, after payment of firm debts, a surplus remains, such surplus, in which each individual partner has an undivided interest, may be applied to the payment of the partners' individual debts. If, after a partner pays his personal debts out of his personal assets, a surplus remains, such surplus may be applied to the payment of firm debts, provided firm assets are insufficient for this purpose.

---

[14] *Whitcomb v. Converse*, 119 Mass. 38; *Rhein v. Pesso*, 194 App. Div. 274, 185 N.Y. Supp. 150.

EXAMPLES:

(1) Jones, Smith and Brown are equal partners. On dissolution, the firm has assets of $50,000 and liabilities of $35,000. The partners thus have a net equity in the firm of $5,000 each. They have no other personal assets, but they owe personal debts of $5,000 each. Under the rule of marshaling assets, the personal creditors of Jones, Smith and Brown cannot resort to the firm assets until the firm creditors (with $35,000 in claims) are first satisfied; that is, each of the partners' personal creditors may resort to each partner's $5,000 equity in the firm for satisfaction of their personal claims.

(2) Suppose that, in Example (1), firm assets were $50,000 and firm liabilities $65,000; that Jones and Smith were insolvent; but that Brown, with personal assets of $15,000, owed personal debts in the same amount. Firm creditors would have no right to resort to Brown's personal assets, because Brown's personal creditors come first.

(3) A and B are partners. A dies. Assets in liquidation amount to 75% of liabilities. A's estate is solvent. B is insolvent. By the rule of marshaling assets, firm creditors may have access to A's assets only after firm assets are exhausted (in this case, to the extent of 25% of their claims), but not until the individual creditors of A's estate have first been paid. Since B's personal creditors may resort to firm assets only after payment of firm debts and since firm assets are insufficient to pay firm debts, B's creditors would receive nothing.

(4) The firm of Baxter, Brady and Childs makes a promissory note to Voorhis. Childs dies before the note is due. On due date, the note is unpaid. If Voorhis sued Baxter, Brady and Childs' executor, the suit against the executor would have to be dismissed. Upon the death of a partner, the firm is dissolved and its assets are administered by the surviving partners as trustees (page 480). Firm creditors must first look to firm assets for payment. Only after firm assets prove insufficient to pay firm debts may firm creditors look to the individual assets of existing or deceased firm members, and even then only after personal debts have been paid.

**What constitutes firm creditor.** A person is not a firm creditor unless value was given by him to, on the credit of, or for the benefit of the firm. Hence, a person giving value to, on the credit of, or for the benefit of a partner or partners, as distinguished from the firm itself, is not a firm creditor.

**Bankruptcy and Partnership.** Where a partnership is declared bankrupt, the separate assets of all partners, as well as of the partnership estate are drawn into bankruptcy, regardless of whether or not the individual members as such are adjudicated bankrupts; that is, the partners are subjected to the payment of partnership debts, regardless of whether all or any of them are declared bankrupt individually. Such individual liability, however, is subject to the prior claims of individual creditors (page 484).

## Questions

1. What is meant by a dissolution of a partnership?
2. Distinguish voluntary from involuntary dissolution.
3. Name four ways in which involuntary dissolution may be brought about.

4. In what five instances must the Court decree dissolution of a partnership?

5. What is the effect of dissolution upon surviving and liquidating partners?

6. Name the three remedies usually available to a partner upon dissolution.

7. Give the order in which assets of an ordinary partnership are distributed upon a voluntary dissolution of the firm.

8. What rules control the adjustment of liabilities among partners upon dissolution?

9. Under what circumstances may partners become personally liable for the debts of the firm?

10. What is meant by the term "marshaling asests"?

## Problems

1. Atwood and Chapin, copartners, are insolvent. Atwood, fraudulently representing the firm to be solvent, induces Morton to become a partner and to make a capital investment of $10,000. Upon discovery of the fraud, what remedies, if any, may Morton pursue?

2. Black and White enter into a ten-year partnership agreement. Black is exceedingly diligent, but White, while attending business during the usual hours, does not unduly exert himself. The partnership prospers, but Black's family and friends, convinced that the firm's success is due almost entirely to Black's efforts, urge him to break off relations with White. Black is willing to do this if he can procure a court order of dissolution, rather than expose himself to a breach of contract suit and possibly substantial damages for terminating a profitable association that has seven years more to go. What is your opinion of this situation?

3. A firm consists of three partners, Dole, Dillon and Williams. The latter is dormant. The firm is dissolved by the withdrawal of Dillon and Williams. Two new partners take the place of the retiring partners, and the firm continues business under the old firm name. At the time of the dissolution, notice thereof was published in the newspapers. The new firm goes into bankruptcy. Dole and the new partners are also insolvent. Two creditors, one of whom had extended credit to the old firm, and the other to the new, sue Dillon and Williams. Judgment for whom, and why?

4. Albert, Burton and Chase were partners. Albert contributed $20,000 to the capital, Burton $10,000 and Chase contributed his skill. The partnership was terminated by the expiration of the time mentioned in the partnership agreement and, after all debts and liabilities to third persons were paid, it was found that $6,000 remained. There had been no capital withdrawals. How should the $6,000 be divided and what further adjustment, if any, should be made?

5. A partnership consists of three members, Jones, Smith and Brown. The firm dissolves. At the time of the dissolution, the firm has assets of $100,000 and liabilities of $70,000. Jones has individual debts aggregating $15,000. His creditors seek to attach the surplus of firm assets to satisfy their debts. What are the rights of the parties?

6. Suppose in the above case, that the firm had assets of $100,000 and liabilities of $130,000, and that firm creditors sue the firm and the partners individually, seeking to hold the partners to the extent of all their firm assets as well as their respective individual assets; and at the same time individual creditors of the respective partners bring suit, seeking to satisfy their claims, not only out of the individual assets of the partners, but also out of their firm assets. How should the rights of the respective creditors be determined?

## PART 4. LIMITED PARTNERSHIPS AND OTHER ASSOCIATIONS

**Joint Effort with Limited Liability.** From the earliest day, merchants have sought to circumvent the legal principle, inescapable in agency and partnerships, that the benefits of joint effort entail the consequences of joint liability. The corporate form of doing business presented one escape, as we shall note in the chapter on Corporations. Other forms of business organizations designed to achieve joint effort with limited responsibility include limited partnerships, business trusts and voluntary or unincorporated associations.

### Limited or Special Partnerships

**Definitions.** A *limited* or *special* partnership is one formed pursuant to special statute[15] permitting certain partners to be silent or inactive and to limit their liability to the respective amounts of their investments. Thus, an agreement to share profits ratably, but losses only as to some partners, constitutes a limited partnership.

A *limited* or *special* partner is one who does not participate to the full in partnership liability. He is permitted to limit his liability to the amount of his investment, provided such limitation is duly specified in the limited partnership certificate.

**Uniform Limited Partnership Act.** A Uniform Limited Partnership Act has been adopted by the majority of the states.

**Limited Partnership Certificate.** Persons desiring to form a limited partnership must sign and swear to a certificate designating the names and residences of the partners, their capital contributions, which partners are general and which special, the specified limitations of special partners, and other pertinent information. This certificate must be filed, recorded and published. The object of these provisions is to insure that any member of the public, including prospective creditors, may be fully informed as to the limitations in liability on the part of the partners composing the firm, so that existing and prospective creditors may be properly protected.

*Limited partnership must include general partner.* A limited partnership, which includes one or more special partners, may also include one or more general partners, but it must include at least one general partner.

**Limited Partner's Contribution.** The contribution of a limited partner must be either in cash or other property. It *cannot consist of services.*

**Limitation on Firm Name.** A limited partnership must not contain the surname of a limited partner, unless it is also the surname of a general partner or unless the business has been previously carried on under a name that included such surname.

---

[15] Limited partnerships were unknown at common law.

**Right to Profits.** A limited partner has the right to receive profits and compensation stipulated in the certificate, either out of partnership property or out of the property of a general partner, provided the rights of outside creditors are not thereby impaired.

**Right to Inspection of Books and Formal Account.** A limited partner has the same right as a general partner to have the partnership books available for inspection at the principal place of business, to demand and receive full information as to partnership affairs and to require a formal account when circumstances render it just and reasonable.

**Right to Return of Capital Contribution.** A limited partner has the right to the return, in whole or in part, of his capital contribution to the firm, upon consent of all members and upon the cancellation or amendment of the partnership certificate, provided that such return does not jeopardize the claims of outside creditors.

Subject to the rights of creditors and to the terms of the partnership certificate, a limited partner may also rightfully demand the return of his contribution upon dissolution, on the date specified in the certificate for its return, or upon giving six months' notice in writing to all other members, if no time is specified in the certificate, either for the return of his contribution or for the dissolution of the partnership.

**Right to Dissolution.** A limited partner may have the firm dissolved and its affairs wound up when:

(a) He rightfully but unsuccessfully demands the return of his contribution, or

(b) The other liabilities of the partnership have not been paid or the partnership property is insufficient for their payment, and the limited partner would otherwise be entitled to the return of his contribution.

**Liability of Limited Partner.** Limited partners, as such, are not personally bound by the obligations of the firm, but their capital contributions are subject to claims of firm creditors, and limited partners cannot claim a return of their capital contributions until the claims of such creditors are satisfied or safeguarded.

EXAMPLE: If a special partner contributes $50,000 as capital and then, either before or after dissolution, withdraws it while creditors' claims are unpaid, such creditors may have recourse to such fund for payment.[16]

***Liability for misstatement in partnership certificate.*** A limited partner is liable for loss sustained by any person doing business with the firm, by reason of a misstatement in the certificate of partnership knowingly made or assented to by a limited partner.

**When Limited Partner May Become Liable as a General Partner.**

---

[16] Some authorities hold that the special partner in such case may be joined in the same suit with the general partners, but by the weight of authority, creditors must first exhaust their remedies against the general partners before seeking to hold the special partner.

If (except as noted on page 487) a limited partner permits his surname to be used in the firm name, he becomes liable as a general partner. Also, a limited partner may become liable as a general partner if he takes an active part in the management of the business.

**Order of Distribution in Limited Partnerships.** The Uniform Partnership Act provides that in settling accounts after dissolution, the liabilities of a limited partnership are discharged in the following order:

(a) Those to outside creditors in the order of priority as provided by law.

(b) Those to limited partners in respect to their share of the profits and other compensation by way of income on their contributions.

(c) Those to limited partners in respect to their capital contributions.

(d) Those to general partners other than for capital and profits (advances, loans, and so on).

(e) Those to general partners in respect to profits.

(f) Those to general partners in respect to capital.

### Business Trusts

**How Organized.** Business trusts are organizations for the collective investment of the funds of numerous individuals in numerous securities. A common form is that known as the Massachusetts Trust, also known as an Investment Trust, or Common Law Trust. Such an association is created by a declaration whereby a management group constitute themselves as trustees in respect to funds or property to be invested or managed by them for the benefit of shareholders, or the holders of participation certificates representing equitable interests or shares in the common enterprise. These shares are issued pursuant to an agreement defining the powers and duties of the trustees and the rights of the beneficiaries or shareholders.

**Corporate Characteristics.** Some investment trusts resemble corporations in that the trustees may be elected by the shareholders at annual meetings (corresponding to the election of directors), and the trustees may elect officers. In many states, indeed, investment trusts are required to incorporate.

**Partnership Characteristics.** On the other hand, some forms of investment trusts closely resemble partnerships, and under the declaration or agreement constituting the trust the participants may actually though unwillingly become liable as partners.

Thus in *Simson et al. v. Klipstein*,[17] the beneficiaries under an investment trust had the ultimate authority by right of electing the trustees, and the court held that this made them liable as partners.

On the other hand, in *Williams et al. v. Inhabitants of Milton*,[18] the

---

[17] 262 F. 823.
[18] 215 Mass. 1, 39 N.E. 414.

property owned by the Boston Personal Property Trust Co., assessed for taxation as a partnership, sought immunity as a trust. The trust agreement gave full power to the trustees, but provided that any alteration or amendment of the trust agreement required the assent of the beneficiaries. The taxing authority argued that this constituted the shareholders partners. However, such amendments also required the assent of the trustees, and they could refuse such assent. The court therefore held that since ultimate authority was vested in the trustees, the association was a *trust*, not a partnership.

## Voluntary or Unincorporated Associations

**Nature and Purpose.** Many voluntary or unincorporated associations exist either by virtue of contract, or by statute prescribing the manner in which such organizations may be formed. As a rule, such organizations are non-profit associations, existing for religious, social, fraternal, educational, philanthropic or other mutual interest purposes, as in the case of labor unions, guilds and similar groups. Frequently such associations are organized along lines which resemble those of a corporation, including the adoption of by-laws and the election of directors and officers.

**Basis of Liability: Agency.** Since these organizations do not exist for profit, they cannot constitute partnerships (page 459). Membership liability for their acts must therefore rest on agency, if at all. Thus if members on joining agree to abide by a specific set of by-laws, and the by-laws provide that all members are bound by acts of the majority, liability may be incurred for acts so authorized. In the absence of such provision, however, a member is not bound by acts of the association's officers if he refrains from approving or votes in opposition to such acts.

In *Ash v. Guie*,[19] the members of a Masonic lodge, an unincorporated association, appointed a committee to erect a large building, authorized it to borrow money, and gave the lenders certificates of indebtedness in the name of the lodge, signed by the officers and sealed with the lodge seal. A holder of one of the certificates brought suit, joining all the members as defendants and alleging that they were partners. The court held that the lodge was not a partnership; that the members could not be held as partners; that only those committeemen and lodge members who participated in the erection of the building by voting for and approving it, or those members who in any way assented to the undertaking or subsequently ratified it, were liable for the amount of the certificate; and that this liability was not as partners, but as principals.

## Questions

1. Other than the corporate method of doing business, what are three forms of business organizations designed to achieve joint effort with limited responsibility?

---

[19] 97 Pa. 493.

2. Define a limited or special partnership.

3. What restriction does the law place on the nature of a limited partner's contribution?

4. What are the rights of a limited partner in respect to (a) profits, (b) inspection of books, (c) return of capital contribution, and (d) dissolution?

5. When may a limited partner become fully liable for the debts of the firm?

6. Give the order of distribution of assets upon the dissolution of a limited partnership.

7. What are business trusts? Name a common form of such trusts.

8. What are some of the corporate, and some of the partnership characteristics of a business trust?

9. State the nature and purpose of a voluntary or unincorporated association.

10. What is the basis of liability with respect to the members of an unincorporated association?

## Problems

1. Ames, Baker and Carr formed a limited partnership. Ames and Baker, the general partners, contribute $25,000 each toward capital; Carr contributes his services. Comment on the regularity or irregularity of this arrangement.

2. Oliver, Burke and Benson form a limited partnership. Oliver and Burke are the general partners, and Benson is a limited partner who has invested $2,500 in the business. Oliver and Burke, however, are preoccupied with another business and Benson is given full management of the firm of Oliver, Burke and Benson. The firm becomes heavily indebted and creditors seek to hold Oliver, Burke and Benson equally liable as general partners. Can they do so? Explain.

3. Farley, as general partner, and Gleason, as special partner, contribute $50,000 and $25,000 respectively to the firm of Farley and Gleason. The articles provide that Gleason is to receive a guaranteed profit of $5,000 a year. For five years the firm loses money. Each year, Gleason demands the promised profit of $5,000 and each year Farley persuades Gleason to wait another year. Finally, at the end of five years, Gleason demands an accounting, sues for the return of his capital, plus $25,000 accrued profits. Farley's defense is that although all creditors are paid, the firm has lost $25,000 over the five-year period. How will the Court decide?

### COURT CASES FOR REVIEW
#### How Did the Court Decide, and Why?

1. The creditors of a partnership filed a petition to force one William Ganaposki into bankruptcy as a member of the firm. Ganaposki opposed the petition and denied that he was a partner. It was shown that although his name had appeared on different checks, drafts and financial statements of the firm, he had never made any contribution to its capital, nor shared in its profits, nor exercised any control in respect to its business. *In re Ganaposki et al.*, 27 Fed. Supp. 41.

2. John Phillips, a poor Scotch immigrant, came to this country many years ago with his wife, four sons and two daughters, and founded a small business. As he prospered, he took in each of his four sons as each reached his majority, and they helped him in his business. The business originally was in the name of John Phillips, although in a few instances bills were made out to John Phillips & Sons. The sons devoted all their time to the business and received a

portion of the profits, although the father repeatedly denied that they owned any interest in the business, saying on one occasion, "Na, na. I will ha' nae sons for partners. . . . They would put me out of the door." One of the sons withdrew from the business and sued for an accounting as a partner. His father resisted. *Phillips v. Phillips*, 49 Ill. 437.

3. Perry advanced $10,000 as a loan to L. W. Counselman & Co., a partnership, and received in turn a promissory note for that amount, together with a written agreement that the firm was to pay him one tenth of the net yearly profits of the business, if such profits exceeded the sum advanced as a loan. Upon Perry's death, his executor was sued by a firm creditor who, on learning the foregoing facts, contended that Perry was a partner. *Meehan v. Valentine*, 145 U.S. 611.

4. Plaintiff, under the name, "Taylor and Company," carried on an individual business. In a subsequent suit against a purchaser for goods sold and delivered, defendant set up, as a defense, that plaintiff was violating the law. *Taylor v. Bell & Bogart Soap Co.*, 18 App. Div. 175, 45 N.Y. Supp. 939.

5. Hutchinson allowed his name to be used with that of Cram under the firm name of Cram & Hutchinson, although in reality he was not a partner and had no interest in the firm. In a subsequent action, Hutchinson was able to show that he in fact was not a partner. Plaintiff insisted that Hutchinson was liable notwithstanding. *Hicks v. Cram*, 17 Vt. 449.

6. The death of one of the partners in the firm of "J. & J. Slater" automatically caused a dissolution of the firm. In a subsequent action by the executrix of the deceased partner for an accounting, plaintiff insisted that the firm name should be sold as an asset, but the surviving partner contended that as surviving partner, he was entitled to the firm name. *Slater v. Slater*, 175 N.Y. 143.

7. Defendant, a member of a business firm, was convicted of grand larceny for allegedly misappropriating $1,000 which he had taken from the firm's bank account. Defendant appealed. *State v. Elsbury*, 63 Nev. 463, 175 Pac. 2d 430.

8. Decedent, as a member of a firm, had been unable to do work of any sort for about one year before his death, thus placing an unusual burden upon the remaining partner, who now seeks extra compensation for his services in an accounting proceeding instituted by the executor of the deceased partner's estate. *Heath v. Waters*, 40 Mich. 457.

9. Defendant, a partner in a banking firm, was authorized to and did invest the sum of $15,000 on behalf of the firm. Although he acted honestly, his judgment was poor and the investment resulted in a substantial loss. The firm now seeks to recoup the loss by charging defendant with responsibility therefor. *Exchange Bank of Leon v. Gardner*, 104 Iowa 176, 73 N.W. 591.

10. Plaintiff and one O'Brien were partners. O'Brien, on behalf of his firm, received certain nonnegotiable vouchers for municipal work done by the firm. O'Brien transferred the vouchers to his father in payment of a *bona fide* individual obligation to his father. Plaintiff sued the father on behalf of the firm for an accounting. *Morrison v. Austin State Bank*, 213 Ill. 472, 72 N.E. 1109.

11. Three persons founded a partnership for the purpose of making and selling soap. One of the partners, without the knowledge of his copartners, borrowed money from a local bank on a note to which he signed the firm name. Upon default, the bank sued the copartners. *Winship et al. v. Bank of the United States*, 5 Peters (U.S.) 529.

12. Plaintiff leased a portion of his land to two brothers as partners in the piggery business, which later was suspended by the local authorities. When one of the brothers went on plaintiff's property to remove some lumber, an

altercation ensued, resulting in a wilful and deliberate assault, with resulting injuries inflicted upon plaintiff, who thereupon sued the partnership for damages. The court dismissed the complaint and the plaintiff appealed. *Polis v. Heizmann*, 276 Pa. 315, 120 A. 269.

13. Two partners who had been transacting business for a long period of time, formed a corporation to which they transferred all the partnership assets. Later, one of the partners, without the knowledge of the other, executed a promissory note to the plaintiff, on which he indorsed the partnership name. Suit is now brought against the firm and the other partner whose name did not appear on the note. *Seufert v. Gille*, 230 Mo. 453, 131 S.W. 102.

14. One of two partners sought a judicial decree of dissolution because of the extended illness of his copartner. The latter had already been physically incapacitated for a period of more than three and a half years. At the trial it was shown that the ill partner was making a gradual recovery, but that the term of the partnership would expire within less than a year and a half. *Barclay v. Barrie*, 209 N.Y. 40.

# 12

# Corporations

**Scope of This Chapter.** In this chapter we deal with that legal instrumentality which has completely revolutionized our modern way of doing business—the artificial person known as a corporation. In Part 1 we analyze the legal nature and attributes of a corporation, the characteristics which have made it so useful and popular as a medium for conducting business, and the various classifications of corporations. In Part 2 we deal with the promotion of a corporation, the steps necessary to bring it into existence, and its organization following incorporation, including the first meeting of incorporators, the first meeting of directors, and the adoption of by-laws. In Part 3 we deal with corporate ownership: subscriptions to and issuance of capital stock, the various classes of capital stock, and the consideration for which it may be issued. In Part 4 we deal with management: the qualifications of directors, the manner of their election, and their duties, powers and liabilities, including tenure, resignations and removal from office; also the election, duties, powers and liabilities of corporate officers. In Parts 5, 6 and 7 we consider the rights and liabilities of stockholders, and in Part 8 the rights, powers and liabilities of the corporation itself in dealing with the rest of the world. Part 9, dealing with insolvency, receivership, succession and dissolution of corporations, concludes the chapter.

## PART 1. NATURE AND CLASSIFICATION

**Law Governing Corporations.** The statutes governing corporations—their formation, powers, liabilities, management, stockholding, dissolution, and so on—vary in the different states, though conforming to a general pattern. To a limited extent, uniformity has been achieved through legislation. There are two uniform statutes dealing with corporations: the Uniform Stock Transfer Act[1] and the Uniform Business Corporation

---

[1] The Uniform Stock Transfer Act, widely adopted throughout the United States, sought to impart to innocent purchasers of stock for value, a measure of protection approaching, but falling far short of the position of a holder in due course of a negotiable instrument. The Uniform Commercial Code (Article 8, Investment Securities) broadens the protection afforded innocent purchasers for value of investment securities, including shares of stock. (See pages 903-904.)

Act.[2] To a surprisingly large extent, the courts have adopted a uniform approach to most of the basic legal problems involved in corporation practice.

## Nature and Characteristics

**Definition and Nature of Corporation.** A corporation, as defined by Chief Justice Marshall, is "an artificial being, invisible, intangible, and existing only in contemplation of law." It is a *fictitious person* adopted as a device whereby groups of individuals, large or small, may concentrate their efforts. It is endowed by law with many of the rights, duties powers and liabilities of a natural person. Being an artificial or fictitious person, it can act only through human agency: *directors,* who are elected by owners or *shareholders,* and who guide its policies and elect its *officers;* the latter, in turn, selecting its administrative *agents* and *employees.*

**Attributes of Corporation.** Corporations, regardless of type or class, have certain attributes that have an important bearing on the rights, powers, duties and liabilities of a corporation. Among these are the following: Creation by government franchise, existence as a legal entity and continuous succession.

**Corporations are Government Creatures.** Corporations are created by governmental authority. They cannot come into existence by mere contract, as in the case of partnerships. The right to exist as a corporation is sometimes referred to as a *primary franchise,* to distinguish it from a *secondary franchise,* such as the right subsequently acquired by certain corporations (page 499) to use public highways or city streets in connection with transportation, waterworks, gas, electric, telephone or telegraph services. A primary franchise is better known as a *charter.*

**Corporation as Legal Entity.** A corporation exists as a complete being, separate and apart from its incorporators, stockholders, directors, officers or employees. Corporate property belongs to the corporation, not to the stockholders; and corporate liabilities are the liabilities of a corporation, not of its stockholders.

EXAMPLES:

(1) If a person owns the entire capital stock of a corporation and nothing else, and such corporation owns nothing but real property, the stockholder does not own real property, but personal property; namely, shares of stock in the corporation.

(2) Button sued Hoffman for certain property belonging to a corporation. Button contended that the property belonged to him because he owned all the

---

[2] Until the past few years, the states were slow to adopt this statute. Idaho substantially adopted it in 1929. Illinois, Minnesota and Washington adopted some of its provisions in 1933, and Kentucky adopted many parts of it in 1946. Then the statute was revamped, improved and republished in 1951 as the Model Business Corporation Act, since which date it has been meeting with readier acceptance.

stock of the corporation that owned the property. The suit was dismissed. Button and the corporation, said the Court, were separate and distinct persons.[3]

Where the legal entity of a corporation is utilized to perpetrate a fraud, the courts may disregard it (page 548).

**Continuous Succession.** A corporation's existence continues, regardless of the death or incapacity of any of its directors, officers or employees, and regardless of changes in stockholder personnel. Corporate existence may continue forever (page 506).

**Purposes for Which Corporations May Be Formed.** A corporation may be formed for any lawful purpose, to do anything that a natural person may do. This rule is subject to certain exceptions (page 551).

**Advantages of Corporate Form of Doing Business.** We have already noted certain basic differences between partnerships and corporations (page 461). Corresponding with these differences are the basic advantages that corporations have over the individual or partnership form of doing business:

(1) *Limitation of liability: debts.* Persons conducting business as partners or individual proprietors may lose their all and go heavily into debt. Persons conducting business in corporate form risk liability only to the extent of the amount invested.

(2) *Limitation of liability: no agency.* Individual proprietors and partners are liable for all acts of their agents within the course and scope of their duties. Partners are additionally liable for the partnership acts of their copartners. Stockholders, as such, are in no sense agents of one another; neither is a stockholder personally liable for the acts of a corporation's directors, officers or employees.

(3) *Flexibility of financing.* Through the medium of widely distributed shares or units of ownership, it is possible to secure corporate financing on a larger scale than is the case with an individual or partnership undertaking.

(4) *Continuity of business.* A corporation, if its charter so provides, may continue business indefinitely, regardless of death or change of stockholders, and regardless of death or change of managing personnel. In the case of partnerships, on the other hand, the firm is terminated by the death or withdrawal of any of its members.

(5) *Transferabilty of interest.* If a person invests in an individual or partnership enterprise, it is not always easy for him to sell his interest in the business, and, when he does, the business as a rule suffers a violent change of management. The admission or withdrawal of a partner, for example, usually dissolves the firm. This is not true of a corporation. Stockholders need not even know one another. In thousands of corporate enterprises, hundreds of thousands of stockholders freely buy and sell their shares without in any way affecting continuity of management.

---

[3] *Button v. Hoffman,* 61 Wis. 20, 20 N.W. 667.

(6) *Concentration of business strength through right to act as entity.* Partnerships, to a greater or less degree, must still act as individuals, rather than as an entity. Corporations, as entities, enable large groups to concentrate their power and to exert more effectively their combined efforts and resources in the conduct of their business. A corporation may own property, make contracts, conduct business, sue and be sued, all as a single person and in its own name.

**Disadvantages of Corporate Form of Doing Business.** Among the disadvantages of the corporate form of doing business are the following:

(1) *Expense.* Persons must pay for the privilege of doing business in corporate form. The cost varies with the size of the corporation, amount of stock authorized and issued, amount of business done, and so on. The initial incorporation and organization expenses, including filing fees, organization taxes, attorney's fees, and so on, are relatively less burdensome on larger than on smaller corporations.

(2) *Taxation.* Many states have franchise taxes which must be paid annually for the privilege of doing business as a corporation. The tax burden, Federal and state, tends to be heavier in the case of corporations than with individuals and partnerships. Excess profits taxes constitute one example. Profits of a partnership, unlike those of a corporation, are apportionable among partners. Special corporate taxes and levies are not uncommon.

(3) *Scope of activity: charter limitations.* Individuals and firms may engage in any legitimate business, as their desires may dictate. A corporation may do only those things that are expressly or impliedly authorized in its charter. (See pages 550-551.)

(4) *Right to do business in other states.* Natural persons, either as individuals or as members of a firm, have the constitutional right to conduct business in any state of the Union. This is not true of corporations. (See pages 549-550.)

(5) *Government supervision.* Partnerships and individuals are free from the necessity imposed upon corporations of filing Federal and state returns concerning their activities, capital stock, director and officer personnel, and so on.

(6) *Right to practice profession.* Corporations, as pointed out on page 553, are generally forbidden to practice the professions.

**Corporations Distinguished from Joint-Stock Associations.** We have already noted certain resemblances and distinctions between joint-stock associations and partnerships (page 462). Joint-stock associations also resemble corporations in certain respects and differ from them in others.

(a) *Resemblances.* Joint-stock associations resemble corporations in the following respects:

(1) *Capital stock.* Joint-stock associations issue shares of stock against capital.

(2) *Continuous succession.* Joint-stock associations enjoy the corporate advantage of continuous succession (page 496).

(3) *Management.* Like corporations, joint-stock associations are managed by directors and officers.

(b) *Differences.* Joint-stock associations differ from corporations, and resemble partnerships, in the following respects:

(1) *Name in which suits may be brought and defended.* In most states a joint-stock association sues or is sued in the names of its members, or in the name of its president or treasurer, not in its registered name.

(2) *Personal liability.* Members of a joint-stock association are individually liable for its debts.

Joint-stock associations are sometimes formed by groups not desiring to incorporate, such as labor unions, trade associations, insurance underwriting groups, stock exchanges and cooperative stores.

## Classification of Corporations

**General Classification.** Corporations may be generally classified as follows:

(1) Public and private
(2) Domestic and foreign
(3) *De jure* and *de facto*
(4) Corporations by estoppel.

*De jure* and *de facto* corporations are discussed on page 502, and corporations by estoppel on page 503.

**Public Corporations.** A public corporation is one created for governmental purposes. Theoretically, every government, Federal, state or local, is a corporation. However, the term "public corporation" is more commonly applied to a governmental division that has received a specific grant of corporate powers in the form of a charter, such as a *municipal* corporation or a *public benefit* corporation.

*Municipal corporations.* A municipal corporation is a political or governmental agency of the state that has been constituted for the local government of the territorial division described and that exercises, by delegation, a portion of the sovereign power for the public good. It is the creation of the legislature, which endows it with certain local governmental functions and imposes upon it the performance of certain duties.[4]

*Public benefit corporations.* Public benefit corporations are organized to construct or operate a public improvement wholly or partly within a state, such as a bridge or a tunnel, the profits from such improvement to inure to the benefit of the state or states thus served.

*Quasi corporations.* The word "quasi" means "as if." Some bodies are not exactly corporations but are treated as if they were; for example,

---

[4] *MacMullen v. City of Middletown*, 187 N.Y. 37, 79 N.E. 863.

a board of county commissioners representing the county, boards of school trustees, boards of education, and the like.

*Quasi public ("public utility") corporations.* A quasi public corporation is one engaged in rendering service of such general public importance as to justify the privilege of *eminent domain* (page 13) and amenability to public regulation under the *police power* (pages 13 and 570).

EXAMPLES: Common carriers, water works, gas, electric, telephone and telegraph companies, and all companies coming generally within the classification of *public service* or *public utility* corporations.

**Private Corporations.** Private corporations are those organized for nongovernmental purposes. They embrace *stock* and *nonstock* corporations.

*Stock corporations.* A stock corporation is one having shares of stock, and authorized by law to distribute dividends to the holders of such shares. Stock corporations are variously classified in the different states, according to statute. Under the New York statute they are classified as follows:

(1) *Moneyed corporations:* Formed under or subject to the Banking Law or the Insurance Law.

(2) *Railroad corporations:* Engaged in railway transportation and organized under the Railroad Law.

(3) *Transportation corporations:* Organized under or subject to the Transportation Corporations Law, and actually embracing nontransportation as well as transportation companies, such as gas, electric, telegraph, telephone, water works, omnibus, ferry, pipeline, freight-terminal and district steam corporations.

(4) *Business corporations:* Engaged in general manufacturing, commercial or industrial activity for profit.

(5) *Co-operative corporations:* Such as producers' or consumers' cooperative stock corporations.

*Nonstock corporations.* Nonstock corporations are those that do not issue stock, such as:

(1) *Religious corporations:* Organized for religious purposes.

(2) *Membership corporations:* Including incorporated clubs, hospitals, colleges, benevolent societies, fire companies, cemetery corporations, bar and medical associations, boards of trade, and so on.

**Domestic and Foreign Corporations.** A corporation doing business in the state where it was incorporated is known in that state as a *domestic* corporation. All other corporations in that state are *foreign* corporations. (See pages 549-550.)

## Questions

1. Just exactly what is a corporation?
2. Name the three essential attributes of a corporation.

3. What are the six basic advantages of the corporate form of doing business?

4. Name six disadvantages of the corporate form of doing business.

5. Name three points of resemblance between corporations and joint stock associations.

6. What are two differences between corporations and joint stock associations?

7. Name the four general classifications of corporations. Explain.

8. Give five different classifications of stock corporations.

9. Name two types of nonstock corporations.

10. Distinguish between a domestic and a foreign corporation.

## Problems

1. Clark sues Stover for trespass. Stover interposes the technical defense that the property allegedly trespassed does not belong to Clark, but to the Clark Corporation. Clark's reply is that he owns all the stock of his corporation. How will the Court decide? Why?

2. Ames, Bond and Crane owned all the stock of the ABC Corporation, which became insolvent and went into bankruptcy. Unable to collect from the corporation, the creditors brought action against the three individual stockholders for recovery of the corporate obligations, on the ground that the corporation was merely a "front" for the stockholders. How was the suit decided? Why?

3. The three sole stockholders of Peerless Coal Company, Inc., were killed in a railroad wreck on their way home from business. In a subsequent suit against the corporation based on breach of contract, it was contended that the coal company had been automatically dissolved by the deaths of all of the stockholders. How did the Court decide? Why?

## PART 2. PROMOTION, INCORPORATION AND ORGANIZATION

**Promotion, Incorporation and Organization Distinguished.** *Promotion* relates to the plans and steps which precede and determine the formation, purpose and structure of a corporation and the way its shares and interests are to be issued and distributed. *Incorporation* relates to the legal steps by which a corporation is brought into existence. *Organization* relates to the legal steps by which a corporation is made to function.

## Promotion

**Promoter Defined.** A promoter is one who undertakes to form a corporation, or cause it to be formed, for a specified purpose or purposes, and who further undertakes to procure for the corporation the capital, rights, property and organization necessary to achieve such purpose or purposes.

**Promoters' Profits.** Promoters are self-appointed agents of the corporation they undertake to form. Before the corporation comes into functioning existence, with directors and officers to safeguard its interests, promoters are in a position to dictate the way the corporation is to be formed, how it is to be organized, how capital is to be raised, the price at which stock is to be sold, and so on. The position of promoters, therefore, in relation to the corporation and to the stockholders, is highly fiduciary. Hence, promoters will not be permitted to take advantage of their position and to make secret profits at the expense of the corporation or its subscribers.

**When Corporation Bound by Promoter's Contracts.** Corporations come into existence unfettered by contract obligations. A corporation is, therefore, not bound by any agreement made by a promoter on its behalf, unless and until the corporation approves the agreement. If the corporation fails to approve the agreement, the promoter alone is bound.

EXAMPLE: The directors of the *XYZ* Corporation, notwithstanding a large net profit, decide not to declare a dividend. Smith claims that prior to incorporation, *K,* one of the promoters, made dividend promises contrary to the present acts of the directors. Such promises, unless subsequently approved by the corporation, are in no way binding upon it.

**Adoption *v.* Ratification.** Since the acts of a promoter are not for himself, but for the proposed corporation, they constitute acts of an agent without an existing principal. Hence, contracts made for a corporation before it comes into existence are said to be *adopted,* rather than ratified, upon subsequent corporate approval.

**Express *v.* Implied Adoption.** Corporate adoption should be reflected in the *minutes* (pages 521 and 535). However, though not so expressed, it may be inferred from corporate conduct.

EXAMPLE: Four promoters retained Morgan as accountant to inaugurate a bookkeeping system for a corporation to be organized. They promised that the corporation would pay Morgan by issuing to him 25 shares of its stock. Upon incorporation, Morgan, with the knowledge and approval of the officers of the corporation (who had been its promoters), performed the services as agreed, but the corporation refused to issue the 25 shares as promised. The Court held that the facts themselves spelled out an adoption.[5]

## Incorporation

**Source of Authority.** The sovereign power to grant corporate charters is vested in the states. The Federal Government has no power to grant corporate charters except as to territory under its jurisdiction, such as the District of Columbia, and except as an incident to the conduct of its own business. Thus, Congress has power to create a corporation as a means of executing a Federal power conferred by the Constitution. Examples are the Federal Deposit Insurance Corporation, Federal Farm Mortgage Corporation, production credit corporations, Federal Savings and Loan Insurance Corporation and the Home Owners' Loan Corporation.

---

[5] *Morgan v. Bon Bon Company,* 222 N.Y. 22, 118 N.E. 205.

Originally, every corporate franchise (page 495) required a special statute. Today, except in special cases, corporations are formed merely by complying with the provisions of a general statute.

**Right to repeal, alter or amend.** In the famous Dartmouth College Case,[6] Chief Justice Marshall held that a charter was a contract, and that no state, having granted a charter, could repeal, alter or amend it without violating the constitutional provision against impairing the obligation of contracts. As a result, most if not all state constitutions provide that corporate charters shall not be granted outright (as in the Dartmouth College Case), but shall be subject to the right of the state at any time to repeal, alter or amend.

**Failure to Comply with Incorporation Laws.** Broadly speaking, corporations cannot come into existence except upon compliance with incorporation laws. To this rule, however, there are several exceptions, including *de facto* as distinguished from *de jure* corporations, and corporations by *estoppel*.

**De Jure and De Facto Corporations.** A *de jure* corporation is one duly and properly formed under the law. A *de facto* corporation is one not so formed, yet deemed in fact to exist for certain purposes, provided the following elements are present:

(1) There is a law in existence under which such a corporation can be formed;

(2) There has been some colorable attempt to comply with such law, i.e., a bona fide attempt to organize; and

(3) There has been an exercise or use of corporate powers.

**Failure to file certificate.** "A corporation ordinarily may have de facto existence although it fails to comply with statutory provisions relating to the filing or recording of the articles or certificate of incorporation, or of the charter, provided there is a bona fide attempt to comply with such requirements and a colorable compliance; otherwise not." [7]

Colorable compliance does not mean substantial compliance; rather, good faith is the test.

EXAMPLE: Three incorporators retain an attorney who prepares a certificate of incorporation. The incorporators execute it, with instructions to one of them to take it to the lawyer for filing. The incorporator forgets to do so; the lawyer assumes that the incorporators have dropped the matter; and in the meantime the other incorporators make various contracts on behalf of the corporation. These facts might justify recognition of *de facto* existence. There was a "colorable" attempt to comply. Bad faith was wholly absent.

**De Facto Corporations: No Personal Liability.** Where the law recognizes the *de facto* existence of a corporation, its officers and employees cannot be personally held for debts incurred on its behalf.

---

[6] *Dartmouth College v. Woodward*, 4 Wheat. (U.S.) 518, 636.

[7] 18 C.J.S. 498.

EXAMPLE: A corporation was duly organized in every respect except that the addresses of the initial subscribers to the stock were inadvertently omitted from the certificate of incorporation. Subsequently, a creditor, denying that the corporation had valid existence, sought to hold the incorporators (who later became directors and officers) personally liable on the debt. Since *de facto* existence cannot be collaterally attacked, the suit must fail.

**Corporations by Estoppel.** Even where the elements of a *de facto* corporation are missing, a corporation may be deemed to exist for the purposes of a given transaction if the principle of *estoppel* (page 877) would make it unjust to allow a denial of corporate existence.

EXAMPLES:

(1) *Where persons purport to act on behalf of a nonexistent corporation, and later seek to deny corporate existence.* Arnold, Bates and Church contract with Dalton in behalf of the *ABC* Company, Inc., which exists as a trade name ("*ABC* Company") but not as a corporation. Dalton sues *ABC* Company, Inc. as a corporation. Arnold, Bates and Church are estopped to deny the corporate existence of such company.

(2) *Where persons deal with a nonexistent corporation as if it existed, then seek to deny liability to such corporation on the ground that it does not exist.* In the preceding illustration, Dalton, if sued by *ABC* Company, Inc., would be estopped to deny its corporate existence.

(3) *Where persons purporting to act for a nonexistent corporation are charged with personal liability when the nonexistence of the corporation is disclosed.* Using the illustration given above, Dalton, after dealing with *ABC* Company, Inc. as if it were a corporation, seeks to hold Arnold, Bates and Church personally liable as partners, or at least as joint principals, on the ground that *ABC* Company, Inc. is not really a corporation. Is Dalton estopped from denying corporate existence and from seeking to hold Arnold, Bates and Church personally liable? Some cases say yes, others no. Majority view: Persons cannot shelter themselves behind the doctrine of estoppel, and escape personal liability, by inducing strangers to contract with a pretended corporation.

**No Existence *De Jure, De Facto,* or by Estoppel: Personal Liability.** "Where an association has no corporate existence either de jure or de facto, and there is no estoppel, it cannot do any act whatever as a legal entity. It cannot take title to real or to personal property, convey real property, * * * acquire rights by contract or otherwise, incur debts or other liabilities either in contract or in tort, sue or be sued." [8] In such cases the associates are personally liable as partners.

**Steps in Formation of Stock Corporation.** The term *incorporation* is generally applied to the steps necessary for the formation of a corporation. These steps may vary slightly with the type of corporation. We may take as an example the formation of a business stock corporation under the New York statute. In the formation of such a corporation three steps are involved:

(1) Preparation of the certificate of incorporation.

---

[8] 18 *C.J.S.* 488.

(2) Filing and payment of taxes and fees.

(3) Organization:

    (a) Meeting of incorporators.

    (b) First meeting of directors.

**Qualifications of Incorporators.** Qualifications of incorporators vary. In New York, any three or more persons of full age may form a corporation, provided two-thirds of them are United States citizens and one of them is a resident of the state.[9]

**Certificate of Incorporation: Contents.** Except for minor variations, the required contents of a certificate of incorporation are fairly uniform in the different states.[10] They usually embrace: (1) Proposed name; (2) purpose; (3) capital stock; (4) principal place of business; (5) duration; (6) directors; (7) subscribers to stock; and (8) designation of agent to accept service of process.

(1) *Corporate name.* Every corporation must have a name. Such name remains the property of the corporation as long as the corporation continues to exist. The corporation may, however, change its name by complying with the statutory requirements for change of name. Under the common law a corporation could have adopted any name. Statutory provisions now place restrictions upon the use of corporate names. These restrictions vary. The most common restrictions relate to (a) similarity, (b) indication of corporate character, and (b) prohibition against certain words as part of the corporate name.

(a) *Similarity of names.* Incorporators generally ascertain in advance from the secretary of state whether the proposed name of the corporation is acceptable. The secretary of state will reject a certificate if the name too closely resembles that of an existing corporation. Approval by the secretary of state constitutes no guaranty that use of the name will not be enjoined by the courts as too similar to an existing name. It is difficult to lay down a fixed rule as to when names will be prohibited as too similar, and when not.

(b) *Words or abbreviations indicating corporate character.* In most states, business corporations must contain words or abbreviations that clearly indicate that the name is that of a corporation, as distinguished from a natural person or a partnership. Such words or abbreviations are "Corporation," "Corp.," "Incorporated," or "Inc."

(c) *Prohibited words.* Ordinary business corporations must not give the impression that they are financial institutions. Hence, such words as "bank," "trust," "surety," and so on, may not be used in the name of an ordinary business corporation. In some states (Pennsylvania, for example)

---

[9] The requirement that one of the incorporators must be a resident of the state obtains in only eighteen of the fifty-three states and territories. The Model Business Corporation Act omits it.

[10] The comment on pages 504 to 507 in reference to the contents of such certificate is substantially applicable to incorporations generally.

FORM 11

# CERTIFICATE OF INCORPORATION
## OF THE
## HAMILTON AUTOMOBILE CO., INC.

(Pursuant to Article Two of the Stock Corporation Law)

We, the undersigned, for the purpose of forming a corporation pursuant to Article two of the Stock Corporation Law of the State of New York, certify:

*First:* The name of the proposed corporation shall be Hamilton Automobile Co., Inc.

*Second:* The purposes for which it is to be formed are to make and deal in automobiles, automobile accessories and supplies, and supplies for whatever purpose used. (Note: usually this clause is expressed at greater length and the corporation is given a wider range of "express" powers.)

*Third:* The amount of the capital stock of the corporation shall be $100,000.

*Fourth:* The capital stock shall consist of 1,000 shares of a par value of $100 each, all of which are to be of the same class.

*Fifth:* The principal office of the corporation shall be located in the City, County, and State of New York and the address to which the Secretary of State shall mail a copy of any process in any action or proceeding against the corporation, which may be served upon him, is 70 Fifth Avenue, New York, N. Y.

*Sixth:* The duration of the corporation shall be perpetual.

*Seventh:* The number of directors shall be not less than three nor more than seven.

*Eighth:* The names and post-office addresses of the directors until the first annual meeting of the stockholders are:

| Name | Post-office address |
| --- | --- |
| Joseph Hall | 98 South Elm Ave., Brooklyn, New York City |
| James McKeon | 108 North Oak Ave., Bronx, New York City |
| Andrew J. Cook | 118 West Poplar Rd., Queens, New York City |

*Ninth:* The names and post-office addresses of the subscribers to the certificate, and the number of shares of stock which each agrees to take are as follows:

| Subscriber | Post-office address | Shares |
| --- | --- | --- |
| Joseph Hall | 98 South Elm Ave., Brooklyn, New York City | 50 |
| James McKeon | 108 North Oak Ave., Bronx, New York City | 2 |
| Andrew J. Cook | 118 West Poplar Road, Queens, New York City | 2 |

*Tenth:* All the subscribers to this certificate are of full age, at least two-thirds of them are citizens of the United States, at least one of them is a resident of the State of New York, and at least one of the persons named as a director is a citizen of the United States and a resident of the State of New York.

*Eleventh:* The Secretary of State is hereby designated as the agent of the corporation upon whom process in any action or proceeding against it may be served.

In witness whereof we have made, signed, and acknowledged this certificate on the 9th day of November, 1950.

(Signed)    JOSEPH HALL
    JAMES McKEON
    ANDREW J. COOK

the statute prohibits the registration of names containing the word "state." Hence, the name "Keystone State Moving Picture Operators Association" was held to violate the statute.[11]

(2) *Purpose: objects and powers of corporations.* The *object* of a

---

[11] *Horowitz v. Beamish*, 323 Pa. 273, 185 A. 760.

corporation is the business purpose for which it is formed; for example, the object of a real estate corporation is to deal in real estate. The *powers* of a corporation are the things that a corporation may do to achieve its object; for example, the power of a real estate corporation to issue a note or purchase land. The franchise or charter granted by the state gives the corporation its power to do business as a corporation for the purposes specified in the charter. The nature of the business to be carried on by the corporation must accordingly be set forth in what is known as the "purpose clause" of the certificate of incorporation, which in reality specifies not only the objects and purposes of the corporation, but its powers as well. *Express powers* are those specifically set forth in the charter. *Implied powers* are those inferred from the express powers as necessarily incidental to corporate existence and the conduct of the business. (See pages 550-551.)

(3) *Capital stock.* The certificate of incorporation must set forth the kinds and amounts of capital stock that the corporation is authorized to issue in exchange for capital. The nature of capital stock, its different classifications and the purposes for which it may be issued are discussed on pages 509 to 517.

(4) *Location.* The location of the principal office of the corporation must be set forth in the certificate because the law requires that corporate books and records be kept at the principal offices of the corporation. Such books and records must be available for inspection by stockholders and judgment creditors, and the officers of the corporation must have a specified place of business where they may be served with process should occasion arise.

(5) *Duration.* Formerly it was the custom to fix a given number of years as the duration of a corporation's existence. It is now common practice to specify in the certificate of incorporation that the duration of corporate existence shall be perpetual.

(6) *Directors.* The certificate must set forth the name and address of each director who is to serve either during the first year or, as is now commonly provided, until the first annual meeting of stockholders. It must also specify the *number* of directors the corporation is to have. There must be a minimum of those, as a rule.

(7) *Subscribers to stock.* The names and addresses of each subscriber to the certificate of incorporation and a statement of the number of shares of stock that he agrees to take, must be set forth in the certificate. There is no specific requirement, however, as to the number of shares that a subscriber must take.

(8) *Designation of agent for service of process.* In suits against a corporation, the summons or other process may be served on an officer, director or managing agent. It has often been difficult to secure service of

process on a corporation because of difficulty in locating an officer. Hence statutes frequently provide that the certificate of incorporation must designate the name of the agent for the corporation upon whom process may be served, or the secretary of state as agent for such purpose.

**Signature and Acknowledgment.** Incorporators must sign the certificate of incorporation at the end, and must acknowledge their signature before a notary public or other person authorized to take oaths. The acknowledgment is for the purpose of authenticating the signature and to prevent forgery.

**Filing the Certificate: Fees and Taxes.** The certificate of incorporation is usually filed with the secretary of state or other corresponding official, and a certified copy filed with the county clerk or corresponding official having charge of the county records in the county where the corporation is to have its principal place of business. Upon such filing and the payment of required fees and taxes, the corporation comes into existence. No corporation may exercise any corporate powers or privileges until such taxes and fees have been paid.

## Organization

**First Meeting of Incorporators.** The first meeting of incorporators is held at a time and place fixed either pursuant to a written call, or by a written "waiver of notice" signed by all the incorporators. If the incorporators are "dummies," that is, nominees of the true parties in interest, they tender assignments of their stock subscriptions to the true stockholders in interest. If the directors are dummies, they tender their resignations and the directors who are actually to serve are elected in their place. It is also customary at the organization meeting for corporate resolutions to be adopted for the purpose of enabling the corporation to start functioning; such as resolutions authorizing the issuance of stock for cash or other property; resolutions for the acquisition of a business or business property in exchange for stock or cash, such as a store, plant, machinery, patents and good will; resolutions designating a bank or banks as depositories of corporate funds; and resolutions covering any other matters necessary to enable the corporation to begin functioning.

**By-Laws.** One of the most important steps in organizing a corporation is to adopt by-laws, which govern the conduct of the corporation by specifying the duties and powers of officers, the time and manner of holding meetings, the fiscal year of the corporation, and so on. At common law, only the members or stockholders could adopt, rescind, alter or amend by-laws. Under the law today, directors are generally authorized to adopt by-laws for the corporation, subject to by-laws, if any, adopted by the members or stockholders. By-laws are binding on the corporation, its officers and directors. They have the binding force of a contract. No by-laws may be adopted, amended or rescinded so as to impair vested rights (see example on page 533).

**First Meeting of Directors.** This usually follows immediately after the first meeting of incorporators. The directors elect officers, and the corporation is then ready to do business.

## Questions

1. Distinguish (a) promotion, (b) incorporation, and (c) organization, as related to the formation of a corporation.
2. What is a promoter's legal relationship to the corporation and its stockholders?
3. When is a corporation bound by a promoter's contract?
4. Distinguish between corporate adoption and ratification.
5. Comment on the decision in the Dartmouth College case with respect to the right of a state to amend or change a corporate charter.
6. Distinguish between a *de jure* and a *de facto* corporation.
7. What three elements must be present in order that a *de facto* corporation may be said to exist?
8. What is a "corporation by estoppel"? Give three illustrations.
9. Name three basic steps in forming a stock corporation.
10. What are the qualifications of an incorporator in your state?
11. Name eight major items in a certificate of incorporation.
12. In what three major respects does the law restrict the use of corporate names?
13. Distinguish between the "objects" and the "powers" of a corporation.
14. What is the purpose of the provision in a certificate of incorporation which designates an agent for service of process?
15. Outline the process of organizing a corporation.

## Problems

1. Darby, a promoter, induces a merchant to subscribe to stock in a corporation about to be formed, on the promise that the corporation will give the merchant a large order for his merchandise. After the corporation is organized, Darby is unable to induce its directors to order the merchandise in question, and the merchant sues the corporation. Who should have judgment? Why?
2. The promoters of a corporation retain an attorney to handle the legal details of organization up to and through the first meeting of incorporators. The attorney submits a bill for his services, but the corporation defends on the ground that it made no agreement with the attorney and adopted no resolution approving payment of his fees. Will the attorney succeed in collecting a fee from the corporation?
3. A duly executed certificate of incorporation is forwarded by an attorney to the secretary of state, but is apparently lost in the mails. The attorney informs the incorporators of this fact, and requests that they execute a new certificate, which they decide to do at a later date. In the meantime, they hold an organization meeting, elect directors and officers, and enter into various contracts. In a suit by the supposed corporation on one of these contracts, the defense of no corporate existence is interposed. How will the court decide?
4. A certificate of incorporation is duly filed with the Secretary of State,

all filing fees and organization taxes are paid, stock is issued, directors and officers are elected, business is commenced, and then it is discovered that the certificate is defective since the notary who took the acknowledgment was not qualified to do so, his term having expired. A debtor against whom this corporation has instituted suit raises the question of the *de facto* existence of the plaintiff. How should the court rule?

5. John James and William Wise, purportedly acting on behalf of "The Wise Corporation" (which does not exist), enter into a contract with Durkin, after opening a substantial bank account in the name of said corporation. The contract being breached, Durkin sues "The Wise Corporation." The answer interposes the defense of no corporate existence. How should the court decide and why?

6. Abraham Able organized a corporation under the name of Able Ladies Apparel Shop, Inc., which became a rival of a much older and long established corporation with the name of Able Stores Corp. Can the latter get relief in equity against the former?

7. A certificate of incorporation of a business stock corporation was signed by four persons, two of whom were over 21 years of age, three of whom were citizens of the United States, and one of such three was a resident of your state. Was the certificate legal, and why?

8. Brown attempted to file a certificate of incorporation of the Brown Trading and Trust Corporation under a Stock Corporation Law. Should the certificate be accepted?

## PART 3. OWNERSHIP: CAPITAL STOCK

**Capital *v*. Capital Stock.** Capital, as applied to corporations, means the value of the property actually received for stock issued by the corporation. Thus, if $50,000 has been paid into the treasury of a corporation against stock issued, the capital of the corporation is $50,000.

Capital stock, in its strict sense, is substantially synonymous with capital. In everyday practice, however, capital stock has come to mean not only the aggregate of a corporation's assets but also a convenient mode of expressing collective ownership. It is because capital stock is supposed to reflect the aggregate of a corporation's assets that the law rigorously insists that it may be issued only in exchange for equivalent value.

Capital stock is fixed, capital assets may vary. If, after a corporation starts business, its net assets remain the same as its capital stock, the result is neither surplus nor deficit. If the net assets exceed the capital stock, there is a surplus; if they shrink below the amount of the capital stock, there is a deficit.

**Share of Stock: Nature of.** A share of stock is the interest or right that the holder has in the corporation. It gives the holder no right to the property of the corporation because that belongs to the corporation itself. In other words, a share of stock is not a physical piece or fraction of the corporate property, but rather a *right or collection of rights* in respect to the corporation.

**Shares of Stock: How Issued.** Shares of stock are issued in the form

# COMMON STOCK CERTIFICATE

*(Front)*

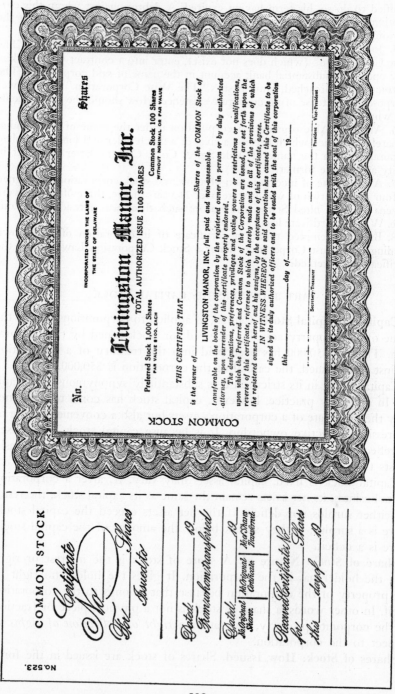

# COMMON STOCK CERTIFICATE

### (Reverse Side)

THE DESIGNATIONS, PREFERENCES, PRIVILEGES AND VOTING POWERS OR RESTRICTIONS OR QUALIFICATIONS OF THE SHARES OF EACH CLASS ARE AS FOLLOWS:—

The authorized shares of stock without par value, may be issued by this corporation from time to time for such consideration as may be fixed from time to time by the Board of Directors; and any and all shares without par value so issued, the consideration for which so fixed has been paid or delivered, shall be fully paid stock and shall not be liable to any further call or assessment thereon, and the holders of such shares shall not be liable for any further payments in respect of such shares.

The holders of the shares of Preferred Stock shall be entitled to receive and the corporation shall be bound to pay thereon, preferential dividends, as and when declared by the Board of Directors, out of the annual net profits of the corporation or out of its net assets in excess of its capital, as determined pursuant and subject to the provisions of the General Corporation Law of the State of Delaware, at the rate of Five (5%) per centum cumulative from the date of issuance and payable semi-annually on the first day of January and July, before any dividends shall be declared or paid upon or set apart for the holders of the shares of Common Stock.

After full dividends at the rate of Five (5%) per centum for the then current year and for all previous years shall have been declared and paid upon or set apart for the holders of the shares of Preferred Stock, additional dividends may be declared or paid or set apart during such year. Such additional dividends if declared, shall be set apart for or paid exclusively to the holders of the shares of Common stock, share and share alike, subject however, to the provisions hereinafter contained to the effect that no dividends shall be paid on the Common Stock until all of the outstanding Preferred Stock has been either redeemed or funds have been set apart for such redemption.

The corporation, through its Board of Directors, and conformable with the General Corporation Law of the State of Delaware, may from time to time redeem the whole or any part of the Preferred stock at the price of One Hundred Dollars ($100) per share, plus any arrearages of dividends thereon that may be due and payable to the date of such redemption. The notice of such redemption shall be mailed not less than thirty (30) days prior to the date upon which the stock is to be redeemed to each holder of stock so to be redeemed, at his address as it appears on the books of the corporation. In the event that less than all of the outstanding Preferred Stock of the corporation is to be redeemed, the amount to be redeemed and the method of effecting such redemption, whether by lot or pro-rata or otherwise, may be determined by the Board of Directors. On and after the date fixed for such redemption the holders of shares so called for redemption shall cease to be entitled to any further dividends on such preferred

stock and the respective holders thereof shall have no right or interest thereon or thereon, by reason of the ownership of such shares, except to receive the said redemption price, plus arrearages of dividends, as a debt without interest, upon presentation and surrender of their certificates therefor.

In the event of any liquidation, dissolution or winding up of the corporation, whether voluntary or involuntary, the holders of the shares of Preferred Stock shall be entitled to receive out of the assets of the corporation (whether from capital or surplus or both) the par amount of their Preferred shares plus any arrearages of dividends that may be due and unpaid thereon to that time, before any distribution shall be made to the holders of the shares of Common Stock, and thereafter the holders of the shares of Common Stock shall be entitled, to the exclusion of the holders of the shares of Preferred stock, to share ratably in all assets of the corporation remaining after such payment to the holders of the shares of Preferred stock. If, upon such liquidation, dissolution or winding up of the corporation, the assets of the corporation shall be insufficient to permit the payment in full to the holders of the shares of Preferred stock of the amount distributable as aforesaid, then the entire assets of the corporation shall be distributed among the holders of the shares of Preferred stock. The foregoing provision of this paragraph shall not, however, be deemed to require the distribution of assets among the holders of the shares of Preferred stock and the holders of the shares of Common stock in the event of a consolidation, merger, lease or sale, which does not in fact result in the liquidation or winding up of the enterprise.

No dividends shall be paid on the Common Stock until all of the outstanding Preferred Stock has been either redeemed or funds have been set apart for such redemption, and any holder of common stock shall have the right to demand the prompt redemption of all outstanding Preferred stock if there are sufficient funds available for such purpose, and in that case and upon such demand, the preferential dividend of Five (5%) percent on such Preferred Stock shall thereafter cease to be payable thereon, and the directors may declare and pay such dividend or dividends upon the Common Stock as will then be advisable from the surplus funds of the corporation.

The corporation shall not issue any Preferred stock, except for actual cash paid to the corporation in the amount of the par value of the Preferred stock so issued.

Subject to the General Corporation Law of the State of Delaware the voting power shall vest exclusively in the holders of the shares of Common Stock.

---

For Value Received,_____ hereby sell, assign, and transfer unto_____

_____ Shares of the Capital Stock represented by the within Certificate, and do hereby irrevocably constitute and appoint _____ Attorney to transfer the said Stock on the books of the within named Company, with full power of substitution in the premises.

Dated_____ 19____

In presence of

of *stock certificates* (see Form 12). These designate the name of the holder, the number and kind of shares issued to him, and the date of issuance. A certificate of stock is not valid unless signed by the proper officers of the company, with corporate seal affixed. Once issued, stock may be transferred in various ways (page 532).

**Bearer shares.** When a certificate of stock is made out to bearer, the shares are known as *bearer shares.*

**Closed corporation: family corporation.** A corporation whose capital stock is held by a limited group is known as a *closed corporation.* When the limited group are members of the same family, the corporation is known as a *family corporation.*

**Par Value and No-Par Value Stock.** Stock that is given a fixed arbitrary value is called *par value stock.* Stock that has no fixed value is known as *no-par value stock.* The rights and privileges of the holders of par value stock are the same as those who hold no-par value stock; that is, the distinction between the two is not a distinction of rights and privileges of the stockholders but of the form of issuance and the stockholder's liability in connection with it (page 516).

**"Authorized," "Issued," "Outstanding," and "Treasury" Stock.** The maximum amount of capital stock that a corporation is authorized by its charter to issue is known as its *authorized* capital stock. Any part of such stock for which a certificate has been made out and delivered is known as *issued* stock. Issued stock in the hands of stockholders is known as *outstanding* stock. Issued stock returned to or reacquired by the corporation is known as *treasury* stock.

**Treasury stock: how acquired.** A corporation may acquire its own stock by purchase, by donation, in extinguishment of a debt, and as a forfeited pledge or collateral.

**Treasury stock purchasable only out of surplus.** A corporation may purchase its own stock only out of surplus. To do otherwise would prejudice the rights of creditors. If a corporation disposed of all its capital assets in buying up all its outstanding stock, there would be nothing left with which to pay creditors.

**No right to vote treasury stock.** A corporation cannot, in any true sense, be a stockholder in itself. Hence, it cannot vote its treasury stock, whether held by the treasurer, trustee, or other official on behalf of the corporation.

**Classes of Stock: In General.** The different classes of ownership interest and the rights, privileges, limitations or liabilities that go with each class are as set forth in the certificate of incorporation. Thus, the capital stock of a company may consist of *common stock* and *preferred stock.* The latter may be *cumulative* or *noncumulative, participating* and *nonparticipating.* Preferred stock may be subclassified as to various preferences, such as *first preferred, second preferred,* and so on. Ordinary stock may likewise have various classifications, such as *Class A, Class B,* and so on. However, none of these designations or classifications has meaning other than that defined in the certificate of incorporation. The usual provisions specifying the rights, privileges, limitations or liabilities of the different classes of stock commonly issued are set forth in the stock classifications which follow.

**Common Stock.** The holder of this class of stock has, as a rule, a right to vote but no right to dividends unless the directors see fit to declare them.

**Preferred Stock.** The holder of this class of stock, as the name implies, is usually given some kind of preference over another class of stock. The usual preferences relate to dividends and the distribution of assets upon dissolution.

*Cumulative preferred stock.* If a dividend is not earned on this class of stock, the obligation to pay it continues or accumulates until it is paid.

EXAMPLE: The *ABC* Corporation has the following stock outstanding: 1000 shares of cumulative $6-a-year preferred and 1000 shares of common. For five years it fails to earn or pay a dividend. In the sixth year it earns a profit of $30,000. The directors propose to distribute $25,000, as back dividends on the preferred, and $5 per share on the common. This they cannot do. All past and current dividends on the cumulative preferred must be paid before any dividend can be paid on the common.

Unless the certificate of incorporation contains language indicating the contrary, dividends on preferred stock will be deemed cumulative.[12]

*Noncumulative preferred.* If a dividend is not earned or declared on this class of stock in any given year, the obligation to pay it ceases. Even if enough is earned for such purpose, the directors may in their discretion pass the dividend, yet in a subsequent year declare and pay a dividend on the common stock without making good the passed dividend.

*Participating and nonparticipating preferred.* If earnings are more than sufficient to pay dividends on the preferred stock, the remainder may be given entirely to the common stock, in which case the preferred stock is nonparticipating; or such remainder may be distributed pro rata to both classes of the stock, in which case the preferred stock is said to "participate" with the common. Whether preferred stock is participating or not may be specifically stated in the articles of incorporation, or implied from language used in defining the stock, or prescribed by statute. In the absence of any indication one way or the other, the authorities are not in accord. Some hold that unless the contrary is indicated, preferred stock is participating: The fact that the dividend is guaranteed creates no inference that it is limited to the guaranteed amount. Other authorities hold that in the absence of provision to the contrary, preferred stock is

---

[12] 18 *C.J.S.* 661-662.

nonparticipating: The guaranty of a fixed return is presumably accepted in lieu of equal participation.

*Preference as to assets on dissolution.* Holders of preferred stock have, as a rule, a preferred right to share in the distribution of assets on dissolution. If net assets on dissolution amount to $100,000, and outstanding preferred and common amount to $100,000 each, all the assets would go to the preferred stockholders, none to the common.

*Voting rights.* Preferred stock has the same voting rights as common unless the certificate of incorporation provides to the contrary. If voting power is vested only in the common, but preferred stock only is issued, the voting power shifts to the preferred. Normally, preferred stock is given no voting power. However, it is not uncommon for the charter to provide that voting power and management pass from the common to the preferred stockholders upon default in payment of preferred dividends.

*Degrees of preference and priority.* Statutes permit corporations to provide in their charters for the issuance of the same class of stock in various degrees of priority, such as *prior preference, ordinary preferred,* and so on, or *first preferred, second preferred,* and similar designations.

**Redeemable ("Callable") Stock.** Stock (usually preferred) is frequently issued subject to redemption at the option of either the corporation, the stockholder, or both, at a fixed price representing a premium above the price originally paid. Stock cannot be redeemed, however, if the rights of creditors are thereby prejudiced. Redeemable stock is sometimes said to be "callable."

EXAMPLES:
(1) 5% prior preference, par $100, callable at $105.
(2) $3 preferred, no par, callable at $55.

**Convertible Stock.** Preferred stockholders may be given an option to exchange their stock for common stock, and vice versa. Likewise, preferred stock may be convertible into bonds, and vice versa.

**Preferred Stock v. Bonds: Relative Advantage in Financing.** For the purpose of financing a new corporation, preferred stock is preferable to bonds in that the latter represent a fixed debt, repayable at a fixed time, with fixed interest obligations, default in which may result in suit, judgment, execution and levy (page 861). Preferred stockholders, on the other hand, are not creditors, but investors.

**Stock Subscriptions.** A stock subscription is a contract to take and pay for a certain number of shares of the capital stock of a corporation already organized or to be organized. Before incorporation, stock of the proposed corporation may be acquired only by subscription; after incorporation, it may be acquired either by subscription, or by purchase from the corporation or another stockholder. Formerly, it was customary to prepare a preliminary subscription list prior to incorporation, to make sure that the necessary capital would be forthcoming. The more common practice today is to organize the corporation first upon nominal subscriptions by the incorporators, and then, upon organization, to issue stock to the real parties in interest, against cash, property, services, the transfer of a business or other value. Then, if more capital is needed, subscriptions are solicited.

**Legal Effect of Stock Subscription.** The legal effect of a stock subscription depends upon its terms. Ordinarily, a subscription is an offer to buy stock. It is not effective until accepted by the corporation; then it becomes a contract and the subscriber becomes a stockholder. A stock subscription should not be confused with a contract to purchase stock.

**Stock Subscription v. Contract to Purchase Stock.** A stock subscription is a definite offer that immediately ripens into a contract upon acceptance, regardless of whether a stock certificate is tendered or the purchase price paid. It is sometimes referred to as a *present subscription.* Upon acceptance of the subscription, the subscriber becomes liable, not merely on his subscription, *but as a stockholder.*

A contract to purchase stock, however, is not a present subscription but an executory agreement to subscribe for stock in the future. Mere acceptance by the corporation is not enough to make the prospective purchaser a stockholder. The purchaser in such case becomes liable *as a stockholder* only when the certificate is tendered and the price paid, and both these conditions are *concurrent* (page 103). If the purchaser refuses to accept and pay for the certificate, he is not liable as a *stockholder* but for breach of contract. If the corporation refuses to tender the certificate, it cannot be compelled to do so, but is liable in damages for failure to do it. If the purchaser fails to pay the entire amount due, he is not entitled to the stock nor to any dividend declared in the meantime.

EXAMPLE: Plaintiff's assignor, a corporation, contracted to buy stock in an existing corporation but failed to pay the entire amount due. Plaintiff sued for dividends declared after purchase. The Supreme Court of Pennsylvania pointed out that the alleged subscriptions were "simply contracts of purchase and sale," and that the failure of the purchaser to complete its part of the bargain "prevented it from acquiring the status of a shareholder." The right to dividends was denied.[13]

**Installment Subscriptions.** Where a stock subscription is payable in installments, a corporation may sue to recover the unpaid balance of the stock subscription with interest from the date of default, or the corporation may declare the shares and all previous payments thereon forfeited. In the former case, the corporation affirms the subscriber's position as a stockholder; in the latter, it repudiates the subscriber as a stockholder,

---

[13] *Schwartz v. Manufacturers' Casualty Insurance Company,* 335 Pa. St. Rep. 130, 6 A. 2d 299.

and thereafter neither the corporation nor a corporate creditor may hold the subscriber liable as a stockholder.

*Required deposit.* Statutes in some states provide that stock subscriptions are unenforceable unless accompanied by a minimum down payment. Some corporate charters contain a like provision. The tendency is to dispense with such requirement.

*Paid-in capital.* The amount of money or property received by a corporation on its stock subscriptions is known as its paid-in capital.

**Consideration for Which Capital Stock May Be Issued.** For the protection of creditors and existing stockholders, the law requires that the capital stock of a corporation shall be issued only for equivalent value. To issue capital stock without corresponding capital contribution is to impair the capital of the corporation.

*Original par value stock* cannot be issued except for its full value in cash, property or services.[14] National bank stock can be issued only for cash. Once par value stock has been issued, it may be sold for any price the stockholder wishes to accept. If a corporation reacquires any of its issued stock, it may reissue such treasury stock for any price it will fetch.

As to what constitutes full value for original issue stock, the judgment of the directors is final, provided it is honest, and not arbitrary or capricious.

EXAMPLES:

(1) You render services connected with the organization of a corporation. At the request of the directors, you accept 100 shares of stock of the corporation, $100 par, as compensation for your services. The value thus placed on your services will be accepted as final, unless dishonest, arbitrary or capricious conduct on the part of the directors can be shown.

(2) If, in Example (1), the stock had been issued after you had submitted a bill for $5000 for your services, the validity of the issue, because of the obvious discrepancy, might subsequently be questioned by a judgment creditor of the corporation, though the corporation itself would be bound by the action of its directors. (See page 545.)

*Original no-par value stock* may be issued for such consideration as represents the fair market value of such shares. As to this, also, the honest judgment of the directors is final. However, such stock must be issued for *some* consideration. Hence, if a new corporation issues no-par value common stock as a bonus with preferred, the transaction is invalid. (See page 545.)

*Watered stock.* Outstanding capital stock, to the extent that it does not represent true value given for it, is said to be diluted or *watered*.

---

[14] Although in some states, directors or stockholders are permitted to fix a price for par value stock at less than par, the rule is the other way. The Model Business Corporation Act provides: "Shares having a par value may be issued for such consideration, *not less than the par value thereof,* as shall be fixed from time to time by the board of directors."

*Blue sky laws.* Laws aimed at preventing the practice of issuing stock for inadequate or fictitious values are known as "blue sky laws." (See page 528.)

## Questions

1. Explain the terms "capital" and "capital stock."
2. How are shares of stock issued?
3. What is meant by a closed corporation?
4. Define (a) common stock, (b) preferred stock, (c) cumulative preferred stock, (d) noncumulative preferred stock, (e) participating preferred stock, (f) nonparticipating preferred stock, (g) par value stock, (h) no-par value stock, (i) authorized stock, (j) issued stock, (k) outstanding stock, and (l) treasury stock.
5. Distinguish between "redeemable" and "convertible" stock.
6. For the purpose of financing a new corporation, why is preferred stock preferable to bonds?
7. (a) Distinguish between a stock subscription and a contract to purchase stock.
   (b) When does one become a stockholder in each case?
8. Where a stock subscription, payable in installments, is not honored on time, what remedies has the corporation against the subscriber?
9. What can you say about the consideration for which a corporation may issue (a) original par value stock, or (b) original no-par value stock?
10. What is meant by (a) watered stock, and (b) blue sky laws?

## Problems

1. Holders of noncumulative preferred stock (Class A), complaining that from 1915 to 1926 they had failed to receive their 5 per cent dividends though earned, sued to restrain the directors of the Continental Railway Company from declaring dividends on its Class B preferred and on its common stock until the back dividends on the Class A preferred were first paid. Judgment for whom and why?
2. Plaintiff contracted to buy stock in an existing corporation but failed to pay the entire amount due. He sued for dividends declared after purchase. May he recover? If so, why? If not, why not?
3. A firm of accountants, on completing an audit for the Zebulon Corporation, submits a bill for $500 to cover the cost of the audit. The Zebulon Corporation, being short of cash, offers to issue to the accountants a block of 50 shares of its common stock, original issue, par value $100. Comment on the regularity of this transaction.

### PART 4. MANAGEMENT: DIRECTORS AND OFFICERS

**General Scheme of Corporate Management.** Since a corporation is a pure fiction, existing only in contemplation of law, it can act only through agents. The ultimate control of a corporation is in the stockholders, but the actual conduct of a corporation's affairs is delegated by the stockholders to general agents, or *directors,* who guide the general policy of the corporation and who in turn delegate to officers the task of actual management. Finally, to carry out the details of business management, the officers hire the necessary employees.

**Relationship of Directors to Corporation.** Although the stockholders elect the directors, the directors, once elected, become the representatives of the corporation itself, not of its stockholders.

The official position of a director is one of trust. As to third parties directors are agents; as to the corporation itself they are chargeable as trustees. The judgment of the directors must be unwarped by personal interest. Any outside consideration received and accepted by them for the discharge of their duties belongs to the corporation. The corporation may not only hold directors liable for breach of their fiduciary duties, but may also hold third parties for inducing directors to breach their duties.

EXAMPLE: Brown, a director of the X Company, received $500 from the Y Company for inducing the X Company to award a certain contract to the Y Company. The X Company, upon discovering the facts, may recover the sum so paid Brown, or it may sue Brown for breach of his fiduciary duty and the Y Company for inducing such breach.

**Number and Qualifications of Directors.** The law in most states puts no maximum on the number of directors a corporation may have, but prescribes a minimum of at least three, as does the Model Business Corporation Act[15] (page 495), which provides "The business of every corporation shall be managed by a board of at least three directors." The qualifications of directors vary in the different states. Two common provisions are that all directors must be of full age and that at least one must be a citizen of the United States and a resident of the state. Most states require either that the directors be stockholders or that they be stockholders unless the articles of incorporation or by-laws otherwise provide.

**Directors: How Chosen.** The original board of directors is generally designated in the certificate of incorporation to serve for the first year or until successors are chosen. Frequently, the original directors are dummies; their resignations are accepted and their successors chosen by stockholders' vote at the organization meeting (page 507). All directors subsequent to the original board are elected by the stockholders. Such vote in some states must be by *plurality;* that is, by the largest number of votes cast as distinguished from a *majority*, which is more than half the votes cast.

**Vacancies on Board: How Filled.** As a rule, vacancies on the board of directors are filled by a vote of stockholders at a special meeting called for this purpose or at the next annual meeting following the vacancy. Directors have no power to fill vacancies on their own board except where such power is conferred by statute, charter or by-law. The statute in

[15] Sec. 33.

many states confers such power. The Model Business Corporation Act provides:[16]

Any vacancy occurring in the board of directors may be filled by the affirmative vote of a majority of the remaining directors though less than a quorum of the board of directors. A director elected to fill a vacancy shall be elected for the unexpired term of his predecessor in office.

In some states the statute provides that vacancies on the board shall be filled as prescribed in the by-laws. Unless a vacancy causes the number of directors to fall below the number required for a quorum, the vacancy does not interfere with the transaction of business and need not be filled until the next annual meeting.

**Acceptance of Office.** No corporation can impose the burdens, duties and responsibilities of office upon any person unless he accepts such office.[17]

EXAMPLE: In *Cameron v. Seaman*,[18] an action was brought against Seaman to enforce the liability of a trustee for failure properly to file an account. Seaman defended on the ground that he was not present at the meeting of stockholders when he was elected, that he had never received written notification of his election, and that when he was orally notified of his election by the president of the corporation, he had stated he would not serve. On these facts, the Court held that Seaman was not liable, since the facts negatived acceptance.

**Principal Duties and Powers of Directors.** Directors function as the original agency by which a corporation expresses its will and achieves its objectives. The principal function of the directors is to establish and guide the policies of the corporation. To accomplish these policies and objectives, the board elects the officers of the corporation, furnishes authority for their major acts and supervises their conduct generally. The board also determines whether to declare dividends, and supervises and approves all major steps and acts initiated and negotiated by the officers.

In the exercise of their duties and powers, directors are guided and limited by the corporation's charter and by-laws and by the governing statutes. Directors have implied power to do what is required for a full discharge of their duties.

Directors have no implied power to be generous with corporate assets, however worthy the objective, unless the expenditure furthers the interests of the corporation.

**Delegation of Duties by Directors: Executive Committees.** Directors must attend personally to their duties as directors. Thus, directors may not vote by proxy. "We know of no principle, applicable to the discharge of corporate functions, by which directors or trustees of the corporation can vote at the meeting of the board of directors or trustees by proxy."[19]

[16] Sec. 36.
[17] *Standard Oil Co. v. Morrison, etc., Co.*, 54 Ill. App. 531.
[18] 69 N.Y. 396.
[19] *Craig Medicine Co. v. Merchants' Bank*, 14 N.Y. Supp. 16, 19 (cited with approval in 274 Fed. 1011).

However, this relates only to *discretionary* powers; *ministerial* or routine duties may and often are delegated by directors to others.[20]

EXAMPLE: A stockholders' agreement provided for the election of six equal stockholders as directors, any five of whom might exclude the sixth, upon submission to arbitration. *Held*, that the directors were not required to abide by the terms of the agreement or to resort to arbitration, because their duties could not be thus delegated to others.[21]

*Executive committee.* In the absence of provision to the contrary, the board of directors may delegate its powers to an executive committee, either subject to subsequent board ratification or with full power to act during intervals between board meetings. Executive committees, however, may not "inaugurate radical reversals of or departures from fundamental policies and methods of conducting the business as prescribed by the directorate." [22]

**Directors Must Act as Board.** The authority of directors must be exercised as a body, not individually. Individual directors, unlike individual officers, have no power to act as agents of the corporation.

EXAMPLE: The charter of a banking corporation gave its board of directors power to alter or amend its by-laws. One of the by-laws provided that no interest should be paid on certificates of deposit payable on demand. Such interest was, however, paid to X, whom the bank later sued for return of interest. X proved at the trial that he had obtained, one at a time, the written consent of a majority of the directors to such payment. Proof of such consent was insufficient. Directors must act as a board.

**Freedom from Interference.** The law requires directors to exercise their own untrammeled discretion in guiding the affairs of the corporation. General supervision and the actual conduct of a corporation's affairs by its directors and officers respectively, are exclusive; that is, they are not subject to outside interference.[23] Thus, a stockholder owning all the stock of a corporation may not override or interfere with the discretion and control of the board of directors, so long as they hold office. "If the action of the board of directors does not express the will and wish of the minority of the shares of stock, the majority has its remedy by retiring the members . . . at the regular time for election of directors." [24] Neither will the courts interfere with the judgment and discretion of directors except for fraud or arbitrary conduct contrary to the interests of the corporation. "As a general rule courts have nothing to do with the internal management of business corporations, but, if the acts of directors

---

[20] *Wheeler v. Layman Foundation,* 188 Ga. 267, 3 S.E. 2d 645; *Lowell Hoit & Co. v. Detig,* 320 Ill. App. 179, 50 N.E. 2d 602.

[21] *In re Allied Fruit & Extract Co.,* 243 App. Div. 52, 276 N.Y.S. 153.

[22] *Fensterer v. Pressure Lighting Co.,* 85 Misc. 621, 149 N.Y.S. 49, 53, citing numerous cases.

[23] *Raynolds v. Diamond Mills Paper Co.,* 69 N.J. Eq. 299, 60 A. 941.

[24] *Lamb v. Lehmann,* 110 Ohio St. 59, 143 N.E. 276.

are so unjust as to be evidence of fraud and intentional wrong, the courts may act. They may not compel directors to act wisely, but may compel them to act honestly." [25]

EXAMPLES:

(1) The controlling stockholders of a corporation agreed to elect certain directors who would act as nominal directors only and who would not take part in the management of the corporation. The Court held such an arrangement illegal. Only directors may direct.[26]

(2) A majority stockholder designates his son as treasurer of the corporation. Certain minority stockholders object. Their objection may be enforced by court action. Only directors may elect officers. Stockholders have no right to interfere except through regular corporate action.[27]

**Meetings of Directors.** Formerly, it was the rule rather than the exception that corporations organized in a given state had to hold their directors' as well as their stockholders' meetings within the state. The rule is now the other way. In practically all states, directors may hold their meetings outside the state upon special authorization contained in a statute, charter, by-law, majority vote of directors or, in some cases, by inference from the fact that there is no statutory provision against it.

*Conduct of meetings.* Directors' meetings need not be conducted by parliamentary rules, but parliamentary usage generally governs. Proposals for action are usually formulated by the chairman, and the order of disposition thereon is generally as follows: (1) Report, (2) motion, (3) discussion, and (4) resolution.

**Minutes.** Directors must see to it that a record of their meetings, known as the *minutes,* is kept by an officer of the corporation duly charged with this duty. Such officer is usually the secretary. The minutes should show the dates of all meetings, the members who attended and the resolutions adopted. If the minutes are in any respect inaccurate, the board of directors may correct them so as to show what action was actually taken at the meeting.

**Compensation of Directors.** Directors as such are not ordinarily entitled to compensation, unless there is some provision in the charter or by-laws of the corporation for this purpose. However, where a director renders services not as director, but in some other capacity—as, for example, where a director renders legal, accounting or engineering services apart from his duties as director—he is entitled to compensation for such services, because it will be implied, in the absence of express contract, that services of this character are not ordinarily rendered gratuitously.

**Disqualification by Personal Interest.** A director, as we have seen,

---

[25] *Jones v. Van Heusen Charles Co.,* 230 App. Div. 694, 696, 246 N.Y. Supp. 204.
[26] *Jackson v. Hooper,* 76 N.J. Eq. 592, 75 A. 568.
[27] *Walsenburg Water Co. v. Moore,* 5 Colo. App. 144, 38 P. 60; *State v. Rosenow,* 174 Wis. 9, 182 N.W. 324. In some states, however, provision may be made for the election of certain officers by the stockholders.

stands in a fiduciary relation to the corporation that he serves. He must not permit himself to act on behalf of the corporation if his act is tainted by self-interest. A director is therefore disqualified to vote at a meeting of the board if he has any personal interest in a matter before the board; neither can his vote, in such case, be counted in making up a quorum. If a director does vote on such matter, the vote cannot be counted in determining the action of the board; and if it has been counted and was decisive, the action of the board may be set aside. It is customary for a director who has a personal interest in a matter under consideration by the board to note on the minutes that he is refraining from voting in respect to the matter. Directors who are also officers should refrain from voting on a resolution fixing their own compensation.

**Tenure of Office: Removal of Directors.** Generally, when a director is elected for a fixed term, such term, except for cause, cannot be abridged without the director's consent. The tendency of statutes today is to limit the tenure of office so as to require periodic re-election. The Model Business Corporation Act provides[28] that where the board consists of nine or more members, they may be divided into classes and elected in rotation.

Where the by-laws specifically provide that a director may be removed at any time, with or without cause, such provision has the binding force of a contract and such director may be removed arbitrarily at any time.

**Holding Over.** Officers and directors whose terms have expired, hold over until their successors are chosen or until they resign or are removed. This applies not only to directors elected at a meeting of stockholders but also to original directors named in a certificate of incorporation.

**De Facto Officers and Directors.** We have already explained the meaning of *de jure* and *de facto* as applied to corporations. Similarly, a *de jure* officer or director is one duly qualified, and duly elected and functioning as such. A *de facto* officer or director is one holding office with ostensible corporate consent and under color of election or appointment, though such election or appointment be irregular. The irregularity may consist in the manner of election, or in some personal disqualification for office, involving age, citizenship, residence, ownership of stock and the like. If a director thus elected accepts office and acts at a directors' meeting, he is said to be a director *de facto*.

EXAMPLE: In *Conaty v. Torghen, et al.,*[29] the only active officer was the secretary, who appointed a president and a treasurer to sign checks as required by the bank. All three were held to be officers *de facto*.

**Resignation.** Since a director holds office until his successor is chosen, it is not always safe for him to assume that his liabilities cease when his

---

[28] Sec. 35.
[29] 46 R.I. 447.

term expires. If a director wishes to terminate his duties and liabilities as such, he must tender his resignation. Directors or officers may resign during office or while holding over, despite a provision that they shall serve for a prescribed term and until their successors are chosen.

**Agreements for Perpetuation in Office: Agreements upon United Action.** Though continuation in office of experienced directors may be desirable from the business standpoint, it is regarded as against public policy to contrive perpetuation in office by agreement or by dispensing with elections.

EXAMPLE: Three directors controlling a majority of the stock of a corporation made an agreement to vote as stockholders and directors for the election of one another, or of such persons as they should respectively nominate, to the offices of president, treasurer and auditor, respectively, so long as each should remain such stockholder and desire such office. The Court held the agreement illegal.[30]

*Stockholders' agreements upon united action.* Although it is contrary to public policy to contrive perpetuation in office, it is not illegal for stockholders to unite upon a common policy or the election of certain directors.[31]

**Officers: Distinguished from Directors.** Although in the broadest sense directors are "officers" of the corporation, in a narrower sense they are clearly distinguishable from officers. The officers of a corporation, unlike its directors, are true agents of the corporation. Each officer may bind the corporation by his individual acts within the actual or apparent scope of his authority. A director, on the other hand, as previously noted (page 520), has no individual authority to act for the corporation.

A director, by virtue of his office as such, cannot legally bind the corporation to a contractual or other obligation.

EXAMPLE: Bundy is the principal stockholder and a director of the Bundy Corporation, but holds no office in the company. He hires Wilson as assistant treasurer for the company under a written contract for two years. Wilson, with full knowledge of Bundy's status, accepts the employment. The treasurer repudiates the employment and Wilson sues the company for breach of contract. The corporation will prevail. Wilson had no right to assume that Bundy, as a director, had authority to bind the corporation by contract.

**Election of Officers: Tenure.** Officers, as previously noted, are elected by the directors. They are usually elected for a definite term fixed in the by-laws, statute or charter. Where such term is fixed, officers are regarded as having *tenure*, which, like other contracts, cannot be disturbed except for cause. If no term is fixed by statute, charter, by-law or other contract, officers are removable at the pleasure of the directors.

---

[30] *Snow v. Church,* 13 App. Div. 108, 42 N.Y. Supp. 1072.
[31] *Manson v. Curtis,* 223 N.Y. 313, 119 N.E. 559; *Brightman v. Bates,* 175 Mass. 105, 55 N.E. 809.

**Usual Corporate Officers.** The usual officers of a corporation are the president, secretary, and treasurer. In addition, convenience and the nature of a corporation's business frequently require the appointment of one or more vice presidents, managing directors, general managers or superintendents, counsel, assistant secretaries, assistant treasurers and auditors. It is not illegal or improper to choose one person for two corporate offices.

**Duties of Officers.** The duties of officers are prescribed in the by-laws, and they vary accordingly. Usually, the by-laws provide as follows:

*President.* The president presides at stockholders' and directors' meetings. As a rule, he must be a director himself. He signs certificates of stock, contracts, drafts, checks, promissory notes and similar commitments on behalf of the corporation.

*Vice President.* The vice president acts in the president's absence, and discharges such other duties as may be designated in the by-laws.

*Secretary.* The secretary records, signs and keeps the minutes of meetings of stockholders and of directors; attends to giving and serving all notices; affixes the corporate seal to certificates of stock and countersigns such certificates (except where the treasurer is charged with such duty of countersignature); and has charge of the stock book, certificate book and other corporate books, papers, documents and records. He also makes up the necessary tax and other reports required by law.

*Treasurer.* The treasurer is the chief financial officer of the corporation and the custodian of its funds and other assets. He is frequently designated as the officer to sign or countersign all promissory notes, bills of exchange, checks and other corporate instruments for the payment of money. He is thus both custodian of the corporation's property and paymaster of its debts. He is likewise the collecting officer of the corporation. He is frequently required to give bond for faithful performance. He must see that the corporate books of account and records of financial transactions are accurately kept, so as to reflect the true financial condition of the company.

**Freedom of Officers from Interference.** Officers, like directors, are immune from interference with the discharge of their duties. They may be removed for cause, or in some cases (page 523) without cause, or upon the expiration of their terms; but so long as they function, they cannot be dictated to by directors or stockholders as to contracts to be signed, employees to be hired or any other details of management.

**Compensation of Officers.** Officers, more frequently than directors (page 521), serve for compensation. Their salaries are fixed by resolution of the board of directors. As noted on page 522, directors who are also officers should refrain from voting on a resolution fixing their own compensation.

**Salaries in Lieu of Dividends.** Where small groups dominate a corporation through stock ownership, it is not uncommon for the dominating stockholders to elect themselves as directors and officers and to vote themselves salaries that should go into surplus available for dividends. Such practice is frequently difficult to combat because of the hesitancy of courts to interfere with the discretion of directors in the internal management of a corporation. However, if salaries are clearly more than a fair and reasonable compensation, or if their payment clearly amounts to bad faith, fraud or a breach of trust, the Court will require restoration of such salaries to the surplus of the corporation.

**Transactions with Corporation.** The rules generally applicable to dealings between principal and agent apply to the relationship between a corporation and its officers and directors. Officers and directors may make contracts with their corporation provided they do so openly and upon full disclosure. If, however, they secretly benefit in their dealings with the corporation, they may be compelled to account for such benefits.

**Profiting at Corporate Expense.** Directors and officers owe primary allegiance to the corporation that they serve. Hence, if a director or officer, either by competing or by driving a hard bargain with his corporation, derives a profit at the corporation's expense, he must account to the corporation for such profit.

EXAMPLE: A piano concern was in financial difficulties. A director knew it, and took advantage of his corporation by buying pianos from it at prices that he knew were inadequate. He kept the majority of the board in ignorance of the terms of the contract. For the profits thus derived by the director out of his dealings with the corporation, the Court held the director accountable to the corporation.[32]

**Taking Personal Advantage of Corporate Opportunities.** Directors and officers must rigidly refrain from taking advantage of corporate opportunities. Even where the corporation rejects a transaction, directors, though acting ostensibly in good faith and with the best of motives, must not avail themselves of the transaction thus rejected. If they do, they will be open to the suspicion that they rejected the transaction on behalf of the corporation so that they could take advantage of the opportunity themselves.

EXAMPLE: The Acoustic Products Company dealt in phonographs, radios and similar apparatus. An offer was made to the company to sell it certain shares in the De Forest Radio Co. that would give the Acoustic Company valuable rights of manufacture. The directors of the Acoustic Company rejected the offer on the ground that the company was financially unable to purchase the stock, which was probably the fact. Later, the same directors formed a syndicate, purchased the stock themselves, and made a substantial profit. The Court, holding that fiduciaries should not be permitted to assume a position in which their individual interests might conflict with those of the corporation, compelled the directors to account to the corporation for these profits.[33]

[32] *Lazenby v. Henderson*, 241 Mass. 177, 135 N.E. 302.
[33] *Irving Trust Company v. Deutsch*, 75 F. 2d 121.

**Dealings in Corporate Stock.** Directors and officers may purchase stock in their corporation or, if they already own it, may dispose of it in any way they see fit. However, if they use their official position to gain advantage for themselves in connection with the issuance, purchase or sale of such stock, they will be compelled to account to the corporation for any profits thus derived.

EXAMPLE: The directors and officers of a corporation whose stock is listed on the stock exchange, having advance knowledge of an extra dividend to be declared, purchase a large block of the company's stock. Later, when the dividend is declared and the stock correspondingly advances in price, they sell their stock at a substantial profit. The directors and officers may be compelled to account for such profits. They are further liable under the Securities Exchange Act of 1934.[34]

**Dealings in Corporate Office.** Directors and officers have no right to engage in transactions, the object of which is to buy or sell corporate office. Any proceeds thereby derived belong to the corporation.

EXAMPLE: The directors and president of a life insurance company receive money from an outsider for procuring the election of the outsider and his friends as directors with control and management of the insurance company. The Court held that the officers and directors had a right to resign, but that money paid for procuring for others their election as directors and control of the company was derived by virtue of office and therefore belonged to the corporation.[35]

**Dual Allegiance: Interlocking Officers and Directors.** The mere fact that a majority of or even all the directors or contracting officers of two corporations are common to both does not render a contract between such corporations void. The contract is merely voidable (page 83) if fraud or unfairness can be shown to have been exercised. However, such transactions are viewed with suspicion by the courts because they place fiduciaries in a position of dual allegiance.[36]

EXAMPLE: Maynard was the dominating stockholder and director of an electric company and of a woolen company. He negotiated a contract by which the electric company was required to furnish power to the woolen company at losing rates. The electric company refused to proceed with the contract and the woolen company sued. The Court, in refusing to enforce the

---

[34] Section 16(b).

[35] *McClure v. Law*, 161 N.Y. 78, citing *Chandler v. Bacon*, 30 Fed. Rep. 538; *Rutland El. L. Co. v. Bates*, 68 Vt. 579; *Farmers & Merchants' Bank v. Downey*, 53 Cal. 466.

[36] *Potter v. Sanitary Co. of America*, 22 Del. Ch. 110, 194 A. 87; *Overfield v. Pennroad Corporation*, D.C. Pa., 42 F. Supp. 586, op. supp. 48 F. Supp. 1008, affd., C.C.A., 146 F. 2d 889; *Godfrey L. Cabot, Inc. v. Gas Products Co.*, 93 Mont. 497, 19 P. 2d 878, 883; *Truman v. Coghlin Machinery & Supply Co.*, 11 Ohio App. 220; *Bonini v. Family Theatre Corporation*, 327 Pa. 273, 194 A. 498; *Olympia Box & Package Co. v. Pacific Veneer Co.*, 123 Wash. 533, 213 P. 24; *Wheeling Dollar Sav. & Trust Co. v. Hoffman*, 127 W.Va. 777, 35 S.E. 2d 84; *State v. Grossman*, 213 Wis. 135, 250 N.W. 832, 833.

contract, held that although Maynard had refrained from voting, it was his duty as a director "to speak out and not reap a profit from the errors of the other directors." He could not "rid himself of the duty to warn and denounce . . . improvidence or oppression . . . visible to his practiced eye." [37]

**Liability for Negligence.** Directors and officers, like agents, are liable to the corporation for loss sustained by it through their negligence in office.

EXAMPLE: A resolution of the X Corporation provided that all checks were to be signed by the treasurer and countersigned by the president or a director. By a series of ingenious excuses the treasurer, from time to time, obtained countersignatures, by directors, of checks payable to cash or to bearer, then misappropriated the proceeds and disappeared. Upon discovery of the misappropriation, the corporation may require the directors to make good their negligence.

What constitutes negligence is a question of fact in each case.

*Liability for misconduct of codirectors.* Directors may be negligent not only with respect to the normal discharge of their duties but also for failure to detect and prevent wrongs by codirectors or to redress such wrongs on behalf of the corporation after they were committed. The nonparticipating directors, in such cases, are jointly and severally liable with the participating directors.

**Liability for Nonexistent or Defectively Organized Corporation.** Persons who purport to act for a nonexistent corporation are in the same position as agents who purport to act for a nonexistent principal: They are personally liable in such transactions (see page 410). A similar rule, as already noted, applies in connection with defectively organized corporations (page 503).

**Liability for Preferential Transfers.** Stockholders and judgment creditors of a corporation may hold directors and officers personally liable to the full extent of any loss sustained if such directors or officers are guilty of preferential transfers.

EXAMPLES:
(1) Transferring corporate property to an officer, director or stockholder in payment of a debt or for any consideration other than full value in cash, where the corporation has previously refused to pay any of its notes or other obligations when due.
(2) Preferring any creditor (except wage earners) over other creditors while the corporation is insolvent.

**Liability for Loans to Stockholders, Directors and Officers.** Statutes commonly forbid directors to make loans of corporate funds to stockholders, directors or officers. The Model Business Corporation Act provides:[38] "No loans shall be made by a corporation to its officers or direc-

---

[37] *Globe Woolen Co. v. Utica Gas & Electric Co.,* 224 N.Y. 483, 121 N.E. 378.
[38] Sec. 42.

tors, and no loans shall be made by a corporation secured by its shares."

**Liability in Connection with Treasury Stock.** Directors incur personal liability if they authorize the acquisition of treasury stock out of capital instead of surplus (page 512). Also, in causing a corporation to acquire or dispose of treasury stock, directors must not prejudice the rights of creditors or stockholders.

**Liability for Declaring Dividends Out of Capital.** Directors may declare dividends only out of surplus. If directors pay dividends out of capital instead of surplus, they may incur liability (a) at law to the corporation, (b) in equity to creditors, and (c) criminally, by statute. A statute may exempt directors from liability where (1) they cause their dissent to be noted in the minutes at the time the dividend is declared, or (2) they were absent when the dividend was declared but communicated their dissent in writing within a reasonable time after learning of the dividend declaration (see page 529), or (3) they can show they had reasonable ground to believe and did believe that the dividend distribution would not impair capital.

**Liability for Failure to File Reports.** States commonly impose personal liability on corporate directors or officers for failure to file or publish reports containing prescribed information as to corporate affairs, or for failing to file such reports within a prescribed time. Even more severe penalties are provided by statute for making fraudulent reports. (See page 529.)

**Liability for Failure to Qualify a Foreign Corporation.** Every state has a right to require foreign corporations doing business in that state to qualify by filing a prescribed certificate and paying a prescribed fee. There are various penalties in the different states for failure to comply with such requirement, the most common of which is to deprive the offending corporation of the right to bring suit on any contracts made in the state. (See page 550.) In a number of states, however, such as Massachusetts, Virginia, Florida, Indiana, Colorado, Idaho and Utah, directors, officers, agents or employees acting on behalf of such corporation are made personally liable for obligations incurred by such foreign corporations, and in some cases for fines imposed on the corporation in such situations.

**Liability in Connection with Fraudulent Practices (Blue Sky Laws).** Reference has been made to the so-called "blue sky laws" in connection with the consideration for which capital stock may be issued (page 517). Many states have statutes that prescribe penalties for fraudulent corporate practices in connection with the issuance of corporate stocks, bonds, notes or other securities. Any officer, director or employee engaged in or connected with such fraudulent practices is subject to severe penalties.

**Liability for Issuing Unauthorized Stocks and Bonds.** Statutes impose heavy penalties on officers for the unauthorized issuance of stocks and bonds. Penal laws commonly prescribe fines, imprisonment, or both for any officer or agent of a corporation who wilfully, knowingly and with intent to defraud, sells, pledges, issues, signs or executes any certificate of stock, bond or other evidence of debt without corporate authority, or contrary to the charter or laws under which the corporation exists, or in excess of corporate authority. They also commonly provide that an officer or director of a stock corporation is guilty of a misdemeanor, punishable by fine, imprisonment, or both, if he issues, participates in issuing or concurs in a vote to issue any increase of capital stock beyond the amount of the capitalization authorized by the charter, or if he sells, agrees to sell or is directly or indirectly interested in selling any share of stock of such corporation, unless at the time of such sale or agreement to sell, he is an actual owner of such share of stock.

**Criminal Misconduct in Connection with Corporate Books and Records.** Penal statutes generally impose fines or imprisonment for misconduct of directors, officers or employees in connection with corporate books and records. For example, statutes commonly provide that a director, officer, agent or employee of a corporation is guilty of a misdemeanor if, in connection with corporate books and records, he knowingly makes false entries, omits material ones, publishes false financial statements, suppresses injunction papers served upon him, refuses or neglects to make official reports or statements required by law, or causes or concurs in any of these acts or omissions.

**Liability for Political Contributions.** Statutes generally prohibit political contributions by a corporation except where the corporation is organized for political purposes. Directors and officers who participate in, aid, abet, advise or consent to such violation are guilty of a misdemeanor and are subject to such penalties as the particular statutes of a state may impose.

**Innocent Directors: Steps for Protection against Liability.** When a majority of the board of directors adopts a resolution that an innocent director believes to be wrong, he should see that his dissent from the resolution is noted in the minutes. Even where a director is absent from the meeting, it is not safe for him to assume that such absence protects him against liability, because while this may be true in many cases, there are some cases where the statute requires such director to put himself on record notwithstanding his absence. For example, the statute may provide that where dividends are declared out of capital instead of surplus, a director absent from the meeting at which such action was taken, if he wishes to relieve himself from liability for such act, must communicate his dissent to the secretary of the corporation or cause his dissent to be entered on the minutes within a reasonable time after he learns of the dividend declaration. Some states prescribe a specific time, such as six months, within which a director must cause his dissent to be noted.

## Questions

1. In what respects may a director be regarded as an agent for the corporation and in what respect may he not be so regarded?

2. What are the legal requirements as to (a) eligibility of directors, and (b) maximum and minimum number?

3. Are directors always chosen by the stockholders? Explain.

4. (a) What determines how vacancies on the board of directors shall be filled? (b) How are such vacancies usually filled? (c) What other provisions may be made for filling vacancies?

5. What statutory provisions, if any, are commonly in force in regard to the tenure of office of directors and the frequency with which elections of directors are to be held?

6. Distinguish between *de facto* and *de jure* officers and directors. Is a corporation bound by the acts of its *de facto* officers and directors (a) in transactions involving third parties, and (b) in transactions involving internal management, such as the election of officers by *de facto* directors?

7. State the general principles governing transactions between a corporation and its officers and directors.

8. Are directors as such entitled to compensation (a) in the absence of provision for same in the charter or by-laws, (b) where provision therefor is contained in the charter or by-laws, and (c) where the director renders services in some capacity other than as director?

9. May directors or officers become creditors of a corporation? Comment and explain.

10. Name and explain twelve ways in which a director may become personally liable for his conduct as such.

## Problems

1. A syndicate is formed for the purpose of organizing a service corporation to operate throughout the United States. It is proposed to designate a board of directors of twenty-one members. The corporation is to operate through subsidiaries in the different states, the subsidiaries to be formed for the limited purpose of local representation and to be governed through boards consisting of a single director for each corporation. Comment on the validity of the proposed corporate enterprises.

2. The by-laws of the Superfine Hardware Corporation provide that directors shall be elected annually by a majority vote of stockholders. At a meeting of stockholders, 1,000 shares are represented. Arthur, Ames and Anderson receive 400 votes, Burns, Black and Baker receive 350 votes, and Crane, Carr and Chase receive 250 votes. Arthur, Ames and Anderson are declared elected, and duly take office. The stockholders who voted for the other directors challenge the validity of the election. Is the election valid? Give reasons.

3. At the annual stockholders' meeting of Homestead Bakeries, Inc., a board of directors was elected for a term of five years. Through neglect, no by-laws have ever been adopted by the corporation. The directors faithfully discharge their duties, but during the fourth year of their term in office their tenure of office is attacked by a stockholder, who insists that a new board be elected, and who brings suit for this purpose. How will the suit be decided? Explain.

4. A director is elected for three years. The by-laws, however, limit the term for which directors may be elected to one year. At the end of two years

the stockholders at a special meeting vote to remove the director. The board consists of twelve directors, and the by-laws contain a further provision that at least one-fourth in number of the directors shall be elected annually. This provision has been duly complied with in all respects. The director, however, brings proceedings in court to compel the stockholders to reinstate him. Will the director succeed?

5. McCann was elected director for a term which would normally not expire until June 30, 1955, in accordance with the by-laws. On November 1, 1954, pursuant to a vote of stockholders, an amended certificate of incorporation was filed which provided that a director could be removed at any time by the board of directors with the approval of two-thirds of the stockholders. Subsequently a directors' meeting was held and a resolution adopted which provided for McCann's removal from office, and this action was duly approved by two-thirds of the stockholders. McCann thereupon brought proceedings to compel the stockholders and directors to reinstate him. How did the court rule?

6. Platt owns 98 per cent of the capital stock of the Platt Power Works, Inc. Platt instructs the board of directors to see to it that his son, just graduated from college, is given the position of assistant secretary of the company, at an annual salary of $5,000. May Platt enforce his request if it is not complied with by the directors? If so, how; if not, why not?

7. A corporation's affairs have been conducted for many years without annual or other meetings of stockholders or directors. George Montgomery, the principal stockholder, a director and president of the corporation, together with four other directors, have continued to serve in their respective capacities throughout this period. George Montgomery finally dies, and the executor of his estate wishes to submit the name of a successor, as president of the corporation, to the existing and remaining members of the board, without holding a new meeting of stockholders to elect a new board of directors. May he do so?

8. The balance sheet of the Excelsior Corporation shows a deficit. The corporation decides to raise money by issuing new stock, so as to expand its operations in a more profitable direction. The board of directors decides to sell some of the corporation's capital assets and to devote the proceeds to the payment of a dividend to be declared so as to expedite the raising of new capital. As a member of the board, you disapprove of this action. What will you do about the matter besides voting to disapprove the resolution?

## PART 5. RIGHTS OF STOCKHOLDERS

**Who Are Stockholders.** A stockholder is one who is recognized as the true owner of stock, either at law, as where the stock is directly held, or in equity, as where the stock is held by one person for the benefit of another.

*Three ways of acquiring stock.* A person may become a stockholder (1) by original issue, (2) by the purchase of treasury stock, and (3) by stock transfer from an existing stockholder.

**When Stockholder's Rights Arise.** One acquires the rights of a stockholder as soon as he becomes the true owner of the stock, either in law or in equity. In the case of a *present subscription*, as we have noted (page 515), one becomes a stockholder when his subscription is accepted, regardless of whether the certificate has been issued or the price paid; whereas in case of a *contract to purchase* stock one does not become a stockholder until discharge of the concurrent conditions of (1) payment and (2) delivery of the certificate. In the case of stock transfers *as between the old and the new stockholder*, the latter acquires the rights of a stockholder as soon as he buys the stock. As between the *corporation and the new stockholder*, the latter is not recognized as a stockholder until the transfer is registered on the corporate books.

EXAMPLE: Ladd on June 4 sells stock to Brown, who has the transfer registered on the books of the corporation June 6. The corporation, having declared a dividend to holders of record June 5, pays Ladd the dividend. Brown has a claim against Ladd, not against the corporation.

**Rights and Privileges of Stockholder.** The rights and privileges of a stockholder embrace: (1) The right to a certificate, (2) the right to transfer the stock, (3) the right to vote, (4) the right to dividends, (5) the right to inspect corporate books, (6) the "pre-emptive" right, and (7) the right upon dissolution to a proportionate share of the net assets. The first three of these are discussed in this Part, the others in the next Part.

**Right to Certificate; Lost Certificates.** A stockholder has the right to a duly authenticated certificate evidencing his stock ownership. If the certificate is lost, stolen or destroyed, the stockholder may compel the corporation to issue a new one upon filing a bond indemnifying the corporation against liability should the old certificate turn up in the hands of an innocent holder for value. Ordinarily, a corporation will issue a new certificate upon an affidavit setting forth the facts in full, accompanied by an indemnity bond. Where the corporation refuses to issue a new certificate in such cases, a court order may be obtained to compel its issuance.

**Right to Transfer Stock.** The right to transfer stock is as important as the right to own it. Stock may be transferred in three ways: (1) By delivering the certificate, duly indorsed on the back; (2) by delivering the certificate accompanied by a separate assignment; and (3) where stock is levied on in execution of a judgment, by delivering the certificate coupled with an assignment by the sheriff or marshal who made the levy. Stock transfers are governed by the Uniform Stock Transfer Act.

**Limitations Upon Right to Transfer Stock.** Although the right to transfer stock is implicit in the right to own it, the law permits reasonable restrictions upon the right. Such restrictions may be imposed by charter, by-law or special contract. Since an innocent purchaser of stock is not bound by such restrictions unless he has notice of them, it is customary to indorse such notice on the stock certificates. Usually, the restrictions concern (a) unpaid stock or (b) a requirement that the stockholder must not sell the stock to outsiders without first offering it to the corporation or existing stockholders on specified terms.

(a) *Unpaid stock: lien.* In the absence of restriction, a stockholder may freely transfer his stock regardless of unpaid installments. The Uniform Stock Transfer Act provides that a corporation has no lien upon stock nor any right to restrict its transfer, unless such lien or right is noted upon the certificate. A corporation, by charter or by-law provision, may reserve the right to refuse to register a stock transfer unless the stock is fully paid. If, notwithstanding such right, the corporation registers the transfer though the stock has not been fully paid, the right to hold the transferor is waived (page 546).

(b) *Pre-emptive options.* Closed corporations frequently provide, by charter, by-law or separate agreement among the stockholders and with the corporation, that no stockholder shall offer his stock to outsiders without first offering it to the corporation or existing stockholders on specified terms. A by-law containing such provision has the force of a contract and cannot be subsequently changed without the consent of all parties concerned.[39]

EXAMPLE: Three incorporators adopted a by-law providing that no stockholder could sell his stock without first offering it for sale to the corporation at the proposed sales price. Twelve years later a majority of the stockholders adopted a resolution repealing the by-law. Plaintiff, a stockholder, was granted an injunction restraining the amendment on the ground that the by-law constituted a valid contract that could not be repealed without the consent of all.[40]

**Right to Vote: Nature of.** A vote is a means of ascertaining the will of a group. The voting rights of stockholders have already been referred to in the discussion of common and preferred stock (pages 513 to 514). The right to vote is governed and determined by (1) the charter, (2) the by-laws, and (3) the controlling statutes.

**Right to Vote as Governed by Charter.** The charter of a corporation usually designates and prescribes the voting privileges of the different classes of stock. If the charter is silent on the subject, preferred and common stockholders have an equal right to vote. Usually, however, the charter provides that only common stockholders shall vote. Often there is a provision that if dividends on the preferred are "passed," the preferred stockholders may take over control until their rights are satisfied. Under the common law, each stockholder, regardless of the number of shares he

[39] *Warner & Swasey Co. v. Rusterholz,* D.C. Minn., 41 F. Supp. 498; *People v. Galskis,* 233 Ill. App. 414; *Doss v. Yingling,* 95 Ind. App. 494, 172 N.E. 801; *U.S. Gypsum Co. v. Houston,* 239 Mich. 249, 214 N.W. 197; *In re Magnetic Mfg. Co.,* 201 Wis. 154, 229 N.W. 544; *Hulse v. Consolidated Quicksilver Mining Corp.,* 65 Idaho 768, 154 P. 2d 149, 153.

[40] *Cowles v. Cowles Realty Co.,* 201 App. Div. 460, 194 N.Y. Supp. 546.

held, was entitled to but one vote. Today, each stockholder is entitled to one vote for each share held.

*Cumulative voting.* Frequently the charter provides for cumulative voting as a device to insure minority representation on the board of directors. By ordinary voting, a stockholder must vote for an entire slate, not for individual directors; that is, he votes for a proposed board of directors as a unit. By cumulative voting, a stockholder may concentrate his voting strength on one or more directors to be elected, instead of spreading his vote over the entire slate. For example, suppose three directors are to be elected by two stockholders, one of whom, Major, owns 70 shares and the other, Minor, 30. By ordinary voting, Major will elect his entire slate. By cumulative voting, each stockholder may multiply the number of shares he owns by the number of vacancies to be filled, to make up his entire voting strength, which he may spread over the entire slate or concentrate on a single director. Thus:

Major: 70 x 3 = 210 votes (which, split three ways, cannot elect all
the directors)
Minor: 30 x 3 = 90 votes (which, concentrated on one director, insures his election)

**Right to Vote: By-Law Provisions.** The by-laws may require that certain corporate acts shall be invalid unless authorized or approved by the stockholders. In such cases, stockholders' approval is required, though not necessarily at a meeting (as in the case of a vote by directors).

EXAMPLE: The by-laws of a corporation provided that approval by 60 per cent of the stockholders was necessary for a sale of capital assets or the purchase of treasury stock. The president, owning one-half of the company's stock, conveyed, on its behalf, a substantial part of its real property in exchange for the rest of the outstanding stock. Such sale of a capital asset and such acquisition of treasury stock were entirely valid, since the transaction was participated in, hence approved by all the stockholders.

**Right to Vote as Governed by Statute.** No charter or by-law provision may conflict with an existing statute governing a stockholder's right to vote. If it does, the provision is invalid. The law provides that certain basic powers of a corporation must by exercised by the stockholders themselves, instead of through directors and officers. The statute may require only a plurality approval for some corporate acts. Still other acts, such as increasing or reducing capital stock, or changing the corporate headquarters, may require a majority approval, while still others, such as mortgaging corporate property, consolidating with another corporation, or dissolving the corporation, may require a two-thirds vote of approval by outstanding stockholders.

However, where stockholders have failed to approve a transaction as required by statute, but have retained the benefits of the transaction, they cannot subsequently question its validity.

EXAMPLE: A mortgage on corporate realty was executed and delivered in the name and on behalf of the corporation by its president and secretary, without further authority. The company received adequate value for the mortgage and retained it. If the stockholders knew and acquiesced in the transaction, they would be estopped to question it, otherwise not.

**Stockholders' Meetings.** Meetings of stockholders may be *regular* or *special*. The annual meeting of stockholders, as fixed in the by-laws, is a regular meeting. A meeting called to vote on some special project is a special meeting. The *minutes*, or the record of the meetings, must be kept in a Minute Book. All stockholders entitled to vote are entitled to a notice of the meetings. This notice must specify the purpose or purposes of the meeting. Meetings must be held at the time and place, if any, fixed by the charter or by-laws, or at any reasonable place (usually required to be within the state of incorporation). However, stockholders may sign a *waiver of notice of meeting*, and this is the usual practice with small corporations, to avoid the trouble of sending out notices of meeting.

**Quorum.** A quorum is the number of votes necessary to validate a meeting. The charter or by-laws of a corporation may fix the number of shares necessary to constitute a quorum, but such provision must not conflict with the law.

EXAMPLE: If the statute provides (as it does in some states) that in the election of directors a stockholders' quorum cannot be fixed at more than a majority, a charter or by-law provision fixing a quorum at two-thirds would be invalid.

The Model Business Corporation Act provides that a majority constitutes a quorum *unless otherwise provided in the articles of incorporation*.

**High-Fraction Voting: Open Issue v. Closed Corporation.** In dealing with open-issue corporations, where the stock is widely held, it is difficult to achieve unanimity or high-fraction votes or quorums, such as two thirds, three fourths, etc. The rule therefore is that a charter or by-law cannot require more than a majority or plurality of stockholders to constitute a quorum, or more than a majority or plurality vote of the quorum to elect directors. Thus, for many years the voting requirement in New York for electing directors has been that it could not exceed a plurality, so that a charter provision requiring unanimous consent for a change of directors was held void.[41] But in 1948, the New York statute was broadened to take into account the practical needs of a closed corporation (page 512), so that the statute now permits a corporation to require more than a plurality and up to unanimity in the election of

---

[41] *In re Boulevard Theater & Realty Company*, 231 N.Y. 615, 132 N.E. 910.

directors, provided the required vote is shown in the certificate of incorporation.

**Proxies.** A proxy is a power of attorney (page 396) given by a stockholder authorizing a designated person to cast the stockholder's ballot. Like any other agency, a proxy may be revoked at any time unless "coupled with an interest" (page 423). Statutes may limit the duration of a proxy. One need not be a stockholder to be a proxy. The authority of a proxy generally is discretionary rather than ministerial (i.e., routine); hence a proxy, unless so authorized, may not appoint another in his place.

**Voting Trusts.** A voting trust is an agreement by which stockholders surrender their voting power and place it irrevocably in the hands of others. Such agreements, in that they vest voting power in the hands of persons having no beneficial interest in the stock, are generally restricted as contrary to public policy. For example, statutes commonly provide that a voting trust agreement is void unless it is limited to a period of ten years.[42] In exchange for the certificates of stock deposited with the voting trustees, the latter issue *voting trust certificates*.

**Minority Stockholders.** Although minority stockholders must abide by the decision of the majority, they may restrain the majority from exercising control (1) to the detriment of the corporation, or (2) for the sole benefit of the majority, or (3) in violation of the charter, by-laws or statute.

EXAMPLES:

(1) A proposal by the majority to transfer valuable corporate assets to a "friendly" competitor, thereby crippling the corporation, may be restrained by the minority.

(2) If a majority seeks to absorb as salaries profits that should go into dividends, a court will overcome its hesitancy in interfering with the judgment of directors and will intervene to provide redress at the instance of a minority stockholder. (See pages 524-525.)

(3) If three individuals, constituting all the stockholders of a corporation, unanimously adopt a by-law that no stockholder may dispose of his shares without first offering them to the company, any subsequent attempt by a majority of the stockholders to repeal such by-law may be thwarted by a single minority stockholder. (See page 533.)

**Minority Stockholders' Suits.** Wrongs to a corporation should be redressed by the corporation itself acting through its directors. Such directors are supposed to reflect the will of the majority as to what is best for the corporation. However, the majority often act for their own benefit and to the detriment of the corporation itself. In such cases a minority stockholder, after first making a demand upon the directors that they bring suit and following their failure to do so, may himself institute suit on behalf of the corporation. Such an action is said to be "derivative" be-

---

[42] This is the provision of the Model Business Corporation Act.

cause the stockholder has no *individual* right of action against directors for neglect and mismanagement entailing loss to the *corporation*. The right of action is in the corporation, which sustains the loss. Hence, when a stockholder brings a "derivative action," he should do so in the name and on behalf of the corporation. The relief usually sought in minority stockholders' suits is to compel directors and officers to account to the corporation for loss because of their negligence, breach of fiduciary duty or other misconduct, and for injunctions to restrain threatened or continued wrongs to the corporation.

## Questions

1. Name three ways in which a person may become a stockholder.
2. Name seven of the more common rights and privileges of a stockholder.
3. Give three ways in which stock may be transferred.
4. Name two of the reasonable restrictions sanctioned by the law with respect to the right to transfer stock.
5. What are the three factors which govern and control the stockholder's right to vote?
6. What is meant by cumulative voting?
7. Certain basic corporate acts require stockholders' approval. Can you name five such acts?
8. What is meant by a quorum as applied to a stockholders' meeting?
9. What is a proxy? A voting trust?
10. Name three situations in which minority stockholders may restrain the majority from exercising control.
11. What procedure may be adopted by a stockholder when the directors refuse to redress a wrong committed against a corporation?

## Problems

1. Three incorporators unanimously adopt a by-law which provides that no stockholder of the corporation shall have the right or power to pledge, sell or otherwise dispose of any shares of stock of the corporation except by will, without first offering such stock for sale to the corporation at the actual price at which it is proposed to sell the stock. Twelve years later a majority of the stockholders adopt a resolution repealing the by-law. Plaintiff, one of the original incorporators, refuses to abide by such majority decision and sues for an injunction. How will such suit be determined, and why?
2. The stockholders of a corporation, reposing full faith and confidence in their board of directors, which consists of a competent group of business men, unanimously adopt a resolution by which they give such directors all discretion in the conduct of corporate affairs. Specifically, the stockholders give the directors full power to do the following things as their honest judgment and discretion may dictate: (1) to arrange for the election of any new directors during the next five years; (2) to increase or reduce the capital stock of the corporation; (3) to change the place of business of the corporation, if deemed advisable; (4) to mortgage any and all of the corporate property; (5) to consolidate the corporation with any other corporation; (6) to sell all the corporate assets if a favorable price in the judgment of the directors can be procured upon such sale; (7) to extend corporate existence which is now fixed

by charter at 25 years; and, if deemed advisable, (8) to dissolve the corporation. Counsel for the company advises that the stockholders' vote for the above purposes having been unanimous, the procedure is entirely regular. Do you agree with this advice? Give reasons.

3. Barry on June 4th sells stock to Logan, who has the transfer registered on the books of the corporation on June 6th. The corporation, having declared a dividend to holders of record on June 5th, pays Barry the dividend. Logan sues Barry and the corporation as co-defendants for the amount of the dividend paid to Barry. How will the suit be decided and why?

4. The by-laws of a corporation provided that approval by 60 per cent of the stockholders was necessary for a sale of capital assets or the purchase of treasury stock. The president, owning one-half of the company's stock, conveyed, on its behalf, a substantial part of its real property in exchange for the rest of the outstanding stock. Was such sale of a capital asset and such acquisition of treasury stock valid? Give reason.

5. A mortgage on corporate property was executed and delivered in the name and on behalf of the corporation by its president and secretary, without further authority. The company received adequate value for the mortgage and retained it. Could the stockholders question such transaction?

## PART 6. RIGHTS OF STOCKHOLDERS (CONCLUDED)

**Summary.** In addition to a stockholder's right to the issuance of a certificate evidencing his ownership, and his right to vote or transfer his stock interest, he has the further right to participate in profits in the form of dividends, to inspect the corporate books, to be given priority or "pre-emption" in subscribing to new stock, and to share proportionately in a distribution of net assets upon dissolution.

**Right to Dividends: Nature and Classification.** A dividend, literally, is a fund to be divided. A dividend on stock is a distribution of profits to stockholders in proportion to their holdings. Dividends may be either *regular* or *extra,* depending upon the regularity with which they are paid, and either *profit* or *liquidation* dividends, the former payable out of profits, the latter out of capital upon liquidation or dissolution.

Dividends may also be classified as to the medium in which they are payable, viz., cash, stock or property. The latter are usually payable in securities, though they may also be payable in merchandise; for example, a dividend by a distilling corporation payable in whiskey. Dividends may also be payable in *scrip,* i.e., certificates entitling the holder to cash, stock, bonds or other property.

**Stock Dividends.** A stock dividend is a dividend payable in stock instead of in cash or property. As in the case of all dividends, it cannot be declared except out of surplus. For tax purposes, stock dividends are treated as capital, not as income.[43] As the United States Supreme Court has pointed out,[44] a stock dividend merely transfers an accumulated sur-

---

[43] *Equitable Trust Co. of New York v. Prentice,* 250 N.Y. 1, 164 N.E. 723; *Eisner v. Macomber,* 252 U.S. 189.

[44] *Eisner v. Macomber, supra.*

plus to the capital account of the corporation. This takes nothing from the property of the corporation and adds nothing to the shareholder. The stockholder receives nothing out of the company's assets for his separate use and benefit, but on the contrary, his investment in the corporation, plus accretions and accumulations, remains the same as it was and continues to be the property of the corporation.[45]

**Right to Dividends: Necessity of Declaration.** Except where dividends are guaranteed, a stockholder has no inherent right to a dividend unless and until it is declared. The declaration of a dividend rests in the sound discretion of the directors (page 540). If a corporation never achieves a surplus, its stockholders never acquire the right to a dividend.

**Dividend Not a Fixed Charge.** If the charter of a corporation makes a dividend mandatory, it is not truly a dividend, but a fixed charge. To be a dividend, it must be discretionary.

EXAMPLE: To encourage purchases, the by-laws of a grocery corporation devised a customer profit-sharing plan in the form of "patronage dividends." By an amendment to the by-laws, the "dividends" were made mandatory. In computing its Federal income tax, these "dividends" were deducted as expense. The by-law amendment was then superseded by a charter amendment which made the dividends discretionary. The corporation continued its practice of deducting these dividends as a fixed charge, but such deductions, amounting to $10,000, were disallowed for the period following the charter amendment, because, having become discretionary instead of mandatory, they were no longer an expense, but a true dividend.[46]

**Dividends Payable Only Out of Surplus.** As previously noted (page 528), dividends are payable only out of surplus, that is, out of an excess of assets over liabilities including capital stock.

EXAMPLE: A corporation has a deficit of $40,000 as of January 1. During the ensuing year it earns a net income of $45,000. During the following year the directors declare a dividend of $10,000 out of the previous year's profits. Such dividend would be illegal.

*Borrowing money to pay dividend.* It is not necessary, for the payment of a dividend, that the corporate surplus be in cash. If funds on hand are insufficient to pay a cash dividend, the corporation may borrow money for such purpose.

EXAMPLE: A realty corporation issues $300,000 worth of stock for an equal amount of cash, with which it buys a building. The building is resold for $350,000, which is promptly reinvested in another building. There are no corporate liabilities except outstanding stock. The corporation may declare a $50,000 dividend payable in new stock, scrip, or cash, and in the latter case may borrow money with which to pay the dividend.

---

[45] The doctrine has been limited, however, to dividends declared in stock of the same class. *Helvering v. Sprouse*, 318 U.S. 604.

[46] *Associated Grocers of Alabama, Inc. v. Willingham, Coll. of Int. Rev.,* 77 F. Supp. 990.

It is regarded as unsound business practice to borrow money for the purpose of paying a dividend; in some states, the practice is prohibited.

*Recovering dividends paid out of capital.* Dividends paid out of capital may be recovered by the corporation. If the directors fail to take steps for such recovery after demand by a stockholder that they do so, the stockholder may institute suit for such purpose in the name and on behalf of the corporation or he may sue in the corporate name to hold the directors accountable for loss entailed by the illegal dividend declaration. Similar steps may be instituted by a judgment creditor of the corporation, acting through a receiver, or by a trustee in bankruptcy, to require restitution of the moneys illegally paid.

Dividends paid out of capital may be followed into the hands of stockholders to the extent necessary to pay the debts of the corporation. The fact that directors are liable in such a case does not exonerate the stockholders from liability. (See page 546).

**Discretion of Directors in Declaring Dividends.** The determination as to whether dividends should be declared is left to the discretion of the directors. As previously shown (page 513), directors may even pass a dividend on noncumulative preferred, though enough is earned for payment of such dividend, if in their discretion they deem such action to be in the interests of the corporation.

**When Stockholders May Compel Dividend.** Ordinarily, stockholders may not compel directors to declare a dividend, though the corporation has a substantial surplus. Courts prefer to leave such matters to the judgment of the directors. However, if a stockholder can show that directors, in withholding dividends, are guilty of dishonesty or abuse of discretion, a court of equity will interfere to compel the directors to declare a dividend.

EXAMPLES:

(1) The *AB* Corporation made profits sufficient for a 5 per cent dividend on its stock, but the directors refused to declare a dividend. A suit by stockholders to compel the directors to declare a dividend would be dismissed unless fraud, bad faith or arbitrary conduct could be shown.

(2) Ford Motor Co. had:

| | |
|---|---:|
| A surplus of | $112,000,000 |
| Annual profits of | 60,000,000 |
| Total liabilities not exceeding | 20,000,000 |
| Cash available for dividends of | 54,000,000 |
| But paid, in dividends, only | 1,200,000 |

A court of equity ordered the directors to pay an additional dividend of $19,000,000, saying: "A business corporation is organized and carried on primarily for the profit of the stockholders." [47]

---

[47] *Dodge v. Ford Motor Co.,* 204 Mich. 459, 170 N.W. 668.

**Dividends on Partly Paid Stock.** As we have seen (page 531), one is entitled to the rights of a stockholder (including the right to dividends) as soon as he becomes a stockholder, which, on a *present subscription* means as soon as the subscription is *accepted*, whether or not the certificate has been issued or the price paid (pages 531-532). To this rule there are two exceptions:

(1) Dividends may be made payable to stockholders *of record* on a given date, and a corporation may refuse to recognize a stockholder as of record until his stock is fully paid.

(2) State statutes[48] may permit a corporation to provide in its charter that dividends on stock that is payable in installments shall be paid only in proportion to the amount actually paid in on the stock.

**Right to Inspect Books.** A stockholder's right to inspect corporate books is two-fold: (1) The common law right to inspect books of account, and (2) the statutory right to inspect the stock book of the corporation. In some states, the common law right to inspect books of account has been confirmed by statute. In most states, the statutory right of inspection is limited to an examination of the stock book of the company showing names, addresses and stock holdings.

*Books of account.* The right of a stockholder to inspect the financial books of his corporation is similar to the right of a partner to inspect the books of account of his firm. However, stockholders are relatively more numerous than partners, their interests are frequently relatively slight, and their stock ownership creates no such fiduciary rights and duties as those involved in partnerships. Hence, applications by stockholders to inspect corporate books of account are less readily granted by the courts than in the case of similar applications by partners. A stockholder's motive in seeking this type of inspection may be questioned. If the inspection is sought for speculative purposes, or for purposes hostile to the interests of the corporation, or to gratify idle curiosity, it will be denied.

*Statutory right to inspect stock book.* In this type of inspection, motive is generally immaterial. The statute, however, may impose certain limitations; for example, it may limit the right of inspection to (1) persons who have been stockholders for a given minimum period (regardless of amount of stock held), or (2) persons who hold at least a given per cent of the outstanding stock (regardless of how long the stock has been held). For this purpose the stock book must be open daily for at least a given number of hours. Inspection may be denied if sought for the purpose of providing a stockholder's list for commercial exploitation.

*Inspection by judgment creditors.* Judgment creditors as well as stockholders have a right in most states to inspect the books of account as well as the stock book for the purpose of enforcing judgments obtained against the corporation.

---

[48] For example, sec. 74 of the New York Stock Corporation Law.

*Remedies and penalties for failure to permit inspection.* Upon refusal to permit inspection, stockholders may obtain a court order compelling inspection, in addition to fines against the officers concerned. ·

**Right to Financial Statements.** Corporate practice in furnishing reports and other information to stockholders varies widely. Many corporations are required to file annual and other reports with state and Federal departments and regulatory commissions. The duty to furnish financial statements to stockholders is not generally prescribed by statute. In some cases, stockholders owning a given percentage of stock are entitled by law to financial statements.

**Pre-emptive right.** A stockholder's pre-emptive right is his right to subscribe to new stock in proportion to his existing holdings, before such stock is offered to the public. By "new" stock is meant *newly authorized stock*, not unissued stock under an existing authorization. A corporation need not offer the new issue to existing holders at par, but may demand more, if it can get more from the public.

EXAMPLES:

(1) The *A* Corporation, with an authorized capital stock of $25,000 (of which $20,000 is issued and outstanding), is about to sell the rest of its authorized stock to *A* at par. *C*, an existing stockholder, demands the right to subscribe to this stock at par in proportion to his present holdings.

(2) Later, the authorized capitalization is increased by $25,000, which is offered to *F* at $150 per share. *C* demands the right to subscribe to this new stock at par in proportion to his existing stock ownership.

*C* will not succeed in either of the above situations. However, in (2) above, *C* will be allowed to subscribe to the new stock at $150 in proportion to his existing holdings.

**Treasury stock.** The pre-emptive right does not generally attach to the sale of treasury stock.[49] Directors, however, may not issue such stock so as to obtain any undue advantage for themselves.[50] In some states, the reissue of treasury stock is regarded as equivalent to an issue of new stock and is subject to the pre-emptive right.

**Preferred stockholders,** as a rule, have no pre-emptive rights: so long as their dividends are paid and net assets are equal in value to the amount of outstanding preferred, such stockholders cannot complain.

**Rights on Dissolution.** Upon dissolution of a corporation, stockholders are entitled to a *pro rata* distribution of net assets after payment of debts. The order of distribution may be in accordance with priorities fixed in the charter, as where it specifies that preferred creditors shall come first, then Class "A" stockholders, then Class "B," and so on. (See "Preference as to assets on dissolution," page 514.)

---

[49] *Crosby v. Stratton,* 17 Colo. App. 212, 68 P. 130; *Thurmond v. Paragon Colliery Co.,* 82 W.Va. 49, 95 S.E. 816.

[50] *Hammer v. Werner,* 239 App. Div. 38, 265 N.Y. Supp. 172.

## Questions

1. What is meant by a dividend on stock?
2. What is a stock dividend?
3. Under what circumstances may stockholders compel the payment of a dividend?
4. Name two exceptions to the rule that one is entitled to the right of dividends as soon as he becomes a stockholder.
5. "A stockholder at all times has the right to inspect any and all books of the corporation." Is this statement true, false, or partly true and partly false? Explain.
6. Under what circumstances may stockholders demand a financial statement of a corporation?
7. What is meant by "a stockholder's pre-emptive right"? Illustrate.

## Problems

1. The X Corporation, having $100,000 in surplus assets, amends its charter by increasing its authorized capital stock from $400,000 to $500,000. It then issues the new stock to existing stockholders. How should such a transaction be designated?
2. A corporation has a deficit of $40,000 at January 1. During the ensuing year, it earns a net income of $45,000. During the following year the directors declare a dividend of $10,000 out of the previous year's profits. Comment on the legality of such action by the Board.
3. The XYZ Corporation is organized with an authorized capital stock of $5,000,000, all of which is issued. At the end of the third year the books of the corporation show a net profit of $800,000. The board of directors meet and decide that instead of declaring a dividend, they will use $600,000 of the net profit for increase in plant and equipment, and keep the remainder in the surplus account as a reserve for future expansion. Smith and several of the other stockholders are incensed and bring suit in equity to compel the directors to declare such dividend as, in the judgment of the court, may seem just and proper. How should the court decide and why?
4. Wilbur Wade is the owner of all the capital stock of the Wade Optical Corporation. The latter corporation competes with the Crystal Optical Works, Inc., a corporation capitalized at $500,000, all issued. Wade buys a block of 100 shares of Crystal Optical Works, Inc., par value $5, and after the lapse of seven months, seeks to compel an inspection of the financial books and records of Crystal Optical Works, Inc. The officers and directors of the latter company refuse to submit its books to inspection, and Wade seeks a court order directing such inspection. Will the injunction be granted or refused? Explain.
5. American Gas and Electric Co. has an authorized capital stock of $7,000,-000, divided into 140,000 shares of the par value of $50 each, half preferred and half common. Of the 70,000 shares of preferred, 33,230 shares have been issued and are outstanding. Of the 70,000 shares of common, 50,000 shares have been issued, leaving, unissued, 36,770 shares of preferred and 20,000 shares of common. The directors adopt a resolution to issue 10,000 shares of the unissued common and to allow the holders of the issued common to subscribe for such new shares ratably at $50 per share (par). The market value of the common stock is $80 per share; the market value of the preferred, $47. Russell, a holder

of 480 shares of preferred stock, insists that he is just as much entitled to subscribe pro rata for the new common stock as the existing holders of the common. He sues to restrain the proposed issue except upon the basis of equality
as between preferred and common. How will suit be decided and why?

## PART 7. LIABILITIES OF STOCKHOLDERS

**Commencement and Termination of Stockholder's Liability.** As we
have seen (page 515), a stockholder's liabilities, like his rights and privileges, come into existence when he becomes a stockholder. *So far as
the corporation is concerned,* just as a stockholder's rights may not be
recognized unless he is a stockholder of record, so his liabilities continue
though he has transferred his stock and is no longer actually a stockholder
at the time such liabilities arise, provided the transfer has not been
recorded on the books of the corporation. This is particularly true of
banking corporations.

EXAMPLE: John Doe transferred 200 shares of stock in the X bank to Richard
Roe, with privilege in the latter to return the stock if unable to sell it within
six months. Richard Roe signed a blank transfer with power of attorney on the
back of the certificate, and two months later returned the certificate to Doe,
who pledged it with another bank to secure a loan. Later, the X bank became
insolvent. Roe had registered his stock upon acquiring it from Doe, but had
neglected to register the retransfer to Doe. The receiver sued Roe on his
"double liability." The Court, holding that Roe should have seen that the retransfer was registered if he wished to avoid his statutory liability as a stockholder, said: "Had a dividend been declared * * * defendant would have been
the one entitled to it * * *. Defendant was clothed with title to the advantages, and in the absence of reasonable diligence to effect a transfer upon the
bank records, should not be heard to repudiate the disadvantages." [51]

Where, however, failure to register is the fault of the corporation or
of the transferee, a stockholder who has made a bona fide sale of his
stock and has done everything in his power to comply with all the requirements ceases to be liable as such.[52]

*Where liability has accrued prior to transfer: statute of limitations.*
Once corporate liability arises, a stockholder cannot escape liability merely
by transferring his stock. However, the statute may protect him in such
cases by fixing a period of limitations. For example, a typical statute[53]
provides that:

No stockholder shall be personally liable for any debt of the corporation not
payable within two years from the time it is contracted, nor unless an action
for its collection shall be brought against the corporation within two years
after the debt becomes due; and no action shall be brought against a stockholder after he shall have ceased to be a stockholder, for any debt of the cor-

---

[51] *Broderick v. Pomerantz,* 148 Misc. 188, 265 N.Y. Supp. 425, 427-8.
[52] *Realty & Rebuilding Co. v. Rea,* 184 Cal. 565, 194 P. 1024; *Andrew v. Sandford,*
212 Iowa 300, 233 N.W. 529, 532; *Schmitt v. Kulamer,* 267 Pa. 1, 110 A. 169.
[53] N.Y. Stock Corporation Law, sec. 73.

poration, unless brought within two years from the time he shall have ceased to be a stockholder.

**Limited Liability of Stockholders.** A stockholder's liability is ordinarily limited to the amount of his investment. Under certain conditions, however, a stockholder may become specially liable (1) to the corporation, (2) to judgment creditors of the corporation, (3) to wage earners, and (4) to the state.

**Liability of Stockholder to Corporation.** As pointed out on page 515, a stockholder is liable to the corporation for the unpaid balance of his stock subscription with interest from the date of default. Stock may be and frequently is issued on a part-payment basis subject to "call." When the call is made, payment must be forthcoming or the corporation may exercise its option to sue for the balance or declare a forfeiture of the stock.

*On original par value stock* issued for less than its full par value, a stockholder is liable to the corporation for the difference.

*On original no par value stock,* a stockholder is liable to the corporation for the difference between the amount paid in and the agreed price, which must be its fair market value (page 516). If the consideration to be paid for such stock is fixed in the articles of incorporation, the subscriber is liable up to this amount.

However, any one of three factors, (1) illegality, (2) estoppel, or (3) waiver, may bar a corporation from recovering against a stockholder in connection with a stock purchase.

(1) *Illegality.* A corporation, including a receiver suing on its behalf, may be barred by illegality from recovering against a stockholder on an unpaid stock subscription.[54]

EXAMPLE: In *Stone v. Young,*[55] two hundred shares of preferred stock, par $100, were issued at a price $20,000, with one hundred shares of no-par common thrown in. After the subscriber paid in $13,000, the corporation became insolvent. A receiver sued for the unpaid balance of $7000. The Court held that since the preferred had to be sold at par, the common was issued for nothing; and since it was illegal to issue stock for no value, the corporation, and hence the receiver, was barred from recovering on the illegal transaction.

(2) *Estoppel.* When a corporation, acting through its directors, makes a bargain with a purchaser of stock, it is bound by the bargain and estopped from claiming that the bargain was unfair or invalid.[56]

EXAMPLES:
(1) A corporation that issues stock as "fully paid and nonassessable," though

---

[54] *Bucher v. Federal Baseball Club of Baltimore,* 130 Md. 635, 101 A. 534; *Drees v. Minnesota Petroleum Co.,* 189 Minn. 608, 250 N.W. 563, 564; *Norfolk Motor Exchange v. Grubb,* 152 Va. 471, 147 S.E. 214.

[55] 210 App. Div. 303, 206 N.Y. Supp. 95.

[56] *Stoecker v. Goodman,* 183 Ky. 330, 290 S.W. 374.

the full value thereof has not been paid, is estopped from thereafter trying to hold the stockholder for the difference.[57]

(2) Stock having a par value of $100 was issued for $25 a share. The corporation agreed with the stockholder that the amount of his investment was to be the limit of his liability. The corporation was adjudicated a bankrupt and the trustee in bankruptcy sued the stockholder for the difference between the par value of the stock and the amount actually paid by the stockholder. The Court, in dismissing the case, held that the trustee stood "in the shoes" of the corporation; and since the corporation was estopped by its bargain, so was the trustee.[58]

(3) *Waiver.* As previously noted (page 533), a corporation may refuse to record a stock transfer on its books unless the stock has been fully paid. Once the corporation records the transfer, however, it waives any claim against the transferor and accepts the new stockholder as a substitute debtor; that is, the transaction amounts to a *novation*[59] (page 99).

*Liability for unlawful dividends.* A stockholder is generally liable to the corporation for illegal dividends received by him. "Generally, dividends paid by a corporation out of capital may be followed into the hands of stockholders to the extent necessary to pay the debts of the corporation, and the liability of directors in such a case does not exonerate the stockholders from liability." [60] If a corporation fails to enforce restitution, a stockholder or judgment creditor may do so.[61]

**Liability of Stockholders to Judgment Creditors of the Corporation.** The statute gives judgment creditors of a corporation a right of action against stockholders who for one reason or another are obligated to the corporation. Such obligations to the corporation represent corporate assets in the form of *choses in action* (page 652); and to the extent that a corporation has assets, judgment creditors are entitled to be satisfied.

There are various types of stockholders' obligations to which a judgment creditor of the corporation may thus resort:

(a) *Unpaid stock subscriptions.* These include not only ordinary unpaid balances on a stock subscription, but also cases where a corporation issues original stock for less than its full value. Although, as noted on pages 545-546, the *corporation* may be barred from bringing suit for such deficiency, a *judgment creditor* is not.

EXAMPLES:
(1) Hurd subscribes for 50 shares of stock of the Basswood Furniture Co. but fails to pay any part of his subscription. Later, the corporation becomes insolvent. The creditors in such case may compel Hurd to make good his subscription.

(2) X purchases from the Y Corporation 50 shares of its preferred stock,

[57] *Thompson v. Knight,* 74 App. Div. 316, 77 N.Y. Supp. 599.
[58] *Southworth v. Morgan,* 205 N.Y. 293, 98 N.E. 490.
[59] *Schmitt v. Kulamer,* 267 Pa. 1, 110 A. 169.
[60] 18 *C.J.S.* 1323.
[61] *Gager v. Paul,* 111 Wis. 638, 87 N.W. 675.

paying its par value. As a bonus, the $Y$ Corporation issues to $X$ 5 shares of its $100 par common stock, the certificate for which carries the printed notation: "Full paid, nonassessable." $X$ can be compelled to pay for this stock in a suit by a judgment creditor, but not in a suit by the corporation or anyone who derives his rights directly from the corporation.

(b) *Watered stock.* Where stock is watered (page 516), the stockholder receiving such stock for less than its true value may be compelled to make good the deficiency to judgment creditors.

(c) *Unlawful dividends.* As already noted, judgment creditors of the corporation may compel stockholders to make restitution to the corporation for unlawful dividends received by them, so that the proceeds of such restitution will be available for the discharge of such judgments.

**Liability to Wage Earners.** In some states, stockholders of a corporation are personally liable for unpaid wages. In such cases, if the wage earner procures a judgment against the corporation for unpaid wages and is unable to collect it, he may hold the stockholder personally for the amount of the judgment.

**Liability Where Foreign Corporation Fails to Register.** A state may compel all foreign corporations doing business therein to file certificates authorizing them to conduct such business, and upon their failure to do so, may impose various penalties, including personal liability of stockholders for corporate debts. (See pages 549 to 550.)

## Questions

1. What does the statute of limitations provide with respect to the termination of a stockholder's liability?
2. Under certain conditions a stockholder may become liable to four separate entities. What are they?
3. What three factors may bar a corporation from recovering against a stockholder in connection with a stock purchase?
4. Name three types of stockholders' obligations to which a judgment creditor may on some occasions resort.
5. Under what circumstances may a stockholder be liable to a wage earner?

## Problems

1. Harding buys 50 shares of $100 par value stock in the Metropolitan Corporation, under an agreement permitting him to pay for the stock in ten equal installments. He pays eight installments, then sells the stock to Bryan, subject to the last two installments which Bryan is to pay. Harding indorses the certificate of stock, and after affixing the required documentary stamps, delivers it to Bryan, who in turn delivers the certificate to the corporation's secretary for cancellation and the issuance of a new certificate. Through the negligence of a clerk in the secretary's office, the stock remains registered in Harding's name. Both the Metropolitan Corporation and Bryan become insolvent. The receiver sues Harding as a stockholder of record owing $1000 on his stock, and Bryan pleads the foregoing facts in defense. Judgment for whom and why?
2. In a state which makes it illegal to issue stock for anything but cash,

property or services of adequate value, the Reckless Corporation issues a $10,000 block of stock to Dorne, who gives his ninety-day note for the purchase price. On due date the note is defaulted, and the Reckless Corporation sues Dorne on the note. Will the corporation succeed?

3. The Generous Corporation issues to A. Shrood Trader, as "fully paid and non-assessable," 100 shares of its original issue common stock. Actually, only 50 per cent of the face value of the stock was paid for. Subsequently, a new management insists on Trader's making good the deficiency on his stock purchase. Trader objects. How will the court decide? Why?

4. Suppose, in the foregoing case, that a judgment was procured against the corporation, which was uncollectible, and that the judgment creditor brought suit to compel Trader to make good the deficiency on his stock purchase. Would your answer be the same? Explain.

5. Blue Sky, Inc., issues $50,000 worth of stock to Van Pelt, its president, for a relatively worthless mine. Later, after additional stock has been sold for cash, the directors cause the mine to be valued on the books of the corporation at $50,000, thereby creating a fictitious surplus; after which they declare a 10 per cent cash dividend to stockholders, including Van Pelt, who owns a majority of the stock. A few months later the corporation goes into bankruptcy. The trustee seeks to compel Van Pelt to restore both the full value of the stock originally purchased by him, as well as the 10 per cent dividend received by him. Will the trustee succeed?

### PART 8. CORPORATE RIGHTS, POWERS AND LIABILITIES

**The Corporation as a Person.** Generally speaking, corporations are endowed by law with the same rights, powers and responsibilities as natural persons. They may buy, own, hold and sell property. They may make contracts. They are liable for their debts, torts and agreements. They may sue and be sued. In short, as pointed out on page 495, a corporation is treated in law as a person in its own right, separate and distinct from the human beings behind it.

However, where the corporate device is used to perpetrate a fraud, the corporate fiction may be disregarded. Moreover, by their very nature, corporations differ from individuals in certain basic respects, namely, as to existence, citizenship, scope of power and amenability to punishment.

**Disregarding the Corporate Fiction: Fraudulent Devices.** Where persons utilize the corporate entity for the achievement of illegal or fraudulent ends, the courts will penetrate the corporate fiction and deal directly with the realities. Thus, persons will not be permitted to evade existing debts and obligations by resorting to the corporate form of doing business.

EXAMPLE: Smith discovered that his government land grants were void. Anticipating a suit to annul the grants on the ground of fraud, Smith formed a corporation and deeded the lands to it, but suppressed the transfer by failing to record his deed to the corporation. The government, assuming that Smith was still the owner, sued Smith, who contrived to drag the lawsuit out for more than six years, by which time the statute of limitations would normally outlaw such government suits against the true owner. Smith then disclosed that he was no longer the true owner. Upon discovery of the facts, the United

States Supreme Court refused to allow Smith's trick to succeed. The corporation, being wholly owned by Smith, was charged with knowledge of the facts and was required to give up the lands.[62]

However, where the corporation is not chargeable with guilty knowledge of the wrong, the Court will not disturb the corporate fiction.

EXAMPLE: Where the owner of a business sells its assets to a corporation but says nothing about its liabilities, and the corporation has no knowledge of such liabilities, the creditors of the old business have no redress against the corporation. But where the corporation was formed or is largely owned by the seller, its separate existence will be disregarded and it will be deemed merely an *alter ego* of the seller.

**Corporate Existence.** The life of a corporation is prescribed in its certificate of incorporation. It is now customary for incorporators to provide for perpetual existence. Failure to do this frequently results in the inconvenience and expense of filing a new certificate for the purpose of extending corporate existence.[63]

**Citizenship: When Corporation Deemed Citizen, When Not.** A corporation is a citizen for some purposes but not for others. For jurisdictional purposes (taxation, for example), a corporation is a citizen of the state where it is incorporated. From the standpoint of Article IV of the United States Constitution ("The Citizens of each State shall be entitled to all the Privileges and Immunities of Citizens in the several States") a corporation is not a citizen. To do business as a foreign corporation in another state and to have the right to sue on such business in such state, it must first procure a certificate from the Secretary of State and pay a fee to that state for the privilege of doing business there.

**Foreign Corporations: License Requirements.** The license requirements for the purpose of authorizing foreign corporations to do business in a given state depend upon the laws of that particular state. The usual procedure is to file an application certifying the corporation's name, date and state of incorporation, the nature of its business, the location of its principal office, the proposed registered office, the names and addresses of officers and directors, the name of the proposed resident agent on whom process may be served, facts in reference to capitalization, value and similar information, together with a certified copy of the certificate of incorporation. This information must be accompanied by a registration fee.

**Foreign Corporations: What Constitutes Doing Business.** It is not easy to define what constitutes "doing business" in a given state. Isolated deals, mail-order transactions and transactions that are purely interstate in char-

---

[62] *Linn & Lane Timber Co. v. United States*, 236 U.S. 574.
[63] The head of a well known accounting firm writes to the author: "Probably it will not be a surprise to you that I have found more than one bond issue the maturity of which was subsequent to the expiration of the charter."

acter have been held clearly not to constitute "doing business." The law generally contemplates a more or less permanent and continuous business establishment, evidenced by the appointment of some local business agent, or by a branch store, or by a listing in a telephone directory, or similar indications that the business that is being done is not merely temporary or isolated.

**Doing Business Without License: Corporate Penalties.** In addition to personal penalties, states may impose fines upon a foreign corporation doing business in a given state without a license. The most common penalty for such infraction is to deprive the offending corporation of the right to sue in such state for moneys due or for any other cause.

EXAMPLE: In *The Truly Warner Company, Inc. v. Kaufman Hats, Inc.*,[64] plaintiff sued defendant for damages sustained by having been kept wrongfully out of a store it had leased on a valuable Chicago corner. The lower court gave plaintiff judgment for $44,921. On appeal the decision was reversed on the ground that plaintiff was a New York corporation, that it had not been qualified as a foreign corporation in Illinois, and that it was doing business in the state and therefore had no right to maintain an action in the Illinois courts.

**Doing Business Without License: Personal Penalties.** As noted on page 528, personal liabilities and penalties are imposed by some states upon stockholders, directors and officers of a foreign corporation doing business in the state without a license. These may include personal liability for corporate debts, fines, and, in some cases, imprisonment.

EXAMPLES:

(1) In *Equitable Trust Co. v. Central Trust Co., et al.*,[65] a Scottish bank had become a stockholder of a corporation by taking its stock in settlement of a debt. The corporation had done business in Tennessee without having qualified as a foreign corporation. The bank in question, as stockholder, was held liable for the company's debts in the state, and judgment was awarded against the bank for the sum of $146,637.39.

(2) In *Critchfield and Co. v. A. Watson Armour, et al.*,[66] a corporation known as the Tireoid Company kept an office in Chicago and employed the services of a Chicago advertising agency. In the course of time the corporation became insolvent. It owed the advertising agency a debt of $15,710.50. The agency discovered that the company was a foreign corporation not qualified to do business in Illinois, and that some of its directors were wealthy Chicago citizens. Suit was brought against these directors personally, and judgment was obtained against them for the full amount of the debt.

**Scope of Corporate Power.** A corporation has only such power as is (1) expressly conferred by charter or (2) reasonably implied therefrom. Acts of a corporation within its express or implied powers are *intra vires;* outside of its express or implied powers, *ultra vires.*

Certain powers, though not expressed in the charter, are implicit in the

---

[64] 352 Ill. 541, 186 N.E. 167.
[65] 145 Tenn. 148, 239 S.W. 171.
[66] 228 Ill. App. 28.

nature of corporate activity, such as perpetual succession; the power to sue and be sued in the corporate name; the power to take, hold, sell and convey real and personal property for corporate purposes; the power to have a corporate seal; the power to make by-laws; and the power to do all acts reasonably necessary to carry out the corporate objects and purposes. Beyond these, the question as to what constitutes an implied power is one on which the courts are at variance.

EXAMPLES:

(1) May a corporation engage in selling *electrical supplies* made by other concerns if its sole object is to *manufacture electrical appliances?* The court has answered this question in the negative.[67]

(2) Does a railroad corporation have implied power to guarantee expenses of a "World's Peace Jubilee and International Music Festival" on the ground that the latter would stimulate railroad traffic? The court said no.[68]

(3) If the Ford Motor Company was formed for the sole purpose of making automobiles, as expressly provided in its certificate of incorporation, could a power be reasonably implied to operate a smelter to make castings from iron ore to be used in its cars? The court held that the company had such an implied power.[69]

(4) Has a corporation with the express power to operate an office building the implied power to operate, in conjunction therewith, a laundry to furnish towels to its tenants, such business being incidental to the efficient operation and management of the building? The court said it has.[70]

(5) Has a laundry corporation, expressly authorized to lease and otherwise deal in real estate and personal property and to do anything to enhance the value of its property and rights, the power to operate a lumber business? The court said it has.[71]

(6) May a lumber manufacturing corporation publish a newspaper? The court held that it could, because such a newspaper may be considered primarily as an advertising medium, useful in promoting sales.[72]

Regardless of the scope of implied corporate powers, the law, on grounds of public policy, limits a corporation in respect to the following rights, powers and functions: (1) The right to become a partner; (2) the right to buy its own stock; (3) the right to buy stock in other corporations; (4) the power to lend money; (5) the power to guarantee obligations; (6) the power to indorse for accommodation; and (7) the right to practice a profession.

(1) *Right of corporation to become partner.* We have already noted (page 460) that a corporation, from its very nature, does not have the power to become a partner, though it may be estopped to deny liability as such. As pointed out in the chapter on "Partnerships and Other Asso-

---

[67] *Powell v. Murray,* 157 N.Y. 717, 53 N.E. 1130.

[68] *Davis v. Old Colony R.R. Co.,* 131 Mass. 258.

[69] *Dodge v. Ford Motor Co.,* 204 Mich. 459, 170 N.W. 668.

[70] *American Coat, Apron and Towel Supply Co. v. Grant Building,* 102 Pa. Super. 373, 157 A. 52.

[71] *People's Wet Wash Laundry Co. v. Debeau,* 80 N.H. 544, 119 A. 706.

[72] *State ex inf. Gentry v. Long-Bell Lumber Co.,* 321 Mo. 461, 12 S.W. 2d 64.

ciations," each partner may bind his copartners by acts within the scope of the partnership. If corporations could become partners, corporate affairs could be controlled by persons who are neither stockholders, directors nor officers, and this would violate the basic principle of corporate management.

(2) *Right of corporation to buy its own stock.* Some states (Washington, Missouri and California, for example) have held that a corporation cannot purchase its own shares of stock either to retire or to reissue them. The better rule, however, is that a corporation may acquire and hold its own stock, provided:

(a) The transaction is fair and made in good faith.

(b) The transaction is free from fraud.

(c) The rights of creditors and other stockholders will not be prejudiced by the purchase.

(d) The purchase is made out of an existing surplus.

(e) The purchase will not cause the corporation to lose its surplus nor to become insolvent.

(f) The corporation is not in the process of dissolution.

*Corporate commitment v. corporate option to buy stock.* An agreement by a corporation that *obligates* it to purchase its own stock in the future, either at a definite time or upon a contingent event, is unenforceable because at such future time the corporation may not have a surplus, in which event it could not be compelled to buy the stock. Since such an agreement would lack mutuality (page 59), it would be void from the start.[73]

(3) *Right of corporation to buy stock in other corporations.* On general principles, a corporation cannot buy stock in another corporation unless such power has been expressly granted to it in its charter or is necessarily implied from its express powers. Many states have statutes that expressly authorize a corporation under certain conditions to purchase and hold stock of other corporations. These statutes, for the most part, provide that any stock corporation (other than a moneyed corporation) may buy stocks or bonds of another corporation provided: (1) The power is expressly conferred by charter; or (2) the corporation whose stock is acquired is engaged in a business similar to that of the acquiring corporation so that the acquisition is reasonably incidental and necessary to the express objects and purposes of the latter; or (3) the corporation whose stock is acquired is one with which the acquiring corporation is authorized to consolidate. In no event may one corporation purchase the stock of another except out of surplus. Also, as noted in the following chapter, stock acquisitions resulting in unreasonable restraints of trade are prohibited.

(4) *Power to lend money.* Ordinarily, a corporation has no power to lend money unless it is authorized to do so by charter pursuant to statute.

---

[73] *Topken, Loring & Schwartz, Inc. v. Schwartz,* 249 N.Y. 206, 163 N.E. 735.

A corporation that lends money as a business is a moneyed corporation, and moneyed corporations are incorporated under special banking statutes. There are situations, however, in which a corporation may find it necessary to lend money as an incidental part of its normal functions and powers.

EXAMPLE: A Kentucky court has held that a corporation authorized to operate a public warehouse for receiving and storing tobacco and to buy, sell and resell the tobacco on commission, has authority to lend money to a customer on his growing crop.[74]

The law makes a distinction between the *practice* of lending money and the granting of a temporary loan as an incidental and necessary part of the corporation's business.

Corporate loans to directors, officers and stockholders are generally prohibited, with penalties for violations. (See page 527.)

(5) *Power to guarantee obligations.* Ordinarily, a corporation has no power to become a guarantor or surety or to lend its credit to another person or corporation. There are, however, two exceptions to this rule: (1) Guaranty and surety bonds issued by a company engaged in such business, and (2) guaranties made in furtherance of corporate business.

EXAMPLE: A parent corporation owns all the capital stock of a building company that is required to procure a completion bond on a building contract. The surety company refuses to issue a completion bond unless the parent corporation guarantees the subsidiary corporation's indemnity to the surety company required in connection with such bond. Such guaranty by the parent corporation would be valid.

(6) *Power to indorse for accommodation.* A corporation cannot indorse negotiable paper for another's accommodation. Any person who accepts a negotiable instrument in reliance upon such indorsement is presumed to do so with knowledge of its invalidity and cannot hold the corporation on such an instrument. However, where a bona fide holder for value takes negotiable paper bearing a corporate indorsement, without notice that such indorsement was made without consideration and was purely for accommodation, he may enforce collection on the instrument.

(7) *Right to practice profession.* We have already pointed out that the law generally prohibits corporations from practicing the learned professions (pages 462 and 497). Statutes generally prohibit corporations from practicing law, medicine, dentistry, architecture and even optometry. A corporation that renders such professional services may recover nothing for them, and if they were tied into an otherwise valid contract, the entire contract fails, though the services were only a small part of the contract. See, in this connection, page 71.

**Corporate Liabilities: Contracts.** A corporation, as previously noted

---

[74] *Holt v. Farmers Loose Leaf Tobacco Warehouse Co.,* 201 Ky. 184, 256 S.W. 6.

(pages 500 to 501) is not liable on contracts made in its behalf prior to its incorporation except where such contracts are expressly or impliedly adopted. Neither is a corporation liable on illegal contracts, though in some cases it may be liable for *ultra vires* acts.

**Illegal v. unauthorized acts.** A distinction must be noted between corporate acts that are invalid because they are prohibited by law, such as crimes and statutory violations generally, and corporate acts that are not invalid in themselves but which are invalid as to the corporation because they are *ultra vires*—beyond the express or implied powers of the corporation.

**Ultra Vires Acts: When Enforceable and When Not.** Not all *ultra vires* acts are unenforceable. A corporation may, in certain cases, be estopped to deny liability on its *ultra vires* acts. Likewise, estoppel may prevent a third party from taking advantage of the *ultra vires* plea. *Ultra vires* contracts may involve the following situations:

(1) *Where neither the corporation nor the third party has performed.* In such situations, neither party can enforce the contract against the other.

EXAMPLE: By agreement with Nassau Bank, Jones subscribed for $90,000 worth of railroad securities, including stock, in which the bank was to have a one-half interest and for which it was to pay one half the purchase price. Jones bought the stock, made a large profit. The bank claimed one half the profits. It had not yet contributed its half of the price, nor had Jones paid over any of the profits. Held: The contract being executory on both sides and the agreement with Jones being *ultra vires* (the bank had no right to invest in railroad stock), such agreement was unenforceable.[75]

(2) *Where both parties have performed.* In such situations, the contract being executed on both sides, neither party may sue to rescind it.

EXAMPLE: A fire insurance company issued a policy insuring against loss of crops by hail, and received the premium. The company later sought to escape liability for loss on the ground that it had no power to insure against loss by hail. Held: that, though the contract was *ultra vires,* the transaction would stand, since it had been executed on both sides.[76]

(3) *Where the contract has been executed on one side but not on the other.* Here, the authorities differ. The Federal and some state courts declare such contracts void, but hold that the party receiving the benefit of the contract must pay the fair and reasonable value of such benefit, regardless of the agreed value under the contract. The majority of states hold that the party receiving full performance is estopped to raise the defense of *ultra vires.*

EXAMPLE: A corporation borrows money for use in an *ultra vires* business, to the knowledge of the lender. It gives its note for the loan, but thereafter

[75] *Nassau Bank v. Jones,* 95 N.Y. 115.
[76] *Denver Fire Ins. Co. v. McClelland,* 9 Colo. 11.

seeks to avoid liability on it because of the *ultra vires* character of the transaction. Held: that the corporation is estopped from setting up such defense.[77]

(4) *Where there has been part performance on both sides.* Here the law generally enforces the contract to the extent that it has been performed but refuses to enforce the unexecuted part.

EXAMPLE: Plaintiff contracted to sell excelsior to defendant corporation for *ultra vires* speculative purposes. After delivering a considerable quantity, plaintiff refused to deliver more. Defendant corporation refused to pay for what had been delivered unless the whole amount was delivered as agreed. Held: that plaintiff was entitled to recover for the excelsior actually delivered, though the contract was *ultra vires,* but that defendant could not recoup damages for failure to complete performance by delivering the balance.[78]

**Corporate Liability for Unauthorized Acts of Officers.** Just as a principal is liable to third parties for acts of a general agent within the *apparent scope* of the latter's duties (page 406), so a corporation is liable to third parties for the acts of its officers—even when such acts are outside the scope of their actual duties as prescribed in the by-laws—provided such acts are customarily delegated to such officers. If such authority is not customarily delegated, third parties have no right to rely on it, as, for example, where the president of a corporation, without specific authority, undertakes to hire an employee for life.

*Restrictions on authority: when third parties bound by.* Third parties are not bound by restrictions contained in by-laws, unless they have actual knowledge of them. They are, however, chargeable with knowledge of *legal restrictions* and of those set forth in the certificate of incorporation. The reason for this is that everyone is supposed to know the law and everyone is supposed to have constructive notice of filed documents. A charter must be publicly filed; by-laws need not be.[79]

*Liability for notes and checks improperly signed.* Even though the by-laws of a corporation provide that some specific officer or officers must sign all checks, notes, and so on, the corporation is liable on instruments signed by an officer without such authority where the corporation, with full knowledge, has received the benefit of the transaction.

EXAMPLE: The by-laws of a corporation provide that the treasurer or, in his absence, the president or vice president shall sign checks, notes, and so on for the company. A note for $10,000 is made out by the company to itself and indorsed in blank. Albert Smith, who is both secretary and treasurer, signs the note as follows: "The X Company, by Albert Smith, Secretary." The note is negotiated at the bank, but on maturity the corporation refuses to pay on the ground that the note is not signed properly. The corporation, having received

---

[77] *Bradley v. Ballard,* 55 Ill. 413.

[78] *Day v. Spiral Springs Buggy Co.,* 57 Mich. 146, 23 N.W. 628.

[79] This rule, however, is not uniform. There are states that refuse to recognize the mere filing of a certificate of incorporation as constructive public notice of its contents.

the benefit of the transaction, is obligated on the instrument regardless of irregularity in signature.

However, where an officer indorses checks payable to the corporation and deposits them in his personal account and the bank collects the proceeds and pays them out on the officer's personal checks, the bank and not the corporation must stand the loss, since the bank in such case is chargeable with knowledge that the funds were diverted from corporate purposes.

**Corporate Torts.** A corporation, like a natural person, is liable for all torts committed by its officers, agents or employees during the course and scope of their corporate duties. It is no defense that the acts or transactions, in connection with which such torts occurred, were *ultra vires*. "It is to be kept in mind that all torts are necessarily *ultra vires*, since if an act is authorized by a valid statute it is for that reason lawful and not a tort." [80]

**Corporate Crimes.** Corporations, like individuals, are capable of committing crimes. These may include statutory offenses, such as making a political campaign contribution, rebating, or violating a labor or an antitrust statute. Corporate crimes may also be of the so-called "common law" variety (page 826), although it has been held that unless the statute so provides, a corporation cannot commit homicide, particularly where the statute defines homicide "as the killing of one human being by *another*." [81] Crimes applicable to human beings only, such as bigamy, cannot, of course, be committed by a corporation. Moreover, since a corporation is a fictitious being, it cannot be imprisoned. Corporate punishment must necessarily take the form of fines, or forfeiture of charter, which is equivalent to corporate death.

## Questions

1. Under what circumstances will the Courts disregard the corporate fiction?
2. Name four basic respects wherein corporations differ from individuals.
3. "A corporation is a citizen for some purposes but not for others." Explain this statement.
4. What are the usual requirements for a foreign corporation to do business in another state?
5. What, in general, constitutes "doing business" in a particular state?
6. What is the usual penalty inflicted upon a foreign corporation that does business in a given state without a license?
7. What personal liabilities are imposed in some states when a foreign corporation does business in such states without a license?
8. What powers not necessarily expressed in the charter are implicit in the nature of corporate activity?

---

[80] *Ziegler v. Denver Hog Serum Co.*, 204 Minn. 156, 283 N.W. 134, 137.
[81] *People v. Rochester Railway and Light Company*, 195 N.Y. 102, 88 N.E. 22.

9. Name seven respects in which the law limits the rights, powers, and functions of a corporation.

10. Why does the law restrict a corporation's right to become a partner?

11. Name six conditions under which a corporation will be permitted to buy its own stock.

12. Differentiate between a corporate commitment and a corporate option to buy its own stock.

13. Under what three conditions may a corporation exercise the right to buy stock in other corporations?

14. Comment on a corporation's right to lend money.

15. Name two exceptions to the rule that a corporation may not guarantee the obligations of others.

16. "*Ultra vires* contracts are not enforceable against the corporation." Is this statement true, false, or partly true and partly false?

17. In what circumstances, if any, may a corporation be liable for the unauthorized acts of its officers?

18. Are the following statements true, false, or partly true and partly false?

(a) "Corporations cannot be liable for torts."

(b) "Corporations cannot be liable for crimes."

## Problems

1. A railroad corporation desires to operate a gravel pit, but is advised by counsel that it has no power to engage in commercial operations. The officers and directors of the railroad corporation then personally organize the Acme Gravel Corporation to operate the pit. The railroad officers and directors hold all the stock in the gravel corporation in their individual names, but they operate the corporation for the benefit of the railroad corporation. A competing gravel concern files a complaint with the Federal Trade Commission against the Acme Gravel Corporation and the railroad corporation, alleging unfair competition. The railroad corporation denies any corporate connection with the gravel corporation. How will the Federal Trade Commission find?

2. The Transcontinental Tool Corporation, through its general sales manager, embarked upon a nation-wide mail-order campaign, and in consequence procured a large order from a customer in Illinois. The customer failed to pay, and the Transcontinental Tool Corporation brought suit in Illinois. The defense was that the plaintiff corporation being a foreign corporation, and having failed to procure a license to do business in Illinois, had no right to bring suit in that state. How did the court decide, and why?

3. Plaintiff, a meat packer, sued defendant, a Troy, New York, butcher, for a balance due for meat sold. The defense was that plaintiff was an Illinois corporation and was doing business in New York without having filed a certificate authorizing it to do so. The plaintiff corporation had an office in the City of Troy, New York, for the sale of meats and provisions and the sales to the butcher were transacted through said office. Defendant moved for a non-suit. How did the court decide, and why?

4. Plaintiff, a Tennessee corporation, having made a $25,000 sale of Mississippi real estate for defendant, presented its bill for $1,250 broker's commission which defendant refused to pay. On suit for commissions, the defense was that plaintiff had failed to qualify in Mississippi as a foreign corporation. How did the court decide? Give reasons.

5. A corporation indorses a promissory note for the accommodation of William Smith. The note is then negotiated to Frank White, a holder in due

course, who is without notice that the indorsement was made without consideration and purely for accommodation. May White enforce collection on the instrument?

6. The First National Bank of Springfield entered into an agreement with Wright by which the bank subscribed for $100,000 worth of railroad securities, including stock, in which the bank was to have a one-half interest and for which it was to pay one half the purchase price. Wright bought the stock and made a handsome profit. The bank tendered one half the purchase price and claimed one half the profits, but Wright refused the tender and refused to pay over any of the profits. The bank sued. How did the court decide, and on what ground?

7. Suppose that the First National Bank of Springfield, in another case, had accepted a deed to real estate in trust, the property to be conveyed at the grantor's direction, and that subsequently upon the grantor's direction, the bank, for a valuable consideration, conveyed title to the parties designated. Suppose, further, that an action is brought to set aside the deed on the ground that the bank had no power to take, hold and convey title for the purposes stated, which was the fact. What would be the disposition of the court, and why?

8. The Non-Appeasement Arms Company was organized to manufacture firearms and munitions. During a lull in government orders the company made up and delivered a quantity of railroad ties on special order. The business was clearly *ultra vires*. The buyer failing to pay the purchase price, the Non-Appeasement Company brought suit. How did the court hold, and on what grounds?

9. The Automatic Gas Producer Co. made two promissory notes signed by the corporation, by its president. The by-laws required that such instruments be countersigned by the treasurer. The instruments were not thus countersigned. The notes were given in payment of services duly rendered and were negotiated in due course to Robert Reed, a bona fide holder, who brings suit against the maker when the latter refuses to pay because of improper execution of the instruments. How did the court decide, and on what theory?

## PART 9. INSOLVENCY, RECEIVERSHIP, SUCCESSION AND DISSOLUTION

**In General.** Corporations, like individuals, may suffer financial misfortune requiring creditor protection and judicial interference. Like those of individuals, also, corporate rights and liabilities may be assumed by successors. But unlike individuals, corporations may legally dissolve their own existence, which after all depends on a legally supported fiction.

### Insolvency

**Insolvency Defined.** Insolvency has various meanings. Under the National Bankruptcy Act, a person is insolvent if the aggregate value of his assets, at a fair valuation, is insufficient to pay his debts (page 712). As defined by courts of equity, however, insolvency means inability to meet one's debts as they mature. If a corporation is unable to meet its debts as they mature, creditors may seek equitable remedies not otherwise available.

**Position of Creditors When Corporation Becomes Insolvent.** Ordinarily, a creditor of a corporation has no right to interfere with its affairs. If creditors are not paid, they may sue the corporation, just as they may sue anyone else. However, when a corporation becomes insolvent or when its insolvency is threatened or imminent, creditors are concerned to the extent that the corporate assets are jeopardized. In such cases, a court of equity may intervene to grant exceptional relief. Such relief may take the form of actions or proceedings on behalf of all creditors ("representative actions") for relief in respect to the following:

(1) Fraudulent and preferential transfers.

(2) Receivership in sequestration proceedings.

(3) Receivership to reach equitable assets.

(4) Receivership to preserve corporate assets.

(5) Receivership to restrain unlawful transfers.

*Creditors' bills.* A *creditor's bill* is a *bill in equity*, meaning a "bill of complaint" or complaint brought in an equity court, seeking some form of equitable remedy available to creditors.

**Fraudulent and Preferential Transfers.** The rule governing fraudulent or preferential transfers by a corporation while insolvent or while in a condition which would result in insolvency by reason of the transfer, is the same as that governing any other fraudulent or preferential transfer. (See page 257.) The law views with particular suspicion any corporate transfer to an officer, director or stockholder, or to any of their relatives, because such transfers frequently prejudice the rights of creditors.

EXAMPLES:

(1) A corporation, the insolvency of which was imminent, sold its bonds to the wife of one of its officers. The proceeds of these bonds were used to pay the corporation's debts to the officer. The Court held that this constituted an illegal preference; that the wife was not an innocent purchaser for value and that the obvious intent was to prefer her husband.[82]

(2) A corporation was organized to build and rent apartments. It leased an apartment to the wife of its president at a rental of one dollar per month. The wife thereupon sublet the premises for a substantial rent. The Court held that this constituted an illegal transfer of corporate property to an officer and that on the insolvency of the corporation, a judgment creditor might compel the wife to account for the rents received.[83]

## Receivership

**Receivership: Nature and Classification of.** Receivership denotes two things: (1) A remedy in equity and (2) a status or condition involving the appointment of a person by a court to take into his custody, control and management the property or funds of another person, or of a business, pending some final action by the court.

*Equity receiverships* are those wherein a receiver is appointed by a

[82] *Davis v. Seneca Falls Mfg. Co. Inc.*, 8 Fed. 2d 546, aff'd 17 Fed. 2d 546.

[83] *Larsen v. Newmark*, 182 App. Div. 724, 117 N.Y. Supp. 268.

court of equity, by virtue of its inherent power to preserve the subject matter of a litigation pending its outcome ("pendente lite").

*Statutory receiverships* are those wherein a receiver is appointed pursuant to a particular statute.

*Temporary receivers* are appointed by the court as custodians to prevent waste of assets until a hearing can be held on the dispute affecting such assets.

*Permanent receivers* are appointed pursuant to a final judgment or order. Their tenure is more permanent and their authority and discretion are wider than in the case of temporary receiverships.

Among the major purposes of a receivership are the following: (a) to sequestrate assets; (b) to reach equitable assets; (c) to preserve corporate assets; and (d) to restrain unlawful transfers.

(a) *To sequestrate assets.* To "sequestrate" assets is to place them in the custody of the court or of a representative of the court, such as a receiver, so as to provide a fund out of which debts may be discharged. A sequestration proceeding may be brought upon application of a judgment creditor who has had an execution returned unsatisfied (page 862). The Court takes possession of the assets for the purpose of applying them ratably in payment of debts.

(b) *To reach equitable assets.* Where a corporation has no tangible assets, but has claims against others that may be realized by instituting suit, a court, upon application of a judgment creditor, may appoint a receiver for the purpose of reaching such equitable assets so that they may be applied to the satisfaction of creditors' claims.

(c) *To preserve corporate assets: equity receivership.* Where impending lawsuits threaten to deluge a corporation with judgments so as to paralyze its continued existence or the conduct of its business, a corporation may, under exceptional circumstances and upon proof that it will serve the best interests of all creditors to do so, appoint a receiver in equity to take charge of corporate affairs until they can be straightened out; and in the meantime, the threatened lawsuits will be restrained so as to permit the receiver to continue to operate the business unmolested by creditors' suits.

(d) *To restrain unlawful transfers.* Under exceptional circumstances, a court may appoint a receiver to prevent a corporation from carrying out a threatened transfer of corporate property that would leave the corporation unable to pay its debts, or, if such transfer has been effected, to cause the transaction to be set aside as a fraudulent transfer.

### Succession: Purchase, Merger, Consolidation and Reorganization

**Succession Defined.** "Succession," literally, is the transmission of the rights and obligations of a deceased person to his heirs. A corporation, being an artificial person, cannot have heirs, but it may have successors. One corporation may succeed to the rights of another (1) by purchase, (2) by merger, (3) by consolidation and (4) by reorganization.

**Succession by Purchase of Assets.** The right of a corporation to buy or sell assets in the normal conduct of its affairs depends, as previously noted, upon its express or implied powers. However, in the purchase or sale of the entire assets of a corporation, there are certain fundamental rules that must be observed:

(1) *The transaction must not be contrary to charter or statute.* The purchase or sale of the entire assets of a corporation must be expressly or impliedly permitted by charter. Moreover, the statute generally requires a minimum vote of stockholders, such as a two-thirds vote (page 534), to validate a sale of entire assets.

(2) *The transaction must not violate public policy: antitrust laws.* Where the purchase and sale of assets will have the necessary effect of creating a monopoly or of restraining trade, the transaction is held contrary to public policy and is generally prohibited by statute. Most states have antitrust statutes reflecting this general policy.

(3) *The transaction must not be in fraud of creditors.* See pages 257 and 258.

**Merger and Consolidation.** Succession by merger and consolidation involves no direct transfer of corporate property but rather of corporate rights as a whole. Consolidations and mergers, though frequently confused, are not the same. Upon a consolidation, a new corporation comes into existence and the prior corporations cease to exist. Upon a merger, the existence of one of the corporations is continued without the formation of a new corporation and the others are absorbed by the surviving corporation, so that the continuing corporation becomes a successor of the merged corporations, subject to the rights and obligations imposed by statute. Neither merger nor consolidation can wipe out the rights of creditors without their consent, and the continuing corporation in the case of a merger, or the new corporation in the case of a consolidation, becomes liable for the debts of the merged or consolidated corporations.

*Unauthorized mergers: rights of dissenting stockholders.* The right of corporations to merge or consolidate is not absolute but may be limited by statute. Statutes commonly provide that one corporation cannot merge others with it unless the business of the merged corporations is similar to that which the merging corporation is expressly or impliedly authorized to transact. Consolidations usually require a two-thirds vote of stockholders. In both mergers and consolidations, dissenting stockholders may require an appraisal of their stock and its purchase by the corporation upon the basis of such appraisal. Antitrust laws further limit the unlawful combination of corporations in restraint of trade, whether by merger, consolidation or otherwise.

**Reorganization.** Reorganization, as applied to a corporation, means a re-arrangement of the interests of creditors and security holders, usually through the formation of a new corporation organized to take over the business of the old. The most common purpose of a corporate reorganization is to scale down capital obligations at a minimum sacrifice to stockholders, bondholders and unsecured creditors, so as to permit the corporation to continue in business instead of "folding up" with the usual losses entailed by a forced liquidation. Corporate reorganizations may be brought about in the following ways:

(1) Voluntarily, by agreement of all parties.

(2) By forced or judicial sale upon foreclosure.

(3) By decree without sale.

(4) By proceedings under the National Bankruptcy Act.

## Dissolution

**Dissolution Defined.** The dissolution of a corporation means the termination of its existence by surrender, cancellation or other extinguishment of its charter so that not only are the corporation's affairs wound up and its assets distributed among creditors and stockholders, but the corporation also ceases to exist as a corporation. A mere sale of a corporation's entire assets, or the appointment of a receiver, or an assignment for the benefit of creditors does not accomplish corporate dissolution.

Dissolution may be *voluntary* or *involuntary*.

**Voluntary Dissolution.** Dissolution is voluntary when brought about by the corporation itself. Such dissolution may arise in any one of the following ways:

(a) *Termination of charter.* The charter of a corporation may provide for a fixed period of corporate existence, upon termination of which the corporation is automatically dissolved.

(b) *Merger or consolidation.* See page 561.

(c) *Filing certificate without judicial proceedings.* Where the charter provides for perpetual existence, the stockholders may voluntarily bring about the surrender of the charter by filing a certificate for this purpose in accordance with the statute. This may be done (1) by incorporators prior to the commencement of business or the issuance of shares, (2) by the written consent of all outstanding stockholders, or (3) by resolution at a stockholders' meeting, upon a minimum required approval (such as a majority or a two-thirds vote of the holders of outstanding stock).

(d) *Judicial proceedings on petition.* Where the required vote of stockholders cannot be obtained and it can be shown to the Court that a dissolution is desirable in the interests of the corporation and its stockholders, judicial proceedings may be instituted by stockholders on petition for an order permitting and directing dissolution. Such petitions are sometimes presented where the corporation is hopelessly deadlocked.

**Involuntary Dissolution.** Involuntary dissolution may be brought about, either (a) at the instance of the state, acting through the attorney-general, or (b) at the instance of a judgment-creditor or stockholder, acting through the attorney-general or directly if the attorney-general refuses to act.

*Quo warranto* (literally, "by what right," or "by what warrant") is the old legal term applied to proceedings by which inquiries are made into the right of a corporation to exist and conduct business as such.

*Dissolution by state.* Dissolution may be brought about at the instance of a state upon any of the following grounds: (1) Non-user, as where a corporation fails to organize, commence business or undertake its duties within a given period; (2) fraud or fraudulent concealment in procuring a charter; (3) violations of a statute; (4) forfeiture, surrender or abuse of the corporate privilege or charter, or (5) a failure to exercise powers or to do or omit some act that amounts to a surrender of corporate rights, such as a continuous failure to pay taxes.

*Dissolution at instance of creditor or stockholder.* Dissolution may be brought about by the attorney-general at the instance of a creditor or stockholder where, for a given period, the corporation has (1) remained insolvent, or (2) neglected or refused to pay and discharge its notes or other evidences of debt, or (3) suspended its ordinary and lawful business.

**Procedure on Dissolution: Distribution of Assets.** As previously noted, the assets of a dissolved corporation belong to the stockholders in the order of their priorities and preferences as fixed in the charter. However, creditors' claims must first be discharged before such assets can be distributed to stockholders. These claims include (1) tax claims, (2) secured claims, and (3) unsecured claims. After all debts are paid, the distribution to stockholders is in order.

*Distribution of assets before paying debts.* Where assets are distributed before all debts are paid, stockholders may be compelled to account for the assets to the extent necessary for payment of such debts. If they are no longer able so to account, directors become liable to the extent that the distribution deprived creditors of their ability to collect.

EXAMPLE: A corporation in financial difficulties sold its assets and distributed the proceeds to the stockholders as a liquidation dividend. Upon an adjudication in bankruptcy, the trustee may compel the stockholders to make good to the creditors.

*Effect of dissolution: survival of rights and liabilities.* Upon dissolution, a corporation ceases to exist as such. It no longer has the customary rights or liabilities of a corporation. It can neither sue nor be sued, hold or convey property, make contracts, or exercise any of the corporate powers provided for by its charter—in short, the corporation, legally speaking, is dead.

However, statutes generally continue a corporation's existence after dissolution for such period and within such limits as may be necessary to complete liquidation and wind up its affairs. As an incident to such purpose, the corporation may prosecute and defend suits, recover contingent or unrealized assets, and dispose of contingent and unmatured liabilities, to the end that all debts may be paid and all net assets distributed among the stockholders. All other corporate transactions entered into after dissolution are void and unenforceable.

## Questions

1. In what respect does the position of a creditor of a corporation differ from that of creditors of ordinary individuals?
2. In what situation may judgment creditors institute representative actions involving insolvent corporations?
3. What is a creditor's bill?
4. Receivership denotes what two characteristics?
5. Name and define four types of receiverships.
6. Name four major purposes of receiverships.
7. Name four ways in which one corporation may succeed to the rights of another.
8. What are the three fundamental rules that must be observed with respect to the purchase or sale of the entire assets of a corporation?
9. Distinguish between a merger and a consolidation.
10. What rights, if any, have dissenting stockholders in a merger or consolidation?
11. What is meant by a corporate reorganization?
12. Name four ways in which a corporate reorganization may be brought about.
13. What is meant by the dissolution of a corporation?
14. Name and describe four ways in which the voluntary dissolution of a corporation may arise.
15. Name five reasons any one of which would serve as ground for an involuntary dissolution by the state.
16. Name three ways in which corporate dissolution may be brought about at the instance of a creditor or a stockholder.
17. Name the order of priority in which creditors' claims must be paid on a dissolution before distribution is made to stockholders.

## Problems

1. The Select Shirt Corporation, after refusing to pay several of its notes when due, transfers its entire account with the Sterling Bank to John Kay, the president of the corporation, against a note which had been issued to said president for a loan in the same amount made some two years before. The company owes a balance of $3,200 for rent on its loft to the owner of the building in which the loft is located. Upon failure to pay this rent, the building sues, obtains judgment, and has execution issued thereon, which is returned in due course unsatisfied. The owner of the building, however, is unable to prove that the corporation is insolvent. Has he any further remedy? Explain.
2. The Reckless Wrecking Corporation, having reached the stage of insol-

vency, decides to salvage some of its assets. Accordingly, the corporation (a) transfers some of its machinery to the principal stockholder; (b) permits a friendly creditor to obtain a judgment for $500 against the corporation; (c) executes and delivers a chattel mortgage on three trucks; (d) pays a bill for material delivered to an innocent creditor unaware of the wrecking company's financial condition; and (e) pays laborers' wages in full. Assuming that the wrecking company's acts are all done with the intent by such corporation of giving a preference, which of the acts, if any, can be set aside?

3. The Seneca Falls Manufacturing Co., Inc., the insolvency of which was imminent, sold securities held by the corporation to the wife of one of its officers. The proceeds of these securities were used to pay the corporation's debts to the officer. Comment on the attitude of the court should this transaction be questioned.

4. Suppose that in 3 above, a creditor succeeded in procuring a judgment setting aside the transaction, but that the judgment could not be satisfied, either as against the corporation, or as against the officer, who has spent the proceeds of the monies obtained by him in the manner indicated, and who was wholly insolvent. If the corporation's board of directors consisted of the husband, wife, and a wealthy brother-in-law, what remedy, if any, would be available to the judgment creditor under the circumstances?

5. Baker obtained a judgment against a corporation. The stockholders and officers of the corporation thereupon formed a new corporation, to which they transferred the assets of the old company. The new company immediately executed a mortgage covering its own property and the property received from the old company. The effect of the transfer of the property from the old company to the new was to suspend and terminate the regular business of the old company. What remedies, if any, were available to Baker?

6. The X Company, Inc., is formed for the purpose of consolidating the A, B and C corporations, and for the further purpose of acquiring certain assets from the D corporation necessary to the conduct of the X Company's business, for which assets the X Company pays in stock. Upon completion of the consolidation, the creditors of the A, B, C and D corporations, being unable to collect from these corporations, respectively, bring suits against the X Company, Inc. How will these suits be decided, and why?

7. A judgment creditor of the Defunct Corporation learns of certain hidden assets belonging to the corporation. May he have a sheriff levy on these assets to satisfy his judgment, or is he required to take other steps in this situation?

8. Impending lawsuits threaten to deluge a corporation with judgments so as to paralyze its continued existence or the conduct of its business. What possible relief may the corporation obtain under the circumstances?

9. Following dissolution of the Gadget Corporation, its former counsel discovers that one of its former debtors, thought to be insolvent, has come into substantial assets. May the dissolved corporation now do anything about this account?

## COURT CASES FOR REVIEW

### How Did the Court Decide, and Why?

1. A *de facto* corporation issued stock in exchange for property. A personal creditor of the seller sought to levy execution on the property thus sold to the corporation, on the ground that the corporation had no valid existence, hence no right to the property. *Thies v. Weible*, 126 Neb. 720, 254 N.W. 420.

2. Plaintiff corporation brought suit against defendant corporation seeking an injunction and money damages for having allegedly used in its business a name similar to plaintiff's. Defendant showed that there was no business competition between itself and the plaintiff. *Burnside Veneer Corp. v. New Burnside Veneer Co.* (Kentucky, 1952), 247 S.W. 2d 524.

3. In a suit for the appointment of a receiver, the existence of a corporation was challenged and the question raised whether the associates who went through the motions of forming a corporation were not liable as partners instead. It appears that a certificate of incorporation had been recorded in the county clerk's office but not filed in the secretary of state's office as required by statute. No fees had been tendered; no payment for capital stock had been made; there had been no meetings of stockholders or directors; no officers had been elected; and the only exercise of corporate powers was the opening of a bank account. *Culkin v. Hillside Restaurant, Inc.*, 126 N.J. Eq. 97, 8 A. 2d 173.

4. Raymond, a stockholder, who was also a director, owed $2,000 to the corporation on his stock. Knowing that the corporation was in financial straits, he transferred his stock for $3 to a waiter in a restaurant and caused the transfer to be registered on the corporate books. The corporation subsequently sued Raymond. How did the Court decide and why? *Rochester and Kettle Falls Land Co. v. Raymond*, 158 N.Y. 576, 53 N.E. 507.

5. The President of X Corporation had power under the by-laws to appoint, remove and fix the compensation of employees. Without express authorization from or ratification by the board of directors, he made a contract on behalf of the corporation to employ Jones for life. This contract was subsequently repudiated by the corporation. *Heaman v. E. N. Rowell Co. Inc.*, 261 N.Y. 229, 185 N.E. 83.

6. A group of men sold out a fish business and, in so doing, agreed not to engage in the fish business in the same locality. Immediately thereafter, they organized a corporation to carry on the fish business in competition with the old concern. The purchasers then sued for an injunction. Judgment for whom and why? *Booth v. Siebold, et al.*, 37 Misc. 101, 74 N.Y. Supp. 776.

7. An oral contract of employment made by defendant with plaintiff provided that the latter, for services rendered as a salesman, should receive as remuneration a division of the profits realized. When the defendant failed to pay, plaintiff sued. Defendant alleged and proved that after entering into such agreement, he had incorporated his business. *Dyer v. Sterett*, 248 S.W. 234 (Tex. Civ. App., 1952).

8. A by-law of a corporation provided that three out of eleven directors of the corporation should be sufficient to constitute a quorum for the transaction of business, although the General Corporation Law provided that in no case could a quorum of the board of directors of a corporation be less than one third of total number of directors. In a subsequent action, it became important to decide which provision should be controlling. *Kerbs v. California Eastern Airways*, 90 A. 2d 652, reargument denied, 91 A. 2d 62.

9. One of two stockholders, each of whom owned 50 per cent of the stock, took over management of the corporation during the absence of the other while in military service, but failed to pay the latter his share of the profits upon his return to civilian life. In a suit by the absentee stockholder against his co-stockholder for an accounting, defendant moved to dismiss the complaint on the ground that the plaintiff had no individual right to sue, but should have sued derivatively, in the name and on behalf of the corporation. *Funk v. Spalding*, 74 Ariz. 219, 246 P. 2d 184.

10. A director entered into an agreement with a contractor whereby, in con-

sideration of an award by the corporation to the contractor of a contract for unloading poles and electrical equipment at a given contract price, the director and contractor would share equally in the amounts paid by the corporation to the contractor. Upon the contractor's subsequent refusal to honor this agreement, the director brought suit, whereupon the contractor interposed a counterclaim for damages. *Schurr v. Weaver*, 53 N.W. 2d 290.

11. Plaintiff, a minority stockholder, after being ousted as director of a corporation, brought suit against the other directors to recover for the corporation, monies allegedly paid out as excessive salaries. Nine years before, plaintiff, an employee of the company, had been elected a director, secretary and treasurer of the corporation, at the instance of the defendant Kimball, who controlled 97 per cent of the stock. Plaintiff had devised and built up a profitable branch of the business, but when Kimball attempted to reduce plaintiff's salary and at the same time to raise his own, plaintiff refused to consent and to sign the minutes of the meeting purporting to authorize such increase, whereupon defendant had plaintiff frozen out as a director and officer, and barred from employment and access to the corporation's place of business, books, and records. Three other employees were elected directors, and together with Kimball, voted themselves increased salaries and profits as extra compensation. *Carr v. Kimball*, 153 App. Div. 825, 139 N.Y. Supp. 253, aff'd 215 N.Y. 634, 109 N.E. 1068.

12. Pursuant to a resolution of the board of directors of a corporation, the president executed a contract with plaintiff, granting him the right to remove peat moss from the corporation's property. After the president's death, the plaintiff, with full knowledge of the board, continued with the contract. In a subsequent suit, the corporation denied liability for services rendered after the president's death. *McCoy v. Pastorius*, 125 Colo. 574, 246 P. 2d 611.

13. A corporation delivered a "bank resolution" designating a specified bank as depositary for corporate funds, and providing that its managing officer could sign checks, drafts and orders against any corporate funds or accounts in the bank. Thereafter the managing officer paid, with corporate checks, personal loans made to him by the bank. The corporation now brings action against the bank for a refund of the total proceeds of the checks thus honored by the bank. *Blue J Feeds, Inc. v. Scottsbluff Nat. Bank*, 156 Neb. 84, 54 N.W. 2d 404.

14. Defendant was convicted of a violation of the labor law prohibiting the employment of any child between the ages of fourteen and sixteen without filing an employment certificate. A girl under sixteen had been found by a factory inspector working in the factory of a corporation for which defendant was superintendent, and no employment certificate had been filed. Although defendant was personally unaware of such employment, the foreman who worked under his direction had hired the girl. Defendant appealed his conviction. *People v. Taylor*, 192 N.Y. 398, 85 N.E. 759.

15. An agreement was entered into involving the management of the New York National League Baseball Club (popularly known as the "Giants") whereby McQuade, Stoneham and McGraw, as owners of a majority of the stock of the corporation, agreed upon certain salaries to be paid them by the corporation, and further agreed to "use their best endeavors" to continue themselves in office as directors and officers of the company. In the course of time, McQuade was dropped. He sued for reinstatement and for damages for breach of contract. *McQuade v. Stoneham*, 263 N.Y. 323, 189 N.E. 234.

16. A stockholder sued on two counts: (1) To compel the directors to declare a dividend, and (2) To restore to the corporate treasury money paid to themselves allegedly in excess of fair and reasonable salaries. The directors and

officers, controlling a majority of the stock, had voted themselves into their positions as officers and directors. The corporation was organized with a capital stock of $300,000, and after ten years had acquired assets of about $600,000, thereby doubling the corporation's capital. *Raynolds v. Diamond Mills Paper Co.*, 69 N.J. Eq. 299, 60 A. 941.

17. Guth, president of Loft, Inc. was desirous of obtaining a substitute syrup in place of that sold by the Coca-Cola Company. At that time, a corporation controlled by Megargel owned a secret formula and trademark for a syrup designated Pepsi-Cola, and was going through bankruptcy. Guth and Megargel together bought the assets of the bankrupt corporation, including the Pepsi-Cola formula and trademark, and transferred them to a corporation organized by them under the name, "Pepsi-Cola Company." In this transaction, and in a subsequent transaction whereby Guth acquired Megargel's interest in the Pepsi-Cola Company and became owner of 91 per cent of its stock, Guth used the assets of Loft, Inc. The board of directors of Loft, Inc. sued Guth on behalf of Loft, Inc. to impress a trust on the shares of Pepsi-Cola stock held by Guth, and for an accounting. *Guth v. Loft, Inc.*, 23 Del. Ch. 255, 5 A. 2d 503.

18. Plaintiff, an Illinois corporation, was engaged in the sale of electrical machines. It sold to customers throughout the country exclusively on catalogue. One day, however, the president of the corporation, anticipating a large order, took a demonstration machine with him to Des Moines, Iowa, where, by personal demonstration, he was enabled to sell a large number of machines, which were paid for partly in cash and partly by notes. The notes not being met at maturity, plaintiff sued. The defense was that plaintiff was doing business in Iowa without a license. How was the case decided, and on what basis? *Actino Laboratories, Inc. v. Lamb*, 278 N.W. 234 (Iowa).

19. A New York City department store advertised that it was offering the facilities of a dental department, with a dentist in charge, where customers could arrange to have their dental work done. Plaintiff went to the department store and arranged for dental work. The work was done and paid for. Thereafter plaintiff complained that the work was so negligently and unskillfully done as to amount to malpractice. Defendant contended that as a corporation it could not engage and was not engaged in the practice of dentistry; that all it did was to lease space to a dentist so that the facilities would be available to such of the customers as desired to take advantage of them; and that in consequence it was not liable for any professional negligence or malpractice by such dentist. *Hannon v. Seigel Cooper Co.*, 167 N.Y. 244, 60 N.E. 597.

# 13

# The Regulation of Business

**Scope of This Chapter.** In this chapter we consider the various ways in which the law seeks to achieve a balance of rights and duties in the field of business. In Part 1, we consider the constitutional basis and scope of government regulation. In Part 2, we consider the various antitrust laws by which Congress and the courts seek to curb, regulate and control any contracts, arrangements or activities which tend to impede the competitive process. In Part 3, we consider the leading antitrust cases bearing on various phases of trade restraints, including price fixing, monopolistic expansion, and cooperative arrangements to limit or restrain the free play of competitive forces. In Part 4, we consider unfair competitive methods and unfair trade practices, including trade infringements (involving trade names, marks, wrappers, packages and containers), price discrimination, false advertising and other unfair business practices.

## PART 1. BASIS AND SCOPE

**Meaning of Regulation.** In a sense, all law is regulation—the regulation of human conduct. The current century, however, has witnessed a growing emphasis on the regulation of business. This has not been due to a lowering of business standards. Neither does it signify a change in our concept that government exists for the individual, not the other way around, and that it should interfere with individual freedom only so far as may be necessary to ensure justice and equal opportunity for all. The growing emphasis on business regulation is due to the growing complexity of our business structure. As society becomes more complex, the need for regulation increases.

**Conditions Requiring Regulation: Formerly, and Now.** Business regulation is not new to our economy. Fully two centuries ago we had statutes and ordinances regulating the quality of merchandise, prices, standards of weight and measure, maximum wages, profits, interest charges, and other incidents of trade. But the regulations then were simple and direct, matching the business problems of the period, when human needs were few and living was simple; when the farmer tilled his own soil and washed at the same pump with his hired man; when the man on the street wore homespun and walked about in the handmade product of the town cobbler; when the artisan in his one-man shop wrought with his own hands, taught his craft to his apprentice, and virtually made him a member of his family.

These things are no more. The business of producing, exchanging and consuming the world's goods has become infinitely complex. The application of steam, gasoline and electricity to the raw materials of the earth has transformed the simple society our ancestors knew into an intricate social structure requiring government supervision at a thousand points of human contact. Mass production and the assembly line have superseded the painstaking product of man's fingers. The consequent outburst of vast production has brought vast wealth, but it has also brought vast problems of government. Industrial combinations must be policed by antitrust statutes. Railroads and other utilities must be regulated as to rates and service. Factory conditions must be supervised, hazardous employment must be safeguarded, sanitary working conditions must be enforced, employer's liability and workmen's compensation insurance must absorb the risks of industrial accidents and occupational diseases.

Not to do these things is no longer a private right, but a public menace. Failure to provide adequate housing to workers invites crime and disease. Sweatshops become the concern of all. Monetary inflation can no longer be dismissed by letting "nature"—the law of supply and demand—take its course. Cycles of depression take too much out of us to be treated as if they were unavoidable, like cyclones and earthquakes. Chronic social and economic diseases such as unemployment, child labor and destitute old age have necessitated corresponding regulatory measures.

In short, our basic concepts of liberty and justice remain unchanged, but the means of preserving them have necessarily become more varied and numerous. The standards of business, if anything, are higher than ever, but the opportunities for wrong-doing, and the consequent need for regulation, have kept pace with the enormous growth and complexity of our business structure.

**Regulatory Powers.** Under our dual system of government, business may be regulated both by a state government, under its sovereign police power, and by the Federal Government, under its constitutional power to regulate interstate commerce. Both these sources of regulatory power have been greatly broadened by judicial interpretation in recent years.

## Regulation Under the Police Power

**Proper Exercise of Police Power.** We have already referred (page 13) to the dominant power of a state to pass laws for the protection and promotion of the health, safety, morals and general welfare of the people. This dominant "police" power is not derived from any constitutional document, but is inherent in the nature of sovereignty. Hence any statute which imposes necessary restraints or limitations on a person's property or business cannot be successfully attacked as unconstitutional if it is a proper exercise of the police power. What constitutes a proper exercise of the police power depends upon whether the particular business sought to be regulated sufficiently touches the public health, safety, morals or general welfare to justify public intervention.

*Public health.* Any regulation of business reasonable and necessary to protect the public health is a proper exercise of the police power. It may concern itself with sanitation, such as drainage and sewer systems, or with reclamation projects, the elimination of stagnant pools or other breeders of disease, irrigation, flood control, conservation, slum clearance and housing projects to eliminate overcrowding in tenements, pure food and drugs, the proper labeling of medicinal compounds, provisions for the inspection of cattle, milk, meat, etc., and a host of similar matters.

*Public safety.* Closely allied to public health is the matter of public safety. Regulation under the police power to assure public safety may include building codes and rules, such as those designed to secure buildings against the hazards of fire and structural defects. It may concern itself with the manufacture, storage and sale of high explosives, compulsory inspection of motor vehicles and aircraft, the fixing of minimum standards of technical fitness and qualification and the requirement of a license to engage in skilled pursuits, such as the practice of medicine, law, engineering, architecture or aviation (see page 837).

*Public morals.* Under this head come the various laws, rules and regulations governing vice, gambling and antisocial enterprises, Sunday laws, and similar restrictions and prohibitions (see pages 837 to 838).

*General welfare.* The broadest and most indefinite area for the proper exercise of the police power is the vague realm known as "the general welfare." It is here that the authorities most frequently conflict.

Some sections of this area may be clearly defined. Regulations designed to prevent fraud in the sale of food, medicines and merchandise generally, to insure the quality of goods offered for sale, to prevent deceitful food imitations or injurious ingredients, to guard against false weights and measures, or to prevent the fraudulent sale of goods in bulk (page 258) are definitely within the police power function. So, also, are state labor laws aimed at safeguarding the health and safety of workers, at preventing them from becoming public charges through inadequate financial provision for the future, and at preventing labor disturbances which disrupt the public economy (see page 442). Similarly, statutes for the conservation of natural resources clearly come within the police power, such as statutes directed at the waste of natural gas, oil or mineral waters, or statutes forbidding the cutting down of standing timber except under prescribed limitations. Even statutes to promote orderliness and public comfort, such as zoning laws and laws restricting the erection of public eyesores, may be regarded as a proper exercise of the police power for the protection of the general welfare.

There are other situations, however, where the propriety of government regulation as an exercise of the police power is by no means clear, because of the debatable question whether the business sought to be regulated has become sufficiently "affected with a public interest" to justify public regulation. The Supreme Court has declared that property becomes "clothed" or "affected" with a public interest "when used in a manner to make it of public consequence and affect the community at large." [1] Whether or not business is so affected is for the legislature to decide, but the courts may nullify such legislation as unconstitutional if it has no real foundation, that is, if the matter is clearly of no public concern.

### Regulation Under the Commerce Clause

**Federal Regulation: Interstate Commerce.** The basis of Federal regulation of business is the so-called "commerce clause" by which the Constitution of the United States empowered Congress to regulate commerce among the states and with foreign nations. This power, like the police power, has been greatly expanded by judicial interpretation; and this expansion applies to all aspects of the commerce power—to questions such as (1) What is commerce, (2) when is it interstate, and (3) how may it be regulated, i.e., what is the nature of government regulation?

**(1) What is Commerce?** The word "commerce" includes everything related to trade or traffic: the buying and selling of any legitimate commodity, whether tangible, such as food, clothing or manufactured products, or intangible, such as stocks, bonds or other choses in action. In more recent years, the term "commerce" has taken on a still broader meaning. It includes not only the business of transmitting news,[2] conducting insurance,[3] and leasing motion picture film,[4] but the manufacture and production of goods for commerce.[5]

**(2) When is Commerce Interstate?** Until recent years no business was regarded as interstate, or subject to Federal regulation, if it was conducted

---

[1] *Louisville & N.R. Co. v. Kentucky,* 161 U.S. 677.

[2] *Associated Press v. National Labor Relations Board,* 301 U.S. 103.

[3] *Prudential Insurance Co. v. Benjamin,* 328 U.S. 408.

[4] *Kappler v. Republic Pictures Corp.,* 59 F. Supp. 112, aff'd 151 F. 2d 543, 327 U.S. 757.

[5] *National Labor Relations Board v. Jones & Laughlin Steel Corp.,* 301 U.S. 1; *National Labor Relations Board v. Freuhauf Trailer,* 301 U.S. 49; *National Labor Relations Board v. Friedman-Marks Clothing Co.,* 301 U.S. 58; *Assoc. Press v. National Labor Relations Board,* 301 U.S. 103. All these cases were argued on February 10, 1937 and decided on April 12, 1937.

wholly within a single state and had no direct relation to interstate commerce.[6] Recent decisions, however, have tended to do away with the distinction between "direct" and "indirect" interstate commerce, and today, apparently any business that "affects" interstate commerce is subject to the commerce clause.[7] The commerce power covers not only the subject matter of interstate commerce itself, but also the agencies and instrumentalities which make such commerce possible, such as highways and highway vehicles, navigable bodies of water and the vessels and water craft which navigate them, railroads, and commercial aircraft. Similarly, agencies engaged in the transmission of electric power by wire, and of intelligence, whether by wire or through the air, including telegraph, telephone, cable, radio broadcasting and television, are subject to regulation under the commerce clause.

(3) **What is the Nature of Government Regulation?** For the most part, government regulation is conducted through commissions and boards. Examples are the State and Federal commissions which regulate carriers and other utilities, the Securities Exchange Commission, and the National Labor Relations Board (whose functions have already been discussed in Chapter 10). The regulation of monopolistic and unfair business practices is governed in part by the Federal Trade Commission and corresponding state agencies, and in part by Federal and State departments of justice.

*Carriers and public utilities generally.* State regulation of carriers and public utilities generally is conducted through state commissions, such as railroad, public utility or public service commissions. Federal regulation of common carriers engaged in interstate transportation by water or rail, including also express companies, pipe lines, sleeping car companies and motor carriers such as buses and trucks, is under the supervision of the Interstate Commerce Commission, the objectives of which have already been set forth on pages 310-311. Regulation of telegraph, telephone, cable, radio and television services is entrusted to the Federal Communications Commission. Electric light, power and gas companies operating on an interstate basis are subject to the supervision and control of the Federal Power Commission.

These various bodies seek to regulate safety, rates, public convenience and service in the public interest.

*Securities and security exchanges.* We have already referred to statutes adopted by many states, known as "blue sky laws," which prescribe penalties for fraudulent corporate practices in connection with the issuance of

---

[6] *Hammer v. Dagenhart,* 247 U.S. 251; *Schechter Poultry Corp. v. United States,* 295 U.S. 495.
[7] *United States v. Wrightwood Dairy Co.,* 315 U.S. 110; *National Labor Relations Board v. Fainblatt,* 306 U.S. 601; *Wickard v. Filburn,* 317 U.S. 111; *Kirschbaum v. Walling,* 316 U.S. 517.

corporate stocks, bonds, notes, or other securities (pages 517 and 528). Congress, also, has adopted laws governing the issuances of securities and the conduct of security exchanges.

*Securities Act (1933).* This act was designed to accomplish two objectives: first, to provide full and fair disclosure to prospective investors of the character of new securities or new offerings, and second, to prevent fraud or misrepresentation in the sale of securities, old and new.

All securities offered for public sale must be registered with the Securities and Exchange Commission (SEC), except: (1) Securities which are offered locally, that is, not sold in interstate commerce or through the mails; (2) Securities not offered to the general public, but to limited groups of private investors; (3) Securities sold by the owner himself, individually or through a broker; and (4) Government securities and those of religious, charitable and fraternal organizations, farmers' cooperative associations, and various non-profit, non-commercial or non-speculative types of securities. The registration certificate must make full disclosure in respect to the issuing corporation, its stockholders and managing personnel, capitalization and financial status.

Registration of securities does not insure investors against loss in their purchase, but supplies facts on which to appraise merits and risks. Neither does registration warrant the accuracy of the facts disclosed. However, persons responsible for filing false information incur the risk of fine, imprisonment, or both; and the issuing company, its responsible directors and other officials, and the underwriters, may be liable in damages to purchasers of registered securities if the disclosures in the registration statement and prospectus are materially defective.

*Securities Exchange Act (1934).* Under this act, companies whose securities are listed on a stock exchange must file registration applications and annual and other reports with national securities exchanges and the SEC. These applications and reports must contain financial and other data prescribed by the Commission for the information of the investing public. Material misstatements or omissions of material facts are grounds for suspension or withdrawal of the security from exchange trading.

The essence of the Securities Exchange Act is full disclosure. Proxies must not be solicited without full disclosure of all facts necessary to a vote for or against. Officers, directors, and large (10 per cent or over) security holders must fully disclose their holdings in the corporation and their dealings in its securities. They may be compelled to account to the corporation for profits based on "inside" information.

The act also prohibits manipulation, misrepresentation, and other fraudulent and deceptive devices in the purchase and sale of securities. It regulates short sales, floor trading, the activities of specialists and odd-lot dealers, and such matters as excessive trading by exchange members.

## Questions

1. What is meant by the "police power" and from what source is it derived?

2. What are some of the more common matters embraced in state regulation of (a) public health, (b) public safety, (c) public morals, and (d) general welfare?

3. What is the constitutional basis for Federal regulation of business generally?

4. Name five types of business activity which fall within the definition of "commerce" for purposes of Federal regulation.

5. When is commerce "interstate," within present-day Supreme Court definitions for purposes of Federal regulation?

6. "The commerce power covers not only the subject matter of interstate commerce, but also the agencies and instrumentalities which make such commerce possible." Give four illustrations.

7. "Government regulation is conducted through commissions and boards." Give four examples.

8. What are the regulatory bodies having supervision, respectively, of (a) interstate carriers, (b) interstate wire, wireless and television services, and (c) interstate electric light, power and gas companies?

9. What are the major functions and objectives of the Securities Act of 1933?

10. What are the major functions and objectives of the Securities Exchange Act of 1934?

## Problems

1. A municipal building department condemns an apartment house as unsafe. All the tenants are forced to vacate. The owner, complaining that the action of the municipal authorities has brought him financial ruin, seeks recompense for what he charges was the unconstitutional condemnation of private property for a public purpose, without just compensation. How will the court decide?

2. During a period of unusual scarcity in the supply of meat, Congress passes a law fixing maximum prices for meats of various kinds and cuts. The act is attacked as unconstitutional. How will the court hold?

3. The National Labor Relations Board seeks to regulate labor conditions in a plant engaged in the manufacture of a product widely sold throughout the country. The owner of the plant resists such interference on the ground that he has never engaged in interstate commerce, but only in manufacturing activities inside of a single factory located in a small-sized community. How will the court decide, and why?

4. The directors and officers of the X Company, fearful of inability to raise sufficient funds for their company from a prospective issue of its stock if all the facts as to current earnings become known, cause false information to be embodied in the company's registration statement filed with the Securities and Exchange Commission. The question now arises as to whether any liability has been incurred in connection with such registration.

5. In connection with a registration application for the listing of a company's securities on a stock exchange, John Brinton, who owns 5,000 shares of the company's 100,000 outstanding shares of stock, requests the company not

to disclose his stock holdings, and the company, in its application, duly honors Brinton's request. Has any liability been incurred in this connection?

6. George Watson, an officer of a corporation whose securities are listed on a stock exchange, is instrumental in inducing the company's board of directors to declare an extra dividend. Before such action is announced, however, Watson purchases a large block of the company's stock, which he sells at a handsome profit when the extra dividend is announced. Except for taxes, may Watson retain this profit? Explain.

## PART 2. RESTRAINT OF TRADE: ANTITRUST LAWS

**Restraint of Trade Defined.** The term "restraint of trade," as used in the law, applies to any interference with free competition. Such interference may take the form of a monopoly or monopolistic combination, or it may take a form considerably short of monopoly but tending toward it. Monopoly and restraint of trade are therefore not one and the same. Every monopoly is a restraint of trade but not every restraint of trade constitutes a monopoly.

**Classification of Monopolies.** Monopolies, broadly classified, may be *public* or *private*. Public monopolies are those which are owned or conducted by the government itself, as in the case of the postal service or a municipal waterworks system. Private monopolies are those which are privately owned.

*Legal v. illegal monopolies.* Private monopolies may be legal or illegal. Legal monopolies are created by government grant or franchise, as in the case of a patent or copyright, or by government recognition of an exclusive right to identify one's product by a given name or mark, as in the case of a trade name, trade mark or service mark. Also included in the legal monopolies are the so-called "natural monoplies," in which competition may be a public nuisance rather than a public benefit. Examples are duplicatory water, gas, electric or telephone systems operating in the same community. Such monopolies, though sanctioned by public policy, are subject to public regulation (pages 572 to 573).

Illegal monopolies are those which are prohibited as contrary to public policy. Unless otherwise stated, all subsequent references to monopolies will relate to this group.

**Forms of Monopoly.** Monopolies may take numerous forms, arising out of the method adopted to effect the monopoly. Various forms resorted to in the past include "corners," the acquisition of assets, the creation of holding companies, mergers and consolidations, trusts, and agreements to act in unison, as in the case of pools and cartels.

*Corners.* A "corner" is the oldest form of monopoly, dating back to Biblical Egypt and probably long before. It consists in buying up some necessity, such as wheat, corn, cotton, meat, coal, and so forth, and re-selling it at whatever price the traffic will bear.

*Purchase of assets.* A form of monopoly similar to a corner is the acquisition by a person, firm or corporation of all or a large part of a competitor's assets, thereby controlling the source of supply of a given product.

*Holding companies, mergers and consolidations.* In the field of corporate enterprise, one of the simpler forms of monopoly is the acquisition by one corporation of the stock of another or others so as to control the latter as a sole or majority stockholder. In many cases, effective control of a corporation may be exercised by substantial stock ownership amounting to less than half the outstanding stock.

We have already referred to mergers and consolidations (page 561). In both cases, the rights of one or more corporations are acquired by another corporation. Where the effect is to eliminate or restrict a preexisting competitive situation, the transaction becomes exposed to antitrust prosecution. A noteworthy example is the Northern Securities case (page 587).

*Trusts.* The term "trust," as applied to monopolies, originated in the scheme by which a majority of the shares of a group of competing corporations were trusteed to a single board of trustees, thereby ensuring "harmonious" management of the competitors.

*Agreements to act in unison: pools and cartels.* Monopolistic arrangements are sometimes brought about by agreements to act in unison in reference to some product or commodity, without the necessity of a common ownership. One example is a "pool," or combination of persons contributing money to a common fund, to be used for the purpose of manipulating the market price of securities, or of some product or commodity, such as wheat, corn, sugar or meat. Another form, employed both in this country and abroad, is the "cartel," a combination of producers joined together to control the production, sale and price of some product, or to allocate among its members specific territories or divisions of the market.

*Monopolies at Common Law.* At common law, all contracts, combinations or agreements which create or tend to create a monopoly are unlawful as being in restraint of trade. However, the common law penalty for agreements in restraint of trade is a refusal to enforce them, except where they are necessary to protect a property right (pages 69 to 70). By the latter part of the 19th century it became apparent that the common law was wholly inadequate to deter the growth of monopolies which seriously threatened our competitive system. Statutory remedies were provided by a series of Congressional acts applicable to interstate commerce, which were reflected in state statutes applicable to intrastate business. These acts and statutes have not only reaffirmed the common law illegality of monopolies, but have made offenders liable criminally for penalties, and civilly for damages sustained by their victims.

The major Federal act aimed at correcting the evils of restraint of trade is the Sherman Antitrust Act, as amended by the Clayton, Robinson-Patman and Miller-Tydings Acts. Supplementing these antitrust laws, the Federal Trade Commission Act was passed to provide an additional arm of enforcement.

**Sherman Antitrust Act (1890).** The Sherman Antitrust Act is the basic antitrust statute applicable to interstate and foreign trade. Its major provisions are embodied in the first two sections. Section 1 declares unlawful "every contract, combination in the form of a trust or otherwise, or conspiracy in restraint of trade or commerce among the several states or with foreign nations." Section 2 declares that every person shall be guilty of a misdemeanor, subject to a fine not exceeding $5000, to imprisonment not exceeding one year, or both, if he shall (a) monopolize, or (b) attempt to monopolize, or (c) combine or conspire with any other person or persons to monopolize any part of our interstate or foreign trade. Government enforcement of these provisions may take the form either of a criminal prosecution, or a civil suit for an injunction. Criminal prosecutions are instituted by the Department of Justice, under the direction of the Attorney General, who may also institute civil suits for an injunction in which the court may make a decree designed to correct the evils disclosed on the trial. In addition to these government actions, the statute gives a right of action for damages to any person injured in his business or property by reason of a violation of the Sherman Act. To counterbalance the difficulty of proving damages in such cases, the law allows three times the amount of damages actually proved, plus attorneys' fees.

**Clayton Act (1914).** The Clayton Act "aims to strike down a monopoly at its inception, when the first step is taken," as distinguished from the Sherman Act, which aims to strike it down "after it has become more virile." [8] Incipient evils aimed at include (1) price discrimination, (2) exclusive dealing ("tying") contracts, (3) stock acquisitions that substantially lessen competition, and (4) interlocking directorates that tend to eliminate active competition among the larger corporate units.

*Price discrimination.* Section 2 of the Clayton Act prohibits price discrimination between different purchasers "where the effect of such discrimination may be to substantially lessen competition or to tend to create a monopoly in any line of commerce." The section was designed to correct the practice of killing off a competitor with a barrage of low prices, then boosting prices back to or beyond the old level. This section proved too rigid to meet the requirements of our complex business structure, and was ultimately amended by the Robinson-Patman Act (pages 580 and 598).

*"Tying" contracts.* Section 3 of the Clayton Act makes it unlawful for a person engaged in interstate commerce to lease or sell goods, machinery, or supplies on condition that the lessee or purchaser shall not

---

[8] *United States v. Besser Mfg. Co.*, 96 F. Supp. 304, 308 (1951).

deal in the goods, machinery, or supplies of a competitor or competitors of the lessor or seller, where the effect "may be to substantially lessen competition or tend to create a monopoly." (See page 592.)

*Stock acquisition of competitors.* Section 7 of the Clayton Act prohibits those stock acquisitions whose effect would be a substantial lessening of competition between the corporations concerned, or to restrain commerce in any section or community, or to create a tendency toward monopoly. Unless such effect can be shown, a complaint filed under this section must fail.

*Interlocking directorates.* Section 8 of the Clayton Act prohibits any director from serving on the boards of two or more corporations then or previously in competition, industrially and geographically, where the resultant elimination of competition would violate the antitrust laws. This provision of the Clayton Act is applicable only where one of the corporations has capital, surplus and undivided profits of more than $1,000,000.

*Enforcement; remedies.* Enforcement of the foregoing provisions is entrusted to the Federal Trade Commission. In addition, private individuals, firms and corporations are no longer confined, as they were under the Sherman Act, to suits for treble damages resulting from statutory violation, but may sue and have injunctive relief against threatened loss or damage because of such violation.

*Federal Trade Commission (1914).* The Federal Trade Commission, established within a few weeks of the adoption of the Clayton Act,[9] has been assigned an expanding role as the watchdog of trade relations. The Commission is charged with the enforcement of the foregoing sections of the Clayton Act. It also administers and enforces the Webb-Pomerene Export Trade Act which exempts export associations from the operation of the antitrust laws, subject to specified safeguards. Its jurisdiction was extended in 1936 over the Robinson-Patman amendments to Section 2 of the Clayton Act, dealing with price discrimination. It was still further broadened in 1938 to cover the Wheeler-Lea Act dealing with false advertisements of food, drugs, cosmetics and devices, together with unfair and deceptive acts and practices. The Wool Products Labeling Act of 1939 added control over the adulteration and mislabeling of wool products. The McCarran Act of 1945 applied the Clayton and Federal Trade Commission Acts to the insurance business except as regulated by state law, and the Lanham Trade-Mark Act of 1947 authorized the Federal Trade Commission to apply to the Commissioner of Patents for cancellation of the registration of trade marks which are deceptive, immoral or scandalous, or which have been fraudulently obtained, or which otherwise violate the law.

---

[9] The Federal Trade Commission Act (38 Stat. 717; 15 U.S.C. 41-51) became effective September 26, 1914. The Clayton Act (38 Stat. 730; 15 U.S.C. 12) was approved October 15, 1914.

**Major Functions.** The major functions of the Federal Trade Commission fall into three categories: (1) Policing trade restraints and unfair competition; (2) Policing unfair trade practices; and (3) Collateral activities, dealing with trade information, investigations, conferences and reports. The first two of these functions are discussed more fully in Part 4 of this chapter.

**Remedies.** A private party has no personal remedy under the Federal Trade Commission Act, except such as is afforded by the correction of an unfair practice. If he seeks treble damages for loss suffered through anti-trust violation, he must proceed directly through the courts under either the Sherman or the Clayton Act. However, any aggrieved party may file a complaint with the Commission, and if the complaint has merit and is of sufficient public concern, the Commission will follow it up and issue a formal complaint.

**Enforcement.** On failure to comply with a final order of the Commission, the law imposes a civil penalty of $5000 for each violation. In cases of false advertising with intent to defraud or mislead, or of falsely advertising an article injurious to health, the law imposes a fine not exceeding $5000, imprisonment not exceeding six months, or both. Repetition of the offense doubles the penalty.

**Robinson-Patman Act (1936).** The Robinson-Patman Act was designed to render more flexible the price discrimination provisions of the Clayton Act. The amendatory act makes it unlawful to discriminate in price between different purchasers of commodities of like grade and quality, where the effect may substantially lessen competition or tend to create a monopoly. Price differences are allowed in the following situations: (1) absence of restraint or monopolistic effect, (2) differences in grade and quality, (3) differences in quantity, (4) changing conditions, (5) necessity to meet competition, and (6) cooperative associations. These are more fully discussed in pages 598 to 601.

**Parties affected.** The statute affects both sides of a price discriminatory transaction. It applies to "any person who either grants or knowingly receives the benefit of such discrimination or to customers of either of them." Processor, manufacturer, middleman, jobber, wholesaler and retailer are all equally guilty if they have knowingly participated in such transaction.

**Enforcement.** On failure to establish an allowable basis for price discrimination, the Federal Trade Commission may issue a "cease and desist" order which (on becoming final) entails a civil penalty of $5000 if disobeyed, and subjects the offender to a government injunction suit and, in certain situations, to a criminal penalty as well. In addition, the offender may become liable in treble damages to any person injured by the price discrimination.

**Miller Tydings Act (1937).** In the absence of statute, a contract whereby a manufacturer, processor or other seller tries to fix a minimum resale price for his goods—trade-marked, trade-named, or otherwise— is unenforceable on common law grounds, as in restraint of trade. Price fixing under the Sherman Act was unqualifiedly condemned,[10] except for the right of a patentee to fix the price of his patented article on the first sale but no further.[11] This prohibition was founded on the principle that price-fixing has no place in a free-enterprise economy, discourages healthy competition and destroys incentive for greater marketing efficiency.

*"Fair trade" laws.* Many manufacturers and merchants complained that this rigid attitude of the law toward price-fixing afforded no protection against destructive price-cutting, and robbed trade marks, trade names and other trade values of the benefits that go with high quality standards. They pointed out that when a standard dollar item can be offered by a zealous dealer below cost as bait for more profitable purchases, other dealers cease stocking the item, and the manufacturer loses his retail outlets, the benefit of his quality standards and the value of his national advertising. Beginning in 1931, all but three states[12] adopted "fair trade" laws permitting manufacturers to fix and enforce minimum resale prices for trade-marked products. The typical statute did two things: (1) It permitted a distributor of branded merchandise to make a contract with a retailer whereby the latter agreed to sell the product at a fixed price; and (2) It provided for enforcement of prices thus fixed, not only against the signers of such contracts, but against all retailers of the same product who had notice of the fixed price, since otherwise, price-cutting non-signers could break the "fair-trade" market.

*Status of non-signers of resale contracts.* The Miller-Tydings Act permits the producer or distributor of an article which bears his trade mark, brand or name, to prescribe a minimum resale price *by contract,* if (1) such contracts are lawful in the state where the resale is to be made, and (2) the article is in free and open competition with other articles of the same commodity. The state statutes permitted a producer or processor not only to fix his resale price by contract, but *by notice* to non-signers. Since the Miller-Tydings Act, however, permitted resale price fixing by *contract only,* the Supreme Court refused to uphold a state statute permitting enforcement against non-signers of such contracts involving interstate products,[13] a ruling that was followed by a Federal amendment[14] conforming more closely to the majority of state statutes. In a subsequent case challenging the amendment as unconstitutional, the

---

[10] *U.S. v. Socony-Vacuum Oil Co.,* 310 U.S. 150, 223.
[11] *Sola Electric Co. v. Jefferson Electric Co.,* 317 U.S. 173.
[12] Missouri, Texas and Vermont; also the District of Columbia.
[13] *Schwegmann Brothers v. Calvert Distillers Corporation, et al.,* 341 U.S. 384 (1951).
[14] H.R. 5767 (McGuire Act), 1952.

Supreme Court refused to review a decision of the United States Court of Appeals upholding the constitutionality of the amendment.[15]

## Questions

1. What is meant by the term "restraint of trade"?
2. Distinguish between (a) public and private monopolies; (b) legal and illegal monopolies.
3. Name and explain five common forms of monopoly.
4. Describe the basic provisions of the Sherman Anti-trust Act. Who may enforce it and what are the forms which such enforcement may take?
5. What was the purpose of the Clayton Act, and what are its four major provisions?
6. What forms of relief are available under the Clayton Act?
7. With respect to the Federal Trade Commission state (a) the matters over which it has jurisdiction, (b) its two major functions, and (c) its collateral activities.
8. What remedies are available under the Federal Trade Commission?
9. What penalties does the law provide in connection with final orders of the Federal Trade Commission?
10. What was the major purpose in adopting the Robinson-Patman Act?
11. "Price discrimination is illegal and the law tolerates no exceptions." Is this statement true, false, or partly true and partly false? Explain.
12. What are the possible penalties for violating the Robinson-Patman Act?
13. What is the major purpose of the Miller-Tydings Act?
14. What is the purpose of "fair trade" laws, and what is the status of such laws and their enforcement today?

## Problems

1. A group of financiers attempt to monopolize interstate trade in a specialized type of electronic equipment. While negotiations are in progress, it becomes evident that the proposed monopoly will prove unavailing because of a new device which will render the electronic equipment in question obsolete. The negotiations are therefore dropped. In the meantime, an antitrust prosecution is commenced against the negotiators, with the threat of an impending fine of $5,000 and imprisonment for one year for each of the participants. The plea interposed is that no monopoly was consummated. How will the court rule?

2. Allen, a small manufacturer of platinum watch cases, is forced out of business by a combination of his competitors. He sues the latter for treble damages. The defendants move to dismiss the suit on the ground that antitrust suits can be brought only by the government, not by private individuals. Will this motion be granted or denied?

3. Baker is being threatened with business failure by persistent and continuous price discrimination against him and in favor of his competitors. He contemplates a suit for treble damages against his supplier, but is fearful he will be out of business before the case can be reached for trial. He would prefer an injunction. Is such relief available to him?

4. Carter is prosecuted under the Robinson-Patman Act for implication in

---

[15] *Schwegmann Brothers v. Eli Lilly & Co.*, 205 F. 2d 788 (1953), certiorari denied, October 19, 1953, 74 Sup.Ct. 71, 346 U.S. 856.

a price discriminatory transaction. His defense is that he received, but did not grant the discriminatory benefits in question, and with respect to the latter, was unaware that the benefits were discriminatory. Will the defense succeed?

## PART 3. RESTRAINT OF TRADE: ANTITRUST CASES

**Need for Clarification: Major Issues.** A clear interpretation of our antitrust laws is of profound concern to business. Businessmen complain that such an interpretation is lacking; that conflicting decisions afford no clear guide; that nothing is so demoralizing to business as uncertainty whether a proposed transaction will win success and commendation or a criminal prosecution. On the other hand, the problems presented for judicial decision have not been simple, and their solutions have frequently reflected changing economic theories and changing public attitudes. Numerous issues have been presented, but the major ones are as follows:

1. *"Rule of reason":* When an act is prohibited by the antitrust laws, does the act in and of itself constitute a violation, or must the courts apply a "rule of reason"—must they consider the surrounding facts and circumstances—in determining innocence or guilt?

2. *Price fixing:* How far may a business go in fixing and maintaining a price for its product?

3. *Business expansion v. monopoly:* To what extent may a business lawfully expand; or, to put it differently, does mere size justify antitrust prosecution?

4. *Cooperation v. conspiracy:* When do business arrangements for united effort constitute lawful cooperation, and when do they become conspiracies in restraint of trade?

Unless otherwise indicated, references in this discussion to "restraint of trade" will relate to interstate, not intrastate trade: space will permit no more than the barest reference to State antitrust cases.

**"Rule of Reason."** The earlier decisions interpreting the Sherman Act held that every contract or combination, reasonable or unreasonable, which directly restrained trade or commerce was unlawful. Later, in *United States v. Standard Oil Company*,[16] Chief Justice White declared that in determining whether a contract or combination was unlawful under the statute, the common law standard of reasonableness had to be applied. The common law, he pointed out, condemned only such restraints as unreasonably restricted competition. To determine whether a restraint was unreasonable, you had to look to the nature of the contract or act, or to the surrounding circumstances. If these showed that the contract or act had been entered into for the purpose and with the effect of impeding the "free flow of commerce," there was a violation, otherwise not. More recently, however, antitrust cases have presented an apparent conflict with the earlier decisions, and with one another. Prosecuting authorities con-

---

[16] 221 U.S. 1 (1912).

tend that *any* restraint of trade is unlawful *per se*, hence violates the statute, and that the "rule of reason" is no longer valid. Antitrust lawyers challenge this. The truth seems to be that consciously or otherwise, the "Rule of Reason" is adhered to by the courts as a rule of evidence. Some forms of restraint are so clearly obstructive of the "free flow of commerce" that resort to outside circumstances is unnecessary. Examples are boycotts, price-fixing agreements, cartels and "exclusion arrangements," that is, arrangements to exclude a competitor from benefits monopolistically held. On the other hand, there are many forms of restraint which a court hesitates to condemn without proof that they unreasonably restrict the "free flow of commerce." The most common example is that of a merger or consolidation: where the evidence shows an appreciable lessening of competition, the court will declare the restraint unlawful, but if the evidence shows no appreciable restraint, the court will not interfere (page 577).

EXAMPLES OF RESTRAINT HELD TO BE REASONABLE:

(1) *Pictorial Review Company v. Curtis Publishing Co.*,[17] where certain distributors were prohibited by a publisher from handling other periodicals than The Ladies Home Journal.

(2) *Pick Mfg. Co. v. General Motors Corp.*,[18] involving contracts requiring dealers to sell and use only General Motors repair parts.

(3) *Federal Trade Commission v. Sinclair Refining Co.*,[19] where Sinclair limited the use of its leased pumps to its own gasoline.

(4) *United States v. Columbia Steel Co., et al.*,[20] involving U.S. Steel's acquisition of Consolidated Steel's assets, where the court concluded the merger would have no unreasonable impact on the affected market.

EXAMPLES OF RESTRAINT HELD TO BE UNREASONABLE:

(1) *International Business Machines Corporation v. U.S.*,[21] where tabulating machines were leased on condition that the lessee buy all his tabulating supplies from the lessor.

(2) *International Salt Co., Inc. v. U.S.*,[22] involving the sale or lease of patented salt dispensing machinery on condition that the purchaser or lessee buy all his salt from the seller or lessor.

(3) *Standard Oil Company of California v. U.S.*,[23] where contracts with 6000 independent dealers bound each of them to buy his petroleum products and automobile accessories from Standard alone, and where the court considered Standard's annual gallonage in deciding that competition had been substantially lessened.

**Price Fixing.** Everyone may fix a price for his product, but when the price is fixed artificially by a combination or conspiracy, prosecution

---

[17] 255 Fed. 206 (1917).
[18] 299 U.S. 3 (1936).
[19] 261 U.S. 463 (1923).
[20] 334 U.S. 495 (1948).
[21] 298 U.S. 131 (1936).
[22] 332 U.S. 392 (1947).
[23] 337 U.S. 293 (1949).

may follow. Price fixing may be (1) horizontal, (2) vertical, or (3) resale.

*Horizontal price fixing.* Horizontal price fixing obtains among competitors, actual or potential. Such price fixing is illegal regardless of motive or surrounding circumstances.

EXAMPLES:

(1) In *American Tobacco Co. v. U.S.*,[24] three cigarette manufacturing corporations entered into an arrangement to refrain from purchasing at any tobacco market unless all three were present. Prosecuted for conspiracy, they urged that the presence of all three as bidders assured the tobacco growers the best prices the market would afford. The Court held this immaterial even if true: the law simply forbade pricing arrangements between competitors.

(2) In *United States v. Socony-Vacuum Oil Co.*,[25] numerous oil companies and individuals were charged with conspiring to raise and maintain gasoline prices, by buying up distress gasoline on the spot market and eliminating it as a market factor. In defense it was urged (1) that the elimination of distress gasoline from the current market had eliminated certain evils of competition which were detrimental to the public, and (2) that there was no substantial restraint of trade. The Court held that these defenses were immaterial to the fact that there was a conspiracy to fix prices, which was illegal. (3) In *United States v. Trenton Potteries Co.*,[26] a group controlling 80% of the business of manufacturing and distributing sanitary pottery in the United States entered into an agreement to fix and maintain uniform prices. Prosecuted for conspiracy, the group urged that the prices agreed upon were entirely reasonable. The court held that the agreement was illegal whether the prices were reasonable or not.

*Vertical price fixing.* Vertical price fixing applies to arrangements between suppliers and dealers, such as between a manufacturer and a jobber or wholesaler, or between the latter and a retailer. Such price fixing is also illegal, but the price must be actually "fixed," by agreement or compulsion, otherwise there is no violation.

EXAMPLES:

(1) Manufacturers may maintain list prices by arrangements with dealers and agents. Such arrangements are not illegal, since the ultimate price is not fixed by contract, but is subject to the dealer's discretion.[27]

(2) A manufacturer may urge his wholesalers, by circulars or otherwise, not to sell his product to price-cutting dealers, provided he does not withhold or threaten to withhold his product from wholesalers who continue to sell to such dealers.[28]

*Resale price fixing.* Resale price fixing is the term commonly applied to vertical price fixing governing resale to the consumer. Like horizontal and vertical price fixing generally, it is illegal *per se*, except where per-

---

[24] 147 F. 2d 93 (1944), rehearing denied, 324 U.S. 891 (1945).
[25] 310 U.S. 150 (1939).
[26] 273 U.S. 392 (1927).
[27] *Spielman Motor Sales Co. v. Dodge*, 8 F. Supp. 437 (1934), modified on other grounds 295 U.S. 89 (1934).
[28] *Great Atlantic & Pacific Tea Co. v. Cream of Wheat Co.*, 227 F. 46 (1915).

mitted under a Fair Trade statute. We have already noted the business considerations which led to the adoption of Fair Trade state statutes (page 581), the Miller-Tydings amendment to the Sherman Act, and the *Schwegmann* case which led to the adoption of an amendment to the Miller-Tydings Act.

*Maximum resale price fixing.* Does the Sherman Act prohibit producers from fixing a *maximum* resale price? The answer to this question is furnished by the court in the case of *Kiefer-Stewart Company v. Joseph E. Seagram & Sons, Inc., et al.,*[29] in which the plaintiff, a wholesale liquor dealer, sued for treble damages under the Sherman Act, charging that respondents had agreed or conspired to sell liquor only to those wholesalers who would agree not to resell at prices above maximum prices fixed by the Seagram and Calvert distilling interests. The court, sustaining the petitioner, held that "such agreements, no less than those to fix minimum prices, cripple the freedom of traders and thereby restrain their ability to sell in accordance with their own judgment."

*Price fixing by buyers.* A combination or agreement among dealers fixing the price they will pay a supplier is just as unlawful a restraint as a price fixing agreement among suppliers. A seller has the same right to competition among buyers as a purchaser has to competition among sellers.[30]

*Price fixing of patented products.* Price control has been frequently exercised through granting or withholding patented products or patent licenses, and through the pooling of patents by cross-licensing or similar arrangements. A patent owner has the exclusive right to make and sell his patented product. He may fix the price on the first sale of his product, or he may license others to manufacture and sell his patented article, and to charge a fixed price for it. But beyond that he may not go. His monopoly gives him no right to violate the antitrust laws. If he attempts to control the price of his product after the first sale, he violates the law. If he licenses others to manufacture and sell his patented article, he may fix the terms and conditions on which the article may be sold, or the price at which and the persons to whom the article may be sold; but he may not require the licensee to fix the terms and prices for subsequent resale by *his* purchasers.[31]

*Patent combinations: pooling and cross-licensing.* Patent owners may combine the use of their patents, may pool them, or cross-license them to one another for most effective output, provided that in so doing they in no way suppress competition or restrain trade, as by fixing prices,

---

[29] 340 U.S. 211 (1951).

[30] *Mandeville Island Farms v. American Crystal Sugar Co.,* 334 U.S. 219 (1948).

[31] *United States v. Bausch & Lomb,* 321 U.S. 707 (1944); *United States v. Masonite Corp., et al.,* 316 U.S. 265 (1942); *United States v. United States Gypsum Company,* 333 U.S. 364 (1948).

dividing and distributing the market, or indulging in any other form of monopolistic practice. Hence a mere patent combination is not illegal *per se*, but is to be judged by the "rule of reason." [32]

**Business Expansion v. Monopoly.** A business may expand by natural, internal growth, as by increased efficiency and economy of production, resulting in a superior product at a lower price, followed by increased demand for its products and a corresponding increase in output and revenue. On the other hand, its size may be externally augmented by merger, consolidation and stock acquisition. The attitude of the courts toward mere growth and size is discussed on pages 588 to 589. So far as concerns external expansion, the antitrust laws apply only where the competitive situation has been altered.

*Combinations: competing v. non-competing units.* There is nothing inherently unlawful in a merger, consolidation, or stock acquisition affecting two or more corporate entities. It is only where such transactions substantially lessen competition and thereby pave the way for monopolistic practices that the law steps in to undo or prevent the actual or threatened evil.

EXAMPLE: Two groups of stockholders, respectively controlling two competing railroad companies, formed a holding company, exchanged their stock for the stock of the holding company, and thereby brought the two competing companies under a single direction. The consolidation was condemned as a conspiracy in restraint of trade.[33]

*Competition must be real or substantial.* Before a combination may be enjoined, there must be (1) proof of prior substantial competition between the acquiring and acquired corporation and (2) a substantial lessening of such competition by reason of the combination.

EXAMPLE: The International Shoe Company purchased the McElwain Shoe Company in order to extend its plant facilities. The latter had been threatened with insolvency. There was no substantial competition between the two companies, since the McElwain Company made a better grade of shoes than the International Company and sold to a different class of customers. The court reversed an order of the Federal Trade Commission restraining the acquisition.[34]

**Integration: Horizontal v. Vertical.** The court has defined "horizontal integration" as a combination under one management of a number of similar industries, and "vertical integration" as a combination under one management of different business functions at more than one level.[35] An example of the former would be that of one railroad company acquiring

---

[32] *Standard Oil Company (Indiana) v. U.S.*, 283 U.S. 163 (1930); *United States v. Line Material Company*, 333 U.S. 287 (1947); *Hartford-Empire Company v. U.S.*, 323 U.S. 386 (1945).

[33] *Northern Securities Co. v. United States*, 193 U.S. 197 (1903).

[34] *International Shoe Company v. Federal Trade Commission*, 280 U.S. 291 (1930).

[35] *U.S. v. New York Great Atlantic & Pacific Tea Co.*, 67 F. Supp. 626.

the stock of another. An example of the latter would be the acquisition by a large automobile manufacturing company of a coal mine, or a steel plant, or a transportation company, to effect economies in the process of manufacture. Since vertical integration rarely involves a lessening of competition, it is rarely declared unlawful. As Mr. Justice Holmes put it: "It is as lawful for one corporation to make every part of a steam engine and to put the machine together as it would be for one to make the boilers and another to make the wheels." [36]

In *United States v. Columbia Steel Co. et al.*,[37] the government sought to enjoin the United States Steel Corporation and its subsidiaries from purchasing the assets of the Consolidated Steel Corporation, which was the largest steel fabricator on the West Coast. The government contended that the purchase was an effort to monopolize the market in fabricated steel products. The evidence showed, however, that United States Steel and its subsidiaries were producing rolled steel products and structural fabrication (building framework, bridges, transmission towers and similar structures), but that they did no plate fabrication (pressure vessels, tanks, welded pipe and similar products). Consolidated Steel Corporation, on the other hand, was engaged only in structural and plate fabrication, and its own sales were only 2 per cent of the sales of United States Steel and subsidiaries. The object of the purchase, according to the latter, was to round out their manufacturing operations by acquiring facilities for plate fabrication (vertical integration). The Supreme Court rejected the government's contentions, saying that the law did not forbid "an expansion of facilities . . . to meet the needs of new markets."

**Mere Size: An Inherent Evil?** Mere size is not necessarily monopolistic. The automobile industry, for example, is made up of a number of industrial giants in active competition with one another. On the other hand, a tiny concern may possess a monopoly of a given product. From the standpoint of our antitrust laws, size becomes significant only when it is coupled with the actual or threatened exercise of monopoly power.

*Earlier decisions.* The earlier cases dealing with large industrial units stressed the distinction between mere size and monopoly power. "The size and power which a combination may grow to and acquire," said the court in one of these cases,[38] "are not limited by the Sherman Act unless actual restraint of competition is shown." Even in cases where industrial organizations were condemned as monopolies, the Court took pains to point out that mere size played no part in the decision. In the *Eastman Kodak* case,[39] for example, defendant was charged with obtain-

---

[36] *U.S. v. Winslow*, 227 U.S. 202 (1913).

[37] 334 U.S. 495 (1948).

[38] *United States v. United States Steel Corporation*, 251 U.S. 417 (1920).

[39] *United States v. Eastman Kodak Co.*, 226 F. 62 (1915), final decree entered 230 F. 522, appeal dism. 255 U.S. 578.

ing control of the only imported raw paper which was standard for the manufacture of photographic "printing-out" paper, and then killing off competition by refusing to sell photographic paper to other manufacturers; after which, it was alleged, the defendant fixed resale prices and secured control of 75 to 80 per cent of the entire interstate trade. The court held that these methods were intended and calculated to, and did, result in an undue and unreasonable restraint of trade. However, in so holding, the court observed that size alone and the extent of a company's business did not violate the statute. The Court took a similar position in the *International Harvester* case.[40]

*Size v. monopoly: trend of more recent decisions.* The more recent cases under the Sherman Act continue to distinguish between mere size and monopoly, but stress the *potential* evils of monopoly as such. Indeed, in the Aluminum case[41] the Court held that where size amounts to a monopoly, it automatically becomes illegal. The moment a monopoly begins to function, said Judge Learned Hand in that case, it must sell something. When it sells something, it must fix its price. Such price is necessarily monopolistic. Hence to the extent that the price is fixed by a monopoly it is a violation of the Sherman Act. In the *Pullman* case,[42] the company had achieved a 100 per cent monopoly of the business of furnishing sleeping cars to the railroads of the United States. This, said the Court, was not mere size: it was monopoly pure and simple, and as such it could not but run counter to the express provisions of the Sherman Act.

*At what point does size become monopoly?* The point at which size becomes monopoly is one that can scarcely be fixed by mathematical computation. Much depends on the market and the degree of domination that can be exercised in a given industry. Yet the courts have tried to fix a rough boundary line between mere size and monopoly. In the Aluminum case, defendant controlled 90% of the entire aluminum industry in the country. "That percentage," said Judge Hand, "is enough to constitute a monopoly; it is doubtful whether sixty or sixty-four per cent would be enough; and certainly thirty-three per cent is not." [43]

**Cooperation v. Conspiracy.** In a broad sense, every conspiracy involves cooperation. Under our antitrust laws, however, the distinction between the two terms is one of purpose. Cooperation implies a lawful, and conspiracy an unlawful concert of action. The thing which makes such concert of action unlawful under the Sherman Act is that its purpose is

---

[40] *United States v. International Harvester Company,* 214 F. 987, def's appeal dism. 248 U.S. 587 (1918), remanded and reappealed 274 U.S. 693 (1927).

[41] *United States v. Aluminum Co. of America,* 148 F. 2d 416 (1945).

[42] *United States v. Pullman Co.,* 50 F. Supp. 123. Subsequent proceedings: 53 F. Supp. 908 (1944); 55 F. Supp. 985 (1944); 55 F. Supp. 985 (1944); 64 F. Supp. 108 (1946); 329 U.S. 748 (1946).

[43] *United States v. Aluminum Co. of America,* supra, p. 424.

to restrain trade. The language of the Sherman Act makes it immaterial whether the purpose is formulated by a "contract," "combination" or "conspiracy": if its aim is to restrain trade, it is unlawful. The test applied by the courts in determining whether a given agreement or association represents lawful cooperation or unlawful conspiracy is whether its objective or consequence is to restrain trade. Typical of the contracts, combinations and associations which have come under judicial scrutiny are those involving group action by trade, industrial or labor groups for the advancement of their respective interests. Where these contemplate or result in a restraint of trade, they are vulnerable; otherwise not.

EXAMPLES:

(1) In *Maple Flooring Manufacturing Association v. United States*,[44] suit was brought under the Sherman Act to dissolve a trade association formed by numerous manufacturers of hard-wood flooring. The activities complained of were as follows: (a) Computation, and distribution to members, of information as to the average cost of their products; (b) Compilation, and distribution to members, of booklets for quick reference showing freight rates from basing points to numerous other points; (c) Periodical gathering of information from members and re-distribution to them in summarized form, on the kind and quantities of flooring sold, dates of sales, prices received, average freight rates, commissions paid, amount and kinds of stock on hand, unfilled orders, monthly production, new orders booked, and similar trade data; (d) Meetings and discussions, but not on fixing prices. The court held that such an association was not an unlawful restraint of trade.

(2) In *Fashion Originators Guild v. Federal Trade Commission*,[45] a group of 176 dress manufacturers banded themselves together to prevent pirating of their styles. Their designs, though not patented or copyrighted, were original and distinctive. The object of the organization was to suppress piracy by competitors who copied the designs and sold them at lower prices. The members registered their designs with the Guild and agreed to boycott retailers who sold the copied garments. The Federal Trade Commission issued a cease and desist order against the Guild, which appealed on the ground that its arrangement was not intended to, nor did it, fix or regulate prices, or parcel out or limit production. The Supreme Court, however, in sustaining the order of the Federal Trade Commission, held that such boycotts were illegal, regardless of their objectives.

***Limiting or excluding competitors.*** However legitimate the purposes of an association may be in other respects, if it practices exclusion of competitors or any other restraint upon persons not members of the association, it violates the Sherman Act as an unlawful conspiracy in restraint of trade.

EXAMPLE: In *Associated Press v. United States (N.Y.)*,[46] a cooperative news gathering association adopted by-laws rigidly limiting applications for membership by competing newspapers. These by-laws, the court held, constituted a

---

[44] 268 U.S. 563 (1924).
[45] 312 U.S. 457 (1941).
[46] 326 U.S. 1 (1944), rehearing denied 326 U.S. 802 (1945).

violation of the anti-trust laws, in that they imposed an unreasonable restraint on interstate commerce in news.

*Agreements not to compete: pools and cartels.* The basic vice of a pool or cartel is the stifling of competition. The first judicial condemnation of this practice under the Sherman Act came in the *Addyston Pipe and Steel* case,[47] where a combination of six shops engaged in making cast iron pipes controlled the market and entered into an agreement to control prices by suppressing competition and public bidding among themselves, except by a prearranged representative who was to make the lowest bid. This arrangement was condemned by the court as a monopoly in restraint of trade.

A more recent instance, on an international scale, was that of *United States v. National Lead Co.*[48] In that case, defendants participated in an international cartel by pooling patents and allocating the right to manufacture and sell titanium pigments and compounds in the United States and abroad. The defendants were enjoined from continuing this practice. The court decree required the granting of compulsory non-exclusive licenses at uniform reasonable royalties.

*Agreements not to sell to one another's customers.* Agreements by producers or distributors to "respect" one another's exclusive customers, and to refrain from soliciting business among them are regarded as conspiracies in restraint of trade.[49]

*Agreements not to sell to specified customer.* Ordinarily, a person may deal or refuse to deal with any other person, business or industrial establishment, as he sees fit. However, a *concerted* refusal to deal with some person or business concern, in the nature of a seller's boycott, may be attacked as an illegal combination or conspiracy.[50] A person who induces such a boycott is likewise liable, though the victim is a violator himself.

EXAMPLE: In *United States v. Univis Lens Co.*,[51] a patent owner demanded that an alleged infringer desist from further infringement, and on the latter's failure to desist, induced licensees to cancel orders placed with the alleged infringer. The court held that such practice constituted a violation of the Sherman Antitrust Act.

*Exclusive dealing contracts.* An exclusive dealing contract is one in which a person or group of persons agrees to buy or sell to a given person or group of persons only. Such contracts are unlawful only where they have the effect of substantially lessening competition or tending to create a monopoly. Thus, a contract may lawfully bind a producer

---

[47] *United States v. Addyston Pipe & Steel Co.*, 85 F. 271, modified and affirmed 175 U.S. 211 (1899).

[48] 332 U.S. 319 (1948).

[49] *Jos. Schlitz Brewing Co. v. Johnson*, 123 F. 2d 1016 (1941).

[50] *Kiefer-Stewart Company v. Joseph E. Seagram & Sons, Inc., et al.*, 340 U.S. 211 (1951).

[51] 41 F. Supp. 258 (1941), modified on other grounds, 316 U.S. 241 (1941).

to sell, and the buyer to purchase, the producer's entire output, or it may lawfully bind a buyer to purchase his entire requirements from a given seller or producer. But if such a contract has the effect of substantially lessening competition or tending to create a monopoly, as by binding the producer not to sell to a competing buyer, or the buyer not to purchase from a competing producer, the law will step in.[52]

*"Tying" contracts.* Section 3 of the Clayton Act, as noted on page 578, makes "tying" agreements unlawful if their effect "may be to substantially lessen competition or tend to create a monopoly." The courts necessarily adopt a "rule of reason" in each case to determine whether the "tying" agreement substantially lessens competition or tends toward monopoly. (See cases cited on page 584, under examples of reasonable and unreasonable restraints.)

*Labor boycotts.* We have already noted the distinction between primary boycotts, in which only those directly concerned participate (such as employees seeking to redress a grievance), and secondary boycotts, in which pressure is brought to bear on others than those directly concerned. The latter type of boycott only is condemned by statute (page 443). A combination of employees to withhold their services from a given employer is not regarded as a combination or conspiracy in restraint of trade under the Federal antitrust laws. However, although the Clayton Act specifically provides that "the labor of a human being is not a commodity or an article of commerce," it does not exempt labor unions from liability under the antitrust laws where they depart from these objectives and engage in an actual combination or conspiracy in restraint of trade. At least, that was the attitude of the courts prior to the adoption of the Norris-LaGuardia Act.

EXAMPLES:

(1) In *Duplex Printing Press Co. v. Deering et al.*,[53] following an unsuccessful strike, organizations of machinists with headquarters in New York City, together with a national organization, entered into a combination to interfere with and restrain plaintiff's interstate trade by means of a secondary boycott. They threatened plaintiff's customers with sympathetic strikes and other forms of loss if the latter purchased or installed plaintiff's presses; they cautioned trucking companies employed by customers not to haul any of the presses; they incited employees of truckers and customers to strike to prevent hauling and installation; they similarly warned repair shops, threatened union men with loss of their cards and with a "scab" blacklisting, and brought similar pressure to bear in other directions. The court held that all this constituted a combination and conspiracy to restrain trade, and that the plaintiff was entitled to an injunction.

---

[52] *Pittsburgh Plate Glass Co. v. Jarrett*, 42 F. Supp. 723 (1942), modified on other grounds, *Jarrett v. Pittsburgh Plate Glass Co.*, 131 F. 2d 674 (1942); *Alexander's Department Stores v. Ohrbach's, Inc.*, 266 App. Div. 535, 42 N.Y. Supp. 2d 703 (1943), appeal dismissed, 291 N.Y. 707, 52 N.E. 2d 595 (1943).
[53] 254 U.S. 443 (1920).

(2) In *Bedford Cut Stone Company v. Journeymen Stone Cutters' Assn. of North America*,[54] a combination of union stone-cutters declared certain building-stone producers as "unfair," and forbade union members to work on the stone in building construction in other states where the stone was extensively bought and used. The result was to induce or coerce those building construction employers, anxious to avoid strikes, to refrain from purchasing such stone. The Court held that this action on the part of the union violated the Sherman Act.

After the passage of the Norris-LaGuardia Act, however, the courts indicated that labor unions were in large part immune from antitrust liability.

EXAMPLES:

(1) In *Apex Hosiery Co. v. Leader, et al.*,[55] members of a labor union sought to unionize a hosiery factory in which but a few of them were employed. In violation of the civil and criminal laws of the state, they forcibly took possession of the plant and held it during a protracted sit-down strike. Much of the machinery was wilfully injured or destroyed. The business of the concern was entirely suspended. Yet the Court refused to interfere.

(2) In *United States v. Hutcheson*,[56] the Court said, in effect, that neither the Sherman nor the Clayton Act could be relied upon to restrain practices otherwise unlawful under these Acts, if these practices were carried on by a labor union.

However, by 1945 public opinion had veered toward holding labor unions equally responsible with business organizations for monopolistic practices, of which a combination or conspiracy in the nature of a boycott is an outstanding example. This change of attitude was reflected in the adoption of the Labor-Management ("Taft-Hartley") Act, which outlawed secondary boycotts, and in current labor decisions. Thus, in *Allen Bradley Co. v. Local Union No. 3*,[57] the Supreme Court took pains to point out that labor unions have no right to claim immunity under antitrust statutes when they depart from the basic purposes of such immunity. In that case, a labor union threatened to strike unless all electrical equipment used by local employers was purchased from local manufacturers. The union persuaded others not to patronize sellers of the boycotted electrical equipment. The Court held that because the union had joined with businessmen in organizing a boycott, it could be restrained along with the businessmen, and was in no position to set up the Norris-LaGuardia Act as a defense.

## Questions

1. What is meant by the judicial doctrine "rule of reason" as applied to alleged violations of the antitrust laws?

---

[54] 274 U.S. 37 (1927).
[55] 310 U.S. 469 (1939).
[56] 312 U.S. 219 (1941).
[57] 325 U.S. 797 (1945).

2. Distinguish "horizontal," "vertical," and "resale" price fixing. To what extent does the law permit any of these forms of price fixing?

3. To what extent does the law limit price fixing of patented products?

4. "Mergers, consolidations and stock acquisitions affecting two or more corporate entities are inherently unlawful." Is this statement true, false, or partly true and partly false? Explain.

5. Distinguish between horizontal and vertical integration. Which of the two is more likely to conflict with our antitrust laws?

6. What is the present attitude of the courts with respect to the distinction between mere size and monopoly? Do the courts give any indication as to what they regard as the point at which size becomes monopoly?

7. How do the courts distinguish between cooperation and conspiracy in restraint of trade?

## Problems

1. A publishing company refuses to appoint distributors for its various publications unless they agree that they will not handle the products of other publishers. The publishing company is prosecuted for violation of the Sherman Antitrust Act. The evidence at the trial indicates that the arrangements in question had no appreciable effect on the publishing market. How should the court decide, and why?

2. A group of produce merchants who mutually agreed that they would not bid on a potato grower's output unless they were all together, were prosecuted under the antitrust laws. Their defense was that their competitive bidding provided a higher price for the potatoes than if only one or two of the merchants were to bid separately. How did the court rule?

3. An automobile manufacturer bought up the assets of a mine owner, a local transportation company, a manufacturer of automobile bodies and a leather processing concern. The manufacturer was prosecuted for violation of the antitrust laws. How should the court decide, and why?

4. A combination of dealers mutually agree on the maximum price they will pay a manufacturer for his products. The manufacturer brings suit for treble damages against the dealers. How will the court decide, and why?

5. A manufacturer enters into a contract with a dealer in a given state by which the dealer agrees to resell the manufacturer's products at prices fixed in a schedule annexed to and made part of the contract. The manufacturer then sends a copy of this contract to all other dealers in the state, requesting them to abide by the prices set forth in the schedule. The statute in this particular state permitted a producer or processor to fix resale prices not only by contract, but by notice to non-signers. One of the dealers handling the products on an interstate basis refuses to adhere to the price schedule. In the ensuing litigation, the question is raised whether the offending dealer was bound by the price schedule in view of the fact that he had made no commitment in respect to it. How was the question decided?

## PART 4. UNFAIR COMPETITION AND UNFAIR TRADE PRACTICES

**Meaning of Unfair Competition: Formerly and Now.** Until recent years the term "unfair competition" was confined to the practice of passing off one's goods as another's, by simulating another's name, mark or otherwise. To constitute unfair competition, there had to be actual competition or no relief was afforded. Later, the courts widened the meaning of unfair competition by stressing the element of unfairness rather than competition, and extending equitable jurisdiction over all cases in which one party fraudulently sought to pass off his goods as those of another. Today, with the rapid growth in trade and the diversity in modern methods of marketing—including mail-order distribution and identifiable packaging, aided by newspaper, magazine, radio and now television advertising, much of it on a national scale—the concept of "unfair competition" has widened far beyond its original scope, to embrace all conceivable forms of unfair business practices.

**Fraud in Relation to Unfair Competition.** Originally, the basis of relief against unfair competition was fraud: deception in palming off one's goods as another's. With the broadening concept that any unfair business practice has an evil effect on the public welfare, the element of fraud is no longer required to warrant relief. Examples are the innocent infringement of a trade mark and the numerous types of unfair business practices that may have nothing to do with fraud, such as the disparagement of a competitor's goods, the improper use of customer lists, the unauthorized disclosure of trade secrets, the intimidation of one's customers or employees, or price cutting with a view to forcing a competitor out of business.

**Restraint of Trade in Relation to Unfair Competition.** Although many forms of unfair competition involve a restraint of trade, the two terms are not identical. To restrain trade is to slow down the competitive game or abandon it altogether to monopolistic control. To indulge in unfair competition is not necessarily to abandon or slow down the competitive game—frequently it sharpens the game—but to play it unfairly. However, unfair competition is often resorted to in achieving a monopoly, and equally often is practiced after a monopoly is achieved.

**Unfair Competition, Unfair Trade Practices and the Federal Trade Commission.** The Clayton Act was aimed at certain practices tending toward monopoly, and the Federal Trade Commission, as the watchdog of trade relations, was charged with the enforcement of sections of the Clayton Act aimed at these practices. However, in directing its enforcement powers against these practices, the Federal Trade Commission is not limited to these practices alone, but may nip in the bud all forms of incipient monopoly or practices tending toward monopoly. Thus the power bestowed on the Federal Trade Commission is much wider than that created by the Clayton Act. Under the Clayton Act, neither the government, in an equity or criminal action, nor a private litigant, seeking treble damages, can succeed without proving the existence of a restraint capable of exercising monopolistic power. But no such limitation is placed on the Federal Trade Commission. The Act creating the Commission forbids *all* unfair methods of competition (though it does not define what *is* unfair competition, but leaves that for the Commission to decide in any case). The Federal Trade Commission Act goes even further. Section 5 not only declares "unfair methods of competition in commerce" unlawful, but it similarly stigmatizes "unfair or deceptive acts or practices in commerce." The Commission is empowered and directed to prevent both forms of unfair dealing. However, with one exception, the statute refrains from defining just what constitutes such acts and practices, thereby borrowing a leaf from the English chancellor who refused to define fraud for fear ways would be found to circumvent it. The exception is the Wheeler-Lea amendment dealing with false advertisements of food, drugs, etc., which are specifically declared to constitute an unfair or deceptive act or practice (page 579).

**Forms of Unfair Competition and Unfair Trade Practices.** Unfair practices may be primarily injurious to one's competitors and incidentally to the public, as in the case of simulating a competitor's design, mark, name or product, or it may be primarily injurious to the public and incidentally to one's competitors, as in the case of fraudulent advertising. Unfair competition and unfair trade practices may take numerous forms. Among those more frequently dealt with by the courts are the following: (1) trade infringements, (2) price discrimination, and (3) false advertising.

## (1) Trade Infringements

**Trade Infringements as Unfair Competition.** The subject of trade values is discussed on pages 673 to 678. The common law has for many years redressed infringements by one person of the trade values of another. In more recent years, however, the remedies for infringement have been greatly broadened by the application of equitable principles to inequitable or unfair practices, and by the creation of the Federal Trade Commission and corresponding state bodies to cope with unfair competitive practices not recognized at common law. As a result, many trade abuses which formerly went unredressed because they fell short of "trade infringements" are now redressed because they constitute unfair competition. At common law, if a businessman wanted to protect his design, mark, name or product, he had to establish (1) distinctiveness and (2) prior use. Today, a businessman may be unable to establish prior use and distinctiveness and yet may enjoin imitation if it constitutes unfair competition. This is particularly true in the case of (a) words or names which have acquired a "secondary meaning," (b) personal names which have acquired trade values, (c) geographical names which have become associated in the public mind with a given product or business, and (d) products marketed in a distinctive trade dress, such as a distinctive wrapper, package or container.

**(a) Secondary Meaning.** Frequently a name or descriptive word may become so identified with a business or product that it acquires a secondary meaning. In such cases, although the name or word cannot be trade-marked, it would constitute a deception for a competitor to imitate it and ride along on its reputation. Such "commercial hitchhiking" [58] may be enjoined as unfair competition.

EXAMPLES:

(1) Although the word "seventeen," being numerically descriptive, cannot be trade-marked, the court on petition of the publisher of *Seventeen*, a girl's fashion journal, enjoined a manufacturer of foundation garments from using the word as well as the number "seventeen" in connection with his garments, on the ground that it had attained a secondary meaning.[59]

(2) Although the words "fifth" and "column" are descriptive and cannot be trade-marked, the court, holding that "The Fifth Column" as the title of a play had acquired a secondary meaning, enjoined as unfair competition the exhibition of a motion picture entitled "Fifth Column Squad." [60]

(b) **Personal Names.** Everyone has a right to use his own name in his business, hence one cannot trade-mark his name so as to prevent others with the same name from exercising the same privilege. However, it constitutes unfair competition for a person to use even his own name in such a way as to appropriate the trade values built up by another person with the same name. Hence, while a person cannot be enjoined from using his own name, he can be enjoined from using it unfairly.

EXAMPLES:

(1) The Waterman Pen, as a name, could not be trade-marked, but since the name was well established and had acquired a secondary meaning, a former employee of the concern named Waterman was enjoined from using his name in the pen business, or as an inscription on its pens, without adding the words, "Not connected with the L. E. Waterman Co." [61]

(c) **Geographical Names.** Geographical names designating origin of product or location of business are descriptive and cannot be appropriated. However, when such names become so established in the public mind in connection with a given product or business as to acquire a secondary meaning, their use by a competitor will be enjoined as unfair competition.

EXAMPLES: Waltham[62] and Elgin[63] watches, and Plymouth cars.[64]

---

[58] "Unfair competition is a species of commercial hitch-hiking which the law finds offensive and therefore prohibits." *Bard-Parker Co. v. Crescent Mfg. Co.*, 174 Misc. 356, 20 N.Y. Supp. 2d 759 (1940).

[59] *Triangle Publications Inc. v. Rohrlich, et al.*, 167 F. 2d 969 (1948).

[60] *Hemingway v. Film Alliance*, 174 Misc. 725, 21 N.Y. Supp. 2d 827 (1940).

[61] *L. E. Waterman Co. v. Modern Pen Co.*, 235 U.S. 88 (1914).

[62] *American Waltham Watch Co. v. United States Watch Co.*, 173 Mass. 85, 53 N.E. 141 (1899).

[63] *Elgin Nat. Watch Co. v. Illinois Watch Case Co.*, 179 U.S. 665 (1900).

[64] *In re Plymouth Motor Corporation*, 46 F. 2d 211 (1931).

(d) **Trade Dress: Wrappers, Packages and Containers.** Where a manufacturer or dealer uses a specific form, style or design for wrapping, packaging or enclosing his product as it goes into the market, he may acquire therein what corresponds to a secondary meaning based on identification with the product or his product. Regardless of technical trademarks, it would constitute unfair competition for a competitor to appropriate such trade values. In determining whether a plaintiff is entitled to an injunction in such cases, the court considers whether the public is likely to be deceived by an imitation, and in determining the latter, the court will not consider any isolated feature, such as form, size, shape or color, but whether, taking the wrapper, package or container as a whole, the public is likely to be deceived.[65]

## (2) Price Discrimination

**What Constitutes Unlawful Price Discrimination.** Discriminatory practices, whatever their nature, are generally regarded as obnoxious. However, price cutting is not necessarily price discrimination, and the sale of an article at a reduced price is not illegal unless it is made for the purpose of discriminating between competitive buyers. Section 2 of the Clayton Act, as noted on page 578, prohibits price discrimination only where its effect may be a substantial lessening of competition or a tendency toward monopoly. Thus, in *Porto Rican American Tobacco v. American Tobacco Co.*,[66] the manufacturer of Lucky Strike cigarettes sold them in Porto Rico at a lower price than in the continental United States. This discrimination was not mere price cutting to meet competition, but was designed to effect a substantial lessening of competition, hence it was duly enjoined.

**Purpose of Robinson-Patman Act.** Notwithstanding basic objections to price discrimination, there are situations where differences in competitive conditions must be recognized in the interest of fairness, and the Robinson-Patman Act attempts to provide for such conditions. This amendment to section 2 of the Clayton Act, as pointed out on page 580, permits price differences in the following situations: (1) absence of trade restraint or monopolistic effect, (2) differences in grade and quality, (3) differences in quantity, (4) changing conditions, (5) necessity to meet competition, and (6) purchases by or on behalf of cooperative associations.

**Absence of Trade Restraint or Monopolistic Effect.** Price discriminations among non-competitive customers are permissible because they have no effect on trade restraint or monopoly; for example, different sugar prices to candy manufacturers and to chemists.

---

[65] *Barbasol Co. v. Jacobs*, 150 F. 2d 336 (1947).
[66] 30 F. 2d 234 (1929).

**Differences in Grade and Quality.** Prices based on differences in grade and quality are not really discriminatory, in the objectionable sense of the term. The law does not compel dealers to sell Grade A eggs at the same price as those of a lower grade, or high grade perfume at the same price as that of a lower quality.

**Differences in Quantity.** Section 2 of the Clayton Act, prior to its Robinson-Patman amendment, seemed to deprive the chain stores, especially grocery and drug chains, of their principal advantage over smaller competitors, namely, their ability to buy more cheaply by direct dealing in large quantities with manufacturers and processors. The advantage was restored by the Robinson-Patman Act, but only in part, because even under the amendment, quantity discounts tending toward trade restraint or monopoly are forbidden: they must be related to differences in the seller's cost of manufacture, sale, or delivery based on different methods or quantities in which commodities are sold or delivered. Business organizations desiring to sell on a quantity discount basis must therefore maintain cost accounting systems reflecting the lower cost of quantity production and marketing.

**Changing Conditions.** The Robinson-Patman Act allows price differences based on deterioration of perishable goods, obsolescence of seasonable goods, "distress" sales under court process, or sales in good faith on discontinuing business or a given line of merchandise.

**Necessity to Meet Competition.** Price differences based in good faith on the necessity of meeting competition are permitted under the statute. Section 2 (b) of the Clayton Act as amended provides that a seller may justify a lower price by showing that it was made in good faith to meet the equally low price of a competitor. This provision of the Clayton Act has been the cause of considerable dispute in the courts, particularly in connection with the so-called "basing-point system."

*Basing-point system.* Under the basing-point system, producers compete for business in geographical areas where competitors nearer the buyer have the advantage of lower freight rates. In order to compete, such producers quote delivered prices low enough to equal the delivered prices of competitors nearer to the prospective customer. Such competition results in differences in the net proceeds of the producing mill on sales of the same product to different customers located in different places. For this reason, cease and desist orders against the basing-point system have been sustained in a number of important cases, notably the Cement Institute case,[67] notwithstanding the defense that such price discrimination was necessary in good faith to meet competition.

**Cooperative Associations.** The Clayton Act, as amended by the Robinson-Patman Act, does not prevent a cooperative association from returning to its members, producers or consumers, the whole or a part of

---

[67] *Federal Trade Commission v. Cement Institute, et al.,* 333 U.S. 683 (1948).

its net earnings or surplus resulting from its operations, in proportion to their purchases or sales from, to or through the association. However, the Act does not compel producers to recognize retail cooperative associations as if they were wholesalers.[68]

**Indirect Price Discrimination: Forbidden Practices.** Any practice by which it is sought to circumvent the law against price discrimination is specifically forbidden. Among these practices are:

(1) Giving rebates under the guise of commissions paid to a fictitious or pretended broker or middleman;

(2) Making payments or allowances to a customer for alleged services or facilities, such as show window demonstrations or other forms of sales promotion or advertising.

Discounts, payments, allowances or credits are permissible only when they represent services actually rendered on a basis proportionately available to all customers.

*Discrimination in form of "commission."* Rebates in the guise of commissions represent a common form of indirect price discrimination, and are condemned as such. Thus, in *Quality Bakers of America v. Federal Trade Commission*,[69] a corporation acting as agent for its stockholders (who were members of an association of bakers) engaged extensively in the purchase of merchandise for its stockholders. It collected commissions or brokerage fees from the sellers of such merchandise and transmitted them (mostly in a form other than cash) to the stockholders. This practice was held to constitute indirect price discrimination.

*Discrimination in form of advertising benefits.* In *Corn Products Refining Co. v. Federal Trade Commission*,[70] a candy company purchased dextrose from the Corn Products Company, which expended large advertising sums for the benefit of the candy company to promote the use of dextrose in making candy. The court held that this constituted indirect discrimination in favor of one purchaser against another.

*Profit sharing.* In *Pittsburgh Plate Glass Co. v. Jarrett*,[71] a profit-sharing plan had been worked out between a glass company and a dealer, which involved no special services rendered by the dealer. The court held the plan illegal under the Clayton Act provision prohibiting the payment or receipt of commissions in sales transactions except for services rendered.

*Furnishing demonstrators.* Where a concern markets its products through a large number of shops and stores, all of whom are able to buy at the same price but only some of whom are given the benefit of subsi-

---

[68] *Mennen Co. v. Federal Trade Commission,* 288 Fed. 774, certiorari denied 262 U.S. 759 (1923).

[69] 114 F. 2d 393 (1940).

[70] 324 U.S. 726 (1945).

[71] 42 F. Supp. 723 (1942) modified on other grounds, *Jarrett v. Pittsburgh Plate Glass Co.*, 131 F. 2d 674 (1942).

dized demonstrators, the practice will be condemned as a form of price discrimination.[72]

### (3) False Advertising and Other Unfair Practices

**Advertising: A Mirror of Business Standards.** Nothing so plainly reflects the standards of a business as the character of its advertising. This is clearly shown by contrasting the advertising standards of a generation ago with those of today.

A generation ago, false advertising was rampant. Magic cure-alls, get-rich-quick schemes, exaggerated claims and dubious bargains crammed our advertising columns and competed for the savings of the unwary. Regard for truth was scant. Some of these advertisements were downright false; others practiced deception by a play on words; still others by typographical or pictorial suggestion.

EXAMPLES:

*Direct Falsity:*

(1) POWER POTION has been known to cure cancer, even in an advanced stage.

(2) STRETCHO will increase your height by at least two inches.

*Deception by Play on Words:*

(1) "How to double your money immediately: send 25 cents." (Answer on receiving 25 cents: "Convert all your money into paper bills and fold over.")

(2) "How to raise turnips successfully: send 50 cents." (Answer on receiving 50 cents: "Take hold of the top, and *lift*.")

*Deception by Typographical or Pictorial Suggestion:*

(1) Offer of gift of attractive article FREE (in large type), conditioned (in miniature type) on buying something else for a substantial payment.

(2) Picture of woman with luxuriant tresses reaching to her feet, accompanied by suggestion that women using LUXURIO will have equally long hair.

Today, the foregoing types of advertising are on the wane. The trend toward honesty is marked. State and Federal laws have expedited the trend. Newspapers, periodicals and other advertising media have grown increasingly scrupulous with respect to the advertising matter they will accept.

**Legal Restraints and Remedies.** Though a growing segment of business is alive to the evils of false advertising, legal restraints have been necessary to bring offenders into line. The common law has dealt with fraud since the earliest day. Our penal laws against false pretenses have been on the statute books for many years. But not until the last generation or

---

[72] 156 F. 2d 132 (1948), certiorari denied 331 U.S. 806 (1946).

two has it come to be fully recognized that the tort of fraud or the crime of false pretenses should be remedied or punished as fully when committed against the public generally[73] through our advertising columns, as when committed face to face.

Today numerous statutes and ordinances prohibit false or fraudulent advertisements. The remedies vary. A victim who has sustained loss through fraudulent advertising may seek civil damages in the courts. In many cases he may cause the offender to be prosecuted criminally. In cases covered by the Federal statute, he may invoke the intervention of the Federal Trade Commission.

**Wheeler-Lea Act.** The Wheeler-Lea Act of 1938 broadened the jurisdiction of the Federal Trade Commission to cover false advertisements of food, drugs, cosmetics, and devices, together with unfair or deceptive acts and practices. The constitutionality of the Act was challenged in the case of *American Medicinal Products Inc. et al. v. Federal Trade Commission*,[74] involving an advertised product known as Re-Duce-Oids as a remedy for obesity. The advertisement, it was held, failed to reveal "that said preparation should only be used under competent medical supervision; that the unsupervised use of said preparation by persons not skilled in the diagnosis and treatment of thyroid conditions may result in . . . the breaking down of muscular and other tissues, as well as fat tissues, causing irritation of nerve tissue, nervousness, irritability, and increased heart rate, with possible irreparable injury to health even to a normal individual." The court, in sustaining the Act, held that petitioners had no constitutional right to disseminate false advertisements.

**What Constitutes False Advertisement.** The art of persuasion, by word and picture, is of the essence of a successful advertisement. Advertisements today rarely contain blunt falsehoods. Many of them do, however, dwell on the boundary line between truth and fiction, making it difficult, in some cases, to decide whether a statement is merely "persuasive," or false and misleading. In reaching a decision in such cases, the courts have emphasized the following rules:

(1) The test of deception is not whether a statement might mislead the knowing, but the credulous.

(2) Misleading suggestions are as objectionable as direct misstatements.

(3) Deception may consist in a failure to tell the whole truth.

(4) The seller has some latitude in "puffing" his goods, but "puffing" must not overflow into misstatement.

(1) *Test of deception.* The test of deception under the false advertising statute is not whether a knowing person would or should have been deceived, nor, as in a common law damage action for fraud, whether the plaintiff had a right to rely on the misstatement, but rather whether

---

[73] *Jackson v. People,* 126 Ill. 139, 18 N.E. 286 (1888).
[74] 136 F. 2d 426 (1943).

the general public reading the advertisement—foolish, wise or otherwise —is likely to be deceived.

In *Charles of the Ritz Distributing Corporation v. Federal Trade Commission,*[75] petitioner sought to review and set aside a cease and desist order issued by the Federal Trade Commission on a complaint charging the petitioner with violating the law by advertising its cosmetic preparation, "Charles of the Ritz Rejuvenescence Cream," and representing that it would rejuvenate and restore the appearance of youth to the skin, regardless of its condition or the user's age. The evidence showed that external applications of cosmetics cannot overcome skin conditions which result from systemic causes, or from physiological changes occurring with the passage of time; that there was no treatment known to medical science by which changes in the condition of the skin could be prevented, or by which an aged skin could be rejuvenated or restored to a youthful condition. In asking that the order be set aside, the petitioner urged that no straight-thinking person could believe that its cream would actually rejuvenate the skin, hence there could be no deception. But the court pointed out that the statute prohibiting false advertising was not adopted for the protection of experts, but for the general public, "which includes the ignorant, the unthinking and the credulous."

(2) *Deception by suggestion.*[76] Just as one may personally convey a misleading suggestion by the tone of his voice, a deceptive gesture, or the lift of an eyebrow, he may likewise embody deceptive suggestions in an advertisement by the size or arrangement of type, with or without pictorial illustration.

In *Parker Pen Co. v. Federal Trade Commission,*[77] an advertisement stated, in sizable type, distinct coloration, and adjacent to the picture of a large blue diamond, that the "blue diamond" fountain pen was guaranteed for life. Some distance away, and in smaller type next to a small blue diamond, the advertisement stated that the guaranty was conditioned on payment of a 35-cent service charge. The court held that such advertisement was deceptive; that the limitation on the guaranty should appear on the advertisement close to the words "guaranteed for life," and in the same size print.

(3) *Failing to tell the whole truth.* It is notorious that critics may unite in condemning a play, yet experts in theatrical advertising, by adroit omissions, may so quote the criticisms as to convey the impression of critical approval. Where such advertisements relate to matters within the jurisdiction of the Federal Trade Commission, they may invite a cease and desist order.

---

[75] 143 F. 2d 676 (1944).
[76] See "Deceptive practices," page 605.
[77] 159 F. 2d 509 (1946).

In *P. Lorillard Co. v. Federal Trade Commission*,[78] a tobacco company advertised that its cigarettes and the smoke from them contained less tars and resins, and were less irritating to the throat than six other leading brands of cigarettes. In support of this claim, the advertisement referred to an article in the *Reader's Digest*, stating: "Reader's Digest assigned a scientific testing laboratory to find out about cigarettes. They tested seven leading cigarettes and Reader's Digest published the results. The cigarette whose smoke was lowest in nicotine was Old Gold. The cigarette with the least throat-irritating tars and resins was Old Gold. On both these major counts Old Gold was best among all seven cigarettes tested." Actually, said the court, in sustaining the Federal Trade Commission's order, the Reader's Digest article went on to point out that the laboratory's findings showed that whatever difference there might be between different cigarettes as to nicotine, tar and resin content "was so small as to be entirely insignificant and utterly without meaning so far as effect upon the smoker is concerned."

(4) *When "puffing" overflows into misstatement.* The law allows an advertiser a certain amount of poetic license in praising his product, but the basic distinction between fact and opinion (page 47) must be observed. Thus in *Gulf Oil Corporation v. Federal Trade Commission*,[79] the advertiser represented that Gulf Livestock Spray afforded complete protection to livestock from all insects and that its use would cause milk production to increase and cows to be healthier. The Federal Trade Commission issued an order forbidding the use of such statements in advertising this insecticide. The Gulf Oil Corporation petitioned the court for a review of this order, arguing that the benefits set forth in the advertisements beyond those actually derived from use of the spray were merely trader's talk or "puffing," hence excusable. The court, however, in refusing to vacate the Commission's order, pointed out that "While a seller has some latitude in 'puffing' his goods, he is not authorized to misrepresent them or to assign to them benefits or virtues they do not possess."

**Miscellaneous Forms of Misrepresentation.** The Federal Trade Commission has dealt with a wide variety of merchandising by misrepresentation through salesmen, newspaper or periodical advertising, circulars, letterheads, show windows or otherwise. A mere list of these would take up several pages. Characteristic of this type of misrepresentation condemned as unfair business practices are the following:

That the proceeds of certain sales would be used for charitable purposes, where there was no intention to do so.
That one's business was "bonded," when it was not.
That a concern of little financial worth was a "Million Dollar Firm."

[78] 186 F. 2d 52 (1950).
[79] 150 F. 2d 106 (1945).

That a new concern was an "old established firm," or a "pioneer in the business."

That the National Association of Delta Theta Chi was a sorority, when actually it was a business concern interested in selling certain books.

That a local concern, as shown by its letterhead, had offices in other cities and countries, such offices being fictitious.

That merchandise was being sold at "factory price," or "below cost," which was contrary to fact.

That a battery solution would "charge old batteries, double the life of any battery, preserve the plates, prevent overcharging or crystallization, would not freeze, and would counteract the corrosive elements . . ."

That various motor attachments, designated as "Vaporizer and Decarbonizer," "Syncro Ignition System," "Circuit Master," "Gas-Miser," "Supercharger," "Hot Spark Transformer," and so forth, would "save gas and oil," "prevent overheating," "clean spark plugs," "remove carbon," "produce smoothness of operation," and so forth.

**Deceptive Practices.** Hardly distinguishable from, but less direct than out-and-out misrepresentation are the devices grouped under the heading "Deceptive Practices" and condemned by the Federal Trade Commission. The essence of these practices is deception, but the method is suggestion rather than representation. (See "Deception by suggestion," page 603.) Examples are as follows:[80]

Marketing a vitamin product under a name containing the word "Guild," thereby suggesting a non-profit organization.

Using the Red Cross name and emblem in selling paper towels, suggesting that such towels are endorsed by the American Red Cross.

Labeling whiskies, "Mac Nab Distilleries Limited," suggesting a Scottish distilling company, when no such company existed.

Using the testimonials of prominent persons in the sale of products, suggesting voluntary approval, without disclosing that the testimonials had been paid for.

**Disparagement.** We shall deal later with disparagement as a tort (pages 814 to 815). In addition to the usual remedy for damages by court action, the Federal Trade Commission has jurisdiction over this tort as an unfair practice in interstate commerce, and has issued many cease and desist orders against this form of unfair competition. Examples are the following:

Statement that a competitive product infringed a valid patent.

Statement that a competitor's hydrogen peroxide contained lime, was dangerous for human use, and was only a weak solution of bleaching powder.

Statement that a competitor's dog food consisted largely of horsemeat.

Statement that other face powders contained gritty substances that would impair beauty and cause users to look older.

Statement that a competitor's decorated china bathroom fixtures would crack with changes of temperature.

Statement that a competitor's electric light bulbs gave 30 per cent less light.

---

[80] Commerce Clearing House, Trade Regulation Service, Vol. 2.

**Coercive and Oppressive Practices.** In Chapter 20, we consider such business torts as wrongful interference with contract, malicious injury to business through competition inspired by malice rather than the desire for gain, and threats which amount to mental harassment and annoyance. The Federal Trade Commission has issued numerous cease and desist orders against similar practices, such as collection letters threatening suit without intending in good faith to sue; pushing the circulation of a trade or other publication by veiled suggestions that unfavorable editorial or other comment might follow on failure to subscribe; acquiring a competitor's trade secrets by unfair means, such as espionage, bribery, and so forth; and enticing employees away from competitors.

**Merchandising by Gambling: Lotteries and Prizes.** Most states prohibit the practice of merchandising by gambling devices such as lotteries, "bingo" games and gifts or prizes based solely on chance rather than as an award for knowledge, ability or skill. However, it is notorious that such laws are not rigidly enforced in many communities, particularly where such gambling devices are employed in aid of some charitable enterprise.

In the field of interstate commerce, the Federal Trade Commission not only has the power to eradicate merchandising by gambling, but it may also prohibit the distribution of any device designed to aid and encourage such merchandising.

*Lucky centers, pushcards and punchboards.* The most common offenders in the latter category have been candies, although chewing gum has been sold by awarding prizes to the "lucky" purchaser of a package containing the right interior color, and hosiery sales have been furthered by "punchboard." In the distribution of candy, various lottery methods have been adopted, all condemned by the Federal Trade Commission.

*"Club plans."* A favorite method of merchandising has been by a so-called "club plan," in which a number of persons pay more or less for a given article of merchandise, the amount paid being determined by lot. The Federal Trade Commission has condemned this type of merchandising, and the court has sustained the Commission.[81]

## Questions

1. "Unfair competition and restraint of trade are necessarily linked together." Is this statement true, false, or partly true and partly false? Explain.

2. "Unfair competition is based on fraud." Is this statement true, false, or partly true and partly false? Explain.

3. Distinguish between the Clayton Act and the Federal Trade Commission Act in respect to what must be shown to establish that a violation has occurred.

4. What are the three forms of unfair competition and unfair trade practices most frequently dealt with by the courts?

---

[81] *Savoy Manufacturing Co. v. Federal Trade Commission*, 152 F. 2d 65 (1945).

5. Give an example of unfair competition in each of the following situations: (a) Imitating a trade name; (b) Using one's own name unfairly; (c) Using a geographical name unfairly; (d) Using a trade wrapper, package or container unfairly.

6. "Price cutting necessarily entails price discrimination, and is unlawful." Is this statement true, false, or partly true and partly false? Explain.

7. Name and explain six situations in which price differences are permissible under the Robinson-Patman Act.

8. What is the "basing-point" system? Is it presently allowable under current court decisions? What justification has been urged in support of the system?

9. Name two practices by which producers and dealers have sought to circumvent the law against price discrimination.

10. What was the purpose of the Wheeler-Lea Act?

11. What is the legal test of deception under current false advertising statutes?

12. Give an illustration of each of the following types of advertising deception forbidden by law: (a) deception by suggestion, (2) failing to tell the whole truth, and (3) "puffing" which overflows into misstatement.

13. Give an illustration of each of the following unfair trade practices: (a) disparagement, (b) coercive and oppressive practices, and (c) merchandising by gambling.

## Problems

1. The manufacturer of "Dyanshine," a shoe polish, sued to enjoin as unfair competition the use of the words "Dye and Shine" applied to a competitor's shoe polish. The competitor challenged the validity of the plaintiff's trade-mark, arguing that it was merely a corruption of the words "dye and shine," hence descriptive of the product and not a valid trade-mark. How did the court decide?

2. Sixty years ago, John P. Smith started a soap business. His soap was known as Smith Soap, was widely advertised at great expense to the owner, and was identified in the public mind with the owner's product. Years later, George Q. Smith, a stranger to John P. Smith, also started a soap business, and referred to his product as Smith Soap. John P. Smith now sues George Q. Smith for an injunction. How will the court decide, and why?

3. A candy company puts out a hard candy of a given shape, wrapped in paper colored a distinctive shade of blue and studded with silver stars. The candy, called "Candy From Heaven," becomes popularly identified not only by name, but by the particular paper in which it is wrapped. Another candy company puts out a similarly shaped hard candy called "Sweets From Heaven," wrapped in a similarly colored and silver-starred paper. The first candy company sues the second candy company for an injunction. How will the court decide, and why?

4. A cooperative association organized to purchase books in quantity and resell them on a cooperative basis to its members, is prosecuted for price discrimination under the Robinson-Patman Act on the ground that, in returning a substantial part of its net earnings and surplus to its members by way of cheaper prices for books purchased, it was guilty of price discrimination in respect to other purchasers who were not members of the association. Will the prosecution succeed? Explain.

5. A producer of cosmetics sold its merchandise to a specially selected list

of department stores, women's specialty shops and drug stores. It furnished wholly or partly subsidized demonstrators to about ten per cent of its customers, thereby giving them a substantial selling advantage over its other customers in the same community. The Federal Trade Commission issued a cease and desist order against the concern, and the latter appealed. What was the decision of the court?

6. A nationwide chain of stores sells groceries to its customers at a substantial reduction compared to the prices of individually owned grocery stores. The latter causes a prosecution against the chain stores to be instituted under the Robinson-Patman Act. The chain store organization is able to show, by its books, that its prices are related to substantial differences in its cost of manufacture, sale and delivery, based on different methods and quantities in which its merchandise is sold and delivered. How will the court decide, and why?

7. The Worldwide Woolen Corporation discontinues handling a given line of woolen blankets which it advertises to the public at a discount of 25 per cent off the price for a similar grade of blankets sold on the regular market. The question arises whether, in so doing, the company risks prosecution under the Robinson-Patman Act.

8. Superior Building Blocks, Inc., in order to compete successfully with similar concerns in different parts of the country widely removed from its main factory on the Atlantic Seaboard, sells its products in the Midwestern and Pacific Coast markets at prices competitive with those of local producers in such markets. These prices are less than those at which the company is selling its product on the Atlantic Seaboard, notwithstanding lower freight rates in the latter market. The company is prosecuted for price discrimination and its defense is that its Midwestern and Pacific Coast prices were necessary to meet competition. How would the court decide, and why?

9. A newspaper prints an advertisement by The Fastbuck Corporation reading: "How to double your money instantly. Send $1.00." An investigation discloses that many dollars are thereby sent to this advertiser, with the following response to all inquiries: "Convert all your money into paper bills and fold over." Do victims of this type of advertising have any recourse, and if so, what?

10. A farm journal prints an advertisement, "How to raise turnips successfully: send 50 cents." The advertiser, on receiving paid responses, advises: "Take hold of the top, and lift." In a prosecution for false advertising, the defense is that the advice given is literally correct. Will the defense succeed?

11. A merchant advertises one of its specialties in placards posted on trains, buses and trolley lines. The placards display an offer headed, in large, boldface type: "FREE—NO CHARGE." At the foot of the advertisement, in minuscule type, the advertisement concludes: "This offer, as stated, is free, except for a small shipping charge of 49 cents." Should a complaint be filed with the Federal Trade Commission, will it receive official attention?

12. A manufacturer advertises a Television Rectifier which "completely does away with your repair bills." The question arises whether the manufacturer, in so doing, incurs any liability. What would you say?

13. The salesmen for Happy Canine Eating, Inc., in selling their product, emphasize the danger "of using dog food such as that put out by the XYZ Dog Food Company, which is made up mostly of decayed animal carcasses." Assuming that the latter statement is untrue, has the XYZ Dog Food Company any remedy under the circumstances?

14. The Business Man's Friend, a new monthly periodical, embarks on an

advertising campaign, during the course of which it writes to many merchants: "We are in a position to write up your business and products, on a friendly basis or otherwise, depending on our judgment of the facts. You may win our warm friendship by a full-page ad." Complaint is made to the Federal Trade Commission. Will the latter act on the complaint?

## COURT CASES FOR REVIEW

### How Did the Court Decide, and Why?

1. In 1933, during a period of economic crisis marked by depression and deflation, the State of New York passed a law fixing *minimum* milk prices to be paid to farmers, wholesalers and retailers, and *minimum* prices to be charged to consumers (nine cents a quart). A small neighborhood grocer, to attract customers, gave away a loaf of bread with two quarts of milk at nine cents a quart. The grocer was jailed for violating the statute. His arrest and conviction were appealed to the Supreme Court on the ground that the statute was an unconstitutional interference with personal liberty. *Nebbia v. New York*, 219 U.S. 502.

2. A small clothing manufacturer sold his products to a clothing contractor conducting business in the same state. The latter, however, shipped the products to customers, some of whom were outside the state. The clothing manufacturer was prosecuted by the National Labor Relations Board for allegedly unfair labor practices. The manufacturer challenged the jurisdiction of the Board on the ground that he did no business outside the state. *National Labor Relations Board v. Fainblatt*, 306 U.S. 601.

3. An Ohio farmer planted twenty-three acres of wheat. This was twelve acres more than his allotment under the Agricultural Adjustment Act. Defendant protested a Federal penalty, on the ground that most of the wheat raised was used locally, not marketed, hence interstate commerce was not involved. *Wickard v. Filburn*, 317 U.S. 111.

4. In a dispute involving wages and hours of porters, elevator operators, and night watchmen in a New York City loft building, the owner challenged the jurisdiction of the Federal Administrator under the Wages and Hour Law. The Wages and Hour Administrator contended that he had jurisdiction because some of the tenants in the building were engaged in interstate commerce and this meant that the building employees were engaged in occupations "necessary to the production" of goods for commerce. *Kirschbaum v. Walling*, 316 U.S. 517.

5. A sugar-beet grower sued for treble damages under the Sherman Act on the following ground: Due to the perishability of his product his only outlet was to three refiners in his area and these three had entered into a contract to pay a uniform price for beets. The refiners contended that they had merely entered into an agreement to pay a price based on the net return per hundred pounds realized by them on their sugar, depending on the sugar content of the individual growers' beet. *Mandeville Island Farms v. American Crystal Sugar Co.*, 334 U.S. 219.

6. An arrangement was made between a distributor of pink-tinted lenses and retail dealers licensed by the distributor, whereby the dealers were bound to sell at locally prevailing prices. The distributor contended that his patent on the license gave him the right to make the arrangement in question. *United States v. Baush & Lomb*, 321 U.S. 707.

7. A number of competing dealers in building material entered into an understanding whereby one of them, which manufactured and sold material

called "hardboard," for which it held a patent, undertook to constitute the others its *del credere* agents for the sale of that product through their respective sales organizations, at prices fixed by the patent owner. *United States v. Masonite Corp., et al.*, 316 U.S. 265.

8. Three oil companies owned patents for "cracking" processes by which the yield of gasoline from crude oil was greatly increased. Another corporation owned a similar patent. All the companies joined in an agreement for the exchange of patent rights and the division of royalties. The government sought an injunction on the ground that the exchange of licenses enabled the corporations to maintain existing royalties in restraint of trade. *Standard Oil Company (Indiana) v. U.S.*, 283 U.S. 163.

9. The Line Material Company and the Southern State Equipment Corporation owned interfering patent applications. Dominant claims were awarded to the Southern State Corporation, and subservient claims to the Line Material Company, making it impossible for any manufacturer to use both patents when later issued, without some form of cross-licensing arrangement. The device disclosed in the subservient patent proved to be the more commercially desirable. Cross-licenses were exchanged. The Line Material Company was given the right by the Southern State Corporation to grant sub-licenses to other manufacturers, these to contain price restrictions in respect to the Southern State patent. The government sought an injunction under the Sherman Act. *United States v. Line Material Company*, 333 U.S. 287.

10. The government brought suit to dissolve the Aluminum Company as a monopoly. The company urged in defense that it had sought no monopoly; that it did not seek, but could not avoid control of the market; that by embracing every opportunity for progress, and by virtue of its experience, trade connections and competent personnel, it had been geared into a great organization, but that it had never used its dominant position to exclude competitors or extract more than a fair profit from consumers. *United States v. Aluminum Co. of America*, 148 F. 2d 416.

11. Suit was brought under the Sherman Act to dissolve a trade association formed by numerous manufacturers of hard-wood flooring. The activities complained of were as follows: (a) Computation, and distribution to members, of information as to the average cost of their products; (b) Compilation, and distribution to members, of booklets for quick reference showing freight rates from basing points to numerous other points; (c) Periodical gathering from and redistribution to members, of information in summarized form on the kind and quantities of flooring sold, dates of sales, prices received, average freight rates, commissions paid, amount and kinds of stock on hand, unfilled orders, monthly production, new orders booked, and similar trade data; (d) Meetings and discussions, but not on fixing prices. *Maple Flooring Manufacturing Association v. U.S.*, 268 U.S. 563.

12. Several brewing companies were charged with conspiracy in restraint of trade, in having agreed not to solicit patronage from or sell draft beer to exclusive customers of any of the other companies in the agreement, and to bind their distributors to such policy. *Jos. Schlitz Brewing Co. v. Johnson*, 123 F. 2d 1016.

13. Seagram refused to sell its product to Kiefer-Stewart, an Indiana wholesaler, because Kiefer-Stewart refused to abide by Seagram's maximum resale prices. Calvert, another manufacturer, was at first willing to sell to Kiefer-Stewart without any fixed sales price agreement, but later decided to go along with Seagram. Seagram and Calvert then sold to other Indiana wholesalers, but

not to Kiefer-Stewart. The company sued for treble damages under the Sherman Act. *Kiefer-Stewart Company v. Joseph E. Seagram & Sons, Inc., et al.,* 340 U.S. 211.

14. The Eastman Kodak Company had established itself as a leading manufacturer of photographic equipment and film. By 1920 it manufactured and sold 94 per cent of the raw film used in motion picture laboratories. In 1921, however, competition from importers of foreign film reduced its sales to 81 per cent. The Eastman Company thereupon acquired three laboratories, and began manufacturing prints itself. The competing importers of foreign film finally agreed to use only American-made film, on condition that the Eastman Company would cease manufacturing prints. The Federal Trade Commission issued a cease and desist order against the agreement, requiring the Eastman Company to divest itself of the laboratories. The Eastman Company appealed. *Federal Trade Commission v. Eastman Kodak Co.,* 274 U.S. 619.

15. Complainant, engaged in the public taxicab business in Providence, R.I., had established a general reputation for safe and satisfactory service. To distinguish its cabs from others, it used the name "Yellow Cab Co." and dressed the cabs in a distinctive color combination. The lower and larger part of the cab body was painted yellow, and the upper part of the body, chassis, hood and fenders were painted black. The complaint alleged that Anastasi, the respondent, was operating public taxicabs in Providence with a color scheme and dress so closely resembling complainant's as to deceive complainant's patrons and the public, thereby reaping the benefit of complainant's reputation and business. The respondent contended that his colors were not yellow and black, but orange and brown. The trial justice, after an inspection and comparison, found that the respondent's "orange" looked very much like yellow, and his "brown" looked quite black. He therefore granted an injunction. *Yellow Cab Co. v. Anastasi,* 46 R.I. 49, 124 A. 735.

16. A department store, taking advantage of its superior economic power to continue or withhold substantial patronage, compelled a manufacturer to stop selling to the purchaser's competitor (to whom the manufacturer had been selling for years). The arrangement was confirmed by agreement. The plaintiff sued for an injunction. *Alexander's Department Stores v. Ohrbach's Inc.,* 266 App. Div. 535, appeal dism. 291 N.Y. 707, 52 N.E. 2d 595.

17. Standard Oil Company of California entered into contracts with 6,000 independent dealers, binding each of them to purchase his petroleum products and automobile accessories from Standard alone. The government attacked Standard's distribution system as a violation of the Sherman and Clayton Acts, in that these contracts "substantially" lessened competition. The evidence showed that Standard's combined sales in 1946 were 23 per cent of the total taxable gallonage sold in seven western states; that Standard's six leading competitors sold another 42.5 per cent of the total taxable gallonage in the area; and that Standard's exclusive dealer contract covered 16 per cent of the retail gasoline stations in the seven states. *Standard Oil Company of California v. U.S.,* 337 U.S. 293.

18. International Business Machines Corp., dominating the market in tabulating machines, leased them on condition that the lease should terminate in case any tabulating cards other than those manufactured by the lessor were used in the leased machines. The government attacked this arrangement as monopolistic. *International Business Machines Corp. v. United States,* 298 U.S. 131.

19. Sinclair Refining Co. limited the use of its leased pumps to its own

gasoline. The Federal Trade Commission issued a cease and desist order, and the Sinclair Company appealed. *Federal Trade Commission v. Sinclair Refining Co.*, 261 U.S. 463.

20. United Shoe Machinery Co., controlling 95 per cent of the shoe machinery production of the country, leased its machines subject to a condition that the lessee had to buy all his sewing and fastening material from the lessor, and that all spare parts likewise had to be obtained from the lessor. The Federal Trade Commission issued a cease and desist order on the ground that the arrangement tended toward a substantial lessening of competition. *United States v. United Shoe Machinery Co.*, 264 Fed. 188, affirmed 258 U.S. 451.

21. International Salt Co., Inc. was engaged in the business of leasing patented salt-dispensing machines. The lease form contained a clause requiring the lessee to purchase from the lessor all unpatented salt used in such machines. The lessor contended that the clause was necessary to minimize the cost of maintenance and assure satisfactory operation; that the sodium chloride content of salt varied; that the patented machines functioned best on salt of average sodium chloride content; and that since the lessor was obligated to maintain and repair the machines, it had to make sure that the best salt was used. The government attacked this arrangement as monopolistic. *International Salt Co., Inc. v. U.S.*, 332 U.S. 392.

22. The manufacturer of Lucky Strike cigarettes sold them in Porto Rico at a lower price than in continental United States. This practice was attacked as discriminatory. *Porto Rican American Tobacco v. American Tobacco Co.*, 30 F. 2d 234.

23. The government brought suit against a group of sugar refiners because of an agreement entered into among them which set up a schedule of uniform and arbitrary differentials for purchases of raw cane sugar, based on the quality of raw sugar as indicated by polarization tests. *United States v. Sugar Institute*, 15 F. Supp. 817, modified on other grounds, *Sugar Institute v. United States*, 297 U.S. 553.

24. The Federal Trade Commission instituted proceedings against a group of cement producers, banded together as the Cement Institute, charging that the cement industry had adopted a basing-point delivered price system which resulted in identical prices for cement at any given point in the United States regardless of distance from the cement mill, and that this was done with a view to destroying competition. The cement people urged that the pricing system was designed in good faith to meet competition, hence allowable under the Robinson-Patman Act. The Commission, however, issued a cease and desist order on testimony that there were differences in net returns from different sales by a particular producer, hence that such price differentials were not designed in good faith to meet individual competitive conditions. The Cement Institute appealed. *Federal Trade Commission v. Cement Institute et al.*, 333 U.S. 683.

25. A manufacturer sold to both wholesalers and retailers. It allowed a discount to wholesalers which it denied to retailers. It classified as retailers, mutual or cooperative corporations organized and owned by retailers, and refused to sell to such organizations at wholesale prices. The Federal Trade Commission issued a cease and desist order, and the manufacturer appealed. *Mennen Co. v. Federal Trade Commission*, 288 Fed. 774, cert. denied 262 U.S. 759.

26. General Motors Corporation issued an advertisement dealing with an installment sales "six per cent" finance plan. Actually, as things worked out, the charge exceeded the straight six per cent simple interest charge. The Fed-

eral Trade Commission issued a cease and desist order and General Motors Corporation appealed. *General Motors Corp. v. Federal Trade Commission,* 114 F. 2d 33, cert. denied 312 U.S. 682.

27. A manufacturer offered prizes in connection with the sale of his candy to dealers. The candy was packed and assembled for resale to consumers, the prizes to be awarded by lottery. Dealers were supplied with display cards describing the proposed lottery method. The Federal Trade Commission issued a cease and desist order against this method of merchandising, and the manufacturer appealed. (*Federal Trade Commission v. R. F. Keppel & Bro., Inc.,* 291 U.S. 304.)

28. Respondents issued a catalog to customers, together with membership cards bearing numbers from 1 to 26 running around the border of each card. The customers distributed these cards to a given number of "members," who agreed to pay 25 cents each week for 26 weeks or until they drew a prize—a $6.50 article listed in the catalog—drawn by lot each week. Those who drew a prize the first week paid only 25 cents. Those who won the second week had paid 50 cents, and those who drew a prize the 26th week had paid the full list price by the time they drew their "prize." The Federal Trade Commission issued a cease and desist order and respondent appealed. (*Savoy Manufacturing Co. v. Federal Trade Commission,* 152 F. 2d 65.)

# 14

# Real Property

**Scope of This Chapter.** In this chapter we consider the nature of property generally; the different kinds of property; land and things connected with it, such as trees, crops, buildings and fixtures; the different kinds of interests or "estates" one may have in real property; the rights or "easements" one may have in the lands of another; and, finally, how persons may acquire and dispose of interests in real property.

## PART 1. PROPERTY IN GENERAL: NATURE AND CLASSIFICATION

**Nature of Property.** Property is a legal relationship of persons to things, which gives persons control over things. It has been broadly defined as "any valuable right or interest protected by law." It is a "natural" or "absolute" right (page 22) guaranteed by the Constitution of the United States (page 23). A country may be rich in resources, but if it abolishes the right of ownership, property as a legal institution ceases to exist.

**Real v. Personal Property.** All property is either real or personal. Real property is anything fixed, permanent and immovable, such as land and things permanently annexed to land. All other property is personal. Although the distinction seems obvious, there are many borderline situations where the distinction is not always so clearly marked. These we shall presently consider.

**Tangible v. Intangible Real Property.** In the field of real property, tangibles embrace lands and things permanently annexed to lands. Such interests are sometimes said to be *corporeal*. Intangible rights in real property, also called *incorporeal* rights, are those not physically perceptible, but recognized to exist in law, such as an easement (page 617).

**Land and Its Contents.** All land, being permanent, constitutes real property. This includes not only surface, but contents, such as soil, clay, rock, minerals, and so on. But if such contents are removed from the land, their permanence is destroyed and they become personal property.

**Natural Products.** Natural products of the soil, while permanently annexed to it, constitute real property; severed, personal. If trees are sold standing, the transaction is a sale of real property; if cut, they are personal. Crops while attached to the soil are real property; if severed, they are personal.

**Buildings.** Buildings remain real property so long as they are annexed to the land with intent of permanence. They cease to be real property upon being removed; as, for example, where a building is sold to a wrecking concern which is to remove it from the land. A building erected upon the land of another by the latter's license and consent is regarded as personalty belonging to the person who erected it and does not pass to a purchaser of the land unless he buys *without notice* of the facts as to separate ownership.

**Fixtures.** Fixtures are chattels affixed to realty. They are *real* or *personal*, depending, respectively, upon whether they are affixed with or without the intent of permanence. Such intent may be expressed by the parties or implied from the character of the annexation. The subject of fixtures is more fully discussed in connection with the rights of Landlord and Tenant (pages 637 to 640).

**Estates Defined and Classified.** The word "estate," broadly, means everything a person owns. As applied to real property, it means the interest one has in lands. Estates may be classified as follows:

(a) *As to their duration:* freehold and less than freehold.

(b) *As to present or future possession:* present and future estates.

(c) *As to their absolute or qualified nature:* absolute and conditional estates.

(d) *As to number and connection of owners:* joint estates, estates in common and estates by the severalty.

(e) *As to courts of jurisdiction:* legal and equitable (trust) estates.

**Freehold Estates: (Fee and Life Estates).** A freehold estate is a major interest in lands, of indefinite duration. The duration may be perpetual, running on indefinitely into the future, and automatically subject to inheritance if not otherwise disposed of by the owner (as by deed or will). Hence such an estate is called a *freehold estate of inheritance*, the most common form of which is an *estate in fee*. A freehold estate may also be one of *less than inheritance*, its duration being measured by someone's life. Hence it is known as a *life estate*.

*Estate in fee.* An estate in fee, or "fee simple," being of unlimited duration, is the largest estate or ownership in real property. It means ownership forever. It is the estate usually granted by deed, conveying title to the grantee "and his heirs forever."

*Life estates* may be created by *act of the parties*, as by deed or will; or by *operation of law*, as in the case of *dower* and *curtesy* (page 621). A life tenant may take from the land wood and timber necessary for fuel, current construction and repairs. This right is known as *estovers;* that is, the owner of a life estate ("life tenant") has the current use of the land. He is therefore responsible for its current maintenance, including taxes and carrying charges. A life tenant must not commit *waste*, which consists of impairment in the permanent value of premises, either by positive act ("active waste") or neglect ("passive waste").

**Less than Freehold Interests: Chattels Real.** Less than freehold estates include (a) estates for years, (b) estates at will, (c) estates by sufferance and (d) statutory tenancies. (See pages 631 to 632.) Such estates represent *personal property interests* in connection with lands, or *chattels real*, as distinguished from freehold estates, which are *real property* interests.

**Present and Future Estates.** A present estate is one wherein the owner has present use or possession of the property. A future estate is one wherein possession is deferred. Thus, when the owner of a house and lot leases it to a tenant, the landlord has a future estate and the tenant a present estate. Future estates may be either in *reversion* or *remainder*.

**Reversion.** A reversion is the balance of a fee which goes back or "reverts" to a grantor after the lapse of a particular precedent estate granted by him.

EXAMPLE: *X* owns an estate in fee, and grants to *A* a life estate. Nothing further being said, the estate in fee would revert to *X* upon the death of *A*, the owner of the life estate. If *X* is dead at the time of *A*'s death, the estate would revert to *X*'s heirs. The estate so reverting would be referred to as a *reversion*. It is a future estate because its enjoyment must await the expiration of the particular precedent estate.

**Remainder.** A remainder is the balance of a larger estate, which goes to some person other than the grantor, after a particular precedent estate expires.

EXAMPLE: *X*, the owner of the fee, grants a life estate to *A*, and the remainder in fee to *B*. *A* has a present estate, namely, the right to present possession for his life; and *B* has the balance in fee in the future, after *A* dies. Such an estate is called a *remainder* rather than a reversion, because it does not revert or *go back* to the grantor, but is the balance or remainder which *goes on* to some person other than the grantor.

**Particular estate.** The estate which precedes a reversion or remainder is referred to as the *particular* estate. In both the above examples, the life estate to *A* is the particular or "precedent" estate.

**Absolute and Conditional Estates.** If an estate is free from any conditions, it is called an *absolute* or *unconditional* estate. Estates subject to conditions or restrictions are *conditional* or *qualified* estates.

**Covenants running with the land** are conditions limiting an estate. They bind not only the original grantee who took subject to such conditions, but also all other subsequent grantees or lessees. Such covenants cannot be "shaken off the land" by deed, will, assignment or transfer, because they are part and parcel of the estate to which they attach.

**Joint Estates.** If two or more persons acquire the same estate at one and the same time, by one and the same title or source of ownership, each having the same degree of interest as the others, and each having the same right of possession as the others, it is called a joint estate. In such a case, if one of the owners ("joint tenants") dies, his interest automatically passes to the others by *survivorship,* which is the characteristic feature of joint estates.

*Tenancy by the entirety.* If husband and wife are joint tenants, the estate is known as a tenancy by the entirety.

*Estates in common.* An estate or tenancy in common is one held by two or more persons, each having an undivided interest which is not subject to survivorship. Thus, each "tenant in common" may sell his interest, or dispose of it by will, to an outside party. If he dies without having disposed of his interest by deed or will, his heirs and not the other "tenants in common" acquire his undivided interest. Under the common law, and prior to the adoption of statutes modeled on the Uniform Partnership Act, real property owned by a partnership was generally held by the partners as tenants in common.

*Estates by the severalty.* When a person owns an interest in property by himself, such interest is known as an estate (or tenancy) by the severalty. Most property is thus held.

**Legal and Equitable (Trust) Estates.** The usual estate one has in property is known as a *legal estate* or *estate at law.* Normally, an owner's interest in property is recognized in an ordinary common law court. However, when one person holds title in real property *for the benefit of another,* the latter's interest is recognized only in a court of equity. Such an estate is therefore referred to as an *equitable,* or *trust* estate. Trust estates are more fully considered in Chapter 19.

**Easement; Distinguished from License.** An easement is a right which one has in the lands of another, either for his own convenience, or for the benefit of his own land. An easement is to be distinguished from a *license* in that the former is a definite interest in lands, whereas the latter is a mere permission or privilege not attaching to the land itself. Since an easement is an interest in lands, it must be created by a writing (pages 86-87), whereas a license may be granted by oral permission.

EXAMPLES OF EASEMENTS:
(1) Rights of way;
(2) the right to use water (in streams, springs, wells, cisterns, and so on);
(3) rights in highways, party walls, light and air.

EXAMPLES OF LICENSES:
(1) Permission to a fruit vendor to put up his stand and sell his wares on the property of another;
(2) the implied license of a contractor engaged to erect a house, or of a laborer to work on the premises, to enter upon the lands in question for such purposes.

*Easements classified.* Easements may be either *in gross* or *appurtenant.* They may also be *public* and *private.*

*Easements in gross.* An easement in gross is one which exists for a person's own convenience and not in conjunction with any lands owned by him. The right of a person to use a public thoroughfare is an easement in gross.

*Appurtenant easements: servient and dominant estates.* An appurtenant easement is one which a person enjoys in conjunction with his own land. The land to which the easement is subject, and which therefore *serves* the land of the person who has the easement, is known as the *servient* estate. The land which is thus served by the easement is known as the *dominant* estate.

EXAMPLES:

(1) Mann sells part of his lands to Nagle, giving Nagle a right of way across his remaining property. Nagle has an *appurtenant* easement. The *dominant* estate is in Nagle, the *servient* estate in Mann.

(2) Lord owns a forty-story building adjoining a six-story building owned by Cushing. Lord acquires from Cushing an easement in light and air over Cushing's building for the benefit of Lord's building. Lord has an *appurtenant* easement. The *dominant* estate is in Lord, the *servient* estate in Cushing.

*Public easements.* Public easements are those enjoyed by the public at large, such as streets and public highways generally. The public has an easement of navigation and fishing in all tidal waters, such as oceans, arms of the sea and navigable rivers with a tide; the adjoining owners own up to the ordinary high water mark. Shore rights are known as *riparian rights.*

*Private easements.* Private easements are those enjoyed by individuals as such, either *in gross,* or as *appurtenant* to lands.

**Creation of easements.** Easements may arise by (a) grant or reservation, (b) natural right, (c) necessity, or (d) prescription.

EXAMPLES:

*Easement by grant: A* gives or sells *B,* by deed or other instrument, a right to cross *A's* land.

*Easement by reservation: A* conveys a part of his land to *B,* and reserves the right to cross the part conveyed in order to get to the highway.

*Easement by natural right: A* and *B* are adjoining owners. Each has an easement by natural right to have his own land supported by the land of the other; for instance, to prevent undermining thereof by unreasonable excavation without taking precaution to shore up the adjoining land, to build a retaining wall, or otherwise to protect the adjoining property against collapse.

*Easement by necessity:* The owner of land along a highway conveys an inside parcel with no access to the highway. The law in such case creates an easement by necessity, giving the grantee a right to cross the grantor's land in order to get to the highway.

*Easement by prescription:* (1) For fifteen consecutive years (the period varies in the different states (see page 621), members of the public indiscriminately cross *A's* lot, openly, "adversely" (without his permission), and notoriously. At the end of the period there arises a public right of way by prescription across *A's* lot.

(2) If *B* alone similarly crossed *A*'s lot, and for the same period, a private easement would arise in favor of *B* alone.

*Extinguishment of easements.* An easement may be lost or extinguished in the following ways: (a) by release; (b) by abandonment of the easement; (c) by adverse obstruction of the easement, as where the servient owner obstructs the easement openly and adversely, canceling it in the same way that it may be created, that is, by adverse use; (d) by union of the dominant and servient estates, as where the owner of the dominant parcel acquires the other parcel, or vice versa, and becomes the owner of both parcels.

## Questions

1. How may property be defined?
2. Distinguish between real and personal property.
3. What is the difference between tangible and intangible real property?
4. "Natural products of the soil constitute real property." Is this statemen true, false, or partly true and partly false?
5. Name five ways in which "estates" as applied to real property may be classified, and the classifications of each.
6. How does an easement differ from a license?
7. Name four different classifications of easements.
8. Name five ways in which an easement may be created, and four in which it may be extinguished.

## Problems

1. Chase owns a two-story frame building. He receives a substantial offer for the building site exclusive of the building. He therefore moves the building to another and less valuable site. While the building is on rollers, Chase dies. His will left all his real property to his son and his personal property to his daughter. Who gets the frame building?

2. Aiken sells all the hay in his field to Bromley for $100, giving Bromley a right to cut and harvest the same. Aiken likewise sells Bromley, for $75, his crop of potatoes, half of which is in barrels and the other half of which is to be dug up by Bromley. The agreement is oral. When Bromley comes to cut the hay, dig up the potatoes and remove the barrels, Aiken refuses to permit him to do so. Bromley sues Aiken for breach of contract. How should the case be decided?

3. A farmer orally agrees to sell 1000 feet of standing timber to a lumberman for $25, the latter to cut and transport the timber. When the lumberman comes to cut the trees and take them away, at the same time tendering the purchase price, the farmer refuses to permit the lumberman to proceed. Has the lumberman a good claim against the farmer?

4. Peters orally agrees, for a consideration of $25 a year, to give his neighbor Clarke a ten-year right of way. When Clarke tenders $25 to Peters for the first year, Peters rejects the tender and refuses to allow Clarke to use the right of way. May Clarke enforce the agreement?

5. Anderson owns a thirty-story building. The adjoining building owned by Baker is six stories in height. Anderson procures from Baker by an appro-

priate grant, an easement in the light and air over Baker's building. Thereafter he purchases Baker's building, and still later sells his own building to Church and the building which he bought from Baker, to Davis. Davis plans to erect a forty-story building and Church seeks an injunction to prevent him from doing so. Will Church succeed?

## PART 2. ACQUIRING AND DISPOSING OF REAL PROPERTY

**Title.** Title means ownership. In real property title is frequently not absolute but qualified by flaws or defects. The law distinguishes between a *perfect* and a *marketable* title.

**Perfect v. marketable title.** A *perfect* title theoretically embraces three elements: (1) right of property, (2) right of possession, and (3) possession. A person may have the right of property (ownership), yet lack a perfect title, as where he leases the property to a tenant and thereby parts with possession and the right of possession. He may have the right of property and the right of possession, but not possession, because a third party without right (say a "squatter") is in possession and must be ousted before the owner can convey a perfect title. Or the owner may have possession but not the right of possession, as where he has leased the premises but retains possession: His title is not perfect to the extent of the outstanding lease.

A *marketable* title, on the other hand, is one free from encumbrances, encroachments, restrictions, doubt as to validity, and so on. The owner may lack possession, or right of possession, or both, yet the title may be marketable. Thus, if the owner sells a fully rented apartment house which is drawing substantial revenue and which the buyer acquires for purposes of investment, the seller's title may not be theoretically "perfect," because the seller has voluntarily parted with possession and right of possession as to the apartments leased; but from the standpoint of marketability, the title may be excellent.

**How Title May Be Acquired.** When someone disposes of title to real property, someone else necessarily acquires it. In considering the different ways in which title to real property may be acquired, we necessarily consider also the different ways in which it may be transferred. Title to real property may be acquired by (a) occupancy, (b) descent (inheritance), (c) marriage, (d) devise (will) and (e) deed. Descent and devise are discussed in Chapter 19.

**Title by Occupancy.** The earliest form of acquiring title to real property was by occupancy ("First come, first served"). Title by occupancy also embraces titles acquired by discovery, by conquest, and by accretion (deposit of silt by streams, or of shore front by the tides). The most common forms of title by occupancy, however, are prescription in relation to easements (page 618) and adverse possession in relation to title.

*Adverse possession* is the occupation of lands in such a way and for such a period that the real owner is barred from recovering title and possession. Where a person "openly, adversely [that is, without the owner's permission] and notoriously" occupies the lands of another for a *consecutive* period of years,[1] such person in wrongful possession, if left undisturbed by the true owner, acquires, at the end of the specified period, a title which is recognized in law, and which the true owner becomes powerless to dispute. In such case the adverse user, though his possession was wrongful up to the end of the prescribed period, may convey good title to another at the end of the prescribed period. To constitute adverse possession, the following elements must be found: (1) The possession must be under some claim of right; (2) it must be hostile to the owner; (3) it must be actual; (4) it must be open, visible and notorious; (5) it must be continuous; and (6) it must be exclusive.

**Title by Marriage.** Under the common law, the interest of a wife or husband in the other's property was known, respectively, as *dower* and *curtesy*. Both interests took the form of life estates (page 615). Dower was a life estate in *one third* of the husband's real property; curtesy, a life interest in *all* the wife's real property. To counterbalance this disproportion, the widow's right of dower could not be defeated save by her own act (as by "signing away" the right, or by adultery), whereas the wife could always cut off the right of curtesy, either by deed or by will, so that the only way a husband's right of curtesy took effect was by the wife's prior death without will, and even then there must have been birth of issue, or curtesy would not take effect. The tendency in recent years has been to abolish the rights of dower and curtesy and to substitute, in their place, fee instead of life interests. In some states, for example, a widow or widower has the option of taking, in lieu of dower or curtesy, respectively, an out-and-out share, by way of inheritance, in the fee of the deceased spouse.

**Title by Deed.** A deed is an instrument by which title to real property is conveyed from one person to another. A deed is not to be confused with a contract of sale. The latter is an agreement to convey title; the deed is the conveyance itself. Frequently, the steps leading to the transfer of title by deed involve (a) an informal contract, or binder; (b) a formal contract; (c) a title search in the interval between the making of the contract and the delivery of the deed; and (d) closing the title by the delivery of the deed on the one hand and payment of the price on the other.

*Informal contract or binder.* When the buyer or seller of real property desires to bind the other party to the bargain, it is customary to write out an informal contract of sale, or binder, to serve until a more formal

---

[1] The period varies. A common period is twenty years. In some states it is fifteen years, in others, even shorter.

contract can be drawn up and signed by the parties. What such a memorandum must contain to be enforceable under the statute of frauds has already been noted (page 88).

*Formal contract of sale.* An informal contract of sale may invite litigation by leaving open possible points of dispute. These should be covered in a formal and complete instrument properly drawn, which should specify: (a) date of contract; (b) parties; (c) exact description of property; (d) amount to be paid down at time of contract; (e) amount payable on delivery of deed; (f) amount of first mortgage subject to which title is taken, and whether or not such mortgage is assumed by the purchaser (see page 694); (g) amount of purchase money mortgage, if any; (h) whether or not premises are taken subject to tenancies in possession; (i) covenants, conditions and restrictions subject to which purchaser is taking title; (j) who shall bear the risk of fire loss, pending closing of title; (k) when and where title is to be closed and deed delivered; and (l) what kind of deed is to be delivered (warranty deed, bargain and sale deed, quitclaim deed, and so on; see pages 623-625).

*Option v. contract.* When a prospective purchaser does not wish to be bound by a contract of sale, he may take an option on the property in the form of an option agreement.

*Searching title.* Between the date of the contract of sale and the date of closing title, it is customary to make a careful search of the public records to guard against prior conveyances, mortgage liens, mechanics' liens, tax liens, judgments and other encumbrances (Chapter 17) not provided for in the contract.

*Abstracts of title.* In communities where title insurance policies are not available, it is customary to procure an abstract of title setting forth a condensed history of the title to the property which is being acquired, so that the purchaser may be assured that his title is good. An abstract of title is taken from the public records affecting the parcel which is being sold, covering prior conveyances and decedent estate transfers showing the chain of title to the grantor, mortgages, mechanics' liens, judgments, taxes and other liens and encumbrances against the property, and similar information bearing on the state of the vendor's title.

*Title insurance.* The function of title insurance has been noted on page 376. When the purchaser orders a policy of title insurance, the title insurance company conducts a title search and reports on it to the purchaser or his attorney in advance of the closing. If flaws appear in the title, the purchaser or his attorney usually gives the seller a reasonable time in which to remedy them. If the flaws are not remedied and the purchaser takes title notwithstanding, the title company will except these defects from its policy of insurance; that is, the purchaser will not be insured against loss from such excepted causes, since the title company makes good only such loss to the policyholder as he sustains from the defects insured against.

*Closing title.* Title is closed by the purchaser making payment and executing such instruments as are required in the contract of sale, and by the seller delivering to the purchaser a valid deed duly executed. If the purchase price is part cash and part mortgage, the buyer may have to execute and deliver a bond and mortgage (page 691) as part payment of the price.

*Purchase money mortgage; junior and senior mortgages.* A mortgage given to secure the unpaid portion of the purchase price is known as a *purchase money mortgage.* If added to an existing mortgage, it is known as a *junior mortgage,* such as a second or third mortgage, as distinguished from a prior mortgage, which would be a *senior mortgage.*

EXAMPLE: Adams sells Baker a house and lot for $20,000, payable as follows: $5000 in cash, of which $1000 is to be paid on the signing of the contract and $4000 on delivery of the deed; $10,000 by the buyer's taking the property subject to an existing first mortgage on the premises; and $5000 by the buyer's executing and delivering to the seller his bond and mortgage in that amount. The latter mortgage is the purchase money mortgage, which is a junior lien on the premises, the $10,000 mortgage being a senior lien.

*Tender; adjournments.* Each party, on the closing of title, must be prepared to make due tender in case the other defaults (page 107). Either party is ordinarily entitled to a reasonable first adjournment of the closing, unless the contract makes time of the essence (page 103).

*Remedies for default.* When either seller or buyer defaults on the closing, the other party may sue at common law for breach of contract, or in equity for specific performance (page 124), or in a single suit for both. Contracts of sale frequently contain a clause (inserted at the seller's request) that if the seller is for any reason (other than his own deliberate default) unable to deliver a good title, the buyer's remedy shall be limited to rescission of the contract and recovery of the amount paid in, plus expenses incurred in the examination of title. Also, if the contract so provides, the buyer has a lien on the property for the amount paid in.

*Kinds of deeds.* There are numerous types of deeds. The most common are:

*Full covenant and warranty deed* (see Form 13), wherein the grantor warrants (1) that he owns the property and has a right to convey it, (2) that the purchaser's title will be protected against attack, (3) that the premises are free from encumbrances except those specified, (4) that the grantor will execute and procure any further documents or assurances necessary to perfect the title, and (5) that the grantor will forever continue to warrant the title.

*Bargain and sale deed,* wherein the seller conveys title without the warranties set forth in a full covenant and warranty deed.

*Quitclaim deed* (see Form 14), wherein the seller does not purport to

No................
Entry Book................. Page..........

## WARRANTY DEED

### GEORGE WILSON AND WIFE
### TO
### JOHN MOORE

STATE OF ILLINOIS,
.....................County
SS.:
I, ......................................., Clerk of the Circuit Court and
Ex-Officio Recorder within and for the County and State aforesaid, do hereby certify
that the within and foregoing instrument of writing was filed for record on the
...............day of................, A. D. 19..., at .....o'clock.....M,
and duly recorded in volume..........of Deeds, on page..........and examined.
.........................................
Clerk.

## WARRANTY DEED

THE GRANTORS, *George Wilson and Grace Wilson, his wife,* of the City of
*Danville,* in the County of *Vermilion,* and State of *Illinois,* for and in considera-
tion of *one dollar and other good and valuable consideration* in hand paid,
CONVEY AND WARRANT to *John Moore,* of the City of *Urbana,* County of
*Champaign,* and State of *Illinois,* the following described Real Estate, to wit:
*Lot Five (5) of Block Six (6) of J. R. Jones' second addition to the City of
Danville,* situated in the County of *Vermilion,* in the State of *Illinois,* hereby
releasing and waiving all rights under and by virtue of the Homestead Exemp-
tion laws of this State.
Dated this *3rd* day of *July,* A.D. 19...
Signed, Sealed, and Delivered in Presence of
*Andrew Smith*
*Marie Smith*

*George Wilson* (Seal)
*Grace Wilson* (Seal)
............ (Seal)

State of *Illinois* } ss.:
*Vermilion* County
I, *Laura Black, a notary public,* in and for said County, in the State aforesaid,
do hereby certify that *George Wilson and Grace Wilson, his wife,* personally
known to me to be the same persons whose names *are* subscribed to the foregoing instrument, as having executed the same, appeared before me this day
in person and acknowledged that *they* signed, sealed, and delivered the said
instrument as *their* free and voluntary act, for the uses and purposes therein set
forth, including the release and waiver of the right of homestead.
Given under my hand and *notarial* seal this *3rd* day of *July,* A.D. 19...
*Laura Black,*
*Notary Public.*

## QUITCLAIM DEED

STATUTORY FORM

THE GRANTOR, *George Wilson* of the City of *Urbana*, in the County of *Champaign*, and State of *Illinois*, for and in consideration of *One and no*/100 Dollars CONVEYS AND QUITCLAIMS TO *John Moore*, of the City of *Urbana*, County of *Champaign*, and State of *Illinois*, all interest in the following described Real Estate, to wit:

*Lot Five (5) of Block Six (6) of J. R. Jones' Second Addition to the City of Urbana*, situated in the County of *Champaign*, in the State of *Illinois*, hereby releasing and waiving all rights under and by virtue of the Homestead Exemption laws of this State.

Dated this *3rd* day of *July*, A.D. 19...

Signed, Sealed, and Delivered in Presence of

. . . . . . . . . . . . . . . . .

. . . . . . . . . . . . . . . . .

*George Wilson* (Seal)

. . . . . . . . . . . (Seal)

. . . . . . . . . . . (Seal)

. . . . . . . . . . . (Seal)

*Champaign County* ⎫
State of *Illinois* ⎬ ss.:

I, *Charles Walker*, *a notary public*, in and for said County, in the State aforesaid, do hereby certify that *George Wilson*, personally known to me to be the same person whose name *is* subscribed to the foregoing instrument, as having executed the same, appeared before me this day in person and acknowledged that *he* signed, sealed, and delivered the said instrument as *his* free and voluntary act, for the uses and purposes therein set forth, including the release and waiver of the right of homestead.

Given under my hand and *notarial* seal this *3rd* day of *July*, A.D. 19...

*Charles Walker,*

*Notary Public.*

convey title, but merely to release any claim that he has to the property in question.

*Execution of deed.* A deed is properly executed when it is (a) signed by the grantor, (b) witnessed or acknowledged, and (c) duly delivered.

*Signature.* Formerly the grantor's signature had to be under seal. This is no longer the general rule in most states.

*Acknowledgment.* To acknowledge an instrument is to declare before a notary public, commissioner of deeds, or similar official that one has executed a certain document. The certificate of such official that such declaration has been duly made is known as the *certificate of acknowledgment*, or acknowledgment.

*Witnessing.* When an instrument is signed but no notary is available, a witness may acknowledge before a notary or commissioner of deeds that he saw the grantor sign. This is what is meant by "witnessing" a deed.

*Delivery.* Without delivery, a deed is ineffective as a conveyance. A deed takes effect from the date of its delivery, not from the date of recording.[2] In the absence of proof to the contrary, the presumption is that a deed was delivered on its date.[3] However, this presumption is subject to rebuttal. It may be shown that the deed was conditionally delivered, so as not to take effect until some subsequent date; or that the deed was delivered on a date subsequent to that indicated in the deed.

*Delivery in escrow.* Delivery in escrow means delivery to a third person instructed to deliver the instrument to the grantee upon compliance with certain conditions, such as payment of purchase price, and so on.

*Recording.* A careful purchaser records a deed immediately upon its delivery so as to "give notice to the world" of his interest. All persons who thereafter acquire any interest or claim in the property do so subject to such notice.

EXAMPLE: If Smith sells me a house and lot by a deed which I do not record, and then sells the same property to you by a deed which you promptly record, the law—as between you and me—gives you a prior right to the house, and my only recourse is to sue Smith. But had I promptly recorded my deed, such recording would have constituted notice to the world, including yourself, of my interest in the property, and your only recourse, under the circumstances, would have been against Smith.

## Questions

1. What three elements does a perfect title theoretically embrace?
2. What is meant by a marketable title?
3. Name five ways in which title to real property may be acquired.
4. What five elements must be present to constitute title to real property by adverse possession?
5. What is the difference between dower and curtesy?
6. Distinguish between a deed and a contract of sale.
7. What are the four steps usually involved in the transfer of title by deed?
8. Name twelve specifications which should be covered by a formal contract of sale.
9. How may a prospective purchaser avail himself of the opportunity of purchasing a parcel of property without signing a contract of sale?
10. What is meant by "searching a title"?
11. What is a purchase money mortgage?
12. What are the three most common types of deeds?
13. Name the five elements in a full covenant and warranty deed.
14. What three elements must be present for the proper execution of a deed?
15. Why is it important for a deed to be recorded?

## Problems

1. Earle takes possession of certain property, title to which is claimed by Stimson. Stimson threatens to sue Earle in ejectment, but delays bringing ac-

---

[2] *In re Cray's Estate*, 353 Pa. 25, 44 A. 2d 286.

[3] *Purdy v. Coar*, 109 N.Y. 488; *People v. Snyder*, 41 N.Y. 397; *Louisville, N. A. R. Co. v. Sumner*, 106 Ind. 55, 5 N.E. 404; *Carnahan v. Gupton*, 109 Mont. 244, 96 P. 2d 513.

tion. After living on the premises openly, adversely and continuously for a period of ten years, Earle abandons the premises. Thereupon Farley takes possession and Stimson likewise threatens to bring an action in ejectment against him, but delays doing so for a period of eleven years. These facts being proved upon the ejectment suit finally brought by Stimson against Farley, who should get judgment and why?

2. Adam and Benson entered into a contract wherein Benson agreed to convey to Adam a certain dwelling house for $25,000. Adam deposited $2,500 on account at the time of the signing of the contract. There was nothing in the contract which required Adam to take title subject to any tenancy or occupancy. At the time fixed for the closing, there was a tenant in possession. Adam refused to take title because of such tenancy. Benson sought a two weeks' adjournment to get the tenant out, claiming that he had an informal agreement with the tenant whereby the latter would leave upon two weeks' notice, and further claiming that this was informally understood between Adam and Benson. Adam refuses the adjournment and sues for the return of the $2,500 deposit. Benson counterclaims for breach of contract in refusing to complete the deal subject to adjournment. How should the case be decided?

3. Martin sells a house and lot to Nolan for $15,000. Nolan takes immediate possession, but does not record his deed. Thereafter Martin delivers another deed to the house and lot to Knapp, who promptly records his deed. Knapp seeks to eject Nolan. Will he succeed?

4. Hand delivers a deed to Lamb duly signed and sealed. Opposite the signature are the names of three witnesses. The County Clerk, however, refuses to record the deed. Can he be compelled to record it?

5. Clifford delivers a warranty deed to Flynn after a complete title search by Flynn and upon the issuance of a title policy. The title proves defective and the title company being in the hands of a receiver, Flynn seeks to hold Clifford, who insists that Flynn's sole remedy is against the title company. Is Clifford right?

## COURT CASES FOR REVIEW

### How Did the Court Decide, and Why?

1. Defendants claimed title by adverse possession. The weight of evidence showed (1) possession for the full statutory period and longer, and (2) testimony that two of the defendants had stated that all the land in their enclosure belonged to the plaintiff. Defendants' claim was contested. *Mass v. Bromberg*, 28 Tex. Civ. A. 145.

2. The owner of a house and lot with a mortgage on it sells the house to a house-mover without the mortgagee's permission. The purchaser moves the house from its location, and while transporting the house on a highway is sued in replevin. The plaintiff's right of action is challenged on the ground that the remedy of replevin is applicable only to personal property. *Dorr v. Dudderar*, 88 Ill. 107.

3. Plaintiff and defendant entered into a contract whereby defendant agreed to convey a certain dwelling house to plaintiff for $7,500. The contract made no reference to existing tenancies. Plaintiff refused to take title on the ground that there was a tenant in possession, and sued to recover back the money paid on the contract. *Haiss v. Schmukler*, 121 Misc. 574, 201 N.Y. Supp. 332.

4. King and others, executors of John J. Alcott, deceased, entered into an agreement with the defendant to convey a piece of land in the City of Albany. Title was to close on September 1, 1899. The deed was tendered by King on

December 6, 1899, and defendant refused to accept it or pay the purchase price, claiming that it was too late. Plaintiff, as trustee under the last will and testament of King, sued for specific performance. *Hun v. Bourdon,* 57 App. Div. 351, 68 N.Y. Supp. 112.

5. Plaintiff claimed title by adverse possession to lands the record title to which was in defendant. It seems that plaintiff had obtained a deed from one who had no title, had recorded the deed, and had paid taxes on the land for the statutory period required as a basis for adverse possession, though plaintiff did not otherwise occupy, use or improve the land. *Perry v. Alford,* 225 N.C. 146, 33 S.E. 2d 665.

6. A deed of land to a church contained a restriction providing that the property was to be used for church purposes only, and upon abandonment of such use, was to revert to the grantor. The grantee erected a church upon the land, which continued to be used as such, but the trustees also executed an oil and gas lease on the land. When the lessee started drilling for oil, the grantor's heirs brought suit to recover possession of the land. *Davis et al. v. Skipper et al.,* 125 Texas 364, 85 S.W. 2d 333.

7. The owner of a tract of land with frontage on a beach conveyed a portion of his land to plaintiff, with use of the beach. The land conveyed did not front on the beach. The grantee claimed the right to cross the grantor's land, and the grantor resisted the claim. *Rice v. Vineyard Grove Co.,* 270 Mass. 81, 169 N.E. 664.

8. For many years, the owner of a building maintained an eave projecting over and above an adjoining owner's land, the period exceeding that for the ripening of an adverse interest in land. The adjoining owner made no protest until he finally objected to the accumulation of snow on the roof which kept falling onto his land. The owner of the building with the projecting eave thereupon asserted that his neighbor could not cause the eave to be removed. *Bishop v. Readsboro Chair Mfg. Co.,* 85 Vt. 141, 81 A. 454.

9. A deed contained a property description which failed to give the measurements of the boundary lines, but which conformed to the description contained in the contract of sale and in every previous deed conveying the land. The purchaser refused to take title and the seller sued. *Wolford v. Jackson,* 123 Va. 280, 96 S.E. 237.

10. The front wall of a brick building encroached upon the street from two thirds of an inch to two inches. The purchaser refused to accept the deed, claiming that the title was unmarketable. The seller contended that the law takes no account of such trifling deviations. *Perlman v. Stellwagen,* 115 Misc. 6, 187 N.Y. Supp. 845.

# 15

# Landlord and Tenant

**Scope of This Chapter.** In this chapter we consider the nature and essentials of the landlord and tenant relation; the different types of tenancy, and the rights, duties and liabilities of landlord and tenant in respect to each other, either as provided for in their contract (lease), or as fixed by law regardless of lease. We note particularly some of the major clauses that should be carefully examined before signing a lease. The chapter is concluded by a discussion of the different ways—voluntary or otherwise—in which a tenancy may be terminated.

## PART 1. NATURE AND ESSENTIALS; TYPES OF TENANCY

**A Relationship That Concerns Us All.** By far the large majority of us live in dwellings owned by others. For this privilege, we pay a life-long rental. Yet most of us enter into this relationship with but two points in mind, namely, the rent and the length of the lease. The other incidents of this important relation are generally ignored, though some of these incidents, if not carefully considered, may give us trouble. Persons who spend most of their lives as tenants should have a basic understanding of the landlord and tenant relationship. Landlords, of course, are equally concerned in this relationship.

## Nature and Essentials of Landlord and Tenant Relationship

**Origin, Nature and Essentials.** The relation of landlord and tenant originated as an outgrowth of the feudal system, under which a serf or less than freeholder, the forerunner of the tenant, *held* or *possessed* the land of his feudal lord, as distinguished from a freeholder, who *owned* the land he occupied. The relationship, from its nature, concerns lands: There can be no *land*lord of personal property.

*Definition.* The relation of landlord and tenant may be defined as that which arises from a contract whereby, for a consideration, one person,

629

known as tenant, occupies the real property of another, known as landlord, exclusively, with his permission, and in subordination to his rights;
the landlord retaining a reversion, the contract being termed a lease, and
the consideration being designated as rent.

**Essentials.** The foregoing definition discloses five essentials to the landlord and tenant relation: (1) a contract, (2) exclusive possession, (3) a
subordinate holding, (4) a reversion in the landlord, and (5) reservation
of rent. (The subject of rent is discussed on page 636.)

**The Contract.** Like all contracts, a lease must possess all the contract
requisites (page 33). The *parties* (*landlord* and *tenant*, or *lessor* and
*lessee*) must be capable in law of making a contract. There must be
*consideration* (rent to the landlord, possession to the tenant). There must
be *mutual assent*. (A "squatter," for example, occupying without the
landlord's consent, is not a tenant.) Finally, there must be *valid subject
matter*. A lease is void if its object or purpose is void. The object or
purpose may be void when the lease is made, or it may become so later.

EXAMPLES:

*Leases void when made:*

(1) Lease for gambling purposes.
(2) "Black market" lease, that is, at a rental above a maximum fixed by an
emergency rent law.

*Lease becoming void after leasing.* A lease provided that the premises were
to be used and occupied for a liquor saloon and no other purpose. The Court
held that the lease was terminated by a law prohibiting the sale of intoxicants.[1]

An owner who leases premises for an unlawful purpose cannot recover
rent for the use of the premises and in addition may become criminally
liable for violating the law.

An oral lease may be voidable under the statute of frauds (page 86),
as where the statute requires every leasing of real property for over a year
to be evidenced by a writing.

**Exclusive Possession.** Not everyone who occupies another's real property, even by consent, is a tenant. To be a tenant, one must have *exclusive
possession*, not mere use alone. That is, one must have an *estate*, or
*interest in the land*. The following classes of persons, lacking exclusive
possession, are not tenants:

(a) *Licensees.* A license is a mere privilege or permission to use lands;
for example, the license of a contractor while he is erecting a building
upon your land, or of an advertiser who pays you for the privilege of
erecting and maintaining a sign on the roof of your building. In the latter
case, if the advertiser failed to remove his sign at the end of a year, he

---

[1] *Kaiser v. Zigler*, 115 Misc. 281, 187 N.Y. Supp. 638.

could not be treated as a "holdover tenant" for another year, because he is a mere licensee.[2]

(b) *Boarders and lodgers.* Unlike a tenant, a boarder and lodger *occupy*, but do not *possess* the rooms they hire: Possession is in the proprietor.[3] Hence, for an unpaid bill, a hotel proprietor or a boardinghouse keeper may hold a guest's or boarder's trunk under a *possessory lien* (page 685); but a landlord, lacking possession, has no possessory lien, hence no right to hold a tenant's property for unpaid rent, except where the common law remedy of "distress" (page 644) is still recognized.

EXAMPLE: The occupant of office space under a lease, and of rooms in a hotel, in the absence of the "distress" remedy, is not subject to seizure of his belongings for rent delinquency under the lease, but is subject to such seizure for nonpayment of his hotel bill.

(c) *Agents, employees, servants, and so on.* An agent, employee or servant who occupies a principal's or employer's property as part of his employment contract, is not a tenant, but a mere licensee, and may be removed at any time.

EXAMPLES: Clergymen, schoolteachers, superintendents, janitors, watchmen or caretakers who occupy premises incidentally to the discharge of their duties.

**Subordinate Holding.** As the freeholder in feudal times owed absolute allegiance to his lord from whom he held his lands, so a tenant today owes allegiance to the title of his landlord. Once he recognizes the landlord's title by accepting a tenancy from him, he cannot thereafter dispute it, or set up a superior claim to it. If a stranger comes in, and by suit against the tenant asserts a title superior to his landlord's, the tenant must promptly notify the landlord. In some states he may be made to forfeit three years' rent for failure to do so.

**Reversion in Landlord.** A reversion, as noted (page 616), is the balance of interest which one retains in an estate, after disposing of part of it to another. Hence, a leasing forever is inconsistent with the landlord and tenant relationship.

### Kinds of Tenancies

**Less Than Freehold Estates Generally.** We have already briefly mentioned, in the discussion of estates, the various classifications of *less than freehold* estates (page 616). As pointed out, such estates are personal property interests, known as "chattels real." They relate to *possession*

---

[2] *United Merchants' Realty & Improvement Co. v. N.Y. Hippodrome,* 133 App. Div. 582, 118 N.Y. Supp. 128.

[3] *People v. Vaughan,* 65 Cal. App. 2d Supp. 844, 150 P. 2d 964; *Carroll v. Cooney,* 116 Conn. 112, 163 A. 599, 600; *Washington Realty Co. v. Harding* (D.C.), Mun. App., 45 A. 2d 785; *Brin v. Sidenstucker,* 232 Iowa 1258, 8 N.W. 2d 423; *Marden v. Radford,* 229 Mo. App. 789, 84 S.W. 2d 947.

rather than *ownership*. They include: (1) estates for years, or tenancies for a fixed period, (2) tenancies at will, (3) tenancies by sufferance, and (4) statutory tenancies.

**Tenancies for Fixed Period** ("Estate for Years"). The term *estate for years* is not to be taken literally. Tenancies for years include all tenancies wherein the term or duration of the estate, however short, is definite and fixed. The tenancy need not be for a given number of years, or even for a year, but may be for a month, or a week, or even a day.

**Tenancies at Will.** A tenancy at will is one for an uncertain period, which is held at the will of either the landlord or the tenant. Either party has a right to terminate the tenancy whenever he pleases. Unless thus terminated, it continues indefinitely. At common law, a tenancy at will could be brought to an end by either party at any time without notice. The tendency of modern decisions, however, is to require notice before such a tenancy can be terminated. A common period of notice in such cases is thirty days.

**Tenancies by Sufferance.** A tenancy by sufferance exists when a tenant has entered into possession rightfully, but holds over wrongfully. Strictly speaking, he is not a tenant at all; yet since he has come into possession rightfully, he cannot be treated as a trespasser. He simply stays in possession until the landlord gets him out. Under the statute in many states, a tenant at sufferance, like a tenant at will, cannot be removed except upon thirty days' notice in writing.

**Statutory Tenancies: Emergency Rent Laws.** What virtually amounts to a statutory tenancy results from a condition where, because of a housing emergency, the state steps in and passes a law depriving a landlord, despite the expiration of a lease, of the right to remove a tenant so long as he pays a reasonable rent. Such an estate is in no way dependent upon the landlord's wishes, but is solely the creature of a statute. Its justification lies in the "police power" or dominant right of the state to take such measures as may be necessary, in any given emergency, to protect the public welfare (page 13). Emergency laws continuing tenancies beyond the period fixed by contract or lease were necessitated by housing shortages during and after the First and Second World Wars.

## Questions

1. Define the relationship of landlord and tenant.
2. What are the five essentials that must be present in a landlord and tenant relationship?
3. How does a tenant differ from (a) a licensee, (b) a boarder, or (c) a lodger?
4. Name the four different types of tenancies.
5. (a) What are statutory tenancies? (b) Do the laws which create them impair the obligation of contracts? (c) Are they unconstitutional? Explain.

## Problems

1. A lease provided that the premises were to be used and occupied for a liquor saloon and for no other purposes. Thereafter a law was enacted prohibiting the sale of intoxicants. When the tenant vacated the premises by reason of his being unable to dispense intoxicating liquors, the landlord instituted this action for breach of contract. How did the Court decide and why?

2. Robinson owns a corner lot. He makes a contract with the Fine Foods Company whereby he agrees to allow them to erect advertising signs upon the lot for a period of one year, expiring September 1st, at an annual rental of $600.00 payable in equal installments of $50.00 each on the 15th day of each month. On August 15th, prior to the expiration of the contract, Robinson writes the company, inquiring if they desire to renew the contract, and they respond that they do not. On September 15th, the advertising signs being still on the premises, Robinson demands rent, claiming that the Fine Foods Company is a holdover tenant for another year. The company refuses to pay and Robinson sues. Judgment for whom, and why?

3. Dr. Gordon, a physician, has a summer home in the country. He hires Perkins, a farmer, to take care of his summer home during the winter months and agrees in exchange therefor to permit Perkins and his wife to live on the premises and to raise such vegetables for themselves as they desire during the year. He further agrees to pay them $200.00 a year. He becomes dissatisfied with Perkins in the spring and orders him to quit the premises at once. Perkins refuses to quit the premises, claiming that he has a lease from year to year and that his term has six months more to run. Judgment for whom and why?

4. A landlord consults you on the following facts: He has a tenant in an unfurnished apartment house who has failed to pay his rent; also a rooming house in which one of the lodgers has failed to pay his room rent. Both tenants are about to move without paying their rent. The landlord desires to know if he can seize a mahogany piano belonging to the tenant in the apartment house as security for the unpaid rent; also a television set belonging to the lodger. What is your advice, and why?

5. The janitor of an apartment house, having rooms in the basement for himself and his family, endeavored to bring another person into the house to reside with him without the consent of his employer who voiced his protest against this procedure. Was the employer's position well taken? Why?

6. A school teacher was given possession by the school district of rooms in the school building for the purpose of enabling him better to perform his duties as a teacher. In subsequent litigation it became important to ascertain if the school teacher was in fact a tenant. How did the Court decide and why?

7. A member of the Order of Elks, having a room in the club house of one of the lodges, brought this action against his lodge for wrongful eviction therefrom on the ground that as a tenant he was entitled to the usual statutory notice provided in connection therewith. Defendant contended that he was a mere lodger. How did the Court decide and why?

8. Farnham, without the owner's consent, squatted upon the latter's land and paid rent therefor, which was accepted. Later, when the owner attempted to eject Farnham as a trespasser and squatter, the latter set up the defense that he was a tenant. How would you decide the question?

# LEASE *

THIS AGREEMENT, made in the City of New York, State of New York, on May 1st, 1952, by Doe Building Corporation, a corporation duly created, organized and existing under, and by virtue of, the laws of the State of New York, and having its principal office at No. 11½ Broadway, Borough of Manhattan, City of New York (herein called the "Landlord"), and Richard Roe, residing at No. 37½ Broadway, Borough of Manhattan, City of New York (herein called the "Tenant"), WITNESSETH:

That the Landlord hereby lets to the Tenant, and the Tenant hereby hires from the Landlord, the building in the Borough of Manhattan, City of New York, known as No. 17½ Broadway, for the term of two (2) years from the 1st day of June, 1952, to be occupied as a private dwelling by the Tenant, and not otherwise, at the yearly rent of two thousand four hundred ($2,400.) dollars, payable in equal monthly instalments of two hundred ($200.) dollars each, in advance, on the first day of each and every month (except that the first of such instalments shall be paid simultaneously with the execution and delivery of this lease), upon the conditions and covenants following:

1. That the Tenant shall pay the rent as aforesaid, as and when the same shall fall due; and each such payment shall be made at the principal office of the Landlord above stated, or at such other place or places as the Landlord hereafter may designate for that purpose by notice mailed to the Tenant at the demised premises.

2. That the Tenant shall, at his own cost and expense,

(a) Take good care of the house and of its fixtures, and shall suffer no waste;

(b) Make and execute all repairs required to the said house, and to the plumbing work, pipes, furnace, range and fixtures belonging thereto;

(c) Keep the water pipes, as well as the connections with the water main, free from ice and other obstructions;

(d) Promptly execute and fulfill all of the ordinances of the City Corporation applicable to said premises, and all orders and requirements made or imposed by the Board of Health, the Fire Department and the Police Department, and all other departments of the city, state or federal government, for the correction, prevention and abatement of nuisances or other grievances in, upon, or connected with, the said premises, or other grievances; and

(e) Pay the water tax or taxes levied, assessed or imposed upon the demised building in each and every year during the term hereby granted.

3. That the Tenant shall

(a) Not call upon the Landlord for any disbursements or outlay during the term of this lease;

(b) Not make any improvements or alterations in or to the demised building without first obtaining the written consent of the Landlord; and all improvements made by the Tenant shall belong to the Landlord and be surrendered to it at the expiration of the term of this lease however occurring; and

(c) At the end, or other expiration, of the term, deliver up the demised premises in good order and condition, damage by the elements excepted.

4. That the Tenant shall not assign this agreement, nor underlet the premises, or any part thereof, without the Landlord's prior written consent; nor shall the Tenant occupy, permit or suffer the same to be occupied for any business, or for any purpose deemed extra-hazardous on account of fire.

5. That the Tenant shall, in case of fire, give immediate notice thereof to the Landlord, who thereupon shall cause the damage to be repaired forthwith; but if the premises shall be so damaged that the Landlord shall decide to rebuild, the term shall cease, and the accrued rent shall be paid up to the time of the fire.

6. That in case of default in any of the conditions or covenants herein contained on the part of the Tenant to be kept, observed and performed, the Landlord may resume possession of the premises, and relet the same for the remainder of the term at the best rent that it can obtain, for the account of the Tenant, who shall pay any deficiency thereby resulting to the Landlord.

---

* Reprinted from *Modern Annotated Forms of Agreement* by Saul Gordon. Published by Prentice-Hall, Inc. Copyright, 1940, 1947, by Saul Gordon.

FORM 15 (continued)

**7.** (a) That the Landlord shall have the right, at least three (3) months prior to the expiration of the term hereby granted, to put up, in some conspicuous part on the exterior of said premises, a notice or notices "For Sale" or "To Let", and applicants shall be admitted, at reasonable hours of the day, to view them until sold or rented.

(b) That the Landlord, or its agents, shall, also, be permitted, at any time during the term, to visit and examine the premises at any reasonable hour of the day.

**8.** That this lease is, and shall remain at all times, subject and subordinate in lien to any and all mortgages now or hereafter a lien or liens upon the said premises.

IN WITNESS WHEREOF, the parties hereto have hereunto set their hands and seals, the day and year first above written.

(Corporate Seal)  
Attest:

John Doe, Jr.  
Secretary

Sealed and delivered in the presence of  
Richard Roe, Jr.  
John Doe, Jr.

Doe Building Corporation,  
By John Doe, President

Richard Roe (L.S.)

**9.** Morton, a tenant, is being sued by his landlord for rent. Morton claims that the landlord has no title to the property, but that in fact the premises are owned by Carter. He sets up this defense in an action for rent. Judgment for whom, and why?

**10.** Upon the termination of a lease, the landlord advises the tenant that he wishes to use the premises for himself and that the tenant must vacate the premises forthwith. The tenant refuses, and the landlord without further notice institutes a summary proceeding to dispossess the tenant. The tenant claims that he is entitled to a thirty day notice before the commencement of any proceeding against him, but the landlord claims that since the latter's lease has expired and he is no longer a tenant, he is not entitled to any preliminary thirty day notice. Who is right and why?

## PART 2. LEASES: RIGHTS, DUTIES AND LIABILITIES

**Importance of Reading Lease.** The practice of signing leases without reading them has already been noted. That this is risky practice may be readily illustrated.

EXAMPLES:

(1) A residence lease contains a provision that "the term of this letting and hiring shall be deemed extended for a further period of one year on the same terms and conditions as those herein expressed, unless the tenant shall notify the landlord to the contrary by registered mail at least five months before expiration of the existing term." The tenant, unaware of this provision, fails to give the required notice. Instead, two months before his lease expires, he finds new quarters and obligates himself under a new lease to another landlord. The tenant is thus simultaneously obligated to two landlords under two separate leases.[4]

(2) A ten-year business lease prohibits the tenant from assigning or subletting the premises without the landlord's written consent. After five years, the

---

[4] Some states have adopted statutes making such automatic renewal clauses ineffective unless the landlord calls the tenant's special attention to them.

tenant receives an offer for his business which would yield him a substantial profit. The seller is unable to avail himself of this profit, however, because the buyer insists on retaining the good will attached to the existing location, and the landlord refuses to consent to an assignment of the lease.

**Major Provisions of Lease.** Among the more important provisions of a lease fixing the rights, duties and liabilities of landlord and tenant are those dealing with (1) the term or duration of the lease, (2) rent, (3) description of premises, (4) use of premises, (5) repairs, (6) destruction or damage to premises by fire or otherwise, (7) fixtures and improvements, (8) taxes, (9) what happens if the premises are condemned for public use, (10) assignment and subletting, (11) liability to third parties injured on the premises, (12) deposit of security, (13) compliance with laws, ordinances, and so forth, and (14) the landlord's obligation of ensuring quiet and undisturbed possession of the premises. (See Form 15.)

**Term or Duration.** Customarily, the term or duration of a lease is fixed in the instrument, specifying exactly the day possession is to begin and to end. Such a lease creates a tenancy "for years" (page 632). Unless otherwise provided, a lease terminates at midnight of the last day. As previously noted, a lease may also be for an indefinite term, such as a tenancy at will. Some statutes provide that where a lease is made for an indefinite term, it will be deemed to expire on a given calendar date; for example, on the following October 1st.

**Rent.** Rent is compensation in money or other value paid by a tenant to his landlord for the use of premises. The obligation to pay rent, like the landlord's covenant of quiet enjoyment and the tenant's covenant not to dispute the landlord's title, is implied in law, whether it is mentioned in the lease or not. Usually it is fixed in the lease. If there is no specific agreement for rent, the law will imply an obligation to pay reasonable value for "use and occupation."

**When rent is payable in advance.** It is customary in a lease to provide that rent shall be payable monthly or at some other interval in advance. In the absence of such provision, rent is not payable in advance.

**Description of Premises.** A tenant gets the use only of such premises as are described in the lease. This includes all facilities necessary to such use: entrances, exits, hallways, elevators, and so on. A lease of an entire floor includes the right to use the outside wall of the floor, unless the lease specifies the contrary. (Leases frequently limit the right to use signs on the outside of a building.)

**Use of Premises.** When a lease is silent on the purpose for which the premises are to be used, the lessee may use the premises for any legal purpose not constituting *waste* (page 616). Most leases contain limitations on the purpose for which the premises may be used; such as covenants in residence leases restricting the use of premises to residential purposes; covenants in business leases that the premises are to be used for a given business purpose and no other; covenants against nuisances, the use of premises as a boardinghouse, and so on.

**Fitness for Use.** The law implies no covenant by the landlord that premises are *fit* for any particular purpose, even if the lease provides that the premises are to be used for a given purpose. If a tenant wishes to be protected by such covenant, he must have it inserted in the lease. However, a landlord is liable for fraud in knowingly making false statements about the condition of premises, or in failing to make disclosure when he should, as by renting premises infected with a contagious disease without disclosing such fact,[5] or by failing to disclose a dangerous condition of the building leased, which caused public authorities to condemn it shortly after the tenant took possession.[6]

**Repairs.** Contrary to common belief, the duty to make repairs is on the tenant, not on the landlord. To this rule, however, there are certain exceptions:

(a) When the landlord assumes the duty by lease.

(b) When the duty is imposed on the landlord by statute, as by tenement house or emergency rent legislation (page 632).

(c) When the landlord has exclusive control of portions of premises used in common, as in the case of common stairways, hallways, roof of buildings, and so on.

(d) When the repairs are of a structural nature.

**Destruction or Substantial Injury to Premises.** At common law, the destruction of leased premises, or any damage to them, substantial or otherwise, did not relieve the tenant of his obligation to pay rent—though the premises became wholly untenantable—unless such destruction or damage was due to the landlord's neglect. This rule has been modified by statute in most states. When a building is completely or substantially destroyed so as to be rendered untenantable, as in the case of a fire, the tenant may quit or surrender possession without further obligation to pay rent, unless (a) the lease otherwise provides, or (b) the damage or destruction is due to the tenant's fault.

**Fixtures and Improvements.** The term *fixtures* has already been defined on page 615. As there noted, fixtures may be *real* or *personal*, depending, respectively, upon whether they are affixed with or without intent of permanence. In the former case, the fixture becomes part of the realty and cannot be removed without the landlord's consent. In the latter case, the fixture, being personalty, may be removed.

*Essential test.* The essential test of removability of a fixture is whether or not its annexation was intended to be permanent. Such intent may be *express*, as where specific provision concerning the ownership of the fixture is made in a lease or other contract; or it may be implied from the

---

[5] *Manor v. Sharon*, 112 Mass. 477.

[6] *Steefel v. Rothschild*, 179 N.Y. 273.

circumstances of the annexation (such as the character of the annexation itself, the purpose of the annexation, its adaptability to permanent use in connection with the premises, or the question of whether its removal will seriously injure the premises). No one of these circumstances is necessarily conclusive: Intent in each case must be determined from *all* the circumstances. Some fixtures are so clearly intended for permanent use that there can be no questioning their nature as real fixtures; for example, the installation of a bathtub. Other fixtures are so clearly intended for temporary use that there can be no questioning their nature as personal fixtures; for example, readily removable machinery used by a tenant in his business.

In many cases, however, it is more difficult to determine the probable intent governing the annexation. In such cases, intent must be determined from all the surrounding circumstances.

*Test as between vendor and vendee.* When the annexation is by the owner, who then sells the property, the question as between seller and buyer (when both claim the fixture) will usually be resolved against the seller, because annexation by an owner is presumed to be permanent.

EXAMPLE: The owner of a house equips his windows with Venetian blinds. In the absence of special circumstances showing the contrary, the blinds will be presumed to go with the house.

*Test as between landlord and tenant.* Since the tenant's use is temporary, annexations made by him are presumed to be for temporary use in connection with the premises, unless there is an express agreement to the contrary in the lease, or an implied intent of permanence shown by the character of the annexation (as by building a fence around the house or adding a porch to it).

EXAMPLE: If a tenant installs Venetian blinds, the presumption is that they are to remain his (in the absence of agreement to the contrary in a lease, or of other facts showing an intent to disclaim ownership).

*Trade fixtures.* Trade fixtures are those annexed or installed for the current business purposes of the tenant and hence obviously not intended for permanent annexation, so that they cannot be deemed part of the realty unless a contrary intention is expressed by the parties. Illustrations of trade fixtures are as follows: mirrors, chairs, and similar installations in a barber shop; refrigerators in a meat market; sewing machinery, cutting tables and benches in a clothing establishment. These, even though affixed to the premises, will be deemed property of the tenant unless otherwise expressly agreed. Since trade fixtures in the absence of agreement to the contrary are deemed the property of the tenant, they are removable by the tenant at the expiration of the lease provided they can be removed without substantial injury to the premises.[7]

---

[7] *Carte-Caldwell v. Berryhill*, 188 Okla. 617, 112 P. 2d 370; *Hopwood v. Green*, 34 N.E. 2d 559, transferred 375 Ill. 167, 30 N.E. 2d 656.

*Ornamental fixtures.* Ornamental fixtures are those affixed by a tenant to a dwelling house for purposes of ornamentation, not being intended, as a rule, for permanent annexation, and being easily separated from the premises without injury thereto; as, for example, special lamps and lighting fixtures, easily removable bathroom appliances, removable mantelpieces, and so on.

*Machinery; heating and cooling systems, and so on.* Whether or not machinery, heating and cooling systems, and similar equipment become part of the building in which they are installed depends upon intent as disclosed by (1) character of the annexation and (2) adaptability for use in the particular premises where they are installed. Each case must be judged on its own facts in the light of these tests.

EXAMPLES:

(1) A tenant installs machinery in a building for the purpose of running a mill. The machinery is put on solid foundations and attached to the property. The Court would probably rule that such fixture became part of the realty.

(2) A tenant in possession of a factory under a lease replaced an old engine belonging to the landlord with a new one belonging to himself, and stored the old engine, intending to put it back on expiration of the lease. When the lease expired, the landlord claimed the new engine. The Court held for the tenant.[8]

(3) A turbine pump installed in a theatre building as part of the theatre's cooling system was held to constitute a real fixture and to have become a permanent part of the premises.[9]

(4) A refrigerating system was installed in a building in such manner as to indicate its adaptability to the realty. From the manner of its installation, and from the fact that damage would be caused if the system were removed, the owner was presumed to have intended that the system installed should become part of the building itself. The court therefore declared this a real fixture.[10]

(5) An oil heating system was installed in a building in place of a coal heating system. The oil tank was cut in half and then placed in position and welded. The rest of the machinery was also placed in position and then bricked up. The Court held that the oil heating system and the bricking became part of the realty.[11]

(6) A water heater actually attached to a building and connected with water pipe was held "immovable."[12]

(7) But a gas burner attached by coupling to a gas pipe extending from the furnace and removable without injuring the premises was declared personalty.[13]

*House fixtures.* House fixtures, such as *gas fixtures, furnaces, ranges, ornamental mantels,* and *fireplaces fastened into the walls, installed hat racks,* and similar things annexed to a house as part of it, and completing

[8] *Andrews v. Day Button Company,* 132 N.Y. 348.
[9] *Rinbrand Well Drilling Co. v. L. & H. Theatres,* 126 N.J.L. 446, 20 A. 2d 358.
[10] *Dolan v. Doherty,* 242 App. Div. 671, 272 N.Y. Supp. 892, modified 242 App. Div. 897, 275 N.Y. Supp. 1004.
[11] *Nicklas v. Pickford,* 160 Misc. 254, 289 N.Y. Supp. 174.
[12] *Scott v. Brennan,* 3 La. App. 452.
[13] *Delaware Hill Development Co. v. Delaware Building Corp.,* 137 Misc. 672, 244 N.Y. Supp. 324.

the interior finish of the house, are fixtures. Their adaptability for permanent use as part of the house shows conclusively that they were annexed with intent to make them fixtures. Radiators are held to be real fixtures.[14] Gas pipes are held to be part of the realty to which they are annexed, but chandeliers and gas fixtures screwed on such pipes for the purpose of using the gas for lighting or heating purposes are treated as personal property.[15] This rule includes gas ranges in residences and apartment houses.[16]

*House furnishings: carpets, shades, radio sets, and so on.* Hall carpets, window shades, curtain poles and ash cans are held to be personal property and not real fixtures.[17] Radio and television sets, though connected up by the tenant to house wires, aerials or antennae, are personalty.

*Failure by tenant to remove fixtures.* A tenant must remove his fixtures during the term of his tenancy, or, if he holds over, before quitting possession of the premises as tenant. If they are on the premises thereafter, they merge with the realty and become the property of the landlord, on the theory of an implied gift. Of course this does not apply where the landlord agrees that the tenant may return at a later time to remove his fixtures.

**Insurance.** In the absence of express agreement in the lease, there is no implied covenant on the part of the tenant to insure the premises. Business leases, especially for the longer terms, frequently provide that the tenant must insure the premises for the landlord's benefit or must keep up insurance already in force, and that in case of loss the insurance money must be applied to rebuilding.

**Taxes.** Unless there is a provision in the lease to such effect, the tenant is not responsible for taxes on the premises. Long term leases usually require the tenant to pay taxes. If taxes remain unpaid for a given period, a tax lien arises (page 689). The foreclosure of a tax lien may wipe out a tenant's interest.

**Condemnation of Leased Premises.** When premises are condemned under the power of eminent domain (page 13), the compensation paid in condemnation proceedings, unless otherwise provided in the lease, must be apportioned between the landlord and the tenant upon the basis of the value of their respective interests; the tenant, for the value of his *present estate* (page 616), and the landlord, for the value of his *reversion* (page 616). Many leases give the landlord the exclusive right to moneys paid in such cases. In business leases, this may represent a substantial sacrifice to the tenant.

**Assignment and Subletting.** Most leases prohibit assignment, or subletting, or both, without the landlord's written consent. A lease prohibiting

---

[14] *Keeler v. Keeler,* 31 N.J. Eq. 181; *Capehart v. Foster,* 61 Minn. 132, 63 N.W. 257.
[15] *Vaughen v. Haldeman,* 33 Pa. St. 522.
[16] *Jarechi v. Philharmonic Soc.,* 79 Pa. St. 403; *McKeage v. Hanover Fire Ins. Co.,* 81 N.Y. 38; *Central Union Gas Co. v. Browning,* 210 N.Y. 10.
[17] *Manning v. Ogden,* 70 Hun. 399; *Cosgrove v. Troescher,* 62 App. Div. 123, 70 N.Y. Supp. 764.

assignment alone does not on that account prohibit subletting, and *vice versa*. An assignment differs from a sublease in three respects:

(1) *As to interest retained by tenant.* An assignment transfers a tenant's entire interest in the premises. A sublease constitutes the tenant a landlord as to a subtenant. If the sublessee fails to pay rent, the tenant may dispossess him. An assignor has no such remedy against his assignee.

(2) *As to how the interest passes.* An assignment may be effected by act of parties (as by contract) or by operation of law (as by death or bankruptcy). A subletting can be effected only by act of parties.

(3) *As to liability on lease.* An assignment creates a *privity of estate* between the original landlord and the assignee. This means that the assignee steps into the shoes of the tenant-assignor and becomes bound by the covenants of the lease to the extent that they "run with the land" but no further. That is, the assignee is not bound by any personal obligation or promise, unless he personally assumes the obligations of the assignor. But so long as the assignee remains in possession, he remains bound by the covenants of the lease, including the covenant to pay rent, not to commit waste, to pay taxes, to make repairs, not to assign or sublet, to insure the premises, and so on. If he fails to pay rent or violates any of the other covenants, the assignor becomes liable as surety, and if he makes good, he may in turn hold the assignee.

A sublessee, on the other hand, is liable only to the lessor on the sublease. He is not liable on the major lease. But if the *tenant* (that is, the sublessor) defaults on the major lease, the landlord may oust the tenant and thereby sweep away the subtenant's rights, since they in turn depend for their existence on the rights of the tenant. As between the original landlord and the sublessee, there is no privity, no relationship of any kind. Neither, in law, knows the other.[18]

**Attornment.** Sometimes a tenant subleases premises and then surrenders his lease to the landlord. In such cases, if the subtenant continues in possession and pays rent directly to the original landlord, and the latter accepts the rent, the sublessee is said to *attorn* to the landlord; that is, he ceases to be a subtenant and becomes the direct tenant of the original landlord.

**Liability to Third Parties for Injuries.** A tenant has exclusive possession. Hence he is liable to third parties for any dangerous or defective condition existing on the premises which may cause injury to such persons. However, if the premises were leased with a nuisance thereon, the landlord would be liable to third parties on account of the nuisance; and the tenant would also be liable if he discovered the nuisance and failed to remedy it within a reasonable time. A landlord is not liable for a nuisance unless it can be shown that he had knowledge of the condition which

---

[18] For a case illustrating the foregoing distinctions, see *Johnson v. Moxley*, 216 Ala. 466, 113 So. 656.

caused the injury, and failed to correct it within a reasonable time. Such defective condition may include defective coal hole covers, sidewalk gratings, areaways, cellar doors, and so on. A tenant is not liable when injury results from a condition of the premises not subject to his exclusive control, as in the case of common hallways, stairways, and so on. A landlord is not relieved from liability to third persons merely because the tenant is liable, too; but as between the landlord and the tenant, he may provide in the lease that if a judgment is recovered by third persons against the landlord for any negligent condition of the premises, the tenant shall bear the loss. This is what is meant by a covenant to "hold the landlord harmless."

**Compliance with Laws and Ordinances.** Most leases contain a clause that the tenant must comply with all federal, state and municipal laws, ordinances, orders and regulations. Such a provision is aimed at preventing a situation where the authorities may impose fines or condemn the building itself because of tenant violations. The provision is not intended to require the tenant to make substantial improvements or building changes, unless so agreed in the lease.

**Deposit of Security.** In many jurisdictions, the courts declare that a landlord is liable as a *trustee* for security deposited with him by a tenant in connection with the lease. This means that a landlord must not commingle such funds with his own.

**Quiet Enjoyment.** When a landlord lets premises he impliedly warrants (a) that he has a paramount right to let the premises, and (b) that neither he, nor any person, nor any condition subject to his control, shall disturb the tenant's right to absolute possession of the premises. These warranties, which the law implies whether they are expressed in a lease or not, constitute the landlord's covenant of "quiet enjoyment." The violation of this covenant, known as "eviction," is discussed on pages 645 to 646.

## Questions

1. Name the more important provisions of a lease fixing the rights, duties and liabilities between landlord and tenant.

2. When is rent payable in advance?

3. When a lease is silent on the purpose for which the premises are to be used, what restrictions, if any, may be invoked against the tenant?

4. Where a lease provides that the premises are to be used for a given purpose, how does such provision affect the landlord with respect to its fitness for purpose?

5. Name four exceptions to the rule that the duty to make repairs is imposed on the tenant.

6. What are two exceptions to the rule that where the rented premises have been so completely or substantially destroyed as to be rendered untenantable, the tenant may quit or surrender possession without further obligation to pay rent?

7. Explain three distinctions between assignment and subletting.
8. What is meant by *attornment?*

## Problems

1. Coffin leases a one-family house to Graham. Nothing is said about repairs in the lease. During the first three months of the tenancy, some plaster falls from the ceiling of one of the rooms. Graham demands that Coffin repair the ceiling and Coffin refuses. Graham then refuses to pay rent. Coffin sues. Judgment for whom, and why?

2. A lease provides that rent shall be $1200.00 per annum "payable in equal monthly installments of $100.00 throughout the duration of the term." On the first day of February, during the term, the tenant defaults in the payment of rent, and on the second day of February, the landlord sues. The tenant sets up that rent is not due until the end of the month, and the landlord insists that it was due on the first of the month, although no provision to this effect appears in the lease. Judgment for whom, and why?

3. A landlord leases certain premises to a tenant for use as a laundry. After the tenant takes possession he finds that the equipment is unsatisfactory for laundry purposes; that there are no adequate facilities for the installation of a boiler and other necessary plumbing fixtures. He thereupon quits the premises. The landlord sues for rent. Judgment for whom, and why?

4. A tenant erects business and residence structures on leased land. The lease says nothing as to ownership of such buildings. Toward the end of the lease the tenant begins to remove the buildings. The landlord sues for an injunction. Who wins, and why?

5. A lease contains a provision that the tenant is to make repairs. The lease covers the entire floor of an office building. Certain beams, supports and steel arches are condemned in the building and directed to be promptly rectified by the municipal authorities. Both landlord and tenant refuse to make the repairs, each claiming that the duty of repair is upon the other. How should the case be decided, and why?

6. Metzger runs a meat market under a lease which gives him exclusive possession of a store on the ground floor of the premises. A customer slips on a piece of fat which has been negligently allowed to remain on the floor, and sustains injuries. The customer sues Metzger and the owner of the premises. How should the case be decided, and why?

7. Cooper orally agrees to lease certain premises to Johnson for a period of 18 months at a monthly rental of $100.00. Johnson takes possession but at the end of the second month vacates the premises. Cooper sues for the balance of the term. Judgment for whom, and why?

8. A lease provides that the tenant shall not assign the demised premises nor any part thereof without first receiving the landlord's consent in writing. The tenant enters into an agreement with Ward by the terms of which he agrees to "demise and sublet the premises for the balance of the tenant's term." The tenant reserves no right of re-entry to the premises. The original landlord promptly moves to dispossess Ward, who sets up that there is no provision in the original lease against subletting. How should the case be decided, and why?

## PART 3. TERMINATION OF TENANCY

**How Tenancy May be Terminated.** A tenancy may be terminated in the following ways: (1) by termination of lease, (2) by forfeiture, (3) by eviction, (4) by surrender, (5) by operation of law, (6) by destruction or substantial injury to the premises, and (7) by condemnation. The last two of these have already been considered (pages 637 and 640).

**Expiration of Lease: "Holdovers."** A tenancy for a fixed period ordinarily terminates upon the expiration of such period. If a tenant "holds over," the landlord may (a) treat the tenant as a trespasser, or (b) sue him for damages and remove him by legal proceedings, or (c) treat the tenant as obligated for an additional year. These remedies of a landlord do not exist when the tenant holds over because of sickness. Neither may a landlord exercise these remedies in the face of emergency rent laws (page 632).

**Forfeiture.** Forfeiture may result from the violation of some provision in the lease, such as nonpayment of rent, using premises for an unauthorized purpose, unauthorized assignment or subletting, and so forth.

*Remedies for nonpayment of rent.* When a tenant fails to pay his rent, the landlord may (1) sue for the rent, as for any other debt, or (2) bring a *summary proceeding* (see below) to dispossess the tenant, or, in some jurisdictions,[19] may do both in one proceeding. Ordinarily, as pointed out on page 631, a landlord, unlike a hotel or boardinghouse keeper, not having possession, has no possessory lien (page 685) against the tenant's furniture and chattels, hence cannot attach or levy upon them for nonpayment of rent, at least, not until he has first brought suit and obtained a money judgment against the tenant. An exception to this rule is found in states which recognize the common law right of "distress."

*Distress proceedings.* Under the common law, a landlord may seize movables found on premises when rent is in arrears, and may hold them until the rent is paid. This remedy is known as *distress*. It has been abolished or greatly curtailed in a majority of the states. Under the common law, *any* movables found on the premises (whether the tenant's or not) were subject to distress; today, in states which still recognize the remedy, only a tenant's own chattels are subject to it. Also, the remedy may no longer be enforced by direct action of the landlord, but by law-enforcement officers acting under a warrant or court order.

*Ejectment v. summary proceedings.* Under the common law, when a person claimed a right to immediate possession of property occupied by another, he had but one legal remedy to oust the person in possession, namely, by a proceeding in *ejectment*. Such proceeding was and still is complicated and long drawn out. It requires, as a rule, the filing of a *lis pendens* (notice of pending action) and involves delay. *Summary* or prompt proceedings are now resorted to by a landlord in dispossessing a tenant. The proceedings are started by a *petition*, upon which a *precept* is issued, which requires the tenant to show cause, within a limited time, why he should not be dispossessed.

*Forcible entry and detainer.* No matter how just the landlord's claim

---

[19] Among them, California, Illinois, New York and Pennsylvania.

against the tenant for possession of the premises, he must not resort to force, but must proceed according to law. If he resorts to force, he is guilty of a misdemeanor, and may further become liable in treble damages. The action brought by a tenant in such cases is known as an action for *forcible entry and detainer*.

**Eviction.** Eviction is a breach of the landlord's covenant of quiet enjoyment (page 642), whereby a tenant is deprived of possession by some wrongful act or omission of the landlord. Originally, eviction meant putting a tenant out of possession in whatever manner and for whatever cause. Even today, a tenant is commonly said to have been *evicted* when what is meant is *dispossessed*, that is, put out of possession by due process.

Eviction may be *actual* or *constructive*.

**Actual Eviction.** Actual eviction is ousting a tenant from possession by some direct act of the landlord, as by forcible expulsion, entry and interruption of possession, locking the tenant out, leasing the premises to another tenant and giving him possession as against the first tenant, or preventing a tenant from using halls, elevators or other means of access.

**Constructive Eviction.** Constructive eviction exists when the tenant is forced to quit the premises, not because of an act which the landlord *commits*, but rather because of an act or condition (under his control) which he *permits*.

EXAMPLES: Any nuisance on the same or adjoining premises over which the landlord has control; stenches from dead rats in the walls of the building; disorderly conduct of other tenants in the building without reasonable effort by the landlord to prevent it; failure to furnish heat, steam or hot water when the landlord is required to do so.

*Acts or conditions beyond the landlord's control* do not constitute constructive eviction; for example, a nuisance in the neighborhood which the landlord is powerless to abate.

*Necessity that tenant promptly quit premises.* If a tenant claims constructive eviction, he must promptly quit the premises. He cannot claim he was forced out, while he remains in.

**Eviction by Paramount Title.** If, after a landlord leases premises, someone else proves that he has a superior title to the premises, and forces the tenant out, the latter has a right of action against the landlord for the consequent damage. This is the type of situation which the landlord's covenant of quiet enjoyment (page 642) clearly contemplates.

**Eviction by Mortgage Foreclosure.** When a tenant leases premises on which a third party holds a mortgage which he subsequently forecloses, the tenant, if forced out by such foreclosure, may sue the landlord for the eviction, unless the premises were leased "subject and subordinate" to the mortgage. When a tenant signs a lease which contains a provision that it is subject to existing or future mortgages, he signs a blanket surrender of the premises in advance in case foreclosure proceedings should be brought in connection with any existing or future mortgages upon the property. Even if the lease contains no such provision, the tenant is subject to existing mortgages on the premises, provided (a) the tenant has actual knowledge of the mortgage, or (b) the tenant has constructive knowledge of the mortgage by reason of its having been recorded (page 694).

EXAMPLE: $X$ mortgages property to $Y$ and thereafter leases it to $Z$. If $Y$ forecloses the mortgage and makes $Z$ a party to the foreclosure proceedings, he may terminate $Z$'s tenancy by the judgment of foreclosure, provided $Z$ had actual or constructive knowledge of the prior mortgage.

**Surrender.** Surrender is a mutual agreement between landlord and tenant, express or implied, to extinguish the tenancy, followed by repossession of the premises on the part of the landlord. Surrender may result from (a) agreement of the parties, or (b) operation of the law.

*Surrender by agreement* may be either express or implied. An express surrender results from the voluntary act of the parties, accompanied by an express agreement. An implied surrender may be based upon facts and circumstances from which an agreement to surrender may be inferred.

*Surrender by operation of law* results when both landlord and tenant take some action with respect to the premises which is inconsistent with the continuance of the term; for example, when the parties make a new lease, or when a tenant relinquishes possession and the landlord enters and occupies the premises for *himself*, or when a tenant returns the key to the landlord who accepts it without reservation.

**Termination of Tenancy by Operation of Law.** A tenancy may be terminated by operation of law, as in the case of death or bankruptcy.

*Death of tenant.* The death of a tenant automatically terminates a tenancy at will, but not a tenancy "for years," that is, a tenancy for any fixed period, unless the lease so provides. Hence, when a tenant dies before the expiration of a lease for a fixed term, his estate is liable for the rent, which becomes a debt chargeable against estate assets.

*Death of landlord.* The death of a landlord has no effect upon a lease except to substitute a new landlord or landlords for the old. Ownership of premises carries with it the right to collect rent: If leased premises are sold, the tenant pays rent to the new owner. Similarly, upon death of a landlord, leased premises pass to new owners, namely, devisees under a will (page 763) or heirs in case of intestacy (page 753). These would be entitled to rent accruing after the landlord's death. Rent accrued and unpaid at the time of the landlord's death would go to the landlord's executor in case of a will, or administrator in case of intestacy, to be distributed in accordance with the will or the law governing intestacy, as the case may be.

*Bankruptcy of landlord.* (See page 725.)

*Bankruptcy of tenant.* (See page 725.)

**Duty of Tenant upon Vacating Premises.** If a tenant fails to remove his belongings within a reasonable time after vacating the premises, he is deemed to have abandoned them by the prevailing rule in a majority of states.[20] However, the landlord need not accept such abandonment but may require the tenant to remove his belongings. If the tenant fails to remove them, the landlord may cause their removal at the tenant's expense,[21] since a tenant, in the absence of a contrary stipulation, must leave the premises as he found them, except for ordinary wear and tear.

## Questions

1. If a tenant holds over after the expiration of a fixed term under his lease, and there is no statute to the contrary, a landlord may pursue any one of three remedies. What are they?

2. In the law of landlord and tenant, what is meant by "distress proceedings"? Are such proceedings common?

3. What is meant by summary proceedings in connection with the possession of premises? How does it differ from ejectment?

4. What is meant by "forcible entry and detainer"? Does it entail any penalty?

5. What is the true legal meaning of eviction? Distinguish between actual and constructive eviction.

6. What is meant by "eviction by paramount title"?

7. What constitutes eviction by mortgage foreclosure?

8. In the law of landlord and tenant, what is meant by surrender? What two forms may it take? Explain each by an illustration.

9. "The death of a tenant automatically terminates the tenancy." Is this statement true, false, or partly true and partly false? Explain.

10. How does the death of a landlord affect a tenant's rights?

## Problems

1. A landlord executes a lease for one year expiring September 30. On the last day of the term the tenant moves out of a portion of his premises, but retains a bedroom for two additional days because of sickness in his family. He then moves out completely. The landlord seeks to hold the tenant for an additional term of one year. Can he prevail? Why?

2. Roberts, a tenant in an apartment house, is being sued for rent, which he refuses to pay on the ground that for the past three months his premises have been overrun with cockroaches so as to make them unlivable. The action for rent is coupled with an action to dispossess Roberts, the tenant, but Roberts refuses to move, and refuses to pay rent, claiming that rent is suspended because of constructive eviction. Judgment for whom, and why?

3. Billings has a lease which expires September 30th. The lease provides that during the last three months of the term the landlord may, during the reasonable hours of the day, exhibit the premises to prospective tenants. Four months prior to the expiration of the lease, the landlord rings the tenant's

---

[20] See page 640, "Failure by tenant to remove fixtures."
[21] *Ide v. Finn*, 196 App. Div. 304, 187 N.Y. Supp. 202; *Lee Chuck v. Quan Wo Chong Co.*, 81 Cal. 222, 22 Pac. 594.

doorbell and requests permission to show a prospective tenant through the premises. Billings refuses this permission. The landlord then pushes Billings aside and shows the prospective tenant through the premises anyway. Billings promptly quits the premises, and in a subsequent action for rent sets up these facts as a complete defense. He also sues for damages on the ground of eviction. How should the case be decided, and why?

4. A tenant goes to his landlord and tells him that he is unable to pay further rent. He thereupon hands him the key to the premises and moves out. Nothing further being said about the matter as between the parties, the landlord re-lets the premises for a rental of $25.00 per month less than that which was paid by the former tenant, and at the end of the term, six months later, sues the tenant for $150.00. Judgment for whom, and why?

5. Morgan executes a five-year lease to Brown, agreeing to give possession 30 days after the date when the lease is signed. Brown puts the lease in his safe, and makes extensive and costly preparations for transferring his plant from another city to the city where the new premises are located. Five days after Morgan executes his lease to Brown, he executes another lease covering the same premises to Smith, giving him immediate possession. Smith goes into possession, and 25 days later Brown attempts to move in but, finding the premises occupied by Smith, brings an action to dispossess him. Smith was unaware that a lease had been executed to Brown. Judgment for whom, and why?

6. A lease provides that "it is hereby mutually understood and agreed that the terms, covenants and conditions of this lease shall be binding upon the parties hereto, their heirs, executors, administrators and assigns." The lease is for a two-year term at a monthly rental of $250.00, and is for residence purposes only. The tenant dies at the end of the first year and the landlord after unsuccessfully endeavoring to lease the premises for the balance of the term, sues the tenant's estate upon the expiration of the term for one year's rent. Judgment for whom, and why?

7. Bidwell agrees to purchase a house from James. After the contract is signed, but before title is closed, Bidwell is permitted to take possession of the house. On the closing of title it appears that there is a defect in James' title and the deal falls through. James demands that Bidwell promptly remove from the premises, claiming that he is a trespasser, and Bidwell refuses. James hires a truckman, and they forcibly put Bidwell out. Bidwell sues. What are the rights of the parties?

8. Certain premises are destroyed by fire during the second year of a five-year lease. The landlord insists upon payment of rent for the balance of the term on the ground that the lease contains no provision with respect to destruction of the premises by fire. The tenant resists payment of the rent. How should the case be decided, and why?

9. Shortly before a tenant's lease expired, the landlord contracted with the Demolition Company to wreck the building by a given date at a given price, less $50 for each day's delay. The tenant, upon vacating, left a big safe on the premises, the removal of which cost the Demolition Company $50 for a day's delay, for which sum the Company sues the tenant. Will it succeed?

## COURT CASES FOR REVIEW

### How Did the Court Decide, and Why?

1. The janitor of an apartment house, having rooms in the basement for himself and family, brought in an outsider, not a member of his family, to reside with him, without his employer's consent. The question arose as to

whether the janitor had a right to do this. *Tucker v. Burt*, 152 Mich. 68, 115 N.W. 722.

2. Plaintiff let to defendant the roof of its building for a term of years, to be used solely for erecting a bulletin board to display advertising, at an annual rental of $2000. Defendant was to have access to the roof for the purpose of erecting and maintaining the sign. At the end of the year, defendant having failed to remove the sign, plaintiff sought to charge defendant as a holdover tenant for another year. *United Merchants' Realty & Improvement Co. v. N.Y. Hippodrome*, 133 App. Div. 582.

3. A realty owner allegedly requested tenant to pay realty taxes, insurance premiums, and the cost of maintaining the realty, and in consideration therefor, it was agreed that the tenant would be permitted to use the premises. While the tenant occupied the premises under such arrangement, the owner died. The owner's heirs sought to dispossess the tenant without notice. The question thereupon arose as to whether the tenant had any status as such, and if so what it was. *Gretkowski v. Wojciechowski*, 97 A. 2d 701.

4. In execution of a judgment against defendant, certain premises owned by him were levied upon and sold to plaintiff at a judicial sale. Defendant refused to surrender possession of the property. The question thereupon arose as to whether defendant had any status at all with respect to the property. *Hunter v. Ranitz*, 88 Ga. App. 182, 76 S.E. 2d 542.

5. Following a dangerous accumulation of snow on a roof, which could have been prevented by the tenant, who had sole possession of the building, and in the absence of a roof-guard to prevent the snow from sliding down on passersby in the street, one of the latter was injured because of the falling snow. The question of the liability of the landlord and tenant respectively was raised by the suit for damages which followed. *Clifford v. American Cotton Mills*, 146 Mass. 471.

6. A tenant brought suit against his landlord for damages caused to his goods by the overflowing of a bathtub on the floor above. Plaintiff established no facts with respect to the condition of the bathtub other than that it overflowed. *Pembroke Sationery Co. v. Rogers*, 41 Utah 411.

7. Tenant's heel got caught in a hole in the floor of a leased apartment. The tenant had given no notice to the landlord of the defective condition of the floor, but the landlord's agent had received such notice from a prior tenant, and had done nothing about it. Following the accident, the landlord promptly made repairs. Tenant then brought this action against the landlord. *Noble v. Marx*, 298 N.Y. 106, 81 N.E. 2d 40.

8. Prior to the expiration of her lease, a tenant notified the landlord that she did not intend to renew. The lease expired on May 1, which was a holiday. The tenant held over until May 4, on the ground that moving vans were unobtainable and one of her boarders was ill and could not safely be moved between May 1 and May 4. The landlord claimed a renewal for another year, and sued for rent accordingly. *Haynes v. Aldrich*, 133 N.Y. 287, 31 N.E. 94.

9. Plaintiff leased a property for three years to Dallas Brewery Co., which in turn leased the premises to the defendant for the remainder of the term, reserving the right of entry for breach of any condition, and the right to pay the rental to the original lessor in case of default by the defendant. The lessor sued defendant for breach of the lease, and from a judgment in favor of the latter, plaintiff appealed. *Davis v. Vidal*, 105 Tex. 444, 151 S.W. 290.

10. An owner leased premises to defendants for a period of ten years, at a monthly rental of $150. After one year, defendants assigned the lease to an assignee who neglected to pay rent for nearly two years. The owner then

sold the premises to plaintiff, together with his right to collect accrued rental. From a judgment for defendants in the lower court, plaintiff appealed. *Samuels v. Ottinger*, 169 Cal. 209, 146 P. 638.

11. Clark leased premises to Ganz. The premises were subject to a mortgage. Clark then sold the property. The new owner defaulted on the mortgage. The mortgage was foreclosed and as a result Ganz was ousted from possession. Ganz sued Clark for damages. *Ganz v. Clark*, 252 N.Y. 92, 169 N.E. 100.

# 16

# Personal Property

**Scope of This Chapter.** In this chapter we consider the legal aspects of personal property, with particular reference to certain of its well known forms. In Part 1 we deal with the major classifications of personal property, and the different ways in which it may be acquired or disposed of—appropriation, discovery, creation, gift, sale, and operation of law, as by death, bankruptcy or the sheriff. In Part 2 we discuss the legal aspects of money, interest and usury. In Part 3 we deal with creative values in the form of patents and copyrights, with some of the more important provisions applicable to both, including the basic requirements for granting a patent, its duration, and how it may be protected; original ideas which can not be patented, and what may be done to protect them; the basic requirements for a copyright, the productions which may be copyrighted, and the period for which a copyright may be granted. Finally, in Part 4, we consider intangible trade values, including trade names, trade marks and trade "dress," such as wrappers, packages and containers; also the Lanham Act provisions for "service," "certification" and "collective" marks.

## PART 1. CLASSIFICATION, ACQUISITION AND DISPOSITION

**Nature of Personal Property; Outline of Discussion.** As noted on page 614, personal property is all property not fixed or immovable. Originally, all such property was designated as *chattels*, a corruption of *cattle*, going back to the days when a freeholder's assets consisted of lands (realty) and cattle (personalty). Today, the concept of personal property has greatly broadened, taking many intangible forms not commonly identified with chattels.

## Classifications of Personal Property

**Major Classifications.** Personal property may be broadly classified as follows:

(*a*) *As to lands:* related or unrelated to lands.
(*b*) *As to tangibility: choses in possession* and *choses in action.*
(*c*) *As to income:* contingent and fixed.

(d) *As to origin of title:* by appropriation, discovery, creation, accession, gift, sale or exchange, will, and operation of law.

**Personal Property in Relation to Lands.** We have already noted such things connected with lands as trees, crops, soil, clay, minerals and so forth (pages 614 to 615). The question when fixtures constitute real property, and when personal, has been discussed on pages 637 and 640. It may be added that fish and game do not constitute property unless actually caught, even when one owns land through which fishing streams flow or animals run wild.

*Chattels real: leases.* The distinction between chattels real and fixtures is occasionally confused. Chattels real embrace all interests in real property less than freehold (page 616). Such interests, though connected with lands, constitute personal property. Hence a life estate is real property, but a ninety-nine-year lease, though it may be more valuable than a life estate, is personal property.

*Emblements.* The right of a tenant to harvest crops planted by him but maturing after his tenancy terminates is referred to as *emblements.* The right exists only when: (1) the crops are annual, not perennial, having been planted or sowed by the tenant; (2) the tenancy is of uncertain duration, such as a life tenancy (page 615), or a tenancy at will (page 632), so that the tenant could not have known, when he planted, that the tenancy would terminate before harvest; and (3) the tenancy does not terminate by the tenant's own act, as where he quits of his own accord or violates a condition which terminates the tenancy.

**Tangibles ("Choses in Possession") v. Intangibles ("Choses in Action").** The distinction between tangible and intangible personal property corresponds roughly to the distinction between tangible and intangible real property (page 614). The terms *tangibles* and *intangibles,* though used chiefly in the law of taxation, correspond broadly to the terms *choses in possession* and *choses in action.*

*Choses in possession* include all things physical, such as money, gold, silver, merchandise and all other forms of personal property which are susceptible to physical possession.

*Choses in action* embrace all things personal which are not susceptible to physical possession and which require some form of action to reduce them to possession, such as contracts, promissory notes, checks, trade acceptances, stocks, bonds, bank accounts, and so on.

**Intangibles Generally.** Numerous forms of intangibles have already been considered: contracts, bills of exchange, promissory notes, checks, bonds, bills of sale, chattel mortgages, trust receipts, warehouse receipts, bills of lading, express receipts, certificates of stock and insurance policies. In this and the subsequent Parts of this chapter we note other forms of intangibles: accounts, income, patents, copyrights, and the various forms of trade values, such as trade marks and trade names. In Chapter 19 we consider intangible rights relating to property left by a decedent, namely, legacies and distributive shares.

**Accounts.** An account is a statement of debit and credit between parties, arising out of contract or a fiduciary relation.

*Open v. liquidated accounts.* An *open* account is one not settled or closed, being open to future adjustment, settlement, modification or determination. A *liquidated* account is one definitely agreed upon between the parties or not subject to dispute because reduced to specific form, as by promissory note, check or otherwise.

*Joint accounts,* in personalty, correspond to joint estates in realty. They are accounts held jointly, as in the case of joint bank accounts, each of the parties having an equal interest with the others, and each having an equal right to draw up to the full amount of the balance.

**Income.** The term *income,* in its broadest sense, includes all forms of return on the use of property. Income may be contingent or fixed.

*Contingent income.* Income based on results, such as business profits, is necessarily contingent, being subject to uncertainties in respect to the volume of business done, expenses and deductions. This is true, also, of rents dependent on results or percentages, rather than those fixed by contract.

*Fixed income.* Income may be fixed by contract, as in lands or chattels leased on a fixed rental, or annuities and pensions.

*Fixed rentals.* As noted in connection with leasehold estates (page 636), the right to income on land (rent), as distinguished from land itself, is personal property. The leasing of chattels, as noted on page 299, constitutes a bailment for the hire of use.

*Annuities.* An annuity is a stated sum payable annually, whether in fee (page 615), for life, or for years. It may be created by contract, as in the case of an insurance policy, or by will, as in the case of a testamentary trust (page 769) establishing a fixed income in favor of a specified beneficiary.

*Pensions.* Pensions are annuities granted by governments and business organizations to individuals, their heirs, representatives or beneficiaries, for services performed, or as a social measure. Examples are pensions to veterans and retired employees, and old age pensions.

## Acquiring and Disposing of Personal Property

**In General.** Title to personal property may be acquired by (a) appropriation, (b) discovery, (c) creation, (d) gift, (e) sale or exchange, (f) will, and (g) operation of the law. The acquisition and disposition of personal property by sale or exchange, and by will, are discussed, respectively, in Chapters 4 and 19.

**Appropriation.** Originally, when all things were free in nature, title to personal property was acquired by simple appropriation, represented by such modern counterparts as hunting and fishing.

*Adverse possession.* Title to personal property, as well as to real property, may be acquired by adverse possession (page 620).

The title to a chattel may be lost by one party and acquired by another by adverse possession for more than the period prescribed, either by the statute providing for title by prescription to personal property, or, in the absence of such a statute, by the statute of limitations relating to the recovery of such property. . . .[1]

**Discovery: Lost Property.** The finder of lost property acquires a title which is good as against the whole world except the true owner. He must, however, make a reasonable effort to locate the owner, though he need not incur expense in so doing. The owner may reclaim his property no matter who has it, including innocent purchasers for value (page 238). Policemen who find lost property may be subject to special regulations requiring them to waive their rights in favor of some worthy cause, such as a policemen's benevolent fund.[2]

**Creation.** A person is entitled to the product of his labor, physical or mental, unless such product is made during the course and as part of his employment. In the latter event, the product belongs to the employer. Examples of personal property thus acquired are too numerous to mention. They include all products of handicraft or manufacture, literary and artistic productions, patents, copyrights, trade-marks and all other evidences of creative effort.

**Gift: Nature and Essentials.** A gift is the voluntary transfer, without consideration, of title in and possession of personal property. To be valid as such, it must be a consummated transaction, not a contemplated transfer or promise to make one. Thus, an *agreement to give*, like any other agreement, is ineffective without consideration, and if such agreement is supported by consideration, it is a contract, not a gift. The essential elements of a gift are: (a) competency of parties, (b) absence of consideration, (c) voluntary character of transaction, (d) transfer of possession, and (e) intent to pass title.

(a) *Parties.* The parties to a gift are *donor* and *donee*. The donor must be legally competent to make a gift, not only as to age and mental capacity, but also as to solvency. If his gift will defeat the rights of creditors, it may be set aside as an unlawful preference (page 721).

EXAMPLES:
(1) A gift by a bankrupt, or by an insolvent person or one rendered insolvent by the gift, may be set aside.

---

[1] 2 *C.J.S.* 884, citing *Merrill v. Bullard*, 59 Vt. 389, 8 A. 157; *Ulmer v. Ulmer*, 53 Ga. App. 417, 186 S.E. 433; *Redmond v. New Jersey Historical Society*, 132 N.J. Eq. 464, 28 A. 2d 189; *Edison Oyster Co. v. Pioneer Oyster Co.*, 22 Wash. 2d 616, 157 P. 2d 302.

[2] *Majewski v. Farley*, 203 App. Div. 77, 196 N.Y. Supp. 508.

(2) It is not within the implied powers of a partner to make gifts of firm property, and the recipient of such a gift takes it subject to the rights of the other partners.

(b) *Absence of consideration,* from the very nature of a gift, is an essential characteristic: If the donor requires or accepts any consideration, the transaction is not a gift.

(c) *Voluntary character.* When the donor has been induced to make the gift through force, fraud, duress or undue influence, the gift may be set aside. But a gift will not be set aside merely because of favoritism or even injustice, so long as it was not induced by fraud or undue influence.

(d) *Transfer of possession.* To validate a gift, there must be immediate change of possession. This means both delivery and acceptance. The delivery may be actual (as by the manual or physical delivery of a ring), or constructive (symbolical), as by the delivery of a key, a bill of sale, a bankbook, or a warehouse receipt.

(e) *Intent to pass title.* There must be a clear and unmistakable intention by the donor to make a gift. Delivery through inadvertence or mistake will not support a gift.

**Gift *Inter Vivos* v. Gift *Causa Mortis*.** A gift *inter vivos*, literally, is one between the living, as in the ordinary case where one person makes a gift to another. A gift *causa mortis* is one made in contemplation of approaching death.

EXAMPLE: Desmond, on his death bed in a hospital, requests his son to bring him the contents of a deposit box, which Desmond then hands back to his son, saying, "They are yours; they are no good to me any more."

*Gift* causa mortis *v. gift to take effect on death.* A gift *causa mortis* is a present transfer, subject to revocability upon the happening of a condition subsequent (page 103), namely, the recovery of the donor. A gift to take effect upon death contemplates a future transfer, effective upon death. Such a gift is ineffective except by last will and testament (page 749).

*Gift* causa mortis *v. gift in contemplation of death.* A gift *causa mortis* is one made in fear of impending death from an existing cause. A gift in contemplation of death is one made with a view to the approaching end of one's life in the normal course of things. The former is made upon the assumption that death is shortly to follow from a specific cause. Such an assumption operates as a condition for the transfer, so that if the condition fails and the donor recovers, the gift is revoked. A gift in contemplation of death, however, is made upon no such condition. The gift, motivated by the normal expectation of death, remains absolute.

*Taxability of transfers in contemplation of death.* It is common knowledge that transfers in contemplation of death are motivated by a desire to avoid taxes and the expense and delay involved in the administration and distribution of decedent estates. If a transfer can be definitely shown to have been made in contemplation of death, it will be subject to a transfer tax.

**Revocability of Gifts.** Gifts *causa mortis*, as we have noted, are conditional, and revocable in case the donor does not die as expected. Gifts *inter vivos*, ordinarily, are absolute and irrevocable. To this rule, however, there are two exceptions:

(a) *Force, fraud, and so on.* If the donor has been induced to make the gift through force, fraud, duress or undue influence, the gift is revocable.

(b) *Conditional gifts.* Conditional gifts are revocable if the conditions are not fulfilled.

EXAMPLE: Gift made in contemplation of marriage, which does not take place.

*Engagement rings.* "The gift of an engagement ring is conditional, and as a general rule the donor is entitled to reclaim it if the engagement is broken.[3] The rule generally applies where the engagement is broken by the donee,[4] where the engagement is terminated by mutual consent,[5] or where the marriage does not occur because of disability of either party which is recognized by law,[6] or because of the death of the donee." [7]

**Title by Operation of Law.** As more fully discussed in Chapter 19, when a person dies "intestate," his property passes "by operation of the law" to certain relatives of the deceased in a given order. If a person becomes bankrupt (Chapter 18), all his property, save for certain personal exemptions, passes by operation of law to a trustee for the benefit of creditors. A person's property may also be taken from him by legal process, as by attachment, and by levy and sale under execution of a judgment (page 861).

## Questions

1. Name the four divisions into which personal property may be broadly classified.
2. What do chattels real embrace?
3. What do emblements embrace?
4. Name the three conditions which are necessary before the right of emblements may be said to exist.
5. Distinguish between choses in possession and choses in action.
6. How would you define an account?
7. Distinguish between an open account and a liquidated account.

---

[3] *Sloin v. Lavine,* 11 N.J. Misc. 899; *Ruehling v. Hornung,* 98 Pa. Super. 535.
[4] *Hutchinson v. Kernitzky,* 23 N.Y. Supp. 2d 650, appeal denied 260 App. Div. 628, 24 N.Y. Supp. 2d 1013.
[5] *Wilson v. Riggs,* 267 N.Y. 570, aff'g 243 App. Div. 33.
[6] *Ruehling v. Hornung,* 98 Pa. Super. 535.
[7] Quoted excerpt and citations therefrom are from 38 C.J.S. 850-851.

8. What does the term "income" embrace?
9. Differentiate between contingent income and fixed income.
10. What is meant by an annuity? Name three common forms of annuity.
11. What is a pension?
12. Name the seven methods by means of which title to personal property may be acquired.
13. Name the five essential elements of a gift.
14. Distinguish between a gift "*inter vivos*" and a gift "*causa mortis.*"
15. Name two exceptions to the rule that gifts "*inter vivos*" ordinarily are absolute and irrevocable.

## Problems

1. The owner of several hundred acres of land died leaving a will wherein he bequeathed all the fish in a running stream to his nephew. On subsequent estate-tax proceedings, a dispute arose between the executor and the State Tax Commission as to the value to be placed on the fish in the stream. The Commission argued that the value had to be ascertained before the tax could be fixed, and the executor argued that the bequest was valueless. What is your opinion?

2. Ajax died leaving all his personal property to his son and his real property to his daughter. Among the assets of the estate was a valuable lease which he held on some real estate and which still had some twenty years to run. Both son and daughter claimed this asset. Who should prevail and why?

3. A wealthy man, among other provisions in his will, gave a life estate in all his realty holdings to his wife, with remainder to his children. In subsequent litigation it became important to determine whether the wife's interest was one of realty or personalty. How would you decide and why?

4. Sloan as lessor and Thompson as lessee entered into an agreement whereby Thompson was to rent, on a stipulated annual rental, several acres of farm land as long as Sloan lived. In September, shortly before the crops (beans, Swiss chard, beets, corn, and so forth) were ready for harvest, Sloan died. Sloan's heirs demanded immediate possession of the farm land, and Thompson insisted he had a right to stay until he had harvested his crops. How should the case be decided?

5. An engagement between a couple was broken by mutual consent. Thereafter the prospective groom sought to have the young lady return to him an engagement ring which he had previously given to her, but this she refused to do. In a subsequent action by the young man for the return of the ring, how should the court decide?

6. An old lady writes her granddaughter: "Cecilia, you know you are my favorite granddaughter. Well, that diamond pendant you have always so much admired—it's yours. As soon as I get back to the city, I will take it out of the vault and give it to you. In the meantime, darling, it's all yours." The old lady dies intestate before she gets back to the city, and her heirs as well as the granddaughter claim the diamond pendant. Who gets the pendant?

## PART 2. MONEY, INTEREST AND USURY

**In General.** The ancients regarded money as a useful device, but barren of productivity. Hence the practice of exacting a consideration for the loan of money was frowned upon, so that charging *any* interest for the use of money was regarded as usury. The modern viewpoint is more realistic, though definitely hostile to excessive interest charges.

## Money

**Definition.** Blackstone defines money as "the universal medium or common standard, by comparison with which the value of all merchandise may be ascertained; or it is a sign which represents the value of all commodities." [8]

**Nature and Function of Money.** Money is a common denominator of value. It is the medium of exchange adopted by civilized nations in place of barter. It is a uniform equation by which all property values may be measured in terms of a given number of units. It includes coins of all kinds, officially recognized as the standard of value, and all forms of obligation negotiable by delivery and approved by the government as circulating units of value.

**Money Essentially a Chattel.** Although money is an expression of value, it is itself a chattel. As stated by the court: "Money is, in all things, a chattel, and subject to the law which governs other chattels, except so far as it has the peculiar attribute of money in carrying its title by delivery from hand to hand, and that exception is only made on grounds of public policy for the protection of those who take it as money." [9]

**Lawful Money.** Only money coined or authorized by Congress is lawful. The Constitution of the United States provides that Congress shall have power "to coin money, regulate the value thereof, and of foreign coin." It also provides that "no state shall coin money, issue bills of credit or make anything but gold and silver coin a legal tender in payment of debts."

## Interest

**Legal v. Lawful Interest.** *Legal* interest is interest at a rate which the law applies to a debt in the absence of specific agreement. *Lawful* interest is the maximum which parties are allowed to charge. In some states, the legal and lawful rates are the same. Other states have a legal, but no maximum or "lawful" rate. In a majority of the states, the lawful rate is higher than the legal. (For examples, see table on pages 662-664).

**Law of What Place Governs Interest.** Whether a given interest rate is lawful or not, and what the rate should be when it is not specifically fixed in the contract, will depend on the law of the place which governs the contract. This, ordinarily, is the state where the contract was made, except when it is to be performed in another state, when the law of the latter will control (see page 95).

---

[8] *Bl. Comm.* 276.
[9] *In re Ketchum*, 1 Fed. 815.

**When Interest Begins.** Interest begins to run from the time agreed upon by the parties, or in the absence of agreement, from the maturity of a debt and the making of a demand. An open and running account, being unliquidated (page 653) and uncertain as to the amount due at any given time, cannot be regarded as a fixed money obligation on which interest will run. Only when an account becomes liquidated or definitely agreed upon, and a due date is established by a demand for payment, will the account mature and become interest-bearing. The establishment of an "account stated" (page 114) will clearly start the running of interest at the *legal* rate, unless otherwise provided by contract.

**When Interest Stops.** Interest stops in the following situations:

(a) *On performance.* Payment of the debt or performance of an obligation generally terminates the obligation, including interest thereon.

(b) *On tender.* If, on or after due date, a debtor tenders the correct amount due and the creditor rejects it, interest stops forthwith.

EXAMPLE: On July 1 Loft, after a series of transactions, tenders $2580 to Croft, who rejects it, claiming that the correct amount due is $2850. A year later Croft, having ascertained that Loft was right, demands $2580 with interest from the original due date. Since Loft tendered the correct amount in the first place, he will not be liable for the interest.

(c) *On impossibility created by war.* A state of war between two countries suspends all peaceful intercourse between their respective nationals residing in their respective countries. Interest on debts as between such nationals is suspended during the war period.

(d) *On impossibility created by creditor.* Interest is suspended when the payment cannot be made because of the creditor's absence from the state without provision for a plan of payment or a person to receive it, and when the debtor is ready, willing and able to pay.

(e) *On moratorium.* The Federal government may, in emergency, declare a *moratorium*, or suspension in payment of debts, including interest.

(f) *On deposit in court.* When a debtor is pressed by conflicting claimants and is uncertain who is entitled to payment, he may deposit the disputed fund in court, leave the disputants to fight it out between them, and thereby absolve himself from further liability as to principal or interest.

**Compound Interest.** Compound interest is interest upon interest; accrued interest being added to principal and the whole treated as new principal for the reckoning of interest.

**Rests.** Rests are periodical balancings of an account, made for the purpose of converting interest into principal and charging the party liable thereon with compound interest.

**Enforceability of compound interest: general rule.** The law does not favor compound interest. Except when authorized by contract or statute, compound interest is generally unenforceable. However, the law distinguishes between agreements in advance to pay compound interest, and agreements to pay interest on principal which includes past due interest. Except when a statute expressly permits it, parties may not contract in advance for the compounding of interest. After interest has accrued, parties may agree to add the accrued interest to principal, thus making a new principal upon which interest is to be computed.

## Usury

**Usury Defined.** Usury is taking, or agreeing to take, directly or indirectly, a greater sum for the use of money than that allowed by law. It can apply only to the loan of money or the forbearance of a debt.

*Subterfuges for usury.* Numerous subterfuges have been adopted to circumvent the usury statutes, among them the following:

(1) Requiring the borrower to form a corporation which is to receive the loan. This subterfuge is usually successful. See page 661.

(2) Requiring the borrower to sign an instrument falsely purporting to show a valid loan, as where (a) the actual amount loaned is $2300 and the borrower signs a note of $2800;[10] or (b) the loan is for six months at 6 per cent interest from July 1st, and the borrower is required to sign a note antedated six months so that the lender may collect a year's interest for a half-year loan; or (c) the lender deducts 10 per cent interest in advance, but the loan recites interest at 6 per cent.

(3) Charging fictitious fees, commissions or service charges, as where (a) the lender, in addition to lawful interest, requires the borrower to pay exorbitant attorney's fees for drawing up papers; or (b) the lender, as the borrower's pretended agent, collects commissions for procuring the loan (from himself); or (c) the lender imposes "service charges" to cover alleged bookkeeping, credit investigation and other "overhead" expenses in connection with the loan.

(4) Requiring the borrower, upon receiving the money, to give back part of it. ("The formal delivery of the whole with the one hand, and the retrenchment of a part of it with the other . . . is . . . simply a device to elude the statute." [11]

(5) Selling property to the borrower on credit at an inflated price, the borrower to raise the amount of the loan by reselling the property; as where *A* lends *B* $1000 by selling him, at a price of $1500, stock worth $1000, to be resold by *B* for the latter amount, *B* remaining liable to *A* for $1500.

(6) Requiring the borrower to sell something at a low price, and to agree to buy it back later at a higher price; as where, simultaneously with

---

[10] *Schoenfelder v. Bremer*, 239 App. Div. 366, 267 N.Y. Supp. 549.
[11] *Oyster v. Longnecker*, 16 Pa. 269, 274.

a $5000 loan at 6%, the borrower is required to sell his farm to the lender for $2000 and to buy it back later for $2500.

(7) Requiring the borrower to pay excessive interest under the guise of rent, as where the lender, instead of taking a mortgage on the borrower's property, buys the property and leases it back to the borrower upon rental (instead of interest) installments until the borrower "repurchases" the property (that is, pays back the loan).

(8) Requiring the borrower to buy property from the lender at an excessive price.

**Remedies and Penalties for Usury.** The remedies and penalties for usury vary with the statutes of the different states. (See table on pages 662-664.) They not infrequently vary with the type of transaction in the same state. The most common penalty is loss of all interest. In some states, usury entails a loss of excess interest only. Some statutes prescribe loss of principal and interest, others double and even treble the usurious interest, recoverable by the borrower. In some states, no penalty at all is prescribed, except for usurious loans to the needy.

**Exemptions from Usury Laws.** On grounds of public policy, certain transactions involving interest charges in excess of the prescribed maximum are exempted from the operation of the usury laws. These include:

(a) *Loans to corporations.* In many states, by special statutory provision, corporations cannot plead usury; neither can an individual guarantor of a usurious corporate obligation, nor a trustee of the estate of a bankrupt corporation.

EXAMPLES:

(1) *A* tried to borrow money from *B* on second mortgage. *B*, to secure 12 per cent interest, required *A* to form a corporation, and to assign the mortgage to the corporation. The loan was then made against the corporation's note secured by the mortgage. *A* then sued to cancel the mortgage for usury. The court refused to grant the relief.[12]

(2) If *A* guaranteed the corporate note, and the mortgage proved worthless, *A* could be held on his guaranty though the note was usurious, since the guarantor of a corporate obligation is in no better position than the corporation to plead usury.[13]

The fact that a corporation was organized for the sole purpose of taking the loan and escaping the usury laws will not enable it to interpose the defense of usury.[14]

(b) *Small loans.* Thirty-six states, besides Hawaii and the District of Columbia, have comprehensive small-loan statutes, mostly modeled after the Uniform Small Loan Law (drafted by the Russell Sage Foundation).

---

[12] *Jenkins v. Moyse*, 254 N.Y. 319, 172 N.E. 521.
[13] *Tennant v. Joerns*, 329 Ill. 34, 160 N.E. 160; *Lane v. Watson*, 51 N.J. Law, 17 A. 117.
[14] *Rabinowich v. Eliasberg*, 159 Md. 655, 152 A. 437.

## LEGAL AND LAWFUL RATES OF INTEREST

| State | Legal Rate (%) | Lawful Rate (%) | ORDINARY LOANS Civil Penalty for Usury (exclusive of any criminal penalty) | SMALL LOANS ($300 or less) Maximum Rate (monthly, unless otherwise stated) |
|---|---|---|---|---|
| Ala. | 6 | 8 | Forfeiture of interest; usurious interest applied on principal | 8% per annum |
| Ariz. | 6 | 8 | Forfeiture of all interest; usurious interest applied on principal | |
| Ark. | 6 | 10 | Forfeiture of interest and principal | 3½% |
| Calif. | 7 | 10 | Three times interest paid in excess of 12% | 10% per annum; Unsecured, 10% per annum; secured, 2½% to $100; 2% on remainder, 2% on all loans where security is insured |
| Colo. | 6 | No limit | No penalty | 10% per annum plus 10% fee plus other charges |
| Conn. | 6 | 12 | Forfeiture of principal and interest | 3% to $100; 2% on remainder |
| Del. | 6 | 6 | Forfeiture of excess | |
| D.C. | 6 | 6 | Forfeiture of interest | 1% |
| Fla. | 6 | 10 | Forfeiture of interest plus double interest; over 25%, forfeiture of interest and principal | 3½% |
| Ga. | 7 | 8 | Forfeiture of interest | 1½% |
| Idaho | 6 | 6 | Forfeiture of interest plus recovery of twice amount of interest | |
| Ill. | 5 | 7 | Forfeiture of interest | 3% to $150; 2½% on remainder |
| Ind. | 6 | 8 | Forfeiture of interest over 6% | 3% to $150; 1½% on remainder plus 50¢ fee on small loans (com. rate) |
| Iowa | 5 | 7 | Forfeiture of principal and interest; State gets 8% of judgment | |
| Kan. | 6 | 10 | Forfeiture of double amount of usurious interest | 3% to $150; 2% on remainder (com. rate) |

## LEGAL AND LAWFUL RATES OF INTEREST (Continued)

| State | Legal Rate (%) | Lawful Rate (%) | ORDINARY LOANS Civil Penalty for Usury (exclusive of any criminal penalty) | SMALL LOANS ($300 or less) Maximum Rate (monthly, unless otherwise stated) |
|---|---|---|---|---|
| Ky. | 6 | 6 | Forfeiture of excess interest | 3½% to $150; 2½% on remainder |
| La. | 5 | 8 | Forfeiture of interest | 3½% |
| Maine | 6 | No limit | Forfeiture of principal and interest if under $300 | 3% to $150, 2½% on remainder, 25¢ minimum charge. If lender unlicensed, 12% per annum |
| Md. | 6 | 6 | Forfeiture of excess interest | 3½% |
| Mass. | 6 | No limit | Forfeiture of interest over 18% on loans under $1000 | Unsecured loans, 3% to $150; 2½% on remainder; chattel and comaker loans, 3% to $150; 2% on remainder; other special classes (com. rate) |
| Mich. | 5 | 7 | Forfeiture of all interest | 3% to $100, 2½% on remainder |
| Minn. | 6 | 8 | Forfeiture of debt and interest | 3% |
| Miss. | 6 | 8 | Forfeiture of interest; if over 20%, forfeiture of debt also | 3% on loans of $100 or less, 2½% on loans of more than $100 |
| Mo. | 6 | 8 | Forfeiture of excess interest and security | |
| Mont. | 6 | 10 | Forfeiture of double interest | 9% per annum plus 10% fee plus examination fee on small loans |
| Neb. | 6 | 9 | Forfeiture of interest | |
| Nev. | 7 | 12 | No penalty; but contract void as to excess over 12% | 2% plus small fee |
| N.H. | 6 | No limit | No penalty | 2½% |
| N.J. | 6 | 6 | Forfeiture of interest and costs | 10% per annum plus 10% fee plus other charges |
| N.Mex. | 6 | 10-12* | Forfeiture of interest | |

* Secured, 10%; unsecured, 12%.

## LEGAL AND LAWFUL RATES OF INTEREST (Continued)

| State | Legal Rate (%) | Lawful Rate (%) | ORDINARY LOANS — Civil Penalty for Usury (exclusive of any criminal penalty) | SMALL LOANS ($300 or less) Maximum Rate (monthly, unless otherwise stated) |
|---|---|---|---|---|
| N.Y. | 6 | 6 | Forfeiture of debt and interest | 2½% to $100; 2% on remainder |
| N.C. | 6 | 6 | Forfeiture of interest plus double interest | |
| N.D. | 4 | 7 | Forfeiture of interest plus double interest | |
| Ohio | 6 | 8 | Forfeiture of excess above 6% | 3% plus $1 fee on small loans |
| Okla. | 6 | 10 | Forfeiture of double interest | 10%, plus various fees |
| Oreg. | 6 | 10 | Forfeiture of principal and interest | 3% |
| Penna. | 6 | 6 | Forfeiture of excess interest | 3% to $150; 2% on remainder |
| R.I. | 6 | 30 | Forfeiture of principal and interest, except secured pawn-broker loans | 3% |
| S.C. | 6 | 7 | Forfeiture of interest plus double interest | |
| S.D. | 6 | 8 | Forfeiture of interest | |
| Tenn. | 6 | 6 | Transaction void; recovery of usurious interest paid | 6% per annum plus fee of 1% per month |
| Tex. | 6 | 10 | Forfeiture of interest plus double interest paid | |
| Utah | 6 | 10 | Forfeiture of debt and interest | 3% |
| Vt. | 6 | 6 | Forfeiture of excess interest | 2½% to $125; 2¼% on remainder |
| Va. | 6 | 6 | Forfeiture of interest | 2% |
| Wash. | 6 | 12 | Forfeiture of interest charged plus double interest | 3% up to $300; 1% on remainder to $500, minimum charge of $1 |
| W.Va. | 6 | 6 | Forfeiture of excess interest | 3½% to $150; 2½% on remainder |
| Wis. | 5 | 10 | Treble amount of usurious interest | 2½% to $100; 2% to $200; 1% on remainder (com. rate) |
| Wyo. | 7 | 10 | Forfeiture of interest | |

The Uniform Law requires those engaged in lending sums of $300 or less at rates above the maximum to be licensed, bonded and supervised by the state banking department. Rates allowed range from 2½ to 3½ per cent a month on unpaid balances. (See table on pages 662 to 664.) Violations bring civil and criminal penalties.

(c) *Special lending agencies and institutions.* Many states exempt certain lending agencies and institutions from the operation of the usury and small-loan statutes, imposing other regulations and restrictions instead. These agencies and institutions include pawnbrokers, industrial banks and loan companies, discount companies, credit unions, building and loan associations and the "personal loan" departments of regular banking institutions.

(d) *Interest taken in advance.* When maximum interest is deducted in advance, it really amounts to a usurious charge on the net loan given. However, most states allow this practice by banks and lending agencies in connection with short term loans (usually not in excess of one year).

(e) *Discount of paper other than the borrower's.* When the borrower discounts another person's note, the parties may agree on any price offered for the paper, provided this is not done as a cloak for usury. The transaction is treated, not as a loan, but as the sale of a *chose in action* (page 652); that is, the borrower *sells* another person's note.

(f) *Charges payable on borrower's default.* Excessive interest, costs of collection, attorney's fees, and so on payable on the borrower's default are not usurious, because the contingency upon which these charges are based is within the debtor's control.[15]

EXAMPLE: A note "with interest after date" at a usurious rate would be void. But a note "with interest at 8% after maturity" (in a state where 6% is the lawful rate) would be valid, because when an excessive rate of interest is made payable only in the event of default in payment of the principal on its due date, there is no usury, since the debtor may relieve himself of all liability by paying the principal and interest theretofore due.[16]

(g) *Miscalculation.* If usury is unintentionally charged as the result of a miscalculation, the penalties involved for usury will be withheld.

(h) *Legitimate service charges.* When service charges, such as financing or carrying charges, expenses for examination of title to property before granting a mortgage loan, broker's commissions, and so on, added to the interest charged on a loan, are legitimate, not mere subterfuges for usury, the loan will not be deemed usurious.

---

[15] See 66 C.J. 202-203, citing Arkansas, Illinois, Indiana, Iowa, Kansas, Kentucky, Massachusetts, Nebraska, New York, North Carolina, Ohio, Oklahoma, Oregon, Virginia and Washington cases.

[16] *Hunt v. Bell*, 129 Ark. 167, 195 S.W. 362; *Easton v. Butterfield Live Stock Co.*, 48 Idaho 153, 279 P. 716; *Sanner v. Smith*, 89 Ill. 123, 31 Am. R. 70; *Conrad v. Gibbon*, 29 Iowa 120; *Patrons' Mut. Fire Ins. Co. of Michigan v. Helli*, 232 Mich. 446, 205 N.W. 169; *Weyrich v. Hobelman*, 14 Neb. 432, 16 N.W. 436; *Diehl v. Becker*, 227 N.Y. 318, 125 N.E. 533; *Ward v. Cornett*, 91 Va. 676, 22 S.E. 494.

(i) *Premium for purchases on credit.* The mere fact that a seller charges a higher price for selling on credit than he does for cash is insufficient to establish usury, unless it can be shown that the transaction is a usurious subterfuge.

## Questions

1. "Money is a *chose in action*." Is this statement true, false, or partly true and partly false?

2. What is "lawful money" in the United States?

3. Distinguish legal interest from lawful interest.

4. When does interest begin to run?

5. When a debt arises between parties living in different states having different interest rates, and the interest rate is not fixed by agreement, what interest rate governs?

6. Name six circumstances which will stop the running of interest.

7. What is (a) compound interest; (b) usury?

8. Name eight methods commonly used to circumvent usury laws.

9. What penalties may be invoked for usury?

10. Name nine types of transactions which involve interest charges in excess of the prescribed maximum, yet are exempted from the operation of the usury laws.

## Problems

1. The maker of a $5,000 note for one year, with interest at 6% payable quarterly, defaults in his interest payments for a whole year, then tenders a new note for $5,000 plus a year's interest. The payee demands a note for the face amount plus interest on the unpaid quarterly interest installments. The maker insists that such a note would be usurious. Who is right? Explain.

2. Talbot, in obtaining a $500,000 loan from Gibbons, is required to buy from Gibbons a $250,000 residence for $278,000, and stock of no value for $80,000. In subsequent litigation between the parties, Talbot raises the defense of usury. Is such defense valid?

3. Ackerman tried to borrow money from Brubaker on a second mortgage. Brubaker, to secure 12 per cent interest, required Ackerman to form a corporation, and to assign the mortgage to the corporation. The loan was then made against the corporation's note secured by the mortgage. Ackerman then sued to cancel the mortgage for usury. Judgment for whom and why?

4. A promissory note made and payable in Florida provides for 9 per cent interest. The legal rate of interest in Florida is 8 per cent, the lawful rate 10 per cent. Is the note valid? If so, why? If not, why not?

5. A note provided for 8 per cent interest after maturity in case of default, in a state where 6 per cent was the lawful rate. The maker defaulted, and the holder sued. The maker raised the defense of usury. How should the court decide and why?

6. A finance company, in addition to charging the highest rate of interest, added the following to the expenses of the borrower: financing and carrying charges, expenses for examination of title and broker's commissions. The borrower now claims that the added expenses made the transaction usurious. Is he right?

7. Anderson held Bailey's note for $5,000. In sending out a notice of interest due, Anderson miscalculated the interest so that it amounted to 12 per cent instead of the legal rate of 6 per cent. Bailey refuses to make payment on the ground of usury. Is his position well taken? Explain.

## PART 3. CREATIVE VALUES: PATENTS AND COPYRIGHTS

**Patents and Copyrights: Stimulants to Progress.** Both patents and copyrights represent monopolistic grants by a sovereign body. Unlike other government monopolies, however, such as the tax monopolies of ancient Rome or the salt monopolies of the French monarchy, and unlike most private monopolies (see page 576), patents and copyrights take nothing from the public for the benefit of a few, but instead, by encouraging new and useful inventions, devices, arts and letters, they stimulate the creation of new wealth, economic and cultural, and thereby enrich the nation.

**Power to Grant Monopolies.** The Constitution of the United States empowered Congress "to promote the Progress of Science and the useful Arts by securing for limited Times to Authors and Inventors the exclusive Right to their respective Writings and Discoveries." Congress from time to time has passed laws granting such exclusive rights.

### Nature of Patent Right

**Definitions.** A patent is an exclusive right granted by the United States Patent Office for a fixed period to an inventor, his heirs and assigns, to make, use and sell an invention or invented product.

*Ordinary v. design patents.* Ordinary patents cover processes, machines, compositions of matter and other articles of manufacture, such as the telephone, the printing press, the automobile or the harvester. "Design" patents cover "any new, original and ornamental design for an article of manufacture," such as a specially designed frame for spectacles, a newly designed doll, or a specially designed fabric.

**Term of Patent.** Ordinary patents are granted for a term of seventeen years. No provision is made for renewal. Design patents are granted for terms of three and one-half, seven or fourteen years, at the option of the applicant, upon payment of fees which vary with the period.

**Necessity for Registration.** The common law recognized no exclusive right in an inventor to make and sell the products of his invention: secrecy was his sole protection. In a mechanical age such as ours, however, secrecy affords scant protection. If an inventor desires exclusiveness in the right to make and sell, he must seek a government patent, and this necessarily involves registration in the Patent Office.

**Registration No Guaranty of Validity.** The registration and issuance of a patent constitute no guaranty of its validity. They merely create a presumption of validity, which may be overthrown in the courts by anyone who can successfully challenge the validity of its issue. Such challenge may be based on proof that the invention was not truly patentable, or, if it was, that the patentee was not the person entitled to the patent.

## Patentability

**Basic Statutory Requisites.** Patentability is determined by the following requisites prescribed in the Patent Act:[17] (1) An invention must be new; (2) It must be useful and practicable; (3) It must be original, and not previously known; and (4) It must not have been either "dedicated" or abandoned.

**(1) Invention Must Be New.** The word "invention" connotes novelty. Under the decisions, novelty is tested, not by what is new to the layman, but to the average artisan or workman in the field. A new skill is not enough.

**Improvements.** The statute further provides that a patent may be granted for "any new and useful *improvement* thereof." Existing patents stimulate improvements. For a small sum, any one can obtain a copy of a patent from the Patent Office. Where one obtains a patent on an improvement of an existing patent, he cannot use it without the consent of the owner of the basic patent, but on the other hand, the owner of the basic patent cannot use the improvement without the consent of its inventor.

**(2) Invention Must Be Useful and Practicable.** A patent will not be granted for a device that serves no useful purpose. "An invention is useful . . . if it is capable of being beneficially used for the purpose for which it was designated. . . . Or, as sometimes stated, if it will operate to perform the function and secure the results intended. . . ."[18]

*New idea or principle alone insufficient.* An invention may represent a brand new idea possessing great utility, but if the patent claim, when submitted (page 670), fails to establish that the invention is *operative* or practicable, a patent will not be granted. Thus a person may have the idea of preventing airplane accidents by an automatic contrivance which would open up a huge parachute device to break the fall of a plane when it loses flying speed or becomes otherwise disabled. Such an idea, though possessing utility, and even assuming it possessed novelty, would not be patentable unless it was implemented with a new practicable device for demonstrating that the idea was operative.

*Protecting an idea.* Suppose you have a useful and important idea, one which may prove of great value: a new way to sell merchandise, a new approach to advertising, or a new system for doing business. The idea, if put into effect, may reap a rich reward. Yet you cannot patent it, since an idea alone, unconnected with "some particular medium or mechanical

---

[17] 35 U.S.C.A. sec. 31.
[18] *Callison v. Dean,* 70 F. 2d 55, 58.

contrivance" by which it "acts on the material world" is not patentable. The weakness of the idea is that once it is disclosed, you cease to have a monopoly of it. Unless a firm is willing to commit itself by contract on some method of payment for the idea if acceptable and used—and most firms are unwilling to do this—you are at a considerable disadvantage in capitalizing on the idea.

One way of protecting an idea to some extent is to submit a letter in advance stating that the writer has a unique and practicable idea with respect to the subject in question, and would like to submit it with the understanding that if found to be of interest, a satisfactory arrangement could be worked out by way of compensation for the idea. This, at least, lays a contractual foundation for a claim, which is less likely to be ignored than a mere claim based on disclosure and utilization.

(3) **Invention Must Be Original, and Not Previously Known or Published.** To be patentable, an invention must not have been known or used by others in this country, nor patented or described in any printed publication in this or any foreign country, before its invention or discovery by the applicant.

*Originality v. priority.* Originality relates to the independence of an invention, priority to the time of its conception and perfection. If two persons, independently of each other, conceive the same invention, the one who first perfects it is entitled to the patent. Prior registration of a previously unknown invention may result in the issuance of a patent, but the patent may be set aside in favor of anyone who can prove that he conceived and perfected the invention first, and that he has neither "dedicated" nor abandoned it.

(4) **Invention Must Have Been Neither Dedicated nor Abandoned.** A person may deliberately dedicate his invention, as in the case of many medical discoveries, or he may unintentionally allow it to go into the "public domain," by making and selling it or allowing it to be made and sold for a year or more prior to his filing an application for a patent. Abandonment may be spelled out from: (1) Willful or inexcusable delay in making or prosecuting a patent application; (2) Failure to complete the patent application within six months of first filing; and (3) Failing to pay the final fee within six months of the date when the patent is allowed.

## Who May Obtain Patent

**In General.** Any person, citizen or alien, provided that he is the true inventor or his assignee, may obtain a patent by taking the proper steps and paying the proper fees. A patent may be issued jointly to two or more persons if they are the joint inventors, or to a corporation if it has acquired the right to the invention.

*Officers, servicemen and government employees.* Any officer, soldier or government employee (except employees of the United States Patent Office) may procure a patent without fee upon stating in his application that the invention may be used by the United States Government without compensation.

**Officers and Employees of Patent Office Barred.** "All officers and employees of the Patent Office shall be incapable, during the period for which they hold their appointments, to acquire or take, directly or indirectly, except by inheritance or bequest, any right or interest in any patent issued by the office." [19]

*Inventions by employees generally.* The respective rights of employer and employee in connection with inventions by employees are discussed on page 436.

## Steps to Procure a Patent

**Preliminary Search.** Before going to the expense of applying for a patent, inventors are well advised to order a preliminary search, which is relatively inexpensive. They may be surprised to learn how many people have already conceived of the idea they thought was their own. A preliminary search, however, will not reveal pending applications for a patent, which are secret.

**Subsequent Steps to Procure Patent.** The inventor must make written application to the Commissioner of Patents, and file a *specification* or written description of the invention or discovery, "and of the manner and process of making, constructing, compounding and using it." Claim and specification must be designed by the inventor and attested by two witnesses. The applicant must also furnish a drawing, specimen or model to illustrate his claim. Finally, he must make oath that he believes himself to be the original or first inventor or discoverer of the art, machine, manufacture, composition, or improvement for which he solicits a patent, and that he does not know, and does not believe, that the same was ever before known or used. These papers must be accompanied with a preliminary fee in advance. The matter is then taken up and considered at the Patent Office in Washington. If, on examination, it appears that the claimant is justly entitled to a patent, the Commissioner will issue the letters patent accordingly, at which time a final fee must be paid.

## Copyrights

**Definition.** A copyright is an exclusive right to print or otherwise multiply copies of an intellectual or artistic production, to publish and sell the same, and to prevent others from doing so.

*Form of expression v. thoughts or ideas.* An author or artist is protected in his copyright only insofar as his *form of expression* is concerned. His

---

[19] 35 U.S.C.A., sec. 4.

thoughts, ideas, themes, emotions or concepts are not protected unless they have been embodied in some form of expression, such as a letter, essay, book or painting.

**Productions Covered by Copyright.** The law protects not only the writers of books, but artists and musical composers as well. The law expressly provides that "any citizen of the United States, or a resident therein, who shall be the author, inventor, designer, or proprietor of any book, map, chart, dramatic or musical composition, engraving, cut, print, photograph or negative thereof, or of a painting, drawing, chromo, statue, statuary, and of models or designs intended to be perfected as works of the fine arts, and his executors, administrators, or assigns, shall, upon compliance with the provisions of this chapter, have the sole liberty of printing, reprinting, publishing, completing, copying, executing, finishing, and vending the same; and in the case of a dramatic composition, of publicly performing or representing it, or causing it to be performed or represented by others; and authors may reserve the right to dramatize or to translate their own works."

*Motion pictures* are copyrightable not only as dramatic productions or photoplays, but also as photographs.

**Matter Not Covered by Copyright.** Matter not covered by copyright includes the following:

*News,* except for the form in which it is written, which is protected;

*Official reports* of a governmental body or government officer;

*Republished works by a foreign author* which have not been protected by a copyright in this country;

*Judicial opinions officially published,* except special arrangements thereof in the form of a textbook or other privately arranged publication;

*Unoriginal works,* not necessarily amounting to plagiarism, such as those representing mere copies of official documents;

*Immoral, indecent, obscene or scandalous matter,* written, photographic or otherwise.

**Common Law Copyright Distinguished from Statutory Copyright.** When a person writes a book, paints a picture, composes a song or makes a drawing, he is entitled, as a matter of common law right, to the exclusive ownership of his creation. He need not publish his work if he does not wish to, and he may prevent others from doing so. If he does publish his work, he loses his common law right. In the process of publication, he may, if he wishes, acquire a statutory copyright in place of his old common law right; but if he fails to take the necessary steps to secure a statutory copyright upon publication, he loses his right in the published work forever.

The distinction between a common law copyright and a statutory copyright has been well summarized by the court.

The owner of the common-law copyright has a perpetual right of property and the exclusive right of first general publication, and may, prior thereto, enjoy the benefit of a restricted publication without forfeiture of the right of general publication. Thus, he may communicate the contents of his work under restrictions without forfeiture of the right. This communication of contents under restriction, known as a restricted or limited publication, is illustrated by lectures to classes of students, dramatic performances before a select audience, exhibitions of paintings in private galleries, private circulation of copies of manuscripts, etc.[20]

**Steps to Procure Statutory Copyright.** The following steps are necessary to perfect a statutory copyright:

(1) Publication of the work must be accompanied by a sufficient inscription, or notice of claim. *Example:* "Copyright, 1954, by Prentice-Hall, Inc."

(2) Promptly after publication, two copies of the published work must be filed in the Copyright Office, accompanied by application for copyright and statutory fee.

**Term of Copyright.** Copyrights are granted for a term of 28 years, with a further right of extending the same for an additional period of 28 years, which may be secured by the author or his widow or children. If neither the owner of the copyright nor his personal representatives or next of kin are in existence when the right of renewal accrues, the copyright lapses.

### Questions

1. How do patents and copyrights differ from other monopolies?
2. Define (a) patent, and (b) patentee.
3. Distinguish ordinary patents from design patents. For how long are they granted?
4. "Registration is essential to the validity of a patent." Is this statement true, false, or partly true and partly false?
5. "Registration guarantees the validity of a patent." Is this statement true, false, or partly true and partly false?
6. Name the four basic requisites to patentability.
7. How is the novelty of an invention tested?
8. How may one protect a new, useful and important idea?
9. How does originality differ from priority with respect to an invention?
10. Name three things which will spell out an abandonment of an invention.
11. Who may obtain a patent?
12. What steps, preliminary and subsequent, are necessary to procure a patent?
13. What is a copyright? Does it offer protection to (a) form of expression, (b) thoughts and ideas, (c) artists, (d) musical composers, (e) news, (f) designs, (g) maps and charts, (h) official reports of governmental bodies, (i) photographs, (j) judicial opinions officially published, (k) motion pictures, (l) designs, (m) paintings, and (n) drawings?

---

[20] *Bobbs-Merrill Co. v. Straus*, 147 Fed. 15, 18-19.

14. Distinguish common law copyright from statutory copyright.

15. What steps are necessary to procure a statutory copyright? For how long is it granted?

## Problems

1. James Watson develops a novel device to improve radio reception. He sells receiving sets with the improvement, and after three years of successful development and use, decides to patent the improvement. May he do so?

2. A famous author writes a letter to a friend who feels that the letter is of such public interest and so well phrased that it ought to be published. Can the friend publish the letter without the author's consent?

3. For many years, Arc Welders, Inc., employed a unique welding process which they had patented. In the course of time the company's business fell off, due to competition from The Magic Welders Corporation, which had obtained a patented improvement on the Arc Welders patent. Arc Welders, Inc. now sue The Magic Welders Corporation for infringement. What will be the outcome of the suit?

4. Blake patents a revolutionary type of marine propeller. Thereafter Nelson files an application for a similar patent, and is informed of Blake's prior patent. Actually, Nelson was the first to perfect the device. As between Blake and Nelson, who is entitled to the patent?

5. Martin Bennett writes a book on basic procedures for improving the lot of the underprivileged throughout the world and thereby arresting the growth of Communism. He publishes the book at his own expense. The book has a good sale and Bennett decides to copyright it. May he do so?

6. Mrs. Willoughby, whose husband has just died, writes to her brother: "Unfortunately, John left me little insurance, and the royalties on his book, which have been enough for both of us to live on, are about to run out, the copyright being in its 28th year, so it looks as if I'll soon be a candidate for the poorhouse." Has Mrs. Willoughby accurately appraised her prospects?

7. A lecturer gives his class permission to take notes, and in fact insists upon their doing so. One of the members of the class edits, publishes and sells the series of lectures. May the lecturer do anything about this?

## PART 4. TRADE VALUES: TRADE NAMES AND TRADE-MARKS

**Intangible Trade Values.** The success of a business frequently depends less on its plant or equipment than on certain intangible trade values, such as a reputation for good faith, honest dealing and the worth of its products. It is important to such a business that its identity be established in the public mind, and that its products or service should not be confused with a competitor's. Such values, though intangible, may constitute precious property. Among the devices adopted for achieving such values are trade names, trade-marks, and trade "dress," such as wrappers, packages or containers.

The law governing trade names and trade-marks concerns itself principally with the following: (1) The nature and characteristics of trade names, trade-marks and trade "dress"; (2) The legal requisites of such trade values; (3) How far the law will protect such trade values; (4) The advantage, if any, of registering a trade name, mark or "dress"; and (5) The remedies for infringement.

## (1) Nature and Characteristics

**Trade Names v. Trade-Marks.** Although trade names and trade-marks are frequently associated together, they differ in nature and purpose. A trade name is used to designate a particular business, or a class of goods. A trade-mark is a sign, symbol or device which is either attached to goods offered for sale, so as to distinguish them from similar goods and identify them with a particular concern, or used (a) in the sale of services, i.e., a *service mark* (page 678); (b) to certify some product, i.e., a *certification mark* (page 678); or (c) to indicate membership in an organization, i.e., a *collective mark* (page 678). A trade name is broader than a trade-mark. A trade name involves both the thing sold and the individuality of the seller or maker; a trade-mark relates chiefly to the article sold,[21] the service rendered, the thing certified, or the organization designated. On the other hand, a trade name may serve as the basis for a trade-mark; for example, the mark, "Cyclops," applied to products of the Cyclops Iron Works.[22]

**Trade Dress.** The term "trade dress" is used to designate labels, wrappers, packages or containers of goods as they go into the market. These, as already noted in Chapter 13 (page 598), whether trade-marked or not, may be protected from unfair imitation by a competitor who tries to pass off his goods as those of the legitimate proprietor.

## (2) Requisites for Protection

**In General.** A person who wishes to protect the use of a name, mark or symbol in connection with his business or product must show two things: (1) Priority of use, and (2) Either distinctiveness, or facts showing that the name or mark, through long use or otherwise, has become so identified with his business or product that its use by another would constitute unfair competition.

**Priority of Use.** To establish one's right to a trade-mark and to prevent others from infringing it, one must show priority of use. He need not show how long he has used the mark, so long as he used it first. The use must be actual, not constructive: one must show that he has actually used the mark in connection with goods actually placed on the market, and that the mark was actually affixed to the goods, or to the package or wrapper containing them.

---

[21] 63 C.J. 331-332.
[22] *Hainque v. Cyclops Iron Works*, 136 Cal. 351, 68 P. 1014.

EXAMPLES: Branding a mark on cork; stamping a mark into a cake of butter, or on the skin of an orange; imprinting a name or mark on a container, or fabricating it into a glass, metal or plastic product.

If a person designs, invents or suggests a particular device as a trademark, but does not use it, and someone else later uses it first, the latter's rights in the device will be superior to those of the person who designed, invented or suggested it.

**Distinctiveness: Words.** A trade-mark, to be valid, must be distinctive. Words in common use cannot be appropriated: the dictionary is the property of all, and everyone has a right to describe his goods or products in the best language available. However, where ordinary or descriptive words are used in an arbitrary or fanciful sense (see below), they become distinctive and may be trade-marked.

Descriptive words may reflect characteristics of the product, or they may be laudatory, generic or geographic.

*Descriptive words reflecting characteristics.* Words which reflect characteristics of common objects or functions are naturally lacking in the distinctiveness essential to a trade-mark.

EXAMPLES: "Automarket"; "Eggcarrier"; "Sportshop"; "All Around Van and Trucking"; "Always Closed," applied to a revolving door; "Rubberoid," applied to roofing; "Copper Clad," applied to copper coated steel wire; "Self-Loading," applied to cartridges.

*Laudatory or commendatory words.* Words indicating excellence, superiority, popularity or serviceability will not be protected.

EXAMPLES: High Standard Hats; Best Sausages; Favorite Cigarettes; Faultless Stockings; Nationwide Candies.

*Generic words.* Words which designate things of a common class, type or nature likewise lack distinctiveness and cannot be trade-marked.

EXAMPLES: Jewelry, groceries, meats, clothing, factories, shops, stores, restaurants, or any names based on such words, such as "Ye Smart Shoppe," "The Corner Restaurant," "The Haberdashery," "The Pastry Shop," "Hamburger Haven," "The Chophouse," "The Oysterhouse."

*Geographical designations as such* are not distinctive. A manufacturer may designate on his product the country, state, city or locality where such product is made, but he cannot trade-mark such designation.

EXAMPLES: Boston Wafers; Coney Island Frankfurters; Columbia Lumber Mills; Jersey Publishing Company.

*Ordinary words used in arbitrary or fanciful sense.* Ordinary words may become distinctive by being used in an arbitrary or fanciful way, as in the case of newly coined or invented words, ordinary words given an arbitrary meaning, and derivative words or word combinations arbitrarily devised or put together.

EXAMPLES: Cuticura (toilet soap); No-To-Bac (tobacco cure); Sapolio (scouring soap); Valvoline (lubricating oil); Uneeda (biscuit).

*Fictitious, mythological or noted names.* "Trade-marks may consist of names of characters in fiction or mythology or of celebrated imaginary or historical persons or things, unless they have been in common use upon the particular kind of product, or . . . have become generic and descriptive of quality owing to the manner of use and the general understanding." [23]

EXAMPLES: Lister (as applied to "Listerine," a name for an antiseptic preparation); Rameses (as applied to cigarettes); Roger Williams (as applied to cotton cloth, or a hotel). But Bismark (as applied to herring) has become generic.

*Distinctive words may become ordinary* through common use; for example, "zipper," "celluloid," cellophane," "linoleum," "aspirin" and "shredded wheat."

**Distinctiveness: Symbols and Devices.** Symbols and devices, like words, must be distinctive or they will not be protected as trade-marks. Any device or symbol which is arbitrary and not merely descriptive may constitute a valid trade-mark.

*Pictures in combination with names* may constitute valid trade-marks.

EXAMPLES:
(1) Picture of Father Knickerbocker and the name "Knickerbocker";
(2) Picture of the White House and the name "Whitehouse."

*Pictures alone* may constitute trade-marks, provided they are used arbitrarily, not descriptively.

EXAMPLE: The figure of a Durham bull in connection with cigarette tobacco may constitute a valid trade-mark, but the figure of a cow in connection with dairy products may not; the former being used arbitrarily (distinctively), the latter descriptively.

*Color.* Color alone cannot be made into a trade-mark. "But a color impressed in a particular design, such as a circle, square, triangle, cross, or star, or used in connection with other characters, may be appropriated as a trade-mark." [24] For example, a trade-mark for a fountain pen, consisting of a red body and two black ends, is invalid,[25] but the use of several colors on a package of brushless shaving cream, in a distinct and arbitrary design, was upheld.[26]

### (3) Extent of Trade-Mark Protection

**Protection Not Absolute.** The monopoly of a trade-mark is not absolute, but limited and prescribed. The principal limitations are those which

---

[23] 63 C.J. 355.
[24] 63 C.J. 359.
[25] *Parker Pen Co. v. Finstone,* 7 F. 2d 753.
[26] *Barbasol Co. v. Jacobs,* 150 F. 2d 336.

relate to (a) the class of goods to which the use of the name is applied, and (b) the territory to which its use has penetrated.

**Limitation to Particular Class of Goods.** The exclusiveness of a trade-mark is limited to the particular class of goods in connection with which the mark has been actually used. The mere fact that one person has adopted and used a trade-mark on his particular class of goods does not prevent the adoption and use of the same trade-mark by others on articles of a different description. Thus, "Ambrosia," as a trade-mark for a particular brand of coffee, may be available to another concern for use in connection with a brand of wine or whiskey, but not in connection with a brand of tea or cocoa.

**Limitation to Territory Penetrated by Use.** A trade-mark may extend over a large area, regardless of territorial or political boundaries, provided it has penetrated such territory by actual use, and not merely by advertisement or publicity. "The mark, of itself, cannot travel to market where there is no article to wear the badge and no trader to offer the article." [27]

## (4) Advantages of Registration

**Registration Prior to Lanham Act.** Prior to the Lanham Act, registration of a trade-mark conferred no new rights, but furnished procedural advantages only. A registrant was still subject to the common law rule that the trade-mark belonged to the first actual user, whether he had registered or not. Registration merely created a presumption of prior use, which could be overcome by proof to the contrary. A registrant might spend millions advertising his trade-mark only to have another person step in and prove a prior right. Registration was limited to manufactured and mercantile products, excluding the values attached to commercial services, to products certified by responsible organizations other than the owners, or to membership in a collective group or association. Registration was denied to descriptive words, geographical designations, personal names, wrappers, packages and containers, no matter how distinctive they had become by advertising or otherwise; the owners in such cases having to rely on equity suits to restrain unfair competition. The owner of a trade-mark could not assign it without selling the entire business in connection with which the trade-mark was used.

**Advantages of Lanham Act.** The Lanham Act, adopted in 1947, established definite rights on registration and broadened its scope. Registration may constitute constructive notice to all. Time may run in favor of a registrant to the point where his claim becomes incontestable. Names and designations formerly excluded because they were originally descriptive, personal or common, may now be registered when they become distinc-

---

[27] 63 C.J. 320.

tive. Registered marks may now be assigned without assigning the entire business in which they are used.

The right to register embraces not only names and marks of manufactured products, but also "service," "certification," and "collective" marks.

*Service marks* are used in the sale or advertising of services, to identify the services of one person and distinguish them from those of others. They include the marks, names, symbols, titles, designations, slogans, character names and distinctive features of radio and television or other advertising used in commerce.

EXAMPLES: Greyhound (bus transportation); Union Pacific (railroad transportation); Spotless (cleaners); Snow White (laundry); Mercury (messenger service); Burns & Allen, The Lone Ranger and Hopalong Cassidy (radio and television entertainment).

*Certification marks* are used in connection with the products or services of persons other than the owner of the mark, to certify such products or services in some respect, such as with respect to regional or other origin, material, mode of manufacture, quality, accuracy or other characteristic, or that such goods or services were made or rendered by a labor union or other organization.

EXAMPLES: Idaho Potatoes; the Good Housekeeping Seal of Approval; Accepted by the Council on Foods and Nutrition, American Medical Association; Union Made Garment, Issued by Amalgamated Clothing Workers of America.

*Collective marks* are used by members of a "cooperative" or by an association or other collective group or organization. They include marks used to indicate membership in a union, association or other organization.

EXAMPLES: Emblems used by members of the "4-H Club," the Farm Bureau Association or the American Legion.

## Questions

1. How does a trade name differ from a trade-mark?
2. What is meant by the term "trade dress"?
3. If a person wishes to protect the use of a name, mark or symbol in connection with his business or product, what two things must he show?
4. When, if at all, may ordinary or descriptive words be registered as trade names?
5. Descriptive words may (a) reflect characteristics, or they may be (b) laudatory, (c) generic or (d) geographic. Give an illustration of each type.
6. Suggest how each of the examples given by you in Question 5 may be altered so as to be acceptable as a trade name.
7. What are the two principal limitations which relate to the monopoly of a trade-mark?
8. Name some of the advantages with respect to the registration of a trade-mark under the Lanham Act.

## Problems

1. A manufacturer sought to register his product under the trade name of "Pocono Pines." Was he allowed to do so?

2. To avoid useless advertising expense, it became important to ascertain if a soap manufacturer might register the trade name "Cashmere Bouquet." How would the court decide, and why?

3. A brewer used the name "Knickerbocker" in conjunction with a picture of Father Knickerbocker indorsed on his containers. He desired to have both the picture and the name registered as a trade-mark. How would the court rule?

4. The Ajax Company used a certain trade-mark in connection with the manufacture of phonographs and radio sets. Subsequently, the Apex Company used a similar trade-mark in connection with the manufacture of television sets. May the former company obtain a restraining order against the latter? If so, why? If not, why not?

5. Plaintiff sought to restrain the defendant from using the word "Oh-Boy" on its candy, claiming that it conflicted with plaintiff's prior use of the same name for his chewing gum. How would the Court decide, and why?

6. Plaintiff had made local use of a trade-mark. In another territory to which plaintiff's trade had not as yet extended, defendant, in good faith and without knowledge of plaintiff's prior use of the mark, was using a similar mark. Plaintiff sought to use his own mark in defendant's territory. May he do so?

## COURT CASES FOR REVIEW

### How Did the Court Decide, and Why?

1. An automobile dealer leased premises as a show room, and installed heavy paneling on the walls and columns of the leased premises. To do this, it was necessary to drill holes in the plaster several inches deep, and to insert wooden plugs in these holes. Thereafter the lessee went into bankruptcy. The trustee undertook to sell the paneling as part of the bankrupt's assets, and the owner of the premises moved the Court for an injunction to restrain the trustee from doing this. *In re Lexington Motors Company*, 294 Fed. 233.

2. A produce merchant leased a building as a warehouse and installed therein a refrigeration room and a heating room which could easily be dismantled without serious harm to the premises. The tenant stayed over at the end of the lease, at which time the premises were sold to a new owner, who ousted the merchant therefrom. The merchant sued to recover the refrigeration room and the heating room, or their value. *Andrews v. Williams*, 115 Colo. 478, 173 P. 2d 882.

3. The agents of defendant, a manufacturer of railroad cross ties, deliberately trespassed upon the timberlands of plaintiff, appropriated some timber, made them into ties and sold them. Upon discovering the facts, plaintiff sued to recover as damages the value of the timber in its improved condition. Defendant argued that the most to which plaintiff was entitled was the value of the timber before it was cut. *Sligo Furnace Co. v. Hobart-Lee Tie Co.*, 153 Mo. App. 442, 134 S.W. 585.

4. The owner of a hotel engaged the services of a decorator to paint several rooms. During the course of his work, the painter found $750 in old bills

under a rug. He turned the money over to the hotel proprietor on the latter's representation that he knew the true owner and would give him the money. Later, when it developed that the money was still in the proprietor's possession, the painter brought this action against him. At the trial, defendant did not contend that he had delivered the money to the true owner, nor even that he knew him, but that he had a right and a duty to keep possession of the money for the true owner, should he show up. *Erickson v. Sinykin et al.*, 223 Minn. 232, 26 N.W. 2d 172.

5. An elderly lady, the owner of a $5,000 Farm Mortgage Bond, desiring to execute a joint assignment of it to herself and her niece, or the survivor of the two, indorsed the assignment in the presence of the niece and a bank officer, which she then delivered to the latter for registration on the books of the Farm Mortgage Corporation. Before the registration could be effected, and without notice to her niece, the aunt changed her mind and revoked the assignment. On the death of the aunt, the niece filed a claim with the executor of the estate for the proceeds of the bond. *In re Scott's Estate*, 148 Neb. 182, 26 N.W. 2d 799.

6. A policeman while off duty found 14 liberty bonds which he took to the station house and turned over to the department for the purpose of finding the true owner. The rules and regulations of the police department provided that if no claimant of personal property appeared within six months, or, in the case of money, within a year, and proved ownership, the property would be turned over to the police pension fund. The patrolman sued to recover the bonds. How did the court decide and why? *Majewski v. Farley*, 203 App. Div. 77, 196 N.Y. Supp. 508.

7. Testator was an intimate friend of the plaintiff. Seriously ill and expecting to die, he sent for plaintiff and gave him a diamond ring. At the time of delivery, he stated that all his affairs were in order, with the exception of the ring, which he then handed over. He subsequently recovered and lived for years thereafter. The question arose as to whether this transaction was a gift *causa mortis* and revocable, or *inter vivos* and irrevocable. *Newell v. Nat. Bank of Norwich*, 214 App. Div. 331, 212 N.Y. Supp. 158.

8. Deceased delivered to defendant, his wife, 90 shares of stock in the Bethlehem Steel Corporation, and at the same time executed an agreement in substance as follows: "I give into the possession of my wife, Jennie Dickson, 90 shares of Bethlehem Steel to hold in her possession, and after my death, they are to become her personal property; but in case I should survive her, they are to be returned to me and become part of my estate." The husband died before the wife. Plaintiff claimed title to the stock as executor of the estate. The wife claimed the stock as a valid gift. How did the court decide and why? *Peoples Trust Co. v. Dickson*, 126 Misc. 580, 214 N.Y. Supp. 73.

9. As the result of a collision between two automobiles, this action was instituted. Defendant claimed that since she had made an oral gift of the car to her daughter, she should be absolved from any liability and the complaint dismissed. No proof was offered as to who had custody, control and management of the car. *Feore v. Trammel*, 213 Ala. 293, 104 So. 808.

10. A loan company, in addition to a lawful interest charge of 10 per cent, imposed upon the borrower: (a) charges paid to a retail credit bureau for a credit report on the borrower, and (b) charges for the services of the manager and other employees of the loan company in investigating, appraising and listing the borrower's property mortgaged to secure the loan. In subsequent litigation between the borrower and lender, the former alleged that the loan

was usurious. *Winston v. Personal Finance Co. of Pine Bluff,* 220 Ark. 580, 249 S.W. 2d 315.

11. A retailer without substantial capital or credit, arranged with defendant to finance him to the extent of 90 per cent of merchandise purchased by him from the defendant for resale, under an agreement whereby the retailer would pay a monthly 1 per cent charge on the value of certain merchandise on display. The retailer in subsequent litigation with the finance company charged that the entire transaction was usurious. *Klett v. Security Acceptance Co.,* 38 Cal. 2d 770, 242 P. 2d 873.

12. Morton made a famous discovery in the fact that the inhalation of ether would create insensibility of pain. He thereupon made an application to patent the idea. How did the Court decide? *Morton v. New York Eye Infirmary,* 17 Fed. Cases (No. 9865), 879, 881.

13. Plaintiff, the owner of a Chevrolet car, communicated with the Chevrolet Motor Co., advising them of a serious defect in the car, that he had a constructive idea on how to correct it, and that he was willing to sell them the idea. The company replied that they could not purchase any such idea until they knew exactly what they were buying. Plaintiff then submitted the idea to them, which he claimed the company thereafter used without giving him any compensation for it, and for which he then brought suit. *Lueddecke v. Chevrolet Motor Co.,* 70 F. 2d 345.

14. An inventor sought a patent for a device which liberated or expanded steam into radiating pipes at a rate controlled by the expansion of a thermostatic device under the heat of discharging steam. Was the device patentable? *Vapor Car Heating Co. v. Gold Car Heating, etc. Co.,* 7 F. 2d 284.

15. The validity of a patent for a gear made of compressed cotton fibers was questioned because of the prior publication of a statement that a firm had sent out a catalog of a silent gear made of fiber of prepared cotton. *Gen. Elec. Co. v. Continental Fiber Co.,* 256 Fed. 660.

16. A patent claim was based on simplicity of construction resulting in greater facility with which the mainspring barrel of a watch could be disassembled and reassembled. The claim was challenged for lack of sufficient utility. *Hills v. Hamilton Watch Co.,* 248 Fed. 499.

17. In a suit for patent infringement, it appeared that the inventor of a cigar pocket, for more than two years before applying for a patent therefor, had made and sold such pockets in the regular course of his business, thereby putting the validity of the patent in issue. *Dittgen v. Racine Paper Co.,* 181 Fed. 394.

18. Plaintiff as agent warranted his principal's exclusive ownership of the stage performance rights in an operetta which he licensed defendant to produce. Actually, the principal's statutory copyright had expired at the time that defendant was licensed to produce the operetta. Two licenses were issued by the plaintiff. Nearly $50,000 in royalties was paid under the first license, and $1,000 under the second license. Defendant then notified plaintiff that it would pay no more royalties, since the copyright of the operetta had expired. Plaintiff brought suit for royalties under the second contract, and defendant counterclaimed for the return of the money paid under both contracts. Plaintiff contended that a licensee is estopped to deny the licensor's title. How did the Court decide, and why? *Tam-Witmark Music Library, Inc. v. New Opera Co.,* 298 N.Y. 163, 81 N.E. 2d 70.

19. A mercantile agency prepared and printed twice a year a book which contained information concerning the business and credit of persons engaged

in the jewelry trade. The agency sent a copy to all those who chose to subscribe under a contract which provided that the printed information should be returned upon the expiration of the subscription. The question was, whether the arrangement constituted a publication so as to divest the agency of its exclusive rights therein under the copyright law? *Jeweller's Mercantile Agency v. Jewellers' Weekly Pub. Co.*, 155 N.Y. 241.

20. Plaintiff sought to register "California Fig Syrup" as a trade name for a laxative medicine, which in fact was not a fig syrup but a compound of senna. Upon refusal to accept the name for registration, plaintiff instituted suit. *California Fig Syrup Co. v. Stearns & Co.*, 73 Fed. 812.

21. Plaintiffs had for many years operated a number of restaurants in Boston designated as "Union Oyster House," when defendant opened one up in the same city under the name "Hi Ho Oyster House." Plaintiffs sought an injunction restraining defendant from using such name or any name containing the words "oyster house." How did the court decide, and why? *Union Oyster House, Inc. v. Hi Ho Oyster House, Inc.*, 316 Mass. 543, 55 N.E. 2d 942.

22. Two companies joined as plaintiffs to restrain Armour and Company from using a red and white label on some of its food products. How did the court rule on plaintiff's request for an injunction? *Campbell Soup Co. & Carnation Milk Co. v. Armour & Co.*, 175 F. 2d 195.

# 17

# Mortgages and Other Liens

**Scope of This Chapter.** In this chapter we consider the charges or liens which may become attached to property as security for the discharge of some obligation. In Part 1 we consider the nature of a lien, and its different classifications, including common law, equitable and statutory liens, general and special liens, and possessory and charging liens—possessory liens embracing such liens as artisans', factors', common carriers' and garage keepers' liens, and charging liens embracing those which do not require possession of the property affected, such as judgments, mortgages, tax liens and mechanics' liens.

In Part 2 we consider in some detail two of the more important types of liens: real estate mortgages and mechanics' liens. In connection with the former, we analyze the nature of a real estate mortgage, its usual provisions, the execution and recording of mortgages, the rights of mortgagor and mortgagee in connection with the assignment of a mortgage, including the importance of an estoppel certificate, and the rights and liabilities of a seller and buyer of real property where the property is subject to an existing mortgage; the extension of a mortgage, its prepayment, and the importance of a prepayment clause; the satisfaction of a mortgage, and the importance of promptly recording the "satisfaction piece" when the mortgage is paid; the steps on foreclosure of a mortgage, and the owner's right or "equity" of redemption. We also consider in Part 2 the rules of particular interest to builders, building contractors and home owners in connection with mechanics' liens.

### PART 1. NATURE AND CLASSIFICATION OF LIENS

**Mortgages in Relation to Liens Generally.** Mortgages represent the most commonly known type of lien. Their essential characteristics, however, cannot be fully understood except in relation to the basic principles governing liens generally.

683

**Nature of Lien.** A lien is a charge imposed on property by which the property is made security. It has been defined by the court as a "right to resort to property in order to enforce a debt or duty." [1] It may or may not be accompanied by actual possession of the property itself.

A lien is not to be confused with ownership. If one has a lien on certain property (for example, a mortgage) and then acquires title to the property, the lien merges into the ownership and ceases to exist. That is, one cannot have a lien on his own property.

The holder of a lien is known as a *lienor*.

**Lien and Pledge Distinguished.** The distinctions between a lien and a pledge have already been noted (page 297). Liens and pledges are alike in that they represent rights of a creditor in the property of a debtor by way of security. However, a pledge without possession is meaningless, but liens may be nonpossessory (page 688) as well as possessory.

**Classification.** Liens may be variously classified as follows:

(1) As to legal origin: *common law, equitable* and *statutory* liens.

(2) As to the debt or debts secured: *general* and *special* (*particular*).

(3) As to right of possession: *possessory* and *nonpossessory* (*charging*).

We shall discuss liens in the order of this classification, including the rights, duties and liabilities of the parties concerned.

## (1) Common Law, Equitable and Statutory Liens

**Common Law Liens.** A common law lien is the right, regardless of statute, to retain possession of personal property until some obligation in connection with it is paid or satisfied. Originally, common law liens were confined to the right which certain mechanics and artisans had to retain a chattel on which they had done some work at the owner's request. Gradually the common law right of lien spread to all cases involving personal property the possession of which is retained by one who has rendered some service in connection with it.

**Equitable Liens.** The so-called "equitable lien" is merely an application of equitable principles to a situation where the remedy at law is inadequate (page 6). The general characteristics of equitable liens are (a) absence of possession in the creditor, and (b) absence of an adequate remedy at law. Common law liens grew out of the fact that the creditor had possession of something belonging to the debtor, which he refused to return until some charge growing out of such possession (for example, repair work done on a chattel by an artisan) was paid or satisfied. (See page 294.) If, in such case, the lienor surrendered possession, he lost his lien (page 687). In the course of time, situations arose where, though possession was in the debtor, it was obviously inequitable to deprive a creditor of the right to have specific property applied to the payment of a debt.

---

[1] *Ancona v. Becker*, 14 Pa. Co. 73, 77.

In such cases, equity imposed a "charging lien" upon the property (page 688). In modern times, the doctrine of equitable liens has been liberally extended to facilitate mercantile transactions and to promote justice.

EXAMPLES:
(1) Right of stoppage in transit (page 254).
(2) Lien of one who lends money against an assignment of future cargoes.
(3) Lien of a vendor of real property for the unpaid purchase price, when the price recited in the deed has not in fact been paid.

**Statutory Liens.** A statutory lien is one created by statute. Many statutory liens are merely "declaratory" of pre-existing liens recognized at common law or in equity. Others represent new rights not previously recognized.

EXAMPLE: Under the common law, the keeper of a livery stable was denied a lien. Such liens and their derivatives (see page 686, "Motor vehicles, motor boats and aircraft") now exist by statute.

Most of the liens discussed in this chapter are statutory liens.

## (2) General and Special (Particular) Liens

**General Liens.** "A general lien is a right to retain a thing, not only for charges specifically arising out of or connected with that identical thing, but also for a general balance of accounts between the parties, in respect to other dealings of the like nature." [2] A general lien is not favored, and the law will refuse to recognize it unless the parties have clearly indicated an intention to create one.

EXAMPLE: When securities are pledged to a banker or broker for the payment of a particular loan or debt, he has no lien upon such securities for a general balance or for the payment of other claims.

**Special or Particular Liens.** A *special* or *particular* lien is a right to retain the property of another for some particular claim or charge upon the identical property retained. Such liens are favored in law. Examples of such liens are furnished in the case of any possessory lien on specific personal property for services rendered in connection with that particular property.

## (3) Possessory and Nonpossessory (Charging) Liens

**Possessory Lien Defined.** A possessory lien is the right to retain possession of another's property until some debt or charge in connection with it has been paid or satisfied. Possessory liens apply to personal property only. This is because personal property is movable and possession is on that account often essential to make the lien effective. This would not be true of real property.

---

[2] Story, *Agency*, sec. 354.

**Essentials of Possessory Lien.** A possessory lien is not valid unless possession is rightfully acquired and retained. If possession is wrongfully acquired, or if the person claiming a lien parts with possession and then wrongfully reacquires it, he does not thereby obtain a possessory lien.

EXAMPLE: Baron takes his car to the Barger Garage for repairs. The bill is $38.50. Baron drives away, promising to pay the bill within a week. A week later Baron leaves the car at the garage to have a flat tire repaired. Barger refuses to surrender the car unless Baron pays the entire bill to date. Baron, upon tendering the cost of repairing the flat tire, may recover possession, because Barger, upon previously surrendering possession, lost his possessory lien for the original repairs and reacquired a particular possessory lien for the cost of the tire repair only. (Barger, of course, though he has lost his possessory lien, may sue Baron for the entire bill due him.)

**Types of Possessory Lien.** Possessory liens are of various types. Some of these we have already considered, including a *vendor's* (*seller's*) *lien* (page 253), an *agent's lien* (page 402), a *warehouseman's lien* (page 302) and an *innkeeper's lien* (page 302). Others are:

*Artisan's lien.* One who has bestowed labor or services upon a chattel has a right to retain possession of it until he is paid for his work; as in the case of a watchmaker, machinist, garage mechanic, garment maker, silk manufacturer or shoemaker.

*Factor's lien on merchandise.* The statute gives a consignee a lien on merchandise shipped to him for any advances made by him to the person in whose name the shipment is made. The statute is designed to protect factors who finance or help finance shipments of merchandise. The factor may reimburse himself for the amount of his lien by pledging or disposing of the merchandise for such purpose.

*Common carrier's lien.* A common carrier has a lien on goods shipped pending payment of transportation charges. The lien is a *special,* or *particular,* not a *general* lien; that is, it attaches to the goods involved in one transaction or one consignment for charges related to that transaction or connected with that consignment and does not extend to charges for other shipments under a separate contract.

*Animal and livery stable keeper's lien.* This lien, as previously noted (page 685) is purely statutory; it did not exist under the common law. A person who keeps animals is known as an "agistor"; for example, one who boards horses, pastures cattle or maintains a dog and cat hospital. The keeper of a livery stable has a lien not only for animals kept, but also for any vehicles stored.

*Motor vehicles, motor boats and aircraft.* A person who keeps a garage, dockyard or hangar for the storage or repair of motor vehicles, motor boats or aircraft, or who furnishes gasoline or other supplies to the owners thereof, has a lien on such vehicles, boats or aircraft for any sum due for such storage, repairs or supplies. This lien exists even if the owner is only a conditional vendee or a mortgagor under a chattel mortgage (page 266).

*Liens of truckmen and draymen.* Every person, firm or corporation engaged in carting or trucking property has a lien on such property for services rendered.

*Lien of motion picture film laboratories.* Motion picture film laboratories have a lien for services rendered in storing, developing, copying, printing or otherwise rendering service in connection with motion picture film.

*Liens of hospitals.* A new type of lien created by statute, of which the New York statute is an illustration, is that which gives hospitals a lien on the proceeds of any lawsuit brought on behalf of an injured person receiving treatment in a hospital, in cases where the injuries are claimed to be the fault of some other person against whom suit is brought for the recovery of damages.

**Waiver of Possessory Liens.** As previously noted, a possessory lienor who parts with possession loses his lien. He also waives his lien if he extends credit or accepts a note or check in payment. However, if he takes a note or check subject to collection, he does not waive his lien until the instrument is paid.

EXAMPLES:

(1) The Polar Fur Company sells a mink coat to a retailer for $2000 and delivers a bill of sale against the retailer's thirty-day note. The company refuses to make delivery, however, until the note is paid, insisting that it has a seller's lien pending payment. The company's position is unsound: It waived its lien when it took the note.

(2) If the Polar Fur Company had taken the retailer's note, or a check, "subject to collection," it would not have waived its lien; delivery could have been lawfully withheld until the note or check was paid.

**Enforcement of Possessory Liens.** The holder of a possessory lien in a chattel may satisfy his lien by a public sale of the chattel. The lienor must give notice of the sale to all persons having an interest in the chattel, and he must give the owner a time limit within which to discharge the lien by payment. If the lien is not discharged, the proposed sale is then duly advertised. The advertisement must describe the property to be sold and must state the name of the owner or person for whose account the property is to be sold and the time and place of sale. At any time before the property is sold, the owner may redeem it by paying the debt and expenses in connection with the lien. If the property is not redeemed and is sold, the lienor may retain from the proceeds of the sale an amount sufficient to satisfy his lien plus expenses. If there is a surplus, he must turn it over to the owner. If there is a deficit, the owner is personally liable for the difference.

**Other Remedies of Lienor.** The lienor need not enforce his lien, but may bring an ordinary action for the recovery of the debt secured by the lien. If the lienor prefers, he may bring an action to foreclose the lien and procure a judgment thereon. Or he may resort to both remedies simultaneously, but in such event, he can have only one satisfaction.

EXAMPLE: If *A* lends *B* $7000 against stock of equal or greater value as collateral, and if, upon the debt becoming due and unpaid, the market value of the stock has declined to $5000, *A* has three alternatives: (1) he may foreclose his lien and cause the stock to be sold, (2) he may sue on the indebtedness, or (3) he may do both. However, he may have but one satisfaction: If his debt has been satisfied, for example, the stock must be returned.

**No Time Limit on Action to Foreclose Possessory Lien.** There is no time limit on an action to foreclose a possessory lien or on the pledgee's right to sell, even though the debt secured by the lien may be barred by the statute of limitations.

EXAMPLE: *A* deposits a gold watch with *B* to secure a $100 loan and gives *B* the right to sell the watch if *A* fails to pay the loan when due. *A* defaults. Ten years pass. *B* may no longer sue on the debt, but he may foreclose the lien and sell the watch.[3]

**Nonpossessory (Charging) Liens: Definition and Nature.** A nonpossessory or charging lien is one not dependent on possession. It usually attaches to real property, because such property is fixed and permanent and actual possession is not so essential to protect the lienor. Examples are (a) judgments, (b) mortgages, (c) mechanics' liens, and (d) tax liens. Instead of requiring possession as a condition for the lien, the statute provides for a means whereby the lienor may give public notice of the lien which he claims in respect to the property concerned. Such notice takes the form of a public record, which all may consult before buying the property affected or before lending money upon such property as security. Real property subject to such lien is said to be subject to "incumbrances."

*Charging liens on personal property.* Although charging liens usually concern real property, they may also affect personal property when possession is impractical and the filing of notice is sufficient to furnish some measure of protection. Examples of charging liens in connection with personal property are: (1) chattel mortgages (page 271); (2) liens on vessels (page 689); (3) liens on monuments, grave stones and cemetery structures, and for labor on stone (page 689). (Mortgages and mechanics liens will be discussed in Part 2 of this chapter.)

**Judgments.** A judgment upon being "docketed" (filed) constitutes a lien against the debtor's real property. The period of the lien varies in the dif-

[3] *Conway v. Caswell*, 121 Ga. 254, 48 S.E. 956; *Pollock v. Smith*, 107 Ky. 509, 54 S.W. 740; *Farmers' Bank v. Iglehart* (Md.), 6 Gill 50; *Townsend v. Tyndale*, 165 Mass. 293, 43 N.E. 107; *Chouteau v. Allen*, 70 Mo. 290; *Hutson v. Title Guarantee and Trust Co.*, 118 Misc. 795, 799, 195 N.Y. Supp. 316; *U.S. v. Mercantile Trust Co.*, 213 Pa. 411, 62 A. 1062; *Connecticut Mut. L. Ins. Co. v. Dunscomb*, 108 Tenn. 724, 69 S.W. 345; *Goldfrank v. Young*, 64 Tex. 432; *Roots v. Mason City Salt Min. Co.*, 27 W.Va. 483.

ferent states. A common period is ten years, with a right to renew for an additional ten years. Ordinarily, the docketing of a judgment creates no lien against the debtor's personal property, unless execution has been issued, as explained on page 861.[4]

**Tax Liens.** A tax lien may be imposed by statute in favor of a governmental authority, Federal, state or local, for the purpose of securing the payment of taxes. Tax liens may be imposed upon either real or personal property; but it is customary for real property taxes to attach only to the real property taxed. If the tax is not paid, the lien may be foreclosed, and upon the subsequent tax sale a purchaser may acquire a valid title if the proceedings have been regular in every respect. Such title is known as a *tax title*.

**Liens on Vessels.** Although vessels constitute personal property, they are by their very nature not readily subject to possessory liens. The law creates a lien against vessels in favor of any person rendering labor or material in building, repairing, fitting, furnishing or equipping a vessel; also for any provisions and stores furnished to the vessel, wharfage, services in loading and unloading, towing, piloting, insurance and even damage caused by the negligence or wilful misconduct of the person navigating the vessel.

**Miscellaneous Charging Liens.** In addition to the charging liens already specified, the law provides for other charging liens in respect to personal property in cases where a possessory lien would be impractical or contrary to public policy. Examples are liens on monuments, gravestones and cemetery structures, and liens for labor on stone.

## Questions

1. What is a lien? How is it distinguished from ownership?
2. Give the three different classifications of a lien.
3. What is meant by (a) a common law lien, (b) an equitable lien, and (c) a statutory lien?
4. Distinguish between a general and a special (particular) lien.
5. (a) What is a possessory lien? (b) What is its outstanding requisite? (c) How may a lienor lose a possessory lien?
6. Give eight illustrations of a possessory lien.
7. (a) How may a possessory lienor enforce his lien? (b) What other remedy has he, if any?
8. Comment on the statute of limitations with respect to the enforcement of a possessory lien.
9. (a) What is a nonpossessory lien? (b) By what other name is it known? (c) Give four illustrations of a nonpossessory lien with respect to real property, and three with respect to personal property.
10. What is meant by a tax title?
11. In whose favor may a lien be acquired against a vessel?

---

[4] *In re Flushing Queensboro Laundry*, 90 F. 2d 601.

## Problems

1. Bates in Chicago sells merchandise on credit to Callan in New York, to be transported via the N.Y. Central Railroad. While the merchandise is on its way to New York City, Bates learns that Callan is insolvent. What type of lien, if any, has Bates with respect to this merchandise?

2. Jones borrows $5,000 from the Ajax National Bank, depositing, as collateral, stock worth $10,000. He pays off the indebtedness of $5,000, but the bank refuses to deliver the stock on the ground that Jones owes the bank $3,000 on another transaction, which is the fact. Jones contends that the bank has no right to keep his stock because of the other transaction. Is his position well taken?

3. Smith takes his car to the Pioneer Garage for repairs. The bill is $42.80. Smith drives away, promising to pay the bill within a week. Thereafter, Smith leaves the car at the garage to have the carbureter adjusted. The garage proprietor refuses to surrender the car unless Smith pays the entire bill to date. What are the respective rights of the parties?

4. Peters buys an automobile "on time," making a down payment of $500, giving twelve notes for the balance secured by a chattel mortgage on the car, and duly receiving possession. Peters keeps his car at Golden's garage. Several months' storage charges accumulate, also charges for repairs. The chattel mortgagee, having received no further payments, seeks to repossess the car, but Golden refuses to surrender it until his charges are paid. Whose position will be sustained by the Court?

5. Blackmore is seriously injured as the result of an automobile accident, and is confined to the City hospital for several months. He has insufficient funds to pay his bill. Thereafter Blackmore recovers a $5,000 judgment against the owner of the car which struck him. In the meantime, the hospital has served a notice on defendant's attorney of its claim for hospitalization in the amount of $850, chargeable against any recovery of damages by Blackmore. The defendant's attorney tenders a check for $4,150 to Blackmore's attorney, who insists that his client is entitled to the full amount of $5,000, with the right to make his own arrangements to pay the hospital. Whose position will the court sustain?

6. The Arctic Fur Company sells a mink coat to a retailer for $3,000 and delivers a bill of sale against the retailer's thirty-day note. The company refuses to make delivery, however, until the note is paid, stating that it has a seller's lien pending payment. How should the court rule on this question?

7. Gordon lends to Moody $10,000 against $10,000 worth of stock as collateral. When the debt falls due, Moody neglects to pay it. The market value of his stock has declined to $8,500. What three alternatives has Gordon under the circumstances?

8. Darby borrows $200 from Craig. He deposits his gold watch with Craig to secure the loan, giving Craig the right to sell the watch if Darby fails to pay the loan when due. Darby defaults. Ten years pass. The statute of limitations on the debt has expired. Has Craig any remedy?

9. Darling delivers goods to a warehouseman and receives a negotiable warehouse receipt for the goods. Yates recovers a judgment against Darling and seeks to levy on Darling's goods in the warehouseman's possession. Can he do so? Explain.

10. Martin delivers two trucks to the Reliable Garage, the first for extensive repairs, the second for brake adjustment. After the work is completed, Martin

calls for the first truck, stating that he needed it in a hurry and would pay the bill later. Later he calls for the second truck, tendering $3.50 for the brake adjustment, and promising to pay the bill on the first truck ($189.85) "in a week or two." Reliable Garage refuses to return the second truck until both bills are paid. What are the rights of the parties?

## PART 2. MORTGAGES AND MECHANICS' LIENS

### Mortgages

**Origin and Nature.** The word "mortgage," literally (from the French, *mort gage*), means "dead pledge." In the early days of the English common law, when a debtor pledged real property to secure a debt, he conveyed title and possession to the creditor, who collected rents, applied them to the debt, and became the absolute owner if the debt was not fully paid when due. The security thus became a dead pledge so far as the debtor was concerned. The hardships and inequities arising out of such transactions caused equity to intervene and to declare that the conveyance, though absolute in form, was really only a lien. Possession was retained by the debtor, but the creditor, upon default, instead of being allowed to declare a complete forfeiture, was permitted to bring a proceeding to shut out or "foreclose" all interests except his own, and upon obtaining judgment, to have the property sold to satisfy the debt; the surplus, if any, being turned over to the debtor.

**Real Estate Mortgage Defined.** Ordinarily, the word "mortgage," standing alone, means a real estate mortgage. Such a mortgage is defined as "the conveyance of an estate by way of pledge for the security of a debt, to become void on payment of it." [5] The debt secured by the mortgage usually takes the form of a bond or note.

*Real estate v. chattel mortgage.* Both real estate and chattel mortgages are charging liens (page 688), and both relate to specific property; the former to realty and the latter to personalty. Since in both cases the lienor does not have possession, he must protect himself against possible claims of innocent third parties; in the former case by recording his mortgage (page 694), and in the latter by either filing or recording (page 273).

*Purchase money mortgages,* and the distinction between *junior* and *senior* mortgages have already been discussed in connection with title closings (page 623).

*Trust deed (trust indenture) v. mortgage.* A trust deed, also variously known as a *deed of trust* and a *trust indenture*, resembles a mortgage in that both are given to secure an obligation, and both create a lien on the property concerned. A mortgage, however, is usually given directly by the debtor to the creditor in the form of a specific lien. A trust deed is given to a third party in the form of a conveyance, to be held by such third party as trustee for the creditor or creditors, the latter frequently consti-

---

[5] Kent, *Commentaries*, p. 133.

tuting a goup participating in the loan by the purchase of bonds in various denominations.

**Parties to mortgage.** The parties to a mortgage are the *mortgagor* who executes the mortgage to secure his obligation and the *mortgagee* to whom the mortgage is executed and delivered to secure the obligation due him.

**Contents of Mortgage.** The usual mortgage recites its date; name and address of the mortgagor and of the mortgagee; the principal amount of indebtedness secured, its due date, and the rate of interest payable thereon, according to the bond or other obligation secured; and a full description of the property mortgaged (see Form 16). In addition, the mortgagor usually covenants with the mortgagee as follows:

(a) *Payment:* that the mortgagor will pay the indebtedness.

(b) *Insurance:* that the mortgagor will keep the buildings on the premises insured against loss by fire for the mortgagee's benefit.

(c) *Injury to premises:* that no building on the premises will be removed or demolished without the mortgagee's consent.

(d) *Default clauses:* that the whole of the principal sum shall become due after default in the payment of any installment of principal when due, or of interest for thirty days, or after default in the payment of any tax, water rate or assessment for thirty days after notice and demand.

(e) *Right to receiver:* that in case of foreclosure the mortgagee shall be entitled to the appointment of a receiver for the collection of rents, and so on.

(f) *Taxes, assessments and water rates:* that the mortgagor will pay all taxes, assessments or water rates.

(g) *Statement upon request:* that the mortgagor, upon request, will furnish a statement of the amount due on the mortgage.

(h) *Warranty of title:* that the mortgagor warrants title to the premises.

**Execution of Mortgage.** The formalities required for the execution of a mortgage differ in the different states. As a rule, the formalities required for the execution of a mortgage, whether made by an individual or a corporation, are the same as those for the execution of a deed.

FORM 16

## REAL ESTATE MORTGAGE

THIS INDENTURE, made this 10th day of May, 1952, between Abner Brooks (unmarried), party of the first part, and hereinafter designated the mortgagor, and Charles Dawson, party of the second part, hereinafter designated the mortgagee.

WHEREAS, the said mortgagor is, by virtue of a bond bearing even date herewith, justly indebted to the said mortgagee in the sum of $25.000 lawful money of the United States, secured to be paid on the 10th day of May, 1954, together with interest thereon, to be computed from the 10th day of May, 1952, at the rate of 6 per cent per annum, and to be paid on the 10th day of November next ensuing the date hereof and semiannually thereafter.

FORM 16 (continued)

default, upon proceedings being commenced for the foreclosure of this mortgage, to apply for the appointment of a receiver of the rents and profits of the said premises without notice, and the mortgagee shall be entitled to the appointment of such a receiver as a matter of right, without consideration of the value of the mortgaged premises as security for the amount due the mortgagee, or the solvency of any person or persons liable for the payment of such amounts.

SEVENTH—And the mortgagor does further covenant and agree that, in default of the payment of any taxes, charges, and assessments which may be imposed by law upon the said mortgaged premises, or any part thereof, it shall and may be lawful for the said mortgagee, without notice to or demand from the mortgagor, to pay the amount of any such tax, charge, or assessment, and any amount so paid the mortgagor covenants and agrees to repay to the mortgagee, with interest thereon, without notice or demand, and the same shall be a lien on the said premises, and be secured by the said bond and by these presents and the whole amount thereby secured, if the mortgagee so elect, become due and payable forthwith, anything herein to the contrary notwithstanding.

EIGHTH—It is hereby further agreed by the parties hereto that if, at any time before said bond is paid, any law be enacted changing the law in relation to taxation so as to affect this mortgage or the debt thereby secured, or the owner or holder thereof, in respect thereto, then said bond and this mortgage shall become due and payable at the expiration of thirty days after written notice requiring the payment of the mortgage debt shall have been given to the owner of the mortgaged premises, anything herein contained to the contrary notwithstanding.

NINTH—The mortgagor, or any subsequent owner of the premises described herein, shall, upon request, made either personally or by registered mail, certify, in writing, to the mortgagee or any proposed assignee of this mortgage, the amount of principal and interest that may be due on this mortgage, and whether or not there are any offsets or defenses to the same, and upon the failure to furnish such certificate after the expiration of six days in case the request is made personally, or after the expiration of thirty days after the mailing of such request in case the request is made by mail, this mortgage shall become due at the option of the holder thereof, anything herein contained to the contrary notwithstanding.

TENTH—It is expressly understood and agreed that the whole of said principal sum and the interest shall become due at the option of the mortgagee, upon failure of any owner of the above described premises to comply with any requirement of any department of the City of New York, within six months after notice in writing of such requirements shall have been given to the then owner of said premises by the mortgagee, anything herein contained to the contrary notwithstanding.

ELEVENTH—Every provision for notice and demand or request contained herein shall be deemed fulfilled by written notice and demand or request personally served on one or more of the persons who shall at the time hold the record title to the premises, or on their heirs or successors, or by registered mail directed to such person or persons or their heirs or successors, at his, their, or its address to the mortgagee last known.

IN WITNESS WHEREOF, the said mortgagor hath signed and sealed this instrument the day and year first above written.

On this 10th day of May, 1952, before me personally came Abner Brooks, to me known and known to me to be the person described in and who executed the foregoing instrument, and he duly acknowledged to me that he executed the said instrument for the purposes therein contained.

ISAAC JOHNSON,
Notary Public No. 1001,
County of New York,
State of New York.

(Notarial Seal)

*Execution of mortgage by corporation.* A mortgage is executed by a corporation through one of its officers duly authorized by the board of directors; and the acknowledgment must recite this fact. A corporate mortgage is usually not valid unless accompanied by a certificate of the secretary evidencing that consent to the execution of such mortgage by the holders of two thirds of the total number of outstanding shares was duly obtained.

**Recording of Mortgage.** A careful mortgagee promptly records his mortgage for the same reason that a careful purchaser promptly records his deed, namely, so that all persons who thereafter acquire any interest or claim in the property will do so subject to the recorded instrument.

EXAMPLE: If Smith, to secure a loan, gives me a mortgage on his house, and then, to secure a second loan from you, gives you another mortgage on the same house which you promptly record, my mortgage will be subordinate to yours, unless you had either actual knowledge of my previous mortgage, by having been informed of it, or else "constructive" knowledge, by reason of the fact that my mortgage was on record when yours was created.

**Rights of Mortgagor and Mortgagee.** A mortgage being a charging lien, the mortgagor continues in possession of the property as owner, notwithstanding the mortgage. The mortgagor's interest in the property, subject to the mortgage, is said to be his *equity*. The rights of the mortgagee are specifically fixed by the terms of the mortgage, including its covenants (page 692). In the absence of specific terms, a mortgagee has the right to receive payment of principal and interest on his mortgage, to have the property stand intact as security, free from damage or diminution, and in case of default to have the property foreclosed and sold to pay the mortgage debt, with interest and court costs, and expenses of foreclosure.

**Assignment of Mortgage.** A mortgagee may assign his mortgage. In such event the assignee acquires only the interest of the assignor, and is subject to any claims or offsets which the mortgagor may have against the latter.

*Estoppel certificate.* An assignee should require the assignor to produce a certificate executed by the mortgagor wherein the latter acknowledges that he has no claims or offsets in connection with the mortgage. Otherwise the assignee takes the risk that such claims may be subsequently asserted by the mortgagor when the assignee requires payment of the mortgage.

**Taking "Subject to" v. Assuming Mortgage.** A person who buys real property with a mortgage on it takes either "subject to" the mortgage, or agrees to assume it, depending on the agreement of the parties. In the former case, his maximum risk is that he may lose the property if the mortgage is foreclosed and sold. On the other hand, by assuming the mortgage, he becomes primarily liable on it as if he had executed the original bond and mortgage.

*Deficiency judgment.* When one is personally liable on a mortgage debt, and the property, on foreclosure, fails to fetch enough at the sale to satisfy the judgment, the mortgagee may enter a "deficiency judgment" and hold the debtor personally for the deficiency.

EXAMPLE: Abel buys a house and lot for $20,000, half of which he pays in cash and half by giving a purchase money bond and mortgage (pages 623 and 691). He then sells the house to Baker, who takes the property *subject* to the mortgage but does not assume it. Later the mortgage is foreclosed and the property sold for $7500, leaving $2500 still due. Abel is personally liable for this deficiency, but Baker is not. Had Baker assumed the mortgage, he would have been liable personally for the deficiency.

**Sale of Mortgaged Premises: Respective Liabilities of Grantor and Grantee.** Upon the sale of mortgaged premises, the grantee takes the land subject to the condition that it is to stand as security for the mortgage debt. At least to the extent of the value of the land, the grantee stands in the position of principal debtor, with the grantor as surety, including the surety's right of subrogation (page 342), that is, his right, in case he pays the mortgage debt himself, to "stand in the shoes" of the mortgagee and to compel reimbursement from the grantee to the extent of the value of the land.

EXAMPLE: In the preceding illustration, the fact that Abel sold the property to Baker was of no concern to the mortgagee: so far as he was concerned, Abel remained liable on the mortgage. If Baker defaulted on the mortgage, and Abel was compelled to pay it, Abel could compel reimbursement by Baker to the extent of the value of the land.

*Liability when grantee assumes mortgage.* When the grantee not only takes subject to the mortgage but assumes it, the mortgagee may hold either the grantee or the grantor for the full amount of the mortgage debt. He may hold the grantee under the Third Party Beneficiary Rule (page 96), because the promise was made to the grantor for the benefit of a third party (the mortgagee), and the grantor as promisee was obligated to such third party beneficiary.[6] If the mortgagee prefers, however, he may hold the grantor, who is liable on the mortgage in the first place. If the grantor has to pay the debt, he in turn may hold the grantee, not only to the extent of the value of the property, but to the full extent of the debt, since the grantee assumed it.

**Extension of Mortgage: Effect of.** The holder of a mortgage may extend its time of payment by executing and delivering an *extension of mortgage* to the mortgagor. When such agreement, upon sufficient consideration, is entered into between the mortgagee and the original mortgagor, the only effect is to postpone the time of payment.

*Modification of mortgage without mortgagor's consent.* Any modification of a mortgage, by agreement between the mortgagee and a subsequent owner without the mortgagor's consent, discharges the mortgagor. Thus,

---

[6] *Vrooman v. Turner*, 69 N.Y. 280.

if the original mortgagor has sold the premises, and an extension agreement is entered into between the mortgagee and a subsequent grantee without the mortgagor's knowledge and consent, the latter, as surety, is discharged, at least to the extent of the value of the land as of the date of the extension agreement; and if the subsequent grantee *assumes* the mortgage, the mortgagor will be discharged as to the entire mortgage debt.

**Prepayment of Mortgage; "Prepayment Clause."** The mortgagee or person entitled to payment of the mortgage cannot be compelled to accept such payment before it falls due according to the terms of the mortgage, unless there is a clause in the mortgage which gives the mortgagor a right to prepay it. Such a clause, known as a "prepayment clause," may prove beneficial to the mortgagor or any subsequent purchaser if the current interest rate falls below the rate fixed in the mortgage.

EXAMPLE: Cole owns an office building on which Davis holds a $100,000 mortgage at 5 per cent interest. The mortgage has five years more to run. Cole can raise a new mortgage on the building for $100,000 at 4 per cent, or a saving in interest of $1000 a year. If the mortgage held by Davis has a prepayment clause, Cole can pay it off with the new mortgage loan, otherwise not, unless Davis consents to the prepayment.

*Accelerating payment.* Mortgages commonly provide that the entire principal sum shall become due after default in the payment of any installment of principal or interest, or of any tax, water rate or assessment, for a given number of days (usually thirty days or less). Such a provision is for the benefit of the mortgagee, and only the mortgagee may take advantage of it. Thus, a mortgagor cannot compel the mortgagee to accept prepayment by deliberately defaulting in the payment of interest.

**Satisfaction of Mortgage.** A mortgage is "satisfied" by payment. A mortgage should not be paid without receiving a sworn certificate by the mortgagee certifying to the fact that the mortgage has been paid. Such certificate is known as a *satisfaction piece*. The satisfaction piece should be promptly recorded, so that the record will show that the property is free and clear of the mortgage.

**Foreclosure of Mortgage.** To "foreclose" is to shut out. When a mortgagee forecloses a mortgage he seeks a judicial decree and judgment shutting out all interests except his own in connection with the mortgaged property. A suit in foreclosure is brought in a court of equity. If successful, it results in a *judgment of foreclosure*. Usually a referee or master is appointed by the court to compute the amount due. The judgment directs that the property be sold at a *foreclosure sale* conducted by an auctioneer under the direction of such referee or master. If the property sells for more than the amount of the mortgage, plus interest, costs, fees and expenses, the surplus, representing the owner's "equity" (page 694), is turned over to him. If the property sells for less than the amount due, a *deficiency* *judgment* is entered and the mortgagor may be required to make good the deficiency.

**Equity of Redemption.** Originally, the owner's *equity of redemption* meant the right in equity, upon paying the debt, to redeem property which the owner had deeded to his creditor. In the course of time, as noted (page 691), equity came to regard such transactions as liens rather than conditional conveyances. The owner was allowed to remain in possession, but the mortgagee was given a right to foreclose and sell the property upon the owner's default. To balance the remedy of foreclosure, equity gives the mortgagor the right, within certain limits, to redeem his property from a forced sale under foreclosure. Such right is now known as the mortgagor's *equity of redemption*. It may be exercised either before judgment of foreclosure, or after judgment and before sale, but not, as a rule, after conveyance upon the foreclosure sale. Only the owner, or some person claiming under him by assignment or sale, may exercise the equity of redemption.

## Mechanic's Liens

**Nature of Mechanic's Lien.** A *mechanic's* lien should not be confused with an *artisan's* lien. It is not really the lien of a mechanic as that word is popularly understood. It relates to work—not necessarily mechanical—and to materials supplied in connection with some permanent improvement to real property.

If a property owner hires a bricklayer and fails to pay him for work done, the bricklayer may sue and get judgment against the owner; but if in the meantime the latter has sold the building and disappeared, the bricklayer's judgment may prove to be of no avail. On the other hand if the bricklayer, within the period prescribed by statute, had filed a *notice of lien* against the premises for the amount due him, such lien, known as a *mechanic's lien*, would have constituted a charge *upon the property*, similar to a mortgage, and if the debt remained unpaid, any purchaser of the property would take it subject to the bricklayer's lien. Similarly, the concern which supplied the bricks to the owner would have a mechanic's lien for any unpaid balance due on the bricks.

Any large corporation, such as a steel company, a cement company or any of the big dealers in building supplies may become entitled to a "mechanic's" lien for materials supplied but not paid for in connection with a building operation. In many states, architects or engineers who have rendered services in connection with a building operation are entitled to a mechanic's lien for the unpaid value of their services.

**Definition; Extent of Lien.** A mechanic's lien may therefore be defined as the charging lien of a laborer, contractor, subcontractor or materialman who performs work or furnishes material for the permanent improvement of real property, at the request or with the consent of the owner, or of his agent, contractor or subcontractor.

From the foregoing definition, the following requisites for a mechanic's lien should be noted:

1. *Permanent improvements to real property.* The lien relates only to *permanent* improvements to *real* property. It would therefore not apply to some temporary task, such as mowing lawn or trimming hedges, as distinguished from beautifying the premises by landscaping. Neither would it apply to work done or material supplied in connection with personal property, such as a printing press.

2. *Subcontractors and materialmen.* A mechanic's lien protects not only a contractor who deals directly with the owner, but also subcontractors who supply or assist the contractor under the latter's agreement with the owner. It is not necessary that such subcontractors or materialmen should have had direct dealings with the owner.

EXAMPLE: Modern Apartments, Inc., enters into an agreement with Modern Builders, Inc., calling for renovation of an apartment house owned by the former. The contract price is $150,000. Modern Builders, Inc., as general contractor, in fulfilling its contract, enters into subcontracts with various foundation and wrecking, steel, cement, carpentry, bricklaying, plastering, painting, plumbing, tile and hardware concerns. These subcontractors and materialmen are entitled to mechanic's liens against the premises for the unpaid amounts due them on the job, up to the full amount due from Modern Apartments, Inc., to Modern Builders, Inc.

**Subordination to Existing Liens.** A mechanic's lien attaches only to the owner's interest in the premises. This interest may be subject to prior liens of third parties. Thus, if Turner buys a house from Todd for $30,000, paying $5,000 in cash and giving Todd a purchase money mortgage for the difference, Turner's interest or "equity" in the premises is $5,000. The $25,000 purchase money mortgage represents a prior lien on the premises. If Turner then orders but fails to pay for $10,000 worth of improvements on the house, any mechanic's liens filed against the premises would be subject and subordinate to Todd's $25,000 mortgage.

**Steps Necessary to Effectuate Lien.** A mechanic's lien does not enlarge the owner's obligation to the lienor. Rather, it serves as notice to all third parties who acquire rights in the premises after the lien arose, that such lien exists and that they take subject to it. To make this lien effective as to third parties, most statutes provide that a written notice of it and the facts on which it is based must be filed in a public place (usually the county clerk's office) within a prescribed period after the work was finished or the material supplied. A common period for such filing is four months. After the notice is filed, the lien takes precedence over all subsequent interests in the premises.

**Bonding and Vacating Lien; Discharge and Satisfaction.** Where a mechanic's lien is filed without right or legal basis, the owner may have it removed from the record by filing a bond or undertaking to make good any judgment that might be entered on the claim; or the owner may instead move for an order vacating the lien on proof that there is no legal basis for it.

Where the claim of a lienor is paid or satisfied, the owner obtains a written acknowledgment to such effect by the lienor, known as a "satisfaction of lien," which, upon public filing, cancels the lien.

**Foreclosure of Lien.** If a mechanic's lien is not vacated, discharged or satisfied, it may be foreclosed, subject to any prior liens. Upon such foreclosure, the premises may be sold, subject, of course, to prior liens. The mechanic's lien is paid out of the proceeds of such sale, and the surplus, if any, is turned over to the owner of the property. The purchaser on such sale takes the premises subject to all prior liens.

**Protection against Claims of Subcontractors.** Subcontractors are entitled to liens against the premises up to the amount of the general contract.

What happens where the owner pays the general contractor but the latter fails to pay the subcontractors? The law generally provides that the owner, before paying the general contractor, must obtain from the latter a sworn statement setting forth all claims of subcontractors and materialmen in connection with the job. If any such claims are or may become due, the owner must retain a sum sufficient to pay them, up to the amount of his contract. Any excess over such claims may be paid over to the general contractor. Payment by the owner without requiring such statement is made at his own risk. If in such case the general contractor fails to pay his subcontractors or materialmen, they may file liens against the premises notwithstanding payment by the owner under his contract.

## Questions

1. How would you define a real estate mortgage? Does it resemble a chattel mortgage in any way?

2. What is the difference between a trust deed and a mortgage?

3. Distinguish between a mortgagor and a mortgagee.

4. What are the principal recitals in a mortgage?

5. What formalities are usually required for the execution of a mortgage?

6. In what respects does the execution of a mortgage by an individual differ from one executed by a corporation?

7. Why is it advisable to record a mortgage?

8. In general, what are the respective rights of a mortgagor and a mortgagee?

9. What rights may be acquired by an assignee of a mortgage?

10. What is an estoppel certificate?

11. What is the difference between the rights and responsibilities of one who takes title "subject to" a mortgage and one who "assumes" the mortgage?

12. What is meant by a deficiency judgment?

13. (a) Where the owner of property mortgages it and later sells it, what are

the respective liabilities of the grantor and grantee in connection with the mortgage? (b) Would such liabilities be affected in any way by the fact that the grantee, instead of taking subject to the mortgage, assumed it? (c) Would they be affected in any way if the terms of the mortgage were modified by the mortgagee and grantee, without the grantor's knowledge or consent?

14. What is meant by the extension of a mortgage?

15. What is meant by (a) a "prepayment" clause in a mortgage; (b) a clause "accelerating payment"?

16. What is meant by (a) satisfaction of mortgage, (b) "satisfaction piece"?

17. Describe briefly the process of foreclosing a mortgage.

18. What is meant by the owner's "equity of redemption"?

19. Explain the nature of a mechanic's lien, including the following: (a) The persons who may seek its protection; (b) The type of work or materials to which it relates; and (c) The subject matter to which it may attach.

20. May a mechanic's lien protect any one other than the contractor who deals directly with the owner? Explain.

21. What steps must be taken to effectuate a mechanic's lien?

22. How may a mechanic's lienor convert his lien into money?

23. What procedure may be adopted by an owner to vacate a mechanic's lien?

24. What liability, if any, may an owner incur if he pays the general contractor, and the latter in turn fails to pay the subcontractors?

## Problems

1. A mortgage is executed by a corporation through one of its officers. It has been duly authorized by its board of directors, and a certificate by the secretary duly attests such fact. The prospective mortgagee, however, refuses to accept the mortgage, insisting that its validity is not established. Is the mortgagee justified in his position?

2. Barton, pressed for funds, executes a first mortgage on his home to Abel, which the latter delays in recording. Subsequently Barton, pressed for additional funds, gives a second mortgage on his home to Baker, who promptly records it. In the event that payment of neither mortgage is made by Barton, whose mortgage would have priority?

3. Chase, the holder of a mortgage on property owned by Dalton, is about to assign the mortgage to Ellis for a valid consideration. What precaution should Ellis take before accepting the assignment? Why?

4. Harvey buys a house for $25,000. He pays in $5,000 of his own money, and borrows the rest from a bank, giving the latter a bond and mortgage for $20,000 in connection with the premises. Later, Harvey sells the house to Dole, subject to the aforesaid mortgage. Still later, the bank forecloses the mortgage for nonpayment of interest and taxes. At the foreclosure sale, the house is sold for $18,000, leaving a deficiency of $2,000. What may the bank do with respect to such deficiency?

5. Suppose in the preceding case that at the time of the sale from Harvey to Dole, the latter had assumed the payment of the mortgage, followed by nonpayment, foreclosure, public sale, and the $2,000 deficiency thereon. Would such facts in any way alter the remedies available to the bank?

6. In connection with the purchase of a home, Johnson executed a $15,000 bond and mortgage with Turner, due in five years. Johnson sold his home to Landon, subject to the mortgage. When the mortgage became due, Turner, at Landon's request, but without Johnson's knowledge, extended payment of the

mortgage for an additional period of five years. Shortly after the execution of the extension agreement, Landon defaults on his interest. Turner forecloses, and at the foreclosure sale, there is a deficiency. Turner seeks to hold Johnson and Landon on the deficiency. How would the court rule?

7. Collins owns an office building on which Dooley holds a $100,000 mortgage at 5 per cent interest. The mortgage has five years more to run. Collins can raise a new mortgage on the building for $100,000 at 4 per cent, thus effecting a saving in interest of $1,000 a year. Under what circumstances, if any, may Collins compel Dooley to accept an immediate payment of his mortgage?

8. The owner of an apartment house enters into an agreement with a general contractor for the renovation of the building at a cost of $150,000. The general contractor in turn hires a number of bricklayers, carpenters, plasterers, plumbers, painters, and so forth to do the necessary work. Although the owner has paid his bill in full to the general contractor, the latter withholds $80,000 from the subcontractors, which he needs in connection with another job. The subcontractors promptly file mechanic's liens for said amount against the owner's premises. The owner moves to vacate said liens, on the ground that he has made payment in full. How will the court decide?

9. Norton retains the services of a general contractor to make necessary repairs to his home, to the extent of $2,500. Before the work is done he finds that he needs another $2,500 to complete the job. Accordingly, he arranges to borrow $2,500 from Ferguson, against a bond and mortgage in that amount. However, Norton has not yet paid any part of his indebtedness to the contractor. Within four months after completing the job, and one day prior to the recording of Ferguson's mortgage, the contractor files a mechanic's lien for the amount due him. As between Ferguson and the contractor, who will have the prior lien?

10. Curran has a past due $10,000 mortgage on his home. The mortgagee threatens foreclosure. Curran does not have the money with which to pay the mortgage, but is trying to raise it by a loan from the bank, to be secured by a new mortgage in place of the old one. The mortgagee finally starts foreclosure proceedings, and obtains a judgment of foreclosure. A week before the scheduled foreclosure sale, the bank agrees to lend Curran the money on a new bond and mortgage. May Curran do anything now to save his home?

## COURT CASES FOR REVIEW

### How Did the Court Decide, and Why?

1. A grantor deeded land to a grantee on the latter's oral promise to reconvey, on repayment by the grantor of a loan made to him by the grantee. The grantor subsequently tendered repayment, but the grantee, pleading the statute of frauds, refused to reconvey. *Emmons v. Emmons*, 64 So. 2d 753 (Miss.).

2. A firm engaged in the manufacture of bricks, having become financially involved, sought and obtained a loan from a former partner, under an agreement whereby the firm was to manufacture brick for him to the value of the amount advanced. Six weeks later the firm went into bankruptcy, whereupon the trustee sued the former partner to recover the value of the brick which he had received within four months prior to bankruptcy, on the ground that the same was a voidable preference. The former partner denied the preference, claiming an equitable lien by virtue of the loan agreement, which was more than four months prior to the bankruptcy. The trustee contended that no lien could arise on property not yet in existence. *Sieg v. Greene*, 225 Fed. 955.

3. A three-year note secured by a mortgage contained the further provision,

"note to be renewed until paid in full." The mortgagors insisted that they were entitled to further renewals beyond the initial renewal period, since the note was renewable until paid in full. *Riepl v. Sardino,* 262 Wis. 670, 56 N.W. 2d 493.

4. A theater was sold to a purchaser who executed a deed of trust to secure payment. The deed of trust obligated the purchaser to protect creditors under the deed of trust by keeping improvements fully insured against loss. It further provided that failure to comply would entitle the creditors to foreclose for payment and satisfaction of the indebtedness. The purchaser defaulted in the payment of insurance premiums. The creditors brought foreclosure proceedings. *Weir v. Boren,* 64 So. 2d 342 (Miss.).

5. A landowner conveyed to a grantee an absolute deed to land, subject to an unrecorded agreement between themselves constituting an encumbrance on the property in favor of the grantor. Later the lands were sold to the county for taxes. The county conveyed the land to a purchaser, by a resale tax deed, valid in all respects on its face. The purchaser had no knowledge of a claim by the heirs of the original owner based on the unrecorded agreement encumbering the original grant. The heirs insisted that since what the county sold was subject to a prior encumbrance, the purchaser took title subject to such encumbrance. *Casker v. Dennis,* 252 P. 2d 1027 (Okla.).

6. On foreclosure by the assignee of a mortgage, the defense was that the assignor (the original mortgagee) had given defendant no consideration for the mortgage. The assignee contended that such defense was insufficient, in view of the fact that plaintiff was an innocent purchaser of the mortgage without notice of what may have transpired between his assignor and the defendant. *Katsoris v. Durham House, Inc.,* 280 App. Div. 718, 117 N.Y. Supp. 2d 156.

7. Casey gave a mortgage on real estate. A subsequent grantee of the property personally assumed the mortgage. After the debt became due, the mortgagee accepted advance interest on the mortgage, without Casey's knowledge or consent. On foreclosure and sale, there was a deficiency, for which the mortgagee sought to hold Casey, who defended on the ground that the payment and acceptance of interest from Casey's grantee prior to its due date amounted to an extension of the mortgage without Casey's consent and thereby relieved him as surety. *Germania Life Ins. Co. v. Casey,* 98 App. Div. 88, 90 N.Y. Supp. 418, aff'd 184 N.Y. 554, 76 N.E. 1095.

8. A lumberman furnished materials to a subcontractor and cash to pay the subcontractor's laborers. He claimed a mechanic's lien on the property involved to the extent of the materials furnished and the cash advanced. *Cooper v. Sparrow,* 259 S.W. 2d 496 (Ark.).

9. A subcontractor placed on record his notice of intention to file a mechanic's lien. The record copy was duly verified by affidavit as required by the statute. The original notice, however, which was served upon the owners, was not verified by affidavit as required by statute. The validity of the lien was challenged. *Associated Lumber & Mfg. Co. v. Mastroianni,* 173 Pa. Super. 310, 98 A. 2d 52.

10. A Louisiana statute provided that a mechanic's lien must be filed within 60 days from the last delivery of material or the last performance of services. Plaintiff, having failed to file within the required period, claimed that the period was extended by the making of certain building changes and the correction of certain building defects. Lift doors had been delivered and installed and adjustments were necessitated by reason of the doors taking on added weight as a result of cleaning, or of absorbing moisture from the elements. The adjustments

further involved oiling moving parts and tightening coil springs. It was contended that these changes constituted "the last delivery of material and the last performance of services," and that the 60 day period thereafter for filing a notice of lien had not expired. *W. M. Bailey & Sons v. Western Geo-physical Co.*, 66 So. 2d 424 (La. App.).

11. The owner of realty entered into an agreement with a general contractor for the erection of a structure on a cost-plus basis. The general contractor then entered into agreements with subcontractors to complete parts of the structure for stipulated sums. Thereafter the general contractor breached the contract and abandoned the structure before the undertaking was finished. The question then arose as to the amounts for which mechanics' liens could be enforced by the subcontractors. *Rebisso, Inc. v. Frick*, 159 Ohio St. 449, 112 N.E. 2d 651.

# 18

# Debtor and
# Creditor

**Scope of This Chapter.** In this chapter we consider the plight of the
hard-pressed debtor, the avenues of legal relief open to him, and the rights
of creditors with respect to one another and their common debtor. In
Part 1 we consider composition agreements between a financially embarrassed debtor and his creditors, and assignments by an insolvent person to
a trustee or other person for the benefit of his creditors. In Part 2 we
consider the nature and purpose of bankruptcy; also petitions in bankruptcy, and the various acts which constitute grounds for a bankruptcy
proceeding.

In Part 3 we consider the administration of a bankrupt's estate, including
the functions and duties of receivers and marshals in bankruptcy proceedings, the election, duties and functions of a trustee, the filing of creditors'
claims, and the payment of dividends in bankruptcy. In Part 4 we consider
the rights, duties and liabilities of the bankrupt, including his right to
counsel, his property exemptions, his duty to attend meetings, testify
under oath, verify claims, execute and deliver necessary papers, file schedules, surrender books and records, and do whatever may be required to
assist in administering the estate and making its assets available for distribution to creditors. In Part 5 we consider the facts which will justify a bankrupt's discharge, and those which will bar it; debts not dischargeable in
bankruptcy; and the provisions of the National Bankruptcy Act for relief
of debtors without the necessity of going through bankruptcy, including,
among others, corporate reorganization and "arrangements."

### PART 1. COMPOSITIONS AND ASSIGNMENTS

**Debtor and Creditor Arrangements Generally.** When a debtor is solvent, his agreements with one or more creditors are of no concern to the
others, since they are protected by the debtor's solvency. But where the
debtor is insolvent, any special arrangement with one creditor necessarily

704

affects the others to the extent that it aggravates the debtor's insolvency. Hence, though a solvent debtor may make such arrangements as he pleases for paying his debts, an insolvent debtor has a limited and dubious choice of alternatives. He may allow himself to be pursued by a succession of suits and judgments; he may file a voluntary petition in bankruptcy; he may be subjected by his creditors to an involuntary petition in bankruptcy; he may petition for an "arrangement" under the Bankruptcy Act (page 741); or he may seek to avoid both bankruptcy and litigated proceedings, either by effecting a composition with his creditors, or by making an assignment of his assets for their benefit.

The latter two alternatives we consider in this Part, and bankruptcy proceedings in the remainder of the chapter.

**Compositions and Assignments Distinguished.** A composition with creditors is an agreement between a financially embarrassed debtor and his creditors, by which the latter agree, upon certain conditions, to release their claims against the debtor in full. The consideration for such an agreement is the mutual forbearances among the creditors to press their claims against the debtor, and an immediate *pro rata* payment by the debtor, or a series of stipulated future payments, frequently evidenced by the debtor's notes and sometimes secured by the deposit of collateral. Generally, the consent of all creditors is required. Generally, also, following the composition agreement and pending its performance, the debtor continues in control of his assets and his business.

An assignment for the benefit of creditors, on the other hand, need not be part of or pursuant to any agreement. It is usually made pursuant to an existing statute. It may, and now usually does consist of the voluntary transfer by an insolvent debtor, to a trustee or assignee, of all the debtor's assets, to be sold or otherwise liquidated for the benefit of such creditors as wish to participate. Not all creditors need participate: those who wish to stay out may pursue other remedies. The debtor ceases to have control of his business or assets, since the essence of an assignment is that his assets must be placed beyond his control.

In view of the basic differences between compositions and assignments, they will be treated separately in the remainder of this discussion.

## Compositions

**Common Law *v.* Statutory Procedure.** Common law agreements for the relief of insolvent debtors have been largely superseded by proceedings under the Bankruptcy Act (pages 712 to 742) and the various state insolvency laws. Such agreements, however, have not become obsolete, and are still resorted to frequently in many states.

**Enforceability of Agreements.** The very essence of a composition agreement is that it shall be fully enforceable, otherwise compositions would be a useless procedure. The requisites of such an agreement are the same as in all contracts (page 33). Particularly important in such agreements, however, is the presence of consideration in some form or other, and the genuineness of mutuality, entailing a high degree of good faith and a corresponding absence of fraud or concealment.

**Consideration.** As pointed out in the chapter on Contracts (page 63), a composition agreement is more than a mere promise to accept a smaller sum for a larger sum due, because it involves mutual forbearances among creditors as well as their promises to the debtor. These forbearances furnish consideration because they represent not only mutual sacrifices, but also a mutual exchange of benefits among creditors, including the potential advantage of rescuing something from a bad financial situation, as against the danger of receiving nothing or next to nothing.

**Mutuality.** No composition agreement is binding on a debtor unless he has accepted it.

EXAMPLE: The following agreement was held to lack mutuality: "We the undersigned agree to take fifty per cent of the amount due us in full, for account against D. M. Stuart. Ellsworth." [1]

A preliminary agreement among creditors alone, however, that they would take a given percentage of their claims as payment in full, is binding upon *them* in advance of debtor acceptance, so that where one or more of the creditors seek to withdraw from such an agreement before the others have had a reasonable opportunity to close the compromise with the debtor, they will be chargeable with a breach of their agreement. On the other hand, if a creditor agrees with other creditors that he will go along with a proposed compromise if all other creditors do likewise, such creditor is not bound unless all other creditors join.

EXAMPLE: In *Greer v. Schriver*,[2] plaintiff, holding notes of the debtor, signed an agreement to take 50 per cent of his claim "on condition that all the creditors should sign." Plaintiff received fifty per cent and gave up his notes, but all the creditors did not sign, and some were paid in full. The court held that plaintiff could recover the balance of his claim.

It is not necessary that all creditors join in a compromise agreement unless the agreement itself so provides.

**Fraud.** A composition agreement must necessarily be based in large part on good faith. The law demands not only the utmost good faith on the part of the debtor in dealing with the creditors, but also on the part of the creditors in dealing with one another. Hence any misrepresentation on the part of the debtor in respect to his assets or affairs, or as to the

---

[1] *Webb v. Stuart*, 59 Me. 356, 357.
[2] 53 Pa. 259.

number of creditors who have already agreed to join, or in respect to anything else which induces a creditor to join in the composition, will, as to such creditor, void the agreement and give the creditor a right to rescind it and either hold the debtor on the original claim, or sue him for damages.

**Secret Preferences.** From the nature of a composition agreement, there is an implied condition that creditors who enter into it, in the absence of express stipulation to the contrary, shall share alike; that no one creditor shall receive more than the others without the latters' assent. Hence any agreement to give one creditor a preference, without the knowledge or consent of the other creditors, is void, and any composition based on it is void so far as the non-participating creditors are concerned. Thus if a debtor induces a creditor to enter into a composition by secretly preferring his claim and promising to pay it in full after the composition, the creditor cannot enforce such promise. Non-participating creditors, upon discovering the preference, may rescind the composition agreement and sue on their claims in full. If the preferential payment is made, it may be subsequently recovered for the benefit of the non-participating creditors, but in such event they are estopped from voiding the composition agreement. Any note, guaranty or other security secretly and preferentially given to induce a creditor to join is unenforceable.

**Conditions.** A creditor may impose such conditions as he sees fit, as a basis for entering into the composition, so long as they do not constitute a fraud or secret preference with respect to the other creditors. The usual conditions are that all creditors shall sign or join in the composition within a limited period, that the creditor's remedies against sureties, indorsers and other joint debtors shall remain unimpaired, and that any security held by the creditor shall be unaffected by the composition.

**Form of Composition Agreement; "Composition Deeds."** The early cases dealing with composition agreements were slow to recognize the doctrine that mutual forbearances by creditors were sufficient to supply consideration. Hence they regarded such agreements as ineffective unless they took the form of a sealed instrument. Hence such agreements are sometimes referred to as "composition deeds."

**Breach.** Where a debtor fails to comply with a composition agreement, as by failing to pay the stipulated installments, the creditors' rights depend upon whether the composition is executory (where the debtor is not released until he has completed his contract), or executed (where the composition releases the debtor from his prior obligations, and substitutes therefor certain stipulated future payments). In the former case, a breach voids the composition and revives the original debt or so much of it as remains unpaid; in the latter case, the creditors' only remedy is damages, which would normally be the unpaid balance under the composition.

## Assignments

**Origin.** Statutory regulation of assignments for the benefit of creditors is comparatively recent. Common law assignments, that is, those not made pursuant to any statute, originated in the desire of a debtor to rid himself of his debts by voluntarily entrusting his property to another, with authority to dispose of it on the best terms obtainable and to distribute the proceeds equitably among the assignor's creditors.

**Status of Assignments Today.** In many states, common law assignments can still be made, even where there are statutes regulating them. Moreover, many of the statutory provisions governing assignments are derived from the common law. A summary of some of the basic principles of common law assignments may therefor be helpful.

**Consent of All Creditors Not Required.** As already noted, assignments, unlike compositions, do not require the assent of all creditors, unless so stipulated in the assignment, or unless the assignment is joined with a composition agreement. When one person entrusts property to another for the benefit of a third, the latter's assent is unnecessary.

**Assignment Must Be Complete and Irrevocable.** A valid assignment for the benefit of creditors must result in a complete and irrevocable transfer of title. If the assignor retains any custody or control over the property, or is given the right to manage it, even for the benefit of creditors, the assignment will not be recognized as valid in all respects. Where assets are transferred under a valid assignment for the benefit of creditors, and no bad faith can be shown, such assets are placed not only beyond the reach of the debtor, but beyond the reach of non-assenting creditors as well. Creditors in such a case who do not wish to participate in the proceeds of an assignment have other remedies, as we shall presently note.

*Necessity of relinquishing custody or management.* The object of the assignment is liquidation. Continued custody or management by the assignor, assignee or anyone else is not in order.

**Preferences.** Under the common law, a debtor, in making an assignment for the benefit of creditors, may give a preference to any creditor or group of creditors, even though other creditors may receive nothing in consequence; the theory being that a person has a right to do what he pleases with his own property. In most states, this right has been restricted by statute or prohibited altogether. In some states, an assignment may provide for preferences to creditors who execute releases of their claims, with the further provision, however, that all other creditors shall have recourse to all other assets. Since frequently no other assets are left, such provision has a tendency to pressure creditors into participating against their will. The only other remedy left to creditors under these circumstances is to file a petition in bankruptcy (page 712), inasmuch as the Bankruptcy Act has exclusive jurisdiction in cases involving the discharge of an insolvent debtor by operation of law.

**Rights of Non-Assenting Creditors.** As stated, creditors need not participate in an assignment proceeding if they do not wish to do so. While they cannot reach assets which have been properly assigned for the benefit of creditors, they have a choice of remedies other than to participate in the proceeds of an assignment. Among these are the following:

(1) *Recourse against surplus.* Non-participating creditors may obtain judgment against the debtor and levy on or attach any surplus after assenting creditors are paid.

(2) *After-acquired property.* Since an insolvent debtor cannot be discharged by operation of law except in bankruptcy, any after-acquired property may be reached by non-assenting creditors.

(3) *Invalidation of general assignment.* If the general assignment has been irregular in some respect, or has failed to comply with requirements, or has been tainted with fraud or bad faith, as in the case of secret preferences, concealed assets, hidden transfers, continued control by the debtor, and the like, a creditor may have the assignment set aside, and may then proceed against the debtor as if no assignment had been made.

(4) *Bankruptcy.* Creditors may petition the debtor into bankruptcy (page 712).

**Statutory Assignments.** The large majority of states have statutes dealing with assignments for the benefit of creditors. In a number of states, the law provides that such assignments can be made only pursuant to statute. Such assignments are said to be purely statutory. Some statutes merely prescribe certain formalities to make the assignment effective, such as that the assignment must be recorded, or that an inventory of the debtor's assets or a schedule of his debts must be filed with the assignment, or that the assignee must file a bond, and so forth. Other statutes go to the extent of placing the assignment, including the conduct and disposition of the estate, under the supervision of the court, so that the entire assignment takes on the character of a judicial proceeding. Among other provisions found in various assignment statutes are the following:

*No preferences.* Most statutes prohibit preferences, voiding either the preferences themselves, or the entire proceeding.

*All assets must be transferred.* The assignor may withhold no assets except those exempted by law.

*Management must be wholly relinquished.* The debtor may retain no custody or control of the assigned property. Intermediate custody, pending liquidation, must be in the hands of the creditors or their representatives (assignees, trustees, creditors' committees, and so forth).

*Discharge of debtor.* State statutes may provide that an assignment for the benefit of creditors shall operate as a release of unpaid balances provided creditors consent thereto; but the power to discharge insolvent debtors by law alone is an exclusive bankruptcy function, vested in Congress by the Constitution of the United States.

## Questions

1. What courses are open to an insolvent debtor?

2. What is meant by a composition with creditors? How does it differ from an assignment for the benefit of creditors?

3. "A common law composition must have the same requisites as any other contract." Is this statement true, false, or partly true and partly false?

4. In respect to a common law composition, illustrate the effect of the presence or absence of (a) consideration, or (b) mutuality.

5. Explain the effect of fraud upon the rights of a creditor who enters into a composition agreement.

6. Where a debtor induces a creditor to enter into a composition agreement by secretly promising preferential treatment, (a) may the creditor enforce such promise, and (b) what are the rights of the other creditors upon discovering such preference?

7. What remedies are open to a creditor upon the debtor's failure to comply with the terms of a composition agreement, (a) where such agreement is executory, and (b) where the agreement is executed?

8. What is meant by a common law assignment?

9. What are some of the factors connected with an assignment that may result in its being declared invalid?

10. How does continued custody or management affect the ultimate object of an assignment?

11. What four remedies may a creditor pursue where he does not wish to join in the execution of an assignment?

12. Name some of the provisions frequently found in statutes governing the execution and enforceability of assignments for the benefit of creditors.

## Problems

1. In the execution of a compromise agreement, a debtor misrepresented the nature and extent of his assets as well as the number of creditors who had already agreed to join. What remedies, if any, have the creditors in connection therewith?

2. In a compromise agreement, a creditor represented that his claim was smaller than it actually was, hoping thereby to reserve the balance of his claim for subsequent payment in full. Will he be bound by his representations?

3. A debtor induced a creditor to enter into a composition by secretly preferring his claim and promising to pay it in full after the composition. (a) What rights, if any, has such creditor with respect to enforcing said promise? (b) When the non-participating creditors discover the preference, what may they do under the circumstances?

4. After the execution of a composition agreement, the debtor failed to pay the stipulated installments as therein provided. The creditors then moved to set aside the composition agreement and to hold the debtor on the original amounts of their respective claims. May they do so?

5. Ninety per cent of a debtor's creditors consented to the execution by the debtor of a general assignment for their benefit. The remaining 10 per cent

who dissented, now move to vacate the said assignment on the ground that the consent of the creditors in connection therewith must be unanimous. Is their contention correct?

6. A debtor in making an assignment for the benefit of creditors, gave a preference to one of them. The remaining creditors voiced their objections to the Court and moved to disallow same. How would the Court decide?

7. Following the execution of an assignment by a debtor and his creditors, wherein the latter all agreed to accept 30 per cent in full payment of their claims, the debtor inherits from a wealthy uncle a large sum of money which would be sufficient to pay off all claims in full. Have the creditors any rights with respect to this inheritance?

## PART 2. BANKRUPTCY: NATURE AND PURPOSE; PETITIONS AND ACTS

**Origin and Development of Bankruptcy Laws.** Ancient Roman law treated insolvency as a crime, punishable by imprisonment, servitude and even death. The *debtor's gaol*, until comparatively recent times, was an established institution. In 18th century England, Parliament offered escape from the debtor's prison upon the surrender of one's assets for the benefit of one's creditors; but the debtor was not discharged as to any deficiency. Gradually, imprisonment for debt was abolished. The legal principle developed that if one surrendered all his worldly goods, he ought to be relieved of *all* his debts. By the time the United States Constitution was adopted, a number of state statutes not only permitted, but *compelled* an insolvent debtor to surrender his assets for the benefit of his creditors. The United States Constitution took all bankruptcy jurisdiction away from the states: first, by prohibiting any state from passing laws impairing the obligation of contracts; second, by vesting all bankruptcy jurisdiction in Congress, which was empowered to pass "uniform laws on the subject of bankruptcies throughout the United States." Congress has passed numerous bankruptcy laws, including revisions and amendments. The latest became effective September 22, 1938.

### Nature and Purpose of Bankruptcy

**Purpose of National Bankruptcy Act.** The essential purpose of the National Bankruptcy Act is two-fold: (1) to give honest but insolvent debtors an opportunity to make a new start in life, and (2) to give all creditors an equal opportunity to share in the debtor's property in proportion to their claims. The recent trend is to broaden the first of these purposes. For example, the Bankruptcy Act of 1938 added liberal provisions whereby honest but unfortunate debtors may make "arrangements" to secure financial respite without incurring the taint of bankruptcy.

**Bankruptcy and Insolvency Distinguished.** Bankruptcy is a legal status. A person is not a bankrupt unless he has been so declared ("adjudicated") in a bankruptcy court. Insolvency, on the other hand, is a financial status. It has two meanings:

*Insolvency in the state or equity sense.* Insolvency in the state or equity sense of the term means inability to meet one's debts as they mature. One may be "worth" a million dollars in frozen assets, yet be insolvent in the equity sense because of inability to meet a $100,000 note when it falls due.

*Insolvency in the bankruptcy sense.* Under the Bankruptcy Act a person is insolvent if the aggregate value of his assets is not at a fair valuation sufficient to pay his debts. Thus, if one's entire assets, liquid or otherwise, are worth $90,000 at a fair valuation, and his liabilities amount to $100,000, he is insolvent in the bankruptcy sense of the term.

*Insolvency laws v. bankruptcy laws.* There are numerous insolvency laws, but there is only one Bankruptcy Act. (See page 711.) The essence of a bankruptcy law is to compel a debtor to surrender his assets for the benefit of his creditors and to afford him a discharge at the end of a court proceeding if he has fully complied with the law. State laws may compel a debtor to surrender assets in individual cases, either upon an attachment or in execution of a judgment (page 861), but they may not compel a debtor to make an involuntary surrender of all his assets for the general benefit of all his creditors; neither may they grant a debtor a statutory discharge from all his debts. These are bankruptcy functions which the United States Constitution vests exclusively in the Federal courts.

## Petitions in Bankruptcy

**Voluntary and Involuntary Petitions: in General.** Bankruptcy proceedings are commenced by the filing of a petition, asking that the Court declare or adjudge some person a bankrupt. In *voluntary* bankruptcy the petitioner asks that he himself be adjudged a bankrupt. When the proceedings are *involuntary*, the petitioner requests that some person other than the petitioner or petitioners be adjudged a bankrupt.

**Voluntary Petitions: Who May File.** Any person (except a municipal, railroad, insurance or banking corporation or a building and loan association) may file a voluntary petition in bankruptcy. The act does not require a voluntary petitioner to be solvent, or to owe any fixed minimum of debt; there is nothing to prevent a solvent person from having his property distributed among his creditors in bankruptcy.

EXAMPLE: A corporation has assets convertible into cash amounting to $285,000. It has outstanding: $100,000 of common stock; $50,000 of preferred stock; $75,000 in bonds; $8000 in taxes; and $150,000 in claims of general creditors. Although the corporation is solvent, having $285,000 in assets as against debts of $233,000 (outstanding stock is not a debt), it may file a voluntary petition and have its property distributed in bankruptcy. The surplus, after administration expenses, would presumably go to the preferred stockholders (page 514). If anything is left, it will go to the common stockholders, *pro rata*.

**Involuntary Petitions: Who May File.** When a person is insolvent and refuses to make an assignment for the benefit of creditors or to take any other action, creditors may bring about a distribution of his assets by filing an involuntary petition in bankruptcy against him. Three or more creditors who have provable claims against any person amounting in the aggregate (in excess of the value of any security held by them) to $500 or over, may file an involuntary petition. If the combined number of creditors is less than twelve, any *one* of such creditors whose claim equals $500 net, in excess of securities, may file the petition.

**Involuntary Petitions: Against Whom May Be Filed.** Any natural person (except a wage earner[3] or farmer) and any moneyed, business or commercial corporation (except a building and loan association, or a municipal, railroad, insurance or banking corporation) owing debts to the amount of $1,000 or over, may be forced into bankruptcy. If a petition is filed against any person or corporation other than those specified, it will be dismissed; for example, a petition against a railroad corporation.

**Petitions by and against Partnerships.** The Bankruptcy Act treats a partnership as an entity (page 495) separate from the partners. An involuntary petition may be filed against the partnership entity alone, or against it and any of the general partners. The petition may be filed either before or after dissolution of the firm but not after a final settlement of partnership affairs. A trustee in bankruptcy may demand a statement of the individual assets of the partners, outside of their firm assets, even though no petition has been filed against the individual partners; and a trustee must keep separate accounts of partnership property and of the individual property of partners.

**Where and How Petitions Are Filed.** Petitions are filed in the office of the Clerk of the United States District Court. If the petition is voluntary, it must be accompanied by a schedule of the petitioner's property showing the amount and kind of property, location, value, list of creditors, and their residences, amounts due each, and so on. The petition, whether voluntary or involuntary, must be under oath.

**Proceedings upon Voluntary Petition.** In voluntary proceedings the bankrupt merely files a petition, accompanied by schedules of his assets and liabilities, and asks for a discharge. In these schedules he lists all his assets in detail, and all his liabilities, actual or contingent. These schedules are under oath, and are executed in triplicate. The three copies are filed in the office of the District Court where the bankrupt lives or has his place of business. Immediately upon filing a voluntary petition, the petitioner is adjudicated a bankrupt. The procedure subsequent to this is the same as in the case of involuntary proceedings after adjudication.

**Proceedings upon Involuntary Petition.** In the case of an involuntary proceeding, three or more creditors, or one creditor, as the case may be (see above), file a petition setting forth that within the preceding four

---

[3] The Bankruptcy Act defines a wage earner as one "who works for wages, salary or hire, at a compensation not exceeding $1,500 per year."

months the alleged bankrupt has committed one or more of the acts of bankruptcy (pages 714 to 716). The alleged bankrupt is served with a "writ of subpoena," which is the equivalent of a summons (page 857). Such service is returnable within ten days. The alleged bankrupt has five days after the return day within which to answer or plead under oath to the petition. If he fails to answer and the petition is in proper form, he is adjudged a bankrupt. If he denies the allegations of the petition, a trial must be had on the issues. The alleged bankrupt may demand a jury trial when solvency is an issue. If, at the trial, the allegations of the petition are sustained, the debtor is declared or "adjudged" a bankrupt; otherwise, the petition is dismissed. To sustain the allegations of the petition, it must be shown that the alleged bankrupt actually did, within the previous four months, commit one of the six acts of bankruptcy.

## Acts of Bankruptcy

**First Act of Bankruptcy: Fraudulent Transfers.** If a person transfers or conceals any part of his property, or permits it to be transferred or concealed, with intent to "hinder, delay or defraud his creditors," he commits an act of bankruptcy. Solvency (Bankruptcy Act definition) is a complete defense to this act.

EXAMPLES:
(1) An insolvent debtor ran away with his assets to avoid criminal prosecution. This was a clear case of concealing assets with intent to hinder, delay and defraud creditors.[4]
(2) An insolvent debtor raised money to pay certain particular creditors by executing and delivering, to a security trust company, a chattel mortgage covering the debtor's entire stock in trade. The execution and delivery of this mortgage were held to have been in bad faith and to have constituted an effort to hinder and delay creditors; hence, an act of bankruptcy.[5]

**Second Act of Bankruptcy: Giving Preference While Insolvent.** A person commits an act of bankruptcy if, *while insolvent,* he transfers any part of his property to one or more creditors with intent to prefer them over other creditors. If a debtor is solvent, he may prefer to pay any one creditor in full, ahead of the others. No injustice is done thereby, since the debtor's solvency assures payment to the other creditors as well. But if an insolvent debtor pays any one creditor in full, he thereby deprives the others of their ratable share.

EXAMPLE: Smith has assets of $50,000 and debts of $100,000. He owes Allen $50,000, Brown $30,000, and Carter $20,000. He pays Carter's debt in full. Since Smith's assets amounted to 50 per cent of his liabilities, Allen, Brown, and Carter were entitled, respectively, to a distribution of $25,000, $15,000 and

---

[4] *In re Filer*, 108 Fed. 209 (D.C., N.Y.).
[5] *In re Pease*, 129 Fed. 446.

$10,000. Smith's preferential payment to Carter deprived Allen and Brown of their ratable shares.

**Third Act of Bankruptcy: Permitting Lien While Insolvent.** A person commits an act of bankruptcy if, *while insolvent*, he permits a creditor to obtain a lien through legal proceedings and fails to vacate or discharge the lien within thirty days, or at least within five days before the date set for any sale or other disposition of the property affected by the lien.

The most common lien which a creditor may be permitted to obtain through legal proceedings is by means of a judgment. However, merely procuring a judgment does not necessarily constitute a lien on all of a debtor's property. In order that a judgment shall constitute a lien on a debtor's real property, it must be duly docketed or filed; and in order that it may constitute a lien against the debtor's personal property, it must as a rule be advanced to the point of issuing execution (page 861) on it to a sheriff or corresponding officer.

**Fourth Act of Bankruptcy: Assignment for Benefit of Creditors.** We have already discussed, in Part 1, the nature and purpose of general assignments for the benefit of creditors. These, as we have noted, are pursuant either to common law or to a state statute. Such proceedings are frequently terminated by a petition in bankruptcy, because a general assignment for the benefit of creditors constitutes an act of bankruptcy and creditors dissatisfied with such an assignment may file a petition in bankruptcy against the assignor. The assignor's solvency in such a situation is immaterial: if the petition is in proper form, the state proceedings are thereby terminated, and a Federal court takes over.

**Fifth Act of Bankruptcy: Appointment of Receiver or Trustee while Insolvent.** If a person, either *while insolvent*, or *while unable to pay debts as they mature*, procures, permits or suffers, voluntarily or involuntarily, the appointment of a receiver or trustee to take charge of his property, he commits an act of bankruptcy. Receivership without insolvency does not constitute an act of bankruptcy. The word "insolvency," under this specified act of bankruptcy, is used in both the equity and bankruptcy meanings of the term (page 712). Moreover, receivership as an act of bankruptcy must be general, not special. For example, if a mortgage on the debtor's property is being foreclosed and a receiver is appointed in connection with the foreclosure, such receivership does not constitute an act of bankruptcy.

**Sixth Act of Bankruptcy: Written Admission.** If a person admits in writing his inability to pay his debts and his willingness to be adjudged a bankrupt, he commits an act of bankruptcy. The clearest admission of willingness to be adjudged a bankrupt is, of course, the filing of a voluntary petition in bankruptcy. However, many persons are unwilling to take the formal step of filing a petition in court, and yet are willing to admit their inability to pay their debts and their willingness to be adjudged a bankrupt.

A written admission, to constitute an act of bankruptcy, must cover both inability to pay debts and willingness to be adjudged a bankrupt. The former, alone, is insufficient. Thus, in one case,[6] a letter written by the secretary and general manager of a corporation informed the employees of its inability to pay their wages. It was claimed that this constituted an act of bankruptcy. The court held that it did not, because the corporation had not admitted its willingness to be adjudged a bankrupt. In another case,[7] an insolvent debtor signed and published a statement of his affairs showing an excess of liabilities over assets. The court held that this was not an act of bankruptcy.

## Questions

1. What is the two-fold purpose of the National Bankruptcy Act?
2. What is the difference between bankruptcy and insolvency?
3. Distinguish between insolvency in the state or equity sense and insolvency in the bankruptcy sense.
4. Distinguish between a voluntary petition and an involuntary petition in bankruptcy.
5. Who may file (a) voluntary petitions; (b) involuntary petitions?
6. Against whom may an involuntary petition in bankruptcy be filed?
7. What effect, if any, does the bankruptcy of an individual partner have upon the partnership itself?
8. Where a partnership is forced into bankruptcy, but no petition has been filed against the individual partners, may a trustee make any demands upon them? Explain.
9. (a) Where are petitions in bankruptcy filed? (b) Where the petition is voluntary, what must it show? (c) What is the immediate effect of filing such petition?
10. (a) What must an involuntary petition in bankruptcy show? (b) How is the alleged bankrupt informed of the petition? (c) What may he do about it? (d) What effect does his action or inaction have upon subsequent proceedings?
11. Is insolvency alone a sufficient basis to force a debtor into bankruptcy? Comment.
12. Name the six acts of bankruptcy.
13. Comment on the materiality of a debtor's solvency where the act charged against him was that he made an assignment for the benefit of creditors.
14. In order to constitute an act of bankruptcy, what two features with respect thereto must a written admission cover?

## Problems

1. Bingham finds himself over-extended in the matter of real estate investments. He has approximately $200,000 tied up in real estate which he is at present unable to sell, and he has a $5,000 note falling due today which he is

---

[6] In re Erie City Airport, 44 F. 2d 673.
[7] In re Berthoud, 231 F. 529, appeal dismissed 238 F. 797.

unable to pay. His total liabilities are in the neighborhood of $75,000. The question arises as to whether Bingham is insolvent, using the term insolvency within the original meaning of the Bankruptcy Act. How would you answer such a question?

2. An involuntary petition in bankruptcy is filed against the Perfection Plastering Co., Inc. There are ten creditors of the company with aggregate claims of $33,250. The petition is filed, however, by only one of the creditors whose claim amounts to $750. Assuming that an act of bankruptcy can be shown to have been committed within four months of the filing of the petition, should the company be adjudicated a bankrupt or should the petition be dismissed? Why?

3. A petition is filed against a partnership concern consisting of seven members, none of whom is alleged to be personally insolvent. The trustee in bankruptcy, however, demands a statement of the individual assets of the partners, which they refuse to furnish. Can the trustee compel the individual partners to furnish such statements?

4. An accountant is employed by the XYZ Corporation at a salary of $5,000 a year. He owes $8,000 to his creditors, three of whom now file an involuntary petition in bankruptcy against him. He moves to dismiss the petition. How will the Court rule and why?

5. A corporation has assets convertible into cash amounting to $285,000. It has outstanding: $100,000 of common stock; $50,000 of preferred stock; $75,000 in bonds; $8,000 in taxes; and $150,000 in claims of general creditors. It files a voluntary petition in bankruptcy. An interested stockholder moves to dismiss the petition on the ground that since the corporation is solvent, it may not file a voluntary petition. How should the Court rule, and why?

6. An insolvent debtor ran away with his assets to avoid criminal prosecution. During subsequent litigation a question arose whether or not this was a case of concealing assets with intent to hinder, delay and defraud creditors. How did the court decide?

7. An insolvent debtor raised money to pay certain particular creditors by executing and delivering to a security trust company, a chattel mortgage covering the debtor's entire stock in trade. Did this constitute an act of bankruptcy? If so, why? If not, why not?

8. A corporation conveyed real estate to a creditor within four months prior to the filing of a petition. The conveyance was made to secure past indebtedness and to obtain future advances. However, there was no proof to indicate that the transfer was made with fraudulent design. Did this constitute an act of bankruptcy?

9. Three months ago, Poor, with assets of $100,000 and liabilities of $200,000, paid off a $10,000 note to Raymond and permitted the Active Corporation to procure and collect a $20,000 judgment against him. How would the Court rule with respect to the commission of an act of bankruptcy?

10. A corporate debtor, while insolvent, aided a creditor in obtaining a judgment against itself by appearing in the suit, signing a confession of judgment, and then facilitating the execution of the judgment by the sheriff. Within four months thereafter, an involuntary petition was filed against the corporation. The corporation opposed the petition, contending that the filing of the confession of judgment, followed by execution, did not constitute a transfer. The lower court sustained the corporation's motion to dismiss the petition. On appeal, what was the court's decision?

11. An insolvent debtor desiring to raise money for the purpose of paying certain particular creditors, executed and delivered to a private banking con-

cern a chattel mortgage covering the debtor's entire stock in trade. Other creditors, objecting to this transaction, file a petition in bankruptcy against the debtor. Will the petition be sustained or dismissed? Why?

12. Good and Andrew have been personal friends and have done business together for many years. Good, however, is slow in paying his bills. Notwithstanding ample assets with which to discharge his debts, he defers payment to creditors who are pressing their claims except as to Andrew, to whom he makes a substantial payment in complete satisfaction of all claims by Andrew against Good. The creditors file a petition in bankruptcy against Good. Will the petition be sustained or dismissed? Give reasons.

13. A merchant becomes insolvent, his debts being greatly in excess of his assets. A newspaper vender who has been delivering newspapers to the merchant for many years, begs the merchant to pay an accumulated bill amounting to $9.50, and the merchant, because of the newspaperman's needy condition, pays the bill. The question now arises whether in view of the merchant's insolvency, he has not committed an act of bankruptcy. How would you answer such question, and why?

14. A judgment is entered against Wayne Bullock in the amount of $32,617. Bullock makes no effort to vacate the judgment and two months later a petition in bankruptcy is filed against him. Bullock's assets, all personal property, total $19,500; liabilities, $25,000. It appears that the judgment creditor had made no effort to collect the judgment. Will the bankruptcy petition be sustained or dismissed? Why?

15. Burns, the proprietor of a hardware store, makes an assignment for the benefit of creditors of all his stock in trade, reserving his furniture and fixtures. Three dissatisfied creditors file a petition against Burns, specifying the assignment as an act of bankruptcy. Will their position be supported by an adjudication? Why?

16. Kelly filed a petition to have the Gray Hat Co., Inc. adjudged an involuntary bankrupt on the ground that within four months from the filing of the petition, said company made an assignment for the benefit of its creditors. The Gray Hat Co., Inc. interposes the defense that it was solvent at the time the general assignment was made and still is solvent. How will the petition be disposed of and why?

## PART 3. ADMINISTRATION OF BANKRUPTCY ESTATE

**In General.** Between the filing of an involuntary petition and the determination of the bankruptcy court as to whether the petition should be dismissed or the debtor adjudicated a bankrupt, there is sometimes danger that the debtor's property may be spirited away and the administration of the bankrupt estate handicapped in case of adjudication. Frequently, too, it becomes necessary to appoint a custodian to protect and preserve the debtor's property pending adjudication. Such custodian may be a receiver or marshal appointed by the court, on petition showing special reasons justifying such appointment.

### Custody: Receivers and Marshals

**Grounds for Appointment of Receiver.** Ordinarily, a receiver in bankruptcy will be appointed only when absolutely necessary to preserve assets; for example, when assets are perishable or unprotected, or likely to be wasted, destroyed, stolen, misappropriated, dissipated, secreted or turned over to favored creditors pending adjudication.

*Receiver v. trustee.* Receivers and trustees differ basically in two respects: (1) A receiver is appointed by the court, whereas a trustee is elected by the creditors; and (2) a receiver's functions are primarily custodial, though he has administrative dutes as well, whereas a trustee's duties are primarily administrative, though he takes over custody as an incident to administration.

**Powers and Duties of Receiver or Marshal.** The receiver or marshal, whenever necessary, may secure an order restraining the bankrupt from transferring any of his property, restraining creditors from attempting to seize any of the debtor's property by legal process or otherwise, and directing the receiver or marshal to seize and hold the property himself pending adjudication. Before the property of an alleged bankrupt can be seized or a receiver appointed pending adjudication, a bond must be given by the person applying for such seizure or appointment, so as to protect the debtor in case it turns out that he was not really bankrupt. Otherwise, he may suffer serious damage without assurance of recompense. Usually, the powers and duties of a receiver or marshal are confined to custody and preservation of assets. All books, papers and records of the alleged bankrupt must be carefully preserved. A receiver or marshal has authority to collect rents, bank accounts or bills receivable owed to the alleged bankrupt. Ordinarily a receiver has authority to take charge of premises and to continue to occupy them under an existing lease, especially when the alleged bankrupt has assets on the premises. If he surrenders the premises, the landlord's damages are limited by statute. (See page 725.)

**Termination of Receivership.** Temporary custody by the receiver or marshal is terminated upon appointment of the trustee in bankruptcy. The receiver must account for all property and income of the bankrupt estate coming into his hands during the period he has custody, as well as all administration and other expenses incurred during the same period. A receivership may also be terminated by dismissal of the petition in bankruptcy, in which event the receiver, upon surrendering custody to the alleged bankrupt, must likewise make full report covering receivership assets, income and expenses.

## Election of Trustee

**Necessity for Administration.** If the debtor is adjudicated a bankrupt, it becomes necessary to administer his estate, that is, to take over and collect the bankrupt's assets, convert it into money and, after payment of fees and expenses, to distribute it among creditors in a prescribed order of priority. For this purpose, creditors elect a trustee to act on their behalf under the general supervision of the referee and subject to court direction.

**Creditors' Meetings.** Not less than ten nor more than thirty days after the adjudication, the referee calls and presides over the first meeting of creditors. Subsequent meetings may be called by the referee whenever required. One fourth or more of the creditors may request that subsequent meetings be called. At the first meeting, creditors file "proofs of claim" (page 722).[8] The referee may allow or disallow any claim.

**Voting by Creditors.** Only creditors whose claims have been allowed may vote at creditors' meetings. Such creditors may vote personally or by a representative. Voting is governed by a majority in number as well as in amount. For example, ten creditors aggregating $20,000 in claims cannot outvote two creditors with a total of $50,000 in claims, and neither can the latter outvote the former, because neither group has a majority in number *and* amount. Claims of $50 or less are counted in computing the amount, but not in computing the number of creditors voting. Secured or priority creditors (pages 723 and 724) may not vote unless the amounts of their claims exceed the values of their securities or priorities.

**Election of Trustee: Creditors' Committee.** The creditors at their first meeting may elect one or three trustees. If they do not elect a trustee, or if the trustee elected fails to qualify, the referee appoints a trustee. The trustee, by operation of law, automatically takes over all the bankrupt's right, title and interest in any of his property, real or personal, tangible or intangible.

The creditors may at their first meeting also designate a committee of not less than three creditors. This committee may consult and advise with the trustee, make recommendations, and submit to the Court any questions affecting the administration of the estate.

## Duties of Trustee

**Duties of Trustee: in General.** Primarily, the trustee's function is to collect and reduce to money, under the direction of the court and as expeditiously as possible, all property, real or personal, tangible or intangible, which may belong to the bankrupt, wherever such property may be located and whoever may be in possession of it. All other duties of the trustee are subordinate and incidental to this one.

**Duty to Examine Bankrupt.** The trustee must examine the bankrupt at the first meeting of creditors, or at other meetings especially fixed for that purpose, unless the bankrupt has already been examined by the referee, receiver or creditors. The trustee must satisfy himself that the bankrupt has withheld no property which should go into the estate, and that he

---

[8] Creditors have six months within which to file their proofs of claim, but only creditors whose claims are filed may vote at meetings.

has not been guilty of a voidable preference, transfer or lien in favor of some particular creditor or creditors.

**Duty to Set Aside Voidable Preferences, Transfers and Liens.** It is a trustee's duty to take the necessary steps to set aside any unlawful preference, transfer or lien. A solvent person, as noted on page 714, may prefer any creditor he pleases; but an insolvent person cannot prefer one creditor before another without causing injury to the latter. Similarly, when an insolvent person transfers any of his property for an inadequate consideration or permits a lien to be placed on his property for the benefit of a favored creditor, he thereby depreciates the value of the estate available to creditors generally.

**Trustee's Duty to Assume or Reject Contract.** The trustee is allowed sixty days after adjudication within which to assume or reject any executory contract (page 83) to which the bankrupt is a party. If the contract has been executed by the other party, that is, if the bankrupt has already received the benefit of the contract, the trustee may neither assume nor reject; the estate is liable, and the other party has a valid claim against the estate.

**Actions by or against Trustee.** A trustee in bankruptcy may bring any action in any court in behalf of the bankrupt estate and for the benefit of creditors, and may conduct such suit, continue it or discontinue it as his own discretion may dictate in the interests of the creditors. For this purpose he may retain an attorney or attorneys to represent him. Formerly, an attorney could not represent a trustee if he also represented a general creditor. This is no longer the law. Trustees may not only bring suit in outside courts, but suit may be brought against them to enforce any claims or rights other than those ordinarily provable by filing a proof of claim in bankruptcy.

**Trustee's Duty to Account.** Within the first month after his appointment, and every two months thereafter, the trustee must render an accounting to the court concerning his administration of the estate. He must make a final report and file his final account, fifteen days before the day fixed for the final meeting of creditors; and he must lay before such final meeting a detailed statement of the administration of the estate.

**Objections; Surcharge; Approval; Discharge.** Any party in interest may object to the trustee's account upon a hearing set for such purpose. The referee sustains such objections if they are meritorious and overrules them if they are not. So long as the bankrupt estate has not been closed and the trustee has not been discharged, his accounts are subject to inspection and audit by the Court. If, by some wrongful act or omission of the trustee, the estate has suffered loss, the trustee may be *surcharged*, or held personally liable for such loss. If a trustee's account is not objected to, and the referee finds it in order, the account will be approved and the trustee discharged. The estate is thereupon closed.

## Creditors' Claims

**Proofs of Claim: Nature, Form and Contents.** A proof of claim in bankruptcy is a statement under oath signed by a creditor setting forth the facts in reference to his claim. These facts include the amount and consideration for the claim; whether the claim is secured, and if so, how; whether any payments have been made on the claim, and if so, what; together with an affirmation that the sum claimed is justly owing from the bankrupt to the creditor. If a claim is founded on a written instrument, the original instrument must be attached.

**Time for Filing Proofs of Claims.** Proofs of claims must be filed with the court or referee within six months after the first date set for the first meeting of creditors. As previously noted, however, if a creditor wants to vote at the first meeting, he must first file his proof of claim. If a creditor fails to file his proof of claim within the time allowed by law, his claim is lost.

**Provable Claims.** Not every claim is provable in bankruptcy. Only those claims which are specifically enumerated in the Bankruptcy Act[9] may be proved, namely, the following:

*Fixed liabilities,* as evidenced by a judgment or a written instrument absolutely owing at the time of the filing of the petition, *whether then payable or not.*

*Liabilities on open account, or on contract,* express or implied, including claims for anticipatory breach of contracts (page 122), and unexpired leases (within the limits referred to on page 725).

*Contingent claims,* including contingent debts and contractual liabilities, and rights to recover damages in negligence actions commenced prior to and pending at the time of the filing of the petition.

*Workmen's compensation awards* against the bankrupt for injuries occurring prior to adjudication.

*Court costs* incurred by a creditor before the filing of the petition, or awarded against a bankrupt who at the time the petition was filed was plaintiff in an action which the trustee later declines to prosecute.

The foregoing claims, which involve money demands, are subject to *reclamations* and *trust claims.* They are also subject to the rights of *secured creditors* and to a fixed order of *priority* in payment.

**Reclamations.** If a person claims specific property in the bankrupt estate as his own, he must bring "reclamation proceedings" for the recovery of such property, instead of filing a proof of claim. If he files a proof of claim, he forfeits his right to the specific property and becomes relegated to the status of a creditor.[10]

---

[9] Section 63.

[10] *Lowell v. Brown,* 280 Fed. 193, aff'd 284 Fed. 936 (reversed on other grounds, 265 U.S. 1).

(See page 416, "Where broker becomes insolvent: rights of customer as to deposited securities.")

**Trust Claims.** When a bankrupt holds property in trust, the beneficiary, as equitable owner, may reclaim the property or its proceeds. The beneficiary is not, strictly speaking, a creditor entitled to priority but a claimant entitled to specific property or a specific fund. (See page 767.)

*Checks drawn prior to bankruptcy.* When the depositor of a bank, prior to his bankruptcy, issues a check which is not presented until after his bankruptcy, the holder has no claim to any specific fund. The mere issuance of a check does not constitute an equitable assignment of the funds drawn against. But if the check has in the meantime been honored, as by certification, or by being credited to the payee on the books of the bank, an equitable assignment takes place, and the holder may establish a specific claim upon the fund represented by the check.

**Secured, "Preferred," and General Creditors Distinguished.** A *secured* creditor is defined by the Bankruptcy Act[11] as "a creditor who has security for his debt upon the property of the bankrupt of a nature to be assignable under this Act or who owns such a debt for which some endorser, surety, or other person secondarily liable for the bankrupt has such security upon the bankrupt's assets."

EXAMPLES: The following are secured creditors under the Bankruptcy Act: (1) one who holds the bankrupt's bond secured by a mortgage, (2) one who holds the bankrupt's note guaranteed by a third party who holds security belonging to the bankrupt.

A "preferred creditor," literally, is one who has been given a preference (page 714). Frequently, however, the term is incorrectly used to designate a *priority creditor*, or one whose claim has priority over the claims of general creditors.

A *general* creditor is one who has no security or priority.

**Rights of Secured Creditors.** Creditors who are fully secured may resort to their security in satisfaction of their claims. If there is anything left after the claim is satisfied, the surplus goes to the trustee in bankruptcy. When the value of the security obviously exceeds the amount of the claim, a creditor has no right to vote at meetings, nor, of course, to dividends in bankruptcy.

*Claims of partially secured creditors.* When a creditor's claim is only partially secured, he is entitled to vote on the basis of his unsecured debt,[12] and may participate in dividends only to such extent.

---

[11] Sec. 1, subd. 28.

[12] "Claims of secured creditors and those who have priority may be temporarily allowed to enable such creditors to participate in the proceedings at creditors' meetings held prior to the determination of the value of their securities or priorities, but shall be thus temporarily allowed for such sums only as to the courts seem to be owing over and above the value of their securities or priorities." *Bankruptcy Act*, sec. 57, subd. e.

**Priorities.** Debts are accorded priority over the claims of general creditors in the following order:

(1) *Actual and necessary costs and expenses of preserving the estate* after the filing of the petition. These include filing fees, expenses of recovering concealed or fraudulently transferred assets, trustee's expenses, attorney's fees, and so on.

(2) *Wage claims* (not exceeding $600 to any claimant) which have been earned within three months before bankruptcy, including claims of full or part time salesmen on salary or commission. The Bankruptcy Act definition of a wage earner refers only to the classification of persons who may be adjudged involuntary bankrupts (page 713) and is not intended to refer to wage earners as creditors. A wage earner, to be entitled to priority, is one who serves in a subordinate capacity "otherwise than in the pursuit of an independent calling" and who, in such service, "remains entirely under the control and direction of the employer." However, the court in laying down this rule held that musicians hired by a bankrupt to play on his roof garden are "servants" entitled to priority on their wage claims.[13] Neither the general manager of a corporation[14] nor a certified public accountant who audits the books of a bankrupt firm[15] is classed as a wage earner entitled to priority.

(3) *Costs and expenses of creditors* for successfully opposing, revoking or setting aside a plan of arrangement, or a wage earner's plan, or a bankrupt's discharge; or in securing the conviction of any person for a bankruptcy offense.

(4) *Tax claims.* Taxes are a prior claim upon a bankrupt estate, and any fiduciary who pays a private debt ahead of taxes runs the risk of being personally liable for such taxes if the estate is unable to pay them. The statute provides[16] that every executor, administrator, assignee or other person who pays, in whole or in part, any debt due by the person or estate for whom or for which he acts, before he satisfies and pays the debt due the United States from such person or estate, shall become answerable personally to the extent of such payments for the debt so due, or for so much of it as remains due and unsatisfied. A trustee is similarly liable for rendering an estate unable to pay state taxes. However, a trustee is not liable if he had no notice of the existence of the tax.[17]

(5) *Debts entitled to priority by Federal law,* and *rent due and owing for actual use and occupancy* (accrued within three months prior to bankruptcy) to a landlord entitled to priority under the laws of a particular state.

---

[13] *In re Caldwell,* 164 Fed. 515 (D.C., Ark.).

[14] *In re Grubbs-Wiley Grocery Co.,* 96 Fed. 183 (D.C., Mo.).

[15] *Matter of Samek & Robel, Inc.,* 5 Am. B. R. (N.S.) 683.

[16] U.S. Rev. St. sec. 3467, 31 U.S.C.A. sec. 192.

[17] *State of Delaware v. Irving Trust Co.,* 92 Fed. (2d) 17 (C.C.A., N.Y.), aff'g 19 Fed. Supp. 231 (D.C., N.Y.); certiorari denied, 302 U.S. 754.

EXAMPLE: Mary Moore, owner of a business corner in Miami, Fla., files a claim for three months' rent as a priority creditor of Universal Drug Shops, Inc., a nationwide chain store organization which has been adjudicated a bankrupt in the Southern District of New York. Since such rent claims are recognized as prior liens under the laws of Florida (though not in New York), the priority will be allowed.

(6) *Debts contracted after the granting of a discharge* or after the confirmation of an arrangement, where the discharge or confirmation is subsequently revoked or set aside for fraud or similar reason.

**Landlord and Tenant Claims.** Bankruptcy claims arising between landlord and tenant have been a source of frequent dispute and conflicting decisions.

*Bankruptcy of landlord:* When the landlord becomes bankrupt, his leasehold interest goes to the trustee in bankruptcy, the same as any other asset, and the tenant's rights are generally unaffected.

*Landlord's claim for rent due and unpaid at time of tenant's bankruptcy.* When, at the time of the tenant's bankruptcy, there is a balance due and accrued for unpaid rentals, the claim for such rent is a fixed liability and is provable as such.

*Claims based on unexpired leases.* Formerly, a landlord's claim against a bankrupt tenant, to be provable, had to be actually due and owing at the time of bankruptcy. Future rents under unexpired leases were generally held to be nonprovable, hence not dischargeable, so that bankrupts frequently found themselves burdened with heavy lease obligations notwithstanding a discharge in bankruptcy. The Bankruptcy Act of 1938 made claims based on unexpired leases provable, hence dischargeable. As noted on page 122, provable claims in bankruptcy include anticipatory breaches of contract. The trustee has sixty days after adjudication within which to approve or reject the bankrupt's executory contracts. Disaffirmance of an unexpired lease may be treated by the landlord as a breach of contract, which constitutes a provable claim. However, the maximum damage which a landlord may claim in such cases, regardless of how much longer the lease still has to run, is a year's rent from the date of surrender of the premises or re-entry by the landlord (whichever occurs first) plus rent previously accrued.

**Unmatured Claims.** As noted on page 722, fixed liabilities evidenced by a judgment or a written instrument are provable claims in bankruptcy, whether they are *then payable or not.*

EXAMPLE: *A* holds *B*'s note due in three years. Six months after date *B* is adjudged bankrupt. *A* may prove his claim, though the note has two and a half years to run. If *A* fails to prove his claim, the debt, being provable, will be discharged in bankruptcy.

**Claims as Offsets.** Section 68 of the Bankruptcy Act provides: "In all cases of mutual debts or mutual credits between the estate of a bankrupt and a creditor the accounts shall be stated and one debt shall be set off against the other, and the balance only shall be allowed or paid."

EXAMPLE: *A* borrows $2000 at the bank, against his note. He leaves $1500 on deposit. In contemplation of filing a petition in bankruptcy, he gives the bank a check for the full amount of his deposit, which the trustee seeks to recover as an unlawful preference. The trustee will not succeed. The check conferred no right on the bank which the bank did not have anyway, that is, a right to offset $1500 of its $2000 claim on the note against its $1500 debt to *A* on the bank account.[18] The fact that *A*'s note was not due is immaterial. Under section 63 of the Bankruptcy Act, a claim based on a written instrument absolutely owing is provable whether due at the time of the petition or not.

The foregoing rule applies only in bankruptcy. A bank cannot ordinarily anticipate the due date of a depositor's note by appropriating the amount of his balance.

**Relative Rights of Partnership and Individual Creditors.** When a partnership is declared bankrupt, the separate assets of all partners, as well as the partnership estate, are drawn into bankruptcy. This applies also where members of a partnership individually and as copartners are adjudged bankrupts. However, the bankruptcy of a partner does not draw in the partnership property except with the consent of the remaining partners, or unless the bankrupt is the sole surviving member of the firm and has control of the partnership assets.[19] In the administration of a bankrupt partnership estate, the Bankruptcy Act recognizes the rule of *marshaling assets*. Firm assets must first be made available for payment of firm debts, and the partners' individual assets for the payment of their respective individual debts. If, after payment of firm debts, a surplus remains, such surplus—in which each individual partner has an undivided interest—may be applied to the payment of the partners' individual debts. If, after a partner pays his personal debts out of his personal assets, a surplus remains, such surplus may be applied to the payment of firm debts, provided firm assets are insufficient for this purpose.

**Objections to and Allowance of Claims.** Ordinarily, the filing of a proof of claim, duly executed and in proper form, constitutes *prima facie* evidence (page 868) of the claim; and the claim will be allowed unless an objection is filed. The allowance of a claim may be objected to by any party interested in the estate. The trustee in bankruptcy *must* object to the allowance of any doubtful claims; and any creditor *may* object. Upon the filing of objections, a hearing is held before the court or referee, and upon the evidence adduced at such hearing, the claim is either allowed or disallowed.

---

[18] *N.Y. County Nat'l Bank v. Massey*, 192 U.S. 138.
[19] *C.J.S.* 428-429.

## Dividends

**Dividends in Bankruptcy.** Dividends in bankruptcy, unlike corporate dividends, represent no profit on one's investment, but rather a share of what is left in a bankrupt's estate after payment of debts and administration expenses. Also unlike corporate dividends, they are payable out of principal, or what is left of it. Dividends in bankruptcy are declared by the referee and paid by the trustee. The first dividend must be declared within thirty days after the first date set for the first meeting of creditors, provided the amount in the estate in excess of the amount necessary to pay debts which have priority, equals 5 per cent or more of claims which have been and probably will be allowed. The first dividend cannot exceed 50 per cent of the surplus over the moneys necessary to pay claims having priority and claims not yet allowed. A final dividend cannot be declared until three months after the first one. The dividend rate must be uniform as to all unsecured creditors.

**Claims Allowed after Dividend Declarations.** The rights of creditors who have received dividends, or in whose favor final dividends have been declared, are not affected by the subsequent proof and allowance of claims. However, before such creditors are paid any further dividends, subsequent claimants are entitled to receive dividends equal in amount to those already received by the others.

**Unclaimed Moneys.** Dividends or other moneys which remain unclaimed for sixty days after the final dividend has been paid and distributed must be paid by the trustee into the bankruptcy court. The trustee must file a list of the names and post-office addresses, as far as known, of the persons entitled to such moneys and the amounts respectively due them. Dividends remaining unclaimed for one year are distributed to creditors whose claims have been allowed and not paid in full. If such claims have been paid in full, the balance is paid to the bankrupt.

## Questions

1. (a) Under what circumstances may a receiver or marshal be appointed? (b) What are the duties of this officer, and how do they differ from those of a trustee? (c) When do the duties of a receiver or marshal cease?

2. In general, what is meant by the administration of a bankrupt's estate?

3. What are procedural steps for calling of the first meeting of creditors?

4. (a) When are creditors' proofs of claim usually filed? (b) Within what time must they be filed? (c) Who may vote at creditors' meetings?

5. What procedure is used in situations involving voting by creditors where one creditor's claim may exceed the claims of all the remaining creditors?

6. What treatment is afforded creditors whose claims amount to $50 or less?

7. When, where and how is a trustee appointed?

8. (a) What, broadly speaking, is the function of a trustee? (b) Name five duties which he may be required to discharge in furtherance of his major function.

9. (a) What is a proof of claim in bankruptcy? (b) What facts must it contain? (c) Is there any additional requirement where the claim is founded on a written instrument?

10. Name five types of provable claims in bankruptcy.

11. Ordinary provable claims are subject to four major classes of rights. What are they?

12. What is meant by a reclamation proceeding?

13. What is meant by a trust claim? What is the status of such a claimant in a bankruptcy proceeding?

14. What is the status of a payee who deposits a check after the drawer has become a bankrupt?

15. What distinctions may be drawn among (a) a secured creditor, (b) a "preferred" creditor and (c) a general creditor?

16. Usually, how are the rights of a fully secured creditor enforced?

17. Where the value of security held by a creditor exceeds the amount of his claim, (a) what happens to the surplus in case of a sale; and (b) how is such a creditor's right to vote affected?

18. Name in order of recognition the six types of claims which are afforded priority.

19. How does the Bankruptcy Act define a wage earner in connection with claims entitled to priority?

20. What risk may a trustee encounter if he pays a private debt of the bankrupt ahead of taxes?

21. How does the bankruptcy of a landlord affect the rights of a tenant with respect to an unexpired lease?

22. What are the rights of a landlord against a bankrupt tenant with respect to: (a) Rent due and unpaid at the time of the tenant's bankruptcy; (b) Rent to become due for the balance of the rental term?

23. What is the position of a creditor with respect to an unmatured claim against a bankrupt debtor?

24. How, if at all, does the bankruptcy of a partnership affect the individual assets of the partners?

25. How, if at all, does the bankruptcy of an individual partner affect the partnership?

26. (a) Who may object to the allowance of a claim in bankruptcy? (b) When *must* a trustee in bankruptcy object? (c) What procedure is adopted where such objections are filed?

27. (a) What is a dividend in bankruptcy? (b) By whom, when and under what circumstances are such dividends declared?

28. How are the rights of those creditors who have already received dividends affected, where claims of other creditors are subsequently allowed?

29. What procedure is adopted where dividends or other moneys remain unclaimed?

## Problems

1. Ball is adjudicated a bankrupt, with liabilities of $50,000. Musgrave, with a claim of $28,000, is the largest creditor. At the first meeting of creditors held within thirty days after adjudication, a creditor objects to Musgrave's voting upon the election of a trustee on the ground that Musgrave has not filed his proof of claim. Musgrave claims that he has at least six months more within which to file his claim. Will the objecting creditor's position be sustained? Explain.

2. In an involuntary proceeding, ten creditors whose claims aggregate $20,000, vote for *A* as trustee. Two creditors whose claims total $50,000, vote for *B* as trustee. What will be the outcome?

3. An insolvent father transfers stock to his son just prior to bankruptcy. This fact is discovered shortly after the father is adjudged a bankrupt. The question arises as to what, if anything, can be done about this transfer, and who should do it?

4. An interested party files objection to the account of the trustee. It appears that the trustee inadvertently overpaid one of the creditors $10,000, and that the creditor cannot now be located. Under the circumstances, has the objecting creditor any other remedy?

5. Potter has an unsecured note given by Crocker which is due three years from date. Six months after making the note, Crocker goes into bankruptcy.

(a) May Potter prove his claim?

(b) Can Potter ignore the bankruptcy proceedings and when the note is due have judgment on the note if Crocker has in the meantime been discharged?

6. Krum, a shipwright, induced the Miller Marine Sales Co. to sell a quantity of marine equipment to Krum on credit. In procuring such credit Krum submitted a balance sheet showing a net worth of $10,000. The truth was that Krum was insolvent. Two weeks later Krum is adjudicated a bankrupt. Krum being still in possession of the equipment purchased from the Miller Marine Sales Co., the latter institutes reclamation proceedings for the return of said equipment. May it do so?

7. Suppose in the previous case that the attorney representing the Miller Marine Sales Co. had filed a proof of claim in bankruptcy on its behalf, and thereafter, upon going into the facts, decided to institute reclamation proceedings instead. What would be the creditor's position in such situation?

8. Walter Baxter is given $10,000 by his widowed sister, to invest for her six-year-old daughter, who has inherited that amount. Before the money is invested, Baxter is adjudged a bankrupt. His net assets, exclusive of the $10,000, total $40,000; his liabilities, $100,000. Creditors insist on a 50 per cent dividend. Baxter insists that the dividend cannot exceed 40 per cent. How will the referee decide?

9. Kahn, the proprietor of a cigar store, cashes a check for Hope for $50. The following day Hope files a voluntary petition in bankruptcy and is promptly adjudicated a bankrupt. Kahn thereafter presents Hope's check to the bank on which it is drawn, and the bank refuses payment because of Hope's bankruptcy. Kahn insists that he is entitled to the specific monies represented by the check, but the trustee subsequently appointed insists that Kahn is only a general creditor. Who is right, and why?

10. Deep Sea Packers, Inc., is adjudicated a bankrupt. Net assets, after estimated costs of preserving the estate and taxes, are approximately $8,000. Liabilities for debts due merchandise and other general creditors are estimated at $80,000. Turner, one of the employees, has a wage claim for $250 based on his share of a fishing haul during the past three weeks. He is told by the ship's clerk, "You'll be lucky if you collect ten cents on the dollar." What are Turner's prospects?

11. Franklin was a stockholder, director and general manager of the Acme Food Products, Inc. The corporation was adjudicated a bankrupt. Franklin files his proof of claim for $1,750, the monthly salary due him as manager. The referee refuses to allow the claim. Should the claim, either in whole or in part, be allowed? Give reasons.

12. The estate of John King, bankrupt, has approximately $40,000 in duly

filed claims and $30,000 in assets converted into cash. Dividends aggregating 50% are later duly declared and paid. The difference, or $10,000, has been expended by the trustee in administration expenses, including, besides ordinary fees and disbursements, the cost of three lawsuits which were necessary in the process of liquidating assets and opposing claims. Thereafter it is discovered that the United States Government has a claim in the amount of $3,800 for unpaid income taxes. What recourse has the government, and against whom?

13. A creditor holds a bankrupt's note for $2,500. The note is secured by collateral worth $1,800. A 40 per cent dividend is declared to general creditors. How much will such creditor receive?

14. At the first meeting of creditors in a bankruptcy proceeding, Collins, to whom the bankrupt is indebted in the amount of $10,000—against which Collins has collateral having a market value of $7,500—seeks to vote his $10,000 claim in the selection of a trustee. The referee refuses to allow Collins any voice in the selection of a trustee, on the ground that he is a secured creditor. Collins appeals from the referee's decision. How will the appeal be decided?

15. A receiver in bankruptcy takes possession of the premises occupied by the tenant. The tenant's lease provides for rent at the rate of $500 per month. After the receiver has been in possession for two months without making any payments to the landlord, the latter brings suit for two months' rent. How will the court decide, and why?

16. A lease to the Cleary Auto Sales Company provides that in case of the tenant's bankruptcy, the landlord may at his option declare the lease forfeited, and in addition thereto, may forthwith recover as damages the aggregate of rentals for the remainder of the term. The Cleary Auto Sales Company is adjudicated a bankrupt. Its lease has three more years to run at an annual rental of $2,400. The Company is also behind two months in rent. The landlord files a claim for $7,600, representing two months' rent plus the aggregate of rentals for the remainder of the term. The trustee contests the claim. Will the claim be wholly allowed, wholly disallowed, or partly allowed and partly disallowed? Explain.

17. Watson borrows $10,000 at his bank against his 90-day note in that amount. He leaves $7,500 on deposit and checks out $2,500 in payment of debts. He reaches the conclusion, however, that he will be unable to stave off his creditors, and gives the bank his check for $7,500, though his note has 70 days more to run before maturity. Two weeks later he is adjudged a bankrupt. In due course the trustee seeks to reclaim $7,500 from the bank as an unlawful preference. Will he succeed?

18. Beckwith, a depositor with the Union Bank, discounts his six months' note with the bank for $2,000. He dies insolvent three months later. There have been no bankruptcy proceedings. Within a few days after Beckwith's death, Jordan qualifies as executor of the estate and immediately upon qualifying, seeks to withdraw the amount of Beckwith's balance from the bank. The bank insists on offsetting the amount of Beckwith's unmatured note against the balance on deposit, and therefore refuses to honor the estate's check for the amount of such balance. The executor seeks to compel the bank to honor the check. May he do so? Explain.

19. The firm of Ford, Samson and Dale, a partnership, is petitioned into bankruptcy. The firm's assets are $300,000; liabilities, $400,000. Ford individually has assets of $50,000 and liabilities of $60,000; Samson individually has assets of $120,000 and liabilities of $40,000; Dale has individual assets of $50,000 and individual liabilities of $40,000.

(a) How will the respective assets be administered in bankruptcy?

(b) What principle of bankruptcy law is involved in such administration?

20. Watson presents a claim against a bankrupt estate within six months after the first date set for the first meeting of creditors, but subsequently to the distribution of the dividend.

(a) Can Watson share in the dividend?

(b) Has Watson any rights if the final dividend has been declared and the estate closed?

21. In a bankruptcy estate involving over 1,300 creditors, the trustee, after payment and distribution of a final dividend, finds that he has $11,263.32 on hand which remains unclaimed.

(a) What should the trustee do under the circumstances?

(b) Assuming that half the above amount remains unclaimed for one year and that all the creditors have been paid their claims in full, what would happen to such undistributed balance?

## PART 4. RIGHTS, DUTIES AND LIABILITIES OF BANKRUPT

**In General.** A bankrupt has certain rights and exemptions which the law allows him, but he is also expected to discharge certain duties. Moreover, he must be careful to avoid committing certain offenses prescribed by the Bankruptcy Act, which may entail criminal as well as civil consequences. Likewise, all persons are charged with knowledge that certain prohibited acts connected with the estate may bring severe penalties by way of fine and imprisonment.

### Rights and Exemptions of Bankrupt

**Right to Counsel.** Whether proceedings be voluntary or involuntary, a bankrupt is entitled to counsel so that he may be duly advised of his legal rights. However, the court may re-examine any fee which the bankrupt pays his attorney in contemplation of bankruptcy, and may require any amount deemed in excess of a reasonable fee to be turned over to the estate as an unlawful preference.

**Exemptions of Bankrupts Generally.** State laws throughout the country prescribe various personal exemptions immune from legal process, such as wearing apparel, wages, jewelry, and so on, and various forms of occupational exemptions, such as growing crops, tools and implements of trade. What may constitute an exemption for one person will not necessarily constitute an exemption for another.

EXAMPLES:

(1) Pianos as part of a stock in trade would not ordinarily be exempt; but a piano used principally in the teaching of music and constituting a part of the household furniture has been held to be exempt.[20]

(2) An ordinary ring, such as a wedding ring, might be exempt, but a diamond ring has been declared not to be exempt.[21]

[20] *Hill v. Binford*, 91 S.W. 2d 488 (Tex. Civ. App.).

[21] *Rivas v. Noble*, 241 Fed. 673, 154 C.C.A. 431 (Fla.); *Langever v. Stitt*, 237 Fed. 83, 150 C.C.A. (Tex.) 285.

**Insurance Exemptions: in General.** The rights of bankrupts in connection with insurance policies depend upon whether the policy covers property or life.

*Property insurance.* The rule governing property insurance is fairly uniform: a bankrupt's property insurance forms part of his estate, and the bankrupt is entitled to no exemption in respect to such insurance.

*Life insurance.* In regard to life insurance, the rule is not uniform. To determine the bankrupt's rights in respect to life insurance, it is necessary to consider whether the bankrupt is himself the policyholder, thus having an interest in the cash surrender value of the policy (page 369), or whether he is the beneficiary under a policy insuring the life of another. Even with this distinction, the rule varies in the different states, and the question of a bankrupt's exemptions is governed by the law of the state where the bankrupt is domiciled.

## Duties and Liabilities of Bankrupt

**Duties of Bankrupt: in General.** The primary duty of a bankrupt is to surrender all his property of whatsoever nature, except property exempt by law. The act charges the bankrupt with specific duties, including attendance at meetings, obedience to court orders, verification of proofs of claim and reporting irregularities therein to the trustee, the execution and delivery of all necessary papers, the preparation of schedules, the submission of a preliminary statement of his affairs, the submission of himself to examination, and the filing of cost inventories when required by the Court.

**Attendance at Creditors' Meetings.** The bankrupt must attend the first meeting of creditors, the hearing upon objections to his discharge, if any, and at such other times as the court may order. Attendance at the first meeting of creditors is particularly important, so that the bankrupt may assist in checking creditors' claims and help to determine, in case of dispute, which creditors are qualified to vote and which are not. The bankrupt must attend both the first meeting of creditors and the hearing on objections, if any, to his discharge, without the necessity of any order being served upon him for this purpose. In all other cases, the bankrupt is not required to attend meetings unless ordered by the Court to do so.

**Verifying Proofs of Claim and Reporting Irregularities.** The bankrupt must examine and report to the trustee concerning the correctness of all proofs of claim filed against his estate. He must immediately inform his trustee of any attempt which comes to his knowledge, by creditors or other persons, to evade the provisions of the Bankruptcy Act. If the bankrupt learns that any person has proved a false claim against the estate, he must make immediate disclosure of this fact to the trustee.

**Execution and Delivery of Papers; Obedience to Court Orders.** The bankrupt must execute and deliver such papers as may be ordered by the

Court, including the execution and delivery to the trustee of any documents necessary to transfer property in foreign countries. He must comply strictly with all orders of the Court. For a failure to do so, he may be arrested and punished for contempt, either by fine, imprisonment or both. In addition, such noncompliance will bar his discharge in bankruptcy.

**Preparation and Filing of Schedules.** The bankrupt must prepare in triplicate, make oath to, and file, within five days after adjudication if he is an involuntary bankrupt, and with his petition if he is a voluntary bankrupt, a schedule of his property showing amount, kind, location, and value of each item, and a list of all creditors—whether their claims be liquidated or unliquidated, fixed or contingent, disputed or admitted—showing their names, residences, amounts due and similar details.

**Preliminary Statement of Affairs: Advance Information before First Meeting.** Prior to 1938 attorneys for creditors desiring to examine a bankrupt at the first meeting of creditors were handicapped by absence of advance information. Examinations were necessarily "fishing expeditions" for possible irregularities, clues to hidden assets, and so on. The Bankruptcy Act of 1938 made it obligatory upon bankrupts to furnish a preliminary statement of affairs in advance of the first meeting, as an intelligent basis upon which to examine the bankrupt. This statement must be filed in triplicate with the court at least five days prior to the first meeting of creditors, on a form prescribed by the Supreme Court. One form governs bankrupts or debtors who are not engaged in business, and another those who are.

The preliminary statement of affairs must be sworn to by the bankrupt or debtor, who must be very careful to make sure that the statements are correct in every detail. If any part of such preliminary statement be false in any respect, or if there has been any concealment of assets, the bankrupt is not only guilty of a bankruptcy offense, but he will be unable to secure his discharge in bankruptcy.

**Examinations.** At the first meeting of creditors, at the hearing upon objections to his discharge, if any, and at such other times as the court may order, the bankrupt must submit to an examination concerning the conduct of his business, the cause of his bankruptcy, his dealings with creditors and others, the amount, kind and whereabouts of his property, and all matters which may affect the administration and settlement of his estate or the granting of his discharge.

**Inventory of Costs.** The court may require a bankrupt to file an inventory of costs as of the date of bankruptcy, as a basis for checking any claim that goods were sold at a loss. In the absence of a cost inventory, where ordered, the Court presumes that the bankrupt's goods were not sold at a loss. Likewise, if the bankrupt fails to produce books and records showing cost of goods sold, he has the burden of proving that sales were made at a loss.

**Liability to Arrest.** A bankrupt is not only liable to arrest and imprisonment for the commission of one of the bankruptcy offenses, but of course he is subject to imprisonment for the commission of any other crime under the laws of any state. Bankruptcy proceedings can in no way be allowed to impede the prosecution of persons for crimes such as larceny, embezzlement, arson, and so on, except that when a person is imprisoned for the commission of such crimes, he may be temporarily taken out of jail for the purpose of attending bankruptcy hearings requiring his presence.

**Death or Insanity of Bankrupts.** The death or insanity of a bankrupt does not abate the proceedings; the estate continues to be administered and is concluded in the same manner, as far as possible, as if the bankrupt had not died or become insane.

## Bankruptcy Offenses

**Persons Liable.** The Bankruptcy Act prescribes various forms of punishment for offenses committed by persons connected, officially or otherwise, with the administration of an estate in bankruptcy. Not only are the persons who actually commit the bankruptcy offenses punishable, but all persons who aid, counsel, procure or induce their commission are themselves guilty of a felony warranting their indictment as principals (not, as formerly, mere accessories to the crime). Thus, attorneys and accountants who, by advice, suggestions or otherwise, knowingly assist a client in respect to any of the offenses referred to below, are equally guilty with their clients of a felony warranting their indictment as principals rather than accessories.

**Miscellaneous Offenses.** A person is punishable by imprisonment for a period not exceeding five years, or by a fine of not more than $5000, or both, upon conviction of the offense of having knowingly and fraudulently:

(1) Concealed from the receiver, custodian, trustee, marshal or other officer of the court charged with control or custody of property, or concealed from creditors in any bankruptcy proceeding, any property belonging to the bankrupt estate; or

(2) Made false oath or account in relation to any proceeding in bankruptcy; or

(3) Presented, under oath, any false claim against the estate, or used any such claim in any bankruptcy proceeding, either personally or by agent or attorney; or

(4) Received property from a bankrupt after the filing of a petition or a proceeding, with intent to defeat the purpose of the law; or

(5) Received or attempted to obtain money, property, compensation, reward or advantage, or a promise of the same, from any person for acting or forbearing to act in any proceeding under the Bankruptcy Act; or

(6) While an agent of any person, or officer of any corporation, and in

contemplation of a bankruptcy proceeding, or with intent to defeat the provisions of the Bankruptcy Act, concealed or transferred any property of such person or corporation; or

(7) After the commencement of a bankruptcy proceeding, or in contemplation thereof, has concealed, destroyed, mutilated, falsified or made a false entry in any document affecting the property or affairs of a bankrupt; or

(8) After the commencement of a bankruptcy proceeding, has withheld from the receiver, custodian, trustee, marshal or other officer of the court, any document affecting the property or affairs of the bankrupt, to the possession of which such officer is entitled.

## Questions

1. Comment on the bankrupt's right to counsel and the payment of a fee to him in advance of the filing of a petition.

2. Name four specific types of exemptions available to a bankrupt.

3. What exemption provisions in law, if any, are made with respect to the bankrupt's rights in property and life insurance?

4. What is the primary duty of a bankrupt?

5. What two meetings must a bankrupt attend without being served a court order requiring him to attend?

6. Name seven other specific duties of a bankrupt.

7. What punishment may be visited upon a bankrupt who wilfully fails to comply with a court order?

8. What must the bankrupt's schedules contain? Within what time must they be filed?

9. What is the purpose of requiring a bankrupt to file a preliminary statement of affairs?

10. What does the examination of a bankrupt usually embrace?

11. What presumption may be raised where the Court orders a bankrupt to file an inventory of costs and he fails to do so?

12. What effect, if any, does a bankruptcy proceeding have with respect to a debtor who is being prosecuted for the commission of a serious crime?

13. How would the death or insanity of a debtor affect the pendency against him of bankruptcy proceedings?

14. "Only persons who actually commit any of the bankruptcy offenses are liable thereunder." Is this statement true, false, or partly true and partly false? Explain.

15. Name eight bankruptcy offenses, and the punishment therefor.

## Problems

1. Mortimer Strauss, a concert pianist, is compelled to discontinue his career as an artist by reason of arthritis which prevents the free use of his hands and fingers. He thereupon opens a retail store for the sale of pianos and musical instruments. In the course of time, owing to financial losses, his stock is reduced to one piano, and upon the filing of a petition in bankruptcy the trustee seeks to compel Strauss to deliver up the piano for the benefit of the estate. Strauss objects. How will the referee rule, and why?

2. Shortly after a debtor had been adjudicated a bankrupt, he became men-

tally ill and was confined to a State institution. The attorney for the bankrupt then made a motion to dismiss the petition on the ground that the insanity of the bankrupt automatically terminated the proceedings. What was the outcome of the motion?

3. An involuntary petition was filed against Mrs. Sarah Jones who was duly declared a bankrupt. As part of the assets of the bankrupt estate, the trustee sought to obtain a wedding ring and a diamond ring in the possession of the debtor. How did the Court rule?

4. A bankrupt failed to attend the first meeting of creditors on the ground that although he had been notified of the meeting, he had not been served with any order requiring him to attend. Was his contention justified?

5. Prior to his adjudication in bankruptcy, a debtor paid his attorney a fee of $10,000 in an estate having assets of $50,000 and liabilities of $100,000. Creditors object to this fee. How will the Court rule?

6. X was indicted and convicted of grand larceny. Thereafter, he was declared a bankrupt in involuntary bankruptcy proceedings. Subsequently, his attorney raised the point that the Court lacked jurisdiction of the bankrupt by reason of his conviction and imprisonment. Is his position well taken?

7. A petition in bankruptcy is filed against John Howard Sims. The schedule of assets filed by Sims excludes $10,000 worth of stock in the *ABC* Corporation held by Watson Parker, a broker's clerk, as nominee for Sims. These facts being disclosed during the course of the bankruptcy proceeding, criminal prosecution is begun against Sims for the offense of having knowingly and fraudulently made a false oath in relation to a proceeding in bankruptcy. Sims defends on the following grounds:

(1) He made no false oath, because it was literally true that he did not hold title to the stock in question;

(2) He was unaware that he was required to include stock not held in his name, and had no intention to misrepresent the facts.

Sims is convicted and appeals. Will the conviction be reversed or sustained? Give reasons.

8. John Silver files a petition for an arrangement. His plan contemplates payment in full to all creditors over a period of five years. Noe, one of the largest creditors, holds out, but on being assured that an arrangement will be privately consummated whereby Noe will receive payment in full within two years, he agrees to vote with the other creditors in approval of the proposed plan, and does so vote. Upon discovery of these facts, the United States attorney prosecutes Noe for fraudulently receiving property of the debtor with intent to defeat the Bankruptcy Act. During the course of the trial, Noe proves that the debtor had arranged to borrow the money with which to anticipate the special payment. To what extent will this evidence affect the result of the prosecution?

9. During the course of bankruptcy proceedings affecting the Xanader Corporation, the accountant for the corporation testified that the books of the corporation had disappeared under the following circumstances: He was taking the books home from New York City to Jersey City to work on them at night. He had the books in a large briefcase. As he leaned over the rail of the ferryboat, the briefcase slipped from his hands and fell into the Hudson River. They could not be recovered.

Assuming that the referee disbelieves the foregoing story, what action, if any, should he take?

## PART 5. DISCHARGE; CORPORATE REORGANIZATION; ARRANGEMENTS

**In General.** The broad policy of the present Bankruptcy Act is not punitive, but remedial. It is to afford meritorious debtors, individual or corporate, an opportunity for rehabilitation, so long as their dealings have been fair and honest: to the honest bankrupt, a discharge; to the hard-pressed corporation, relief by way of statutory reorganization; to hard-pressed individuals as well as corporations who wish to avoid the stigma of bankruptcy, relief by way of "arrangements."

### Discharge of Bankrupt

**In General.** Under the old Bankruptcy Act a bankrupt could apply for a discharge after the expiration of one month and within twelve months subsequent to adjudication. As a matter of practice the bankrupt, choosing his own time in applying for a discharge, often waited until creditors had lost interest, so that there would be little chance of opposition. Under the Bankruptcy Act as amended in 1938, after the bankrupt has been examined, the court itself fixes the time for filing objections to a discharge. Notice must be given to all interested parties. The United States Attorney, when requested by the court, must examine into any case to ascertain whether there are probable grounds for denying a discharge. If he finds such grounds, he must oppose the discharge. Under the old practice there were often such grounds, but not so often a creditor willing to foot the bill for sustaining them.

**Acts Which Will Bar Discharge.** A bankrupt will be unable to obtain his discharge in bankruptcy if it can be shown that he has been guilty of any of the following acts:

(a) *Committed a bankruptcy offense.* (Pages 734 to 735.)

(b) *Destroyed, mutilated, falsified, concealed or failed to keep or preserve books of account or records* from which his financial condition and business transactions might be ascertained, unless in the opinion of the Court such act or omission was justified.

(c) *False statements.* If the bankrupt has obtained money or property on credit, or obtained an extension or renewal of credit, by a false statement in writing as to his financial condition, he will be denied a discharge.

(d) *Removing, destroying or concealing property.* If the bankrupt has transferred, removed, destroyed or concealed any of his property *within twelve months prior to the filing of the petition in bankruptcy*, or has permitted the same to be removed, destroyed or concealed with intent to hinder, delay or defraud creditors, he cannot obtain a discharge in bankruptcy.

(e) *Prior discharge or composition.* The act bars a discharge if the bankrupt "has within six years prior to bankruptcy been granted a discharge, or had a composition or an arrangement by way of composition or a wage earners' plan by way of composition[22] confirmed under this Act." Such prior discharge or composition will constitute a bar whether the subsequent bankruptcy proceedings are voluntary or involuntary.

(f) *Refusal to obey court order or answer material question.* The act bars a discharge to a bankrupt if in the course of a proceeding he has "refused to obey any lawful order of, or to answer any material question approved by, the court."

(g) *Failure to explain loss or deficiency.* The act bars a discharge to a bankrupt if he "has failed to explain satisfactorily any losses of assets or deficiencies of assets to meet his liabilities."

**Debts Not Dischargeable.** The effect of a discharge in bankruptcy is to release the bankrupt of all civil obligations provable in bankruptcy, with the exceptions noted below. As indicated on page 725, only debts which are provable in bankruptcy (page 722) are dischargeable. If this were not so, many creditors would not only be unable to prove their claims in bankruptcy, but would likewise be barred from proving their claims after the bankrupt's discharge. The most common instance of a debt not provable, hence not dischargeable in bankruptcy, is one arising out of goods sold, money loaned or services rendered after the commencement of a bankruptcy proceeding. Again, in some situations claims have potential existence during bankruptcy and do not acquire actual existence until after discharge. Since such claims are not provable, they are not dischargeable.

EXAMPLE: A bankrupt surety is discharged on his unmatured bond. A cosurety is later required to pay the bond when it matures. The cosurety seeks to hold the discharged bankrupt for his contributory share (page 343). The former bankrupt pleads his discharge as a defense. Such defense will not avail; the cosurety's claim for contribution was not in existence during bankruptcy.

However, not all debts which are provable are necessarily on that account dischargeable. The following classes of provable debts are not dischargeable in bankruptcy, and will survive as obligations notwithstanding the bankrupt's discharge:

(a) *Taxes.* The act provides that taxes shall not be dischargeable in bankruptcy. These include not only Federal taxes, but also taxes levied by any state, county, district or municipality.

(b) *Liability for obtaining money or property by false pretenses or representations.* It matters not whether the false representations were made orally or in writing, nor whether they were made directly to the creditor seeking to have the debt excluded from the discharge. If the statement was made to a mercantile agency, for example, the claim is not dischargeable.[23]

---

[22] Under Chapter XIII of the Bankruptcy Act of 1938.
[23] *Katzenstein v. Reid & Co.*, 41 Tex. Civ. App. 106, 91 S.W. 360.

(c) *Liability for wilful and malicious injury to person or property.* The court may determine whether the injury in question was wilful or malicious.

EXAMPLES:
(1) A judgment for assault and battery.
(2) Wilful and malicious hypothecation by a broker of securities owned by a customer outright (not on margin).

(d) *Liability for maintenance or support of wife or child.* Claims of this character concern not only the parties themselves, but the state as well. Hence public policy requires that such obligations should not be dischargeable in bankruptcy.

(e) *Alimony.* Liability for alimony due or to become due is not dischargeable.

(f) *Certain torts.* Liabilities for seduction, or for breach of promise of marriage accompanied by seduction, or for criminal conversation, are not dischargeable.

(g) *Debts not duly scheduled.* The act provides that debts shall not be dischargeable in bankruptcy if they "have not been duly scheduled in time for proof and allowance, with the name of the creditor, if known to the bankrupt, unless such creditor had notice or actual knowledge of the proceedings in bankruptcy." In the absence of such a provision, a creditor might well be prejudiced by failure to learn of the bankruptcy in time to permit him to file his proof of claim within the time allowed by law.

(h) *Debts created by fraud, embezzlement, and so on in official or fiduciary capacity.* The act renders nondischargeable all debts of a bankrupt which "were created by his fraud, embezzlement, misappropriation or defalcation while acting as an officer or in any fiduciary capacity."

EXAMPLES:
(1) Failure by postmaster to account for government funds.
(2) Liability of sheriff for profits made out of government moneys entrusted to him for the safekeeping, care and feeding of prisoners.
(3) Liability of officer of a corporation who, with knowledge of its insolvency, transferred corporate assets to himself and his son to liquidate their own claims against the corporation. (See page 559.)

(i) *Wages.* Debts due for wages which have been earned within three months before the date of commencement of the bankruptcy proceedings are not dischargeable.

(j) *Employees' security deposits.* A bankrupt is not discharged as to any moneys deposited with him by an employee as security for faithful performance.

**Revival of Debt Discharged in Bankruptcy.** As noted on pages 61 and 88, a subsequent or new promise, *in writing*, to pay a debt discharged in bankruptcy revives the debt. When a person orally agrees to revive a debt discharged in bankruptcy and then gives a note pursuant to such agreement, the statute of frauds is satisfied, because the note would represent a promise in writing to pay a debt discharged in bankruptcy and would be enforceable.[24]

**Revocation of Discharge.** The Bankruptcy Act provides[25] that "The court may, upon the application of parties in interest who have not been guilty of undue laches, filed at any time within one year after a discharge shall have been granted, revoke it if it shall be made to appear that it was obtained through the fraud of the bankrupt, that the knowledge of the fraud has come to the petitioners since the granting of the discharge and that the actual facts did not warrant the discharge."

## Provisions for Debtor Relief

**Earlier Provisions.** The economic depression which followed the financial crash of 1929 revealed the necessity for lightening the burden of debtors stricken by abnormal conditions. In 1933 Congress added a new chapter, Chapter VIII, to the Bankruptcy Act of 1898, making provision for the relief of debtors. Section 74 of Chapter VIII gave debtors an opportunity to work their way out of their financial difficulties by judicially controlled compositions or extension agreements. Section 75 gave farmers a similar opportunity. Section 77 provided machinery whereby railroads engaged in interstate commerce could effect reorganizations under judicial direction. In 1934 Congress extended the relief provisions of Chapter VIII by adding two new sections, 77A and 77B. The latter section provided for corporate reorganizations.

**Extension of Debtor Relief: the Chandler Act.** The amendments of 1933 and 1934 proved to be but temporary makeshifts. In 1938 a new act —the Chandler Act—radically amended the Bankruptcy Act of 1898 and superseded the amendments of 1933 and 1934. The objects sought to be achieved by the Act of 1938 were to simplify and improve the procedure whereby honest but insolvent debtors may secure relief without incurring the stigma of bankruptcy, and to extend the relief to a wider class of debtors. The Act provided a new approach to corporate reorganizations, a new procedure for debtor arrangements, and a wider degree of creditor-control.

## Corporate Reorganizations

**In General.** The nature and purpose of corporate reorganizations generally and the different ways of bringing them about other than through bankruptcy have already been discussed (page 562). For many years corporate reorganization through bankruptcy was brought about through the filing of a petition in bankruptcy, followed by a composition, or settle-

---

[24] *Stokes v. Sanders*, 181 App. Div. 249, 168 N.Y. Supp. 409.
[25] Sec. 15.

ment, upon which the corporate assets were sold to a new corporation which often had the same name as the old, with a corporate setup designed to conform to the composition agreement and the original scheme of reorganization. The 1934 amendment of the Bankruptcy Act, particularly section 77B, provided a plan of corporate reorganization which, on majority acceptance and court approval, could overcome a recalcitrant minority. In practice, however, the administration of corporate reorganizations under section 77B revealed glaring abuses, calling for change.

**Outstanding Features of Corporate Reorganization under Present Bankruptcy Act.** The Bankruptcy Act of 1938 was designed, among other things, to establish a new procedure for corporate reorganization (embodied in Chapter X of the Act). Every petition for corporate reorganization must show in the petition why adequate relief cannot be had by an "arrangement" proceeding (page 742). This is to prevent corporate reorganizations from being used by insolvent corporations with no chance of reorganization, solely for the purpose of settlement or delay. In every case where a debtor corporation's scheduled liabilities are $250,000 or over, the court must, and in every other case the court may, appoint a disinterested trustee. The disinterested trustee's attorney must likewise be disinterested. Such trustee must on his own initiative examine the affairs of the debtor corporation and the conduct of its business, so as to ascertain the reasons for its failure, the probability of success in the event of reorganization, and any other facts that will help the court in passing on reorganization plans. The Securities and Exchange Commission is empowered to prepare advisory reports on reorganization plans for the use of the court. Creditors and stockholders may propose reorganization plans of their own and may compel the furnishing of data on which to base a program of action. Compensation, fees and expenses are stringently regulated. No person, without the consent of the court, may solicit the acceptance of any plan of reorganization until after the court or judge has approved the plan.

## Arrangements

**Definition and Purpose: Extension of Debtor Relief.** An "arrangement" is defined by the Bankruptcy Act as "any plan of a debtor for the settlement, satisfaction, or extension of the time of payment of his unsecured debts, upon any terms." The provisions for arrangements embodied in the present Bankruptcy Act are an outgrowth of emergency relief provisions adopted by Congress in 1933, whereby debtors were given an opportunity to work their way out of their financial difficulties without the stigma of bankruptcy, by judicially controlled composition or extension agreements. Chapter XI of the act is designed for ordinary debtors, Chapter XII for real property arrangements, and Chapter XIII for wage earners' plans.

**Compositions, Arrangements and Common-Law Settlements, Distinguished.** Arrangements are really an outgrowth of compositions in bankruptcy, which were formerly provided for in section 12 of the Bankruptcy Act. The basic purpose of an arrangement is the same as that which governed compositions under the old act: to effect a compromise with unsecured creditors by offering them a settlement which would yield them as much benefit as a full proceeding in bankruptcy without, however, the delays and expense of such proceeding; and at the same time to enable the debtor, freed from his financial burdens, to resume his normal status and activities.

A common-law settlement is one effected by contract between a debtor and his creditors. It offers the advantage of simplicity and freedom from the taint of bankruptcy. However, common-law settlements have always labored under a fundamental handicap: the power of a minority, or even one creditor, to block a full settlement. Compositions in bankruptcy under the old act and arrangements under the present act were designed to overcome this handicap. By a composition in bankruptcy, a willing majority had power to override a rebellious minority; and this advantage has been carried over into the provisions for arrangements under the present act.

Arrangements, however, offer an important advantage over compositions, which they have superseded. Although compositions in bankruptcy could be effected either before or after adjudication, they had to be consummated within the framework of the bankruptcy court. An arrangement, on the other hand, may be effected either during the course of a bankruptcy proceeding, or without any proceeding in bankruptcy at all.

**Who May Take Advantage of Arrangements.** Any person who can become a bankrupt may file a petition for an arrangement. This includes individuals, partnerships and corporations.

## Questions

1. Enumerate seven acts which will bar a bankrupt's discharge.
2. What is the effect of a discharge in bankruptcy?
3. Mention ten classes of provable debts which are not dischargeable in bankruptcy.
4. How may a debt be revived though discharged in bankruptcy?
5. Under what circumstances may a discharge in bankruptcy be revoked?
6. Summarize the general provisions for corporate reorganization under the Bankruptcy Act, with particular reference to (a) purpose, (b) disinterested trustees, (c) participation by the Securities and Exchange Commission, (d) participation by creditors and stockholders, and (e) soliciting acceptances of the plan.
7. Summarize the general provisions for "arrangements" under the Bankruptcy Act, with particular reference to (a) nature and purpose, and (b) persons who may take advantage of them.
8. In what respect does an arrangement differ from and constitute an improvement over the relief formerly available by way of (a) common law settlements, and (b) compositions in bankruptcy?

## Problems

1. The court having fixed a time for filing objections to a bankrupt's discharge, such objections are filed on the following grounds:

(a) The bankrupt has burned all his books.

(b) The bankrupt was asked at a creditors' meeting to explain the following shrinkage in values, but was unable to do so: The bankrupt's inventory, a month before his adjudication, showed $13,000, but at the time of adjudication, it had depreciated to $2,000, though there were no sales during the intervening period.

(c) The bankrupt had concealed $5,000 worth of property from the trustee.

(d) The bankrupt had been granted a discharge seven months before.

(e) The bankrupt had refused to speak to the trustee's attorney or to answer any of his questions when the attorney first visited the bankrupt at his place of business and made certain inquiries concerning the estate.

Assuming that the above objections can be sustained by proof, which of them, if any, will bar a discharge?

2. A bankrupt, on the hearing for his discharge in bankruptcy, sought to explain away a large portion of his loss by stating that he had sold goods at less than wholesale cost over a period of a year because "it was necessary to meet competition." His turnover during the year was $28,000, and his "loss" was $5,000. He offered no other explanation. Was the discharge granted?

3. Slade is adjudged an involuntary bankrupt, and in due course secures a discharge in bankruptcy. Subsequent to this discharge, the following creditors bring suit against him for the collection of their respective claims:

(a) His wife, who seeks to enforce arrears in alimony.

(b) The U.S. Government, which seeks to enforce taxes unpaid for two years prior to the discharge.

(c) A creditor, who secured a judgment based on the negligent operation of Slade's automobile.

(d) An employee, in connection with moneys deposited by him as security for the faithful discharge of his duties as cashier.

(e) A salesman, for damages sustained by reason of assault and battery committed by the bankrupt upon the salesman prior to the commencement of bankruptcy proceedings.

Discuss the respective claims, stating which are and which are not dischargeable in the bankruptcy, and why.

4. Kimmell obtained a loan of $13,000 from a friend by making certain oral representations which were later proven to have been false. He procured additional credit of $7,000 from a merchandising establishment without making any direct representations as to his credit, except to observe, "Look me up in Proudstreet's if you want to see where I stand financially." This the merchandising creditor did, and was advised by the mercantile agency that according to a statement which had been submitted to them three months before, Kimmell had a net worth of $40,000. The statement thus submitted included $35,000 of inflated assets. Following Kimmell's discharge in bankruptcy, his friend and the merchandising creditor both seek judgments on their respective claims. Will they recover? Give reasons.

5. The officer of an insolvent corporation transferred certain assets to himself allegedly for corporate expenses on behalf of the corporation. Thereafter a creditor procures judgment against the corporation and upon learning the

facts, brings a judgment creditor's action against the officer for the value of the corporate assets transferred, which action is terminated favorably to the judgment creditor. Thereupon the officer files a petition in bankruptcy. Upon the hearing for a discharge, the judgment creditor files objections and sets up the foregoing facts. Will the objections be sustained or dismissed? Explain.

6. John Doe, doing business as a merchant, borrowed money from his bank, which he failed to repay prior to his becoming insolvent. He subsequently went through bankruptcy and was discharged. Believing himself morally, if not legally, indebted to the bank, he executed and delivered to the bank, subsequent to the date of his discharge, a note in payment of his debt. When the note became due, Doe declined to pay it, on the ground that the note was executed without consideration, since it was given to cover a debt that he owed to the bank prior to his discharge in bankruptcy. The bank brought suit to enforce payment of the note. Will it succeed?

7. The XYZ Corporation have debts of $100,000 and assets of $50,000. The directors hold a meeting, and after a complete survey of the business, reach the conclusion that if given time, the corporation can work its way out of its difficulties. They therefore adopt a resolution to file a petition for corporate reorganization. Comment on this resolution.

8. An involuntary petition in bankruptcy is filed against The Smiley Corporation. During the course of the bankruptcy proceedings, Winston Smiley, president of the corporation, inquires whether it would not be possible to work out a corporate reorganization, but is advised by his attorney that in view of the bankruptcy proceedings it is too late for corporate reorganization. Is this advice sound?

## COURT CASES FOR REVIEW

### How Did the Court Decide, and Why?

1. The creditors of a financially embarrassed debtor executed the following statement in connection with a composition agreement: "We, the undersigned, creditors of Edward Ware, of Waterville . . . hereby agree to accept 30 per cent of our actual net claims against him, the amounts of which are correctly stated against our respective names in full discharge thereof. . . ." During subsequent litigation, the question arose whether this agreement was binding on the debtor. *Guilford First Nat. Bank v. Ware*, 95 Me. 388, 50 A. 24.

2. A bank president agreed that the bank would, along with all other creditors of the partnership, accept one third of its claim against the firm. Upon failure of all creditors to accept the proposed compromise agreement, the bank refused to be bound thereby. *Mermis v. Waldo*, 91 F. 2d 385.

3. The president of a creditor company arranged a meeting of creditors and acted as sponsor for a proposed settlement. He told the creditors that he thought 20 per cent was all "we" could get and that this was better than bankruptcy. He failed to disclose, however, that three brothers of the debtor had guaranteed payment in full to the president of the debtor's obligations at the end of six months. Thereafter, the company sought to hold the brothers on their guaranty. *Consolidated Cos. v. Angellos*, 170 So. 556 (La. App.), reinstating 166 So. 910.

4. An involuntary petition in bankruptcy was filed against X by one creditor. Nearly all of the claims were small in amount and were for current expenses. X moves to dismiss the petition on the ground that he had more than twelve creditors. *In re Luther*, 63 Fed. Supp. 83.

5. An involuntary petition in bankruptcy was filed against a country golf

club which appeared in the proceeding and consented to be so adjudicated. The club was a membership organization, not founded for profit, but existing only for the pleasure of its members. After the adjudication, two creditors moved to vacate the adjudication on the ground that an involuntary petition may not be filed against a membership corporation. *In re Elmsford Country Club*, 50 F. 2d 238.

6. A petition was filed against a partnership doing business under the name of Stovall Grocery Company. Several acts of bankruptcy were alleged, one of which was that C. C. Stovall, a member of the firm, had conveyed and transferred his undivided half interest in a certain lot to his wife, and that such conveyance was made without consideration, and with intent to hinder, delay, and defraud his creditors and the creditors of the firm. *In re Stovall Grocery Co.*, 161 F. 882.

7. *A* and *B* were partners. *A* filed a petition on behalf of the partnership for voluntary adjudication as a bankrupt. The petition was opposed by *B* who alleged that he, *B*, personally was solvent. *A* replied that since a partnership was a separate entity and since its assets were insufficient to pay its debts, the individual solvency of the partners was immaterial. *B* moved to dismiss the petition. *Mason v. Mitchell*, 135 F. 2d 599.

8. A restaurant operator, upon voluntary adjudication in bankruptcy, without permission of the bankruptcy court, turned over furniture and equipment to the conditional vendor who had sold it to him. Although the trustee did not elect, within 60 days after adjudication, to assume or reject the bankrupt's contract with the conditional vendor, he now seeks to obtain the proceeds of the sale. *Costello v. Golden*, 196 F. 2d 1017, affirming *In re Pagliaro*, 99 Fed. Supp. 548.

9. A firm consisting of two persons was duly adjudicated bankrupt. The partners in their statement of affairs answered one of the questions to the effect that no financial statement had been given by them. The answer was false. Upon the hearing of objections to a discharge, the partners urged that their statement of affairs had been prepared by their manager and, although they had signed it, they were personally ignorant of the misstatement. *In re Lovich*, 34 Fed. Supp. 85.

10. A bankrupt in his schedules sets forth that the residence and occupation of Guasti and Bernard, holders of a judgment against him, were "Unknown—Oklahoma." As a matter of fact, the bankrupt knew the exact residence of said creditors, and the latter had no knowledge of the bankruptcy proceeding until long after its termination. Upon discovering the facts subsequent to the bankrupt's discharge, the creditors sued the bankrupt. *Miller v. Guasti*, 226 U.S. 170.

11. Vincent Papale presented an air rifle to Tony, his thirteen and a half year old son. Tony went about the neighborhood shooting at cats, birds and his own playmates, in consequence of which one of his playmates lost the sight of one eye. Subsequently Papale filed a petition in bankruptcy and received a discharge. Thereafter suit was brought against Papale based upon the personal injuries sustained because of Tony's careless use of the air rifle. Papale set up his discharge as a defense. *In re Papale*, 17 Fed. Supp. 146.

12. Certain loan companies objected to a bankrupt's discharge upon the ground that he had made false statements to them in obtaining loans. It appeared that the misrepresentations were not material and that the loan companies did not rely on them. *In re Anderson*, 104 Fed. Supp. 599.

13. Creditors opposed a bankrupt's application for discharge on the ground that he had concealed property with the intent to hinder, delay and defraud

creditors. Although he had previously testified that he had no property except a car which was mortgaged to a bank, it seems that some nine months prior thereto, he had made a down payment of $2,000 on the contemplated purchase of some real property under contract for the sum of $12,000. In order to obtain the down payment, he borrowed on his life insurance, also on a car, and from his mother-in-law. *In re Walter*, 67 Fed. Supp. 925.

14. A landlady placed a claim for rent in the hands of her attorney for collection, but was informed by the latter that the tenant intended to file a petition in bankruptcy. The attorney learned through a notice to creditors that such a petition had been filed. However, he himself filed no proof of claim on behalf of his client for unpaid rent; neither was the landlady listed in the schedules as a creditor. The landlady now seeks to recover damages for unpaid rent. *Rosenfield v. Moore*, 112 N.Y.S. 2d 18.

15. *A*, although insolvent, purchased goods on credit from *B*. Thereafter, *B* obtained a judgment against *A* for the value of the merchandise. Still later, *A* went into bankruptcy and listed *B* as a creditor. After *A*'s discharge, *B* instituted garnishee proceedings against *A*, who now seeks to vacate such proceedings on the ground that the indebtedness has been discharged through bankruptcy. *B* replies that *A*'s failure to disclose his insolvent condition at the time he bought the merchandise amounted to obtaining the goods by false pretenses, and therefore that the indebtedness was not discharged in bankruptcy. *Davison-Paxon Co. v. Caldwell*, 115 F. 2d 189, cert. denied, 313 U.S. 564.

16. On application for a discharge in bankruptcy, a bankrupt furrier showed a loss of assets during an accounting period which ran to $38,000, with a deficiency in assets of $20,000. The bankrupt sought to explain the shrinkage by stating that a robbery had occurred. He made no effort, however, to establish the quantity or the value of furs or of any other property abstracted and carried away by the robbers. *In re Margolis*, 23 Fed. Supp. 735.

17. Knapp & Spencer Company, together with two other creditors, filed a petition in bankruptcy against Fuller. The petitioning creditors procured the appointment of a receiver pending adjudication and the election of a trustee. The receiver took possession and among the assets found an item of $4,000 in cash belonging to the bankrupt. Thereupon, the Knapp & Spencer Company brought about a settlement with the bankrupt by which the receivership was to be dropped and the money turned over, first to the bankrupt, then by him to the petitioning creditors. The three creditors secured an order discharging the receiver and returned the money to the bankrupt, who thereupon paid the money over to the creditors pursuant to the settlement. The bankruptcy proceedings, however, had not been dismissed. Certain other creditors, who were not included in the settlement, intervened in the bankruptcy proceeding, procured an adjudication, and had a trustee appointed. The trustee procured an order from the referee requiring the three creditors to return the settlement money to the estate. From this order of the referee, the three creditors appealed. (*Knapp & Spencer Co. v. Drew*, 160 Fed. 413.)

18. Katharine Lavine filed a voluntary petition in bankruptcy. She had three creditors in all. One of these in due course was eliminated. With the consent of the other two creditors, the petitioner moved to dismiss her petition and to vacate the order of adjudication. The trustee objected on the ground that the petitioner had committed perjury before the referee and that she should not be allowed to withdraw her petition, because to permit her to do so would prevent a prosecution for perjury. *In re Lavine*, 20 Fed. Supp. 362.

19. The preferred stockholders of a corporation, whose dividends had accu-

mulated with respect thereto, filed a petition under the Bankruptcy Act for reorganization of said corporation. A receiver who had previously qualified in an equity proceeding moved to dismiss the petition. *In re Pittsburgh Terminal Coal Corp.*, 30 Fed. Supp. 106, affirmed 109 F. 2d 1020 and 130 F. 2d 872.

# 19

# Wills and Estates

**Scope of This Chapter.** This chapter concludes Book I, devoted to the discussion of our rights and duties. It concerns the disposition of a person's worldly goods upon his death, either in accordance with his own wishes, where he leaves a will, or in accordance with certain rules of distribution, where he leaves no will. In Part 1 of this chapter we consider the rights of persons to dispose of their property upon their death, and discuss the persons who may make a last will and testament, the property which may be thus transferred, the persons to whom it may be transferred, and the limitations imposed by law upon the right to make such transfers. We also consider how a will must be executed and how it may be revoked; the different kinds of wills; the way a will is construed and put into effect, and the laws of inheritance, that is, the rules which govern the disposition of a person's property when he dies without leaving a will.

In Part 2 we consider the actual administration of a decedent's estate, by executors in case there is a will, and by administrators in case there is no will, with the object of collecting the decedent's assets, paying his debts and taxes, and making distribution. In Part 3 we consider estate administration where distribution is deferred pending the fulfilment of some trust. In that connection, we shall consider some of the general principles affecting all trusts, including those created by will.

### PART 1. WILLS AND INHERITANCE

**Status of Property upon a Person's Death.** When a person dies, some disposition must be made of his property. Such person is known in law as a *decedent*. If he has left a will, he is said to have died *testate;* and if such will is valid, the decedent's property is disposed of in accordance with the will. If the decedent leaves no will, he is said to have died *intestate*, and he is sometimes referred to as *the intestate*. In such cases the law steps in and directs the disposition of his property.

### Wills

**Will Defined: Testator.** A will is a disposition of property, real or personal, to take effect upon the death of the person who makes it, who is known as a *testator*.

A disposition to take effect *prior* to death is not a will, though designated as such.

EXAMPLE: John Ward, about to enter an Old Men's Home, delivers his savings to the superintendent and signs a statement reading: "This is my last Will. I give everything I have to the Old Men's Home. They will take care of me." Ward dies the next day. The transfer is subsequently attacked as an improperly executed will. The attack must fail. The instrument effecting the transfer is not a will, and did not have to be executed as such, because it did not purport to transfer anything after death.

On the other hand, an instrument which does purport to effect a transfer after death, though designated as a contract, deed or otherwise, is a will, and if not executed with all the legal formalities applicable to wills, is ineffective. Thus an agreement between two parties which provides that the survivor is to take certain property on the death of the other is in effect a purported will, invalid unless properly executed.

**Who May Make Will.** Each state has a right to prescribe the qualifications of persons who wish to make a will. Although there are numerous variations, most of the states substantially conform to the following pattern of qualifications:

All persons except idiots, persons of unsound mind and infants may dispose of real property by will; and every person of the age of eighteen years and upwards, of sound mind and memory, and no others, may dispose of personal property by will. The age limitation applies to the testator's age at the time of making the will, not at the time of death. Hence, if one makes a will while he is an infant nineteen years of age, disposing of real and personal property, and then dies at the age of twenty-three, the will is valid as to the personalty but not as to the realty.

**Freedom of Transfer by Will: Restraints.** Ordinarily, a person may freely transfer any of his property to any person or persons selected by him. To this rule, however, there are certain exceptions. These involve (a) rights of a surviving spouse, (b) after-born children, (c) charitable bequests, (d) witnesses to a will, and (e) the rule against perpetuities.

(a) *Rights of surviving spouse.* In the states which still observe the common law rule, a testator's right to dispose of his property by will is subject to *dower* but not to *curtesy* (page 621). Many states have abolished the common law rights of *dower* and *curtesy*, and have substituted, in their place, the absolute right of a surviving spouse, as an heir, to take a fixed percentage of the estate, real and personal. (See page 621.)

(b) *After-born children.* When a person makes a will and makes no mention of, or provision for after-born children, a child born to the testator after the making of the will is entitled to receive the same share that he or she would have received had the parent died intestate (page 754). This includes after-adopted children, who, for the purpose of this rule, are treated as born at the date of adoption. The law presumes that a parent intends to provide for his children by will. If, however, a parent having a child makes a will without providing for such child, the law will not presume that the parent forgot his child; the child will be deemed cut off by the will.

(c) *Charitable bequests.* No person may leave more than half of his net estate to charity if he leaves a surviving spouse, child or other descendant, or parent.

(d) *Witnesses to will.* When a witness is named as a beneficiary under a will, and the will cannot be proved without his testimony, he will not be allowed to take under the will. Neither can he refuse to testify for the sake of protecting his interest. However, if the witness is to share in the estate whether the will be proved or not, he will take either by will, or by intestacy, whichever will give him the *lesser* amount.

EXAMPLE: The testator's brother is a necessary witness to a will which gives him $10,000. If there were no will, he would receive $5000. He may be compelled to testify to the will, but is entitled only to $5000. If, by intestacy, he would be entitled to $15,000, he would have to testify, but would receive only $10,000.

(e) *Rule against perpetuities.* The law places a limitation upon the maximum period for which a person may tie up his estate and control its disposition by will. (See pages 770-771.)

**Formal Requisites of Will.** Generally speaking, any writing to take effect at death may constitute a will. However, statutes vary as to the formal requisites of such a writing. Some states merely require a simple statement of the testator's wishes, duly signed by the testator. Others require certain additional formalities, in the absence of which the will cannot be proved. The following formalities are not uncommon: (a) the will must be signed by the testator at the end; (b) the testator must sign in the presence of the attesting witnesses or he must acknowledge his signature to each of the attesting witnesses; (c) at the time of affixing or acknowledging his signature, the testator must declare the instrument to be his last will and testament; and (d) there must be at least two witnesses, each of whom must sign his name at the testator's request. Although most states require two witnesses, some require three, and three are advisable, since one or more of the witnesses may predecease the testator, or be difficult to locate. (See Form 17.)

**Codicils.** A codicil is a testamentary disposition subsequent to a will, by which the will is altered, explained, added to, subtracted from, or confirmed by way of republication, but in no case totally revoked.[1] The term *will* includes all codicils. A codicil must be executed with the same formalities as those applying to wills.

**Witnesses to will: statutory penalties.** Witnesses to a will need not know its contents. Difficulties in locating witnesses for probate have led

---

[1] *Black's L. Dic.*, 212.

FORM 17

# SIMPLE FORM OF WILL

## LAST WILL AND TESTAMENT OF JOHN DOE

I, JOHN DOE, of the City of_____, in the County of Suffolk and State of_____,_____, being of sound and disposing mind and memory, and not acting under duress, menace, fraud or undue influence of any person whatsoever, do make, publish and declare this instrument to be my Last Will and Testament, intending hereby to dispose of all the property over which I shall at my death have a right of disposition, by appointment, will, or otherwise and I do hereby cancel, revoke and annul all former wills and testaments or codicils by me at any time made.

*First:* I direct that all my just debts, funeral and testamentary expenses be paid as soon after my death as can conveniently be done.

*Second:* I give and bequeath to my son RICHARD my gold watch and chain and all my other personal jewelry and effects.

*Third:* I give and bequeath to my said son RICHARD the sum of ten thousand dollars.

*Fourth:* All the rest, residue and remainder of my estate, real and personal, of whatsoever character and wheresoever situated, of which I shall die seized or possessed or to which I shall be in any way entitled at the time of my death, I give, devise and bequeath to my wife, HANNAH DOE, absolutely, if she shall survive me, and if my said wife shall not be living at the time of my death I give, devise and bequeath my residuary estate to my son RICHARD absolutely.

*Fifth:* I nominate and appoint THOMAS BROWN to be the executor of this my last will and testament, and I direct that my said executor shall not be required to give any bond or security for the proper discharge of his duties.

IN TESTIMONY WHEREOF I hereunto set my hand and seal on this_____day of _____, in the year Nineteen Hunded and_____

_____(L.S.)

(Signature)

The foregoing instrument, consisting of_____ pages, including this page, was, at the date hereof, signed, sealed, published and declared by JOHN DOE, the testator above named, at _____ in the State of_____ as and for his last will and testament, in our presence, who, in his presence, at his request, and in the presence of each other, have hereunto set our names as witnesses.

| *Names* | *Addresses* |
|---|---|
| _____ | _____ |
| _____ | _____ |
| _____ | _____ |

(Signed by three witnesses)

to statutes making it mandatory for witnesses to add their addresses to their signatures. For example, a witness who omits his address may be required by statute to pay $50 or some similar sum to a person who sustains expense or other loss because of the omission.

*Attestation clause.* In addition to witnesses' signatures, it is customary for a will to contain an "attestation clause," reciting that the will was signed, published and declared by the testator as and for his last will and testament, and that the witnesses thereupon, at the testator's request, and in his presence, and in the presence of one other, subscribed their names as attesting witnesses and their respective places of residence. Such clause is not always essential to the validity of a will, but it has weight in showing proper execution.

**Date: Sundays and legal holidays.** A will should be dated, for practical reasons, but a date is not essential to its validity. A will or codicil may be executed any day, including Sundays and legal holidays.

**Holographic Wills.** A holographic will is one entirely in the handwriting of the testator. Although there is a strong presumption favoring the validity of holographic wills, such wills must nevertheless be executed, as a rule, with the same formalities as those governing ordinary wills. In many states,[2] however, the formalities of attestation and subscription by witnesses are unnecessary to the validity of holographic wills.

**Nuncupative Wills.** A nuncupative will is an oral will. It is invalid unless made by a soldier or sailor in actual military service or a mariner at sea. There must be at least two witnesses to prove a nuncupative will. In many states, a nuncupative will can dispose of personal property only. In some states, the statute provides that a nuncupative will becomes invalid a year after discharge from the military or naval service, unless the testator lacks testamentary capacity at such time, in which event it becomes invalid a year after he regains testamentary capacity.

**Revocation of Will.** A will may be revoked by act of the testator, as by making a subsequent will, or by destruction, cancellation, and so on; or by operation of law, as by marriage or divorce.

(a) *Revocation by subsequent will.* A will is effective only if it is the testator's *last* will and testament. Hence if a person makes a will, and then makes a later one, the former will is automatically revoked by the latter.

(b) *Revocation by destruction, mutilation, cancellation or obliteration,* provided the same is deliberate and intentional, revokes the will. If one accidentally tears up a will or throws it into a fire, or spills a bottle of ink on it, no revocation is shown, and the will may be established if it can be proved by proper evidence.

(c) *Marriage.* At common law, an unmarried woman's will was revoked by subsequent marriage, but not an unmarried man's. This rule has been modified by statute. Generally, regardless of sex, if a testator marries after making a will, and then dies, the will is deemed revoked as to the surviving spouse, unless provision for the latter has been made by an "ante-

[2] Including Arizona, California, Idaho, Kentucky, North Carolina, Oklahoma, Pennsylvania, Texas and Virginia, as well as the District of Columbia. In New York, attestation of a holographic will is dispensed with only when made by a soldier or sailor in actual service or a mariner at sea.

nuptial" or a premarital agreement in writing. If no such provision has been made, the surviving spouse may take as if the testator had died intestate.

(d) *Divorce.* In the absence of a statute to the contrary, divorce alone does not revoke a testator's will. Divorce accompanied by a property settlement has been held to spell out an implied revocation.

**Probate of Will.** To probate a will is to prove it. Proceedings for the probate of a will are instituted by a petition. Generally, a petition to probate a will may be presented by any person designated in the will as executor, devisee, legatee, testamentary trustee or guardian, or by the general guardian of an infant devisee or legatee, or by a creditor of the decedent, or by any party to an action involving the estate. Before the will can be admitted to probate, proof must be given, through the attesting witnesses, that the will was duly executed, that the testator when he executed it was in all respects competent to make a will, and that he was under no restraint when making the will.

**Construction of Will.** The parties interested in a will may request the appropriate court to construe the meaning of doubtful clauses in a will. Often a court must construe a will in litigation concerning it. In construing a will, the court seeks to give effect to the true intention of the testator so far as it can be gathered from the contents of the will and the surrounding circumstances.

## Inheritance: Descent and Distribution

**Inheritance.** The term *inheritance* has nothing to do with a will. It relates to the rules of law by which the real property of a decedent passes *in the absence of a will*, either to his heirs, or his "personal representatives."

**Heirs.** The term *heirs*, under the common law, designates all those persons who by law are entitled to the real property of a person who dies intestate. Under the early common law, this meant the decedent's eldest son, in accordance with the rule of *primogeniture* (descent to the eldest son). Originally, a decedent had no right to violate this rule of inheritance by even attempting to dispose of his real property by will. Today, the distinction between real and personal property, for purposes of intestate succession, has been abolished in many states.

**Personal Representatives and Next of Kin.** The term *personal representatives* generally means executors and administrators. However, under the common law, the term was employed to designate all those entitled to share in the unbequeathed *personalty* of a decedent, as distinguished from his *realty*. Thus, a surviving spouse, being entitled to share in the decedent's unbequeathed personalty, was a "personal representative"; but not being entitled to outright ownership in the realty, but only to a life interest, such as dower or curtesy (page 621), the surviving spouse could not be an "heir." Neither could a surviving spouse be classed as "next of kin," because "next of kin" involved kinship, and included all those who were related by blood to the decedent; for example, children, parents, brothers, sisters, and so on. Thus, under the common law, a decedent's personal representatives include a surviving spouse *plus* next of kin. Many states have abolished the distinction between heirs and personal representatives. In such states, a surviving spouse takes an outright share of the decedent's property, regardless of whether it is real or personal.

**Procedure on Intestacy.** When a person dies intestate, it becomes necessary to apply to the court for authority to administer his estate. Such application takes the form of a petition for *letters of administration* (page 758), upon the issuance of which the administrator takes possession of, administers and distributes the estate.

*Property in different states: law applicable.* When the intestate leaves real and personal property in several states, the real property passes in accordance with the law of the state where it is situated (*lex situs*), and the personal property is distributed in accordance with the law of the decedent's domicile.

**Order of Intestate Succession.** The order of intestate succession varies in the different states. Some states, in distributing intestate property, still preserve the distinction between real property and personal property, giving the former to heirs (page 753), and the latter to personal representatives (page 753). In other states, as noted (see above), the distinction between real and personal property has been abolished. The prevailing rule of priority governing intestate succession (except for a surviving spouse) has been summarized as Down, Up and Across; that is:

*First,* down to *descendants,* including children, grandchildren, great grandchildren, and so on, and if none such survive, then,

*Second,* up to *ascendants,* including parents, grandparents, great grandparents, and so on, and if none such survive, then,

*Third,* across to *collaterals,* that is, brothers and sisters, or their children (nephews and nieces), or brothers and sisters of parents (that is, uncles and aunts), or their children (that is, cousins).

The foregoing order of distribution is subject to the surviving spouse's share. This, in states which retain the common law principle, may consist of *dower* or *curtesy,* or it may represent an outright share, such as an outright one-third where children, grandchildren or great-grandchildren survive; a given sum plus one-half of the remainder where there are parents but no lineal descendants; a larger sum plus one-half of the remainder where there are no lineal descendants or parents, but where there are collateral relatives, such as brothers and sisters, nephews and nieces, and so forth.

## Questions

1. Define a will. Who may make one? May a person be qualified to make a will for some purposes and not for others? Explain.

2. "A person may freely transfer any of his property to any person or persons selected by him." Name and explain exceptions.

3. Explain the meaning of the following terms in connection with the formal execution of a will: (a) signature, (b) acknowledgement, and (c) declaration.

4. Are the following wills valid: (a) an undated will, (b) a will made on Sunday or a legal holiday?

5. (a) What are the requirements in your state in respect to the necessity for witnesses and their number and competency? (b) Do witnesses to a will have to know its contents? (c) Define attestation clause. What is its purpose? What is the effect of omitting such a clause from a will?

6. Define a holographic will. What advantages, if any, do such wills have in your state?

7. Define a nuncupative will. Under what conditions is a nuncupative will permitted in your state? Are nuncupative wills as effective in disposing of property as ordinary wills?

8. Define codicil. What formalities are required for the proper execution of a codicil?

9. Comment on a testator's right to revoke a will. Name and explain the different ways in which a will may be revoked.

10. Define probate. What is meant by a probate proceeding?

11. What is meant by the construction of a will? When is it resorted to?

12. Define inheritance as distinguished from the distribution of property by will.

13. What, broadly speaking, is the usual order of intestate distribution?

14. When a person dies intestate, what, briefly, are the steps that must be taken to transfer his property to those who are entitled to it by law?

## Problems

1. Helen James entered into a contract for the purchase of property. The contract required a series of installment payments over a period of two years. One month after she entered into the contract, she married. After her marriage, she entered into an agreement with her husband whereby he was to continue payments required under the purchase contract. The agreement between them provided that if he died first, the wife was to get the property in accordance with the contract of purchase; but that if the wife died first, the husband was to take title. The agreement was duly executed. It was not witnessed, however, the parties having been advised by counsel that although wills, under the law of that state, were required to be witnessed, contracts were valid regardless of witnesses. Upon the death of the wife, her personal representatives challenged the husband's exclusive right to take title. How was the case decided and why?

2. A, an infant, was 19 years old at the time he executed his last will and testament disposing of realty and personalty. At the time of his death, A was 23 years old. Is the will in all respects valid? Give reasons.

3. Under the last will and testament of Mortimer Watrous, a wealthy stockbroker, the following bequests are made governing an estate of $5,000,000 left by the decedent: (a) $2,000,000 in trust for the Midwestern Museum of

Fine Arts; (b) $1,000,000 to The Society for the Advancement of Peace and International Cooperation; (c) $1,000,000 to the Mercy Hospital; and (d) $1,000,000 to be distributed among two sons and one daughter of the deceased. Comment on the enforcibility of the provisions of this will.

4. Peter Dorne instructs his attorney to draw up a will leaving one-third of his estate to his widow and two-thirds to his two sons by a former marriage. He goes to his attorney's office to execute the will and takes with him his two sons who act as attesting witnesses to the will. Thereafter Dorne dies. After the will is probated, the widow challenges the right of the two sons to take under the will. Is the widow's position well taken? Explain.

5. A husband and wife intended to execute mutual wills, each making provision for the other. They executed the two instruments simultaneously in the presence of the same subscribing witnesses, who attested both instruments. By mistake, however, each spouse signed the instrument prepared for the other. Upon the wife's death her will, which had been mistakenly signed by her husband, was offered for probate. How did the case come out? Why?

6. The last will of Philip Green is duly executed in accordance with the formalities required by law. The will consists of sixty typewritten pages. It sets up a series of trusts for the benefit of five grandchildren. One of the grandchildren predeceases the testator, who thereupon adds a codicil at the foot of the will as follows: "Helen Dixie Green, my granddaughter, having died, it is my wish that her share of the trusts shall go to my four other grandchildren in equal portions." This codicil was then signed, "Philip Green." State whether or not the change thus made would become effective upon Green's death.

7. James Slavery, having a wife and two children, executes a will leaving everything to his wife. On his death the children contest the will on the ground that the law presumes that a parent intends to take care of his children, and the will contained no specific provision indicating an intent to cut the children off from any part of their father's estate. How will the court decide, and why?

8. An aged spinster, on her death bed in a hospital, reaches for paper, writes out two pages of directions as to how her property is to be distributed, but hesitates to call on her nurses to act as witnesses because she does not want them to know the contents of her will. If you were present, what would you tell her?

## PART 2. ESTATE ADMINISTRATION: EXECUTORS AND ADMINISTRATORS

**Purpose of Estate Administration.** In general, the purpose of estate administration is to carry out the legitimate directions of the testator in the case of a will, and regardless of the existence of a will to discover and collect assets, to conserve them pending distribution, to pay all proper claims and taxes, and to make ultimate distribution to those entitled to it. In the case of a will without trust provision, distribution follows the payment of debts, taxes and expenses. When the will creates a trust, distribution is deferred (so far as concerns the principal of the trust) until the terms of the trust are fulfilled. The purposes and functions of estate administration are discharged by executors or administrators in the case of outright distribution, and by testamentary trustees (that is, trustees named in a will) where distribution is deferred pending fulfillment of a trust.

**Executors and Administrators, Defined and Distinguished.** An executor is a person named in a will to execute or carry out its terms. An administrator is a person named by a court to administer the estate of a person who dies intestate. The authority of an executor is derived from the testator himself; of an administrator, from the Court. The duties of an executor differ from those of an administrator, in that the former are defined by the will, and the latter by law. An executor must pay the debts of the estate and distribute the assets as directed by the will; an administrator must pay the debts of the estate and distribute the assets as required by law under the rules of intestate succession (page 754). An executor may be exempted by will from the requirement of filing a bond; an administrator is required by law to furnish a bond in any event.

**Executors and Administrators: Who Are Competent to Act.** Generally speaking, all persons competent to make a will are competent to act as executors and administrators. The statute usually prohibits certain classes of persons from acting as an executor or administrator, such as (a) persons hostile to or adversely interested in the estate, (b) persons indebted to the estate, (c) persons without means, such as bankrupts or insolvents, (d) illiterate persons, (e) nonresident aliens, (f) nonresidents who are not by law required to give a bond, (g) persons under the age of twenty-one years, (h) adjudged incompetents, (i) felons and (j) persons incompetent to execute the duties of such trust by reason of drunkenness, dishonesty, improvidence or want of understanding.

**Classification of Administrators.** There are six classes of administrators:

(1) *Ordinary* administrator, appointed by the court in the usual situation, where a person dies intestate.

(2) *Administrator with the will annexed,* a person appointed by the court to carry out the terms of a will which fails to designate an executor.

(3) *Administrator* de bonis non, or substitute administrator appointed by the court when an administrator for some reason or other fails to qualify, or dies, or becomes incapacitated.

(4) *Temporary administrator,* or one appointed by the court on application of a creditor or person interested in the estate when, for any cause, delay occurs in the granting of letters testamentary, or letters of administration, or in probating a will.

(5) *Ancillary administrator,* or one appointed in another state than the one where the will is probated, by reason of the fact that the testator or intestate leaves property in such other state.

(6) *Public administrator,* appointed in a case where there is no personal representative or next of kin in the jurisdiction willing or competent to act as administrator.

**Administrators: Priorities in Right of Appointment.** In establishing the right to appointment as administrator, personal representatives (page 753) of the deceased are generally entitled to priority in a given order. The order, which may vary slightly in the different states, is generally as follows:

(a) Surviving husband or wife.

(b) Children.

(c) Grandchildren.

(d) Father or mother.

(e) Brothers or sisters.

(f) Any other next of kin entitled to share in the distribution of the estate, preference being given to the person entitled to take the largest share in the estate.

(g) If any or all of the above persons are infants, or have been adjudged incompetents, or have died, and if no competent adult entitled to take or share in the estate and having a prior right to appointment will accept it, administration may be granted to the general guardian of an infant, the committee of an incompetent, or the legal representative of a deceased distributee.

**Creditors as Administrators.** A creditor may be appointed as an administrator when all persons otherwise entitled, including the public administrator, fail or refuse to qualify. Next of kin are unlikely to apply for letters of administration when it becomes evident that the estate is inadequate to yield a surplus over debts. In such circumstances, unless a creditor applied for letters of administration, creditors' claims would be lost for want of an administrator.

**Qualifying for Duty: Oath; Bond; Objections.** An executor or administrator is not qualified to act as such until he has executed and filed the written oath required by statute, and until he has filed his bond. An executor, as noted on page 757, may be exempted from filing a bond where the will so provides. Any person interested in the estate may, prior to qualification, file objections to the designation of a proposed executor or administrator, on any of the grounds listed on page 757, or because such designation conflicts with the order of priority shown above.

**"Letters."** The authority officially granted to an executor or administrator to act as such, takes the form of "letters." *Letters testamentary* are granted to an executor, *letters of administration* to an administrator. When the deceased leaves property in another state, *ancillary letters* must be issued before such property may be taken over and distributed; *ancillary letters testamentary*, when there is a will, and *ancillary letters of administration* when there is no will.

**Fiduciary Character of Estate Management.** "An executor or administrator occupies a position of the highest trust and confidence and is required to use reasonable diligence and act in entire good faith in performing the duties of his trust. He is not a guarantor or insurer of the safety of the estate, nor is he expected to be infallible, but the prudence, care, and judgment which one of fair average capacity and ability exercises in the transaction of his own business or, as sometimes stated, the prudence, care, and judgment of fiduciaries ordinarily capable under like circumstances furnish the standard by which his conduct is to be judged." [3]

**Duties Prior to Appointment and Qualification.** Although an executor or administrator has no official authority prior to qualifying as such, he may be called upon to make certain necessary arrangements, such as those for burial of the deceased, before qualifying for his duties. When a person dies, it is customary to ascertain, first, whether he left a will, and if so, the identity of the executor named in the will. If there is a will, all preliminary steps are taken by or on behalf of the executor named; otherwise, application must be made for the appointment of an administrator.

*Safe deposit box.* If the testator maintained a safe deposit box, it may be necessary to obtain a court order permitting some party interested to gain access to the box. Such permission is governed by statute. In New York, for example, permission is not granted unless ten days' notice of the time and place of obtaining such access is given to the Tax Commission. A representative of the Tax Commission must be given an opportunity to examine the securities, deposits or assets contained in the safe deposit box at the time it is opened. A safe deposit company may become liable for unpaid taxes and a penalty of not less than $5000, nor more than $25,000, for permitting access to the safe deposit box of a decedent without proper authority and without due notice to the Tax Commission.

**Discovery and Collection of Assets.** An executor or administrator must take all steps necessary to discover and collect all the assets of the decedent in order that there may be a complete distribution of the decedent's property and goods. If necessary, he may bring a suit in equity for discovery against any person who, he has reason to believe, has in his possession or under his control any assets belonging to the estate. If the decedent had any contract or other property rights or *choses in action* (page 652), the executor or administrator may bring suit for the recovery on behalf of the estate; and upon recovering such judgment, the proceeds become part of the assets of the estate.

*Bank accounts; stocks and bonds.* One of the first steps of an executor or administrator in the collection of assets is to transfer all bank balances standing in the decedent's name, to the name of the estate, followed by the name and designation of the executor or administrator. Before effecting the change, banks usually require a waiver from the tax department, a certified copy of the letters which have been issued (page 758), and sometimes a death certificate. Similarly, stocks and bonds in the decedent's name are transferable on the books of the corporation to the name of the estate and executor or administrator, upon requirements similar to those governing the transfer of bank accounts.

*Insurance.* When life insurance is payable to a named beneficiary other

[3] 24 C.J. 48.

than the estate, it does not pass through the estate, but is payable directly to such beneficiary. When, however, the insurance is payable to the estate, the executor or administrator must promptly present proof of loss (death), with such other documents as the insurance company may require.

When a testator's property is covered by insurance policies, the executor must cause such policies to be transferred promptly to the name of the estate or the executor acting on its behalf, so that the policies will be enforceable in case of loss.

**Right to Continue Business.** Ordinarily, an executor or administrator may not continue a decedent's business, and if he does so, he becomes chargeable with all losses incurred and profits made.[4] His duty is to collect, convert and distribute with reasonable dispatch. In doing this, however, an executor or administrator must act with discretion; he may continue the business for the purpose of collecting existing commitments, and to the extent reasonably necessary to avoid too drastic a loss.

*Specific authority by will.* An executor may be specifically authorized by will to continue the decedent's business. In such case, he will not be liable for losses, if he acted "in good faith and with ordinary prudence." [5]

*Partnerships.* As noted on page 479, death dissolves a partnership, unless the partnership agreement specifically provides to the contrary. Partners may provide in their articles of copartnership, or by will, that upon death of any partner, his interest in the firm shall continue, through his executor, for a specified period or a specified purpose.

**Contracts on Behalf of Estate.** Contracts of an executor or administrator, though made on behalf and in the interests of the estate, are not binding on the estate until they are approved by the court, usually by order approving the executor's account (page 764). Estate fiduciaries cannot be regarded as agents of the estate; an agent must have a principal, and in no sense can an "estate" be regarded as a principal, since it is neither a natural nor an artificial person. Estate fiduciaries are really trustees for the estate beneficiaries. As such, they are primarily liable on estate contracts. They have no authority to satisfy these contracts out of estate assets except upon approval by the court. Such approval will depend upon whether the contract was necessary for a proper administration of the estate, or to carry out existing commitments.

Persons dealing with an executor or administrator are charged with knowledge of their legal limitations.

*Borrowing money.* An executor or administrator who borrows money for the estate is personally liable therefor. However, if the money was needed and used for estate purposes, the estate may be properly charged

---

[4] 33 *C.J.S.* 1171. See, especially, *Carter v Carter*, 247 Ala. 409, 24 So. 2d 759.
[5] 33 *C.J.S.* 1175.

with the loan, and the executor or administrator may be credited with it accordingly.

**Legal, Accounting and Other Services.** An executor or administrator may engage such legal, accounting and other assistance in the administration of the estate as is reasonably necessary. What is or is not reasonably necessary will depend on the nature, character and size of the estate, the ease of collecting and administering the assets, the necessity of bringing legal proceedings, the existence of substantial accounting problems, and so on.

**Liability for Torts.** Since executors and administrators cannot be regarded as agents for an estate (page 760), they cannot by their torts impose liability upon the estate but are personally liable for their torts though committed while they were acting on behalf of the estate.[6]

EXAMPLE: A decedent, at the time of his death, had property in his possession as bailee, which the executor subsequently refused to give up. The owner sued the executor as such, for conversion (page 803). The Court held that the action must be brought against the executor personally, not as representative of the estate.[7]

**Liability for Shrinkage in Assets.** An executor is liable for shrinkage in estate assets only when such shrinkage is due to his neglect or violation of duty. Thus, an executor, like a trustee, is limited by law to certain investments (page 778), though such investments should be temporary only, pending administration and liquidation of the estate. If he invests estate assets otherwise than as provided by law, he is personally liable for any consequent loss or shrinkage. An executor must not allow estate funds to remain unnecessarily idle; if he does, he is chargeable with interest he might have earned in the interim. Whether they are unnecessarily idle, that is, whether to keep funds readily available or to deposit them in interest-bearing accounts, is largely a matter of discretion with the executor.

An executor is not liable for shrinkage in estate assets, if he complies with the specific wishes of the testator in retaining existing assets without converting them into safer or more liquid form. (See page 778.)

**Commingling Funds.** An executor or administrator must keep estate funds and property separate and apart from his own account. If he fails to do so, he is liable by statute in many states for a misdemeanor; and in addition he is liable for any loss or shrinkage of such funds, by bank failure or otherwise, while the funds are so commingled. Improper designation of a deposit may be tantamount to commingling.

[6] *State, for the Use of Skinner v. Redding,* Del. Super., 45 A. 2d 507; *Ernest G. Beaudry, Inc., v. Freeman,* 73 Ga. App. 736, 38 S.E. 2d 40; *Christensen v. Frankland,* 324 Ill. App. 391, 58 N.E. 2d 289, 292; *Ostheimer v. McNutt,* Ind. App., 116 Ind. App. 649, 66 N.E. 2d 142; *Premium Cut Beef Co. v. Karp,* 318 Mass. 229, 61 N.E. 2d 112; *Brown v. Mack,* 185 Misc. 368, 56 N.Y. Supp. 2d 910.

[7] *Watson v. Moriarty,* 59 N.Y. 573.

*Designating deposit in fiduciary capacity.* An executor or administrator depositing estate funds should designate the deposit in his fiduciary capacity. If the deposit is made in his individual name, without any designation of the trust, he is liable for any loss which results from such disposition of the funds, regardless of any question of negligence or innocent intent.

**Property Available for Payment of Debts: Real v. Personal.** Although all property in the estate is subject to debts, personal property must be applied first, and then the realty. A testator, however, may, if he wishes, direct otherwise. Hence if a testator wishes his real property to be applied first in payment of debts, or equally with his personal property, he should so provide in his will; otherwise, devisees may benefit at the expense of the legatees (page 763). In some states, an administrator is given specific statutory authority to take possession of real property, manage it and collect rents, thereby giving creditors protection which does not exist at common law where real property, under intestacy, goes directly to heirs without passing through the estate.

**Time Limit for Presenting Claims.** Statutes in the different states generally fix a time limit within which creditors must file their claims, or be without remedy against an executor or administrator as to assets which have been distributed. For example, in some states, if a claim is not presented within seven months from the date letters were issued, the executor or administrator is not chargeable for any assets or moneys paid in satisfaction of other claims, or to any beneficiaries or distributees of the estate. In such states, the executor or administrator, if he wishes, may shorten this period by advertising for claims.

**Actions and Proceedings against Estate.** Just as an executor or administrator may bring suit on behalf of an estate for the recovery of a judgment in its favor, so creditors and claimants generally may sue the executor or administrator, as representing the estate, in connection with any cause of action against the decedent which survives his death. For example, if a decedent breached a contract, his estate is liable. However, statutes generally require that a creditor must first get leave of the probate court before he may sue an executor or administrator on a claim against the estate. If no executor or administrator has been appointed, a creditor may, as previously noted (page 758), petition for letters himself.

**Payment of Debts and Claims: Order of Priority.** The order of priority in the payment of debts of an estate is now governed by statute, which may vary as to detail in the different states. Administration expenses always come first. Then, generally, come claims preferred by Federal and state laws, government claims, secured claims, and, finally all others.

**Distribution of Estate: Net Assets.** Only net assets after payment of debts are distributable. Debts have priority over legacies. "A testator must be just before he is generous." Thus, if there are not enough assets in the estate to pay expenses, debts and legacies in the amounts specified in a will, the legatees' shares will be reduced proportionately.

*Provisions for distribution exclusive of taxes.* Taxes must be apportioned among all beneficiaries. A testator may, however, make provision for bequests exclusive of taxes, by directing that taxes shall be payable out of the residuary estate.

EXAMPLE: "I direct that the legacy to Mary Smith shall be paid without deduction therefrom of any taxes, but that estate taxes payable thereon shall be payable out of my residuary estate." [8]

**Devises and Legacies (Bequests).** A *devise* is a disposition of real property by will. The recipient of a devise is a *devisee*. A *legacy* is a disposition of personal property by will. It is also known as a *bequest*. The recipient of a legacy is known as a *legatee*. Legacies are of various types.

*General legacies.* A legacy is general when it does not dispose of a particular thing or things.

EXAMPLES:
(1) A bequest of $5000.
(2) A bequest of "Ten Upland Water Company bonds of the par value of $1000 each."

A general legacy begins to bear interest when it is payable, not before.

*Specific legacy.* A legacy is specific when it disposes of a particular thing or things.

EXAMPLES:
(1) A legacy of some keepsake or item of jewelry, such as a watch or a diamond ring.
(2) A bequest of "*my* ten Upland Water Company bonds of the par value of $1000 each."

*Lapsed legacy.* A lapsed legacy is one payable to a legatee who dies before the testator or before the legacy is payable. Under the common law, such legacy would fail. Today, such legacy would not fail if the legatee is either a child, grandchild, brother or sister of the testator, provided such legatee, upon predeceasing the testator, leaves a child or other descendant surviving.

*Residuary devisees and legatees.* A residuary devisee or legatee is one to whom, respectively, the balance or residue of real or personal property is devised or bequeathed, after the making of general and specific devises or bequests.

**Accounting and Settlement.** The nature of the estate determines the general nature of the accounting records which should be maintained by

---

[8] Or "shall be borne proportionately by all my devisees and legacies" (where the testator does not wish to burden the residuary legatee unduly).

an executor or administrator, in order that he may properly record and reflect the assets entrusted to him and his administration of such assets and the affairs of the estate. (See page 761.) The extent of these records will depend on the degree of accountability necessitated by the nature and extent of the estate. An executor or administrator has concluded his duties when he has distributed the estate property, after he has paid all expenses and taxes, and has paid, compromised or caused to be legally dismissed all claims against the estate. Upon the conclusion of such duties, it is customary for the executor or administrator to render an accounting and to procure an order or decree for the judicial settlement of such accounts as final and binding upon all parties. Such an order may be procured only after notice to all parties interested in the estate. Upon procuring such judicial settlement, the executor or administrator may have his bond canceled, and the estate is thereby closed. If the testator has set up trusts to be administered, the executor, in making distribution, will transfer the trust property to the trustee.

## Questions

1. Estate administration may involve either outright or deferred distribution. Which of these is the concern of the following: (a) executors, (b) administrators, (c) testamentary trustees?

2. What, basically, is the function and process of estate administration?

3. Explain four distinctions between executors and administrators.

4. Who are competent to act as executors and administrators? Name ten classes of persons prohibited from acting as an executor or an administrator.

5. Name six classes of administrators.

6. What is the usual order of priority in establishing the right to appointment as an administrator?

7. What is meant by "letters" as applied to executors and administrators, and what are the full designations used in such connection?

8. What authority may an executor or administrator have prior to qualifying as such?

9. Discuss the steps which an executor or administrator must take in discovering and collecting assets, with particular reference to bank accounts, stocks, bonds and insurance.

10. When, if ever, may an executor or administrator continue the decedent's business?

11. What contracts may an executor or administrator enter into on behalf of the estate?

12. What principles should govern an executor or administrator in respect to the following: (a) bringing lawsuits, (b) engaging legal, accounting, and other services, (c) borrowing money?

13. What is the liability of executors and administrators for (a) torts committed by them while acting for the estate; (b) shrinkage of estate assets; (c) commingling of estate with personal funds?

14. What is the law of your state in respect to the availability of property, real and personal, for the payment of estate debts?

15. What is the order of priority in the payment of debts and claims against a decedent estate?

16. What is the effect of a failure to present claims against an estate within the time allowed by law?

17. Distinguish between: (a) devises and bequests; (b) general and specific legacies.

## Problems

1. John Benson dies intestate, leaving a very substantial estate. The following personal representatives, through their attorneys, seek priority in being designated as Benson's administrator:

(a) A father;

(b) An infant son;

(c) A non-resident brother;

(d) A daughter who owes the estate $50,000;

(e) A widow who has been adjudged incompetent;

(f) A mother whose eyesight has been impaired to a point where she is unable to read or write;

(g) A sister who is without means.

Which of the above would have priority in being appointed as administrator of the estate of John Benson?

2. Among the papers found in Carter's safe upon his death was a life insurance policy for $20,000 payable to his wife as beneficiary. Carter's son by a prior marriage is named executor under his father's last will and testament. He demands that the insurance policy be turned over to him so that it may be presented by him to the Insurance Company with proper proof of loss. The wife's attorney insists on handling the matter himself. Who is entitled to handle the matter and why?

3. Janet Weems, a wealthy widow, leaves a will designating as executor her impecunious nephew, of whom she was very fond. Her brother, a responsible businessman, seeks to have the nephew disqualified. Will he succeed in doing this?

4. Walter Beegle is designated executor under the last will and testament of James Beegle, his brother. Walter is thoroughly familiar with James Beegle's affairs, having put James through college in the latter's earlier days. The principal assets of the estate consist of liquid funds in the amount of $20,000, which Walter Beegle transfers to his own bank account, expecting in due course to account therefor to the beneficiaries of James Beegle's estate, after payment of debts. The bank in which Beegle's funds are thus deposited, including those of his brother's estate, becomes insolvent through mismanagement and dishonesty of its directors. Prior to that, the bank had forfeited its right to Federal Deposit Insurance, so that the depositors, including Beegle, sustained almost an entire loss on their accounts. Beegle has other substantial means, but refuses to make good to the beneficiaries of his brother's estate on the ground that the loss of the estate moneys was not due to any fault on his part. On a proceeding to surcharge Walter Beegle, how should the surrogate rule, and why?

5. Don Kramer, executor of the estate of Thurlow Wilson, advertises for claims, pays all claimants after due proof thereof, except for the claim of one Mantel, who delays filing his claim until a year after the executor advertised for claims. By the time Mantel's claim is filed, the estate has been distributed and the legatees have disappeared. Mantel seeks to hold Kramer liable for not having withheld the amount of his claim prior to closing the estate. Will Mantel succeed? Give reasons.

6. An executor finds that he has $15,000 available in the estate with which

to pay the following claims: (a) a promissory note for $10,000; (b) a judgment for $5,000; (c) a claim for unpaid customs duty on jewelry which had been brought into the country by the decedent three years before his death, the claim amounting to $22,500; (d) a claim for $8,000 based on state property taxes; (e) a claim for $16,000 unpaid Federal income tax. How will the executor apply the estate assets to the payment of these claims?

7. Jerome Mason, a small-town merchant, dies leaving as his sole assets the stock, furniture and fixtures of his business establishment, valued at approximately $10,000. Under his last will and testament, Mason left everything to his only child, a needy daughter in poor health and unable to work. Mason had only one creditor, a wealthy wholesaler named Taylor, to whom he was indebted in the sum of $10,000. The respective claims of the daughter and Taylor are urged upon the executor. What should the executor do under the circumstances?

8. Brady, a wholesale grocer, ordered a large quantity of perishable fruit. A week after his death the fruit was unloaded at the dock, awaiting shipping directions and payment of accrued charges. The executor issued shipping instructions to the produce merchant, and agreed to make payment upon prompt delivery of the fruit. He also arranged with the produce merchant for new shipments over the succeeding three months' period. These commitments were later challenged by a beneficiary of the estate in a proceeding to surcharge the executor for a loss on the resale of all the fruit in question. How did the probate court rule?

9. Morgan leaves one legacy to his brother, another to his friend, and the rest, or residuary estate, to his grandchildren. Both the brother and the friend predecease Morgan, and each leaves a son. What disposition should the court make (a) as to the friend's legacy, and (b) as to the brother's legacy? Explain.

10. A testator owns a large variety of securities. Among numerous bequests in his will is one which provides: "To my granddaughter I leave 5 shares of A.T.&T. stock and my twenty shares of Upland stock." He sells all his securities a month before he dies. The granddaughter claims the equivalent of 5 shares of A.T.&T. stock and 20 shares of Upland stock. How will the court rule?

## PART 3. ESTATE ADMINISTRATION: TRUSTS

**Trusts in Relation to Estate Administration.** Most wills provide for an outright distribution after payment of debts and expenses. However, persons who accumulate wealth are prone to direct that it be kept intact as long as possible. Often they wish to defer distribution of principal for someone's lifetime, or until certain next of kin mature, or for other reasons. In such cases, they establish trusts, with provision for a trustee to succeed the executor and to administer the trust fund until such time as the will directs final distribution. Estate administration by a trustee is therefore governed by a different purpose from that which governs executors and administrators. The function of an executor or administrator is to collect assets and pay debts and legacies. The trustee's function is primarily to invest, manage and distribute income on the trust fund created by the will, in accordance with the terms of the trust, and upon its conclusion to dispose of the principal or corpus as directed. A proper understanding of estate administration by trustees presupposes a general understanding of basic trust principles. An outline of the law governing trusts is therefore essential in considering estate administration by trustees.

## Definitions and Distinctions

**Nature of Trust.** A trust involves property held by one person for the benefit of another, the latter having a right in equity to compel the person in whom the confidence is reposed to discharge the obligations imposed in respect to the property. A trust may therefore be defined as a confidence reposed in one person with respect to property held by him for the benefit of another.

**Parties to Trust.** Every trust involves three parties: the person who creates it, called the *donor* (also known as *trustor*, *settlor*, *creator*, *founder*); the person in whom legal title is vested, known as the *trustee*; and the person for whose benefit the trust is created, known as the *beneficiary*, or *cestui que trust*.

**Trust Property: Legal and Equitable Interests.** Every trust involves two estates or interests in the subject matter of the trust: the *legal* estate, or interest held by the trustee for administrative purposes, and the *equitable* estate, or interest of the beneficiary which entitles him to the benefits of the trust. The latter is enforceable only in a court of equity.

EXAMPLES:

(1) *A* conveys certain real property to *X* in trust for *B*. *X*, the trustee, has the legal title, that is, the title recognized in a court of law, but *B* has the *beneficial* or *equitable* title, that is, the title recognized in a court of equity.

(2) *A* establishes a fund with the University Trust Company for the benefit of the Metropolitan University. The Trust Company, as trustee, has the *legal* (administrative) interest and the university the *equitable* (beneficial) interest.

**Trust Distinguished from Ordinary Obligation.** A trust differs from an ordinary obligation in several respects:

(1) *Nature of obligation.* A debtor merely owes his creditor a debt. The relationship is that of a simple contract or business obligation. A trustee owes his beneficiary the highest degree of faith in the discharge of the trust. The relationship is fiduciary.

(2) *Liability for loss.* If trust property is lost or destroyed without the trustee's fault, the trustee is not liable for it; but a debtor remains liable regardless of fault.

(3) *Rights of creditors in case of insolvency.* When a debtor becomes insolvent, general creditors are entitled only to a *pro rata* share of his assets. If a trustee becomes insolvent, the beneficiary has a prior right to so much of the trustee's assets as represent trust property or its proceeds.

EXAMPLE: *A* becomes insolvent. His debts amount to $100,000. He has assets of $60,000, all on deposit in a bank, including $10,000 in trust for *B*. Creditors demand sixty cents on the dollar. *B* demands his $10,000 in full. *B* will prevail.

**When Bank Deposits Constitute Trust Funds.** Ordinary bank deposits do not constitute trust funds. They merely establish the relationship of debtor and creditor. However, when a bank accepts a special deposit, it becomes the depositor's trustee. In such case, if the bank were to fail, the special depositor would be entitled to a preference.

## Classification of Trusts

**Express and Implied Trusts.** Express trusts are those created by direct and positive acts of the parties, in words, oral or written. Implied trusts are those which, without being expressed, may be inferred from the nature of the transaction. Implied trusts are either *resulting* or *constructive*. (See page 775.)

**Executory and Executed Trusts.** Executory trusts are those wherein the donor's intentions are imperfectly or incompletely expressed, or not fully declared, so that something remains to be done in order to complete and perfect the trust.

EXAMPLES:
(1) A promise to create a trust.
(2) Directions given for the execution of some future conveyance or settlement of trust property subject to further instructions.
(3) A conveyance of property in trust, subject to subsequent instructions.

In an executed trust, the terms of the trust are fully and perfectly declared, the donor has given complete directions for settling his estate, and no further act is necessary to effectuate the trust.

EXAMPLE: A deed or will creating a trust in terms so clear and certain that a trustee has nothing to do but to carry out the provisions of the instrument.

**Other Types of Trusts.** There are numerous other classifications of trust, among them the following:

*Active v. passive trusts.* An *active* trust, also known as a *special* or *operative* trust, is one which imposes active duties upon the trustee in executing the trust. A *passive* trust, also known as a *simple, technical, dry* or *naked* trust, is one in which the trustee is a mere passive holder of the property with no duties to perform. (See page 770.)

*Discretionary v. ministerial trusts.* Discretionary trusts are those in which the administration of the trust is left to the sole discretion of the trustee; for example, where a trustee may decide how much, if anything, a beneficiary is to receive. Ministerial trusts are those which involve no discretion on the part of the trustee and merely require that he specifically carry out certain explicit instructions.

*Shifting trusts.* Shifting trusts are so created that, under specified contingencies, they may operate in favor of beneficiaries additional to or substituted for those first named. (See page 772.)

*Spendthrift trusts.* Spendthrift trusts are those created with a view to providing a fund for the maintenance of an improvident person, by securing the fund against such person's improvidence or incapacity. (See page 773.)

*Living* (inter vivos) *v. testamentary trusts.* A living trust is one that is created and comes into existence during the lifetime of the donor. Testamentary trusts are those created by will.

## Express Trusts: Requisites and Restrictions

**Requisites: in General.** The requisites of a valid express trust include:

(1) *Subject matter,* or trust *res,* which must be sufficiently identified or identifiable so that it can be appropriated to the trust, and which must represent a legitimate property interest not contrary to law or public policy.

(2) *Parties:* These include the donor, trustee and beneficiary (page 767). A donor and beneficiary are absolutely essential to the trust; but equity will not permit a trust in other respects valid to fail for want of a trustee, and will in such case appoint a trustee.

(a) *Who may be donor.* Every person competent to dispose of his property by contract, deed or will has the power likewise to dispose of it by creating a trust in such property. Since infants cannot dispose of real property by deed or will, they cannot create a trust in such property.

(b) *Who may be trustee.* Any person may be a trustee if he has the capacity to do what the trust requires. (See page 776.)

(c) *Who may be beneficiary.* Any person may be a beneficiary regardless of age or sex and regardless of physical or mental capacity. Trusts without specific beneficiaries are void, excepting charitable trusts, which necessarily can have no specific beneficiary.

(3) *Consideration.* When the trust is wholly executory, that is, when there is merely an agreement to create a trust not yet in existence, consideration is essential, or the trust is ineffective. An executed trust, like a gift, requires no consideration.

(4) *Certainty.* It is a requisite of every express trust that the intent to create a trust shall be clearly expressed. The declaration of trust must be sufficiently explicit to designate with reasonable certainty the subject matter, purpose and beneficiary of the trust. Otherwise, the trust is impossible of execution.

Examples:

(1) A trust for the benefit of certain persons, *or either of them,* is void for uncertainty of beneficiaries.

(2) A trust created by a testatrix for the purpose of keeping her burial plot in good condition is void for want of a beneficiary.

(3) A trust for the building of a school house was declared void for uncertainty.[9]

---

[9] *Emory etc. College v. Schoemaker,* 92 Va. 320, 23 S.E. 765.

**Restrictions: in General.** In addition to the above, the law imposes other essential requirements and restrictions. Among these are the requirements as to *form* in certain cases (for example, that a contract to create a trust must be in writing under the statute of frauds), the requirement that a trust must have an *active purpose* (eliminating "passive" trusts), the "rule against perpetuities" (to prevent tying up property for overlong periods of time), and the rule against the accumulation of income beyond the period measured by a person's minority.

**Trusts and the Statute of Frauds.** As a general rule, trusts need not be *created* by a writing, but must be *manifested and proved* by a writing. This means that even when a trust comes into existence without a writing, it will be sustained if it can be established by a subsequent writing. The writing need be signed only by the donor. It need not be in any particular form, so long as it sufficiently designates the property, the beneficiary and the purpose of the trust. If the writing does not designate a trustee, the court will appoint one. A person complies with the statute of frauds if he declares in writing that he holds property, in any form, for the benefit of another.

*Exceptions to statute of frauds.* There are two exceptions to the rule that an oral trust is invalid: (1) when an oral trust has been fully or partly executed and (2) implied trusts, including resulting and constructive trusts (pages 775 to 776).

**Trust Must Be "Active."** A trust wherein the trustee has no active duty to perform and is merely a temporary holder of title—a channel through whom title flows—is ineffective as a trust, and legal title in such cases passes automatically to the beneficiaries. Passive trusts have been generally abolished throughout the country.

EXAMPLES:
(1) Trust wherein the right to both possession and profits vests in the beneficiary.
(2) Trust for the grantor's sole use.
(3) Trust for the sole purpose of conveying title.

**Specific Purposes for Which Trusts in Real Property May Be Created.** Some states, notably Michigan, New York and Wisconsin, have abolished all uses and trusts in lands except such as are expressly authorized by statute. Among such purposes are the following: (1) To sell real property for the benefit of creditors; (2) To sell, mortgage or lease real property so as to establish an income for named beneficiaries, or to pay off some claim against the property; (3) To receive the rents and profits, and apply them to some person's use; (4) To receive the rents and profits, and to accumulate them for a period of time not exceeding the minority of an infant; (5) To further some religious, educational, charitable or benevolent purpose.

**Rule against Perpetuities: Purpose of Rule.** The object of the rule against perpetuities is to prevent tying up title to property in such a way that for an unreasonable period of time, no one can be pointed to as the person who has the absolute right to transfer title and possession. Such tying up of title is referred to as *suspending the absolute power of alienation*. The rule generally provides that the *absolute power of alienation* is suspended when there are no persons in existence by whom an absolute fee in possession (pages 615 and 616) can be conveyed. Absolute ownership may be suspended in two ways:

(1) By creating a contingent or uncertain future estate.

EXAMPLE: Life estate to Jones, remainder to the person who shall be Mayor of the City of New York in 1980. Such remainder is contingent, not vested. It suspends until 1980 the *absolute power of alienation*.

(2) By creating a trust for a specific period. The law does not permit the *power of alienation* or transfer to be suspended for fixed periods but prefers to measure the period by human lives. Hence a trust for ten years in *X* as trustee for the benefit of *A* would fail.

**Rule against Perpetuities: Maximum Period of Suspension.** The longest possible period during which the absolute power of alienation may be suspended, whether by future estate or by trust, is a period not measured by time, but by *two lives in being plus the period of minority*.

EXAMPLE: Life estates in Allen and Baker, remainder to Curtis, an infant born on the day the estate is created; with the provision that if Curtis dies before he is twenty-one or marries before he is twenty-one, or if any other prescribed condition occurs or fails to occur during such twenty-one year period, then the remainder is to go to Dalton. This is the maximum period during which alienation may be suspended: the lives of *A* and *B* and the minority of *C*.

In some states, the maximum period of suspension of the power of transfer is two lives in being without the added minority period.

**Trusts in Personal Property: Rule against Accumulations.** The rule against perpetuities applies to trusts in both real and personal property, but trusts in personal property are further subject to the rule against accumulations, namely, that where such trusts provide for accumulations of interest upon principal they are void unless they are limited to the period of infancy.

### Express Trusts: How Created

**In General.** Broadly, there are two ways in which an express trust may be created: (1) by a disposition *inter vivos*, or living trust, namely, one which becomes effective during the donor's lifetime and (2) by a testamentary disposition, which becomes effective after the donor's death (page 769). In the case of a living trust, the donor's disposition may be *revocable* or *irrevocable*, depending upon the terms of the trust. A testamentary trust, of course, becomes irrevocable upon the donor's death, though its benefits may shift upon contingencies named in the trust. (See "Shifting Trusts," page 768.) Prior to the testator's death, however, the trust may be revoked at any time, since a will is revocable at the testator's election (page 752).

A person may subject property to a trust in one of two ways: (1) he may transfer the property subject to a trust and (2) he may constitute himself trustee, without any transfer, by a declaration of trust.

**Transfer of Property: Living (*Inter Vivos*) Trusts.** Real property may be transferred subject to a trust in three ways: (a) by deed, subject to trust provisions embodied in the instrument itself; (b) by deed, simultaneously with a trust instrument which sets forth the trust purposes and provisions of the conveyance; (c) by deed to a grantee who in turn agrees to hold or convey the property to the use of another. The same methods may apply to personal property transfers for trust purposes.

**Transfer of Property: Testamentary Trusts.** Although most wills provide for an outright distribution, many wills, especially by wealthy testators, contain trust provisions of one sort or another. Testamentary trusts may be created (a) by a devise of real property for trust purposes (b) by gift of a specific sum of money in trust, (c) by gift of income-producing personalty, such as securities and (d) by gift to a trustee of all or part of the residuary estate in trust for named beneficiaries.

**Settlor Constituting Himself Trustee.** An express trust may be created without transfer, by a simple declaration by the owner that thenceforth he holds such property in trust for the benefit of some other person or persons named.

EXAMPLE: The owner of securities agreed to hold them for the account of a correspondent to secure drafts drawn by the owner against the correspondent. The Court held that such agreement made the owner a trustee in respect to such securities.[10]

*Promises to convey or transfer: tentative trusts.* The declaration must not take the form of a voluntary *promise to convey or transfer*, for such promise, as we have seen (page 769), is ineffective without consideration. Neither must it take a form sometimes referred to as a *tentative trust*, in which the settlor remains the true owner notwithstanding an ostensible declaration of trust. A common illustration of this is a bank account opened by one person as trustee for another.

*Bank deposit in name of one person as trustee for another.* Where one person (Abel) opens a bank account in his own name as trustee for another (Baker), no true trust is created because the depositor—so long as he retains the passbook—remains the true owner of the account. Abel's creditors, not Baker's, may resort to the account. This would not be the

---

[10] *Sexton v. Kessler,* 172 Fed. 535.

case if the account constituted a true trust. However, if Abel transfers the passbook, or dies without revoking the account, Baker becomes entitled to it. (Baker's death prior to Abel's would have no effect on Abel's rights, so long as Abel retained his passbook.) This type of trust is referred to in some jurisdictions as a *Totten Trust*.[11]

## Express Trusts: Purposes

**In General.** Trusts in real property, as stated (page 770), are limited in many states to certain specified purposes. Trusts in personal property may be created for any purpose not contrary to law. Among some of the more common forms are: (a) trusts for married women, (b) family settlement trusts, (c) spendthrift trusts, (d) charitable trusts, (e) insurance trusts, (f) investment trusts, (g) voting trusts (described on page 536), and (h) trusts for the benefit of creditors.

**Trusts for Married Women.** Formerly, trusts for married women were devised because of the latters' common law disabilities (page 24) and the fear that the husband, who upon marriage acquired control of his wife's property, might use it for his own benefit. The principal function of a married woman's trust today is to protect her from her husband's influence exercised by persuasion, sympathy or otherwise against her own interests and for the husband's benefit. The trustee stands in the way of such influence.

**Family Settlement Trusts.** The most common type of trust is one by which a person provides for a settlement or distribution of his property to his family through the medium of a trustee empowered to manage trust property, collect and pay out income, and ultimately distribute the principal or "corpus." Although such trusts are usually testamentary, they are sometimes set up by a husband as part of a divorce settlement, by stipulation embodied in the decree. Family settlement trusts, in addition to providing for the support and maintenance of a donor's family, may specify particular purposes for which trust moneys shall be used, as in the case of a trust providing for a daughter's dowry, or the education of children or grandchildren.

**Spendthrift Trusts.** A spendthrift trust, as noted on page 768, is one which provides a fund for the maintenance of an improvident person, by securing the fund against his improvidence or incapacity. Such trusts, as a rule, provide for the payment of the income to the beneficiary, but prohibit him from alienating (selling or assigning) his interest, or anticipating the income (as by borrowing against it), or subjecting it, in advance of payment, to the claims of his creditors. A person may not immunize *himself* against the claims of creditors by setting up a spendthrift trust *for his own benefit;* but if he sets up a spendthrift trust for someone

---

[11] From *Matter of Totten*, 179 N.Y. 112,

else, the court may sustain it, not out of consideration for the beneficiary, but because a donor has a right to control his bounty. The fund may be effectively placed beyond the reach of creditors by a provision that the trustees in whom the spendthrift fund is vested may *in their discretion* apply the whole or some portion of the income to the support of the beneficiary. The tendency in some states is to regard spendthrift trusts as contrary to public policy in thwarting the just claims of creditors; but even in those states, such trusts are recognized to a limited extent. For example, trusts may provide that in the case of bankruptcy or insolvency the income will cease and be payable to another.[12]

**Charitable Trusts.** Charitable trusts have two essential characteristics: (a) they are created for an indefinite number of unascertained persons and (b) they have, for their object, some public benevolence. If either of these elements is lacking, the trust is not charitable. Charitable trusts are generally grouped into four classes: (1) religious, (2) educational, (3) eleemosynary, and (4) governmental.

EXAMPLES:

*Religious trust:* A bequest "to the Evangelical Baptist Benevolent and Missionary Society for the benefit of Poor Churches of the City of Boston and Vicinity."

*Educational trust:* A devise in trust for the establishment of a college.

*Eleemosynary trust:* A bequest to a trustee for the use and benefit of the poor widows and children under ten years of age in a given community.

*Governmental trust:* A legacy in trust to the town of New Rochelle for the purpose of erecting a town house for the transaction of town business.

*Cy pres doctrine.* The term "cy pres" means, literally, "as nearly as possible." When the purpose of a charitable trust becomes impossible of fulfillment in accordance with the donor's intentions, the court may, in exceptional cases, adapt the charity as nearly as possible so as to give approximate effect to the intention of the donor.

EXAMPLE: A bequest was made in trust for propaganda against Negro slavery. After slavery was abolished, the heirs of the honor claimed the fund. The court, under its cy pres power, ruled that the trust fund, if administered for the benefit of the colored race, would approximate the donor's intentions.[13]

**Insurance Trusts.** Trusts are frequently established in the proceeds of a life insurance policy, either by the terms of the policy itself, or by an express declaration of trust, or by an agreement between the assured and a designated beneficiary that the latter shall apply and pay over to a third person part or all of the proceeds.

**Investment Trusts.** Investment trusts are organizations for the collective investment of the funds of numerous individuals in numerous securities. They have taken three forms: (1) the Massachusetts or business trust,

---

[12] *Bramball v. Ferris,* 14 N.Y. 41.
[13] *Jackson v. Phillips,* 14 Allen (Mass.) 539.

holding securities in trust and issuing participation certificates giving the owners equitable interests in the stocks held in trust, (2) corporations which issue stock or debentures and invest the proceeds in widely diversified securities, and (3) corporations which deposit stocks with a trustee and issue certificates of interest in such stocks. With the enactment of statutes requiring investment trusts to incorporate, the last form of investment trust is the most prevalent.

**Trusts for the Benefit of Creditors.** Trusts for the benefit of creditors may take various forms:

(a) *Trusts to sell real property* for the benefit of creditors are sometimes set up by debtors who are "land poor," though more frequently they are incidental to a general assignment for the benefit of creditors (page 705).

(b) *Trust deeds,* which have been described on page 691.

(c) *Deposit of bonds in reorganization proceedings,* with bondholders' committees who function as trustees in connection with such bonds, for the purpose of achieving united action in respect to a plan of reorganization (page 562).

(d) *Statutory trusts* created by Federal or state statute, as in the case of trustees in bankruptcy (page 720).

## Implied Trusts: Resulting and Constructive

**Nature of Implied Trusts.** Implied trusts are creatures of equity to prevent injustice. They may be inferred from (a) conduct or (b) the nature and circumstances of the transaction. They include *resulting* and *constructive* trusts.

*Resulting and constructive trusts distinguished.* Resulting trusts are presumed to exist from the supposed intention of the parties as indicated by their conduct and the nature of the transaction. Constructive trusts, on the other hand, are construed to exist, regardless of the actual or presumed intention of the parties, often, indeed, directly contrary to such intention, so as to defeat the designs of those who, acting in a fiduciary capacity, seek by fraud or otherwise to gain some unfair advantage.

**How Resulting Trusts May Arise.** Resulting trusts may arise in any situation where the legal title to property is in the name of a person not justly entitled to it. Equity may intervene in such cases to establish the rights of the true or equitable owner.

EXAMPLES:

(1) I give you $10,000 to buy certain property in my name and you buy the property in your own name. Equity will declare that you hold the property as a trustee for my benefit.

(2) I transfer property to you with the mutual understanding that the transfer is in trust; but the understanding is inadequately, imperfectly or illegally expressed, so that it fails as an express trust. Equity will not permit you to

benefit from such failure, but will declare you to hold as a resulting trustee.

(3) A trustee or other fiduciary invests trust funds for his personal benefit. As to any profits so derived, he is a resulting trustee.

*Effect of resulting trust.* A resulting trust is a passive or naked trust (page 768). In consequence, the trustee's function is merely that of obeying a decree of court requiring him to transfer the property in question, with all accruing benefits, to the true beneficial owner. (See page 770.)

**Basis of Constructive Trusts.** The basis of a constructive trust is fraud, actual or constructive; hence constructive trusts are sometimes referred to as trusts *ex maleficio*.

*Actual fraud* consists in deception by direct misrepresentation or concealment. It may take a thousand forms, too numerous to mention. A simple example is furnished where one obtains a conveyance of land from an illiterate person, by misrepresenting the nature of the transaction. Such fraudulent grantee holds title as constructive trustee for the benefit of the illiterate grantor.

*Constructive fraud* consists in any act or omission contrary to good faith or good conscience, to the injury of another. It may arise out of the nature of the transaction, as where one person disposes of property to another for a consideration so grossly inadequate as to create the inference of fraud; or it may arise out of a relationship of parties which gives one of them an advantage over the other, or which requires exceptional good faith because of such relationship, as in the case of husband and wife, parent and child, brother and sister, attorney and client, principal and agent, guardian and ward, partner and copartner, executor or administrator and the beneficiaries of an estate.

**Statute of Frauds Inapplicable to Resulting and Constructive Trusts.** The statute of frauds applies only to express trusts; that is, to the way in which such trusts shall be expressed. It therefore has no applicability to resulting and constructive trusts, which are created, not by acts of parties, but by operation of law to insure justice.

## Qualifications and Duties of Trustees

**Qualifications of Trustees.** Any person may be a trustee who has legal capacity to make contracts and to do the acts required by the terms of the trust. Hence, even infants, idiots and lunatics may be trustees if their disability does not interfere with their capacity to execute the trust. Some states provide that no person may act as a testamentary trustee if he is an infant, an adjudged incompetent, a nonresident alien, a felon or a person incompetent to execute the duties of the trust by reason of drunkenness, dishonesty, improvidence or want of understanding. A corporation may be a trustee when so authorized by its charter, or when the trust is necessarily incidental to its express powers; but an unincorporated association may not act as trustee except in the case of a charitable trust. A person cannot be trustee for himself.

**Bond and Oath.** A trustee before entering upon his duties is frequently required to file a bond and take a prescribed oath. Such is the case when a trustee is named in a will, or appointed by a surrogate or probate court when the trustee named in a will dies or renounces the trust, or becomes incompetent, or is otherwise disqualified.

**Executors and Testamentary Trustees: Separation of Functions.** Though the persons named in a will as executor and as trustee are often one and the same, their functions are separate and distinct. The basic function of an executor, as noted on page 759, is to collect, convert, and distribute with reasonable dispatch. The basic function of a trustee is to administer the trust in accordance with its terms. When the executor's duties are completed, he must make such distribution in trust as the will directs. Occasionally, the duties of executor and trustee merge, in which event, generally, single commissions only are allowed. If the testator creates a trust but names no trustee, or the trustee dies, renounces or is disqualified, the executor must set up a trust fund, retain it in his custody, and attend to such administrative duties in respect to it as may be necessary pending court appointment of a trustee. Frequently an executor, as such, transfers to himself, as trustee, the property and funds devised and bequeathed in trust. In doing this and in all matters affecting his separate duties as executor and as trustee, he must keep separate books of account.

**Powers, Rights, Duties and Liabilities of Trustees: in General.** The powers, rights, duties and liabilities of trustees may be specifically defined in a trust instrument, such as a will, deed or trust agreement. In addition, the law imposes upon trustees the duty to exercise the highest degree of good faith, care and skill—beyond that of an ordinary agent or fiduciary. A trustee is not, however, an insurer; he is required merely to exercise reasonable judgment. He must keep his beneficiary duly informed; must seek advice of counsel when in doubt; and he must avoid placing himself in any position where his personal interest will conflict with the duties of his trust.

**Trustee with Conflicting Interests.** As noted, the law imposes upon a trustee the duty of exercising the highest degree of good faith in the discharge of his duties. He must not accept the trust if it will conflict with other interests, or with his own. In the discharge of his duties, he must avoid situations where his own interests conflict with those of his trust. When such conflicting interests become unavoidable, he must not prefer his own interests to the detriment of the trust.

*Mingling individual with trust funds.* We have already noted (page 761) that an executor, administrator, guardian or testamentary trustee who commingles estate funds with his own is not only guilty of a misdemeanor, but is liable to the estate for any loss or shrinkage while the funds are so commingled. This would be true regardless of the trustee's good faith.

*Personal transactions with estate.* A trustee cannot deal with the estate to his personal advantage. Except for his lawful commissions, he is permitted to derive no profit from his trust, whether by dealing in trust property, selling his own property to the estate, buying estate property (through "dummies" or otherwise) at public or private sale, or lending estate moneys to himself or to members of his family.

**Management of Trust Property: in General.** The basic function of a testamentary trustee is to assume custody, invest, manage and distribute. He assumes custody of the trust property, either initially, or upon taking it over from the executor; and if there are any uncollected assets, he collects them, by suit if necessary. The functions of investment, management and distribution, including any power to mortgage, pledge, lease or sell, are governed by the donor's wishes, subject to established rules of law.

*Authority to incur and pay debts.* A trustee may incur such expenses as are reasonably necessary for the preservation of trust property and the protection of beneficiaries.

*Power to mortgage or pledge trust property.* A trustee ordinarily has no power to mortgage or pledge trust property unless such authority is conferred by the trust instrument.

*Power to lease trust property.* Trustees may lease trust property on such terms, conditions and rentals as are reasonable and customary for that class of property in the particular vicinity.[14]

**Trust Investments.** The rules of law governing the investment of trust funds and property are designed to afford maximum protection to beneficiaries on a conservative basis. As a rule, trust moneys may be invested only in a legally prescribed class of securities, commonly designated "legals." The tendency of recent statutes is to liberalize the law in relation to fiduciary investments: to avoid the rigidity of statutory tests, to give the trustees wider discretion in the choice of securities and to charge them with a corresponding degree of responsibility.

*Where trustee is given discretion as to investments.* A trustee authorized to make or continue an investment in securities not prescribed by statute is not liable for losses, provided he exercises fidelity, diligence and prudence.

EXAMPLE: A will provides: "My said trustee is authorized to hold and possess, or dispose of and convey, any and all of my securities." Among the securities in the estate are 200 shares of Pain Killer stock. The trustee, over a period of years, sold 100 shares of this stock and held the rest, which subsequently shrank greatly in value. The trustee would not be liable for such loss provided he exercised fidelity, diligence and prudence.

---

[14] 65 C.J. 971.

***Where trustee is instructed to sell and invest proceeds.*** Where a trustee is instructed to sell property and invest the proceeds, and fails to do so, he may be liable for subsequent shrinkage and loss.

EXAMPLE: Failure to sell a farm and invest the proceeds, as directed in the will, renders an executor, and the trustee after him, liable for loss of income.

***Lending on mortgage: duty to investigate solvency of mortgagor.*** When a trustee lends trust funds on mortgage, he must investigate the solvency of the mortgagor as well as the adequacy of the security, because if the mortgaged property depreciates in value, the trustee should be able to fall back on the solvency of the borrower.

### Accounting and Settlement: Principal and Income

**Nature of Accounting.** The term *accounting*, as a proceeding, is not to be confused with the mere rendering of an *account*. The latter is purely informatory. It consists in the preparation and verification of a statement by the fiduciary, in narrative form supplemented by schedules, reflecting his stewardship in the administration of the estate. An accounting in the legal sense is a proceeding. It usually includes an account. It is *voluntary* when made at the instance of the fiduciary himself, *involuntary* when the fiduciary is compelled by the court to make it, either at the instance of someone interested in the estate, or by the court of its own motion. In such a proceeding, the fiduciary submits his account for judicial approval. The trustee charges himself with all principal and income received and all gains in respect to them, and he credits himself with all expenditures on behalf of the estate, with any shrinkage or loss of estate assets, and with all distributions under the trust.

**Objections.** The account as thus rendered may be challenged by persons interested, who raise issues in respect to it by filing *objections*. If principal or income has been improperly charged, the Court will direct an adjustment.

**Settlement.** If the account is found to be correct, it is judicially *settled* by a decree approving the acts of the fiduciary as set forth in the account. A judicial settlement is binding and conclusive upon all parties served with notice of the proposed settlement and as to all matters embraced in the settlement decree.

**Commissions.** A testamentary trustee's commissions are usually fixed by statute. Such commissions are generally based on all sums of principal and interest received and paid out.

**Principal and Income: in General.** Trusts frequently provide for income to go to certain persons for life, or for a fixed period embraced by lives in being (page 771), with the remainder, or *corpus* (principal), to go to someone else on completion of the income period. The recipient of the income is commonly referred to as the life tenant or life beneficiary, as distinguished from the remainderman, who is entitled to the principal or *corpus*. The interests of the two frequently conflict. A trustee must carefully distinguish between them.

Generally speaking, the principal or *corpus* of a trust includes property originally coming into the trustee's hands, plus its increase in value, or any new form of investment which such property may take, or any proceeds from the sale of such property, including profits realized on such sale. Income includes any earnings derived from the use and management of trust property, or from a business held in trust. In short, the trust property itself belongs to the remainderman, its yield to the life beneficiary.

**Invasion of Principal.** Testators are sometimes well advised to incorporate a provision in the will, authorizing the trustee, in his discretion, to "invade the principal" for the purpose of supplying a possible deficiency of income. Interest rates, in the unforeseeable future, may decline almost to the vanishing point; income-producing property may lose its yield; and a widow or infant for whom a testator may have thought he had generously provided, may find herself or himself in actual need while the trustee conserves a frozen principal. The power to invade the principal in such cases, to be exercised only when necessary, rescues the beneficiaries from their plight.

## Termination of Trusts

**How Trusts May Be Terminated.** Trusts, in general, including living as well as testamentary trusts, may be terminated (a) by fulfillment, (b) by merger, and (c) by failure of purpose.

(a) *Fulfillment.* A trust ceases when its terms are fulfilled and there is no further reason for its continuance.

(b) *Merger.* When the legal and equitable interests under a trust become vested in the same person, the equitable interest merges into the legal and the trust ceases. For example, if a brother is designated as a trustee for the benefit of himself and his sister, or the survivor of the two, and the sister dies, both legal and beneficial interests under the trust become merged, the trust ceases, and the brother becomes sole owner without any further need for a trustee.

(c) *Failure of purpose.* When the purpose of a trust fails or becomes impossible of fulfillment, and the cy pres doctrine (page 774) cannot be invoked, the trust ceases and the estate passes to the persons who would otherwise have been entitled but for the trust.

**Removal of Trustee.** A court of equity has inherent jurisdiction over trusts. This includes jurisdiction in all actions to declare or establish a trust, and likewise the right to supervise, regulate and control the proper discharge of the duties of a trust, as well as the power to remove the trustee for cause. Among the causes for the removal of a trustee are: (a) adverse personal interest of the trustee which may conflict with his duties or with the interests of beneficiaries; (b) personal unfitness because of incompetence, ill health, intemperance, mental infirmity, old age, dishonesty or improvidence; (c) misconduct and mismanagement; (d) abandonment or neglect of trust; (e) disobedience of court orders or of instructions in a trust instrument; (f) unexcused failure to pay principal or income to beneficiaries; (g) making illegal and unsafe investments, or investments in direct violation of the trust instrument; (h) taking a personal profit; and (i) failure to keep proper accounts or neglecting or refusing to file accounts.

**Resignation and Discharge of Trustee.** A trustee, after accepting office, cannot discharge himself from liability by a mere resignation and abandonment of his trusteeship. His resignation must be tendered for cause, or upon the termination of the trust, and it must be duly accepted and approved by the Court or by general consent of all persons interested. However, when a trustee acts without compensation, or without agreement as to time, he may resign as a matter of personal convenience; otherwise, he must have a good reason for resigning.

## Questions

1. Define trust. Name the parties to a trust, and describe their functions in relation to it.

2. What is the distinction between a legal estate and an equitable estate?

3. Name and illustrate three ways in which a trust differs from an ordinary obligation.

4. "Bank deposits are trust funds." Is this statement true, false, or partly true and partly false? Explain.

5. Distinguish between (a) express and implied trusts, (b) executory and executed trusts, (c) active and passive trusts, (d) discretionary and ministerial trusts, (e) living and testamentary trusts.

6. Define (a) shifting trusts, and (b) spendthrift trusts.

7. Who may be (a) donor of a trust, (b) the trustee, and (c) the beneficiary?

8. "A trust requires no consideration, to be valid." Is this statement true, false, or partly true and partly false?

9. What are the four requisites of a valid express trust? Illustrate each.

10. Distinguish between an *inter vivos*, and a testamentary, trust.

11. "Trusts need not be *created* by a writing, but must be *manifested and proved* by a writing." Explain this statement.

12. Give two exceptions to the rule that an oral trust is invalid.

13. What is the general effect of a passive trust? Illustrate.

14. Name and explain the different purposes for which trusts in real property may be created under the laws of your state.

15. Explain the rule against perpetuities, with particular reference to (a) its purpose, (b) the two ways in which absolute ownership may be suspended, and (c) the maximum period of suspension permissible under the law.

16. Does the rule against perpetuities apply to personal property? What is the rule against accumulations? To what form of property does it apply?

17. From the standpoint of the purposes for which they may be created, name and explain eight common forms of trusts in personal property.

18. What are the two essential characteristics of a charitable trust?

19. Charitable trusts are generally grouped into four classes. Name and give an example of each.

20. Explain and illustrate the cy pres doctrine.

21. Distinguish between insurance and investment trusts.

22. Distinguish between a resulting and a constructive trust, and give an example of each.

23. Generally, what are the qualifications of a trustee?

24. Summarize the basic functions of a testamentary trustee. Comment on the power of a trustee (a) to incur expenses, and (b) to mortgage or pledge trust property.

25. When, if ever, may a trustee use his own discretion in making estate investments? What is the usual situation in this connection?

26. Distinguish between an accounting and the rendering of an account in connection with a trust estate. How may an accounting be challenged? What is meant by settling an account in connection with a trust estate?

27. Name three ways in which a trust may be terminated.

## Problems

1. Allen deposits with Brown five bonds, each in the amount of $1,000, with instructions to Brown, confirmed in writing, to pay over the interest to Allen's wife, and the principal, upon maturity, to Allen's son. At the same time that the bonds are delivered, Allen loans $1,000 in cash to Brown, which Brown deposits together with the bonds in an office safe. During the night a thief steals the bonds and money without Brown's fault. Allen seeks to charge Brown with liability on the bonds and the loan. Can he do so? Explain.

2. A father signs a written instrument declaring that on his son's 25th birthday he intends to establish a trust fund for the benefit of his son. On the son's 25th birthday, the father prepares the trust instrument, signs it, and is about to go to the bank with it, in order to open the necessary account and deliver the instrument to the trust officer of the bank, when he takes sick and dies two hours later. The instrument signed by the father has disappeared. However, three witnesses can testify to its contents and execution, and on the strength of this testimony, the son seeks to have the trust fund declared for his benefit. The father's estate defends. Judgment for whom, and why?

3. A father bought land and placed his daughter in possession. He subsequently wrote her a letter that he had given the land to her and that it was hers forever. There was no consideration for the transfer or for the declaration by the father. The father thereafter seeks to recover the property. How should the case be decided, and why?

4. A deed of trust is executed to Albert as trustee "for the benefit of Albert and Bronson, or either of them." Subsequently an action is brought in equity to compel the execution of the trust. How should the court decide, and why?

5. A testatrix creates a trust instrument which reads in its entirety as follows: "I hereby establish a trust fund of $1,000, the income of which is to be devoted to keeping my burial plot in good condition." Is this a valid trust?

6. Horace Hilton, a San Francisco merchant, wrote to Marion Hilton, his cousin, president of the Gotham Finance Company in New York: "If you can let me have $20,000 for six months, I will send you my note in this amount,

and I will earmark 250 shares of Pacific Tel. & Tel. in my private safe as security for repayment." Marion Hilton extended the loan, but Horace Hilton not only failed to repay it, but sold his shares of Pacific Tel. & Tel. Co. The question now arises, may Horace Hilton be held for breach of trust?

7. Carter conveys all his real property to a corporation of which he is sole stockholder. He thereafter orally declares, prior to his death and in the presence of witnesses, that "If I never get around to making a will, I want it understood and I want you to remember that I am holding all the stock of my real estate corporation for the benefit of my son." Following Carter's death intestate, the son seeks to impress a trust upon the corporate stock and the widow, a stepmother, resists the claim of the son on the ground that no valid trust has been created by reason of the Statute of Frauds. What are the rights of the parties?

8. Upon the death of Orrin Leffingwell, a holographic will is discovered in which he leaves everything in trust for the benefit of his widow for life, the remainder in trust to his daughter, thereby excluding a son, who contests the will on the ground that a trust without a trustee is null and void. Will the son succeed, or not?

9. Martin Fuller transfers property to James Billup as trustee for the benefit of his niece, pursuant to a duly executed trust instrument described as "irrevocable." Thereafter, Fuller seeks to revoke the trust on the ground that there was no consideration therefor, which was the fact. Will he succeed? Explain.

10. A trust instrument creates a life estate, "with remainder to the next Republican governor of this state." Is this a valid trust?

11. A husband opens a bank account in trust for his wife. Prior to his death, he causes the account to be transferred to the name of his sister as beneficiary. Upon his death, the wife sues the executor of the state to have the bank account declared to be in trust for her on the ground that the same was irrevocable. How should the case be decided, and why?

12. A depositor opens a savings bank account in trust for a named beneficiary. The depositor dies before the beneficiary without having revoked the trust by withdrawal or otherwise. The beneficiary seeks the proceeds and the depositor's personal representatives refuse to acquiesce in the transfer of the monies on deposit on the ground that the depositor had retained the bank book up to the date of his death. In an action between the beneficiary and the personal representatives of the depositor, who will succeed, and why?

13. A will devised certain property to a nephew in trust for life, with the provision that the interest of the nephew should cease on the recovery of any judgment against him and should then go to his wife or to any other person the executors might name. Bailey, a creditor, secures a judgment against the nephew. The executors thereupon transfer the interest to the nephew's wife and Bailey seeks to set aside the transfer. Will he succeed?

14. Dole is the president and principal stockholder of the Dole Manufacturing Corporation. Ewing, a competent man with a good business record, is Dole's general manager. Ewing owns no stock in the Dole Corporation, but has a substantial though secret stock interest in the Farwell Manufacturing Corporation, which competes with the Dole Corporation. In his last will and testament, Dole leaves the bulk of his estate, consisting of stock in the Dole Corporation, in trust for the benefit of his widow, designating Ewing as trustee. On Dole's death, Ewing makes frank disclosure of his stock interest in the Farwell Corporation, but promises to administer the trust under Dole's will faithfully and to the best of his ability. Mrs. Dole seeks to remove Ewing nonetheless. Will she succeed?

## COURT CASES FOR REVIEW

### How Did the Court Decide, and Why?

1. A will left more than one-half of the estate after payment of debts to charity, the residue being left to the decedent's widow. The amount of the excess over one-half was $110.29. It was contended on behalf of the widow that the disposition in question resulted in the entire estate passing to her as next in line, by intestacy. *Bowker's Estate*, 157 Misc. 341, 283 N.Y. Supp. 564.

2. A letter to decedent's brother-in-law stated that if anything should happen to the writer "you Will all Find My Bisnes Fix and in the Citszen Bank Still looks like Rain made ida over every thing." Upon the writer's death this letter was offered for probate. No question was raised as to insufficiency of formal execution, but as to whether the letter in other respects constituted a sufficient will. *Watts' Estate*, 117 Mont. 505, 160 P. 2d 492.

3. A member of the Marine Corps serving in the Pacific wrote to his father in part as follows: "This war is a dangerous business at best and while I have been Lucky so far one never knows. So I am going to give you all the dope on what you are to do in the event of my getting in the way of a well aimed slug." The letter, after disposing of various items of insurance, closed as follows:

This letter will serve as your authority for the transfer of the money to you It has been read and my signature witnessed by a Commissionsd (sic) Officer of the Marine Crop. (sic) serving with the Armed Forcses (sic) overseas.

As ever, love.
your son
James D Cummings

I have Witnessed this signature
J.M. Venard 2nd Leiut. (sic) USMCR

The soldier died shortly after in the attack at Guam Island on July 24, 1944. The question arose as to whether this letter constituted a valid will. *Phoenix Mut. Life Ins. Co. v. Cummings*, 67 F. Supp. 159.

4. Letters of Administration were granted to the widow of a deceased sailor on a petition alleging that he had died intestate. The mother of the deceased sought to revoke such letters on the ground that the deceased had made a nuncupative will favoring the mother, while he was on shore in New York. It appeared from the petition that the deceased had vainly sought leave from the master of his ship to visit his friends and relatives in New York, and the proof showed that he had actually left the ship without permission and in defiance of orders, and had remained away more than two days. The deceased lost his life in the sinking of the steamship "Lake Osweya" which sailed from New York Harbor on February 16, 1942 and was torpedoed and sunk on February 19, 1942. *McDonald's Estate*, 179 Misc. 284, 37 N.Y. Supp. 2d 945.

5. Following the death of his first wife, the deceased made a will devising the greater part of his estate to his three sisters in Italy. Two and one-half years later, he married his second wife. Three years later he died, survived by his second wife and a child born seven months after his death. The executor offered the will for probate. A guardian *ad litem* for the infant opposed. *Pascucci v. Alsop*, 147 F. 2d 880.

6. Cora Carter, widow and executrix of the estate of John H. Carter, Sr., entered into an agreement as such executrix, continuing the old partnership as a new firm. There was no provision for such continuance in the articles of copartnership, nor in the will; neither was such authority sought or granted in any court proceeding. Subsequently creditors sought to charge the estate

with debts and obligations incurred as a result of the continuance of the old partnership by said executrix. It was contended on behalf of others interested in the estate that Cora Carter should be personally liable for these debts and obligations. *Carter v. Carter*, 247 Ala. 409, 24 So. 2d 759.

7. Three persons orally agreed that if any one of them should be the purchaser of a lot of land at an administrator's sale, they would all be equally interested in the purchase; and that when the purchaser received the deed, he was to reconvey one-third to each of his associates. Thereafter one of the parties received the deed but refused to reconvey to his associates, setting up as a defense, in an action by them to enforce an alleged trust, that the agreement, being oral, was unenforceable under the Statute of Frauds. *Farnham v. Clements*, 151 Me. 426.

8. While the testator was confined in a hospital, his brother, at the testator's request, procured a lawyer to prepare a will. The brother was made one of the beneficiaries of the will. The will was attacked for undue influence. *Wright v. Stevens*, 246 S.W. 2d 817 (Mo.).

9. The competency of a testator was questioned and the validity of his will was attacked because of a statement made by the testator that his deceased wife appeared and told him to leave his property to his brother. The testator actually left his property chiefly to his brother instead of an only daughter. *In re Sandman's Estate*, 121 Cal. App. 9, 8 P. 2d 499.

10. A testatrix, fatally ill, requested her daughter to destroy her will, stating that she did not want to die with the will in existence. The daughter said she would rather not do this without first advising with her father, a lawyer and probate judge. The father told the testatrix to put her mind at rest; that the will would never be set up. The will was put back in the box. The testatrix died twelve hours later. The question then arose whether the will had actually been revoked. *Jones v. Jones*, 143 Tenn. 596, 228 S.W. 405.

11. A deed was handed over to a depositary with instruction to deliver it to the grantee at the grantor's death, unless otherwise directed in the meantime. Upon the grantor's death a dispute arose whether title had been effectually transferred. It was contended on behalf of the estate that the attempted transfer represented an ineffective will. *Jorgensen v. Jorgensen*, 51 N.W. 2d 632.

12. A will gave the residue of an estate to certain persons to distribute to any of the testatrix' close friends with the request that special generosity be shown to a designated maid of the testatrix. The question arose whether this was a valid bequest in trust. *In re Rowlands' Estate*, 73 Ariz. 337, 241 P. 2d 781.

13. A testator in his will created a trust for the benefit of two infants. The trust provided that the income be reinvested until the two beneficiaries had elected to attend a private educational institution. The trust was attacked as invalid. *In re Welty's Estate*, 24 Leh. L.J. 322.

14. A testatrix wrote "This will is null and void" across and through the dispositive provisions of her will, then added the date and her signature. The question arose as to what effect this had on the will. *In re Robinson's Will*, 201 Misc. 439, 103 N.Y. Supp. 2d 967.

15. A testator left his estate to his brother. Following his brother's death, he crossed out his brother's name wherever it appeared in the will and wrote in the name of the brother's son. He made no other change in the will. The question arose as to what effect this had on the will. *In re Swanson's Estate*, 74 D. & C. 358.

# BOOK II
# Wrongs

*In Book I we considered the rights and duties that make up the substance of the law. The violation of any of these rights and duties constitutes a wrong. Wrongs are either civil or criminal, depending, respectively, on whether they invade private or public rights and duties. Among the more common civil wrongs are torts and breaches of contract. The latter we discussed in the chapter on contracts. The subject of torts and crimes will be dealt with in Book II.*

# 20

# Torts

**Scope of This Chapter.** In this chapter we consider invasions of our so-called natural, or absolute, rights, invasions commonly known as torts. In Part 1 we consider the nature of a tort, how it differs from a breach of contract, what elements must be present to constitute a tort, and the circumstances which may render certain persons immune from liability for certain torts. In Part 2 we consider torts that invade our personal security, personal liberty and personal well-being, as distinguished from those that primarily affect our property; including assault and battery on one's person, assault on one's reputation, as in libel or slander, upon his liberty, as in false imprisonment, and upon his right of security, as in malicious prosecution, abuse of process or interference with privacy.

In Part 3 we consider those torts that primarily affect one's property, such as trespass, conversion, nuisance and waste. In Part 4 we consider omissions of reasonable care, known as negligence, which may affect either one's person, or his property, or both. Finally, in Part 5, we consider certain property wrongs which are commonly encountered in business, hence frequently referred to as "business wrongs," including fraud and deceit, slander of title, disparagement, wrongful interference with contract, malicious injury to business, and threatening letters, with a passing reference to copyright, trade-mark and trade name infringements, and unfair competition.

### PART 1. GENERAL PRINCIPLES

**Torts: Nature and Distinctions.** The word "tort" is derived from the Latin *tortum*, meaning crooked, or twisted, as opposed to that which is straight. It consists in the violation of a natural, or non-contract right, such as a violation of the right of personal security by assault and battery, or by negligence, or of personal liberty by false imprisonment, or of property by conversion, waste or trespass.

*Tort v. crime.* A tort is a private wrong, that is, it invades a private right. It exposes the wrongdoer to a private or civil suit for damages to compensate for the loss caused by the wrong. A crime is a public wrong, that is, it invades a public right. It exposes the wrongdoer to prosecution by the people collectively, and to the imposition of a penalty, such as a fine, imprisonment, or even death.

The same act, however, may constitute both a tort and a crime. Thus, if Baxter beats Carpenter with a club, causing the latter physical injury, suffering and medical expense accompanied by substantial loss of earnings, Baxter may not only be prosecuted criminally, with consequent fine or imprisonment, but he may also be forced to pay Carpenter substantial money damages in a civil suit for the tort.

**Tort v. breach of contract.** As noted in Chapter 1, rights and duties are reciprocal, that is, your rights as to me are my duties toward you, and vice versa. Since one man's right is the other man's duty, a tort, which invades a natural right, likewise invades a natural or non-contractual duty, that is, an involuntary duty existing regardless of contract. A breach of contract, on the other hand, represents the violation of a duty voluntarily assumed by contract.

Here, too, the same act may constitute both a tort and a breach of contract. A trucking concern may assume by contract the duty of safely transporting a quantity of china. Regardless of contract, however, the concern must exercise care in discharging its duty. Should the shipment be damaged through negligence, the owner could sue the trucking concern for breach of contract, or for the tort of negligence, or for both, electing which remedy to pursue on the trial.

**Elements of Tort.** The principal elements of a tort are (1) a wrongful act or omission, and (2) a resulting injury or loss. Unless the two concur, no tort is committed.

EXAMPLES:
(1) Adams utters slanderous words about Barnes in the presence of Carr who, however, is deaf.
(2) Dalton, intoxicated, drives his car with reckless abandon through a crowded thoroughfare, but no one is hurt.
Neither of the above situations will support an action in tort, since the wrong was not accompanied by damage or injury.

**Wrong Without Damage.** Where a wrong is committed without resulting damage (*injuria absque damno*), the act or omission, however wrongful, is not actionable as a tort.

In some situations, however, the law will conclusively presume damage from the mere commission of the wrong. Thus, though no damage can be shown, the law will conclusively presume damage from the mere act of trespass, assault, or battery, and in the absence of proof of damage, will award nominal damages (see page 848). On the other hand, proof of actual damage is necessary to sustain a suit for fraud and deceit, negligence, and (in most cases) libel and slander.

**Damage Without Wrong.** Damage may be sustained without actionable wrong (*damnum absque injuria*), that is, one may be damaged without legal injury, or legal recourse. This may be due to one of three causes:

(1) The loss or injury was not caused or contributed to by human agency;

(2) The loss or injury may have been caused by some act or omission which was in no way wrongful; or

(3) The act, though wrongful, was one for which the law affords no remedy, either because (a) the injured party consented or contributed to the injury, or (b) public policy surrounds the wrongdoer with some privilege or immunity in connection with the act.

**Acts Not Caused by Human Agency.** "There is a large class of cases, in which injury is suffered by a party, where the law gives no redress. If a tree growing upon the land of one is blown down upon the premises of another, and in its fall injures his shrubbery, or his house, or his person, he has no redress against him upon whose land the tree grew. . . . If the house of A accidentally take fire, and the flames spread and consume the house of B, the latter has no claim of indemnity upon A. . . . In these cases the injury arises from a fortuitous occurrence beyond the control of man. . . . The party suffering must submit to it, as a providential dispensation." [1]

**Blameless Acts or Omissions.** If a remedy is to be afforded for an injury, some form of wrong, deliberate or negligent, must characterize the act or omission. Thus, one may back away from a mad dog or an onrushing vehicle and thereby involuntarily injure a person to the rear, but since such injury would have been caused by an involuntary and spontaneous act clearly free from fault, no action will lie to redress the injury. If a person opens up a competing establishment across the way from one which has enjoyed a thriving trade for years, and which now suffers loss because of the competition, no remedy will lie, since the loss was occasioned by no wrongful act.

**Assumption of Risk of Injury.** If a person invites danger or voluntarily assumes the risk of injury, as where he enters the prize ring, participates in a rodeo or football game, ignores the cry of "Fore!" on the golf links, or sits in an unscreened ball park behind home plate, he abandons the right to complain if he is injured. These situations are governed by the legal maxim, *volenti non fit injuria*, which, freely translated, means that one who consents cannot sustain legal injury.

**Contributing to Risk of Injury.** Where a person's own conduct causes or contributes to his injury, he is without legal remedy, since he brought about or helped bring about his own misfortune. If a person assaults another, is bested in the argument, and severely beaten, he has no cause to

---

[1] *Sheldon v. Sherman*, 42 N.Y. 484.

complain. If a person recklessly drives his automobile head-on into a truck, he can obtain neither recompense for his injuries nor damages for the wreck of his vehicle, though the driver of the truck was equally reckless.

**Privilege or Immunity.** Generally speaking, everyone is liable for his torts, whether committed personally or through another. The law, however, on grounds of public policy, extends certain privileges and immunities to certain persons in the discharge of certain acts.

**Public Bodies.** "The King can do no wrong." This common law concept is carried over into the concept of governmental sovereignty. The United States Government and all state governments, as sovereign bodies within their respective spheres, are immune from suits by citizens except where they consent thereto, as they often do.[2]

*Public servants: executive, legislative and judicial.* Executive officers are immune from liability to private individuals for wrongs committed in the discharge of their public duties, since such wrongs are public, not private. Hence if the President of the United States signs an executive order which allegedly invades a private property right, or if a member of his cabinet or other executive officer, while in the performance of his duties, is guilty of negligence resulting in loss to some person or persons, no civil redress will lie for the tort.

Members of Congress and of state legislatures are exempt from civil liability for things done or said in the discharge of their legislative duties. This exemption does not apply to wrongful acts by legislative agents or servants.

Judges cannot be held civilly for what they say or do in the discharge of their judicial duties, even when their conduct is malicious or corrupt, "or a judge could not be either respected or independent if his motives for his official actions or his conclusions, no matter how erroneous, could be put in question at the instance of every malignant or disappointed suitor."[3]

However, government officers are not immune from liability for torts having no relation to public duty. A government officer who commits assault in the heat of a private argument, or who, while driving his car, negligently runs over a pedestrian, is just as liable for his tort as any private citizen.

*Municipal corporations.* Incorporated cities and villages function in a dual capacity. They discharge purely governmental functions, such as police, health, fire, sanitation, public parks, etc., and they also function as corporate agencies in the construction, maintenance and use of streets, sidewalks, sewers, waterworks, bridges, tunnels, ferries, and similar public, quasi-public and quasi-commercial services. As to the purely governmental functions, municipalities enjoy the same immunity from tort liability as

---

[2] The Federal Tort Claims Act, for example, allows actions in tort against the Government, and authorizes adjustments without suit up to $1,000.

[3] *Grove v. Van Duyn*, 44 N.J.L. 654, 656.

governments generally; but as to their corporate functions, they are answerable in damages for their torts the same as other corporations.

*Charitable and public benefit corporations.* The earlier cases tended to exempt charitable and public benefit corporations, including hospitals, churches, schools and social service organizations, from liability for torts, on the theory that they were supported in large part by donations in the nature of a trust, which should not be dissipated by damage payments in tort actions. The more recent view of the courts is that such immunity exacts an unjust sacrifice from persons injured by the servants of charity.[4] However, in fixing the liability of a hospital to its patients, a distinction is made between professional services and administrative or ministerial acts. If a hospital has exercised due care in the selection of a properly qualified professional staff, it is not liable for a tort committed on a patient by physicians, nurses or others in the performance of their professional duties. The hospital "undertakes, not to heal or attempt to heal through the agency of others, but merely to supply others who will heal or attempt to heal on their own responsibility." [5] But if such professional personnel, acting for the hospital, commit a tort of an administrative or non-professional nature, such as mistakenly treating the wrong patient, the hospital is liable.

**Intent as an Element of Tort.** In tort, as in crime, a distinction must be made between motive and intent; between the inducement for doing an act and the resolve to do it. In most torts, motive is immaterial. A person with the best of motives may negligently cause grievous injury, or may deprive another of his property in the honest belief that the property is his own, or may cause the arrest of an innocent citizen in the mistaken belief he is apprehending a criminal. On the other hand, there are some torts in which motive may be material in determining liability. Among these are fraud and deceit, slander, libel, malicious prosecution and malicious interference with contract.

A wrongdoer is deemed to have intended the natural consequences of his acts. If he aims a blow at *A* and strikes *B* instead, it is no defense to a suit by *B* that the blow was intended for *A*.

**Torts of Agents and Employees: *Respondeat Superior*.** We have already indicated (page 409) that a principal is liable for his agent's torts if they are committed during the course of the agent's duties and within the scope of his authority. A similar rule, referred to in law as the doctrine of *respondeat superior*, applies to the liability of employers for the torts of their employees. Except for immunities grounded in public policy, as in the case of executive, legislative and judicial officers engaged in the discharge of governmental duties, employees who commit torts in the dis-

---

[4] *Silva v. Providence Hospital of Oakland,* 14 Cal. 2d 762, 775, 97 P. 2d 798, 805.
[5] *Matter of Bernstein v. Beth Israel Hospital,* 236 N.Y. 268, 270, 140 N.E. 694.

charge of their duties are not exempt merely because their employers are liable.

**Proximate and Remote Cause.** The "proximate" cause of an injury is the one from which the injury results in direct sequence, without the intervention of a voluntary independent cause.[6] In torts deliberately committed, such as assault and battery, it is not so necessary to inquire into the distinction between the proximate and the remote cause of an injury, because the proximate cause in such cases is usually obvious. However, in actions involving negligence, the proximate cause is not always easy to determine. If a person digs a pit and two persons engage in a scuffle at the edge of it, in the course of which one pushes the other in, the proximate cause of any consequent injury is obviously not the digging of the pit but the intervention of a voluntary independent act—pushing a person in. But if, instead, a pedestrian, seeing the pit, walks around it, and in doing so slips on some mud from the pit that had frozen within the hour, sustaining, in his fall, cuts from a red lantern which had been shattered by mischievous boys, the question as to whether the digging of the pit was the proximate cause of the consequent injuries is less easy to determine. Since the question of proximate cause must be resolved by the facts in each case, it is a question for the jury.

## Questions

1. Exactly what is a tort?
2. Distinguish between a tort and a crime.
3. Distinguish between a tort and a breach of contract.
4. "The same act may constitute both a tort and a crime." Is this a correct or an incorrect statement of the law? Explain.
5. Every tort involves at least two elements. What are they? Illustrate.
6. Explain what is meant by a wrong without damage. Give an example.
7. Explain what is meant by damage without wrong. Give three types of situations in which this can occur.
8. Name and illustrate three exceptions to the rule that everyone is liable for his torts.
9. "Motive is immaterial in determining whether a tort has been committed." Is this statement true, false, or partly true and partly false?
10. What is meant by the doctrine of *respondeat superior?*
11. In the law of torts, what is the distinction between proximate and remote cause?

## Problems

1. Carr, while driving in an intoxicated condition, runs down Davis, causing him serious injury and prolonged confinement in a hospital. Carr is convicted of the crime of reckless driving, and is sentenced to six months' imprisonment and a $5,000 fine. Upon leaving prison, he is sued by Davis for $25,000 damages. Carr's defense is double jeopardy: that he cannot be prosecuted twice for the same offense. Is the defense good or bad? Explain.

---

[6] 62 C.J. 1115.

2. Johnson misses $500 in cash which he has left in his private safe. He calls in Dun, his confidential secretary (the only other person besides himself with access to the safe), and demands, "What have you done with that money?" and when Dun starts to stammer, calls him an embezzler and a petty thief, and dismisses him. Later, he finds the money in the safe under a sheaf of papers, where he had put it. Dun sues Johnson for slander. Will he win? Why or why not?

3. Earle, who was born with a deformed hip, is negligently struck by an automobile owned and operated by Hull. Earle is rushed to the hospital, operated on as a free patient by a skilled surgeon, and ultimately leaves the hospital with a normal hip and in better physical condition than ever before. Nevertheless, he sues Hull for damages. Has Hull any defense? Explain.

4. Celestial Beam, a racehorse owned by Connover, becomes frightened by a thunderclap during a storm, breaks out of his stall, escapes the enclosure, and runs into and tramples a child, injuring him severely. The child's parent sues Connover. Will he win? Give reasons.

5. A driver loses control of his car, which mounts the curb and speeds over the sidewalk in the direction of Adams, who backs away, and in so doing knocks down Bowers, an aged man, who later sues Adams for his injuries. Who will win, and why?

6. George Grunto, a wrestler, is manhandled by his opponent during a match and sustains a leg fracture in consequence. When he leaves the hospital, he sues his opponent for damages. How will the case be decided? Explain.

7. Congressman Smith, during the course of a debate on the floor of the House, refers to Congressman Jones as a "cheap chiseler." A House clerk repeats this charge to numerous friends. Several days later, Congressman Jones meets Congressman Smith on the street and assaults him. Jones sues Smith and the House clerk for slander, and Smith sues Jones for assault. How will these suits be determined? Explain.

8. The Town of Elyria repaves Main Street, but due to defective supervision, a large hole is left in the asphalt, over which Mary Ryan trips and falls, sustaining serious injuries. Mary Ryan sues the Town of Elyria. The Town's defense is that a governmental authority is immune from suit based on tort. Will the defense be sustained or dismissed? What is the reason for your answer?

9. Dr. Knox, a physician of recognized standing in attendance at the Mercy Hospital, after 22 hours of consecutive duty on an emergency case, is asked to give a sedative to another patient. By mistake, the doctor gives the patient an overdose of strychnine, from which the patient later dies. Shortly thereafter Dr. Knox likewise dies, in a street accident. The patient's estate sues the hospital. What will be the outcome of this suit, and why?

10. Roberts calls Judd a liar. Judd aims a blow at Roberts, who sidesteps it. The blow strikes Forman instead. Forman sues Judd, whose defense is that he intended to strike Roberts, not Forman. How will the court decide? Explain.

11. Carter digs a pit. Dawson and Engel engage in a scuffle at the edge of the pit, during the course of which Dawson pushes Engel into the pit. Engel sues Carter and Dawson. How will the case be decided? Give your reasons.

12. A contracting concern engaged in repairing a road leaves a protective barrier in front of a defective stretch, with a red lantern as a night warning. The lantern is defective and goes out. Mischievous children have rolled a rock into the enclosure inside the barrier. Williams backs his car through the barrier and over the rock, breaking his rear axle. He sues the contracting concern for damages. Will he win? Explain.

## PART 2. PERSONAL WRONGS

**Nature and Classification of Personal Wrongs.** Although all torts are personal in that they invade personal rights, some are peculiarly personal, such as those which invade personal security, personal liberty, or personal well being, as distinguished from those which primarily affect one's property. Included among these personal wrongs are an assault and battery upon one's person, an assault upon one's reputation, as in libel or slander, upon his liberty, as in false imprisonment, and upon his right of security, as in malicious prosecution, abuse of process or interference with privacy.

**Assault and Battery.** The terms "assault" and "battery" are commonly coupled together. They are not, however, identical. An assault is an unlawful offer or attempt to use force coupled with the present ability to use it. A battery is the actual use of force itself.

*Threats: when may constitute assault.* Threats alone are insufficient to constitute an assault: they must be accompanied by an evident intent to carry the threat into execution.

EXAMPLE: Pointing a pistol (loaded or unloaded) at another in such manner as to raise a well-grounded fear of bodily injury.[7]

No real assault can be said to take place unless there is reasonable ground for apprehension.

EXAMPLE: Shaking a finger at a distance of eight feet from another and saying, "For two cents I'd toss you out of the window."

*Battery: what constitutes.* A battery, as stated, is the actual exercise of force, either directly, as by striking another, or indirectly, as by throwing, striking a horse one is riding, or frightening the animal so as to cause him to start. The force must be intentional: accidental contact, though violent, is not a battery. On the other hand, the barest touch, if deliberate, rude and insolent, is actionable as a battery. Good motive is not necessarily an excuse: a surgeon is liable for assault and battery if—except in emergency —he operates on a patient without his consent.

*Justification.* An assault is justifiable if committed in defense of one's self, family, neighbor or property; but in no case must the force used exceed that necessary to repel the aggression. Law officers and persons assisting or directed by them may use such force as is necessary in discharging their duty. A private citizen may use force in preventing or arresting the commission of a felony, or in delivering the offender to a public officer competent to receive him in custody. A parent or his authorized agent, or a guardian, master or teacher may use force within reasonable limits to restrain or correct a child or ward. A railroad conductor or similar employee and any person assisting him may use rea-

---

[7] 6 C.J.S. 799-800, and cases cited.

sonable force in expelling a violent, dangerous or offensive passenger threatening the well being of other passengers in public vehicles. A person may use force in preventing persons of unsound mind from committing acts dangerous to themselves or others.

Neither challenges to a fight nor abusive language will justify one in inflicting injury on another. The same holds true for provocative taunts, gestures of derision, advice of counsel, mistaken identity, intoxication and uncontrollable anger.

**False Imprisonment.** The term "false imprisonment" is not limited to a wrongful confinement in prison, but includes every form of unlawful restraint of a person's liberty, whether by force, threats, fear or fraud. Any exercise of force by which a person is deprived of his liberty and compelled to remain where he does not wish to remain or to go where he does not wish to go, is an imprisonment. This offense may constitute a crime as well as a tort.

*False arrest.* False imprisonment is frequently confused with false arrest, which is merely one form of false imprisonment. A false arrest must be committed under color of legal authority or legal process. A false imprisonment may be committed without any pretense of legal authority.

EXAMPLES:
(1) The foreman of a mill refused to unlock the mill doors during working hours to permit departure of a mill hand seeking to go home because of illness. The court held that this might constitute false imprisonment, but not false arrest.[8]

(2) An officer, without a warrant and because of personal anger, arrested a person for a breach of the peace, but failed to sustain the charge. He was held liable in damages for false arrest.[9]

*Motive and malice immaterial.* Neither motive nor malice is material on the issue whether there was justification for the false imprisonment, although either may be important on the issue of exemplary damages, that is, damages imposed as a warning to others. Hence, neither ill will nor wrongful intention is a necessary element of false imprisonment: one can be guilty of false imprisonment through an honest mistake.

*Lawful detention.* There can be no *false* imprisonment where the detention is lawful, as in the case of a proper restraint by parents, school authorities, or officers of the law engaged in a proper discharge of their duties. However, regardless of the lawfulness of an arrest, an officer of the law may be guilty of false imprisonment if he detains a person for an unreasonable time without taking him before a judicial officer so that charges may be formulated against him.[10]

**Malicious Prosecution.** Malicious prosecution has been defined as a

---

[8] *Davis & Alcott Co. v. Boozer,* 215 Ala. 116, 110 So. 28.

[9] *Smith v. Dulion,* 113 La. 882, 37 So. 864.

[10] *Kaufman v. Brown,* 93 Cal. App. 2d 508, 209 P. 2d 156.

prosecution that begins in malice, without probable cause to believe it can succeed, and which finally ends in failure.[11] Ordinarily, public policy favors free access to the courts, civil or criminal, provided one honestly believes that he has a just grievance, or that a crime has been committed. If one had to risk retaliation for every honest but mistaken effort to right a wrong, the result would be to encourage wrongdoing. Hence, the law generally does not favor malicious prosecution actions, and a plaintiff who brings such an action will fail unless he can show that the prior prosecution or civil suit was instituted maliciously, that it was brought without probable cause, that it was decided in his favor, and that it had caused him actual damage.

*Want of probable cause.* For a defendant to prevail in a malicious prosecution action, it is not necessary to show that he had actual cause to institute the proceeding complained of, but only "probable cause." This means, in criminal cases, such grounds for belief as would induce the court to infer that the prosecution was undertaken from public motives, and in civil cases such grounds for belief, supported by facts and circumstances, as might lead a cautious, reasonable and prudent man honestly (though mistakenly) to conclude that his action was legal, just and proper. Hence, if a party, before instituting the suit complained of, was advised by counsel, after a full and fair disclosure of the facts, that he had a just and meritorious case, he will be deemed to have had probable cause, though the advice was bad and the action was dismissed.

*Termination of prior proceeding.* One cannot complain of a malicious prosecution unless he was wronged thereby, and he cannot establish the wrong unless the proceeding has been finally terminated in his favor.

*Damage.* The plaintiff in a malicious prosecution action must show that the prior proceeding caused him to sustain some money or property damage, or some injury to his person or reputation.[12]

**Defamation: Libel and Slander.** Strictly speaking, libel and slander are different means for perpetrating the tort known as defamation, namely, an attack upon a person's reputation. *Libel* consists of written, printed or other graphic defamation, such as by sign, mark, picture, effigy or movie reel, as distinguished from *slander*, or defamation by the spoken word.

Not every attack on a person's reputation is subject to legal action. To be actionable, the defamatory words or acts must have been (1) injurious, (2) published, (3) false, and (4) free from privilege.

*Injury: words actionable per se.* Some words are recognized on their face as injurious. These are said to be actionable per se; that is, damage will be presumed from the mere use of the word. Other words are harmless in their ordinary sense, yet may be shown by extraneous proof to have been defamatory, and to have caused special damage because of their

---

[11] *Zebrowski v. Bobinski,* 278 N.Y. 332, 16 N.E. 2d 355, 356.
[12] 54 C.J.S. 956.

special meaning under the circumstances in which they were uttered. or may not be, and to found an action on it, it may be necessary to prove that the use of the word under the circumstances resulted in special damage to the plaintiff.

**Publication.** No matter how defamatory words may be, whether orally uttered, written or printed, they are not actionable unless "published," that is, communicated to a third person or persons. Such communication must have been by or at the direction of the defendant, acting wholly without the plaintiff's direction, authorization or consent, and the person or persons to whom the defamatory words were communicated must have understood their meaning.

**Radio broadcasts.** Does a radio broadcast, if defamatory, constitute libel, or slander? The answer given by the courts is, that if the broadcast is read from a script, it is libel, otherwise slander.[13]

**Republication or repetition.** The republication or repetition of defamatory matter constitutes a separate wrong from the original publication. It is no defense to a person who republishes a libel or repeats a slander that it was previously published by someone else. However, the person who first publishes defamatory matter is ordinarily not responsible for its subsequent republication or repetition unless he authorized or induced it.

**Falsity.** In the absence of statute, defamatory words are not actionable unless they are false. In other words, in an action for libel or slander, truth is a good defense. However, the burden of proving that the defamatory words were true is on the defendant, because in the absence of proof to the contrary, the law presumes that the words are false. Hence if neither party offers proof on the point at the trial, the plaintiff will prevail.

**Intent** is immaterial to an action for defamation. The law looks to the consequences of the publication, not the motive or intent of the publisher.

**Privilege.** We have already referred (page 792) to certain privileges and immunities from tort liability extended to certain persons in the discharge of certain acts. As a defense to a civil action for libel or slander, the law recognizes that there are situations in which one should be permitted to write and speak freely without the risk of damages for libel or slander.

**"Fair comment."** The doctrine which exempts "fair comment" from liability for defamation is based on a different principle from that of privileged communications. Justification for the latter, even where defamatory, rests on the nature of the occasion. In the case of fair comment or criticism, the language is not defamatory because it is not directed to the

---

[13] *Sorensen v. Wood*, 123 Neb. 348, 243 N.W. 82, appeal dismissed *KFAB Broadcasting Co. v. Sorensen*, 290 U.S. 599; *Hartmann v. Winchell*, 296 N.Y. 296, 73 N.E. 2d 30; *Hryhorijiv (Grigorieff) v. Winchell*, 180 Misc. 574, 45 N.Y. Supp. 2d 31.

person himself, but to his work, and deals only with such things as invite public attention or call for public comment or criticism. The doctrine of "fair comment" is most frequently concerned with public men, public officers, candidates for office, works of art or literature, and commodities, wares and merchandise offered to the general public.

**Breach of Privacy.** Violation of the "right to be let alone," as the right of privacy has been called,[14] "consists in the interference with another's seclusion by subjecting him to unwarranted and undesired publicity." [15] The right of privacy differs from the right to freedom from defamation in two respects: (1) It directly concerns one's own peace of mind rather than his reputation among others; and (2) Truth is a good defense to an action for defamation, but not to an action for breach of privacy.

*How right may be violated.* The right of privacy can be violated only by printings, writings, pictures, or other permanent publications or reproductions, and not by word of mouth.

*When right non-existent.* The right of privacy ceases to exist "where a person has become so prominent that by his very prominence he has dedicated his life to the public, and thereby waived his right to privacy. There can be no privacy in that which is already public." [16] The right of privacy does not exist in the dissemination of news and news events, nor in the discussion of events of the life of a person in whom the public has a rightful interest, nor where the information would be of public benefit, as in the case of a candidate for public office.

## Questions

1. Distinguish between assault and battery.

2. "A threat of forcible injury to a person constitutes an assault." Is this statement true, false, or partly true and partly false? Explain.

3. "The exertion of force upon another, accompanied by actual physical contact, will constitute a battery regardless of injury or intent." Is this statement true, false, or partly true and partly false? Discuss fully.

4. Give six illustrations of justifiable assault.

5. "False imprisonment and false arrest are synonymous." Is this statement true, false, or partly true and partly false? Explain.

6. "Neither motive nor malice is material in determining damages for false imprisonment." Is this statement true, false, or partly true and partly false? Explain.

7. May an officer of the law be liable for false imprisonment? If not, why not? If so, under what circumstances?

8. Define malicious prosecution so as to include its three constituent elements.

9. Define and distinguish the two major forms of defamation.

10. Words or acts are not defamatory unless four conditions are present. What are the conditions?

[14] 21 R.C.L. 1197, 1198.
[15] 21 R.C.L. 1198-1200.
[16] *Melvin v. Reid*, 112 Cal. App. 285, 297 P. 92.

11. What is meant by words being "actionable per se"? Illustrate.

12. When may radio broadcasts constitute libel, and when slander?

13. "Intent is immaterial to an action for defamation." Is this statement true, false, or partly true and partly false?

14. What is the so-called doctrine of "fair comment," and with what situations is it chiefly concerned?

15. In respect to the right of privacy, state: (a) the nature of the right, (b) two ways in which it differs from defamation, (c) the different ways in which the right may be violated, and (d) in what situations the right does not exist.

## Problems

1. Rufnik, a quick-tempered man, after repeatedly chasing his neighbor's chickens out of his garden, walks up to his neighbor, a small, nervous man, and sticking his fist under his neighbor's nose, shouts: "One of these days I'll wring the neck of every one of your chickens, and when I get through, I'll wring your neck!" The neighbor has a nervous breakdown. After he recovers, he sues Rufnik for assault. How will the case be decided? Why?

2. Speed, in his desire to board a bus, pushes Blake out of his way. Blake slips, falls, and is hurt. He sues Speed for his injuries. Speed's defense is that the force was unintentional. How will the court decide, and why?

3. Warren calls Brown a "phony," and Brown knocks Warren down. Warren sues Brown for assault and battery. Brown pleads justification. Who wins, and why?

4. An employer locked his office and refused to let his secretary go home until she had finished all her correspondence. The secretary became ill in consequence. She now sues her employer on two counts: (1) false imprisonment, and (2) false arrest. The employer moves to dismiss both counts. How will the court decide? Give reasons.

5. Lee, employed in Baker's jewelry store, marries a banker's daughter. On the banker's suggestion and with his financial support, Lee opens a jewelry store across the street from Baker, who thereupon sues the banker for wrongful interference with contract. While that suit is pending, the banker sues Baker for malicious prosecution. Baker's defense is fourfold: (a) His suit against the banker is still pending; (b) The suit does not constitute a "prosecution"; (c) He had "probable cause" because he acted on the advice of counsel; and (d) The banker could not show he had sustained any damage from Baker's suit. How and on what legal grounds were these defenses disposed of?

6. Roberts and Williams, copartners, while alone in their office, have a heated altercation during which Roberts calls Williams "a low-down thief and embezzler." Williams sues Roberts for slander. Who will win? Why?

7. Frank Jones tells a newspaper columnist: "Rumor has it that Bob Smith's absence from the movie lot and his usual haunts was connected with vertical bars and a suit for non-support." The columnist repeats this statement in his newspaper and is sued by Bob Smith for libel. His defense is that he was merely repeating what Frank Jones had said. Will the defense be sustained?

8. Suppose in the above case that Bob Smith in his libel suit joined Frank Jones as a codefendant. Will Jones be held equally liable with the columnist? Explain.

9. Jim and Tim are identical twins. It is hard to tell them apart. Jim is convicted of embezzlement, and Tim, a model citizen, moves to Peoria, where he obtains a good position with a bank. Johnson, on a business visit from

Tim's home town to Peoria, sees Tim in the bank, and reports to a friend that Tim had been convicted of embezzlement. The friend conveys this information to the bank, which discharges Tim. Tim sues Johnson for slander. Johnson's defense is that he had made an honest and natural mistake. How will the case be decided? Give your reasons.

10. Lemon, a well known critic, writes of Horace Howe's new novel: "It is the worst collection of trash that has found its way between covers." Sales of the novel promptly drop. Howe sues Lemon for damages. What will be the decision? Explain.

## PART 3. PROPERTY WRONGS

**In General.** Wrongs directly connected with one's property rather than his person include trespass, conversion, nuisance and waste.

**Trespass.** Technically, any unlawful act committed with violence upon the person of another constitutes a trespass. However, the term "trespass" is most commonly applied to an unlawful interference with one's possession of real property. To constitute such trespass, it is not necessary that an actual enclosure be breached. The law draws an imaginary line around one's real property, and says, in effect, "You cannot cross this line without permission of the owner or person in lawful possession." Any violation of this rule is regarded as a forcible interference with possession, though no actual force is used. Hence, merely walking over another's land may constitute trespass, however slight the damage.

Trespass may be committed on, above or below the surface of another's real property. An example of trespass on the surface would be to cut timber on another's land; of trespass above the surface, flying over another's land without the owner's permission or governmental authority; of trespass below the surface, diverting a water main so that it floods one's cellar.

*Intent immaterial.* A trespasser's intent is immaterial. Regardless of motive or intent, and whether his act was deliberate or not, he commits trespass if he invades possession without permission or license, except where he is forced by some emergency upon the land of another. Thus a person may commit trespass by mistake.

*Entry by thing instead of by person.* One may commit entry through objects instead of in person, by projecting anything into, over or upon another's land; for example, felling trees so that they fall on another's land, pumping water, or casting earth, garbage or other substances upon a neighbor's land.

*Trespass by officers of the law.* One is not licensed to commit trespass merely because he is an officer of the law. Law enforcement officers are as liable for trespass as private citizens if they invade one's premises without legal right.

*Justification.* Although there is no justification for trespass, there can be no trespass where circumstances may justify entry upon another's premises, as in any of the following cases:

(1) Consent of the owner, either by express invitation, or by implied permission, as in the case of visits by friends, relatives, tradesmen or repairmen;

(2) Legal authority, as by legal process, civil or criminal;

(3) Emergencies, as where a road becomes impassable, making it necessary to pass over adjoining land, or where a storm imperils life and compels one to put to shore.

**Conversion.** Like trespass, conversion is an offense against the right of possession. Unlike trespass, conversion relates only to personal property. It consists not merely in an *interference* with the right of possession, but in an *assumption of such right* by exclusive dominion over the property itself.

*Elements of conversion.* The basic element of conversion is the deliberate and wrongful exercise of dominion over personal property: deliberate in that the exercise of dominion is intentional, and wrongful in that the right to exercise it is in another. Motive is immaterial; so are questions of good or bad faith, knowledge or ignorance, care or carelessness.

*Replevin.* When the relief sought is the *return of the chattel*, instead of damages for its retention, the action is in *replevin*.

**Nuisance.** Literally, the term "nuisance" means annoyance. More particularly, it is a wrong arising (a) from using one's property in such a way as to diminish the enjoyment of another's property, or (b) from such unlawful, improper or indecent personal conduct as to produce material annoyance, inconvenience, discomfort or injury to another person, or to the public.

Originally, one could not complain of nuisance unless the act or condition complained of caused injury to his *property*. This is no longer true. Any property use or personal conduct which renders the enjoyment of life uncomfortable, or which is indecent or offensive to the senses, may constitute a nuisance.

EXAMPLES:

(1) Improper use of property: Larkin, not satisfied with his right to the continued flow of a natural stream through his land, widens it into a deep pond, thereby depleting the flow to his neighbor downstream.

(2) Improper personal conduct: Habitually playing a saxophone in a crowded neighborhood during the small hours of the night, or continuous drunken and disorderly conduct offensive to neighbors and their families.

*Damage as an essential element.* Mere annoyance is not enough to constitute nuisance. Unless one can show substantial injury resulting from the annoyance, he can neither recover damages because of it, nor restrain its continuance. However, if there has been a physical invasion of, or interference with another's property, the presence or absence of actual damage is immaterial.

*Public v. private nuisance.* A nuisance is public if it affects rights enjoyed by the public in common, such as the right to a park, street or alley. A nuisance is private if it affects a single individual or group of individuals in the enjoyment of some private right not common to the public. The same act may constitute both a public and a private nuisance, such as an obstruction which blocks free access to a public street and a private entrance. A private citizen cannot enjoin a public nuisance unless it is also a private nuisance, that is, unless he sustains special damage of his own because of the nuisance.

*Nuisance at law v. nuisance in fact.* A nuisance at law (per se) is an act, omission or use of property which is of itself hurtful to health, tranquility or morals, or which outrages the decency of a community, hence is not permissible or excusable under any circumstances.[17] A nuisance in fact (per accidens) is an act, omission or use of property which becomes a nuisance by reason of the surrounding circumstances. Thus, the maintenance of a factory or garage, in itself entirely proper and legitimate, may constitute a nuisance in a residential district. Noises which may be unobjectionable by daytime may become exceedingly objectionable at night. Picketing, if it is peaceful and unaccompanied by coercion, duress or intimidation, is lawful, but when accompanied by coercion or intimidation for the purpose of interfering with one's business, it becomes a private nuisance.[18] Most nuisances are such because of the circumstances in which they occur. An attempt to classify such nuisances "would be almost the equivalent of an attempt to classify the infinite variety of ways in which one may be annoyed or impeded in the enjoyment of his rights." [19]

*Remedies.* The remedies for nuisance depend upon whether it is public or private.

A public nuisance is indictable, subjecting the perpetrator to criminal prosecution. Any private person may *by his own act* abate such a nuisance, provided he suffers special damage from it himself.

A person injured by a private nuisance may not abate the nuisance by his own act and without resorting to law, unless he can do so without disturbing the public peace. He has, however, other remedies. He may sue at law for damages; or in equity to abate or enjoin the nuisance and recover as well.

Where a person resorts to "summary abatement," that is, where he acts

---

[17] *Ehrlick v. Com.,* 125 Ky. 742, 746, 102 S.W. 289; *Remsberg v. Iola Portland Cement Co.,* 73 Kan. 66, 68, 84 P. 548.

[18] *Bomes v. Providence Local No. 223,* 51 R.I. 500, 155 A. 581; *Vegelahn v. Guntner,* 167 Mass. 92, 44 N.E. 1077.

[19] 46 C.J. 690, citing *Choctaw, etc., R. Co. v. Drew,* 37 Okl. 396, 130 P. 1149.

on his own to abate a nuisance, he must avoid unnecessary damage, and unless the nuisance is maintained on his own premises, he must give reasonable notice of his intention to abate the nuisance.

EXAMPLE: Summary abatement of nuisance. "The person aggrieved may kill a dog which haunts his premises, and by barking and howling becomes a nuisance, cut off branches of a neighbor's trees overhanging his land, remove a part of an adjoining owner's wall which overhangs his premises, or cut off the eaves of a building overhanging his property." [20]

*Waste.* We have already referred to waste in connection with life estates (page 616). Where a tenant for life, for years, or for any other more or less temporary period has the present use of premises the permanent ownership (fee) of which is in another, such tenant must so use the premises that—apart from ordinary wear and tear—it will suffer no permanent deterioration or injury. An act or omission by the tenant which results in permanent injury to the premises constitutes waste. Waste may be voluntary ("active") or involuntary ("permissive").

*Voluntary (active) waste* consists in some deliberate act of destruction or injury, such as pulling a house down, cutting down shade or ornamental trees, removing substantial and permanent fixtures, opening new mines or quarries upon the premises, or taking soil, clay, rock, oil or minerals therefrom.

*Involuntary (permissive) waste* "consists in the neglect or omission to prevent injury to the inheritance or freehold, as, for example, the suffering of buildings to fall into decay from neglect, or to be destroyed by fire through negligence." [21]

## Questions

1. As the term is most commonly applied in law, what is the essence of the wrong called "trespass"?

2. May a person commit trespass by mistake?

3. May a law enforcement officer commit trespass? Explain.

4. Name three situations in which entry upon another's premises does not constitute a tort.

5. What is the basic nature of the tort constituting conversion?

6. In what way does conversion resemble trespass? In what way does it differ from trespass?

7. To what extent is conversion affected by (a) good faith or bad faith, (b) knowledge or ignorance, (c) care or negligence?

8. In what two ways may the tort of nuisance arise?

9. Distinguish between (a) public and private nuisance, and (b) nuisance at law (per se) and nuisance in fact. Illustrate each distinction.

10. Distinguish between voluntary (active) and involuntary (permissive) waste.

---

[20] 46 C.J. 755, 756, citing cases.
[21] 67 C.J. 611.

## Problems

1. At various times and places, various persons did the following things:
   (a) Strung wire 20 or 30 feet above the surface of another's land;
   (b) Took water from another's spring;
   (c) Broadened the base of a building foundation so that it extended into the soil of an adjacent owner;
   (d) Merely thrust his arm into the space over a neighbor's land;
   (e) Hunted and fished on another's property without the owner's consent;
   (f) Entered another's dwelling-house without permission or license;
   (g) Dug holes and set telegraph poles without the owner's permission;
   (h) Allowed his roof and a branch of one of his trees to overhang his neighbor's property;
   (i) Mowed part of a neighbor's lawn by mistake;
   (j) Included, by mistake, a small strip of another's land within one's own fence; and
   (k) While standing on one's own land, painted an advertisement on another's wall, without permission.
State whether any or all the above acts constituted a tort, and if so, what tort.

2. A construction company, while blasting on White's land, caused fragments of rock to fall on the adjacent land owned by Brown. Brown sues the contracting company for trespass. The company's defense is that inanimate objects cannot commit trespass. How will the case be decided, and why?

3. A sheriff enters Baxter's logging camp in search of an illegal still. Baxter protests that the sheriff has no right to enter his premises without a warrant, and later seeks advice as to whether he has a cause of action against the sheriff. What would you say on this point?

4. Page innocently buys stolen goods, which he insists on retaining in the belief that the goods are his. Has the owner a cause of action against Page? Explain.

5. Adams chops down trees which he believes to be on his own land, though actually they are on his neighbor's land. Then he sells the lumber. Has Adams committed any tort or torts, and if so, what?

6. Two cases appear on the court calendar: *Camp v. Ladd* and *Fink et al. v. Watrous Chemical Company*. In the first case, Camp complains that Ladd, not satisfied with his right to the continued flow of a natural stream through his land, dammed it up, thereby causing an overflow onto Camp's land. In the second case, Fink and others, whose property is watered by Hollow Brook, complain that the Watrous Chemical Company, whose plant is upstream, continuously empties its factory waste into the stream. Assuming that the facts are as alleged, is there a valid cause of action in either or both cases, and if so, what is its nature?

7. Ernest Hope practices on his saxophone day and night. His neighbor claims that this constitutes a nuisance per se, and seeks an injunction. Will he succeed? Explain.

## PART 4. NEGLIGENCE

**Meaning of Negligence.** In everyday use, the word "negligence" means carelessness. In its legal sense, negligence is a breach of duty to use such care as a reasonably prudent man would use under a given set of circumstances. Negligence differs from most torts in that the wrong is wholly unintentional. A deliberate act, however wrongful, is not negligent. Neither motive nor intent is an element of negligence: the essence of the wrong is lack of due care regardless of motive or intent.

**Negligence Distinguished from Nuisance.** Negligence entails a wrongful injury or damage resulting from lack of due care. Nuisance "is a condition, and not an act or failure to act of the person responsible for the condition." [22] Failure to adjust or correct a leaky gas valve is negligence; the consequent stench may constitute a nuisance. The condition constituting a nuisance is not necessarily occasioned by lack of due care, but often by deliberation and intent, as, for example, where the owner of premises knowingly maintains a malodorous chemical plant in a residential district. In a negligence action, however, the damage or injury is necessarily occasioned by lack of due care.

**Negligence Per Se.** "Negligence per se" is defined as "an act or omission which is contrary to positive law, or so opposed to the dictates of common prudence that it can be said, without hesitation or doubt, that no careful person would have been guilty thereof." [23]

**Willful and Wanton Negligence.** The terms "willful" and "wanton," applied to negligence, are really misnomers, since negligence is the opposite of willfulness, and wantonness suggests conduct which is not only deliberate but unrestrained. However, the courts use the expression "willful and wanton negligence" as signifying such reckless disregard of consequences as to constitute "the legal equivalent of willful misconduct and intentional wrong." [24]

EXAMPLE: If a freight train is approaching a tunnel, and railroad employees are aware of the presence of a trespasser riding backwards on top of one of the cars, but fail to warn him, the railroad company would be chargeable with wilful and wanton negligence in the consequent death of the trespasser.

**Actionable Negligence.** Not all negligence is actionable. Negligence, to be actionable, involves three elements: (1) a duty to use care toward another, (2) a breach of such duty, and (3) resulting damage or injury.

**Duty to Use Care.** There is no absolute duty to use care. The very word "duty" implies the existence of someone to whom the duty is owing. A person alone on a desert island cannot be guilty of negligence, since there is no one toward whom he must be careful. Even in the most crowded community, one may negligently cause substantial injury or loss yet if he owes no duty of care toward the injured party, he is not chargeable with liability.

---

[22] 46 C.J. 663.
[23] 45 C.J. 633.
[24] *Bailey v. North Carolina R. Co.*, 149 N.C. 169, 175, 62 S.E. 912.

EXAMPLE: A robber, attempting to hold up a motorist, points a gun at the approaching vehicle. The motorist, intending to step on the brake, negligently steps on the accelerator instead, killing the robber. The motorist would not be liable for the accident, since he owed no duty of care to the robber.

**Incapacity as Affecting Due Care.** The degree of care which must be exercised by or toward a normal person naturally differs from the care required from or toward a person laboring under some disability, such as that of infancy, old age, physical or mental incapacity or intoxication.

*Infants* are chargeable with a degree of care commensurate with their age and understanding. Thus, infants of tender years are generally not chargeable with negligence. Their liability for the exercise of care arises and keeps pace with their growth toward maturity. On the other hand, the degree of care required *toward* an infant is merely that which is to be expected in the light of their known characteristics. One who drives a motor vehicle through a street on which children are at play would be expected to exercise greater circumspection than if the street were peopled by adults.

*Old age.* Infirmities incident to old age impose a corresponding duty of exercising more caution and vigilance than would be required in the case of persons not thus handicapped.

*Physical or mental incapacity.* Persons who are physically or mentally handicapped are held to the same standard of care as others. The law imposes no special standards of care to be exercised by a lunatic, or by the blind, sick, crippled or infirm, but measures their duty by the general standard.[25] On the other hand, "where one has actual or imputed knowledge that another, who may be injured by his act or omission, is afflicted with some physical incapacity which may affect his ability to observe or avoid danger, such as blindness, defective eyesight, deafness, or lameness, the fact of such incapacity is a matter proper for consideration in determining whether or not sufficient care has been exercised with respect to such person."[26]

*Intoxication* is not of itself negligence, and the care required of an intoxicated person is the same as that of a prudent man when sober. However, as to the care required of others *toward* an intoxicated person, the law imposes such duty as the fact of intoxication requires. A motorist, for example, seeing an intoxicated person staggering in front of him, would have to exercise corresponding care not to run him down.

**Parents: Liability for Negligence of Children.** Although parents are not liable for the negligence of their children, they may be guilty of negligence if children inflict damage or injury on others which could have been avoided by the exercise of reasonable care on the part of the parent. Thus, if a father allows his boy to use an air rifle in a crowded street, in

---

[25] *Williams v. Hays,* 143 N.Y. 442, 38 N.E. 449.
[26] 45 C.J. 701.

consequence of which a playmate loses the sight of one eye, the parent would be liable, not for the boy's negligence, but his own. (See page 26.)

**Owners of Vehicles.** The owner of a motor vehicle is of course liable for injuries or damages caused by his own negligence. As for his liability for the negligence of others who drive his vehicle, the common law rule is that such liability exists only when the vehicle is driven by his permission, or in furtherance of his business. This liability, however, has been extended by statute in many states, which may provide that authority is presumed to exist when a vehicle is driven by members of the owner's family, or by his employees even when deviating from their duties.

**Ownership or Possession of Premises.** The owner of lands or buildings, or the person having occupancy or possession of them, may incur liability for negligence toward persons who come upon the premises, whether as tenants, licensees, invitees, or even trespassers.

**Tenants.** In the absence of fraud, concealment, or covenant in the lease, a landlord is not liable to a tenant for injuries due to the defective condition or faulty construction of the premises. To hold the landlord liable, it is not enough to show that by the exercise of reasonable care he *could have* discovered the defective condition, but it must be shown that he *knew* of the defect.[27]

EXAMPLE: A landlord had surrendered control of a gas water heating system to a tenant, who operated it thereafter for herself and other tenants. When the tenant tried to light the heater it exploded. The explosion was due to defects in the fixtures. The court held that in the absence of fraud or concealment by the landlord, he was not liable for the personal injuries caused by the explosion.[28]

(As to the duty of maintaining the premises in safe condition, and the respective liabilities of landlord and tenant for negligent injuries to third parties, see pages 641-642.)

**Invitees.** An invitee of premises is a person who has been expressly or impliedly invited by the owner or person in possession to come upon the premises. Invitations may be implied from the conduct of the person in possession, or from the nature of the premises. Examples are: persons hired to work on premises; customers whose patronage is presumably solicited from the fact that a store is maintained for the sale of merchandise to the public; persons delivering required supplies or rendering required service to the person in possession, such as suppliers delivering groceries, milk or butter, mail carriers, or service employees of telephone, gas or electric companies. Where persons are thus invited upon premises, the owner or occupant owes an affirmative duty to exercise ordinary care in keeping the premises reasonably safe. He is not an insurer, that is, he is not liable merely because injuries are sustained on his premises, but he is lia-

[27] See 52 C.J.S. sec. 417 and cases there cited.
[28] *Brooks v. Peters,* 157 Fla. 141, 25 So. 2d 205.

ble for injuries sustained because of a defective or negligent condition of which he knows, or which has existed so long that by the exercise of reasonable care he had the opportunity to discover the defect and to remedy it.[29]

*Licensees.* Licensees are persons who enter one's lands, home or place of business, not by his express or implied invitation, but by his passive acquiescence, or by legal authority. Examples are: bill collectors, process servers, peddlers, persons seeking shelter, as from a storm, persons making inquiries, or desiring to use a private telephone, or to sit down and rest, or applicants for employment (other than those who were invited to apply, either personally or through a "Help Wanted" column).

A licensee occupies a position half-way between that of an invitee and a trespasser. Since his entry upon the premises is not by invitation, but upon his own initiative, he takes upon himself all risk as to the condition of the premises, and the owner or person in possession owes him no duty of care. If the licensee sustains injury because of a defective condition of the premises, he cannot hold the owner or occupier for negligence. However, once the presence of a licensee is known, there is a duty to use reasonable care to avoid injuring him.

EXAMPLE: Where the owner of property knows of a pitfall or other secret danger on the premises, and sees a licensee about to come into contact with it, he is under a duty to give warning of the danger.[30]

A proprietor must refrain from willful or wanton negligence toward actual or potential licensees. He must leave nothing in the nature of a trap or pitfall, intentionally or unintentionally, where the presence of a licensee may be reasonably anticipated.

*Trespassers.* A landowner owes no duty to keep his premises safe for trespassing. Neither does he have to warn possible trespassers of hidden defects or dangers on his land. However, if a trespasser is actually discovered on the premises in a position of peril, there is a duty to exercise ordinary care to avoid injuring him.

A proprietor is also liable, even to a trespasser, for willful or wanton negligence. He must set no spring guns, traps or pitfalls for a trespasser. "The liability for spring guns and mantraps arises from the fact that the defendant has . . . expected the trespasser and prepared an injury that is no more justified than if he had held the gun and fired it." [31]

*Infant trespassers; attractive nuisance doctrine.* "An infant who enters upon premises, having no legal right to do so, either by permission, invitation or license or relation to the premises or its owner, is as essentially a trespasser as an adult." [32] However, the courts in many states, following

---

[29] *Daddetto v. Barbiera,* 4 N.J. Super. 479, 67 A. 2d 691.
[30] *Rollestone v. Cassirer,* 3 Ga. A. 161, 59 S.E. 442.
[31] *United Zinc, etc. Co. v. Britt,* 258 U.S. 268.
[32] *Briscoe v. Henderson Lighting etc. Co.,* 148 N.C. 396, 411, 62 S.E. 600.

and extending a precedent set by an early English case,[33] have adopted what is known as the doctrine of "attractive nuisance," namely, that where one maintains upon his premises a condition, device or instrumentality dangerous to children because of their natural inability to apprehend the danger, and sufficiently attractive to lure them to the danger, and where the situation is such as to suggest to the landowner the probability of such allurement and of a resulting accident, such landowner is charged with liability to such child trespasser if he fails to take reasonable precautions against such injuries. A notable example is the Defective Turntable Case.[34]

**Manufacturers.** Ordinarily, manufacturers are liable only to those with whom they directly deal, that is, those with whom they have a contractual relation. As to third parties, they owe no duty, contractual or otherwise. Thus the lunchroom waitress referred to on page 250, who bit into a nail baked into a cake, was non-suited when she attempted to hold the company which baked the cake, from whom *her employer*, not she, had bought it.[35] However, a manufacturer of articles which are inherently dangerous, or which may become dangerous through some defect in manufacture, owes a duty to all persons into whose hands the articles may come or by whom they may be used "to exercise care and caution commensurate with the peril." [36] Examples of articles inherently dangerous are poisons, poisonous or dangerous drugs, poisonous chemicals, or ingredients necessary to the preparation of certain soaps, face creams and hair dyes which are poisonous unless properly neutralized. In the category of articles that may become dangerous because of some defect in manufacture are carbonated beverages bottled in defective or overcharged containers.

**Knowledge of Duty.** In order that a person may be charged with negligence, or violation of the duty of care, he must have had knowledge of the duty, or must be chargeable with such knowledge. In other words, a person is not liable for negligence unless he either had knowledge or should have had knowledge of the fact which gave rise to the duty and its breach. Thus, in the case of manufacturers chargeable with liability in connection with articles dangerous because of some defect in manufacture, it must be shown that the manufacturer had knowledge of this defect, or by the exercise of reasonable care should have had knowledge of it. If the defect were such that it could not have been discovered, by inspection, tests or otherwise, the manufacturer would not be liable.

**Duty to Anticipate Consequences of Neglect.** The law does not require one to anticipate all *possible* consequences of his acts or omissions,

---

[33] *Lynch v. Nurdin*, 1 Q.B. 29, 41 ECL 422.
[34] *Sioux City, etc. R. Co. v. Stout*, 17 Wall. 657. Because of this leading case, the attractive nuisance doctrine is sometimes called the Doctrine of the Turntable Cases.
[35] *Chysky v. Drake Bros. Co.*, 235 N.Y. 468, 139 N.E. 576.
[36] 45 C.J. 888, citing cases.

but it does impose a duty to exercise reasonable care in anticipating the *probable* consequences of his neglect.

**Res ipsa loquitur.** Ordinarily, one who charges another with negligence must prove it; that is, negligence is not presumed without initial proof. An important exception to this rule is the doctrine of *res ipsa loquitur*, which means, literally, "the thing speaks for itself." Inanimate objects cannot commit negligence by themselves. Where a person has charge of something that does not ordinarily happen in the absence of negligence, the very happening of the accident constitutes proof of negligence.

**Contributory Negligence.** As noted in Part 1 (page 791), where a person's own conduct contributes to his injury, he is without legal remedy, since he brought about or helped bring about his own misfortune. If a defendant charged with negligence can show that the plaintiff was guilty of contributory negligence, the plaintiff in most jurisdictions cannot recover.[37]

Contributory negligence is immaterial if the injury would have happened though the plaintiff had not been negligent, or if the defendant, after discovering the danger to which plaintiff was exposed by his own negligence, could have avoided the accident by the exercise of due care under the circumstances. This latter rule is sometimes referred to as the doctrine of "the last clear chance."

**"Last clear chance."** The doctrine of "the last clear chance" is based on the humanitarian principle that even where the plaintiff himself is negligent, the defendant should be charged with liability if by the exercise of ordinary care he might have avoided the consequences of plaintiff's negligence.

## Questions

1. What constitutes negligence in the legal sense?
2. "Negligence is more culpable when it is deliberate." Comment on this statement.
3. Name and explain two ways in which negligence differs from nuisance.
4. What is meant by negligence per se?
5. "There is no such thing as wilful and wanton negligence." Is this statement true, false, or partly true and partly false? Explain.
6. What are the three elements of actionable negligence?
7. "There is no absolute duty to use care." Is this statement true, false, or partly true and partly false? Explain.
8. What is the degree of care which the law requires (a) of infants toward others, (b) of others toward infants, (c) of the physically or mentally handicapped toward others, (d) of others toward the physically or mentally handicapped; (e) of intoxicated persons toward others, and (f) of others toward intoxicated persons?

---

[37] Some jurisdictions have adopted the doctrine of "comparative negligence," awarding lesser damages to the plaintiff, instead of none, where his contributory negligence was substantially less than the defendant's.

9. "Parents are liable for their children's negligence." Is this statement true, false, or partly true and partly false? Explain.

10. To what extent is the owner of premises liable for negligence in respect to (a) tenants, (b) invitees, (c) licensees, and (d) trespassers?

11. What is the doctrine of "attractive nuisance"?

12. "A manufacturer is not liable for negligence in respect to defective products except to those with whom he directly deals." Is this statement true, false, or partly true and partly false? Explain.

13. Explain what is meant by each of the following terms and give an illustration of each: (a) "Res ipsa loquitur," and (b) "Last clear chance."

14. What is the effect of contributory negligence? When is it immaterial?

## Problems

1. Hull, a new driver, runs into Tracey's car, which is parked against the curb in a space allowed by law. Tracey sues Hull for negligence. On the trial, he proves the above facts. Hull's attorney moves to dismiss, on the ground that Tracey failed to show in what respect Hull was negligent. How will the court decide, and on what basis?

2. A thug robs Dr. Peterkin, a chemist, taking his wallet and a metal case apparently made of silver. The case is actually made of a non-corrosive metal and contains a powerful explosive. Later the thug accidentally drops the case, which explodes, killing the thug. The thug's estate sues Dr. Peterkin on the ground that he should have warned the thug of the contents of the case. How will the court decide? Explain.

3. Two days before arriving at full age, Wilfred Green, while driving his car, runs into a pedestrian, causing him severe injury. The pedestrian sues Wilfred Green and his father for negligence. Both defendants move to dismiss on the ground that as a matter of law, they are not liable for negligence. How should the court decide, and why?

4. Gilpin, while driving his car at fifty miles an hour, the legal limit, sees an obviously intoxicated pedestrian ahead of him, blows his horn, and without retarding his speed, attempts to pass the pedestrian. The latter, however, lurches helplessly toward the car, which strikes and kills him. In an action by his estate against Gilpin for wrongful death, Gilpin's attorney asks the court to charge the jury that Gilpin owed the deceased no greater care under the circumstances than if the deceased had been sober. Should the court so charge? Explain.

5. Roper has a two-story cottage. He rents the second story to Bundy. A violent storm causes a serious roof leak in the cottage, and dangerously wets the plaster on the ceiling beneath the roof. Bundy reports the roof leak, but says nothing about the ceiling. Roper sends a carpenter to attend to the roof, which is duly repaired. A week later a large section of plaster falls on Mrs. Bundy, seriously injuring her. Bundy and Mrs. Bundy sue Roper for negligence. Who wins and why?

6. One evening late in December, Jimmy Peters, aged 5, leaves a roller skate on the sidewalk in front of the family cottage. The milkman, following his usual 5 A.M. routine, is about to deliver the usual two quarts of milk at the Peters' front door, when he steps on the roller skate, falls and sustains a broken ankle. He sues Peters in negligence. Peters' defense is threefold: (a) He did not know that the skate was there; (b) He was not responsible for what Jimmy did, because he was away at work when Jimmy left the skate on the sidewalk; and (c) Even though it was dark at the time, and the milkman could not see

the skate, Peters owed him no duty of care. How did the court dispose of these defenses and why?

7. Marvin digs a pit for a septic tank between his house and his chicken coop. Pending arrival of the tank, he covers the pit with roofing paper. That evening a trespasser, discovered near the chicken coop, starts running away and falls into the pit, sustaining serious injuries. When he recovers, he sues Marvin for negligence on two counts: (a) Marvin owed a duty to put up a sign, or a night lantern, to warn possible trespassers of the existence of the covered pit; and (b) Marvin, by the exercise of reasonable care, could have warned the trespasser in time to prevent the injury, but failed to do so (which was the fact). Marvin's attorney moves to dismiss both these counts on the ground that as a matter of law, they stated no cause of action for negligence. How did the court dispose of these defenses, and on what basis?

8. A locomotive engineer approaching a grade crossing notices a car nearing the crossing at a rapid rate of speed. The driver of the car is apparently unaware of the approaching train and fails to slow down. The engineer, aware of the situation, could have slowed down to avoid hitting the car, but failed to do so. As a result, the driver was fatally injured. His estate sues the railroad company, and the latter interposes the defense of contributory negligence. How should the court charge the jury on this point?

## PART 5. BUSINESS WRONGS

**In General.** In the somewhat arbitrary classification of "business wrongs" we include certain property wrongs which are commonly encountered in business practice. These embrace fraud and deceit, slander of title, disparagement, wrongful interference with contract, malicious injury to business, business threats and intimidation, patent, copyright, trade-mark and trade name infringements, and unfair competition.

**Fraud and Deceit.** We have previously considered the subject of fraud in connection with contracts (pages 44 to 48). We shall also later refer to various criminal offenses involving the element of fraud. The act of deception, whether for the purpose of inducing a contract, or for any other purpose, constitutes a tort, for which damages may be recovered.

**Disparagement.** We have already dealt with disparagement as an unfair trade practice (Chapter 13). Disparagement differs from defamation in that it relates to property rather than to persons. There are two kinds of disparagement: (1) Disparagement of title (commonly referred to as "slander of title"), and (2) Disparagement of quality (commonly referred to as "trade libels").

**Disparagement of title (slander of title).** The courts have defined slander of title as a "false and malicious statement disparaging a person's title to property to his special damage." [38] The word "slander" in this connection is not limited to the spoken word, because the statement constituting a slander of title may be oral or written. There can be no slander of title, however, unless the statement is both false and malicious, and unless it results in special damage to the owner.

---

[38] *Billingsley v. Townsend*, 132 Ohio St. 603, 9 N.E. 2d 690, 691.

EXAMPLE: Mason honestly but mistakenly believes that he is the owner of property which actually belongs to Parker. This challenge to Parker's title causes Parker to sustain damage in not being able to dispose of the property. If Parker sues Mason for slander of title, the case will be dismissed. Mason's conduct was not malicious.

*Disparagement of quality (trade libels).*[39] Anyone who circulates or "publishes" an untrue statement of fact (not opinion) which disparages the quality of another person's merchandise or other property, causing loss through impairment in the salability of such merchandise or property, is liable for such loss if it could have been reasonably anticipated by the disparager. In this type of disparagement, malice or honest mistake is immaterial.

In disparagement, as in defamation, one may plead privilege (pages 792 to 793). Thus, if you are merely trying to protect a third party against loss, you may express a reasonable belief that a product is inferior, especially where you are under a legal, moral or civic duty to offer such protection, as in the case of a parent, a close friend, a person who responds to an inquiry, or a civic, business or research bureau issuing commodity advice to consumers.

*Remedies for disparagement.* In addition to the usual common law remedy for damages for the tort of disparagement, the Federal Trade Commission may issue cease and desist orders against it. (See page 605.)

**Wrongful Interference with Contract.** Any wrongful interference with an existing contract, by obstructing, delaying or preventing its performance, or rendering its performance less valuable to the injured party, gives the latter a cause of action for such tortious interference. The most common example of such interference is the act of inducing a person to breach an existing contract commitment.

*Inducing breach of contract.* A person who "induces a party to a contract to break it, intending thereby to injure another person or to get a benefit for himself commits an actionable wrong unless there is sufficient justification for interference."[40]

EXAMPLES: (1) Plaintiff, a tourist agency, obtained a contract with a hotel corporation for exclusive representation in the New England states. Defendant, another tourist agency, with knowledge of the contract, induced the hotel corporation to extend the same rights to defendant. Defendant contended that it acted without malice and in good faith, and was only pursuing its legitimate right to compete. Held, for plaintiff.[41]

(2) See Example (2) on page 67.

In the case cited in Example (1), above, the court pointed out that absence of malice does not justify inducing a person to breach a contract.

---

[39] The word "libel," in this connection, is not to be construed in its strictly legal sense, but includes spoken as well as written or printed matter.

[40] 15 R.C.L. 54.

[41] *Beekman v. Marsters*, 195 Mass. 205, 80 N.E. 817.

The act is wrongful where done intentionally, and with knowledge of the existing contract. The fact that it is selfish rather than malicious does not render it any the less wrongful. The court further pointed out that it is one thing to compete for a contract not yet awarded, but a wholly different thing—constituting actionable wrong—to procure a contract for one's self by inducing the breach of another contract.

*Justification.* There are situations, however, where one may advise another, in good faith and on justifiable grounds, to refrain from the performance of a contract. A physician may advise a patient to abandon a concert tour for reasons of health. An attorney may advise a client to abandon a contract if he believes (even mistakenly) that its performance will violate the law. A father, solicitous for his son's welfare, will not be liable if he persuades his son to cancel a stock subscription.

**Malicious Injury to Business.** The law recognizes the right of everyone to engage freely in a business of his own choosing, even if the competition thus offered causes loss to similar establishments. But where one embarks on a competitive venture, not for business reasons, but for the malicious and willful purpose of injuring another person already engaged in such venture, he is merely using his own venture as an instrumentality for achieving a wrongful purpose. Thus, in *Tuttle v. Buck*,[42] defendant, a wealthy banker, threatening to destroy plaintiff's business and run him out of the community, opened up a competitive barber shop, and hired a barber to run it at ruinously low charges for the purpose of diverting business away from plaintiff's shop. The court held that such conduct constituted "a wanton wrong and an actionable tort."

**Threatening Letters.** Business concerns in general and collection agencies in particular, in attempting to make collections by mail, will be well advised to remember the distinction between collection demands and collection threats. A creditor is within his rights in making vigorous and insistent demands for payment and in stating that non-payment will be followed by suit. However, threats which amount to mental harassment and annoyance are not only prohibited by penal statutes (see page 831, "Extortion"), but are also recognized as inflicting a type of injury for which damages are recoverable.

*Illustrative cases.* There is no exact definition for an actionable threat, but the attitude of the courts is reflected in the following cases:

(1) In *Barnett v. Collection Service Company*,[43] defendant sent plaintiff, an employed widow, a series of letters threatening to sue, and to "bother" plaintiff's employer "until he is so disgusted with you he will throw you out the back door. . . . We will tie you up tighter than a drum." Plaintiff became nervous and unable to work, suffered mental pain, cried and had to go to bed. Judgment was awarded plaintiff because defendant's acts had been done for the "purpose of harassing and annoying the appellee mentally."

---

[42] 107 Minn. 145, 119 N.W. 946.
[43] 214 Iowa 1303, 242 N.W. 25.

(2) In *LaSalle Extension University v. Fogarty*,[44] plaintiff, who had signed an application for a correspondence course, received some thirty letters, which varied from mild reminders and threats to garnish wages to accusations of moral turpitude "well calculated to coerce the defendant into payment." Plaintiff was allowed to recover for worry, humiliation and loss of sleep, on the theory that the letters were written for the purpose of harassing him until he paid.

**Infringements: Patents, Copyrights, Trade-Marks and Trade Names.** Ownership of a patent, copyright, trade-mark or trade name is just as much entitled to protection as any other property right. The violation of a property right is a tort, regardless of the nature of the property. The particular nature of the property right in patents, copyrights, trade marks and trade names has already been discussed (pages 667 to 678). Trade infringements were dealt with in Chapter 13, Part 4.

**Unfair Competition.** The subject of unfair competition has already been discussed in a previous chapter (pages 594 to 601).

## Questions

1. "Fraud may be the basis of an action or prosecution involving a contract, a tort or a crime." Is this statement true, false, or partly true and partly false?
2. How does disparagement differ from defamation?
3. There are two kinds of disparagement. What are they?
4. What is meant by "slander of title"?
5. Can a written or printed statement constitute slander of title?
6. If a statement is false but not malicious, may it constitute slander of title?
7. What is meant by a "trade libel"?
8. May an oral statement constitute a trade libel?
9. Give an example of a wrongful interference with contract.
10. "The sending of any letter containing a threat constitutes a tort." Is this statement true, false, or partly true and partly false?

## Problems

1. In execution of a judgment by White against Gray, a sheriff levies on a tractor which he finds in Black's possession, and which he believes to be Gray's. The fact is that Black had borrowed Gray's tractor, and White had so informed the sheriff. Actually, however, Black had returned Gray's tractor, and had bought a new tractor exactly identical with Gray's. At the sheriff's sale of Black's tractor, Black warns the bidders that the tractor is his. As a result, no one bids on the tractor. The sheriff sues Black for slander of title. Will he succeed?

2. King, residing in a small community, has purchased a new television set. Mott, his neighbor has had a similar set for some time. King is transferred by his employer to a new position in another community where they do not have television. He therefore attempts to sell his television set. Mott, however, warns everyone in the community that he has had "lots of trouble" with his set, and that anyone thinking of buying King's set "had better think twice." As a result, King is unable to sell his set except for a fraction of what he paid for it. He sues King for damages. Will he recover?

---

[44] 126 Neb. 457, 253 N.W. 424.

3. Butterworth agrees to buy a used station wagon from Shane. Fisher, who would like to sell his own station wagon, tells Butterworth he is familiar with Shane's station wagon, and that it has a weak transmission. Butterworth repudiates his agreement with Shane and buys Fisher's vehicle instead. Shane sues Fisher, whose defense is that what he did was not malicious, but "simply business, that's all." How will the court decide, and why?

4. A physician advises his patient to abandon a concert tour for reasons of health. The patient, a famous pianist, is under contract with a well known impresario to make the tour, but follows his physician's advice. The impresario has incurred substantial expense in arranging and publicizing the tour. He sues the physician for wrongful interference with his contract. Judgment for whom, and why?

5. Richards, a wealthy tourist driving through Tompkins Corners, stops for gas and oil at the only service station in town. Huff, the proprietor, is slow, surly, and offensive to Richards. Several weeks later, Richards opens a new service station across the street from Huff's, puts a bright young mechanic in charge, and takes most of the business away from Huff, who sues Richards. Who will win, and why?

6. Wurry, a merchant whose business has fallen off considerably, receives a letter from the Energetic Collection Agency, demanding payment of an unpaid bill for merchandise, and threatening suit if the bill is not promptly paid. Wurry becomes nervous and unable to attend to business, with the result that his business goes into bankruptcy, and he loses everything he owns. He now sues the collection agency for damages. How will the case be decided, and why?

## COURT CASES FOR REVIEW

### How Did the Court Decide, and Why?

1. A restaurant employee picked up a gasoline lamp, which had become improperly lit, to carry it outside. While proceeding to the door, he was severely burned, and threw the lamp, causing it to explode and injure a third person, who sued the proprietor. *Donahue v. Kelly*, 181 Pa. 93, 37 A. 186.

2. Plaintiff was successfully operated on for the removal of a kidney at the defendant hospital. Her recovery progressed to a point where she was to be discharged within 48 hours. During this interval an interne and a nurse entered her room to give plaintiff a blood transfusion supplied by "her daughter." The plaintiff protested she had no daughter, but the nurse and interne went ahead anyway. The transfusion was given by mistake: it was intended for another patient. Plaintiff had a chill and a rising temperature, suffered severe headaches, and later became mentally ill and spent some time in a hospital for the insane. Plaintiff sued the hospital for damages. *Necolayff v. Genesee Hospital*, 270 App. Div. 648, 61 N.Y. Supp. 2d 832, aff'd 296 N.Y. 936.

3. "Shepherd threw a lighted squib, composed of gunpowder, into a markethouse, where a large concourse of people were assembled; it fell on the standing of *Y*, and to prevent injury, it was thrown off his standing, across the market, where it fell on another standing; from thence, to save the goods of the owner, it was thrown to another part of the market-house, and in so throwing it, it struck the plaintiff in the face, and, bursting, put out one of his eyes." (From opinion of Court in *Guille v. Swan*, 19 Johns. 381, referring to *Scott v. Shepherd*, 2 Black. Rep. 892.) Plaintiff sued Shepherd for damages.

4. Plaintiffs sued the receiver of the Erie Railway Company for damages

because of the negligence of defendant's employees resulting in destruction by fire of plaintiffs' barn and its contents. The defense was that the acts of the employees were not the proximate cause of the fire. One of defendant's freight cars containing barrels of oil had been insufficiently blocked. As a result, the barrels rolled off the car downhill and collided with a locomotive, which sparked into the running oil that escaped from the damaged barrels. The oil caught fire, ran into a brook and ignited the plaintiffs' barn. *Kuhn v. Jewett*, 32 N.J. Eq. 647.

5. A telephone wire attached to a 39-foot chimney extended across the street to the top of a building 100 feet high. The boom of a derrick used in hoisting materials struck the wire and pulled the chimney over. Plaintiff, injured by the falling bricks, sued the telephone company. *Leeds v. New York Tel. Co.*, 178 N.Y. 118, 70 N.E. 219.

6. In each of the following situations the court was called upon to decide whether the acts in question constituted an assault:

(a) Approaching plaintiff with an iron poker and ordering him off the premises, where plaintiff merely came to resume employment. *Hrnicek v. Chicago, M. & St. P. Ry. Co.*, 187 Iowa 1145, 175 N.W. 30.

(b) Conduct of defendant who, in violent manner, with walking stick in view, forced plaintiff against his will to sign a paper, threatening to "whip hell out of him" if he did not sign. *Trogden v. Terry*, 172 N.C. 540, 90 S.E. 583.

(c) Approaching another angrily, with a threatening gesture, and saying, "I would knock you down if it were not for your gray hairs." See *Ross v. Michael*, 246 Mass. 126, 140 N.E. 292.

7. A woman patient, after consulting with her family physician and with a surgeon, decided to submit to an operation on her right ear. The surgeon, skilled in his profession, administered an anesthetic, then examined both ears, and found the left ear more seriously diseased than the right, whereupon, after consultation with the family physician who was in attendance, he operated on the left ear. The operation was skillfully done. The right ear, which turned out to be less diseased than previously thought, was not operated on. The patient sued the surgeon for assault and battery. *Mohr v. Williams*, 95 Minn. 261, 104 N.W. 12.

8. A customer in a store, mistakenly suspected of shoplifting, was restrained and searched by a store clerk. The customer sued for false imprisonment. On the trial the store clerk's honesty of purpose and intention was completely established. *Hurst v. Montgomery Ward & Co.*, 145 S.W. 2d (Mo. App.) 992.

9. Plaintiff instituted a criminal proceeding under a Mississippi statute known as the Bad Check Law, for the purpose of collecting a debt. Thereafter, defendant sued plaintiff for malicious prosecution. The question at issue was whether malice could be inferred from the circumstances. *Grenada Coca Cola Co. v. Davis*, 168 Miss. 826, 151 So. 743.

10. In the following cases, the court was called upon to decide whether the words in question were libelous or slanderous per se:

(a) Charging that plaintiffs, if not members of the Communist party, were at least sympathetic to its objectives, fellow-travelers and pinks. *Spaniel v. Pegler*, 70 F. Supp. 926.

(b) Reference to plaintiff in a caption over a newspaper publication of his photograph, as an American "Quisling." *Sanctuary v. Thackrey*, 189 Misc. 724, 72 N.Y. Supp. 2d 104.

(c) A written publication accusing one of being a Communist. *Mencher v. Chesley*, 297 N.Y. 94, 75 N.E. 257.

(d) An oral statement that plaintiff was a Communist, and that the whole neighborhood knew that plaintiff and her husband were Communists. *Keefe v. O'Brien*, 203 Misc. 113, 116 N.Y. Supp. 2d 286.

(e) Assertion that a person is a "dirty rat." *Parker v. Kirkland*, 298 Ill. App. 340, 18 N.E. 2d 709.

(f) Assertion that a person is "too dirty" (as ground for refusing to serve him in a cafeteria). *Larson v. R. B. Wrigley Co.*, 183 Minn. 28, 235 N.W. 393.

11. In the following cases, the court was called upon to decide whether the words in question were actionable as libel or slander:

(a) A statement charging several persons with acting in concert in the commission of a crime. The statement was communicated only to the persons so charged. *Miller v. Pusey*, Pa. Com. Pl. 20 Erie Co. 362.

(b) Plaintiff's attorney wrote defendant requesting facts on a matter in controversy. Defendant replied by letter containing the defamatory words complained of. *Wells v. Belstrat Hotel Corporation*, 212 App. Div. 366, 208 N.Y. Supp. 625.

(c) A physician wrote his patient disclosing the report of a reputable laboratory that the patient had a disreputable disease. The letter was read aloud by the patient to the latter's mother, and its contents were overheard by a casual bystander for whose presence the physician was not responsible. *Shoemaker v. Friedberg*, 80 Cal. App. 2d 911, 183 P. 2d 318.

(d) Allegedly defamatory words were spoken in a foreign language, which no one present understood. *Economopoulis v. A. G. Pollard Co.*, 218 Mass. 294, 105 N.E. 896.

12. After plaintiff's family had retired, a police officer, without warrant or intent to make an arrest, but merely to see and "give a talking to" to a woman of bad character erroneously supposed to be inside, effected an entry by threatening, if the door was not voluntarily opened, to burst it open. Plaintiff sued the police officer for trespass. *Bailey v. Ragatz*, 50 Wis. 554, 7 N.W. 564.

13. Plaintiff, caught in a severe storm, moored his vessel to a private dock at an island in Lake Champlain. Defendant, owner of the island, unmoored the vessel and cast it adrift, by reason of which the vessel was damaged. *Ploof v. Putnam*, 81 Vt. 471, 71 A. 188.

14. In the following cases action was brought for conversion:

(a) A carrier misdelivered a valuable painting to a person other than the true consignee and owner. *Hassam v. Platt*, 163 App. Div. 366, 147 N.Y. Supp. 544.

(b) A young man bought a new automobile from a dealer, made a down payment, took possession, then returned the car for mechanical adjustments. His father called on the dealer and paid the balance. The dealer, without authorization from the son, delivered the car to the father, who insisted on keeping it. *Sullivan & O'Brien, Inc. v. Kennedy*, 107 Ind. App. 457, 25 N.E. 2d 267.

15. A property owner created an artificial lake or pond with sloping banks of white sand within a few feet of a public highway, in a settled community where there were many children of tender years. This was left unguarded and unprotected. A child two and a half years old, attracted by the sandy slopes, fell into the pond and was drowned. The family sued. *Allen v. William P. McDonald Corp.*, Fla., 42 So. 2d 706.

16. Plaintiff bought a car from a dealer. He sustained injuries because of a defective wheel, for which he sued the automobile manufacturer. *MacPherson v. Buick Motor Co.*, 217 N.Y. 382, 111 N.E. 1050.

17. Suit was brought against the owner of an airplane and the pilot in charge under the following circumstances: Owing to a violent windstorm, defendant's

parked airplane was caused to roll along the apron of the flying field and to collide with plaintiff's parked plane, damaging the latter. The evidence showed that the wind velocity was 60 to 70 miles an hour; that such wind could not have moved defendant's plane had its parking brakes been locked and functioning; and that the pilot of defendant's plane had ample warning of the storm's approach. Defendant pleaded an "Act of God." *Southern Air Transport v. Gulf Airways*, 215 La. 366, 40 So. 2d 787.

18. Plaintiff, a bartender, sustained injuries from an explosion of one of the bottles in a case of beer delivered by defendant. The evidence showed that neither the case nor the bottle had received rough or unnatural handling after delivery. *Fick v. Pilsener Brewing Co.*, 151 Ohio St. 555, 86 N.E. 2d 616.

19. Defendant trust company wanted certain land owned by plaintiff. To force plaintiff to sell the land to defendant, or to make it difficult for plaintiff to sell to another, defendant's president recorded an instrument falsely indicating that plaintiff had bought the land as defendant's agent. Plaintiff sued for slander of title. *Dowse v. Doris Trust Co.* (Utah), 208 P. 2d 956.

20. A collection agency undertook to collect from plaintiff an alleged debt of $61.80. Defendant sent plaintiff three letters. These stated, among other things: (a) That defendant was a member of a nation-wide organization with branches in every locality; (b) That it kept credit reports of millions of customers and its members; (c) "This unpaid account may jeopardize your credit standing. We do not want to enter it against your record if we can help it"; (d) "We earnestly suggest that you protect your credit and avoid needless expense"; (e) "Do you realize how your continued neglect of this account is going to affect your credit standing?" (f) "Wherever you go, whatever you do, a bad credit record will follow you like a shadow"; (g) "Your future credit standing depends on your prompt payment of this account. Further neglect on your part will necessitate drastic action." The final letter stated the account had to be paid within seven days, and threatened suit, attachment and garnishment. Plaintiff's complaint alleged that he had been suffering from arterial hypertension, had lost his sense of sight, and was slowly recovering when these letters threw him into a relapse, aggravated his condition, and caused him to suffer physically and mentally, with accompanying doctor's bills and inability to attend to his business. The complaint was challenged for legal insufficiency and dismissed. Plaintiff appealed. *Clark v. Associated Retail Credit Men of Washington, D.C.*, 105 F. 2d 62.

# 21

# Crimes

**Scope of This Chapter.** In this chapter we consider some of the basic principles of criminal law of interest and importance to every student of business law, not only as such, but as a well-informed member of his community. In Part 1 we consider the elements which must be present in every crime, what persons may be deemed parties to a crime, and the major classifications of crime. In Part 2 we consider the crimes that may be classed as offenses against the person, such as homicide, assault and battery, false imprisonment (including kidnapping and child stealing), robbery, arson, extortion and criminal libel.

In Part 3 we consider property, business and miscellaneous offenses, including crimes against property such as theft in its various forms (larceny, embezzlement, obtaining money or goods by false pretenses, and so forth), receiving stolen goods, burglary and malicious mischief; commercial crimes such as forgery, counterfeiting, combinations in restraint of trade, unfair competition, falsification of records and false financial statements; and various miscellaneous crimes and violations, such as perjury, bribery, bigamy and offenses arising out of regulatory legislation of a social and economic nature.

## PART 1. ELEMENTS: CLASSIFICATION

**Criminal Law.** "Law and order," so-called, would be impossible but for rules governing human aggression in a civilized community. These rules, commanding certain acts, prohibiting others, and prescribing penalties for infraction, constitute what is known as criminal law. Originally based on precedent expressed in judicial decisions, they are now for the most part formulated in statutes.

## Elements of Crime

**In General.** Although crimes are defined as public wrongs, or offenses against the people, not every public offense constitutes a crime. An offense must possess the following elements to charge the offender with criminal responsibility: (1) The offender must have had sufficient capacity to understand the nature of his act; (2) The act must have been accompanied by criminal intent, or by a recklessness equivalent in law to criminal intent; and (3) The act must have been completed, or at least attempted, not merely contemplated.

**(1) Capacity to Commit Crime.** Where physical or mental capacity to commit a crime is lacking, the offense, however wrongful, is not criminal.

*Infants of tender years* are deemed incapable of understanding the nature of a criminal act. Thus under the common law an infant under the age of seven years is conclusively presumed to be incapable of crime; between the ages of seven and fourteen, he is presumed to be incapable of possessing guilty knowledge unless the contrary can be shown; over the age of fourteen, he is deemed to have the same capacity to commit a crime as an adult. The tendency of modern statutes is to treat juvenile delinquency as in a class by itself, requiring correction rather than punishment.

*Insanity* or *feeble-mindedness,* in such degree as to render a person incapable of knowing right from wrong, constitutes a complete defense to a criminal charge.

*Intoxication.* Ordinarily, voluntary intoxication affords no defense to a criminal charge. If a motorist kills a pedestrian, it is no defense to the charge of homicide that he was intoxicated while driving. There are, however, numerous statutes which provide that evidence of intoxication may be considered by a jury in determining the purpose, motive or intent with which the crime was committed. Thus if one breaks into a home while hopelessly intoxicated, his physical condition at the time may be considered in deciding whether he was pursuing a burglarious intent, or merely trespassing. And where a particular motive or intent is a necessary element of a particular crime, the intoxicated condition of the accused becomes material in determining whether it was possible for him, in such condition, to entertain such motive or intent.

EXAMPLE: In *Edwards v. State,*[1] a drunken occupant of a taxicab struck the driver on the head with a bottle, removed the driver from the cab, then parked the cab near his mother's home, where he went to sleep. He did not awaken until the owner had recovered the cab. It was held that the occupant was not guilty of larceny, since he was too intoxicated to entertain an intent to steal.

Involuntary intoxication, induced by duress, fraud or stratagem,[2] has been held to afford a valid defense to a criminal charge, especially where it renders the victim unable to understand what he is doing.

*Married women.* Under the common law, there was a presumption that if a married woman committed a crime in the presence of her husband, she was coerced. This is no longer true except in one or two states.

---

[1] 178 Miss. 696, 174 So. 57.

[2] For example, inducing a person to drink medicinal alcoholic preparations to such an extent that he could not tell right from wrong. *Choate v. State,* 19 Okl. Cr. 169, 197 P. 1060.

*Corporations* at common law were deemed incapable of committing crime. This concept no longer prevails, though certain crimes from their very nature can be committed only by natural persons (bigamy, for example). The courts have generally held that corporations cannot commit murder. (See page 556.)

**(2) Criminal Intent.** Intent is a necessary element of some crimes; other acts may be made criminal regardless of intent. A person cannot commit murder unintentionally, but his act may be so reckless of life as to constitute manslaughter. On the other hand, purely accidental killing, as in the case of a golfer killed by a ball, would not be classed as criminal. Criminal intent, in law, does not mean the purpose to commit a crime, but knowingly doing a forbidden act, regardless of whether the offender knows it is forbidden. Thus if you and I own identical automobiles parked alongside of each other, and I mistakenly drive off in your car, there is no intent to appropriate, hence no theft. But if I knowingly sell mislabeled food, I am criminally liable though I was unaware of the law forbidding the act.

*Ignorance of the law; advice of counsel.* Ignorance of the law, as everyone knows, furnishes no exemption from criminal responsibility.[3] Neither is it a defense to a criminal charge that the accused acted on the advice of counsel. To hold otherwise, as the court has put it,[4] would be to place the advice of counsel above the law.

*Ignorance of fact; mistakes.* Where ignorance of a fact, or a mistake in reference to it, necessarily means absence of malice or criminal intent, it will exempt one from criminal responsibility (except where an act is made a crime by statute regardless of malice or criminal intent).

EXAMPLES:
(1) Killing an intruder in the reasonable but mistaken belief that he is a burglar;
(2) Receiving goods in ignorance of the fact that they were stolen;
(3) Passing a counterfeit bill in ignorance of the fact that it is counterfeit;
(4) Remarrying in the mistaken belief that one's wife is dead.

*Motive v. intent.* "Although sometimes confused, motive and intent are not synonymous. A motive is an inducement for doing some act; it gives birth to a purpose. The resolve to commit an act constitutes the intent."[5] One may commit a crime with the most laudable of motives.

EXAMPLE: In a prosecution for removing a fence from around a graveyard, the defendant pleaded good motive: he wanted to build a better fence. The court rejected this defense, saying: "It is a well settled principle of law, that when a man does the thing prohibited, with the intent which the law forbids, it will not avail him that he also intended an ultimate good."[6]

---

[3] 16 C.J. 84.
[4] *Needham v. State*, 55 Okl. Cr. 430, 32 P. 2d 92.
[5] *People v. Kuhn*, 232 Mich. 310, 205 N.W. 188, 189.
[6] *Phillips v. State*, 29 Tex. 226, 236.

(3) **Commission v. Contemplation of Criminal Act.** To render one liable for a criminal act, the act must have been committed, or at least attempted, not merely contemplated. Thus if one buys a weapon intending to persuade another to use it illegally, no crime will have been committed if the buyer abandons his purpose.

*Criminal attempt.* An attempt has been defined as an act done with the intent to commit a crime, tending but failing to accomplish it.[7] To use the previous illustration, if the purchaser of a weapon hands it over to another for a criminal purpose, which is either thwarted, or abandoned by the recipient, the act of handing the weapon over for criminal use constitutes a criminal attempt and is punishable as such.[8]

*Mistaken attempts to commit crime.* A person is liable for criminal attempt if he does an act which, if successful, would be criminal, though the act itself is thwarted by a circumstance rendering consummation impossible; for example, shooting at a spot where one mistakenly believes his victim to be, or picking an empty pocket in the belief it contains a wallet. But one is not liable for a criminal attempt if he does an act which he *mistakenly believes to be criminal,* as where he kills a deer in the mistaken belief that the deer season has closed, or where he buys goods from the true owner in the mistaken belief that the goods are stolen.

## Parties to Crime

**Persons Included.** A person is a party to a crime if he (1) commits it, (2) does some act which forms part of it, (3) assists in its commission or in doing some act which forms part of it, or (4) directly or indirectly counsels or procures any person to commit the offense or to do any act which forms part of it.[9] In felonies, parties are classed either as principals or accessories; in treason and misdemeanors, all parties, if guilty at all, are principals.

**Principals and Accessories.** A principal is one who actually perpetrates the crime (sometimes classed as a principal in the *first degree*), or who, being actually or constructively present, aids and abets its commission[10] (sometimes classed as a principal in the *second degree*).

An accessory is one "who procures, counsels, commands or abets the principal, and is absent when the latter commits the crime" (referred to at common law as an *accessory before the fact*), "or who, after the crime has been committed, receives, relieves, comforts or assists the perpetrator" (known at common law as an *accessory after the fact*).[11] Since an acces-

---

[7] *State v. McLeavey,* 157 Minn. 408, 196 N.W. 645.
[8] *State v. Bowers,* 35 S.C. 262, 14 S.E. 488.
[9] 22 C.J.S. 143.
[10] *People v. Bunkers,* 2 Cal. App. 197, 84 P. 364, 370.
[11] *Hitt v. Commonwealth,* 131 Va. 752, 109 S.E. 597.

sory after the fact is not connected with the crime itself, but with the principal, his offense is separate and distinct from the principal crime.

These classifications and distinctions have in whole or in part been affirmed by statute in some states, and modified or abolished in others.

**Compounding Felonies.** Compounding felonies or other crimes consists in taking money or reward on an engagement, express or implied, to conceal a crime, withhold evidence, or discontinue or delay prosecution; except where compromise is allowed by law.

*Forgiveness by employer: when may constitute compounding felony.* An employer may forgive an employee's theft, allow restitution, and give him another chance; but if the employer makes restitution part of a bargain for not prosecuting, he is guilty of compounding the offense.

### Classifications of Criminal Law

**Major Classifications.** Criminal law may be classified as to function (*substantive* and *procedural*); as to source (*common law* and *statutory*); and as to jurisdiction (*Federal* and *state*). Crimes may also be classified as to whether they are inherently wrong, or merely regulatory (*malum in se* and *malum prohibitum*), as to their gravity (*treason, felonies, misdemeanors* and *breaches of the public peace*), and as to the character of the offense.

**Substantive v. Procedural Criminal Law.** Substantive criminal law sets forth the acts or omissions which constitute crimes, and prescribes penalties for their commission. Criminal procedure deals with the rules whereby a person charged with crime is brought to justice and his guilt or innocence established.

**Common Law Crimes.** Originally, common law crimes were those prescribed by precedent only. They were punishable mostly by death. As late as the seventeenth century, there were seven common law felonies in England: homicide, rape, burglary, arson, robbery, theft and mayhem. Except for mayhem and petty larceny (stealing something worth less than twelvepence), these were capital offenses. Though now embodied in penal statutes, these crimes are still referred to as the "common law crimes." Strictly speaking, however, common law crimes embrace all acts or omissions which were originally crimes under the common law.

**Statutory Crimes.** Practically all crimes are now statutory, in the sense that they are defined by statute. Some states have specifically abrogated the common law with respect to crime and have substituted criminal codes, usually with the provision that no act or omission shall be deemed criminal or punishable except as prescribed by statute.

**Federal Crimes.** Federal law dealing with crime, unlike state law, is derived from Constitutional grant instead of the common law. The Constitution of the United States gives Congress power to provide laws and procedure for the punishment of counterfeiting, piracies and felonies on the high seas, offenses against the Law of Nations and infractions of rules and regulations prescribed for the land and naval forces of the United States. Accordingly, Congress has passed many laws prescribing penalties for acts or omissions in these matters, and these have been compiled into the Criminal Code of the United States.

**State Crimes; Penal Codes.** State crimes are those subject to state jurisdiction. For all crimes not subject to Federal jurisdiction, state sovereignty is exclusive. Penal statutes of the different states, commonly known as *penal codes*, define and prescribe penalties for a multitude of criminal acts.

**Criminal Jurisdiction: Extradition and Change of Venue.** Crimes must be prosecuted in the place where they are committed. No state can punish for a crime unless it was committed in that state. If a criminal flees the jurisdiction, it is customary, though not compulsory, for the state or foreign country where the criminal is apprehended to surrender the fugitive to the jurisdiction where the crime was committed. This procedure is known as *extradition*.

Inside the state, the county where the crime is committed is the county where the criminal must be tried, unless it can be shown that justice requires trial in another county, in which case a *change of venue* may be directed.

**Malum in se v. malum prohibitum.** A crime is said to be *malum in se* if it is wrong in itself because of its evil nature, as in the case of homicide, burglary and robbery. It is said to be *malum prohibitum* if it is wrong solely because it is prohibited, as in the case of a traffic violation, or the violation of an anti-smoking ordinance.

**Treason.** Under our dual system of sovereignty, treason may be committed either against the United States, or any State. Treason against the United States, as defined in the Constitution, consists in "levying war against them, or in adhering to their enemies, giving them aid and comfort." The Constitution further provides that no person shall be convicted of treason except on the testimony of two witnesses to the same act, or on confession in open court.

**Felonies v. Misdemeanors.** Broadly speaking, felonies are crimes punishable by death, or by imprisonment in the state penitentiary. Indictable offenses not amounting to felonies are misdemeanors.

**Breach of the Public Peace.** In a sense, all crimes constitute a breach of the public peace. However, the term is more specifically applied to public disturbances which have a tendency to terrorize or frighten, such as brandishing a weapon in public, street fighting, riots, breaking into another's home by force, disturbing a public meeting, and similar acts of interference with public tranquility.

**Crimes Classified According to Nature of Offense.** It would be impracticable to attempt here even the barest outline of the vast catalogue of crime listed according to the nature of the offense. They are frequently grouped under three main heads: (1) Offenses against the person; (2) Offenses involving property; and (3) Commercial crimes. The classification, of course, is artificial. All offenses, public or private, personal, property or "commercial," affect some person or persons in the first instance. However, the classification has a convenient basis. *Offenses against the person* are intended to designate crimes involving one's person rather than his property (though the same crime may equally affect one's person *and* his property, as in the case of robbery, arson, extortion and libel). *Commercial crimes* relate to offenses committed in the course or under the guise of commerce.

A broader term, *business crimes,* is sometimes used to embrace certain offenses involving one's property and the so-called commercial crimes.

## Questions

1. What three elements must be present in an offense to charge the offender with criminal liability?

2. To what extent is criminal liability chargeable to: (a) infants, (b) the insane or feeble-minded, (c) intoxicated persons, (d) married women, and (e) corporations?

3. "Criminal intent, in law, may consist either in the purpose to commit a crime, or knowingly doing a forbidden act, regardless of whether it is known to be forbidden." Is this statement true, false, or partly true and partly false?

4. When will ignorance of a fact or a mistake in reference to it exempt one from criminal responsibility, and when not?

5. "There can be no crime without an evil motive." Is this statement true, false, or partly true and partly false? Illustrate your answer.

6. Distinguish between (a) contemplation of a criminal act and (b) criminal attempt. Will either or both constitute a crime?

7. Name four situations in which a person may be held as a party to a crime.

8. With respect to the commission of a crime, distinguish between principals and accessories.

9. Distinguish between an accessory before the fact and an accessory after the fact.

10. How does one compound a felony?

11. Distinguish between extradition and change of venue.

12. "Treason may be committed either against the United States, or any State." Is this statement true, false, or partly true and partly false?

13. Distinguish between *malum in se* and *malum prohibitum.* Give two illustrations of each.

14. Distinguish between felonies and misdemeanors.

## Problems

1. In a state where it is a criminal offense to serve liquor to a minor, Frank Gay, a minor, enters a tavern, orders a highball, and is duly served by the bartender, who is promptly arrested by a detective who had witnessed the

proceedings. The bartender's defense is twofold: (1) That he did not know Gay was a minor, and (2) That he did not know of the law which prohibited him from thus serving minors. How will the court dispose of these defenses?

2. A decree of divorce grants custody of an only child to the mother. The father, who feels that the mother is not properly taking care of the child, spirits the child away during the mother's absence, and takes the child to a distant state, whence the father is ultimately extradited to the original jurisdiction. Charged with kidnapping, the father pleads that he acted under the advice of counsel. Will the defense prevail? Explain.

3. Which of the following acts, if any, constitute a crime:

(a) Killing an intruder in the reasonable but mistaken belief that he is a burglar;

(b) Receiving goods in ignorance of the fact that they were stolen;

(c) Passing a counterfeit bill in ignorance of the fact that it is counterfeit;

(d) Remarrying in the mistaken belief that one's wife is dead;

(e) During a neighbor's absence, demolishing his chicken coop as a public eyesore (which it was).

4. I. C. Redd, in a fit of rage, buys a pistol, intending to shoot his neighbor with it, then leave for parts unknown. He thinks it over during the night, and changes his mind. Later, the weapon is discovered in Redd's possession, and he is arrested for unlawful possession of firearms. He explains how he came to buy the weapon, and is indicted for criminal attempt to commit homicide. Will he be convicted?

5. Suppose that in the above case Redd had delivered the weapon to a gangster whom he had hired to commit the crime in question, and that the gangster, apprehended before he could commit the crime, implicated Redd: would your answer be the same as in Problem 4? Explain.

6. Alec Smart, purportedly a sailor "just off the boat," sells E. Z. Mark an allegedly smuggled "Smyrna rug," at "a fraction of its true value." Actually, the rug is made in New Jersey, and is worth half of what Mark pays for it. Can Mark be prosecuted for criminal attempt—either as principal or as accessory—to violate the law in respect to smuggling?

7. Barton and Thomas, employed in the jewelry department of the Mammoth Department Store, are caught in the act of severally pilfering various items from their respective showcases. After thorough questioning by the store manager, the latter recommended to the proprietor that Barton, who was exceedingly contrite over his misdeeds, and whose family was in great need, be forgiven, but that Thomas be told that if he did not make good his pilfering, he would be prosecuted. These facts having come to the attention of the public authorities, the store proprietor himself is prosecuted. State the nature of such prosecution, and whether it is well founded.

8. Irving Ingrate is convicted of treason on the testimony of an F.B.I. investigator. Ingrate protests his innocence and appeals. How should the appeal be decided?

### PART 2. OFFENSES AGAINST THE PERSON

**Summary.** Included in offenses against the person are homicide in its various forms, assault and battery, and false imprisonment; also offenses relating to one's property as well as his person, namely, robbery, arson, extortion and libel.

**Homicide.** The killing of one human being by another, by direct act, procurement, or omission, is broadly designated "homicide." Homicide may constitute murder in various degrees, and manslaughter; and in some cases it may be justifiable.

*Murder in the first degree.* The most heinous form of homicide is murder in the first degree, consisting of deliberate and premeditated homicide, committed with *malice aforethought,* and punishable by death except where capital punishment is abolished.

*Manslaughter* is the unlawful killing of another without malice. It may be *voluntary,* as in cases where the act is committed with a real design and purpose to kill, but through the violence of sudden passion occasioned by great provocation; or *involuntary,* where death is caused by some unlawful act without the intention of taking life, as in the case of persons who cause death through the faulty construction of a building or bridge, or the negligent operation of a train, machine or motor vehicle.

*Justifiable homicide.* Homicide may be justifiable, as in self-defense, warfare or capital punishment, or in cases where killing becomes absolutely necessary to prevent or resist the commission of a felony, to arrest a felon, or to prevent his escape. *Excusable,* as distinguished from *justifiable,* homicide is accidental killing without negligence, as in the case of a man killed by an axehead which flew off the handle of an axe that appeared to be in good condition.

**Assault and Battery.** We have already noted that in the law of torts, the terms "assault" and "battery" are commonly used to designate a single type of offense but actually represent separate and distinct offenses. This is equally true in the law of crimes.

A criminal *assault* is an intent to do violence, coupled with the ability to do it and some act or step toward doing it, but without actual physical contact; such as frightening another by pointing a gun at him, or making a violent leap or threatening gesture toward another, suggestive of harm, but unaccompanied by physical contact.

In a *battery,* the intent to do violence must be coupled with physical contact of some sort, as by striking, kicking, pushing, beating with club or other object, hitting with a missile, spitting or throwing water. Malice is not essential: an attempt to kiss another without the latter's consent, or to discipline a college freshman by *hazing,* may constitute a battery.

*Wounding; mayhem.* A battery resulting in severe physical injury is sometimes referred to as the crime of *wounding.* If it results in injury to another's arms, legs, eyes or other organs, it is frequently designated as *mayhem.*

*Civil v. criminal assault.* The same act may constitute both a civil and a criminal assault; in the former case, as a tort, it subjects the offender to a suit for damages by the person injured, and in the latter to criminal prosecution, punishable by fine, imprisonment, or both.

**False Imprisonment.** We have already defined false imprisonment as related to the law of torts (page 797). The definition is equally applicable to the law of crimes.

**Kidnapping.** Where false imprisonment is accompanied by moving a person from one place to another, whether for the purpose of exacting a ransom, or for any other purpose, the crime is known as *kidnapping*. The *Lindbergh Act*[12] makes it a crime to transport any kidnapped or abducted person in interstate commerce.

**Child stealing** is a form of kidnapping, though differing from the latter in that consent of the victim is no defense. Parents not entitled to custody are frequently guilty of this offense.

**Robbery.** The crime of robbery consists in taking and carrying away, from another's person, money or goods in the latter's possession, by force and violence, or by assault and putting in fear, and with intent to steal.

**Larceny from the person** is a similar taking away of property, but without force or violence, as by picking another's pocket, or by stealing from a person who is asleep.

**Arson.** Under the common law, arson consisted in the malicious and wilful burning of another's house, involving danger to life. It now includes the burning of one's own dwelling, though in the possession of another, for an illegal purpose (for example, to collect insurance), and it also includes personal as well as real property. Unless the burning is wilful and malicious, it does not constitute arson; for example, a person is not guilty of arson if he starts a fire to clear his land and thereby unintentionally burns a dwelling, either his own or another's.

**Extortion.** At common law, extortion meant exaction by a public official of an extra consideration for discharging his official duty. Statutes now include, in extortion, the obtaining of promises, signatures or property by the wrongful use of force, fear, or show of official authority. Unlike robbery, extortion may be committed without force, or even duress: the suggestion of unpleasant consequences for failure to comply will suffice.

EXAMPLES:
(1) Threatening to collect a bill by "calling on you in our Collection Wagon" (a picture of which is enclosed, showing a large red van bearing the sign "WE BEAT THE DEAD BEATS").
(2) Obtaining money, property, promise or signature by threatening an unlawful injury.
(3) Threatening to expose a secret, or to impute or expose some crime, disgrace or deformity.

**Libel.** This offense, like many others, may be criminal as well as civil. Libel has been defined as "a malicious publication, expressed either in printing or writing, or by signs and pictures, tending either to blacken the memory of one dead or the reputation of one who is alive, and expose

---

[12] Enacted by Congress after the kidnapping and murder of the baby Charles Lindbergh.

him to public hatred, contempt, or ridicule." [13] Although the line between civil and criminal libel is not clearly drawn, the usual basis of criminal libel is its injurious effect on the public as well as upon the person libeled, or its tendency to create a breach of the public peace.

## Questions

1. Name three types of crime against one's person and four relating to one's property as well as his person.

2. "Murder in the first degree is the killing of one human being by another, by direct act, procurement or omission." Is this statement true, false, or partly true and partly false?

3. "Manslaughter is the unlawful killing of another without malice." Is this statement true, false, or partly true and partly false?

4. Distinguish between justifiable and excusable homicide. Give three illustrations of each.

5. "Kidnapping is false imprisonment accompanied by moving a person from one place to another, regardless of purpose." Is this statement true, false, or partly true and partly false?

6. "Larceny from the person is the taking away of property from one's person, by force, violence, assault or putting in fear, with intent to steal."

7. "Extortion may be committed without force, or even duress." Is this statement true, false, or partly true and partly false?

8. Can one commit criminal libel in any other way than by the written or printed word?

## Problems

1. The following facts were established in a case involving the alleged killing of Dodd by Dalrymple: Dalrymple and Dodd, partners, quarreled in a tavern over the division of profits. Later, Dalrymple, who had been drinking excessively, drove to Dodd's home. Knowing Dodd's wife was away, and that Dodd was alone, Dalrymple left his car, with motor running, entered Dodd's home, was heard to quarrel loudly with Dodd, and, following three shots, was seen to re-enter his car, in which he fled the jurisdiction. The jury had to decide whether Dalrymple was guilty of murder in the first, or a lesser degree. How did it decide?

2. R. U. Frisch was arrested for attempting to kiss a young lady without her consent. He was charged with criminal assault. It was conceded, however, that there was no malice in what he was doing. How did the magistrate decide, and on what basis?

3. Three college sophomores forcibly shaved a freshman's head and painted the letter "F" on his scalp. The sophomores were prosecuted for criminal assault and battery. Their defense was that it was all in fun. The magistrate refused to accept this defense and the sophomores appealed. Was the decision affirmed or reversed? Give reasons.

4. Willie Lightfinger picks the pocket of a passenger on a bus, and on alighting from the bus, is apprehended with the passenger's wallet in his possession. He is taken to the police station, where he is booked for robbery. Will he be convicted?

5. Ladd, tiring of his country home, sets fire to it. The home is completely

---

[13] *Bl. Law Dict.*, 3d Ed.

destroyed. Charged with arson, he pleads two defenses: (a) He cannot commit arson in respect to his own property, and (b) His act was not motivated by any illegal purpose. The prosecuting attorney moves to dismiss both defenses. How will the court rule?

6. Teresa Tardy, discharged by her employer as his secretary, demands a letter of recommendation, threatening to reveal alleged income tax irregularities unless she obtains such letter. The employer charges Miss Tardy with attempted extortion. Can the charge be sustained?

7. Oliver Oversmart, a newspaper columnist, prints an article which falsely blackens the memory of Latham's father. Latham asks his attorney if there is anything he can do about this. What was the attorney's advice?

## PART 3. PROPERTY, BUSINESS AND MISCELLANEOUS OFFENSES

**Basis of Classification.** Such designations as "property crimes" and "business crimes" are necessarily somewhat arbitrary. Strictly speaking, there is no such thing as a crime against property or against business, since only persons, either individually or collectively, can suffer a wrong. However, the classification is adopted as a convenient one for designating crimes committed in connection with business or commercial transactions.

### Crimes Against Property

**Summary.** The so-called "crimes against property" relate to theft, burglary, robbery and malicious mischief. Robbery has already been noted as a crime against the person. It is also frequently classified as a crime against property.

**Theft.** The word "theft" embraces all forms of wrongful taking of another's personal property with intent to appropriate it. Statutes frequently include, in the designation, the specific crimes of larceny, embezzlement and obtaining money under false pretenses.

*Larceny* is taking and carrying away another's personal property with intent to appropriate it. The law commonly distinguishes between *grand* and *petit* larceny, depending, respectively, upon whether the property stolen has a value above or below a given minimum.

*Embezzlement* is theft by one who has lawful possession of another's money or personal property and wrongfully misappropriates it.

**Obtaining money or goods by false pretenses.** The core of this crime is in obtaining something of value through fraudulent misrepresentation, either by actual misstatement, or by creating a false impression. The thing or things obtained may be money, goods, securities, signatures or indorsements to commercial paper, or anything else of value. In this category come all forms of fraudulent schemes, "confidence" games, fake advertising, false impersonations and swindles, classed generally as *frauds and cheats*. Among the more common forms of frauds and cheats are the following:

*Fictitious partnership names.* A person who transacts business by using the name, as partner, of one not interested as such, or by using the designation "and company" or "& Co." when no actual partner is represented thereby is, in many states, guilty of a misdemeanor.

*Frauds on hotel keepers,* by obtaining credit or accommodations through false pretenses.

*Circulating false rumors* about the market price of stocks, bonds, and so on.

*Fraudulently obtaining employment* by false letters of recommendation

*False representation or advertisements of employment opportunities* by way of inducement to persons seeking employment.

*Selling tickets for balls and entertainments* without authority from the institution or organization concerned.

*Transactions affecting securities,* such as reporting or publishing fictitious transactions, false statements or advertisements, manipulation of prices, or trading by brokers against customers' orders ("bucketing").

*Hypothecating or selling a customer's securities,* by a broker, without the customer's consent, except where the broker has a lien on the securities for an unpaid purchase price. (See page 416.)

*Issuing fraudulent checks, drafts or orders.* (See page 212.)

Many penal statutes make specific reference to various types of frauds and cheats, with specific penalty provisions.

**Receiving Stolen Goods.** The act of receiving stolen goods is a crime in itself if committed by one who knowingly buys or conceals such goods or aids in concealing them with intent to deprive the owner of possession.

**Burglary.** Burglary is breaking and entering into the premises of another with intent to commit some crime. Entry at night in an occupied dwelling aggravates the offense.

**Malicious Mischief.** This crime relates to the deliberate, wilful and wanton damage or destruction of another's property, such as poisoning a neighbor's dog, contaminating a neighbor's well or stream, or defacing or destroying public signs or advertisements.

**Commercial Crimes.** In the category of the so-called "commercial crimes" may be listed forgery, counterfeiting, combinations in restraint of trade, unfair competition, falsifying records and false financial statements.

**Forgery.** The essence of forgery is the false making or altering of an instrument having legal value, with intent to defraud by imposing or changing legal liability on the instrument. It is not forgery to make or alter an instrument which has no legal value (for example, to change the amount of an unsigned note), or to create or change no legal liability in connection with a writing (for example, to sign another's name to a congratulatory message).

**Counterfeiting.** By Federal and State laws, counterfeiting includes the making, passing, or possession with intent to pass, of counterfeit coins, currency, obligations or other securities of the United States, such as national bank currency, United States bonds, notes, certificates or other commercial paper, as well as stamps and other evidences of value insured under the law. Counterfeiting also includes the possession of any die, plate or other material for the making of counterfeit money.

*Restraint of trade and unfair competition.* The criminal penalties prescribed by Congress in connection with restraint of trade and unfair competition have already been discussed in Chapter 13.

*Falsifying records.* Most states prescribe severe penalties for falsifying books and records. A typical statute[14] provides that a person is guilty of forgery in the third degree punishable by imprisonment for not more than five years if:

(a) As an individual, officer, or employee of a corporation, association or partnership, he falsifies or unlawfully and corruptly alters, erases, obliterates or destroys any accounts, books of account, records or other writing pertaining to the business of said individual, corporation, and so on;

(b) With intent to defraud or to conceal any larceny or misappropriation by any person of any money or property, he does any of the following things:

(1) Alters, erases, obliterates, or destroys an account, book of accounts, record, or writing, belonging to, or appertaining to the business of, a corporation, association, public office or officer, partnership or individual; or,

(2) Makes a false entry in any such account or book of accounts; or,

(3) Wilfully omits to make true entry of any material particular in any such account or book of accounts, made, written, or kept by him or under his direction.

Similar alterations are declared to constitute forgery in the third degree if made:

(a) With intent to defraud creditors, or

(b) To conceal a crime, or

(c) To conceal from creditors or stockholders or other persons interested, matters materially affecting the financial condition of any individual, corporation, association or partnership, or

(d) To provide a basis for obtaining credit.

The foregoing provisions do not generally apply to a clerk, bookkeeper or other employee who, without personal profit or gain, merely executes the orders of his employer.

The effect of these penal provisions is to aggravate crimes which are accompanied by false record entries.

EXAMPLE: Two cashiers steal different sums from their corporate employer. *A* takes currency received by him as the proceeds of a note receivable which

---

[14] N.Y. Penal Law, sec. 889.

has never been entered on the corporation's books. *B* takes currency from the cash drawer and makes an entry charging the withdrawal on the corporation's books to an expense account. *A* is guilty of larceny by embezzlement, but *B* is guilty not only of larceny but of forgery in the third degree.

*False financial statements.* Penal statutes throughout the country generally prescribe fines and imprisonment for obtaining credit by false financial statements. The following classes of persons may be liable under such statutes:

(a) A person who, to secure credit, knowingly makes or causes to be made a false written statement concerning the financial condition or ability to pay of himself or of some other person, firm or corporation in which he is interested or for whom he is acting;

(b) A person who, knowing that such a statement has been made concerning himself or some other person, firm or corporation in which he is interested or for whom he is acting, procures money, property or credit on the faith of such statement; and

(c) A person who, knowing that a written statement has been made concerning the financial condition or ability to pay of himself or some other person, firm or corporation in which he is interested or for whom he is acting, represents on a later day that such statement theretofore made, if then again made, would be then true, when in fact, said statement, if then made, would be false, and who procures money, property or credit upon the faith of such oral or written statement.

## Miscellaneous Crimes and Violations

**Summary.** In addition to the crimes briefly referred to under the foregoing classifications, there are a number of others which do not readily lend themselves to any particular classification. Among these are perjury, bribery and bigamy; also offenses arising out of regulatory legislation of a social and economic nature. These include laws dealing with narcotics, liquor and cigarettes, gambling and gambling devices, the maintenance of professional and technical standards, business licenses and certificates, public safety, sanitation, consumer protection, Sunday laws, and various bankruptcy crimes.

**Perjury.** At common law, the crime of perjury can be committed only in the course of a suit or judicial proceeding. Statutes have extended this definition so as to include false swearing wherever an oath is required or allowed by law, such as affidavits and depositions required to be made in tax returns, pension proceedings, customs transactions and various other administrative or non-judicial proceedings.

**Bribery.** Under the common law, bribery is giving or receiving anything of value, including any valuable service intended to influence the discharge of a legal duty, the gist of the offense being the tendency to pervert justice.[15] The term bribery now includes any giving, offering, receiving or asking of a reward as inducement to influence official action.

**Bigamy.** The crime of bigamy consists in willfully and intentionally contracting a second marriage, or going through the form of a second marriage, while the first marriage, to the knowledge of the offender, is still undissolved. The crime is more pointedly defined as the state of a man who has two wives, or a woman who has two husbands, living at the same time.[16]

**Prohibition of Anti-Social Enterprises.** The law severely regulates or prohibits the sale of narcotics, the sale of liquor or cigarettes to minors, and, in general, the more flagrant form of gambling.

*Gambling and gambling devices; lotteries and "bank nights."* Gambling and betting, whether by cards, dice ("crap-shooting") or otherwise, including the maintenance of slot, card or dice machines, for gambling purposes, are prohibited in many states; likewise lotteries (the sale of chances to win prizes) and "bank nights" (stimulating motion picture and other attendances by offering cash prizes to the holders of "lucky numbers").

**Professional and Technical Standards.** Many statutes aim to protect the public against incompetent or unscrupulous professional or technical services, by regulations in respect to licensing, disciplinary proceedings, suspension or revocation of a license, penalties for practicing without a license, and so on. These services concern attorneys, certified public accountants, physicians, nurses, dentists, pharmacists, osteopaths, veterinarians, optometrists, architects, civil engineers, surveyors, embalmers, chiropractors, chiropodists and others engaged in rendering professional or technical service to the public generally. Of special note are the provisions relative to unlawful practice of the law, medicine and accountancy.

*Unlawful practice of law.* Anyone may be his own lawyer, but if he acts or holds himself out as authorized to act as a lawyer for another, or if he engages in the practice of furnishing legal advice or drawing up legal papers other than on his own behalf without having been admitted to the practice of the law, he is guilty of practicing law unlawfully and punishable accordingly.

*Champerty* consists in carrying on a lawsuit in another's name, but at one's own expense, with a view to profiting out of the proceeds.

*Maintenance* is meddling to instigate or conduct a lawsuit for another, regardless of whether one profits from this practice.

*Unlawful practice of medicine.* Heavy fines, penalties and even imprisonment may be incurred for practicing medicine or surgery without a license.

*Unlawful practice of accountancy.* Legislation governing the practice of accountancy in the United States is far from uniform. Usually it pro-

---

[15] *People v. Peters*, 265 Ill. 122.
[16] *State v. Lindsey*, 26 N.M. 526, 194 P. 877,

vides for restrictions on the use of the designation "Certified Public Accountant" or "C.P.A.," rather than on the practice of accountancy itself. A minority of states have adopted statutes restricting practice to state-licensed public accountants.

*Business licenses, certificates of approval, and so on.* Statutes may prescribe penalties for engaging in certain businesses without prior public approval, where such businesses are of sufficient public concern to justify such regulation. Examples are the requirement for obtaining government approval before engaging in the banking or insurance business, or in public utilities, such as waterworks, railroad, bus or other transportation services, electric light, telephone or similar public service enterprises. Licenses are commonly required in connection with collection and employment agencies, theaters, hospitals, hotels, investment companies, mining or oil properties, cold storage plants, and so on. State statutes commonly prescribe penalties for doing business under a fictitious or trade name without first registering such name and disclosing the true name of the proprietor.

*Public safety.* Numerous statutes concerned with public safety prohibit or restrict the sale and possession of firearms; regulate factory conditions, child labor and the employment of women in industry; prescribe rules governing the ownership and operation of motor vehicles and the regulation of traffic; impose regulations to protect against fire hazards; and fix building safety requirements, such as building plans, specifications as to building materials, elevator inspections and similar building precautions.

*Sanitation.* Many statutes, including local ordinances, deal with plumbing and sewage disposal, meat, fruit and vegetable canneries, food handling and packing under prescribed sanitary conditions by employees free from contagious diseases, purity of foods and drugs and proper labeling and disclosure of their contents, barbers and barber shops, beauty parlors, the sale of secondhand mattresses or upholstered furniture containing padding or stuffing, and numerous other items affecting public health and sanitation.

**Consumer Protection: True Weights, Measures and Labels.** A variety of statutes and local ordinances prescribe standards governing the size of containers, true weights and measures and similar items helpful in protecting consumers against unscrupulous manufacturers, producers and dealers. Congress has passed laws prescribing the size of various measures, such as barrels, baskets and containers of fruits, vegetables and produce. It has also prohibited the use of deceptive labels on containers or receptacles of food and drugs, and in particular requires that dangerous or potentially injurious ingredients contained in food and drugs be clearly marked on the label.

**Sunday Laws.** We have already referred to Sunday laws in our discussion of Contracts (pages 76 to 78). State laws and particularly local ordinances aim at restricting business activities on Sunday. Violations are generally punishable by fines. Exceptions are usually made in the case of services and supplies of "public convenience and necessity," such as medical and surgical attendance, emergency repairs, church subscriptions, Sunday newspapers, drugs, motion picture and other entertainment, and (subject to local regulation) dairy, delicatessen and other foods within limited hours. (See pages 77 to 78.)

**Bankruptcy Crimes.** The Bankruptcy Act prescribes penalties for a variety of illegal business practices connected with bankruptcy. These are referred to in the chapter on Debtor and Creditor (pages 734 to 735).

## Questions

1. Distinguish between larceny and robbery.

2. Penal statutes in different states commonly provide that certain acts in connection with the following constitute a crime. What are the acts? (a) Fictitious partnership names; (b) Frauds on hotel keepers; (c) Circulating certain types of rumors; (d) Obtaining employment by letters of recommendation; (e) Advertisement of employment opportunities; (f) Selling tickets for balls and entertainments; (g) Certain transactions affecting securities; (h) Issuing checks.

3. How would you define malicious mischief? Give three illustrations.

4. What is the essence of the crime of forgery?

5. "By Federal and state laws, counterfeiting includes the making or passing of imitated coins, currency, obligations or other securities of a constituted governmental authority." Is this statement true, false, or partly true and partly false?

6. "The crime of perjury can be committed only in the course of a prosecution, suit or judicial proceeding." Is this statement true, false, or partly true and partly false?

7. What acts are embraced in the crime of bribery as commonly defined today?

8. How would you define bigamy?

9. Describe some of the common provisions embodied in our penal statutes today designed to achieve the following objectives: (a) Maintenance of standards of skill and competence in businesses which are of sufficient public concern to justify public regulation; (b) Public safety; (c) Sanitation; (d) Consumer protection.

10. Name five forms of forgery by falsification of records and three forms of falsification of financial statements which may render one liable for fines and imprisonment.

## Problems

1. Franklin hires a new bookkeeper who, unknown to Franklin, has a criminal record. One evening after Franklin has gone home the bookkeeper, while putting the books away in the safe, notices that the cash drawer is open and withdraws $200 therefrom. He is later indicted and tried for embezzlement. Will he be convicted?

2. The following facts were established on a trial: (a) Defendant received stolen goods, and (b) he resold them. Defendant's attorney moves to dismiss. How will the court decide and why?

3. Tired and weary at the end of a day's quest for shelter, Dusty Dan

finally arrives at a shack in the woods which to his knowledge had been abandoned years before. Two months previously, however, the owner had decided to use the place himself as a summer retreat. Dusty enters the shack after nightfall, makes for a bunk in the rear, is overpowered and captured by the owner and two of his friends, and is then turned over to the sheriff, charged with burglary in the first degree for breaking and entering into the premises of another at night while such premises were occupied. Will the prosecution prevail?

4. Adams, after a vigorous fight with Brown for public office, wins the election. Brown is bitter over his defeat. Merrill, a practical joker, sends Adams a congratulatory telegram and signs Brown's name to it. When Brown learns of this he files charges against Merrill for forgery. Will these charges be sustained?

5. I. M. Shifty is caught picking a passenger's pocket in a public conveyance. He is searched and discovered to be in possession of a counterfeit twenty-dollar bill. Can Shifty be convicted of any other crime besides that of larceny?

6. A representative of the Internal Revenue Office, while checking Mullin's income tax return, discovers that Mullin has falsified his books and records. The Internal Revenue agent advises the district attorney's office. Apart from income tax prosecution, with what state crime can Mullin be charged?

7. Horn is seeking a loan from a private lending agency. The latter retains its auditor to check Horn's books, with a view to ascertaining his financial worth. The auditor prepares a financial statement which he asks Horn to sign. Horn signs the statement in reliance on the accuracy of the audit. Actually the audit shows Horn to be worth $50,000 more than the facts truly support. The error is due to a mistake in computation. Horn obtains the loan but is later unable to repay it. The lending agency institutes criminal proceedings. Will Horn be convicted or discharged?

8. The Landlords' Protective Corporation hires a group of lawyers as part of its regular staff and advertises to property owners generally that it is prepared "to handle any and all kinds of rent cases on behalf of property owners." A question arises as to whether this type of activity is within the law. What is your opinion?

9. A tenant handles his own rent case successfully, and later states to a friend, who is confronted with a similar situation, "Don't worry, I'll handle your case. I've been through the same situation and I know all about it." The tenant handles his friend's case successfully. He is about to organize a Tenants' Protective Association when the district attorney examines into the two prior proceedings. What will be the district attorney's conclusion as to the regularity of each of such proceedings?

## COURT CASES FOR REVIEW

### How Did the Court Decide and Why?

1. Defendant made up his mind to kill a certain person, then fortified himself with liquor, became drunk, and killed the man. Charged with murder in the first degree, he interposed the defense that while the intoxication may have been premeditated, the act of killing could not be. *State v. Robinson*, 20 W.Va. 713.

2. Defendant killed an intruder in his house, believing—mistakenly but reasonably—that the intruder was a burglar. In the subsequent prosecution for the killing the accused interposed mistake of fact as a defense. *Levet's Case*, 1 Hale P.C. 474.

3. In a prosecution for bigamy, the accused interposed the defense that he believed on the advice of counsel that he had the right to marry. *State v. Goodenow*, 65 Me. 30.

4. The accused procured another person to commit a robbery. The latter killed the victim to conceal the robbery. The accused was charged with being an accessory before the fact of the murder. *Watts v. State*, 5 W.Va. 532.

5. The accused, charged with shooting his uncle, pleaded self-defense in that the uncle, while intoxicated, had thrown a rock at him, then drawn his gun with intent to shoot the accused. It appeared that the rock had safely passed the accused when the latter did the shooting, and that the uncle did not attempt to draw his own gun until after the accused drew his. *Ledford v. Commonwealth*, 267 Ky. 289, 102 S.W. 2d 38.

6. Defendant was charged with kidnapping under a statute providing that a person who wilfully seizes, confines, inveigles, or kidnaps another, with intent to cause him, without authority of law, to be confined or imprisoned within the state, is guilty of kidnapping. The act complained of was that defendant, a labor union member, took an employee by the arm, forced her to enter a cab, and took her to union headquarters, where she was told that unless she joined the union she would be unable to remain at her job. *People v. Kuntzsch*, 64 N.Y. Supp. 2d 116.

7. The enforcement officer of a highway department, under the guise of collecting a fine and costs, collected money from a delinquent automobile owner in excess of the legal license taxes. The question arose as to whether the facts justified the particular crime with which the officer was charged. *Cox v. State*, 33 Okl. Cr. 436, 244 P. 206.

8. Defendant presented a money order to the paying official in a post office. The money order was payable to another person, whose name, however, was exactly identical to defendant's own name. Defendant signed his name as if he were the person for whom the money was intended. Defendant was charged with forgery. *United States v. Long*, 30 F. 678.

9. The accused solicited a bribe on the promise to procure the release of a party who had been arrested. On the trial, it appeared that the person was not guilty of the crime for which he was arrested. *State v. Worsham*, 154 Wash. 575, 283 P. 167.

10. Defendant entered upon the premises of another with the intention of committing a robbery. While displaying a deadly weapon, he was met by resistance on the part of his intended victim. The resistance was pressed with such vigor that the would-be robber had no opportunity to abandon his plan or withdraw from the resulting conflict. The intended victim was killed while the would-be robber was attempting to escape or to save himself from death or bodily harm. The defendant, charged with murder in the first degree, pleaded absence of premeditation. *State v. Owen* (Idaho), 253 P. 2d 203.

11. The accused entered a retail store with intent to commit larceny. At gunpoint, he demanded money of the storekeeper. When the storekeeper denied having any money, he was bludgeoned over the head with a pistol. The accused was charged with three separate crimes: (1) burglary, (2) robbery, and (3) assault with a deadly weapon. It was contended on behalf of the accused that his acts constituted but one crime. It appeared that the pistol was a type for which ammunition was never obtained, and was not obtainable. *People v. White* (Calif.), 253 P. 2d 108.

12. The accused was prosecuted for the offense of burning a building with intent to defraud the insurance company. His defense was that he believed

the insurance policy on the building to be in force, whereas it was actually invalid. *Brower v. State* (Miss.), 64 So. 2d 576.

13. Defendants, operators of a "wire service," were charged with conspiracy to aid and abet others in the commission of the crime of bookmaking. Their defense was that while they were aware that their operations aided bookmaking, they were unaware of the existence of a statute prohibiting bookmaking. *People v. McLaughlin,* 111 Cal. App. 2d 781, 245 P. 2d 1076.

14. A party desiring to purchase steel deposited $75,000 with a corporation for this purpose. The evidence established that the relationship between the corporation and the depositor of the money was that of debtor and creditor, not that of agent and principal. The corporate officers were charged with converting the money to their own use, and were prosecuted for embezzlement. *People v. Becker,* 414 Ill. 291, 111 N.E. 2d 491.

15. A certified public accountant was called in by a corporate taxpayer to advise on the question whether it could pay past-due sales taxes for prior years, in one year when it had a large income, and then deduct these payments in its Federal income tax return for that year. The accountant did no accounting work for the corporation, had nothing to do with the corporation's books or its tax return, and confined himself solely to advising as to what view the tax authorities, and ultimately the courts, would take on the question involved. The question arose as to whether the accountant's conduct constituted a penal violation. *Application of New York County Lawyers' Association,* 273 App. Div. 524, aff'd 299 N.Y. 728, 87 N.E. 2d 451.

16. A railroad section boss padded his time-roll by crediting a subordinate with more days than were actually worked. He was convicted of forging an order for the payment of money, and appealed. *De Rose v. People,* 64 Colo. 332, 171 P. 359.

# BOOK III
# Enforcement

*Thus far, we have considered what our rights, duties and wrongs are. We now consider how our rights and duties are enforced and our wrongs redressed.*

# 22

# Civil Procedure

**Scope of This Chapter.** In this chapter we consider the civil (non-criminal) procedure for safeguarding and enforcing rights and duties, and restraining or redressing wrongs. In Part 1 we consider the civil remedies available for this purpose, including those which are "extra legal," or self-applied, and those which are provided by the courts, both at common law and in equity. In Part 2 we present a picture of our judicial system: the nature and functions of a court, the factors that determine which court has jurisdiction of a particular dispute, and the different kinds of courts in this country—Federal, State, and local.

In Part 3, after examining the preliminary steps of a lawsuit leading up to the trial, such as process, attachments, pleadings, demurrers and preliminary motions, we step inside the courtroom to observe a trial in action, from the call of the calendar to impanelling a jury, "opening" the case, direct examination of the witnesses, cross-examination and redirect examination, "resting" the case, summation by counsel, the judge's charge, the jury's verdict, the judgment, and the proceedings which follow the trial, including execution of the judgment, supplementary proceedings and possible appeal. In Part 4 we discuss the rules of evidence given in a court room: admissible and inadmissible testimony; objections of counsel and rulings by the court; when testimony is relevant, competent and material, and when it is not; who has the burden of proof; things which need not be proved; evidence illegally obtained, as by search and seizure without warrant, or by wire-tapping; prima facie and conclusive evidence, direct and circumstantial evidence, hearsay evidence and opinion evidence; hypothetical questions; and "privileged" communications on which a witness cannot be compelled to testify, such as those between a husband and wife, attorney and client, physician and patient, and clergyman or priest and penitent. In Part 5 we consider the bars which the law may raise to a prospective litigant: the statute of limitations, laches, estoppel and moratoria.

## PART 1. REMEDIES

**Nature of Law Enforcement.** Law enforcement consists in compelling obedience to the rules of conduct prescribed by society for the government of its members. These rules are of two kinds: (1) Those which reveal our rights and duties (*substantive* law), and (2) Those which prescribe our remedies (*adjective* law). We have already considered the major divisions of our rights and duties (Book I) and the major types of wrongs, both civil and criminal (Book II). We come now to the remedies for enforcing rights and duties and for redressing, restraining or penalizing wrongs.

**Enforcement Procedure.** Enforcement procedure may be either civil or criminal, depending upon the nature of the wrong to be redressed. Civil procedure deals with means and method for safeguarding or enforcing individual rights and restraining or redressing individual wrongs. Criminal procedure deals with the means and method for safeguarding public rights and restraining, or imposing punishment for, public wrongs. We shall deal with the former in this chapter and the latter in Chapter 23.

**Classification of Remedies.** Broadly, all remedies are either "extra legal" or "legal." Extra legal remedies are those which a person applies directly without seeking legal assistance. Legal remedies are those which a person seeks through legal channels. This broad classification requires further clarification and subdivision.

## Extra Legal Remedies

**In General.** Ordinarily, a person who suffers wrong is not allowed to take the law into his own hands, but must seek redress through established legal procedure. In a number of situations, however, the law allows a person, either on his own initiative or in cooperation with others, to apply his own remedy if the situation requires it. Examples are (1) self-defense, (2) retaking, (3) entry, (4) abatement of nuisance, (5) distress, (6) accord and satisfaction and (7) arbitration and award. The first five of these remedies are exclusively self-applied. The last two, which call for cooperation with others, have been discussed on pages 113 to 114, and 125 to 126, respectively.

**Self-Defense.** The remedy of self-defense consists in using requisite force to protect one's person, family or property against some threatened injury. The degree of allowable force is less where property is involved than where personal injury is threatened.

**Retaking.** The common law remedy of retaking, also known as "recapture," or "reprisal," related to a situation where the owner was deprived of his goods or chattels and was allowed to follow and retake them if he could do so without jeopardizing the public peace. This extralegal remedy is permissible only in extreme cases.

**Entry.** Where one is ousted of his lands by another, who takes possession, the law affords the former the remedy of *entry*, that is, of going peaceably upon his own land for the purpose of retaking possession. Here, too, if the remedy cannot be exercised without disturbing the public peace, the owner must resort to legal procedure to enforce his rights.

**Abatement of Nuisance.** As pointed out on page 804, a person injured by a private nuisance may summarily abate it without resort to law, provided he can do so without disturbing the public peace. (For examples, see pages 803 and 805.)

**Distress.** The common law remedy of distress relates to the seizure by one person of chattels belonging to another, to ensure satisfaction for some wrong committed by the latter. Examples are the seizure of a neighbor's cattle or chickens until the damage done by them has been compensated, or the seizure of a tenant's chattels on nonpayment of rent. These remedies have been largely abolished.

## Legal Remedies: In General

**Civil and Penal Remedies Distinguished.** Legal remedies, or those applied through legal procedure, are of two kinds, civil and penal. The object of a civil remedy is to prevent or redress a private wrong. The object of a penal remedy is to protect the public against criminal acts by prescribing punishment for their commission.

## Civil Remedies: In General

**Common Law and Equitable Remedies Distinguished.** We have already noted the distinction between common law and equity jurisdiction (pages 6 to 7), and the fact that equity owes its origin to the inadequacy, in many circumstances, of the remedy available at common law. These separate classes of remedies were originally sought through separate tribunals or courts. Though the distinction in jurisdiction is still carefully preserved, the distinction in tribunals no longer exists in many jurisdictions; that is, in many states both legal and equitable remedies may be administered in the same courts and by the same judicial personnel.

## Civil Remedies: Common Law

**Ordinary _v._ Extraordinary Remedies.** Common law remedies are sometimes classed as ordinary and extraordinary. Ordinary common law remedies provide relief by way of restoration and recompense. Extraordinary common law remedies deal mainly with such writs of ancient origin as mandamus, quo warranto, prohibition and habeas corpus.

**Restoration: Replevin and Ejectment.** When the owner of a chattel has been or is being wrongfully deprived of its possession and benefit, the common law will award him a judgment of replevin (page 803), requiring that possession of the specific chattel be restored to him. The same is true of real property: where the owner is being wrongfully deprived of possession he may seek ejectment (page 644).

**Recompense: Damages.** Where the purpose of a remedy is to provide recompense for wrongful injury, the common law may award a money judgment which is supposed to measure the loss occasioned by the wrong. For example, where restoration of a chattel is impossible, impracticable or undesirable, an action for conversion (page 803) may provide a money equivalent for the owner's loss of possession.

Damages represent the most widely applied remedy at common law by way of recompense. We have already defined damages occasioned by the breach of a contract. Such damages may be general, special or liquidated (page 123). From the standpoint of purpose, damages may also be classed as nominal, compensatory and exemplary. Nominal damages (frequently expressed as "six cents") may be awarded to vindicate a right in the absence of actual loss. Compensatory damages are supposed to represent the money equivalent of the loss sustained. Exemplary or punitive damages ("smart money") are damages by way of punishment, as in the case of a wilful, malicious or wanton injury.

**Mandamus.** Mandamus (literally, "We command") is the name of a writ which was originally issued by the King and is now issued by a court of superior jurisdiction. It may be directed to a corporation or any of its officers, or to an executive, administrative or judicial officer of government, or to an inferior court, commanding the performance of a particular act. The writ may be *peremptory*, commanding absolute obedience, or *alternative*, requiring the defendant either to obey the writ or show cause why he should not do so.[1]

**Quo Warranto.** The writ of "quo warranto" (literally "by what authority") was originally issued by the King to inquire into an alleged usurpation of office. It now takes the form of an "information," resembling a criminal proceeding, though actually a civil remedy for trying the title to a corporate or other franchise, or to a public or corporate office.

**Prohibition.** A writ of prohibition is an order issued by a superior court to an inferior court, commanding the latter to desist from further proceedings in a case, for lack of jurisdiction.

**Habeas Corpus.** This basic remedy safeguarding the right of personal liberty has already been discussed in our first chapter (page 23).

## Civil Remedies: Equity

**Specific Equitable Remedies.** It would be impracticable to attempt here more than a bare reference to some of the better known equitable remedies. Many of them we have already considered elsewhere. Mainly, they deal with (1) the *prevention of wrongs*, such as injunctions (page 6); (2) *Contractual regulation and enforcement*, such as specific performance (page 124), reformation (page 6), and rescission (page 7); (3) *prop-*

---

[1] *Bl. Law Dict.*, 3d Ed., 1152.

*erty rights,* such as mortgage foreclosure (page 696), partition (page 6), accounting (page 482), trusts (page 767), receivership (page 559) and "quieting title"; and (4) *remedies dealing solely with procedure,* such as bills of peace (page 6), interpleader and *ne exeat.*

**"Quieting Title."** There are many situations where one has good title to property, notwithstanding some contrary claim or impediment that constitutes a "cloud" upon the owner's right. If the owner wishes to "remove the cloud," he may bring a suit in equity to establish his rights and thereby to "quiet title" to his property.

**Interpleader.** Where two or more persons lay claim to property or funds in the hands of someone who has no interest in the matter except as a stakeholder, the latter, instead of deciding in favor of one contestant at the risk of being sued by the other, may file a bill in equity "interpleading" the contestants, removing himself from the dispute, and letting the court decide which contestant is right.

**Ne Exeat.** The writ of *ne exeat* ("Let him not leave") is issued by a court of equity where it is feared that the defendant may leave the jurisdiction and thereby defeat the decree of the court. The writ commands the sheriff to apprehend the defendant and keep him in custody unless he gives bond to abide by the decree.

## Penal Remedies

**Nature and Purpose.** The object of a penal remedy is to protect society against criminal acts by prescribing penalties designed to deter their commission or repetition. Such penalties may take the form of capital punishment, imprisonment and fines.

**Capital Punishment.** Capital punishment is punishment by death. It is the usual penalty for treason and first degree murder. In most states it takes the form of death by hanging; in New York and a number of other states, by electrocution. Some states have abolished capital punishment in favor of life imprisonment.

**Imprisonment.** The more serious offenses not punishable by death are commonly punishable by imprisonment. The period of imprisonment varies with the gravity of the offense.

**Fines.** The penalty for most misdemeanors consists of fines, either alone, or in conjunction with imprisonment. In many situations the lesser offenders are given the alternative of paying a fine or suffering imprisonment; for example, "Ten dollars or ten days."

## Questions

1. What is the object of law enforcement?
2. Distinguish between civil procedure and criminal procedure.
3. What is the difference between an "extralegal" remedy and a "legal" remedy?

4. "One who suffers a wrong is not allowed to take the law into his own hands." Is this statement true, false, or partly true and partly false? Explain.

5. What is the object of a civil remedy?

6. What is the object of a penal remedy?

7. Ordinary common law remedies provide relief by way of restoration and recompense. Distinguish between these two forms of remedy.

8. Explain the following extraordinary remedies at common law: (a) mandamus, (b) quo warranto, (c) prohibition, and (d) habeas corpus.

9. Explain the following equitable remedies: (a) specific performance, (b) reformation, (c) rescission, (d) partition, (e) quieting title, (f) interpleader, (g) ne exeat.

10. Name and explain the three major types of penal remedy.

## Problems

1. Jones threatens to strike Smith. Smith shoots and kills Jones to prevent the threatened injury, and is indicted for murder. Smith's plea is self-defense. Should Smith be convicted? Explain.

2. Johnson buys an antique clock, but loses or misplaces it on his way home. A week later he sees a similar clock on the mantelpiece of a neighbor whom he is visiting. He insists the clock is his, but the neighbor disputes this. He then forcibly removes the clock from his neighbor's possession, insisting that the law gives him such right. Comment on Johnson's legal position.

3. During Dorsey's absence abroad for many years, Lane has taken possession of Dorsey's summer cottage. When Dorsey returns to this country, he demands that Lane vacate the premises, which Lane refuses to do, claiming that he has acquired title by adverse possession. Dorsey then decides to hire several muscular assistants to help him dispossess Lane. Is Dorsey well advised in respect to this plan?

4. Judge William erroneously decides that he has no jurisdiction over an important dispute. He therefore refuses to hear the litigants on the merits of his case, determine the facts, or proceed in any way in reference to the dispute. The litigant's attorney advises the litigant he has a specific remedy by appeal to a higher court. What is the remedy?

5. A state attorney general disputes the right of Gadgets, Inc., to function as a corporation. What is the name of the proceeding to which the attorney general may resort?

6. Several neighbors cross Broderick's land on their way to the railroad station. They insist that they have acquired the right to do so. Broderick's attorney advises that if Broderick is sure of his position, he may sue for an injunction. Broderick states that he is not sure of his position, but would like to have it established definitely at law, nevertheless. What remedy may Broderick pursue?

7. Motley buys a diamond bracelet at a public auction. About to leave on a trip, he asks Folsom, a business man, to keep the bracelet for him in Folsom's safe during Motley's absence. Folsom later shows the bracelet to a customer, who insists the bracelet is his—that he lost it some time before. Motley, on his return, demands the bracelet, and the customer threatens suit unless Folsom gives *him* the bracelet. What should Folsom do?

8. Potter, shortly before leaving on his vacation, leaves his pedigreed dog with Slater. During Potter's absence, Slater becomes attached to the dog and refuses to return him to Potter on the latter's return. Potter learns that Slater,

fearing litigation, is about to leave the jurisdiction. Has Potter an effective remedy under the circumstances?

## PART 2. COURTS

**In General.** What is the nature of a court of law? When does it have jurisdiction? From the standpoint of what they do, and when and where they do it, what are the different kinds of courts that make up our judicial system? These questions we shall endeavor to answer briefly in this Part. What goes on in these courts we shall indicate in Part 3.

**Nature and Functions of Court.** A court consists of a body sitting in judgment on a dispute between two or more parties, or on a question whether someone has violated the law. Such body consists of a presiding judge or justices, a jury in trials of fact, and various other officers, such as a clerk who keeps the records of the court, administers the oath to witnesses, and calls the calendar of cases; a court stenographer who takes down the minutes of the trial; and a court attendant (sometimes called *bailiff*) who announces the opening and closing of each court session, and keeps order in the courtroom.

It is not the function of a court to enforce the law, but to declare it as it applies to the parties before it.

Court sessions are generally held in a courtroom, but they may be held anywhere, as at the bedside of a dying witness.

**Jurisdiction.** A court has jurisdiction when it has the power to render a binding decision. If it has jurisdiction, its decision, unless reversed on appeal, is binding for all time (*res adjudicata*) as to the same facts and parties. If the court does not have jurisdiction over the parties, or the dispute, its decision is ineffective. The jurisdiction of a court may depend on the following factors:

1. *Governmental division or territorial boundaries:* A Federal court has no jurisdiction over a purely intrastate dispute, nor a state court over a Federal matter. A New Jersey court has no jurisdiction over non-residents living in New Mexico, neither may a summons out of a New York City Court be served on a party in Buffalo.

2. *Amount of money involved:* The jurisdiction of many inferior courts is limited to disputes involving amounts not exceeding a prescribed maximum.

3. *Nature of the dispute:* A probate or surrogate's court has no jurisdiction over negligence cases, neither may a criminal court try an action for breach of contract.

4. *Residence of parties:* Statewide courts are commonly divided into counties, circuits or districts, with the requirement that parties must submit their disputes in the county, circuit or district where one or both of them reside.

5. *Location of property in suit:* A dispute involving real property lo-

cated in a given county or district must usually be tried by a court in that county or district.

**Original v. Appellate Jurisdiction.** Jurisdiction is original when the court may try an issue in the first instance; appellate, when it reviews the judgment of a court below. Some courts have both original and appellate jurisdiction.

**Judicial System in United States.** To understand the judicial system in this country, we must bear in mind our dual system of government. Under the Federal Constitution the states, originally sovereign, delegated certain powers to the Federal Government, reserving all undelegated powers to themselves. Thus we have a dual system of courts, each with a separate and well-defined jurisdiction of its own.

## Federal Courts

**Source of Authority.** The Constitution of the United States provides that the judicial power of the Federal Government shall be vested in a Supreme Court, "and in such inferior courts as Congress may from time to time ordain and establish." [2] Acting under this authority, Congress has established United States courts of appeals and United States district courts. These, with the Supreme Court, are known as "constitutional courts."

In addition, Congress has found it necessary from time to time, in order to determine matters not within the scope of the judicial power created by the Constitution, to create other tribunals known as "legislative courts." These include the United States Court of Claims, the United States Court of Customs and Patent Appeals, the United States Customs Court and a system of Territorial Courts.

**Supreme Court of the United States.** The Supreme Court of the United States is the highest court in the land. Although created by the Constitution, its organization is determined by Congress. Its present organization consists of a Chief Justice and eight Associate Justices, appointed for life by the President with the consent of two-thirds of the Senate.

The Supreme Court has both original and appellate jurisdiction.

*Original jurisdiction.* The original jurisdiction of the United States Supreme Court is limited to "all cases affecting ambassadors, other public ministers and consuls, and those in which a state shall be a party." [3]

*Appellate jurisdiction.* The appellate jurisdiction of the Supreme Court embraces:

1. Appeals in all cases arising under the United States Constitution, laws of the United States and treaties.

2. Appeals in admiralty cases. These involve breaches of contract relat-

---

[2] Article III, sec. 1.
[3] Constitution, Art. III, sec. 2.

ing to maritime affairs, torts on the high seas or navigable waters, and maritime liens.

3. Appeals in controversies to which the United States is a party. This includes prosecution for Federal offenses, suits to enforce penalties and forfeitures for violation of revenue, postal and similar laws, and breach of contract.

4. Appeals in controversies between states and the citizens of another state or foreign country. These relate to cases where the state is suing, not defending a suit; because in the latter case, a state, being sovereign in all respects not delegated to the United States Constitution, cannot be sued by any citizen without the state's consent.

5. Appeals in controversies between citizens of different states

6. Appeals in controversies affecting State land grants.

**United States Court of Appeals.** In 1891, Congress set up a system of intermediate appellate courts, to relieve the Supreme Court of the volume of appeals from cases decided by the trial (United States District) courts. These appellate courts, formerly known as the Circuit Courts of Appeal, are now designated United States Courts of Appeal. They hear all appeals from the United States district courts, except in the case of capital and infamous crimes, which go up on appeal direct to the United States Supreme Court. They also review and enforce orders of many Federal administrative bodies, such as the Securities and Exchange Commission, the National Labor Relations Board and appealable decisions of the Tax Court of the United States.

The United States is divided into eleven judicial circuits, each with its own United States court of appeals. Each of the 48 states as well as the District of Columbia is assigned to one of these circuits. The Territories, likewise, are assigned to various of the circuits. Each court of appeals has from three to nine circuit judges, depending upon the volume of judicial work. Normally, each court of appeals hears cases in divisions of three judges.

**United States District Courts.** The United States district courts are the Federal trial courts: the courts of original jurisdiction. Each state has at least one district court; some of the larger states have as many as four. There are district courts, also, in Alaska, Hawaii, Puerto Rico, the Virgin Islands and the Canal Zone. The district courts have jurisdiction over bankruptcy proceedings; Federal crimes and torts; Federal prosecutions for penalties, forfeitures, and so forth; admiralty cases; patent and copyright litigation; controversies between citizens of different states, or between citizens and aliens; cases under the immigration, interstate commerce, postal and Federal revenue laws; and all questions generally arising under the Constitution, laws or treaties of the United States.

**United States Court of Claims.** The Court of Claims was established in

1855 to provide a means for determining the validity of certain kinds of claims against the United States which formerly could be obtained only by special act of Congress. The Court decides all suits filed with it against the United States and all claims referred by Congress and the executive departments.

**United States Court of Customs and Patent Appeals.** This court, created in 1910 to decide certain questions arising under the customs laws, was given jurisdiction in 1929 to review certain patent and trade-mark cases. It reviews decisions of the Customs Court on classifications and duties governing imported merchandise, decisions of the Patent Office on patent applications and interferences, and legal questions on the findings of the Tariff Commission as to unfair practices in import trade.

**United States Customs Court.** This court reviews appraisals of imported merchandise, and all decisions of collectors of customs. As stated, its decisions are subject to review by the United States Court of Customs and Patent Appeals.

## State Courts

**General Pattern.** There is no uniform system of state courts. What is more, there is a confusing variety of nomenclature: the names by which the courts are designated offer no sure guide as to the true status of a particular court with respect to the state's judicial system. Bearing this fact in mind, we may discern a general pattern in the judicial establishments of the different states.

Each state has a court of final appeal, superior courts of general original jurisdiction, inferior courts of original jurisdiction, and courts of special jurisdiction, such as probate courts, land courts, etc. Some states have intermediate courts of appeal, corresponding to the United States courts of appeal.

**Courts of Final Appeal.** Each state has a court of last resort from which there is no appeal except on questions involving the Constitution of the United States (which may be appealed to the Supreme Court of the United States). These courts are generally designated as the Supreme Court of the state, though they are otherwise designated in some of the states.[4]

**Courts of Intermediate Appeal.** In most states, the court of final appeal hears appeals directly from the courts of general original jurisdiction. In some states, however, as in California, Illinois, Indiana, Missouri, New York and Texas, provision is made for a court of intermediate appeal.

**Superior Courts of Original Jurisdiction.** The superior courts of general (statewide) original jurisdiction are usually established on a statewide

---

[4] For example, Court of Appeals in Kentucky, Maryland, and New York, Supreme Court of Errors in Connecticut, Supreme Judicial Court in Maine and Massachusetts, and Supreme Court of Appeals in Virginia and West Virginia.

basis. They are variously known as Superior Court, Circuit Court, District Court, Court of Common Pleas, and even, in some states (for example, New York), as the Supreme Court. It is in these courts that the most important cases are brought. Though statewide, the courts are divided, for the convenience of litigants, into circuits and districts. In some of the more populous states, there is one such court in each county. These courts generally afford equitable as well as legal (common law) relief, though some states, such as Arkansas, Delaware, Mississippi and Vermont, still retain separate chancery courts for the hearing of equity cases. Many of these courts, also, have criminal jurisdiction.

**Inferior Courts.** Best known, perhaps, of our inferior, or minor, courts are the Justices Courts. These are to be found in most townships. They are conducted by justices of the peace with extremely limited jurisdiction over civil cases, such as those involving not more than $100 or $200, and minor violations of the law. In a somewhat higher category are the numerous city and municipal courts established in the larger communities, chiefly for the trial of civil cases involving amounts up to a specified maximum.

**Special Courts.** Every state has special courts of one kind or another. The most common of these are the probate courts, dealing with the estates of deceased persons, guardianships and similar matters. These courts are variously known as probate, orphans', and surrogate's courts. In some states, such jurisdiction is vested in the county courts.

A number of states[5] have a court of claims, similar to the Federal Court of Claims, to try claims against the state. Some states, also, make provision for the registration of land titles, in connection with which land courts are established.

**Criminal Courts.** In some states, jurisdiction over criminal cases is vested in the statewide courts of original jurisdiction; in others, such jurisdiction may lie in special criminal courts; and in still others, such jurisdiction may be given to the county courts, or may be divided between county courts for certain specified crimes and statewide courts for the most serious crimes, such as murder and manslaughter. Minor offenses may be triable before city magistrates and in police courts, in the larger communities, and before justices of the peace in the smaller communities. Such courts may also conduct preliminary hearings on major offenses to determine whether the accused should be released or held for the grand jury.

## Questions

1. Name the usual officers who constitute a court and briefly describe their respective functions.
2. What is meant by a court having jurisdiction?
3. Name five factors that may determine a court's jurisdiction.

---

[5] Examples are Illinois, Michigan, and New York.

4. To what classes of cases does the original jurisdiction of the Supreme Court of the United States extend?

5. Name six classes of cases to which the appellate jurisdiction of the Supreme Court of the United States extends.

6. Describe briefly the jurisdiction and functions of the following Federal courts: (a) United States Court of Appeals; (b) United States District Court; (c) United States Court of Claims; (d) United States Court of Customs and Tax Appeals; (e) United States Customs Court.

7. Name and describe a court of limited jurisdiction found in most townships.

8. All states have courts dealing with the estates of deceased persons. By what name or names are these courts commonly known?

## Problems

1. The State of New York has a claim against the State of New Jersey for money advanced in building a bridge across the Hudson. It desires to litigate the claim. In what court should the suit be brought?

2. The legislature of one of our states adopted a statute last year making it a crime to deal in raw materials directly useful in the manufacture of atomic bombs. George H. Oder, an unsavory character with a long criminal record, is convicted of having dealt extensively in such materials four years ago. His conviction is sustained by the highest court in the state. The question now arises whether Oder has any further remedy? What is your opinion?

3. Dobson sues Earle in the Circuit Court of Florida, a court of original jurisdiction in that state, for a patent infringement. He has complete proof of the validity of his patent and of Earle's infringement. Will he succeed?

4. Two distinguished Senators, each from a different state, have a dispute. Neither wishes to have the case decided in the court of the state represented by the other. They finally decide to submit the dispute to the United States Supreme Court in the first instance. Is that course proper? Explain.

## PART 3. LAWSUITS AND APPEALS

**Summary of Judicial Process.** When one person claims to have been wronged by another, his remedy is to bring the latter into court so that both parties may be heard and the remedy sought either granted or denied. This process involves three stages: (1) Preliminary proceedings before the case gets into court, (2) Court proceedings, and (3) Proceedings after trial to effectuate the judgment. If either party is dissatisfied with the decision of the court, the judicial process may involve a fourth stage, namely, an appeal.

### Preliminary Proceedings

**Service of Process.** The first step in a lawsuit is to bring the defendant into the jurisdiction of the court. This is done by "service of process," whereby the defendant is notified of plaintiff's claim and required to appear in court, either personally or by attorney, to answer the plaintiff's complaint on penalty of having judgment entered against him if he fails to do so. This practice dates back to the early days of the English common law, when a writ, or court order, would be issued under the great seal in the name of the King directing the sheriff of the county where the wrong was allegedly committed to command the defendant to satisfy the plaintiff's claim or appear in court to defend the action. Today, the procedure for starting a civil suit varies in the different states. Some states retain the basic forms of the common law, others have abandoned them in favor of a simplified code, and still others maintain some features of both forms of procedure. As a result, there are three ways in which an action may be started today:

(1) First a writ is filed with the clerk of the court, who issues a summons on the writ and has it served on the defendant by a sheriff or other officer. The writ is then "returned" with a notation that it has been duly served, and on the day fixed for the defendant to appear, the plaintiff's statement of his grievances is filed, so that the defendant or his attorney may inspect, copy and reply to it.

(2) The plaintiff first files a petition, complaint or statement of his claim, accompanied by a request (*praecipe*) for the issuance of a summons, which is then served on defendant by a sheriff or other officer, together with a copy of plaintiff's petition, complaint or statement of claim.

(3) First a summons is issued by the attorney for the plaintiff in his capacity as an officer of the court. The summons is then served on the defendant by any process server, with or without plaintiff's statement of his claim.

**How process may be served.** There are three ways in which a summons may be served: (1) personally, (2) by substitution, and (3) by publication.

(1) *Personal service.* Normally, a summons must be served personally, that is, by handing it to the defendant or by leaving it with him in his presence.

(2) *Substituted service.* Substituted service may be resorted to where the defendant, a resident, is avoiding service so that it cannot be made. On complete proof of such fact, the court may make an order allowing service by leaving one copy of the summons and court order at the defendant's residence, and by mailing him another copy.

(3) *Service by publication.* Service by publication is resorted to only against non-residents. It confers jurisdiction *in rem,* not *in personam;* that is, it is effective only as to the defendant's property located in the state, not as to the defendant himself. If such property amounted to $1,000, a $50,000 judgment based on such service would be collectible only to the amount of $1,000, no matter how much property the defendant had elsewhere. Service by publication must be accompanied by a sheriff's at-

tachment of the defendant's property inside the state. One copy of the summons and court order authorizing such service must be published and another copy mailed, as prescribed in the order.

**Attachment.** The remedy of attachment is employed not only in connection with service by publication on non-residents with property in the state, but also against residents whose conduct may render a subsequent judgment ineffective. In such situations, a sheriff may seize the property at the outset of the suit, to make sure that if a judgment is rendered there will be property in hand to satisfy it. Although the remedy is freely applied in some states, in most states it is regarded as drastic, and allowed against residents only in exceptional situations involving fraudulent conduct designed to defeat the effect of a judgment. For example, to procure an order of attachment against a resident, it is generally necessary to show that the defendant has departed from the state with intent to defraud creditors, or to avoid service, or that he keeps himself concealed with like intent, or that for the purpose of procuring credit, he has made a false statement in writing as to his financial condition.

Attachments may be had in actions for a sum of money only.

**Pleadings.** The "pleadings" are the mutual written assertions and denials by the parties to the action. They are set forth in categorical form so as to raise distinct issues of fact for a trial. They must be pertinent to the issues, and they must spell out a legal wrong or a legal defense, otherwise they may be stricken out on motion by the opposite party.

Under the common law, the pleadings presented a long drawn-out process of mutual statement and counter-statement in an effort to narrow the dispute to a single issue. Today, these pleadings have been greatly simplified. The plaintiff serves and files a categorical statement constituting his *complaint*, or *declaration*. To this, the defendant may enter his *answer*, or *plea*. Such answer or plea may *traverse* or deny the facts alleged by the plaintiff, or it may admit the facts, but allege new facts which would nullify the legal effect of plaintiff's claim, such as that the claim is unenforceable under the statute of frauds (page 85), or barred by the statute of limitations (page 874). The defendant's answer may also set up a counterclaim by the defendant against the plaintiff, to which the plaintiff may enter a *reply*.

**Demurrers and Motions to Dismiss.** If either party takes the position that one or more allegations by the other party, even if true, are legally insufficient, he may *demur* to them (in some jurisdictions), or *move to dismiss* them (in others), with a view to striking out such allegations from the pleadings. Thus, if plaintiff sues for slander, and alleges that defendant spoke defamatory words of plaintiff, without alleging that such words were heard by another person, such allegation, being insufficient in law, may be stricken out on motion, and if it cannot be truthfully alleged that the words *were* heard by another, the case ends then and there.

**Placing Case on Calendar.** Upon the issues presented by the pleadings, either party may have the case placed on the calendar of the court for trial. When the case is reached in due course, the parties are notified and the case proceeds to trial.

## Court Proceedings

**Call of Calendar.** When the court session opens the clerk proceeds to *call the calendar*, that is, to announce the cases awaiting trial in their order. In designating these cases the plaintiff's name appears first, followed by the word *versus* (usually abbreviated *v.*), meaning *against*, followed by the defendant's name. These cases are *answered* by the attorneys for the parties, who either announce that they are ready, or apply for an adjournment or "continuance" on some ground, the sufficiency of which is passed upon the court if the other party is unwilling to consent to the adjournment.

**The Jury.** The constitutional right to a jury trial has already been briefly discussed (page 15). Juries are either *petit* (small) or *grand* (large). A petit jury is usually composed of twelve persons. A grand jury may be composed of any number from twelve to twenty-three. The function of a petit jury is to sit in the trial of a case. The function of a grand jury is to hear criminal charges against individuals and to find true bills of indictment against them if the jury believes a trial should be had.

**Impanelling a Jury.** When a case reaches trial, the judge directs the attorneys to *impanel* a jury, if the trial of the case calls for a jury (as it does in most ordinary law—as distinguished from equity—actions). Citizens are called for jury duty by a writ, known as a *venire*. When the list of jurymen is returned to the court, it is known as a *panel*. To impanel a jury is to draw a jury from the panel to try a given case. The clerk calls the first twelve names from pieces of paper drawn by lot, and the jurymen whose names are called take their seats in the *jury box*. The juryman whose name is first called and accepted is usually the foreman. He presides over the proceedings in the juryroom and announces the jury's verdict.

**Challenges.** In impaneling a jury the attorneys question the jurymen to make sure that they are absolutely impartial. If bias is indicated, a juryman may be excused on a *challenge to the favor*, where the questioning shows that a juryman favors one side or the other, or on a *challenge for cause*, where the questioning shows an obvious disqualification, such as family or business relationship with one side or the other. There is usually no limit to the number of such challenges allowed either party: one is entitled to an *impartial* jury. In addition, either side has a limited number of *peremptory*, or arbitrary, challenges. If all the peremptory challenges have been used up and no bias can be shown, a party must proceed with the jury as impanelled.

**"Opening" to the Jury.** The plaintiff has the affirmative burden of establishing his case. It is he, therefore, who must take the initiative upon the trial. Usually, his attorney "opens" to the jury as soon as it is sworn in, that is, he gives the jury a summary of what he expects to prove by his witnesses. The defendant's attorney may likewise make an opening statement for his side of the case.

**The Testimony.** The testimony of the witnesses is governed by rules of evidence which have been established to ensure justice. These rules are discussed in Part 4 of this chapter. After the opening statements, the plaintiff's attorney calls his witnesses to the stand. These have come to court either voluntarily, or else in response to a *subpoena*. The plaintiff himself may take the stand as a witness on his own behalf. The examination of a witness may be *direct, cross* and *redirect.*

*Direct examination.* The witnesses are not permitted to volunteer testimony, but must respond to direct and specific questions by counsel. The plaintiff presents his case by the testimony of his witnesses on direct examination, and the defendant establishes his defense in the same way.

*Cross-examination.* As each witness finishes his direct examination, the attorney on the other side may cross-examine him to bring out inconsistencies, or testimony favorable to the other side, or else to discredit or destroy the credibility of the witness. Thus the attorney for the defendant may cross-examine the plaintiff's witnesses, and vice versa.

*Redirect examination.* If the attorney for either party believes that the testimony of one of his witnesses has been shaken or weakened by cross-examination, he may re-examine the witness in an effort to re-establish the soundness of his testimony and the merit of his client's position.

*Objections by counsel.* Counsel for either side may object to any question put to the witness by counsel for the other. He may also object to any answer given by the witness. The court may either sustain or overrule the objection, and in the case of an answer already given, the court may direct that the answer be stricken out and that the jury disregard it, though in such case the damage has already been done because the jury has heard the answer and cannot completely forget it. Counsel is required to state the reasons for his objection, otherwise the court may overrule it. Objections by counsel and rulings on them by the court are governed by the rules of evidence.

**"Resting" the Case.** When all the plaintiff's witnesses have been examined and cross-examined, his attorney rests his case by announcing to the court that "plaintiff rests." If all the facts adduced by the plaintiff fail to establish the wrong alleged in his complaint or declaration, the court may dismiss the case on motion by defendant's attorney; otherwise, the defendant must proceed with his witnesses. When the defendant's witnesses have concluded their testimony, the defendant's attorney likewise announces that defendant "rests." If the testimony of the defendant's witnesses leaves no doubt that plaintiff's case is without merit, the court may then and there dismiss the case on motion. Otherwise, he directs counsel to proceed with "summation."

**Summation by Counsel.** Following the testimony on both sides, it is customary for counsel to "sum up" the testimony supporting his client's position. In most jurisdictions, the defendant's attorney sums up first, the plaintiff's attorney having the last word.

**The Judge's Charge.** After the summation, the judge *charges* the jury, that is, he instructs them on the law applicable to the facts disclosed by the testimony. If counsel for either or both parties feel that the judge's charge is insufficient or inadequate in one or more respects, they may request the judge to amplify or qualify his charge accordingly.

**The Jury's Verdict.** Having been instructed by the court, the jury retires to a private room, to deliberate and decide upon a verdict. The jury may decide for the plaintiff, though not necessarily for the full amount sought, or it may decide for the defendant, or it may fail to reach a verdict. When the jury reaches a verdict, the foreman so advises the court attendant, who escorts the jury back to the courtroom, where the verdict is announced in open court.

**Judgment.** A judgment is the official decision of the court, based on the jury's verdict, or if there is no jury, on the law and facts as found by the judge. Such judgment, to be effective, must be *entered*, or filed and recorded by the clerk in the proper book or *docket*. If the judgment calls for the payment of money or the doing of some other act, such money must be paid or such act done, otherwise *execution* may issue or, in an equity case, contempt proceedings may follow.

The person in whose favor a judgment is entered is known as a *judgment creditor*. The person against whom it is entered is known as a *judgment debtor*.

## Proceedings After Trial

**Execution against Property; Levy.** If the judgment debtor fails or refuses to comply with the judgment, a sheriff or marshal may be directed to *execute* the judgment. The sheriff or marshal may thereupon seize or *levy* upon the judgment debtor's property, sell it at public auction, and apply the proceeds in payment of the judgment.

**Execution against Income (Garnishment).** Where a judgment debtor has no property but has income due him, such as salary, wages or dividends, execution may issue against such income. Execution against salary or wages is commonly referred to as *garnishment*, and such proceedings are referred to as *garnishment proceedings*.

**Property Exempt from Execution.** Statutes commonly exempt certain property of a judgment debtor from levy under execution. These statutes vary widely in the different states. Generally, they exempt wearing apparel, the tools of one's trade, livestock, household goods and all but a given fraction (usually 10 per cent) of an employee's wages.

**Supplementary Proceedings.** A sheriff or marshal endeavoring to execute a judgment may be unable to locate any property belonging to the judgment debtor, or any income due him. In such case he returns the execution *nulla bona* ("no goods," or "unsatisfied"). The judgment creditor may then seek to examine the judgment debtor under oath with a view to discovering the existence of property which may be applied in payment of the judgment. Such steps, governed by statute, are referred to as *supplementary proceedings*.

## Appeals

**In General.** We have already referred to the functions of an appellate court (pages 852 to 853). Either party to a lawsuit, if dissatisfied with the decision of the court below, may have it reviewed on appeal. Such review may involve some motion unconnected with the trial of a case, such as a motion directed to the pleadings, or it may involve the trial itself, or the judgment based upon the trial.

**Record on Appeal.** An appellate court hearing numerous appeals cannot be expected to decide a case on oral argument alone. The court must have before it a record of the proceedings which it is to review. The practice in connection with records on appeal is not uniform in the different states. Where the appeal relates to the pleadings only, the record may be confined to such pleadings, and to the decision and opinion of the court below with respect to them, together with copies of any affidavits on which relief was sought. In the case of a trial, the record may consist of a complete stenographic transcript, usually printed, of the testimony and other proceedings on the trial; or it may consist of a more limited digest of so much of the trial proceedings as the appellate court is asked to review. Thus, a case may go up for review on "a bill of exceptions" setting out the rulings, the objections and so much of the testimony as is pertinent to the rulings and objections.

**Briefs of Counsel.** Supplementing the record, the attorneys on appeal are required to submit briefs, also generally printed, setting forth the matters under review and the points of law supporting the respective positions of the parties. Such points of law are supported by the citation of previous cases or precedents favoring the respective positions of the parties. These are woven together by appropriate argument of counsel. In some cases, a court will insist on oral argument; in others, oral argument will not be permitted; and in still others, such argument is optional with counsel.

**Disposition of Appeal.** The appellate court may affirm or reverse the decision appealed from, or it may order a new trial where it is of the opinion that errors were committed which prejudiced the rights of the appellant, or party appealing. Such disposition takes the form of a *decision*, which may or may not be accompanied by an opinion. The decision may be either unanimous, or by a "divided court." In the latter event, opinions may be rendered setting forth the majority and minority views of the court. The majority view only is recognized as the binding opinion of the appellate court.

## Questions

1. What is meant by "service of process"? What is its purpose?
2. Name and describe three ways in which a summons may be served.
3. What is meant by the remedy of attachment? What is its purpose?
4. Does the remedy of attachment apply equally to resident and non-resident defendants?
5. What is meant by the "pleadings"? What is their purpose?
6. What is meant by a demurrer? What is its effect? What similar remedy is employed in some jurisdictions?
7. What is meant by the "call of the calendar"?
8. Distinguish between petit and grand juries.
9. What is meant by (a) a jury panel, and (b) impanelling a jury?
10. Explain the following terms: jury challenge, challenge to the favor, challenge for cause, peremptory challenge.
11. What is meant by "opening to the jury"?
12. What is the difference between a summons and a subpoena?
13. Define: (a) direct examination, (b) cross-examination, (c) redirect examination.
14. Under what circumstances may counsel offer objections during the course of a trial? What must a court do in respect to such objections?
15. What is meant by: (a) "resting" the case, (b) summation, (c) charging the jury?
16. What are the possible results of a jury's deliberation, and who announces the result?
17. What is meant by a judgment? What is its legal effect? What is meant by entering a judgment?
18. Define: (a) judgment creditor, (b) judgment debtor.
19. What is meant by a levy upon execution?
20. Distinguish between execution against property and execution against income. What common term is employed to designate the latter?
21. What property is generally exempt from execution?
22. Describe the process known as supplementary proceedings.
23. What is meant by a record on appeal?
24. Name three possible results of an appeal.

## Problems

1. Burk, a defendant, has left for a vacation in South America. A process server learns of the South American hotel where defendant is stopping, mails him a copy of a summons in an action against him, and on receiving no answer, files an affidavit of service, on which plaintiff enters a judgment by default.

On defendant's return from South America, the sheriff seeks to garnishee his salary in execution of the judgment. What remedy has defendant?

2. You have a simple debt claim against Charles Munson, a resident of your community, but you fear that if you start suit against him, he may put his property beyond the reach of a judgment. You therefore decide to commence suit against Munson by attachment. Can you do so?

3. Baker, a resident of Indiana, owns a small fishing shack on a Wisconsin lake. The property is assessed at $900. You have a claim against Baker for $7,500. Your attorney writes Baker at his place of business in Indianapolis demanding payment, which is refused. You thereupon institute attachment proceedings against Baker, by attaching his fishing shack and serving him thereafter by publication. Baker, who is on vacation in Mexico, puts in no defense. The question now arises whether you may enter up a judgment against Baker for $7,500 and proceed to collect it in Indianapolis. How would you answer this question?

4. Suit is brought against you on a declaration or complaint alleging the following facts: You are the landlord of certain premises. On a given day, Jones, while walking on the sidewalk in front of your premises, slipped and fell, sustaining a fracture of the hip, accompanied by prolonged pain and suffering, and incurring substantial medical and nursing bills, all to his damage in the sum of $25,000, for which he asks judgment against you. Is there any way this suit can be terminated in your favor without a trial? Explain.

5. In the trial of a lawsuit in a given jurisdiction, plaintiff is allowed six peremptory challenges. He uses them up, then discovers that a prospective juror, who has entered the box in the place of the last juror dismissed, is a brother-in-law of defendant. What is plaintiff's position with respect to the jury as now set up?

6. In the trial of a negligence case, plaintiff's attorney asks the defendant on cross-examination, "Weren't you once indicted for bootlegging?" The defendant's attorney objects, but the court refuses to rule one way or another. Has defendant any recourse under the circumstances?

7. Owing to general business conditions, a dentist is unable to collect several large bills due him from patients, and in consequence is unable to pay his own bills. In a suit by one of his creditors, judgment is obtained and execution issued against the dentist. The sheriff is about to levy on the dentist's office equipment. Has the dentist any recourse?

8. Execution is issued on a judgment against Samuel Slick. The sheriff, however, is unable to find any property belonging to Slick. Has the judgment creditor any further remedy? Explain.

### PART 4. EVIDENCE

**Nature of Evidence.** Evidence is the means by which a fact is established. In law, it is the means by which a civil claim or a criminal charge is proved or disproved.

**Rules of Evidence.** In the course of the centuries, the law has evolved certain rules governing the submission of evidence on a trial. The object of these rules is to arrive at the truth of a civil dispute or a criminal charge, in an orderly and expeditious manner, by allowing only such evidence as is pertinent and authentic, and by excluding all other evidence before a jury is allowed to hear and speculate on it. These rules are numerous and somewhat technical to the layman who comes into contact with them in a courtroom and is sometimes bewildered by the objections of counsel to this or that item of testimony. Mainly, these objections concern either the form or the substance of the evidence sought to be adduced.

## Objections as to Form

**In General.** Objections as to form may relate either to the questions asked by counsel, or to the answers given by the witness. Such questions may be ambiguous or confusing, or they may be "leading," or they may call, not for a fact, but for an opinion or conclusion. The answers may likewise be objectionable because they state conclusions instead of facts, or because they are not responsive to the question.

**Ambiguous or Confusing Questions.** A question may be objectionable on the ground that it is ambiguous or confusing, either because it is not precise, or because it combines two or more questions into one, or because it assumes something not yet proved.

EXAMPLES:
(1) Did you see defendant on the day in question, and what was he doing, or if you did not see him on that occasion, when did you see him?
(2) Under what circumstances did you bring this action?
(3) Have you stopped beating your wife?
(4) Were you present when defendant struck plaintiff in the face?

**Leading Questions.** A leading question is one which suggests an answer. With some exceptions, an attorney is not permitted to ask leading questions.

EXAMPLE: Is it a fact that you paid plaintiff $231.85 in cash on the fifteenth of last month?

**Opinions or Conclusions.** A question which calls for, and an answer which gives the witness' conclusion or opinion, instead of facts, is objectionable.[6]

EXAMPLES:
(1) Was plaintiff a person of careless habits?
(2) His manner was quite objectionable.
(3) He was very shrewd in business matters.
(4) Would you say he was negligent in the way he was driving his car?

**Responsiveness.** Counsel is entitled to a direct answer to his question. Evasive or garrulous witnesses who fail to give direct answers may be compelled to do so.

EXAMPLES:
(1) *Question:* Didn't you have a talk with plaintiff's attorney prior to this trial?
   *Answer:* I may and I may not have.

---

[6] Except where "opinion evidence" is allowed (page 872).

(2) *Question:* How deep, would you say, was the water in plaintiff's cellar?

*Answer:* Well, if you were to compare it to the Johnstown flood, I would say it wasn't so deep. I know, because I was in the Johnstown flood. I remember. . . . (At this point, counsel would be justified in moving to strike out the answer as unresponsive, and asking the court to require a direct answer.)

## Objections as to Substance

**In General.** We shall presently consider the different substantial classifications of evidence—direct, circumstantial, documentary, primary, secondary and so forth. Whatever the nature and classification of the evidence offered, it must conform to three requisites as to substance, or it will be open to objection:

(1) It must be relevant.

(2) It must be competent.

(3) It must be material.

**(1) Relevance.** Evidence is relevant if it tends to prove or disprove the fact at issue.[7]

EXAMPLE: On the issue whether a motorist exceeded a super-highway speed limit of 60 miles an hour, his activity as a good citizen would be irrelevant, but the sluggishness of his motor would be relevant.

**(2) Competence.** Evidence may be relevant, but if it lacks competence, it is inadmissible. "By 'competent' evidence is meant that which the very nature of the thing to be proved requires as the fit and appropriate proof in the particular case."[8] Thus, in a breach of contract action, testimony on the contents of a written contract may be relevant, but if the contract itself is available, the testimony will be incompetent and hence inadmissible, because the contract itself will be the proper, or best evidence (page 870).

**(3) Materiality.** As a practical matter, it is not always feasible or desirable to lay before a judge or jury all the facts having any relevance to the issues, however slight. A court must decide what is material as well as relevant, to avoid an unnecessary waste of time. Generally speaking, evidence is material if it goes to the substance of the dispute or has an effective bearing on the outcome.

## Burden of Proof

**Nature of Burden of Proof.** The *burden of proof* is on the party holding the affirmative (usually the plaintiff); that is, he must go forward with enough proof so that if nothing were shown to the contrary, he would win. When he does this, he puts the burden on the defendant. If the de-

---

[7] *Smith v. Lehigh Valley R.R. Co.*, 177 N.Y. 379, 69 N.E. 729.
[8] 31 C.J.S. 505.

fendant fails to meet the burden with equal proof to the contrary, the plaintiff is entitled to judgment. If the defendant meets the burden and the plaintiff fails to present additional proof to outweigh the defendant's, the case is dismissed. In a criminal case, the burden of proof is on the prosecution and remains so throughout the trial.

**What Proof Necessary to Sustain Burden.** The amount of proof necessary to sustain a legal position cannot be fixed except in general terms.

In a civil case, the party having the affirmative sustains the burden if he establishes his case by a "fair preponderance" or "weight" of the evidence. Such preponderance is measured by the quality rather than the quantity of the evidence.

In a criminal case, the prosecution is required to prove the defendant's guilt "beyond a reasonable doubt."

## Things Which Need Not Be Proved

**In General.** There are certain things which require no proof in a court proceeding, among them the following: (1) things which a court or judge will "judicially notice," (2) things which are presumed as a matter of law, and (3) things which are admitted.

**Judicial Notice.** Certain matters of common knowledge need not be proved; the court will take "judicial notice" of them. One does not have to prove, for example, well-known facts in history, or that a well-known public official occupies a well-known public office; the location of streets or avenues in the local community; that whiskey is intoxicating; that there are 12 inches to the foot or 16 ounces to the pound. A court is likewise presumed to know the law of his own jurisdiction.

**Presumptions.** A presumption is an inference justifying a legal conclusion. For example, the unexplained absence of a person from the place of his regular abode for a given period may justify the legal conclusion that he is dead. Presumptions may be *prima facie* or *conclusive*.

*Prima facie presumptions.* A *prima facie* or *rebuttable* presumption is an inference that the law will draw without proof, unless and until the contrary can be shown; for example, that one is presumed to be innocent until proven guilty, or that a letter duly mailed reached its destination.

*Conclusive presumption.* A *conclusive* presumption is one drawn with such finality that the law will accept no proof to the contrary; for example, that a debt is extinguished after a given lapse of time (statute of limitations), or that infants under seven years of age are incapable of crime.

**Admissions.** An admission is a statement made by a party, in the form of a confession, concession or voluntary acknowledgment, in support of a position contended for by the prosecution in a criminal trial, or by an adversary in a civil dispute. The admission may be express (in words), or implied, from some act. It may take the form of a statement made out of court; it may be embodied in a pleading or stipulation; or it may be made by a party on the witness stand or by his attorney in open court.

## Evidence Illegally Obtained

**In General.** Largely because of the Fourth Amendment (page 14), evidence obtained by search and seizure without a warrant cannot be used against a defendant in a Federal proceeding. Thus, if a defendant in a Federal case is accused of burglary and the theft of a diamond bracelet, and a search of his premises without a warrant discloses a burglar's kit and the missing bracelet, such evidence cannot be used against the defendant on the trial. A similar rule prevails in some but not most of the states.

**Wire-tapping.** The Federal Communications Act[9] forbids any "person not authorized by the sender" to intercept a telephone conversation and disclose its contents. The Supreme Court, however, has sustained the admissibility of such evidence in state courts where not prohibited by state statute.[10] Some states restrict but do not prohibit the use of wire-tapped evidence. New York, for example, permits such evidence if obtained under a court order.

## Classifications of Evidence

**Prima Facie Evidence.** Prima facie evidence, as distinguished from *prima facie presumptions*, is evidence which, standing alone, unexplained or uncontradicted, establishes the proposition or conclusion to support which it is introduced. For example, *prima facie* evidence of a debt is evidence which, if not controverted by evidence to the contrary, establishes the existence of the debt.

**Conclusive Evidence.** Conclusive evidence is evidence which is incontrovertible (a) as a matter of law, such as the presumption of ownership from adverse use (page 620), or (b) as a matter of fact, such as evidence from which only one reasonable conclusion can be drawn.

**Direct Evidence.** Direct evidence consists of testimony by persons who saw, heard or sensed the matter in controversy, so that they can testify on direct knowledge. "If, for example, it is desired to ascertain whether the accused has lost his right hand and wears an iron hook in place of it, one source of belief on the subject would be the testimony of witnesses who had seen the arm." [11]

**Indirect or Circumstantial Evidence.** Indirect or circumstantial evidence is evidence which tends to establish a fact, not by direct proof of

---

[9] 15 U.S.C. 21; 47 U.S.C. 35, 151-609.
[10] *Schwartz v. State of Texas*, 344 U.S. 199.
[11] *Wigmore on Evidence*, sec. 1150.

its existence but by indirect proof from which a logical inference may be drawn. To use Wigmore's illustration again, the mark of the hook on something carried by the accused would furnish circumstantial evidence that the accused wore a hook in place of his hand.

**Real Evidence.** Real evidence is that derived from personal observation by the court and jury. Again using Wigmore's illustration, if the jury inspected the accused's arm and saw the hook, this would constitute real evidence.

**Privileged Communications.** Because of their peculiarly confidential relationships, certain parties are made incompetent by law to testify as to "privileged" communications between them.

*Attorney and client.* An attorney or counsellor at law is not allowed to disclose a communication made to him by his client or his advice to the client thereon. This includes any clerk, stenographer or other person employed by the attorney, such as an interpreter. The client, however, may waive this privilege, and if he does, the attorney may be compelled to testify.

*Physician and patient.* Physicians are forbidden to disclose information acquired in a professional capacity, unless the patient waives the privilege.

*Clergyman and penitent.* Confessions or admissions made to a clergyman or priest in his professional capacity are privileged. (Some states refuse to recognize this privilege.)

*Husband and wife.* At common law, the husband or wife of a party to an action was wholly incompetent to testify as a witness. Statutes have largely qualified this rule. Husband and wife may now generally testify for or against each other except as to confidential matters between them. Neither may testify against the other in divorce actions except to prove the marriage or to disprove accusations or defenses to accusations.

**Communications Not Privileged.** The mere fact that a communication is imparted in confidence does not make it privileged. Hence confidential information imparted to or acquired by bookkeepers, detectives, merchants, bankers, agents, copartners or business employees generally cannot be refused on the witness stand, though to disclose it voluntarily might constitute a breach of contract or breach of faith. "No pledge of privacy nor of secrecy can avail against the demand for truth in a court of justice." [12]

*Newspaper editors and reporters.* "The rule of privileged communications does not apply to communications to a newspaper editor or reporter, for, although there is a canon of journalistic ethics forbidding the disclosure of a newspaper's source of information, it is subject to qualification and must yield when in conflict with the interests of justice. Accordingly, a witness before the grand jury on a complaint for libel published in a newspaper may be required to disclose the name of the writer, which

---

[12] *Ibid.*, sec. 2286.

he admits he knows, over the objection that it is an office regulation that the editors of the paper are not to give the name of the writer of articles published in it." [13]

*Accountants.* Under the common law (that is, in the absence of statute), there is no privilege with regard to communications made to an accountant. "The information given to the witness and to the accountants in his employ for the purpose of making financial statements and doing other work characteristically performed by accountants is not privileged, despite the fact that the witness may also have rendered legal advice on the basis of such data." [14] However, in some states communications to accountants in their confidential capacity have been made privileged by statute. In Illinois the statute provides: "A public accountant shall not be required by any court to divulge information which has been obtained by him in his confidential capacity as a public accountant." [15] Other states which have adopted similar statutes are: Colorado, Florida, Iowa, Maryland and New Mexico.[16]

**Primary or Best Evidence.** Primary evidence is the best evidence of which a case, in its nature, is susceptible.[17] If a witness is personally available for testimony, his own direct testimony on a pertinent fact is the best evidence. A writing itself is the primary or best evidence of its contents.

*Best evidence rule.* Testimony on the contents of a document is inadmissible if the document is available, because the document itself is the best evidence.

EXAMPLE: A party sues for trespass in cutting down his trees. If he is asked, on direct examination, "Do you own the farm?" the question is objectionable because the deed to the farm is the best evidence. Whenever it becomes necessary to prove the contents of a document, it must be produced or its absence accounted for.

**Secondary Evidence.** If a witness is not personally available for testimony, as in a case where he resides outside the jurisdiction or is dead, secondary evidence may be used; as, in the case of nonresidents, depositions properly taken, or, in the case of a deceased person, testimony by another (not interested in the event) on what such deceased person had said that is competent and material to the issue. If it can be proved that

---

[13] 70 C.J. 377-8.

[14] *In re Fisher*, 51 Fed. (2d) 424, 425.

[15] Illinois Revised Statutes, Ch. 110½, sec. 51, as amended July 22, 1943.

[16] In 1938, a Committee of the American Bar Association on Improvements in the Law of Evidence recommended "that the legislatures refuse to create any new privileges for secrecy of communications in any occupation; and particularly we recommend against any further recognition of (A) Privilege for information obtained by *Accountants;* (B) Privilege for information obtained by *Social Workers;* (C) Privilege for information obtained by *Journalists*."

[17] *Landon v. Morehead*, 34 Okl. 701, 126 P. 1027, 1032.

an original writing is lost, destroyed, or physically unavailable, secondary evidence of its contents is admissible, either by producing a copy with proof that it corresponds to the original or by oral testimony on the contents of the original writing.

**Hearsay Evidence.** Hearsay evidence is evidence on a fact based, not on the witness's own knowledge or observation of the fact, but on what someone else told him about it. Such evidence is objectionable because it cannot be tested by oath or cross-examination. The witness cannot swear or respond on cross-examination as to the truth of the alleged fact, but only as to the truth of someone having told him about it; for example, in the suit for trespass previously referred to, if the question were asked, "Did you see the defendant chop down the trees?" the answer, "No, but my wife saw it and told me about it" would have to be stricken out as hearsay.

*Exceptions to hearsay evidence rule: "res gestae."* There are numerous exceptions to the hearsay evidence rule. These are mostly based on the *res gestae* doctrine, that words spoken or written about an event, and so soon after it that there was no time to fabricate, may be regarded as part of the event itself, so that, though hearsay, they may be testified to by another as evidence of the fact.

EXAMPLE: On a trial for the murder of a man shot in church from the outside, the deceased, looking out of the window, was heard to say just before he was shot that the defendant "is outside there, fixing to shoot me." Testimony as to these words, though hearsay, was admissible as part of the *res gestae*.[18]

Other exceptions to the hearsay rule are confessions, admissions against interest and the declarations of a testator. Exceptions of particular interest to students of business law include: book entries, statistical tables, charts and analyses, and expert testimony.

*Book entries: the shop book rule.* Declarations in the form of book entries are hearsay, but when made in the regular course of business they carry some presumption that they reflect the facts they record. Such a presumption is of course *prima facie* only: subject to rebuttal.

This rule of evidence is known as "the shop book rule." It is hedged about by a variety of conditions, some of which have been retained in some states, dropped in others. Basically, in order that a book entry or record may be accepted as evidence of the fact recorded, it must be shown that it was made in the regular course of the business, profession or calling concerned, and that it was the regular practice to make such book entry or record at the time of the act recorded or within a reasonable time thereafter.

*Statistical tables.* Standard statistical tables commonly accepted as au-

---

[18] *Means v. State*, 10 Tex. A. 16.

thentic may be admissible as proof of the facts therein tabulated. Examples are mortality tables, stock exchange quotations, census tables, and so on.[19]

*Charts and analyses.* As an aid to the court, statistical charts and analyses of properly established facts are frequently admitted into evidence, provided a proper foundation is laid for their admissibility, showing how they were prepared, who prepared and checked them, and so on.

*Opinion evidence: expert testimony.* Ordinarily, a witness may testify on facts only; his opinions are inadmissible. However, an important exception is furnished in the case of experts, who may either (a) testify to specialized facts only and let the jury draw its own conclusions or (b) testify to specialized facts and give their expert conclusions as well. The latter category includes testimony by doctors, lawyers, certified public accountants, scientists, engineers, merchants with knowledge of values, fingerprint and handwriting experts, and all persons generally who possess specialized knowledge of the subject under inquiry.

*Qualifying the expert.* The attorney who puts an expert on the stand must first "qualify" him, that is, ask questions the answers to which will show that the witness is qualified to testify as an expert. A medical expert, for example, will be examined on his education, training, and experience. An accountant will show that he has been duly certified by an official examining board.

*Hypothetical questions.* Experts are not called to testify upon the particular facts of a case, but upon their opinion on an assumed state of facts, which must have some relevance to the facts under inquiry. Such testimony is elicited by putting a *hypothetical question* to the witness reflecting the facts which counsel assumes to have been proved on the trial and then asking the expert his opinion on such an assumed state of facts.

## Questions

1. Give a short definition of evidence as used in the law.
2. You are asked to explain in simple terms the basic purpose underlying the rules of evidence. How would you explain it?
3. In the course of a protracted trial numerous questions were objected to because of their form, and numerous other objections were interposed as to substance. Name five types of questions objectionable as to form, and three types objectionable as to substance.
4. Give an illustration of a question objectionable on the following grounds: (a) It is ambiguous or confusing, (b) It is leading, (c) It calls for an opinion or conclusion, (d) It is not responsive.
5. Give an illustration of a question objectionable on the following grounds: (a) It is not relevant, (b) It is not competent, (c) It is not material.
6. What is meant by the burden of proof?

---

[19] In a recent case, the author introduced in evidence a statistical compilation showing relative popularity ratings of different types of radio programs, taken from a standard statistical publication commonly used in radio advertising.

7. Distinguish between the evidence required to establish the plaintiff's case in a civil suit, and the prosecution's case in a criminal proceeding.

8. Name and explain three things which need not be proved.

9. Distinguish between a prima facie and a conclusive presumption.

10. To what extent may evidence illegally obtained be used in a criminal prosecution?

11. Explain and illustrate the following types of evidence: (a) prima facie, (b) conclusive, (c) direct, (d) indirect or circumstantial, (e) real, (f) primary or best, (g) secondary, and (h) hearsay.

12. In the law of evidence, what is meant by a privileged communication? Give four classes of such communications.

13. Give five illustrations of communications which are not privileged.

14. Name and explain four types of exceptions to the hearsay evidence rule.

## Problems

1. State which of the following questions or statements on a trial are admissible and which objectionable, and in the latter cases, state the grounds on which they are objectionable:

(a) "Would you say he was driving cautiously, or recklessly?"

(b) "He appeared to be quite excited."

(c) "Did defendant admit to you that he had borrowed $50 from you on two separate occasions?"

(d) "State the circumstances under which you met defendant, and how did he impress you when you first met him; also what conversation you had with him or any of his associates prior to last Tuesday."

(e) "Q. Didn't you discuss this matter with plaintiff yesterday? A. Possibly."

(f) (In an action for goods sold and delivered:) "Didn't you have a quarrel with defendant prior to commencing suit?"

(g) "Mr. Defendant, I show you this copy of an agreement between you and plaintiff, the original of which, I regret to say, I left in my office, and I ask you if this is not a correct copy of such agreement."

(h) I show you a paper and ask if that is not your signature at the bottom of the paper. (The paper is a letter from plaintiff to defendant, admitting payment of a debt for which defendant is now suing.)

(i) After plaintiff is sworn and has stated his name and address, plaintiff's attorney asks him, "Are you the plaintiff in this action?"

(j) "Q. Will you state positively that this is not your handwriting? A. I'm not a handwriting expert."

(k) "Q. How come you remember mailing this letter a year ago, out of thousands mailed by you since? A. My lawyer told me at the time to be sure to remember it because some fool lawyer might ask me about it some day on the witness stand."

2. In an action on a promissory note, there is conflicting testimony as to whether the note was actually delivered. The Court charges the jury that if they find that the plaintiff has established his case beyond a reasonable doubt, they must find for plaintiff, otherwise for defendant. Plaintiff's attorney excepts to the charge. The jury finds for the defendant. Plaintiff appeals. How will the appellate court decide?

3. In an action for breach of contract, defendant moves to dismiss because the contract called for work on the Fourth of July. The court denied the motion and defendant appealed. In argument on appeal, it was admitted by plaintiff that the statute of the state in question made contracts illegal if they

called for performance on a legal holiday, but plaintiff pointed out that no proof was offered that the Fourth of July was a legal holiday. How did the appellate court decide?

4. Defendant in a Federal case is accused of the theft of a diamond ring, which was found in defendant's bedroom by a detective who searched the premises one night during defendant's absence. On the trial, defendant objects when the assistant United States attorney offers the ring in evidence, on the ground that such evidence, obtained without a search warrant, was inadmissible. How should the court rule?

5. A bookkeeper is entrusted by the head of a firm with secret information relating to profits on a highly competitive item. A former employee sues the firm for a share of the profits based on an agreement, and serves a subpoena on the bookkeeper, requiring him to testify in reference to the profits of the firm, including the secretly imparted information. The firm's attorney objects. How will the court rule?

6. In a boundary dispute, the plaintiff starts describing his boundary lines, while refreshing his memory from a copy of the deed, the original of which is in his safe. Defendant's attorney objects. How should the court rule?

7. Plaintiff sues defendant for goods sold and delivered. Plaintiff's delivery boy is in the military service, hence is not available. Plaintiff therefore offers, through his bookkeeper, to introduce his sales record as proof of the transaction. The record is based on entries made by the bookkeeper at the time defendant's order was filled. Defendant's attorney objects on the ground that the evidence is hearsay. How should the court rule?

8. In a suit for damages based on the collapse of a bridge, plaintiff put a well known bridge engineer on the stand, questioned him as to his experience, and asked him whether a bridge under certain specified conditions might not be likely to collapse. The question is objected to as calling for a conclusion. How should the court rule?

## PART 5. BARS TO RECOVERY

**In General.** One may be wronged, yet have no remedy under certain circumstances where the law raises a bar to recovery. Remedies may be barred where one waits too long to seek redress, as in a case where a suit is barred by a *statute of limitations* or by *laches;* or where the suit is inconsistent with prior conduct, as in the case of *estoppel;* or where a statute bars or postpones a remedy to provide relief to a debtor in a public emergency, as in the case of a *moratorium.*

### Statute of Limitations

**Definition and Object.** The "statute of limitations" is really a collection of statutory provisions, fixing a limited period of time within which to sue. Upon the expiration of such period, a cause of action is said to be "outlawed." The object of statutes of limitation is to expedite the prosecution of legitimate causes of action and to discourage the bringing of stale claims. The theory underlying such statutes is that it is the general experience of mankind that claims which are valid are not usually allowed to remain neglected, and that a lapse of years, without any attempt to enforce a demand, creates a presumption against its original validity, or that it has ceased to exist. Furthermore, the neglect of a plaintiff is advanced as an additional ground for barring him from enforcing his remedy. The basic principle on which such statutes are most generally justified is that they tend to prevent fraudulent and stale claims from springing up at great distances of time and surprising parties or their representatives, when all the proper vouchers or evidences which might be introduced in defense of the claim, or the facts which might bear upon the claim, have become obscure. Under such circumstances, such factors as lapse of time, defective memory, death, or removal of witnesses might constitute serious impediments to justice.

**Statutory Period.** The period of the statute of limitations varies with the type of action and the state having jurisdiction. It would be impracticable to list here the numerous variations in the different states or the different types of actions involving different periods in the different states. The most common period for open accounts, promissory notes and contracts generally is six years. Some states allow only a three-year period on open accounts. Many states allow 10 or even 20 years on contracts under seal, although many others have dropped the common law distinction between ordinary contracts and contracts under seal. Some states distinguish between written and oral contracts, allowing a shorter period for the latter.

*Torts.* Statutes of limitations governing torts are usually for a lesser period than for contracts. A common period is three years, with an even lesser period for some types of torts, such as malpractice (page 404).

*Federal statutes: tax delinquencies.* In addition to the state statutes of limitations, various statutory periods are provided by Federal law. For example, the statute of limitations on Federal Income Tax assessments, or for a proceeding in court without an assessment, is three years from the date when the return was filed. The statutory period for a proceeding in court or for a *distraint* (seizure of personal property) *after* an assessment has been made is six years additional. In case of a false or fraudulent return, or no return at all, the statutory period is "suspended" (does not run).

*Criminal prosecutions.* Generally, time does not run against prosecutions for murder, kidnapping or embezzlement of public moneys. For other felonies, the period varies from three to five years. For misdemeanors, it is generally one or two years from the time the act was committed.

**When Statutory Period Starts.** The period of the statute of limitations starts to run when a cause of action "accrues" (that is, when one's right to sue begins). This, in a debt action, is the date when the debt is due and unpaid; in an action on contract, when the breach occurs; in a fraud action, when the fraud was or should have been discovered; in a tort action, when the tort is committed.

*Promissory notes.* In an action on an ordinary promissory note (page 148) due at some future time, the statute starts to run, not from the date of the note, but from the date of its maturity.

*Demand notes.* A demand note (page 139) is due forthwith. The statute of limitations begins to run from the date of the note. This is the prevailing rule throughout the country.[20]

**Suspending the Statute of Limitations.** Factors which suspend the statutory period are: (a) disability of the plaintiff to sue (such as infancy or insanity) and (b) absence of the defendant from the jurisdiction so that he is not amenable to process. In the former case, it would be unjust to count time against one unable to sue, and in the latter, to wipe out a debt in favor of one who placed himself in a position where he could not be sued.

**Tolling the Statute of Limitations.** To "toll" the statute of limitations is to start it running all over again, though the entire period or some part of it has already run. Factors which will toll the statute are: (1) Written acknowledgment, and (2) Payment on account.

(1) *Written acknowledgment.* A written acknowledgment of the debt, from which the inference of a new promise to pay may be drawn, revives the statute for the full period, starting with the date of the acknowledgment. But such acknowledgment must contain nothing inconsistent with the debtor's intention to pay. If it is accompanied by a refusal to pay, or by the contention, "The claim is outlawed, so you can't collect," or a declaration of unwillingness or inability to pay, or an offer to compromise, it will not toll the statute. The effect of a written acknowledgment in reviving the debt is not dependent on consideration.

(2) *Payment on account.* Payment on account, either of principal or interest, from which a promise to pay the debt may be implied, revives the debt. Thus, payment of interest by the maker of a promissory note tolls the statute anew against the *maker*[21] but *not against an indorser,* unless he has authorized or consented to such payment.[22]

**Claims Not Barred by Statute of Limitations.** Certain claims are not subject to the statute of limitations, including, among others:

(a) An action upon a bill, note or other evidence of debt circulating as money.

(b) An action brought by the Federal Government, or by a state, except where the government specifically prescribes a time limit.

(c) Enforcement of an existing property right or lien. For example, if I own a diamond ring, your possession of it for more than six years will

---

[20] 10 *C.J.S.* 744.
[21] *Stevens v. Lord,* 84 Hun 353, aff'd 146 N.Y. 398.
[22] *McMullen v. Rafferty,* 89 N.Y. 456.

not defeat my title; or if I pledged it with you more than six years ago, you would still have the right to foreclose.[23]

(d) Federal Income Tax delinquencies, where a false or fraudulent return, or no return at all, is filed.

(e) Prosecutions for murder, kidnapping, or embezzlement of public moneys.

## Laches

**Basis of Laches.** Where a person delays in bringing suit, but the delay does not equal the period of the statute of limitations, a court of equity may yet hold that the claimant was guilty of unreasonable delay in pursuing his remedy, and may thus bar the claimant by reason of such delay, or *laches*. The underlying basis of laches is the inequity that may result to a defendant from delay in bringing suit. "A person may not withhold his claim awaiting the outcome of a doubtful enterprise and, after the enterprise has resulted in financial success favorable to the claimant, assert his interest, especially where he has thus avoided the risks of the enterprise." [24]

To plead laches, one must show that he has suffered some prejudice by the delay.

## Estoppel

**Basis and Classification.** We have already observed the principle of estoppel as applied to agency (page 399), partnerships (page 464) and corporations (page 503). There are many cases where one wronged is not guilty of delay in seeking redress, yet is barred or *estopped* from bringing suit by reason of previous conduct. Estoppel thus operates as a bar to prevent a person from taking a position inconsistent with one he has previously taken, where such inconsistency will work an injustice to an innocent person who relied on the position previously taken.

Three kinds of estoppel are: (1) equitable estoppel, (2) estoppel by judicial record, (3) estoppel by deed.

**Equitable Estoppel.** *Equitable estoppel* (estoppel *in pais*) is one raised against a person who, having taken a given position (by assertion, denial, or failure to speak when there was a duty to speak), will not be allowed to reverse his position in such a way as to injure a person who relied on the position previously taken. It is this type of estoppel on which ostensible agencies, partnerships and corporations are based.

**Estoppel by Judicial Record.** Where a person sues on one theory on

[23] *Conway v. Caswell*, 121 Ga. 254, 48 S.E. 956; *Pollack v. Smith*, 107 Ky. 509, 54 S.W. 740; *Townsend v. Tyndale*, 165 Mass. 293, 43 N.E. 107; *U.S. v. Mercantile Trust Co.*, 213 Pa. 411; *Connecticut Mut. L. Ins. Co. v. Dunscomb*, 108 Tenn. 724; *Goldfrank v. Young*, 64 Tex. 432; *Roots v. Mason City Salt Min. Co.*, 27 W.Va. 483.
[24] *Alexander v. Phillips Petroleum Co.*, 130 F. 2d 593.

which a judgment is entered and later seeks to proceed on another theory contrary to the judgment, he will be estopped from doing so by the prior judgment. A judicial record "imports absolute verity, and all parties thereto are estopped from denying its truth." [25] For example, after a judgment is rendered, the facts established thereby may not be denied by any party to the action, except by way of appeal. Other examples are: admissions by a party in court;[26] agreed facts upon the basis of which a trial is had; stipulations of counsel; and affidavits made by a party to a judicial proceeding (which the affiant, or party making the affidavit, is not later allowed to deny).

**Estoppel by Deed.** Estoppel by deed exists where a person recites certain facts, assurances or covenants in a deed, which he later seeks to dispute.

EXAMPLE: I sell you a house, which I do not own. I give you a full covenant and warranty deed, in which I warrant, among other things, that I have title. You take possession. Later, I obtain actual title from the true owner, who gives me a deed so that I become the true owner. I then seek to eject you on the ground that I am now the true owner, and you are not. My ejectment proceedings would fail: I would be estopped by my prior deed from now disputing what I formerly warranted, namely, that when I sold you the property, I was then the true owner.

A person who invokes the doctrine of estoppel must show that he has been misled by the prior representation and that he will be damaged if the person who made it is permitted to reverse himself.[27]

## Moratoria

**Definition and Legal Basis.** A moratorium is a suspension of legal remedies against debtors, usually authorized by law in times of emergency or financial distress. Though the Constitution of the United States provides that no state may pass a law impairing the obligation of contracts (which include debts), such constitutional provision is subject to the implied reservation of state sovereignty and its inherent power to protect itself in times of emergency, commonly known as the "police power" (pages 13 and 570). Among the more noteworthy examples of moratorium laws in this country are the statutory restrictions on mortgage foreclosures during the financial depression of the 1930's and Federal legislation barring actions against soldiers and sailors on active duty.

---

[25] 21 C.J. 1064.

[26] *New Jersey Suburban Water Co. v. Town of Harrison,* 122 N.J. Law 189, 3 A. 2d 623.

[27] *Mitchell v. Friedlander,* 246 Ala. 115, 19 So. 2d 394; *Frost Motor Co. v. Pierce,* 72 Ga. App. 447, 33 S.E. 2d 910; *Corn Belt Bank v. Baker,* 190 Okl. 278, 122 P. 2d 989.

## Questions

1. Define the nature and object of a statute of limitations.
2. Generally speaking, when does the period of a statute of limitations begin? How would you apply this rule (a) to a debt action, (b) to an action on contract, (c) to an action based on fraud, (d) to a tort action, (e) to an action on a time note, and (f) to an action on a demand note?
3. What two factors may suspend the operation of a statute of limitations?
4. (a) What is meant by "tolling" the statute of limitations? (b) What two factors may toll the statute?
5. Name three classes of claims or prosecutions that are not barred by the statute of limitations.
6. Define laches and explain its underlying basis.
7. What is the underlying basis for the doctrine of estoppel?
8. Explain and illustrate (a) equitable estoppel; (b) estoppel by judicial record; (c) estoppel by deed.
9. In addition to the underlying basis for estoppel, what must a person show to invoke the doctrine of estoppel in respect to himself?
10. Define and explain the legal basis for a moratorium.

## Problems

1. Dole borrowed money from Kent, and for a period of six years kept promising to repay it, though Kent never demanded the money until a year after the expiration of the six-year period. At that time, Dole refused to pay, and when sued, set up the defense that the six-year statute of limitations on debt actions in his state had outlawed the claim. Kent's position is that the debt did not become due and the statute did not start to run until he demanded the money. Who is right?
2. Arthur loans Bates $500. Bates gives Arthur two notes to evidence the loan, one due on demand, the other a year after date. Six and a half years later the notes remained unpaid and Arthur sues on both of them. Assuming that the statute of limitations in the jurisdiction is six years, may Arthur recover if Bates sets up the statute of limitations as a defense?
3. Colonel Hill, about to leave on a foreign mission, executes a power of attorney to Bronson, authorizing Bronson to sell Colonel Hill's house for not less than $25,000, and to deliver a deed to the house in the Colonel's name. Bronson sells the house for $30,000, but reports to the Colonel that the price was $25,000, and retains the difference. Colonel Hill does not discover the facts until seven years later, when he sues Bronson for $5,000 plus interest. Bronson's defense is that the applicable six-year statute of limitations has expired. Who wins and why?
4. Dr. Leland performs a surgical operation on Mrs. Peabody for an internal ailment. Mrs. Peabody continues to ail for several years thereafter, when she dies. An autopsy discloses the presence of a pair of surgical scissors in Mrs. Peabody's abdomen. Her estate sues Dr. Leland for malpractice, and the surgeon's defense is that the two-year statute applicable to malpractice actions in that state has expired. How will the court decide?
5. Eight years ago, Watson breached an important contract with you, causing you substantial damage. Shortly thereafter Watson left for South America, returning about a month ago. You immediately brought suit against

Watson, whose defense now is the statute of limitations. Assuming that the period of the statute in your jurisdiction is six years, have you any remedy?

6. Three prisoners at the dock, charged respectively with murder, kidnaping, and embezzlement of public funds, have retained attorneys. All three have entered pleas of the statute of limitations. Will the pleas be sustained?

7. A western landowner sells a parcel of undeveloped land by reference to a map. The parcel is designated as Parcel A on the map, and is so referred to in the deed. Actually, the parcel intended to be sold was Parcel B, regarded as a more valuable parcel. The seller discovers the error, but decides to do nothing about it. Three years later, Parcel A is discovered to contain valuable ore. The seller promptly moves for reformation, to rectify the error. The buyer opposes. How will the court decide?

8. Brown bids at a public auction for various lots acquired by a city through foreclosure of a tax lien. Later, Brown's attorney advises Brown that the tax lien proceedings were defective for failure to serve foreclosure papers on a mortgagee, and that the title acquired by Brown was questionable. Brown later conveys the lot to Graham by warranty deed. Thereafter Brown has his attorney obtain an assignment of mortgage from the mortgagee who had not been served in the tax lien foreclosure proceedings, and thereupon, as assignee of the mortgage, starts a mortgage foreclosure proceeding against Graham. What remedy has Graham?

## COURT CASES FOR REVIEW

### How Did the Court Decide, and Why?

1. Crawford was driving along the road with a load of meat when a neighbor overtook him, demanded some meat, and without waiting for a reply, started to help himself. Crawford tried to snatch the meat back; the neighbor made a pass at Crawford with his knife; and Crawford picked up a heavy fence rail, hit the neighbor on the head with it, and inflicted a blow from which the neighbor died. At the trial Crawford pleaded self-defense. The prosecution, while admitting that Crawford was entitled to resist the taking, contended that since the meat was already taken, Crawford had no right to use the force he did to get the meat back; that in so doing, he was not exercising his right of self-defense. *Crawford v. State*, 90 Ga. 701, 17 S.E. 628.

2. Plaintiff, claiming an undivided interest in an automobile with defendant, sued the latter in conversion. He sought attachment under a statute providing that a warrant of attachment may be procured by showing that defendant is about to remove his property from the state with intent to defraud creditors. The affidavit on which he sought attachment set forth that defendant had stated to plaintiff that he intended to move to Texas, where his sister resided, and to take his automobile with him. *Brush v. Brush*, 111 N.Y. Supp. 2d 715.

3. In a will contest brought in the Federal District Court, it was conceded that the parties were residents of different states, yet it was contended that the court was without jurisdiction. *Mitchell v. Nixon*, 200 F. 2d 50.

4. The accused was convicted under a statute declaring that a person is guilty of bigamy if he or she has a spouse living, and either marries another spouse, or lives with him or her as such within the state. The state proved that the accused entered into a second marriage in a sister state, but there was no evidence that he had lived with his second wife within the state where he was convicted. The accused appealed on the ground that the court had no jurisdiction. *Willis v. State*, 63 So. 2d 184.

5. A non-resident came into the state as a witness in a trial. He was served

with a summons in the state where he attended the trial, six days after the trial was completed. He sought to have the process set aside on the ground that a person cannot be served with process in a given state if, as a non-resident, he comes into the state as a necessary party or witness. *McKinney v. Northwest Tractor & Equipment*, 249 P. 2d 401 (Wash.).

6. In a burglary prosecution, the attorney for the defendant, not wanting to use up his peremptory challenges, challenged a prospective juror for cause on the following ground: The prospective juror had stated that his place of business had been robbed four times, though he added that this would not create any prejudice against the defendant. The court rejected the attorney's challenge, and defendant appealed. *State v. Martinz*, 220 La. 899, 57 So. 2d 888.

7. Plaintiff's attorney, in an action arising out of an automobile accident, requested the court, prior to examining the jury, to require disclosure by the defense attorney of the name of the liability insurance company involved but not named as a defendant, so as to allow plaintiff's attorney to ask the jury both as a whole, and individually, whether they, or any of them, were employed by, or interested in, any insurance company issuing liability policies, and to ask each juror whether he or his wife carried liability insurance on their automobile. The request was denied. Plaintiff's attorney took an exception and appealed. *Dunipace v. Martin*, 73 Ariz. 415, 242 P. 2d 543.

8. Counsel in defending an action against the City for personal injuries stated to the jury, in effect, that any money awarded plaintiff would have to come out of taxes. This comment was objected to by plaintiff's counsel as prejudicial. *Williams v. City of Anniston*, 257 Ala. 191, 58 So. 2d 115.

9. In his suit against the defendant, plaintiff's pleading, without going into any factual detail, merely alleged that the defendant had exercised undue influence over the plaintiff. The question arose as to whether this pleading was sufficient to create a triable issue. *Federman v. Stanwyck*, 108 N.E. 2d 333, aff'd 108 N.E. 2d 339.

10. In an action against a railroad for a motorist's death, counsel for the administratrix argued that if it were clear that the motorist was at fault, as the railroad claimed, the jury would not be sitting in court listening to counsel arguing the case. This comment was challenged as prejudicial, improper, and ground for appeal. *Fissette v. Boston & Maine R.R. Co.*, 96 A. 2d 303.

11. Plaintiff sued to enjoin a sheriff's sale of personal property taken from plaintiff's possession under the following circumstances: An execution had been issued to the sheriff under a judgment against the plaintiff. The sheriff, in making his levy, entered the plaintiff's home—by force, according to the plaintiff, peaceably according to the sheriff and as found by the trial judge. On appeal, the court affirmed the finding of the court below, then drew a distinction between what the sheriff could do in getting into the house, and what he could do once he got in. What was the distinction? *Vanden Bogert v. May*, 334 Mich. 606, 55 N.W. 2d 115.

12. In the course of a trial the question arose as to whether it was necessary to prove the following facts: (1) That the year 1932 and succeeding years (prior to World War II) were marked by a financial depression, during which lands generally were not readily marketable; and (2) That a particular tract of land was not desirable at a specified time. *Ramsey v. Ramsey*, 253 S.W. 2d 219 (Ark.).

13. A witness for defendant sought to testify with reference to a purported telephone conversation with plaintiff's agent. The testimony was objected to on two grounds: (1) Conversations over the telephone are not competent, and (2) It was not established that the party in question was plaintiff's agent or had

authority to act for plaintiff. *Linch v. Carlson,* 156 Neb. 308, 56 N.W. 2d 101.

14. In an action for damages from a head-on collision of trucks to which there were no living eye witnesses, the evidence consisted substantially of testimony by an expert based upon inferences drawn from tire marks, measurements, positions of the trucks after the collision, and so forth. This testimony was attacked as incompetent. *Phoenix Refining Co. v. Powell,* 251 S.W. 2d 892 (Tex. Civ. App.).

15. The owner of land subject to a mortgage gave a deed to his mineral rights in the land, subject to the rights of a mortgagee. The mineral grant contained unconditional covenants of warranty. Later, the mortgage was foreclosed, and the grantor of the mineral rights, having acquired title from the purchaser at the foreclosure sale, claimed full rights in the land, including the mineral rights which he had previously granted, on the ground that he had acquired all the rights of the mortgagee, to which the mineral rights had been subject. *Triangle Royalty Corp. v. Graves,* 242 P. 2d 740 (Okla.).

16. The following questions arose upon prosecution of the defendant for liquor violations:

(a) Whether proof that a beverage did not exceed 3.2 per cent by weight in alcoholic content would be automatically accepted by the court as proof that it contained no more than the statutory 0.5 per cent by volume under an existing law,

(b) Whether the court would take judicial notice that moonshine is unlawfully manufactured whiskey,

(c) Whether the court would take judicial notice that beer is a fermented liquor,

(d) Whether the court would take judicial notice that a beverage has a certain alcoholic content upon proof that it is beer. *State v. Henry,* 254 S.W. 2d 307 (Mo.).

17. On cross-examination of a witness, certain questions were asked without objection. On appeal, counsel for the first time argued that the questions were not properly within the scope of cross examination. *People v. Coleman,* 256 P. 2d 338 (Calif.).

18. Defendants were prosecuted for conspiracy to violate the Espionage Act by communicating to the Union of Soviet Socialist Republics various documents, writings, sketches, notes and other information relating to the national defense of the United States, with intent and reason to believe that it would be used to the advantage of the Soviet Union. Evidence was offered that the defendants had expressed a preference for Russian social and economic organization over that of this country. This evidence was objected to on the ground that it was incompetent and irrelevant. Defendants also objected on the same ground to testimony by a witness that the American Communist Party was part of and subject to the Communist International, that said party received orders from Russia to propagandize, spy, and sabotage, and that party members were compelled to go along with such orders. *United States v. Rosenberg,* 195 F. 2d 583.

19. Suit was instituted in 1951 to recover for services rendered during the period from 1946 to 1948, to decedent who died in 1950. Suit was based on the decedent's promise that the claimant would be taken care of for her services at deceased's death. It was contended on behalf of the estate that the suit was barred by a three-year statute of limitations. *In re Whittington's Estate,* 64 So. 2d 580 (Miss.).

20. Suit was brought against a surgeon for malpractice on the ground that he had left a broken needle in the patient during a surgical operation. The

defense sought dismissal on the ground that suit was not brought within two years after the patient first was informed of the existence of the needle, and that the statute of limitations governing the action was two years. Plaintiff brought out that the surgeon knowingly withheld the information that he had left the needle in the patient's abdomen during the surgical operation. *Kroll v. VandenBerg*, 336 Mich. 306, 57 N.W. 2d 897.

21. A daughter was lulled into a false sense of security by promises of her mother and assurances by her stepfather that she would receive her full interest in her deceased father's estate. Ten years after she reached full age and about six years after her mother's death, the daughter brought suit against the stepfather to compel recognition of her interest, and an accounting therefor. The stepfather, without showing irreparable injury because of the delay, urged laches as a defense. *Duhlhammer v. Schneider*, 252 P. 2d 807.

22. A pawnbroker was convicted by a Texas court, partly on the basis of tapped telephone conversations, of complicity in a jewel robbery. He applied to the Supreme Court for a review (*certiorari*) on the ground that the Federal Communications Act forbids any person not authorized by the sender, to intercept a telephone conversation and disclose its contents. The prosecuting attorney contended that the Federal Act was inapplicable to Texas, which had adopted no such prohibition. *Schwartz v. State of Texas*, 344 U.S. 199.

# 23

# Criminal Procedure

**Scope of This Chapter.** In this final chapter we briefly indicate the steps in the process of apprehending and trying a person charged with the commission of a crime. These include arrest, with or without warrant; the preliminary hearing, to determine whether to hold the prisoner for trial or release him for lack of evidence; the commitment, with or without bail, or the release on bail pending trial; the accusation, by complaint, information, presentment or indictment; the arraignment and plea, followed by sentence, on a guilty plea, and by trial, sentence and execution, if the accused is guilty, or discharge, in the case of a not-guilty verdict.

**In General.** A person charged with a crime, whether merely suspected, or actually caught in the act, must be brought to the bar of justice and given a fair trial. Since the trial procedure in a criminal case varies only in detail from that of a civil case, and such detail belongs rather in the field of technical practice than in a study of commercial law, we shall omit it from this discussion. Likewise, we shall omit repetition of the Constitutional safeguards afforded every person accused of a crime. These were discussed in our opening chapter (pages 13 to 18) dealing with searches and seizures, the necessity for informing the accused by presentment or indictment of the exact nature of the offense with which he is charged, the right to a speedy and public trial by an impartial jury, to assistance of counsel and compulsory process for obtaining witnesses, and to be confronted with hostile witnesses, as well as the safeguards against excessive bail, fines, cruel and unusual punishments, double jeopardy and self-incrimination.

In this chapter, therefore, we shall confine our discussion to the preliminary steps leading to a criminal trial. These are matters of common interest on which no well informed person can afford to be ignorant.

**Preliminary Steps: Outline.** The preliminary steps in bringing a criminal to justice are substantially uniform, with minor variations depending upon the necessity, or lack of it, for making an arrest, the nature and gravity of the offense, statutory differences in different jurisdictions, and similar factors. Such steps, broadly, may involve the following: (1) Arrest, with or without a warrant; (2) Preliminary hearing before a magistrate or other judicial officer; (3) Commitment, usually with provision for bail; (4) Accusation, by complaint, information, presentment or indictment; and (5) Arraignment and plea. These steps lead to the ultimate goal of trial, sentence and execution, or, in the case of a not-guilty verdict, discharge.

## Arrest Without Warrant

**Who May Make Arrest.** It is commonly but erroneously believed that only peace officers may make an arrest. Actually, private persons as well as peace officers may make an arrest. The degree of latitude in making the arrest, however, is not the same in both cases.

(1) *Arrest by private persons.* A private person may make an arrest in either of two situations: (a) where a felony has been committed and he has reasonable ground for believing that the person he is about to arrest has committed it; and (b) where a misdemeanor threatening violence or a breach of the peace is, or is about to be, committed in his presence.

A private person attempting arrest not only runs the risk of personal injury if the arrest is resisted, but he may also find himself the subject of a civil suit for false arrest (page 797) if the arrest was unwarranted. When in doubt, therefore, it is safer in such cases for a private person to invoke the aid of a peace officer if one is available.

(2) *Arrest by peace officer.* There are three situations in which a peace officer may make an arrest without a warrant: (a) When a crime—felony or misdemeanor—is committed in his presence and he makes an immediate arrest; (b) When a felony has been committed and he knows or has reasonable ground to believe that the person arrested committed it; and (c) When he has reasonable ground to believe that a felony has been committed and that the person he is about to arrest has committed it.

It should be noted that although a private person cannot make an arrest without a warrant unless a felony or misdemeanor has been or is being actually committed, a peace officer can make such arrest where *he has reasonable ground for believing* that a felony has been committed.

**What Constitutes Arrest.** Arrest does not necessarily require forceful restraint, such as by the use of handcuffs or otherwise. It may take place by a mere touching or taking hold of a party accompanied by the statement that he is under arrest, or even by the statement alone, followed by submission. In the absence of a statement or explanation, or some evidence of authority to make the arrest, such as a peace officer's uniform or badge, a party may resist arrest as an unwarranted interference with his liberty.

## Arrest With Warrant

**Nature of Warrant.** A warrant of arrest is a written order issued and signed by a magistrate, directed to a peace officer or some other person specially named, commanding him to arrest the body of a person accused of an offense and named in the order.[1] A warrant may not be issued in blank, to be served on someone in the discretion of the arresting officer. Where, however, the identity, though not the name of a party is known, a "John Doe" warrant may be issued and executed.

**Executing the Warrant.** Once a warrant is issued by the proper magistrate, a peace officer need not hesitate to make an arrest within his territorial jurisdiction. To do so, he may, if necessary, enter or break into a building; and in case one flees from arrest, the officer may use any reasonable means to halt the flight, even shooting to kill if there is no other way to halt the fugitive. In the latter event, however, an officer risks subsequent conviction for homicide should a jury hold that the killing was unnecessary.

**Basis for Warrant: Preliminary Complaint or Affidavit.** Ordinarily, a magistrate has no right to issue a warrant without a sworn complaint or affidavit to support it. The usual practice is for someone to complain to the magistrate that a certain person has committed a certain offense. If the magistrate, upon examining the complainant, is reasonably satisfied that the offense was committed, and that the person in question committed it, he has the complainant sign and swear to a complaint or affidavit embodying the substance of the complainant's story, and upon this complaint or affidavit he directs the issuance of a warrant. In two situations, however, a magistrate may issue a warrant without a supporting complaint or affidavit, namely, where a crime is committed in his presence, and where a bench warrant is justified.

**Bench Warrant.** A bench warrant differs from an ordinary warrant in that it is issued, not by a judge as an individual magistrate, but by a court as such, through its presiding officer. It may be issued in the following situations: (1) for contempt, (2) where an indictment is found, and (3) to bring in a person who has failed to obey a summons or subpoena.

**Summons in Lieu of Warrant.** In many jurisdictions, a magistrate may issue a summons instead of a warrant, commanding the person named therein to appear in court on a given day to answer a given charge. Such process may be issued instead of a warrant only in the case of lesser offenses or those which may be tried *summarily* by the magistrate (page 888). As noted, if the defendant fails to respond to the summons, a bench warrant may bring him in.

*Traffic "tickets."* In the case of traffic violations, the authority to issue a summons or "ticket" is commonly delegated to a peace officer, who may serve it either personally on the owner or operator of the vehicle, or affix it to the vehicle if it is unattended.

---

[1] *Brown v. State*, 109 Ala. 70, 20 So. 103.

## Preliminary Examination Upon Arrest

**Necessity for Immediate Examination.** Each year, many persons arrested turn out to be innocent. Statutes generally provide that upon arrest, the prisoner must not be unduly sequestered, privately questioned, or subjected to undue force, violence or other abuse, but must be immediately brought before the nearest magistrate for a preliminary examination. Such a hearing is not a trial, but a procedure to safeguard against a possible abuse of power.

**Procedure upon Preliminary Examination.** Upon the preliminary hearing, the magistrate examines into the situation only so far as may be necessary to determine whether there is sufficient evidence to justify prosecution. If not, the prisoner is released. If the evidence indicates that the prisoner should be held for trial, the magistrate orders him bound over, and fixes bail (except where the offense is non-bailable, as in capital or life offenses). If bail is given, the prisoner is released until the trial. If no bail is furnished, the prisoner is returned to custody, to await trial.

Where the prisoner is held, subsequent steps take the form either of a summary trial, in the case of lesser offenses, or a more formal proceeding, where the offense is of a more serious nature. First, however, the defendant must be fully advised of the charge against him, and must have an opportunity to plead to it.

## Accusation: Information, Presentment, Indictment

**Right of Accused to Be Informed of Charge.** We have already noted the basic constitutional principle that where a person is prosecuted for an offense, he must be clearly informed of the charge against him (page 14). Such accusation may take the form of an *information*, an *indictment* or a *presentment*. The latter two terms have already been defined (page 15).

**Information.** Where, following a preliminary examination, the accused is held over, the record on the hearing, including the testimony of witnesses and all papers in the case, may be forwarded to the clerk of the court having charge of subsequent proceedings. On this record, the prosecution may draw up an *information*, setting forth in clear and precise language the nature of the offense which the accused will be required to answer.

*Nolle prosequi* (*"nolle pros."*). Where the prosecuting attorney believes the evidence insufficient to warrant prosecution, he may, with the consent of the court, make a formal entry by which he declares that he "will no further prosecute." The accused is thereupon discharged.

**Indictment.** Where the specific charge is drawn up not only on the basis of a preliminary hearing, but on additional evidence presented to the grand jury with the assistance of the prosecuting attorney, it is known as an *indictment*. If the accused is at large, the indictment is presented to a judge, who orders a warrant of arrest to issue (or a summons where it is believed the defendant will respond to it), and in such case, a preliminary examination is dispensed with.

**Presentment.** A grand jury may undertake an investigation on its own initiative and draw up a statement representing to the court that a public offense has been committed and that there is reasonable ground for believing that a particular individual, named or described in the statement, committed it. Such a statement is known as a *presentment*.

## Arraignment and Plea

**Purpose of Arraignment.** The formal accusation against an accused, whether in the form of an information, indictment or presentment, corresponds to the complaint in a civil action (page 858) which the defendant is required to answer. The purpose of an arraignment is to call the accused to the bar of the court, where the accusation is read to him and he is required to plead to it, unless he elects to demur to the indictment.

**Pleas.** The accused may plead guilty or not guilty. If he pleads guilty, a trial becomes unnecessary. If he pleads not guilty, the case is set down for trial. If he declines to plead, a not-guilty plea is entered.

**Demurrer.** It sometimes happens that an indictment is insufficient on its face as a matter of law. In such case, the accused may demur (page 858) to the indictment, and if the demurrer is sustained, the indictment is dismissed and the prisoner freed. Such action is unlikely unless the accused has taken advantage of his Constitutional right to be represented by counsel.

## Trial, Sentence and Execution

**Trial.** Article VI of the Bill of Rights sums up a person's Constitutional rights connected with a criminal trial: "In all criminal prosecutions, the accused shall enjoy the right to a speedy and public trial, by an impartial jury of the State and district wherein the crime shall have been committed . . . and to be informed of the nature and cause of the accusation; to be confronted with the witnesses against him; to have compulsory process for obtaining witnesses in his favor, and to have the assistance of counsel for his defense."

*Summary trials.* Statutes relating to minor offenses authorize summary or quick trials before a magistrate or justice of the peace without a jury. Cases so tried are of the type not inherently criminal, such as those involving vagrancy, traffic or disorderly conduct charges. The accusation in such cases usually takes the form of an affidavit or complaint in lieu of an indictment or presentment.

**Sentence.** Where the accused pleads guilty, or is found guilty after trial, it is customary to defer sentence for a short interval to allow time for investigation, report and recommendation by a probation officer, and for pleas of leniency by counsel and character witnesses. Sentence is pronounced in the presence of defendant and his counsel, and of the prosecuting attorney or someone associated with him in the prosecution.

**Execution.** The execution of a sentence in a criminal case corresponds to the execution of a judgment in a civil case (page 861). It consists in the carrying out, by a sheriff or corresponding officer, of the punishment directed by the court in its sentence. For this purpose a warrant of commitment, directing imprisonment, or a warrant of execution in the case of a death sentence, fixing the date and manner of execution, is issued to the executing officer, and unless the sentence is followed by an appeal and stay of execution, it is duly carried out.

## Questions

1. Under what circumstances may a private person make an arrest?
2. What risk does a private person incur in making an arrest?
3. There are three situations in which a peace officer may make an arrest without a warrant. What are they?
4. "An arrest is a forceful restraint of one's person." Would you accept this as a correct statement? Explain.
5. When may a person resist arrest as an unwarranted interference with his liberty?
6. What is the exact nature of a warrant of arrest?
7. How far may a peace officer go in executing a warrant of arrest?
8. What, ordinarily, must a magistrate do before issuing a warrant of arrest? Are there any exceptions?
9. What is a bench warrant, and when may it be issued?
10. "An arrest, with or without a warrant, is the only known procedure for requiring a person to appear in a criminal court to answer a given charge." Is this a correct or incorrect statement of the law? Explain.
11. What prompt action does the law require after the making of an arrest? Describe the procedure involved in such action, and its possible consequences.
12. Distinguish and explain the following terms used in criminal procedure: (a) information, (b) indictment, and (c) presentment.
13. What is the nature and purpose of an arraignment?
14. What are the possible pleas on arraignment, and what subsequent steps do they entail?
15. When may a person demur to an indictment, and what are the possible results of such action?
16. What is meant by a summary trial of a criminal charge, and under what circumstances may such a trial be had?
17. What is the usual procedure in connection with the sentencing of a person found guilty of a criminal charge?
18. What is meant by the execution of a sentence?

## Problems

1. Mrs. Green opens the window of her apartment and cries, "Help, a burglar!" Smith, a passerby, seeing a man running out of the apartment house, attempts to arrest him, and is severely injured in so doing. Later, it turns out that the "burglar" was a painter who had mistaken the apartment, and the person whom Smith tried to arrest was a tenant rushing to an appointment. Smith sues the tenant for assault and battery. Who wins and why?

2. To expedite an arrest, a magistrate issues a warrant in blank and gives it to a detective to serve, with instructions that as soon as the detective learns the identity of the criminal, he is to fill in the latter's name on the warrant. The detective, having ascertained that Peter Mugg committed the crime, fills in Mugg's name on the warrant, serves it on Mugg and arrests him. Mugg's attorney seeks to void the warrant. Will he succeed?

3. A peace officer, armed with a warrant for the arrest of Johnson, tries to apprehend him. Johnson, a powerful man, knocks the peace officer down and is in the act of escape when the latter shoots and kills Johnson. The peace officer is prosecuted for homicide. Will he be convicted?

4. A leading merchant telephones his former attorney, now a magistrate, that one of the merchant's employees has just been caught in the act of embezzlement. The merchant asks, "May I arrest the employee until the police come?" and the magistrate replies, "Never mind, Jim, I'll issue a warrant and send over an officer with it." Was the magistrate's course of action proper?

5. Frank and Hank are twins. Frank is arrested for a crime committed by Hank, who has disappeared. Frank assures the arresting officer he can readily establish his innocence and the mistaken identity, but the police officer advises Frank that he will have to remain in jail for two weeks, until the magistrate gets back from his vacation. Comment on this situation.

## COURT CASES FOR REVIEW

### How Did the Court Decide, and Why?

1. An arrest was challenged as improper for having been made without a warrant, under the following circumstances: The police officer had arrested the accused in a public vestibule. The accused was visibly in possession of lottery paraphernalia. It was contended on behalf of the accused that the evidence had been obtained by illegal search and seizure and without a search warrant. *Eisenstein v. State*, 92 A. 2d 739.

2. Police officers had observed a number of automobiles stopping for short intervals near an automobile parked on a highway in front of defendant's home. Upon investigation the officers found defendant trying to hide behind the parked automobile. Through the automobile windows, the officers saw approximately one-half case of whiskey in bottles. They searched the automobile and arrested the defendant for possessing intoxicating liquor in dry territory for the purpose of sale. The arrest was challenged as an improper search and seizure without warrant. *Click v. Comm.*, 247 S.W. 2d 371 (Ky.).

3. Defendant was charged with having been guilty of assault and battery in resisting an arrest, though the force used in resisting the arrest did not exceed that used in making the arrest. The officers had entered defendant's home and arrested him while he was seated doing nothing, though he had allegedly beaten his wife before the police arrived. Defendant challenged the validity

of the arrest without a warrant. *Ronemous v. State*, 87 Ga. App. 900, 74 S.E. 2d 676.

4. The question arose as to defendant's remedy under the following circumstances: An information was filed against him for assault with a deadly weapon, without alleging the type of weapon used. *People v. Collins*, 255 P. 2d 59.

5. An information was filed against the accused charging reckless driving. It recited no facts revealed by the informant's investigation as deputy sheriff, but merely that it was based upon such investigation, upon statements of third parties, and upon admission of the accused that he was driving 70 miles an hour. A warrant was issued on this information, and the warrant was challenged as insufficiently based. *People v. Mezzatesta*, 203 Misc. 253, 115 N.Y. Supp. 2d 498.

6. A wife gave her husband a check in one county to be used by him in purchasing produce in a second county. The wife knew, but the husband did not, that there were insufficient funds to meet the check. Prosecution was instituted against the wife in the second county. The wife was convicted, and appealed. Her contention was that the second county had no jurisdiction over the offense. *Chadwick v. State*, 87 Ga. App. 900, 75 S.E. 2d 260.

7. The following sentence was imposed on defendant: He was to spend 30 nights in the county jail. He was to be checked into the jail by 7 P.M. daily except on a stated date, when he was to be checked in at 8 P.M., and he was to be checked out daily at 7 A.M. except on Saturdays and Sundays. He was also to pay a fine which was to be imposed before the end of the 30-day period. The validity of this sentence was attacked. *Ex parte Emmons*, 256 P. 2d 476.

8. Plaintiff requested permission to conduct his own trial. He lost. On appeal, he complained that, regardless of his request, an assignment of counsel was mandatory under the Constitution, and he should have been requested to accept the assistance of counsel. *People v. Collins*, 255 P. 2d 59.

9. In a prosecution for carrying concealed weapons, the court denied the defendant's motion to suppress evidence alleged to have been improperly procured, and defendant appealed on the following grounds:

(a) There was no evidence that the occupants of an automobile in which the weapons were alleged to have been concealed had committed any crime;

(b) There was no evidence that the occupants had committed a misdemeanor in the presence of the police officers;

(c) There was no evidence that the officers even had a suspicion that the occupants had committed a felony;

(d) The officers had no warrant for the arrest of the occupants;

(e) The officers did not even know of any crime that had been committed in the locality, yet they arrested the occupants, searched the automobile, and then found pistols under the front seat. *State v. Cuezze*, 249 S.W. 2d 373 (Mo.).

10. Defendant was charged with having operated a motor vehicle upon a public highway without being of age, and without being licensed. The trial judge did not inform the defendant that upon conviction, not only would he be liable to a penalty, but in addition his license might be suspended or revoked; neither did the judge inform the defendant that a plea of guilty was equivalent to conviction at the trial. Defendant was convicted, and appealed. *People v. Grogan*, 260 N.Y. 138, 183 N.E. 273.

# Appendix

## Uniform Commercial Code:
## A Digest

**Background and Purpose.** In 1940, the fiftieth annual meeting of the National Conference of Commissioners on Uniform State Laws[1] adopted a proposal to prepare a uniform commercial code that would modernize and coordinate the Uniform Sales Act, The Uniform Negotiable Instruments Law and all other uniform commercial law statutes which had been formulated by the Conference and adopted by the various states. The following year the American Law Institute joined in sponsoring the proposal. Work on the Code, begun in 1945, was brought to substantial completion in 1952 for submission to the various States.

The basic purpose of the Code is to develop greater precision, certainty and uniformity in the rules of law governing commercial transactions. This it seeks to do in three ways: (1) By modernizing and coordinating our existing commercial law statutes, and relating them more closely to modern business practice; (2) By eliminating differences which have arisen in the different states because of different judicial interpretations of our uniform statutes; and (3) By supplying new statutory provisions to fill in the gap where new types of business transactions are not covered by an applicable statute.

**(1) Modernization and coordination.** Our commercial law statutes go back to the days when crackers still came out of a barrel; when the assembly line was unknown, and modern motors, radio and television still lay in the future. The various uniform statutes which had been adopted were formulated separately as if each belonged in a separate vacuum. The Uniform Commercial Code seeks to integrate and coordinate these statutes realistically in the light of modern mercantile and industrial practices. It recognizes that a single transaction may cut across statutory provisions contained in the Uniform Sales Act, the Uniform Conditional Sales Act, the Uniform Bills of Lading Act, the Uniform Negotiable Instruments Law, the Uniform Warehouse Receipt Act and others.

Let us consider a contract made to buy and sell goods. The goods may be physically shipped by rail on issuance of a bill of lading, or they may be raw goods or finished inventory in a warehouse, bought and sold without moving an inch, on a mere exchange or delivery of warehouse receipts. The goods have to be paid for. This payment may be by check, or by sight or time draft, or by trade acceptance or other negotiable instrument, against delivery of a bill

---
[1] See page 19.

of lading or warehouse receipt. On the other hand, the goods may be purchased on open account, or on installments accompanied by promissory notes secured by a conditional sale or chattel mortgage. The seller himself may have required financing—by letter of credit, by trust receipt, or otherwise— or he may be required to assign his accounts receivable on the transaction as security for the bank loan. These various phases of a single commercial transaction are now covered by separate statutes dealing with sales, conditional sales, bills of lading, warehouse receipts or other documents of title, negotiable instruments, chattel mortgages, trust receipts, letters of credit and other mercantile paper. It is the purpose of the Code to provide a single statute for the various facets of this type of commercial transaction.

(2) **Re-creating uniformity.** The original design of the uniform statutes was to eliminate the confusion caused by conflicting judicial decisions and statutes in the various jurisdictions throughout the country. The passage of time, however, has brought a new jungle of conflicting decisions. There are dozens of sections of the Uniform Sales Act, on the meaning of which courts in different parts of the country have reached diametrically opposite conclusions. By actual count, for example, there are 80 sections of the Uniform Negotiable Instruments Law that have different meanings in different states resulting from different court interpretations of the same statutory language.[2] The New Commercial Code seeks to re-establish and broaden the uniformity which the uniform commercial acts were originally designed to achieve.

(3) **New provisions to fill legal gaps.** Numerous business situations have developed since the uniform commercial acts were first conceived. These have left important gaps not covered or inadequately covered by the uniform statutes. Examples are the rapidly growing application of letters of credit to domestic as well as foreign transactions, and the numerous types of secured transactions resorted to in business practice today, which have become subject to a multitude of conflicting and confusing rules.

**Framework and Scope.** The Uniform Commercial Code is one of the most extensive pieces of legislation ever undertaken. It consists of several hundred sections, most of them consisting of several subsections. When adopted,[3] it will supersede the Uniform Negotiable Instruments Law, the Uniform Sales Act, the Uniform Bills of Lading Act, the Uniform Warehouse Receipts Act, the Uniform Stock Transfer Act and the Uniform Trust Receipts Act, as well as the model statutes which have been based on the Uniform Conditional Sales Act and the Uniform Chattel Mortgage Act. In addition the Code makes provision for many situations not covered by any statute and regulated wholly by court decisions, and for some situations not even covered by the latter. Forty per cent of the Code's article on Sales relates to matter not covered by any previous statute.

The Code is divided into ten articles as follows:

1. General Provisions
2. Sales
3. Commercial Paper
4. Bank Deposits and Collections
5. Documentary Letters of Credit

---

[2] William A. Schnader, *The New Commercial Code: Modernizing Our Uniform Commercial Acts*, 36 A.B.A.J. 182 (March 1950).

[3] There is of course no way of knowing when the Code will be generally adopted. The best guess the author can make is that adoption by a majority of the States will not come before 1960.

6. Bulk Transfers
7. Warehouse Receipts, Bills of Lading and Other Documents of Title
8. Investment Securities
9. Secured Transactions, Sales of Accounts, Contract Rights and Chattel Paper
10. Effective Date and Repealer

"Official Comments." Copious comments follow each section. These are designed to furnish a guide to the intention of the framers of the Code, thereby minimizing the area within which the courts of different states may give varying interpretations to the language of the Code. The comments to each section also specify which parts of prior uniform commercial statutes are replaced by the Code section, and if prior statutory language has been rephrased, the reasons for the rephrasing. These comments are designated in the Code itself as "Official Comments," and the Code specifically provides[4] that the comments "may be consulted by the courts to determine the underlying reasons, purposes and policies of this act and may be used as a guide in its construction and application."

## ARTICLE 1. GENERAL PROVISIONS

**Major Provisions.** Three provisions affecting commercial law generally are of special note as indicating the modern approach of the Uniform Commercial Code to present-day business practices. These deal with (1) Overlapping jurisdiction, (2) Legal recognition of the "commercial decencies," and (3) Statutory recognition of a course of dealing and the usages of trade as part of every commercial contract.

(1) **Overlapping jurisdictions.** Under existing practice a single transaction may involve a variety of jurisdictions. Say a resident buyer in Chicago makes a contract with a textile finisher in New Jersey for the purchase of a quantity of rayon fabric in a Virginia warehouse. The New Jersey firm requests that a credit be opened with a New York bank against presentation of a warehouse receipt. Delivery is to be f.o.b. Wilmington, Delaware, where the goods themselves are to be subject to inspection and approval. A dispute arises and litigation follows. The court may now have to consider the validity of the contract under New Jersey law (the place of the contract); questions affecting payment on presentation of the warehouse receipt, under New York law; the validity of the receipt itself, under Virginia law; questions as to delivery, inspection and approval, under Delaware law; and, possibly, questions as to the passing of title, which may have to be construed under the law of one of the several States mentioned. Under the Uniform Commercial Code, any State adopting the Code and having any substantial connection with the transaction could take jurisdiction of the entire dispute and decide all these questions under one statute, namely, the Uniform Commercial Code.

(2) **Obligation of good faith; the "commercial decencies."** The Code specifically enacts into law the obligation of good faith by providing that "Every contract within this Act imposes an obligation of good faith in its performance." [5] The Official Comment under this section is that "This Act adopts the principle of those cases which see a commercial contract not as an 'arm's length' adversary venture," but as one of mutual interest when successful, and as

---

[4] Sec. 1-102.
[5] Sec. 1-203.

"involving due regard for commercial decencies when the expected favorable outcome fails."

(3) **Course of dealing and usages of trade.** The Code specifically enacts[6] that "The parties to a contract are bound by any course of dealing between them and by any usage of trade of which both are or should be aware, and parties engaged in a particular vocation or trade are bound by its usages."

## ARTICLE 2. SALES

**Scope.** This Article of the Code covers generally the same field now covered by the Uniform Sales Act. The approach, however, is along the lines of fair mercantile practice which characterizes the Code as a whole. Not all matters now covered by the Uniform Sales Act, however, are included in this Article. For example, documents of title are covered by Article 7 of the Code. Investment securities are provided for in Article 8. Conditional sales, so far as they concern the sales aspect, remain in Article 2, but the security aspect of conditional sales is omitted from this Article and is covered by Article 9.

**Major Changes.** The major changes found in Article 2 affecting the present law of sales relate to the shift in emphasis from questions affecting title, to the contractual picture as a whole—the rights, duties and obligations of the contract of sale. This necessitated a modification of the rules governing the formation of the contract. The Code also introduces new rules with respect to the statute of frauds governing contracts of sale; the parol evidence rule; the construction and interpretation of sales contracts; the subject of warranties; the remedies of seller and buyer; and miscellaneous provisions, such as those relating to the sale of personalty affixed to lands and the period of the statute of limitations.

**Formation of Contract: Mutual Assent.** The principal changes governing mutual assent in the formation of a contract have to do with: (1) Agreements to abide by an offer for a reasonable time ("firm offers"); (2) The effect of counteroffers; (3) The medium of communicating an acceptance; (4) The manner of acceptance; and (5) What constitutes acceptance.

(1) **Agreement to hold an offer open (firm offers): merchants v. non-merchants.** The established common law rule is that an agreement to hold an offer open is not binding unless supported by a consideration. Some states have modified this rule by statute to the effect that such agreements, if in writing, are binding without consideration. The Code modifies both rules by distinguishing between merchants and non-merchants. It provides[7] that a signed, written offer by a merchant to buy or sell goods with the assurance that such offer will be held open, will be irrevocable for a reasonable time, or for a stated period, but in no event longer than three months. The same rule would apply to a non-merchant offeror only where there is "full understanding of the nature and effect of the offer made."

(2) **Effect of counteroffers.** Under existing law, a counteroffer kills the offer. The Code modifies this rule. It provides that "additional or different terms are to be construed as proposals for addition to the contract and between merchants become part of the contract unless they materially alter it or notice of objection to them is given within a reasonable time after they are received." [8]

(3) **Medium of communicating acceptance.** The generally established common law rule is to the effect that where an offer is made by mail, wire or other

---

[6] Sec. 1-205.
[7] Sec. 2-205.
[8] Sec. 2-207.

intermediate agency, an acceptance delivered or deposited with the offeror's agency is binding, regardless of when the agency communicates the acceptance to the offeror. If the acceptance is delivered to some other agency than the offeror's, it is ineffective until actually communicated to the offeror. This rule will no longer hold good under the Code, which provides that unless the offeror particularly stipulates to the contrary, his offer can be accepted in any manner or by any medium reasonable under the circumstances.[9]

(4) **Manner of acceptance.** Under existing law, disputes frequently revolve around the point of time when title passes in a given transaction. This frequently involves a painstaking study of voluminous correspondence in an effort to determine where title lay when merchandise was lost or destroyed. The Code adopts the common-sense approach. It provides that a contract for the sale of goods may be made in any manner sufficient to show an agreement. Conduct by both parties which recognizes the existence of a contract is sufficient to establish such contract even though the precise moment of its making cannot be determined.

(5) **What constitutes acceptance.** The Code makes rather significant changes in the law with respect to what may constitute the acceptance of an offer in a sales transaction. This may involve (a) the acceptance of an order for shipment, (b) shipment of wrong goods, (c) commencing performance without prior confirmation of acceptance.

(a) *Acceptance of order for shipment.* At present an offer may call for acceptance either by an act or a promise, in which case it cannot be accepted otherwise. This frequently leads to uncertainty as to what the offeror wants by way of acceptance, an uncertainty which is cleared up under the Code by a provision that "an order or other offer to buy goods for prompt or current shipment can be accepted either by such shipment or by a prompt promise thereof." [10]

(b) *Shipment of wrong goods as an acceptance.* Under the Uniform Sales Act, shipment, to constitute an acceptance, must exactly conform with the offer. The Code provides that unless the seller states the contrary, a shipment sent in response to an order to which it does not conform is an acceptance and at the same time a breach.[11]

(c) *Commencing performance as acceptance.* Under the present law if an offer calls for an act as the acceptance, the mere commencing to perform is not an acceptance, where confirmation of the acceptance in advance of actual performance is indicated. The Uniform Code provides that the beginning of a requested performance can be a reasonable mode of acceptance, but in such case an offeror who is not notified of acceptance within a reasonable time may treat the offer as having lapsed for non-acceptance.

(d) *Auction sales.* Under the Uniform Sales Act a sale by auction is complete when the auctioneer announces its completion by the fall of the hammer or in some other customary manner. Until such announcement is made any bidder may retract his bid and the auctioneer may withdraw the goods from sale unless the auction has been announced to be without reserve. Under the proposed Code, where an auction is without reserve, the goods cannot be withdrawn, and neither may a bid be retracted, regardless of the falling of a hammer or similar signal.

**Formation of Contract: Consideration.** The dwindling influence of considera-

---

[9] Sec. 2-206.
[10] Sec. 2-206.
[11] Sec. 2-206.

tion is evident in the Code. As previously indicated, firm offers for a given period no longer require consideration under the Code, whether the offer is made orally or confirmed in writing. A similar tendency is evident in the Code provisions relating to (1) price, and (2) the modification of an existing contract.

(1) **Price.** Under existing law, an "agreement to agree" on a price in the future is unenforceable. This would no longer be true under the Code, which provides that "The parties if they so intend can conclude a contract for sale even though the price is not settled. In such a case the price is a reasonable price at the time of delivery if (a) nothing is said as to price; or (b) the price is left to be agreed by the parties and they fail to agree; or (c) the price is to be fixed in terms of some agreed market or other standard as set or recorded by a third person or agency and it is not so set or recorded." [12] The parties may, however, specifically agree that the contract is not to be deemed consummated unless and until the price is agreed upon.

(2) **Modification of contract.** Generally, under the present law, an existing contract cannot be modified without new consideration. The Code allows a modification of a contract to be binding without consideration therefor.

**Subject Matter of Contract.** Under existing law, the courts, in voiding contracts for invalid subject matter, have gone no further than to reject it for illegality, or the circumstance that it is contrary to public policy. The proposed Code goes further: It empowers a court to refuse to enforce a contract or any clause of it that it deems unconscionable.[13]

**Statute of Frauds.** The statute of frauds provision in relation to contracts for the sale of personal property, as adopted in most states, fixes a maximum price or value at which oral contracts of sale will be permitted. Such maximum varies in the different states. The figure set by the Uniform Sales Act is $500. Many states have set the figure at substantially less. (See page 231.) The Uniform Commercial Code sets the amount at the same figure as that fixed in the Uniform Sales Act, namely, $500. The Code, however, has relaxed the stringency of the memorandum required to satisfy the statute of frauds. It provides that such memorandum will be sufficient if it (1) contains evidence sufficient to justify a court in holding that a contract for the sale of goods has been entered into, (2) is signed by the party to be charged or his agent, and (3) specifies the quantity of goods involved.[14]

**Parol Evidence Rule.** Under existing law, oral evidence of usage or custom would be inadmissible to vary a writing unless the writing were ambiguous. The Code would permit such evidence even where the writing is unambiguous.

**Construction and Interpretation.** The Code clears up, by more precise definitions, the somewhat conflicting interpretations which have been given to the terms, "f.o.b.," "f.a.s.," "c.i.f.," and "c. & f.," going beyond the mere words which these abbreviations respectively denote (free on board; free alongside ship; cost, insurance, and freight; and cost and freight), and their applicability in determining when title passes, to the larger aspect of the duties of the parties in such situations.

**Warranties.** Notwithstanding any contrary contractual provision, the Code would extend the benefit of any express or implied warranty "to any natural person whose relationship to the buyer is such as to make it reasonable to ex-

---

[12] Sec. 2-305(1).

[13] Sec. 2-302.

[14] Sec. 2-201.

pect that such person may use, consume or be affected by the warranty." [15] Moreover, under the Code, direct action for breach of warranty may be maintained against any seller in the chain of distribution with or without joining any subsequent seller in the chain as an additional defendant, thereby eliminating the necessity for privity in such cases. (See page 250.)

**Remedies of Seller.** The Code introduces a number of changes in the seller's remedies, in case of the buyer's insolvency,[16] wrongful rejection of merchandise, or default.[17]

**Buyer's insolvency: further deliveries.** The Code gives the seller the right to refuse further deliveries except for cash upon discovery of the buyer's insolvency.

**Stoppage in transit.** Upon discovery of the buyer's insolvency, the seller may exercise his usual right of stoppage in transit. However, under the Code, the seller's right of stoppage by reason of repudiation or default of the buyer would be limited to carload, truckload or planeload lots, or larger shipments, but would not be so limited in cases involving the buyer's insolvency.[18]

**Reclamation.** On discovery of buyer's insolvency, the seller may reclaim his goods from the buyer within ten days of the buyer's receipt of the goods, except where such goods have been transferred to an innocent purchaser for value and in good faith.[19]

**Right to resell.** In the case of a buyer's default or wrongful rejection of merchandise, the seller's right to resell under the Code would no longer be restricted, as it is under existing law, to cases where the goods are perishable, or where the right has been expressly reserved, or where the buyer has been in default an unreasonable time, but would be available upon *any* breach of the buyer, including an anticipatory breach.[20]

**Buyer's Remedies.** The buyer's remedies are likewise broadened under the Code.[21] The buyer who has justifiably rejected goods or revoked his acceptance is given a "security interest" in the seller's goods which are in the buyer's possession or control, for the amount the buyer has paid, plus expenses. The buyer may realize on this security interest by reselling the goods in like manner as an aggrieved seller, except that he is not allowed to keep any profit resulting from the resale.

**Sale of Personalty Affixed to Lands.** Under existing law, the sale of personalty annexed to lands, such as timber, minerals, clay, stone, and so forth, will constitute a sale of personal property only where the agreement contemplates the severance of such property from the land prior to the sale. This would no longer be the rule under the Code, which provides that such property will be considered personalty when sold with the understanding that it is to be severed by the seller.[22]

**Statute of Limitations.** The Code provides a major change in the statute of limitations applicable to the breach of a contract of sale, by reducing the six-year period generally prevailing at present, to four years.[23]

---

[15] Sec. 2-318.
[16] Sec. 2-702.
[17] Sec. 2-706.
[18] Sec. 2-705(1).
[19] Sec. 2-702(2).
[20] Sec. 2-706.
[21] Sec. 2-711.
[22] Sec. 2-107(1).
[23] Sec. 2-725.

## ARTICLE 3. NEGOTIABLE INSTRUMENTS

**In General.** The Uniform Commercial Code has enacted numerous modifications of the existing provisions under the Uniform Negotiable Instruments Law. These are, however, necessarily detailed in nature. No effort will be made to enumerate all the changes. Some of the more significant ones will be briefly outlined.

**Requisites of Negotiability: Fixed or Determinable Future Time.** In referring to the requisites of negotiability with respect to the time of payment of an instrument, the Code provides that an instrument must be paid at a "definite" time instead of at a "determinable" future time.[24]

**Restrictive Indorsements.** Under the Uniform Negotiable Instruments Act, a restrictive indorsee can neither become, nor transfer the rights of, a holder in due course. This would no longer be true under the Code: A restrictive holder would have the rights of any purchaser of negotiable paper, except that he must do with the instrument as the indorsement directs. Later holders would be affected by such indorsements only where they are on notice of a fiduciary's breach of duty.[25]

**Presumption of Delivery: Incomplete Instruments.** Under the Uniform Negotiable Instruments Law, when an *incomplete* instrument leaves one's possession, there is no presumption of delivery, even as to a holder in due course. Under the Uniform Commercial Code, this distinction is rejected. Non-delivery even of an incomplete instrument is a personal defense, ineffective against a holder in due course.[26]

**Negligence Inviting Alteration.** We have already noted our belief (page 170) that most courts would agree that if blank spaces are so negligently left as to invite alteration, a holder in due course could collect an instrument so altered. The Code adopts this view.[27]

**Time Allowed Drawee to Accept.** The conflict of authority under existing law with respect to the time allowed a drawee to accept a bill of exchange, and the effect of his retention, destruction or refusal to return the bill, have already been discussed (page 186). The Code resolves this seeming conflict by treating a failure to return the bill as a dishonor.[28]

**Promises to Accept.** Under the Uniform Negotiable Instruments Act, promises by a drawee to accept a draft or check, as well as collateral acceptances by a separate writing, are treated as actual acceptances. This would no longer be true under the Code, which requires that the acceptance must be written *on the draft*.[29]

**Acceptance and Payment for Honor.** The provisions of the Uniform Negotiable Instruments Act with respect to acceptances and payments for honor have been omitted from the Uniform Commercial Code.

**Acquiring Rights of Holder in Due Course without Being One.** We have previously noted the existing rule (page 162) that a person may acquire the rights of a holder in due course without being one, provided he was not a party to any fraud or illegality affecting the instrument. This rule would be

---

[24] Sec. 3-109.
[25] Sec. 3-206.
[26] Secs. 3-115, 3-305, 3-407.
[27] Sec. 3-406.
[28] Sec. 3-410.
[29] Sec. 3-410.

modified by the Code, which provides that any holder who *knows* of the fraud or learns of it before negotiation to a holder in due course cannot be protected by reacquisition.[30]

**Liability of Indorser: Necessity of Presentment and Notice.** There has been some wavering on the part of the drafters of the Code with respect to the necessity for presentment and notice of dishonor as prerequisites to holding the indorser on a note. Originally, such prerequisite was eliminated, then reinstated, and the indications are that the rule may be re-established by requiring presentment and notice of dishonor as under the law at present.

**Time within Which Checks Must Be Presented for Payment.** Under the Uniform Negotiable Instruments Act[31] "a check must be presented for payment within a reasonable time after its issue, or the drawer will be discharged from liability thereon to the extent of the loss caused by the delay." That statute does not define a "reasonable time," but it is commonly accepted that a check must be started through banking channels not later than the next business day after receipt by the payee.[32] The Uniform Commercial Code allows a period of 30 days.[33]

**Holder v. Drawer Procuring Certification.** Under the existing rule, where the *holder* of a check procures its certification, the drawer and all indorsers are discharged, but where the *drawer* procures the certification, he remains liable thereon. The Code does away with this distinction: the drawer is relieved of liability in either situation.

## ARTICLE 4. BANK DEPOSITS AND COLLECTIONS

**In General.** This Article has been adopted from various sources, including many of the rules of the American Bankers Association's Bank Collection Code, principles and rules of the Deferred Posting and other statutes, the decisions of the courts and existing banking procedures.

**Cut-off Hour.** Under the Code, a cut-off hour of not earlier than 2 P.M. is allowed, so as to give bank employees full opportunity to perform their clerical work, and yet allow the bank to remain open for banking business.

**Miscellaneous Provisions.** Other provisions of this Article with respect to bank deposits and collections:

(1) *Provision for an extra banking day*, and various other time indulgences, to allow a collecting bank to waive, modify or extend time limits imposed by this Act;

(2) *Direct transmissions* in forwarding and presenting items for payment to a payer bank, but not to persons other than a bank;

(3) *Permission to remit by check*, instead of money, thereby facilitating and expediting remittances;

(4) *Deferred posting*, by providing a deadline at the close of the following banking day, instead of at midnight of the same day, thereby allowing an extra day for posting.

Further elaboration on the numerous other provisions of this Article would be of primary interest to the banking profession, and will therefore not be included in this digest.

---

[30] Sec. 3-201.
[31] Sec. 186.
[32] *Hawkes v. Bd. of Ed. Town of Pelham*, 241 App. Div. 880, 272 N.Y. Supp. 24.
[33] See 3-503.

## ARTICLE 5. DOCUMENTARY LETTERS OF CREDIT

**In General.** This Article bears directly on the full commitment of a bank in a separate instrument to honor drafts upon fulfillment of certain conditions—in short, with letters of credit. Originally confined to foreign transactions, the use of this credit mechanism has grown substantially and achieved considerable importance. While much of this importance is still related to foreign trade, there has been a substantial resort to documentary letters of credit in domestic trade. This Article sets forth the basic rules covering such letters of credit.

**Subject Matter Covered.** The matters covered by this Article can be classified into four major groups:

(1) General nature of letters of credit;

(2) Rights and duties of the issuing bank and other banks;

(3) Rights and duties of the beneficiary under a letter of credit, i.e., the seller; and

(4) Rights and duties of the customer, that is, the buyer.

**Parties to Letter of Credit.** The Code, in its Official Comment to Section 5-102, states that a letter of credit is a contract between the beneficiary (seller) and the bank. However, Section 5-106 of the Code provides for its establishment as to three parties, the beneficiary (seller), the bank, and the customer (buyer), and further provides that such establishment cannot be modified or cancelled except by agreement of all three parties.

## ARTICLE 6. BULK TRANSFERS

**Existing Provisions.** The existing provisions of the Uniform Bulk Sales Law have already been generally indicated (page 258). The statute has been regarded as largely innocuous because of its vagueness with respect to what constitutes a bulk transfer, and its lack of "teeth" in respect to the creditor protection it was designed to achieve.

**Definition of Bulk Transfers.** The existing definition of a bulk transfer[34] has given rise to considerable litigation. The Uniform Commercial Code has supplied a more accurate definition. It provides:[35]

A bulk transfer is any transfer in bulk and not in the ordinary course of the transferor's business of a major part of the materials, supplies, merchandise or other inventory . . . of an enterprise subject to this Article, or of so much thereof that what remains, together with the transferor's other assets exclusive of the consideration received for the transfer is inadequate to enable the transferor to meet his debts as they mature.

Thus the test of what constitutes a bulk transfer is brought closer to the statute's objective, that such transfer, and what the seller gets for it, shall not strip the seller of his ability to meet his debts when they mature.

**Auctioneers.** The present statute for some reason seems to have omitted inclusion of sales in bulk by auctioneers. The Code requires an auctioneer to give notice of the auction to the seller's creditors, and to see to it that the proceeds are applied to the seller's debts.[36]

---

[34] The existing definition of a bulk transfer is a sale, transfer or assignment "in bulk of any part of the whole of a stock of merchandise or of fixtures . . . otherwise than in the ordinary course of trade and in the regular prosecution of (the seller's) business."

[35] Sec. 6-102.

[36] Sec. 6-108(3).

**Personal Liability of Transferor.** This Article places on the transferee of a bulk sale the duty to see that the proceeds of the sale are properly applied to the claims of the creditors.[37] Not until the Code has been in use for some time will the manner of enforcing such liability be ascertained from judicial decisions on the point.

## ARTICLE 7. WAREHOUSE RECEIPTS, BILLS OF LADING AND OTHER DOCUMENTS OF TITLE

**In General.** This Article covers the ground now embraced in the Uniform Bills of Lading Act, the Uniform Warehouse Receipts Act, and the few sections of the Uniform Sales Act, that are now largely duplicated by provisions in the Warehouse Receipts Act and the Bills of Lading Act. The purpose of this Article is to bring into a single statute all the laws relating to documents of title, that is, documents which represent title to personal property entrusted to others for various purposes, such as storage, transportation or others. Notwithstanding the wide acceptance among the states of the various Uniform Acts mentioned, numerous conflicts have arisen in the decisions of the various courts throughout the country bearing on this important group of commercial transactions. The Uniform Commercial Code recognizes the interrelation of these subjects and has sought to relate them in such a way that a minimum opportunity for conflicting interpretations will be presented in the course of practice. There is no attempt to emasculate the intrinsic character of bills of lading, warehouse receipts or other documents of title, but the effort has been to make them so flexible as to be adaptable to any of the existing documents of title in use in present business practice, as well as any forms of business transactions that are likely to arise in the future in this field of commercial practice.

**Omission of Criminal Provisions.** The Uniform Code has followed the pattern of the existing uniform statutes on the subjects named, with the exception that it has omitted their criminal provisions. It was felt by the framers that there was no point in duplicating provisions of existing penal statutes by embodying them in a purely commercial code.

## ARTICLE 8. INVESTMENT SECURITIES

**In General.** This Article deals with bearer and registered bonds formerly covered by the Uniform Negotiable Instruments Act, certificates of stock formerly covered by the Uniform Stock Transfer Act, and additional types of investment paper not heretofore covered at all in any uniform statute. It does not cover commercial paper falling within the scope of the article on secured commercial transactions, such as conditional sales, chattel mortgages, trust receipts and the like.

**Rights of Purchasers.** Of special note are the special provisions of this Article of the Uniform Code covering the rights of purchasers. Since the buyer of investment securities almost invariably acts through a broker or investment house, seldom deals directly with the seller, and rarely sees the evidence of the investment securities he buys or sells (except when these are physically delivered to him), the Code attempts to give special protection to the buyer against certain defenses which the issuer might interpose. The effort is to give the maximum protection to an innocent purchaser and to impose on the issuer the burden of making sure that the security has been validly issued.

**Miscellaneous Provisions.** This Article deals further with purchases made

---

[37] Sec. 6-106(1).

after maturity, lost and stolen securities, broker and customer registration of transfer, and various other provisions designed to afford protection to purchasers of investment securities.

## ARTICLE 9. SECURITY TRANSACTIONS, SALES OF ACCOUNTS, CONTRACT RIGHTS, AND CHATTEL PAPER

**In General.** This Article covers the field now dealt with by conditional sales acts, chattel mortgage acts and the Uniform Trust Receipts Act. Among the security devices covered by this Article are pledges, assignments, chattel mortgages, common law trusts, trust deeds, factor's liens, equipment trusts (other than railway rolling stock), conditional sale contracts, bailment leases, trust receipts, title retention contracts and leases intended as security.

**Policy and Purposes.** The policy and purposes of this Article are in line with the general policy and purposes of uniform statutes, except that instead of seeking to harmonize conflicts in existing statutes, the Commercial Code seeks in this case to integrate the law of secured transactions, and to abolish so much of this law as is derived from outworn forms and practices. It seeks to supply up-to-date provisions covering the problems inherent in secured financing as a unit, whether the subject matter be consumer goods, equipment, farm products, inventory or accounts receivable. In short, the provisions of this Article, upon adoption of the Code, are designed to simplify and unify the handling of personal property of any kind on a part-payment plan.

## ARTICLE 10. EFFECTIVE DATE AND REPEALER

This Article merely makes provision for the date when the Act becomes effective in any State which adopts it, with further provision for the repeal of any and all other acts and parts of acts inconsistent with the Uniform Commercial Code as thus adopted.

# Glossary

**Abatement.** An action to end any act detrimental to the public such as a suit to enjoin a plant from permitting the escape of noxious vapors.

Lessening—Term generally applied to lessening or suppressing a nuisance.

**Abstract of title.** A condensed history of the title to property, based on the records.

**Acceleration.** Speeding up a legal obligation, as when an agreement provides that on failure to make a given payment, the entire series of payments shall fall due.

**Acceptance.** In Contracts—The act of the offeree in agreeing to the terms of an offer.

In Negotiable Instruments—An agreement by the drawee indorsed on a bill of exchange draft, agreeing to pay it.

**Accord.** Acquiescence by both sides to a dispute.

**Accord and satisfaction.** Accord followed by its execution.

**Adjudicate.** To determine judicially, or by a judgment.

**Administrator.** A person appointed by the court to administer the estate and distribute the property of a decedent who fails to leave a will designating an executor.

**Adverse possession.** Open, notorious, and continuous possession of another's property, without the latter's permission, a possession which may ultimately supplant the owner's title.

**Affidavit.** A statement sworn to before a notary.

**Agency coupled with an interest.** An agency in which the agent has a proprietary interest.

**Agent.** One acting for another, called principal, in dealing with third parties.

**Artisan's lien.** The lien of a mechanic or other skilled worker in connection with something on which he has bestowed labor or materials, giving him a right to retain possession of it until paid.

**Assignee.** The transferee of a right.

**Assignment.** Transfer of a right.

**Attachment.** A legal proceeding accompanying an action in court by which a plaintiff may acquire a lien on a defendant's property as a security for the payment of any judgment which the plaintiff may recover.

**Attorney at law.** A person licensed to practice law.

**Attorney in fact.** A person designated as an agent by a written authority or "power."

**Bail.** Security deposited in court as assurance that an accused will stand trial on a given day.

**Bailee.** A person into whose possession personal property is delivered.

**Bailment.** The delivery of personal property to another for a special purpose, on condition that the property will be returned pursuant to agreement.

**Bailor.** One who delivers a bailment.

**Bank draft.** A check, drawn by one bank on another, payable on demand.

**Bench.** A term often used to designate a court or the judges of a court.

**Beneficiary.** A person (not a promisee) to receive a benefit, as under a contract, trust, insurance policy, will, or other instrument.

**Bequest.** A disposition of personal property by will.

**Bilateral contract.** A contract formed by the exchange of mutual promises.

**Bill of exchange.** "An unconditional order in writing addressed by one person to another, signed by the person giving it, requiring the person to whom it is addressed to pay on demand, or at a fixed or determinable future time, a sum certain in money to order or to bearer." (Uniform Negotiable Instruments Law.)

**Bill of lading.** A contract signed by a carrier or his agent to deliver goods described in the contract to the person or persons designated by the shipper.

**Bill of sale.** A writing transferring title to personal property.

**Binder.** A tentative but binding commitment, as by the owner of real property, or by a fire insurance company.

**Bond.** A promise under seal to pay money. The term is generally used to designate the promise made by a corporation, either public or private, to pay money to bearer. U.S. Government Bonds; Illinois Central Railroad Bonds. The term also describes an obligation by which one person promises to answer for the debt or default of another—a surety bond.

**Book account.** A record of the debits and credits between persons evidenced by entries in a book. The record usually contains detailed statements of the transactions between the parties. It indicates rights and duties and is an assignable chose in action.

**Boycott.** A concerted effort to persuade people not to deal with a particular person or organization nor to buy a certain product. X company's employees are on strike. Retailer A's employees strike when Retailer A purchases goods from X Company. A's employees are boycotting X Company.

**By-laws.** The rules adopted by the members or the board of directors of a corporation or other organization for its government. These rules must not be contrary to the law of the land, and they affect only the rights and duties of the members of the corporation or organization. They are not applicable to third persons.

**Call.** An assessment upon a subscriber for partial or full payment on shares of unpaid stock of a corporation. The term may also mean the power of a corporation to make an assessment, notice of an assessment, or the time when the assessment is to be paid.

**Capital.** The net assets of an individual enterprise, partnership, joint stock company, corporation, or business institution, including not only the original investment but also all gains and profits realized from the continued conduct of the business.

**Capital stock.** The expressed equity of the stockholders in corporate assets resulting from their investments before the latter have been influenced by profits and losses.

It may be a sum fixed by the corporate charter.

**Carrier.** A person or corporation engaged in the business of transportation.

**Case law.** Law consisting of court opinions and decisions.

**Cashier's check.** A bill of exchange drawn by the cashier of a bank, for and upon the bank.

**Cause of action.** Grounds for a lawsuit.

**Caveat emptor.** "Let the buyer beware"—the purchase is at the buyer's risk.

**Caveat venditor.** "Let the seller beware"—the seller, in some situations, is liable to the buyer if the goods delivered are different in kind, quality, use, and purpose than those described in the contract of sale.

**Certificate of deposit.** A receipt given by a bank for money and so worded as to constitute a promissory note payable to the order of the depositor or bearer. It may be negotiable in form.

**Certificate of stock.** Written certification by officers of a corporation, under corporate seal, of the ownership of a certain number of shares in a corporation.

**Certified check.** A check drawn on a bank and accepted by it.

**Cestui que trust.** The beneficiary of a trust.

**Charter.** As applied to a corporation, the franchise or right to function as a corporation.

**Chattel.** The word chattel is derived from the word "cattle." It is a very broad term and includes every kind of property that is not real property.

**Chattel mortgage.** A formal instrument executed by a debtor called the mortgagor transferring an interest in a chattel to a creditor called a mortgagee, for the purpose of giving security for a debt.

**Check.** A check is a bill of exchange or draft drawn on a bank and payable on demand.

**Chose in action.** Words used to define the "right" one person has to recover money or property from another by a judicial proceeding. Such right arises out of contract, claims for money, debts and rights against property. Notes, drafts, stock certificates, bills of lading, warehouse receipts, insurance policies are illustrations of choses in action. They are called tangible choses. Book accounts, simple debts and obligations not evidenced by formal writing are called intangible choses. Choses in action are transferred by assignment.

**Circumstantial evidence.** If from certain facts and circumstances which, according to the experience of mankind, an ordinary, intelligent person may infer that other connected facts and circumstances must necessarily exist, the latter facts and circumstances are considered proven by circumstantial evidence. Proof of fact $A$ from which fact $B$ may be inferred is proof of fact $B$ by circumstantial evidence.

**Civil action.** A proceeding in a law court or a suit in equity by one person against another for the enforcement or protection of a private right or the prevention of a wrong. It includes actions on contract, ex delicto, and all suits in equity. Civil action is in contradistinction to criminal action in which the state prosecutes a person for breach of a duty.

**Claimant.** One who makes a claim.

**Clearing house.** An association of banks in the same community which has for its purpose the daily exchange of debits and credits between the several banks in order to make payment of balances disclosed by such debits and credits.

**Cloud on title.** Words used to express the idea that there is some evidence of record by which another person than the owner claims some interest in the latter's property.

**Code.** A collection or compilation of the statutes passed by the legislative body of a state.

**Codicil.** An addition to or a change in an executed last will and testament.

**Co-insurer.** A person or company sharing in the risk under a fire insurance policy.

**Collateral.** Security placed with a creditor to assure performance of an obligation.

**Combination in restraint of trade.** The union of the capital and skill of two or more persons or corporations for the purpose of restraining trade and limiting competition by agreeing to divide markets, maintain prices, limit production, and not to compete.

**Commercial law.** That branch of the law used to designate the rules that determine the rights and duties of persons engaged in trade and commerce.

**Commission merchant.** An agent or factor employed to sell "goods, wares, and merchandise" consigned or delivered to him by his principal, for a compensation called a commission.

**Common carrier.** One who is engaged in the business of transporting personal property from one place to another for a compensation. Such person is bound to carry for all who tender their goods and the price for transportation.

**Common law.** Law based on precedent expressed in judicial decisions, from the early English days down to the present in this country.

**Community property.** All property acquired after marriage by husband and wife other than separate property acquired by devise, bequest, or from the proceeds of non-community property. Community property is a concept of property ownership by husband and wife inherited from the civil law. The husband and wife are somewhat like partners in their ownership of property acquired during marriage.

**Complaint.** The first paper a plaintiff files in a court in a lawsuit. It is called a pleading. It is a statement of the facts upon which the plaintiff rests his cause of action.

**Composition of creditors.** An agreement among creditors and with their debtor by which they agree to take a lesser amount in complete satisfaction of the total debt due.

**Compromise.** An agreement between two or more persons, usually opposing parties in a lawsuit, to settle the matters of the controversy without further resort to hostile litigation.

**Condemnation proceedings.** An action or proceeding in court for the purpose of taking private property for public use.

**Conditional sale.** A sale in which title is retained by the vendor as security for the purchase price, although possession is surrendered to the buyer.

**Condition precedent.** A condition that must be filled before one becomes entitled to some right.

**Conditions concurrent.** Conditions concurrent are conditions that are mutually dependent and must be performed at the same time by the parties to the contract.

**Condition subsequent.** A condition that survives a given transaction.

**Confession of judgment.** A voluntary submission to the jurisdiction of the court by a debtor permitting judgment to be taken against him without a formal trial. Such permission often appears in promissory notes giving consent that judgment may be taken immediately upon default.

**Confusion of goods.** The intermingling of the goods of two or more persons by either of the owners to such extent that the several portions cannot be distinguished. The person so commingling has the duty of distinguishing his own property or losing it.

**Consideration.** Something of value given for a promise to make the promise binding.

**Consignee.** A person to whom a shipper usually directs a carrier to deliver goods. Such person is generally the buyer of goods and is called a consignee on a bill of lading.

**Consignment.** The delivery, sending, or transferring of property, "goods, wares, and merchandise" into the possession of another, usually for the purpose of sale. Consignment may be a bailment or an agency for sale.

**Consignor.** The person who delivers freight to a carrier for shipment is called a consignor or shipper and he is the one who directs the bill of lading to be executed by the carrier. Such a person may be the consignor-consignee, if the bill of lading is made to his own order.

**Constitution.** The Constitution of the United States constitutes the rules of organization of the United States and enumerates the powers and duties of the Federal government thereby created. The constitutions of the several states prescribe the organization of each of the states and in general enumerate those powers not delegated to the Federal government.

**Constructive delivery.** Although physical delivery of personal property has not occurred, yet by the conduct of the parties, it may be inferred that as between them possession and title has passed. *A* sells large and bulky goods to *B*. Title and possession may pass by the act and conduct of the parties.

**Continuing guaranty.** An undertaking by one person to another person to answer from time to time for moneys to be loaned or goods to be sold to a third person. The term refers to the future liability of the principal for a series of future transactions. It is usually revocable upon actual notice as to all future transactions.

**Conveyance.** A formal written instrument usually called a deed by which the title or other interests in land (real property) is transferred from one person to another. The word expresses also the fact that the title to real property has been transferred from one person to another.

**Corporation.** A collection of individuals created by statute as a legal person, vested with powers and capacity to contract, own, control, convey property, and transact business within the limits of the powers granted.

**Corporation de facto.** A corporation recognized for practical purposes as being in existence, though it has failed to effect a regular incorporation.

**Corporation de jure.** A corporation that has been formed by complying with the mandatory requirements of the law authorizing such a corporation.

**Corporeal.** Pertaining to physical things that are susceptible to the senses, such as lands and buildings, as distinguished from intangibles, such as a right of way.

**Costs.** An allowance authorized by statute to the successful party in a lawsuit.

**Counter-claims.** A claim of the defendant by way of cross-action that the defendant is entitled to recover from the plaintiff.

**Covenant.** A promise in writing under seal. It is often used as a substitute for the word contract.

**Cumulative voting.** A stockholder in voting for a director may cast as many votes for one candidate for given office as there are offices to be filled multiplied by the number of shares of his stock, or he may distribute this same number of votes among the other candidates as he sees fit.

**Currency.** Lawful money in current circulation. The terms "currency" and "current funds" now seem to include not only coin, silver, United States Notes, and Treasury Notes, but also silver certificates, Federal Reserve notes, and National Bank notes.

**Curtesy.** A husband's right under certain conditions to have and possess his wife's real property on her death, for the rest of his own life.

**Damages.** A sum of money the court imposes upon a defendant as compensation for the plaintiff because the defendant has injured the plaintiff by the breach of a legal duty.

**Debenture.** A term used to name corporate obligations that are sold as invest-ments. It is similar to a corporate bond. It is not like corporate stock.

**Debt.** Any obligation to pay money. Ordinarily the term debt means a sum of money due by reason of a contract expressed or implied. Broadly, the word may include obligations other than to pay money, such as the duty to render services or deliver goods.

**Declaration.** At common law a word used to name the plaintiff's first pleading in which are set out the facts upon which the cause of action is based. The word "complaint" is used synonymously with declaration.

**Decree.** The judgment of the chancellor (judge) in a suit in equity. Like a judgment at law, it is the determination of the rights between the parties, and is in the form of an order that requires the decree to be carried out. An order that a contract be specifically enforced is a decree.

**Deed.** A written instrument in a special form signed, sealed, and delivered, that is used to pass the legal title of real property from one person to another. See *Conveyance.* In order that the public may know about the title to real property, deeds are recorded in the Deed Record office of the county where the land is situated.

**De facto.** Arising out of, or founded upon fact, although merely apparent or colorable. A de facto officer is one who assumes to be an officer under some color of right, acts as an officer, but in point of law is not a real officer. See *Corporation de facto.*

**Defalcation.** A person occupying a trust or fiduciary relation who, by reason of his own fault, is unable to account for funds left in his hands, has com-mitted a defalcation. The word often means to embezzle or misappropriate funds.

**Defamation.** The use of words that are generally understood to impute some disreputable conduct or moral delinquency about the person of whom they are spoken.

**Defendant.** A person who has been sued in a court of law; the person who an-swers the plaintiff's complaint. The word is applied to the defending party in civil actions. In criminal actions, the defending party is referred to as the accused.

**Deficiency judgment.** A judgment for the amount by which proceeds from property sold on foreclosure fail to meet the amount of the mortgage debt and expenses of litigation.

**Del credere agency.** An agency providing higher commissions because the agent guarantees the account.

**Demurrage.** Demurrage is a sum, provided for in a contract of shipment, to be paid for the delay or detention of vessels or railroad cars beyond the time agreed upon for loading or unloading.

**Demurrer.** A procedural method used in a lawsuit by which the defendant admits all the facts alleged in the plaintiff's complaint, but denies that such facts state a cause of action. It raises a question of law on the facts, which must be decided by the court.

**Dependent covenants (promises).** Covenants wherein the performance of one promise must occur before the performance of the other promise. In a cash sale, the buyer must pay the money before the seller is under a duty to deliver the goods.

**Descent.** The transfer of the title to property to a person, by virtue of his being a lineal heir.

**Devise.** A gift, usually of real property, by a last will and testament.

**Devisee.** The person who receives title to real property by will.

**Dictum.** An expression of an idea, argument, or rule in the written opinion of a judge, that has no bearing on the issues involved and which is not essential for their determination. It lacks the force of a decision in a judgment.

**Directed verdict.** If it is apparent to reasonable men and the court that the plaintiff by his evidence has not made out his case, the court may instruct the jury to bring in a verdict for the defendant, or himself direct a verdict for the defendant. If, however, different inferences may be drawn from the evidence by reasonable men, then the court cannot direct a verdict.

**Dishonor.** Failure or refusal to discharge an obligation on an instrument.

**Dividend.** A dividend is a stockholder's pro rata share in the profits of a corporation. Dividends are declared by the board of directors of a corporation. Dividends are cash, script, property, and stock.

**Divorce.** The dissolution by a court, for proper cause, of the marital relationship.

**Domicile.** That place that a person intends as his fixed and permanent home and establishment and to which, if he is absent, he intends to return. A person can have but one domicile. The old one continues until the acquisition of a new one; thus, while in transit the old domicile exists. One can have more than one residence at a time, but only one domicile. The word is not synonymous with residence. See *Residence*.

**Dominion.** As applied to the delivery of property by one person to another, the word means the separation by the transferor or donor from all control over the possession and ownership of the property, and the endowing of the transferee or donee with such control of possession and ownership.

**Donee beneficiary.** If a promisee is under no duty to a third party, but for a consideration secures a promise from a promisor for the purpose of making a gift to a third party, such third party is a donee beneficiary. *A*, promisee for a premium paid, secures a promise from the insurance company, the promisor, to pay *A*'s wife $10,000 upon *A*'s death. *A*'s wife is a donee beneficiary.

**Dower.** A right for life held by a married woman in part of the lands owned by her husband and which right becomes vested upon his death.

**Draft.** "An unconditional order in writing addressed by one person to another, signed by the person giving it, requiring the person to whom it is addressed to pay on demand or at a fixed or determinable future time a sum certain in money to order or bearer." A draft is a bill of exchange. A draft has three parties; the drawer, who draws the paper; the party to whom payable, the payee; and the person upon whom it is drawn, the drawee. A check is a draft.

**Due bill.** A simple written acknowledgment of a debt. "I.O.U. $10, (signed by) *A.B.*" is a due bill.

**Due care.** The words express that standard of conduct which is exercised by an ordinary, reasonable, prudent person. See *Negligence*.

**Due process of law.** A system of law by which one is fully and fairly heard before he can be deprived of a right.

**Duress.** Forceful interference with volition, by bodily injury or threat, or other painful prospect threatened for noncompliance.

**Earnest.** "Earnest money" is a term used to describe money that one contracting party gives to another at the time of entering into the contract in order to "bind the bargain" and which will be forfeited by the donor if he fails to carry out the contract. Generally, in real estate contracts, such money is used as part payment of the purchase price.

**Earnings.** Earnings as applied to a natural person are the rewards or income gained for labor and services. **Earnings** is a broader term than wages. The term "wages" is applied generally to compensation for manual labor, skilled and unskilled, paid at fixed times and determined by the day, week, or month. Earnings as applied to a corporation or business establishment may mean either the gross or net receipts of the ordinary business operation over a specified period.

**Easement.** An easement is an interest in land—a right that one person has to some profit, benefit, or use in or over the land of another. Such right is created by a deed, or it may be acquired by prescription (the continued use of another's land for a statutory period).

**Ejectment.** An action to recover the possesion of real property. It is now generally defined by statute, and is a statutory action.

**Eleemosynary.** A word used to classify corporations and institutions engaged in public charitable work, such as a hospital or children's home owned and operated by a church.

**Embezzlement.** The fraudulent appropriation by one person, acting in a fiduciary capacity, of the money or property of another.

**Eminent domain.** The right that resides in the United States, state, county, city, school, or other public body, to take private property for public use, upon the payment of just compensation. Eminent domain is to be distinguished from governmental power to take private property by limiting its use in order to eliminate nuisances. Abating a nuisance is the exercise of police power. No compensation is given for limiting the use of property under the police power.

**Entire contract.** A contract, which by its terms requires full and complete performance on one side in return for the full and complete performance on the other. The term "entire contract" is used in contradistinction to the term "divisible contract," wherein a part of the performance required may be set over against a part of the performance on the other side.

**Entirety (estate by).** Property acquired by husband and wife whereby upon the death of one, the survivor takes the whole estate. The estate is called "entirety" because the law regards the husband and wife as one.

**Entity.** The word means "in being" or "existing." The artificial person created when a corporation is organized is "in being" or "existing" for legal purposes; thus, an entity. It is separate from the stockholders. The estate of a deceased person while in administration is an entity. A partnership for many legal purposes is an entity. The marriage status is an entity.

**Equity.** Because the law courts in early English law did not always give an adequate remedy, an aggrieved party sought redress from the king. Since this appeal was to the king's conscience, he referred the case to his spiritual adviser, the chancellor. The chancellor decided the case according to rules of fairness, honesty, right, and natural justice. From this there developed the rules in equity.The laws of trusts, divorce, rescission of contracts for fraud, injunction, and specific performance, are enforced in courts of equity.

**Equity of redemption.** The right a mortgagor has to redeem or get back his property after it has been forfeited for non-payment of the debt it secured. By statute, within a certain time before final foreclosure decree, a mortgagor has the privilege, by paying the amount of the debt, interest, and costs, of redeeming his property.

**Error.** A mistake in fact or law committed by the court in the trial of a case. Such mistake may be the basis of an appeal to a higher court. The admitting of improper evidence is "error of law occurring at the trial." Assumption that a fact exists when it does not is error of fact.

**Escrow.** An agreement under which a grantor, promisor, or obligor places the instrument upon which he is bound with a third person called escrow holder, until the performance of a condition or the happening of an event stated in the agreement permits the escrow holder to make delivery or performance to the grantee, promisee, or obligee.

**Estate.** A word used to name all the property of a living, deceased, bankrupt, or insane person. It is also applied to the property of a ward. In the law of taxation, wills, and inheritance, the word has a broad meaning.

**Estoppel.** A principle by which the law will not permit one person to cause another to give up some right, or to change his status, by denying a previous assertion or representation.

**Et uxor.** The words mean "and wife." Sometimes used in the name of cases. *Smith v. Jones et ux.*

**Eviction.** An action to expel a tenant from the estate of the landlord. Interfering with the tenant's right of possession or enjoyment amounts to an eviction. Eviction may be actual or constructive. Premises made uninhabitable because the landlord maintains a nuisance is constructive eviction.

**Exception.** Dissent by counsel from judge's ruling. An objection taken by an attorney at a trial because of some ruling made by the court upon a matter of law. It forms the basis of an appeal to a higher court.

**Execution.** Execution of a judgment is the process by which the court through the sheriff enforces the payment of the judgment received by the successful party. The sheriff by a "writ" levies upon the unsuccessful party's property and sells it to pay the judgment creditor.

**Executor (of an estate).** The person, named or appointed in a will by a testator (the one who makes the will), who by authority of the will has the power to administer the estate upon the death of the testator and to dispose of it according to the intention of the testator. The terms executor and administrator are not synonymous. An executor is appointed by the deceased to administer an estate. An administrator is appointed by the court to administer the estate of a person who dies without having made a will. See *Intestate.*

**Executory (contract).** Until the performance required in a contract is completed, it is said to be executory as to that part not executed.

**Exemplary damages.** A sum assessed by the jury in a tort action (over and above the compensatory damages) as punishment in order to make an example of the wrongdoer, and to deter like conduct by others. Injuries caused by willful, malicious, wanton, and reckless conduct, will subject the wrongdoer to exemplary damages.

**Exemption.** A person who is free or excused from a duty imposed by some rule of law, statutory or otherwise. A workman against whom a judgment has been secured is by statute exempt from a writ of execution upon his working tools. A portion of a soldier's pay is exempt from the imposition of federal income tax.

**Express warranty.** When a seller makes some positive representation concerning the nature, quality, character, use, and purpose of goods, which induces the buyer to buy, and the seller intends the buyer to rely thereon, the seller has made an express warranty.

**Factor.** A factor is an agent for the sale of merchandise. He may hold possession of the goods in his own name or in the name of his principal. He is authorized to sell and to receive payment for the goods. The law concerning factors is codified in some states by legislation, and is called "Factors' Acts." See *Agent.*

**Factor's lien.** A lien or right that a factor has to keep the possession of goods consigned to him for the purpose of reimbursing himself for all advances previously made to the consignor.

**Failure of consideration.** A phrase used to describe the situation in which one person to a contract has failed to fulfill or comply with his promise, giving the other party either a cause of action for damages or an excuse for non-performance.

**F.A.S.** The abbreviation means the seller places goods on the wharf alongside the ship's tackle. Without evidence to the contrary, legal title and risk of loss passes to the buyer at the moment the goods are so placed. F.A.S. means literally "free alongside steamer."

**Featherbedding.** A term used in labor relations to describe the situation in which demand is made for the payment of wages when a particular service is not rendered.

**Fee simple estate.** A term describing the total interest a person may have in land. Such an estate is not qualified by any other interest and passes upon the death of the owner to the heirs free from any conditions.

**Fellow servants.** Persons working together at a common task and controlled by the same master or employer.

**Felony.** At common law, a felony was a criminal offense, and upon conviction the criminal forfeited his land and goods to the crown and was subject to death. Today by statute, the term includes all those criminal offenses that are punishable by death or imprisonment.

**Fiction of law.** An assumption, or supposition, that something is true and exists, that in actual fact does not exist. "It is used as a rule of convenience, but cannot be used to work a wrong." To say a corporation is a person is a fiction at law. It is of great public convenience to use the idea that a corporation may act as a person. If the corporation wrongfully uses this artificial or fictitious person, the courts will "look behind the corporate veil or person," to the natural persons using the fiction, and hold them personally liable.

**Fictitious payee.** "When a negotiable instrument is payable to the order of a name that does not purport to be the name of any person or to the order of a nonexisting person; or, the maker or drawer does not intend the payee to have an interest in the paper, then the payee is a fictitious payee."

**Fiduciary.** In general a person is a fiduciary when he occupies a position of trust or confidence in relation to another person or his property. Trustees, guardians, and executors are illustrations of persons occupying fiduciary positions.

**Fiscal.** The term applies to the money or financial affairs and management of institutions, public and private. Fiscal officer is the treasurer. Fiscal year is the period within which budgets operate and the time when books are closed. A fiscal year may be from July 1 to June 30.

**Fixtures.** Personal property which, on becoming attached to realty, may become part of the realty. When personal property becomes realty is not easily answered. The following tests are used: (1) the mode of annexation; (2) the intention of the parties; (3) the kind of chattel and its use, called adaptation; (4) the relationship existing between the parties. As between a landlord and tenant, a cooling system placed in the leased premises by the tenant may or may not be a fixture. The statute of the state should be consulted.

**Floating policy.** An insurance policy that covers a class of goods located in a particular place which the insured has on hand at the time the policy was issued, but which goods at the time of fire may not be the identical items that were on hand at the time the policy was issued. A fire policy covering the inventory of a grocery store is an example.

**F.O.B.** The abbreviation means the seller places goods without cost to the buyer on a ship, car, truck, or other conveyance ready to go forward. Without evidence to the contrary, legal title and risk of loss pass to the buyer at the time the goods are placed on the means of transportation. "F.O.B." literally means "free on board."

**Forbearance.** Giving up the right to enforce what one honestly believes to be a valid claim in return for a promise is called forbearance and is sufficient "consideration" to make binding a promise.

**Forced sale.** A sale of a debtor's property by public officials to secure money to pay the debtor's creditors is a forced sale. Sales by sheriff after judgment, foreclosure, and so forth, are illustrations.

**Foreign bill of exchange.** A draft drawn by the resident of one state or country on a resident of another state or country is a foreign bill of exchange.

**Foreign corporation.** A corporation organized in one state is a foreign corporation to another state.

**Forgery.** Forgery is the false writing or alteration of an instrument with the fraudulent intent of deceiving and injuring another. Writing, without his consent, another's name upon a check for the purpose of securing money, is a forgery.

**Franchise.** A right conferred or granted by a legislative body. It is a contract right and cannot be revoked without cause. A franchise is more than a license. A license is only a privilege and may be revoked. A corporation exists by virtue of a "franchise." A corporation secures a franchise from the city council to operate a water works within the city. See *License.*

**Franchise tax.** A tax on the right of a corporation to do business under its corporate name.

**Fraudulent conveyance.** A conveyance of property by a debtor for the intent and purpose of defrauding his creditors. Such conveyance is of no effect, and such property may be reached by the creditors through appropriate legal proceedings.

**Freehold.** An estate in fee or one for life is a "freehold." A freeholder is usually a person who has a property right in the title to real estate amounting to an estate of inheritance (in fee), or one who has title for life, or for an indeterminate period. A grant by a city to a corporation to use the sidewalks for 30 years is not a freeholder. "Householder" is not synonymous with "freeholder." See *Householder.*

**Funded debt.** The term applies to a debt where provision is made for a method of paying off the debt and its interest at fixed periods. A funded debt of a municipality is one where provision is made for the annual raising by tax of the sum necessary to pay the interest and principal as they respectively mature.

**Fungible goods.** The term fungible goods "means goods of which any unit is from its nature of mercantile usage treated as equivalent of any other unit." Grain, wine, and similar items, are examples.

**Futures.** Contracts for the sale and delivery of commodities in the future, made with the intention that no commodity be delivered or received immediately.

**Garnishee.** A person upon whom a garnishment is served. He is a debtor of a defendant and has money or property which the plaintiff is trying to reach in order to satisfy a debt due from the defendant.

**Garnishment.** A proceeding by which a plaintiff seeks to reach the credits of the defendant that are in the hands of a third party, the garnishee. A garnishment is distinguished from an attachment in that by an attachment an officer of the court takes actual possession of property by virtue of his writ. In a garnishment, the property or money is left with the garnishee until final adjudication.

**Gift causa mortis.** A gift made in anticipation of death. The donor must have been in sickness and have died as expected; otherwise, no effective gift has been made. If the donor survives, the gift is revocable.

**Gift inter vivos.** A gift inter vivos is an effective gift made during the life of the donor. By a gift inter vivos, property vests immediately in the donee at the time of delivery; whereas, a gift causa mortis is made in contemplation of death and is effective only upon the donor's death.

**Good title.** A title free from encumbrance, such as mortgages and liens, as disclosed by a complete abstract of the title taken from the records in the recorder's office.

**Grant.** A term used in deeds for the transfer of the title to real property. The words "convey," "transfer," and "grant" as operative words in a deed to pass title are equivalent. The words "grant, bargain, and sell" in a deed, in absence of statute, mean that the grantor promises he has good title to transfer free from incumbrances and that he warrants it to be such.

**Grantee.** A grantee is a person to whom a grant is made. One named in a deed to receive title.

**Grantor.** A grantor is a person who makes a grant. The grantor executes the deed by which he divests himself of title.

**Gross negligence.** The want of even slight care.

**Guardian.** A person appointed by the court to look after the property rights and person of minors, insane, and other incompetents or legally incapacitated persons.

**Guardian ad litem.** A special guardian appointed for the sole purpose of carrying on litigation and preserving the interests of a ward. He exercises no control or power over property.

**Hearsay evidence.** Evidence that is learned from someone else. It does not derive its value from the credit of the witness testifying but rests upon the veracity of another person. It is not good evidence because there is no opportunity to cross-examine the person who is the source of the testimony.

**Heirs.** Those persons upon whom the statute of descent casts the title to real property upon the death of the ancestor. See Statutes of descent of state. See *Descent*.

**Holder in due course.** "A person who takes a negotiable instrument under the following conditions: (1) That it is complete and regular on its face; (2) That he becomes the holder of it before it was overdue and without notice that it had been previously dishonored, if such was the fact; (3) That he took it in good faith and for value; (4) That at the time it was negotiated to him he had no notice of any infirmity in the instrument or defect in the title of the person negotiating it."

**Holding company.** A corporation organized for the purpose of owning and holding the stock of other corporations. Share holders of underlying corporations receive in exchange for their stock, upon an agreed value, the shares in the holding corporation.

**Homestead.** A parcel of land upon which a family dwells or resides, and which to them is home. The statute of the state or federal government should be consulted to determine the meaning of the term as applied to debtor's exemptions, federal land grants, and so forth.

**Householder.** The term has different meanings as applied to the right to serve on the jury, or to have property exempt from execution for personal debts. See *Freeholder*. Consult statute of state.

**Impanel.** The word means to list the persons who are to be drawn for jury service. It applies not only to the general list returned by the sheriff to serve for a term of court, but also to the list used by the clerk for a particular case.

**In personam.** A legal proceeding, the judgment of which binds the defeated party to a personal liability.

**In rem.** A legal proceeding, the judgment of which binds, affects, or determines the status of property.

**In statu quo.** The conditions existing at the time of the commencement of an action, or, in case of rescission of contract, the position of the parties just prior to the creation of the contract.

**Inalienable.** The word means not capable of transfer or sale. The right to sue for a tort is inalienable. Contracts for personal services are inalienable choses in action. The word means non-assignable.

**Inchoate.** Incomplete situations out of which rights and duties may later arise. It also means "as yet not perfect." For example: A wife's dower is inchoate until her husband's death.

**Incontestable.** As applied to insurance, a clause in an insurance policy which states that after a certain period of time the policy may not be contested except for non-payment of the premiums.

**Incorporeal.** Not manifest to the senses. The right of an owner of land to take the water of a stream for irrigation is an incorporeal hereditament.

**Incumbrance.** A burden on either the title to land or thing, or upon the land or thing itself. A mortgage or other lien is an incumbrance upon the title. A right of way over the land is an incumbrance upon the land and affects its physical condition.

**Indenture.** A deed executed by both parties, as distinguished from a deed poll which is executed only by the grantor.

**Independent contractor.** The following elements are essential to establish the relation of independent contractor in contradistinction to principal and agent. An independent contractor must: (1) exercise his independent judgment as to the means used to accomplish the result; (2) be free from control or orders from any other person; (3) be responsible only under his contract for the result obtained.

**Indictment.** An indictment is a finding by a grand jury that it has reason to believe the accused is guilty as charged. It informs the accused of the offense with which he is charged in order that he may prepare his defense. It is a pleading in a criminal action.

**Indorsement.** Writing one's name upon paper for the purpose of transferring the title. When a payee of a negotiable instrument writes his name on the back of the instrument, such writing is an indorsement.

**Information.** An allegation made by a prosecuting officer to a magistrate that a person has committed a crime. See *Indictment*.

**Inherit.** To acquire as an heir. The word is used in contradistinction to acquiring property by will. See *Descent*.

**Inheritance.** An inheritance denotes an estate that descends to heirs. See *Descent*.

**Injunction.** A writ of judicial process issued by a court of equity by which a party is required to do a particular thing or to refrain from doing a particular thing.

**Injunction pendente lite.** A provisional remedy granted by a court of equity before a hearing upon the merits of a suit, for the purpose of preventing the doing of any act whereby the rights in the controversy may be materially changed.

**Insolvent.** An insolvent debtor is one whose property is insufficient to pay all his debts. Within the Bankruptcy Act, "Whenever the aggregate of his property . . . shall not at a fair valuation be sufficient in amount to pay his debts."

**Insurable interest.** A person has an insurable interest in a person or property if he will be directly and financially affected by the death of the person or the loss of the property.

**Insurance.** By an insurance contract, one party, for an agreed premium, binds himself to another, called the insured, to pay to the insured a sum of money conditioned upon the loss of life or property of the insured.

**Intent.** A state of mind that exists prior to or contemporaneous with an act. A purpose or design to do or forbear to do an act. It cannot be directly proven, but is inferred from known facts.

**Interim certificate.** An instrument negotiable by statute in some states, payable in stocks or bonds, and given prior to the issuance of the stocks or bonds in which payable.

**Interlocutory decree.** A decree of a court of equity that does not settle the complete issue, but settles only some intervening part, awaiting a final decree.

**Intestate.** The intestate laws are the laws of descent or distribution of the estate of a deceased person. A person dies intestate who has not made a will.

**Irreparable damage or injury.** Irreparable does not mean such injury as is beyond the possibility of repair, but it does mean that it is so constant and frequent in occurrence that no fair or reasonable redress can be had in a court of law. Thus, the plaintiff must seek a remedy in equity by way of an injunction.

**Issue (in a will).** The word, as applied to a will, means descendants of whatever degree.

**Issue (in pleading).** The purpose of pleadings in a court proceeding is to find the "issue": that is, a point which is affirmed on one side and denied on the other.

**Issue (bonds and securities).** As applied to bonds and securities, the word means those bonds and securities that are created and delivered at the same time.

**Joint adventure.** When two persons enter into a single enterprise for their mutual benefit without the intention of continuous pursuit, they have entered a joint adventure. They are essentially partners.

**Joint contract.** If two or more persons promise upon the same consideration for the same purpose to another party, they are joint obligors to the other party to the contract and have formed a joint contract.

**Joint ownership.** The interest of each of the parties in property has no existence in absence of the interest of the other. The parties together own the total interest. *A*, *B*, and *C* as a unit own the property.

**Joint tenants.** Two or more persons to whom are deeded land in such manner that they have "one and the same interest, accruing by one and the same conveyance, commencing at one and the same time and held by one and the same undivided possession." Upon the death of one joint tenant, his property passes to the surviving joint tenant or tenants.

**Joint tort-feasors.** When two persons commit an injury with a common intent, they are joint tort-feasors.

**Judgment (in law).** A judgment is the decision, pronouncement, or sentence rendered by a court upon an issue in which it has jurisdiction.

**Judgment in personam.** A judgment against a person directing the defendant to do or not to do something, is a judgment in personam. See *In personam.*

**Judgment in rem.** A judgment against a thing, as distinguished from a judgment against a person. See *In rem.*

**Judicial sale.** A judicial sale is a sale authorized by a court that has jurisdiction to grant such authority. Such sales are conducted by an officer of the court. See *Sale.*

**Jurisdiction.** The authority conferred upon a court by the constitution to try cases and determine causes.

**Laches.** Laches is a term used in equity to name that conduct which is neglect to assert one's rights, or to do what by the law a person should have done and did not do. Such failure on the part of one to assert a right will give an equitable defense to another party.

**L.S.** The letters are an abbreviation for the Latin phrase "locus sigilli," meaning place of the seal.

**Lease.** A contract by which one person divests himself of possession of lands or chattels and grants such possession to another for a period of time. The relationship where land is involved is called landlord and tenant.

**Leasehold.** The land held by a tenant under a lease.

**Legacy.** Personal property disposed of by will. Sometimes the term is synonymous with bequest. The word "devise" is used in connection with real property distributed by will. See *Bequest, Devise.*

**Legal tender.** Any money which, if received, will discharge a debt. See *Money, Currency.*

**Legatee.** A person to whom a legacy is given by will.

**Letter of credit.** A letter of credit is a letter containing a request that the party to whom it is addressed pay the bearer or person named therein money, sell him commodities on credit, or give him something of value, with the intention that the addressee later seek payment from the writer of the letter. It is used by a buyer to secure goods without the necessity of having cash in hand.

**Letters testamentary.** The orders or authority granted by a probate court to an executor.

**Levy (taxes).** The word as applied to taxation means to impose or assess, to charge and collect, a sum of money against a person or property for public purposes.

**Levy (writ of).** The literal meaning is the seizure of the defendant's property by the sheriff to satisfy the plaintiff's judgment. The word sometimes means that a lien has attached to land and other property of the defendant by virtue of a judgment.

**Libel.** The malicious publication of a defamation of a person by printing, writing, signs, or pictures, for the purpose of injuring the reputation and good name of such person. "The exposing of a person to public hatred, contempt, or ridicule."

**License (privilege).** A license is a mere personal privilege given by the owner to another to do designated acts upon the land of the owner. It is revocable at will, creates no estate in the land, and such licensee is not in possession. "It is a mere excuse for what otherwise would be a trespass."

**License (governmental regulation).** A license is a privilege granted by a state or city upon the payment of a fee, which confers authority upon the licensee to do some act or series of acts, which otherwise would be illegal. A license is not a contract and may be revoked for cause. It is a method of governmental regulation exercised under the police power. Examples: license to keep dogs in the city, to sell commodities in the street.

**Lien.** A right one person, usually a creditor, has to keep possession of or control the property of another for the purpose of satisfying a debt. There are many kinds of liens: Judgment liens, attorney's liens, innkeeper's liens, logger's liens, vendor's liens. Consult statute of state for types of liens. See *Judgment.*

**Limitation of actions.** Statutes of limitations exist for the purpose of bringing to an end old claims because witnesess die, memory fails, papers are lost, and the evidence is inadequate; thus stale claims are barred. Such statutes are called statutes of repose. Within a certain period of time, action on claims must be brought; otherwise, they are barred. The period varies from 2 to 20 years.

**Lineal descendant.** One descended in a direct line, such as son, grandson, great grandson, etc.

**Liquidated.** A claim is liquidated when it has been made fixed and certain by the parties concerned.

**Liquidated damages.** A fixed sum agreed upon between the parties to a contract, to be paid as ascertained damages by that party who breaches the contract. If the sum is excessive, the courts will declare it to be a penalty and unenforceable.

**Liquidation.** The process of winding up the affairs of a corporation or firm for the purpose of paying its debts and disposing of its assets. Such may be done voluntarily or under the orders of a court.

**Lis pendens.** The words mean, "pending the suit nothing should be changed." The court having control of the property involved in the suit, issues notice *lis pendens*, that persons dealing with the defendant regarding the subject matter of the suit, do so subject to final determination of the action.

**Maintenance (in lawsuits).** The assisting of either party to a lawsuit by a person who has no interest therein. An officious intermeddling in a lawsuit.

**Mala in se.** Acts that are bad in themselves and are void of any legal consequences. A contract to do immoral acts is illegal and void because *mala in se.* Such acts are in contradistinction to acts *mala prohibita*, which are illegal because prohibited by statute.

**Malfeasance.** Knowingly performing an unlawful act.

**Malicious prosecution.** The prosecution of another at law with malice and without probable cause to believe that such legal action will be successful.

**Mandamus.** A writ issued by a court of law, in the name of the state, directed to some inferior court, officer, corporation, or person commanding them to do a particular thing that appertains to their office or duty.

**Mandatory injunction.** An injunctive order issued by a court of equity that compels affirmative action by the defendant.

**Marketable title.** A title of such character that no apprehension as to its validity would occur to the mind of a reasonable and intelligent person. The title to goods in litigation, subject to incumbrances, in doubt as to a third party's right, or subject to lien, is not marketable.

**Marshaling assets.** A principle in equity for a fair distribution of a debtor's assets among his creditors. For example, when a creditor of *A*, by reason of prior right, has two funds *X* and *Y* belonging to *A* out of which he may satisfy his debt, but *B*, also a creditor of *A*, has a right as to *X* fund, the first creditor will be compelled to exhaust *Y* fund before he will be permitted to participate in *X* fund.

**Master in chancery.** An officer appointed by the court to assist the court of equity in taking testimony, computing interest, auditing accounts, estimating damages, ascertaining liens, and doing such other tasks incidental to a suit, as the court may require. The power of a master is merely advisory and his task largely fact-finding.

**Material alteration.** Any alteration of a written instrument that affects the identity of the parties or changes the legal obligations and rights of the parties is material.

**Maxim.** A proposition of law which because of its universal approval needs no proof or argument, and its mere statement gives it authority. Example: "A principal is bound by the acts of his agent, when the agent is acting within the scope of his authority."

**Mechanic's lien.** A mechanic's lien is created by statute to secure laborers for their wages. Such lien has for its purpose to subject the land of an owner to a lien for material and labor expended in the construction of buildings, which buildings having been placed on the land become a part thereof by the law of accession.

**Merger.** Two corporations are merged when one corporation continues in existence and the other loses its identity by its absorption into the first. Merger must be distinguished from consolidation, in which case both corporations are dissolved, and a new one created which takes over the assets of the dissolved corporations.

**Ministerial duty.** The performance of a prescribed duty that requires the exercise of no judgment or discretion. A sheriff performs ministerial duties.

**Minutes.** Official notes of a proceeding, such as the minutes of a court clerk, or of a meeting of stockholders.

**Misdemeanor.** A criminal offense, less than a felony, that is not punishable by death or imprisonment. Consult the local statute.

**Misfeasance.** The improper performance of a duty imposed by law or contract which injures another person. It is distinguished from nonfeasance which means doing nothing of an imposed duty.

**Mitigation of damages.** A plaintiff is entitled to recover damages caused by the defendant's breach, but the plaintiff is also under a duty to avoid increasing or enhancing such damages. Such is called a duty to mitigate damages. If a seller fails to deliver the proper goods on time, the buyer, where possible, must buy other goods, thus mitigating damages.

**Monopoly.** The exclusive control of the supply and price of a commodity that may be acquired by a franchise or patent from the government, or, a monopoly is the ownership of the source of a commodity or the control of its distribution.

**Mortgage.** A conveyance or transfer of an interest in property for the purpose of creating a security for a debt. The mortgage becomes void upon payment of the debt, although the recording of a release is necessary to clear the title of the mortgaged property.

**Motive.** The reason or cause why a person does a particular act. Intent, on the other hand, is the purpose to use a particular means or to do a particular act to reach a particular result.

**Mutual and dependent covenants.** A covenant in a contract is a promise. The performances promised may be either mutual or concurrent, dependent or independent. If the performances promised are to be at the same time, such are mutual acts. If one performance is required to be done before another, the performances are dependent. Thus, if the first performance does not occur, the second promised performance is excused.

**Mutual assent.** In every contract each party must agree to the same thing. Each must know what the other intends; they must mutually assent or be in agreement.

**Mutuality.** A word used to describe the situation in every contract that it must be binding on both parties. Each party to the contract must be bound to the other party to do something by virtue of the legal duty created.

**Negligence.** The failure to do that which an ordinary, reasonable, prudent man would do, or the doing of some act which an ordinary, prudent man would not do. Reference must always be made to the situation, the circumstances and the knowledge of the parties.

**Negotiate.** To transfer an instrument from one person to another in such manner as to make the transferee the holder thereof.

**Net.** The word indicates that something has been deducted; charges, freight, storage, and the like.

**Net assets.** The property or effects of a firm, corporation, institution, or estate, remaining after all its obligations have been paid.

**Nolle prosequi.** A discharge of a particular indictment against the accused by the court upon request of the prosecuting officer. It is not an acquittal nor a pardon. The accused may be indicted again and tried for the same offense.

**Nolo contendere.** This plea by an accused in a criminal action is an implied confession of the offense charged. It virtually equals a plea of guilty. A judgment of conviction follows such plea.

**Nominal damages.** A small sum assessed as sufficient to award the case and cover the costs. In such case, no actual damages have been proven.

**Non compos mentis.** Incapacity to comprehend the nature of one's act—applies to one who does not possess understanding sufficient to comprehend the nature, extent, and meaning of his contracts or other legal obligations.

**Nonfeasance.** The failure to perform a legal duty. See *Misfeasance*.

**Nonresident.** The citizen of another state.

**Nonsuit.** A judgment given against a plaintiff who has not proved his case, or fails to proceed with the trial after the case is at issue.

**Notary.** A public officer authorized to administer oaths by way of affidavits and depositions; also to attest deeds and other formal papers in order that such papers may be used as evidence and be qualified for recording.

**Novation.** The substitution of one obligation for another. When debtor *A* is substituted for debtor *B*, and by agreement with the creditor *C*, debtor *B* is discharged, a novation has occurred.

**Nuisance.** The word nuisance is generally applied to any continuous conduct that causes annoyance, inconvenience, and damage to person or property. It usually applies to the unreasonable and wrongful use of property which produces material discomfort, hurt, and damage to the person or property of another. Example: Fumes from a factory.

**Oath.** A pledge given by a person that what he is about to say is true, and that such statement is made under a responsibility to God. If taken before a court and the statements are not true, the oath-taker has committed perjury. If statements are untrue and the oath is not taken before a court, the oath-taker is guilty of false swearing.

**Obligee.** A creditor or promisee.

**Obligor.** A debtor or promisor.

**Option.** A right secured by a contract to accept or reject an offer to purchase property at a fixed price within a fixed time. It is an irrevocable offer sometimes called a "paid for offer."

**Ordinance.** An ordinance is, generally speaking, the legislative act of a municipality. A city council is a legislative body and passes ordinances that are the laws of the city.

**Overt act.** Overt means open. An overt act is any motion, gesture, conduct, or demonstration that evidences a present design to do a particular act that will lead to a desired result.

**Par value.** The words mean "face value." The par value of stocks and bonds on the date of issuance is the principal. At a later date, the par value is the principal plus interest.

**Parole.** The release of a convict from prison on certain conditions to be observed by him, and a suspension of his sentence while he is at liberty.

**Partition.** Court proceedings brought at the request of a party in interest, that real property be taken by the court and divided among the respective owners as their interests appear. If the property is incapable of division in kind, then the property is to be sold and the money divided as each interest appears.

**Partnership.** An agreement under which two or more persons agree to carry on a business for profit.

**Passbook.** A book in which a bank enters the deposits made by a depositor, and which is retained by the depositor.

**Patent.** A grant made by the Register of Patents of the United States under the authority of federal legislation to an inventor, which gives the patentee the exclusive right to make, use, and sell the patented article. The word "patent" is also used to name the original grant of title to public lands. Such patent is a government deed of public lands to the first grantee.

**Penal bond.** A bond given by an accused, or by another person in his behalf, for the payment of money if the accused fails to appear in court on a certain day.

**Pendente lite.** A Latin phrase which means "pending during the progress of a suit at law."

**Per curiam.** A decision by the full court in which no opinion is given.

**Peremptory challenge.** An objection, by a party to a lawsuit, to a person serving as a juror and for which no reason need be given.

**Perjury.** False swearing upon an oath properly administered in some judicial proceeding. See *Oath*.

**Perpetuity.** The taking of any subject matter out of the channel of commerce by limiting its capacity to be sold for a period of time longer than that of a life or lives in being and 21 years thereafter plus the period of gestation.

**Personal representative.** The administrator or executor of a deceased person. The term also means the heir, next of kin, or descendant of a deceased person. The meaning of the term must be ascertained from the context.

**Personal service.** The term means that the sheriff actually delivered to the defendant in person a service of process.

**Picket.** A workman, member of a trade union on strike, posted in front of a struck place of employment for the purpose of publicizing that the workmen are on strike.

**Plaintiff.** In an action at law, the complaining party or the one who commences the action is called the plaintiff. He is the person who seeks a remedy in court.

**Plea.** An allegation or answer in a court proceeding.

**Pleading.** The process by which the parties in a lawsuit arrive at an issue.

**Pledge.** The deposit or placing of personal property as security for a debt or other obligation with a person called the pledgee. The pledgee has the implied power to sell the property if the debt is not paid. If the debt is paid, the right to possession returns to the pledgor.

**Police power.** The inherent power in government to preserve itself, and to promote the safety, health, morals, and welfare of its citizens.

**Policy of insurance.** In insurance law, the word policy means the formal document delivered by the insurance company to the insured, which evidences the rights and duties between the parties.

**Polling jury.** To poll the jury is to call the name of each juror and inquire what his verdict is before such is made a matter of record.

**Pre-emption.** The right to make a first purchase. The privilege of being first. The word has many applications. At early common law the king had the right to buy provisions for his household in preference to others. In the United States, the government pre-empted land as against settlers.

**Preference.** The term is used most generally in bankruptcy law. Where a bankrupt makes payment of money to certain creditors enabling them to obtain a greater percentage of their debts than other creditors in the same class, and the payment is made within four months prior to the filing of a bankruptcy petition, such payment constitutes illegal and voidable preference. An intention to prefer such creditors must be shown. An insolvent person may lawfully prefer one creditor to another, if done in good faith and without intent to defraud others.

**Preferred stock.** Stock that entitles the holder to dividends from earnings before the owners of common stock can receive a dividend.

**Presumption.** A fact assumed by law.

**Prima facie.** The words literally mean "at first view." Thus, that which first appears seems to be true. A prima facie case is one that stands until contrary evidence is produced.

**Privity.** Mutual and successive relationship to the same interest. Offeror and offeree, assignor and assignee, grantor and grantee are in privity. Privity of estate means that one takes title from another. In contract law, privity denotes parties in mutual legal relationship to each other by virtue of being promisees and promisors. At early common law, third party beneficiaries and assignees were said to be "not in privity."

**Probate.** The word means proof of a will by the proper court.

**Process.** In court proceeding, a process is an instrument issued by the court in the name of the state before or during the progress of the trial, under the seal of the court, directing an officer of the court to do, act, or cause some act to be done incidental to the trial.

**Proximate cause.** The cause that sets other causes in operation. The responsible cause of an injury.

**Proximate damage.** Damages that are direct, immediate, and the natural result of negligence or wrong and which damages might reasonably have been expected.

**Proxy.** Authority to act for another: used by absent stockholders or members of legislative bodies to have their votes cast by others.

**Punitive damages.** Damages by way of punishment allowed for an injury caused by a wrong that is willful and malicious.

**Purchase money mortgage.** A mortgage given for money borrowed at the time of the sale of land to pay the purchase price of the property mortgaged. In some states a deficiency judgment is not permitted upon the foreclosure of a purchase money mortgage.

**Qualified acceptance.** A qualified acceptance varies the terms of the bill and the holder may treat the bill as dishonored.

**Quantum meruit (in pleading).** An allegation that the defendant owes the plaintiff for work and labor a sum for as much as the plaintiff reasonably is entitled.

**Quasi-contracts.** The term "quasi-contracts" is used to define a situation where a legal duty arises that does not rest upon a promise but does involve the payment of money. In order to do justice by a legal fiction, the court enforces the duty as if a promise in fact exists. Thus, if *A* gives *B* money by mistake, *A* can compel *B* to return the money by an action in quasi-contract.

**Quit claim.** A deed that releases a right or interest in land, but which does not include any covenants of warranty. The grantor transfers only that which he has.

**Quo warranto.** A proceeding in court by which the state, city, or county or other governmental body tests or inquires into the legality of the claim of any person to a public office, franchise, or privilege. It is a proceeding to oust persons from public office.

**Receiver.** An officer of the court appointed on behalf of all parties to the litigation to take possession of, hold, and control the property involved in the suit, for the benefit of the party who will be determined to be entitled thereto.

**Rescission.** When both parties to a contract agree to return to the same position as before the creation of the agreement, with a return to each of the consideration given and received, the contract has been rescinded, and rescission has occurred.

**Recognizance.** A recognizance is a contract of record or obligation made before a court by which the parties thereto obligate themselves to perform some act. It is different from a bail bond, in that a bail bond is under seal and creates a new debt. A recognizance is in the nature of a conditional judgment and acknowledges the existence of a present obligation to the state.

**Recoupment.** A right to deduct from the plaintiff's claim any payment or loss that the defendant has suffered by reason of the plaintiff's wrongful act. The words mean "to cut back."

**Re-insurance.** A contract of re-insurance is where one insurance company agrees to indemnify another insurance company in whole or in part against risks which the first company has assumed. The original contract of insurance and the re-insurance contract are distinct contracts. There is no privity between the original insured and the re-insurer.

**Release.** The voluntary relinquishment of a right, lien, or any obligation. A release need not be under seal, nor does it necessarily require consideration. The words "release, remise, and discharge" are often used together to mean the same thing.

**Replevin.** A remedy given by statute for the recovery of the possession of a chattel. Only the right to possession can be tried in such action.

**Requirements contract.** If a party to a contract agrees to purchase his "requirements," he thereby agrees to purchase what he will need in his regular course of business and not what he may choose to order.

**Res.** A Latin word that means "thing."

**Res adjudicata.** The doctrine of "res adjudicata" means that a controversy once having been decided or adjudged upon its merits is forever settled so far as the particular parties involved are concerned. Such a doctrine avoids vexatious lawsuits.

**Respondent superior.** Latin words that mean the master is liable for the acts of his agent.

**Restraining order.** An order issued by a court of equity in aid of a suit to hold matters in abeyance until parties may be heard. A temporary injunction is a restraining order.

**Retainer.** The payment in advance to an attorney to cover future services and advice is called a retainer.

**Right of action.** The words are synonymous with "cause of action"; a right to enforce a claim in a court.

**Riparian.** A person is a riparian owner if his land is situated beside a stream of water, either flowing over or along the border of the land.

**Satisfaction.** The term "satisfaction" in legal phraseology means the release and discharge of a legal obligation. Such satisfaction may be partial or full performance of the obligation. The word is used with accord. Accord means a promise to give a substituted performance for a contract obligation; satisfaction means the acceptance by the obligee of such performance.

**Scienter.** Knowledge by a defrauding party of the falsity of a representation. In a tort action of deceit, knowledge that a representation is false must be proved.

**Scrip.** As applied to corporation law, "scrip" is a written certificate or evidence of a right of a person to obtain shares in a corporation.

**Seal.** A seal is to show that an instrument was executed in a formal manner. At early common law sealing legal documents was of great legal significance. A promise under seal was binding by virtue of the seal. Today under most statutes any stamp, wafer, mark, scroll, or impression made, adopted, and affixed, is adequate. The printed word "seal" or the letters "L.S." is sufficient.

**Seller's lien.** The right of a seller to retain possession of goods until the price is paid. Such right does not exist where goods are sold on credit.

**Set-off.** A matter of defense, called a cross-complaint, used by the defendant for the purpose of making a demand on the plaintiff and which arises out of contract, but is independent and unconnected with the cause of action set out in the complaint. See *Counter-claims* and *Recoupment*.

**Severable contract.** A contract the performance of which is divisible. Two or more parts may be set over against each other. Items and prices may be apportioned to each other without relation to the full performance of all of its parts.

**Share of stock.** A proportional part of the rights in the management and assets of a corporation. It is a chose in action. The certificate is the evidence of the share.

**Sheriff.** A public officer whose authority and duties are created by legislation. His duties are to execute and administer the law.

**Situs.** Situs means place, situation. The place where a thing is located. The "situs" of personal property is the domicile of the owner. The "situs" of land is the state or county where it is located.

**Slander.** Slander is an oral utterance that tends to injure the reputation of another. See *Libel.*

**Specialty.** The word "specialty" in commercial law means a promise under seal to pay money—a bond. In early law there were two kinds of "specialties." "Common law specialties" were formal instruments under seal—bonds and covenants; "mercantile specialties" included bills and notes, insurance policies, and other unsealed commercial papers.

**Specific performance.** Actual performance, decreed by a court of equity where the remedy available is an ordinary law action (for example, damages) would be inadequate.

**Stare decisis.** Translated, the term means "stand by the decision." The law should adhere to decided cases.

**Stock dividend.** The issue by a corporation of new shares of its own stock to its shareholders as dividends.

**Subrogation.** The substitution of one person in another's place, whether as a creditor or as the possessor of any lawful right, so that the substituted person may succeed to the rights, remedies, or proceeds of the claim. It rests in equity on the theory that, where a party is compelled to pay a debt for which another is liable, such payment should vest the paying party with all the rights the creditor has against the debtor. For example: X insurance company pays Y for an injury to Y's car by reason of Z's negligent act. X insurance company will be subrogated to Y's cause of action against Z.

**Substantial performance.** The complete performance of all the essential elements of a contract. The only permissible omissions or deviations are those which are trivial, inadvertent, and inconsequential. Such performance will not justify repudiation. Compensation for defects may be substituted for actual performance. See *Breach*.

**Substantive law.** A word applied to that law which regulates and controls the rights and duties of all persons in society. It is used in contradistinction to the term adjective law, which means the rules of court procedure or remedial law which prescribe the methods by which substantive law is enforced.

**Succession.** The word means the transfer by operation of law of all the rights and obligations of a deceased person to those who are entitled to take.

**Succession tax.** This tax is not a burden on property, but a tax upon the privilege of taking property, whether by will or descent.

**Summons.** A writ issued by a court to the sheriff directing him to notify the defendant that the plaintiff claims to have a cause of action against the defendant and that he is required to answer. If the defendant does not answer, judgment will be taken by default.

**Suretyship.** A promise by which a person binds himself to answer for the "debt, default, or miscarriage of another," and agrees with the obligor's creditor to satisfy the obligation if the debtor does not.

**Surrender.** The abandonment of leased premises by a tenant. If a landlord accepts the abandonment as a termination of the lease a surrender has occurred.

**Talisman.** A juror summoned to fill up a panel for the trial of a particular case. Such person is not bound to serve the term.

**Tender.** To offer money in satisfaction of a debt or obligation by producing the same and expressing to the creditor a willingness to pay. See *Legal tender*.

**Tenement.** The word has historical significance as applied to real property. In a broad sense it means an estate in land or some interest connected therewith, such as houses, rents, profits, and rights, to which a holder of the title is entitled. It is used with the word "hereditaments."

**Tenure.** The word is used to designate the means by which title is held to real property. For example, "tenure in fee simple," "tenure for life." It also is used to indicate the time limit of a person's right to public office. "Term" means limited time. "Tenure" means indefinite.

**Term of court.** That period of time prescribed by statute within which a court may legally hold its sessions and transact its business.

**Testament.** A testament is the declaration of a person's intention as to what disposition he desires to be made of his property after his death. The word is synonymous with will. The word is so used because a will is a testimonial of one's intention.

**Testamentary capacity.** A person is said to have testamentary capacity when he understands the nature of his business, the value of his property, knows those persons who are natural objects of his bounty, and comprehends the manner in which he has provided for the distribution of his property.

**Testator.** A male person who has died leaving a will. A female person is called a testatrix.

**Tort.** A wrongful act committed by one person against another person or his property. It is the breach of a legal duty imposed by law other than by contract. The word tort means "twisted" or "wrong." *A* assaults *B*, thus commits a tort.

**Trademark.** No complete definition can be given for a trademark. Generally it is any sign, symbol, mark, word, or arrangement of words in the form of a label adopted and used by a manufacturer or distributor to designate his particular goods, and which no other person has the legal right to use. Originally, the design or trademark indicated origin, but today it is used more as an advertising mechanism.

**Trading partnership.** A partnership engaged in the business of buying and selling commodities.

**Treasury stock.** Stock of a corporation which has been issued by the corporation for value, but which is later returned to the corporation by way of gift or purchase or otherwise. It may be returned to the trustees of a corporation for the purpose of sale.

**Trespass.** An injury to the person, property, or the rights of another person committed by actual force and violence, or under such circumstances that the law will imply that the injury was caused by force or violence.

**Trust.** A relationship between persons by which one holds property for the use and benefit of another. The relationship is called fiduciary. Such rights are enforced in a court of equity. The person trusted is called a trustee. The person for whose benefit the property is held is called a beneficiary or *cestui que trustent.*

**Trustee in bankruptcy.** An agent of the court authorized to liquidate the assets of the bankrupt, protect them, and to bring them to the court for final distribution for the benefit of the bankrupt and all the creditors.

**Ultra vires.** Literally the words mean "beyond power." The acts of a corporation are *ultra vires* when they are beyond the power or capacity of the corporation as granted by the state in its character.

**Undertaking.** A so called informal bond without a seal is called an "undertaking."

**Unilateral contract.** A promise for an act or an act for a promise; a single enforceable promise. *A* promises *B* $10 if *B* will mow *A*'s lawn. *B* mows the lawn. *A*'s promise now binding is a unilateral contract. See *Bilateral contract.*

**Valuable consideration.** Any consideration that will support a simple contract. A classic definition is, "valuable consideration consists of some right, interest, profit, or benefit or value accruing to the promisor, and some forbearance, detriment, loss, or responsibility given or suffered by the promisee."

**Valued policy.** As used in fire insurance, a valued policy is one in which the sum to be paid in case of loss is fixed by the terms of the policy. No reference can be made to the real value of the property that is lost.

**Vendee.** A purchaser of property. The term is generally applied to the purchaser of real property. The word "buyer" is usually applied to the purchaser of chattels.

**Vendor.** The seller of property. The term is usually applied to the seller of real property. The word "seller" is applied to the seller of personal property.

**Vendor's lien.** An unpaid seller's right to hold possession of property until he has recovered the purchase price. See *Seller's lien.*

**Venire.** To come into court; a writ used to summon a jury. The word is used sometimes to mean jury.

**Venue.** The geographical area over which a court presides. Venue designates the county in which the action is tried. Change of venue means moved to another county.

**Verify.** To fix, determine, or establish a fact by a statement under oath. A corporate secretary verifies, by oath, that a statement is an exact copy of part of the minutes of a corporate meeting.

**Vested.** The word generally applies to the title to or interests in land. The word strictly means "there is an immediate right of present enjoyment, or a present fixed right of future enjoyment." A life estate is a vested interest. Dower right of a wife, however, is not vested until the death of the husband.

**Vis major.** The force of nature, sometimes called "act of God," which excuses persons from liability. If the ordinary exertion of human skill and prudence cannot avoid the effect of the force of nature, then an obligor may be excused under the doctrine of impossibility of performance.

**Voidable.** That which is valid until one party, who has the power of avoidance, exercises such power. An infant has the power of avoidance of his contract. A defrauded party has the power to avoid his contract. Such contract is voidable.

**Voucher.** A written instrument that bears witness or "vouches" for something. Generally a voucher is an instrument showing services have been performed, or goods purchased, and is presented to a disbursing officer authorizing him to make payment and charge the proper account.

**Wager.** A relationship between persons by which they agree that a certain sum of money or thing owned by one of them will be paid or delivered to the other upon the happening of an uncertain event, which event is not within the control of the parties and rests upon chance. Consult state statutes.

**Waive (verb).** To "waive" at law, is to relinquish or give up intentionally a known right or to do an act which is inconsistent with the claiming of a known right.

**Waiver (noun).** The intentional relinquishment or giving up of a known right. It may be done by express words or conduct which involve any acts inconsistent with an intention to claim the right. Such conduct creates an estoppel on the part of the claimant. See *Estoppel.*

**Warehouse receipt.** An instrument showing that the signer has in his possession certain described goods for storage, and which obligates the signer, the warehouseman, to deliver the goods to a specified person or to his order or bearer upon the return of the instrument. Consult Uniform Warehouse Receipts Act.

**Warrant (noun).** An order in writing in the name of the state and signed by a magistrate directed to an officer commanding him to arrest a person.

**Warranty.** An undertaking, either expressed or implied, that a certain fact regarding the subject matter of a contract is presently true or will be true. The word has particular application in the law of sales of chattels. The word relates to title and quality. The word should be distinguished from "guaranty" which means a contract or promise by one person to answer for the performance of another. See *Suretyship, Guarantor.*

**Waste.** Damage to the real property so that its value as security is impaired.

**Watered stock.** Corporate stock issued by a corporation for property at an over valuation, or stock issued for which the corporation receives nothing in payment therefor.

**Wharfage.** A charge against a vessel for lying at a wharf. It is used synonymously with "dockage" and "moorage."

**Will (testament).** The formal instrument by which a person makes disposition of his property to take effect upon his death. See *Testament*.

**Writ.** An instrument in writing under seal in the name of the state, issued out of a Court of Justice at the commencement of, or during a legal proceeding, directed to an officer of the court commanding him to do some act, or requiring some person to do or refrain from doing some act pertinent or relative to the cause being tried.

**Zoning ordinance.** An ordinance passed by a city council by virtue of the police power which regulates and prescribes the kind of buildings, residences, or businesses that shall be built and used in different parts of a city.

# Index

# Index

Liens (*cont.*):
 bonding, 698
 charging, 685, 688
 classified, 683
 common carrier, 686
 common law, 684
 defined, 920
 discharge, 699
 draymen, 687
 employee, 448
 equitable, 684
 factor's, 420, 686, 914
 foreclosure, 688
 foreclosures, 699
 general, 685
 hospitals, 687
 judgment, 688
 livery stable keeper, 686
 merchandise, 686
 mechanic's, 697, 921
 mortgages (*See* Mortgages)
 mortgages distinguished, 683
 motion pictures, 687
 motor boats, 686
 nature, 683
 nonpossessory, 688
 particular, 685
 pledge distinguished, 297, 684
 possessory, 631, 685, 687
 real estate broker, 414
 satisfaction, 698
 sellers, 253, 926
 ships, 689
 special, 685
 statutes, 685
 stock, 533
 subcontractors, 699
 tax, 640, 689
 truckmen, 687
 vacating, 698
 vehicles, 696
 vendors, 929
 vessels, 689
 warehouseman's, 302
Life insurance, 366 et seq.
Limitations, statutes of:
 claims barred, 876
 Commercial Code, 899
 crimes, 875
 debt barred by, 88
 define, 874
 notes, 876
 period of, 875
 suspending, 876
 taxes, 875
 tolling, 876
 torts, 875
Limited partners, 463
Limited partnerships, 487 et seq.

Limited payment life insurance, 367
Lindbergh Act, 831
Lineal descendant, 920
Liquidated, 920
Liquidated accounts, 653
Liquidated damages, 123
Liquidation, 920
Lis pendens, 920
Litigation (*See* Lawsuits)
Livery stable keeper liens, 686
Living trusts, 769
Loans:
 corporate, 527, 552, 661
 insurance, 369 et seq.
 partners, 475
 partnership, 471
 small, 661
 usurious, 661
Lockouts, 444
Lodgers, 631
Lost articles, 237
Lost certificates, 532
Lost property, 654
Lotteries, 606, 837
L.S., 919
Lucky centers, 606
Luxuries, 54
Lyttleton, 4

## M

Machinery, 639
Mail, payment by, 106
Maintenance, 69, 837, 920
Maker, 137, 175
Malicious mischief, 834
Malicious prosecution, 797
Malpractice, 404
Malum in se, 827
Malum prohibitum, 827
Mandamus, 848
Mandatory injunction, 6
Manslaughter, 830
Manufacturer's negligence, 811
Margin, 72, 415
Marine insurance, 359 et seq.
Marketable title, 620, 920
Marriage:
 brokerage, 69
 common law, 24
 contracts, 85, 87, 97
 duty of support, 24
 earnings, 24
 infants, 55
 interference with, 69
 parent's consent, 26
 savings, 24
 Sunday, 78
 title by, 621
 wills, 752